THE NORTON READER
Fifteenth Edition

THE NORTON READER
An Anthology of Nonfiction

FIFTEENTH EDITION

MELISSA A. GOLDTHWAITE, *General Editor*
Saint Joseph's University

JOSEPH BIZUP
Boston University

ANNE E. FERNALD
Fordham University

JOHN C. BRERETON
University of Massachusetts, Boston

W·W·NORTON & COMPANY
NEW YORK · LONDON

W. W. Norton & Company has been independent since its founding in 1923, when William Warder Norton and Mary D. Herter Norton first published lectures delivered at the People's Institute, the adult education division of New York City's Cooper Union. The firm soon expanded its program beyond the Institute, publishing books by celebrated academics from America and abroad. By midcentury, the two major pillars of Norton's publishing program—trade books and college texts—were firmly established. In the 1950s, the Norton family transferred control of the company to its employees, and today—with a staff of five hundred and hundreds of trade, college, and professional titles published each year—W. W. Norton & Company stands as the largest and oldest publishing house owned wholly by its employees.

Editor: Sarah Touborg
Project Editor: Layne Broadwater
Assistant Editor: Madeline Rombes
Editorial Assistant: Emma Peters
Managing Editor, College: Marian Johnson
Production Manager: Stephen Sajdak
Media Editor: Samantha Held
Media Project Editor: Cooper Wilhelm
Media Editorial Assistant: Katie Bolger
Managing Editor, College Digital Media: Kim Yi
Ebook Production Manager: Danielle Lehman
Marketing Manager, composition: Lib Triplett, Michele Dobbins
Design Director: Rubina Yeh
Designer: Juan Paolo Francisco
Director of College Permissions: Megan Schindel
Permissions Clearing: Margaret Gorenstein
Photo Editor: Cat Abelman
Composition: Westchester Publishing Services
Manufacturing: LSC Communications, Crawfordsville

Permission to use copyrighted material is included in the credits section of this book, which begins on page 945.

Library of Congress Cataloging-in-Publication Data

Names: Goldthwaite, Melissa A., 1972– editor. | Bizup, Joseph, 1966– editor. | Fernald, Anne E., editor. | Brereton, John C., 1943– editor.
Title: The Norton reader : an anthology of nonfiction / Melissa A. Goldthwaite, Joseph Bizup, Anne E. Fernald, John C. Brereton.
Description: Fifteenth edition. | New York : W. W. Norton & Company, [2020] | Includes bibliographical references and index.
Identifiers: LCCN 2019042787 | ISBN 9780393690231 (paperback) | ISBN 9780393441277 (epub)
Subjects: LCSH: College readers. | Exposition (Rhetoric)—Problems, exercises, etc. | English language—Rhetoric—Problems, exercises, etc. | Report writing—Problems, exercises, etc.
Classification: LCC PE1122 .N68 2020 | DDC 808/.0427—dc23
LC record available at https://lccn.loc.gov/2019042787

ISBN: 978-0-393-69023-1 (pbk)

W. W. Norton & Company, Inc., 500 Fifth Avenue, New York, NY 10110
wwnorton.com

W. W. Norton & Company Ltd., 15 Carlisle Street, London W1D 3BS

1 2 3 4 5 6 7 8 9 0

BRIEF CONTENTS

CONTENTS

* *New to this edition*

* *New to this edition*

* *New to this edition*

3. SELF AND SOCIETY   129

* *New to this edition*

* *New to this edition*

* *New to this edition*

* *New to this edition*

5. Food   229

* *New to this edition*

* *New to this edition*

SEE ALSO

* *New to this edition*

7. Education 324

New to this edition

* *New to this edition*

* *New to this edition*

* *New to this edition*

* *New to this edition*

* *New to this edition*

See Also

11. Media and Communication   555

* *New to this edition*

* *New to this edition*

* *New to this edition*

* *New to this edition*

* *New to this edition*

* *New to this edition*

* *New to this edition*

* *New to this edition*

* *New to this edition*

*   *New to this edition*

* *New to this edition*

* *New to this edition*

PREFACE

The Norton Reader began as an attempt to introduce students to the essay as a genre and to create an anthology of excellent nonfiction writing. This new edition continues that tradition, offering a wide selection of essays on a broad range of subjects and including examples of the kinds of writing students are most often assigned, from profiles and arguments to narratives and analyses. With 145 selections in the Full Edition and 90 in the Shorter Edition, *The Norton Reader* offers depth, breadth, and variety for teaching the essay as it has developed over time, including selections from the classic to the contemporary.

As always, *The Norton Reader* has aimed to uphold a tradition of anthologizing excellent prose, starting with Arthur Eastman, the founding editor, who insisted that essays be selected for the quality of their writing. As he put it, "Excellence would be their pillar of smoke by day, of fire by night." With this vision, the original editors of *The Norton Reader* chose classic essays that appealed to modern readers and that are now recognized as comprising the essay canon. We have aimed to continue this practice yet have also adapted the *Reader* to new pedagogies and have updated it by adding new writers whose work appeals to new generations of student readers. We believe that the essays in this volume are well written, focus on topics that matter, and demonstrate what all of us tell our students about good writing.

NEW TO THIS EDITION

- Sixty new readings from a diverse array of today's most influential and exciting voices, including Colson Whitehead, Emma González, Viet Thanh Nguyen, Tara Westover, Jose Antonio Vargas, Chimamanda Ngozi Adichie, Fariha Róisín, Daisy Hernández, Roxane Gay, Barbara Ehrenreich, and many others.

- Three new chapters—Self and Society; Where We Live, What We Live For; and In Conversation—will inspire and inform students' reading and writing about issues that matter. The final chapter of readings, In Conversation, offers a unique cluster of contemporary essays around timely topics: gun control, free speech, and the brain science behind bias and behavior.

- New chapter introductions give students a stimulating overview of the readings, with questions and connections to consider. And a refreshed table of contents shows the lively intersection of personal writing with civic conversations and academic ideas. These features help students connect the relevance of their individual experiences to the broader cultural context.

- A new introductory chapter, Reading *The Norton Reader*, includes an annotated example of active reading, advice on reading with a purpose, and guidance on reading different genres.

- Three essays, two of which are new to this edition, are now documented in MLA, APA, and Chicago styles. See Gerald Graff's "Hidden Intellectualism" on page 360, Ben Yagoda's "Your Lying Mind" on page 860, and Nicholas Tampio's "Look Up from Your Screen" on page 325.

HALLMARK FEATURES OF *THE NORTON READER*

- *The Norton Reader* offers the greatest breadth and depth of any composition reader, with an abundance of contemporary essays anchored by classic and canonical selections. For example, a new selection from Tara Westover's best seller, *Educated*, appears alongside Frederick Douglass's *Learning to Read* in the Education chapter. And in Self and Society, James Baldwin's essay *Stranger in the Village* is in conversation with the new essay it inspired from Teju Cole, *Black Body: Rereading James Baldwin's "Stranger in the Village."*

- Apparatus provides just enough detail—but not so much as to overwhelm the essays themselves. Contextual notes indicate when and where the essay was published; annotations explain unfamiliar persons, events, and concepts; study questions for all essays prompt analysis, discussion, and writing; and biographical information about the authors appears at the end of the book.

- Four expanded indexes organize the readings according to genre, rhetorical mode, date of publication, and additional themes. This feature helps teachers structure courses that meet crucial goals of the WPA Outcomes Statement, which urges that students learn to write in several genres, identify conventions of format and structure, and understand how genres shape reading and writing.

ALSO AVAILABLE FOR INSTRUCTORS AND STUDENTS

- *The Norton Reader* ebook, now available for both versions of *The Norton Reader*, lets you and your students highlight and annotate within the digital text. Links make it easy to navigate between—and make connections among—the readings.

- The book's website, Nortonreader.com, makes *The Norton Reader* uniquely searchable and easy to use. Instructors and students can sort readings by theme, genre, rhetorical mode, and more to find just the reading they're looking for, and then open it in the ebook with one click.

- InQuizitive for Writers supplements *The Norton Reader* with activities to help students learn to edit sentences and work with sources. Question-specific feedback and links to the *Little Seagull Handbook* provide students with extra instruction for these crucial first-year writing skills.

- For instructors, *The Guide to* The Norton Reader includes new sample syllabi, suggested classroom activities, and general advice on planning your course—including new coverage on the teaching of reading and advice on how to make the most out of Nortonreader.com. The *Guide* also includes teaching suggestions and writing assignments to accompany each reading.

- Comprehensive LMS-ready resources provide additional support, including documentation guidelines, model student papers, and customizable grammar and language quizzes.

ACKNOWLEDGMENTS

John Brereton began his association with *The Norton Reader* when the house editor for the book, Carol Hollar-Zwick, invited him to write a review of the eighth edition. John pointed to the high quality of the essays in *The Norton Reader*, but he also noted that some of them seemed a bit dated. He suggested updating the book, making it more contemporary and diverse. On the strength of that review and his reputation as a teacher and scholar, John was invited to join the editorial team—which included Linda Peterson and Joan Hartman—for the ninth edition, published in 1996. That edition included a new chapter, "Cultural Critique," and essays such as "In the Kitchen" by Henry Louis Gates Jr., "On Being a Cripple" by Nancy Mairs, and "More Room" by Judith Ortiz Cofer. For nearly a quarter of a century, John has continued to search for quality essays and to include new voices and perspectives in seven editions of *The Norton Reader*. We appreciate John's intelligence, collegiality, and many contributions to the ninth through fifteenth editions.

The editors would like to express appreciation and thanks to the many teachers who provided reviews and invaluable feedback for this edition: Robin Amaro (Cypress Bay High School), Joseph Berenguel (Asnuntuck Community College), Deborah Bertsch (Columbus State Community College), Paul Bounds (San Jacinto College South), Carla Bradley (Drury University), Mary Dalton (Dreher High School), Gita DasBender (Seton Hall University), Michael DeStefano (Fairfield University), Emily Dial-Driver (Rogers State University), Janet Duckham (Ladue Horton Watkins High School), Michael Duffy (Moorpark College), Christine Ethier (Camden County College–Blackwood Campus), Lori Franklin (Northern New Mexico College), Eva Fritsch (Fontana Unified School District), Jordan Heil (Saint Joseph's University), Danielle Johannsen (University of Minnesota Crookston), Edmund Jones (Seton Hall), Susanna Lankheet (Lake Michigan College), Kevin LaPlante (Walled Lake Northern High School), Jessica Lindberg (Georgia Highlands College), Martha Michieka (East Tennessee State University), Caitlin Murphy-Grace (Camden County College–Blackwood Campus), Ruth Prakasam (Suffolk University), Lee Romer Kaplan (Solano Community College), Katie Stoynoff (University of Akron), and Cory Youngblood (East Los Angeles College).

We would also like to thank the many teachers who provided input on previous editions: Sadaf Alam (San Jacinto College), Deborah Bertsch (Columbus State Community College), Patricia Bjorklund (Southeastern Community College), Jessica Brown (City College of San Francisco), Lee Carmouche (Houston Community College), Jessie Casteel (San Jacinto Community College), James M. Chesbro (Fairfield University), Delicia Daniels (Houston Community College), Gita DasBender (Seton Hall University), Syble Davis

(Houston Community College), Michael DeStefano (Fairfield University), Michael Duffy (Moorpark College), Charles Ellenbogen (John F. Kennedy—Eagle Academy), Craig Fehrman (Indiana University), Rebecca Fleming (Columbus State Community College), Lori Franklin (Northern New Mexico College), David Gorin (Yale University), Stacey Higdon (Houston Community College), Sonya Huber (Fairfield University), John Isles (City College of San Francisco), Crystal Johnson (Houston Community College), Kristi Krumnow (San Jacinto College), John Kwist (Georgia Highlands College), Susanna Lankheet (Lake Michigan College), Andrea Laurencell Sheridan (SUNY Orange), Jessica Lindberg (Georgia Highlands College), Iswari Pandey (California State University at Northridge), Rolf Potts, Sonya Prince (San Jacinto College), Mark Ridge (Rust College), Guy Shebat (Youngstown State University), and Kim Shirkhani (Yale University).

We also thank Katharine Ings for her copyediting; Susan McColl for her proofreading; and Michael Fleming for his work on the author biographies that appear in the back of the book. At W. W. Norton we thank Editorial Assistant Emma Peters for her superb project coordination and editing of our chapter introductions; Stephen Sajdak, Layne Broadwater, Madeline Rombes, Ashley van der Grinten, and Juan Paolo Francisco for their expert help with editing, design, and production; Samantha Held, Katie Bolger, Danielle Lehmann, Matthew Vitale, and Michael Hicks for their wonderful work on the website, ebook, and instructor resources; Megan Schindel, Margaret Gorenstein, and Cat Abelman for their expert permissions work; Debra Morton Hoyt for the new cover design; and our editors past and present: Jennifer Bartlett, Carol Hollar-Zwick, Julia Reidhead, Marilyn Moller, and Ariella Foss. We are grateful to the Norton travelers who represent the book on campus so energetically, and to our talented marketers and specialists, Lib Triplett, Elizabeth Pieslor, and Michele Dobbins. A special thanks to our new editor Sarah Touborg, whose kindness, savvy, and collaborative spirit helped shape this new edition.

READING THE NORTON READER

Reading and the Rhetorical Situation

How do specific people, experiences, and environments help shape identity? How might we live and eat in more sustainable ways? How do sports influence our lives and culture? If technology inevitably shapes us, how might we use it to solve some of the world's greatest problems? How might we listen, view art, and understand one another better? How do we have true conversations with others, speaking and listening when we hold different beliefs? These are just a few of the questions and issues explored by essays in *The Norton Reader*. Whether you read many or just a few of the selections, we hope that you will find them thought provoking. We also hope you will use them to inform and improve your own writing; in this anthology you will find readings that model a wide range of genres and styles from a diverse group of writers.

The pieces collected here come from a variety of publications, from graphic memoirs and daily newspapers to blogs, online magazines, science journals, and books. In an anthology like *The Norton Reader*, all of these selections appear in the same format, with the same typeface and layout; most have annotations to explain references and allusions; and all have questions to urge you to think about major issues and themes.

To help in the reading process, we provide information about the context in which the essay first appeared. We also suggest some ways to read the different kinds of essays. In the next chapter, "Writing with *The Norton Reader*" (pp. xliii–lxv) we provide guidance to help you with your own writing. Among the goals of a college anthology like this one are to help make your reading enrich, inspire, and improve your writing.

When you begin reading an essay that your instructor assigns, ask yourself some or all of the following questions. These questions—about audience, author, purpose, and genre—will help you understand the essay, consider its original context, analyze its meaning or effect, recognize its organization and rhetorical strategies, and imagine how you might use similar strategies for your own writing.

WHO IS THE AUDIENCE?

An *audience* consists of those to whom the essay is directed—the people who read the article, listen to the speech, or view the text. The question about audience might be posed in related ways: For whom did the author write? What readers does the author hope to reach? What readers did the author actually reach?

Sometimes the audience is national or international, as in an editorial for a newspaper like the *Washington Post* or the *New York Times*. Often, the audience shares a common interest, as might the readers of an environmental magazine or the buyers of books on food or history. To help you understand the original audience for each essay, we provide *contextual notes* at the bottom of the first page of each essay. These contextual notes give information about when and where the essay first appeared and, if it began as a talk, when and where it was delivered and to what audience. As editors, we could swamp you with information about publication and authorship, but we prefer to include more essays and keep contextual information focused on the original audience and publication history—that is, on where the essay appeared, who read it, and (if we know) what reaction it received.

For example, the contextual note for Chris Wiewiora's "This Is Tossing" (p. 236) tells you that it appeared in *MAKE*, a small-circulation magazine from Chicago that attracts readers who enjoy fiction, essays, art, and poetry. In contrast, Dan Barber's "What Farm-to-Table Got Wrong" (p. 267) appeared as an op-ed in the *New York Times*, a daily newspaper with a huge national readership. Wiewiora could assume that his audience would like reading personal memoirs, whereas Barber knew that he needed to speak to a large, diverse national audience of people holding different opinions on matters of education, politics, religion, and the environment. Recognizing these audiences gives a window into the writers' choices, strategies, and styles.

Wiewiora begins in the present tense, putting the reader in the moment:

> It's 10A.M. An hour before Lazy Moon Pizzeria opens. You have an hour—this hour—to toss. You're supposed to have 11 pies by 11A.M. One hour. (236)

He puts the reader in the place of the dough tosser, providing a sense of purpose and urgency.

Barber, too, begins by putting the reader in a specific moment:

> It's spring again. Hip deep in asparagus—and, soon enough, tomatoes and zucchini—farm-to-table advocates finally have something from the farm to put on the table.
> . . . Today, almost 80 percent of Americans say sustainability is a priority when purchasing food. The promise of this kind of majority is that eating local can reshape landscapes and drive lasting change.
> Except it hasn't. (267)

But unlike Wiewiora, who keeps his reader in the position of dough tosser, Barber quickly moves to his main argument: that the farm-to-table movement has not created sustainable changes in the American food system. The expectations of the two different audiences explain, in part, the writers' different approaches and styles.

Sometimes contextual notes give information about where the selection was published and how it was received—another way to understand the audience. Maya Angelou's "Graduation" (p. 372) comes from her autobiography *I Know Why the Caged Bird Sings* (1969); Angelou then continued writing her life story in six sequential volumes, concluding with *Mom & Me & Mom* (2013)—a sequence that testifies to her book's success and its appeal to a wide variety of readers.

In each contextual note, we try to explain a little about the magazines, newspapers, and books that printed these essays—whether it's *MAKE*, a small literary journal published twice a year; the *New York Times Magazine,* a Sunday supplement of the daily newspaper; or *I Know Why the Caged Bird Sings*, a free-standing book.

Although the contextual notes provide some clues about the original audience for each piece, you might also think about yourself and your classmates as the current audience. What has changed since the essay was originally published? What experiences or knowledge do you bring to your reading of the essay? Are there ways in which you feel you're not the best audience for a specific essay? Understanding the ways you are or are not the best audience for an essay can help you articulate your response, can enliven class discussions, and can give you ideas for your own writing.

WHO IS THE AUTHOR?

If the audience consists of those who read the essays, the *author* is the person who writes them. Through their writing, authors tend to introduce themselves to their audiences, revealing personal experiences, preferences, and beliefs that bear on the subject at hand. In "My Life as an Undocumented Immigrant" (p. 50), the title gives us an important fact about the author Jose Antonio Vargas and his perspective: he is an undocumented immigrant, and he is going to share that experience with readers.

Not all authors are as direct as Vargas. You don't really need to know that Brian Doyle was editor of *Portland Magazine* and the author of several novels to appreciate his meditation on hearts—from those belonging to tiny hummingbirds to huge whales to humans—in "Joyas Voladoras" (p. 435). Nor do you need to know that Florence Williams, author of "ADHD Is Fuel for Adventure" (p. 333), also wrote a book about breasts. Such biographical facts are interesting but not essential to understanding the essays included.

Because we believe that essayists prefer to introduce themselves and reveal details of personality and experience that they consider most relevant, we do not preface each essay with a biographical note. We think they, as authors, should step forward and we, as editors, should stand back and let them speak. But if you want to learn more about the writer of an essay, you can check the "Author Biographies" section at the end of this book. Putting this information at the end of the book gives you a choice. You may already know something about an author and not wish to consult this section, or you may wish to know more about the authors before you read their writing. Or you may just prefer to encounter the authors on their own terms, letting them identify themselves within the essay. Sometimes knowing who authors are and where their voices come from helps readers grasp what they say—but sometimes it doesn't.

What Is the Rhetorical Context and Purpose?

The *rhetorical context*, sometimes called *rhetorical situation* or *rhetorical occasion*, refers to the context—social, political, biographical, historical—in which writing takes place and becomes public. The term *purpose*, in a writing class, refers to the author's goal—whether to inform, to persuade, to entertain, to analyze, or to do something else through the essay. We could also pose this question as follows: what goals did the writer have in composing and publishing the essay? What effect did the author wish to have on the audience?

For some selections, the rhetorical context is indicated by the *title*. Abraham Lincoln's "Second Inaugural Address" (p. 734) and John F. Kennedy's "Inaugural Address" (p. 736) were speeches that marked the beginning of their presidencies. An inauguration represents a significant moment in a leader's—and the nation's—life. The speech given on such an occasion requires a statement of the president's goals for the next four years. In addition to the title, you can discover more about the rhetorical context of a president's inaugural speech in the *opening paragraphs*. Lincoln, for example, refers back to his first inaugural address and the "impending civil war" (734); then he acknowledges that the war continues and that he prays "this mighty scourge of war may speedily pass away" (735). In the midst of the American Civil War, Lincoln knows that he must, as president, address the political conflict that faces the nation, offer hope for its resolution, and set the moral tone for the aftermath. That's his purpose.

Like the presidential speech, many essays establish the rhetorical context in their opening paragraphs. Editorials and op-eds begin with a "hook"—an opening reference to the issue at hand or the news report under consideration. You might even say that the editorial writer "creates" the rhetorical context and shows us the purpose straight away. Kwame Anthony Appiah opens his op-ed "Go Ahead, Speak for Yourself" (p. 130), with the lines, "'As a white man,' Joe begins, prefacing an insight, revelation, objection or confirmation he's eager to share—but let's stop him right there. Aside from the fact that he's white, and a man, what's his point?" (130) Readers know that Appiah is writing about speaking as a member of a group, and in the title and opening, he establishes his position right up front (he wants others to speak for themselves rather than use some aspect of their social identity to gain or undermine authority).

If an essay does not establish a rhetorical context in its opening paragraphs, you can find additional information in the *contextual note* (described above) or in the *footnotes* to each essay (described below). For example, the contextual note for Barack Obama's "Eulogy for Clementa Pinckney" (p. 811) is:

> On June 17, 2015, a twenty-one-year-old shooter entered Mother Emanuel African Methodist Episcopal Church in Charleston, South Carolina, and murdered nine people, including the senior pastor, Reverend Clementa Pinckney, also a state senator. President Barack Obama delivered this eulogy for Reverend Pinckney on June 26, 2015. (811)

Although the title establishes the genre, neither the title nor the opening paragraphs reveal the context of Reverend Pinckney's death, a context that would have been clear to the original audience and becomes clear to the reader later in the eulogy but is important to understand before reading the piece. The footnotes (marked with small numerals) give further details.

Here is some additional information about *footnotes* and how to use them as you read an essay: Explanatory footnotes are a common feature of a textbook. When the original authors wrote the footnotes themselves, we indicate that in the text. In Terry Tempest Williams's essay, for example, we state that all notes are the author's unless indicated otherwise (469). This tells you that the author wished to cite an expert, add information, or send the reader to another source. In most cases, however, we have written the footnotes to help with difficult words, allusions, and references. We provide information about people, places, works, theories, and other unfamiliar things that the original audience may have known. For example, for Maya Angelou's "Graduation" (p. 372) we footnote Gabriel Prosser and Nat Turner, but not Abraham Lincoln and Christopher Columbus. Many of Angelou's readers would have known that Prosser and Turner were executed leaders of slave rebellions in the nineteenth century. But because not all readers today know (or remember) this part of American history, we add a footnote.

Although reading the footnotes can facilitate the making of meaning, it can never take the place of reading carefully. Reading is an active process. Experienced readers take responsibility for that action—reading critically, constructing meaning, interpreting what they read. If our footnotes help you read critically, then use them; if they interfere, then just continue reading the main text and skip over them.

Just as authors have a purpose in writing, readers have a purpose for reading. You will read differently depending on your purpose. Are you reading a piece to prepare for classroom discussion? If so, you might consider your position on or experience with the topic being written about. You might assess the author's argument and support or mark the parts of the essay that seem most and least successful in getting across a point. If your purpose is to gain inspiration as a writer, you might note the stylistic elements (metaphors, similes, varying sentence length, precision of language, and so on) and the rhetorical strategies the writer uses. If you're reading more than one essay on the same topic, you might compare and contrast the authors' positions and approaches. Later in this chapter, we provide sample annotations to model active reading.

WHAT IS THE GENRE AND ITS CONVENTIONS?

Genre is a term used by composition and literature teachers to refer to kinds of writing that are expected to have common features and certain conventions of style, presentation, and subject matter. Essay genres include the memoir and the profile, the visual analysis and the op-ed, the literacy narrative and the lyric essay, among others. For the essay, genre partially determines the form's content and organization, but it should never do so in a "cookie-cutter" way.

Conventions are practices or customs commonly used in a genre—like a handshake for a social introduction. Genre and convention are linked concepts, the one implying the other. Articles in a scientific journal (a genre) begin with a title and an abstract (conventions) and include sections about the methodology and the results (also conventions). Op-eds, by convention, begin with a "hook"; profiles of people or places include a physical description of the subject; literacy narratives include a key episode in the acquisition of reading or writing skills; lyric essays are often written in sections or organized by association rather than by employing explicit transitions. But in reading and writing essays, conventions should not be thought of as rigid rules; rather, they should be seen as guidelines, strategies, or special features.

As you read an essay, think about its form: what it includes, how the writer presents the subject, what features seem distinctive. If you read a pair or group of essays assigned by your teacher, you might ask yourself whether they represent the same genre or are noticeably different. If they are the same, you will recognize similar features; if they are different, you will notice less overlap.

The Norton Reader includes four categories of genres, some of which overlap in particular cases:

- **Narrative genres** tell stories. They include personal essays, memoirs, graphic memoirs, and literacy narratives. If you're reading a narrative, note how the author structures the story. Does the narrative begin with a dramatic moment, unfold in chronological order, or have a different structure? What is the balance between scene (putting the reader in the moment) and reflection (making sense of an experience)? What is the effect of the organization the writer chose?

- **Descriptive genres** give details about how a person, place, or thing looks, sounds, and feels, often in a larger framework. These include profiles of people and places, essays about nature and the environment, lyric essays, reportage, and pieces of humor and satire. If you're reading a descriptive genre, note the author's use of language and sensory imagery. What strategies does the writer use to draw the reader in—to make a person, place, or situation come alive for the reader?

- **Analytic genres** examine texts, images, and cultural objects and trends. They include reflection, textual analysis, visual analysis, and cultural analysis. If you're reading an analytical genre, consider the ways that the author looks closely at a text, image, object, or trend and breaks it down into parts in order to understand the whole. What insight does the analysis provide? How does it make you look differently at the subject?

- **Argumentative genres** take positions and use reasons and evidence to support them. These include evaluations and reviews, proposals, op-eds, and speeches. If you're reading an argumentative genre, identify the author's main point, which may come in a thesis statement or may be implied less directly. Once you know the argument, consider the author's support. What evidence does the writer use? Are the sources reputable? Is the reasoning sound? Does the author respond to counterarguments? Is the argument persuasive? Why or why not?

For more detailed information on some of the common genres included in *The Norton Reader* and some features to consider as you read and write, see pp. xlvi–lv.

What Are Rhetorical Strategies?

Writers use a range of strategies in order to develop and organize their material. Here are some of the most common rhetorical strategies:

- **Describing** appeals to the senses to describe something or someone.
- **Narrating** provides an account of actions or events that occur over a period of time.
- **Exemplifying** provides examples to illustrate a claim or idea.
- **Classifying and dividing** groups people or things on the basis of shared qualities.
- **Explaining or analyzing a process** breaks a process or concept into its component parts.
- **Comparing and contrasting** considers the similarities and differences between or among people, places, things, or ideas.
- **Defining** attempts to give the essential meaning of something.
- **Analyzing cause and effect** considers the reasons something happened (cause) and determines the results (effect).
- **Arguing** makes a claim and provides evidence to support that claim.

Sometimes authors use rhetorical strategies to structure an entire piece. Kathy Fish, for example, uses definition to structure her lyric essay "Collective Nouns for Humans in the Wild" (p. 425). But writers most often use a combination of rhetorical strategies to develop and present their ideas. For example, Maya Angelou in "Graduation" (p. 372) blends narration and description as she tells the story of her graduation from high school. And Marion Nestle uses cause and effect analysis as well as exemplification to make an argument in "Superfoods Are a Marketing Ploy" (p. 271). As you read the essays included in *The Norton Reader*, notice how the writers develop and organize their material— and see if you can get ideas for your own writing. For more details on rhetorical strategies, see pp. lv–lix.

Strategies for Critical Reading

The previous pages gave an overview of different questions to consider when reading, from thinking about the intended audience to recognizing genres and rhetorical strategies. Here we offer some general tips for approaching the reading your instructor assigns.

Preview the essay

Think about the essay's title, read its opening paragraph, and skim the essay to get a sense of its organization and genre. Look at the contextual note on the first page, and try to imagine the experience, issue, or debate that motivated the essayist to write. Previewing is a technique widely used for college reading, but not all writing teachers encourage it. Some teachers explain that it helps readers focus on key issues; others discourage previewing, pointing out that a good essay—like a good novel or movie—can be ruined by knowing the ending. Whether you preview or not might depend on the genre of essay you're reading. While you might want to know an author's argument before reading more carefully, you also might want to allow a personal or lyric essay to unfold—to see where the author takes you.

Annotate in the margin

As you read, note points that seem interesting and important, forecast issues that you think the writer will address, and pose questions of your own. Note the rhetorical strategies and literary features the writer uses. Imagine that you're having a conversation with the author. Respond to their ideas with some of your own. Most essayists want active readers who think about what the essay says, implies, and urges as a personal response or course of action. Similarly, note points that you don't understand or that you find ambiguous. Puzzling over a sentence or a passage with your classmates can lead to crucial points of debate or provide inspiration for your own writing. Mark your queries and use them to energize class discussion. Here, for example, is a sample annotation of the first eleven paragraphs of David French's "What Critics Don't Understand about Gun Culture."

My wife knew something was (amiss) when the car blocked our driveway. She was outside our house, playing with our kids on our trampoline, when a car drove slowly down our rural Tennessee street. As it reached our house, it pulled partially in the driveway, and stopped.

The first sentence tells us something is wrong.

A man got out and walked up to my wife and kids. Strangely enough, at his hip <u>was an empty gun holster</u>. She'd never seen him before. She had no idea who he was. He demanded to see me.

Why is it strange that the holster is empty? Would it be better if there were a gun in the holster?

I wasn't there. I was at my office, a 50-minute drive from my house. My wife didn't have her phone with her. She didn't have one of our guns with her outside. She was alone with our three children. Even if she had her phone, the police were minutes away. My wife <u>cleverly defused the confrontation</u> before it escalated, but we later learned that this same person had been seen, hours before, slowly driving through the parking lot of our kids' school.

What did she say? Would the situation have escalated if she had a gun?

That wasn't the first disturbing incident in our lives, nor would it be the last. My wife is a sex-abuse survivor and was almost choked to death in college by a furious boyfriend. In just the last five years, we've faced <u>multiple threats</u>—so much so that neighbors have expressed concern for our safety, and theirs. They didn't want an angry person to show up at their house by mistake. We've learned the same lesson that so many others have learned. There are evil men in this world, and sometimes they wish you harm.

This detail makes me feel sympathetic to his wife.

Why? What makes this family a target when their neighbors are not?

Miles's law states, "Where you stand is based on where you sit." In other words, <u>your political opinions are shaped by your environment and your experience</u>. We're products of our place, our time, and

Yes—and that's why we should try new things and meet new people.

our people. Each of these things is far more important to shaping hearts and minds than any think piece, any study, or certainly any tweet. And it strikes me that many millions of Americans don't truly understand how "gun culture" is built, how the process of first becoming a gun owner, then a concealed-carrier, changes your life.

It starts with the consciousness of a (threat.) Perhaps not the kind of (threat) my family has experienced. Some people experience more. Some less. And some people don't experience a (threat) at all— but they're aware of those who do. With the consciousness of a (threat) comes the awareness of a vulnerability. The police can only protect the people you love in the most limited of circumstances (with those limits growing ever-more-severe the farther you live from a city center). You want to stand in that gap.

The repetition of "threat" heightens the sense of fear in this paragraph.

So you take a big step. You walk into a gun store. Unless you're the kind of person who grew up shooting, this is where you begin your encounter with American gun culture. The first thing you'll notice—and I've seen this without fail—is that the person behind that counter is ready to listen. They want to hear your experience. They'll share their own. They'll point you immediately to a potential solution. Often the person behind the counter is a veteran. Often they're a retired cop. Always they're well-informed. Always they're ready to teach.

Author switches to 2nd person ("you") here to put the reader in the position of someone wanting to buy a gun.

Author assumes that all gun store workers are like this. Is it true?

Your first brush with this new world is positive, but it's just a start. The next place the responsible adult goes is to the gun range, a place that's often located in the store. Sometimes you buy the gun and walk straight to the range. You put on eye pro-

Is everyone with access to a gun a responsible adult?

tection. You put on ear protection. And if you're honest with yourself, you're nervous.

But, again, there's a person beside you. They show you how to load the gun. They teach you the basics of marksmanship. They teach you gun safety. Always treat the gun as if it's loaded, even if you think you know it's not. Keep your finger off the trigger unless you intend to fire the weapon. Only point it at objects you intend to shoot.

Author uses the 2nd person here to help teach the reader about gun safety.

You do it. You fire. It's loud, but if the salesman has done his job, then he's matched you with a gun you can handle. In an instant, the gun is demystified. You buy a box of ammunition and shoot it all. Then you buy another box. For most people there's an (undeniable thrill) when they realize that they can actually master so potent a tool.

I'm not sure about the use of "thrill" and "fun" here. Would most people really be this eager?

But something else happens to you, something that's deeper than the (fun of shooting) a paper target. Your thought-process starts to change. Yes, if someone tried to break into your house, you know that you'd call 911 and pray for the police to come quickly, but you also start to think of exactly what else you'd do. If you heard that "bump" in the night, how would you protect yourself until the police arrived? You're surprised at how much safer you feel with the gun in the house. ●

Does everyone feel safer with a gun in their house? Aren't there people who worry about their children finding the gun? Is everyone prepared to shoot another person? I don't always identify with the "you." Maybe I'd feel differently if the author had used first person ("I") throughout the essay.

Analyze any illustrations

Many of the essays in *The Norton Reader* include illustrations from their original publications. Think about how the essays and the images "speak" to each other. Consider whether the images enrich, highlight, or possibly challenge the essay. Does the image primarily illustrate the essay, or does it emphasize a feature unexplained by the essayist? Does the image enrich and make clearer one aspect of the writing, or does it minimize certain aspects of the subject, perhaps aspects you find important? What do you see in the images that the essayist discusses or explains? What do you see that the writer overlooks or minimizes? Thinking about images can help you clarify the author's argument or reveal points the author may have missed.

Summarize the essay

Write a summary of the essay. If you're summarizing an argument or analysis, begin by making a list of its key points and identifying the evidence used in support of each; then try to state briefly, in your own words, the "gist" or core of the essay. The goal is to condense the argument and evidence, while remaining faithful to the author's meaning. If you're summarizing a narrative or descriptive essay, summarize the meaning or effect you think the writer wanted to get across and list the strategies the author used to communicate that meaning or effect to readers. Your summary will be useful when you discuss the essay in class or write about it in a paper.

Keep a reading journal

Buy a class notebook or keep an electronic journal for reflections on the essays you read. For each essay, take notes, record your responses, write questions about what puzzles you, and jot down what you might want to write about in an essay of your own. Make note of sentences or passages that you like and that you might want to use as models for your own writing. You may also want to list questions that the essayist raises and answers, as well as write down questions that you think the essayist has overlooked.

Use the study questions

Review the questions that follow each essay in *The Norton Reader* and think about the issues—the subject, the structure, the language—that they cover. We include these questions to help you become an active reader, to focus attention on key issues, and to make suggestions for doing or writing something.

- Some questions ask you to locate or mark an essay's structural features, the patterns that undergird and clarify meaning. Narrative, description, exposition, persuasion, and argument can follow conventional shapes—

but can also distort them—and your ability to recognize these shapes will improve your comprehension.

- Other questions ask you to paraphrase meanings or extend them—that is, to express the meaning in your own words, to amplify points by providing your own examples, or to reframe points by connecting them with points in other essays.

- Still other questions ask you to notice special features or conventions that contribute to meaning: the author's choice of title, the author's voice (or persona), the author's assumptions about audience (and how the author speaks to the audience), and the author's choice of style and forms of expression.

- At least one question, usually the last, asks you to write. Sometimes we ask you to demonstrate comprehension by writing about something from your experience or reading that extends an essay and enforces its argument. Sometimes we invite you to express disagreement or dissent by writing about something from your experience or knowledge that qualifies the author's argument or calls it into question. We may ask you to compare or contrast two authors' positions—especially when their positions seem opposed. Or we may ask you to adapt one of the essay's rhetorical strategies to a topic of your own choice and to make the essay even more your own by basing it on personal experience.

Reread the essay

If possible, read the essay a second time before you discuss it with your peers or write about it in an essay of your own. If you're short on time, reread the key passages and paragraphs that you marked in marginal notes. Ask yourself what you see the second time that didn't register with you on first reading.

Reading need not be only a private activity; it can also become communal and cooperative. Writing down your thoughts or taking part in conversations with others can clarify your own and others' interpretation of the essays. What interests and motives does each reader bring to particular essays? What are responsive and responsible readings? Are there irresponsible readings, and how do we decide? All these questions—and others—can emerge as private reading moves into the more public arena of the classroom.

Readers write, writers read. Making meaning by writing is the flip side of making meaning by reading, and we hope to engage you in both processes. But in neither process are meanings passed from hand to hand like nickels, dimes, and quarters. Instead, they are constructed—as a quilt or a house or an institution. We hope that these suggestions for reading will lead you to engaged and fruitful writing.

WRITING WITH *THE NORTON READER*

Writing in Academic Contexts

We hope that the selections included in *The Norton Reader*, as well as your class discussions, inspire you to write. Much of the writing you will do in a composition course will start with an assignment from your instructor. Perhaps you will be asked to respond to some of the essays in *The Norton Reader*—to expand on something a writer has said; to agree, disagree, or both with a claim a writer has made; or to do some research to extend an author's argument and say something new about it. Or you may be assigned a particular genre or kind of writing—a literacy narrative, a profile of a person or place, a visual or textual analysis, or an argumentative paper—and asked to use selections in this book as models of these kinds of writing. We have selected the readings because they are full of important ideas you can react to, either by agreeing or disagreeing, and also because the essays represent excellent examples of good writers at their best.

What follows is a brief guide for writing with *The Norton Reader*. We'll look at knowing your purpose, addressing your audience, finding a subject, determining what genre to employ, using rhetorical strategies, and understanding the writing process.

KNOWING YOUR PURPOSE

Your *purpose* is, put simply, the goal for your writing. What do you want to achieve? What points do you want to make? What idea or cause motivates you to write? Anything you can do to sharpen your thinking and infuse your writing with a clear sense of purpose will be for the better: you will find it easier to stay focused and help your readers see your key point and main ideas about your subject.

What are some common purposes writers have? The authors of the essays in *The Norton Reader* had informing, persuading, entertaining, or expressing as some of their purposes. So, too, your writing will have a primary purpose, usually defined in an assignment by words such as "explain," "describe," "analyze," "argue." Each is a signal about the purpose for your writing.

For instance, if an assignment asks you to *analyze* the persuasiveness of David French's "What Critics Don't Understand about Gun Culture" (p. 893), then your purpose is to explain the claims French makes, examine the evidence he uses to support them, discuss points or perspectives he might have included, and develop a thesis about the reasons for the essay's persuasiveness. If an assignment asks you to *argue* for or against French's claim about gun ownership, then your purpose is to take a side, defending or refuting his claims and using evidence from your own knowledge and from reputable sources to support your argument.

Use these questions to think about your purpose for writing:

- What does the assignment ask you to do? Is the goal to inform readers, entertain them, argue a point, or express an idea or feeling? Beyond a general purpose, what does the assignment require in terms of a specific purpose?

- How does your purpose affect your choice of a subject? What do you know about the subject? How can you find out more about this subject?

- How can you connect to your readers? What will they want or need to know? How do you want them to respond to your writing?

ADDRESSING YOUR AUDIENCE

Just as the authors in *The Norton Reader* aimed their essays at different *audiences*—readers of books, newspapers, magazines, literary journals, and scholarly publications, as well as activists, ordinary citizens, and churchgoers—so you need to imagine your audience as you write. Too wide an audience—"the general public"—and you run the risk of making your essay too diffuse, trying to reach everyone. Too narrow an audience—"my friend Zach"—and you run the risk of being too specific.

How can you imagine an audience of your own? One way is to look around your writing classroom: that's your immediate audience, the people who are taking the course with you and your instructor. Another way is to think about your home community: your family, your neighbors, and the people of your town or city. If you're taking an online class, what do you know about your classmates as a result of web-based discussions or drafts they've shared? Think of your audience as readers like yourself, with some of the same knowledge of the world and some of the same tastes. Consider your audience's range of reference: historical events they have witnessed firsthand, movies and TV shows they know about or have seen, and the books they have read or heard of. Think of them as willing to be convinced by whatever you write, but in need of good evidence.

Inevitably, some writers find that imagining an audience composed only of class members seems too restrictive. That's fine; feel free to invoke another audience, say, a group of people who share a certain passion, perhaps for a team, a sport, a game, or a type of music or film. (But remember to take into account your instructor, who may need some filling in about the special knowledge you share with your audience.)

Use these questions to guide you in thinking about audience:

- What readers are you hoping to reach?

- What information can you assume your readers know? What information do you need to explain?

- In what ways will you need to adjust the style of your writing—the language, tone, sentence structure and complexity, and examples—to meet the needs of your audience?

FINDING A SUBJECT

Like the audience and purpose for your writing, the *subject* of your writing—what you write about—will often be assigned by your instructor. Some assignments are very specific, such as this study question following Stephen King's "On Writing" (p. 383): "Write about a time someone responded to your writing in a way that helped you learn to be a better writer. What kinds of comments and edits did that person make? Why was that response helpful to you?" Other assignments may be more general, such as this writing prompt that follows Scott Russell Sanders's profile of his father, "Under the Influence" (p. 35): "Drawing on your memories of a family member, write an essay about a problem that person had and its effect on your life." This broader assignment requires you to determine the person you wish to discuss, the problem you wish to analyze, and the larger effect the person and problem had on your life.

Some assignments give you even more leeway in choosing a subject, leaving you with the inevitable question "What should I write about?" In this case, write about what you know or care about, drawing on knowledge you've already gleaned about a subject from personal experience, your reading, or research. Your knowledge does not have to be totally new, but your perspective on a subject needs to come from you—a real person writing about a subject that matters.

How do you find what you know or care about? One way is to raise questions about an essay you've read:

- What is the author's main point? Do you agree or disagree with the main point?

- Has the author said enough about the subject? What gaps or omissions do you see, if any?

- Are the author's examples and evidence convincing? If not, why not? Can you provide a more compelling example, additional evidence, or a counterexample?

- Does this reading "speak" to anything else you've read in *The Norton Reader*? Can you explain how this reading connects to the other? Do the readings agree or disagree?

- Is this reading true to your own experience? Has anything like this happened to you, or have you ever observed anything like this?

You can also choose a subject by reflecting on your own experience:

- Has someone you know affected your life in some way—by teaching you, by serving as an example (good or bad), or by changing your attitude?

- Is there a place that you can describe to others, telling them what makes it unique or special to you?

- Is there a subject you feel strongly about, something you believe others need to learn about—for example, a program on your campus or in your neighborhood, a controversial item of national significance, or a matter of global importance?

- Have you had an experience that has taught you something valuable, influenced the way you live, or made you think differently about life, school, work, family, or friends? Readers will be interested in the details of the experience, including how it affected you and what you have learned.

DETERMINING A GENRE

Like the purpose, audience, and subject of your writing, the *genre* of your writing may be prescribed in your instructor's assignment. *The Norton Reader* contains a variety of essay genres. What follows is an explanation of narrative, descriptive, analytic, and argumentative genres, as well as the subcategories within them.

Narrative genres

These genres tell a story through *narrative*, using vivid details about people, events, and conflicts or crises. They also reflect on the meaning of the stories, offering the reader an interpretation or explanation of what occurred. Common narrative genres include the memoir, personal essay, and literacy narrative.

Memoir   Told from the first-person point of view, the *memoir* is an account of important events or people from an author's life. It includes selected details and descriptions that show how the author feels about and remembers the events or people. Often, memoirs are book-length reflections that span a number of years in the author's life. *The Norton Reader* includes several selections from longer memoirs: Tara Westover's remembrance of a classroom lecture during her first year of college from *Educated* (p. 351), Maya Angelou's chapters on her high school graduation and an important boxing match from *I Know Why the Caged Bird Sings* (p. 302 and p. 372), and Langston Hughes's account of a memorable experience in church from *The Big Sea* (p. 809).

Memoirs can also be essay-length reflections on a significant event or person; such memoirs are also considered personal essays. If you are asked to write a memoir for class, it will likely be one of these shorter pieces, perhaps one in which you narrate an event or series of events that helped shaped you or your understanding of yourself.

Another form of autobiographical writing, the *graphic memoir* renders the author's experience in visual and textual form. This form often includes a narrative storyline, dialogue, and drawings that emphasize elements of the story or sometimes provide information not directly available in the written narrative.

In the selection from *Fun Home* (p. 13), Alison Bechdel uses narrative and drawings to show features of the home in which she was reared and to reveal and reflect upon her relationship with her father. When you read graphic memoirs, and if you choose to create your own, pay close attention to the ways in which images and words are connected—and whether one feature of the text provides information not included elsewhere.

Personal essay   Focusing on a significant personal experience in the writer's past, the *personal essay* draws out the meaning as the writer tells the story and reflects on the experience. Sometimes a personal essay is called a *memoir* or *autobiographical essay*. Its key features include a dramatic event or a tension/conflict; vivid details and narration; and an interweaving of narration with reflection on and interpretation of the essayist's experience.

If you are assigned Roxane Gay's "What Fullness Is" (p. 136) or George Orwell's "Shooting an Elephant" (p. 728), you will immediately spot the dramatic event or conflict. For Gay, it is the decision to undergo weight-loss surgery. For Orwell, it is the day when he, a young British official in Burma, must shoot an elephant that has gone "must." Gay introduces the tension in three sentences: "I capitulated to a procedure after more than 15 years of resistance and had a sleeve gastrectomy at the UCLA Ronald Reagan Hospital in January 2018. I told only a few people; I did not tell my family. I felt—in equal parts—hope, defeat, frustration, and disgust" (137). In the remainder of the essay she reflects on how the experience of being obese and of having surgery affected her sense of self, her identity. Orwell builds up to the dramatic moment more slowly, taking us through the thoughts and events that lead to his pulling the trigger. As he tells his story, Orwell reflects on the motivations for his action and reaches a point of insight:

> And it was at this moment, as I stood there with the rifle in my hands, that I first grasped the hollowness, the futility of the white man's dominion in the East. (731)

These two essayists handle the conventions of their personal essays differently, with different narrative styles and different pacing, but they both focus on a significant event and draw out its significance in the course of the essay.

Literacy narrative   A subcategory of the personal essay, the *literacy narrative* focuses on learning to read or write. Like other narrative genres, it uses personal experience, requires vivid details, and gives a clear indication of the narrative's significance.

If you read Frederick Douglass's "Learning to Read" (p. 346) or Benjamin Franklin's "Learning to Write" (p. 389), you will encounter two classic versions of the literacy narrative. For Douglass, a slave, reading was a forbidden, illegal activity, so to learn to read he was "compelled to resort to various stratagems" (346), as he phrases it. Douglass's literacy narrative includes rich details about his life as a slave, the strategies he used to acquire literacy, and the essential value that reading held for someone who did not want to remain "*a slave for life"* (348). For Franklin, a young man trained as a printer, writing became a means to raise himself in his social and professional world, and his narrative explains some of the tactics that allowed him to succeed. As you read Douglass or Franklin, watch for the details they choose to include and the anecdotes they recount as important to their stories. Other literacy narratives in *The Norton Reader* include Tara Westover's "from *Educated*" (p. 351), Gerald Graff's "Hidden Intellectualism" (p. 360), and Stephen King's "On Writing" (p. 383), which illustrate with fascinating, sometimes painful, details the meaning of reading, writing, and education in American culture.

Descriptive genres

These genres use *description* to let the reader know how a person, place, or thing looks, sounds, feels, or maybe even smells. But they do more: they give a dominant impression, interpret a person's actions, offer a reflection on the significance of place, or in some other way put the objective details into a larger framework. Descriptive genres in *The Norton Reader* include the profile of a person, profile of a place, nature and environmental writing, lyric essays, reportage, and humor and satire.

Profile of a person An in-depth exploration of an individual or a group of people, the *profile of a person* uses firsthand knowledge, interviews, and/or research to present its subject. Since readers like to read about interesting subjects, it is sometimes assumed that the person must be interesting beforehand. But really it's the writer who makes the person interesting by discovering special characteristics or qualities through interviews or observation; by finding an interesting angle from which to present the subject; and by including engaging details, anecdotes, or dialogue to enliven the portrait.

Profiles can be freestanding essays or parts of books. Tom Wolfe's "Yeager" (p. 94) is a portrait of the astronaut Chuck Yeager and part of Wolfe's book about the first American astronauts in space, *The Right Stuff*. When you read this essay, you will see that Wolfe does not begin with date of birth, place of birth, parents, and education (though those details eventually make it into the profile). Instead, Wolfe lets us *hear* Yeager's voice by imitating its sound and style. Then Wolfe suggests the importance of Yeager's place in American aviation by describing how every American pilot tries to imitate this man with "the right stuff" (95). The profile features tales about Yeager's daring, often reckless, escapades—even as it narrates the story of how Yeager made history by breaking the sound barrier.

Taté Walker, in "The (Native) American Dream" (p. 538), profiles two indigenous women who are leaders in teaching others to live more sustainably. Monycka Snowbird raises her own animals and grows her own plants, working with community organizations to educate others on urban food production and indigenous food systems. Karen Ducheneaux works with her community to build sustainable housing: ecodomes and straw bale buildings powered by renewable resources. Walker quotes these women and emphasizes the ways in which they are both drawing from their traditional roots as indigenous people. Although Walker shows how her subjects are similar, she also shows the different challenges they face with Snowbird living in an urban environment and Ducheneaux living in a rural area.

Profile of a place   Places can also become the focus of a profile. The features of a *profile of a place* involve discovering the special characteristics or qualities of the place; finding an interpretive framework in which to present it; and including engaging details, anecdotes, or dialogue to enliven the essay. Since places can't speak, the essayist must speak for them and say enough about them to make them come alive.

Essayists recreate places through description. Ian Frazier, in "Take the F" (p. 103), uses a subway line (the F Sixth Avenue Local) to locate his Brooklyn neighborhood on the New York City grid, but he also engages the five senses—sight, sound, smell, taste, and touch—to give non–New Yorkers a feel for the place.

E. B. White describes a place far different from Brooklyn, New York. In "Once More to the Lake" (p. 120) he recalls a camp in Maine where he spent time both as a child and as an adult, using lists such as the following one:

> . . . the fade-proof lake, the woods unshatterable, the pasture with the sweetfern and the juniper forever and ever, summer without end; this was the background, and the life along the shore was the design, the cottages with their innocent and tranquil design, their tiny docks with the flagpole and the American flag floating against the white clouds in the blue sky, the little paths over the roots of the trees leading from camp to camp and the paths leading back to the outhouses and the can of lime for sprinkling, and at the souvenir counters at the store the miniature birch-bark canoes and the post cards that showed things looking a little better than they looked. (122)

He also uses comparisons and contrasts to show how this place has changed and how it has remained the same over the course of decades.

If a profile includes both person and place, as White's essay does, it is what the writer Anne Fadiman calls a "Character in Context" piece. Many times, we learn about someone by seeing that person in a characteristic space; the place defines the person, the person defines the place. Judith Ortiz Cofer's "More Room" (p. 86) shows readers Cofer's grandmother's house, *la casa de Mamá*. Yet her profile is also about her grandmother, whose "room is the heart of the house" (86). As Cofer describes the changes in the house—and how they came to be—readers learn more about the character of her grandmother.

Nature and environmental writing   This type of writing can refer generally to any composition about nature and can be a profile of a place or some part of the environment, such as plants or animals. (Think of *nature and environmental writing* as profiling not a person but the desert, a bear, a dragonfly, or a weed.) You will find some of these essays in the "Nature and Environment" and "Where We Live, What We Live For" chapters of this book.

In "Under the Snow" (p. 443) John McPhee focuses on a wildlife biologist, Gary Alt, who studies bears; as he describes Alt's research, McPhee includes many scientific facts about the life cycle of bears, including their breeding and feeding practices, their natural habitat, and hibernation patterns. In "Joyas Voladoras" (p. 435) Brian Doyle, too, writes about parts of the natural world. But Doyle's purpose is to consider the hearts of birds and mammals and their metaphorical significance, including the human heart with its capacity to be "bruised and scarred, scored and torn, repaired by time and will, patched by force of character" (437).

Many kinds of writing about nature and the environment in *The Norton Reader* raise questions about science, human nature, and threats to the environment and its inhabitants. Look for them in Terry Tempest Williams's "The Clan of One-Breasted Women" (p. 469), Sandra Steingraber's "Tune of the Tuna Fish" (p. 476), Alan Lightman's "Our Place in the Universe" (p. 490), Cormac Cullinan's "If Nature Had Rights" (p. 549), Elizabeth Kolbert's "The Siege of Miami" (p. 512), and Edward Abbey's "The Great American Desert" (p. 455).

Lyric essays   Often meditations on topics or ideas, *lyric essays* are like poems: They include close attention to language and frequently used literary elements such as metaphor, simile, repetition, attention to sound, and personification. They may use sections or may be organized by association rather than by employing logical traditions. Some lyric essayists also use nonstandard punctuation or fragments. For example, Kathy Fish often eliminates verbs in her lyric piece "Collective Nouns for Humans in the Wild" (p. 425), helping readers focus on groups of people and the sometimes surprising names associated with them.

Reportage   Although it often includes analysis and evaluation and makes an argument, the primary purpose of *reportage* is to relate information. *The Norton Reader* focuses on reports that inform readers about a particular topic or issue, and there are many essays that do just that. In "The Siege of Miami" (p. 512), an example of both reportage and environmental writing, Elizabeth Kolbert reports on recurrent flooding in South Florida and local efforts to deal with its effects. In the process, she educates readers on the larger issue of sea level rise due to climate change.

Humor and satire   Both of these approaches use hyperbole and far-fetched comparisons or descriptions to make a larger point. Sometimes the point of *humor* and *satire* is to show the abuses of a government or political policy, as in the case of Jonathan Swift's "A Modest Proposal" (p. 711), which offers that the poor sell their children as food to the rich to fix Ireland's depressed economy. Other times the purpose is to show a different kind of irony, as Sloane Crosley does in "Wheels Up" (p. 207) when she writes an irreverent essay that positions a woman in a wheelchair as the antagonist. Crosley pokes fun at social conventions, raising questions about typical behaviors and stereotypes that underpin urban social interactions.

Humor and satire can be used in any genre of writing. Mark Twain uses humor and satire in his speech "Advice to Youth" (p. 627), both providing advice and undermining it: "Always obey your parents, when they are present" (628).

Some writers use self-deprecating humor, as Nancy Mairs and JJ Goode do in their personal essays "On Being a Cripple" (p. 148) and "Single-Handed Cooking" (p. 240), respectively, when they describe the serious yet sometimes humorous challenges of living with a disability. Such uses of humor can make a reader more receptive to a writer or speaker, showing that even those addressing serious topics can have a good laugh.

Humor and satire often push the limits of what is acceptable or expected in communication. Since what's funny to one person might be offensive to others, if you use humor in your writing, be aware of potential consequences. Humor can make audiences more receptive to you, but it can also make audiences less receptive if you unintentionally offend someone you're trying to persuade. Of course, writers of satire often intentionally ridicule and shame with the purpose of improvement or change. Still, having your teacher, classmates, or friends read drafts of your humorous and satirical writing can help you gauge responses, making sure your humor has the intended effect.

Analytic genres

Genres that engage in *analysis* carefully and methodically examine a text, an image, a cultural object, or a social trend by breaking it into parts, closely reading its components, and noting how the parts work in relation to the whole. In *The Norton Reader* you will find examples of reflection, textual analysis, visual analysis, and cultural analysis.

Reflection   A form of personal analysis, *reflection* explores the ways in which an experience, practice, idea, or event relates to you and what you can learn from it. Reflection can be done in response to your reading, a past event or series of events, or something you or someone else has done. For example, your teacher might ask you to reflect on your writing process for a specific assignment, to think about what you learned from the process and what you might do differently for the next assignment. Or your teacher might ask you to write a cover letter for a final portfolio of your work for the entire term; in this type of reflection, you might consider why you chose the pieces you did, how you revised those assignments, what you did well, and what you could have done differently. You might also be asked to write a reflection essay on a selection you've read for class and to consider how you made sense of the author's position or ideas in the context of your own experience, ideas, or other reading.

Reflection is also a part of writing a personal essay or a literacy narrative, and you will see many examples of reflection in *The Norton Reader*, especially in "Home and Family" and "Education." In "Under the Influence" (p. 35), Scott Russell Sanders reflects on the effects of having an alcoholic father, "trying to understand the corrosive mixture of helplessness, responsibility, and shame"

(36). In "Salvation" (p. 809), Langston Hughes reflects on a childhood experience in church, contemplating why he pretended to have an experience he didn't have. In "On Being a Cripple" (p. 148), Nancy Mairs reflects on her life with multiple sclerosis. In each of these examples, the author chooses one aspect of experience and seeks to make sense of it through writing, offering readers an interpretation of that experience.

At times, reflection is also a part of writing an argument. In "Is Google Making Us Stupid?" (p. 556), Nicholas Carr starts by reflecting on his own experience of reading online before moving to accounts of other people's experiences and studies of the effects of online reading. Reflection provides a context for the argument and helps establish the author's purpose and ethos or character.

Textual analysis   Also called *close reading*, *textual analysis* focuses on written words. It examines words and phrases for explicit and implicit meanings; it looks for similes (comparisons using *like* or *as*) and metaphors (comparisons without explicit connectors) to reveal patterns of association and meanings; and it interprets the whole text on the basis of these methodical, individual observations. The *text* may be anything from the Bible or Koran, to poems and novels, to ads, billboards, or official memos. In "If Nature Had Rights" (p. 549) Cormac Cullinan considers the importance of close reading and textual analysis in interpreting laws—and creating new ones.

Visual analysis   Like textual analysis, *visual analysis* looks for explicit and implicit meanings; searches for patterns of association; and interprets the whole object on the basis of these methodical, individual observations. Instead of a written text, visual analysis focuses on an image, a photograph, a painting, or another phenomenon. Some visual analyses have as their goal the explanation of the image itself. In "Song Schematics" (p. 781), Michael Hamad creates a visual essay to analyze a sensory process: listening to music. He arranges words and symbols on the page to analyze the process of listening to a Phish song—and his essay invites a visual analysis by readers. In *The Norton Reader* you will find essays that combine textual and visual analysis or that use images to trigger both kinds of analysis. (Watch for essays that include photographs, drawings, graphs, and other visual material.)

Cultural analysis   This genre, called both *cultural analysis* and *cultural critique*, takes an object, trend, fad, or other phenomenon as the subject of its analysis. It uses the strategies of textual and visual analysis described above, adding personal response and research, if desirable, to explain and interpret. Examples of this form appear in the chapter "Cultural Analysis."

What kinds of cultural objects and trends do essayists analyze? Almost anything and everything, it seems. Malcolm Gladwell in "Java Man" (p. 197) chooses caffeine as his subject, Margaret Atwood uses the form of a lyric essay to explore "The Female Body" (p. 203), and the scholar Henry Louis Gates Jr. analyzes hairstyles popular in his youth (p. 213)—how they were created; how movie stars, singers, and black icons popularized them; and why the styles remain so important for him. Other essayists analyze social practices. For example, Barbara Kingsolver takes sexual harassment and systems of patriarchal power as her topic in "#MeToo Isn't Enough" (p. 225).

Argumentative genres

Forms of modern *argument* have their roots in classical Greece and Rome—that is, they go back at least 2,500 years. The Greek philosopher Aristotle held that there were really only two essential parts of an argument: (1) the statement of the case and (2) the proof of the case. But he conceded that in practice most orators added two other parts: an introduction and a conclusion.

Roman rhetoricians like Quintilian refined and expanded this simple Aristotelian approach to include five or six parts:

(1) *exordium*: the introduction

(2) *narratio*: the statement or exposition of the case under discussion

(3) *divisio*: the outline of the points or steps in the argument

(4) *confirmatio*: the proof of the case (sometimes called *probatio*)

(5) *confutatio*: the refutation of opposing arguments

(6) *peroratio*: the conclusion

Yet Roman rhetoricians also acknowledged that, for any given argument, orators might want to omit parts. (They might, for example, omit *divisio* if the steps of the argument were simple.) And orators would often rearrange the parts of their speeches. They might, for instance, refute an opponent's arguments before advancing their own case.

Unless you participate in a debating society, you—like most modern college students—won't see this formal version of classical argument very often. In "The Declaration of Independence" (p. 702), however, Thomas Jefferson used the tactics of classical rhetoric as revived in the eighteenth century. Today, we hear its legacy in public speeches and see traces of it in newspaper editorials. The Greek and Roman philosophers weren't so much prescribing a genre as they were describing common argumentative practices. It makes sense that, if you want to argue your case effectively, you need to introduce it, outline the key points, present your evidence, and refute your opponent's position—all the steps they described. You will find these steps in the argumentative genres considered below: evaluations and reviews, proposals, op-eds, and speeches.

Evaluation and review   These genres combine analysis and argument, using clear criteria as the basis for both *evaluation* and *review*. When you write an evaluation, you make and support an argument about quality, whether something is good or bad, effective or ineffective. The criteria the author uses depend on the subject being analyzed. For example, in evaluating a website, you might focus on design and usability. Is it easy to navigate? Do the organization and design fit the content of the site? Are the visuals appropriate to the subject? In reviewing a restaurant, you might consider the quality of the food and service, the value and price, and the atmosphere and décor. In "Be Nice" (p. 630), Matt Dinan uses Aristotle's theories to evaluate "niceness" as a social virtue.

Proposal   Evaluation and review often provide the groundwork for a *proposal*. A proposal includes a clear statement of what is being proposed, a plan for action, and an explanation of desired outcomes. Your instructor may ask you to write a proposal for a long paper or project that you will undertake. If so, you will likely do a review of other essays, books, or articles on your topic before proposing your own project, one that will be different from the literature you've reviewed. Another kind of proposal you might be assigned is to define a problem and its effects and then to propose a workable solution or approach to that problem.

Op-ed   This genre, which is located "opposite" the "editorial" page of a newspaper, focuses on issues of public interest and encourages ordinary citizens to contribute their perspectives, opinions, and arguments to the public debate. *Op-eds* begin with a "hook"—a link to a recent event or news article that grabs readers' attention—as the introduction or lead. Specific features, or conventions, include a forthright statement of position, evidence in support, often a counterargument or rebuttal of the opposition, and sometimes a formal conclusion.

Dan Barber's "What Farm-to-Table Got Wrong" (p. 267) features most of these conventions. Barber begins by setting a seasonal scene: crowds descending on a local farmers' market and food co-op for fresh produce. He follows with his argument: "For all its successes, farm-to-table has not, in any fundamental way, reworked the economic and political forces that dictate how our food is grown and raised." He then provides evidence for his argument that "Big Food is getting bigger, not smaller" (267). Barber continues with a proposal to work with farmers who are caring for the soil by rotating crops. In doing so, consumers would need to diversify their diets, eating the crops farmers grow for the health of the soil.

Speech   Because *speeches* derive directly, if also distantly, from the classical tradition of argument, they often show its formal features. Many speechwriters introduce the issue at hand, state their position, offer evidence in support and counterarguments against, and sum up—sometimes with a high rhetorical flourish. These modern tactics are based on the older classical conventions.

Elizabeth Cady Stanton, the nineteenth-century feminist, shows her knowledge of American public oratory in "Declaration of Sentiments and Resolutions" (p. 708). Stanton's declaration, presented at the first U.S. women's rights convention, is modeled on Thomas Jefferson's seminal American "The Declaration of Independence" (p. 702). A century later, Martin Luther King Jr., one of the great civil rights leaders and orators of modern America, continues the tradition in "Letter from Birmingham Jail" (p. 739). He makes the case for civil disobedience, taking his audience through the steps of his thinking and quietly refuting those who disagree. It is no coincidence that these important American speeches and documents use the formal conventions of argument:

in so doing, the speakers demonstrate their education, ability, and right to debate the pressing issues of their day.

As you read arguments in various chapters of *The Norton Reader*, consider where and why authors use conventions of argument and where and why they turn to conventions often associated with other genres. In the end, the goal is to make an effective argument, to convince the reader of the validity of your evidence, or urge the listener to take a prescribed course of action.

If you have some leeway in choosing the genre in which you will write, consider what genre best fits your purpose, audience, and subject:

- What goal do you have for your writing? What genre is most appropriate for that goal?

- Who will read your writing? What genre will best convey the point of your writing to your readers?

- What are you writing about? What genre is well suited to your subject?

To gain more understanding of these genres, read plenty of examples, analyze the forms and strategies their authors use, and then try out a genre on your own. There's no better way to understand how a genre works than to try your hand at writing it.

USING RHETORICAL STRATEGIES

As you plan your essay, you will want to think about the *rhetorical strategies* by which you will present your ideas and evidence to readers. These strategies, sometimes called *rhetorical modes* or *techniques*, help a writer organize evidence, arrange facts into a sequence, and provide clusters of information necessary for conveying a purpose or an argument. You might choose to *analyze* the cause of an outcome; *compare* one thing to another; *classify* your facts into categories; *define* a key term; *describe* a person, place, or phenomenon; *explain* how a process works; or *narrate* a pertinent event or experience.

Sometimes, the writing assignment that your instructor gives will determine the strategy: For example, an assignment to compare Matt de la Peña's "Why We Shouldn't Shield Children from Darkness" (p. 768) with Kate DiCamillo's "Why Children's Books Should Be a Little Sad" (p. 771) will require that you use a compare/contrast strategy. Your teacher might ask you to *argue* against or for sadness in children's literature. Or you might be asked to *narrate* an experience of reading or watching a movie as a child and *describe* the effects of the sad moments in that text or film.

Many essays use a mix of strategies. You might want to define a key term in an opening paragraph, narrate a story to make a point in the next paragraph, and analyze cause and effect in yet another. Except for very short pieces, most writers use several rhetorical strategies in an essay, choosing the ones that best fit their material.

Following are some rhetorical strategies that you will encounter in *The Norton Reader* and that you will want to use in your own writing.

Describing

When writers *describe* a person, place, or thing, they indicate what it looks like and often how it feels, smells, sounds, or tastes. As a strategy, describing involves showing rather than telling, helping readers see rather than giving them a formal definition, making the subject come alive rather than remaining abstract. When you describe, you want to choose precise verbs, specific nouns, vivid adjectives—unless your subject is dullness itself.

As a writer, you will use description in many kinds of assignments: in profiles of people and places to provide a key to their essence, in visual analysis to reveal the crucial features of a painting or photograph, in cultural critique to highlight the features of the object or phenomenon you will analyze, and in scientific lab reports to give details of an experiment. Almost no essay can be written without at least some description, and many essays rely on this strategy as a fundamental technique. In *The Norton Reader* you will find study questions in almost every section that ask you to describe: "Describe a 'treasure' someone found and held on to," "Take a flower or tree and write a close-up description of it," "Describe some particular experience that raises a large social question"—these are just a few examples of writing assignments that ask for description.

Narrating

Telling stories may be the most fundamental of all rhetorical strategies. We use *narration* to tell stories about ourselves, about our families, and about friends and neighbors. We tell stories to make a point, to illustrate an argument, to offer evidence or counterevidence, and sometimes even to substitute for an argument. As these uses suggest, narrating appears in many genres: from memoirs and personal essays, to op-eds and formal speeches. Narrating is basic to essay writing.

As you plan a paragraph or segment of narration, think about sequence: the order in which the events occurred (chronological order) or an order in which the events might be most dramatically presented (reverse chronological order or the present moment with flashback). Often, sequential order is easier for the reader to comprehend, but sometimes beginning *in medias res* (at the present moment *in the middle of things*) and then flashing back to the past creates a more compelling story. Consider incorporating time markers—not only dates, but also sequential phrases: early one evening, later that night, the next morning. And use transitions and transitional words: first, then, meanwhile, later, finally. When you've finished narrating your event or episode, reread it and ask: What have I left out that the reader needs to know? What might I omit because the reader doesn't need to know it?

Exemplifying

This strategy involves a main idea and either an extended example or a series of examples that illustrate—or *exemplify*—that idea. In "Superfoods Are a Marketing Ploy" (p. 271), for instance, Marion Nestle uses the example of blueberries to illustrate her argument. Often, exemplification is combined with other rhetorical modes of development, as is the case in Henry Louis Gates Jr.'s essay "In the Kitchen" (p. 213). Much of Gates's essay involves narration and description as he reflects on different hairstyles, processes, and products in African American culture. Yet he also provides numerous examples—especially of African American celebrities—in order to illustrate his ideas.

Classifying and dividing

This strategy involves either *classifying* things by putting them into groups or *dividing* up a large block into smaller units. While this strategy might seem better suited to a biology lab than to a writing class, it works well for organizing facts that seem chaotic or for handling big topics that at first glance seem overwhelming. Classifying and dividing allow the writer—and the reader—to get control of a potentially unwieldy topic by breaking it into smaller units of analysis. For example, in "The End of Forgetting" (p. 565), Sherry Turkle divides her piece into sections, showing human beings interacting with different forms of technology.

You will find that classifying and dividing is helpful in writing all genres of analysis: textual, visual, and cultural. You will also find that it can help in argumentative genres because it enables you, as a writer or speaker, to break down a complex argument into parts or to group pieces of evidence into similar categories.

Explaining or analyzing a process

With this rhetorical strategy, the writer *explains* how something is done: how to write, how to Dumpster dive, or how to toss a pizza. Sometimes, writers use this strategy in historical essays to show or *analyze* how something was done in the past. As these examples suggest, explaining a process can be useful in a range of genres: from a literacy narrative that explains learning to read, to a cultural analysis that offers a method for dealing with harassment, to a reflection that explores a symbolic way to make a religious tradition more inclusive.

To make a process accessible to the reader, you will need to identify the main steps or stages and then explain them in order, one after the other. Sequence matters. In preparing to write a paragraph explaining a process, it might help to list the steps as a flowchart or as a cookbook recipe—and then turn your list into a paragraph (or more) of fully elaborated prose.

Comparing and contrasting

Comparisons look for similarities between things; *contrasts* look for differences. In most uses of this rhetorical strategy, you will want to consider both similarities and differences—that is, you will want to compare *and* contrast. That's because most things worth comparing have something in common, even if they also have significant differences. You may end up finding more similarities than differences, or vice versa, but when using this strategy, think about both.

Comparison-contrast may be used for a single paragraph or for an entire essay. It tends to be set up in one of two ways: block or point-by-point. In the block technique, the writer gives all the information about one item and then follows with all the information about the other. Think of it as giving all the A's, then all the B's. Usually, the order of the information is the same for both. In the point-by-point technique, the writer focuses on specific points of comparison, alternating A, B, A, B, A, B, and so on until the main points have been covered.

Comparing and contrasting is an excellent strategy to use in writing a report, making an argument in an op-ed, or giving a speech to persuade your audience to take a specific course of action. You can set forth the pros and cons of different programs, political policies, or courses of action, leading up to the recommendation you endorse and believe is the more effective.

Defining

This rhetorical strategy involves telling your reader what something is—and what it is not. *Defining* enables you to make sure that both you and your readers understand what you mean by a key term. It may lead to redefining a common term to have a more precise meaning or giving nuance to a term that is commonly used too broadly. Defining and redefining are useful strategies in argumentative writing; they help the writer reshape the thinking of the audience and see a concept in a new light.

This strategy is not as simple as looking up a word in a dictionary, though often that is a good place to begin; you may discover that a word or term meant something 100 years ago that it no longer means or that its meaning varies from one context to another. Citing one of these definitions can help in composing your essay. But defining as a rhetorical strategy may also include giving examples or providing descriptions.

Analyzing cause and effect

Focusing on *causes* helps a writer think about why something happened; focusing on *effects* helps a writer think about what might happen or has happened already. Cause is oriented toward the future; effect looks to the past. But you can use this strategy by working in either direction: from present to future, or from present to the past.

If you were writing about global warming and intending to show its harmful effects, you might lay out your evidence in this sequence:

Cause → leads to → these effects.

If you were writing about a student's actions and trying to identify the pressures that led to those actions, you might reverse the direction:

Effects ← are the result of ← these causes.

Analyzing a cause (or causes) is a crucial strategy for genres such as cultural analysis and op-eds. But you can also use this strategy in a personal essay or reflection, where you might analyze the effects of a childhood experience on your later life, or in a profile of a person, where you might seek the sources (the causes) of the person's adult personality or achievements.

Making an argument

This strategy requires you take a position on—to *make an argument* about—a topic of debate. That is, you need to choose a topic and make a claim about which reasonable people might disagree. Once you take a position on the question or issue at hand, you need to support that position and answer potential objections from those who would disagree with you. Support for an argument can come in many forms—quotations from experts, statistics, facts—but all these forms of evidence must be interpreted, not simply dropped in. Often, after making an argument, a writer proposes a better alternative.

In "What Farm-to-Table Got Wrong" (p. 267), Dan Barber argues that the farm-to-table movement has not "reworked the economic and political forces that dictate how our food is grown and raised" (267). He provides support for his claim through statistics and through expert opinion by interviewing a farmer. He proposes, instead of farm-to-table practices that he once supported, a diversified diet and deeper understanding of how agriculture works.

STRATEGIES FOR WRITING

If you were to watch a writer at work, either yourself or someone else, you might see that the task of writing often occurs in stages, which is often referred to as the *writing process*. You generate ideas, write a draft, revise the draft (sometimes once, often many times), edit (make sentence- or word-level changes), and finally, proofread (check to see that the grammar, spelling, and formatting are correct). Along the way, you develop a main point and find examples and evidence to support that point. The next few pages will walk you through these different stages of the writing process.

Generate ideas

For many people, the hardest part of writing is looking at the blank page or empty screen. What can you say? How can you even get started? Sometimes your task is made easier when your instructor gives you a specific assignment, asks a particular question, or uses one of the prompts included in *The Norton Reader*. Here's the writing prompt that follows Nancy Mairs's "On Being a Cripple" (p. 148):

> Mairs deliberately chooses to call herself a "cripple." Select a person or group that deliberately chooses its own name or description and explain in an essay the rationale behind the choice. (158)

You can respond to this assignment by examining your own memory for stories you've heard, incidents you've witnessed, or people you've met, or you may need to do some research in order to have enough to say. Use one or more of the following techniques to mine your memory or generate ideas:

- Freewrite for several minutes to discover what you already know and think about a subject.

- Group or cluster related ideas.

- Read some articles about the subject. Take notes on what you read.

- Ask questions about the subject, starting with *who, what, when, why,* and *how.*

Different writers develop different ways of finding their material, so experiment with a variety of techniques until you discover one or more that work for you.

Develop a main point or thesis

Most writing you will be assigned in college courses requires a central claim, often called a *thesis*. Most papers contain a thesis statement, often stated in the introduction, that tells readers the main point that will be supported, developed, and extended in the body of the paper.

Sometimes the thesis statement will be an arguable claim supported by evidence, such as Jane McGonigal's claims in "Be a Gamer, Save the World" (p. 604) that computer games "consistently fulfill genuine human needs that the real world fails to satisfy" and that "they may prove to be a key resource for solving some of our most pressing real-world problems" (604).

At other times, the main point of your writing won't be stated so plainly. Instead, it will be implied or evident to the reader, but you won't be trying to argue a claim with evidence. If you're writing in a narrative or descriptive genre, for example, you'll have a main point, of course, particularly if you're writing a historical narrative or creating a profile of a person or place. You will make a claim about the reasons something happened or about the reasons for a person's or place's distinctive characteristics, as Scott Russell Sanders does in "Under the Influence" (p. 35):

> My father drank. He drank as a gut-punched boxer gasps for breath, as a starving dog gobbles food—(35)

Those two sentences, in which Sanders uses similes to describe his father, paint an unflattering picture of his character. The reader can assume that Sanders does not look favorably upon drinking to excess.

Gather evidence

What counts as adequate *evidence* for your claim or thesis? If you're writing an argument, you might use interviews, previously published studies, facts, and statistics. Quoting authorities on the topic can also lend support to your argument.

In other kinds of writing, evidence is drawn more often from personal experience than from secondary sources. In a literacy narrative, for example, the evidence will be in the examples and details of the story you tell about a formative time in your education. In a profile of a person, the evidence will also take the form of examples—the descriptive details about the person's personality, accomplishments, talents, weaknesses, looks, and behavior; anecdotes or stories about the person's life; or testimony from people who've observed the person closely. Evidence is also often drawn directly from reading. In a textual analysis, the evidence will be examples that demonstrate the text's structure, style, and language.

Organize your ideas

How you *organize your ideas* in a piece of writing depends to a large extent on your genre and purpose. Jose Antonio Vargas organizes "My Life as an Undocumented Immigrant" (p. 50) as a chronological memoir, narrating his story of leaving the Philippines when he was twelve and showing his time growing up in the United States, first being unaware he was an undocumented immigrant and then living with the fear of being found out, even as he worked hard and established his journalism career. He covers eighteen years of his life—starting with his mother putting him on a plane in the Philippines and ending with a call to his mother, asking for details of that "goodbye" nearly eighteen years earlier. Rebecca Solnit organizes "How to Be a Writer" (p. 402) in the form of a list. She begins each item on the list in bold text, allowing readers to skim the basic advice but also to read each paragraph for more detailed information.

For many of the essays you write in college—often arguments or analyses, you will use the familiar format of an introduction, body, and conclusion, with separate paragraphs in the body for each major piece of evidence. The introduction often connects your ideas to what your readers already know and seeks to interest them in what you have to say. In the body of an essay, you may want to place your most compelling piece of evidence first, or you may want it to come last to tie matters up for the reader. (But don't hide your best bit of evidence by placing it in the middle.) In the conclusion, you try to wrap things up, finish your line of reasoning, and send your readers off with a final thought.

Write multiple drafts

Even the most experienced writers know they can't do everything at once: find or invent material, assess its usefulness, arrange it in paragraphs, and write it out in well-formed sentences. If you try to produce a good essay at one sitting, in a single draft, you are likely to thin out your material, lock yourself into a structure that may not work and that you don't have time to change, and write sentences that won't fully convey your meaning or intention. In the end, writing a few drafts—in short periods spaced over more than a day—will produce a better essay, one that is thoughtful and deserving of a respectable grade. Here are some tips for drafting in stages:

- Get started by composing a rough draft or small sections of a draft. Don't feel obliged to start with the introduction and write straight through to the conclusion. If you don't know where to begin, write a section you know you want to include, then move to another. As you compose, you will begin to find out what you mean, what is important to your argument or your story, what is missing, and what needs to be revised. Think of composing a rough draft as a way of discovering what you want to say.

- If you get stuck, try focused freewriting. That is, write all you can in response to a particular point or about a particular idea, not stopping for five minutes. After you're done, read what you've written, looking for your thoughts on the subject. You may have come up with key notions or put yourself in touch with useful ideas.

- If you're writing an argument or analysis, write a single paragraph for each key piece of evidence you have to support your thesis. Later on you can refine these paragraphs, combining some and breaking up others.

- At any point in this process, print out a clean version of your draft, read it through, and make changes. Add to, subtract from, rearrange, and revise the parts of your essay.

Acknowledge the words and ideas of others

Your writing should reflect your own thinking, of course, but you'll often incorporate the ideas and actual words of others. Synthesizing and citing the work of others will show your readers that you have consulted reputable sources and will make readers more open to your argument. It may help you to think of anything you write as part of a dialogue you are having with other writers and scholars; just be sure to credit the other writers and scholars whose words and ideas you borrow, so your readers can follow the dialogue and know who said what.

When you cite information from another source in your writing, you must credit the source. First, give other authors credit by acknowledging their work in your text. If you cite someone's exact words, put them in quotation marks, or, if you quote more than four lines, indent them without quotation marks. Tell your readers where you got the words by including the author's name in your text and putting the page number of the book or article in parentheses right after the quote. Here is an example of a direct quotation with appropriate MLA citation:

According to Nestle, "No one food makes a diet healthful" (271).

If you paraphrase a source, that is, if you use another person's idea but not the exact words, you still need to cite the source of that idea, even though you have expressed it in your own words. Here is an example of a paraphrase:

Nestle, a nutritionist, argues that people should eat a variety of healthy, minimally processed foods, and she critiques marketers and food producers who claim some foods are Superfoods (271).

At the end of your paper on a separate page, list all the sources you have quoted and paraphrased. Many style guides provide directions for formatting source material. The guide used most frequently in English classes is the *MLA Handbook*, published by the Modern Language Association. At the end of each essay, we have included an MLA citation so that you can easily cite the essays you've used in your paper. These citations reflect the 2016 guidelines in the eighth edition of the handbook.

Sometimes writers in a hurry are tempted to absorb others' writing wholesale into their papers. This is *plagiarism*. Plagiarism is unethical because it involves the theft of another writer's words and ideas; in college courses, it is a guarantee of failure when discovered. Avoid plagiarizing at all costs. If you have fallen behind on a writing assignment, tell your instructor. You will often find that teachers will accept a late submission, and even if you are graded down for submitting the paper late, that is better than using others' ideas and words without attribution.

Get responses and revise

Although writers can and often do compose and *revise* alone, we all need helpful *responses*, whether from professional editors, classmates, or friends. Many writing classes encourage that process, teaching students to draft and revise independently but also enabling them to put less-than-final drafts forward for responses from the instructor and fellow students. Examples and arguments that seem clear to the writer may seem forced or exaggerated to another reader. In peer groups, listen to readers who disagree with you, who find your position slanted, overstated, or not fully convincing. Be responsive to their comments, and qualify interpretations or further explain points that they do not understand.

Here are some all-purpose questions that you can use to review a draft on your own or in a peer group. Whether you're talking with classmates face-to-face in small groups or responding by writing electronically, the questions should probably be asked in the order below, since they move from larger elements to smaller ones.

Introduction   Treat the introduction as a promise by asking, "Does this essay keep the promises the introduction makes?" If it doesn't, either the introduction or the essay needs to be revised. Try to determine where the problem lies: Is the introduction off track? Do any of the paragraphs wander off topic? Does the introduction promise an organization that isn't followed?

Content   Does this essay include enough material? As you read your own work and that of your classmates, look for examples and details that transmit meaning and engage your interest, understanding, and imagination. Check for adequate and persuasive evidence and multiple illustrative examples that clarify main points. If you or your readers think you need more evidence, examples, or information, revise accordingly.

Evidence and source material If the paper is an argument or analysis, do you interpret the material clearly and connect examples to the main argument? Your essay, and those you read as a peer reviewer, should specify the meanings of the examples you use; don't expect the examples to speak for themselves. A case in point is the use of quotations. How many are there? How necessary are they? How well are they integrated? What analysis or commentary follows each? Watch for quotations that are simply dropped in, without enough introduction or "placing" so that the reader can understand their significance. Quotations should be well integrated, clearly explaining who is speaking, where the voice is coming from, and what to attend to.

Organization and transitions Are the main and supporting points of this essay well organized? Writing puts readers in possession of material in a temporal order: that is, readers read from start to finish. Sometimes material that appears near the end of an essay might work better near the beginning; sometimes material that appears near the beginning might better be postponed. Pay attention to transitions between and within paragraphs; if they are unclear, the difficulty may lie in the organization of the material.

Tone Is the tone of the essay appropriate for its purpose and its audience? Whether the tone is lighthearted, serious, reasoned, funny, enraged, thoughtful, or anything else, it needs to be appropriate to the purpose of the essay and sensitive to the expectations of the audience. Be aware of how formal your writing should be and whether contractions, abbreviations, and slang are acceptable.

Sentences Which sentences unfold smoothly and which sentences might cause readers to stumble? If working in a group, ask your classmates to help you rephrase a sentence or write the thought in new words. Remember, you're trying to reach readers just like your peers, so take their questions and reactions seriously.

Learning to be a responsive reader of essays in *The Norton Reader* can teach you to respond helpfully to the essays of peer writers in your composition class—and to improve your own. Large and small elements of the composing process are reciprocal. Learn to work back and forth among wholes and parts, sections and paragraphs, introductions and conclusions. As shape and meaning come together, you can begin to refine smaller elements: sentences, phrases, specific words. You can qualify your assertions, complicate your generalizations, and tease out the implications of your examples.

Edit, proofread, and format the final draft

After you have revised the structure of your writing, you should devote time to editing and proofreading. This work is best done after giving the paper a rest and coming to it afresh. You may be tempted to move directly to the proofreading stage, thus shortchanging the larger, more important revision work described above. So long as the larger elements of an essay need repair, it's too soon to work on the smaller ones, so save the tinkering for last. When you're satisfied with the overall shape of your essay, turn to the work of tightening your writing by eliminating unnecessary repetition and awkward phrases; correcting grammar, punctuation, and spelling; and putting your work in its final form. Be sure you know what style and format your work should take, be it that of an academic paper with set margins, double-spacing, and a works cited page, or some other format. Ask your instructor if you are unsure about any of these, and make the necessary changes. Then, like other writers, you will need to stop—not because there isn't more to be done but because you have other things to do.

THE NORTON READER
Fifteenth Edition

1 HOME AND FAMILY

Home is the place where, when you have to go there,
They have to take you in.
—ROBERT FROST

Many readers will be familiar with these lines from Robert Frost's poem "The Death of the Hired Man," but some might not know the full narrative of Frost's poem. Silas, "the hired man," had over the years exploited his position working for his employers, coming and going to his own advantage, often leaving his employment when his help was most needed, and then returning when he was near death. Silas had a brother, but he did not return to his biological family when he was about to die. Frost's poem, like the essays here, helps readers consider the nature of home and family. Is there anyone who has "to take you in"?

The writers in this chapter explore an array of experiences and ideas. Joan Didion and Chang-rae Lee ponder what it means to return after leaving one's family home. Alison Bechdel contemplates how family and physical homes are connected. Several writers consider what we inherit from family members—Didion reflects on ways of interacting; Lee on methods of cooking; Durga Chew-Bose on physical features; and Scott Russell Sanders on tendencies toward addiction. Writers Jose Antonio Vargas and Viet Thanh Nguyen also question how we determine or define home: Is home your country of origin, where you live, or where you have citizenship? Who determines the answer to that question? What are the effects of growing up in a homeland that doesn't legally recognize you as a citizen? And Lars Eighner asks what becomes important when you have no physical home and your dog is your family.

The readings in this chapter are personal essays, the authors' first-person accounts of their own experiences of home and family. Even though the genre is the same, the strategies—form, tone, organization, focus—that the authors use differ. In "Fun Home," cartoonist Bechdel, for example, tells readers about her family home and father in a graphic memoir, using drawings and references to Greek mythology. Journalist Vargas, in contrast, gives a direct chronological account of leaving the Philippines when he was twelve and growing up in the United States in "My Life as an Undocumented Immigrant." As you read, look for the similarities and differences between how the writers tell their stories of home and family. What similar strategies can you use in your own writing?

After reading these essays, think about the stories you have to tell about your own home or family. How do you define "home"? Is it a particular house, a group of people, a country? Have you ever returned home after a significant time away? Did you see your home or family differently after that absence and return? How do you define "family"? Is it biological relationship—or more expansive than that? What trait or behavior of a particular family member most affected you or your relationship with that person? Have you considered the ways in which laws and policies affect the home lives and family structures of immigrants and refugees? Have you ever been—literally or figuratively—without a home?

JOAN DIDION
On Going Home

I AM HOME for my daughter's first birthday. By "home" I do not mean the house in Los Angeles where my husband and I and the baby live, but the place where my family is, in the Central Valley of California. It is a vital although troublesome distinction. My husband likes my family but is uneasy in their house, because once there I fall into their ways, which are difficult, oblique, deliberately inarticulate, not my husband's ways. We live in dusty houses ("D-U-S-T," he once wrote with his finger on surfaces all over the house, but no one noticed it) filled with mementos quite without value to him (what could the Canton dessert plates mean to him? how could he have known about the assay scales, why should he care if he did know?), and we appear to talk exclusively about people we know who have been committed to mental hospitals, about people we know who have been booked on drunk-driving charges, and about property, particularly about property, land, price per acre and C-2 zoning and assessments and freeway access. My brother does not understand my husband's inability to perceive the advantage in the rather common real-estate transaction known as "sale-leaseback," and my husband in turn does not understand why so many of the people he hears about in my father's house have recently been committed to mental hospitals or booked on drunk-driving charges. Nor does he understand that when we talk about sale-leasebacks and right-of-way condemnations we are talking in code about the things we like best, the yellow fields and the cottonwoods and the rivers rising and falling and the mountain roads closing when the heavy snow comes in. We miss each other's points, have another drink and regard the fire. My brother refers to my husband, in his presence, as "Joan's husband." Marriage is the classic betrayal.

Or perhaps it is not any more. Sometimes I think that those of us who are now in our thirties were born into the last generation to carry the burden of "home," to find in family life the source of all tension and drama. I had by all objective accounts a "normal" and a "happy" family situation, and yet I was almost thirty years old before I could talk to my family on the telephone without crying after I had hung up. We did not fight. Nothing was wrong. And yet some nameless anxiety colored the emotional charges between me and the place that I came from. The question of whether or not you could go home again was

From Slouching Towards Bethlehem *(1968), Joan Didion's first work of nonfiction, which includes essays analyzing American culture in the 1960s.*

a very real part of the sentimental and largely literary baggage with which we left home in the fifties; I suspect that it is irrelevant to the children born of the fragmentation after World War II. A few weeks ago in a San Francisco bar I saw a pretty young girl on crystal[1] take off her clothes and dance for the cash prize in an "amateur-topless" contest. There was no particular sense of moment about this, none of the effect of romantic degradation, of "dark journey," for which my generation strived so assiduously. What sense could that girl possibly make of, say, *Long Day's Journey into Night*?[2] Who is beside the point?

That I am trapped in this particular irrelevancy is never more apparent to me than when I am home. Paralyzed by the neurotic lassitude engendered by meeting one's past at every turn, around every corner, inside every cupboard, I go aimlessly from room to room. I decide to meet it head-on and clean out a drawer, and I spread the contents on the bed. A bathing suit I wore the summer I was seventeen. A letter of rejection from *The Nation,* an aerial photograph of the site for a shopping center my father did not build in 1954. Three teacups hand-painted with cabbage roses and signed "E.M.," my grandmother's initials. There is no final solution for letters of rejection from *The Nation* and teacups hand-painted in 1900. Nor is there any answer to snapshots of one's grandfather as a young man on skis, surveying around Donner Pass in the year 1910. I smooth out the snapshot and look into his face, and do and do not see my own. I close the drawer, and have another cup of coffee with my mother. We get along very well, veterans of a guerrilla war we never understood.

Days pass. I see no one. I come to dread my husband's evening call, not only because he is full of news of what by now seems to me our remote life in Los Angeles, people he has seen, letters which require attention, but because he asks what I have been doing, suggests uneasily that I get out, drive to San Francisco or Berkeley. Instead I drive across the river to a family graveyard. It has been vandalized since my last visit and the monuments are broken, overturned in the dry grass. Because I once saw a rattlesnake in the grass I stay in the car and listen to a country-and-Western station. Later I drive with my father to a ranch he has in the foothills. The man who runs his cattle on it asks us to the roundup, a week from Sunday, and although I know that I will be in Los Angeles I say, in the oblique way my family talks, that I will come. Once home I mention the broken monuments in the graveyard. My mother shrugs.

I go to visit my great-aunts. A few of them think now that I am my cousin, or their daughter who died young. We recall an anecdote about a relative last seen in 1948, and they ask if I still like living in New York City. I have lived in Los Angeles for three years, but I say that I do. The baby is offered a horehound drop, and I am slipped a dollar bill "to buy a treat." Questions trail off, answers are abandoned, the baby plays with the dust motes in a shaft of afternoon sun.

It is time for the baby's birthday party: a white cake, strawberry-marshmallow ice cream, a bottle of champagne saved from another party. In the eve-

5

1. Methamphetamine.
2. Tragedy by playwright Eugene O'Neill (1956), based on the shame and deception that haunted his own family.

ning, after she has gone to sleep, I kneel beside the crib and touch her face, where it is pressed against the slats, with mine. She is an open and trusting child, unprepared for and unaccustomed to the ambushes of family life, and perhaps it is just as well that I can offer her little of that life. I would like to give her more. I would like to promise her that she will grow up with a sense of her cousins and of rivers and of her great-grandmother's teacups, would like to pledge her a picnic on a river with fried chicken and her hair uncombed, would like to give her *home* for her birthday, but we live differently now and I can promise her nothing like that. I give her a xylophone and a sundress from Madeira, and promise to tell her a funny story.

MLA CITATION

Didion, Joan. "On Going Home." *The Norton Reader: An Anthology of Nonfiction*, edited by Melissa A. Goldthwaite et al., 15th ed., W. W. Norton, 2020, pp. 2–4.

QUESTIONS

1. Joan Didion speaks of herself at home as "paralyzed by the neurotic lassitude engendered by meeting one's past at every turn" (paragraph 3). What about the essay helps explain these feelings?

2. Consider the metaphors Didion uses to describe the relationship she has with her family (for example, "guerrilla war" in paragraph 3), and the body language she uses to describe interactions with family members (for example, "My mother shrugs" in paragraph 4). Based on your analysis of Didion's use of language, how would you characterize her family relationships?

3. In paragraph 6 Didion says she would like to give her daughter "*home* for her birthday, but we live differently now." In an essay, explain whether or not you think parents today can give their children "home." Include examples to support your argument.

CHANG-RAE LEE
Coming Home Again

HEN MY MOTHER began using the electronic pump that fed her liquids and medication, we moved her to the family room. The bedroom she shared with my father was upstairs, and it was impossible to carry the machine up and down all day and night. The pump itself was attached to a metal stand on casters, and she pulled it along wherever she went. From anywhere in the house, you could hear the sound of the wheels clicking out a steady time over the grout lines of the slate-tiled foyer, her main thor-

Published in the New Yorker *(1995), a weekly magazine of "reportage, commentary, criticism, essays, fiction, satire, cartoons, and poetry."*

oughfare to the bathroom and the kitchen. Sometimes you would hear her halt after only a few steps, to catch her breath or steady her balance, and whatever you were doing was instantly suspended by a pall of silence.

I was usually in the kitchen, preparing lunch or dinner, poised over the butcher block with her favorite chef's knife in my hand and her old yellow apron slung around my neck. I'd be breathless in the sudden quiet, and, having ceased my mincing and chopping, would stare blankly at the brushed sheen of the blade. Eventually, she would clear her throat or call out to say she was fine, then begin to move again, starting her rhythmic *ka-jug*; and only then could I go on with my cooking, the world of our house turning once more, wheeling through the black.

I wasn't cooking for my mother but for the rest of us. When she first moved downstairs she was still eating, though scantily, more just to taste what we were having than from any genuine desire for food. The point was simply to sit together at the kitchen table and array ourselves like a family again. My mother would gently set herself down in her customary chair near the stove. I sat across from her, my father and sister to my left and right, and crammed in the center was all the food I had made—a spicy codfish stew, say, or a casserole of gingery beef, dishes that in my youth she had prepared for us a hundred times.

It had been ten years since we'd all lived together in the house, which at fifteen I had left to attend boarding school in New Hampshire. My mother would sometimes point this out, by speaking of our present time as being "just like before Exeter," which surprised me, given how proud she always was that I was a graduate of the school.

My going to such a place was part of my mother's not so secret plan to   5
change my character, which she worried was becoming too much like hers. I was clever and able enough, but without outside pressure I was readily given to sloth and vanity. The famous school—which none of us knew the first thing about—would prove my mettle. She was right, of course, and while I was there I would falter more than a few times, academically and otherwise. But I never thought that my leaving home then would ever be a problem for her, a private quarrel she would have even as her life waned.

Now her house was full again. My sister had just resigned from her job in New York City, and my father, who typically saw his psychiatric patients until eight or nine in the evening, was appearing in the driveway at four-thirty. I had been living at home for nearly a year and was in the final push of work on what would prove a dismal failure of a novel. When I wasn't struggling over my prose, I kept occupied with the things she usually did—the daily errands, the grocery shopping, the vacuuming and the cleaning, and, of course, all the cooking.

When I was six or seven years old, I used to watch my mother as she prepared our favorite meals. It was one of my daily pleasures. She shooed me away in the beginning, telling me that the kitchen wasn't my place, and adding, in her half-proud, half-deprecating way, that her kind of work would only serve to weaken me. "Go out and play with your friends," she'd snap in Korean, "or better yet, do your reading and homework." She knew that I had already done both, and that as the evening approached there was no place to go save her small and tidy kitchen, from which the clatter of her mixing bowls and pans would ring through the house.

I would enter the kitchen quietly and stand beside her, my chin lodging upon the point of her hip. Peering through the crook of her arm, I beheld the movements of her hands. For *kalbi*,[1] she would take up a butchered short rib in her narrow hand, the flinty bone shaped like a section of an airplane wing and deeply embedded in gristle and flesh, and with the point of her knife cut so that the bone fell away, though not completely, leaving it connected to the meat by the barest opaque layer of tendon. Then she methodically butterflied the flesh, cutting and unfolding, repeating the action until the meat lay out on her board, glistening and ready for seasoning. She scored it diagonally, then sifted sugar into the crevices with her pinched fingers, gently rubbing in the crystals. The sugar would tenderize as well as sweeten the meat. She did this with each rib, and then set them all aside in a large shallow bowl. She minced a half-dozen cloves of garlic, a stub of gingerroot, sliced up a few scallions, and spread it all over the meat. She wiped her hands and took out a bottle of sesame oil, and, after pausing for a moment, streamed the dark oil in two swift circles around the bowl. After adding a few splashes of soy sauce, she thrust her hands in and kneaded the flesh, careful not to dislodge the bones. I asked her why it mattered that they remain connected. "The meat needs the bone nearby," she said, "to borrow its richness." She wiped her hands clean of the marinade, except for her little finger, which she would flick with her tongue from time to time, because she knew that the flavor of a good dish developed not at once but in stages.

Whenever I cook, I find myself working just as she would, readying the ingredients—a mash of garlic, a julienne of red peppers, fantails of shrimp—and piling them in little mounds about the cutting surface. My mother never left me any recipes, but this is how I learned to make her food, each dish coming not from a list or a card but from the aromatic spread of a board.

10   I've always thought it was particularly cruel that the cancer was in her stomach, and that for a long time at the end she couldn't eat. The last meal I made for her was on New Year's Eve, 1990. My sister suggested that instead of a rib roast or a bird, or the usual overflow of Korean food, we make all sorts of finger dishes that our mother might fancy and pick at.

We set the meal out on the glass coffee table in the family room. I prepared a tray of smoked-salmon canapés,[2] fried some Korean bean cakes, and made a few other dishes I thought she might enjoy. My sister supervised me, arranging the platters, and then with some pomp carried each dish in to our parents. Finally, I brought out a bottle of champagne in a bucket of ice. My mother had moved to the sofa and was sitting up, surveying the low table. "It looks pretty nice," she said. "I think I'm feeling hungry."

This made us all feel good, especially me, for I couldn't remember the last time she had felt any hunger or had eaten something I cooked. We began to

1. Korean-style beef ribs.
2. Appetizers, usually toast, crackers, or bread slices with toppings.

eat. My mother picked up a piece of salmon toast and took a tiny corner in her mouth. She rolled it around for a moment and then pushed it out with the tip of her tongue, letting it fall back onto her plate. She swallowed hard, as if to quell a gag, then glanced up to see if we had noticed. Of course we all had. She attempted a bean cake, some cheese, and then a slice of fruit, but nothing was any use.

She nodded at me anyway, and said, "Oh, it's very good." But I was already feeling lost and I put down my plate abruptly, nearly shattering it on the thick glass. There was an ugly pause before my father asked me in a weary, gentle voice if anything was wrong, and I answered that it was nothing, it was the last night of a long year, and we were together, and I was simply relieved. At midnight, I poured out glasses of champagne, even one for my mother, who took a deep sip. Her manner grew playful and light, and I helped her shuffle to her mattress, and she lay down in the place where in a brief week she was dead.

My mother could whip up most anything, but during our first years of living in this country we ate only Korean foods. At my harangue-like behest, my mother set herself to learning how to cook exotic American dishes. Luckily, a kind neighbor, Mrs. Churchill, a tall, florid young woman with flaxen hair, taught my mother her most trusted recipes. Mrs. Churchill's two young sons, palish, weepy boys with identical crew cuts, always accompanied her, and though I liked them well enough, I would slip away from them after a few minutes, for I knew that the real action would be in the kitchen, where their mother was playing guide. Mrs. Churchill hailed from the state of Maine, where the finest Swedish meatballs and tuna casserole and angel food cake in America are made. She readily demonstrated certain techniques—how to layer wet sheets of pasta for a lasagna or whisk up a simple roux,[3] for example. She often brought gift shoeboxes containing curious ingredients like dried oregano, instant yeast, and cream of mushroom soup. The two women, though at ease and jolly with each other, had difficulty communicating, and this was made worse by the often confusing terminology of Western cuisine ("corned beef," "deviled eggs"). Although I was just learning the language myself, I'd gladly play the interlocutor, jumping back and forth between their places at the counter, dipping my fingers into whatever sauce lay about.

I was an insistent child, and, being my mother's firstborn, much too prized. My mother could say no to me, and did often enough, but anyone who knew us—particularly my father and sister—could tell how much the denying pained her. And if I was overconscious of her indulgence even then, and suffered the rushing pangs of guilt that she could inflict upon me with the slightest wounded turn of her lip, I was too happily obtuse and venal to let her cease. She reminded me daily that I was her sole son, her reason for living, and that if she were to lose me, in either body or spirit, she wished that God would mercifully smite her, strike her down like a weak branch.

In the traditional fashion, she was the house accountant, the maid, the launderer, the disciplinarian, the driver, the secretary, and, of course, the cook.

15

3. Thickening agent for sauces and soups.

She was also my first basketball coach. In South Korea, where girls' high school basketball is a popular spectator sport, she had been a star, the point guard for the national high school team that once won the all-Asia championships. I learned this one Saturday during the summer, when I asked my father if he would go down to the schoolyard and shoot some baskets with me. I had just finished the fifth grade, and wanted desperately to make the middle school team the coming fall. He called for my mother and sister to come along. When we arrived, my sister immediately ran off to the swings, and I recall being annoyed that my mother wasn't following her. I dribbled clumsily around the key, on the verge of losing control of the ball, and flung a flat shot that caromed wildly off the rim. The ball bounced to my father, who took a few not so graceful dribbles and made an easy layup. He dribbled out and then drove to the hoop for a layup on the other side. He rebounded his shot and passed the ball to my mother, who had been watching us from the foul line. She turned from the basket and began heading the other way.

"*Um-mah*,"[4] I cried at her, my exasperation already bubbling over, "the basket's over *here!*"

After a few steps she turned around, and from where the professional three-point line must be now, she effortlessly flipped the ball up in a two-handed set shot, its flight truer and higher than I'd witnessed from any boy or man. The ball arced cleanly into the hoop, stiffly popping the chain-link net. All afternoon, she rained in shot after shot, as my father and I scrambled after her.

When we got home from the playground, my mother showed me the photograph album of her team's championship run. For years I kept it in my room, on the same shelf that housed the scrapbooks I made of basketball stars, with magazine clippings of slick players like Bubbles Hawkins and Pistol Pete and George (the Iceman) Gervin.

20   It puzzled me how much she considered her own history to be immaterial, and if she never patently diminished herself, she was able to finesse a kind of self-removal by speaking of my father whenever she could. She zealously recounted his excellence as a student in medical school and reminded me, each night before I started my homework, of how hard he drove himself in his work to make a life for us. She said that because of his Asian face and imperfect English, he was "working two times the American doctors." I knew that she was building him up, buttressing him with both genuine admiration and her own brand of anxious braggadocio, and that her overarching concern was that I might fail to see him as she wished me to—in the most dawning light, his pose steadfast and solitary.

In the year before I left for Exeter, I became weary of her oft-repeated accounts of my father's success. I was a teenager, and so ever inclined to be dismissive and bitter toward anything that had to do with family and home. Often enough, my mother was the object of my derision. Suddenly, her life seemed so small to me. She was there, and sometimes, I thought, *always* there, as if she were confined to the four walls of our house. I would even complain about her cooking. Mostly, though, I was getting more and more impatient with

4. Korean for "mommy."

the difficulty she encountered in doing everyday things. I was afraid for her.
One day, we got into a terrible argument when she asked me to call the bank,
to question a discrepancy she had discovered in the monthly statement. I asked
her why she couldn't call herself. I was stupid and brutal, and I knew exactly
how to wound her.

"Whom do I talk to?" she said. She would mostly speak to me in Korean,
and I would answer in English.

"The bank manager, who else?"

"What do I say?"

"Whatever you want to say."   25

"Don't speak to me like that!" she cried.

"It's just that you should be able to do it yourself," I said.

"You know how I feel about this!"

"Well, maybe then you should consider it *practice*," I answered lightly, using
the Korean word to make sure she understood.

Her face blanched, and her neck suddenly became rigid, as if I were throt-   30
tling her. She nearly struck me right then, but instead she bit her lip and ran
upstairs. I followed her, pleading for forgiveness at her door. But it was the one
time in our life that I couldn't convince her, melt her resolve with the blan-
dishments of a spoiled son.

When my mother was feeling strong enough, or was in particularly good spirits, she would roll her machine into the kitchen and sit at the table and watch
me work. She wore pajamas day and night, mostly old pairs of mine.

She said, "I can't tell, what are you making?"

"*Mahn-doo*[5] filling."

"You didn't salt the cabbage and squash."

"Was I supposed to?"   35

"Of course. Look, it's too wet. Now the skins will get soggy before you can
fry them."

"What should I do?"

"It's too late. Maybe it'll be OK if you work quickly. Why didn't you ask
me?"

"You were finally sleeping."

"You should have woken me."   40

"No way."

She sighed, as deeply as her weary lungs would allow.

"I don't know how you were going to make it without me."

"I don't know, either. I'll remember the salt next time."

"You better. And not too much."   45

We often talked like this, our tone decidedly matter-of-fact, chin up, just this
side of being able to bear it. Once, while inspecting a potato fritter batter I was
making, she asked me if she had ever done anything that I wished she hadn't
done. I thought for a moment, and told her no. In the next breath, she wondered

5. Korean dumplings, usually filled with cabbage and meat.

aloud if it was right of her to have let me go to Exeter, to live away from the house while I was so young. She tested the batter's thickness with her finger and called for more flour. Then she asked if, given a choice, I would go to Exeter again.

I wasn't sure what she was getting at, and I told her that I couldn't be certain, but probably yes, I would. She snorted at this and said it was my leaving home that had once so troubled our relationship. "Remember how I had so much difficulty talking to you? Remember?"

She believed back then that I had found her more and more ignorant each time I came home. She said she never blamed me, for this was the way she knew it would be with my wonderful new education. Nothing I could say seemed to quell the notion. But I knew that the problem wasn't simply the *education*; the first time I saw her again after starting school, barely six weeks later, when she and my father visited me on Parents Day, she had already grown nervous and distant. After the usual campus events, we had gone to the motel where they were staying in a nearby town and sat on the beds in our room. She seemed to sneak looks at me, as though I might discover a horrible new truth if our eyes should meet.

My own secret feeling was that I had missed my parents greatly, my mother especially, and much more than I had anticipated. I couldn't tell them that these first weeks were a mere blur to me, that I felt completely overwhelmed by all the studies and my much brighter friends and the thousand irritating details of living alone, and that I had really learned nothing, save perhaps how to put on a necktie while sprinting to class. I felt as if I had plunged too deep into the world, which, to my great horror, was much larger than I had ever imagined.

50   I welcomed the lull of the motel room. My father and I had nearly dozed off when my mother jumped up excitedly, murmured how stupid she was, and hurried to the closet by the door. She pulled out our old metal cooler and dragged it between the beds. She lifted the top and began unpacking plastic containers, and I thought she would never stop. One after the other they came out, each with a dish that traveled well—a salted stewed meat, rolls of Korean-style sushi. I opened a container of radish kimchi[6] and suddenly the room bloomed with its odor, and I reveled in the very peculiar sensation (which perhaps only true kimchi lovers know) of simultaneously drooling and gagging as I breathed it all in. For the next few minutes, they watched me eat. I'm not certain that I was even hungry. But after weeks of pork parmigiana and chicken patties and wax beans, I suddenly realized that I had lost all the savor in my life. And it seemed I couldn't get enough of it back. I ate and I ate, so much and so fast that I actually went to the bathroom and vomited. I came out dizzy and sated with the phantom warmth of my binge.

And beneath the face of her worry, I thought, my mother was smiling.

From that day, my mother prepared a certain meal to welcome me home. It was always the same. Even as I rode the school's shuttle bus from Exeter to Logan airport, I could already see the exact arrangement of my mother's table.

I knew that we would eat in the kitchen, the table brimming with plates. There was the *kalbi*, of course, broiled or grilled depending on the season. Leaf

6. Spicy Korean relish.

lettuce, to wrap the meat with. Bowls of garlicky clam broth with miso and tofu and fresh spinach. Shavings of cod dusted in flour and then dipped in egg wash and fried. Glass noodles with onions and shiitake. Scallion-and-hot-pepper pancakes. Chilled steamed shrimp. Seasoned salads of bean sprouts, spinach, and white radish. Crispy squares of seaweed. Steamed rice with barley and red beans. Homemade kimchi. It was all there—the old flavors I knew, the beautiful salt, the sweet, the excellent taste.

After the meal, my father and I talked about school, but I could never say enough for it to make any sense. My father would often recall his high school principal, who had gone to England to study the methods and traditions of the public schools, and regaled students with stories of the great Eton man. My mother sat with us, paring fruit, not saying a word but taking everything in. When it was time to go to bed, my father said good night first. I usually watched television until the early morning. My mother would sit with me for an hour or two, perhaps until she was accustomed to me again, and only then would she kiss me and head upstairs to sleep.

During the following days, it was always the cooking that started our conversations. She'd hold an inquest over the cold leftovers we ate at lunch, discussing each dish in terms of its balance of flavors or what might have been prepared differently. But mostly I begged her to leave the dishes alone. I wish I had paid more attention. After her death, when my father and I were the only ones left in the house, drifting through the rooms like ghosts, I sometimes tried to make that meal for him. Though it was too much for two, I made each dish anyway, taking as much care as I could. But nothing turned out quite right— not the color, not the smell. At the table, neither of us said much of anything. And we had to eat the food for days. 55

I remember washing rice in the kitchen one day and my mother's saying in English, from her usual seat, "I made a big mistake."

"About Exeter?"

"Yes. I made a big mistake. You should be with us for that time. I should never let you go there."

"So why did you?" I said.

"Because I didn't know I was going to die." 60

I let her words pass. For the first time in her life, she was letting herself speak her full mind, so what else could I do?

"But you know what?" she spoke up. "It was better for you. If you stayed home, you would not like me so much now."

I suggested that maybe I would like her even more.

She shook her head. "Impossible."

Sometimes I still think about what she said, about having made a mistake. 65
I would have left home for college, that was never in doubt, but those years I was away at boarding school grew more precious to her as her illness progressed. After many months of exhaustion and pain and the haze of the drugs, I thought that her mind was beginning to fade, for more and more it seemed that she was seeing me again as her fifteen-year-old boy, the one she had dropped off in New Hampshire on a cloudy September afternoon.

I remember the first person I met, another new student, named Zack, who walked to the welcome picnic with me. I had planned to eat with my parents—my mother had brought a coolerful of food even that first day—but I learned of the cookout and told her that I should probably go. I wanted to go, of course. I was excited, and no doubt fearful and nervous, and I must have thought I was only thinking ahead. She agreed wholeheartedly, saying I certainly should. I walked them to the car, and perhaps I hugged them, before saying goodbye. One day, after she died, my father told me what happened on the long drive home to Syracuse.

He was driving the car, looking straight ahead. Traffic was light on the Massachusetts Turnpike, and the sky was nearly dark. They had driven for more than two hours and had not yet spoken a word. He then heard a strange sound from her, a kind of muffled chewing noise, as if something inside her were grinding its way out.

"So, what's the matter?" he said, trying to keep an edge to his voice.

She looked at him with her ashen face and she burst into tears. He began to cry himself, and pulled the car over onto the narrow shoulder of the turnpike, where they stayed for the next half hour or so, the blank-faced cars droning by them in the cold, onrushing night.

70   Every once in a while, when I think of her, I'm driving alone somewhere on the highway. In the twilight, I see their car off to the side, a blue Olds coupe with a landau top, and as I pass them by I look back in the mirror and I see them again, the two figures huddling together in the front seat. Are they sleeping? Or kissing? Are they all right?

MLA CITATION

Lee, Chang-rae. "Coming Home Again." *The Norton Reader: An Anthology of Nonfiction*, edited by Melissa A. Goldthwaite et al., 15th ed., W. W. Norton, 2020, pp. 4–12.

QUESTIONS

1. Because Chang-rae Lee begins his essay at a late stage of his mother's illness, he often flashes back to earlier points in their relationship. Mark the flashbacks in the text and explain the purpose of each.

2. Details of food and cooking appear throughout the essay—for example, in paragraphs 8 and 9, 11–13, and 32–36. Besides giving us a flavor of Korean food, what function do these details serve?

3. Lee titles his essay "Coming Home Again," whereas Joan Didion titles hers "On Going Home" (pp. 2–4). What different connotations do "coming home" and "going home" suggest? How do these differences emerge in the personal accounts of each writer?

4. Write a personal essay about "coming home" or "going home."

Alison Bechdel

from *Fun Home*

OLD FATHER, OLD ARTIFICER

From Fun Home: A Family Tragicomic (2006), *a graphic memoir that chronicles Alison Bechdel's childhood and relationship with her father.*

LIKE MANY FATHERS, MINE COULD OCCASIONALLY BE PREVAILED ON FOR A SPOT OF "AIRPLANE."

AS HE LAUNCHED ME, MY FULL WEIGHT WOULD FALL ON THE PIVOT POINT BETWEEN HIS FEET AND MY STOMACH.

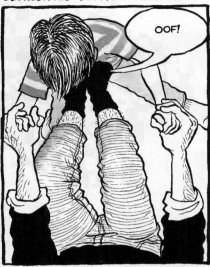

OOF!

IT WAS A DISCOMFORT WELL WORTH THE RARE PHYSICAL CONTACT, AND CERTAINLY WORTH THE MOMENT OF PERFECT BALANCE WHEN I SOARED ABOVE HIM.

IN THE CIRCUS, ACROBATICS WHERE ONE PERSON LIES ON THE FLOOR BALANCING ANOTHER ARE CALLED "ICARIAN GAMES."

CONSIDERING THE FATE OF ICARUS[1] AFTER HE FLOUTED HIS FATHER'S ADVICE AND FLEW SO CLOSE TO THE SUN HIS WINGS MELTED, PERHAPS SOME DARK HUMOR IS INTENDED.

UH-OH!

IN OUR PARTICULAR REENACTMENT OF THIS MYTHIC RELATIONSHIP, IT WAS NOT ME BUT MY FATHER WHO WAS TO PLUMMET FROM THE SKY.

BUT BEFORE HE DID SO, HE MANAGED TO GET QUITE A LOT DONE.

HIS GREATEST ACHIEVEMENT, ARGUABLY, WAS HIS MONOMANIACAL RESTORATION OF OUR OLD HOUSE.

AGAIN!

THIS RUG IS FILTHY. GO GET THE VACUUM CLEANER.

AND THEN GET ME MY TACK HAMMER. THAT STRIP OF MOLDING IS LOOSE.

1. Son of Daedalus in Greek mythology. Daedalus crafted wings made of feathers and wax for himself and his son Icarus so they could escape from Crete, where they had been imprisoned in the Labyrinth (which Daedalus had created) by King Minos. Daedalus warned Icarus not to fly too close to the sun, which could cause his wings to melt, but Icarus did not heed his father's warning. When he flew too close to the sun, his wings failed and he drowned.

WHEN OTHER CHILDREN CALLED OUR HOUSE A MANSION, I WOULD DEMUR. I RESENTED THE IMPLICATION THAT MY FAMILY WAS RICH, OR UNUSUAL IN ANY WAY.

IN FACT, WE WERE UNUSUAL, THOUGH I WOULDN'T APPRECIATE EXACTLY HOW UNUSUAL UNTIL MUCH LATER. BUT WE WERE NOT RICH.

IT'S JUST A HOUSE.

ALISON!

WHAT?

SEND TAMMI HOME. YOU HAVE WORK TO DO.

THE GILT CORNICES, THE MARBLE FIREPLACE, THE CRYSTAL CHANDELIERS, THE SHELVES OF CALF-BOUND BOOKS--THESE WERE NOT SO MUCH BOUGHT AS PRODUCED FROM THIN AIR BY MY FATHER'S REMARKABLE LEGERDEMAIN.

WASH THESE OLD CURTAINS SO WE CAN PUT UP THE HAND-EMBROIDERED LACE ONES I FOUND IN MRS. STRUMP'S ATTIC.

2. Master craftsman in Greek mythology who created the Labyrinth on the island of Crete.

FOR IF MY FATHER WAS ICARUS, HE WAS ALSO DAEDALUS--THAT SKILLFUL ARTIFICER, THAT MAD SCIENTIST WHO BUILT THE WINGS FOR HIS SON AND DESIGNED THE FAMOUS LABYRINTH...

THIS IS THE WALLPAPER FOR MY ROOM?

...AND WHO ANSWERED NOT TO THE LAWS OF SOCIETY, BUT TO THOSE OF HIS CRAFT.

BUT I **HATE** PINK! I **HATE** FLOWERS!

TOUGH TITTY.

HISTORICAL RESTORATION WASN'T HIS JOB.

(TWELFTH-GRADE ENGLISH)

ARCHI-TECTURAL DIGEST

IT WAS HIS PASSION. AND I MEAN PASSION IN EVERY SENSE OF THE WORD.

LIBIDINAL. MANIC. MARTYRED.

OUR GOTHIC REVIVAL HOUSE HAD BEEN BUILT DURING THE SMALL PENNSYLVANIA TOWN'S ONE BRIEF MOMENT OF WEALTH, FROM THE LUMBER INDUSTRY, IN 1867.

BUT LOCAL FORTUNES HAD DECLINED STEADILY FROM THAT POINT, AND WHEN MY PARENTS BOUGHT THE PLACE IN 1962, IT WAS A SHELL OF ITS FORMER SELF.

THE SHUTTERS AND SCROLLWORK WERE GONE. THE CLAPBOARDS HAD BEEN SHEATHED WITH SCABROUS SHINGLES.

THE BARE LIGHTBULBS REVEALED DINGY WARTIME WALLPAPER AND WOODWORK PAINTED PASTEL GREEN.

ALL THAT WAS LEFT OF THE HOUSE'S LUMBER-ERA GLORY WERE THE EXUBERANT FRONT PORCH SUPPORTS.

BUT OVER THE NEXT EIGHTEEN YEARS, MY FATHER WOULD RESTORE THE HOUSE TO ITS ORIGINAL CONDITION, AND THEN SOME.

JESUS! THIS MUST BE THE PATTERN FOR THE ORIGINAL BARGEBOARD!

HE WOULD PERFORM, AS DAEDALUS DID, DAZZLING DISPLAYS OF ARTFULNESS.

3. A 1946 film starring actors James Stewart and Donna Reed that has become a classic Christmas movie in the United States.

BUT IN THE MOVIE WHEN JIMMY
STEWART COMES HOME ONE NIGHT
AND STARTS YELLING AT EVERYONE...

...IT'S OUT OF THE ORDINARY.

HOLD IT STRAIGHT.

TOMMY, STOP THAT! JANIE, HAVEN'T YOU LEARNED THAT SILLY TUNE YET?

ONE OF MY BROTHERS

THE NEEDLES ARE SHARP!

GODDAMN IT!

YOU PLAY IT OVER AND OVER--NOW STOP IT! **STOP IT!**

DAEDALUS, TOO, WAS INDIFFERENT TO
THE HUMAN COST OF HIS PROJECTS.

DON'T HIT ME!

HE BLITHELY BETRAYED THE KING, FOR EXAMPLE, WHEN THE QUEEN ASKED HIM TO
BUILD HER A COW DISGUISE SO SHE COULD SEDUCE THE WHITE BULL.

GEORGE, WHY MUST YOU TORTURE THE CHILDREN?

KUH-CLINK!

INDEED, THE RESULT OF THAT SCHEME--A HALF-BULL, HALF-MAN MONSTER--INSPIRED DAEDALUS'S GREATEST CREATION YET.

HE HID THE MINOTAUR[4] IN THE LABYRINTH-- A MAZE OF PASSAGES AND ROOMS OPEN-ING ENDLESSLY INTO ONE ANOTHER...

...AND FROM WHICH, AS STRAY YOUTHS AND MAIDENS DISCOVERED TO THEIR PERIL...

...ESCAPE WAS IMPOSSIBLE.

THEN THERE ARE THOSE FAMOUS WINGS. WAS DAEDALUS REALLY STRICKEN WITH GRIEF WHEN ICARUS FELL INTO THE SEA?

OR JUST DISAPPOINTED BY THE DESIGN FAILURE?

4. Mythical creature with the body of a man and head of a bull.

SOMETIMES, WHEN THINGS WERE GOING WELL, I THINK MY FATHER ACTUALLY ENJOYED HAVING A FAMILY.

OR AT LEAST, THE AIR OF AUTHENTICITY WE LENT TO HIS EXHIBIT. A SORT OF STILL LIFE WITH CHILDREN.

AND OF COURSE, MY BROTHERS AND I WERE FREE LABOR. DAD CONSIDERED US EXTENSIONS OF HIS OWN BODY, LIKE PRECISION ROBOT ARMS.

PUT HOT, SOAPY WATER IN THE SINK AND GET SOME CLEAN RAGS.

IN THIS REGARD, IT WAS LIKE BEING RAISED NOT BY JIMMY BUT BY MARTHA STEWART.[5]

IN THEORY, HIS ARRANGEMENT WITH MY MOTHER WAS MORE COOPERATIVE.

WHAT DO YOU THINK OF THIS GAS CHANDELIER?

BORDELLO.

AUCTION CATALOG

IN PRACTICE, IT WAS NOT.

5. TV personality, author, and businesswoman (b. 1941) whose TV shows, books, and magazine provide advice for crafting, decorating, cooking, and entertaining.

WE EACH RESISTED IN OUR OWN WAYS, BUT IN THE END WE WERE EQUALLY POWERLESS BEFORE MY FATHER'S CURATORIAL ONSLAUGHT.

MY BROTHERS AND I COULDN'T COMPETE WITH THE ASTRAL LAMPS AND GIRANDOLES AND HEPPLEWHITE SUITE CHAIRS. THEY WERE PERFECT.

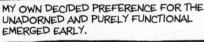

I GREW TO RESENT THE WAY MY FATHER TREATED HIS FURNITURE LIKE CHILDREN, AND HIS CHILDREN LIKE FURNITURE.

MY OWN DECIDED PREFERENCE FOR THE UNADORNED AND PURELY FUNCTIONAL EMERGED EARLY.

I WAS SPARTAN TO MY FATHER'S ATHENIAN.   MODERN TO HIS VICTORIAN.

BUTCH TO HIS NELLY.   UTILITARIAN TO HIS AESTHETE.

I DEVELOPED A CONTEMPT FOR USE-LESS ORNAMENT. WHAT FUNCTION WAS SERVED BY THE SCROLLS, TASSELS, AND BRIC-A-BRAC THAT INFESTED OUR HOUSE?

IF ANYTHING, THEY OBSCURED FUNCTION. THEY WERE EMBELLISHMENTS IN THE WORST SENSE.

PLING KLINK

THEY WERE LIES.

INCIPIENT YELLOW LUNG DISEASE

MY FATHER BEGAN TO SEEM MORALLY SUSPECT TO ME LONG BEFORE I KNEW THAT HE ACTUALLY HAD A DARK SECRET.

MOM SAYS HURRY UP.

"BRONZING STICK"

HE USED HIS SKILLFUL ARTIFICE NOT TO MAKE THINGS, BUT TO MAKE THINGS APPEAR TO BE WHAT THEY WERE NOT.

MASS WILL BE OVER BEFORE WE GET THERE.

THAT IS TO SAY, IMPECCABLE.

HE APPEARED TO BE AN IDEAL HUSBAND AND FATHER, FOR EXAMPLE.

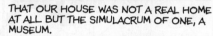

IT'S TEMPTING TO SUGGEST, IN RETRO-SPECT, THAT OUR FAMILY WAS A SHAM.

THAT OUR HOUSE WAS NOT A REAL HOME AT ALL BUT THE SIMULACRUM OF ONE, A MUSEUM.

YET WE REALLY WERE A FAMILY, AND WE REALLY DID LIVE IN THOSE PERIOD ROOMS.

STILL, SOMETHING VITAL WAS MISSING.

WELL?

ME, AGE 4

MY BROTHER CHRISTIAN, AGE 3

AN ELASTICITY, A MARGIN FOR ERROR.

HOW DID THIS VASE GET SO CLOSE TO THE EDGE OF THE TABLE?

BUT I DIDN'T DO ANYTHING!

MOST PEOPLE, I IMAGINE, LEARN TO ACCEPT THAT THEY'RE NOT PERFECT.

BUT AN IDLE REMARK ABOUT MY FATHER'S TIE OVER BREAKFAST COULD SEND HIM INTO A TAILSPIN.

PEACE, MAN.

ALSO AN ENGLISH TEACHER

MY MOTHER ESTABLISHED A RULE.

IF WE COULDN'T CRITICIZE MY FATHER, SHOWING AFFECTION FOR HIM WAS AN EVEN DICIER VENTURE.

WE WERE NOT A PHYSICALLY EXPRESSIVE FAMILY, TO SAY THE LEAST. BUT ONCE I WAS UNACCOUNTABLY MOVED TO KISS MY FATHER GOOD NIGHT.

HAVING LITTLE PRACTICE WITH THE GESTURE, ALL I MANAGED WAS TO GRAB HIS HAND AND BUSS THE KNUCKLES LIGHTLY...

...AS IF HE WERE A BISHOP OR AN ELEGANT LADY, BEFORE RUSHING FROM THE ROOM IN EMBARRASSMENT.

THIS EMBARRASSMENT ON MY PART WAS A TINY SCALE MODEL OF MY FATHER'S MORE FULLY DEVELOPED SELF-LOATHING.

HIS SHAME INHABITED OUR HOUSE AS PERVASIVELY AND INVISIBLY AS THE AROMATIC MUSK OF AGING MAHOGANY.

IN FACT, THE METICULOUS, PERIOD INTERIORS WERE EXPRESSLY DESIGNED TO CONCEAL IT.

MIRRORS, DISTRACTING BRONZES, MULTIPLE DOORWAYS. VISITORS OFTEN GOT LOST UPSTAIRS.

GRACIOUS, I ALMOST WALKED RIGHT INTO THIS!

MY MOTHER, MY BROTHERS, AND I KNEW OUR WAY AROUND WELL ENOUGH, BUT IT WAS IMPOSSIBLE TO TELL IF THE MINOTAUR LAY BEYOND THE NEXT CORNER.

PERMANENT LINOLEUM SCAR

AND THE CONSTANT TENSION WAS HEIGHT-ENED BY THE FACT THAT SOME ENCOUN-TERS COULD BE QUITE PLEASANT.

HIS BURSTS OF KINDNESS WERE AS INCAN-DESCENT AS HIS TANTRUMS WERE DARK.

...AND AT EACH PULL THE ELEPHANT'S CHILD'S NOSE GREW LONGER AND LONGER.

♪ ...WON'T YOU BE MY PONY GIRL? MARRY ME, CARRY ME, FAR ACROSS THE SEA. ♪

DON'T TURN OUT THE HALL LIGHT.

ALTHOUGH I'M GOOD AT ENUMERATING MY FATHER'S FLAWS, IT'S HARD FOR ME TO SUSTAIN MUCH ANGER AT HIM.

I EXPECT THIS IS PARTLY BECAUSE HE'S DEAD, AND PARTLY BECAUSE THE BAR IS LOWER FOR FATHERS THAN FOR MOTHERS.

STOP SPLASHING!

IN MY EYES!

HOLD STILL, DAMMIT!

MY MOTHER MUST HAVE BATHED ME HUNDREDS OF TIMES. BUT IT'S MY FATHER RINSING ME OFF WITH THE PURPLE METAL CUP THAT I REMEMBER MOST CLEARLY.

THE SUFFUSION OF WARMTH AS THE HOT WATER SLUICED OVER ME...

...THE SUDDEN, UNBEARABLE COLD OF ITS ABSENCE.

WAS HE A GOOD FATHER? I WANT TO SAY, "AT LEAST HE STUCK AROUND." BUT OF COURSE, HE DIDN'T.

AGAIN!

IT'S TRUE THAT HE DIDN'T KILL HIMSELF UNTIL I WAS NEARLY TWENTY.

BUT HIS ABSENCE RESONATED RETRO-ACTIVELY, ECHOING BACK THROUGH ALL THE TIME I KNEW HIM.

MAYBE IT WAS THE CONVERSE OF THE WAY AMPUTEES FEEL PAIN IN A MISSING LIMB.

HE REALLY WAS THERE ALL THOSE YEARS, A FLESH-AND-BLOOD PRESENCE STEAMING OFF THE WALLPAPER, DIGGING UP THE DOGWOODS, POLISHING THE FINIALS...

...SMELLING OF SAWDUST AND SWEAT AND DESIGNER COLOGNE.

BUT I ACHED AS IF HE WERE ALREADY GONE.

MLA CITATION

Bechdel, Alison. "From *Fun Home*." *The Norton Reader: An Anthology of Nonfiction*,
    edited by Melissa A. Goldthwaite et al., 15th ed., W. W. Norton, 2020,
    pp. 13–34.

QUESTIONS

1. Alison Bechdel compares her father to both Daedalus and Icarus from Greek mythology. She also mentions Daedalus's Labyrinth and the Minotaur. Trace the references to the Daedalus and Icarus myths throughout. What is Bechdel trying to get across about her father by making these comparisons?

2. Consider Bechdel's use of foreshadowing. For example, in panel 4, she writes, ". . . it was not me but my father who was to plummet from the sky," and in panel 8 she states that her family was unusual, though she "wouldn't appreciate exactly how unusual until much later." What was her father's secret? Where does she reveal it?

3. In a graphic memoir, the images are as important as the words. What do you learn from Bechdel's images that you might not have picked up from her words?

4. Write a piece about a family member or a home (or both). Like Bechdel, use allusions to myth or some other well-known story. If you are comfortable drawing, consider making your text a graphic essay.

SCOTT RUSSELL SANDERS
Under the Influence

MY FATHER DRANK. He drank as a gut-punched boxer gasps for breath, as a starving dog gobbles food—compulsively, secretly, in pain and trembling. I use the past tense not because he ever quit drinking but because he quit living. That is how the story ends for my father, age sixty-four, heart bursting, body cooling and forsaken on the linoleum of my brother's trailer. The story continues for my brother, my sister, my mother, and me, and will continue so long as memory holds.

In the perennial present of memory, I slip into the garage or barn to see my father tipping back the flat green bottles of wine, the brown cylinders of whiskey, the cans of beer disguised in paper bags. His Adam's apple bobs, the liquid gurgles, he wipes the sandy-haired back of a hand over his lips, and then, his bloodshot gaze bumping into me, he stashes the bottle or can inside his jacket, under the workbench, between two bales of hay, and we both pretend the moment has not occurred.

Originally published in Harper's Magazine *(1989), an American monthly covering politics, society, culture, and the environment.*

"What's up, buddy?" he says, thick-tongued and edgy.

"Sky's up," I answer, playing along.

5   "And don't forget prices," he grumbles. "Prices are always up. And taxes."

In memory, his white 1951 Pontiac with the stripes down the hood and the Indian head on the snout jounces to a stop in the driveway; or it is the 1956 Ford station wagon, or the 1963 Rambler shaped like a toad, or the sleek 1969 Bonneville that will do 120 miles per hour on straightaways; or it is the robin's-egg blue pickup, new in 1980, battered in 1981, the year of his death. He climbs out, grinning dangerously, unsteady on his legs, and we children interrupt our game of catch, our building of snow forts, our picking of plums, to watch in silence as he weaves past into the house, where he slumps into his overstuffed chair and falls asleep. Shaking her head, our mother stubs out the cigarette he has left smoldering in the ashtray. All evening, until our bedtimes, we tiptoe past him, as past a snoring dragon. Then we curl in our fearful sheets, listening. Eventually he wakes with a grunt, Mother slings accusations at him, he snarls back, she yells, he growls, their voices clashing. Before long, she retreats to their bedroom, sobbing—not from the blows of fists, for he never strikes her, but from the force of words.

Left alone, our father prowls the house, thumping into furniture, rummaging in the kitchen, slamming doors, turning the pages of the newspaper with a savage crackle, muttering back at the late-night drivel from television. The roof might fly off, the walls might buckle from the pressure of his rage. Whatever my brother and sister and mother may be thinking on their own rumpled pillows, I lie there hating him, loving him, fearing him, knowing I have failed him. I tell myself he drinks to ease an ache that gnaws at his belly, an ache I must have caused by disappointing him somehow, a murderous ache I should be able to relieve by doing all my chores, earning A's in school, winning baseball games, fixing the broken washer and the burst pipes, bringing in money to fill his empty wallet. He would not hide the green bottles in his tool box, would not sneak off to the barn with a lump under his coat, would not fall asleep in the daylight, would not roar and fume, would not drink himself to death, if only I were perfect.

I am forty-two as I write these words, and I know full well now that my father was an alcoholic, a man consumed by disease rather than by disappointment. What had seemed to me a private grief is in fact a public scourge. In the United States alone some ten or fifteen million people share his ailment, and behind the doors they slam in fury or disgrace, countless other children tremble. I comfort myself with such knowledge, holding it against the throb of memory like an ice pack against a bruise. There are keener sources of grief: poverty, racism, rape, war. I do not wish to compete for a trophy in suffering. I am only trying to understand the corrosive mixture of helplessness, responsibility, and shame that I learned to feel as the son of an alcoholic. I realize now that I did not cause my father's illness, nor could I have cured it. Yet for all this grown-up knowledge, I am still ten years old, my own son's age, and as that boy I struggle in guilt and confusion to save my father from pain.

Consider a few of our synonyms for *drunk*: tipsy, tight, pickled, soused, and plowed; stoned and stewed, lubricated and inebriated, juiced and sluiced; three sheets to the wind, in your cups, out of your mind, under the table; lit up, tanked up, wiped out; besotted, blotto, bombed, and buzzed; plastered, polluted, putri-fied; loaded or looped, boozy, woozy, fuddled, or smashed; crocked and shit-faced, corked and pissed, snockered and sloshed.

It is a mostly humorous lexicon, as the lore that deals with drunks—in jokes and cartoons, in plays, films, and television skits—is largely comic. Aunt Matilda nips elderberry wine from the sideboard and burps politely during supper. Uncle Fred slouches to the table glassy-eyed, wearing a lamp shade for a hat and mur-muring, "Candy is dandy but liquor is quicker." Inspired by cocktails, Mrs. Some-body recounts the events of her day in a fuzzy dialect, while Mr. Somebody nibbles her ear and croons a bawdy song. On the sofa with Boyfriend, Daugh-ter giggles, licking gin from her lips, and loosens the bows in her hair. Junior knocks back some brews with his chums at the Leopard Lounge and stumbles home to the wrong house, wonders foggily why he cannot locate his pajamas, and crawls naked into bed with the ugliest girl in school. The family dog slurps from a neglected martini and wobbles to the nursery, where he vomits in Baby's shoe.

It is all great fun. But if in the audience you notice a few laughing faces turn grim when the drunk lurches on stage, don't be surprised, for these are the children of alcoholics. Over the grinning mask of Dionysus,[1] the leering mask of Bacchus,[2] these children cannot help seeing the bloated features of their own parents. Instead of laughing, they wince, they mourn. Instead of cel-ebrating the drunk as one freed from constraints, they pity him as one enslaved. They refuse to believe *in vino veritas*,[3] having seen their befuddled parents skid away from truth toward folly and oblivion. And so these children bite their lips until the lush staggers into the wings.

My father, when drunk, was neither funny nor honest; he was pathetic, frightening, deceitful. There seemed to be a leak in him somewhere, and he poured in booze to keep from draining dry. Like a torture victim who refuses to squeal, he would never admit that he had touched a drop, not even in his last year, when he seemed to be dissolving in alcohol before our very eyes. I never knew him to lie about anything, ever, except about this one ruinous fact. Drowsy, clumsy, unable to fix a bicycle tire, throw a baseball, balance a gro-cery sack, or walk across the room, he was stripped of his true self by drink. In a matter of minutes, the contents of a bottle could transform a brave man into a coward, a buddy into a bully, a gifted athlete and skilled carpenter and shrewd businessman into a bumbler. No dictionary of synonyms for *drunk* would soften the anguish of watching our prince turn into a frog.

Father's drinking became the family secret. While growing up, we children never breathed a word of it beyond the four walls of our house. To this day, my brother and sister rarely mention it, and then only when I press them. I did not confess the ugly, bewildering fact to my wife until his wavering walk and slurred

1. Greek name for the god of wine and intoxication.
2. Roman name for the god of wine and intoxication.
3. Latin for "in wine is truth."

speech forced me to. Recently, on the seventh anniversary of my father's death, I asked my mother if she ever spoke of his drinking to friends. "No, no, never," she replied hastily. "I couldn't bear for anyone to know."

The secret bores under the skin, gets in the blood, into the bone, and stays there. Long after you have supposedly been cured of malaria, the fever can flare up, the tremors can shake you. So it is with the fevers of shame. You swallow the bitter quinine[4] of knowledge, and you learn to feel pity and compassion toward the drinker. Yet the shame lingers in your marrow, and, because of the shame, anger.

15   For a long stretch of my childhood we lived on a military reservation in Ohio, an arsenal where bombs were stored underground in bunkers, vintage airplanes burst into flames, and unstable artillery shells boomed nightly at the dump. We had the feeling, as children, that we played in a mine field, where a heedless footfall could trigger an explosion. When Father was drinking, the house, too, became a mine field. The least bump could set off either parent.

The more he drank, the more obsessed Mother became with stopping him. She hunted for bottles, counted the cash in his wallet, sniffed at his breath. Without meaning to snoop, we children blundered left and right into damning evidence. On afternoons when he came home from work sober, we flung ourselves at him for hugs, and felt against our ribs the telltale lump in his coat. In the barn we tumbled on the hay and heard beneath our sneakers the crunch of buried glass. We tugged open a drawer in his workbench, looking for screwdrivers or crescent wrenches, and spied a gleaming six-pack among the tools. Playing tag, we darted around the house just in time to see him sway on the rear stoop and heave a finished bottle into the woods. In his good night kiss we smelled the cloying sweetness of Clorets, the mints he chewed to camouflage his dragon's breath.

I can summon up that kiss right now by recalling Theodore Roethke's[5] lines about his own father in "My Papa's Waltz":

> The whiskey on your breath
> Could make a small boy dizzy;
> But I hung on like death:
> Such waltzing was not easy.

Such waltzing was hard, terribly hard, for with a boy's scrawny arms I was trying to hold my tipsy father upright.

For years, the chief source of those incriminating bottles and cans was a grimy store a mile from us, a cinder block place called Sly's, with two gas pumps outside and a moth-eaten dog asleep in the window. A strip of flypaper, speckled the year round with black bodies, coiled in the doorway. Inside, on rusty metal shelves or in wheezing coolers, you could find pop and Popsicles, ciga-

---

4. Drug used to treat malaria, made from the bark of the South American cinchona tree.
5. American poet (1908–1963) whose father also drank a lot.

rettes, potato chips, canned soup, raunchy postcards, fishing gear, Twinkies, wine, and beer. When Father drove anywhere on errands, Mother would send us kids along as guards, warning us not to let him out of our sight. And so with one or more of us on board, Father would cruise up to Sly's, pump a dollar's worth of gas or plump the tires with air, and then, telling us to wait in the car, he would head for that fly-spangled doorway.

Dutiful and panicky, we cried, "Let us go in with you!"

"No," he answered. "I'll be back in two shakes."   20

"Please!"

"No!" he roared. "Don't you budge, or I'll jerk a knot in your tails!"

So we stayed put, kicking the seats, while he ducked inside. Often, when he had parked the car at a careless angle, we gazed in through the window and saw Mr. Sly fetching down from a shelf behind the cash register two green pints of Gallo wine. Father swigged one of them right there at the counter, stuffed the other in his pocket, and then out he came, a bulge in his coat, a flustered look on his red face.

Because the Mom and Pop who ran the dump were neighbors of ours, living just down the tar-blistered road, I hated them all the more for poisoning my father. I wanted to sneak in their store and smash the bottles and set fire to the place. I also hated the Gallo brothers, Ernest and Julio, whose jovial faces shone from the labels of their wine, labels I would find, torn and curled, when I burned the trash. I noted the Gallo brothers' address, in California, and I studied the road atlas to see how far that was from Ohio, because I meant to go out there and tell Ernest and Julio what they were doing to my father, and then, if they showed no mercy, I would kill them.

While growing up on the back roads and in the country schools and cramped   25 Methodist churches of Ohio and Tennessee, I never heard the word *alcoholism*, never happened across it in books or magazines. In the nearby towns, there were no addiction treatment programs, no community mental health centers, no Alcoholics Anonymous chapters, no therapists. Left alone with our grievous secret, we had no way of understanding Father's drinking except as an act of will, a deliberate folly or cruelty, a moral weakness, a sin. He drank because he chose to, pure and simple. Why our father, so playful and competent and kind when sober, would choose to ruin himself and punish his family, we could not fathom.

Our neighborhood was high on the Bible, and the Bible was hard on drunkards. "Woe to those who are heroes at drinking wine, and valiant men in mixing strong drink," wrote Isaiah. "The priest and the prophet reel with strong drink, they are confused with wine, they err in vision, they stumble in giving judgment. For all tables are full of vomit, no place is without filthiness." We children had seen those fouled tables at the local truck stop where the notorious boozers hung out, our father occasionally among them. "Wine and new wine take away the understanding," declared the prophet Hosea. We had also seen evidence of that in our father, who could multiply seven-digit numbers in his head when sober, but when drunk could not help us with fourth-grade math.

Proverbs warned: "Do not look at wine when it is red, when it sparkles in the cup and goes down smoothly. At the last it bites like a serpent, and stings like an adder. Your eyes will see strange things, and your mind utter perverse things." Woe, woe.

Dismayingly often, these biblical drunkards stirred up trouble for their own kids. Noah made fresh wine after the flood, drank too much of it, fell asleep without any clothes on, and was glimpsed in the buff by his son Ham, whom Noah promptly cursed. In one passage—it was so shocking we had to read it under our blankets with flashlights—the patriarch Lot fell down drunk and slept with his daughters. The sins of the fathers set their children's teeth on edge.

Our ministers were fond of quoting St. Paul's pronouncement that drunkards would not inherit the kingdom of God. These grave preachers assured us that the wine referred to during the Last Supper was in fact grape juice. Bible and sermons and hymns combined to give us the impression that Moses should have brought down from the mountain another stone tablet, bearing the Eleventh Commandment: Thou shalt not drink.

The scariest and most illuminating Bible story apropos of drunkards was the one about the lunatic and the swine. Matthew, Mark, and Luke each told a version of the tale. We knew it by heart: When Jesus climbed out of his boat one day, this lunatic came charging up from the graveyard, stark naked and filthy, frothing at the mouth, so violent that he broke the strongest chains. Nobody would go near him. Night and day for years this madman had been wailing among the tombs and bruising himself with stones. Jesus took one look at him and said, "Come out of the man, you unclean spirits!" for he could see that the lunatic was possessed by demons. Meanwhile, some hogs were conveniently rooting nearby. "If we have to come out," begged the demons, "at least let us go into those swine." Jesus agreed. The unclean spirits entered the hogs, and the hogs rushed straight off a cliff and plunged into a lake. Hearing the story in Sunday school, my friends thought mainly of the pigs. (How big a splash did they make? Who paid for the lost pork?) But I thought of the redeemed lunatic, who bathed himself and put on clothes and calmly sat at the feet of Jesus, restored—so the Bible said—to "his right mind."

30   When drunk, our father was clearly in his wrong mind. He became a stranger, as fearful to us as any graveyard lunatic, not quite frothing at the mouth but fierce enough, quick-tempered, explosive; or else he grew maudlin and weepy, which frightened us nearly as much. In my boyhood despair, I reasoned that maybe he wasn't to blame for turning into an ogre. Maybe, like the lunatic, he was possessed by demons. I found support for my theory when I heard liquor referred to as "spirits," when the newspapers reported that somebody had been arrested for "driving under the influence," and when church ladies railed against that "demon drink."

If my father was indeed possessed, who would exorcise him? If he was a sinner, who would save him? If he was ill, who would cure him? If he suffered, who would ease his pain? Not ministers or doctors, for we could not bring ourselves to confide in them; not the neighbors, for we pretended they had never seen him drunk; not Mother, who fussed and pleaded but could not budge him; not my brother and sister, who were only kids. That left me. It did not matter that I, too, was only a child, and a bewildered one at that. I could not excuse myself.

On first reading a description of delirium tremens—in a book on alcoholism I smuggled from the library—I thought immediately of the frothing lunatic and the frenzied swine. When I read stories or watched films about grisly meta-morphoses—Dr. Jekyll becoming Mr. Hyde,[6] the mild husband changing into a werewolf, the kindly neighbor taken over by a brutal alien—I could not help seeing my own father's mutation from sober to drunk. Even today, knowing bet-ter, I am attracted by the demonic theory of drink, for when I recall my father's transformation, the emergence of his ugly second self, I find it easy to believe in possession by unclean spirits. We never knew which version of Father would come home from work, the true or the tainted, nor could we guess how far down the slope toward cruelty he would slide.

How far a man *could* slide we gauged by observing our back-road neighbors—the out-of-work miners who had dragged their families to our corner of Ohio from the desolate hollows of Appalachia, the tight-fisted farmers, the surly mechanics, the balked and broken men. There was, for example, whiskey-soaked Mr. Jenkins, who beat his wife and kids so hard we could hear their screams from the road. There was Mr. Lavo the wino, who fell asleep smok-ing time and again, until one night his disgusted wife bundled up the children and went outside and left him in his easy chair to burn; he awoke on his own, staggered out coughing into the yard, and pounded her flat while the children looked on and the shack turned to ash. There was the truck driver, Mr. Sampson, who tripped over his son's tricycle one night while drunk and got so mad that he jumped into his semi and drove away, shifting through the dozen gears, and never came back. We saw the bruised children of these fathers clump onto our school bus, we saw the abandoned children huddle in the pews at church, we saw the stunned and battered mothers begging for help at our doors.

Our own father never beat us, and I don't think he ever beat Mother, but he threatened often. The Old Testament Yahweh was not more terrible in his wrath. Eyes blazing, voice booming, Father would pull out his belt and swear to give us a whipping, but he never followed through, never needed to, because we could imagine it so vividly. He shoved us, pawed us with the back of his hand, as an irked bear might smack a cub, not to injure, just to clear a space. I can see him grabbing Mother by the hair as she cowers on a chair during a nightly quarrel. He twists her neck back until she gapes up at him, and then he lifts over her skull a glass quart bottle of milk, the milk running down his forearm; and he yells at her, "Say just one more word, one goddamn word, and I'll shut you up!" I fear she will prick him with her sharp tongue, but she is terrified into silence, and so am I, and the leaking bottle quivers in the air, and

6. London physician and his evil alter ego, in Robert Louis Stevenson's novella *Strange Case of Dr. Jekyll and Mr. Hyde* (1886).

milk slithers through the red hair of my father's uplifted arm, and the entire scene is there to this moment, the head jerked back, the club raised.

35   When the drink made him weepy, Father would pack a bag and kiss each of us children on the head, and announce from the front door that he was moving out. "Where to?" we demanded, fearful each time that he would leave for good, as Mr. Sampson had roared away for good in his diesel truck. "Someplace where I won't get hounded every minute," Father would answer, his jaw quivering. He stabbed a look at Mother, who might say, "Don't run into the ditch before you get there," or, "Good riddance," and then he would slink away. Mother watched him go with arms crossed over her chest, her face closed like the lid on a box of snakes. We children bawled. Where could he go? To the truck stop, that den of iniquity? To one of those dark, ratty flophouses in town? Would he wind up sleeping under a railroad bridge or on a park bench or in a cardboard box, mummied in rags, like the bums we had seen on our trips to Cleveland and Chicago? We bawled and bawled, wondering if he would ever come back.

He always did come back, a day or a week later, but each time there was a sliver less of him.

In Kafka's[7] *The Metamorphosis,* which opens famously with Gregor Samsa waking up from uneasy dreams to find himself transformed into an insect, Gregor's family keep reassuring themselves that things will be just fine again, "When he comes back to us." Each time alcohol transformed our father, we held out the same hope, that he would really and truly come back to us, our authentic father, the tender and playful and competent man, and then all things would be fine. We had grounds for such hope. After his weepy departures and chapfallen returns, he would sometimes go weeks, even months without drinking. Those were glad times. Joy banged inside my ribs. Every day without the furtive glint of bottles, every meal without a fight, every bedtime without sobs encouraged us to believe that such bliss might go on forever.

Mother was fooled by just such a hope all during the forty-odd years she knew this Greeley Ray Sanders. Soon after she met him in a Chicago delicatessen on the eve of World War II and fell for his butter-melting Mississippi drawl and his wavy red hair, she learned that he drank heavily. But then so did a lot of men. She would soon coax or scold him into breaking the nasty habit. She would point out to him how ugly and foolish it was, this bleary drinking, and then he would quit. He refused to quit during their engagement, however, still refused during the first years of marriage, refused until my sister came along. The shock of fatherhood sobered him, and he remained sober through my birth at the end of the war and right on through until we moved in 1951 to the Ohio arsenal, that paradise of bombs. Like all places that make a business of death, the arsenal had more than its share of alcoholics and drug addicts and other varieties of escape artists. There I turned six and started school and woke into a child's flickering awareness, just in time to see my father begin sneaking swigs in the garage.

7. Franz Kafka (1883–1924), Prague-born novelist and short-story writer.

He sobered up again for most of a year at the height of the Korean War, to celebrate the birth of my brother. But aside from that dry spell, his only breaks from drinking before I graduated from high school were just long enough to raise and then dash our hopes. Then during the fall of my senior year—the time of the Cuban missile crisis, when it seemed that the nightly explosions at the munitions dump and the nightly rages in our household might spread to engulf the globe—Father collapsed. His liver, kidneys, and heart all conked out. The doctors saved him, but only by a hair. He stayed in the hospital for weeks, going through a withdrawal so terrible that Mother would not let us visit him. If he wanted to kill himself, the doctors solemnly warned him, all he had to do was hit the bottle again. One binge would finish him.

Father must have believed them, for he stayed dry the next fifteen years. It was an answer to prayer, Mother said, it was a miracle. I believe it was a reflex of fear, which he sustained over the years through courage and pride. He knew a man could die from drink, for his brother Roscoe had. We children never laid eyes on doomed Uncle Roscoe, but in the stories Mother told us he became a fairy-tale figure, like a boy who took the wrong turning in the woods and was gobbled up by the wolf. 40

The fifteen-year dry spell came to an end with Father's retirement in the spring of 1978. Like many men, he gave up his identity along with his job. One day he was a boss at the factory, with a brass plate on his door and a reputation to uphold; the next day he was a nobody at home. He and Mother were leaving Ontario, the last of the many places to which his job had carried them, and they were moving to a new house in Mississippi, his childhood stomping grounds. As a boy in Mississippi, Father sold Coca-Cola during dances while the moonshiners peddled their brew in the parking lot; as a young blade, he fought in bars and in the ring, seeking a state Golden Gloves championship; he gambled at poker, hunted pheasants, raced motorcycles and cars, played semiprofessional baseball, and, along with all his buddies—in the Black Cat Saloon, behind the cotton gin, in the woods—he drank. It was a perilous youth to dream of recovering.

After his final day of work, Mother drove on ahead with a car full of begonias and violets, while Father stayed behind to oversee the packing. When the van was loaded, the sweaty movers broke open a six-pack and offered him a beer.

"Let's drink to retirement!" they crowed. "Let's drink to freedom! to fishing! hunting! loafing! Let's drink to a guy who's going home!"

At least I imagine some such words, for that is all I can do, imagine, and I see Father's hand trembling in midair as he thinks about the fifteen sober years and about the doctors' warning, and he tells himself *God damnit, I am a free man,* and *Why can't a free man drink one beer after a lifetime of hard work?* and I see his arm reaching, his fingers closing, the can tilting to his lips. I even supply a label for the beer, a swaggering brand that promises on television to deliver the essence of life. I watch the amber liquid pour down his throat, the alcohol steal into his blood, the key turn in his brain.

Soon after my parents moved back to Father's treacherous stomping ground, my wife and I visited them in Mississippi with our five-year-old daughter. Mother 45 had been too distraught to warn me about the return of the demons. So when I climbed out of the car that bright July morning and saw my father napping in the hammock, I felt uneasy, for in all his sober years I had never known him to sleep in daylight. Then he lurched upright, blinked his bloodshot eyes, and greeted us in a syrupy voice. I was hurled back helpless into childhood.

"What's the matter with Papaw?" our daughter asked.

"Nothing," I said. "Nothing!"

Like a child again, I pretended not to see him in his stupor, and behind my phony smile I grieved. On that visit and on the few that remained before his death, once again I found bottles in the workbench, bottles in the woods. Again his hands shook too much for him to run a saw, to make his precious miniature furniture, to drive straight down back roads. Again he wound up in the ditch, in the hospital, in jail, in treatment centers. Again he shouted and wept. Again he lied. "I never touched a drop," he swore. "Your mother's making it up."

I no longer fancied I could reason with the men whose names I found on the bottles—Jim Beam, Jack Daniels—nor did I hope to save my father by burning down a store. I was able now to press the cold statistics about alcoholism against the ache of memory: ten million victims, fifteen million, twenty. And yet, in spite of my age, I reacted in the same blind way as I had in childhood, ignoring biology, forgetting numbers, vainly seeking to erase through my efforts whatever drove him to drink. I worked on their place twelve and sixteen hours a day, in the swelter of Mississippi summers, digging ditches, running electrical wires, planting trees, mowing grass, building sheds, as though what nagged at him was some list of chores, as though by taking his worries on my shoulders I could redeem him. I was flung back into boyhood, acting as though my father would not drink himself to death if only I were perfect.

50   I failed of perfection; he succeeded in dying. To the end, he considered himself not sick but sinful. "Do you want to kill yourself?" I asked him. "Why not?" he answered. "Why the hell not? What's there to save?" To the end, he would not speak about his feelings, would not or could not give a name to the beast that was devouring him.

In silence, he went rushing off the cliff. Unlike the biblical swine, however, he left behind a few of the demons to haunt his children. Life with him and the loss of him twisted us into shapes that will be familiar to other sons and daughters of alcoholics. My brother became a rebel, my sister retreated into shyness, I played the stalwart and dutiful son who would hold the family together. If my father was unstable, I would be a rock. If he squandered money on drink, I would pinch every penny. If he wept when drunk—and only when drunk—I would not let myself weep at all. If he roared at the Little League umpire for calling my pitches balls, I would throw nothing but strikes. Watching him flounder and rage, I came to dread the loss of control. I would go through life without making anyone mad. I vowed never to put in my mouth or veins any chemical that would banish my everyday self. I would never make a scene, never lash out at the ones I loved, never hurt a soul. Through hard work, relentless work, I would achieve something dazzling—in the classroom, on the basketball floor, in the science lab, in the pages of books—and my achievement would distract the world's eyes from his humiliation. I would become a worthy sacrifice, and the smoke of my burning would please God.

It is far easier to recognize these twists in my character than to undo them. Work has become an addiction for me, as drink was an addiction for my father. Knowing this, my daughter gave me a placard for the wall: WORKAHOLIC. The labor is endless and futile, for I can no more redeem myself through work than I could redeem my father. I still panic in the face of other people's anger, because his drunken temper was so terrible. I shrink from causing sadness or disappointment even to strangers, as though I were still concealing the family shame. I still notice every twitch of emotion in the faces around me, having learned as a child to read the weather in faces, and I blame myself for their least pang of unhappiness or anger. In certain moods I blame myself for everything. Guilt burns like acid in my veins.

I am moved to write these pages now because my own son, at the age of ten, is taking on himself the griefs of the world, and in particular the griefs of his father. He tells me that when I am gripped by sadness he feels responsible; he feels there must be something he can do to spring me from depression, to fix my life. And that crushing sense of responsibility is exactly what I felt at the age of ten in the face of my father's drinking. My son wonders if I, too, am possessed. I write, therefore, to drag into the light what eats at me—the fear, the guilt, the shame—so that my own children may be spared.

I still shy away from nightclubs, from bars, from parties where the solvent is alcohol. My friends puzzle over this, but it is no more peculiar than for a man to shy away from the lions' den after seeing his father torn apart. I took my own first drink at the age of twenty-one, half a glass of burgundy. I knew the odds of my becoming an alcoholic were four times higher than for the sons of nonalcoholic fathers. So I sipped warily.

I still do—once a week, perhaps, a glass of wine, a can of beer, nothing   55
stronger, nothing more. I listen for the turning of a key in my brain.

MLA CITATION

Sanders, Scott Russell. "Under the Influence." *The Norton Reader: An Anthology of Nonfiction*, edited by Melissa A. Goldthwaite et al., 15th ed., W. W. Norton, 2020, pp. 35–45.

QUESTIONS

1. Scott Russell Sanders frequently punctuates his memories of his father with information from other sources—dictionaries, medical encyclopedias, poems and short stories, the Bible. What function do these sources perform? How do they enlarge and enrich Sanders's essay?

2. Why does Sanders conclude his essay with paragraphs 53–55? What effect do they create that would be lost without them?

3. Drawing on your memories of a family member, write an essay about a problem that person had and its effect on your life.

DURGA CHEW-BOSE
Tan Lines

COME SUMMER, my reluctance kicks in. It's as if the sheer persistence of a July day—the sun's glare, its flecked appraisal of pavement and trees, those bonus evening hours—solicits from me an essential need to withdraw. Thankfully, writing is an indoor sport. Sometimes I go stretches of days without much sun, and even in the swell of midsummer I maintain what could be characterized as my winter pallor. Though pallor might not be accurate. How might I describe my brownness, my very fair brownness, that following winter appears even more fair? What's the opposite of *glowing*? Dull? Drab? Run-down? Blah?

These questions are not as good-humored as they seem but are fixed instead to my tendency for self-scrutiny, activated long ago when I came to understand my sense of belonging—my *who-ness*—as two-pronged. The beautiful dilemma of being first-generation and all that it means: a reflection of theirs and mine, of source and story. A running start toward blending in among mostly white childhood friends who were rarely curious about my olive-brown skin, the dark shine of my hair, my chestnut eyes. We were kids, after all. We were one another's chorus, encountering parents—and the *elsewhere* that entailed for me—only in consonant environments: a birthday party, ballet recitals, rides to the movies in my parents' burgundy Toyota Previa.

In terms of family, this elsewhere—my parents' *who-ness*—was abundant yet imperceptible. It was my home. Where I ate and slept, and wore big T-shirts to bed, and watched TV, and played Parcheesi, and fought with my brother, and savored the leeway of a Saturday morning, and where I would get scolded for tossing my jacket on the divan, or be corrected for answering a question with "I don't care" instead of "I don't mind."

And, come summer, I reexperience with particular clarity these accumulations of a home, not merely through memory's piping but in actions. Despite New York City's stifling weather, how the air distorts into a muggy mass, I drink hot tea and eat hot soup. It cools me down. Because in that sly way science naturally alloys with what we inherit, I've been told since childhood that hot liquids provide remedial chill. This slight reprieve on especially sticky days, I like to imagine, is a discreet reminder that my parents are not always but sometimes right. That the knowledge they've imparted to my brother and me is not purely an expression of love but firm testimony of their own provenance, and how what keeps us close reveals itself not just in facsimile but, over time, in what kindly amounts in kernels. An everyday tip, a turn of phrase and its unusual construction, reminders to not sit on my bed with "outside clothes," for instance, or how in the summer my body yields to the season's balm with what I've come to regard as heritable agency.

From Too Much and Not the Mood *(2017), Durga Chew-Bose's collection of lyric essays about identity and culture.*

Those beads of sweat that collect on my nose are entirely my Mama's. The   5
annual, deep-healing effects of humidity on my dry skin; that's hers as well. If
friends come over to my apartment and I offer them "some tea," those two
words conjure my father's anticipant inflection on scorching weekend afternoons when he sits on our porch having proudly just fixed something without
needing to replace it, like the broken nozzle of our gardening hose or the loose
legs of a chair.

In my case, inheritance has never simply been what trickles down through
traditions but is also the work required to disallow how those traditions fade.
To recover the various genetic dispatches like those from my grandfather Felix,
whom I met once, long ago, in Kolkata,[1] in a kitchen, I think, of which I
remember little except for the color green. A tablecloth, maybe. A moss stain
on a concrete wall. Perhaps the whole memory is enameled green because for
no discernible reason some colors naturally coat nostalgia with geography.
India, for me, has always been protected in a layer of green.

There is also my paternal grandfather, whom I never met, and his wife, my
grandmother Thama, whom I did. And there is my other grandmother, who
died when my mother was a teenager. Her skin was far darker than mine, a
trait I noted as I studied one photo album in particular, confusing the musty
scent of protective parchment sheets with what I imagined she herself might
have smelled like. I remember foolishly wondering as a child if my much
lighter skin was an outcome of brown girls growing up in cold climates. A dis-
cordance that epitomized how split I felt between life at home and life outside,
overcome and enamored by my white friends and every so often experiencing
waves of assimilation met by lulls of wanting nothing more than to seek lineage, move backward, claim the brownness of my skin as I only knew how:
through family.

I became more aware of my skin, as most of us do with our bodies, in adolescence, and especially when summer arrived. Halter tops. Shoulder blades.
Crop tops. Sweat stains. Denim skirts. Shorts. A growth spurt marked by how
my knees now knocked my bike's handlebars as I pedaled to the park. The
many ways we learned to twist and tie our T-shirts so they'd ride up our stomachs or whorl around our waists. Bathing suits. Boys. The convention of boys
in the summer; how, suddenly, they memorialized the season. Still, I became
heedful of the sun's currency on my body. The sun's signature on my skin and
how the contrast of tan lines carried merit. That I was expected to feel virtuous was strange to me. I tanned fast. Brown to dark umber in a matter of
hours. But what struck me was this: it was as if my white friends were wearing
their tanned skin—bathing in it—as opposed to living in it. The thrill of
becoming temporarily dark was, for them, an advantage. It would take me a
decade or so, longer even, to consider or be faced with what dark skin means
in the world and how my relationship to my skin is further complicated by how
fair it is and the access it allows me, and oh, what a luxury to be allowed a
decade or more of girlhood in the first place.

1. Formerly known as Calcutta, capital of the Indian state of West Bengal.

The level of excitement among my New York friends, in the summer, has now hit a fever pitch and results in one thing: plans. So many plans. An incessancy of plans. An ambush of them, really. Unspent from winter's reserve, these nascent leisure hours develop into a vague inertia where we sip slushy tequila or inestimable glasses of rosé, or where I park myself on a roof in Brooklyn and characterize the faraway hedge of buildings as "a view," and where I squint at my phone or the same paragraph in my book and feel indebted to the car passing below blasting *that song*.

10   And let's not forget the beach. Here, among families and unaccustomed sounds like splashing water and seagulls squawking, we zone out, obscure the sun with shades and funny hats, nap in quick spells, signal over friends and scoot over to make room on our towels and blankets. Summer is many things, but it is, certainly, the season for scooting over. Plans and scooting over.

As new–to–New York adults, living here without history but with the audacity to claim space, these mini migrations from rooftops to small stretches of sand, to the fire escape at sunset where we climb out and gawk and attempt the impossible—to acquire the sky's display in a few inches of touch screen—somehow constitute *spending time*.

Now picture what happens when my skin tans. *When it doesn't.* When over the years my white friends have lathered themselves with Hawaiian Tropic and announced with a sense of crusading enterprise their plans to "sit out and bake." When they've spent long weekends at a wedding in Palm Springs or a house on Fire Island, coming back to the city with burns they bemoan, only to quickly and quite airily reevaluate: *Well, at least now I have my base layer.*

Trace back to high school and then college, when my white friends would return from spring break, from all-inclusive resort vacations or a week at their cottage. Without fail, the most common occurrence—one that has persisted through adulthood—is this: my friend will place her arm next to mine, grow visibly thrilled, and exclaim that her skin is now darker than mine.

The things I've heard: I'm *almost* as brown as you. I'm darker than you now. We match. I'm lucky I tan easily. You *look* like you tan easily. You don't even have to work for your tan.

15   I'll stop after these two: I'm basically black. I wish I had your color.

Since the average white person's spectrum of darkness is limited, the language of tanning is appropriative at best. Witlessness masquerades as admiration, co-option as obtusely worded praise. Compliments, in some cases, can feel like audits.

Growing up brown in mostly white circles means learning from a very young age that language is inured to prejudicial glitches. Time and again, I have concealed my amazement. The semantics of ignorance are oddly extensive and impossible to foresee. Close friends of mine goof. There is, after all, no script. As Wesley Morris[2] recently wrote, "For people of color, some aspect of friendship with white people involves an awareness that you could be dropped through a trapdoor of racism at any moment." Zero notice met with my own long-harvested ability to recoup, ignore, smile, move on.

2. American journalist (b. 1975).

What leaves me uneasy is the covetous near-pricing of quick-tanning skin, so long as the experience is short-lived or euphemistic—a certificate of travel, a token of escape, time off. Proof of having *been away*. Like the watch you forgot to leave by your hotel bedside, that you wore to the beach as you dozed off at noon and then again at three—even that goofy tan becomes, for what it's worth, a holiday trophy. A mark, in some cases, of status.

As a kid, I accepted the compliments my skin would receive from, for instance, the mother offering me orange wedges after a soccer practice, or as I reapplied sunscreen at the local pool. I was, as most children are, innocent to the syntax of difference. How some obscure the act of othering with adulation. The luxury of privilege is so vast that praise is presumed to conceal bias.

But that was then. That was before I could place what was so upsetting to me about the mothers at soccer practice. The mothers at the pool who were looking at my body. Feeling watched yet accepting their compliments, and politely smiling, created a tenseness inside of me I couldn't yet parse. And anyway, it was hot, and the water was cool, and why were these mothers I barely knew talking to me at all?

I have two bathing suits. Well, two that I wear. A one-piece, navy. A two-piece, black. A couple of summers ago I was Gchatting with a friend as we both shopped online for new suits. Bathers, I call them. It must have been late winter or early spring because, from what I remember, we were typing in errant ALL CAPS, singular to anticipating a summer that threatens to never come. *Gonna FINALLY buy a bike; can't WAIT to not wear socks; I wish we knew someone with a POOL.* At one point she linked me to an all-white one-piece bather that scooped low in the back. *I could NEVER wear this,* she typed. *But it'll look SO good on you, especially when you're tanned.*

I've come to interpret comments like my friend's consideration of my skin, how it darkens in these summer months (first inside my elbows, as a boyfriend once pointed out to me), as plain enough. Depending on my mood, I regard or disregard them because I've grown up hearing, as most girls have: She is *this*. Looks great in *that*.

That my skin "goes well" with paler shades has never discouraged me from wearing black, which I ordinarily do. My brown skin, it turns out, means growing accustomed to uninvited sartorial *should*: You should wear yellow. More red, pale blues, and pink.

In the summer, my skin might bronze or redden and even freckle. It silhouettes my scars and turns sweat at four p.m. into liquid gold. But it might also, as if in defiance, preserve its paleness. On the brightest days, I go to the movies. Occasionally a museum. In bed, I sleep pushed up against the cold wall, or on the opposite side, with one leg dangling. For nearly five months, everyone leaves their windows open. Available to me are the season's many sounds. Even alone indoors, I am in the company of others. One neighbor is humming a song she was listening to earlier in the day. Another has started smoking again, cigarettes she never finishes. And another is on the phone; speaking to someone, that same someone, always, who I've long suspected must be mute. Sometimes I'll only leave my apartment once the sun is no longer hitting at an angle; when it's merely *there*, capable, reasonable.

25   But of course there are those days when I'm out, and it feels good. I return
home in the evening, and my eyes need a few seconds to square with that interior
grainy dullness. I'll catch glimpses of not just myself but my hands, and the
length of my fingers: my mother's. Or how my cheeks, now ruddy, have rounded
my long face, and briefly, there he is in my reflection. My father's smile. His
father's jawline. My brother's too. The manner of a person passed down in how
the light sculpts a face and how shadows are not just cast but connect me to that
framed picture of my grandmother when she was young. The sun still has hours
before setting. My skin is warm. It does not cool. The heat is in the seams.

MLA CITATION

Chew-Bose, Durga. "Tan Lines." *The Norton Reader: An Anthology of Nonfiction*, edited
by Melissa A. Goldthwaite et al., 15th ed., W. W. Norton, 2020, pp. 46–50.

QUESTIONS

1. When describing her white friends' comments on tanning and skin color, Durga
Chew-Bose writes, "Since the average white person's spectrum of darkness is limited,
the language of tanning is appropriative at best. Witlessness masquerades as admiration, co-option as obtusely worded praise. Compliments, in some cases, can feel
like audits" (paragraph 16). How does Chew-Bose develop the theme of compliments
masquerading as bias in this essay? Which examples best illustrate that bias?

2. Lyric essays often combine elements of poetry—such as lists of sensory images
and sometimes sentence fragments or the use of nonstandard punctuation. Trace
Chew-Bose's use of sensory images and fragments in this essay. Which uses of
these elements are most effective? Why?

3. Chew-Bose considers what she inherits from her family members—both physical
features and habits or preferences. Write a lyric essay in which you reflect on the
physical features and habits you have inherited from one or more family members.

JOSE ANTONIO VARGAS

My Life as an Undocumented Immigrant

 NE AUGUST MORNING nearly two decades ago, my mother woke
me and put me in a cab. She handed me a jacket. "Baka malamig
doon" were among the few words she said. ("It might be cold
there.") When I arrived at the Philippines' Ninoy Aquino International Airport with her, my aunt, and a family friend, I was
introduced to a man I'd never seen. They told me he was my

Published in the New York Times Magazine *(2011), this essay received the June 2011
Sidney Award, which recognizes excellence in socially-conscious journalism.*

uncle. He held my hand as I boarded an airplane for the first time. It was 1993, and I was 12.

My mother wanted to give me a better life, so she sent me thousands of miles away to live with her parents in America—my grandfather (Lolo in Tagalog[1]) and grandmother (Lola). After I arrived in Mountain View, Calif., in the San Francisco Bay Area, I entered sixth grade and quickly grew to love my new home, family, and culture. I discovered a passion for language, though it was hard to learn the difference between formal English and American slang. One of my early memories is of a freckled kid in middle school asking me, "What's up?" I replied, "The sky," and he and a couple of other kids laughed. I won the eighth-grade spelling bee by memorizing words I couldn't properly pronounce. (The winning word was "indefatigable.")

One day when I was 16, I rode my bike to the nearby D.M.V. office to get my driver's permit. Some of my friends already had their licenses, so I figured it was time. But when I handed the clerk my green card as proof of U.S. residency, she flipped it around, examining it. "This is fake," she whispered. "Don't come back here again."

Confused and scared, I pedaled home and confronted Lolo. I remember him sitting in the garage, cutting coupons. I dropped my bike and ran over to him, showing him the green card. "Peke ba ito?" I asked in Tagalog. ("Is this fake?") My grandparents were naturalized American citizens—he worked as a security guard, she as a food server—and they had begun supporting my mother and me financially when I was 3, after my father's wandering eye and inability to properly provide for us led to my parents' separation. Lolo was a proud man, and I saw the shame on his face as he told me he purchased the card, along with other fake documents, for me. "Don't show it to other people," he warned.

I decided then that I could never give anyone reason to doubt I was an   5
American. I convinced myself that if I worked enough, if I achieved enough, I would be rewarded with citizenship. I felt I could earn it.

I've tried. Over the past 14 years, I've graduated from high school and college and built a career as a journalist, interviewing some of the most famous people in the country. On the surface, I've created a good life. I've lived the American dream.

But I am still an undocumented immigrant. And that means living a different kind of reality. It means going about my day in fear of being found out. It means rarely trusting people, even those closest to me, with who I really am. It means keeping my family photos in a shoebox rather than displaying them on shelves in my home, so friends don't ask about them. It means reluctantly, even painfully, doing things I know are wrong and unlawful. And it has meant relying on a sort of 21st-century underground railroad of supporters, people who took an interest in my future and took risks for me.

---

1. One of two official languages spoken in the Philippines. Its standardized form is Filipino.

Last year I read about four students who walked from Miami to Washington to lobby for the Dream Act, a nearly decade-old immigration bill that would provide a path to legal permanent residency for young people who have been educated in this country. At the risk of deportation—the Obama administration has deported almost 800,000 people in the last two years—they are speaking out. Their courage has inspired me.

There are believed to be 11 million undocumented immigrants in the United States. We're not always who you think we are. Some pick your strawberries or care for your children. Some are in high school or college. And some, it turns out, write news articles you might read. I grew up here. This is my home. Yet even though I think of myself as an American and consider America my country, my country doesn't think of me as one of its own.

10   My first challenge was the language. Though I learned English in the Philippines, I wanted to lose my accent. During high school, I spent hours at a time watching television (especially "Frasier," "Home Improvement," and reruns of "The Golden Girls") and movies (from "Goodfellas" to "Anne of Green Gables"), pausing the VHS to try to copy how various characters enunciated their words. At the local library, I read magazines, books, and newspapers—anything to learn how to write better. Kathy Dewar, my high-school English teacher, introduced me to journalism. From the moment I wrote my first article for the student paper, I convinced myself that having my name in print—writing in English, interviewing Americans—validated my presence here.

The debates over "illegal aliens" intensified my anxieties. In 1994, only a year after my flight from the Philippines, Gov. Pete Wilson was re-elected in part because of his support for Proposition 187, which prohibited undocumented immigrants from attending public school and accessing other services. (A federal court later found the law unconstitutional.) After my encounter at the D.M.V. in 1997, I grew more aware of anti-immigrant sentiments and stereotypes: they don't want to assimilate, they are a drain on society. They're not talking about me, I would tell myself. I have something to contribute.

To do that, I had to work—and for that, I needed a Social Security number. Fortunately, my grandfather had already managed to get one for me. Lolo had always taken care of everyone in the family. He and my grandmother emigrated legally in 1984 from Zambales, a province in the Philippines of rice fields and bamboo houses, following Lolo's sister, who married a Filipino-American serving in the American military. She petitioned for her brother and his wife to join her. When they got here, Lolo petitioned for his two children—my mother and her younger brother—to follow them. But instead of mentioning that my mother was a married woman, he listed her as single. Legal residents can't petition for their married children. Besides, Lolo didn't care for my father. He didn't want him coming here too.

But soon Lolo grew nervous that the immigration authorities reviewing the petition would discover my mother was married, thus derailing not only her chances of coming here but those of my uncle as well. So he withdrew her petition. After my uncle came to America legally in 1991, Lolo tried to get my mother here through a tourist visa, but she wasn't able to obtain one. That's when she decided to send me. My mother told me later that she figured she would follow me soon. She never did.

The "uncle" who brought me here turned out to be a coyote,[2] not a relative, my grandfather later explained. Lolo scraped together enough money—I eventually learned it was $4,500, a huge sum for him—to pay him to smuggle me here under a fake name and fake passport. (I never saw the passport again after the flight and have always assumed that the coyote kept it.) After I arrived in America, Lolo obtained a new fake Filipino passport, in my real name this time, adorned with a fake student visa, in addition to the fraudulent green card.

Using the fake passport, we went to the local Social Security Administration office and applied for a Social Security number and card. It was, I remember, a quick visit. When the card came in the mail, it had my full, real name, but it also clearly stated: "Valid for work only with I.N.S. authorization."

When I began looking for work, a short time after the D.M.V. incident, my grandfather and I took the Social Security card to Kinko's, where he covered the "I.N.S. authorization" text with a sliver of white tape. We then made photocopies of the card. At a glance, at least, the copies would look like copies of a regular, unrestricted Social Security card.

Lolo always imagined I would work the kind of low-paying jobs that undocumented people often take. (Once I married an American, he said, I would get my real papers, and everything would be fine.) But even menial jobs require documents, so he and I hoped the doctored card would work for now. The more documents I had, he said, the better.

While in high school, I worked part time at Subway, then at the front desk of the local Y.M.C.A., then at a tennis club, until I landed an unpaid internship at The Mountain View Voice, my hometown newspaper. First I brought coffee and helped around the office; eventually I began covering city-hall meetings and other assignments for pay.

For more than a decade of getting part-time and full-time jobs, employers have rarely asked to check my original Social Security card. When they did, I showed the photocopied version, which they accepted. Over time, I also began checking the citizenship box on my federal I-9 employment eligibility forms. (Claiming full citizenship was actually easier than declaring permanent resident "green card" status, which would have required me to provide an alien registration number.)

This deceit never got easier. The more I did it, the more I felt like an impostor, the more guilt I carried—and the more I worried that I would get caught. But I kept doing it. I needed to live and survive on my own, and I decided this was the way.

Mountain View High School became my second home. I was elected to represent my school at school-board meetings, which gave me the chance to meet and befriend Rich Fischer, the superintendent for our school district.

2. A paid person who smuggles someone across the U.S.-Mexican border in violation of U.S. immigration laws.

I joined the speech and debate team, acted in school plays, and eventually became co-editor of The Oracle, the student newspaper. That drew the attention of my principal, Pat Hyland. "You're at school just as much as I am," she told me. Pat and Rich would soon become mentors, and over time, almost surrogate parents for me.

After a choir rehearsal during my junior year, Jill Denny, the choir director, told me she was considering a Japan trip for our singing group. I told her I couldn't afford it, but she said we'd figure out a way. I hesitated, and then decided to tell her the truth. "It's not really the money," I remember saying. "I don't have the right passport." When she assured me we'd get the proper documents, I finally told her. "I can't get the right passport," I said. "I'm not supposed to be here."

She understood. So the choir toured Hawaii instead, with me in tow. (Mrs. Denny and I spoke a couple of months ago, and she told me she hadn't wanted to leave any student behind.)

Later that school year, my history class watched a documentary on Harvey Milk, the openly gay San Francisco city official who was assassinated. This was 1999, just six months after Matthew Shepard's body was found tied to a fence in Wyoming. During the discussion, I raised my hand and said something like: "I'm sorry Harvey Milk got killed for being gay. . . . I've been meaning to say this. . . . I'm gay."

25   I hadn't planned on coming out that morning, though I had known that I was gay for several years. With that announcement, I became the only openly gay student at school, and it caused turmoil with my grandparents. Lolo kicked me out of the house for a few weeks. Though we eventually reconciled, I had disappointed him on two fronts. First, as a Catholic, he considered homosexuality a sin and was embarrassed about having "ang apo na bakla" ("a grandson who is gay"). Even worse, I was making matters more difficult for myself, he said. I needed to marry an American woman in order to gain a green card.

Tough as it was, coming out about being gay seemed less daunting than coming out about my legal status. I kept my other secret mostly hidden.

While my classmates awaited their college acceptance letters, I hoped to get a full-time job at The Mountain View Voice after graduation. It's not that I didn't want to go to college, but I couldn't apply for state and federal financial aid. Without that, my family couldn't afford to send me.

But when I finally told Pat and Rich about my immigration "problem"—as we called it from then on—they helped me look for a solution. At first, they even wondered if one of them could adopt me and fix the situation that way, but a lawyer Rich consulted told him it wouldn't change my legal status because I was too old. Eventually they connected me to a new scholarship fund for high-potential students who were usually the first in their families to attend college. Most important, the fund was not concerned with immigration status. I was among the first recipients, with the scholarship covering tuition, lodging, books, and other expenses for my studies at San Francisco State University.

As a college freshman, I found a job working part time at The San Francisco Chronicle, where I sorted mail and wrote some freelance articles. My ambition was to get a reporting job, so I embarked on a series of internships.

First I landed at The Philadelphia Daily News, in the summer of 2001, where I covered a drive-by shooting and the wedding of the 76ers star Allen Iverson. Using those articles, I applied to The Seattle Times and got an internship for the following summer.

But then my lack of proper documents became a problem again. The 30 Times's recruiter, Pat Foote, asked all incoming interns to bring certain paperwork on their first day: a birth certificate, or a passport, or a driver's license plus an original Social Security card. I panicked, thinking my documents wouldn't pass muster. So before starting the job, I called Pat and told her about my legal status. After consulting with management, she called me back with the answer I feared: I couldn't do the internship.

This was devastating. What good was college if I couldn't then pursue the career I wanted? I decided then that if I was to succeed in a profession that is all about truth-telling, I couldn't tell the truth about myself.

After this episode, Jim Strand, the venture capitalist who sponsored my scholarship, offered to pay for an immigration lawyer. Rich and I went to meet her in San Francisco's financial district.

I was hopeful. This was in early 2002, shortly after Senators Orrin Hatch, the Utah Republican, and Dick Durbin, the Illinois Democrat, introduced the Dream Act—Development, Relief, and Education for Alien Minors. It seemed like the legislative version of what I'd told myself: If I work hard and contribute, things will work out.

But the meeting left me crushed. My only solution, the lawyer said, was to go back to the Philippines and accept a 10-year ban before I could apply to return legally.

If Rich was discouraged, he hid it well. "Put this problem on a shelf," he 35 told me. "Compartmentalize it. Keep going."

And I did. For the summer of 2003, I applied for internships across the country. Several newspapers, including The Wall Street Journal, The Boston Globe, and The Chicago Tribune, expressed interest. But when The Washington Post offered me a spot, I knew where I would go. And this time, I had no intention of acknowledging my "problem."

The Post internship posed a tricky obstacle: It required a driver's license. (After my close call at the California D.M.V., I'd never gotten one.) So I spent an afternoon at The Mountain View Public Library, studying various states' requirements. Oregon was among the most welcoming—and it was just a few hours' drive north.

Again, my support network came through. A friend's father lived in Portland, and he allowed me to use his address as proof of residency. Pat, Rich, and Rich's longtime assistant, Mary Moore, sent letters to me at that address. Rich taught me how to do three-point turns in a parking lot, and a friend accompanied me to Portland.

The license meant everything to me—it would let me drive, fly, and work. But my grandparents worried about the Portland trip and the Washington internship. While Lola offered daily prayers so that I would not get caught, Lolo told me that I was dreaming too big, risking too much.

40   I was determined to pursue my ambitions. I was 22, I told them, responsible for my own actions. But this was different from Lolo's driving a confused
teenager to Kinko's. I knew what I was doing now, and I knew it wasn't right.
But what was I supposed to do?

I was paying state and federal taxes, but I was using an invalid Social
Security card and writing false information on my employment forms. But
that seemed better than depending on my grandparents or on Pat, Rich, and
Jim—or returning to a country I barely remembered. I convinced myself all
would be O.K. if I lived up to the qualities of a "citizen": hard work, self-
reliance, love of my country.

At the D.M.V. in Portland, I arrived with my photocopied Social Security
card, my college I.D., a pay stub from The San Francisco Chronicle, and my
proof of state residence—the letters to the Portland address that my support
network had sent. It worked. My license, issued in 2003, was set to expire
eight years later, on my 30th birthday, on Feb. 3, 2011. I had eight years to succeed professionally, and to hope that some sort of immigration reform would
pass in the meantime and allow me to stay.

It seemed like all the time in the world.

My summer in Washington was exhilarating. I was intimidated to be in a major
newsroom but was assigned a mentor—Peter Perl, a veteran magazine writer—
to help me navigate it. A few weeks into the internship, he printed out one of my
articles, about a guy who recovered a long-lost wallet, circled the first two paragraphs, and left it on my desk. "Great eye for details—awesome!" he wrote.
Though I didn't know it then, Peter would become one more member of my
network.

45   At the end of the summer, I returned to The San Francisco Chronicle. My
plan was to finish school—I was now a senior—while I worked for The Chronicle as a reporter for the city desk. But when The Post beckoned again, offering me a full-time, two-year paid internship that I could start when I graduated
in June 2004, it was too tempting to pass up. I moved back to Washington.

About four months into my job as a reporter for The Post, I began feeling
increasingly paranoid, as if I had "illegal immigrant" tattooed on my forehead—
and in Washington, of all places, where the debates over immigration seemed
never-ending. I was so eager to prove myself that I feared I was annoying some
colleagues and editors—and worried that any one of these professional journalists could discover my secret. The anxiety was nearly paralyzing. I decided
I had to tell one of the higher-ups about my situation. I turned to Peter.

By this time, Peter, who still works at The Post, had become part of management as the paper's director of newsroom training and professional development. One afternoon in late October, we walked a couple of blocks to Lafayette
Square, across from the White House. Over some 20 minutes, sitting on a
bench, I told him everything: the Social Security card, the driver's license, Pat
and Rich, my family.

Peter was shocked. "I understand you 100 times better now," he said. He
told me that I had done the right thing by telling him, and that it was now our

shared problem. He said he didn't want to do anything about it just yet. I had just been hired, he said, and I needed to prove myself. "When you've done enough," he said, "we'll tell Don and Len together." (Don Graham is the chairman of The Washington Post Company; Leonard Downie Jr. was then the paper's executive editor.) A month later, I spent my first Thanksgiving in Washington with Peter and his family.

In the five years that followed, I did my best to "do enough." I was promoted to staff writer, reported on video-game culture, wrote a series on Washington's H.I.V./AIDS epidemic, and covered the role of technology and social media in the 2008 presidential race. I visited the White House, where I interviewed senior aides and covered a state dinner—and gave the Secret Service the Social Security number I obtained with false documents.

I did my best to steer clear of reporting on immigration policy but couldn't always avoid it. On two occasions, I wrote about Hillary Clinton's position on driver's licenses for undocumented immigrants. I also wrote an article about Senator Mel Martínez of Florida, then the chairman of the Republican National Committee, who was defending his party's stance toward Latinos after only one Republican presidential candidate—John McCain, the co-author of a failed immigration bill—agreed to participate in a debate sponsored by Univision, the Spanish-language network.

It was an odd sort of dance: I was trying to stand out in a highly competitive newsroom, yet I was terrified that if I stood out too much, I'd invite unwanted scrutiny. I tried to compartmentalize my fears, distract myself by reporting on the lives of other people, but there was no escaping the central conflict in my life. Maintaining a deception for so long distorts your sense of self. You start wondering who you've become, and why.

In April 2008, I was part of a Post team that won a Pulitzer Prize for the paper's coverage of the Virginia Tech shootings a year earlier. Lolo died a year earlier, so it was Lola who called me the day of the announcement. The first thing she said was, "Anong mangyayari kung malaman ng mga tao?"

What will happen if people find out?

I couldn't say anything. After we got off the phone, I rushed to the bathroom on the fourth floor of the newsroom, sat down on the toilet, and cried.

In the summer of 2009, without ever having had that follow-up talk with top Post management, I left the paper and moved to New York to join The Huffington Post. I met Arianna Huffington at a Washington Press Club Foundation dinner I was covering for The Post two years earlier, and she later recruited me to join her news site. I wanted to learn more about Web publishing, and I thought the new job would provide a useful education.

Still, I was apprehensive about the move: many companies were already using E-Verify, a program set up by the Department of Homeland Security that checks if prospective employees are eligible to work, and I didn't know if my new employer was among them. But I'd been able to get jobs in other newsrooms, I figured, so I filled out the paperwork as usual and succeeded in landing on the payroll.

While I worked at The Huffington Post, other opportunities emerged. My H.I.V./AIDS series became a documentary film called "The Other City," which opened at the Tribeca Film Festival last year and was broadcast on Showtime. I began writing for magazines and landed a dream assignment: profiling Facebook's Mark Zuckerberg for The New Yorker.

The more I achieved, the more scared and depressed I became. I was proud of my work, but there was always a cloud hanging over it, over me. My old eight-year deadline—the expiration of my Oregon driver's license—was approaching.

After slightly less than a year, I decided to leave The Huffington Post. In part, this was because I wanted to promote the documentary and write a book about online culture—or so I told my friends. But the real reason was, after so many years of trying to be a part of the system, of focusing all my energy on my professional life, I learned that no amount of professional success would solve my problem or ease the sense of loss and displacement I felt. I lied to a friend about why I couldn't take a weekend trip to Mexico. Another time I concocted an excuse for why I couldn't go on an all-expenses-paid trip to Switzerland. I have been unwilling, for years, to be in a long-term relationship because I never wanted anyone to get too close and ask too many questions. All the while, Lola's question was stuck in my head: What will happen if people find out?

60   Early this year, just two weeks before my 30th birthday, I won a small reprieve: I obtained a driver's license in the state of Washington. The license is valid until 2016. This offered me five more years of acceptable identification—but also five more years of fear, of lying to people I respect and institutions that trusted me, of running away from who I am.

I'm done running. I'm exhausted. I don't want that life anymore.

So I've decided to come forward, own up to what I've done, and tell my story to the best of my recollection. I've reached out to former bosses and employers and apologized for misleading them—a mix of humiliation and liberation coming with each disclosure. All the people mentioned in this article gave me permission to use their names. I've also talked to family and friends about my situation and am working with legal counsel to review my options. I don't know what the consequences will be of telling my story.

I do know that I am grateful to my grandparents, my Lolo and Lola, for giving me the chance for a better life. I'm also grateful to my other family—the support network I found here in America—for encouraging me to pursue my dreams.

It's been almost 18 years since I've seen my mother. Early on, I was mad at her for putting me in this position, and then mad at myself for being angry and ungrateful. By the time I got to college, we rarely spoke by phone. It became too painful; after a while it was easier to just send money to help support her and my two half-siblings. My sister, almost 2 years old when I left, is almost 20 now. I've never met my 14-year-old brother. I would love to see them.

65   Not long ago, I called my mother. I wanted to fill the gaps in my memory about that August morning so many years ago. We had never discussed it. Part of me wanted to shove the memory aside, but to write this article and face the facts of my life, I needed more details. Did I cry? Did she? Did we kiss goodbye?

My mother told me I was excited about meeting a stewardess, about getting on a plane. She also reminded me of the one piece of advice she gave me for blending in: If anyone asked why I was coming to America, I should say I was going to Disneyland.

MLA CITATION

Vargas, Jose Antonio. "My Life as an Undocumented Immigrant." *The Norton Reader: An Anthology of Nonfiction*, edited by Melissa A. Goldthwaite et al., 15th ed., W. W. Norton, 2020, pp. 50–59.

QUESTIONS

1. Jose Antonio Vargas describes many of the challenges of living as an undocumented immigrant in America. Which challenges stand out to you? Why?

2. In this account of his life in America, Vargas extends definitions of home and family, showing how a support network can become a kind of family. Which people in Vargas's life behaved most like family? How do you define family? Does your definition include those who are not biologically related?

3. Vargas defines what it means to him to be a U.S. citizen: "hard work, self-reliance, love of my country" (paragraph 41). Write an essay in which you reflect on what it means to be a citizen of the country you call home.

VIET THANH NGUYEN

from *The Displaced*

I WAS ONCE A REFUGEE, although no one would mistake me for being a refugee now. Because of this, I insist on being called a refugee, since the temptation to pretend that I am not a refugee is strong. It would be so much easier to call myself an immigrant, to pass myself off as belonging to a category of migratory humanity that is less controversial, less demanding, and less threatening than the refugee.

I was born a citizen and a human being. At four years of age I became something less than human, at least in the eyes of those who do not think of refugees as being human. The month was March, the year 1975, when the northern communist army captured my hometown of Ban Me Thuot in its final invasion of the Republic of Vietnam, a country that no longer exists except in the imagination of its global refugee diaspora of several million people, a country that most of the world remembers as South Vietnam.

From The Displaced: Refugee Writers on Refugee Lives *(2018), a collection of seventeen essays written by refugees from Afghanistan, Bosnia, Chile, Ethiopia, Mexico, and other countries.*

Looking back, I remember nothing of the experience that turned me into a refugee. It begins with my mother making a life-and-death decision on her own. My father was in Saigon, and the lines of communication were cut. I do not remember my mother fleeing our hometown with my ten-year-old brother and me, leaving behind our sixteen-year-old adopted sister to guard the family property. I do not remember my sister, who my parents would not see again for nearly twenty years, who I would not see again for nearly thirty years.

My brother remembers dead paratroopers hanging from the trees on our route, although I do not. I also do not remember whether I walked the entire one hundred eighty-four kilometers to Nha Trang, or whether my mother carried me, or whether we might have managed to get a ride on the cars, trucks, carts, motorbikes, and bicycles crowding the road. Perhaps she does remember but I never asked about the exodus, or about the tens of thousands of civilian refugees and fleeing soldiers, or the desperate scramble to get on a boat in Nha Trang, or some of the soldiers shooting some of the civilians to clear their way to boats, as I would read later in accounts of this time.

5   I do not remember finding my father in Saigon, or how we waited for another month until the communist army came to the city's borders, or how we tried to get into the airport, and then into the American embassy, and then finally somehow fought our way through the crowds at the docks to reach a boat, or how my father became separated from us but decided to get on a boat by himself anyway, and how my mother decided the same thing, or how we eventually were reunited on a larger ship. I do remember that we were incredibly fortunate, finding our way out of the country, as so many millions did not, and not losing anyone, as so many thousands did. No one, except my sister.

For most of my life, I did remember soldiers on our boat firing onto a smaller boat full of refugees that was trying to approach. But when I mentioned it to my older brother many years later, he said the shooting never happened.

I do not remember many things, and for all those things I do not remember, I am grateful, because the things I do remember hurt me enough. My memory begins after our stops at a chain of American military bases in the Philippines, Guam, and finally Pennsylvania. To leave the refugee camp in Pennsylvania, the Vietnamese refugees needed American sponsors. One sponsor took my parents, another took my brother, a third took me.

For most of my life, I tried not to remember this moment except to note it in a factual way, as something that happened to us but left no damage, but that is not true. As a writer and a father of a son who is four years old, the same age I was when I became a refugee, I have to remember, or sometimes imagine, not just what happened, but what was felt. I have to imagine what it was like for a father and a mother to have their children taken away from them. I have to imagine what it was that I experienced, although I do remember being taken by my sponsor to visit my parents and howling at being taken back.

I remember being reunited with my parents after a few months and the snow and the cold and my mother disappearing from our lives for a period of time I cannot recall and for reasons I could not understand, and knowing vaguely that it had something to do with the trauma of losing her country, her family, her property, her security, maybe her self. In remembering this, I know that I am also foreshadowing the worst of what the future would hold, of what would happen to her in the decades to come. Despite her short absence, or maybe her long one, I remember enjoying life in Harrisburg, Pennsylvania, because children can enjoy things that adults cannot so long as they can play, and I remember a sofa sitting in our backyard and neighborhood children stealing our Halloween candy and my enraged brother taking me home before venturing out by himself to recover what had been taken from us.

I remember moving to San Jose, California, in 1978 and my parents opening the second Vietnamese grocery store in the city and I remember the phone call on Christmas Eve that my brother took, informing him that my parents had been shot in an armed robbery, and I remember that it was not that bad, just flesh wounds, they were back at work not long after, and I remember that the only people who wanted to open businesses in depressed downtown San Jose were the Vietnamese refugees, and I remember walking down the street from my parents' store and seeing a sign in a store window that said ANOTHER AMERICAN DRIVEN OUT OF BUSINESS BY THE VIETNAMESE, and I remember the gunman who followed us to our home and knocked on our door and pointed a gun in all our faces and how my mother saved us by running past him and out onto the sidewalk, but I do not remember the two policemen shot to death in front of my parents' store because I had gone away to college by that time and my parents did not want to call me and worry me.

I remember all these things because if I did not remember them and write them down then perhaps they would all disappear, as all those Vietnamese businesses have vanished, because after they had helped to revitalize the downtown that no one else cared to invest in, the city of San Jose realized that downtown could be so much better than what it was and forced all those businesses to sell their property and if you visit downtown San Jose today you will see a massive, gleaming, new city hall that symbolizes the wealth of a Silicon Valley that had barely begun to exist in 1978 but you will not see my parents' store, which was across the street from the new city hall. What you will see instead is a parking lot with a few cars in it because the city thought that the view of an empty parking lot from the windows and foyer of city hall was more attractive than the view of a mom-and-pop Vietnamese grocery store catering to refugees.

As refugees, not just once but twice, having fled from north to south in 1954 when their country was divided, my parents experienced the usual dilemma of anyone classified as an *other*. The other exists in contradiction, or perhaps in paradox, being either invisible or hypervisible, but rarely just visible. Most of the time we do not see the other or see right through them, whoever the other may be to us, since each of us—even if we are seen as others by some—have our own others. When we do see the other, the other is not truly human to us, by very definition of being an other, but is instead a stereotype, a joke, or a horror. In the case of the Vietnamese refugees in America, we embodied the specter of the Asian come to either serve or to threaten.

Invisible and hypervisible, refugees are ignored and forgotten by those who are not refugees until they turn into a menace. Refugees, like all others, are unseen until they are seen everywhere, threatening to overwhelm our borders, invade our cultures, rape our women, threaten our children, destroy our economies. We who do the ignoring and forgetting oftentimes do not perceive it to be violence, because we do not know we do it. But sometimes we deliberately ignore and forget others. When we do, we are surely aware we are inflicting violence, whether that is on the schoolyard as children or at the level of the nation. When those others fight back by demanding to be seen and heard—as refugees sometimes do—they can appear to us like threatening ghosts whose fates we ourselves have caused and denied. No wonder we do not wish to see them.

MLA CITATION

Nguyen, Viet Thanh. "From *The Displaced*." *The Norton Reader: An Anthology of Nonfiction*, edited by Melissa A. Goldthwaite et al., 15th ed., W. W. Norton, 2020, pp. 59–62.

QUESTIONS

1. Viet Thanh Nguyen insists on calling himself a refugee even though no one would mistake him for a refuge now (paragraph 1). Why does he make this choice? How might this choice affect how people view other refugees? What parts of the essay inform your answer?

2. Nguyen tells his story through what he remembers, what he does not remember, and what he tries not to remember. Trace Nguyen's use of the word "remember" throughout this essay. Which parts of his experience seem most important for him to remember? Why? How does he emphasize those experiences?

3. Nguyen writes, "I remember all these things because if I did not remember them and write them down then perhaps they would all disappear" (paragraph 11). Is there an important story from your family's history that you want to remember? Interview those family members who would remember the event and write down your own memories. Write an essay that uses your own and your family members' memories to reconstruct the details of a significant event.

LARS EIGHNER
On Dumpster Diving

L ONG BEFORE I BEGAN DUMPSTER DIVING I was impressed with Dumpsters, enough so that I wrote the Merriam-Webster research service to discover what I could about the word *Dumpster*. I learned from them that it is a proprietary word belonging to the Dempster Dumpster company. Since then I have dutifully capitalized the word, although it was lowercased in almost all the citations Merriam-Webster photocopied for me. Dempster's word is too apt. I have never heard

From Travels with Lizbeth: Three Years on the Road and on the Streets *(1993), an account of Lars Eighner's life as a homeless person.*

these things called anything but Dumpsters. I do not know anyone who knows the generic name for these objects. From time to time I have heard a wino or hobo give some corrupted credit to the original and call them Dipsy Dumpsters.

I began Dumpster diving about a year before I became homeless.

I prefer the word *scavenging* and use the word *scrounging* when I mean to be obscure. I have heard people, evidently meaning to be polite, use the word *foraging,* but I prefer to reserve that word for gathering nuts and berries and such, which I do also according to the season and the opportunity. *Dumpster diving* seems to me to be a little too cute and, in my case, inaccurate because I lack the athletic ability to lower myself into the Dumpsters as the true divers do, much to their increased profit.

I like the frankness of the word *scavenging,* which I can hardly think of without picturing a big black snail on an aquarium wall. I live from the refuse of others. I am a scavenger. I think it a sound and honorable niche, although if I could I would naturally prefer to live the comfortable consumer life, perhaps— and only perhaps—as a slightly less wasteful consumer, owing to what I have learned as a scavenger.

While Lizbeth[1] and I were still living in the shack on Avenue B as my savings ran out, I put almost all my sporadic income into rent. The necessities of daily life I began to extract from Dumpsters. Yes, we ate from them. Except for jeans, all my clothes came from Dumpsters. Boom boxes, candles, bedding, toilet paper, a virgin male love doll, medicine, books, a typewriter, dishes, furnishings, and change, sometimes amounting to many dollars—I acquired many things from the Dumpsters.

I have learned much as a scavenger. I mean to put some of what I have learned down here, beginning with the practical art of Dumpster diving and proceeding to the abstract.

What is safe to eat?

After all, the finding of objects is becoming something of an urban art. Even respectable employed people will sometimes find something tempting sticking out of a Dumpster or standing beside one. Quite a number of people, not all of them of the bohemian type, are willing to brag that they found this or that piece in the trash. But eating from Dumpsters is what separates the dilettanti from the professionals. Eating safely from the Dumpsters involves three principles: using the senses and common sense to evaluate the condition of the found materials, knowing the Dumpsters of a given area and checking them regularly, and seeking always to answer the question, "Why was this discarded?"

Perhaps everyone who has a kitchen and a regular supply of groceries has, at one time or another, made a sandwich and eaten half of it before discovering mold on the bread or got a mouthful of milk before realizing the milk had turned. Nothing of the sort is likely to happen to a Dumpster diver because he

1. Lars Eighner's dog.

is constantly reminded that most food is discarded for a reason. Yet a lot of perfectly good food can be found in Dumpsters.

10   Canned goods, for example, turn up fairly often in the Dumpsters I frequent. All except the most phobic people would be willing to eat from a can, even if it came from a Dumpster. Canned goods are among the safest of foods to be found in Dumpsters but are not utterly foolproof.

Although very rare with modern canning methods, botulism is a possibility. Most other forms of food poisoning seldom do lasting harm to a healthy person, but botulism is almost certainly fatal and often the first symptom is death. Except for carbonated beverages, all canned goods should contain a slight vacuum and suck air when first punctured. Bulging, rusty, and dented cans and cans that spew when punctured should be avoided, especially when the contents are not very acidic or syrupy.

Heat can break down the botulin, but this requires much more cooking than most people do to canned goods. To the extent that botulism occurs at all, of course, it can occur in cans on pantry shelves as well as in cans from Dumpsters. Need I say that home-canned goods are simply too risky to be recommended.

From time to time one of my companions, aware of the source of my provisions, will ask, "Do you think these crackers are really safe to eat?" For some reason it is most often the crackers they ask about.

This question has always made me angry. Of course I would not offer my companion anything I had doubts about. But more than that, I wonder why he cannot evaluate the condition of the crackers for himself. I have no special knowledge and I have been wrong before. Since he knows where the food comes from, it seems to me he ought to assume some of the responsibility for deciding what he will put in his mouth. For myself I have few qualms about dry foods such as crackers, cookies, cereal, chips, and pasta if they are free of visible contaminates and still dry and crisp. Most often such things are found in the original packaging, which is not so much a positive sign as it is the absence of a negative one.

15   Raw fruits and vegetables with intact skins seem perfectly safe to me, excluding of course the obviously rotten. Many are discarded for minor imperfections that can be pared away. Leafy vegetables, grapes, cauliflower, broccoli, and similar things may be contaminated by liquids and may be impractical to wash.

Candy, especially hard candy, is usually safe if it has not drawn ants. Chocolate is often discarded only because it has become discolored as the cocoa butter de-emulsified. Candying, after all, is one method of food preservation because pathogens do not like very sugary substances.

All of these foods might be found in any Dumpster and can be evaluated with some confidence largely on the basis of appearance. Beyond these are foods that cannot be correctly evaluated without additional information.

I began scavenging by pulling pizzas out of the Dumpster behind a pizza delivery shop. In general, prepared food requires caution, but in this case I knew when the shop closed and went to the Dumpster as soon as the last of the help left.

Such shops often get prank orders; both the orders and the products made to fill them are called *bogus*. Because help seldom stays long at these places, pizzas are often made with the wrong topping, refused on delivery for being cold, or baked incorrectly. The products to be discarded are boxed up because inventory is kept by counting boxes: A boxed pizza can be written off; an unboxed pizza does not exist.

I never placed a bogus order to increase the supply of pizzas and I believe   20
no one else was scavenging in this Dumpster. But the people in the shop became suspicious and began to retain their garbage in the shop overnight. While it lasted I had a steady supply of fresh, sometimes warm pizza. Because I knew the Dumpster I knew the source of the pizza, and because I visited the Dumpster regularly I knew what was fresh and what was yesterday's.

The area I frequent is inhabited by many affluent college students. I am not here by chance; the Dumpsters in this area are very rich. Students throw out many good things, including food. In particular they tend to throw everything out when they move at the end of a semester, before and after breaks, and around midterm, when many of them despair of college. So I find it advantageous to keep an eye on the academic calendar.

Students throw food away around breaks because they do not know whether it has spoiled or will spoil before they return. A typical discard is a half jar of peanut butter. In fact, nonorganic peanut butter does not require refrigeration and is unlikely to spoil in any reasonable time. The student does not know that, and since it is Daddy's money, the student decides not to take a chance. Opened containers require caution and some attention to the question, "Why was this discarded?" But in the case of discards from student apartments, the answer may be that the item was thrown out through carelessness, ignorance, or wastefulness. This can sometimes be deduced when the item is found with many others, including some that are obviously perfectly good.

Some students, and others, approach defrosting a freezer by chucking out the whole lot. Not only do the circumstances of such a find tell the story, but also the mass of frozen goods stays cold for a long time and items may be found still frozen or freshly thawed.

Yogurt, cheese, and sour cream are items that are often thrown out while they are still good. Occasionally I find a cheese with a spot of mold, which of course I just pare off, and because it is obvious why such a cheese was discarded, I treat it with less suspicion than an apparently perfect cheese found in similar circumstances. Yogurt is often discarded, still sealed, only because the expiration date on the carton had passed. This is one of my favorite finds because yogurt will keep for several days, even in warm weather.

Students throw out canned goods and staples at the end of semesters and   25
when they give up college at midterm. Drugs, pornography, spirits, and the like are often discarded when parents are expected—Dad's Day, for example. And spirits also turn up after big party weekends, presumably discarded by the newly reformed. Wine and spirits, of course, keep perfectly well even once opened, but the same cannot be said of beer.

My test for carbonated soft drinks is whether they still fizz vigorously. Many juices or other beverages are too acidic or too syrupy to cause much concern, provided they are not visibly contaminated. I have discovered nasty molds in vegetable juices, even when the product was found under its original seal; I recommend that such products be decanted slowly into a clear glass. Liquids always require some care. One hot day I found a large jug of Pat O'Brien's Hurricane mix. The jug had been opened but was still ice cold. I drank three large glasses before it became apparent to me that someone had added the rum to the mix, and not a little rum. I never tasted the rum, and by the time I began to feel the effects I had already ingested a very large quantity of the beverage. Some divers would have considered this a boon, but being suddenly intoxicated in a public place in the early afternoon is not my idea of a good time.

I have heard of people maliciously contaminating discarded food and even handouts, but mostly I have heard of this from people with vivid imaginations who have had no experience with the Dumpsters themselves. Just before the pizza shop stopped discarding its garbage at night, jalapeños began showing up on most of the thrown-out pizzas. If indeed this was meant to discourage me, it was a wasted effort because I am a native Texan.

For myself, I avoid game, poultry, pork, and egg-based foods, whether I find them raw or cooked. I seldom have the means to cook what I find, but when I do I avail myself of plentiful supplies of beef, which is often in very good condition. I suppose fish becomes disagreeable before it becomes dangerous. Lizbeth is happy to have any such thing that is past its prime and, in fact, does not recognize fish as food until it is quite strong.

Home leftovers, as opposed to surpluses from restaurants, are very often bad. Evidently, especially among students, there is a common type of personality that carefully wraps up even the smallest leftover and shoves it into the back of the refrigerator for six months or so before discarding it. Characteristic of this type are the reused jars and margarine tubs to which the remains are committed. I avoid ethnic foods I am unfamiliar with. If I do not know what it is supposed to look like when it is good, I cannot be certain I will be able to tell if it is bad.

30   No matter how careful I am I still get dysentery at least once a month, oftener in warm weather. I do not want to paint too romantic a picture. Dumpster diving has serious drawbacks as a way of life.

I learned to scavenge gradually, on my own. Since then I have initiated several companions into the trade. I have learned that there is a predictable series of stages a person goes through in learning to scavenge.

At first the new scavenger is filled with disgust and self-loathing. He is ashamed of being seen and may lurk around, trying to duck behind things, or he may try to dive at night. (In fact, most people instinctively look away from a scavenger. By skulking around, the novice calls attention to himself and arouses suspicion. Diving at night is ineffective and needlessly messy.)

Every grain of rice seems to be a maggot. Everything seems to stink. He can wipe the egg yolk off the found can, but he cannot erase from his mind the stigma of eating garbage.

That stage passes with experience. The scavenger finds a pair of running shoes that fit and look and smell brand-new. He finds a pocket calculator in perfect working order. He finds pristine ice cream, still frozen, more than he can eat or keep. He begins to understand: People throw away perfectly good stuff, a lot of perfectly good stuff.

At this stage, Dumpster shyness begins to dissipate. The diver, after all, has the last laugh. He is finding all manner of good things that are his for the taking. Those who disparage his profession are the fools, not he.   35

He may begin to hang on to some perfectly good things for which he has neither a use nor a market. Then he begins to take note of the things that are not perfectly good but are nearly so. He mates a Walkman with broken earphones and one that is missing a battery cover. He picks up things that he can repair.

At this stage he may become lost and never recover. Dumpsters are full of things of some potential value to someone and also of things that never have much intrinsic value but are interesting. All the Dumpster divers I have known come to the point of trying to acquire everything they touch. Why not take it, they reason, since it is all free? This is, of course, hopeless. Most divers come to realize that they must restrict themselves to items of relatively immediate utility. But in some cases the diver simply cannot control himself. I have met several of these pack-rat types. Their ideas of the values of various pieces of junk verge on the psychotic. Every bit of glass may be a diamond, they think, and all that glisters, gold.

I tend to gain weight when I am scavenging. Partly this is because I always find far more pizza and doughnuts than water-packed tuna, nonfat yogurt, and fresh vegetables. Also I have not developed much faith in the reliability of Dumpsters as a food source, although it has been proven to me many times. I tend to eat as if I have no idea where my next meal is coming from. But mostly I just hate to see food go to waste and so I eat much more than I should. Something like this drives the obsession to collect junk.

As for collecting objects, I usually restrict myself to collecting one kind of small object at a time, such as pocket calculators, sunglasses, or campaign buttons. To live on the street I must anticipate my needs to a certain extent: I must pick up and save warm bedding I find in August because it will not be found in Dumpsters in November. As I have no access to health care, I often hoard essential drugs, such as antibiotics and antihistamines. (This course can be recommended only to those with some grounding in pharmacology. Antibiotics, for example, even when indicated are worse than useless if taken in insufficient amounts.) But even if I had a home with extensive storage space, I could not save everything that might be valuable in some contingency.

I have proprietary feelings about my Dumpsters. As I have mentioned, it is   40
no accident that I scavenge from ones where good finds are common. But my limited experience with Dumpsters in other areas suggests to me that even in poorer areas, Dumpsters, if attended with sufficient diligence, can be made to yield a livelihood. The rich students discard perfectly good kiwifruit; poorer people discard perfectly good apples. Slacks and Polo shirts are found in the one place; jeans and T-shirts in the other. The population of competitors rather

than the affluence of the dumpers most affects the feasibility of survival by scavenging. The large number of competitors is what puts me off the idea of trying to scavenge in places like Los Angeles.

Curiously, I do not mind my direct competition, other scavengers, so much as I hate the can scroungers.

People scrounge cans because they have to have a little cash. I have tried scrounging cans with an able-bodied companion. Afoot a can scrounger simply cannot make more than a few dollars a day. One can extract the necessities of life from the Dumpsters directly with far less effort than would be required to accumulate the equivalent value in cans. (These observations may not hold in places with container redemption laws.)

Can scroungers, then, are people who must have small amounts of cash. These are drug addicts and winos, mostly the latter because the amounts of cash are so small. Spirits and drugs do, like all other commodities, turn up in Dumpsters and the scavenger will from time to time have a half bottle of a rather good wine with his dinner. But the wino cannot survive on these occasional finds; he must have his daily dose to stave off the DTs. All the cans he can carry will buy about three bottles of Wild Irish Rose.

I do not begrudge them the cans, but can scroungers tend to tear up the Dumpsters, mixing the contents and littering the area. They become so specialized that they can see only cans. They earn my contempt by passing up change, canned goods, and readily hockable items.

45   There are precious few courtesies among scavengers. But it is common practice to set aside surplus items: pairs of shoes, clothing, canned goods, and such. A true scavenger hates to see good stuff go to waste, and what he cannot use he leaves in good condition in plain sight.

Can scroungers lay waste to everything in their path and will stir one of a pair of good shoes to the bottom of a Dumpster, to be lost or ruined in the muck. Can scroungers will even go through individual garbage cans, something I have never seen a scavenger do.

Individual garbage cans are set out on the public easement only on garbage days. On other days going through them requires trespassing close to a dwelling. Going through individual garbage cans without scattering litter is almost impossible. Litter is likely to reduce the public's tolerance of scavenging. Individual cans are simply not as productive as Dumpsters; people in houses and duplexes do not move so often and for some reason do not tend to discard as much useful material. Moreover, the time required to go through one garbage can that serves one household is not much less than the time required to go through a Dumpster that contains the refuse of twenty apartments.

But my strongest reservation about going through individual garbage cans is that this seems to me a very personal kind of invasion to which I would object if I were a householder. Although many things in Dumpsters are obviously meant never to come to light, a Dumpster is somehow less personal.

I avoid trying to draw conclusions about the people who dump in the Dumpsters I frequent. I think it would be unethical to do so, although I know many people will find the idea of scavenger ethics too funny for words.

Dumpsters contain bank statements, correspondence, and other documents, just as anyone might expect. But there are also less obvious sources of information. Pill bottles, for example. The labels bear the name of the patient, the name of the doctor, and the name of the drug. AIDS drugs and antipsychotic medicines, to name but two groups, are specific and are seldom prescribed for any other disorders. The plastic compacts for birth-control pills usually have complete label information.

Despite all of this sensitive information, I have had only one apartment resident object to my going through the Dumpster. In that case it turned out the resident was a university athlete who was taking bets and who was afraid I would turn up his wager slips.

Occasionally a find tells a story. I once found a small paper bag containing some unused condoms, several partial tubes of flavored sexual lubricants, a partially used compact of birth-control pills, and the torn pieces of a picture of a young man. Clearly she was through with him and planning to give up sex altogether.

Dumpster things are often sad—abandoned teddy bears, shredded wedding books, despaired-of sales kits. I find many pets lying in state in Dumpsters. Although I hope to get off the streets so that Lizbeth can have a long and comfortable old age, I know this hope is not very realistic. So I suppose when her time comes she too will go into a Dumpster. I will have no better place for her. And after all, it is fitting, since for most of her life her livelihood has come from the Dumpster. When she finds something I think is safe that has been spilled from a Dumpster, I let her have it. She already knows the route around the best ones. I like to think that if she survives me she will have a chance of evading the dog catcher and of finding her sustenance on the route.

Silly vanities also come to rest in the Dumpsters. I am a rather accomplished needleworker. I get a lot of material from the Dumpsters. Evidently sorority girls, hoping to impress someone, perhaps themselves, with their mastery of a womanly art, buy a lot of embroider-by-number kits, work a few stitches horribly, and eventually discard the whole mess. I pull out their stitches, turn the canvas over, and work an original design. Do not think I refrain from chuckling as I make gifts from these kits.

I find diaries and journals. I have often thought of compiling a book of literary found objects. And perhaps I will one day. But what I find is hopelessly commonplace and bad without being, even unconsciously, camp. College students also discard their papers. I am horrified to discover the kind of paper that now merits an A in an undergraduate course. I am grateful, however, for the number of good books and magazines the students throw out.

In the area I know best I have never discovered vermin in the Dumpsters, but there are two kinds of kitty surprise. One is alley cats whom I meet as they leap, claws first, out of Dumpsters. This is especially thrilling when I have Lizbeth in tow. The other kind of kitty surprise is a plastic garbage bag filled with some ponderous, amorphous mass. This always proves to be used cat litter.

City bees harvest doughnut glaze and this makes the Dumpster at the doughnut shop more interesting. My faith in the instinctive wisdom of animals is always shaken whenever I see Lizbeth attempt to catch a bee in her mouth, which she does whenever bees are present. Evidently some birds find Dumpsters profitable, for birdie surprise is almost as common as kitty surprise of the first kind. In hunting season all kinds of small game turn up in Dumpsters, some of it, sadly, not entirely dead. Curiously, summer and winter, maggots are uncommon.

The worst of the living and near-living hazards of the Dumpsters are the fire ants. The food they claim is not much of a loss, but they are vicious and aggressive. It is very easy to brush against some surface of the Dumpster and pick up half a dozen or more fire ants, usually in some sensitive area such as the underarm. One advantage of bringing Lizbeth along as I make Dumpster rounds is that, for obvious reasons, she is very alert to ground-based fire ants. When Lizbeth recognizes a fire-ant infestation around our feet, she does the Dance of the Zillion Fire Ants. I have learned not to ignore this warning from Lizbeth, whether I perceive the tiny ants or not, but to remove ourselves at Lizbeth's first pas de bourrée. All the more so because the ants are the worst in the summer months when I wear flip-flops if I have them. (Perhaps someone will misunderstand this. Lizbeth does the Dance of the Zillion Fire Ants when she recognizes more fire ants than she cares to eat, not when she is being bitten. Since I have learned to react promptly, she does not get bitten at all. It is the isolated patrol of fire ants that falls in Lizbeth's range that deserves pity. She finds them quite tasty.)

By far the best way to go through a Dumpster is to lower yourself into it. Most of the good stuff tends to settle at the bottom because it is usually weightier than the rubbish. My more athletic companions have often demonstrated to me that they can extract much good material from a Dumpster I have already been over.

60   To those psychologically or physically unprepared to enter a Dumpster, I recommend a stout stick, preferably with some barb or hook at one end. The hook can be used to grab plastic garbage bags. When I find canned goods or other objects loose at the bottom of a Dumpster, I lower a bag into it, roll the desired object into the bag, and then hoist the bag out—a procedure more easily described than executed. Much Dumpster diving is a matter of experience for which nothing will do except practice.

Dumpster diving is outdoor work, often surprisingly pleasant. It is not entirely predictable; things of interest turn up every day and some days there are finds of great value. I am always very pleased when I can turn up exactly the thing I most wanted to find. Yet in spite of the element of chance, scavenging more than most other pursuits tends to yield returns in some proportion to the effort and intelligence brought to bear. It is very sweet to turn up a few dollars in change from a Dumpster that has just been gone over by a wino.

The land is now covered with cities. The cities are full of Dumpsters. If a member of the canine race is ever able to know what it is doing, then Lizbeth knows that when we go around to the Dumpsters, we are hunting. I think of scavenging as a modern form of self-reliance. In any event, after having survived nearly ten years of government service, where everything is geared to the lowest common denominator, I find it refreshing to have work that rewards initiative and effort. Certainly I would be happy to have a sinecure again, but I am no longer heartbroken that I left one.

I find from the experience of scavenging two rather deep lessons. The first is to take what you can use and let the rest go by. I have come to think that there is no value in the abstract. A thing I cannot use or make useful, perhaps by trading, has no value however rare or fine it may be. I mean useful in a broad sense—some art I would find useful and some otherwise.

I was shocked to realize that some things are not worth acquiring, but now I think it is so. Some material things are white elephants that eat up the possessor's substance. The second lesson is the transience of material being. This has not quite converted me to a dualist, but it has made some headway in that direction. I do not suppose that ideas are immortal, but certainly mental things are longer lived than other material things.

Once I was the sort of person who invests objects with sentimental value. 65 Now I no longer have those objects, but I have the sentiments yet.

Many times in our travels I have lost everything but the clothes I was wearing and Lizbeth. The things I find in Dumpsters, the love letters and rag dolls of so many lives, remind me of this lesson. Now I hardly pick up a thing without envisioning the time I will cast it aside. This I think is a healthy state of mind. Almost everything I have now has already been cast out at least once, proving that what I own is valueless to someone.

Anyway, I find my desire to grab for the gaudy bauble has been largely sated. I think this is an attitude I share with the very wealthy—we both know there is plenty more where what we have came from. Between us are the rat-race millions who nightly scavenge the cable channels looking for they know not what.

I am sorry for them.

MLA CITATION

Eighner, Lars. "On Dumpster Diving." *The Norton Reader: An Anthology of Nonfiction*, edited by Melissa A. Goldthwaite et al., 15th ed., W. W. Norton, 2020, pp. 62–71.

QUESTIONS

1. How does Lars Eighner organize his essay? What might such an organization imply?

2. Eighner's simple, understated tone suggests that anyone can adapt to Dumpster diving with a little practice. Why do you think he uses such a tone?

3. Write about someone who, as Eighner criticizes in his closing paragraphs, "invests objects with sentimental value" (paragraph 65). Let your description reveal whether or not you agree with Eighner.

2 PEOPLE AND PLACES

> You never really understand a person until you consider things from his point of view . . . until you climb into his skin and walk around in it.
>
> —HARPER LEE

In Harper Lee's *To Kill a Mockingbird*, Atticus Finch famously invites his children, Scout and Jem, to consider things from another person's point of view. The essays in this chapter are all written to help us climb into another person's skin, to imagine their life and what matters to them. One of the surest ways to consider things from a different point of view is to visit a new place. Whether through a profile of a person or a place, these essays offer you the chance to learn about an abundant range of people—the celebrated and accomplished as well as the ordinary—and a wide range of places—urban, suburban, and rural—without leaving your favorite reading spot.

Nigerian novelist Chimamanda Ngozi Adichie opens the chapter with "The Danger of a Single Story." Part of what makes Adichie's experiences so valuable is that, as a middle-class, educated African woman, she has accidentally underestimated people, as she did with the family of her parents' house boy, and she herself has seen others underestimate her, as happened when she met her college roommate in the United States.

Adichie profits from a diverse upbringing, from an African childhood reading British books, to an American university education, to life as an internationally acclaimed novelist. But even without all of that experience, it is possible to comprehend the wide range of stories at play within a single community. In "Working at Wendy's," Joey Franklin takes account of each of his co-workers at a fast food restaurant in a college town and shows how many stories are contained in even just one shift there. In "More Room," Judith Ortiz Cofer takes us to Puerto Rico and lets us peek inside her grandparents' house to see how her elders navigated their love of family and God.

Literary profiles can offer a powerfully nuanced account of another person. Unlike profiling within the context of security or government, where someone is seen for their broad likeness to a category, usually race or gender, literary profiles explore the unique characteristics of a single person. A profile is not an interview, although interviews may be used as source material. The two included here—Tom Wolfe's profile of astronaut Chuck Yeager and Jack Hamilton's profile of musician Aretha Franklin—highlight each individual's context and what makes them stand out from the crowd.

Although every essay here has something to say about both people and place, the second half of this chapter emphasizes the *where* more than the *who*. These essays show us a range of ways of thinking about place. Ian Frazier describes moving through space on a subway and Colson Whitehead describes how a city becomes transformed in a sudden rainstorm. In these essays, as well as in Jhumpa Lahiri's ode to her home state of Rhode Island and E. B. White's memories of returning to a summer cottage in Maine, the act of description itself rises to the point of the essay. Carefully chosen details, selected to render both the place and the author's relation to it, help us imagine places we may never see. So skilled are these writers that we may see place completely through their eyes without at first recognizing how their perspective colors the details they have chosen.

As you read these essays, reflect on your own relationships with people and places. Who has made an impact on your life—a family member, a mentor, a historical figure— and what about them is extraordinary in your eyes? Are you drawn to write about familiar places that you've called home, or new places that surprised or delighted or horrified you in some way? Consider how your perspective on these people and places is different from what someone else's might be. Or consider how your perspective has changed over time: Did an experience change the way you feel about someone? Is home different after you left for a time and returned? Whether you write about people or places, focus on significant and vivid details; use your own writing to let your reader climb into your skin and walk around.

CHIMAMANDA NGOZI ADICHIE
The Danger of a Single Story

I'M A STORYTELLER. And I would like to tell you a few personal stories about what I like to call "the danger of the single story." I grew up on a university campus in eastern Nigeria. My mother says that I started reading at the age of two, although I think four is probably close to the truth. So I was an early reader, and what I read were British and American children's books.

I was also an early writer, and when I began to write, at about the age of seven, stories in pencil with crayon illustrations that my poor mother was obligated to read, I wrote exactly the kinds of stories I was reading: All my characters were white and blue-eyed, they played in the snow, they ate apples, and they talked a lot about the weather, how lovely it was that the sun had come out. Now, this despite the fact that I lived in Nigeria. I had never been outside Nigeria. We didn't have snow, we ate mangoes, and we never talked about the weather, because there was no need to.

My characters also drank a lot of ginger beer, because the characters in the British books I read drank ginger beer. Never mind that I had no idea what ginger beer was. And for many years afterwards, I would have a desperate desire to taste ginger beer. But that is another story.

This text has its origins as a widely viewed TED Talk. Nigerian novelist Chimamanda Ngozi Adichie (b. 1977) is the author of many books, including novels Purple Hibiscus *(2003),* Americanah *(2013), and the book-length essay* We Should All Be Feminists *(2014).*

What this demonstrates, I think, is how impressionable and vulnerable we are in the face of a story, particularly as children. Because all I had read were books in which characters were foreign, I had become convinced that books by their very nature had to have foreigners in them and had to be about things with which I could not personally identify. Now, things changed when I discovered African books. There weren't many of them available, and they weren't quite as easy to find as the foreign books.

But because of writers like Chinua Achebe and Camara Laye,[1] I went through a mental shift in my perception of literature. I realized that people like me, girls with skin the color of chocolate, whose kinky hair could not form ponytails, could also exist in literature. I started to write about things I recognized. Now, I loved those American and British books I read. They stirred my imagination. They opened up new worlds for me. But the unintended consequence was that I did not know that people like me could exist in literature. So what the discovery of African writers did for me was this: It saved me from having a single story of what books are.

5   I come from a conventional, middle-class Nigerian family. My father was a professor. My mother was an administrator. And so we had, as was the norm, live-in domestic help, who would often come from nearby rural villages. So, the year I turned eight, we got a new house boy. His name was Fide. The only thing my mother told us about him was that his family was very poor. My mother sent yams and rice, and our old clothes, to his family. And when I didn't finish my dinner, my mother would say, "Finish your food! Don't you know? People like Fide's family have nothing." So I felt enormous pity for Fide's family.

Then one Saturday, we went to his village to visit, and his mother showed us a beautifully patterned basket made of dyed raffia that his brother had made. I was startled. It had not occurred to me that anybody in his family could actually make something. All I had heard about them was how poor they were, so that it had become impossible for me to see them as anything else but poor. Their poverty was my single story of them.

Years later, I thought about this when I left Nigeria to go to university in the United States. I was nineteen. My American roommate was shocked by me. She asked where I had learned to speak English so well, and was confused when I said that Nigeria happened to have English as its official language. She asked if she could listen to what she called my "tribal music," and was consequently very disappointed when I produced my tape of Mariah Carey. She assumed that I did not know how to use a stove.

What struck me was this: She had felt sorry for me even before she saw me. Her default position toward me, as an African, was a kind of patronizing, well-meaning pity. My roommate had a single story of Africa: a single story of catastrophe. In this single story, there was no possibility of Africans being

---

1. Both pioneering African novelists. From Nigeria, Achebe (1930–2013) was the author of *Things Fall Apart* (1958). From Guinea, Laye (1928–1980) was the author of *The Dark Child* (originally published in French as *L'Enfant Noir*) (1953).

similar to her in any way, no possibility of feelings more complex than pity, no possibility of a connection as human equals.

I must say that before I went to the U.S., I didn't consciously identify as   10
African. But in the U.S., whenever Africa came up, people turned to me. Never mind that I knew nothing about places like Namibia.[2] But I did come to embrace this new identity, and in many ways I think of myself now as African. Although I still get quite irritable when Africa is referred to as a country, the most recent example being my otherwise wonderful flight from Lagos two days ago, in which there was an announcement on the Virgin flight about the charity work in "India, Africa, and other countries."

So, after I had spent some years in the U.S. as an African, I began to understand my roommate's response to me. If I had not grown up in Nigeria, and if all I knew about Africa were from popular images, I too would think that Africa was a place of beautiful landscapes, beautiful animals, and incomprehensible people, fighting senseless wars, dying of poverty and AIDS, unable to speak for themselves and waiting to be saved by a kind, white foreigner. I would see Africans in the same way that I, as a child, had seen Fide's family.

This single story of Africa ultimately comes, I think, from Western literature. Now, here is a quote from the writing of a London merchant called John Lok, who sailed to West Africa in 1561 and kept a fascinating account of his voyage. After referring to the black Africans as "beasts who have no houses," he writes, "They are also people without heads, having their mouth and eyes in their breasts."

Now, I've laughed every time I've read this. And one must admire the imagination of John Lok. But what is important about his writing is that it represents the beginning of a tradition of telling African stories in the West: A tradition of sub-Saharan Africa as a place of negatives, of difference, of darkness, of people who, in the words of the wonderful poet Rudyard Kipling,[3] are "half devil, half child."

And so, I began to realize that my American roommate must have throughout her life seen and heard different versions of this single story, as had a professor, who once told me that my novel was not "authentically African." Now, I was quite willing to contend that there were a number of things wrong with the novel, that it had failed in a number of places, but I had not quite imagined that it had failed at achieving something called African authenticity. In fact, I did not know what African authenticity was. The professor told me that my characters were too much like him, an educated and middle-class man. My characters drove cars. They were not starving. Therefore they were not authentically African.

2. Country on the Atlantic coast of southern Africa. Its capital, Windhoek, is 5,800 km (3,600 miles) from Lagos, the capital of Nigeria.

3. Indian-born British novelist and poet (1865–1936), known for his writing set in the British colonies in books such as *The Jungle Book* (1894) and *Kim* (1901). Kipling was unusual among supporters of Empire for having a powerful love of and respect for other cultures that existed alongside his sense of English superiority.

15   But I must quickly add that I too am just as guilty in the question of the single story. A few years ago, I visited Mexico from the U.S. The political climate in the U.S. at the time was tense, and there were debates going on about immigration. And, as often happens in America, immigration became synonymous with Mexicans. There were endless stories of Mexicans as people who were fleecing the healthcare system, sneaking across the border, being arrested at the border, that sort of thing.

I remember walking around on my first day in Guadalajara, watching the people going to work, rolling up tortillas in the marketplace, smoking, laughing. I remember first feeling slight surprise. And then, I was overwhelmed with shame. I realized that I had been so immersed in the media coverage of Mexicans that they had become one thing in my mind, the abject immigrant. I had bought into the single story of Mexicans and I could not have been more ashamed of myself. So that is how to create a single story, show a people as one thing, as only one thing, over and over again, and that is what they become.

It is impossible to talk about the single story without talking about power. There is a word, an Igbo[4] word, that I think about whenever I think about the power structures of the world, and it is "nkali." It's a noun that loosely translates to "to be greater than another." Like our economic and political worlds, stories too are defined by the principle of nkali: How they are told, who tells them, when they're told, how many stories are told, are really dependent on power.

Power is the ability not just to tell the story of another person, but to make it the definitive story of that person. The Palestinian poet Mourid Barghouti writes that if you want to dispossess a people, the simplest way to do it is to tell their story and to start with, "secondly." Start the story with the arrows of the Native Americans, and not with the arrival of the British, and you have an entirely different story. Start the story with the failure of the African state, and not with the colonial creation of the African state, and you have an entirely different story.

I recently spoke at a university where a student told me that it was such a shame that Nigerian men were physical abusers like the father character in my novel. I told him that I had just read a novel called "American Psycho"[5]—and that it was such a shame that young Americans were serial murderers.

20   Now, obviously I said this in a fit of mild irritation. But it would never have occurred to me to think that just because I had read a novel in which a character was a serial killer that he was somehow representative of all Americans. This is not because I am a better person than that student, but because of America's cultural and economic power, I had many stories of America. I had read Tyler and Updike and Steinbeck and Gaitskill.[6] I did not have a single story of America.

4. Principal language of the 50 million Igbo people of southeastern Nigeria. Adichie's family is Igbo.
5. Novel (1991) by Bret Easton Ellis about Patrick Bateman, an investment banker and serial killer.
6. Anne Tyler (b. 1941), John Updike (1932–2009), John Steinbeck (1902–1968), and Mary Gaitskill (b. 1954), all white American novelists.

When I learned, some years ago, that writers were expected to have had really unhappy childhoods to be successful, I began to think about how I could invent horrible things my parents had done to me. But the truth is that I had a very happy childhood, full of laughter and love, in a very close-knit family.

But I also had grandfathers who died in refugee camps. My cousin Polle died because he could not get adequate healthcare. One of my closest friends, Okoloma, died in a plane crash because our fire trucks did not have water. I grew up under repressive military governments that devalued education, so that sometimes, my parents were not paid their salaries. And so, as a child, I saw jam disappear from the breakfast table, then margarine disappeared, then bread became too expensive, then milk became rationed. And most of all, a kind of normalized political fear invaded our lives.

All of these stories make me who I am. But to insist on only these negative stories is to flatten my experience and to overlook the many other stories that formed me. The single story creates stereotypes, and the problem with stereotypes is not that they are untrue, but that they are incomplete. They make one story become the only story.

Of course, Africa is a continent full of catastrophes: There are immense ones, such as the horrific rapes in Congo[7] and depressing ones, such as the fact that 5,000 people apply for one job vacancy in Nigeria. But there are other stories that are not about catastrophe, and it is very important, it is just as important, to talk about them.

I've always felt that it is impossible to engage properly with a place or a person without engaging with all of the stories of that place and that person. The consequence of the single story is this: It robs people of dignity. It makes our recognition of our equal humanity difficult. It emphasizes how we are different rather than how we are similar.

So what if before my Mexican trip, I had followed the immigration debate from both sides, the U.S. and the Mexican? What if my mother had told us that Fide's family was poor and hardworking? What if we had an African television network that broadcast diverse African stories all over the world? What the Nigerian writer Chinua Achebe calls "a balance of stories."

What if my roommate knew about my Nigerian publisher, Muhtar Bakare, a remarkable man who left his job in a bank to follow his dream and start a publishing house? Now, the conventional wisdom was that Nigerians don't read literature. He disagreed. He felt that people who could read, would read, if you made literature affordable and available to them.

Shortly after he published my first novel, I went to a TV station in Lagos to do an interview, and a woman who worked there as a messenger came up to me and said, "I really liked your novel. I didn't like the ending. Now, you must write a sequel, and this is what will happen . . . ." And she went on to tell me what to write in the sequel. I was not only charmed, I was very moved. Here was a woman, part of the ordinary masses of Nigerians, who were not sup-

25

---

7. From the mid-1990s (shortly after the end of the genocide in neighboring Rwanda) to the present day, estimates suggest that over 200,000 women have been raped in Congo as part of ongoing civil war.

posed to be readers. She had not only read the book, but she had taken ownership of it and felt justified in telling me what to write in the sequel.

Now, what if my roommate knew about my friend Funmi Iyanda, a fearless woman who hosts a TV show in Lagos, and is determined to tell the stories
that we prefer to forget? What if my roommate knew about the heart procedure that was performed in the Lagos hospital last week? What if my roommate knew about contemporary Nigerian music, talented people singing in
English and Pidgin, and Igbo and Yoruba and Ijo,[8] mixing influences from
Jay-Z to Fela to Bob Marley to their grandfathers.

30   What if my roommate knew about the female lawyer who recently went to
court in Nigeria to challenge a ridiculous law that required women to get their
husband's consent before renewing their passports? What if my roommate
knew about Nollywood,[9] full of innovative people making films despite great
technical odds, films so popular that they really are the best example of Nigerians consuming what they produce? What if my roommate knew about my
wonderfully ambitious hair braider, who has just started her own business selling hair extensions? Or about the millions of other Nigerians who start businesses and sometimes fail, but continue to nurse ambition?

Every time I am home I am confronted with the usual sources of irritation
for most Nigerians: our failed infrastructure, our failed government, but also
by the incredible resilience of people who thrive despite the government,
rather than because of it. I teach writing workshops in Lagos every summer,
and it is amazing to me how many people apply, how many people are eager to
write, to tell stories.

My Nigerian publisher and I have just started a non-profit called Farafina
Trust, and we have big dreams of building libraries and refurbishing libraries
that already exist and providing books for state schools that don't have anything in their libraries, and also of organizing lots and lots of workshops, in
reading and writing, for all the people who are eager to tell our many stories.

Stories matter. Many stories matter. Stories have been used to dispossess
and to malign, but stories can also be used to empower and to humanize. Stories
can break the dignity of a people, but stories can also repair that broken dignity.

35   The American writer Alice Walker[10] wrote this about her Southern relatives who had moved to the North. She introduced them to a book about the
Southern life that they had left behind: "They sat around, reading the book
themselves, listening to me read the book, and a kind of paradise was regained."

I would like to end with this thought: That when we reject the single story,
when we realize that there is never a single story about any place, we regain a
kind of paradise.

Thank you.

8. Among the major native languages of Nigeria (a nation where over 500 languages
are spoken).

9. Colloquial name for the Nigerian film industry.

10. African American author (b. 1944). The book she refers to here is *Mules and Men*
by Zora Neale Hurston.

MLA CITATION

Adichie, Chimamanda Ngozi. "The Danger of a Single Story." *The Norton Reader: An Anthology of Nonfiction*, edited by Melissa A. Goldthwaite et al., 15th ed., W. W. Norton, 2020, pp. 73–78.

QUESTIONS

1. What, according to Chimamanda Ngozi Adichie, is the danger of telling only one story about a certain place or type of people? Look at the examples she uses to support her claim. Which are the most persuasive to you?

2. In some of her anecdotes, the author is guilty of having made an assumption about another person, in others, it's another person who's made an assumption about her. Choose one of each and compare them. What can we learn from Adichie's experience of being on both sides of this issue?

3. This essay had its origins as a TED Talk. Now that you have read it, watch the video of Adichie delivering it. What changes when you see and hear her? Can you tell from the prose that it was written to be heard as much as—perhaps more than—read?

4. Write about a time when you were confronted with the danger of a single story, either because of your (false) assumptions about someone or theirs about you.

JOEY FRANKLIN
Working at Wendy's

I T'S 8:45 P.M., and I am standing in front of the counter at Wendy's. It smells of French fries and mop water. In my right hand I hold my résumé. I don't know if I need a résumé to apply for the Wendy's night shift, but I bring it anyway. It anchors me as I drift toward the sixteen-year-old kid behind the counter and ask to speak to his manager.

"One mandarin orange salad?" the boy asks.

"Uh, no. Actually, I'd like to speak to the *manager*." As the cashier retreats to the back of the store, I recognize a large kid with curly hair working the fryer—he used to play football with some of the members of my Boy Scout troop. He looks up at me, and I avert my eyes. Part of me wants to turn around and leave before the manager comes out. A couple in their twenties walks into the restaurant behind me. I step away from the counter and pretend to read the menu, holding my résumé close to my chest. The urge to leave increases. Just then the manager comes out and asks, "You here about the night shift?"

Joey Franklin wrote this essay when he was an English major at Brigham Young University in Provo, Utah. It was published in Twentysomething Essays by Twentysomething Writers *(2006), a collection of writings from the winners of a national contest organized by the publishing company Random House.*

As I hand the manager my résumé, I realize it is a mistake. He doesn't want to know my service experience, or my academic references, or my GPA. All he wants to know is if I can spell my name correctly.

5   "Er, the application is over there," the manager says, handing me back my résumé and pointing to a file folder mounted on the wall next to the counter. I take the application to an empty table in the corner of the restaurant and hunch over it, wishing I had a drink, or a hamburger, or something to put on the table beside me.

The next day I go for an interview with the hiring manager. I sit down at a table in the lobby and answer two questions: "What hours do you want to work?" and "When can you start?"

When he was sixteen, my brother, Josh, got his first job at McDonald's. He lasted two weeks before deciding the greasy uniform and salty mop water weren't worth $5.25 an hour. His manager used to show off rejected applications to the other employees in the back of the store. Most were high school dropouts looking for spending money, but a few had college degrees. One application was from a doctor who had recently left his practice because he "couldn't handle the mortality rate."

I think about that doctor now as I sit in a small back room at Wendy's. I have just watched thirty minutes of training videos about customer service, floor mopping, heavy lifting, and armed robbery. Chelsea, the training manager, hands me two neatly folded uniforms and a brand-new hat. Holding the hat in my hand, I look out into the kitchen at my new coworkers. At the fryer is the large high school kid I remember from the night before. A skinny brown-haired Asian-looking boy who must be about nineteen years old is washing dishes. Two girls are at the front of the store taking orders, and the manager is on the phone with an angry customer. "Can I do this?" I ask myself, and put on my hat.

Chelsea is pregnant. During our training session, I guess she is about six months along. It turns out she is due in three days. "This is my last week on the day shift," she says. "After the baby is born, I'll be back on nights." This is her first child, she explains, and says she is looking forward to being a mom. She smiles as she pats her stomach and asks about my son.

10   "Eighteen months," I tell her, "a real handful." I explain that I want to work nights so I can take care of my son during the day while my wife finishes her last semester of college. I ask about the pay, but I already know her answer. "We start at five-seventy-five," she says, "but the night guys get six." I ask her what she thinks about $7. She says she'll see what she can do.

Chelsea trains me on Tuesday and goes into labor on Wednesday. I don't see her again for three weeks.

Kris Livingston's mom ran the register at the Taco Bell on the corner of Lombard Street and Allen Boulevard in a poorer section of Beaverton, Oregon. Her name was Dawn. She was divorced and had three boys. She shared a three-bedroom apartment with another single mom and her own five children. They listened to Snoop Dogg and Ice-T, drank forty-ounce malt liquors, and walked over two miles round-trip every Saturday to watch the neighborhood boys play basketball at Schiffler Park.

On welfare-check days, Dawn went grocery shopping and brought home twelve-packs of Pepsi, stacks of frozen steaks, crinkly bags of potato chips, several gallons of 2-percent milk, and bag after bag of Malt-O-Meal cereal. The week before welfare checks came, they ate eggs and instant ramen—lots of ramen.

Her son Kris was my best friend in sixth grade. We often walked to Taco Bell together to visit his mother. She usually bought us a taco while we sat in a booth in the corner of the store and talked about bicycles, girls, and football. Once, on the way home from visiting his mom, Kris said, "She used to sell drugs, you know. We had plenty of money, and nobody thought she was a bad mom then."

My first night on the job, I work with Dave. He is seventeen years old, five-ten, and keeps his hair short, like a soldier. He goes to an alternative high school if he wakes up in time and is looking forward to enlisting in the military when he turns eighteen. His dad, who recently remarried and moved, told Dave he would have to find his own place to live. When Dave isn't sleeping on his friends' couches, he lives in his car, a 1982 Volkswagen Rabbit with a hole in the floor just beneath the gas pedal. 15

Dave works with me a few nights a week and knows the business well. He's quick with a mop, can make all the sandwiches blindfolded, and has the entire computer memorized. When he's not working, he hangs out in the restaurant lobby trying to steal Frosties and old fries when no one is looking. The manager says she will give him food if he needs it and asks that he not steal anymore. "Asking gets you nowhere," he says, and keeps stealing.

Because I live just two blocks from the store, I recognize a disproportionate number of the late-night drive-through customers. Mostly, I see parents of the scouts I work with, or other scout leaders, and occasionally a friend from school. When they pull up to the window and see me in the Wendy's hat and head-phones, the following conversation ensues:

"Joey, I didn't know you worked here! How's it going?"

"Good, good. Just flipping burgers."

"Hey, you've got to do what you've got to do." 20

Then I explain the job is temporary, and it's the only job in town that allows me to work at night so I can watch my son during the day while my wife fin-ishes school. I tell them in another month I'll be back in school and working at a better-paying, less humiliating campus job.

One evening a fellow scout leader comes through, and after an exchange similar to the one described above, he says, "Hey, more power to ya. I know a lot of people who think they're above that." He thanks me as I hand him his triple cheeseburger, and he drives around the corner and out of sight.

At 250 pounds, Danny really fills out his uniform. He played varsity football for the local high school, has earned his Eagle Scout award, and knows his way around a car engine. On several occasions he has changed spark plugs, jumped batteries, and even replaced brakes on the cars of fellow employees, usually right in the store parking lot.

Wendy's is the first job Danny has ever had. With six months' experience, he is the senior employee and is being considered for a management position. He brings in about $1,000 a month, much of which he gives to his grandmother. At closing, he always saves the good salads for me and talks the manager into letting me go home early. He likes listening to Metallica, working on his Trans Am, and talking with Tonya, a high school junior who also works at the store.

25   While I'm washing my hands in the bathroom at work, a well-groomed twenty-something man standing at the sink next to me starts a conversation. "Do you like working the night shift?" he asks.

"It's not bad," I say, shaking my wet hands over the sink.

"How long have you worked here?"

"Two weeks."

"Have you ever thought about college?" he asks. I want to tell him I'm in the top 5 percent of students at my college, that I am two semesters away from graduating, and that I'm on my way to grad school to get a Ph.D. in English literature. Instead, I shrug and tell him the same line I tell everyone: "Oh yeah, I'm just working here until my wife finishes." He doesn't believe me. To him, I look like another wasted life, another victim. He thinks I got my girlfriend pregnant, that I never graduated from high school, that I can't do any better than flip burgers at two in the morning. He feels sorry for my kids.

30   "I only applied here because I knew I would get hired," says Sara the first night I work with her. She is a nineteen-year-old single mother with a sixteen-month-old boy. She is very tall and wears her long brown hair in a ponytail pulled through the hole in the back of her Wendy's hat. I ask her why she needed a job so bad.

"I had to get one," she tells me. "My parole officer said it was the only way to stay out of jail." I start at this and then ask, "Why were you in jail?"

"Drugs," she says, and pauses, testing me. "I was wearing my boyfriend's jacket, and the cops found a heroin pipe in the pocket." I ask how long she was in jail. "One year," she tells me. "I just got out a month ago."

When I was in fifth grade, my dad got a job delivering pizza. As an eleven-year-old, pivoting on that blurry edge between boyhood and adolescence, I found myself bragging to my friends about the prospect of free pizza and then wishing I hadn't told them anything about my father's job. He worked a few nights a week, and when he came home, his uniform smelled like steaming cardboard and burnt cheese, but he always brought home pizza.

Oren is nineteen years old and works at Wendy's to pay for a cell-phone bill and to get out of the house. His parents are devout Mormons and think he is a disgrace to their entire family. He wants to sell marijuana because he believes he can do nothing else. "I don't do anything well," he tells me one night while washing dishes. "I don't know what I want to do with my life." He asks Sara to find some pot for him to sell.

Oren's mother is Japanese, born and raised, and speaks to her children in 35 her native tongue. That means Oren speaks Japanese and has family connections in Japan.

Oren also owns an AK-47 and likes to go up into the canyons and shoot jackrabbits. He showed me a picture once of a rabbit carcass out in the desert, its innards all blown out and dangling for the camera.

Tonight, while working the grill, Danny tells me he has never been on a date. "Girls don't like me," he says as he flips a row of sizzling, square quarter-pound patties. I can tell he believes it. Danny, by his own admission, is the kind of guy whom girls like for support. He is a gentleman, he asks thoughtful questions, and he's always willing to talk. He thinks his weight and his scruff turn girls off. He tells me he is going to ask Tonya to a movie this weekend but isn't sure she'll say yes. Later, Tonya comes into the store, and Danny disappears with her for a few minutes out in the lobby. He comes back with a large smile on his face and says, "I've got a date this weekend, can you work for me?"

I don't like when Dave works the front line with me. I can't make sandwiches very fast yet, and he gets tired of waiting. More than once he pushes me aside to finish an order. If he sees me hesitate on a step, he barks at me, "Red, green, red, green! Ketchup, pickle, tomato, lettuce! Come on, Joe, it's not that hard."

Later, while I'm mopping the floor at closing, Dave comes by and takes the mop from my hand. "Like this," he says, scrubbing the tile vigorously. He thrusts the mop back in my hands and walks away, rolling his eyes.

Chelsea is back at work tonight for the first time since having her baby. She 40 appears fairly happy, and I am surprised at how well adjusted she seems to being a working mom. The phone rings several times, and Chelsea takes the calls in her office. She tells me her husband has lots of questions about putting the baby to bed. After the lobby closes, Chelsea disappears into the bathroom for nearly half an hour. This happens every time I work with her. I wonder if she is sick. Then I notice the breast pump in a case on her desk. Another employee tells me Chelsea has been expressing milk in one of the bathroom stalls on her breaks.

Danny and Tonya have been dating for two weeks. He shows up for his shift an hour early to see her before she gets off. They sit in the lobby holding hands and talking for almost the entire hour. When they're not in the store together, she sends text messages to his phone, which I catch him reading while he stands at the grill.

Tonight Danny approaches me while I'm opening boxes of French fries. He wants advice on how to ask Tonya to her junior prom. "I want to do something romantic," he says. I suggest Shakespeare's eighteenth sonnet. He has never heard of it. "'Shall I compare thee to a summer's day . . .'" I recite. "She'll love it." I print off the sonnet at home and bring it to work for him the next day. He writes it in a card and delivers it with flowers. Two weeks later, in a rented tux at Tonya's junior prom, Danny gets his first kiss.

I call my dad tonight. He asks about school, about my son, and about work. I tell him about Wendy's.

"What? Who?" he says.

45 "Me. I got a job at Wendy's." Long pause. "I needed a job I could do at night." More silence. "It's not so bad." Still silence. "I work from nine P.M. to one A.M. a few nights a week."

Just when I think the line must be disconnected, Dad clears his throat and asks, "What happened to your computer job?"

"The guy ran out of work for me."

"Oh." More silence. I imagine he looks around the room to make sure no one is listening before he says, "Wendy's? When did that happen?" I want to tell him that it didn't *happen,* that it wasn't an accident, but I am stuck wondering how to make him understand, and at the same time wondering why I should have to explain anything at all. I wonder what his reaction would be if I had chosen to get more student loans instead of the part-time job. I choose to say nothing. Then I offer him my employee discount on fries next time he is in town. He says he'll take me up on it.

When I come into the store tonight, Dave is talking loudly to some employees gathered in the lobby. I ask what all the laughing is about. They tell me that last night Dave and Oren siphoned all the gas out of Dave's stepmother's four-wheeler, and then they urinated on her car handles.

50 Everyone dreads working with Chelsea. When she is not in her office counting the till or on the phone with her husband, she sits on the front counter and complains about her mother-in-law. She does very little to help prep the store for closing, and we rarely get out before two A.M.

Tonight she tells me about her mother-in-law's most recent visit. "I cleaned the house for hours before she came," Chelsea says, nursing a Diet Coke. "And the first thing she says when she gets there is how disgusting the place looks. She won't even eat my cooking." According to Chelsea, her mother-in-law has hated her ever since she got engaged. She wouldn't even visit except that Chelsea has a baby now, and the mother-in-law feels obligated. Chelsea's mother-in-law is disappointed that she is still working. "A mother's place is in the home," she says to Chelsea. "Your kids will be ruined."

Tonight Waymon Hamilton comes through the drive-up window with his family. Waymon lives around the corner from me, and his two sons are in my scout troop, but they spend most of their free time traveling around the state playing premier Little League baseball. They order a few value meals, some drinks, and they ask how I'm doing. There is no hint of concern or condolence in their voices, and I appreciate it.

I hand them their food and watch them drive away. Most people know Waymon the way I know him, as a dedicated father who works hard at a thankless job to provide for his family. His unassuming nature and warm smile are what I see when I think about him. Few people know him as the fleet-footed running back who helped Brigham Young University win Holiday Bowls in 1981 and 1983. Few people know he holds several BYU scoring records, including second place for touchdowns in a season, third in career touchdowns, and fifth for both season and career points scored. I didn't even know he played college football until someone mentioned it at a scout meeting. I once worked all day with Waymon, putting in a new driveway for a neighbor, and he never mentioned his football days once. He told me about his boys, about teaching public school in California, and about pouring lots of concrete.

After the store closes, I come home, take off my uniform, and climb into bed with my wife. She rolls over, tells me she loves me, and murmurs something about the smell of French fries. I kiss her on the cheek and close my eyes. It is winter, but the house is warm. My son is asleep in the next room. There is food in the fridge, and I have a job that pays an honest wage. In the morning I will make breakfast and send my wife off to school. And then, after the dishes are done, if the weather permits, my son and I will take a walk to the park.

MLA CITATION

Franklin, Joey. "Working at Wendy's." *The Norton Reader: An Anthology of Nonfiction*, edited by Melissa A. Goldthwaite et al., 15th ed., W. W. Norton, 2020, pp. 79–85.

QUESTIONS

1. What is Joey Franklin's attitude toward working at Wendy's? How does he demonstrate it? In answering these questions, look especially at the conclusion of the essay and at the details he chooses about how others respond to him.

2. Franklin uses considerable detail to develop his coworkers as characters (see paragraph 13 for an example). Which details do you find especially effective? Why?

3. Most of this essay is written in the present tense (with past-tense reflections about former jobs held by family members). What is the effect of Franklin's use of this verb tense? How would the essay differ if he wrote the entire essay in past tense?

4. Write an essay about a job you've held. Use dialogue and details to develop characters.

JUDITH ORTIZ COFER
More Room

M Y GRANDMOTHER'S HOUSE is like a chambered nautilus; it has many rooms, yet it is not a mansion. Its proportions are small and its design simple. It is a house that has grown organically, according to the needs of its inhabitants. To all of us in the family it is known as *la casa de Mamá*.[1] It is the place of our origin; the stage for our memories and dreams of Island life.

I remember how in my childhood it sat on stilts; this was before it had a downstairs. It rested on its perch like a great blue bird, not a flying sort of bird, more like a nesting hen, but with spread wings. Grandfather had built it soon after their marriage. He was a painter and housebuilder by trade, a poet and meditative man by nature. As each of their eight children were born, new rooms were added. After a few years, the paint did not exactly match, nor the materials, so that there was a chronology to it, like the rings of a tree, and Mamá could tell you the history of each room in her *casa*, and thus the genealogy of the family along with it.

Her room is the heart of the house. Though I have seen it recently, and both woman and room have diminished in size, changed by the new perspective of my eyes, now capable of looking over countertops and tall beds, it is not this picture I carry in my memory of Mamá's *casa*. Instead, I see her room as a queen's chamber where a small woman loomed large, a throne-room with a massive four-poster bed in its center which stood taller than a child's head. It was on this bed where her own children had been born that the smallest grandchildren were allowed to take naps in the afternoons; here too was where Mamá secluded herself to dispense private advice to her daughters, sitting on the edge of the bed, looking down at whoever sat on the rocker where generations of babies had been sung to sleep. To me she looked like a wise empress right out of the fairy tales I was addicted to reading.

Though the room was dominated by the mahogany four-poster, it also contained all of Mamá's symbols of power. On her dresser instead of cosmetics there were jars filled with herbs: *yerba buena, yerba mala*,[2] the making of purgatives and teas to which we were all subjected during childhood crises. She had a steaming cup for anyone who could not, or would not, get up to face life on any given day. If the acrid aftertaste of her cures for malingering did not get you out of bed, then it was time to call *el doctor*.

5   And there was the monstrous chifforobe she kept locked with a little golden key she did not hide. This was a test of her dominion over us; though my cousins and I wanted a look inside that massive wardrobe more than anything, we never

From Judith Ortiz Cofer's book, Silent Dancing: A Partial Remembrance of a Puerto Rican Childhood *(1990), which won the 1991 PEN/Martha Albrand Special Citation for Nonfiction.*

1. Spanish for "Mama's house." All translations that follow are of Spanish words.
2. "Good herbs, bad herbs."

reached for that little key lying on top of her Bible on the dresser. This was also where she placed her earrings and rosary at night. God's word was her security system. This chifforobe was the place where I imagined she kept jewels, satin slippers, and elegant sequined, silk gowns of heart-breaking fineness. I lusted after those imaginary costumes. I had heard that Mamá had been a great beauty in her youth, and the belle of many balls. My cousins had other ideas as to what she kept in that wooden vault: its secret could be money (Mamá did not hand cash to strangers, banks were out of the question, so there were stories that her mattress was stuffed with dollar bills, and that she buried coins in jars in her garden under rosebushes, or kept them in her inviolate chifforobe); there might be that legendary gun salvaged from the Spanish-American conflict over the Island. We went wild over suspected treasures that we made up simply because children have to fill locked trunks with something wonderful.

On the wall above the bed hung a heavy silver crucifix. Christ's agonized head hung directly over Mamá's pillow. I avoided looking at this weapon suspended over where her head would lay; and on the rare occasions when I was allowed to sleep on that bed, I scooted down to the safe middle of the mattress, where her body's impression took me in like a mother's lap. Having taken care of the obligatory religious decoration with a crucifix, Mamá covered the other walls with objects sent to her over the years by her children in the States. *Los Nueva Yores*[3] were represented by, among other things, a postcard of Niagara Falls from her son Hernán, postmarked, Buffalo, N.Y. In a conspicuous gold frame hung a large color photograph of her daughter Nena, her husband and their five children at the entrance to Disneyland in California. From us she had gotten a black lace fan. Father had brought it to her from a tour of duty with the Navy in Europe (on Sundays she would remove it from its hook on the wall to fan herself at Sunday mass). Each year more items were added as the family grew and dispersed, and every object in the room had a story attached to it, a *cuento*[4] which Mamá would bestow on anyone who received the privilege of a day alone with her. It was almost worth pretending to be sick, though the bitter herb purgatives of the body were a big price to pay for the spirit revivals of her story-telling.

Mamá slept alone on her large bed, except for the times when a sick grandchild warranted the privilege, or when a heartbroken daughter came home in need of more than herbal teas. In the family there is a story about how this came to be.

When one of the daughters, my mother or one of her sisters, tells the *cuento* of how Mamá came to own her nights, it is usually preceded by the qualifications that Papá's exile from his wife's room was not a result of animosity between the couple, but that the act had been Mamá's famous bloodless coup for her personal freedom. Papá was the benevolent dictator of her body and her life who had had to be banished from her bed so that Mamá could better serve her family. Before the telling, we had to agree that the old man was not

3. "The New Yorkers."
4. "Tale."

to blame. We all recognized that in the family Papá was as an *alma de Dios*,[5] a saintly, soft-spoken presence whose main pleasures in life, such as writing poetry and reading the Spanish large-type editions of *Reader's Digest*, always took place outside the vortex of Mamá's crowded realm. It was not his fault, after all, that every year or so he planted a babyseed in Mamá's fertile body, keeping her from leading the active life she needed and desired. He loved her and the babies. Papá composed odes and lyrics to celebrate births and anniversaries and hired musicians to accompany him in singing them to his family and friends at extravagant pig-roasts he threw yearly. Mamá and the oldest girls worked for days preparing the food. Papá sat for hours in his painter's shed, also his study and library, composing the songs. At these celebrations he was also known to give long speeches in praise of God, his fecund wife, and his beloved island. As a middle child, my mother remembers these occasions as a time when the women sat in the kitchen and lamented their burdens, while the men feasted out in the patio, their rum-thickened voices rising in song and praise for each other, *compañeros*[6] all.

It was after the birth of her eighth child, after she had lost three at birth or in infancy, that Mamá made her decision. They say that Mamá had had a special way of letting her husband know that they were expecting, one that had begun when, at the beginning of their marriage, he had built her a house too confining for her taste. So, when she discovered her first pregnancy, she supposedly drew plans for another room, which he dutifully executed. Every time a child was due, she would demand, *more space, more space*. Papá acceded to her wishes, child after child, since he had learned early that Mamá's renowned temper was a thing that grew like a monster along with a new belly. In this way Mamá got the house that she wanted, but with each child she lost in heart and energy. She had knowledge of her body and perceived that if she had any more children, her dreams and her plans would have to be permanently forgotten, because she would be a chronically ill woman, like Flora with her twelve children: asthma, no teeth, in bed more than on her feet.

10   And so, after my youngest uncle was born, she asked Papá to build a large room at the back of the house. He did so in joyful anticipation. Mamá had asked him special things this time: shelves on the walls, a private entrance. He thought that she meant this room to be a nursery where several children could sleep. He thought it was a wonderful idea. He painted it his favorite color, sky blue, and made large windows looking out over a green hill and the church spires beyond. But nothing happened. Mamá's belly did not grow, yet she seemed in a frenzy of activity over the house. Finally, an anxious Papá approached his wife to tell her that the new room was finished and ready to be occupied. And Mamá, they say, replied: "Good, it's for *you*."

And so it was that Mamá discovered the only means of birth control available to a Catholic woman of her time: sacrifice. She gave up the comfort of Papá's sexual love for something she deemed greater: the right to own and

5. Literally, "soul of God"; a thoroughly good person.
6. "Companions."

control her body, so that she might live to meet her grandchildren—me among them—so that she could give more of herself to the ones already there, so that she could be more than a channel for other lives, so that even now that time has robbed her of the elasticity of her body and of her amazing reservoir of energy, she still emanates the kind of joy that can only be achieved by living according to the dictates of one's own heart.

MLA CITATION

Cofer, Judith Ortiz. "More Room." *The Norton Reader: An Anthology of Nonfiction*, edited by Melissa A. Goldthwaite et al., 15th ed., W. W. Norton, 2020, pp. 86–89.

QUESTIONS

1. At the end of the essay, Judith Ortiz Cofer explains in fairly direct terms why her grandmother wanted "more room." Why do you think she uses narration as the primary mode in the rest of the essay? What does she gain by first narrating, then explaining?

2. Cofer uses many similes (comparisons with "like" or "as") and metaphors (comparisons without specific connectors)—for example, in paragraph 1 she says that her grandmother's house was "like a chambered nautilus" and in paragraph 5 that her grandmother's Bible was "her security system." Discuss the use of one or two such comparisons that you find particularly effective.

3. What are the possible meanings of the title?

4. Write about a favorite or mysterious place you remember from childhood.

JACK HAMILTON
Aretha Franklin Was the Defining Voice of the 20th Century

ARETHA FRANKLIN'S WAS THE VOICE of the 20th century. No other singer left such a definitive mark on the course of popular music—simply put, there is singing before Aretha Franklin, and there is singing after her. Her combination of technique, precision, nuance, and sheer power was approached by vanishingly few others—Ray Charles and Sam Cooke, two of Franklin's greatest influences, come to mind—but Franklin also possessed a peerless intuition for forging profound intimacy with a vast range of listeners, an aston-

This essay was published in Slate, *an online magazine that covers culture, politics, and current affairs, on the occasion of Franklin's death (August 16, 2018).*

ishing gift for such a rarefied talent. She had the voice of a god and, just as importantly, the heart and mind of a human visionary, and her late-1960s emergence into superstardom, as a virtuoso black woman steeped in the musical and cultural life of the church, was a watershed in American culture.

It's a cliché to describe someone as "destined for greatness," but the words fit Franklin as well as they have any artist. She was the daughter of the nationally famous Rev. C. L. Franklin, raised in a household frequented by guests like Mahalia Jackson, Martin Luther King Jr., and Cooke[1] himself. She was a musical prodigy and, with her father's encouragement, began a gospel recording career at the age of 14. At age 18 she was signed to Columbia Records by the legendary talent scout John Hammond, who'd already nurtured the careers of artists like Benny Goodman, Count Basie, and Billie Holiday. (Less than two years after signing Franklin, Hammond signed a young folk singer named Robert Zimmerman,[2] who continues to record for Columbia under a pseudonym.)

Columbia's botching of Franklin's early career is one of the more well-worn cautionary tales in the annals of popular music. Ignorant of the depths of her talent, the story goes, Columbia tried to force her into being a watered-down Dinah Washington clone, squandering her for a half-decade by having her sing banal trifles and fusty standards. There's some truth to this, but it's also not totally fair to the parties involved. For starters, Franklin's Columbia albums are quite good and occasionally truly great. They just weren't very popular, largely because neither Columbia nor Franklin's career advisers foresaw the forces that would inexorably alter the musical and social landscape of pop music from 1960 (when Franklin signed with Columbia) to 1966 (when Columbia finally dropped her), forces that included Motown, the Beatles, Stax, and James Brown, to name just a few. In fact, Motown founder Berry Gordy allegedly tried to woo the Detroit-raised Franklin to his upstart label early in her career but the Rev. Franklin rejected the overtures, believing Gordy's fledgling family-operated independent was a woefully insufficient home for his daughter's enormous talents. The reverend was right, of course, until he was wrong.

What happened next is history. The venerable American R&B label Atlantic Records, whose vice president Jerry Wexler was salivating at the untapped potential of Franklin, signed her with the intention of turning her into a pop superstar. Wexler made the shrewd decision to put Franklin in front of a piano in the studio, tapping a crucial component of her musicality that Columbia had often neglected to showcase. (Franklin was an absolutely extraordinary pianist: On many of her Atlantic recordings, the piano is the most memorable and thrilling non-vocal instrument, no small feat given that she was playing alongside some of the best session musicians on earth.) It was on the Atlantic label that Aretha Franklin suddenly went from veteran recording artist with a years-long track record of commercial underperformance to an overnight sensation.

1. Three African American leaders from different but intersecting fields: Mahalia Jackson (1911–1972), gospel singer; Martin Luther King Jr. (1929–1968), Baptist minister and leader of the civil rights movement; Sam Cooke (1931–1964), soul singer.
2. Singer-songwriter Bob Dylan (b. 1941), born Robert Zimmerman.

In 1967 and 1968 alone, Franklin charted nine Top Ten Pop hits, including the No. 1 smash "Respect," a cover of a recent Otis Redding hit that Franklin transformed into one of the most famous pieces of music ever recorded. ("That little girl stole my song," Redding is said to have remarked, correctly.)

If there's one aspect of Franklin's story that I think is often overlooked, particularly by younger generations, it's just how huge she was. In the late 1960s—a period that we can generally agree was pretty great for music—Aretha Franklin was probably the most famous solo artist on earth. Poets and essayists rhapsodized over her. In June 1968, she appeared on the cover of *Time* magazine. She would get incessantly name-dropped in contexts that had almost nothing to do with music, simply because she was all anyone wanted to talk about. She released a recording of "Let It Be" before the Beatles had released theirs, because Paul McCartney had sent Jerry Wexler an acetate demo of the song in hopes she'd sing it. She of course continued to make astonishingly great music well into the 1970s, particularly the live gospel double-LP *Amazing Grace* from 1972, a hugely ambitious and deeply personal piece of work that became the highest-selling album of her career. These years also found Franklin foregrounding her own political commitments more explicitly, frequently expressing solidarity with civil rights activists and cultural-nationalist movements and gravitating toward material that emphasized these stances. (Her 1972 recording of Nina Simone and Weldon Irvine's "(To Be) Young, Gifted and Black," found on the phenomenal album that bears its name, is one of Franklin's most powerful performances.)

Even at the height of her stardom, a lot of people got Aretha Franklin wrong. She was often held up as both singular emblem and apotheosis of an entire black musical tradition, and (usually white) writers tried to force her into the mold of stereotypical beliefs of what that tradition was, often through a romantic exoticism rife with racist fantasies of social and emotional pathology. This type of writing stung and deeply angered Franklin—not only because it was condescending and presumptuous, but also because it was simply incorrect. Franklin wasn't some idealized stereotype magically brought to life, but rather a testament to a rich multiplicity of black American life that many white commentators—even well-meaning ones—have long tended to ignore. Here was a young woman whose trajectory had gone from prodigy to showbiz kid to pro's pro to has-been to superstar, all before her 25th birthday. Aretha Franklin wasn't some mystical vessel but rather a cosmopolitan and fully formed artist in devastating command of her craft. She was exceptional in every sense, and had become that way through a combination of genius and her own tireless work.

Franklin's most famous recordings—"Respect," "Chain of Fools," "Baby I Love You," "(You Make Me Feel Like) A Natural Woman," and so many others—are so fundamental to American popular music that they're basically the air we breathe. I don't remember the first time I heard Aretha Franklin, much in the way I don't remember the first time I saw a sunset or ate a bowl of ice cream. Living in a world with Aretha Franklin's music is one of the great privileges of being a human being. And yet this presents its own challenge on a day like today, when we should strive to get deeper than even that type of familiarity, which is itself a testament to a world-altering artist.

One of my favorite Franklin recordings is a demo of "I Never Loved a Man (The Way I Love You)," which is from sometime in 1966 but wasn't officially released until 2007, on the clunkily titled yet essential 2-CD set *Rare & Unreleased Recordings from the Golden Reign of the Queen of Soul.* "I Never Loved a Man" was, of course, the song that finally broke Aretha Franklin into stardom and changed American music, hitting the Top 10 on the Pop chart (and No. 1 over on R&B) in early 1967. The recorded version that everyone knows, featuring the famed Muscle Shoals rhythm section and Spooner Oldham's humming Wurlitzer piano riff, is sometimes cited as the apotheosis of Southern soul.[3] (The story behind that recording is legendary unto itself, and I won't go into it here, other than to say that a number of years ago the critic Matt Dobkin wrote an excellent book about the recording of the song and the album that shares its name.)

The demo bears only a passing resemblance to the hit. For starters, it's remarkably austere—to my ears, the only personnel on the track are Franklin on piano and vocal, an upright bass player, and a drummer. The song's famous Wurlitzer part—improvised by Oldham on the spot—isn't present, although you can almost hear hints of it in Franklin's own piano performance, like it's floating around in some great musical ether just waiting to be born from *someone's* fingers. At one point before she starts singing, Franklin coughs, just once, as if to let you know she's a normal human just like you before spending the next three minutes or so proving otherwise.

10   "I Never Loved a Man" was written by Ronnie Shannon, and it's a simple song. Its chord changes evoke a blues, but its form is even more spacious and skeletal than the traditional 12-bar form. It's a song that entirely depends on a singer, someone who can take its lyrical themes of snake-bitten masochism and render them with the appropriate mix of swagger, humor, and sensuality to allow the song to rise above what it is at its most literal: a song about an abusive relationship. In the hands of a mediocre singer, "I Never Loved a Man" would simply be a song about being wounded, and really, who wants to listen to that? It's a song that needs Aretha Franklin, and at this moment she needs it.

There's a charming tentativeness to that 1966 demo, as is usually the case with such recordings. The bass player and the drummer are striving for atmosphere more than emphasis, feeling their way through the form, evidently unsure of whether they're really going for it or just fooling around. Aretha is unmistakably going for it, but she's also having *fun*: Her vocal sounds exploratory in the best way, playing around with phrasing, dancing around some words and pitches while landing on others like a hammer, throwing in perfectly executed melismatic runs when her footing gets sure enough. Some of these experiments will make their way into the take she'll record in Muscle Shoals, the one that soon will change her life, and everyone else's.

3. Dewey Lindam "Spooner" Oldham (b. 1943), songwriter, producer, keyboardist, and session musician working out of Muscle Shoal Sound Studio in northwest Alabama. He and his musicians, mostly white, were central to creating the sound of Southern soul and rhythm and blues.

What is there, unmistakably, is the sound of genius and a ferociously ambitious perseverance. Here is a woman who's spent her late teens and early 20s—prime years for many singers—languishing at a record label that didn't understand what to do with her while her generational peers were changing the entire landscape of music, all the while knowing she's more talented than any of them. But she knows she's still got a chance, and that this song might be part of it, and the result is the very mix of urgency, command, and deep joy that will soon become the hallmark of her art. Every time she hits that refrain—"I ain't never loved a man/ the way that I love you"—she wrings new meanings and implications out of it, until a phrase that at first seemed almost offhand in its folksy simplicity now seems impossibly alluring and complex.

All of this is already there on a recording that, by design, barely anyone would ever hear. It's nowhere near as great as the finished, studio version—a distinction it shares with literally almost every other piece of music ever recorded—but it's a gift in its own right, an actual rough draft of musical history. It's like peeking through the keyhole of a new world, the one that Aretha Franklin would soon give us. Living in that world has never felt more like a privilege.

MLA CITATION

Hamilton, Jack. "Aretha Franklin Was the Defining Voice of the 20th Century." *The Norton Reader: An Anthology of Nonfiction*, edited by Melissa A. Goldthwaite et al., 15th ed., W. W. Norton, 2020, pp. 89–93.

QUESTIONS

1. In paragraph 2, Jack Hamilton says that Aretha Franklin was "destined for greatness," but then he goes on to describe some of the obstacles she faced in her career. What does Hamilton suggest about how she was able to overcome them?

2. Franklin wrestled with the tension between offering public support to political causes, such as the civil rights movement (paragraph 5), and her discomfort with being labeled as an "emblem and apotheosis of an entire black musical tradition" (paragraph 6). How can artists navigate that tension? How have other artists approached this dilemma?

3. Listen to one of the Aretha Franklin songs that Hamilton writes about more than once and see if you can hear the qualities that he describes. What else do you hear in the song? How does knowing more about Franklin's life and art inform your listening?

4. Hamilton moves from an overview of Franklin's career to a close analysis of one song. Write a profile of one of your favorite artists (preferably someone with more than two albums) in which you follow a similar structure.

TOM WOLFE
Yeager

NYONE WHO TRAVELS VERY MUCH ON AIRLINES in the United States soon gets to know the voice of *the airline pilot*. . . . coming over the intercom . . . with a particular drawl, a particular folksiness, a particular down-home calmness that is so exaggerated it begins to parody itself (nevertheless!—it's reassuring) . . . the voice that tells you, as the airliner is caught in thunderheads and goes bolting up and down a thousand feet at a single gulp, to check your seat belts because "it might get a little choppy" . . . the voice that tells you (on a flight from Phoenix preparing for its final approach into Kennedy Airport, New York, just after dawn): "Now, folks, uh . . . this is the captain. . . . ummmm . . . We've got a little ol' red light up here on the control panel that's tryin' to tell us that the *land*in' gears're not . . . uh . . . *lock*in' into position when we lower 'em . . . Now . . . I don't believe that little ol' red light knows what it's *talk*in' about—I believe it's that little ol' red light that iddn' workin' right" . . . faint chuckle, long pause, as if to say, *I'm not even sure all this is really worth going into—still, it may amuse you* . . . "But . . . I guess to play it by the rules, we oughta *humor* that little ol' light. . . . so we're gonna take her down to about, oh, two or three hundred feet over the runway at Kennedy, and the folks down there on the ground are gonna see if they caint give us a *vis*ual inspection of those ol' landin' gears"—with which he is obviously on intimate ol'-buddy terms, as with every other working part of this mighty ship—"and if I'm right . . . they're gonna tell us everything is copa*cet*ic all the way aroun' an' we'll jes take her on in" . . . and, after a couple of low passes over the field, the voice returns: "Well, folks, those folks down there on the ground—it must be too early for 'em or somethin'—I 'spect they still got the *sleep*ers in their eyes. . . . 'cause they say they caint tell if those ol' landin' gears are all the way down or not . . . But, you know, up here in the cockpit we're convinced they're all the way down, so we're jes gonna take her on in. . . . And oh" . . . *(I almost forgot)* . . . "while we take a little swing out over the ocean an' empty some of that surplus fuel we're not gonna be needin' anymore—that's what you might be seein' comin' out of the wings—our lovely little ladies . . . if they'll be so kind . . . they're gonna go up and down the aisles and show you how we do what we call 'assumin' the position'" . . . another faint chuckle *(We do this so often, and it's so much fun, we even have a funny little name for it)* . . . and the stewardesses, a bit grimmer, by the looks of them, than *that voice*, start telling the passengers to take their glasses off and take the ballpoint pens and other sharp objects out of their pockets, and they show them *the position*, with the head lowered. . . . while down on the field at Kennedy the little yellow emergency trucks start roaring across the field—and even though in your pounding heart and your sweating palms and your broiling brainpan you *know*

From The Right Stuff (1979), *Tom Wolfe's account of American test pilots and the first U.S. astronauts, which was made into a 1983 movie. "Yeager" refers to Chuck Yeager, a famous Air Force general and an accomplished pilot.*

this is a critical moment in your life, you still can't quite bring yourself to be*lieve* it, because if it were . . . how could *the captain,* the man who knows the actual situation most intimately . . . how could he keep on drawlin' and chucklin' and driftin' and lollygaggin' in that particular voice of his—

Well!—who doesn't know that voice! And who can forget it!—even after he is proved right and the emergency is over.

That particular voice may sound vaguely Southern or Southwestern, but it is specifically Appalachian in origin. It originated in the mountains of West Virginia, in the coal country, in Lincoln County, so far up in the hollows that, as the saying went, "they had to pipe in daylight." In the late 1940's and early 1950's this up-hollow voice drifted down from on high, from over the high desert of California, down, down, down, from the upper reaches of the Brotherhood into all phases of American aviation. It was amazing. It was *Pygmalion*[1] in reverse. Military pilots and then, soon, airline pilots, pilots from Maine and Massachusetts and the Dakotas and Oregon and everywhere else, began to talk in that poker-hollow West Virginia drawl, or as close to it as they could bend their native accents. It was the drawl of the most righteous of all the possessors of the right stuff: Chuck Yeager.

Yeager had started out as the equivalent, in the Second World War, of the legendary Frank Luke of the 27th Aero Squadron in the First. Which is to say, he was the boondocker, the boy from the back country, with only a high-school education, no credentials, no cachet or polish of any sort, who took off the feedstore overalls and put on a uniform and climbed into an airplane and lit up the skies over Europe.

Yeager grew up in Hamlin, West Virginia, a town on the Mud River not   5
far from Nitro, Hurricane Whirlwind, Salt Rock, Mud, Sod, Crum, Leet, Dollie, Ruth, and Alum Creek. His father was a gas driller (drilling for natural gas in the coalfields), his older brother was a gas driller, and he would have been a gas driller had he not enlisted in the Army Air Force in 1941 at the age of eighteen. In 1943, at twenty, he became a flight officer, i.e., a non-com who was allowed to fly, and went to England to fly fighter planes over France and Germany. Even in the tumult of the war Yeager was somewhat puzzling to a lot of other pilots. He was a short, wiry, but muscular little guy with dark curly hair and a tough-looking face that seemed (to strangers) to be saying: "You best not be lookin' me in the eye, you peckerwood, or I'll put four more holes in your nose." But that wasn't what was puzzling. What was puzzling was the way Yeager talked. He seemed to talk with some older forms of English elocution, syntax, and conjugation that had been preserved up-hollow in the Appalachians. There were people up there who never said they disapproved of anything, they said: "I don't hold with it." In the present tense they were willing to *help* out, like anyone else; but in the past tense they only *holped.* "H'it weren't nothin' I hold with, but I holped him out with it, anyways."

1. Play (1912) by George Bernard Shaw, in which a teacher of phonetics attempts to transform a Cockney flower girl into an elegant lady by means of transforming her speech.

In his first eight missions, at the age of twenty, Yeager shot down two German fighters. On his ninth he was shot down over German-occupied French territory, suffering flak wounds; he bailed out, was picked up by the French underground, which smuggled him across the Pyrenees into Spain disguised as a peasant. In Spain he was jailed briefly, then released, whereupon he made it back to England and returned to combat during the Allied invasion of France. On October 12, 1944, Yeager took on and shot down five German fighter planes in succession. On November 6, flying a propeller-driven P-51 Mustang, he shot down one of the new jet fighters the Germans had developed, the Messerschmitt-262, and damaged two more, and on November 20 he shot down four FW-190s. It was a true Frank Luke–style display of warrior fury and personal prowess. By the end of the war he had thirteen and a half kills. He was twenty-two years old.

In 1946 and 1947 Yeager was trained as a test pilot at Wright Field in Dayton. He amazed his instructors with his ability at stunt-team flying, not to mention the unofficial business of hassling. That plus his up-hollow drawl had everybody saying, "He's a natural-born stick 'n' rudder man." Nevertheless, there was something extraordinary about it when a man so young, with so little experience in flight test, was selected to go to Muroc Field in California for the XS-1 project.

Muroc was up in the high elevations of the Mojave Desert. It looked like some fossil landscape that had long since been left behind by the rest of terrestrial evolution. It was full of huge dry lake beds, the biggest being Rogers Lake. Other than sagebrush the only vegetation was Joshua trees, twisted freaks of the plant world that looked like a cross between cactus and Japanese bonsai. They had a dark petrified green color and horribly crippled branches. At dusk the Joshua trees stood out in silhouette on the fossil wasteland like some arthritic nightmare. In the summer the temperature went up to 110 degrees as a matter of course, and the dry lake beds were covered in sand, and there would be windstorms and sandstorms right out of a Foreign Legion movie. At night it would drop to near freezing, and in December it would start raining, and the dry lakes would fill up with a few inches of water, and some sort of putrid prehistoric shrimps would work their way up from out of the ooze, and sea gulls would come flying in a hundred miles or more from the ocean, over the mountains, to gobble up these squirming little throwbacks. A person had to see it to believe it: flocks of sea gulls wheeling around in the air out in the middle of the high desert in the dead of winter and grazing on antediluvian crustaceans in the primordial ooze.

When the wind blew the few inches of water back and forth across the lake beds, they became absolutely smooth and level. And when the water evaporated in the spring, and the sun baked the ground hard, the lake beds became the greatest natural landing fields ever discovered, and also the biggest, with miles of room for error. That was highly desirable, given the nature of the enterprise at Muroc.

10   Besides the wind, sand, tumbleweed, and Joshua trees, there was nothing at Muroc except for two Quonset-style hangars, side by side, a couple of gaso-

line pumps, a single concrete runway, a few tarpaper shacks, and some tents. The officers stayed in the shacks marked "barracks," and lesser souls stayed in the tents and froze all night and fried all day. Every road into the property had a guardhouse on it manned by soldiers. The enterprise the Army had undertaken in this godforsaken place was the development of supersonic jet and rocket planes.

At the end of the war the Army had discovered that the Germans not only had the world's first jet fighter but also a rocket plane that had gone 596 miles an hour in tests. Just after the war a British jet, the Gloster Meteor, jumped the official world speed record from 469 to 606 in a single day. The next great plateau would be Mach 1, the speed of sound, and the Army Air Force considered it crucial to achieve it first.

The speed of sound, Mach 1, was known (thanks to the work of the physicist Ernst Mach) to vary at different altitudes, temperatures, and wind speeds. On a calm 60-degree day at sea level it was about 760 miles an hour, while at 40,000 feet, where the temperature would be at least sixty below, it was about 660 miles an hour. Evil and baffling things happened in the transonic zone, which began at about .7 Mach. Wind tunnels choked out at such velocities. Pilots who approached the speed of sound in dives reported that the controls would lock or "freeze" or even alter their normal functions. Pilots had crashed and died because they couldn't budge the stick. Just last year Geoffrey de Havilland, son of the famous British aircraft designer and builder, had tried to take one of his father's DH 108s to Mach 1. The ship started buffeting and then disintegrated, and he was killed. This led engineers to speculate that the shock waves became so severe and unpredictable at Mach 1, no aircraft could survive them. They started talking about "the sonic wall" and "the sound barrier."

So this was the task that a handful of pilots, engineers, and mechanics had at Muroc. The place was utterly primitive, nothing but bare bones, bleached tarpaulins, and corrugated tin rippling in the heat with caloric waves; and for an ambitious young pilot it was perfect. Muroc seemed like an outpost on the dome of the world, open only to a righteous few, closed off to the rest of humanity, including even the Army Air Force brass of command control, which was at Wright Field. The commanding officer at Muroc was only a colonel, and his superiors at Wright did not relish junkets to the Muroc rat shacks in the first place. But to pilots this prehistoric throwback of an airfield became . . . shrimp heaven! the rat-shack plains of Olympus!

Low Rent Septic Tank Perfection . . . yes; and not excluding those traditional essentials for the blissful hot young pilot: Flying & Drinking and Drinking & Driving.

Just beyond the base, to the southwest, there was a rickety windblown 1930's-style establishment called Pancho's Fly Inn, owned, run, and bartended by a woman named Pancho Barnes. Pancho Barnes wore tight white sweaters and tight pants, after the mode of Barbara Stanwyck in *Double Indemnity*.[2] She was only forty-one when Yeager arrived at Muroc, but her face was so

15

2. Film (1944) featuring a femme fatale housewife played by Stanwyck.

weatherbeaten, had so many hard miles on it, that she looked older, especially
to the young pilots at the base. She also shocked the pants off them with her
vulcanized tongue. Everybody she didn't like was an old bastard or a sonofabitch. People she liked were old bastards and sonsabitches, too. "I tol' 'at ol'
bastard to get 'is ass on over here and I'd g'im a drink." But Pancho Barnes was
anything but Low Rent. She was the granddaughter of the man who designed
the old Mount Lowe cable-car system, Thaddeus S. C. Lowe. Her maiden name
was Florence Leontine Lowe. She was brought up in San Marino, which
adjoined Pasadena and was one of Los Angeles' wealthiest suburbs, and her first
husband—she was married four times—was the pastor of the Pasadena Episcopal Church, the Rev. C. Rankin Barnes. Mrs. Barnes seemed to have few of
the conventional community interests of a Pasadena matron. In the late 1920's,
by boat and plane, she ran guns for Mexican revolutionaries and picked up the
nickname Pancho. In 1930 she broke Amelia Earhart's[3] air-speed record for
women. Then she barnstormed around the country as the featured performer
of "Pancho Barnes's Mystery Circus of the Air." She always greeted her public
in jodhpurs and riding boots, a flight jacket, a white scarf, and a white sweater
that showed off her terrific Barbara Stanwyck chest. Pancho's desert Fly Inn
had an airstrip, a swimming pool, a dude ranch corral, plenty of acreage for
horseback riding, a big old guest house for the lodgers, and a connecting building that was the bar and restaurant. In the barroom the floors, the tables, the
chairs, the walls, the beams, the bar were of the sort known as extremely
weatherbeaten, and the screen doors kept banging. Nobody putting together
such a place for a movie about flying in the old days would ever dare make it
as dilapidated and generally go-to-hell as it actually was. Behind the bar were
many pictures of airplanes and pilots, lavishly autographed and inscribed,
badly framed and crookedly hung. There was an old piano that had been
dried out and cracked to the point of hopeless desiccation. On a good night a
huddle of drunken aviators could be heard trying to bang, slosh, and navigate
their way through old Cole Porter[4] tunes. On average nights the tunes were
not that good to start with. When the screen door banged and a man walked
through the door into the saloon, every eye in the place checked him out. If
he wasn't known as somebody who had something to do with flying at Muroc,
he would be eyed like some lame goddamned mouseshit sheepherder from
Shane.[5]

The plane the Air Force wanted to break the sound barrier with was
called the X-1 at the outset and later on simply the X-1. The Bell Aircraft Corporation had built it under an Army contract. The core of the ship was a
rocket of the type first developed by a young Navy inventor, Robert Truax,
during the war. The fuselage was shaped like a 50-caliber bullet—an object
that was known to go supersonic smoothly. Military pilots seldom drew major
test assignments; they went to highly paid civilians working for the aircraft

3. Pioneering aviator (1897–1937) and the first woman to fly solo across the Atlantic Ocean.
4. American composer of popular music (1891–1964), including Broadway show tunes.
5. Classic Western movie (1953).

corporations. The prime pilot for the X-1 was a man whom Bell regarded as the best of the breed. This man looked like a movie star. He looked like a pilot from out of *Hell's Angels*.[6] And on top of everything else there was his name: Slick Goodlin.

The idea in testing the X-1 was to nurse it carefully into the transonic zone, up to seven-tenths, eight-tenths, nine-tenths the speed of sound (.7 Mach, .8 Mach, .9 Mach) before attempting the speed of sound itself, Mach 1, even though Bell and the Army already knew the X-1 had the rocket power to go to Mach 1 and beyond, if there *was* any *beyond*. The consensus of aviators and engineers, after Geoffrey de Havilland's death, was that the speed of sound was an absolute, like the firmness of the earth. The sound barrier was a farm you could buy in the sky. So Slick Goodlin began to probe the transonic zone in the X-1, going up to .8 Mach. Every time he came down he'd have a riveting tale to tell. The buffeting, it was so fierce—and the listeners, their imaginations aflame, could practically see poor Geoffrey de Havilland disintegrating in midair. And the goddamned aerodynamics—and the listeners got a picture of a man in ballroom pumps skidding across a sheet of ice, pursued by bears. A controversy arose over just how much bonus Slick Goodlin should receive for assaulting the dread Mach 1 itself. Bonuses for contract test pilots were not unusual; but the figure of $150,000 was now bruited about. The Army balked, and Yeager got the job. He took it for $283 a month, or $3,396 a year; which is to say, his regular Army captain's pay.

The only trouble they had with Yeager was in holding him back. On his first powered flight in the X-1 he immediately executed an unauthorized zero-g roll with a full load of rocket fuel, then stood the ship on its tail and went up to .85 Mach in a vertical climb, also unauthorized. On subsequent flights, at speeds between .85 Mach and .9 Mach, Yeager ran into most known airfoil problems—loss of elevator, aileron, and rudder control, heavy trim pressures, Dutch rolls, pitching and buffeting, the lot—yet was convinced, after edging over .9 Mach, that this would all get better, not worse, as you reached Mach 1. The attempt to push beyond Mach 1—"breaking the sound barrier"—was set for October 14, 1947. Not being an engineer, Yeager didn't believe the "barrier" existed.

October 14 was a Tuesday. On Sunday evening, October 12, Chuck Yeager dropped in at Pancho's, along with his wife. She was a brunette named Glennis, whom he had met in California while he was in training, and she was such a number, so striking, he had the inscription "Glamorous Glennis" written on the nose of his P-51 in Europe and, just a few weeks back, on the X-1 itself. Yeager didn't go to Pancho's and knock back a few because two days later the big test was coming up. Nor did he knock back a few because it was the weekend. No, he knocked back a few because night had come and he was a pilot at Muroc. In keeping with the military tradition of Flying & Drinking, that was what you did, for no other reason than that the sun had gone down. You went to Pancho's and knocked back a few and listened to the screen doors banging

6. Movie (1930) about aviation during World War I.

and to other aviators torturing the piano and the nation's repertoire of Familiar Favorites and to lonesome mouseturd strangers wandering in through the banging doors and to Pancho classifying the whole bunch of them as old bastards and miserable peckerwoods. That was what you did if you were a pilot at Muroc and the sun went down.

20   So about eleven Yeager got the idea that it would be a hell of a kick if he and Glennis saddled up a couple of Pancho's dude-ranch horses and went for a romp, a little rat race, in the moonlight. This was in keeping with the military tradition of Flying & Drinking and Drinking & Driving, except that this was prehistoric Muroc and you rode horses. So Yeager and his wife set off on a little proficiency run at full gallop through the desert in the moonlight amid the arthritic silhouettes of the Joshua trees. Then they start racing back to the corral, with Yeager in the lead and heading for the gateway. Given the prevailing conditions, it being nighttime, at Pancho's, and his head being filled with a black sandstorm of many badly bawled songs and vulcanized oaths, he sees too late that the gate has been closed. Like many a hard-driving midnight pilot before him, he does not realize that he is not equally gifted in the control of all forms of locomotion. He and the horse hit the gate, and he goes flying off and lands on his right side. His side hurts like hell.

The next day, Monday, his side still hurts like hell. It hurts every time he moves. It hurts every time he breathes deep. It hurts every time he moves his right arm. He knows that if he goes to a doctor at Muroc or says anything to anybody even remotely connected with his superiors, he will be scrubbed from the flight on Tuesday. They might even go so far as to put some other miserable peckerwood in his place. So he gets on his motorcycle, an old junker that Pancho had given him, and rides over to see a doctor in the town of Rosamond, near where he lives. Every time the goddamned motorcycle hits a pebble in the road, his side hurts like a sonofabitch. The doctor in Rosamond informs him he has two broken ribs and he tapes them up and tells him that if he'll just keep his right arm immobilized for a couple of weeks and avoid any physical exertion or sudden movements, he should be all right.

Yeager gets up before daybreak on Tuesday morning—which is supposed to be the day he tries to break the sound barrier—and his ribs still hurt like a sonofabitch. He gets his wife to drive him over to the field, and he has to keep his right arm pinned down to his side to keep his ribs from hurting so much. At dawn, on the day of a flight, you could hear the X-1 screaming long before you got there. The fuel for the X-1 was alcohol and liquid oxygen, oxygen converted from a gas to a liquid by lowering its temperature to 297 degrees below zero. And when the lox, as it was called, rolled out of the hoses and into the belly of the X-1, it started boiling off and the X-1 started steaming and screaming like a teakettle. There's quite a crowd on hand, by Muroc standards. . . . perhaps nine or ten souls. They're still fueling the X-1 with the lox, and the beast is wailing.

The X-1 looked like a fat orange swallow with white markings. But it was really just a length of pipe with four rocket chambers in it. It had a tiny cockpit and a needle nose, two little straight blades (only three and a half inches thick at the thickest part) for wings, and a tail assembly set up high to avoid the "sonic wash" from the wings. Even though his side was throbbing and his right arm felt practically useless, Yeager figured he could grit his teeth and get through the flight—except for one specific move he had to make. In the rocket launches, the X-1, which held only two and a half minutes' worth of fuel, was carried up to twenty-six thousand feet underneath a B-29. At seven thousand feet, Yeager was to climb down a ladder from the bomb bay of the B-29 to the open doorway of the X-1, hook up to the oxygen system and the radio microphone and earphones, and put his crash helmet on and prepare for the launch, which would come at twenty-five thousand feet. This helmet was a homemade number. There had never been any such thing as a crash helmet before, except in stunt flying. Throughout the war pilots had used the old skin-tight leather helmet-and-goggles. But the X-1 had a way of throwing the pilot around so violently that there was danger of getting knocked out against the walls of the cockpit. So Yeager had bought a big leather football helmet—there were no plastic ones at the time—and he butchered it with a hunting knife until he carved the right kind of holes in it, so that it would fit down over his regular flying helmet and the earphones and the oxygen rig. Anyway, then his flight engineer, Jack Ridley, would climb down the ladder, out in the breeze, and shove into place the cockpit door, which had to be lowered out of the belly of the B-29 on a chain. Then Yeager had to push a handle to lock the door airtight. Since the X-1's cockpit was minute, you had to push the handle with your right hand. It took quite a shove. There was no way you could move into position to get enough leverage with your left hand.

Out in the hangar Yeager makes a few test shoves on the sly, and the pain is so incredible he realizes that there is no way a man with two broken ribs is going to get the door closed. It is time to confide in somebody, and the logical man is Jack Ridley. Ridley is not only the flight engineer but a pilot himself and a good old boy from Oklahoma to boot. He will understand about Flying & Drinking and Drinking & Driving through the goddamned Joshua trees. So Yeager takes Ridley off to the side in the tin hangar and says: Jack, I got me a little ol' problem here. Over at Pancho's the other night I sorta . . . dinged my goddamned ribs. Ridley says, Whattya mean . . . *dinged?* Yeager says, Well, I guess you might say I damned near like to . . . *broke* a coupla the sonsabitches. Whereupon Yeager sketches out the problem he foresees.

Not for nothing is Ridley the engineer on this project. He has an inspiration. He tells a janitor named Sam to cut him about nine inches off a broom handle. When nobody's looking, he slips the broomstick into the cockpit of the X-1 and gives Yeager a little advice and counsel.   25

So with that added bit of supersonic flight gear Yeager went aloft.

At seven thousand feet he climbed down the ladder into the X-1's cockpit, clipped on his hoses and lines, and managed to pull the pumpkin football helmet over his head. Then Ridley came down the ladder and lowered the door into place. As Ridley had instructed, Yeager now took the nine inches of broomstick and slipped it between the handle and the door. This gave him just enough mechanical advantage to reach over with his left hand and whang the thing shut. So he whanged the door shut with Ridley's broomstick and was ready to fly.

At 26,000 feet the B-29 went into a shallow dive, then pulled up and released Yeager and the X-1 as if it were a bomb. Like a bomb it dropped and shot forward (at the speed of the mother ship) at the same time. Yeager had been launched straight into the sun. It seemed to be no more than six feet in front of him, filling up the sky and blinding him. But he managed to get his bearings and set off the four rocket chambers one after the other. He then experienced something that became known as the ultimate sensation in flying: "booming and zooming." The surge of the rockets was so tremendous, forced him back into his seat so violently, he could hardly move his hands forward the few inches necessary to reach the controls. The X-1 seemed to shoot straight up in an absolutely perpendicular trajectory, as if determined to snap the hold of gravity via the most direct route possible. In fact, he was only climbing at the 45-degree angle called for in the flight plan. At about .87 Mach the buffeting started.

On the ground the engineers could no longer see Yeager. They could only hear . . . that poker-hollow West Virginia drawl.

30 "Had a mild buffet there . . . jes the usual instability . . ."

Jes the usual instability?

Then the X-1 reached the speed of .96 Mach, and that incredible caint-hardlyin' aw-shuckin' drawl said:

"Say, Ridley . . . make a note here, will ya?" *(if you ain't got nothin' better to do)* ". . . elevator effectiveness *regained.*"

Just as Yeager had predicted, as the X-1 approached Mach 1, the stability improved. Yeager had his eyes pinned on the machometer. The needle reached .96, fluctuated, and went off the scale.

35 And on the ground they heard . . . that voice:

"Say, Ridley . . . make another note, will ya?" *(if you ain't too bored yet)* ". . . there's somethin' wrong with this ol' machometer. . . ." (faint chuckle) ". . . it's gone kinda screwy on me. . . ."

And in that moment, on the ground, they heard a boom rock over the desert floor—just as the physicist Theodore von Kármán had predicted many years before.

Then they heard Ridley back in the B-29: "If it is, Chuck, we'll fix it. Personally I think you're seeing things."

Then they heard Yeager's poker-hollow drawl again:

40 "Well, I guess I am, Jack. . . . And I'm still goin' upstairs like a bat."

The X-1 had gone through "the sonic wall" without so much as a bump. As the speed topped out at Mach 1.05, Yeager had the sensation of shooting straight through the top of the sky. The sky turned a deep purple and all at once the stars and the moon came out—and the sun shone at the same time. He had reached a layer of the upper atmosphere where the air was too thin to contain reflecting dust particles. He was simply looking out into space. As the X-1 nosed over at the top of the climb, Yeager now had seven minutes of . . . Pilot Heaven . . . ahead of him. He was going faster than any man in history, and it was almost silent up here, since he had exhausted his rocket fuel, and he was so high in such a vast space that there was no sensation of motion. He was master of the sky. His was a king's solitude, unique and inviolate, above the dome of the world. It would take him seven minutes to glide back down and land at Muroc. He spent the time doing victory rolls and wing-over-wing aerobatics while Rogers Lake and the High Sierras spun around below.

MLA CITATION

Wolfe, Tom. "Yeager." *The Norton Reader: An Anthology of Nonfiction*, edited by Melissa A. Goldthwaite et al., 15th ed., W. W. Norton, 2020, pp. 94–103.

QUESTIONS

1. Before recounting Yeager's personal history or the story of breaking the sound barrier, Tom Wolfe begins with the voice of an airline pilot. Why does he begin this way? What connection does the first paragraph have with the rest of the essay?

2. Wolfe interweaves Yeager's personal history with a more public, official history of the space program. Make a flowchart or diagram to show how this interweaving works.

3. Write an essay that interweaves some part of your personal history with some larger, public story.

IAN FRAZIER
Take the F

Brooklyn, New York, has the undefined, hard-to-remember shape of a stain. I never know what to tell people when they ask me where in it I live. It sits at the western tip of Long Island at a diagonal that does not conform neatly to the points of the compass. People in Brooklyn do not describe where they live in terms of north or west or south. They refer instead to their neighborhoods and to the nearest subway lines. I live on the edge of Park Slope, a neighborhood by the crest of a low ridge that runs through the borough. Prospect Park is across the street. Airplanes in the landing pattern for LaGuardia Airport sometimes fly right over my building; every few minutes, on certain sunny days, perfectly detailed airplane shadows slide down my building and up the building opposite in a blink. You can see my building from the plane—it's on the left-hand side of Prospect Park, the longer patch of green you cross after the expanse of Green-Wood Cemetery.

First published as "Letter from Brooklyn" in the New Yorker *(1995), later included in his book* Gone to New York: Adventures in the City *(2005).*

We moved to a co-op apartment in a four-story building a week before our daughter was born. She is now six. I grew up in the country and would not have expected ever to live in Brooklyn. My daughter is a city kid, with less sympathy for certain other parts of the country. When we visited Montana, she was disappointed by the scarcity of pizza places. I overheard her explaining—she was three or four then—to a Montana kid about Brooklyn. She said, "In Brooklyn, there is a lot of broken glass, so you have to wear shoes. And, there is good pizza." She is stern in her judgment of pizza. At the very low end of the pizza-ranking scale is some pizza she once had in New Hampshire, a category now called New Hampshire pizza. In the middle is some okay pizza she once had at the Bronx Zoo, which she calls zoo pizza. At the very top is the pizza at the pizza place where the big kids go, about two blocks from our house.

Our subway is the F train. It runs under our building and shakes the floor. The F is generally a reliable train, but one spring as I walked in the park I saw emergency vehicles gathered by a concrete-sheathed hole in the lawn. Firemen lifted a metal lid from the hole and descended into it. After a while, they reappeared, followed by a few people, then dozens of people, then a whole lot of people—passengers from a disabled F train, climbing one at a time out an exit shaft. On the F, I sometimes see large women in straw hats reading a newspaper called the *Caribbean Sunrise*, and Orthodox Jews bent over Talmudic texts[1] in which the footnotes have footnotes, and groups of teenagers wearing identical red bandannas with identical red plastic baby pacifiers in the corners of their mouths, and female couples in porkpie hats, and young men with the silhouettes of the Manhattan skyline razored into their short side hair from one temple around to the other, and Russian-speaking men with thick wrists and big wristwatches, and a hefty, tall woman with long, straight blond hair who hums and closes her eyes and absently practices cello fingerings on the metal subway pole. As I watched the F train passengers emerge among the grass and trees of Prospect Park, the faces were as varied as usual, but the expressions of indignant surprise were all about the same.

Just past my stop, Seventh Avenue, Manhattan-bound F trains rise from underground to cross the Gowanus Canal. The train sounds different—lighter, quieter—in the open air. From the elevated tracks, you can see the roofs of many houses stretching back up the hill to Park Slope, and a bumper crop of rooftop graffiti, and neon signs for Eagle Clothes and Kentile Floors, and flat expanses of factory roofs where seagulls stand on one leg around puddles in the sagging spots. There are fuel-storage tanks surrounded by earthen barriers, and slag piles, and conveyor belts leading down to the oil-slicked waters of the canal. On certain days, the sludge at the bottom of the canal causes it to bubble. Two men fleeing the police jumped in the canal a while ago; one made it across, the other quickly died. When the subway doors open at the Smith–Ninth Street stop, you can see the bay and sometimes smell the ocean breeze. This stretch of elevated is the highest point of the New York subway system. To the

1. Rabbinic discussions of law, ethics, philosophy, and history collected in the Talmud, a key text of Judaism.

south you can see the Verrazano-Narrows Bridge, to the north the World Trade towers. For just a few moments, the Statue of Liberty appears between passing buildings. Pieces of a neighborhood—laundry on clotheslines, a standup swimming pool, a plaster saint, a satellite dish, a rectangle of lawn—slide by like quickly dealt cards. Then the train descends again; growing over the wall just before the tunnel is a wisteria bush, which blooms pale blue every May.

I have spent days, weeks on the F train. The trip from Seventh Avenue to midtown Manhattan is long enough so that every ride can produce its own mini-society of riders, its own forty-minute Ship of Fools.[2] Once a woman an arm's length from me on a crowded train pulled a knife on a man who threatened her. I remember the argument and the principals, but mostly I remember the knife—its flat, curved wood-grain handle inlaid with brass fittings at each end, its long, tapered blade. Once a man sang the words of the Lord's Prayer to a mournful, syncopated tune, and he fitted the mood of the morning so exactly that when he asked for money at the end the riders reached for their wallets and purses as if he'd pulled a gun. Once a big white kid with some friends was teasing a small old Hispanic lady, and when he got off the train I looked at him through the window and he slugged it hard next to my face. Once a thin woman and a fat woman sitting side by side had a long and loud conversation about someone they intended to slap silly: "Her butt be in the *hospital!*" "Bring out the ar-*tillery!*" The terminus of the F in Brooklyn is at Coney Island, not far from the beach. At an off hour, I boarded the train and found two or three passengers and, walking around on the floor, a crab. The passengers were looking at the crab. Its legs clicked on the floor like varnished fingernails. It moved in this direction, then that, trying to get comfortable. It backed itself under a seat, against the wall. Then it scooted out just after some new passengers had sat down there, and they really screamed. Passengers at the next stop saw it and laughed. When a boy lifted his foot as if to stomp it, everybody cried, "Noooh!" By the time we reached Jay Street–Borough Hall,[3] there were maybe a dozen of us in the car, all absorbed in watching the crab. The car doors opened and a heavyset woman with good posture entered. She looked at the crab; then, sternly, at all of us. She let a moment pass. Then she demanded, "*Whose* is *that?*" A few stops later, a short man with a mustache took a manila envelope, bent down, scooped the crab into it, closed it, and put it in his coat pocket.

The smells in Brooklyn: coffee, fingernail polish, eucalyptus, the breath from laundry rooms, pot roast, Tater Tots. A woman I know who grew up here says she moved away because she could not stand the smell of cooking food in the hallway of her parents' building. I feel just the opposite. I used to live in a converted factory above an army-navy store, and I like being in a place that smells like people live there. In the mornings, I sometimes wake to the smell of toast, and I still don't know exactly whose toast it is. And I prefer living in a borough

2. Ancient Western allegory depicting a ship with human passengers who are mad, frivolous, or witlessly ignorant of their fate.
3. Station on the New York City subway system.

of two and a half million inhabitants, the most of any borough in the city. I think of all the rural places, the pine-timbered canyons and within-commuting-distance farmland, that we are preserving by not living there. I like the immensities of the borough, the unrolling miles of Eastern Parkway and Ocean Parkway and Linden Boulevard, and the disheveled outlying parks strewn with tree limbs and with shards of glass held together by liquor bottle labels, and the tough bridges—the Williamsburg and the Manhattan—and the gentle Brooklyn Bridge. And I like the way the people talk; some really do have Brooklyn accents, really do say "dese" and "dose." A week or two ago, a group of neighbors stood on a street corner watching a peregrine falcon on a building cornice contentedly eating a pigeon it had caught, and the sunlight came through its tail feathers, and a woman said to a man, "Look at the tail, it's so ah-range," and the man replied, "Yeah, I soar it." Like many Americans, I fear living in a nowhere, in a place that is no-place; in Brooklyn, that doesn't trouble me at all.

Everybody, it seems, is here. At Grand Army Plaza, I have seen traffic tie-ups caused by Haitians and others rallying in support of President Aristide,[4] and by St. Patrick's Day parades, and by Jews of the Lubavitcher sect celebrating the birthday of their Grand Rebbe with a slow procession of ninety-three motor homes—one for each year of his life. Local taxis have bumper stickers that say "Allah Is Great"; one of the men who made the bomb that blew up the World Trade Center used an apartment just a few blocks from me. When an election is held in Russia, crowds line up to cast ballots at a Russian polling place in Brighton Beach. A while ago, I volunteer-taught reading at a public elementary school across the park. One of my students, a girl, was part Puerto Rican, part Greek, and part Welsh. Her looks were a lively combination, set off by sea-green eyes. I went to a map store in Manhattan and bought maps of Puerto Rico, Greece, and Wales to read with her, but they didn't interest her. A teacher at the school was directing a group of students to set up chairs for a program in the auditorium, and she said to me, "We have a problem here—each of these kids speaks a different language." She asked the kids to tell me where they were from. One was from Korea, one from Brazil, one from Poland, one from Guyana, one from Taiwan. In the program that followed, a chorus of fourth and fifth graders sang "God Bless America," "You're a Grand Old Flag," and "I'm a Yankee-Doodle Dandy."

People in my neighborhood are mostly white, and middle class or above. People in neighborhoods nearby are mostly not white, and mostly middle class or below. Everybody uses Prospect Park. On summer days, the park teems with sound—the high note is kids screaming in the water sprinklers at the playground, the midrange is radios and tape players, and the bass is idling or speeding cars. People bring lawn furniture and badminton nets and coolers, and then they barbecue. Charcoal smoke drifts into the neighborhood. Last year, local residents upset about the noise and litter and smoke began a campaign to outlaw barbecuing in the park. There was much unfavorable comment about "the barbecuers." Since most of the barbecuers, as it happens, are black

4. Jean-Bertrand Aristide (b. 1953), president of Haiti briefly in 1991, and again from 1994 to 1996 and 2001 to 2004.

or Hispanic, the phrase "Barbecuers Go Home," which someone spray-painted on the asphalt at the Ninth Street entrance to the park, took on a pointed, unkind meaning. But then park officials set up special areas for barbecuing, and the barbecuers complied, and the controversy died down.

Right nearby is a shelter for homeless people. Sometimes people sleep on the benches along the park, sometimes they sleep in the foyer of our building. Once I went downstairs, my heart pounding, to evict a homeless person who I had been told was there. The immediate, unquestioning way she left made me feel bad; later I always said "Hi" to her and gave her a dollar when I ran into her. One night, late, I saw her on the street, and I asked her her last name (by then I already knew her first name) and for a moment she couldn't recall it. At this, she shook her head in mild disbelief.

There's a guy I see on a bench along Prospect Park West all the time. Once I walked by carrying my year-old son, and the man said, "Someday he be carrying you." At the local copy shop one afternoon, a crowd was waiting for copies and faxes when a man in a houndstooth fedora came in seeking signatures for a petition to have the homeless shelter shut down. To my surprise, and his, the people in the copy shop instantly turned on him. "I suppose because they're poor they shouldn't even have a place to sleep at night," a woman said as he backed out the door. On the park wall across the street from my building, someone has written in black marker:

10

COPS PROTECT CITIZENS
WHO PROTECT US FROM COPS.

Sometimes I walk from my building downhill and north, along the Brooklyn waterfront, where cargo ships with scuffed sides and prognathous bows lean overhead. Sometimes I walk by the Brooklyn Navy Yard, its docks now too dormant to attract saboteurs, its long expanses of chain-link fence tangled here and there with the branches of ailanthus trees growing through. Sometimes I head southwest, keeping more or less to the high ground—Bay Ridge—along Fifth Avenue, through Hispanic neighborhoods that stretch in either direction as far as you can see, and then through block after block of Irish. I follow the ridge to its steep descent to the water at the Verrazano Narrows; Fort Hamilton, an army post dating from 1814, is there, and a small Episcopal church called the Church of the Generals. Robert E. Lee once served as a vestryman of this church, and Stonewall Jackson was baptized here. Today the church is in the shade of a forest of high concrete columns supporting an access ramp to the Verrazano-Narrows Bridge.

Sometimes I walk due south, all the way out Coney Island Avenue. In that direction, as you approach the ocean, the sky gets bigger and brighter, and the buildings seem to flatten beneath it. Dry cleaners advertise "Tallis[5] Cleaned Free with Every Purchase Over Fifteen Dollars." Then you start to see occasional lines of graffiti written in Cyrillic.[6] Just past a Cropsey Avenue billboard welcoming visitors to Coney Island is a bridge over a creek filled nearly to the

5. Jewish prayer shawl.
6. Alphabet used for Russian and other Slavic languages.

surface with metal shopping carts that people have tossed there over the years. A little farther on, the streets open onto the beach. On a winter afternoon, bundled-up women sit on the boardwalk on folding chairs around a portable record player outside a restaurant called Gastronom Moscow. The acres of trash-dotted sand are almost empty. A bottle of Peter the Great vodka lies on its side, drops of water from its mouth making a small depression in the sand. A man with trousers rolled up to his shins moves along the beach, chopping at driftwood with an axe. Another passerby says, "He's vorking hard, that guy!" The sunset unrolls light along the storefronts like tape. From the far distance, little holes in the sand at the water's edge mark the approach of a short man wearing hip boots and earphones and carrying a long-handled metal detector. Treasure hunters dream of the jewelry that people must have lost here over the years. Some say that this is the richest treasure beach in the Northeast. The man stops, runs the metal detector again over a spot, digs with a clamming shovel, lifts some sand, brushes through it with a gloved thumb, discards it. He goes on, leaving a trail of holes behind him.

I like to find things myself, and I always try to keep one eye on the ground as I walk. So far I have found seven dollars (a five and two ones), an earring in the shape of a strawberry, several personal notes, a matchbook with a 900 number to call to hear "prison sex fantasies," and two spent .25-caliber shells. Once on Carroll Street, I saw a page of text on the sidewalk, and I bent over to read it. It was page 191 from a copy of *Anna Karenina*.[7] I read the whole page. It described Vronsky leaving a gathering and riding off in a carriage. In a great book, the least fragment is great. I looked up and saw a woman regarding me closely from a few feet away. "You're reading," she said wonderingly. "From a distance, I t'ought you were watchin' ants."

My favorite place to walk is the Brooklyn Botanic Garden, not more than fifteen minutes away. It's the first place I take out-of-towners, who may not associate Brooklyn with flowers. In the winter, the garden is drab as pocket lint, and you can practically see all the way through from Flatbush Avenue to Washington Avenue. But then in February or March a few flowerings begin, the snowdrops and the crocuses, and then the yellow of the daffodils climbs Daffodil Hill, and then the magnolias—star magnolias, umbrella magnolias, saucer magnolias— go off all at once, and walking among them is like flying through cumulus clouds. Then the cherry trees blossom, some a soft and glossy red like makeup, others pink as a dessert, and crowds fill the paths on weekends and stand in front of the blossoms in their best clothes and have their pictures taken. Security guards tell people, "No eating, no sitting on the grass—this is a garden, not a park." There are traffic jams of strollers and kids running loose. One security guard jokes into his radio, "There's a pterodactyl on the overlook!" In the pond in the Japanese Garden, ducks lobby for pieces of bread. A duck quacks, in Brooklynese, "Yeah, yeah, yeah," having heard it all before.

7. Novel by the Russian writer Leo Tolstoy, published in serial installments between 1873 and 1877.

Then the cherry blossoms fall, they turn some paths completely pink next to the grass's green, and the petals dry, and people tread them into a fine pink powder. Kids visit on end-of-school-year field trips, and teachers yell, "Shawon, get back on line!" and boys with long T-shirts printed from neck to knee with an image of Martin Luther King's face run by laughing and swatting at one another. The yellow boxes that photographic film comes in fall on the ground, and here and there an empty bag of Crazy Calypso potato chips. The lilacs bloom, each bush with a scent slightly different from the next, and yellow tulips fill big round planters with color so bright it ascends in a column, like a searchlight beam. The roses open on the trellises in the Rose Garden and attract a lively air traffic of bees, and June wedding parties, brides and grooms and their subsidiaries, adjust themselves minutely for photographers there. A rose called the Royal Gold smells like a new bathing suit and is as yellow.

In our building of nine apartments, two people have died and six have been born since we moved in. I like our neighbors—a guy who works for Off-Track Betting, a guy who works for the Department of Correction, a woman who works for Dean Witter, an in-flight steward, a salesperson of subsidiary rights at a publishing house, a restaurant manager, two lawyers, a retired machinist, a Lebanese-born woman of ninety-five—as well as any I've ever had. We keep track of the bigger events in the building with the help of Chris, our downstairs neighbor. Chris lives on the ground floor and often has conversations in the hall while her foot props her door open. When our kids are sick, she brings them her kids' videos to watch, and when it rains she gives us rides to school. One year, Chris became pregnant and had to take a blood-thinning medicine and was in and out of the hospital. Finally, she had a healthy baby and came home, but then began to bleed and didn't stop. Her husband brought the baby to us about midnight and took Chris to the nearest emergency room. Early the next morning, the grandmother came and took the baby. Then for two days nobody heard anything. When we knocked on Chris's door we got no answer and when we called we got an answering machine. The whole building was expectant, spooky, quiet. The next morning I left the house and there in the foyer was Chris. She held her husband's arm, and she looked pale, but she was returning from the hospital under her own steam. I hugged her at the door, and it was the whole building hugging her. I walked to the garden seeing glory everywhere. I went to the Rose Garden and took a big Betsy McCall rose to my face and breathed into it as if it were an oxygen mask.

15

MLA CITATION

Frazier, Ian. "Take the F." *The Norton Reader: An Anthology of Nonfiction*, edited by Melissa A. Goldthwaite et al., 15th ed., W. W. Norton, 2020, pp. 103–09.

QUESTIONS

1. According to Ian Frazier, Brooklynites identify themselves by neighborhood and subway line (paragraph 1). In addition to his subway line, how does Frazier describe

where he lives? What techniques help him present his Brooklyn neighborhood to readers who are nonresidents?

2. Frazier engages all of the senses—sight, sound, smell, taste, and touch—to portray his Brooklyn home. Choose one example of each that stands out to you. How do these examples create a sense of place?

3. Like Jhumpa Lahiri in "Rhode Island" (pp. 110–19), Frazier wishes to establish the uniqueness of his home. What features seem to be unique? What features seem universal? What relation do you see between the unique and the universal?

4. Write an essay about your neighborhood, using techniques identified in questions 1 and 2.

JHUMPA LAHIRI
Rhode Island

R HODE ISLAND IS NOT AN ISLAND. Most of it is attached to the continental United States, tucked into a perfect-looking corner formed by the boundaries of Connecticut to the west and Massachusetts above. The rest is a jagged confusion of shoreline: delicate slivers of barrier beach, numerous inlets and peninsulas, and a cluster of stray puzzle pieces, created by the movement of glaciers, nestled in the Narragansett Bay. The tip of Watch Hill, in the extreme southwest, extends like a curving rib bone into the Atlantic Ocean. The salt ponds lining the edge of South Kingstown,[1] where I grew up, resemble the stealthy work of insects who have come into contact with nutritious, antiquated paper.

In 1524, Giovanni Verrazzano[2] thought that the pear-shaped contours of Block Island, nine miles off the southern coast, resembled the Greek island of Rhodes. In 1644, subsequent explorers, mistaking one of Rhode Island's many attendant islands—there are over thirty of them—for another, gave the same name to Aquidneck Island, famous for Newport, and it has now come to represent the state as a whole. Though the name is misleading it is also apt, for despite Rhode Island's physical connection to the mainland, a sense of insularity prevails. Typical to many island communities, there is a combination of those who come only in the warm months, for the swimming and the clamcakes, and those full-time residents who seem never to go anywhere else.

Published in State by State: A Panoramic Portrait of America (2008), *a collection edited by Matt Weiland and Sean Wilsey to show the regional diversity of the United States. All fifty contributors wrote about their home states, exploring the intersections of personal, regional, and national history.*

1. Small town in the southern part of the state and home to the University of Rhode Island.
2. Italian explorer (1485–1528) working for King Francis I of France, who sailed the North American coast between South Carolina and Newfoundland.

Jacqueline Kennedy Onassis and Cornelius Vanderbilt[3] were among Rhode Island's summer people. Given its diminutive proportions there is a third category: those who pass through without stopping. Forty-eight miles long and thirty-seven wide, it is a brief, unavoidable part of the journey by train between Boston and New York and also, if one chooses to take I-95, by car.

Historically it has harbored the radical and the seditious, misfits and minorities. Roger Williams, the liberal theologian who is credited with founding Rhode Island in 1636, was banished from the Massachusetts Bay Colony by, among others, Nathaniel Hawthorne's great grandfather.[4] Williams's unorthodox views on matters religious and otherwise made him an enemy of the Puritans. He eventually became and remained until his death a Seeker, rejecting any single body of doctrine and respecting the good in all branches of faith. Rhode Island, the thirteenth of the original thirteen colonies, had the greatest degree of self-rule, and was the first to renounce allegiance to King George in 1776. The Rhode Island Charter of 1663 guaranteed "full liberty in religious concernments," and, to its credit, the state accommodated the nation's first Baptists, its first Quakers, and is the site of its oldest synagogue, dedicated in 1763. A different attitude greeted the indigenous population, effectively decimated by 1676 in the course of King Philip's War.[5] Rhode Island is the only state that continues to celebrate, the second Monday of every August, VJ Day, which commemorates the surrender of Japan after the bombings of Hiroshima and Nagasaki. On a lesser but also disturbing note, it has not managed to pass the bottle bill, which means that all those plastic containers of Autocrat Coffee Syrup, used to make coffee milk (Rhode Island's official beverage), are destined for the purgatory of landfills.

Though I was born in London and have Indian parents, Rhode Island is the reply I give when people ask me where I am from. My family came in the summer of 1970, from Cambridge, Massachusetts, so that my father could begin work as a librarian at the University of Rhode Island. I had just turned three years old. URI is located in the village of Kingston, a place originally called Little Rest. The name possibly stems from accounts of Colonial troops pausing on their way to fight the Narragansett tribe on the western banks of Worden Pond, an event known as the Great Swamp Massacre.[6] We lived on Kingston's

3. Jacqueline Kennedy Onassis (1929–1994), wife of U.S. president John Fitzgerald Kennedy and later of Greek shipping magnate Aristotle Onassis; Cornelius Vanderbilt (1794–1877), American multimillionaire who made his wealth from steamships and railroads, and built "The Breakers," a summer house in Newport, Rhode Island.

4. Roger Williams (c. 1603–1683) was banished by Colonel John Hawthorne (1641–1717), the judge most famous for presiding over the Salem witch trials in 1692. His descendant was the novelist Nathaniel Hawthorne (1804–1864).

5. King Philip's War (1675–1676), sometimes called Metacom's Rebellion after the Native American leader whom the English called "King Philip," was fought between the Native American inhabitants of New England and the English settlers.

6. Pivotal battle in King Philip's War, fought in November 1675 between the colonial militia and the Narragansett tribe.

main historic tree-lined drag, in a white house with a portico and black shutters. It had been built in 1829 (a fact stated by a plaque next to the front door)
to contain the law office of Asa Potter, who was at one point Rhode Island's
secretary of state, and whose main residence was the larger, more spectacular
house next door. After Asa Potter left Rhode Island to work in a bank in New
York, the house became the site of a general store, with a tailor's shop at the
front. By 1970 it was an apartment house owned by a fellow Indian, a professor
of mathematics named Dr. Suryanarayan.

5   My family was a hybrid; year-rounders who, like the summer people, didn't
fundamentally belong. We rented the first floor of the house; an elderly American woman named Miss Tay lived above us, alone, and her vulnerable, solitary
presence was a constant reminder, to my parents, of America's harsh ways. A
thick iron chain threaded through wooden posts separated us from our neighbors, the Fishers. A narrow path at the back led to a brown shingled shed I
never entered. Hanging from one of the outbuildings on the Fishers' property
was an oxen yoke, an icon of old New England agriculture, at once elegant and
menacing, that both intrigued and scared me as a child. Its bowed shape caused
me to think it was a weapon, not merely a restraint. Until I was an adult, I never
knew exactly what it was for.

Kingston in those days was a mixture of hippies and Yankees and professors
and students. The students arrived every autumn, taking up all the parking spaces,
crowding the tables in the Memorial Union with their trays of Cokes and French
fries, one year famously streaking on the lawn outside a fraternity building. After
commencement in May, things were quiet again, to the point of feeling deserted. I
imagine this perpetual ebb and flow, segments of the population ritually coming
and going, made it easier for my foreign-born parents to feel that they, too, were
rooted to the community in some way. Apart from the Suryanarayans, there were
a few other Indian families, women other than my mother in saris walking now
and then across the quad. My parents sought them out, invited them over for Bengali[7] dinners, and consider a few of these people among their closest friends today.

The gravitational center of Kingston was, and remains, the Kingston Con-
gregational Church ("King Kong" to locals), where my family did not worship
but where I went for Girl Scout meetings once a week, and where my younger
sister eventually had her high-school graduation party. Across the street from
the church, just six houses down from ours, was the Kingston Free Library. It
was constructed as a courthouse, and also served as the state house between
1776 and 1791. The building's staid Colonial bones later incorporated Victorian flourishes, including a belfry and a mansard roof. If you stand outside and
look up at a window to the right on the third floor, three stern white life-sized
busts will stare down at you through the glass. They are thought to be like-
nesses of Abraham Lincoln, Oliver Wendell Holmes, and John Greenleaf Whit-

7. From the historic region now in northern India and southern Bangladesh.

tier.[8] For many years now, the bust of Lincoln has worn a long red-and-white striped hat, *Cat in the Hat*[9]–style, on its head.

From my earliest memories I was obsessed with the library, with its creaky, cramped atmosphere and all the things it contained. The books used to live on varnished wooden shelves, the modest card catalog contained in two bureau-sized units, sometimes arranged back to back. Phyllis Goodwin, then and for decades afterward the children's librarian, conducted the story hours I faithfully attended when I was little, held upstairs in a vaulted space called Potter Hall. Light poured in through enormous windows on three sides, and Asa Potter's portrait, predominantly black apart from the pale shade of his face, presided over the fireplace. Along with Phyllis there were two other women in charge of the library—Charlotte Schoonover, the director, and Pam Stoddard. Charlotte and Pam, roughly my mother's generation, were friends, and they both had sons about my age. For many years, Charlotte, Pam, and Phyllis represented the three graces to me, guardians of a sacred place that seemed both to represent the heart of Kingston and also the means of escaping it. They liked to play Corelli or Chopin on the little tape recorder behind the desk, but ordered Patti Smith's *Horses* for the circulating album collection.[10]

When I was sixteen I was hired to work as a page at the library, which meant shelving books, working at the circulation desk, and putting plastic wrappers on the jackets of new arrivals. A lot of older people visited daily, to sit at a table with an arrangement of forsythia or cattails at the center, and read the newspaper. I remember a tall, slightly harried mother with wire-rimmed glasses who would come every two weeks with many children behind her and a large canvas tote bag over her shoulder, which she would dump out and then fill up again with more volumes of *The Borrowers* and Laura Ingalls Wilder[11] for the next round of collective reading. Jane Austen was popular with the patrons, enough for me to remember that the books had red cloth covers. I was an unhappy adolescent, lacking confidence, boyfriends, a proper sense of myself. When I was in the library it didn't matter. I took my cue from the readers who came and went and understood that books were what mattered, that they were above high school, above an adolescent's petty trials, above life itself.

8. Abraham Lincoln (1809–1865), president of the United States during the Civil War; Oliver Wendell Holmes (1841–1935), legal theorist and associate justice of the U.S. Supreme Court from 1902 until 1932; John Greenleaf Whittier (1807–1892), American Quaker poet.

9. Children's book (1957) that launched the career of Dr. Seuss.

10. Arcangelo Corelli (1653–1713), Italian composer; Frédéric François Chopin (1810–1849), Polish composer and pianist; Patti Smith (b. 1946), American musician, poet, and visual artist.

11. *The Borrowers* (1952), the first in a series of children's books by Mary Norton about little people who live in the houses of big people and "borrow" things; Laura Ingalls Wilder (1867–1957), author of the popular "Little House" series for children.

10   By this time we no longer lived in Kingston. We had moved, when I was eight and my sister was one, to a house of our own. I would have preferred to stay in Kingston and live in an enclave called Biscuit City, not only because of the name but because it was full of professors and their families and had a laid-back, intellectual feel. Instead we moved to a town called Peace Dale, exactly one mile away. Peace Dale was a former mill town, an area where the university didn't hold sway. Our housing development, called Rolling Acres, was a leafy loop of roads without sidewalks. The turn into the neighborhood, off the main road, is between a John Deere showroom[12] and a bingo hall. Our house, a style called Colonial Garrison according to the developer's brochure, was historical in name only. In 1975 it was built before our eyes—the foundation dug, concrete poured, pale yellow vinyl siding stapled to the exterior.

        After we moved into that house, something changed; whether it was my growing older or the place itself, I was aware that the world immediately outside our door, with its red-flagged mailboxes and children's bicycles left overnight on well-seeded grass, was alien to my parents. Some of our neighbors were friendly. Others pretended we were not there. I remember hot days when the mothers of my American friends in the neighborhood would lie in their bikinis on reclining chairs, chatting over wine coolers as my friends and I ran through a sprinkler, while my fully dressed mother was alone in our house, deep-frying a carp or listening to Bengali folk songs. In Rolling Acres we became car-bound. We couldn't walk, as we had been able to do in Kingston, to see a movie on campus, or buy milk and bread at Evan's Market, or get stamps at the post office. While one could walk (or run or bike) endlessly around the looping roads of Rolling Acres, without a car we were cut off from the rest of the world. When my parents first moved to Rhode Island, I think they both assumed that it was an experiment, just another port of call on their unfolding immigrant journey. The fact that they now owned a house, along with my father getting tenure, brought the journey to a halt. Thirty-seven years later, my parents still live there. The Little Rest they took in 1970 has effectively become the rest of their lives.

The sense of the environment radically shifting from mile to mile holds true throughout Rhode Island, almost the way life can vary block by block in certain cities. In South Kingstown alone there is a startling mixture of the lovely and the ugly—of resort, rural, and run-of-the-mill. There are strip malls, most of them radiating from a frenetic intersection called Dale Carlia corner, and no one who lives in my town can avoid negotiating its many traffic lights and lanes on a regular basis. There are countless housing developments, filled with energy-efficient split-levels when I was growing up, these days with McMansions. There are several Dunkin' Donut shops (Rhode Island has more per capita than any other state). There are also quiet farms where horses graze, and remote, winding roads through woods, flanked by low stone walls. There are places to buy antiques and handmade pottery. Along South Road is a sloping, empty field that resem-

12. For the sale of John Deere tractors and other agricultural equipment.

bles the one where Wyeth painted *Christina's World*.[13] There is a house on Route 108, just after the traffic light on 138, with the most extraordinary show of azaleas I have ever seen. And then, of course, there are the beaches.

We did not live on the ocean proper, but it was close enough, about five miles away. The ocean was where we took all our visitors from Massachusetts (which was where the majority of my parents' Bengali friends lived), either to Scarborough, which is the state beach, or to Point Judith Light. They used to sit on the grassy hill speaking a foreign tongue, sometimes bringing a picnic of packaged white bread and a pot of *aloo dum*.[14] On the way back they liked to stop in the fishing village of Galilee, where the parking lots of the shops and restaurants were covered with broken seashells. They did not go to eat stuffies, a local delicacy made from quahogs and bread crumbs, but to see if the daily catch included any butterfish or mackerel, to turn into a mustard curry at home. Occasionally my mother's best friend from Massachusetts, Koely Das, wanted to get lobsters or crabs, but these, too, received the curry treatment, a far, fiery cry from a side of melted butter.

The Atlantic I grew up with lacks the color and warmth of the Caribbean, the grandeur of the Pacific, the romance of the Mediterranean. It is generally cold, and full of rust-colored seaweed. Still, I prefer it. The waters of Rhode Island, as much a part of the state's character, if not more, as the land, never asked us questions, never raised a brow. Thanks to its very lack of welcome, its unwavering indifference, the ocean always made me feel accepted, and to my dying day, the seaside is the only place where I can feel truly and recklessly happy.

My father, a global traveler, considers Rhode Island paradise. For nearly four 15 decades he has dedicated himself there to a job he loves, rising through the ranks in the library's cataloging department to become its head. But in addition to the job, he loves the place. He loves that it is quiet, and moderate, and is, in the great scheme of things, uneventful. He loves that he lives close to his work, and that he does not have to spend a significant portion of his life sitting in a car on the highway, or on a crowded subway, commuting. (Lately, because my parents have downsized to one car, he has begun to take a bus, on which he is frequently the sole passenger.) Though Rhode Island is a place of four proper seasons, he loves that both winters and summers, tempered by the ocean breezes, are relatively mild. He loves working in his small garden, and going once a week to buy groceries, coupons in hand, at Super Stop&Shop. In many ways he is a spiritual descendant of America's earliest Puritan settlers: thrifty, hard-working, plain in his habits. Like Roger Williams, he is something of a Seeker, aloof from organized religions but appreciating their philosophical worth. He also embodies the values of two of New England's greatest thinkers,

13. Andrew Wyeth (1917–2009), Maine artist whose most famous work, *Christina's World* (1948), shows a woman in a field of golden grass struggling to reach a farmhouse at the top of the hill.
14. Potato curry.

demonstrating a profound lack of materialism and self-reliance that would have made Thoreau and Emerson proud.[15] "The great man is he who in the midst of the crowd keeps with perfect sweetness the independence of solitude," Emerson wrote. This is the man who raised me.

My mother, a gregarious and hard-wired urbanite, has struggled; to hear her recall the first time she was driven down from Massachusetts, along I–95 and then a remote, lightless stretch of Route 138, is to understand that Rhode Island was and in many ways remains the heart of darkness for her. She stayed at home to raise me and my sister, frequently taking in other children as well, but apart from a stint as an Avon Lady she had no job. In 1987, when my sister was a teenager, my mother finally ventured out, directing a day care and also working as a classroom assistant at South Road Elementary School, which both my sister and I had attended. One day, after she'd been working at the school for a decade, she started to receive anonymous hate mail. It came in the form of notes placed in her mailbox at school, and eventually in her coat pocket. There were nine notes in total. The handwriting was meant to look like a child's awkward scrawl. The content was humiliating, painful to recount. "Go back to India," one of them said. "Many people here do not like to see your face," read another. By then my mother had been a resident of Rhode Island for twenty-seven years. In Rhode Island she had raised two daughters, given birth to one. She had set up a home and potted geraniums year after year and thrown hundreds of dinner parties for her ever-expanding circle of Bengali friends. In Rhode Island she had renounced her Indian passport for an American one, pledged allegiance to the flag. My mother was ashamed of the notes, and for a while, hoping they would stop, she kept them to herself.

The incident might make a good start to a mystery novel, the type that always flew out of the Kingston Free Library: poison-pen letters appearing in a quaint, sleepy town. But there was nothing cozily intriguing about the cold-blooded correspondence my mother received. After finding the note in her coat pocket (it was February, recess time, and she had been expecting to pull out a glove), she told the school principal, and she also told my family what was going on. In the wake of this incident, many kind people reached out to my mother to express their outrage on her behalf, and for each of those nine notes, she received many sympathetic ones, including words of support from the former president of the university, Francis Horn. The majority of these people were Americans; one of the things that continues to upset my mother was that very few members of Rhode Island's Indian community, not insignificant by then, were willing to stand by her side. Some resented my mother for creating controversy, for drawing attention to their being foreign, a fact they worked to neutralize. Others told her that she might not have been targeted if she had worn skirts and trousers instead of saris and bindis. Meetings were held at the elementary school, calling for increased tolerance and sensitivity. The story was covered by the *Providence Journal-*

---

15. Henry David Thoreau (1817–1862), American writer; see "The Battle of the Ants" (pp. 725–27) and "Where I Lived, and What I Lived For" (pp. 481–89); Ralph Waldo Emerson (1803–1882), American writer and philosopher.

Bulletin and the local television news. Montel Williams[16] called our house, wanting my mother to appear on his show (she declined). A detective was put on the case, but the writer of the notes never came forward, was never found. Over ten years have passed. South Road School has shut down, for reasons having nothing to do with what happened to my mother. She worked for another school, part of the same system, in West Kingston, and has recently retired.

I left Rhode Island at eighteen to attend college in New York City, which is where, following a detour up to Boston, I continue to live. Because my parents still live in Rhode Island I still visit, though the logistics of having two small children mean they come to me these days more often than I go to them. I was there in August 2007. My parents, children, sister, and I had just been to Vermont, renting a cabin on a lake. There was a screened-in porch, a Modern Library first edition of *To the Lighthouse*[17] in the bookcase, and a severe mouse problem in the kitchen. In the end the mice drove us away, and during the long drive back to my parents' house, I was aware how little Vermont and Rhode Island, both New England states, have in common. Vermont is dramatically northern, rural, mountainous, landlocked. Rhode Island is flat, briny, more densely populated. Vermont is liberal enough to sanction gay marriage but feels homogenous, lacking Rhode Island's deep pockets of immigration from Ireland, Portugal, and Italy. Rhode Island's capital, Providence, was run for years by a Republican Italian, Buddy Cianci. In 1984 he was convicted of kidnapping his then-estranged wife's boyfriend, beating him with a fire log, and burning him with a lighted cigarette. In 1991 he ran again for mayor, and the citizens of Rhode Island handed him 97 percent of the vote.

It was hotter in Rhode Island than it had been in Vermont. The Ghiorse Beach Factor, courtesy of John Ghiorse, the meteorologist on Channel 10, was a perfect 10 for the weekend we were there. On my way to buy sunscreen at the CVS pharmacy in Kingston, I stopped by the library, excited to see the sign outside indicating that the summer book sale was still going on. The library has been expanded and renovated since I worked there, the circulation desk much larger now and facing the entering visitor, with a computer system instead of the clunky machine that stamped due date cards. The only familiar thing, apart from the books, was Pam. "Just the dregs," she warned me about the book sale. As we were catching up, an elderly couple with British accents approached. "Excuse me," the woman interrupted. "Can you recommend something decent? I'm tired of murder mysteries and people being killed. I just want to hear a decent family story." Pam led her away to the books on tape section, and I went upstairs to Potter Hall to look at the sale. It was just the dregs, as Pam had said, but I managed to find a few things I'd always meant to read—a paperback copy of Donna Tartt's *The Secret History*, and *Monkeys* by Susan Minot. The curtained stage that used to be at one end of the room, on which I had performed, among

16. Montel Williams (b. 1956) hosted an Emmy Award–winning daytime talk show from 1991 to 2008.
17. Novel (1927) by Virginia Woolf set in a summer house by the sea.

other things, the role of the Queen of Hearts in *Alice in Wonderland*, was gone, so that the space seemed even bigger. The grand piano was still there, but Asa Potter's portrait was at the Museum of Fine Arts in Boston, Pam later explained, for repairs. She told me she was thinking of retiring soon, and that Phyllis, who had retired long before, had discovered a late-blooming talent for portrait painting. "It's a quirky place," Pam reflected when I asked her about Rhode Island, complaining, "There's no zoning. No united front." And practically in the same breath, proudly: "Kingston is the melting pot of the state."

20   In the afternoon I took my children, along with my mother and sister, to Scarborough. The beach was packed, the tide high and rough. As soon as we set down our things, a wave hit us, forcing us to pick up a drenched blanket and move. Scarborough is a large beach with a paved parking lot that feels even larger. The parking lot itself is also useful in the off-season, for learning how to drive. Scarborough lacks the steep, dramatic dunes and isolated aura of lower Cape Cod, a stretch of New England coastline I have come, in my adult life, to love more than the beach of my childhood. The sand at Scarborough is extremely fine and gray and, when moist, resembles wet ash. A large tide pool had formed that day, and it was thick with young muddied children lying on their bellies, pretending to swim. My son darted off to chase seagulls. The breeze blew impressively in spite of the sultry weather, justifying Ghiorse's ten out of ten. In the distance I could see Point Judith Light. The giant billboard for Coppertone, the Dr. T. J. Eckleburg of my youth,[18] has vanished, but I imagined it was still there—the model's toasted bikini-clad seventies body sprawled regally, indifferently, above the masses.

An announcement on the loudspeaker informed us that a little girl was lost, asking her to meet her mother under the flag on the boardwalk. Another announcement followed: The men's hot water showers were temporarily out of service. The population was democratic, unpretentious, inclusive: ordinary bodies of various sizes and shades, the shades both genetic and cultivated, reading paperback bestsellers and reaching into big bags of chips. I saw no *New Yorker* magazines being read, no heirloom tomato sandwiches or organic peaches being consumed. A trio of deeply tanned adolescent boys tripped past, collectively courting, one could imagine, the same elusive girl. The sun began to set, and within an hour the crowd had thinned to the point where a man started to drag his metal detector through the sand, and the only kids in the tide pool were my own. As we were getting up to go, our bodies sticky with salt, it occurred to me that Scarborough Beach on a summer day is one of the few places that is not a city but still manages, reassuringly, to feel like one. Two days later, I headed home with my sister and my children to Brooklyn. On our way through West Kingston to catch the highway, a lone green truck selling Dell's, Rhode Island's beloved frozen lemonade, beckoned at an otherwise desolate intersection, but

18. Lahiri alludes to a billboard in F. Scott Fitzgerald's novel *The Great Gatsby* (1925), which shows the eyes of Dr. T. J. Eckleburg, "blue and gigantic—their irises are one yard high."

my sister and I drove on, accepting the fact that we would not taste Dell's for another year.

As long as my mother and father live, I will continue to visit Rhode Island. They are, respectively, in their late sixties and seventies now, and each time I drive by the local funeral home in Wakefield, I try to prepare myself. Just after I'd finished a draft of this essay, early one November morning, my mother had a heart attack at home. An Indian doctor at Rhode Island Hospital, Arun Singh, performed the bypass operation that has saved her life. When I was a child, I remember my mother often wondering who, in the event of an emergency or other crisis, would come running to help us. During the weeks when I feared she might slip away, everyone did. Our mailbox was stuffed with get-well cards from my mother's students, the refrigerator stuffed with food from her friends. My father's colleagues at the library took up a collection to buy my family Thanksgiving dinner. Our next door neighbor, Mrs. Hyde, who had seen the ambulance pulling up to our house, crossed over to our yard as I was heading to the hospital one day, and told me she'd said a special prayer for my mother at her church.

Due to my parents' beliefs, whenever and wherever they do die, they will not be buried in Rhode Island soil. The house in Rolling Acres will belong to other people; there will be no place there to pay my respects. At the risk of predicting the future, I can see myself, many years from now, driving up I–95, on my way to another vacation on the Cape. We will cross the border after Connecticut, turn off at exit 3A for Kingston, and then continue along an alternative, prettier route that will take us across Jamestown and over the Newport Bridge, where the sapphire bay spreads out on either side, a breathtaking sight that will never grow old. There will no longer be a reason to break the journey in Little Rest. Like many others, we will pass through without stopping.

MLA CITATION

Lahiri, Jhumpa. "Rhode Island." *The Norton Reader: An Anthology of Nonfiction*, edited by Melissa A. Goldthwaite et al., 15th ed., W. W. Norton, 2020, pp. 110–19.

QUESTIONS

1. One purpose of the collection in which Jhumpa Lahiri's essay appeared is to show the diversity of the fifty American states. How does Lahiri achieve this purpose? What details does she provide that are unique to Rhode Island or New England?

2. Lahiri is a novelist who alludes to other authors and their writing. Choose one allusion to a novel or short story, and explain how this reference enriches Lahiri's narrative.

3. Lahiri gives both her personal history and a brief history of the state in which she grew up. What connections might be drawn between the personal and the regional? Consider both the explicit and implicit connections.

4. Write an account of the region or state in which you grew up, integrating some of its history with your personal experience.

E. B. WHITE
Once More to the Lake

ONE SUMMER, ALONG ABOUT 1904, my father rented a camp on a lake in Maine and took us all there for the month of August. We all got ringworm from some kittens and had to rub Pond's Extract on our arms and legs night and morning, and my father rolled over in a canoe with all his clothes on; but outside of that the vacation was a success and from then on none of us ever thought there was any place in the world like that lake in Maine. We returned summer after summer—always on August 1st for one month. I have since become a salt-water man, but sometimes in summer there are days when the restlessness of the tides and the fearful cold of the sea water and the incessant wind which blows across the afternoon and into the evening make me wish for the placidity of a lake in the woods. A few weeks ago this feeling got so strong I bought myself a couple of bass hooks and a spinner and returned to the lake where we used to go, for a week's fishing and to revisit old haunts.

I took along my son, who had never had any fresh water up his nose and who had seen lily pads only from train windows. On the journey over to the lake I began to wonder what it would be like. I wondered how time would have marred this unique, this holy spot—the coves and streams, the hills that the sun set behind, the camps and the paths behind the camps. I was sure the tarred road would have found it out and I wondered in what other ways it would be desolated. It is strange how much you can remember about places like that once you allow your mind to return into the grooves which lead back. You remember one thing, and that suddenly reminds you of another thing. I guess I remembered clearest of all the early mornings, when the lake was cool and motionless, remembered how the bedroom smelled of the lumber it was made of and of the wet woods whose scent entered through the screen. The partitions in the camp were thin and did not extend clear to the top of the rooms, and as I was always the first up I would dress softly so as not to wake the others, and sneak out into the sweet outdoors and start out in the canoe, keeping close along the shore in the long shadows of the pines. I remembered being very careful never to rub my paddle against the gunwale for fear of disturbing the stillness of the cathedral.

The lake had never been what you would call a wild lake. There were cottages sprinkled around the shores, and it was in farming country although the shores of the lake were quite heavily wooded. Some of the cottages were owned by nearby farmers, and you would live at the shore and eat your meals at the farmhouse. That's what our family did. But although it wasn't wild, it was a

Originally appeared in "One Man's Meat," E. B. White's column for Harper's Magazine *(1941), an American monthly covering politics, society, culture, and the environment; later included in* One Man's Meat *(1942), a collection of his columns about life on a Maine saltwater farm, and then in* Essays of E. B. White *(1977).*

fairly large and undisturbed lake and there were places in it which, to a child at least, seemed infinitely remote and primeval.

I was right about the tar: it led to within half a mile of the shore. But when I got back there, with my boy, and we settled into a camp near a farmhouse and into the kind of summertime I had known, I could tell that it was going to be pretty much the same as it had been before—I knew it, lying in bed the first morning, smelling the bedroom, and hearing the boy sneak quietly out and go off along the shore in a boat. I began to sustain the illusion that he was I, and therefore, by simple transposition, that I was my father. This sensation persisted, kept cropping up all the time we were there. It was not an entirely new feeling, but in this setting it grew much stronger. I seemed to be living a dual existence. I would be in the middle of some simple act, I would be picking up a bait box or laying down a table fork, or I would be saying something, and suddenly it would be not I but my father who was saying the words or making the gesture. It gave me a creepy sensation.

We went fishing the first morning. I felt the same damp moss covering the worms in the bait can, and saw the dragonfly alight on the tip of my rod as it hovered a few inches from the surface of the water. It was the arrival of this fly that convinced me beyond any doubt that everything was as it always had been, that the years were a mirage and there had been no years. The small waves were the same, chucking the rowboat under the chin as we fished at anchor, and the boat was the same boat, the same color green and the ribs broken in the same places, and under the floor-boards the same fresh-water leavings and débris—the dead hellgrammite,[1] the wisps of moss, the rusty discarded fish-hook, the dried blood from yesterday's catch. We stared silently at the tips of our rods, at the dragonflies that came and went. I lowered the tip of mine into the water, tentatively, pensively dislodging the fly, which darted two feet away, poised, darted two feet back, and came to rest again a little farther up the rod. There had been no years between the ducking of this dragonfly and the other one—the one that was part of memory. I looked at the boy, who was silently watching his fly, and it was my hands that held his rod, my eyes watching. I felt dizzy and didn't know which rod I was at the end of.

We caught two bass, hauling them in briskly as though they were mackerel, pulling them over the side of the boat in a businesslike manner without any landing net, and stunning them with a blow on the back of the head. When we got back for a swim before lunch, the lake was exactly where we had left it, the same number of inches from the dock, and there was only the merest suggestion of a breeze. This seemed an utterly enchanted sea, this lake you could leave to its own devices for a few hours and come back to, and find that it had not stirred, this constant and trustworthy body of water. In the shallows, the dark, water-soaked sticks and twigs, smooth and old, were undulating in clusters on the bottom against the clean ribbed sand, and the track of the mussel was plain. A school of minnows swam by, each minnow with its small individual shadow, doubling the attendance, so clear and sharp in the sunlight. Some

5

1. Larvae of the dobsonfly.

of the other campers were in swimming, along the shore, one of them with a cake of soap, and the water felt thin and clear and unsubstantial. Over the years there had been this person with the cake of soap, this cultist, and here he was. There had been no years.

Up to the farmhouse to dinner through the teeming, dusty field, the road under our sneakers was only a two-track road. The middle track was missing, the one with the marks of the hooves and the splotches of dried, flaky manure. There had always been three tracks to choose from in choosing which track to walk in; now the choice was narrowed down to two. For a moment I missed terribly the middle alternative. But the way led past the tennis court, and something about the way it lay there in the sun reassured me; the tape had loosened along the backline, the alleys were green with plantains and other weeds, and the net (installed in June and removed in September) sagged in the dry noon, and the whole place steamed with midday heat and hunger and emptiness. There was a choice of pie for dessert, and one was blueberry and one was apple, and the waitresses were the same country girls, there having been no passage of time, only the illusion of it as in a dropped curtain—the waitresses were still fifteen; their hair had been washed, that was the only difference—they had been to the movies and seen the pretty girls with the clean hair.

Summertime, oh summertime, pattern of life indelible, the fade-proof lake, the woods unshatterable, the pasture with the sweetfern and the juniper forever and ever, summer without end; this was the background, and the life along the shore was the design, the cottages with their innocent and tranquil design, their tiny docks with the flagpole and the American flag floating against the white clouds in the blue sky, the little paths over the roots of the trees leading from camp to camp and the paths leading back to the outhouses and the can of lime for sprinkling, and at the souvenir counters at the store the miniature birch-bark canoes and the post cards that showed things looking a little better than they looked. This was the American family at play, escaping the city heat, wondering whether the newcomers in the camp at the head of the cove were "common" or "nice," wondering whether it was true that the people who drove up for Sunday dinner at the farmhouse were turned away because there wasn't enough chicken.

It seemed to me, as I kept remembering all this, that those times and those summers had been infinitely precious and worth saving. There had been jollity and peace and goodness. The arriving (at the beginning of August) had been so big a business in itself, at the railway station the farm wagon drawn up, the first smell of the pine-laden air, the first glimpse of the smiling farmer, and the great importance of the trunks and your father's enormous authority in such matters, and the feel of the wagon under you for the long ten-mile haul, and at the top of the last long hill catching the first view of the lake after eleven months of not seeing this cherished body of water. The shouts and cries of the other campers when they saw you, and the trunks to be unpacked, to give up their rich burden. (Arriving was less exciting nowadays, when you sneaked up in your car and parked it under a tree near the camp and took out the bags and in five minutes it was all over, no fuss, no loud wonderful fuss about trunks.)

Peace and goodness and jollity. The only thing that was wrong now, really,   10
was the sound of the place, an unfamiliar nervous sound of the outboard motors.
This was the note that jarred, the one thing that would sometimes break the
illusion and set the years moving. In those other summertimes all motors were
inboard; and when they were at a little distance, the noise they made was a seda-
tive, an ingredient of summer sleep. They were one-cylinder and two-cylinder
engines, and some were make-and-break and some were jump-spark,[2] but they
all made a sleepy sound across the lake. The one-lungers throbbed and fluttered,
and the twin-cylinder ones purred and purred, and that was a quiet sound too.
But now the campers all had outboards. In the daytime, in the hot mornings,
these motors made a petulant, irritable sound; at night, in the still evening when
the afterglow lit the water, they whined about one's ears like mosquitoes. My boy
loved our rented outboard, and his great desire was to achieve singlehanded
mastery over it, and authority, and he soon learned the trick of choking it a little
(but not too much), and the adjustment of the needle valve. Watching him I
would remember the things you could do with the old one-cylinder engine with
the heavy flywheel, how you could have it eating out of your hand if you got
really close to it spiritually. Motor boats in those days didn't have clutches, and
you would make a landing by shutting off the motor at the proper time and
coasting in with a dead rudder. But there was a way of reversing them, if you
learned the trick, by cutting the switch and putting it on again exactly on the
final dying revolution of the flywheel, so that it would kick back against compression and begin reversing. Approaching a dock in a strong following breeze, it
was difficult to slow up sufficiently by the ordinary coasting method, and if a boy
felt he had complete mastery over his motor, he was tempted to keep it running
beyond its time and then reverse it a few feet from the dock. It took a cool nerve,
because if you threw the switch a twentieth of a second too soon you would
catch the flywheel when it still had speed enough to go up past center, and the
boat would leap ahead, charging bull-fashion at the dock.

We had a good week at the camp. The bass were biting well and the sun
shone endlessly, day after day. We would be tired at night and lie down in the
accumulated heat of the little bedrooms after the long hot day and the breeze
would stir almost imperceptibly outside and the smell of the swamp drift in
through the rusty screens. Sleep would come easily and in the morning the red
squirrel would be on the roof, tapping out his gay routine. I kept remembering
everything, lying in bed in the mornings—the small steamboat that had a long
rounded stern like the lip of a Ubangi, and how quietly she ran on the moonlight sails, when the older boys played their mandolins and the girls sang and
we ate doughnuts dipped in sugar, and how sweet the music was on the water
in the shining night, and what it had felt like to think about girls then. After
breakfast we would go up to the store and the things were in the same place—
the minnows in a bottle, the plugs and spinners disarranged and pawed over by
the youngsters from the boys' camp, the fig newtons and the Beeman's gum.
Outside, the road was tarred and cars stood in front of the store. Inside, all was
just as it had always been, except there was more Coca-Cola and not so much

2. Methods of ignition timing so that an engine functions properly.

Moxie and root beer and birch beer and sarsaparilla. We would walk out with a bottle of pop apiece and sometimes the pop would backfire up our noses and hurt. We explored the streams, quietly, where the turtles slid off the sunny logs and dug their way into the soft bottom; and we lay on the town wharf and fed worms to the tame bass. Everywhere we went I had trouble making out which was I, the one walking at my side, the one walking in my pants.

One afternoon while we were there at that lake a thunderstorm came up. It was like the revival of an old melodrama that I had seen long ago with childish awe. The second-act climax of the drama of the electrical disturbance over a lake in America had not changed in any important respect. This was the big scene, still the big scene. The whole thing was so familiar, the first feeling of oppression and heat and a general air around camp of not wanting to go very far away. In midafternoon (it was all the same) a curious darkening of the sky, and a lull in everything that had made life tick; and then the way the boats suddenly swung the other way at their moorings with the coming of a breeze out of the new quarter, and the premonitory rumble. Then the kettle drum, then the snare, then the bass drum and cymbals, then crackling light against the dark, and the gods grinning and licking their chops in the hills. Afterward the calm, the rain steadily rustling in the calm lake, the return of light and hope and spirits, and the campers running out in joy and relief to go swimming in the rain, their bright cries perpetuating the deathless joke about how they were getting simply drenched, and the children screaming with delight at the new sensation of bathing in the rain, and the joke about getting drenched linking the generations in a strong indestructible chain. And the comedian who waded in carrying an umbrella.

When the others went swimming my son said he was going in too. He pulled his dripping trunks from the line where they had hung all through the shower, and wrung them out. Languidly, and with no thought of going in, I watched him, his hard little body, skinny and bare, saw him wince slightly as he pulled up around his vitals the small, soggy, icy garment. As he buckled the swollen belt suddenly my groin felt the chill of death.

MLA CITATION

White, E. B. "Once More to the Lake." *The Norton Reader: An Anthology of Nonfiction*, edited by Melissa A. Goldthwaite et al., 15th ed., W. W. Norton, 2020, pp. 120–24.

QUESTIONS

1. E. B. White includes many details to describe his impressions of the lake when he went there as a child and when he returns as an adult—for example, about the road, the dragonfly, and the boat's motor. What are some other details, and what do they tell us about what has changed or stayed the same?

2. White's last sentence often surprises readers. Go back through the essay and pick out sections, words, or phrases that seem to prepare for the ending.

3. Write about revisiting a place that has special meaning for you, including details of your early memories and reflections on your more recent visit.

COLSON WHITEHEAD

Rain

OUT ON the street they hardly notice the clouds before it starts raining. The rain comes down in sheets. Drenched all at once, not drop by drop. The first drop is the pistol at the start of the race and at that crack people move for shelter, any ragtag thing, they huddle under ripped awnings, the doorway of the diner, suddenly an appetite for coffee. Pressed up against buildings as if on the lam. Little sprints and dashes between horizontal cover. Dry here. Surely it will stop soon, they think. They can wait it out. It cannot last forever.

SUSPECTING such an eventuality, the umbrella salesmen emerge to make deals. They wait all week for this and have ample supply of one-dollar bills. The virtues of their merchandise are self-evident. She carries an umbrella every day no matter what the news says because you can never tell and is vindicated by moisture. It pops open. The doused press down on reluctant buttons and the mechanisms pop open. Underneath their personal domes, they are separated from the peasants. To be this easily isolated from all worry. The silver tips dart and jab for eye sockets. Probability says many are blinded by pointy umbrella spokes and you are surely the next victim. At the corner he wrestles with a ghost for the soul of his umbrella. The gust gains the upper hand as he waits for the light to change and the umbrella is ripped inverse. Many are lost. The wounded, the fallen in this struggle, poke out of trash cans, abandoned, black fabric rippling against split chrome ribs. This is their lot. Either in the trash can or forgotten in the restaurant, the movie theater, the friend's foyer, spreading their slow puddles across floors. Forming an attachment to an umbrella is the shortest route to heartbreak in this town. Any true accounting would reveal that there are only twenty umbrellas in this city, in constant movement from palm to palm. Bunch of Lotharios.[1] So do we learn loss from umbrellas.

THE NEW RIVERS along curbs shove newspaper and grit to gutters. Too big to squeeze through grates the garbage bobs in place like the unstylish waiting for night-club doors to open. The liquid sinks below. The alligators don't mind. Eventually a clog sends a puddle advancing. A sliver of moon, the surface of the puddle is tormented by brief craters. Each drop explodes and extends the surface of the puddle. Doing their part for the water cycle, the bus wheels

---

Colson Whitehead (b. 1969) won the Pulitzer Prize for his novel The Underground Railroad *(2016). This essay comes from his 2003 essay collection,* The Colossus of New York.

1. A man who shamelessly seduces women, from the name of a character in Miguel de Cervantes' novel, *Don Quixote* (1605).

return the puddle to air again. Complacent beneath her umbrella she is thoroughly soaked when she stands too close to the curb. The enemy came from below. The metropolitan transit authority reinforces old lessons: every puddle wants to hug you. If not heavy motor vehicles then it is the children in their bright red boots detonating puddles on people. Knock it off.

IT FINDS the nape of your neck easily. It traces the length of your spine greedily. The long list of errands shrinks into what people can do in the least amount of water. So much for the dry cleaning. All over town the available number of cabs shrinks as thin fingers tilt and quiver at the edges of traffic. The bastard one block upriver gets it before you can stick a hand out, just as you are someone else's bastard one block downriver. Epithets are tossed against the flow of traffic, upon the unbeknownst. Everybody just wants to get home, so they make calculations and jockey. What's a better block for a cab. East or west, up a street or down. Schemes multiply and divide the longer you stand there. The supercomputer of cab-catching. Sixth Avenue is uptown and Seventh is down, important variables. The time of day, the direction and force of the wind, sun spots, that Pacific typhoon, all important considerations in the acquisition of a cab. She hailed it because she thought it was empty, but it speeds by with smug fares in the backseat who do not even notice her. Day like this all it takes is a little cab fare in your pocket to become royalty.

5   COUPLES FORCED into doorways kiss, coached by the cinema. One of them says one two three and they make a break out of the latest slim refuge. They are reminded after a few steps of how cold the rain is. They stop at the next outpost to catch their breath and forget how cold the rain is. This is the start of her long illness. The wrapping would be ruined by the water so he holds the present under his coat, lending to his belly the contours of an absurd pregnancy. She hides in the bus stand. She hasn't taken the bus in years and feels a secret terror. Pressed up against other people: what's the point of money. In shelter they make plans. He doesn't know where he is supposed to be because the paper got wet and now the address is a smudge. Lost at intersections. Look at all the trenchcoats—it is the detectives' convention come at last to take care of all our loose ends. Up in all the windows, leaning on the sills, the dry people look down on the street and think, Glad I'm not out in that. As if they are without problems. Open half an inch, the window in the next room is still open wide enough to get the floor wet before they notice.

A MAN of liberal convictions, he got this umbrella by pledging money to public radio. It sends the message that he supports public radio. Has a matching tote bag. Now no one will suspect she has been crying. After a block it is evident that they both will not fit under the compact umbrella and one must make do with a dry shoulder. Is this the end of their love. The weekend outdoorsman strides through in his appropriate gear, this is no cliff face or ravine, and he is well equipped. Her glasses are too wet to see through so she takes them off and squints through precipitation. When she gets inside she'll use up napkins.

Unable to decide which side of the bed is more comfortable, the windshield wipers toss and turn. Sleepless like rivers. How swiftly the newspaper becomes a sodden brick over his head. It doesn't keep him dry at all despite clichés. From street level as he looks up into the clouds each advancing drop is elongated, a comet, until it hits his cheek and crashes. On his lips it doesn't taste so bad. One drop hits his eye and stings more than mere water should. He blinks. Sooty streaks trail under windowsills. Every building a coquette, a face powdered by industry. This so-called cleansing leaves behind more than it washes away. But then few things are as advertised.

NEW SOCKS tint soaked toes blue. The shoes take forever to dry. Last time it rained he put them under the radiator and hours later they were warped and twisted, as if it were agony to let the water go. Next time he will remember the water repellent spray. It is available at local pharmacies. Secure in her foresight, she wonders about the etymology of the word galoshes. Of course it is a ridiculous thing to walk around with plastic bags tied over your shoes, but do you know how much these things cost. The puddle at the curb is deeper than it looks, an ancient loch. Trying to jump over it you fall short and the lagoon spills into your shoes. Tonight the bunched balls of his socks will dry and stiffen into dingy fists, and roll under the bureau, where they will hide for months and foment.

HE CLIMBS UP the steps and realizes that while he was in the subway the whole world changed. It's all gray. Pull lapels tight. Only the gargoyles seem happy, up there on the roofs. If you're lucky when you die, you become one and get to hang out here forever. He says, You think the money they get paid, the weathermen would get it right for a change. Remembering only disasters. The stock boy rips up cardboard boxes to lay down in the entrance of the store. All our vain gestures. It makes the boss happy, it's how they did it in the old days. The newspaper vendor takes all these wet bills in stride. But no one wants to buy a wet newspaper. The stacks got wet before he could cover them up. In the competing store across the street the news piles up underneath a transparent tarp. Survival of the fittest, but of course he is not saddled with an idiot nephew. In the phone booth preparing for the next sortie. Lay all that money out for the hairdresser and now this. They will drag their feet across doormats and track floors nonetheless. Identical twins wear identical yellow slickers, out of which identical noses poke. What's this in the raincoat pocket. Apparently the last time it rained he saw a romantic comedy.

AT THE CORNER it's worse, thrown into their faces like needles or proof. The wind whips it around. Once they find a parking space they decide to wait it out and make out, tilting the car seats back to uncomfortable angles. A nipple gives against a thumb. Once the engine is off they can make out the rain's true incantation on the roof of the car and clench each other tighter. Safe here. The talk always comes around to the weather. Underneath the scaffolding the conversations among strangers range from grunts to bona fide connections.

Quite serendipitous. It leaks. From block to block the people display an assortment of strides, every station between a walk and a run. Each has a personal strategy of how best to move in this. The best of them gave up long ago. The best of them cease stooping, stand up straight, stop dodging, take it as it comes. Apparently they are supposed to get wet, so they give in. It is like letting go of something and a small miracle wrung from accident. Walking slowly and naturally in this downpour, they are avoided by the more sensible, who walk swiftly around them, unsettled by these strange creatures. Citizens of a better city.

10   IT STOPS. From the river you can see the clouds haunch over adjacent boroughs. What transpired is a problem for sewers now, out of sight and out of mind. Snapping the umbrella open and closed as if it will scare the water off. It pulsates like a jellyfish in bleak fathoms. She tries to button the strap on her umbrella but keeps losing the snap in the folds. Now her hands are all wet. Some people think it's a trick and keep their umbrellas open for blocks just in case. They walk out of the movie theater and say to each other, Did it rain, pointing at puddles. Yes, they are sure of it, something happened and they missed it.

MLA CITATION

Whitehead, Colson. "Rain." *The Norton Reader: An Anthology of Nonfiction*, edited by
    Melissa A. Goldthwaite et al., 15th ed., W. W. Norton, 2020, pp. 125–28.

QUESTIONS

1. In paragraph 2, Colson Whitehead personifies umbrellas. What kind of personality does he give them? What surprises you about these descriptions? Do you imagine umbrellas as having a different personality—or any personality at all?

2. Whitehead jokes that "the alligators don't mind" (paragraph 3), referring to an urban legend that alligators live in the city sewers. What is the effect of that joke on the tone of the piece overall? Where else do you find humor in the essay?

3. This essay is organized organically through the evolution of a rainstorm, from the first drops to the moment an umbrella is no longer needed. Go through the essay again and name the phases of a rain storm, according to Whitehead. Add some categories of your own.

4. There is a narrative voice in this essay, but the narrator does not describe himself. What clues does the narrator offer as to his personality?

5. Write an essay about how a place that you know well changes when the weather suddenly changes.

3 SELF AND SOCIETY

> No man is an island, entire of itself; every man is a piece of the
> continent, a part of the main. If a clod be washed away by the
> sea, Europe is the less, as well as if a promontory were, as well
> as if a manor of thy friend's or of thine own were: any man's
> death diminishes me, because I am involved in mankind, and
> therefore never send to know for whom the bell tolls; it tolls for
> thee.
>
> —JOHN DONNE

Written almost four hundred years ago, while Donne was in the throes of illness, these words are a quintessential affirmation of our shared humanity. None of us, Donne insists, is autonomous; all of us are part of the greater human whole he terms "mankind." On the other hand, we cannot read Donne's words today without also noticing and questioning how they universalize human experience. In this chapter's terms, while every "self" is necessarily involved in "society," we must also recognize that the nature of this involvement varies with our differences.

Donne considers the relationship between "self" and "society" abstractly; the authors represented in this chapter explore it concretely, through their personal histories and experiences. The chapter begins with an op-ed by philosopher Kwame Anthony Appiah that challenges the too-easy way in which assertions of identity—typically of race or ethnicity, gender or sexual orientation, or social class—can be exploited to purchase rhetorical authority. None of us, he cautions, can authoritatively speak for a whole category of people ("As a such-and-such, I . . ."); we do much better when we presume to speak for ourselves. Appiah is not suggesting that our identities are irrelevant to our points of view (how could they be?) but rather that they are too multiple and complex to allow any direct correspondence between collective identity and individual perspectives or experiences. Framed by this corrective, the chapter proceeds through a varied series of readings that are nonetheless united by several common themes: how our physical bodies shape, without entirely defining, both our sense of self and the ways we are perceived by others; how society pressures us to conform to certain neutral or expected or "normal" ways of being; and how we might act to live more fulfilling lives and contribute to a more just society.

These readings fall into two interrelated clusters. The first of these focuses on women's experiences of their bodies, especially in their non-normative aspects. In her 1851 speech "Ain't I a Woman?" African American abolitionist Sojourner Truth invokes her experiences with physical labor, with childbearing, with the brutality of slavery, to argue for "women's rights" and "negroes' rights." Roxane Gay, in "What Fullness Is," delivers a frank account of her weight-loss surgery and her ambivalence about it. Gwendolyn Ann Smith, in "We're All Someone's Freak," affirms her identity as a transgender woman and, more generally, condemns the common impulse of all of us to look down on others. Nancy Mairs, in "On Being a Cripple," describes her life with multiple sclerosis, acknowledging her illness as a defining aspect of her life even as she expresses her hatred for it. Barbara Ehrenreich, in "Why I'm Giving Up Preventive Care," rejects the conventional wisdom that as we age we should subject ourselves to batteries of tests and procedures intended to forestall our inevitable deaths. The second of these clusters likewise focuses on embodiment, specifically the racial embodiment of black men. It begins with James Baldwin's iconic 1953 essay "Stranger in the Village," which recounts his experience as a black, gay man living for a time in a small Swiss village. Teju Cole, in "Black Body," both examines his experience visiting that same village sixty years later through the lens of Baldwin's essay and interprets Baldwin's essay through the lens of that experience. Garnette Cadogan's "Black and Blue" recounts his experiences "walking while black" in the cities of Kingston, Jamaica; New Orleans; and New York. The chapter's final reading, travel writer Pico Iyer's lyrical essay "The Humanity We Can't Relinquish," invites you to ponder the essence and boundaries of what Iyer calls our "shared humanness" and to recognize both its fragility and resilience.

As you read these pieces, use them as Cole uses Baldwin's "Stranger in the Village," to reflect on your own place in society. How would you describe your identity or identities? What social pressures have you faced, and how have you responded to them? Have you ever been judged or stereotyped or even persecuted because of who you are or who you were perceived to be? What did you do? Consider not just your personal experiences but the larger society: What hierarchies of value does society enforce? How are you privileged and constrained by your position in society? What might you do not just to live in society but to make it better for all?

KWAME ANTHONY APPIAH

Go Ahead, Speak for Yourself

S A WHITE MAN," JOE BEGINS, prefacing an insight, revelation, objection or confirmation he's eager to share—but let's stop him right there. Aside from the fact that he's white, and a man, what's his point? What does it signify when people use this now ubiquitous formula ("As a such-and-such, I . . .") to affix an identity to an observation?

First published as an op-ed in the New York Times *on August 10, 2018.*

Typically, it's an assertion of authority: As a member of this or that social group, I have experiences that lend my remarks special weight. The experiences, being representative of that group, might even qualify me to represent that group. Occasionally, the formula is an avowal of humility. It can be both at once. ("As a working-class woman, I'm struggling to understand Virginia Woolf's blithe assumptions of privilege.") The incantation seems indispensable. But it can also be—to use another much-loved formula—problematic.

The "as a" concept is an inherent feature of identities. For a group label like "white men" to qualify as a social identity, there must be times when the people to whom it applies act as members of that group, and are treated as members of that group. We make lives as men and women, as blacks and whites, as teachers and musicians. Yet the very word "identity" points toward the trouble: It comes from the Latin *idem*, meaning "the same." Because members of a given identity group have experiences that depend on a host of other social factors, they're not the same.

Being a black lesbian, for instance, isn't a matter of simply combining African-American, female and homosexual ways of being in the world; identities interact in complex ways. That's why Kimberlé Crenshaw, a feminist legal theorist and civil-rights activist, introduced the notion of intersectionality, which stresses the complexity with which different forms of subordination relate to one another. Racism can make white men shrink from black men and abuse black women. Homophobia can lead men in South Africa to rape gay women[1] but murder gay men. Sexism in the United States in the 1950s kept middle-class white women at home and sent working-class black women to work for them.

Let's go back to Joe, with his NPR mug and his man bun. (Or are you picturing a "Make America Great Again" tank top and a high-and-tight?)[2] Having an identity doesn't, by itself, authorize you to speak on behalf of everyone of that identity. So it can't really be that he's speaking for all white men. But he can at least speak to what it's like to live as a white man, right?

Not if we take the point about intersectionality. If Joe had grown up in Northern Ireland[3] as a gay white Catholic man, his experiences might be rather different from those of his gay white Protestant male friends there—let alone those of his childhood pen pal, a straight, Cincinnati-raised reform Jew.[4] While identity affects your experiences, there's no guarantee that what you've learned from them is going to be the same as what other people of the same identity have learned.

We've been here before. In the academy during the identity-conscious 1980s, many humanists thought that we'd reached peak "as a." Some worried

5

---

1. Known as "corrective rape," because it is intended to "cure" those subjected to it of their orientations.
2. "Make America Great Again," Donald J. Trump's campaign slogan during his 2016 U.S. presidential campaign; high-and-tight, military-inspired hairstyle.
3. Part of the United Kingdom; in the twentieth century, Northern Ireland suffered decades of conflict between its Protestant majority and Catholic minority populations.
4. A liberal form of Judaism.

that the locution had devolved into mere prepositional posturing. The literary theorist Barbara Johnson wrote, "If I tried to 'speak as a lesbian,' wouldn't I be processing my understanding of myself through media-induced images of what a lesbian is or through my own idealizations of what a lesbian should be?" In the effort to be "real," she saw something fake. Another prominent theorist, Gayatri Chakravorty Spivak, thought that the "as a" move was "a distancing from oneself," whereby the speaker became a self-appointed representative of an abstraction, some generalized perspective, and suppressed the actual multiplicity of her identities. "One is not just one thing," she observed.

It's because we're not just one thing that, in everyday conversation, "as a" can be useful as a way to spotlight some specific feature of who we are. Comedians do a lot of this sort of identity-cuing. In W. Kamau Bell's[5] recent Netflix special, "Private School Negro," the "as a" cue, explicit or implicit, singles out various of his identities over the course of an hour. Sometimes he's speaking as a parent, who has to go camping because his kids enjoy camping. Sometimes he's speaking as an African-American, who, for ancestral reasons, doesn't see the appeal of camping ("sleeping outdoors on purpose?"). Sometimes—as in a story about having been asked his weight before boarding a small aircraft—he's speaking as "a man, a heterosexual, cisgender Dadman." (Hence: "I have no idea how much I weigh.")

The switch in identities can be the whole point of the joke. Here's Chris Rock,[6] talking about his life in an affluent New Jersey suburb: "As a black man, I'm against the cops, but as a man with property, well, I need the cops. If someone steals something, I can't call the Crips!"[7] Drawing attention to certain identities you have is often a natural way of drawing attention to the contours of your beliefs, values or concerns.

10   But caveat auditor: Let the listener beware. Representing an identity is usually volunteer work, but sometimes the representative is conjured into being. Years ago, a slightly dotty countess I knew in the Hampstead area of London used to point out a leather-jacketed man on a park bench and inform her companions, with a knowing look, "He's the head gay." She was convinced that gays had the equivalent of a pontiff or prime minister who could speak on behalf of all his people.

Because people's experiences vary so much, the "as a" move is always in peril of presumption. When I was a student at the University of Cambridge in the 1970s, gay men were très chic: You couldn't have a serious party without some of us scattered around like throw pillows. Do my experiences entitle me to speak for a queer farmworker who is coming of age in Emmett, Idaho? Nobody appointed me head gay.

If someone is advocating policies for gay men to adopt, or for others to adopt toward gay men, what matters, surely, isn't whether the person is gay but whether the policies are sensible. As a gay man, you could oppose same-sex

5. American comedian, author, and media personality (b. 1973).
6. American comedian (b. 1965).
7. Predominantly African American street gang.

marriage (it's just submitting to our culture's heteronormativity, and anyway monogamy is a patriarchal invention) or advocate same-sex marriage (it's an affirmation of equal dignity and a way to sustain gay couples). Because members of an identity group won't be identical, your "as a" doesn't settle anything. The same holds for religious, vocational and national identities.

And, of course, for racial identities. In the 1990s the black novelist Trey Ellis wrote a screenplay, "The Inkwell," which drew on his childhood in the milieu of the black bourgeoisie. A white studio head (for whom race presumably eclipsed class) gave it to Matty Rich, a young black director who'd grown up in a New York City housing project. Mr. Rich apparently worried that the script wasn't "black enough" and proposed turning the protagonist's father, a schoolteacher, into a garbage man. Suffice to say, it didn't end well. Are we really going to settle these perennial debates over authenticity with a flurry of "as a" arrowheads?

Somehow, we can't stop trying. Ever since Donald Trump eked out his surprising electoral victory,[8] political analysts have been looking for people to speak for the supposedly disgruntled white working-class voters who, switching from their former Democratic allegiances, gave Mr. Trump the edge.

But about a third of working-class whites voted for Hillary Clinton. Nobody explaining why white working-class voters went for Mr. Trump would be speaking for the millions of white working-class voters who didn't. One person could say that she spoke as a white working-class woman in explaining why she voted for Mrs. Clinton just as truthfully as her sister could make the claim in explaining her support for Mr. Trump—each teeing us up to think about how her class and race might figure into the story. No harm in that. Neither one, however, could accurately claim to speak for the white working class. Neither has an exclusive on being representative. 15

So we might do well to ease up on "as a"—on the urge to underwrite our observations with our identities. "For me," Professor Spivak once tartly remarked, "the question 'Who should speak' is less crucial than 'Who will listen?'"

But tell that to Joe, as he takes a sip of kombucha—or is it Pabst Blue Ribbon?[9] All right, Joe, let's hear what you've got to say. The speaking-as-a convention isn't going anywhere; in truth, it often serves a purpose. But here's another phrase you might try on for size: "Speaking for myself . . ."

MLA CITATION

Appiah, Kwame Anthony. "Go Ahead, Speak for Yourself." *The Norton Reader: An Anthology of Nonfiction*, edited by Melissa A. Goldthwaite et al., 15th ed., W. W. Norton, 2020, pp. 130–33.

8. Donald J. Trump (b. 1946), 45th president of the United States, was widely projected to lose the 2016 presidential election to Hillary Clinton (b. 1947), the first female candidate for president from a major political party.

9. Kombucha, fermented beverage of Chinese origin, today marketed and consumed as a health drink; Pabst Blue Ribbon, American beer traditionally with blue-collar associations, later popular with hipsters.

QUESTIONS

1. In this essay, Kwame Anthony Appiah objects to a common form of argument from authority, in which a speaker or writer prefaces a statement with an assertion of identity: "As a such-and-such, I . . ." (paragraph 1). How does this form of argument work, and what are Appiah's objections to it?

2. Throughout his essay, Appiah returns repeatedly to the example of "Joe" (paragraph 1). What details about "Joe" does Appiah share? How does Appiah use this example to push his readers to examine their own stereotypes and assumptions about identity?

3. In the final paragraph of his essay, just before reiterating the exhortation in his title, Appiah acknowledges, "The speaking-as-a convention isn't going anywhere; in truth it often serves a purpose" (paragraph 17). What purpose does that convention serve? Why does Appiah offer this concession as he brings his essay to a close?

4. Why is legal scholar Kimberlé Crenshaw's idea of "intersectionality" (paragraph 4) so important to Appiah's argument? In an essay of your own, use this concept to analyze a time in which you used, or experienced another speaker using, the "speaking-as-a" convention.

SOJOURNER TRUTH
Ain't I a Woman?

1851 VERSION

I WANT TO SAY A FEW WORDS about this matter. I am a woman's rights [sic]. I have as much muscle as any man, and can do as much work as any man. I have plowed and reaped and husked and chopped and mowed, and can any man do more than that? I have heard much about the sexes being equal. I can carry as much as any man, and can eat as much too, if I can get it. I am as strong as any man that is now. As for intellect, all I can say is, if a woman have a pint, and a man a quart—why can't she have her little pint full? You need not be afraid to give us our rights for fear we will take too much,— for we can't take more than our pint'll hold. The poor men seems to be all in confusion, and don't know what to do. Why children, if you have woman's rights,

Sojourner Truth (c. 1797–1883), born Isabella Baumfree, was an African American abolitionist and women's rights activist. On May 28, 1851, at the Women's Rights Convention in Akron, Ohio, Truth delivered an extemporaneous speech that is most often titled "Ain't I a Woman?" Since what was passed down is a reported version of what Truth said, the speech is a composite of her words and the recollections of two individuals who witnessed it. Two versions appear here—the first recorded version of the speech reported by editor Marius Robinson in the Anti-Slavery Bugle *in 1851 and another, more famous version published by the abolitionist, writer, and speaker Frances Dana Gage in the* National Anti-Slavery Standard *on May 2, 1863.*

give it to her and you will feel better. You will have your own rights, and they won't be so much trouble. I can't read, but I can hear. I have heard the Bible and have learned that Eve caused man to sin. Well, if woman upset the world, do give her a chance to set it right side up again. The Lady has spoken about Jesus, how he never spurned woman from him, and she was right. When Lazarus died, Mary and Martha came to him with faith and love and besought him to raise their brother. And Jesus wept and Lazarus came forth. And how came Jesus into the world? Through God who created him and the woman who bore him. Man, where was your part? But the women are coming up blessed be God and a few of the men are coming up with them. But man is in a tight place, the poor slave is on him, woman is coming on him, he is surely between a hawk and a buzzard.

MLA CITATION

Truth, Sojourner. "Ain't I a Woman?" 1851. *The Norton Reader: An Anthology of Nonfiction*, edited by Melissa A. Goldthwaite et al., 15th ed., W. W. Norton, 2020, pp. 134–35.

1863 VERSION

WELL, CHILDREN, WHERE THERE IS SO MUCH RACKET there must be something out of kilter. I think that 'twixt the negroes of the South and the women at the North, all talking about rights, the white men will be in a fix pretty soon. But what's all this here talking about?

That man over there says that women need to be helped into carriages, and lifted over ditches, and to have the best place everywhere. Nobody ever helps me into carriages, or over mud-puddles, or gives me any best place! And ain't I a woman? Look at me! Look at my arm! I have ploughed and planted, and gathered into barns, and no man could head me! And ain't I a woman? I could work as much and eat as much as a man—when I could get it—and bear the lash as well! And ain't I a woman? I have borne thirteen children, and seen most all sold off to slavery, and when I cried out with my mother's grief, none but Jesus heard me! And ain't I a woman?

Then they talk about this thing in the head; what's this they call it? [member of audience whispers, "intellect"] That's it, honey. What's that got to do with women's rights or negroes' rights? If my cup won't hold but a pint, and yours holds a quart, wouldn't you be mean not to let me have my little half measure full?

Then that little man in black there, he says women can't have as much rights as men, 'cause Christ wasn't a woman! Where did your Christ come from? Where did your Christ come from? From God and a woman! Man had nothing to do with Him.

If the first woman God ever made was strong enough to turn the world upside down all alone, these women together ought to be able to turn it back, and get it right side up again! And now they is asking to do it, the men better let them.

Obliged to you for hearing me, and now old Sojourner ain't got nothing more to say.

MLA CITATION

Truth, Sojourner. "Ain't I a Woman?" 1863. *The Norton Reader: An Anthology of Nonfiction*, edited by Melissa A. Goldthwaite et al., 15th ed., W. W. Norton, 2020, p. 135.

QUESTIONS

1. Sojourner Truth uses both comparison and contrast to develop her speech. How does she compare herself to a man? In what ways does she believe she is not like a man? What do these similarities and differences tell us about how she understands gender?

2. Discuss Truth's use of the Bible to challenge the limitations others try to impose on her. How does her use of biblical allusions support her argument?

3. In his op-ed "Go Ahead, Speak for Yourself" (pp. 130–33) Kwame Anthony Appiah uses legal scholar Kimberlé Crenshaw's concept of "intersectionality" to consider the complexity with which a single individual's various identities interact (paragraph 4). How does this concept help you understand the two versions of Truth's speech?

4. Write an essay comparing the two versions of Truth's speech. What do they have in common, and how do they differ? Which version do you think would have been more persuasive to its original audience? Which version is more persuasive to you?

ROXANE GAY

What Fullness Is

T HE FIRST WEIGHT-LOSS SURGERY was performed during the 10th century, on D. Sancho, the king of León, Spain. He was so fat that he lost his throne, so he was taken to Córdoba, where a doctor sewed his lips shut. Only able to drink through a straw, the former king lost enough weight after a time to return home and reclaim his kingdom.

The notion that thinness—and the attempt to force the fat body toward a state of culturally mandated discipline—begets great rewards is centuries old.

Modern weight-loss surgery began in the 1950s, when surgeons employing various techniques caused their patients fairly distressing problems, like severe diarrhea, dehydration, kidney stones, gallstones, and even death—but, generally, the patients lost weight. Surgeons have since refined their techniques, using a range of restriction or malabsorption methods to force the human body to lose weight. They have tried wiring patients' jaws shut to force weight loss through liquid diets. They have stapled stomachs into smaller pouches to restrict caloric intake. They have developed gastric bands and balloons to

Originally published in 2018 on the social journalism and blog site Medium.

restrict the amount of food that can enter the stomach. But it was the first laparoscopic gastric bypass—in which the gastrointestinal tract is routed around a person's stomach—performed in 1994, that enabled bariatric surgery to go more mainstream by way of minimal invasion.

Some of these interventions have succeeded for people, and some have failed, because not even surgical intervention can overcome the reasons why many people gain and then struggle to lose weight. Some bodies and minds simply cannot be brought to heel.

I capitulated to a procedure after more than 15 years of resistance and   5 had a sleeve gastrectomy at the UCLA Ronald Reagan Hospital in January 2018. I told only a few people; I did not tell my family. I felt—in equal parts—hope, defeat, frustration, and disgust.

The first time I contemplated weight-loss surgery, it was at the bidding of my parents. My father and I went to an orientation seminar at the Cleveland Clinic[1] and learned about gastric bypass. There were graphic, deeply disturbing videos and a question-and-answer session. I submitted myself to a clinical assessment about the problem of my body. It wasn't the right time, I decided. I could be better, eat less, move more.

And over the next several years, I certainly tried to, intermittently or constantly, depending on how you look at it. I continued a near-lifetime of disordered eating, and restriction, and overeating. Sometimes I was motivated enough to work out. Sometimes I wasn't. Mostly I was overwhelmed by inertia. I had a desire to lose weight but an inability—or, perhaps, unwillingness—to force myself toward the deprivation required for the significant weight loss the world told me I needed.

The truth is that my desire for weight loss has long been about satisfying other people more than myself, finding a way to fit more peacefully into a world that is not at all interested in accommodating a body like mine. And the dominant cultural attitude toward fatness is that the fat body is a medical problem, a drain on society, an aesthetic blight. As a fat person, I am supposed to want to lose weight. I am supposed to be working on the problem of my body. I am supposed to apply discipline to physical unruliness. I'm not supposed to be fine with my body. I am not supposed to yearn, simply, for people to let me be, to see me, accept me, and treat me with dignity exactly as I am.

I am, however, sometimes fine with my body. I am fine with my curves, the solidity of me. I am strong and tall. I enjoy the way I take up space, that I have presence. I have someone who appreciates my body and only hates everything I must deal with by virtue of living in this world in this body.

Sometimes I hate my body, the unruliness of it. I hate all my limitations. I   10 hate my lack of discipline. I hate how my unhappiness is never enough to truly motivate me to regain control of myself, once and for all. I hate the way I hunger but never find satisfaction. I want and want and want but never allow myself to reach for what I truly want, leaving that want raging desperately beneath the surface of my skin.

1. Major hospital and medical research center in Ohio.

And the moment I step outside the safety of my home, I hate how visible I am, how people treat me, how they stare and comment both loudly and under their breath, how rude children remind me I'm fat and their rude parents say nothing, how I have to think and overthink where I go and how I will fit into any given space. I do not know how to carry myself with confidence when I go out into the world. Any sense of self I have is often shattered within minutes, and then I am all insecurities and fears, wishing myself into a more socially acceptable form.

And given my career trajectory, there are pictures and videos of me everywhere. I hate these images, cringe when I see them, and then hate myself for cringing, for not seeing myself with kindness. Trolls make memes of my pictures and post them to internet message boards with cruel captions. They tweet these memes at me. They remind me, every chance they get, that I am fat: more than, but less than. Every single day, I am confronted by how people really see me. I am confronted by the fact that no matter what I achieve, I will always be fat first. I will always have this weakness; it will always be easily exploited.

If you're not one statistic, though, you're another. According to the American Society for Bariatric and Metabolic Surgery, 216,000 people received a bariatric procedure in 2016. Doctors tout weight-loss surgery as the gold standard for weight loss, though a relatively small number of the estimated one-third of Americans who are considered obese actually get the surgery.

Many doctors have used that exact phrase with me—"the gold standard"—over the years. They told me that this surgery will save my life, and that if I didn't get the surgery, I wouldn't live until 40. When I turned 40, they told me that if I didn't get the surgery, I wouldn't live until 50.

15   This surgery is touted as the only real option for the morbidly and supermorbidly obese. It is not a question of if a fat person will get weight-loss surgery, but when.

Of course, weight-loss surgery is extraordinarily expensive, and many insurance policies will not cover it. The out-of-pocket cost in the United States is high enough that many people travel to Mexico and Malaysia to get it for a fraction of the cost. My insurance company will cover weight-loss surgery—but only after you've gone through six months of medically supervised weight loss; you have to prove that you deserve to have yourself cut open.

Given my schedule, this six-month waiting period was a requirement I was never going to be able to meet, so I ended up paying for the surgery out of pocket. I suppose I should be grateful that I could afford to do so, but mostly, I'm bitter. The expense was breathtaking.

If there is a silver lining, the expense also removed a lot of bureaucratic red tape. I was able to schedule my surgery and address all the presurgical requirements with relative ease once the surgeon realized he didn't have to deal with an insurance company. Health care is as wantonly susceptible to the ills of capitalism as everything else.

After more than 15 years of refusing it, I made the decision to get weight-loss surgery on an ordinary day. At home in Lafayette, Indiana, a young man

yelled at me to move my fat black ass while I was crossing a grocery store parking lot to my car. It was the last straw.

I tried to hold my head high, shuffled as quickly as I could, put my grocer-   20
ies in my car, and sat behind the steering wheel. I sat there, shaking, wishing
I could have been as quick in that moment to put him in his place as I would
have been online. I wanted to call someone for comfort, but I was at a silent
impasse with the only person to whom I could talk. Instead, I pressed my head
against the steering wheel and sobbed. When I collected myself, I drove home
and went to bed. I hoped I might not wake up, but I did.

The most common weight-loss procedures today are the gastric bypass
and the gastric sleeve. These procedures are usually done laparoscopically in a
matter of hours, with the patient under general anesthesia. In gastric bypass,
the stomach is reduced, creating a small pouch, which is then connected farther down the small intestine. Sleeve gastrectomy is slightly less drastic and
the more common procedure performed. The stomach size is reduced and
reshaped into a slender tube, restricting how much a person can eat. In these
procedures, patients also lose their appetites as a result of reduced ghrelin, a
hormone that stimulates appetite.

In both procedures, the patient's anatomy is irreversibly changed, and
they lose a significant amount of weight quickly. Both procedures result in
malnutrition, requiring patients to take multivitamins and other supplements
for the rest of their lives. Other risks and complications include hair loss,
ulcers, leaks, gastric bleeding, bowel obstruction, gallstones, and dehydration.
These are all fairly horrifying risks, but (the medical establishment has
decided) they are less horrifying than the medical risks of fatness. People who
choose weight-loss surgery trade one kind of health for another.

After such drastic weight loss, many patients need expensive, extensive
plastic surgery to deal with the excess skin. The TLC network even has a
show—spun off from My 600-Lb Life—called Skin Tight, about people who
have lost a significant amount of weight and want to get skin-removal surgery,
altering their anatomy once again.

And with the growing popularity of bariatric surgery, an entire industry
has risen around it—supplements, special foods, dishware, and more. There
are online forums, YouTube channels, bariatric eating blogs, and other such
communities. Where there is money to be made, capitalism finds a way.

The morning after I decided to get weight-loss surgery, I called a local   25
bariatric surgeon and made an appointment for a consultation. A few hours
later, the program administrator called me back and told me I would need to
lose 75 pounds before they would even consider operating on me. I immediately felt hopeless: If I could lose 75 pounds on my own, I wouldn't be considering surgery. The surgeon, the coordinator told me, was involved in some
kind of study and only wanted good outcomes; he did not inspire me with
confidence. I was told to watch some online videos about the surgery and fill
out a lot of paperwork and then we could get started.

After a few days of allowing myself to wallow in defeat, I got a recommendation from a friend and found an excellent surgeon in Los Angeles (where I

also live) who did inspire with me confidence. This surgeon was very frank; I just stared and nodded. He told me at our first appointment in December that surgery was my best option. He remarked that it was good that I carried most of my weight in my lower body, because it would be easier for him to do the surgery. I was an unruly body for him to fix, nothing less, nothing more. He asked me to try losing some weight before the surgery to reduce the size of my liver, but he wasn't too prickly or unrealistic about it. Just don't gain any more weight, he said.

I looked at my work calendar for 2018 and realized I had a small window within which to do this surgery and recover. Before I lost my nerve, I rescheduled the two events I had in January and told my doctor I wasn't going to be able to wait six weeks before flying again post-surgery, as recommended. In a matter of hours, I was scheduled for surgery in early January.

I was then weighed and measured. I had blood drawn and an EKG and an echocardiogram performed. I attended a three-hour workshop where I learned more about the surgery, how to prepare, what the initial weeks and after the surgery would be like, and so on. A nutritionist cautioned us not to visit online forums about bariatric surgery, and I heeded her advice (until I didn't). I received a binder full of information, much of it rather starkly depressing about the "lifestyle changes" that would be demanded of me both before and after the surgery. I bought vitamins and whey protein and tried to wrap my mind around the vastly different way I'd have to be eating in just a few weeks. I saw a psychologist who would determine if I was emotionally prepared for the surgery. After 45 minutes, she determined that I was and charged me $300 for the consultation.

During every part of the preoperative process, I doled out obscene sums of money to a range of medical providers. And every night, I stared at the ceiling, wondering if I would actually go through with it. I chastised myself for allowing myself to get to this point, for lacking the discipline to lose weight by any other means.

30   I had made a drastic decision to change my body, but I did not suddenly develop a healthier relationship toward food. In the weeks leading up to my surgery, I tried to eat all the foods I thought that I was probably never going to be able to eat again, paying particular and loving attention to fried foods and soda. A few nights before surgery, friends and I went to my favorite steakhouse, and I enjoyed a Caesar salad and a finely marbled rib eye with mashed potatoes and green beans almondine and butter cake with fresh whipped cream and gin and tonics with a splash of grenadine. I savored every single bite, often with my eyes closed. I mourned what I was losing, or what I thought I was losing.

The morning of the surgery, I went to the hospital, checked in, and was weighed and escorted to a long row of hospital beds just waiting for patients who would submit themselves to surgical blades for one reason or another. I was hungry and thirsty and nervous. I told the friend accompanying me that the gown the hospital provided probably wouldn't fit me, and she said that couldn't possibly happen, given the nature of my impending procedure. I was right: The gown was indeed too small, and, at six in the morning, I was too tired and too defeated to even laugh or feel any kind of satisfaction for understanding just how shortsighted this world is when it comes to different kinds of bodies.

As I do whenever I'm going under general anesthesia, I told the anesthesiologist to give me extra, because I've seen the movie *Awake*.[2] I was wracked with guilt about not telling my family, and then worried that I was probably going to die and my parents would find out in such a terrible way. As I worried, I was strapped to the operating table, and then, mercifully, I lost consciousness. I don't remember anything about the surgery, and I'm thankful for that because it means that the drugs worked. When I woke up, a nurse was peering at me and then broke into a smile. She said, "I know who you are! My girlfriend and I love your books." I was still pretty out of it, so I muttered, "Please don't tell the internet I'm here."

I care too much what people think. I hate that about myself. Before and after my surgery, I worried what people would think if and when they found out. Each time I went to the doctor's office, I prayed no one would recognize me, and rarely were those prayers answered. I'm just a writer, but I am recognized in public with alarming frequency. "What are you doing here?" a fan asked one afternoon as I walked into the UCLA Medical Center, and I smiled and said, "Routine checkup."

I worried that people would think I betrayed fat positivity,[3] something I do very much believe in even if I can't always believe in it for myself. I worried that everyone who responded so generously to my memoir, *Hunger*, would feel betrayed. I worried I would be seen as betraying myself. I worried I would be seen as taking the easy way out, even though nothing about any of this has been easy, not one thing. I worried.

The surgeon made five neat incisions across my torso and stitched them from the inside so I would eventually have minimal scarring. As I came to my senses, I felt each of those incisions, throbbing gently, reminding me that something invasive had happened to my body. The worst part of the first few hours after the surgery was that I couldn't drink anything until the following morning: I had a brand-new stomach, and a whole lot of stitches holding that brand-new stomach together, so it was best to leave this newly delicate anatomy alone.

As the hours wore on, I felt desiccated. I wanted water more than I have ever wanted anything in my life. I could satisfy myself only with a tiny sponge dipped in ice to dab on my lips and tongue. When no one was looking, I took tiny sips of the melted water pooling at the bottom of my Styrofoam cup—I did.

The hospital buzzed around me. Nurses doted on me. My surgeon stopped by and told me everything had gone well. My liver was nice and small, he said with a smile, and commended me for losing weight before the procedure. I felt a swell of pride and then hated myself for that swell, for being so pedestrian as to take pleasure in the sort of validation that goes against so much of what I believe about how bodies should be allowed to be.

35

---

2. A 2007 thriller whose plot hinges on a heart-surgery patient remaining conscious while under anesthesia.
3. The fat acceptance movement, which arose in the 1960s, resists the stigmatization of fat people and promotes positive attitudes toward fatness.

There was a TV, but I couldn't bother to focus on it. I was on excellent pain medication that I controlled with a little remote, so it was all very pleasant, less the torment of the desert of my mouth. The woman next door also had weight-loss surgery, and she talked loudly about how she was a changed woman. It was like she was trying to prove she deserved the surgery, that she was a better woman now. It was aggravating because I did not feel at all changed; I did not have a new outlook on life.

Every few hours, I got up and walked around so as to avoid blood clots. I dozed. I chatted drowsily with loved ones watching over me. Eventually, I passed out, all praise to Dilaudid. Late the next afternoon, I went home, where I could have only water, clear broth, Gatorade, and sugar-free Jell-O for three days.

40   For the two weeks after that, I could have only liquids like more Gatorade, juices, soups, thinned yogurt. From weeks two to four, I could eat only soft foods. My new diet was as horrible and boring and bland as you might imagine, but it was also manageable. Anything is manageable if it isn't forever.

Slowly, I started coming to terms with how quickly my relationship to food was changing and how disordered my relationship to food had been and for so long. I had to think—carefully—about what I ate and how. I became full after only a few bites. I had to think about protein and making sure I was getting enough. (I never did, because I'm a very picky eater and the protein shakes made me gag.) I wasn't hungry, but I was starving.

That incident in the parking lot was also an accumulation of frustrations and heartache I no longer wanted to carry—doctors not taking me seriously and always trying to "treat" my weight before anything else, never fitting in spaces I wanted to be in, the obsessive rituals I developed around deciding if and how I could go out in public, feeling unfit and hating exercise because everything was so arduous, having such limited fashion options, the familial concern that was a yoke I couldn't ever get out from under, the societal concern that was a yoke I couldn't ever get out from under, the nagging worry that my weight would eventually come between me and the one person in my life who has never made me feel anything but good in my body, the nagging worry that, eventually, my luck would run out and all the terrible things that doctors had long been warning me about would come to pass.

I had to face the extent of my unhappiness and how much of that unhappiness was connected to my body. I had to accept that I could change my fat body faster than this culture will change how it views, treats, and accommodates fat bodies. And I had to do so while recognizing that losing weight wasn't actually going to make me happier—which may have been the bitterest part of all.

That's how I found myself going back to therapy after nearly a decade away—a decade of telling myself that I was fine and fixed and emotionally whole. The nutritionist affiliated with my surgeon gave me a recommendation, and I made an appointment. Within the first five minutes, I knew it wasn't going to work: She stared at me for long, intensely awkward lengths of time. At the beginning of the session, she was simply silent, and I was not at all sure what I was supposed to do with that silence.

45   After two sessions, I decided to try someone else. He was a brash, handsome older man who got under my skin, forcing me to face uncomfortable

truths, forcing me to get comfortable with feeling my feelings—something I've avoided for most of my life. At some point during many of our sessions, he says, "You're mad at me," and I pretend I am not and he knows I am lying, and onward we go, doing the necessary work of breaking me down so that, some-day, I might build myself back up again.

The dominant narrative around weight-loss surgery is that it changes your life and makes everything better. It's a lovely fantasy that, by cutting yourself open and having parts of yourself removed, everything that weighed you down will be lifted. But it is only a fantasy.

People who have weight-loss surgery are more likely to commit suicide. Many married people get divorced after the surgery because their spouses cannot cope with the changes, so much so that "bariatric divorce" is a thing. The psychologist I saw for my presurgical evaluation warned that the first year is really difficult, and many patients end up suffering from depression and regretting the surgery. The second year is better, she said, trying to reassure me after my face fell. And she was right: I am depressed and miserable. I am cold all the time and exhausted because I'm only eating between 1,200 and 1,500 calories.[4] I am filled with regrets because everything has changed, but everything is exactly the same.

I am losing a significant amount of weight very quickly—that's what the scale shows, on those rare occasions when I am not too afraid to get on the scale, terrified I've done all this, spent all this money, only to not lose weight. My clothes are looser. My shoes are inexplicably loose. My ring is loose. I fit into my car in a way I never have. I fit into chairs better. I fit everywhere bet-ter, and it's still so early.

But I can't believe that I am losing weight, despite all this evidence. I've told my person—more than once—that someone is messing with me, sabotaging my sanity by adjusting my seat in the car, stretching out my clothes and shoes to trick me. I am assured such is not the case, that my body is actually changing. For a few moments, I am quieted, and then the doubt creeps back in.

When I look in the mirror, I see no difference—none at all. No one, save   50
for a couple people, has openly acknowledged any weight loss, if they've even noticed, which is a relief and a frustration and a reminder of just how much weight I have to lose. I don't want any weight loss to be acknowledged (or, worse, celebrated), but I also very much do.

I've replaced one set of anxieties with another. I worry I'm eating too much and stretching my new stomach (something I was warned about, repeat-edly and vigorously). I have brief moments where I allow myself to imagine hiking Runyon Canyon[5] or wearing a fabulous outfit because it is available in my size or going to see a musical without making special arrangements . . . and then I tell myself to get ahold of myself. I tell myself not to want. I tell myself that I've failed to discipline my body before and I will probably fail this time, too. I tell myself these things because I've carried this weight for almost 30 years and it is terrifying to face who I could be without it.

4. The U.S. Department of Agriculture (USDA) recommends that adult women con-sume 1,600–2,000 calories per day.
5. Runyon Canyon Park, Los Angeles, California.

I had weight-loss surgery, but I am still the same person who went under the knife. I still have that yawning cavern inside of me that I want to fill with food, only now I cannot fill it with food. I'm rarely hungry, but I am ravenous. Want continues to rage desperately beneath the surface of my skin. I turned to food when I was sad and happy and lonely and scared and anxious. I turned to food, and away from everything else; it was my comfort and my friend. Food helped me survive something I did not think I would survive. Food numbed the uncomfortable feelings I very much did not want to feel.

And then, that comfort was gone. I've lost the best friend I never had the courage to acknowledge but who was my constant, loyal companion nonetheless. I am left holding the shattered pieces of whatever has been left behind, trying to assemble them into something new, something that serves me better.

The forced restriction brought about by the surgery is maddening. Yes, I eat, but I physically cannot overeat. At restaurants, waitstaff interrogate me about all the food I leave on my plate. At home, I eat sad, tiny portions (or, given what I used to eat, what feel like tiny portions). After a few bites of anything, the discomfort begins, and then that discomfort evolves into pain.

55   Sometimes, when I am feeling rebellious, I try to ignore that pain and try to surrender to my desire to eat with abandon. My body reminds me that rebellion will not be tolerated. For the first time in as long as I can remember, I am empty, but I know what fullness is, and I hate this knowing.

MLA CITATION

Gay, Roxane. "What Fullness Is." *The Norton Reader: An Anthology of Nonfiction*, edited by Melissa A. Goldthwaite et al., 15th ed., W. W. Norton, 2020, pp. 136–44.

QUESTIONS

1. In her essay, Roxane Gay takes the occasion of her weight-loss surgery to examine "the dominant cultural attitude toward fatness" (paragraph 8) as well as her complex feelings about her own weight and body. From her first paragraph to her last, she approaches these topics through language of discipline and rebellion. Why does she choose such language?

2. What role does race play in Gay's essay?

3. Gay's relationship to food changed as a result of her weight-loss surgery. What was it before her surgery, and what is it after? What does Gay mean when she writes, "I'm rarely hungry, but I am ravenous" (paragraph 52)? Consider her title and concluding sentence: "For the first time in as long as I can remember, I am empty, but I know what fullness is, and I hate this knowing" (paragraph 55). What is this "fullness," and why does she hate knowing it?

4. In this essay, Gay explores her ambivalence about her weight-loss surgery and its consequences. Using Gay's essay as a model, write an essay about a major decision you have made about which you have mixed or complex feelings.

GWENDOLYN ANN SMITH
We're All Someone's Freak

BEING TRANSGENDER GUARANTEES you will upset someone. People get upset with transgender people who choose to inhabit a third gender space rather than "pick a side." Some get upset at transgender people who do not eschew their birth histories. Others get up in arms with those who opted out of surgical options, instead living with their original equipment. Ire is raised at those who transition, then transition again when they decide that their initial change was not the right answer for them. Heck, some get their dander up simply because this or that transgender person simply is not "trying hard enough" to be a particular gender, whatever that means. Some are irked that the Logo program *RuPaul's Drag Race* shows a version of transgender life different from their own. Meanwhile, all around are those who have decided they aren't comfortable with the lot of us, because we dared to change from one gender expression or identity to some other.

To hell with that.

You see, I have learned not only that I have to do what I have to do to be happy regardless of the struggles I may face, but also that I am the only person responsible for my own comfort or discomfort about my gender. I may wrinkle my nose about what someone else might do, but ultimately what others do cannot change who I am.

I had an unusual request from a friend of mine some time back: I was asked not to mention that I was a friend of hers. You see, I'm transgender. More than this, it's hardly a secret that I'm transgender—I am professionally transgender, as well as the founder of Trans Day of Remembrance. Her fear was that if someone knew that I knew her, then it would automatically be assumed that she was transgender, too.

It was a difficult thing to hear that my very existence was perceived as being enough to harm a person I called a friend. I try to harm no one in my daily affairs—yet here I was, being told that all I need to do to cause someone difficulty is to call them a friend.

I asked many of my friends who are transgender, in the wake of this incident, if they too would be uncomfortable being identified publicly as friends of mine. I consider these people close friends, I said, and still if this inadvertent outing would cause them trouble, I promised I would disclaim them immediately. Oddly, no one else seemed all that perturbed. I did not address this with my non-transgender friends, but maybe I should; presumably it will be a great shock to discover that merely being acquainted with me has the potential to cast doubt on their birth gender.

5

This essay first appeared in the Bay Area Reporter *(2006), a free weekly newspaper based in San Francisco, California, that caters to the LGBT community; it was reprinted in* Gender Outlaws: The Next Generation *(2010), a volume edited by Kate Bornstein and S. Bear Bergman that "collects and contextualizes the work of this generation's trans and genderqueer forward thinkers."*

One of the first lessons I was taught at some of my earliest transgender support group meetings (more years ago than I usually would wish to admit) was that being in a group of transgender people exponentially raises the risk of being read as transgender. If you want to remain hidden, I was told, avoid others like you. Large group events would always require remote locations where we could all be hidden away; the concept of meeting with your transgender siblings just anywhere was taboo. This was a world just a step away from secret handshakes and coded catch-phrases.

Much later, I learned that this divide-and-conquer strategy had been common in the older, university-based transsexuality programs of the 1970s. Associating with other transgender people could get you drummed out of the program. After all, you were supposed to be associating with those in your preferred gender, making strides down the road to Normal, not hanging about with others trying to take paths similar to yours.

While those gatekeeping systems are long gone, their survivors live on. Worse, these individuals, themselves transsexual, perpetuate the enforcement of the system they were required to navigate. If you don't fit the gender-norming rules they were expected to observe, you are a subject of derision, worthy of little more than the ridicule of your would-be peers. They have learned to construct a hierarchical order of who is acceptable and who is not.

10   Let me break it down this way: some lesbians and gays feel that their issues are more important than transgender issues, because transgender people are freaks. Some transgender people—often, but not only, transsexuals—view transsexual issues as more important than the issues of, say, cross-dressers. Some among the more genderqueer portions of our community look down upon those who opt to live in a more "normatively gendered" space. There are even groups that cross-dressers feel superior to: sissies, drag kings and queens, "little girls," and so on. Yes, I'm sure that we could follow even each of these groups and find that, eventually, everyone has someone they view as a freak.

This is a human phenomenon, and one which occurs especially, it seems, among marginalized groups. Trekkers versus trekkies versus people in Klingon costumes, or furries versus fursuiters versus, oh, plushies. I'm sure if I looked at model railroaders, I'd probably find that HO gauge fans look down at N scale,[1] or something like that. The taxonomies are endless, often circular, and are usually graded to a fineness that would be invisible to any outsider. We just want to identify the "real" freaks, so we can feel closer to normal. In reality, not a single one of us is so magically normative as to claim the right to separate out the freaks from everyone else. We are all freaks to someone. Maybe even—if we're honest—to ourselves.

In the end, we find ourselves with one of two choices: do we push others like us away, to best fit in? Or do we seek out our kin, for comfort and company? For that matter, if we are all someone's "freak," does this mean we are all each other's "normal" too—and worthy of embrace?

---

1. Names of scales—or sizes—of model trains; the scale refers to the train's relationship to life-scale measurements.

These are questions I have asked myself, time and time again. I confess to having a phase during which I did not associate with other transgender people, for fear I would be guilty by association, or even get "tranny cooties." Maybe I was afraid I would see things in my own being I was not ready to face, or was afraid of challenging my own assumptions. I found it to be a very limiting way to live, and have chosen to embrace those I might see as my siblings.

Yes, even those who might be having a hard time embracing me.

This isn't to say that there's no such thing as defamation, or that everything   15
is acceptable. Far from it. There is always a need to watch for attacks on us as a whole. We can't ignore right-wing demagogues who insist that the word of the doctor who proclaims a child's sex at birth somehow holds more sway over the reality of the body than the word of the person who inhabits it. Yet just as anyone can call me whatever they want it is up to me to decide whether I care to answer. More than this, it should be irrelevant to me what any other transgender person opts to do. Their action does not somehow change who I am. It cannot.

I know what I am. I know that I've chosen to identify as a transgender woman, and that I am—by and large—happy with where I am in this world. I'm far from perfect, and I could give you a list as long as my arms of the things I'd love to change. Nevertheless, I am still here, and I am still me, and no one can change that without my permission.

At the same time, even though I am happy to identify as a transgender woman, I also applaud those who are seeking to redefine the notions of gender and are carving out spaces of their own. My own comfort is such that I'm glad to see other people out there challenging the assumptions and to know that their challenges do not necessarily pose a threat to my beliefs. Who knows— maybe my beliefs could stand a good challenge once in a while, and they might end up broader than they were before.

We live in a world of incredible variations, where there are some 200,000 species of moths and butterflies to be found in this planet, where one can find snowy ice caps and boiling cauldrons of lava, and where biodiversity is the very thing that keeps the whole complex system in tune. The notion of classifying things and then claiming that only this or that is a *proper* version of some being is a distinctly human construct, full of arrogance and hubris. When those of us who are gender outlaws of any stripe seek to set definitions on our realness, to determine who is somehow "normal" amongst us, it seems all the more crazy.

I assume it is some sort of human failing that makes us always need to shun someone who we perceive as "more different than thou." Some simply need to feel better about themselves by despising someone further down the chain from them. Nevertheless, this does not seem to help move us further along in the world at large.

We can worry about who is this and who is that, we can argue about who   20
does or doesn't belong. We can talk about how much more legitimate one or another of us is. In the end, we are all somebody's freak—and basic human dignity is not a privilege of the lucky superior few, but a right of all or none.

MLA CITATION

Smith, Gwendolyn Ann. "We're All Someone's Freak." *The Norton Reader: An Anthology of Nonfiction*, edited by Melissa A. Goldthwaite et al., 15th ed., W. W. Norton, 2020, pp. 145–47.

QUESTIONS

1. In paragraph 12, Gwendolyn Ann Smith claims that we seek out other "freaks" like us or try to blend in with the mainstream. What examples does she provide throughout her essay to support this claim?

2. Why, according to Smith, do some people get upset by transgender people? How might her ideas relate to Roxane Gay's observations in "What Fullness Is" (pp. 136–44) about society's longstanding efforts "to force the fat body toward a state of culturally mandated discipline" (paragraph 2)?

3. Smith argues that everyone is someone else's freak (paragraph 11), and conversely that everyone makes a freak out of someone else. Write an essay in which you discuss this reciprocal relationship in a social setting you know well.

NANCY MAIRS

On Being a Cripple

> To escape is nothing. Not to escape is nothing.
> —LOUISE BOGAN

THE OTHER DAY I was thinking of writing an essay on being a cripple. I was thinking hard in one of the stalls of the women's room in my office building, as I was shoving my shirt into my jeans and tugging up my zipper. Preoccupied, I flushed, picked up my book bag, took my cane down from the hook, and unlatched the door. So many movements unbalanced me, and as I pulled the door open I fell over backward, landing fully clothed on the toilet seat with my legs splayed in front of me: the old beetle-on-its-back routine. Saturday afternoon, the building deserted, I was free to laugh aloud as I wriggled back to my feet, my voice bouncing off the yellowish tiles from all directions. Had anyone been there with me, I'd have been still and faint and hot with chagrin. I decided that it was high time to write the essay.

First, the matter of semantics. I am a cripple. I choose this word to name me. I choose from among several possibilities, the most common of which are "handicapped" and "disabled." I made the choice a number of years ago, without thinking, unaware of my motives for doing so. Even now, I'm not sure what

From Plaintext (1986), *Nancy Mairs's book of personal essays about life with multiple sclerosis.*

those motives are, but I recognize that they are complex and not entirely flattering. People—crippled or not—wince at the word "cripple," as they do not at "handicapped" or "disabled." Perhaps I want them to wince. I want them to see me as a tough customer, one to whom the fates/gods/viruses have not been kind, but who can face the brutal truth of her existence squarely. As a cripple, I swagger.

But, to be fair to myself, a certain amount of honesty underlies my choice. "Cripple" seems to me a clean word, straightforward and precise. It has an honorable history, having made its first appearance in the Lindisfarne Gospel[1] in the tenth century. As a lover of words, I like the accuracy with which it describes my condition: I have lost the full use of my limbs. "Disabled," by contrast, suggests any incapacity, physical or mental. And I certainly don't like "handicapped," which implies that I have deliberately been put at a disadvantage, by whom I can't imagine (my God is not a Handicapper General), in order to equalize chances in the great race of life. These words seem to me to be moving away from my condition, to be widening the gap between word and reality. Most remote is the recently coined euphemism "differently abled," which partakes of the same semantic hopefulness that transformed countries from "undeveloped" to "underdeveloped," then to "less developed," and finally to "developing" nations. People have continued to starve in those countries during the shift. Some realities do not obey the dictates of language.

Mine is one of them. Whatever you call me, I remain crippled. But I don't care what you call me, so long as it isn't "differently abled," which strikes me as pure verbal garbage designed, by its ability to describe anyone, to describe no one. I subscribe to George Orwell's thesis that "the slovenliness of our language makes it easier for us to have foolish thoughts."[2] And I refuse to participate in the degeneration of the language to the extent that I deny that I have lost anything in the course of this calamitous disease; I refuse to pretend that the only differences between you and me are the various ordinary ones that distinguish any one person from another. But call me "disabled" or "handicapped" if you like. I have long since grown accustomed to them; and if they are vague, at least they hint at the truth. Moreover, I use them myself. Society is no readier to accept crippledness than to accept death, war, sex, sweat, or wrinkles. I would never refer to another person as a cripple. It is the word I use to name only myself.

I haven't always been crippled, a fact for which I am soundly grateful. To be whole of limb is, I know from experience, infinitely more pleasant and useful than to be crippled; and if that knowledge leaves one open to bitterness at my loss, the physical soundness I once enjoyed (though I did not enjoy it half enough) is well worth the occasional stab of regret. Though never any good at sports, I was a normally active child and young adult. I climbed trees, played   5

1. Illustrated manuscript of the four gospels of the New Testament (c. 700 C.E.) done by Irish monks; English commentaries were added in the tenth century.
2. Quotation from "Politics and the English Language" (1946) by George Orwell, British essayist and novelist; see pp. 415–24.

hopscotch, jumped rope, skated, swam, rode my bicycle, sailed. I despised team sports, spending some of the wretchedest afternoons of my life, sweaty and humiliated, behind a field-hockey stick and under a basketball hoop. I tramped alone for miles along the bridle paths that webbed the woods behind the house I grew up in. I swayed through countless dim hours in the arms of one man or another under the scattered shot of light from mirrored balls, and gyrated through countless more as Tab Hunter and Johnny Mathis[3] gave way to the Rolling Stones, Creedence Clearwater Revival, Cream. I walked down the aisle. I pushed baby carriages, changed tires in the rain, marched for peace.

When I was twenty-eight I started to trip and drop things. What at first seemed my natural clumsiness soon became too pronounced to shrug off. I consulted a neurologist, who told me that I had a brain tumor. A battery of tests, increasingly disagreeable, revealed no tumor. About a year and a half later I developed a blurred spot in one eye. I had, at last, the episodes "disseminated in space and time" requisite for a diagnosis: multiple sclerosis. I have never been sorry for the doctor's initial misdiagnosis, however. For almost a week, until the negative results of the tests were in, I thought that I was going to die right away. Every day for the past nearly ten years, then, has been a kind of gift. I accept all gifts.

Multiple sclerosis is a chronic degenerative disease of the central nervous system, in which the myelin that sheathes the nerves is somehow eaten away and scar tissue forms in its place, interrupting the nerves' signals. During its course, which is unpredictable and uncontrollable, one may lose vision, hearing, speech, the ability to walk, control of bladder and/or bowels, strength in any or all extremities, sensitivity to touch, vibration, and/or pain, potency, coordination of movements—the list of possibilities is lengthy and, yes, horrifying. One may also lose one's sense of humor. That's the easiest to lose and the hardest to survive without.

In the past ten years, I have sustained some of these losses. Characteristic of MS are sudden attacks, called exacerbations, followed by remissions, and these I have not had. Instead, my disease has been slowly progressive. My left leg is now so weak that I walk with the aid of a brace and a cane; and for distances I use an Amigo, a variation on the electric wheelchair that looks rather like an electrified kiddie car. I no longer have much use of my left hand. Now my right side is weakening as well. I still have the blurred spot in my right eye. Overall, though, I've been lucky so far. My world has, of necessity, been circumscribed by my losses, but the terrain left me has been ample enough for me to continue many of the activities that absorb me: writing, teaching, raising children and cats and plants and snakes, reading, speaking publicly about MS and depression, even playing bridge with people patient and honorable enough to let me scatter cards every which way without sneaking a peek.

Lest I begin to sound like Pollyanna, however, let me say that I don't like having MS. I hate it. My life holds realities—harsh ones, some of them—that

---

3. Hunter (1931–2018), American actor and singer popular in the 1960s; Mathis (b. 1935), American singer popular in the 1950s and 1960s and well known for his love ballads.

no right-minded human being ought to accept without grumbling. One of them is fatigue. I know of no one with MS who does not complain of bone-weariness; in a disease that presents an astonishing variety of symptoms, fatigue seems to be a common factor. I wake up in the morning feeling the way most people do at the end of a bad day, and I take it from there. As a result, I spend a lot of time *in extremis*[4] and, impatient with limitation, I tend to ignore my fatigue until my body breaks down in some way and forces rest. Then I miss picnics, dinner parties, poetry readings, the brief visits of old friends from out of town. The offspring of a puritanical tradition of exceptional venerability, I cannot view these lapses without shame. My life often seems a series of small failures to do as I ought.

I lead, on the whole, an ordinary life, probably rather like the one I would have led had I not had MS. I am lucky that my predilections were already solitary, sedentary, and bookish—unlike the world-famous French cellist I have read about, or the young woman I talked with one long afternoon who wanted only to be a jockey. I had just begun graduate school when I found out something was wrong with me, and I have remained, interminably, a graduate student. Perhaps I would not have if I'd thought I had the stamina to return to a full-time job as a technical editor; but I've enjoyed my studies.

In addition to studying, I teach writing courses. I also teach medical students how to give neurological examinations. I pick up freelance editing jobs here and there. I have raised a foster son and sent him into the world, where he has made me two grandbabies, and I am still escorting my daughter and son through adolescence. I go to Mass every Saturday. I am a superb, if messy, cook. I am also an enthusiastic laundress, capable of sorting a hamper full of clothes into five subtly differentiated piles, but a terrible housekeeper. I can do italic writing and, in an emergency, bathe an oil-soaked cat. I play a fiendish game of Scrabble. When I have the time and the money, I like to sit on my front steps with my husband, drinking Amaretto and smoking a cigar, as we imagine our counterparts in Leningrad and make sure that the sun gets down once more behind the sharp childish scrawl of the Tucson Mountains.

This lively plenty has its bleak complement, of course, in all the things I can no longer do. I will never run again, except in dreams, and one day I may have to write that I will never walk again. I like to go camping, but I can't follow George and the children along the trails that wander out of a campsite through the desert or into the mountains. In fact, even on the level I've learned never to check the weather or try to hold a coherent conversation: I need all my attention for my wayward feet. Of late, I have begun to catch myself wondering how people can propel themselves without canes. With only one usable hand, I have to select my clothing with care not so much for style as for ease of ingress and egress, and even so, dressing can be laborious. I can no longer do fine stitchery, pick up babies, play the piano, braid my hair. I am immobilized by acute attacks of depression, which may or may not be physiologically related to MS but are certainly its logical concomitant.

10

4. Latin for "in the last straits." Here it means "at the limits of endurance."

These two elements, the plenty and the privation, are never pure, nor are the delight and wretchedness that accompany them. Almost every pickle that I get into as a result of my weakness and clumsiness—and I get into plenty—is funny as well as maddening and sometimes painful. I recall one May afternoon when a friend and I were going out for a drink after finishing up at school. As we were climbing into opposite sides of my car, chatting, I tripped and fell, flat and hard, onto the asphalt parking lot, my abrupt departure interrupting him in mid-sentence. "Where'd you go?" he called as he came around the back of the car to find me hauling myself up by the door frame. "Are you all right?" Yes, I told him, I was fine, just a bit rattly, and we drove off to find a shady patio and some beer. When I got home an hour or so later, my daughter greeted me with "What have you done to yourself?" I looked down. One elbow of my white turtleneck with the green froggies, one knee of my white trousers, one white kneesock were blood-soaked. We peeled off the clothes and inspected the damage, which was nasty enough but not alarming. That part wasn't funny: The abrasions took a long time to heal, and one got a little infected. Even so, when I think of my friend talking earnestly, suddenly, to the hot thin air while I dropped from his view as though through a trap door, I find the image as silly as something from a Marx Brothers movie.

I may find it easier than other cripples to amuse myself because I live propped by the acceptance and the assistance and, sometimes, the amusement of those around me. Grocery clerks tear my checks out of my checkbook for me, and sales clerks find chairs to put into dressing rooms when I want to try on clothes. The people I work with make sure I teach at times when I am least likely to be fatigued, in places I can get to, with the materials I need. My students, with one anonymous exception (in an end-of-the-semester evaluation), have been unperturbed by my disability. Some even like it. One was immensely cheered by the information that I paint my own fingernails; she decided, she told me, that if I could go to such trouble over fine details, she could keep on writing essays. I suppose I became some sort of bright-fingered muse. She wrote good essays, too.

15   The most important struts in the framework of my existence, of course, are my husband and children. Dismayingly few marriages survive the MS test, and why should they? Most twenty-two- and nineteen-year-olds, like George and me, can vow in clear conscience, after a childhood of chicken pox and summer colds, to keep one another in sickness and in health so long as they both shall live. Not many are equipped for catastrophe: the dismay, the depression, the extra work, the boredom that a degenerative disease can insinuate into a relationship. And our society, with its emphasis on fun and its association of fun with physical performance, offers little encouragement for a whole spouse to stay with a crippled partner. Children experience similar stresses when faced with a crippled parent, and they are more helpless, since parents and children can't usually get divorced. They hate, of course, to be different from their peers, and the child whose mother is tacking down the aisle of a school auditorium packed with proud parents like a Cape Cod dinghy in a stiff breeze jolly well stands out in a crowd. Deprived of legal divorce, the child can at least deny the

mother's disability, even her existence, forgetting to tell her about recitals and PTA meetings, refusing to accompany her to stores or church or the movies, never inviting friends to the house. Many do.

But I've been limping along for ten years now, and so far George and the children are still at my left elbow, holding tight. Anne and Matthew vacuum floors and dust furniture and haul trash and rake up dog droppings and button my cuffs and bake lasagna and Toll House cookies with just enough grumbling so I know that they don't have brain fever. And far from hiding me, they're forever dragging me by racks of fancy clothes or through teeming school corridors, or welcoming gaggles of friends while I'm wandering through the house in Anne's filmy pink babydoll pajamas. George generally calls before he brings someone home, but he does just as many dumb thankless chores as the children. And they all yell at me, laugh at some of my jokes, write me funny letters when we're apart—in short, treat me as an ordinary human being for whom they have some use. I think they like me. Unless they're faking. . . .

Faking. There's the rub. Tugging at the fringes of my consciousness always is the terror that people are kind to me only because I'm a cripple. My mother almost shattered me once, with that instinct mothers have—blind, I think, in this case, but unerring nonetheless—for striking blows along the fault-lines of their children's hearts, by telling me, in an attack on my selfishness, "We all have to make allowances for you, of course, because of the way you are." From the distance of a couple of years, I have to admit that I haven't any idea just what she meant, and I'm not sure that she knew either. She was awfully angry. But at the time, as the words thudded home, I felt my worst fear, suddenly realized. I could bear being called selfish: I am. But I couldn't bear the corroboration that those around me were doing in fact what I'd always suspected them of doing, professing fondness while silently putting up with me because of the way I am. A cripple. I've been a little cracked ever since.

Along with this fear that people are secretly accepting shoddy goods comes a relentless pressure to please—to prove myself worth the burdens I impose, I guess, or to build a substantial account of goodwill against which I may write drafts in times of need. Part of the pressure arises from social expectations. In our society, anyone who deviates from the norm had better find some way to compensate. Like fat people, who are expected to be jolly, cripples must bear their lot meekly and cheerfully. A grumpy cripple isn't playing by the rules. And much of the pressure is self-generated. Early on I vowed that, if I had to have MS, by God I was going to do it well. This is a class act, ladies and gentlemen. No tears, no recriminations, no faintheartedness.

One way and another, then, I wind up feeling like Tiny Tim,[5] peering over the edge of the table at the Christmas goose, waving my crutch, piping down God's blessing on us all. Only sometimes I don't want to play Tiny Tim. I'd rather be Caliban,[6] a most scurvy monster. Fortunately, at home no one much

5. Crippled, frail young boy saved by Ebenezer Scrooge's generosity in Charles Dickens's novel *A Christmas Carol* (1843).
6. Son of the witch Sycorax in William Shakespeare's play *The Tempest* (c. 1611).

cares whether I'm a good cripple or a bad cripple as long as I make vichyssoise with fair regularity. One evening several years ago, Anne was reading at the dining-room table while I cooked dinner. As I opened a can of tomatoes, the can slipped in my left hand and juice spattered me and the counter with bloody spots. Fatigued and infuriated, I bellowed, "I'm so sick of being crippled!" Anne glanced at me over the top of her book. "There now," she said, "do you feel better?" "Yes," I said, "yes, I do." She went back to her reading. I felt better. That's about all the attention my scurviness ever gets.

20   Because I hate being crippled, I sometimes hate myself for being a cripple. Over the years I have come to expect—even accept—attacks of violent self-loathing. Luckily, in general our society no longer connects deformity and disease directly with evil (though a charismatic once told me that I have MS because a devil is in me) and so I'm allowed to move largely at will, even among small children. But I'm not sure that this revision of attitude has been particularly helpful. Physical imperfection, even freed of moral disapprobation, still defies and violates the ideal, especially for women, whose confinement in their bodies as objects of desire is far from over. Each age, of course, has its ideal, and I doubt that ours is any better or worse than any other. Today's ideal woman, who lives on the glossy pages of dozens of magazines, seems to be between the ages of eighteen and twenty-five; her hair has body, her teeth flash white, her breath smells minty, her underarms are dry; she has a career but is still a fabulous cook, especially of meals that take less than twenty minutes to prepare; she does not ordinarily appear to have a husband or children; she is trim and deeply tanned; she jogs, swims, plays tennis, rides a bicycle, sails, but does not bowl; she travels widely, even to out-of-the-way places like Finland and Samoa, always in the company of the ideal man, who possesses a nearly identical set of characteristics. There are a few exceptions. Though usually white and often blonde, she may be black, Hispanic, Asian, or Native American, so long as she is unusually sleek. She may be old, provided she is selling a laxative or is Lauren Bacall. If she is selling a detergent, she may be married and have a flock of strikingly messy children. But she is never a cripple.

Like many women I know, I have always had an uneasy relationship with my body. I was not a popular child, largely, I think now, because I was peculiar: intelligent, intense, moody, shy, given to unexpected actions and inexplicable notions and emotions. But as I entered adolescence, I believed myself unpopular because I was homely: my breasts too flat, my mouth too wide, my hips too narrow, my clothing never quite right in fit or style. I was not, in fact, particularly ugly, old photographs inform me, though I was well off the ideal; but I carried this sense of self-alienation with me into adulthood, where it regenerated in response to the depredations of MS. Even with my brace I walk with a limp so pronounced that, seeing myself on the videotape of a television program on the disabled, I couldn't believe that anything but an inchworm could make progress humping along like that. My shoulders droop and my pelvis thrusts forward as I try to balance myself upright, throwing my frame into a bony S. As a result of contractures, one shoulder is higher than the other and I carry one arm bent in front of me, the fingers curled into a claw. My left arm and leg have wasted into pipe-stems, and I try always to keep them covered. When I think about how my body must look to others, especially to men, to whom I have been trained to display myself, I feel ludicrous, even loathsome.

At my age, however, I don't spend much time thinking about my appearance. The burning egocentricity of adolescence, which assures one that all the world is looking all the time, has passed, thank God, and I'm generally too caught up in what I'm doing to step back, as I used to, and watch myself as though upon a stage. I'm also too old to believe in the accuracy of self-image. I know that I'm not a hideous crone, that in fact, when I'm rested, well dressed, and well made up, I look fine. The self-loathing I feel is neither physically nor intellectually substantial. What I hate is not me but a disease.

I am not a disease.

And a disease is not—at least not singlehandedly—going to determine who I am, though at first it seemed to be going to. Adjusting to a chronic incurable illness, I have moved through a process similar to that outlined by Elisabeth Kübler-Ross in *On Death and Dying.*[7] The major difference—and it is far more significant than most people recognize—is that I can't be sure of the outcome, as the terminally ill cancer patient can. Research studies indicate that, with proper medical care, I may achieve a "normal" life span. And in our society, with its vision of death as the ultimate evil, worse even than decrepitude, the response to such news is, "Oh well, at least you're not going to *die.*" Are there worse things than dying? I think that there may be.

I think of two women I know, both with MS, both enough older than I to have served me as models. One took to her bed several years ago and has been there ever since. Although she can sit in a high-backed wheelchair, because she is incontinent she refuses to go out at all, even though incontinence pants, which are readily available at any pharmacy, could protect her from embarrassment. Instead, she stays at home and insists that her husband, a small quiet man, a retired civil servant, stay there with her except for a quick weekly foray to the supermarket. The other woman, whose illness was diagnosed when she was eighteen, a nursing student engaged to a young doctor, finished her training, married her doctor, accompanied him to Germany when he was in the service, bore three sons and a daughter, now grown and gone. When she can, she travels with her husband; she plays bridge, embroiders, swims regularly; she works, like me, as a symptomatic-patient instructor of medical students in neurology. Guess which woman I hope to be.

At the beginning, I thought about having MS almost incessantly. And because of the unpredictable course of the disease, my thoughts were always terrified. Each night I'd get into bed wondering whether I'd get out again the next morning, whether I'd be able to see, to speak, to hold a pen between my fingers. Knowing that the day might come when I'd be physically incapable of killing myself, I thought perhaps I ought to do so right away, while I still had the strength. Gradually I came to understand that the Nancy who might one

25

7. An influential 1969 book by Swiss American psychiatrist Elisabeth Kübler-Ross positing five stages of grief.

day lie inert under a bedsheet, arms and legs paralyzed, unable to feed or bathe herself, unable to reach out for a gun, a bottle of pills, was not the Nancy I was at present, and that I could not presume to make decisions for that future Nancy, who might well not want in the least to die. Now the only provision I've made for the future Nancy is that when the time comes—and it is likely to come in the form of pneumonia, friend to the weak and the old—I am not to be treated with machines and medications. If she is unable to communicate by then, I hope she will be satisfied with these terms.

Thinking all the time about having MS grew tiresome and intrusive, especially in the large and tragic mode in which I was accustomed to considering my plight. Months and even years went by without catastrophe (at least without one related to MS), and really I was awfully busy, what with George and children and snakes and students and poems, and I hadn't the time, let alone the inclination, to devote myself to being a disease. Too, the richer my life became, the funnier it seemed, as though there were some connection between largesse and laughter, and so my tragic stance began to waver until, even with the aid of a brace and a cane, I couldn't hold it for very long at a time.

After several years I was satisfied with my adjustment. I had suffered my grief and fury and terror, I thought, but now I was at ease with my lot. Then one summer day I set out with George and the children across the desert for a vacation in California. Part way to Yuma I became aware that my right leg felt funny. "I think I've had an exacerbation," I told George. "What shall we do?" he asked. "I think we'd better get the hell to California," I said, "because I don't know whether I'll ever make it again." So we went on to San Diego and then to Orange, up the Pacific Coast Highway to Santa Cruz, across to Yosemite, down to Sequoia and Joshua Tree, and so back over the desert to home. It was a fine two-week trip, filled with friends and fair weather, and I wouldn't have missed it for the world, though I did in fact make it back to California two years later. Nor would there have been any point in missing it, since in MS, once the symptoms have appeared, the neurological damage has been done, and there's no way to predict or prevent that damage.

The incident spoiled my self-satisfaction, however. It renewed my grief and fury and terror, and I learned that one never finishes adjusting to MS. I don't know now why I thought one would. One does not, after all, finish adjusting to life, and MS is simply a fact of my life—not my favorite fact, of course—but as ordinary as my nose and my tropical fish and my yellow Mazda station wagon. It may at any time get worse, but no amount of worry or anticipation can prepare me for a new loss. My life is a lesson in losses. I learn one at a time.

30   And I had best be patient in the learning, since I'll have to do it like it or not. As any rock fan knows, you can't always get what you want. Particularly when you have MS. You can't, for example, get cured. In recent years researchers and the organizations that fund research have started to pay MS some attention even though it isn't fatal; perhaps they have begun to see that life is something other than a quantitative phenomenon, that one may be very much alive for a very long time in a life that isn't worth living. The researchers

have made some progress toward understanding the mechanism of the disease: It may well be an autoimmune reaction triggered by a slow-acting virus. But they are nowhere near its prevention, control, or cure. And most of us want to be cured. Some, unable to accept incurability, grasp at one treatment after another, no matter how bizarre: megavitamin therapy, gluten-free diet, injections of cobra venom, hypothermal suits, lymphocytopheresis, hyperbaric chambers. Many treatments are probably harmless enough, but none are curative.

The absence of a cure often makes MS patients bitter toward their doctors. Doctors are, after all, the priests of modern society, the new shamans, whose business is to heal, and many an MS patient roves from one to another, searching for the "good" doctor who will make him well. Doctors too think of themselves as healers, and for this reason many have trouble dealing with MS patients, whose disease in its intransigence defeats their aims and mocks their skills. Too few doctors, it is true, treat their patients as whole human beings, but the reverse is also true. I have always tried to be gentle with my doctors, who often have more at stake in terms of ego than I do. I may be frustrated, maddened, depressed by the incurability of my disease, but I am not diminished by it, and they are. When I push myself up from my seat in the waiting room and stumble toward them, I incarnate the limitation of their powers. The least I can do is refuse to press on their tenderest spots.

This gentleness is part of the reason that I'm not sorry to be a cripple. I didn't have it before. Perhaps I'd have developed it anyway—how could I know such a thing?—and I wish I had more of it, but I'm glad of what I have. It has opened and enriched my life enormously, this sense that my frailty and need must be mirrored in others, that in searching for and shaping a stable core in a life wrenched by change and loss, change and loss, I must recognize the same process, under individual conditions, in the lives around me. I do not deprecate such knowledge, however I've come by it.

All the same, if a cure were found, would I take it? In a minute. I may be a cripple, but I'm only occasionally a loony and never a saint. Anyway, in my brand of theology God doesn't give bonus points for a limp. I'd take a cure; I just don't need one. A friend who also has MS startled me once by asking, "Do you ever say to yourself, 'Why me, Lord?'" "No, Michael, I don't," I told him, "because whenever I try, the only response I can think of is 'Why not?'" If I could make a cosmic deal, who would I put in my place? What in my life would I give up in exchange for sound limbs and a thrilling rush of energy? No one. Nothing. I might as well do the job myself. Now that I'm getting the hang of it.

MLA CITATION

Mairs, Nancy. "On Being a Cripple." *The Norton Reader: An Anthology of Nonfiction*, edited by Melissa A. Goldthwaite et al., 15th ed., W. W. Norton, 2020, pp. 148–57.

QUESTIONS

1. How does Nancy Mairs organize her essay? What connects the different parts to each other?

2. What stereotypes of "disabled" people does Mairs expect us to believe in? How does she set out to counter them?

3. Mairs deliberately chooses to call herself a "cripple." Select a person or group that deliberately chooses its own name or description and explain in an essay the rationale behind the choice.

BARBARA EHRENREICH
Why I'm Giving Up on Preventive Care

IN THE LAST FEW YEARS, I HAVE GIVEN UP on the many medical measures—cancer screenings, annual exams, Pap smears, for example—expected of a responsible person with health insurance. This was not based on any suicidal impulse. It was barely even a decision, more like an accumulation of micro-decisions: to stay at my desk and meet a deadline or show up at the primary care office and submit to the latest test to gauge my biological sustainability; to spend the afternoon in the faux-cozy corporate environment of a medical facility or to go for a walk. At first I criticized myself as a slacker and procrastinator, falling behind on the simple, obvious stuff that could prolong my life. After all, this is the great promise of modern scientific medicine: You do not have to get sick and die (at least not for a while), because problems can be detected "early" when they are readily treatable. Better to catch a tumor when it's the size of an olive than that of a cantaloupe.

I knew I was going against my own long-standing bias in favor of preventive medical care as opposed to expensive and invasive high-tech curative interventions. What could be more ridiculous than an inner-city hospital that offers a hyperbaric chamber but cannot bestir itself to get out in the neighborhood and test for lead poisoning? From a public health perspective, as well as a personal one, it makes far more sense to screen for preventable problems than to invest huge resources in the treatment of the very ill.

I also understood that I was going against the grain for my particular demographic. Most of my educated, middle-class friends had begun to double down on their health-related efforts at the onset of middle age, if not earlier. They undertook exercise or yoga regimens; they filled their calendars with upcoming medical tests and exams; they boasted about their "good" and "bad" cholesterol counts, their heart rates and blood pressure. Mostly they understood the task of aging to be self-denial, especially in the realm of diet, where

Exerpted in Yes! *magazine from Barbara Ehrenreich's book* Natural Causes: An Epidemic of Wellness, the Certainty of Dying, and Killing Ourselves to Live Longer *(2018).*

one medical fad, one study or another, condemned fat and meat, carbs, gluten, dairy, or all animal-derived products. In the health-conscious mind-set that has prevailed among the world's affluent people for about four decades now, health is indistinguishable from virtue, tasty foods are "sinfully delicious," while healthful foods may taste good enough to be advertised as "guilt-free." Those seeking to compensate for a lapse undertake punitive measures like fasts, purges, or diets composed of different juices carefully sequenced throughout the day.

I had a different reaction to aging: I gradually came to realize that I was old enough to die, by which I am not suggesting that each of us bears an expiration date. There is of course no fixed age at which a person ceases to be worthy of further medical investment, whether aimed at prevention or cure. The military judges that a person is old enough to die—to put him or herself in the line of fire—at age 18. At the other end of life, many remain world leaders in their seventies or even older, without anyone questioning their need for lavish continuing testing and care. Zimbabwe's former president, Robert Mugabe, recently turned 90, and has undergone multiple treatments for prostate cancer.

If we go by newspaper obituaries, however, we notice that there is an age at   5
which death no longer requires much explanation. Although there is no general editorial rule on these matters, it is usually sufficient when the deceased is in their 70s or older for the obituary writer to invoke "natural causes." It is sad when anyone dies, but no one can consider the death of a septuagenarian "tragic," and no one will demand an investigation.

Once I realized I was old enough to die, I decided that I was also old enough not to incur any more suffering, annoyance, or boredom in the pursuit of a longer life. I eat well, meaning I choose foods that taste good and that will stave off hunger for as long as possible, like protein, fiber, and fats. I exercise—not because it will make me live longer but because it feels good when I do. As for medical care: I will seek help for an urgent problem, but I am no longer interested in looking for problems that remain undetectable to me. Ideally, the determination of when one is old enough to die should be a personal decision, based on a judgment of the likely benefits, if any, of medical care and—just as important at a certain age—how we choose to spend the time that remains to us.

At the same time, I had always questioned whatever procedures the health care providers recommended; in fact I am part of a generation of women who insisted on their right to raise questions without having the word "uncooperative," or worse, written into their medical records. So when a few years ago my primary care physician told me that I needed a bone density scan, I of course asked him why: What could be done if the result was positive and my bones were found to be hollowed out by age? Fortunately, he replied, there was now a drug for that. I told him I was aware of the drug, both from its full-page magazine ads as well as from articles in the media questioning its safety and efficacy. Think of the alternative, he said, which might well be, say, a hip fracture, followed by a rapid descent to the nursing home.

So I grudgingly conceded that undergoing the test, which is noninvasive and covered by my insurance, might be preferable to immobility and institutionalization. The result was a diagnosis of "osteopenia," or thinning of the bones, a condition that might have been alarming if I hadn't found out that it is shared by nearly all women over the age of 35. Osteopenia is, in other words, not a disease but a normal feature of aging. A little further research, all into readily available sources, revealed that routine bone scanning had been heavily promoted and even subsidized by the drug's manufacturer. Worse, the favored medication at the time of my diagnosis has turned out to cause some of the very problems it was supposed to prevent—bone degeneration and fractures. A cynic might conclude that preventive medicine exists to transform people into raw material for a profit-hungry medical-industrial complex.

My first major defection from the required screening regimen was precipitated by a mammogram. No one likes mammography, which amounts to a brute-force effort to render the breasts transparent. First, a breast is flattened between two plates, then it is bombarded with ionizing radiation, which is, incidentally, the only environmental factor known for sure to cause breast cancer. I'd been fairly dutiful about mammograms since having been treated for breast cancer at the turn of the millennium, and now, about 10 years later, the gynecologist's office reported that I'd had a "bad mammogram." I spent the next few anxious weeks undergoing further tests, in the midst of which I managed to earn a ticket for "distracted driving." Naturally I was distracted— by the looming decision of whether I would undergo debilitating cancer treatments again, or just let the disease take its course this time.

10   It turned out, after I'd been through a sonogram and fought panic in a coffin-like MRI tube, that the "bad mammogram" was a false positive resulting from the highly sensitive new digital forms of imaging. That was my last mammogram. Lest this seem like a reckless decision, I was supported in it by a high-end big-city oncologist, who viewed all my medical images and said that there would be no need to see me again, which I interpreted as ever again.

After this, every medical or dental encounter seemed to end in a tussle. Dentists—and I have met a number of them in my moves around the country— always wanted a fresh set of X-rays, even if the only problem was a chip in the tip of a tooth. All I could think of was the X-ray machines every shoe store had offered in my youth, through which children were encouraged to peer at the bones of their feet while wiggling their toes. The fun ended in the 1970s, when these "fluoroscopes" were eventually banned as dangerous sources of radiation. So why should I routinely expose my mouth, which is much more cancer-prone than the feet, to high annual doses of roentgens? If there was some reason to suspect underlying structural problems, okay, but just to satisfy the dentist's curiosity or meet some abstract "standard of care"—no.

In all these encounters, I was struck by the professionals' dismissal of my subjective reports—usually along the lines of "I feel fine"—in favor of the occult findings of their equipment. One physician, unprompted by any obvious signs or symptoms, decided to measure my lung capacity with the new hand-held instrument he'd acquired for this purpose. I breathed into it, as instructed, as hard as I could, but my breath did not register on his screen. He fiddled with the instrument, looking deeply perturbed, and told me I seemed to be suffering from a pulmonary obstruction. In my defense, I argued that I do at least 30 minutes of aerobic exercise a day, not counting ordinary walking, but I was too polite to demonstrate that I was still capable of vigorous oral argument.

My dentist, oddly enough, suggested, during an ordinary filling, that I be tested for sleep apnea. How a dentist got involved in what is normally the domain of ear, nose, and throat specialists, I do not know, but she recommended that the screening be done at a "sleep center," where I would attempt to sleep while heavily wired to monitoring devices, after which I could buy the treatment from her: a terrifying skull-shaped mask that would supposedly prevent sleep apnea and definitely extinguish any last possibility of sexual activity. But when I protested that there is no evidence I suffer from this disorder—no symptoms or detectable signs—the dentist said that I just might not be aware of it, adding that it could kill me in my sleep. This, I told her, is a prospect I can live with.

As soon as I reached the age of 50, physicians had begun to recommend—and in one case even plead—that I have a colonoscopy. As in the case of mammograms, the pressure to submit to a colonoscopy is hard to avoid. Celebrities promote them, comics snicker about them. During March, which is Colorectal Cancer Awareness Month, an 8-foot-high inflatable replica of a colon tours the country, allowing the anally curious to stroll through and inspect potentially cancerous polyps "from the inside." But if mammography seems like a refined sort of sadism, colonoscopies mimic an actual sexual assault. First the patient is sedated—often with what is popularly known as the "date rape drug," Versed—then a long flexible tube, bearing a camera on one end, is inserted into the rectum and all the way up through the colon. What repelled me even more than this kinky procedure was the day of fasting and laxatives that was supposed to precede it, to ensure that the little camera encounters something other than feces. I put this off from year to year, until I finally felt safe in the knowledge that since colon cancer is usually slow-growing, any cancerous polyps I contain are unlikely to flourish until I am already close to death from other causes.

Then my internist, the chief physician in a midsized group practice, sent out a letter announcing that he was suspending his ordinary practice in order to offer a new level of "concierge care" for those willing to cough up an extra $1,500 a year beyond what they already pay for insurance. The elite care would include 24-hour access to the doctor, leisurely visits, and, the letter promised, all kinds of tests and screenings in addition to the routine ones. This is when my decision crystallized: I made an appointment and told him face-to-face that, one, I was dismayed by his willingness to drop his less-than-affluent patients, who appeared to make up much of the waiting room population. And, two, I didn't want more tests; I wanted a doctor who could protect me from unnecessary procedures. I would remain with the masses of ordinary, haphazardly screened patients.

15

Of course all this unnecessary screening and testing happens because doctors order it, but there is a growing rebellion within the medical profession. Over-diagnosis is beginning to be recognized as a public health problem, and is sometimes referred to as an "epidemic." It is an appropriate subject for international medical conferences and evidence-laden books like *Overdiagnosed: Making People Sick in the Pursuit of Health* by H. Gilbert Welch and his Dartmouth colleagues Lisa Schwartz and Steve Woloshin. Even health columnist Jane Brody, long a cheerleader for standard preventive care, now recommends that we think twice before undergoing what were once routine screening procedures. Physician and blogger John M. Mandrola advises straightforwardly:

> Rather than being fearful of not detecting disease, both patients and doctors should fear health care. The best way to avoid medical errors is to avoid medical care. The default should be: I am well. The way to stay that way is to keep making good choices—not to have my doctor look for problems.

With age, the cost/benefit analysis shifts. On the one hand, health care becomes more affordable—for Americans, anyway—at age 65, when a person is eligible for Medicare. Exhortations to undergo screenings and tests continue, with loved ones joining the chorus. But in my case, the appetite for medical interactions of any kind wanes with each passing week. Suppose that preventive care uncovered some condition that would require agonizing treatments or sacrifices on my part—disfiguring surgery, radiation, drastic lifestyle limitations. Maybe these measures would add years to my life, but it would be a painful and depleted life that they prolonged.

As it is now, preventive medicine often extends to the end of life: 75-year-olds are encouraged to undergo mammography; people already in the grip of one terminal disease may be subjected to screenings for others. At a medical meeting, someone reported that a 100-year-old woman had just had her first mammogram, causing the audience to break into a "loud cheer."

20   One reason for the compulsive urge to test and screen and monitor is profit, and this is especially true in the United States, with its heavily private and often for-profit health system. How is a doctor—or hospital or drug company—to make money from essentially healthy patients? By subjecting them to tests and examinations that, in sufficient quantity, are bound to detect something wrong or at least worthy of follow-up. Gilbert and his coauthors offer a vivid analogy, borrowed from an expert in fractal geometry: "How many islands surround Britain's coasts?" The answer of course depends on the resolution of the map you are using, as well as how you are defining an "island." With high-resolution technologies like CT scans, the detection of tiny abnormalities is almost inevitable, leading to ever more tests, prescriptions, and doctor visits. And the tendency to over-test is amplified when the doctor who recommends the tests has a financial interest in the screening or imaging facility that he or she refers people to.

It's not only a profit-hungry medical system that drives over-testing and over-diagnosis. Individual consumers, that is, former and potential patients, may demand the testing and even threaten a malpractice suit if they feel it is being withheld. In the last couple of decades, "patient advocacy" groups have sprung up to "brand" dozens of diseases and publicize the need for screening. Many have their own celebrity spokespersons—Katie Couric for colorectal cancer, Rudy Giuliani for prostate cancer[1]—and each sports its own distinctive colored ribbon—pink for breast cancer, purple for testicular cancer, black for melanoma, a "puzzle pattern" for autism, and so on—as well as special days or months for concentrated publicity and lobbying efforts. The goal of all this is generally "awareness," meaning a willingness to undergo the appropriate screening, such as mammograms and PSA tests.

There are even sizable constituencies for discredited tests. When the U.S. Preventive Services Task Force[2] decided to withdraw its recommendation of routine mammograms for women under 50, even some feminist women's health organizations, which I had expected to be more critical of conventional medical practices, spoke out in protest. A small band of women, identifying themselves as survivors of breast cancer, demonstrated on a highway outside the task force's office, as if demanding that their breasts be squeezed. In 2008, the same task force gave PSA testing a grade of "D," but advocates like Giuliani, who insisted that the test had saved his life, continued to press for it, as do most physicians.

Many physicians justify tests of dubious value by the "peace of mind" they supposedly confer—except of course on those who receive false positive results. Thyroid cancer is particularly vulnerable to over-diagnosis. With the introduction of more high-powered imaging techniques, doctors were able to detect many more tiny lumps in people's necks and surgically remove them, whether surgery was warranted or not. An estimated 70 to 80 percent of thyroid cancer surgeries performed on U.S., French, and Italian women in the first decade of the 21st century are now judged to have been unnecessary. In South Korea, where doctors were especially conscientious about thyroid screening, the number rose to 90 percent. (Men were also over-diagnosed, but in far lower numbers.) Patients pay a price for these surgeries, including a lifelong dependence on thyroid hormones, and since these are not always fully effective, the patient may be left chronically "depressed and sluggish."

So far I can detect no stirrings of popular revolt against the regime of unnecessary and often harmful medical screening. Hardly anyone admits to personally rejecting tests, and one who did—science writer John Horgan in a Scientific American[3] blog on why he will not undergo a colonoscopy—somewhat undercut his well-reasoned argument by describing himself as an "anti-testing nut." Most people joke about the distastefulness of the recommended procedures, while gamely submitting to whatever is expected of them.

1. Katie Couric (b. 1957), American television news anchor and author; Rudolph Giuliani (b. 1944), mayor of New York City (1994–2001), who in 2018 became a personal attorney for U.S. President Donald J. Trump.

2. Panel of volunteer medical experts that rates the effectiveness of preventive care procedures and advises the U.S. Congress on research priorities in preventive medicine.

3. Popular magazine for a general audience about all aspects of science.

But there's a significant rebellion brewing on another front. Increasingly, we read laments about the "medicalization of dying," usually focused on a formerly frisky parent or grandparent who had made clear her request for a natural, nonmedical death, only to end up tethered by cables and tubes to an ICU bed. Physicians see this all the time—witty people silenced by ventilators, the fastidious rendered incontinent—and some are determined not to let the same thing happen to themselves. They may refuse care, knowing that it is more likely to lead to disability than health, like the orthopedist who upon receiving a diagnosis of pancreatic cancer immediately closed down his practice and went home to die in relative comfort and peace. A few physicians are more decisively proactive, and have themselves tattooed "NO CODE" or "DNR," meaning "do not resuscitate." They reject the same drastic end-of-life measures that they routinely inflict on their patients.

25   In giving up on preventive care, I'm just taking this line of thinking a step further: Not only do I reject the torment of a medicalized death, but I refuse to accept a medicalized life, and my determination only deepens with age. As the time that remains to me shrinks, each month and day becomes too precious to spend in windowless waiting rooms and under the cold scrutiny of machines. Being old enough to die is an achievement, not a defeat, and the freedom it brings is worth celebrating.

MLA CITATION

Ehrenreich, Barbara. "Why I'm Giving Up on Preventive Care." *The Norton Reader: An Anthology of Nonfiction*, edited by Melissa A. Goldthwaite et al., 15th ed., W. W. Norton, 2020, pp. 158–64.

QUESTIONS

1. Barbara Ehrenreich rejects a piece of conventional wisdom: that "responsible" people, especially as they age, should receive regular "preventive care," or medical procedures intended not to treat disease but to catch and prevent it (paragraph 1). What arguments does she make against preventive care? Do you find any of them more persuasive than others? If so, why?

2. What is Ehrenreich's attitude toward aging? How does this attitude inform her argument against preventive care?

3. Consider Ehrenreich's examples. Is she fair to the health care industry? Why or why not?

4. Like Ehrenreich, Roxane Gay in her essay "What Fullness Is" writes about her medical treatments, in Gay's case, her weight-loss surgery (pp. 136–44). Compare Ehrenreich's and Gay's perceptions of their bodies. How are they similar? different? What might these writers say to one another in a conversation?

5. Using Ehrenreich's contrarian essay as a model, write an essay that questions a widely held value, belief, or assumption.

JAMES BALDWIN
Stranger in the Village

F ROM ALL AVAILABLE EVIDENCE no black man had ever set foot in this tiny Swiss village before I came. I was told before arriving that I would probably be a "sight" for the village; I took this to mean that people of my complexion were rarely seen in Switzerland, and also that city people are always something of a "sight" outside of the city. It did not occur to me—possibly because I am an American—that there could be people anywhere who had never seen a Negro.

It is a fact that cannot be explained on the basis of the inaccessibility of the village. The village is very high, but it is only four hours from Milan and three hours from Lausanne. It is true that it is virtually unknown. Few people making plans for a holiday would elect to come here. On the other hand, the villagers are able, presumably, to come and go as they please—which they do: to another town at the foot of the mountain, with a population of approximately five thousand, the nearest place to see a movie or go to the bank. In the village there is no movie house, no bank, no library, no theater; very few radios, one jeep, one station wagon; and at the moment, one typewriter, mine, an invention which the woman next door to me here had never seen. There are about six hundred people living here, all Catholic—I conclude this from the fact that the Catholic church is open all year round, whereas the Protestant chapel, set off on a hill a little removed from the village, is open only in the summertime when the tourists arrive. There are four or five hotels, all closed now, and four or five *bistros,* of which, however, only two do any business during the winter. These two do not do a great deal, for life in the village seems to end around nine or ten o'clock. There are a few stores, butcher, baker, *épicerie,*[1] a hardware store, and a money-changer—who cannot change travelers' checks, but must send them down to the bank, an operation which takes two or three days. There is something called the *Ballet Haus,* closed in the winter and used for God knows what, certainly not ballet, during the summer. There seems to be only one schoolhouse in the village, and this for the quite young children; I suppose this to mean that their older brothers and sisters at some point descend from these mountains in order to complete their education—possibly, again, to the town just below. The landscape is absolutely forbidding, mountains towering on all four sides, ice and snow as far as the eye can reach. In this white wilderness, men and women and children move all day, carrying washing, wood, buckets of milk or water, sometimes skiing on Sunday afternoons. All week long

First published in Harper's Magazine *(1953) and then included in* Notes of a Native Son *(1955), James Baldwin's collection of essays that describes and analyzes the experience of being black in America and Europe.*

1. French for "grocery shop."

boys and young men are to be seen shoveling snow off the rooftops, or drag-ging wood down from the forest in sleds.

The village's only real attraction, which explains the tourist season, is the hot spring water. A disquietingly high proportion of these tourists are cripples, or semi-cripples, who come year after year—from other parts of Switzerland, usually—to take the waters. This lends the village, at the height of the season, a rather terrifying air of sanctity, as though it were a lesser Lourdes.[2] There is often something beautiful, there is always something awful, in the spectacle of a person who has lost one of his faculties, a faculty he never questioned until it was gone, and who struggles to recover it. Yet people remain people, on crutches or indeed on deathbeds; and wherever I passed, the first summer I was here, among the native villagers or among the lame, a wind passed with me—of astonishment, curiosity, amusement, and outrage. That first summer I stayed two weeks and never intended to return. But I did return in the winter, to work; the village offers, obviously, no distractions whatever and has the fur-ther advantage of being extremely cheap. Now it is winter again, a year later, and I am here again. Everyone in the village knows my name, though they scarcely ever use it, knows that I come from America—though, this, apparently, they will never really believe: black men come from Africa—and everyone knows that I am the friend of the son of a woman who was born here, and that I am staying in their chalet. But I remain as much a stranger today as I was the first day I arrived, and the children shout *Neger! Neger!* as I walk along the streets.

It must be admitted that in the beginning I was far too shocked to have any real reaction. In so far as I reacted at all, I reacted by trying to be pleasant—it being a great part of the American Negro's education (long before he goes to school) that he must make people "like" him. This smile-and-the-world-smiles-with-you routine worked about as well in this situation as it had in the situa-tion for which it was designed, which is to say that it did not work at all. No one, after all, can be liked whose human weight and complexity cannot be, or has not been, admitted. My smile was simply another unheard-of phenomenon which allowed them to see my teeth—they did not, really, see my smile and I began to think that, should I take to snarling, no one would notice any differ-ence. All of the physical characteristics of the Negro which had caused me, in America, a very different and almost forgotten pain were nothing less than miraculous—or infernal—in the eyes of the village people. Some thought my hair was the color of tar, that it had the texture of wire, or the texture of cotton. It was jocularly suggested that I might let it all grow long and make myself a winter coat. If I sat in the sun for more than five minutes some daring creature was certain to come along and gingerly put his fingers on my hair, as though he were afraid of an electric shock, or put his hand on my hand, astonished that the color did not rub off. In all of this, in which it must be conceded there was the charm of genuine wonder and in which there was certainly no ele-ment of intentional unkindness, there was yet no suggestion that I was human: I was simply a living wonder.

2. Site of visions of the Virgin Mary and now a prominent pilgrimage destination.

I knew that they did not mean to be unkind, and I know it now; it is neces- 5
sary, nevertheless, for me to repeat this to myself each time that I walk out of
the chalet. The children who shout *Neger!* have no way of knowing the echoes
this sound raises in me. They are brimming with good humor and the more
daring swell with pride when I stop to speak with them. Just the same, there
are days when I cannot pause and smile, when I have no heart to play with
them; when, indeed, I mutter sourly to myself, exactly as I muttered on the
streets of a city these children have never seen, when I was no bigger than these
children are now: *Your* mother *was a nigger.* Joyce is right about history being
a nightmare[3]—but it may be the nightmare from which no one *can* awaken.
People are trapped in history and history is trapped in them.

There is a custom in the village—I am told it is repeated in many villages—
of "buying" African natives for the purpose of converting them to Christianity.
There stands in the church all year round a small box with a slot for money,
decorated with a black figurine, and into this box the villagers drop their
francs. During the *carnaval* which precedes Lent, two village children have
their faces blackened—out of which bloodless darkness their blue eyes shine
like ice—and fantastic horsehair wigs are placed on their blond heads; thus
disguised, they solicit among the villagers for money for the missionaries in
Africa. Between the box in the church and the blackened children, the village
"bought" last year six or eight African natives. This was reported to me with
pride by the wife of one of the *bistro* owners and I was careful to express astonishment and pleasure at the solicitude shown by the village for the souls of
black folks. The *bistro* owner's wife beamed with a pleasure far more genuine
than my own and seemed to feel that I might now breathe more easily concerning the souls of at least six of my kinsmen.

I tried not to think of these so lately baptized kinsmen, of the price paid
for them, or the peculiar price they themselves would pay, and said nothing
about my father, who having taken his own conversion too literally never, at
bottom, forgave the white world (which he described as heathen) for having
saddled him with a Christ in whom, to judge at least from their treatment of
him, they themselves no longer believed. I thought of white men arriving for
the first time in an African village, strangers there, as I am a stranger here,
and tried to imagine the astounded populace touching their hair and marvel-
ing at the color of their skin. But there is a great difference between being
the first white man to be seen by Africans and being the first black man to be
seen by whites. The white man takes the astonishment as tribute, for he
arrives to conquer and to convert the natives, whose inferiority in relation to
himself is not even to be questioned; whereas I, without a thought of conquest, find myself among a people whose culture controls me, has even, in a
sense, created me, people who have cost me more in anguish and rage than
they will ever know, who yet do not even know of my existence. The astonishment with which I might have greeted them, should they have stumbled

3. James Joyce (1882–1941), Irish novelist; Stephen Dedalus, a character in Joyce's
novel *Ulysses*, says, "History is a nightmare from which I am trying to escape."

into my African village a few hundred years ago, might have rejoiced their hearts. But the astonishment with which they greet me today can only poison mine.

And this is so despite everything I may do to feel differently, despite my friendly conversations with the *bistro* owner's wife, despite their three-year-old son who has at last become my friend, despite the *saluts* and *bonsoirs*[4] which I exchange with people as I walk, despite the fact that I know that no individual can be taken to task for what history is doing, or has done. I say that the culture of these people controls me—but they can scarcely be held responsible for European culture. America comes out of Europe, but these people have never seen America, nor have most of them seen more of Europe than the hamlet at the foot of their mountain. Yet they move with an authority which I shall never have; and they regard me, quite rightly, not only as a stranger in their village but as a suspect latecomer, bearing no credentials, to everything they have—however unconsciously—inherited.

For this village, even were it incomparably more remote and incredibly more primitive, is the West, the West onto which I have been so strangely grafted. These people cannot be, from the point of view of power, strangers anywhere in the world; they have made the modern world, in effect, even if they do not know it. The most illiterate among them is related, in a way that I am not, to Dante, Shakespeare, Michelangelo, Aeschylus, Da Vinci, Rembrandt, and Racine; the cathedral at Chartres says something to them which it cannot say to me, as indeed would New York's Empire State Building, should anyone here ever see it. Out of their hymns and dances come Beethoven and Bach. Go back a few centuries and they are in their full glory—but I am in Africa, watching the conquerors arrive.

10 The rage of the disesteemed is personally fruitless, but it is also absolutely inevitable; this rage, so generally discounted, so little understood even among the people whose daily bread it is, is one of the things that makes history. Rage can only with difficulty, and never entirely, be brought under the domination of the intelligence and is therefore not susceptible to any arguments whatever. This is a fact which ordinary representatives of the *Herrenvolk*,[5] having never felt this rage and being unable to imagine, quite fail to understand. Also, rage cannot be hidden, it can only be dissembled. This dissembling deludes the thoughtless, and strengthens rage and adds, to rage, contempt. There are, no doubt, as many ways of coping with the resulting complex of tensions as there are black men in the world, but no black man can hope ever to be entirely liberated from this internal warfare—rage, dissembling, and contempt having inevitably accompanied his first realization of the power of white men. What is crucial here is that, since white men represent in the black man's world so heavy a weight, white men have for black men a reality which is far from being reciprocal; and hence all black men have toward all white men an attitude which is

4. French for "hellos" and "good evenings."
5. German for "master race."

designed, really, either to rob the white man of the jewel of his naïveté, or else to make it cost him dear.

The black man insists, by whatever means he finds at his disposal, that the white man cease to regard him as an exotic rarity and recognize him as a human being. This is a very charged and difficult moment, for there is a great deal of will power involved in the white man's naïveté. Most people are not naturally reflective any more than they are naturally malicious, and the white man prefers to keep the black man at a certain human remove because it is easier for him thus to preserve his simplicity and avoid being called to account for crimes committed by his forefathers, or his neighbors. He is inescapably aware, nevertheless, that he is in a better position in the world than black men are, nor can he quite put to death the suspicion that he is hated by black men therefore. He does not wish to be hated, neither does he wish to change places, and at this point in his uneasiness he can scarcely avoid having recourse to those legends which white men have created about black men, the most usual effect of which is that the white man finds himself enmeshed, so to speak, in his own language which describes hell, as well as the attributes which lead one to hell, as being as black as night.

Every legend, moreover, contains its residuum of truth, and the root function of language is to control the universe by describing it. It is of quite considerable significance that black men remain, in the imagination, and in overwhelming numbers in fact, beyond the disciplines of salvation; and this despite the fact that the West has been "buying" African natives for centuries. There is, I should hazard, an instantaneous necessity to be divorced from this so visibly unsaved stranger, in whose heart, moreover, one cannot guess what dreams of vengeance are being nourished; and, at the same time, there are few things on earth more attractive than the idea of the unspeakable liberty which is allowed the unredeemed. When, beneath the black mask, a human being begins to make himself felt one cannot escape a certain awful wonder as to what kind of human being it is. What one's imagination makes of other people is dictated, of course, by the laws of one's own personality and it is one of the ironies of black-white relations that, by means of what the white man imagines the black man to be, the black man is enabled to know who the white man is.

I have said, for example, that I am as much a stranger in this village today as I was the first summer I arrived, but this is not quite true. The villagers wonder less about the texture of my hair than they did then, and wonder rather more about me. And the fact that their wonder now exists on another level is reflected in their attitudes and in their eyes. There are the children who make those delightful, hilarious, sometimes astonishingly grave overtures of friendship in the unpredictable fashion of children; other children, having been taught that the devil is a black man, scream in genuine anguish as I approach. Some of the older women never pass without a friendly greeting, never pass, indeed, if it seems that they will be able to engage me in conversation; other women look down or look away or rather contemptuously smirk. Some of the men drink with me and suggest that I learn how to ski—partly, I gather, because they cannot imagine what I would look like on skis—and want to know if I am married, and ask questions about my *métier*.[6] But some of the men have accused *le sale nègre*[7]—behind my back—of stealing wood and there is already in the eyes of some of them that peculiar, intent, paranoiac malevolence which one sometimes surprises in the eyes of American white men when, out walking with their Sunday girl, they see a Negro male approach.

There is a dreadful abyss between the streets of this village and the streets of the city in which I was born, between the children who shout *Neger!* today and those who shouted *Nigger!* yesterday—the abyss is experience, the American experience. The syllable hurled behind me today expresses, above all, wonder: I am a stranger here. But I am not a stranger in America and the same syllable riding on the American air expresses the war my presence has occasioned in the American soul.

15   For this village brings home to me this fact: that there was a day, and not really a very distant day, when Americans were scarcely Americans at all but discontented Europeans, facing a great unconquered continent and strolling, say, into a marketplace and seeing black men for the first time. The shock this spectacle afforded is suggested, surely, by the promptness with which they decided that these black men were not really men but cattle. It is true that the necessity on the part of the settlers of the New World of reconciling their moral assumptions with the fact—and the necessity—of slavery enhanced immensely the charm of this idea, and it is also true that this idea expresses, with a truly American bluntness, the attitude which to varying extents all masters have had toward all slaves.

But between all former slaves and slave-owners and the drama which begins for Americans over three hundred years ago at Jamestown,[8] there are at least two differences to be observed. The American Negro slave could not suppose, for one thing, as slaves in past epochs had supposed and often done, that he would ever be able to wrest the power from his master's hands. This was a supposition which the modern era, which was to bring about such vast changes in the aims and dimensions of power, put to death; it only begins, in unprecedented fashion, and with dreadful implications, to be resurrected today. But even had this supposition persisted with undiminished force, the American Negro slave could not have used it to lend his condition dignity, for the reason that this supposition rests on another: that the slave in exile yet remains related to his past, has some means—if only in memory—of revering and sustaining the forms of his former life, is able, in short, to maintain his identity.

This was not the case with the American Negro slave. He is unique among the black men of the world in that his past was taken from him, almost literally, at one blow. One wonders what on earth the first slave found to say to the first dark child he bore. I am told that there are Haitians able to trace their ancestry back to African kings, but any American Negro wishing to go back so far will find his journey through time abruptly arrested by the signature on the

6. French for "occupation" or "profession."
7. French for "the dirty Negro."
8. Founded in 1607, the first lasting English settlement in North America.

bill of sale which served as the entrance paper for his ancestor. At the time—to say nothing of the circumstances—of the enslavement of the captive black man who was to become the American Negro, there was not the remotest possibility that he would ever take power from his master's hands. There was no reason to suppose that his situation would ever change, nor was there, shortly, anything to indicate that his situation had ever been different. It was his necessity, in the words of E. Franklin Frazier,[9] to find a "motive for living under American culture or die." The identity of the American Negro comes out of this extreme situation, and the evolution of this identity was a source of the most intolerable anxiety in the minds and the lives of his masters.

For the history of the American Negro is unique also in this: that the question of his humanity, and of his rights therefore as a human being, became a burning one for several generations of Americans, so burning a question that it ultimately became one of those used to divide the nation. It is out of this argument that the venom of the epithet *Nigger!* is derived. It is an argument which Europe has never had, and hence Europe quite sincerely fails to understand how or why the argument arose in the first place, why its effects are frequently disastrous and always so unpredictable, why it refuses until today to be entirely settled. Europe's black possessions remained—and do remain—in Europe's colonies, at which remove they represented no threat whatever to European identity. If they posed any problem at all for the European conscience it was a problem which remained comfortingly abstract: in effect, the black man, as a *man* did not exist for Europe. But in America, even as a slave, he was an inescapable part of the general social fabric and no American could escape having an attitude toward him. Americans attempt until today to make an abstraction of the Negro, but the very nature of these abstractions reveals the tremendous effects the presence of the Negro has had on the American character.

When one considers the history of the Negro in America it is of the greatest importance to recognize that the moral beliefs of a person, or a people, are never really as tenuous as life—which is not moral—very often causes them to appear; these create for them a frame of reference and a necessary hope, the hope being that when life has done its worst they will be enabled to rise above themselves and to triumph over life. Life would scarcely be bearable if this hope did not exist. Again, even when the worst has been said, to betray a belief is not by any means to have put oneself beyond its power; the betrayal of a belief is not the same thing as ceasing to believe. If this were not so there would be no moral standards in the world at all. Yet one must also recognize that morality is based on ideas and that all ideas are dangerous—dangerous because ideas can only lead to action and where the action leads no man can say. And dangerous in this respect: that confronted with the impossibility of remaining faithful to one's beliefs, and the equal impossibility of becoming free of them, one can be driven to the most inhuman excesses. The ideas on which American beliefs are based are not, though Americans often seem to think so,

9. African American sociologist (1894–1962).

ideas which originated in America. They came out of Europe. And the establishment of democracy on the American continent was scarcely as radical a
break with the past as was the necessity, which Americans faced, of broaden-
ing this concept to include black men.

20   This was, literally, a hard necessity. It was impossible, for one thing, for
Americans to abandon their beliefs, not only because these beliefs alone seemed
able to justify the sacrifices they had endured and the blood that they had spilled,
but also because these beliefs afforded them their only bulwark against a moral
chaos as absolute as the physical chaos of the continent it was their destiny to
conquer. But in the situation in which Americans found themselves, these beliefs
threatened an idea which, whether or not one likes to think so, is the very warp
and woof of the heritage of the West, the idea of white supremacy.

Americans have made themselves notorious by the shrillness and the brutality with which they have insisted on this idea, but they did not invent it; and
it has escaped the world's notice that those very excesses of which Americans
have been guilty imply a certain, unprecedented uneasiness over the idea's life
and power, if not, indeed, the idea's validity. The idea of white supremacy rests
simply on the fact that white men are the creators of civilization (the present
civilization, which is the only one that matters; all previous civilizations are simply "contributions" to our own) and are therefore civilization's guardians and
defenders. Thus it was impossible for Americans to accept the black man as one
of themselves, for to do so was to jeopardize their status as white men. But not
so to accept him was to deny his human reality, his human weight and complexity, and the strain of denying the overwhelmingly undeniable forced Americans
into rationalizations so fantastic that they approached the pathological.

At the root of the American Negro problem is the necessity of the American white man to find a way of living with the Negro in order to be able to live
with himself. And the history of this problem can be reduced to the means used
by Americans—lynch law and law, segregation and legal acceptance, terrorization and concession—either to come to terms with this necessity, or to find a
way around it, or (most usually) to find a way of doing both these things at once.
The resulting spectacle, at once foolish and dreadful, led someone to make the
quite accurate observation that "the Negro-in-America is a form of insanity
which overtakes white men."

In this long battle, a battle by no means finished, the unforeseeable effects
of which will be felt by many future generations, the white man's motive was the
protection of his identity; the black man was motivated by the need to establish an
identity. And despite the terrorization which the Negro in America endured
and endures sporadically until today, despite the cruel and totally inescapable
ambivalence of his status in his country, the battle for his identity has long ago
been won. He is not a visitor to the West, but a citizen there, an American; as
American as the Americans who despise him, the Americans who fear him,
the Americans who love him—the Americans who became less than themselves, or rose to be greater than themselves by virtue of the fact that the challenge he represented was inescapable. He is perhaps the only black man in the
world whose relationship to white men is more terrible, more subtle, and more
meaningful than the relationship of bitter possessed to uncertain possessors.

His survival depended, and his development depends, on his ability to turn his peculiar status in the Western world to his own advantage and, it may be, to the very great advantage of that world. It remains for him to fashion out of his experience that which will give him sustenance, and a voice.

The cathedral at Chartres, I have said, says something to the people of this village which it cannot say to me; but it is important to understand that this cathedral says something to me which it cannot say to them. Perhaps they are struck by the power of the spires, the glory of the windows; but they have known God, after all, longer than I have known him, and in a different way, and I am terrified by the slippery bottomless well to be found in the crypt, down which heretics were hurled to death, and by the obscene, inescapable gargoyles jutting out of the stone and seeming to say that God and the devil can never be divorced. I doubt that the villagers think of the devil when they face a cathedral because they have never been identified with the devil. But I must accept the status which myth, if nothing else, gives me in the West before I can hope to change the myth.

Yet, if the American Negro has arrived at his identity by virtue of the abso- 25 luteness of his estrangement from his past, American white men still nourish the illusion that there is some means of recovering the European innocence, of returning to a state in which black men do not exist. This is one of the greatest errors Americans can make. The identity they fought so hard to protect has, by virtue of that battle, undergone a change: Americans are as unlike any other white people in the world as it is possible to be. I do not think, for example, that it is too much to suggest that the American vision of the world—which allows so little reality, generally speaking, for any of the darker forces in human life, which tends until today to paint moral issues in glaring black and white— owes a great deal to the battle waged by Americans to maintain between themselves and black men a human separation which could not be bridged. It is only now beginning to be borne in on us—very faintly, it must be admitted, very slowly, and very much against our will—that this vision of the world is dangerously inaccurate, and perfectly useless. For it protects our moral high-mindedness at the terrible expense of weakening our grasp of reality. People who shut their eyes to reality simply invite their own destruction, and anyone who insists on remaining in a state of innocence long after that innocence is dead turns himself into a monster.

The time has come to realize that the interracial drama acted out on the American continent has not only created a new black man, it has created a new white man, too. No road whatever will lead Americans back to the simplicity of this European village where white men still have the luxury of looking on me as a stranger. I am not, really, a stranger any longer for any American alive. One of the things that distinguishes Americans from other people is that no other people has ever been so deeply involved in the lives of black men, and vice versa. This fact faced, with all its implications, it can be seen that the history of the American Negro problem is not merely shameful, it is also something of an achievement. For even when the worst has been said, it must also be added that the perpetual challenge posed by this problem was always, somehow, perpetually met. It is precisely this black-white experience which may prove of indispensable value to us in the world we face today. This world is white no longer, and it will never be white again.

MLA CITATION

Baldwin, James. "Stranger in the Village." *The Norton Reader: An Anthology of Nonfiction*, edited by Melissa A. Goldthwaite et al., 15th ed., W. W. Norton, 2020, pp. 165–74.

QUESTIONS

1. James Baldwin was an American, but he lived for many years in France. Consider the role of geography in this essay. How does Baldwin use his experience in the Swiss village to comment on America?

2. Trace the use of the word "stranger" over the course of the essay. How does Baldwin's use of the word evolve as the essay develops?

3. Baldwin relates the white man's language and legends about black men to the "laws" of the white man's personality. What conviction about the source and the nature of language does this essay suggest?

4. Describe some particular experience that raises a large social question or shows the workings of large social forces. How might Baldwin help in the problem of connecting the particular and the general?

5. Baldwin writes, "There is a dreadful abyss between the streets of this village and the streets of the city in which I was born, between the children who shout *Neger!* today and those who shouted *Nigger!* yesterday—the abyss is experience, the American experience" (paragraph 14). There is no word in contemporary American public discourse that is more fraught than the "N-word." Write an essay that explores the contemporary news media's handling of this word. Focus your essay by analyzing one or more specific examples.

TEJU COLE

Black Body

T HEN THE BUS began driving into clouds, and between one cloud and the next we caught glimpses of the town below. It was suppertime and the town was a constellation of yellow points. We arrived thirty minutes after leaving that town, which was called Leuk. The train to Leuk had come in from Visp, the train from Visp had come from Bern, and the train before that was from Zürich, from which I had started out in the afternoon. Three trains, a bus, and

First published in the New Yorker *(2014) as "Black Body: Rereading James Baldwin's 'Stranger in the Village.'" Reprinted in Cole's collection* Known and Strange Things *(2016).*

a short stroll, all of it through beautiful country, and then we reached Leuk-erbad[1] in darkness. So Leukerbad, not far in terms of absolute distance, was not all that easy to get to. August 2, 2014: it was James Baldwin's birthday. Were he alive, he would be turning ninety. He is one of those people just on the cusp of escaping the contemporary and slipping into the historical—John Coltrane would have turned eighty-eight in the same year; Martin Luther King, Jr., would have turned eighty-five—people who could still be with us but who feel, at times, very far away, as though they lived centuries ago.[2]

James Baldwin left Paris and came to Leukerbad for the first time in 1951. His lover Lucien Happersberger's family had a chalet in a village up in the mountains. And so Baldwin, who was depressed and distracted at the time, went, and the village (which is also called Loèche-les-Bains) proved to be a refuge for him. His first trip was in the summer, and lasted two weeks. Then he returned, to his own surprise, for two more winters. His first novel, *Go Tell It on the Mountain*, found its final form here. He had struggled with the book for eight years, and he finally finished it in this unlikely retreat. He wrote something else, too, an essay called "Stranger in the Village"; it was this essay, even more than the novel, that brought me to Leukerbad.

"Stranger in the Village" first appeared in *Harper's Magazine* in 1953, and then in the essay collection *Notes of a Native Son* in 1955. It recounts the expe-rience of being black in an all-white village. It begins with a sense of an extreme journey, like Charles Darwin's in the Galápagos or Tété-Michel Kpomassie's in Greenland.[3] But then it opens out into other concerns and into a different voice, swiveling to look at the American racial situation in the 1950s. The part of the essay that focuses on the Swiss village is both bemused and sorrowful. Baldwin is alert to the absurdity of being a writer from New York who is consid-ered in some way inferior by Swiss villagers, many of whom have never traveled. But, later in the essay, when he writes about race in America, he is not at all bemused. He is angry and prophetic, writing with a hard clarity and carried along by a precipitous eloquence.

I took a room at the Hotel Mercure Bristol the night I arrived. I opened the windows to a dark view in which nothing was visible, but I knew that in the darkness loomed the Daubenhorn mountain. I ran a hot bath and lay neck-deep in the water with my old paperback copy of *Notes of a Native Son*. The tinny sound from my laptop was Bessie Smith singing "I'm Wild About That Thing," a filthy blues number and a masterpiece of plausible deniability: "Don't hold it, baby, when I cry / Give me every bit of it, else I'll die." She could be sing-ing about a trombone. And it was there in the bath, with his words and her

---

1. Swiss town about which James Baldwin writes in "Stranger in the Village."
2. John Coltrane (1926–1967), American jazz saxophonist; Martin Luther King Jr. (1929–1968), American civil rights leader.
3. The English naturalist Charles Darwin (1809–1882) visited the Galápagos Islands during the second expeditionary voyage of the HMS *Beagle* (1831–1836); born in Togo, Tété-Michel Kpomassie (b. 1941) spent more than a decade working his way from Africa, through Europe, to Greenland.

voice, that I had my body-double moment: here I was in Leukerbad, with Bessie Smith singing across the years from 1929; and I am black like him; and I am slender; and have a gap in my front teeth; and am not especially tall (no, write it: short); and am cool on the page and animated in person, except when it is the other way around; and I was once a fervid teenage preacher (Baldwin: "Nothing that has happened to me since equals the power and the glory that I sometimes felt when, in the middle of a sermon, I knew that I was somehow, by some miracle, really carrying, as they said, 'the Word'—when the church and I were one"); and I, too, left the church; and I call New York home even when not living there; and feel myself in all places, from New York City to rural Switzerland, the custodian of a black body, and have to find the language for all of what that means to me and to the people who look at me. The ancestor had briefly taken possession of the descendant. It was a moment of identification. In that Swiss village in the days that followed, that moment guided me.

5   "From all available evidence no black man had ever set foot in this tiny Swiss village before I came," Baldwin wrote. But the village has grown considerably since his visits, more than sixty years ago. They've seen blacks now; I wasn't a remarkable sight. There were a few glances at the hotel when I was checking in, and in the fine restaurant just up the road; there are always glances. There are glances in Zürich, where I spent the summer, and there are glances in New York City, which has been my home for fourteen years. There are glances all over Europe and in India, and anywhere I go outside Africa. The test is how long the glances last, whether they become stares, with what intent they occur, whether they contain any degree of hostility or mockery, and to what extent connections, money, or mode of dress shield me in these situations. To be a stranger is to be looked at, but to be black is to be looked at especially. ("The children shout *Neger! Neger!* as I walk along the streets.") Leukerbad has changed, but in which way? There were, in fact, no bands of children on the street, and few children anywhere at all. Presumably the children of Leukerbad, like children the world over, were indoors, frowning over computer games, checking Facebook, or watching music videos. Perhaps some of the older folks I saw in the streets were once the very children who had been so surprised by the sight of Baldwin, and about whom, in the essay, he struggles to take a reasonable tone: "In all of this, in which it must be conceded that there was the charm of genuine wonder and in which there was certainly no element of intentional unkindness, there was yet no suggestion that I was human: I was simply a living wonder." But now the children or grandchildren of those children are connected to the world in a different way. Maybe some xenophobia or racism is part of their lives, but part of their lives, too, are Beyoncé, Drake, and Meck Mill, the music I hear pulsing from Swiss clubs on Friday nights.

Baldwin had to bring his records with him in the fifties, like a secret stash of medicine, and he had to haul his phonograph up to Leukerbad, so that the sound of the American blues could keep him connected to a Harlem[4] of the

4. Neighborhood in New York City and a historical center of African American culture.

spirit. I listened to some of the same music while I was there, as a way of being with him: Bessie Smith singing "I Need a Little Sugar in My Bowl" ("I need a little sugar in my bowl / I need a little hot dog on my roll"), Fats Waller singing "Your Feet's Too Big." I listened to my own playlist as well: Bettye Swann, Billie Holiday, Jean Wells, *Coltrane Plays the Blues*, the Physics, Childish Gambino. The music you travel with helps you to create your own internal weather. But the world participates, too: when I sat down to lunch at the Römerhof restaurant one afternoon—that day, all the customers and staff were white— the music playing overhead was Whitney Houston's "I Wanna Dance with Somebody." History is now and black America.

At dinner, at a pizzeria, a table of British tourists stared at me. But the waitress was part black, and at the hotel one of the staff members at the spa was an older black man. "People are trapped in history, and history is trapped in them," Baldwin wrote. But it is also true that the little pieces of history move around at tremendous speed, settling with a not-always-clear logic, and rarely settling for long. And perhaps more interesting than my not being the only black person in the village is the plain fact that many of the other people I saw were also foreigners. This was the biggest change of all. If, back then, the village had a pious and convalescent air about it, the feel of "a lesser Lourdes," it is much busier now, packed with visitors from other parts of Switzerland, and from Germany, France, Italy, and all over Europe, Asia, and the Americas. It has become the most popular thermal resort in the Alps. The municipal baths are full. There are hotels on every street, at every price point, and there are restaurants and luxury-goods shops. If you wish to buy an eye-wateringly costly watch at 4,600 feet above sea level, it is now possible to do so.

The better hotels have their own thermal pools. At the Hotel Mercure Bristol, I took an elevator down to the spa and sat in the dry sauna. A few minutes later, I slipped into the pool and floated outside in the warm water. Others were there, but not many. A light rain fell. We were ringed by mountains and held in the immortal blue.

In her brilliant *Harlem Is Nowhere*, Sharifa Rhodes-Pitts writes, "In almost every essay James Baldwin wrote about Harlem, there is a moment when he commits a literary sleight-of-hand so particular that, if he'd been an athlete, sportscasters would have codified the maneuver and named it 'the Jimmy.' I think of it in cinematic terms, because its effect reminds me of a technique wherein camera operators pan out by starting with a light shot and then zoom out to a wide view while the lens remains focused on a point in the distance." This move Rhodes-Pitts describes, this sudden widening of focus, is present even in his essays that are not about Harlem. In "Stranger in the Village," there's a passage about seven pages in where one can feel the rhetoric revving up, as Baldwin prepares to leave behind the calm, fabular atmosphere of the opening section. Of the villagers, he writes:

> These people cannot be, from the point of view of power, strangers any-
> where in the world; they have made the modern world, in effect, even if

they do not know it. The most illiterate among them is related, in a way
I am not, to Dante, Shakespeare, Michelangelo, Aeschylus, Da Vinci, Rembrandt, and Racine; the cathedral at Chartres says something to them
which it cannot say to me, as indeed would New York's Empire State Building, should anyone here ever see it. Out of their hymns and dances come
Beethoven and Bach. Go back a few centuries and they are in their full
glory—but I am in Africa, watching the conquerors arrive.

What is this list about? Does it truly bother Baldwin that the people of Leukerbad are related, through some faint familiarity, to Chartres? That some distant genetic thread links them to the Beethoven string quartets? After all, as
he argues later in the essay, no one can deny the impact "the presence of the
Negro has had on the American character." He understands the truth and the
art in Bessie Smith's work. He does not, and cannot—I want to believe—rate
the blues below Bach. But there was a certain narrowness in received ideas of
black culture in the 1950s. In the time since then, there has been enough
black cultural achievement from which to compile an all-star team: there's
been Coltrane and Monk and Miles, and Ella and Billie and Aretha. Toni Morrison, Wole Soyinka, and Derek Walcott happened, as have Audre Lorde, and
Chinua Achebe, and Bob Marley. The body was not abandoned for the mind's
sake: Alvin Ailey, Arthur Ashe, and Michael Jordan happened, too. The source
of jazz and the blues also gave the world hip-hop, Afrobeat, dancehall, and
house. And, yes, by the time James Baldwin died, in 1987, he, too, was recognized as an all-star.

10   Thinking further about the cathedral at Chartres, about the greatness of
that achievement and about how, in his view, it included blacks only in the
negative, as devils, Baldwin writes that "the American Negro has arrived at his
identity by virtue of the absoluteness of his estrangement from his past." But
the distant African past has also become much more available than it was in
1953. It would not occur to me to think that, centuries ago, I was "in Africa,
watching the conquerors arrive." But I suspect that for Baldwin this is, in part,
a piece of oratory, a grim cadence on which to end a paragraph. In "A Question
of Identity" (another essay collected in *Notes of a Native Son*), he writes, "The
truth about that past is not that it is too brief, or too superficial, but only that
we, having turned our faces so resolutely away from it, have never demanded
from it what it has to give." The fourteenth-century court artists of Ife[5] made
bronze sculptures using a complicated casting process lost to Europe since
antiquity, and which was not rediscovered there until the Renaissance. Ife
sculptures are equal to the works of Ghiberti or Donatello. From their precision and formal sumptuousness we can extrapolate the contours of a great
monarchy, a network of sophisticated ateliers, and a cosmopolitan world of
trade and knowledge. And it was not only Ife. All of West Africa was a cultural
ferment. From the egalitarian government of the Igbo to the goldwork of the
Ashanti courts, the brass sculpture of Benin, the military achievement of the

5. Yoruba city that by the eleventh century was the capital of an extensive kingdom.

Mandinka Empire[6] and the musical virtuosi who praised those war heroes, this was a region of the world too deeply invested in art and life to simply be reduced to a caricature of "watching the conquerors arrive." We know better now. We know it with a stack of corroborating scholarship and we know it implicitly, so that even making a list of the accomplishments feels faintly tedious, and is helpful mainly as a counter to Eurocentrism.

There's no world in which I would surrender the intimidating beauty of Yoruba-language poetry for, say, Shakespeare's sonnets, or one in which I'd prefer chamber orchestras playing baroque music to the koras[7] of Mali. I'm happy to own all of it. This carefree confidence is, in part, the gift of time. It is a dividend of the struggle of people from earlier generations. I feel little alienation in museums, full though they are of other people's ancestors. But this question of filiation tormented Baldwin. He was sensitive to what was great in world art, and sensitive to his own sense of exclusion from it. He made a similar list in the title essay of *Notes of a Native Son* (one begins to feel that lists like this had been flung at him during arguments): "In some subtle way, in a really profound way, I brought to Shakespeare, Bach, Rembrandt, to the stones of Paris, to the Cathedral at Chartres, and the Empire State Building a special attitude. These were not really my creations, they did not contain my history; I might search them in vain forever for any reflection of myself. I was an interloper; this was not my heritage." The lines throb with sadness. What he loves does not love him in return.

This is where I part ways with Baldwin. I disagree not with his particular sorrow but with the self-abnegation that pinned him to it. Bach, so profoundly human, is my heritage. I am not an interloper when I look at a Rembrandt portrait. I care for them more than some white people do, just as some white people care more for aspects of African art than I do. I can oppose white supremacy and still rejoice in Gothic architecture. In this, I stand with Ralph Ellison:[8] "The values of my own people are neither 'white' nor 'black,' they are American. Nor can I see how they could be anything else, since we are people who are involved in the texture of the American experience." And yet I (born in the United States more than half a century after Baldwin) continue to understand, because I have experienced in my own body the undimmed fury he felt about racism. In his writing there is a hunger for life, for all of it, and a strong wish to not be accounted nothing (a mere nigger, a mere *neger*) when he knows himself to be so much. And this "so much" is neither a matter of ego about his writing nor an anxiety about his fame in New York or in Paris. It is about the incontest-

6. Igbo, a people inhabiting southeastern Nigeria; Ashanti, a people inhabiting southern Ghana and a West African empire originating in the late seventeenth century; Benin, a West African kingdom from the thirteenth through the nineteenth centuries; Mandinka Empire, also Wassoulou Empire, created through military conquest in the late nineteenth century.

7. 21-stringed musical instrument.

8. American novelist (1914–1994), author of *Invisible Man* (1952).

able fundamentals of a person: pleasure, sorrow, love, humor, and grief, and the complexity of the interior landscape that sustains those feelings. Baldwin was astonished that anyone anywhere should question these fundamentals—thereby burdening him with the supreme waste of time that is racism—let alone so many people in so many places. This unflagging ability to be shocked rises like steam off his written pages. "The rage of the disesteemed is personally fruitless," he writes, "but it is also absolutely inevitable."

Leukerbad gave Baldwin a way to think about white supremacy[9] from its first principles. It was as though he found it in its simplest form there. The men who suggested that he learn to ski so that they might mock him, the villagers who accused him behind his back of being a firewood thief, the ones who wished to touch his hair and suggested that he grow it out and make himself a winter coat, and the children who, "having been taught that the devil is a black man, scream[ed] in genuine anguish" as he approached: Baldwin saw these as prototypes (preserved like coelacanths) of attitudes that had evolved into the more intimate, intricate, familiar, and obscene American forms of white supremacy that he already knew so well.

It is a beautiful village. I liked the mountain air. But when I returned to my room from the thermal baths, or from strolling in the streets with my camera, I read the news online. There I found an unending sequence of crises: in the Middle East, in Africa, in Russia, and everywhere else, really. Pain was general. But within that larger distress was a set of linked stories, and thinking about "Stranger in the Village," thinking with its help, was like injecting a contrast dye into my encounter with the news. The American police continued shooting unarmed black men, or killing them in other ways. The protests that followed, in black communities, were countered with violence by a police force that is becoming indistinguishable from an invading army. People began to see a connection between the various events: the shootings, the fatal choke hold,[10] the stories of who was not given lifesaving medication. And black communities were flooded with outrage and grief.

15   In all of this, a smaller, much less significant story (but one that nevertheless signified), caught my attention. The mayor of New York and his police chief have a public-policy obsession with cleaning, with cleansing, and they decided that arresting members of the dance troupes that perform in moving subway cars was one of the ways to clean up the city.[11] I read the excuses for this becoming a priority: some people feared being seriously injured by an

9. Ideology asserting the superiority of white people that has its origins in seventeenth-century European race theory and anthropology.

10. In 2014, Eric Garner, an African American man, died after being subjected to a choke hold by a New York City police officer.

11. Bill de Blasio (b. 1961) has been mayor of New York City since 2014; William Bratton (b. 1947) was New York City police commissioner from 1994 to 1996 and then again from 2014 to 2016. He embraced the "broken windows theory" of policing, which emphasizes the aggressive policing of minor crimes as a way of preventing more serious crime.

errant kick (it has not happened, but they sure feared it), some people considered the dancing a nuisance, some policymakers believed that going after mis-
demeanors is a way of preempting major crimes. And so, to combat this menace
of dancers, the police moved in. They began chasing, and harassing, and
handcuffing. The "problem" was dancers, and the dancers were, for the most
part, black boys. The newspapers took the same tone as the government: a
sniffy dismissal of the performers. And yet these same dancers are a bright
spark in the day, a moment of unregulated beauty, artists with talents unimaginable to their audience. What kind of thinking would consider their abolition
an improvement in city life? No one considers Halloween trick-or-treaters a
public menace. There's no law enforcement against people selling Girl Scout
cookies or against Jehovah's Witnesses.[12] But the black body comes prejudged,
and as a result it is placed in needless jeopardy. To be black is to bear the brunt
of selective enforcement of the law, and to inhabit a psychic unsteadiness in
which there is no guarantee of personal safety. You are a black body first,
before you are a kid walking down the street or a Harvard professor who has
misplaced his keys.[13]

William Hazlitt,[14] in an 1821 essay entitled "The Indian Jugglers," wrote
words that I think of when I see a great athlete or dancer: "Man, thou art a
wonderful animal, and thy ways past finding out! Thou canst do strange
things, but thou turnest them to little account!—To conceive of this effort of
extraordinary dexterity distracts the imagination and makes admiration
breathless." In the presence of the admirable, some are breathless not with
admiration but with rage. They object to the presence of the black body (an
unarmed boy in a street, a man buying a toy, a dancer in the subway, a
bystander) as much as they object to the presence of the black mind. And
simultaneous with these erasures is the unending collection of profit from
black labor and black innovation. Throughout the culture, there are imitations
of the gait, bearing, and dress of the black body, a vampiric "everything but the
burden" co-option of black life.

Leukerbad is ringed by mountains: the Daubenhorn, the Torrenthorn, the
Rinderhorn. A high mountain pass called the Gemmi, another 2,800 feet above
the village, connects the canton of Valais with the Bernese Oberland. Through
this landscape—craggy, bare in places and verdant elsewhere, a textbook
instance of the sublime—one moves as though through a dream. The Gemmi
Pass is famous for good reason, and Goethe was once there, as were Byron,

12. Girl Scouts have traditionally raised money for their organization by selling cookies door-to-door; Jehovah's Witnesses, a Christian denomination known for door-to-
door evangelization.

13. In 2012, Trayvon Martin, an unarmed African American teenager, was shot by
George Zimmerman, who claimed he was acting in self-defense; in 2009, African American professor Henry Louis Gates Jr. was arrested at his home in Cambridge, Massachusetts, after a neighbor called police to report that his home was being broken into.

14. English critic and essayist (1778–1830).

Twain, and Picasso.[15] The pass is mentioned in a Sherlock Holmes adventure, when Holmes crosses it on his way to the fateful meeting with Professor Moriarty at Reichenbach Falls.[16] There was bad weather the day I went up, rain and fog, but that was good luck, as it meant I was alone on the trails. While there, I remembered a story that Lucien Happersberger told about Baldwin going out on a hike in these mountains. Baldwin had lost his footing during the ascent, and the situation was precarious for a moment. But Happersberger, who was an experienced climber, reached out a hand, and Baldwin was saved. It was out of this frightening moment, this appealingly biblical moment, that Baldwin got the title for the book he had been struggling to write: *Go Tell It on the Mountain*.

If Leukerbad was his mountain pulpit, the United States was his audience. The remote village gave him a sharper view of what things looked like back home. He was a stranger in Leukerbad, Baldwin wrote, but there was no possibility for blacks to be strangers in the United States, or for whites to achieve the fantasy of an all-white America purged of blacks. This fantasy about the disposability of black life is a constant in American history. It takes a while to understand that this disposability continues. It takes whites a while to understand it; it takes nonblack people of color a while to understand it; and it takes some blacks, whether they've always lived in the United States or are latecomers like myself, weaned elsewhere on other struggles, a while to understand it. American racism has many moving parts, and has had enough centuries in which to evolve an impressive camouflage. It can hoard its malice in great stillness for a long time, all the while pretending to look the other way. Like misogyny, it is atmospheric. You don't see it at first. But understanding comes.

"People who shut their eyes to reality simply invite their own destruction, and anyone who insists on remaining in a state of innocence long after that innocence is dead turns himself into a monster." The news of the day (old news, but raw as a fresh wound) is that black American life is disposable from the point of view of policing, sentencing, economic policy, and countless terrifying forms of disregard. There is a vivid performance of innocence, but there's no actual innocence left. The moral ledger remains so far in the negative that we can't even get started on the question of reparations. Baldwin wrote "Stranger in the Village" more than sixty years ago. Now what?

MLA CITATION

Cole, Teju. "Black Body." *The Norton Reader: An Anthology of Nonfiction*, edited by Melissa A. Goldthwaite et al., 15th ed., W. W. Norton, 2020, pp. 174–82.

---

15. Johann Wolfgang von Goethe (1749–1832), preeminent German writer; Lord Byron (1788–1824), English Romantic poet; Mark Twain, pen name of Samuel Clemens (1835–1910), American novelist, journalist, and satirist; Pablo Picasso (1881–1973), Spanish modernist painter.

16. See the short story "The Final Problem" (1893) by Sir Arthur Conan Doyle.

QUESTIONS

1. When it was first published in the *New Yorker*, Teju Cole's essay was subtitled "Rereading James Baldwin's 'Stranger in the Village.'" How does Cole "reread" Baldwin's classic essay (pp. 165–74)? How does his experience as the "custodian of a black body" (paragraph 4) compare with Baldwin's? What does Cole's engagement with Baldwin allow him to recognize or understand that he might not have otherwise?

2. Cole is troubled by Baldwin's stance toward what has traditionally been called European or Western culture, writing "This is where I part ways with Baldwin" (paragraph 14). What about Baldwin's stance troubles Cole? What stance does he adopt instead?

3. Cole's many references to music form a kind of "soundtrack" to his essay. How does he mix periods and musical genres? What role does this soundtrack play in his essay?

4. Cole ends his essay with a question: "Now what?" Why might he have chosen to conclude this way?

5. Using Cole's essay as a model, write an essay of your own in which you use an interpretation of one of the essays in this chapter of *The Norton Reader* to examine similarly an aspect of your identity and relationship to some element of society.

GARNETTE CADOGAN
Black and Blue

> "My only sin is my skin. What did I do, to be so black and blue?"
> —FATS WALLER, "(What Did I Do to Be So) Black and Blue?"

> "Manhattan's streets I saunter'd, pondering."
> —WALT WHITMAN, "Manhattan's Streets I Saunter'd, Pondering"

MY LOVE FOR WALKING started in childhood, out of necessity. No thanks to a stepfather with heavy hands, I found every reason to stay away from home and was usually out—at some friend's house or at a street party where no minor should be—until it was too late to get public transportation. So I walked.

The streets of Kingston, Jamaica, in the 1980s were often terrifying—you could, for instance, get killed if a political henchman thought you came from

First published in Freeman's *under the title "Walking While Black" (2015) and included in the essay collection* The Fire This Time: A New Generation Speaks about Race *(2016), edited by Jesmyn Ward.*

the wrong neighborhood, or even if you wore the wrong color. Wearing orange showed affiliation with one political party and green with the other, and if you were neutral or traveling far from home you chose your colors well. The wrong color in the wrong neighborhood could mean your last day. No wonder, then, that my friends and the rare nocturnal passerby declared me crazy for my long late-night treks that traversed warring political zones. (And sometimes I did pretend to be crazy, shouting non sequiturs when I passed through especially dangerous spots, such as the place where thieves hid on the banks of a storm drain. Predators would ignore or laugh at the kid in his school uniform speaking nonsense.)

I made friends with strangers and went from being a very shy and awkward kid to being an extroverted, awkward one. The beggar, the vendor, the poor laborer—those were experienced wanderers, and they became my nighttime instructors; they knew the streets and delivered lessons on how to navigate and enjoy them. I imagined myself as a Jamaican Tom Sawyer,[1] one moment sauntering down the streets to pick low-hanging mangoes that I could reach from the sidewalk, another moment hanging outside a street party with battling sound systems, each armed with speakers piled to create skyscrapers of heavy bass. These streets weren't frightening. They were full of adventure when they weren't serene. There I'd join forces with a band of merry walkers, who'd miss the last bus by mere minutes, our feet still moving as we put out our thumbs to hitchhike to spots nearer home, making jokes as vehicle after vehicle raced past us. Or I'd get lost in Mittyesque[2] moments, my young mind imagining alternate futures. The streets had their own safety: Unlike at home, there I could be myself without fear of bodily harm. Walking became so regular and familiar that the way home became home.

The streets had their rules, and I loved the challenge of trying to master them. I learned how to be alert to surrounding dangers and nearby delights, and prided myself on recognizing telling details that my peers missed. Kingston was a map of complex, and often bizarre, cultural and political and social activity, and I appointed myself its nighttime cartographer. I'd know how to navigate away from a predatory pace, and to speed up to chat when the cadence of a gait announced friendliness. It was almost always men I saw. A lone woman walking in the middle of the night was as common a sight as Sasquatch;[3] moonlight pedestrianism was too dangerous for her. Sometimes at night as I made my way down from hills above Kingston, I'd have the impression that the city was set on "pause" or in extreme slow motion, as though as I descended I was cutting across Jamaica's deep social divisions. I'd make my way briskly past the mansions in the hills overlooking the city, now transformed into a carpet of dotted lights under a curtain of stars, saunter by middle-class subdivisions hidden behind high walls

1. Tom Sawyer, a character in several novels by Mark Twain (1835–1910), is an adolescent boy characterized by his boisterousness and fertile imagination.
2. Walter Mitty, a character from "The Secret Life of Walter Mitty" (1939) by James Thurber, is a timid man given to heroic fantasies and daydreams.
3. A mythical ape-like creature, the subject of repeated "sightings" in North America.

crowned with barbed wire, and zigzagged through neighborhoods of zinc and wooden shacks crammed together and leaning like a tight-knit group of limbo dancers. With my descent came an increase in the vibrancy of street life—except when it didn't; some poor neighborhoods had both the violent gunfights and the eerily deserted streets of the cinematic Wild West. I knew well enough to avoid those even at high noon.

I'd begun hoofing it after dark when I was ten years old. By thirteen I was   5
rarely home before midnight, and some nights found me racing against dawn. My mother would often complain, "Mek yuh love street suh? Yuh born a hospital; yuh neva born a street." ("Why do you love the streets so much? You were born in a hospital, not in the streets.")

I left Jamaica in 1996 to attend college in New Orleans, a city I'd heard called "the northernmost Caribbean city." I wanted to discover—on foot, of course—what was Caribbean and what was American about it. Stately mansions on oak-lined streets with streetcars clanging by, and brightly colored houses that made entire blocks look festive; people in resplendent costumes dancing to funky brass bands in the middle of the street; cuisine—and aromas—that mashed up culinary traditions from Africa, Europe, Asia, and the American South; and a juxtaposition of worlds old and new, odd and familiar: Who wouldn't want to explore this?

On my first day in the city, I went walking for a few hours to get a feel for the place and to buy supplies to transform my dormitory room from a prison bunker into a welcoming space. When some university staff members found out what I'd been up to, they warned me to restrict my walking to the places recommended as safe to tourists and the parents of freshmen. They trotted out statistics about New Orleans' crime rate. But Kingston's crime rate dwarfed those numbers, and I decided to ignore these well-meant cautions. A city was waiting to be discovered, and I wouldn't let inconvenient facts get in the way. These American criminals are nothing on Kingston's, I thought. They're no real threat to me.

What no one had told me was that I was the one who would be considered a threat.

Within days I noticed that many people on the street seemed apprehensive of me: Some gave me a circumspect glance as they approached, and then crossed the street; others, ahead, would glance behind, register my presence, and then speed up; older white women clutched their bags; young white men nervously greeted me, as if exchanging a salutation for their safety: "What's up, bro?" On one occasion, less than a month after my arrival, I tried to help a man whose wheelchair was stuck in the middle of a crosswalk; he threatened to shoot me in the face, then asked a white pedestrian for help.

I wasn't prepared for any of this. I had come from a majority-black country   10
in which no one was wary of me because of my skin color. Now I wasn't sure who was afraid of me. I was especially unprepared for the cops. They regularly stopped and bullied me, asking questions that took my guilt for granted. I'd never received what many of my African-American friends call "The Talk": No parents had told me how to behave when I was stopped by the police, how to

be as polite and cooperative as possible, no matter what they said or did to me. So I had to cobble together my own rules of engagement. Thicken my Jamaican accent. Quickly mention my college. "Accidentally" pull out my college identification card when asked for my driver's license.

My survival tactics began well before I left my dorm. I got out of the shower with the police in my head, assembling a cop-proof wardrobe. Light-colored oxford shirt. V-neck sweater. Khaki pants. Chukkas. Sweatshirt or T-shirt with my university insignia. When I walked I regularly had my identity challenged, but I also found ways to assert it. (So I'd dress Ivy League style, but would, later on, add my Jamaican pedigree by wearing Clarks Desert Boots, the footwear of choice of Jamaican street culture.) Yet the all-American sartorial choice of white T-shirt and jeans, which many police officers see as the uniform of black troublemakers, was off-limits to me—at least, if I wanted to have the freedom of movement I desired.

In this city of exuberant streets, walking became a complex and often oppressive negotiation. I would see a white woman walking towards me at night and cross the street to reassure her that she was safe. I would forget something at home but not immediately turn around if someone was behind me, because I discovered that a sudden backtrack could cause alarm. (I had a cardinal rule: Keep a wide perimeter from people who might consider me a danger. If not, danger might visit me.) New Orleans suddenly felt more dangerous than Jamaica. The sidewalk was a minefield, and every hesitation and self-censored compensation reduced my dignity. Despite my best efforts, the streets never felt comfortably safe. Even a simple salutation was suspect.

One night, returning to the house that, eight years after my arrival, I thought I'd earned the right to call my home, I waved to a cop driving by. Moments later, I was against his car in handcuffs. When I later asked him—sheepishly, of course; any other way would have asked for bruises—why he had detained me, he said my greeting had aroused his suspicion. "No one waves to the police," he explained. When I told friends of his response, it was my behavior, not his, that they saw as absurd. "Now why would you do a dumb thing like that?" said one. "You know better than to make nice with police."

A few days after I left on a visit to Kingston, Hurricane Katrina slashed and pummeled New Orleans.[4] I'd gone not because of the storm but because my adoptive grandmother, Pearl, was dying of cancer. I hadn't wandered those streets in eight years, since my last visit, and I returned to them now mostly at night, the time I found best for thinking, praying, crying. I walked to feel less alienated—from myself, struggling with the pain of seeing my grandmother terminally ill; from my home in New Orleans, underwater and seemingly abandoned; from my home country, which now, precisely because of its childhood familiarity, felt foreign to me. I was surprised by how familiar those streets felt. Here was the corner where the fragrance of jerk chicken greeted me, along with the warm tenor and peace-and-love message of Half Pint's[5] "Greetings," broad-

4. Category 5 hurricane that devasted New Orleans in 2005.
5. Jamaican singer (b. 1961), born Lindon Andrew Roberts.

cast from a small but powerful speaker to at least a half-mile radius. It was as if I had walked into 1986, down to the soundtrack. And there was the wall of the neighborhood shop, adorned with the Rastafarian colors red, gold, and green along with images of local and international heroes Bob Marley, Marcus Garvey, and Haile Selassie.[6] The crew of boys leaning against it and joshing each other were recognizable; different faces, similar stories. I was astonished at how safe the streets felt to me, once again one black body among many, no longer having to anticipate the many ways my presence might instill fear and how to offer some reassuring body language. Passing police cars were once again merely passing police cars. Jamaican police could be pretty brutal, but they didn't notice me the way American police did. I could be invisible in Jamaica in a way I can't be invisible in the United States.

Walking had returned to me a greater set of possibilities. And why walk, if not to create a new set of possibilities? Following serendipity, I added new routes to the mental maps I had made from constant walking in that city from childhood to young adulthood, traced variations on the old pathways. Serendipity, a mentor once told me, is a secular way of speaking of grace; it's unearned favor. Seen theologically, then, walking is an act of faith. Walking is, after all, interrupted falling. We see, we listen, we speak, and we trust that each step we take won't be our last, but will lead us into a richer understanding of the self and the world.

In Jamaica, I felt once again as if the only identity that mattered was my own, not the constricted one that others had constructed for me. I strolled into my better self. I said, along with Kierkegaard,[7] "I have walked myself into my best thoughts."

When I tried to return to New Orleans from Jamaica a month later, there were no flights. I thought about flying to Texas so I could make my way back to my neighborhood as soon as it opened for reoccupancy, but my adoptive aunt, Maxine, who hated the idea of me returning to a hurricane zone before the end of hurricane season, persuaded me to come to stay in New York City instead. (To strengthen her case she sent me an article about Texans who were buying up guns because they were afraid of the influx of black people from New Orleans.)

This wasn't a hard sell: I wanted to be in a place where I could travel by foot and, more crucially, continue to reap the solace of walking at night. And I was eager to follow in the steps of the essayists, poets, and novelists who'd wandered that great city before me—Walt Whitman, Herman Melville, Alfred Kazin, Elizabeth Hardwick. I had visited the city before, but each trip had felt like a tour in a sports car. I welcomed the chance to stroll. I wanted to walk alongside Whitman's ghost and "descend to the pavements, merge with the crowd, and gaze

6. Rastafari, religion and political movement arising in Jamaican in the 1930s; Bob Marley (1945–1981), Jamaican musician and Rastafarian regarded as a national hero; Marcus Garvey (1887–1940), Jamaican-born leader of the Pan-African movement, which asserted the unity of all peoples of African descent; Haile Selassie (1892–1975), emperor of Ethiopia revered as a prophet or the messiah in Rastafari.

7. Danish philosopher and theologian (1813–1855).

with them." So I left Kingston, the popular Jamaican farewell echoing in my mind: "Walk good!" *Be safe on your journey,* in other words, *and all the best in your endeavors.*

I arrived in New York City, ready to lose myself in Whitman's "Manhattan crowds, with their turbulent musical chorus!"[8] I marveled at what Jane Jacobs praised as "the ballet of the good city sidewalk" in her old neighborhood, the West Village.[9] I walked up past midtown skyscrapers, releasing their energy as lively people onto the streets, and on into the Upper West Side, with its regal Beaux Arts[10] apartment buildings, stylish residents, and buzzing streets. Onward into Washington Heights, the sidewalks spilled over with an ebullient mix of young and old Jewish and Dominican-American residents, past leafy Inwood, with parks whose grades rose to reveal beautiful views of the Hudson River, up to my home in Kingsbridge in the Bronx, with its rows of brick bungalows and apartment buildings nearby Broadway's bustling sidewalks and the peaceful expanse of Van Cortlandt Park. I went to Jackson Heights in Queens to take in people socializing around garden courtyards in Urdu, Korean, Spanish, Russian, and Hindi. And when I wanted a taste of home, I headed to Brooklyn, in Crown Heights, for Jamaican food and music and humor mixed in with the flavor of New York City. The city was my playground.

20   I explored the city with friends and then with a woman I'd begun dating. She walked around endlessly with me, taking in New York City's many pleasures. Coffee shops open until predawn; verdant parks with nooks aplenty; food and music from across the globe; quirky neighborhoods with quirkier residents. My impressions of the city took shape during my walks with her.

As with the relationship, those first few months of urban exploration were all romance. The city was beguiling, exhilarating, vibrant. But it wasn't long before reality reminded me I wasn't invulnerable, especially when I walked alone.

One night in the East Village, I was running to dinner when a white man in front of me turned and punched me in the chest with such force that I thought my ribs had braided around my spine. I assumed he was drunk or had mistaken me for an old enemy, but found out soon enough that he'd merely assumed I was a criminal because of my race. When he discovered I wasn't what he imagined, he went on to tell me that his assault was my own fault for running up behind him. I blew off this incident as an aberration, but the mutual distrust between me and the police was impossible to ignore. It felt elemental. They'd enter a subway platform; I'd notice them. (And I'd notice all the other black men registering their presence as well, while just about every-

8. From American poet Walt Whitman's poem "Give Me the Splendid Silent Sun" (1867).

9. From writer and activist Jane Jacobs's book *The Death and Life of Great American Cities* (1961).

10. Style of architecture influential in the late nineteenth century.

one else remained oblivious to them.) They'd glare. I'd get nervous and glance. They'd observe me steadily. I'd get uneasy. I'd observe them back, worrying that I looked suspicious. Their suspicions would increase. We'd continue the silent, uneasy dialogue until the subway arrived and separated us at last.

I returned to the old rules I'd set for myself in New Orleans, with elaboration. No running, especially at night; no sudden movements; no hoodies; no objects—especially shiny ones—in hand; no waiting for friends on street corners, lest I be mistaken for a drug dealer; no standing near a corner on the cell phone (same reason). As comfort set in, inevitably I began to break some of those rules, until a night encounter sent me zealously back to them, me having learned that anything less than vigilance was carelessness.

After a sumptuous Italian dinner and drinks with friends, I was jogging to the subway at Columbus Circle—I was running late to meet another set of friends at a concert downtown. I heard someone shouting and I looked up to see a police officer approaching with his gun trained on me. "Against the car!" In no time, half a dozen cops were upon me, chucking me against the car and tightly handcuffing me. "Why were you running?" "Where are you going?" "Where are you coming from?" "I said, why were you running?!" Since I couldn't answer everyone at once, I decided to respond first to the one who looked most likely to hit me. I was surrounded by a swarm and tried to focus on just one without inadvertently aggravating the others.

It didn't work. As I answered that one, the others got frustrated that I wasn't 25
answering them fast enough and barked at me. One of them, digging through my already-emptied pockets, asked if I had any weapons, the question more an accusation. Another badgered me about where I was coming from, as if on the fifteenth round I'd decide to tell him the truth he imagined. Though I kept saying—calmly, of course, which meant trying to manage a tone that ignored my racing heart and their spittle-filled shouts in my face—that I had just left friends two blocks down the road, who were all still there and could vouch for me, to meet other friends whose text messages on my phone could verify that, yes, sir, yes, officer, of course, officer, it made no difference.

For a black man, to assert your dignity before the police was to risk assault. In fact, the dignity of black people meant less to them, which was why I always felt safer being stopped in front of white witnesses than black witnesses. The cops had less regard for the witness and entreaties of black onlookers, whereas the concern of white witnesses usually registered on them. A black witness asking a question or politely raising an objection could quickly become a fellow detainee. Deference to the police, then, was sine qua non for a safe encounter.

The cops ignored my explanations and my suggestions and continued to snarl at me. All except one of them, a captain. He put his hand on my back, and said to no one in particular, "If he was running for a long time he would have been sweating." He then instructed that the cuffs be removed. He told me that a black man had stabbed someone earlier two or three blocks away and they were searching for him. I noted that I had no blood on me and had told his fellow officers where I'd been and how to check my alibi—unaware that it was even an alibi, as no one had told me why I was being held, and of course, I hadn't dared ask. From what I'd seen, anything beyond passivity would be interpreted as aggression.

The police captain said I could go. None of the cops who detained me thought an apology was necessary. Like the thug who punched me in the East Village, they seemed to think it was my own fault for running.

Humiliated, I tried not to make eye contact with the onlookers on the sidewalk, and I was reluctant to pass them to be on my way. The captain, maybe noticing my shame, offered to give me a ride to the subway station. When he dropped me off and I thanked him for his help, he said, "It's because you were polite that we let you go. If you were acting up it would have been different." I nodded and said nothing.

30   I realized that what I least liked about walking in New York City wasn't merely having to learn new rules of navigation and socialization—every city has its own. It was the arbitrariness of the circumstances that required them, an arbitrariness that made me feel like a child again, that infantilized me. When we first learn to walk, the world around us threatens to crash into us. Every step is risky. We train ourselves to walk without crashing by being attentive to our movements, and extra-attentive to the world around us. As adults we walk without thinking, really. But as a black adult I am often returned to that moment in childhood when I'm just learning to walk. I am once again on high alert, vigilant.

Some days, when I am fed up with being considered a trouble-maker upon sight, I joke that the last time a cop was happy to see a black male walking was when that male was a baby taking his first steps. On many walks, I ask white friends to accompany me, just to avoid being treated like a threat. Walks in New York City, that is; in New Orleans, a white woman in my company some-times attracted more hostility. (And it is not lost on me that my woman friends are those who best understand my plight; they have developed their own vigi-lance in an environment where they are constantly treated as targets of sexual attention.) Much of my walking is as my friend Rebecca once described it: A pantomime undertaken to avoid the choreography of criminality.

Walking while black[11] restricts the experience of walking, renders inaccessible the classic Romantic[12] experience of walking alone. It forces me to be in con-stant relationship with others, unable to join the New York flaneurs[13] I had read about and hoped to join. Instead of meandering aimlessly in the footsteps of Whitman, Melville, Kazin, and Vivian Gornick,[14] more often, I felt that I was tiptoeing in Baldwin's—the Baldwin who wrote, way back in 1960, "Rare,

11. A play on "driving while black," which refers to the racial profiling of drivers by police.

12. Nineteenth-century literary, artistic, musical, and intellectual movement empha-sizing emotion, individual subjectivity, and the imagination.

13. From the French *flâneur*, meaning "idler" or "stroller."

14. Authors and essayists Herman Melville (1819–1891), Alfred Kazin (1915–1998), and Vivian Gornick (b. 1935) have all written about walking in New York City.

indeed, is the Harlem citizen, from the most circumspect church member to the most shiftless adolescent, who does not have a long tale to tell of police incompetence, injustice, or brutality. I myself have witnessed and endured it more than once."[15]

Walking as a black man has made me feel simultaneously more removed from the city, in my awareness that I am perceived as suspect, and more closely connected to it, in the full attentiveness demanded by my vigilance. It has made me walk more purposefully in the city, becoming part of its flow, rather than observing, standing apart.

But it also means that I'm still trying to arrive in a city that isn't quite mine. One definition of home is that it's somewhere we can most be ourselves. And when are we more ourselves but when walking, that natural state in which we repeat one of the first actions we learned? Walking—the simple, monotonous act of placing one foot before the other to prevent falling—turns out not to be so simple if you're black. Walking alone has been anything but monotonous for me; monotony is a luxury.

A foot leaves, a foot lands, and our longing gives it momentum from rest to rest. We long to look, to think, to talk, to get away. But more than anything else, we long to be free. We want the freedom and pleasure of walking without fear—without others' fear—wherever we choose. I've lived in New York City for almost a decade and have not stopped walking its fascinating streets. And I have not stopped longing to find the solace that I found as a kid on the streets of Kingston. Much as coming to know New York City's streets has made it closer to home to me, the city also withholds itself from me via those very streets. I walk them, alternately invisible and too prominent. So I walk caught between memory and forgetting, between memory and forgiveness. 35

MLA CITATION

Cadogen, Garnette. "Black and Blue." *The Norton Reader: An Anthology of Nonfiction*, edited by Melissa A. Goldthwaite et al., 15th ed., W. W. Norton, 2020, pp. 183–91.

QUESTIONS

1. In his essay, Garnette Cadogan recounts and reflects on his encounters with the police as a black man walking in three cities: Kingston, then New Orleans, then New York. How do the police perceive black men, and how do they perceive themselves? What do Cadogan's experiences in these cities have in common? How do they differ?

2. This essay was originally titled "Walking While Black" but was later retitled "Black and Blue." How does this change shift the focus of the essay?

3. Writing of his early excursions in Kingston, Cadogan portrays himself as an astute observer and analyst: "I learned how to be alert to surrounding dangers and

15. From Baldwin's essay "Fifth Avenue, Uptown" (1960).

nearby delights, and prided myself on recognizing telling details that my peers missed" (paragraph 4). What does this characterization of his boyhood imply about his purpose as an author?

4. In all three cities, Cadogan takes steps to mitigate the perception that he is a threat. What are some of the things he tries? Why? How successful are his efforts?

5. Like Teju Cole in his essay "Black Body," Cadogan expresses an affinity with James Baldwin (paragraph 32), whose essay "Stranger in the Village" also appears in this chapter of *The Norton Reader* (pp. 165–74). Write a dialogue among these three writers in which they discuss their experiences as black men in public spaces. What do you imagine them saying to each other? As much as you can, use direct quotations from their essays to allow them to speak in their own voices.

PICO IYER

The Humanity We Can't Relinquish

NARA, JAPAN—WE'D JUST EMERGED from a long and rather liquid dinner on a barge along the Taedong River, in the heart of North Korea's showpiece capital of Pyongyang.[1] Two waitresses had finished joining our English tour guide, Nick, in some more than boisterous karaoke numbers. Now, in the bus back to the hotel, one young local guide broke into a heartfelt rendition of "Danny Boy."[2] His charming and elegant colleague, Miss Peng—North Korea is no neophyte when it comes to trying to impress visitors—was talking about the pressures she faced as an unmarried woman of 26, white Chanel clip glinting in her hair. Another of our minders—there were four or five for the 14 of us, with a camera trained on our every move for what we were assured was a "souvenir video"—kept saying, "You think I'm a government spy. Don't you?"

But I was back in North Korea because nowhere I'd seen raised such searching questions about what being human truly involves. Nowhere so unsettled my easy assumptions about what "reality" really is. The people around me clearly wept and bled and raged as I did; but what did it do to your human instincts to be told that you could be sentenced, perhaps to death, if you displayed a picture of your mother—or your granddaughter—in your home, instead of a photo of the Father of the Nation? Did being human really include not being permitted to leave your hometown, and not being allowed to say what you think?

I've never doubted that humanity is a privilege, even if we, as the animals who think, are also the creatures who agitate, plot and fantasize. Govern-

First published as an op-ed in the New York Times *on August 12, 2018.*

1. The Democratic People's Republic of Korea, or North Korea, is an insular, totalitarian state established in 1948.
2. Irish ballad.

ments try to suppress this at times, and many of us in the freer world now imprison ourselves by choosing to live through screens, or to see through screens, like the Buddhist demagogue Ashin Wirathu who, in defiance of the shared humanness that the Buddha worked so hard to elucidate, compares his Muslim neighbors in Myanmar to wolves and jackals.[3] More and more of us these days seem to be living at post-human speeds determined by machines, to the point where we barely have time for kids or friends. But if we're feeling less than human—or pretending we can engineer mortality away—for most of us it's a choice we're making, and can unmake tomorrow.

In my home of more than 30 years, Japan, nobody thinks twice about being married by a robot or apologizing to a pencil after you throw it across a room. My neighbors rattle on cheerfully about "2.5 dimensional characters" and "demi-humans"; their government has appointed the mouthless cartoon cutie Hello Kitty and a 22nd-century blue robotic cat named Doraemon as cultural ambassadors.[4] Lines between animate and inanimate run differently in an animist Shinto[5] universe where—you see this in the beautiful films of Hayao Miyazaki[6]—every blade of grass or speck of dust is believed to have a spirit.

In Japan, as in its neighbor North Korea, a human is often taken to be part of a unit, a voice in a choir; her job may be to be invisible, inaudible and all but indistinguishable from those around her. At the Family Romance company in Tokyo, 1,200 actors stand ready to impersonate, for a price, a child's absent father, for years on end, or a wife's adulterous lover. The Henn-na Hotel in Nagasaki describes itself as the world's "first hotel staffed by robots."

But all this means only that the boundaries of what it is to feel human emotion are stretched, to the point of including motes of pollen or the railway carriages people bring presents for. Even the dead are treated as human in Japan. After my mother-in-law passed away in February, her closest relatives never stopped chattering to her, setting out a glass of her favorite beer next to her coffin, applying blush to her waxen cheeks. My wife still puts food out for her father five years after he was placed into the earth; this month our son will return home because his departed grandfather and grandmother are believed to be visiting for three days then as well.

To me this only confirms the visceral sense many of us have that holiness and humanness may be more closely entwined than we imagine. Speaking to

5

3. Myanmar is a predominantly Buddhist, Southeast Asian country in which Muslims are a persecuted minority.
4. Hello Kitty, an iconic cartoon character created in 1974 by the Japanese company Sanrio; Doraemon, the title character in a Japanese manga series by Hiroshi Fujimoto (1933–1996) and Motoo Abiko (b. 1934), childhood friends who wrote under the name Fujiko F. Fujio.
5. Japan's traditional, indigenous religion, emphasizing ritual and involving worship of *kami* or spirits that inhabit all natural things.
6. Japanese filmmaker and manga artist (b. 1941) whose works often have environmental themes.

the Dalai Lama[7] for 44 years now, I'm often most touched when he stresses how mortal he is, sometimes impatient, sometimes grieving, just like all the rest of us. I keep returning to the novels of Graham Greene[8] because he reminds us that a "whisky priest" can get drunk, neglect every duty, even father a child, yet still rise to a level of kindness and selflessness that a pious cardinal might envy. It's in our vulnerability, Greene knew, that our strength truly lies (if only because our capacity to feel for everyone else lies there, too).

For more than 30 years now I've been traveling—to Yemen, to Easter Island, to Ethiopia—to see what humanness might be, beneath differences of custom and circumstance and race. I've watched young mothers dodging bullets, children living in garbage dumps, those whom disease has left far from most of the capacities and restraints we associate with being human. If circumstances change, however, I never doubt that the humanness of just about every one can be recovered.

The first time I visited North Korea, 24 years before my evening on the barge, my guide led me, during my last afternoon in the city, up a hill. It was just the two of us. Below were the cutting-edge (if often uninhabited) sky-scrapers, the amusement parks and spotless, wide boulevards his government had created out of what, only 35 years before, had been rubble, a demolished city in which, North Koreans claim, only two buildings remained upright.

10   My guide wasn't unworldly; he'd studied for three years in Pakistan and spoke Urdu and English. He knew that his sense of what it is to lead a human life was very different from mine. But what he said was, "Don't listen to my propaganda. Just tell your friends back in America what you've seen here."

Was he going off script for a moment—or only offering an even craftier set of lines his directors had given him? I couldn't tell. But I could feel that he was appealing to something human in me and whatever understanding two humans can share, even if they come from opposite worlds. Official Pyong-yang seems the last word in inhumanity to me, but as my guide kept waving and waving goodbye while I passed through immigration, I felt with fresh power how no one can fully deprive us of our humanity but ourselves.

MLA CITATION

Iyer, Pico. "The Humanity We Can't Relinquish." *The Norton Reader: An Anthology of Nonfiction*, edited by Melissa A. Goldthwaite et al., 15th ed., W. W. Norton, 2020, pp. 192–94.

7. Leader of the *Dge-lugs-pa* or "Yellow Hat" order of Tibetan Buddhism, who until 1959 was also the head of the government of Tibet. The fourteenth Dalai Lama (b. 1935) was exiled from Tibet in 1959 and is recognized internationally as a moral authority and spiritual leader.

8. English novelist (1904–1991) whose works have strongly Catholic themes.

QUESTIONS

1. Pico Iyer, in his title phrase, writes about the common "humanity we can't relinquish," but he never explicitly defines what this shared "humanity" is. Why not? Can you infer from his essay what Iyer might understand "humanity" or "humanness" to be?

2. Iyer writes, "I've never doubted that humanity is a privilege" (paragraph 3) and, later, that "holiness and humanness may be more closely entwined than we imagine" (paragraph 7). What does he mean by these statements?

3. Why is travel so important to Iyer? Several other essays in this chapter of *The Norton Reader*—James Baldwin's "Stranger in the Village," Teju Cole's "Black Body," and Garnette Cadogan's "Black and Blue"—also concern travel. How do the insights Iyer arrives at through his travels compare with Baldwin's, Cole's, or Cadogan's?

4. Choose one sentence from Iyer's essay that resonates with you. Write an essay in which you use that sentence to illuminate an episode from your own life in which you learned something about what it means to be human.

4 CULTURAL ANALYSIS

> One day you turn and "social studies" has become "Chilean
> fiefdoms of the fourteenth century" and that's how you know
> you're in college.
>
> —SLOANE CROSLEY

People love to make generalizations almost as much as they love to pick them apart. We gather data, observe ourselves and our neighbors, and absorb stereotypes only to find ourselves continually confronted by new information that throws our prior assumptions into check. Even so, a generalization can help us make an educated guess while navigating the world and a good one has the flexibility to acknowledge that not every single example will fit the mold. The work of cultural analysis examines broad social trends at the same time as it admits that individuals vary widely: in short, the essays here are in the business of making good generalizations.

This chapter's essays all engage in cultural analysis. While the word "culture" originated with *agri*culture, in this context, it has come to connote how we develop and grow together as a society. Analyzing these social surroundings can be challenging in part because it can be hard to see the assumptions that we rely upon daily. Drawing upon methods from anthropology, sociology, literary analysis, history, the law, and more, the writers of these essays take on what they observe to be widespread assumptions or practices and investigate them—analyzing not only how they work, but whom they leave out, and what they signify.

One of the challenges every writer faces when writing about something as open-ended as culture is the challenge of scale. Sometimes writers take on topics so vast that readers have trouble finding their own point of entry. Other times writers take things down to such an atomistic level of detail that it can be difficult to discern the larger import of the example. The writers in this chapter are all masters of scale. Each in their different way, with passion, humor, gravity, and rage, draws links between small, often overlooked details and capacious and resonant cultural observations. As you read through the essays in this chapter, notice how much their tone varies from one to the next.

Each essay here takes a specific phenomenon and uses that as the lens through which to examine something larger. Margaret Atwood offers a range of vignettes about women's bodies, including her ambivalence about her daughter having a Barbie doll. Henry Louis Gates Jr. offers a glimpse into the world of black barber shops and home salons. Both Patricia Williams and Barbara Kingsolver take injustices they witness and transform them into passionate pleas for greater racial and gender justice, under the law and in society. And the essays that do not primarily take on these massive topics of race and gender—Malcolm Gladwell on our love of coffee, Sloane Crosley on city etiquette, and Tim Kreider on anxiety—are also important for their insights into the way we work and live now. These essays each have at their core the ability to draw together large cultural trends and small, finely observed details in a manner that has much to teach us about the way we live now and how we examine—and write about—our culture.

After reading these essays, think about your own experience with culture. How do you define the different cultures you belong to? You might choose one culture—whether it's a religion or a sport or your regional culture. What behaviors, beliefs, or objects are significant to that culture? What details or experiences can you use to ground your observations about this culture? Consider the challenge of scale: How can you compress—or expand—all that you need to say to fit a single essay? Starting small and specific can help you reach a broader conclusion.

MALCOLM GLADWELL

Java Man

T HE ORIGINAL COCA-COLA was a late-nineteenth-century concoction known as Pemberton's French Wine Coca, a mixture of alcohol, the caffeine-rich kola nut, and coca, the raw ingredient of cocaine. In the face of social pressure, first the wine and then the coca were removed, leaving the more banal modern beverage in its place: carbonated, caffeinated sugar water with less kick to it than a cup of coffee. But is that the way we think of Coke? Not at all. In the nineteen-thirties, a commercial artist named Haddon Sundblom had the bright idea of posing a portly retired friend of his in a red Santa Claus suit with a Coke in his hand, and plastering the image on billboards and advertisements across the country. Coke, magically, was reborn as caffeine for children, caffeine without any of the weighty adult connotations of coffee and tea. It was—as the ads with Sundblom's Santa put it—"the pause that refreshes." It added life. It could teach the world to sing.

One of the things that have always made drugs so powerful is their cultural adaptability, their way of acquiring meanings beyond their pharmacology. We think of marijuana, for example, as a drug of lethargy, of disaffection. But in Colombia, the historian David T. Courtwright points out in "Forces of Habit," "peasants boast that cannabis helps them to *quita el cansancio* or reduce fatigue; increase their *fuerza* and *ánimo*, force and spirit; and become *incansable*, tireless." In Germany right after the Second World War, cigarettes briefly and suddenly became the equivalent of crack cocaine. "Up to a point, the majority of the habitual smokers preferred to do without food even under extreme conditions of

First published in the New Yorker *(2001), a weekly magazine of "reportage, commentary, criticism, essay, fiction, satire, cartoons, and poetry," to which Malcolm Gladwell has been a regular contributor.*

nutrition rather than to forgo tobacco," according to one account of the period. "Many housewives . . . bartered fat and sugar for cigarettes." Even a drug as demonized as opium has been seen in a more favorable light. In the eighteen-thirties, Franklin Delano Roosevelt's grandfather Warren Delano II made the family fortune exporting the drug to China, and Delano was able to sugar-coat his activities so plausibly that no one ever accused his grandson of being the scion of a drug lord. And yet, as Bennett Alan Weinberg and Bonnie K. Bealer remind us in their marvellous book "The World of Caffeine," there is no drug quite as effortlessly adaptable as caffeine, the Zelig of chemical stimulants.

At one moment, in one form, it is the drug of choice of café intellectuals and artists; in another, of housewives; in another, of Zen monks; and, in yet another, of children enthralled by a fat man who slides down chimneys. King Gustav III, who ruled Sweden in the latter half of the eighteenth century, was so convinced of the particular perils of coffee over all other forms of caffeine that he devised an elaborate experiment. A convicted murderer was sentenced to drink cup after cup of coffee until he died, with another murderer sentenced to a lifetime of tea drinking, as a control. (Unfortunately, the two doctors in charge of the study died before anyone else did; then Gustav was murdered; and finally the tea drinker died, at eighty-three, of old age—leaving the original murderer alone with his espresso, and leaving coffee's supposed toxicity in some doubt.) Later, the various forms of caffeine began to be divided up along sociological lines. Wolfgang Schivelbusch, in his book "Tastes of Paradise," argues that, in the eighteenth century, coffee symbolized the rising middle classes, whereas its great caffeinated rival in those years—cocoa, or, as it was known at the time, chocolate—was the drink of the aristocracy. "Goethe, who used art as a means to lift himself out of his middle class background into the aristocracy, and who as a member of a courtly society maintained a sense of aristocratic calm even in the midst of immense productivity, made a cult of chocolate, and avoided coffee," Schivelbusch writes. "Balzac, who despite his sentimental allegiance to the monarchy, lived and labored for the literary marketplace and for it alone, became one of the most excessive coffee-drinkers in history. Here we see two fundamentally different working styles and means of stimulation—fundamentally different psychologies and physiologies." Today, of course, the chief cultural distinction is between coffee and tea, which, according to a list drawn up by Weinberg and Bealer, have come to represent almost entirely opposite sensibilities:

Coffee Aspect	Tea Aspect
Male	Female
Boisterous	Decorous
Indulgence	Temperance
Hardheaded	Romantic
Topology	Geometry
Heidegger	Carnap
Beethoven	Mozart
Libertarian	Statist
Promiscuous	Pure

That the American Revolution began with the symbolic rejection of tea in Boston Harbor, in other words, makes perfect sense. Real revolutionaries would naturally prefer coffee. By contrast, the freedom fighters of Canada, a hundred years later, were most definitely tea drinkers. And where was Canada's autonomy won? Not on the blood-soaked fields of Lexington and Concord but in the genteel drawing rooms of Westminster, over a nice cup of Darjeeling and small, triangular cucumber sandwiches.

All this is a bit puzzling. We don't fetishize the difference between salmon eaters and tuna eaters, or people who like their eggs sunny-side up and those who like them scrambled. So why invest so much importance in the way people prefer their caffeine? A cup of coffee has somewhere between a hundred and two hundred and fifty milligrams; black tea brewed for four minutes has between forty and a hundred milligrams. But the disparity disappears if you consider that many tea drinkers drink from a pot, and have more than one cup. Caffeine is caffeine. "The more it is pondered," Weinberg and Bealer write, "the more paradoxical this duality within the culture of caffeine appears. After all, both coffee and tea are aromatic infusions of vegetable matter, served hot or cold in similar quantities; both are often mixed with cream or sugar; both are universally available in virtually any grocery or restaurant in civilized society; and both contain the identical psychoactive alkaloid stimulant, caffeine."

It would seem to make more sense to draw distinctions based on the way caffeine is metabolized rather than on the way it is served. Caffeine, whether it is in coffee or tea or a soft drink, moves easily from the stomach and intestines into the bloodstream, and from there to the organs, and before long has penetrated almost every cell of the body. This is the reason that caffeine is such a wonderful stimulant. Most substances can't cross the blood-brain barrier, which is the body's defensive mechanism, preventing viruses or toxins from entering the central nervous system. Caffeine does so easily. Within an hour or so, it reaches its peak concentration in the brain, and there it does a number of things—principally, blocking the action of adenosine, the neuromodulator that makes you sleepy, lowers your blood pressure, and slows down your heartbeat. Then, as quickly as it builds up in your brain and tissues, caffeine is gone—which is why it's so safe. (Caffeine in ordinary quantities has never been conclusively linked to serious illness.)

But how quickly it washes away differs dramatically from person to person. A two-hundred-pound man who drinks a cup of coffee with a hundred milligrams of caffeine will have a maximum caffeine concentration of one milligram per kilogram of body weight. A hundred-pound woman having the same cup of coffee will reach a caffeine concentration of two milligrams per kilogram of body weight, or twice as high. In addition, when women are on the Pill, the rate at which they clear caffeine from their bodies slows considerably. (Some of the side effects experienced by women on the Pill may in fact be caffeine jitters caused by their sudden inability to tolerate as much coffee as they could before.) Pregnancy reduces a woman's ability to process caffeine still further.

5

The half-life of caffeine in an adult is roughly three and a half hours. In a pregnant woman, it's eighteen hours. (Even a four-month-old child processes caffeine more efficiently.) An average man and woman sitting down for a cup of coffee are thus not pharmaceutical equals: in effect, the woman is under the influence of a vastly more powerful drug. Given these differences, you'd think that, instead of contrasting the caffeine cultures of tea and coffee, we'd contrast the caffeine cultures of men and women.

But we don't, and with good reason. To parse caffeine along gender lines does not do justice to its capacity to insinuate itself into every aspect of our lives, not merely to influence culture but even to create it. Take coffee's reputation as the "thinker's" drink. This dates from eighteenth-century Europe, where coffeehouses played a major role in the egalitarian, inclusionary spirit that was then sweeping the continent. They sprang up first in London, so alarming Charles II that in 1676 he tried to ban them. It didn't work. By 1700, there were hundreds of coffeehouses in London, their subversive spirit best captured by a couplet from a comedy of the period: "In a coffeehouse just now among the rabble I bluntly asked, which is the treason table." The movement then spread to Paris, and by the end of the eighteenth century coffeehouses numbered in the hundreds—most famously the Café de la Régence, near the Palais Royal, which counted among its customers Robespierre, Napoleon, Voltaire, Victor Hugo, Théophile Gautier, Rousseau, and the Duke of Richelieu.[1] Previously, when men had gathered together to talk in public places, they had done so in bars, which drew from specific socioeconomic niches and, because of the alcohol they served, created a specific kind of talk. The new coffeehouses, by contrast, drew from many different classes and trades, and they served a stimulant, not a depressant. "It is not extravagant to claim that it was in these gathering spots that the art of conversation became the basis of a new literary style and that a new ideal of general education in letters was born," Weinberg and Bealer write.

It is worth noting, as well, that in the original coffeehouses nearly everyone smoked, and nicotine also has a distinctive physiological effect. It moderates mood and extends attention, and, more important, it doubles the rate of caffeine metabolism: it allows you to drink twice as much coffee as you could otherwise. In other words, the original coffeehouse was a place where men of all types could sit all day; the tobacco they smoked made it possible to drink coffee all day; and the coffee they drank inspired them to talk all day. Out of this came the Enlightenment. (The next time we so perfectly married pharmacology and place, we got Joan Baez.)[2]

10   In time, caffeine moved from the café to the home. In America, coffee triumphed because of the country's proximity to the new Caribbean and Latin American coffee plantations, and the fact that throughout the nineteenth century duties were negligible. Beginning in the eighteen-twenties, Courtwright tells us, Brazil "unleashed a flood of slave-produced coffee. American

1. French politicians, authors, or nobility.
2. American folksinger and political activist (b. 1941).

per capita consumption, three pounds per year in 1830, rose to eight pounds by 1859."

What this flood of caffeine did, according to Weinberg and Bealer, was to abet the process of industrialization—to help "large numbers of people to coordinate their work schedules by giving them the energy to start work at a given time and continue it as long as necessary." Until the eighteenth century, it must be remembered, many Westerners drank beer almost continuously, even beginning their day with something called "beer soup." (Bealer and Weinberg helpfully provide the following eighteenth-century German recipe: "Heat the beer in a saucepan; in a separate small pot beat a couple of eggs. Add a chunk of butter to the hot beer. Stir in some cool beer to cool it, then pour over the eggs. Add a bit of salt, and finally mix all the ingredients together, whisking it well to keep it from curdling.") Now they began each day with a strong cup of coffee. One way to explain the industrial revolution is as the inevitable consequence of a world where people suddenly preferred being jittery to being drunk. In the modern world, there was no other way to keep up. That's what Edison[3] meant when he said that genius was ninety-nine per cent perspiration and one per cent inspiration. In the old paradigm, working with your mind had been associated with leisure. It was only the poor who worked hard. (The quintessential preindustrial narrative of inspiration belonged to Archimedes,[4] who made his discovery, let's not forget, while taking a bath.) But Edison was saying that the old class distinctions no longer held true— that in the industrialized world there was as much toil associated with the life of the mind as there had once been with the travails of the body.

In the twentieth century, the professions transformed themselves accordingly: medicine turned the residency process into an ordeal of sleeplessness, the legal profession borrowed a page from the manufacturing floor and made its practitioners fill out time cards like union men. Intellectual heroics became a matter of endurance. "The pace of computation was hectic," James Gleick writes of the Manhattan Project[5] in "Genius," his biography of the physicist Richard Feynman. "Feynman's day began at 8:30 and ended fifteen hours later. Sometimes he could not leave the computing center at all. He worked through for thirty-one hours once and the next day found that an error minutes after he went to bed had stalled the whole team. The routine allowed just a few breaks." Did Feynman's achievements reflect a greater natural talent than his less productive forebears had? Or did he just drink a lot more coffee? Paul Hoffman, in "The Man Who Loved Only Numbers," writes of the legendary twentieth-century mathematician Paul Erdős that "he put in nineteen-hour days, keeping himself fortified with 10 to 20 milligrams of Benzedrine or Ritalin, strong espresso and caffeine tablets. 'A mathematician,' Erdős was fond of saying, 'is a machine for turning coffee into theorems.'" Once, a friend bet Erdős five hundred dollars that he could not quit amphetamines for a month. Erdős took the bet and won, but, during his time of abstinence, he found himself incapable of

3. Thomas Alva Edison (1847–1931), American inventor.
4. Greek mathematician and inventor (c. 290–80 B.C.E.–c. 212 B.C.E.).
5. Project that built the atomic bomb.

doing any serious work. "You've set mathematics back a month," he told his friend when he collected, and immediately returned to his pills.

Erdős's unadulterated self was less real and less familiar to him than his adulterated self, and that is a condition that holds, more or less, for the rest of society as well. Part of what it means to be human in the modern age is that we have come to construct our emotional and cognitive states not merely from the inside out—with thought and intention—but from the outside in, with chemical additives. The modern personality is, in this sense, a synthetic creation: skillfully regulated and medicated and dosed with caffeine so that we can always be awake and alert and focussed when we need to be. On a bet, no doubt, we could walk away from caffeine if we had to. But what would be the point? The lawyers wouldn't make their billable hours. The young doctors would fall behind in their training. The physicists might still be stuck out in the New Mexico desert. We'd set the world back a month.

That the modern personality is synthetic is, of course, a disquieting notion. When we talk of synthetic personality—or of constructing new selves through chemical means—we think of hard drugs, not caffeine. Timothy Leary used to make such claims about LSD, and the reason his revolution never took flight was that most of us found the concept of tuning in, turning on, and dropping out to be a bit creepy. Here was this shaman, this visionary—and yet, if his consciousness was so great, why was he so intent on altering it? More important, what exactly were we supposed to be tuning in to? We were given hints, with psychedelic colors and deep readings of "Lucy in the Sky with Diamonds," but that was never enough. If we are to re-create ourselves, we would like to know what we will become.

15   Caffeine is the best and most useful of our drugs because in every one of its forms it can answer that question precisely. It is a stimulant that blocks the action of adenosine, and comes in a multitude of guises, each with a ready-made story attached, a mixture of history and superstition and whimsy which infuses the daily ritual of adenosine blocking with meaning and purpose. Put caffeine in a red can and it becomes refreshing fun. Brew it in a teapot and it becomes romantic and decorous. Extract it from little brown beans and, magically, it is hardheaded and potent. "There was a little known Russian émigré, Trotsky by name, who during World War I was in the habit of playing chess in Vienna's Café Central every evening," Bealer and Weinberg write, in one of the book's many fascinating café yarns:

> A typical Russian refugee, who talked too much but seemed utterly harmless, indeed, a pathetic figure in the eyes of the Viennese. One day in 1917 an official of the Austrian Foreign Ministry rushed into the minister's room, panting and excited, and told his chief, "Your excellency . . . Your excellency . . . Revolution has broken out in Russia." The minister, less excitable and less credulous than his official, rejected such a wild claim and retorted calmly, "Go away. . . . Russia is not a land where revolutions break out. Besides, who on earth would make a revolution in Russia? Perhaps Herr Trotsky from the Café Central?"

The minister should have known better. Give a man enough coffee and he's capable of anything.

MLA CITATION

Gladwell, Malcolm. "Java Man." *The Norton Reader: An Anthology of Nonfiction*, edited by Melissa A. Goldthwaite et al., 15th ed., W. W. Norton, 2020, pp. 197–203.

QUESTIONS

1. How serious do you think Malcolm Gladwell is when he says that we're all drugged on caffeine? How can you tell?

2. Gladwell creates a binary between coffee and tea. Describe another binary between two closely similar forms—such as seashore vs. mountains; Coke vs. Pepsi; skis vs. snowboards. How do binaries work? What limitations do you see in the binary you created or in Gladwell's?

3. Gladwell offers several hypotheses for caffeine's success as the drug of choice for the modern world. Which one do you find most persuasive, and why?

4. Write a description of some of the rituals that you or someone you know indulges in with coffee or tea.

MARGARET ATWOOD

The Female Body

> ". . . entirely devoted to the subject of 'The Female Body.' Knowing how well you have written on this topic . . . this capacious topic . . ."
> —LETTER FROM *Michigan Quarterly Review*

1.

IAGREE, IT'S A HOT TOPIC. But only one? Look around, there's a wide range. Take my own, for instance.

I get up in the morning. My topic feels like hell. I sprinkle it with water, brush parts of it, rub it with towels, powder it, add lubricant. I dump in the fuel and away goes my topic, my topical topic, my controversial topic, my capacious topic, my limping topic, my nearsighted topic, my topic with back problems, my badly-behaved topic, my vulgar topic, my outrageous topic, my aging topic, my topic that is out of the question and anyway still can't spell, in its

This essay was originally published in a 1990 special issue of the Michigan Quarterly Review, *a print journal of essays, poetry, and short stories. The issue was entirely devoted to the female body.*

oversized coat and worn winter boots, scuttling along the sidewalk as if it were flesh and blood, hunting for what's out there, an avocado, an alderman, an adjective, hungry as ever.

2.

The basic Female Body comes with the following accessories: garter belt, panti-girdle, crinoline, camisole, bustle, brassiere, stomacher, chemise, virgin zone, spike heels, nose ring, veil, kid gloves, fish-net stockings, fichu, bandeau, Merry Widow, weepers, chokers, barrettes, bangles, beads, lorgnette, feather boa, basic black, compact, Lycra stretch one-piece with modesty panel, designer peignoir, flannel nightie, lace teddy, bed, head.

3.

The Female Body is made of transparent plastic and lights up when you plug it in. You press a button to illuminate the different systems. The Circulatory System is red, for the heart and arteries, purple for the veins; the Respiratory System is blue; the Lymphatic System is yellow; the Digestive System is green, with liver and kidneys in aqua. The nerves are done in orange and the brain is pink. The skeleton, as you might expect, is white.

5   The Reproductive System is optional, and can be removed. It comes with or without a miniature embryo. Parental judgment can thereby be exercised. We do not wish to frighten or offend.

4.

He said, I won't have one of those things in the house. It gives a young girl a false notion of beauty, not to mention anatomy. If a real woman was built like that she'd fall on her face.

She said, If we don't let her have one like all the other girls she'll feel singled out. It'll become an issue. She'll long for one and she'll long to turn into one. Repression breeds sublimation. You know that.

He said, It's not just the pointy plastic tits, it's the wardrobes. The wardrobes and that stupid male doll, what's his name, the one with the underwear glued on.

She said, Better to get it over with when she's young. He said, All right but don't let me see it.

10   She came whizzing down the stairs, thrown like a dart. She was stark naked. Her hair had been chopped off, her head was turned back to front, she was missing some toes and she'd been tattooed all over her body with purple ink, in a scrollwork design. She hit the potted azalea, trembled there for a moment like a botched angel, and fell.

He said, I guess we're safe.

5.

The Female Body has many uses. It's been used as a door-knocker, a bottle-opener, as a clock with a ticking belly, as something to hold up lampshades, as a nutcracker, just squeeze the brass legs together and out comes your nut. It bears torches, lifts victorious wreaths, grows copper wings and raises aloft a ring of neon stars; whole buildings rest on its marble heads.

It sells cars, beer, shaving lotion, cigarettes, hard liquor; it sells diet plans and diamonds, and desire in tiny crystal bottles. Is this the face that launched a thousand products? You bet it is, but don't get any funny big ideas, honey, that smile is a dime a dozen.

It does not merely sell, it is sold. Money flows into this country or that country, flies in, practically crawls in, suitful after suitful, lured by all those hairless pre-teen legs. Listen, you want to reduce the national debt, don't you? Aren't you patriotic? That's the spirit. That's my girl.

She's a natural resource, a renewable one luckily, because those things wear   15
out so quickly. They don't make 'em like they used to. Shoddy goods.

6.

One and one equals another one. Pleasure in the female is not a requirement. Pair-bonding is stronger in geese. We're not talking about love, we're talking about biology. That's how we all got here, daughter.

Snails do it differently. They're hermaphrodites, and work in three's.

7.

Each female body contains a female brain. Handy. Makes things work. Stick pins in it and you get amazing results. Old popular songs. Short circuits. Bad dreams.

Anyway: each of these brains has two halves. They're joined together by a thick cord; neural pathways flow from one to the other, sparkles of electric information washing to and fro. Like light on waves. Like a conversation. How does a woman know? She listens. She listens in.

The male brain, now, that's a different matter. Only a thin connection. Space   20
over here, time over there, music and arithmetic in their own sealed compart-ments. The right brain doesn't know what the left brain is doing. Good for aiming though, for hitting the target when you pull the trigger. What's the target? Who's the target? Who cares? What matters is hitting it. That's the male brain for you. Objective.

This is why men are so sad, why they feel so cut off, why they think of themselves as orphans cast adrift, footloose and stringless in the deep void. What void? she asks. What are you talking about? The void of the Universe, he says, and she says Oh and looks out the window and tries to get a handle on it, but it's no use, there's too much going on, too many rustlings in the leaves, too many voices, so she says, Would you like a cheese sandwich, a piece of cake, a cup of tea? And he grinds his teeth because she doesn't understand, and wanders off, not just alone but Alone, lost in the dark, lost in the skull, searching for the other half, the twin who could complete him.

Then it comes to him: he's lost the Female Body! Look, it shines in the gloom, far ahead, a vision of wholeness, ripeness, like a giant melon, like an apple, like a metaphor for *breast* in a bad sex novel; it shines like a balloon, like a foggy noon, a watery moon, shimmering in its egg of light.

Catch it. Put it in a pumpkin, in a high tower, in a compound, in a chamber, in a house, in a room. Quick, stick a leash on it, a lock, a chain, some pain, settle it down, so it can never get away from you again.

MLA CITATION

Atwood, Margaret. "The Female Body." *The Norton Reader: An Anthology of Nonfiction*, edited by Melissa A. Goldthwaite et al., 15th ed., W. W. Norton, 2020, pp. 203–06.

QUESTIONS

1. Although Margaret Atwood describes her own body in this essay (especially paragraph 2), she describes herself as an object, rather than a subject. What difference does that change make?

2. In section five, Atwood lists a range of objects made in the shape of women's bodies. What does she suggest these objects connote about women and how society views women's bodies?

3. Although this essay neither makes an explicit argument nor has a thesis statement, it does have a definite point of view. What is the implicit argument of Atwood's piece?

4. This essay is written in sections and the tone, approach, and method shifts from section to section. Make a list of all the approaches you can find. What is the overall effect of this abundance?

5. Write an updated essay about the female (or male) body. Following Atwood's example, experiment with more than one approach and perspective.

SLOANE CROSLEY

Wheels Up

I AM RUNNING LATE FOR THE AIRPORT, trying to catch a cab on my street corner. A woman in a wheelchair and her date, a man, arrive at the corner seconds after me. They pretend not to see me and I pretend not to see them, which is the kind of cutthroat strategy New Yorkers employ when embarking on otherwise benign activities. It's partially to avoid conflict and partially to claim innocence in the event of the finger. As the minutes pass and no cabs come, the tension grows. I make a big show of checking the time and rotating my suitcase back and forth. At long last, a cab drifts in our direction. Under normal circumstances the cab would be mine. I have the clear lead. But this particular vehicle is the model with the sliding doors, designated for handicapped access. Seeing as how my plane will definitely crash if I steal a cab from a woman in a wheelchair, I step aside.

"Here," I say, "you guys take it."

"Thanks so much," says the man.

And for a whole three seconds, everyone in this scenario feels very good about themselves. The lack of fanfare is a kind of fanfare in itself, a celebration that society has not yet broken down into breadlines and ATM-based riots. We do not throw our handicapped under the bus. We move to the back of the bus for them.

The cab door gapes open on its tracks. The man leans down and puts a   5
hand on each armrest of the wheelchair. He kisses the woman sweetly in what I assume is a casual assertion of their love. Then he unhands the chair and springs into the cab by himself. He waves at her from the open window. The cab wheels off in one direction, the woman in the other.

One of the very few things of which I am certain is that it's not possible to be handicapped by association. Being in the social orbit of a person in a wheelchair does not entitle you to special accommodations and it certainly does not entitle you to someone else's cab. In a huff, I tug my luggage to the next block, thinking about how this man is the worst person to have ever lived. Meanwhile, the woman is just ahead of me. I begin to judge her, too. Physical impediments are nontransferable, but social ones are. You are who you kiss goodbye.

We stay the course for a couple of blocks. She's covering twice as much ground. It's unclear if she's fleeing the scene or just more adept at slicing through crowds. But I try to catch up with her. Should an available cab arrive, I plan on announcing my urgent destination to the driver so that *certain* people might feel very guilty indeed.

We pass a liquor store where someone has tied up a dog outside. The dog, a bright-eyed mutt, sits with his legs stretched out on the pavement. Without so much as a swerve, the woman wheels over his tail. The dog jumps up and lets out a high-pitched yelp. The woman keeps going. Bystanders are transformed

The opening essay to Crosley's 2018 collection, Look Alive Out There.

into witnesses. Upon hearing his pet's cry, the dog's owner comes charging out of the store, looking for answers. The store's cashier stands in the doorway. Everyone hesitates to finger the culprit.

"That woman," I say, pointing. "She wheeled over his tail."

10   The man's face morphs from enraged to sympathetic as he registers this lady, forever seated, waiting for a traffic light to change.

"Oh," he says, backing down, "she probably didn't realize."

The dog, by now, has recovered from the incident. But I have not.

"No," I correct him, "she realized—she just didn't care."

The man shrugs. The dog plows his wet nose into his owner's palm. The whole point of pets is to have a living annex of your personality filled with all the qualities you'd like to have but don't. Instant forgiveness is one of those qualities. If this guy is going to be so magnanimous, it seems redundant that he should even have a dog.

"She's in a *wheelchair*," the cashier pipes up behind me. "What's the matter with you?"

MLA CITATION

Crosley, Sloane. "Wheels Up." *The Norton Reader: An Anthology of Nonfiction*, edited by Melissa A. Goldthwaite et al., 15th ed., W. W. Norton, 2020, pp. 207–08.

QUESTIONS

1. This short essay charts shifting expectations of etiquette, or polite behavior. In so doing, it raises some ethical questions of how we should behave in public with each other. How does Sloane Crosley navigate the various social conundrums she encounters in her efforts to snag a taxi?

2. The cashier chastises Crosley for speaking ill of a person in a wheelchair. What are the advantages of special social rules for people with physical disabilities? How should they change, if at all, if we find out the person is unkind?

3. Study the first paragraph of the essay, in which Crosley delineates the ordinary rules for priority in hailing a cab, adding the variables that, to her mind, apply in this instance, and write a short paper describing the ordinary social rules and some of their variations for a ritual in your life (e.g., cutting in on an exercise machine at the gym, getting a parking space in a crowded mall).

TIM KREIDER

The "Busy" Trap

I F YOU LIVE IN AMERICA in the 21st century you've probably had to listen to a lot of people tell you how busy they are. It's become the default response when you ask anyone how they're doing: "Busy!" "*So* busy." "*Crazy* busy." It is, pretty obviously, a boast disguised as a complaint. And the stock response is a kind of congratulation: "That's a good problem to have," or "Better than the opposite."

Notice it isn't generally people pulling back-to-back shifts in the I.C.U. or commuting by bus to three minimum-wage jobs who tell you how busy they are; what those people are is not busy but *tired. Exhausted. Dead on their feet.* It's almost always people whose lamented busyness is purely self-imposed: work and obligations they've taken on voluntarily, classes and activities they've "encouraged" their kids to participate in. They're busy because of their own ambition or drive or anxiety, because they're addicted to busyness and dread what they might have to face in its absence.

Almost everyone I know is busy. They feel anxious and guilty when they aren't either working or doing something to promote their work. They schedule in time with friends the way students with 4.0 G.P.A.'s make sure to sign up for community service because it looks good on their college applications. I recently wrote a friend to ask if he wanted to do something this week, and he answered that he didn't have a lot of time but if something was going on to let him know and maybe he could ditch work for a few hours. I wanted to clarify that my question had not been a preliminary heads-up to some future invitation; this *was* the invitation. But his busyness was like some vast churning noise through which he was shouting out at me, and I gave up trying to shout back over it.

Even *children* are busy now, scheduled down to the half-hour with classes and extracurricular activities. They come home at the end of the day as tired as grown-ups. I was a member of the latchkey generation and had three hours of totally unstructured, largely unsupervised time every afternoon, time I used to do everything from surfing the *World Book Encyclopedia*[1] to making animated films to getting together with friends in the woods to chuck dirt clods directly into one another's eyes, all of which provided me with important skills and insights that remain valuable to this day. Those free hours became the model for how I wanted to live the rest of my life.

The present hysteria is not a necessary or inevitable condition of life; it's   5
something we've chosen, if only by our acquiescence to it. Not long ago I Skyped with a friend who was driven out of the city by high rent and now has an artist's residency in a small town in the south of France. She described herself as

Written as part of a series on anxiety in the New York Times *opinion pages (2012). Tim Kreider is a cartoonist and essayist.*

1. First published in 1917 and popular in the 1950s and 1960s, this encyclopedia for schoolchildren provided information in accessible language and included many illustrations.

happy and relaxed for the first time in years. She still gets her work done, but it doesn't consume her entire day and brain. She says it feels like college—she has a big circle of friends who all go out to the café together every night. She has a boyfriend again. (She once ruefully summarized dating in New York: "Everyone's too busy and everyone thinks they can do better.") What she had mistakenly assumed was her personality—driven, cranky, anxious and sad— turned out to be a deformative effect of her environment. It's not as if any of us wants to live like this, any more than any one person wants to be part of a traffic jam or stadium trampling or the hierarchy of cruelty in high school— it's something we collectively force one another to do.

Busyness serves as a kind of existential reassurance, a hedge against emptiness; obviously your life cannot possibly be silly or trivial or meaningless if you are so busy, completely booked, in demand every hour of the day. I once knew a woman who interned at a magazine where she wasn't allowed to take lunch hours out, lest she be urgently needed for some reason. This was an entertainment magazine whose raison d'être[2] was obviated when "menu" buttons appeared on remotes, so it's hard to see this pretense of indispensability as anything other than a form of institutional self-delusion. More and more people in this country no longer make or do anything tangible; if your job wasn't performed by a cat or a boa constrictor in a Richard Scarry[3] book I'm not sure I believe it's

2. French for "reason for being."
3. Children's book writer and illustrator (1919–1994) whose books used animals— cats, rats, rabbits, and pigs—and sometimes worms for characters.

necessary. I can't help but wonder whether all this histrionic exhaustion isn't a way of covering up the fact that most of what we do doesn't matter.

I am not busy. I am the laziest ambitious person I know. Like most writers, I feel like a reprobate who does not deserve to live on any day that I do not write, but I also feel that four or five hours is enough to earn my stay on the planet for one more day. On the best ordinary days of my life, I write in the morning, go for a long bike ride and run errands in the afternoon, and in the evening I see friends, read or watch a movie. This, it seems to me, is a sane and pleasant pace for a day. And if you call me up and ask whether I won't maybe blow off work and check out the new American Wing at the Met or ogle girls in Central Park or just drink chilled pink minty cocktails all day long, I will say, what time?

But just in the last few months, I've insidiously started, because of professional obligations, to become busy. For the first time I was able to tell people, with a straight face, that I was "too busy" to do this or that thing they wanted me to do. I could see why people enjoy this complaint; it makes you feel important, sought-after and put-upon. Except that I hate actually being busy. Every morning my in-box was full of e-mails asking me to do things I did not want to do or presenting me with problems that I now had to solve. It got more and more intolerable until finally I fled town to the Undisclosed Location from which I'm writing this.

Here I am largely unmolested by obligations. There is no TV. To check e-mail I have to drive to the library. I go a week at a time without seeing anyone I know. I've remembered about buttercups, stink bugs and the stars. I read. And I'm finally getting some real writing done for the first time in months. It's hard to find anything to say about life without immersing yourself in the world, but it's also just about impossible to figure out what it might be, or how best to say it, without getting the hell out of it again.

Idleness is not just a vacation, an indulgence or a vice; it is as indispensable to the brain as vitamin D is to the body, and deprived of it we suffer a mental affliction as disfiguring as rickets. The space and quiet that idleness provides is a necessary condition for standing back from life and seeing it whole, for making unexpected connections and waiting for the wild summer lightning strikes of inspiration—it is, paradoxically, necessary to getting any work done. "Idle dreaming is often of the essence of what we do," wrote Thomas Pynchon[4] in his essay on sloth. Archimedes' "Eureka" in the bath, Newton's apple, Jekyll & Hyde and the benzene ring:[5] history is full of stories of inspirations that come in idle moments and dreams. It almost makes you wonder whether loafers, goldbricks and no-accounts aren't responsible for more of the world's great ideas, inventions and masterpieces than the hardworking.

"The goal of the future is full unemployment, so we can play. That's why we have to destroy the present politico-economic system." This may sound like

10

---

4. American novelist (b. 1937).

5. Discoveries—Archimedes' method for calculating the volume of an object with an irregular shape, Isaac Newton's discovery of the principle of gravity, Robert Louis Stevenson's dream that led to his famous novel, and Friedrich August Kekulé's reverie of a snake with its tail in its mouth—that connect moments of daydreaming with originality, invention, and productivity.

the pronouncement of some bong-smoking anarchist, but it was actually Arthur C. Clarke,[6] who found time between scuba diving and pinball games to write "Childhood's End" and think up communications satellites. My old colleague Ted Rall[7] recently wrote a column proposing that we divorce income from work and give each citizen a guaranteed paycheck, which sounds like the kind of lunatic notion that'll be considered a basic human right in about a century, like abolition, universal suffrage and eight-hour workdays. The Puritans turned work into a virtue, evidently forgetting that God invented it as a punishment.

Perhaps the world would soon slide to ruin if everyone behaved as I do. But I would suggest that an ideal human life lies somewhere between my own defiant indolence and the rest of the world's endless frenetic hustle. My role is just to be a bad influence, the kid standing outside the classroom window making faces at you at your desk, urging you to just this once make some excuse and get out of there, come outside and play. My own resolute idleness has mostly been a luxury rather than a virtue, but I did make a conscious decision, a long time ago, to choose time over money, since I've always understood that the best investment of my limited time on earth was to spend it with people I love. I suppose it's possible I'll lie on my deathbed regretting that I didn't work harder and say everything I had to say, but I think what I'll really wish is that I could have one more beer with Chris, another long talk with Megan, one last good hard laugh with Boyd. Life is too short to be busy.

MLA CITATION

Kreider, Tim. "The 'Busy' Trap." *The Norton Reader: An Anthology of Nonfiction*, edited by Melissa A. Goldthwaite et al., 15th ed., W. W. Norton, 2020, pp. 209–12.

QUESTIONS

1. Tim Kreider writes against the American penchant for "busyness" and in favor of idleness. What reasons does he give for being against "busyness"?

2. In paragraph 7, Kreider claims, "I am the laziest ambitious person I know." What details of the essay reveal his ambition? What anecdotes of other writers and inventors support his case?

3. Both Kreider, in paragraph 10, and Gladwell (paragraph 11) contrast the contemporary obsession with busyness with the legend of Archimedes eureka moment in the bathtub. What does that story mean for each essay? What stories about discovery do you cherish, and what do they reveal about your beliefs about idleness and busyness?

4. Take a position against Kreider's and argue for the value of keeping busy. You might include examples from your own life or the lives of friends and family.

6. British science and science fiction writer, inventor, and TV host (1917–2008) best known for coauthoring the screenplay for *2001: A Space Odyssey*.
7. American columnist and political cartoonist (b. 1963).

HENRY LOUIS GATES JR.

In the Kitchen

E ALWAYS HAD A GAS STOVE IN THE KITCHEN, in our house in Piedmont, West Virginia, where I grew up. Never electric, though using electric became fashionable in Piedmont in the sixties, like using Crest toothpaste rather than Colgate, or watching Huntley and Brinkley rather than Walter Cronkite.[1] But not us: gas, Colgate, and good ole Walter Cronkite, come what may. We used gas partly out of loyalty to Big Mom, Mama's Mama, because she was mostly blind and still loved to cook, and could feel her way more easily with gas than with electric. But the most important thing about our gas-equipped kitchen was that Mama used to do hair there. The "hot comb" was a fine-toothed iron instrument with a long wooden handle and a pair of iron curlers that opened and closed like scissors. Mama would put it in the gas fire until it glowed. You could smell those prongs heating up.

I liked that smell. Not the smell so much, I guess, as what the smell meant for the shape of my day. There was an intimate warmth in the women's tones as they talked with my Mama, doing their hair. I knew what the women had been through to get their hair ready to be "done," because I would watch Mama do it to herself. How that kink could be transformed through grease and fire into that magnificent head of wavy hair was a miracle to me, and still is.

Mama would wash her hair over the sink, a towel wrapped around her shoulders, wearing just her slip and her white bra. (We had no shower—just a galvanized tub that we stored in the kitchen—until we moved down Rat Tail Road into Doc Wolverton's house, in 1954.) After she dried it, she would grease her scalp thoroughly with blue Bergamot hair grease, which came in a short, fat jar with a picture of a beautiful colored lady on it. It's important to grease your scalp real good, my Mama would explain, to keep from burning yourself. Of course, her hair would return to its natural kink almost as soon as the hot water and shampoo hit it. To me, it was another miracle how hair so "straight" would so quickly become kinky again the second it even approached some water.

My Mama had only a few "clients" whose heads she "did"—did, I think, because she enjoyed it, rather than for the few pennies it brought in. They would sit on one of our red plastic kitchen chairs, the kind with the shiny metal legs, and brace themselves for the process. Mama would stroke that red-hot iron—which by this time had been in the gas fire for half an hour or more—slowly but firmly through their hair, from scalp to strand's end. It made a scorching,

Originally published in the New Yorker *(1994) in advance of the publication of Henry Louis Gates Jr.'s memoir,* Colored People *(1994).*

1. Newscasters of the 1960s: Chet Huntley and David Brinkley were on NBC; Walter Cronkite was on CBS.

crinkly sound, the hot iron did, as it burned its way through kink, leaving in its wake straight strands of hair, standing long and tall but drooping over at the ends, their shape like the top of a heavy willow tree. Slowly, steadily, Mama's hands would transform a round mound of Odetta[2] kink into a darkened swamp of everglades. The Bergamot made the hair shiny; the heat of the hot iron gave it a brownish-red cast. Once all the hair was as straight as God allows kink to get, Mama would take the well-heated curling iron and twirl the straightened strands into more or less loosely wrapped curls. She claimed that she owed her skill as a hairdresser to the strength in her wrists, and as she worked her little finger would poke out, the way it did when she sipped tea. Mama was a south-paw, and wrote upside down and backward to produce the cleanest, roundest letters you've ever seen.

5   The "kitchen" she would all but remove from sight with a handheld pair of shears, bought just for this purpose. Now, the kitchen was the room in which we were sitting—the room where Mama did hair and washed clothes, and where we all took a bath in that galvanized tub. But the word has another meaning, and the kitchen that I'm speaking of is the very kinky bit of hair at the back of your head, where your neck meets your shirt collar. If there was ever a part of our African past that resisted assimilation, it was the kitchen. No matter how hot the iron, no matter how powerful the chemical, no matter how stringent the mashed-potatoes-and-lye formula of a man's "process," neither God nor woman nor Sammy Davis, Jr.,[3] could straighten the kitchen. The kitchen was permanent, irredeemable, irresistible kink. Unassimilably African. No matter what you did, no matter how hard you tried, you couldn't de-kink a person's kitchen. So you trimmed it off as best you could.

When hair had begun to "turn," as they'd say—to return to its natural kinky glory—it was the kitchen that turned first (the kitchen around the back, and nappy edges at the temples). When the kitchen started creeping up the back of the neck, it was time to get your hair done again.

Sometimes, after dark, a man would come to have his hair done. It was Mr. Charlie Carroll. He was very light-complected and had a ruddy nose—it made me think of Edmund Gwenn, who played Kris Kringle in *Miracle on 34th Street*. At first, Mama did him after my brother, Rocky, and I had gone to sleep. It was only later that we found out that he had come to our house so Mama could iron his hair—not with a hot comb or a curling iron but with our very own Proctor-Silex steam iron. For some reason I never understood, Mr. Charlie would conceal his Frederick Douglass–like mane[4] under a big white Stetson hat. I never saw him take it off except when he came to our house, at night, to have his hair pressed. (Later, Daddy would tell us about Mr. Charlie's most

2. Odetta Holmes (1930–2008), singer of blues and spirituals in the 1950s and a lead-ing figure in the American folk revival of the 1960s.
3. Singer, dancer, and entertainer (1925–1990) with notably "processed" hair.
4. Douglass (1817–1895) was an escaped slave turned abolitionist; photographs show him with a lion-like mane of hair.

prized piece of knowledge, something that the man would only confide after his hair had been pressed, as a token of intimacy. "Not many people know this," he'd say, in a tone of circumspection, "but George Washington was Abraham Lincoln's daddy." Nodding solemnly, he'd add the clincher: "A white man told me." Though he was in dead earnest, this became a humorous refrain around our house—"a white man told me"—which we used to punctuate especially preposterous assertions.)

My mother examined my daughters' kitchens whenever we went home to visit, in the early eighties. It became a game between us. I had told her not to do it, because I didn't like the politics it suggested—the notion of "good" and "bad" hair. "Good" hair was "straight," "bad" hair kinky. Even in the late sixties, at the height of Black Power, almost nobody could bring themselves to say "bad" for good and "good" for bad. People still said that hair like white people's hair was "good," even if they encapsulated it in a disclaimer, like "what we used to call 'good.'"

Maggie would be seated in her high chair, throwing food this way and that, and Mama would be cooing about how cute it all was, how I used to do just like Maggie was doing, and wondering whether her flinging her food with her left hand meant that she was going to be left-handed like Mama. When my daughter was just about covered with Chef Boyardee Spaghetti-O's, Mama would seize the opportunity: wiping her clean, she would tilt Maggie's head to one side and reach down the back of her neck. Sometimes Mama would even rub a curl between her fingers, just to make sure that her bifocals had not deceived her. Then she'd sigh with satisfaction and relief: No kink . . . yet. Mama! I'd shout, pretending to be angry. Every once in a while, if no one was looking, I'd peek, too.

I say "yet" because most black babies are born with soft, silken hair. But   10
after a few months it begins to turn, as inevitably as do the seasons or the leaves on a tree. People once thought baby oil would stop it. They were wrong.

Everybody I knew as a child wanted to have good hair. You could be as ugly as homemade sin dipped in misery and still be thought attractive if you had good hair. "Jesus moss," the girls at Camp Lee, Virginia, had called Daddy's naturally "good" hair during the war. I know that he played that thick head of hair for all it was worth, too.

My own hair was "not a bad grade," as barbers would tell me when they cut it for the first time. It was like a doctor reporting the results of the first full physical he has given you. Like "You're in good shape" or "Blood pressure's kind of high—better cut down on salt."

I spent most of my childhood and adolescence messing with my hair. I definitely wanted straight hair. Like Pop's. When I was about three, I tried to stick a wad of Bazooka bubble gum to that straight hair of his. I suppose what fixed that memory for me is the spanking I got for doing so: he turned me upside down, holding me by my feet, the better to paddle my behind. Little *nigger,* he had shouted, walloping away. I started to laugh about it two days later, when my behind stopped hurting.

When black people say "straight," of course, they don't usually mean literally straight—they're not describing hair like, say, Peggy Lipton's (she was the white girl on *The Mod Squad*), or like Mary's of Peter, Paul & Mary[5] fame; black people call that "stringy" hair. No, "straight" just means not kinky, no matter what contours the curl may take. I would have done *anything* to have straight hair—and I used to try everything, short of getting a process.[6]

15   Of the wide variety of techniques and methods I came to master in the challenging prestidigitation of the follicle, almost all had two things in common: a heavy grease and the application of pressure. It's not an accident that some of the biggest black-owned companies in the fifties and sixties made hair products. And I tried them all, in search of that certain silken touch, the one that would leave neither the hand nor the pillow sullied by grease.

I always wondered what Frederick Douglass put on *his* hair, or what Phillis Wheatley[7] put on hers. Or why Wheatley has that rag on her head in the little engraving in the frontispiece of her book. One thing is for sure: you can bet that when Phillis Wheatley went to England and saw the Countess of Huntingdon she did not stop by the Queen's coiffeur on her way there. So many black people still get their hair straightened that it's a wonder we don't have a national holiday for Madame C. J. Walker, the woman who invented the process of straightening kinky hair. Call it Jheri-Kurled or call it "relaxed," it's still fried hair.

I used all the greases, from sea-blue Bergamot and creamy vanilla Duke (in its clear jar with the orange-white-and-green label) to the godfather of grease, the formidable Murray's. Now, Murray's was some *serious* grease. Whereas Bergamot was like oily jello, and Duke was viscous and sickly sweet, Murray's was light brown and *hard*. Hard as lard and twice as greasy, Daddy used to say. Murray's came in an orange can with a press-on top. It was so hard that some people would put a match to the can, just to soften the stuff and make it more manageable. Then, in the late sixties, when Afros came into style, I used Afro Sheen. From Murray's to Duke to Afro Sheen: that was my progression in black consciousness.

We used to put hot towels or washrags over our Murray-coated heads, in order to melt the wax into the scalp and the follicles. Unfortunately, the wax also had the habit of running down your neck, ears, and forehead. Not to mention your pillowcase. Another problem was that if you put two palmfuls of Murray's on your head your hair turned white. (Duke did the same thing.) The challenge was to get rid of that white color. Because if you got rid of the white stuff you had a magnificent head of wavy hair. That was the beauty of it: Murray's was so hard that it froze your hair into the wavy style you brushed it into. It looked really good if you wore a part. A lot of guys had parts *cut* into their hair by a barber, either with the clippers or with a straight-edge razor. Especially if you had kinky hair—then you'd generally wear a short razor cut, or what we called a Quo Vadis.

5. Folksinging group famous in the 1960s for "Puff the Magic Dragon."
6. Hair-straightening chemical treatment.
7. America's first published African American woman writer (1753–1784).

We tried to be as innovative as possible. Everyone knew about using a stocking cap, because your father or your uncle wore one whenever something really big was about to happen, whether sacred or secular: a funeral or a dance, a wedding or a trip in which you confronted official white people. Any time you were trying to look really sharp, you wore a stocking cap in preparation. And if the event was really a big one, you made a new cap. You asked your mother for a pair of her hose, and cut it with scissors about six inches or so from the open end—the end with the elastic that goes up to the top of the thigh. Then you knotted the cut end, and it became a beehive-shaped hat, with an elastic band that you pulled down low on your forehead and down around your neck in the back. To work well, the cap had to fit tightly and snugly, like a press. And it had to fit that tightly because it *was* a press: it pressed your hair with the force of the hose's elastic. If you greased your hair down real good, and left the stocking cap on long enough, voilà: you got a head of pressed-against-the-scalp waves. (You also got a ring around your forehead when you woke up, but it went away.) And then you could enjoy your concrete do. Swore we were bad, too, with all that grease and those flat heads. My brother and I would brush it out a bit in the mornings, so that it looked—well, "natural." Grown men still wear stocking caps—especially older men, who generally keep their stocking caps in their top drawers, along with their cufflinks and their see-through silk socks, their "Maverick" ties, their silk handkerchiefs, and whatever else they prize the most.

A Murrayed-down stocking cap was the respectable version of the process,   20 which, by contrast, was most definitely not a cool thing to have unless you were an entertainer by trade. Zeke and Keith and Poochie and a few other stars of the high-school basketball team all used to get a process once or twice a year. It was expensive, and you had to go somewhere like Pittsburgh or D.C. or Uniontown—somewhere where there were enough colored people to support a trade. The guys would disappear, then reappear a day or two later, strutting like peacocks, their hair burned slightly red from the lye base. They'd also wear "rags"—cloths or handkerchiefs—around their heads when they slept or played basketball. Do-rags, they were called. But the result was straight hair, with just a hint of wave. No curl. Do-it-yourselfers took their chances at home with a concoction of mashed potatoes and lye.

The most famous process of all, however, outside of the process Malcolm X describes in his "Autobiography," and maybe the process of Sammy Davis, Jr., was Nat King Cole's[8] process. Nat King Cole had patent-leather hair. That man's got the finest process money can buy, or so Daddy said the night we saw Cole's TV show on NBC. It was November 5, 1956. I remember the date because everyone came to our house to watch it and to celebrate one of Daddy's buddies' birthdays. Yeah, Uncle Joe chimed in, they can do shit to his hair that the average Negro can't even *think* about—secret shit.

---

8. Singer and jazz pianist (1919–1965).

Nat King Cole was *clean*. I've had an ongoing argument with a Nigerian friend about Nat King Cole for twenty years now. Not about whether he could sing—any fool knows that he could—but about whether or not he was a hand-kerchief head for wearing that patent-leather process.

Sammy Davis, Jr.'s process was the one I detested. It didn't look good on him. Worse still, he liked to have a fried strand dangling down the middle of his forehead, so he could shake it out from the crown when he sang. But Nat King Cole's hair was a thing unto itself, a beautifully sculpted work of art that he and he alone had the right to wear. The only difference between a process and a stocking cap, really, was taste; but Nat King Cole, unlike, say, Michael Jackson, looked *good* in his. His head looked like Valentino's[9] head in the twenties, and some say it was Valentino the process was imitating. But Nat King Cole wore a process because it suited his face, his demeanor, his name, his style. He was as clean as he wanted to be.

I had forgotten all about that patent-leather look until one day in 1971, when I was sitting in an Arab restaurant on the island of Zanzibar surrounded by men in fezzes and white caftans, trying to learn how to eat curried goat and rice with the fingers of my right hand and feeling two million miles from home. All of a sudden, an old transistor radio sitting on top of a china cupboard stopped blaring out its Swahili music and started playing "Fly Me to the Moon," by Nat King Cole. The restaurant's din was not affected at all, but in my mind's eye I saw it: the King's magnificent sleek black tiara. I managed, barely, to blink back the tears.

MLA CITATION

Gates, Henry Louis, Jr. "In the Kitchen." *The Norton Reader: An Anthology of Nonfiction*, edited by Melissa A. Goldthwaite et al., 15th ed., W. W. Norton, 2020, pp. 213–18.

Questions

1. "Kitchen" has two meanings here; write a brief explanation of the significance of both uses of the word in Henry Louis Gates Jr.'s essay.

2. Why do you think Gates alludes to so many celebrities (mostly from the 1950s and 1960s) and brand-name products? Note his preferences and progression. What is the significance of the allusions and brand names?

3. Gates observes, "If there was ever a part of our African past that resisted assim-ilation, it was the kitchen" (paragraph 5). What does *assimilation* mean in the con-text of this sentence? What do you think it means generally? What does the essay imply about Gates's stance on African American assimilation?

4. Write an essay in which you use memories from childhood—including sensory details, popular allusions, and brand-name products—to describe some element of your culture or identity.

9. Rudolph Valentino (1895–1926), film star known, among other things, for his slicked-back hair.

PATRICIA WILLIAMS

The Death of the Profane:
The Rhetoric of Race and Rights

UZZERS ARE BIG IN NEW YORK CITY. Favored particularly by smaller stores and boutiques, merchants throughout the city have installed them as screening devices to reduce the incidence of robbery: if the face at the door looks desirable, the buzzer is pressed and the door is unlocked. If the face is that of an undesirable, the door stays locked. Predictably, the issue of undesirability has revealed itself to be a racial determination. While controversial enough at first, even civil-rights organizations backed down eventually in the face of arguments that the buzzer system is a "necessary evil," that it is a "mere inconvenience" in comparison to the risks of being murdered, that suffering discrimination is not as bad as being assaulted, and that in any event it is not all blacks who are barred, just "17-year-old black males wearing running shoes and hooded sweatshirts."[1]

The installation of these buzzers happened swiftly in New York; stores that had always had their doors wide open suddenly became exclusive or received people by appointment only. I discovered them and their meaning one Saturday in 1986. I was shopping in Soho and saw in a store window a sweater that I wanted to buy for my mother. I pressed my round brown face to the window and my finger to the buzzer, seeking admittance. A narrow-eyed, white teenager wearing running shoes and feasting on bubble gum glared out, evaluating me for signs that would pit me against the limits of his social understanding. After about five seconds, he mouthed "We're closed," and blew pink rubber at me. It was two Saturdays before Christmas, at one o'clock in the afternoon; there were several white people in the store who appeared to be shopping for things for *their* mothers.

I was enraged. At that moment I literally wanted to break all the windows of the store and *take* lots of sweaters for my mother. In the flicker of his judgmental gray eyes, that saleschild had transformed my brightly sentimental, joy-to-the-world, pre-Christmas spree to a shambles. He snuffed my sense of humanitarian catholicity, and there was nothing I could do to snuff his, without making a spectacle of myself.

I am still struck by the structure of power that drove me into such a blizzard of rage. There was almost nothing I could do, short of physically intruding upon him, that would humiliate him the way he humiliated me. No words, no

A chapter in Patricia Williams's book The Alchemy of Race and Rights (1991), *which probes the roots of racism through anecdotes, personal accounts, and scholarly analysis. All notes in the essay are the author's.*

1. "When 'By Appointment' Means Keep Out," *New York Times*, December 17, 1986, p. B1. Letter to the Editor from Michael Levin and Marguerita Levin, *New York Times*, January 11, 1987, p. E32.

gestures, no prejudices of my own would make a bit of difference to him; his refusal to let me into the store—it was Benetton's, whose colorfully punnish ad campaign is premised on wrapping every one of the world's peoples in its cottons and woolens—was an outward manifestation of his never having let someone like me into the realm of his reality. He had no compassion, no remorse, no reference to me; and no desire to acknowledge me even at the estranged level of arm's-length transactor. He saw me only as one who would take his money and therefore could not conceive that I was there to give him money.

5   In this weird ontological imbalance, I realized that buying something in that store was like bestowing a gift, the gift of my commerce, the lucre of my patronage. In the wake of my outrage, I wanted to take back the gift of appreciation that my peering in the window must have appeared to be. I wanted to take it back in the form of unappreciation, disrespect, defilement. I wanted to work so hard at wishing he could feel what I felt that he would never again mistake my hatred for some sort of plaintive wish to be included. I was quite willing to disenfranchise myself, in the heat of my need to revoke the flattery of my purchasing power. I was willing to boycott Benetton's, random white-owned businesses, and anyone who ever blew bubble gum in my face again.

My rage was admittedly diffuse, even self-destructive, but it was symmetrical. The perhaps loose-ended but utter propriety of that rage is no doubt lost not just to the young man who actually barred me, but to those who would appreciate my being barred only as an abstract precaution, who approve of those who would bar even as they deny that they would bar *me*.

The violence of my desire to burst into Benetton's is probably quite apparent. I often wonder if the violence, the exclusionary hatred, is equally apparent in the repeated public urgings that blacks understand the buzzer system by putting themselves in the shoes of white storeowners—that, in effect, blacks look into the mirror of frightened white faces for the reality of their undesirability; and that then blacks would "just as surely conclude that [they] would not let [themselves] in under similar circumstances."[2] (That some blacks might agree merely shows that some of us have learned too well the lessons of privatized intimacies of self-hatred and rationalized away the fullness of our public, participatory selves.)

On the same day I was barred from Benetton's, I went home and wrote the above impassioned account in my journal. On the day after that, I found I was still brooding, so I turned to a form of catharsis I have always found healing. I typed up as much of the story as I have just told, made a big poster of it, put a nice colorful border around it, and, after Benetton's was truly closed, stuck it to their big sweater-filled window. I exercised my first-amendment right to place my business with them right out in the street.

So that was the first telling of this story. The second telling came a few months later, for a symposium on Excluded Voices sponsored by a law review. I wrote an essay summing up my feelings about being excluded from Benet-

2. *New York Times*, January 11, 1987, p. E32.

ton's and analyzing "how the rhetoric of increased privatization, in response to racial issues, functions as the rationalizing agent of public unaccountability and, ultimately, irresponsibility." Weeks later, I received the first edit. From the first page to the last, my fury had been carefully cut out. My rushing, run-on rage had been reduced to simple declarative sentences. The active personal had been inverted in favor of the passive impersonal. My words were different; they spoke to me upside down. I was afraid to read too much of it at a time— meanings rose up at me oddly, stolen and strange.

A week and a half later, I received the second edit. All reference to Benet- 10 ton's had been deleted because, according to the editors and the faculty adviser, it was defamatory; they feared harassment and liability; they said printing it would be irresponsible. I called them and offered to supply a footnote attesting to this as my personal experience at one particular location and of a buzzer system not limited to Benetton's; the editors told me that they were not in the habit of publishing things that were unverifiable. I could not but wonder, in this refusal even to let me file an affadavit, what it would take to make my experience verifiable. The testimony of an independent white bystander? (a requirement in fact imposed in U.S. Supreme Court holdings through the first part of the century).[3]

Two days *after* the piece was sent to press, I received copies of the final page proofs. All reference to my race had been eliminated because it was against "editorial policy" to permit descriptions of physiognomy. "I realize," wrote one editor, "that this was a very personal experience, but any reader will know what you must have looked like when standing at that window." In a telephone conversation to them, I ranted wildly about the significance of such an omission. "It's irrelevant," another editor explained in a voice gummy with soothing and patience; "It's nice and poetic," but it doesn't "advance the discussion of any principle . . . This is a law review, after all." Frustrated, I accused him of censorship; calmly he assured me it was not. "This is just a matter of style," he said with firmness and finality.

Ultimately I did convince the editors that mention of my race was central to the whole sense of the subsequent text; that my story became one of extreme paranoia without the information that I am black; or that it became one in which the reader had to fill in the gap by assumption, presumption, prejudgment, or prejudice. What was most interesting to me in this experience was how the blind application of principles of neutrality, through the device of omission, acted either to make me look crazy or to make the reader participate in old habits of cultural bias.

That was the second telling of my story. The third telling came last April, when I was invited to participate in a law-school conference on Equality and Difference. I retold my sad tale of exclusion from Soho's most glitzy boutique, focusing in this version on the law-review editing process as a consequence of an ideology of style rooted in a social text of neutrality. I opined:

---

3. See generally *Blyew v. U.S.*, 80 U.S. 581 (1871), upholding a state's right to forbid blacks to testify against whites.

Law and legal writing aspire to formalized, color-blind, liberal ideals. Neutrality is the standard for assuring these ideals; yet the adherence to it is often determined by reference to an aesthetic of uniformity, in which difference is simply omitted. For example, when segregation was eradicated from the American lexicon, its omission led many to actually believe that racism therefore no longer existed. Race-neutrality in law has become the presumed antidote for race bias in real life. With the entrenchment of the notion of race-neutrality came attacks on the concept of affirmative action and the rise of reverse discrimination suits. Blacks, for so many generations deprived of jobs based on the color of our skin, are now told that we ought to find it demeaning to be hired, based on the color of our skin. Such is the silliness of simplistic either-or inversions as remedies to complex problems.

What is truly demeaning in this era of double-speak-no-evil is going on interviews and not getting hired because someone doesn't think we'll be comfortable. It is demeaning not to get promoted because we're judged "too weak," then putting in a lot of energy the next time and getting fired because we're "too strong." It is demeaning to be told what we find demeaning. It is very demeaning to stand on street corners unemployed and begging. It is downright demeaning to have to explain why we haven't been employed for months and then watch the job go to someone who is "more experienced." It is outrageously demeaning that none of this can be called racism, even if it happens only to, or to large numbers of, black people; as long as it's done with a smile, a handshake and a shrug; as long as the phantom-word "race" is never used.

The image of race as a phantom-word came to me after I moved into my late godmother's home. In an attempt to make it my own, I cleared the bedroom for painting. The following morning the room asserted itself, came rushing and raging at me through the emptiness, exactly as it had been for twenty-five years. One day filled with profuse and overwhelming complexity, the next day filled with persistently recurring memories. The shape of the past came to haunt me, the shape of the emptiness confronted me each time I was about to enter the room. The force of its spirit still drifts like an odor throughout the house.

The power of that room, I have thought since, is very like the power of racism as status quo: it is deep, angry, eradicated from view, but strong enough to make everyone who enters the room walk around the bed that isn't there, avoiding the phantom as they did the substance, for fear of bodily harm. They do not even know they are avoiding; they defer to the unseen shapes of things with subtle responsiveness, guided by an impulsive awareness of nothingness, and the deep knowledge and denial of witchcraft at work.

The phantom room is to me symbolic of the emptiness of formal equal opportunity, particularly as propounded by President Reagan, the Reagan Civil Rights Commission and the Reagan Supreme Court. Blindly formalized constructions of equal opportunity are the creation of a space that is filled in by a meandering stream of unguided hopes, dreams, fantasies, fears, recollections. They are the presence of the past in imaginary, imagistic form—the phantom-roomed exile of our longing.

It is thus that I strongly believe in the efficacy of programs and paradigms like affirmative action. Blacks are the objects of a constitutional omission which has been incorporated into a theory of neutrality. It is thus that omission is really a form of expression, as oxymoronic as that sounds: racial omission is a literal part of original intent; it is the fixed, reiterated prophecy of the Founding Fathers. It is thus that affirmative action is an affirmation; the affirmative act of hiring—or hearing—blacks is a recognition of individuality that re-places blacks as a social statistic, that is profoundly interconnective to the fate of blacks and whites either as sub-groups or as one group. In this sense, affirmative action is as mystical and beyond-the-self as an initiation ceremony. It is an act of verification and of vision. It is an act of social as well as professional responsibility.

The following morning I opened the local newspaper, to find that the event of my speech had commanded two columns on the front page of the Metro section. I quote only the opening lines: "Affirmative action promotes prejudice by denying the status of women and blacks, instead of affirming them as its name suggests. So said New York City attorney Patricia Williams to an audience Wednesday."[4]

I clipped out the article and put it in my journal. In the margin there is a note   15
to myself: eventually, it says, I should try to pull all these threads together into yet another law-review article. The problem, of course, will be that in the hierarchy of law-review citation, the article in the newspaper will have more authoritative weight about me, as a so-called "primary resource," than I will have; it will take precedence over my own citation of the unverifiable testimony of my speech.

I have used the Benetton's story a lot, in speaking engagements at various schools. I tell it whenever I am too tired to whip up an original speech from scratch. Here are some of the questions I have been asked in the wake of its telling:

Am I not privileging a racial perspective, by considering only the black point of view? Don't I have an obligation to include the "salesman's side" of the story?

Am I not putting the salesman on trial and finding him guilty of racism without giving him a chance to respond to or cross-examine me?

Am I not using the store window as a "metaphorical fence" against the potential of his explanation in order to represent my side as "authentic"?

How can I be sure I'm right?   20

What makes my experience the real black one anyway?

Isn't it possible that another black person would disagree with my experience? If so, doesn't that render my story too unempirical and subjective to pay any attention to?

Always a major objection is to my having put the poster on Benetton's window. As one law professor put it: "It's one thing to publish this in a law review, where no one can take it personally, but it's another thing altogether to put your own interpretation right out there, just like that, uncontested, I mean, with nothing to counter it."*

---

4. "Attorney Says Affirmative Action Denies Racism, Sexism," *Dominion Post* (Morgantown, West Virginia), April 8, 1988, p. B1.

* At the end of her essay, Williams added these observations. "These questions put me on trial—an imaginary trial where it is I who have the burden of proof—and proof being nothing less than the testimony of the salesman actually confessing yes yes I am a racist. These questions question my own ability to know, to assess, to be objective. And of course, since anything that happens to me is inherently subjective, they take away my power to know what happens to me in the world. Others, by this standard, will always know better than I. And my insistence on recounting stories from my own perspective will be treated as presumption, slander, paranoid hallucination, or just plain lies.

"Recently I got an urgent call from Thomas Grey of Stanford Law School. He had used this piece in his jurisprudence class, and a rumor got started that the Benetton's story wasn't true, that I had made it up, that it was a fantasy, a lie that was probably the product of a diseased mind trying to make all white people feel guilty. At this point I realized it almost didn't make any difference whether I was telling the truth or not—that the greater issue I had to face was the overwhelming weight of a disbelief that goes beyond mere disinclination to believe and becomes active suppression of anything I might have to say. The greater problem is a powerfully oppressive mechanism for denial of black self-knowledge and expression. And this denial cannot be separated from the simultaneously pathological willingness to believe certain things about blacks—not to believe them, but things about them.

"When students in Grey's class believed and then claimed that I had made it all up, they put me in a position like that of Tawana Brawley [a black woman who falsely claimed she was abducted and raped by white men (eds.)]. I mean that specifically: the social consequence of concluding that we are liars operates as a kind of public absolution of racism—the conclusion is not merely that we are troubled or that I am eccentric, but that we, as liars, are the norm. Therefore, the nonbelievers can believe, things of this sort really don't happen (even in the face of statistics to the contrary). Racism or rape is all a big fantasy concocted by troublesome minorities and women. It is interesting to recall the outcry in every national medium, from the *New York Post* to the *Times* to the major networks, in the wake of the Brawley case: who will ever again believe a black woman who cries rape by a white man? Now shift the frame a bit, and imagine a white male facing a consensus that he lied. Would there be a difference? Consider Charles Stuart, for example, the white Bostonian who accused a black man of murdering his pregnant wife and whose brother later alleged that in fact the brothers had conspired to murder her. Most people and the media not only did not claim but actively resisted believing that Stuart represented any kind of 'white male' norm. Instead he was written off as a troubled weirdo, a deviant—again even in the face of spousal-abuse statistics to the contrary. There was not a story I could find that carried on about 'who will ever believe' the next white man who cries murder."

MLA CITATION

Williams, Patricia. "The Death of the Profane: The Rhetoric of Race and Rights." *The Norton Reader: An Anthology of Nonfiction*, edited by Melissa A. Goldthwaite et al., 15th ed., W. W. Norton, 2020, pp. 219–24.

QUESTIONS

1. Patricia Williams's essay is about how the "objective," "neutral" forms writing often takes can drain away the significance of a particular person's story. Can you find examples of this phenomenon in other writings you have read? Or can you find examples of it on TV or radio talk shows, for instance?

2. How does Williams move from the Benetton story to her larger point?

3. How would you characterize the tone of Williams's essay? Does any of her original rage remain?

4. What do you think of Williams's posting her reaction on the Benetton window? Write your opinion of the function and effectiveness of this action.

BARBARA KINGSOLVER
#MeToo Isn't Enough

I N EACH OF MY DAUGHTERS' LIVES came the day in fifth grade when we had to sit on her bed and practice. I pretended to be the boy in class who was making her sick with dread. She had to look right at me and repeat the words until they felt possible, if not easy: "Don't say that to me. Don't do that to me. I hate it." As much as I wanted to knock heads around, I knew the only real solution was to arm a daughter for self-defense. But why was it so hard to put teeth into that defense? Why does it come more naturally to smile through clenched teeth and say "Oh, stop," in the mollifying tone so regularly, infuriatingly mistaken for flirtation?

Women my age could answer that we were raised that way. We've done better with our daughters but still find ourselves right here, where male puberty opens a lifelong season of sexual aggression, and girls struggle for the voice to call it off. The *Mad Men* cliché of the boss cornering his besotted secretary is the modern cliché of the pop icon with his adulating, naked-ish harem in a story that never changes: attracting male attention is a woman's success. Rejecting it feels rude, like refusing an award. It feels ugly.

Now, all at once, women are refusing to accept sexual aggression as any kind of award, and men are getting fired from their jobs. It feels like an earthquake. Men and women alike find ourselves disoriented, wondering what the rules are. Women know perfectly well that we hate unsolicited sexual attention, but navigate a minefield of male thinking on what "solicit" might mean. We've spent so much life-force on looking good but not too good, being professional but not unapproachable, while the guys just got on with life. And what of the massive costs of permanent vigilance, the tense smiles, declined work assignments and lost chances that are our daily job of trying to avoid assault? Can we get some backpay?

I think we're trying to do that now, as the opening volleys of #MeToo smack us with backlash against backlash. Patriarchy persists because power does not willingly cede its clout; and also, frankly, because women are widely complicit in the assumption that we're separate and not quite equal. If we're woke, we inspect ourselves and others for implicit racial bias, while mostly failing to recognize explicit gender bias, which still runs rampant. Religious faiths that subordinate women flourish on every continent. Nearly every American educational institution pours the lion's share of its athletics budget into the one sport that still excludes women—American football.

Most progressives wouldn't hesitate to attend a football game, or to   5
praise the enlightened new pope—the one who says he's sorry, but women

The #MeToo movement was founded in 2006 by Tarana Burke in an effort to help survivors of sexual violence, especially black girls, find solidarity, healing, and community. #MeToo returned to the headlines in 2018 in the wake of multiple sexual assault allegations against Hollywood producer Harvey Weinstein. This essay was first published in the British newspaper The Guardian, *January 16, 2018.*

still can't lead his church, or control our reproduction.[1] In heterosexual weddings, religious or secular, the patriarch routinely "gives" his daughter to the groom, after which she's presented to the audience as "Mrs New Patriarch," to joyous applause. We have other options, of course: I kept my name in marriage and gave it to my daughters. But most modern brides still embrace the ritual erasure of their identities, taking the legal name of a new male head of household, as enslaved people used to do when they came to a new plantation owner.

I can already hear the outcry against conflating traditional marriage with slavery. Yes, I know, the marital bargain has changed: women are no longer chattels. Tell me this giving-away and name-changing are just vestiges of a cherished tradition. I'll reply that some of my neighbors here in the south still fly the Confederate flag—not with hate, they insist, but to honor a proud tradition. In either case, a tradition in which people legally control other people doesn't strike me as worth celebrating, even symbolically.

If any contract between men required the non-white one to adopt the legal identity of his Caucasian companion, would we pop the champagne? If any sport wholly excluded people of color, would it fill stadiums throughout the land? Would we attend a church whose sacred texts consign Latinos to inferior roles? What about galas where black and Asian participants must wear painful shoes and clothes that reveal lots of titillating, well-toned flesh while white people turn up comfortably covered?

No wonder there is confusion about this volcano of outrage against men who objectify and harass. Marriage is not slavery, but a willingness to subvert our very names in our primary partnership might confound everyone's thinking about where women stand in our other relationships with men. And if our sex lives aren't solely ours to control, but also the purview of men of the cloth, why not employers too? We may ache for gender equality but we're rarely framing or fighting for it in the same ways we fight for racial equality. The #MeToo movement can't bring justice to a culture so habituated to misogyny that we can't even fathom parity, and women still dread losing the power we've been taught to use best: our charm.

Years ago, as a college student, I spent a semester abroad in a beautiful, historic city where the two sentences I heard most in English, usually conjoined, were "You want to go for coffee?" and "You want to have sex with me, baby?" I lived near a huge public garden where I wished I could walk or study, but couldn't, without being followed, threatened and subjected to jarring revelations of some creep's penis among the foliages. My experiment in worldliness had me trapped, fuming, in a tiny apartment.

10   One day in a fit of weird defiance I tied a sofa cushion to my belly under a loose dress and discovered this was the magic charm: I could walk anywhere, unmolested. I carried my after-class false pregnancy to the end of the term,

1. Pope Francis (b. 1936, Jorge Mario Bergoglio), leader of the Roman Catholic church since 2013, reaffirmed the Church's opposition to both the ordination of women and the use of birth control in 2016.

happily ignored by predators. As a lissome 20-year-old I resented my waddly disguise, but came around to a riveting truth: being attractive was less useful to me than being free.

Modern women's magazines promise we don't have to choose, we can be sovereign powers and seductresses both at once. But study the pictures and see an attractiveness imbued with submission and myriad forms of punitive self-alteration. Actually, we have to choose: not one or the other utterly, but some functional point between these poles. It starts with a sober reckoning of how much we really need to be liked by the universe of men. Not all men confuse "liking" with conquest, of course—just the handful of jerks who poison the well, and the larger number who think they are funny. Plus the majority of the U.S. male electorate, who put a boastful assaulter in charge of us all.

This is the point. The universe of men does not merit women's indiscriminate grace. If the #MeToo revolution has proved anything, it's that women live under threat. Not sometimes, but all the time.

We don't have unlimited options about working for male approval, since here in this world that is known as "approval." We also want to be loved, probably we want it too much. But loved. Bear with us while we sort this out, and begin to codify it in the bluntest terms. Enduring some guy's copped feel or a gander at his plumbing is so very much not a Valentine. It is a letter bomb. It can blow up a day, an interview, a job, a home, the very notion of safety inside our bodies.

It shouldn't be this hard to demand safety while we do our work, wear whatever, walk where we need to go. And yet, for countless women enduring harassment on the job, it is this hard, and escape routes are few. The path to freedom is paved with many special words for "hideously demanding person" that only apply to females.

Chaining the links of our experiences behind a hashtag can help supply the courage to be unlovely while we blast an ugly reality into the open. The chain doesn't negate women's individuality or our capacity to trust men individually, nor does it suggest every assault is the same. Raped is not groped is not catcalled on the street: all these are vile and have to stop, but the damages are different. Women who wish to be more than bodies can use our brains to discern context and the need for cultural education. In lieu of beguiling we can be rational, which means giving the accused a fair hearing and a sentence that fits the crime. (Let it also be said, losing executive power is not the death penalty, even if some people are carrying on as if it were.) Polarization is as obstructive in gender politics as in any other forum. Sympathetic men are valuable allies.

Let's be clear: no woman asks to live in a rape culture:[2] we all want it over, yesterday. Mixed signals about female autonomy won't help bring it down, and neither will asking nicely. Nothing changes until truly powerful offenders start to fall. Feminine instincts for sweetness and apology have no skin in this

15

---

2. Sociological term coined in the 1970s (see, for example, the 1975 film *Rape Culture*) to describe the way that mass media and popular culture make sexual violence seem normal and even glamorous.

game. It's really not possible to overreact to uncountable, consecutive days of being humiliated by men who say our experience isn't real, or that we like it actually, or are cute when we're mad. Anger has to go somewhere—if not out then inward, in a psychic thermodynamics that can turn a nation of women into pressure cookers. Watching the election of a predator-in-chief seems to have popped the lid off the can. We've found a voice, and now is a good time to use it, in a tone that will not be mistaken for flirtation.

Don't say that to me. Don't do that to me. I hate it.

MLA CITATION

Kingsolver, Barbara. "#MeToo Isn't Enough." *The Norton Reader: An Anthology of Nonfiction*, edited by Melissa A. Goldthwaite et al., 15th ed., W. W. Norton, 2020, pp. 225–28.

QUESTIONS

1. In paragraph 1, Barbara Kingsolver describes teaching her daughters how to say no to unwanted sexual touching. How effective do you think this is as part of sexual education? How does it compare to what you have been taught about how to say no to unwanted sexual aggression?

2. Kingsolver begins to enumerate "the massive costs of permanent vigilance" (paragraph 3). How would you describe those costs? What are other examples of how women "pay" for being women? What is the cost to men?

3. Kingsolver ends the essay by repeating her advice to her daughters, this time to the culture at large. How does the repetition of the line "Don't say that to me. Don't do that to me. I hate it" (paragraph 17) affect the essay's conclusion?

4. Choose one of the areas that Kingsolver identifies as a cultural space where women remain unequal. Research some of the statistical differences between how women and men are treated in that area and write an essay describing the ongoing challenges and suggesting how we might work toward more equal relations.

5 FOOD

Our three basic needs, for food and security and love, are so
mixed and mingled and entwined that we cannot straightly
think of one without the others.

—M. F. K. FISHER

In her foreword to *The Gastronomical Me*, M. F. K. Fisher writes in answer to those who ask her, "Why do you write about food, and eating and drinking? Why don't you write about the struggle for power and security, and about love, the way others do?" Her answer, in part, as quoted in the epigraph above is that writing about food involves a hunger for love, security, and warmth. As you read the selections in this chapter, you'll be reading about food, but you'll also be reading about topics and ideas that intersect with food: work, art, disability, ethnicity, culture, religion, the environment, health, and advertising.

Although the genres the authors use differ—from Teresa Lust's personal essay to Kate Holbrook's academic argument to Dan Barber's op-ed—many of the strategies they use are similar. In writing about food, nearly all writers use description, sensory detail, and specific examples. Some authors use detail to show the physical act of preparing food, as Chris Wiewiora does in "This Is Tossing" when he describes "the dough not only slapping but also rotating between your palms in a figure eight, an infinity symbol, an hourglass." His use of strong verbs and metaphors helps readers see and feel the process of tossing pizza dough. Likewise, JJ Goode uses similar strategies in describing the challenge of cooking with one arm.

Many of the authors included in this chapter use sensory detail to make food sound appealing. Diana Abu-Jaber describes her grandmother's "cookies covered with sugar crystals like crushed rubies, the beckoning finger of vanilla." That same precision, however, can also show less appetizing qualities—even of food many people love—as when Anthony Bourdain describes "sodium-loaded pork fat, stinky triple-cream cheeses, the tender thymus glands and distended livers of young animals." Whether you wish to show the beauty or ugliness, the challenge or joy of cooking and eating, close attention to details and well-chosen verbs heighten the readers' experience, giving them a taste of someone else's experience.

Even when writing about larger issues rather than particular dishes or cooking techniques, the authors in this chapter pay close attention to details, and they provide specific examples. To support her argument that the dietary codes of the Church of Jesus Christ of Latter-day Saints and of the Nation of Islam were shaped by American sensibilities and values, Holbrook analyzes specific recipes associated with each group. In making a larger argument about sustainable food practices, Barber relates the knowledge he gained about soil from visiting Lakeview Organic Grain Farm. Marion Nestle, in "Superfoods Are a Marketing Ploy," uses the example of the marketing of wild blueberries in order to show that "superfoods" is an advertising concept rather than a nutritionally accurate term.

As the essays in this chapter illustrate, culture, religion, history, tradition, economics, ability, health, and location all affect what we eat, how we prepare food, and how we relate to others and to the environment. Whether you're writing a personal essay that shows how your family's ethnicity or culture influenced the food you ate or you're making an argument about how religion and culture are entwined, you're likely—as Fisher asserts—writing about some mix of larger issues: food, security, love. Choosing specific dishes or moments to illustrate larger ideas or claims helps ground your audience and clarifies both experience and ideas. In considering topics for your own writing, you might choose some of these questions: Have you ever worked in a restaurant? If so, what experiences stand out in your memory—and why? What foods or traditions from your family differ from those of your friends' families? What can you learn from those differences? What restrictions do you place on your own eating—and why? Are those restrictions related to religion, environmental concerns, health concerns, or something else? Is there research that informs, supports, or contradicts your experience with food? How does marketing inform the dietary choices you make?

ANTHONY BOURDAIN

Don't Eat before Reading This

GOOD FOOD, GOOD EATING, is all about blood and organs, cruelty and decay. It's about sodium-loaded pork fat, stinky triple-cream cheeses, the tender thymus glands and distended livers of young animals. It's about danger—risking the dark, bacterial forces of beef, chicken, cheese, and shellfish. Your first two hundred and seven Wellfleet oysters may transport you to a state of rapture, but your two hundred and eighth may send you to bed with the sweats, chills, and vomits.

Gastronomy is the science of pain. Professional cooks belong to a secret society whose ancient rituals derive from the principles of stoicism in the face of humiliation, injury, fatigue, and the threat of illness. The members of a tight, well-greased kitchen staff are a lot like a submarine crew. Confined for most of their waking hours in hot, airless spaces, and ruled by despotic leaders, they often acquire the characteristics of the poor saps who were press-ganged into the royal navies of Napoleonic times—superstition, a contempt for outsiders, and a loyalty to no flag but their own.

First published in the New Yorker *(1999). Bourdain expanded the article, later publishing* Kitchen Confidential: Adventures in the Culinary Underbelly *(2000), a memoir about working in the restaurant industry.*

A good deal has changed since Orwell's[1] memoir of the months he spent as a dishwasher in "Down and Out in Paris and London." Gas ranges and exhaust fans have gone a long way toward increasing the life span of the working culinarian. Nowadays, most aspiring cooks come into the business because they want to: they have chosen this life, studied for it. Today's top chefs are like star athletes. They bounce from kitchen to kitchen—free agents in search of more money, more acclaim.

I've been a chef in New York for more than ten years, and, for the decade before that, a dishwasher, a prep drone, a line cook, and a sous-chef. I came into the business when cooks still smoked on the line and wore headbands. A few years ago, I wasn't surprised to hear rumors of a study of the nation's prison population which reportedly found that the leading civilian occupation among inmates before they were put behind bars was "cook." As most of us in the restaurant business know, there is a powerful strain of criminality in the industry, ranging from the dope-dealing busboy with beeper and cell phone to the restaurant owner who has two sets of accounting books. In fact, it was the unsavory side of professional cooking that attracted me to it in the first place. In the early seventies, I dropped out of college and transferred to the Culinary Institute of America. I wanted it all: the cuts and burns on hands and wrists, the ghoulish kitchen humor, the free food, the pilfered booze, the camaraderie that flourished within rigid order and nerve-shattering chaos. I would climb the chain of command from *mal carne* (meaning "bad meat," or "new guy") to chefdom—doing whatever it took until I ran my own kitchen and had my own crew of cutthroats, the culinary equivalent of "The Wild Bunch."[2]

A year ago, my latest, doomed mission—a high-profile restaurant in the Times Square area—went out of business. The meat, fish, and produce purveyors got the news that they were going to take it in the neck for yet another ill-conceived enterprise. When customers called for reservations, they were informed by a prerecorded announcement that our doors had closed. Fresh from that experience, I began thinking about becoming a traitor to my profession.

Say it's a quiet Monday night, and you've just checked your coat in that swanky Art Deco update in the Flatiron district, and you're looking to tuck into a thick slab of pepper-crusted yellowfin tuna or a twenty-ounce cut of certified Black Angus beef, well-done—what are you in for?

The fish specialty is reasonably priced, and the place got two stars in the Times. Why not go for it? If you like four-day-old fish, be my guest. Here's how things usually work. The chef orders his seafood for the weekend on Thursday night. It arrives on Friday morning. He's hoping to sell the bulk of it on Friday and Saturday nights, when he knows that the restaurant will be busy, and he'd like to run out of the last few orders by Sunday evening. Many fish purveyors

5

1. George Orwell (1903–1950), English novelist and writer of nonfiction; see "Politics and the English Language" (pp. 415–424) and "Shooting an Elephant" (pp. 728–733).
2. American Western film (1969) known for its violence and the willingness of the characters to do whatever was necessary in order to survive.

don't deliver on Saturday, so the chances are that the Monday-night tuna you want has been kicking around in the kitchen since Friday morning, under God knows what conditions. When a kitchen is in full swing, proper refrigeration is almost nonexistent, what with the many openings of the refrigerator door as the cooks rummage frantically during the rush, mingling your tuna with the chicken, the lamb, or the beef. Even if the chef has ordered just the right amount of tuna for the weekend, and has had to reorder it for a Monday delivery, the only safeguard against the seafood supplier's off-loading junk is the presence of a vigilant chef who can make sure that the delivery is fresh from *Sunday* night's market.

Generally speaking, the good stuff comes in on Tuesday: the seafood is fresh, the supply of prepared food is new, and the chef, presumably, is relaxed after his day off. (Most chefs don't work on Monday.) Chefs prefer to cook for weekday customers rather than for weekenders, and they like to start the new week with their most creative dishes. In New York, locals dine during the week. Weekends are considered amateur nights—for tourists, rubes, and the well-done-ordering pretheatre hordes. The fish may be just as fresh on Friday, but it's on Tuesday that you've got the good will of the kitchen on your side.

People who order their meat well-done perform a valuable service for those of us in the business who are cost-conscious: they pay for the privilege of eating our garbage. In many kitchens, there's a time-honored practice called "save for well-done." When one of the cooks finds a particularly unlovely piece of steak—tough, riddled with nerve and connective tissue, off the hip end of the loin, and maybe a little stinky from age—he'll dangle it in the air and say, "Hey, Chef, whaddya want me to do with *this*?" Now, the chef has three options. He can tell the cook to throw the offending item into the trash, but that means a total loss, and in the restaurant business every item of cut, fabricated, or prepared food should earn at least three times the amount it originally cost if the chef is to make his correct food-cost percentage. Or he can decide to serve that steak to "the family"—that is, the floor staff—though that, economically, is the same as throwing it out. But no. What he's going to do is repeat the mantra of cost-conscious chefs everywhere: "Save for well-done." The way he figures it, the philistine who orders his food well-done is not likely to notice the difference between food and flotsam.

Then there are the People Who Brunch. The "B" word is dreaded by all dedicated cooks. We hate the smell and spatter of omelettes. We despise hollandaise, home fries, those pathetic fruit garnishes, and all the other cliché accompaniments designed to induce a credulous public into paying $12.95 for two eggs. Nothing demoralizes an aspiring Escoffier[3] faster than requiring him to cook egg-white omelettes or eggs over easy with bacon. You can dress brunch up with all the focaccia, smoked salmon, and caviar in the world, but it's still breakfast.

Even more despised than the Brunch People are the vegetarians. Serious cooks regard these members of the dining public—and their Hezbollah-like[4] splinter faction, the vegans—as enemies of everything that's good and decent in the human spirit. To live life without veal or chicken stock, fish cheeks, sausages, cheese, or organ meats is treasonous.

Like most other chefs I know, I'm amused when I hear people object to pork on nonreligious grounds. "Swine are filthy animals," they say. These people have obviously never visited a poultry farm. Chicken—America's favorite food—goes bad quickly; handled carelessly, it infects other foods with salmonella; and it bores the hell out of chefs. It occupies its ubiquitous place on menus as an option for customers who can't decide what they want to eat. Most chefs believe that supermarket chickens in this country are slimy and tasteless compared with European varieties. Pork, on the other hand, is cool. Farmers stopped feeding garbage to pigs decades ago, and even if you eat pork rare you're more likely to win the Lotto than to contract trichinosis. Pork tastes different, depending on what you do with it, but chicken always tastes like chicken.

3. Auguste Escoffier (1846–1935), famous French chef who directed the kitchens at the Savoy Hotel and the Carlton Hotel in London.
4. Shi'a Islamist militant group that is considered a terrorist organization by the United States and several other countries.

Another much maligned food these days is butter. In the world of chefs, however, butter is in everything. Even non-French restaurants—the Northern Italian; the new American, the ones where the chef brags about how he's "getting away from butter and cream"—throw butter around like crazy. In almost every restaurant worth patronizing, sauces are enriched with mellowing, emulsifying butter. Pastas are tightened with it. Meat and fish are seared with a mixture of butter and oil. Shallots and chicken are caramelized with butter. It's the first and last thing in almost every pan: the final hit is called "*monter au beurre.*" In a good restaurant, what this all adds up to is that you could be putting away almost a stick of butter with every meal.

If you are one of those people who cringe at the thought of strangers fondling your food, you shouldn't go out to eat. As the author and former chef Nicolas Freeling notes in his definitive book "The Kitchen," the better the restaurant, the more your food has been prodded, poked, handled, and tasted. By the time a three-star crew has finished carving and arranging your saddle of monkfish with dried cherries and wild-herb-infused *nage* into a Parthenon or a Space Needle, it's had dozens of sweaty fingers all over it. Gloves? You'll find a box of surgical gloves—in my kitchen we call them "anal-research gloves"—over every station on the line, for the benefit of the health inspectors, but does anyone actually use them? Yes, a cook will slip a pair on every now and then, especially when he's handling something with a lingering odor, like salmon. But during the hours of service gloves are clumsy and dangerous. When you're using your hands constantly, latex will make you drop things, which is the last thing you want to do.

15 Finding a hair in your food will make anyone gag. But just about the only place you'll see anyone in the kitchen wearing a hat or a hairnet is Blimpie. For most chefs, wearing anything on their head, especially one of those picturesque paper toques—they're often referred to as "coffee filters"—is a nuisance: they dissolve when you sweat, bump into range hoods, burst into flame.

The fact is that most good kitchens are far less septic than your kitchen at home. I run a scrupulously clean, orderly restaurant kitchen, where food is rotated and handled and stored very conscientiously. But if the city's Department of Health or the E.P.A. decided to enforce every aspect of its codes, most of us would be out on the street. Recently, there was a news report about the practice of recycling bread. By means of a hidden camera in a restaurant, the reporter was horrified to see returned bread being sent right back out to the floor. This, to me, wasn't news: the reuse of bread has been an open secret—and a fairly standard practice—in the industry for years. It makes more sense to worry about what happens to the leftover table butter—many restaurants recycle it for hollandaise.

What do I like to eat after hours? Strange things. Oysters are my favorite, especially at three in the morning, in the company of my crew. Focaccia pizza with robiola cheese and white truffle oil is good, especially at Le Madri on a summer afternoon in the outdoor patio. Frozen vodka at Siberia Bar is also good, particularly if a cook from one of the big hotels shows up with beluga. At Indigo, on Tenth Street, I love the mushroom strudel and the daube of beef. At my own place, I love a spicy boudin noir that squirts blood in your mouth; the braised fennel the way my sous-chef makes it; scraps from duck confit; and fresh cockles steamed with greasy Portuguese sausage.

I love the sheer weirdness of the kitchen life: the dreamers, the crackpots, the refugees, and the sociopaths with whom I continue to work; the ever-present smells of roasting bones, searing fish, and simmering liquids; the noise and clatter, the hiss and spray, the flames, the smoke, and the steam. Admittedly, it's a life that grinds you down. Most of us who live and operate in the culinary underworld are in some fundamental way dysfunctional. We've all chosen to turn our backs on the nine-to-five, on ever having a Friday or Saturday night off, on ever having a normal relationship with a non-cook.

Being a chef is a lot like being an air-traffic controller: you are constantly dealing with the threat of disaster. You've got to be Mom and Dad, drill sergeant, detective, psychiatrist, and priest to a crew of opportunistic, mercenary hooligans, whom you must protect from the nefarious and often foolish strategies of owners. Year after year, cooks contend with bouncing paychecks, irate purveyors, desperate owners looking for the masterstroke that will cure their restaurant's ills: Live Cabaret! Free Shrimp! New Orleans Brunch!

In America, the professional kitchen is the last refuge of the misfit. It's a   20
place for people with bad pasts to find a new family. It's a haven for foreigners—Ecuadorians, Mexicans, Chinese, Senegalese, Egyptians, Poles. In New York, the main linguistic spice is Spanish. "*Hey, maricón! chupa mis huevos*" means, roughly, "How are you, valued comrade? I hope all is well." And you hear "*Hey, baboso!* Put some more brown jiz on the fire and check your meez before the sous comes back there and fucks you in the *culo!*," which means "Please reduce some additional *demi-glace*, brother, and reëxamine your *mise en place*, because the sous-chef is concerned about your state of readiness."

Since we work in close quarters, and so many blunt and sharp objects are at hand, you'd think that cooks would kill one another with regularity. I've seen guys duking it out in the waiter station over who gets a table for six. I've seen a chef clamp his teeth on a waiter's nose. And I've seen plates thrown—I've even thrown a few myself—but I've never heard of one cook jamming a boning knife into another cook's rib cage or braining him with a meat mallet. Line cooking, done well, is a dance—a highspeed, Balanchine collaboration.

I used to be a terror toward my floor staff, particularly in the final months of my last restaurant. But not anymore. Recently, my career has taken an eerily appropriate turn: these days, I'm the chef de cuisine of a much loved, old-school French brasserie/bistro where the customers eat their meat rare, vegetarians are scarce, and every part of the animal—hooves, snout, cheeks, skin, and organs—is avidly and appreciatively prepared and consumed. Cassoulet, pigs' feet, tripe, and charcuterie sell like crazy. We thicken many sauces with foie gras and pork blood, and proudly hurl around spoonfuls of duck fat and butter, and thick hunks of country bacon. I made a traditional French pot-au-feu a few weeks ago, and some of my French colleagues—hardened veterans of the business all—came into my kitchen to watch the first order go out. As they gazed upon the intimidating heap of short ribs, oxtail, beef shoulder, cabbage, turnips, carrots, and potatoes, the expressions on their faces were those of religious supplicants. I have come home.

MLA CITATION

Bourdain, Anthony. "Don't Eat before Reading This." *The Norton Reader: An Anthology of Nonfiction*, edited by Melissa A. Goldthwaite et al., 15th ed., W. W. Norton, 2020, pp. 230–35.

QUESTIONS

1. From the title, "Don't Eat before Reading This," to the opening sentence that references "blood and organs, cruelty and decay" (paragraph 1), Anthony Bourdain makes clear that his essay about working in restaurants will not gloss over the darker side of food preparation and eating. What was his purpose in being straight-forward about even the unsavory parts of running a kitchen? What did you learn about eating out from reading this essay?

2. Bourdain often uses similes and metaphors to show something about a group of people. For example, he describes kitchen staff as "a submarine crew" (paragraph 2), top chefs as "star athletes" (paragraph 3), and vegans as a "Hezbollah-like splin-ter faction" (paragraph 11). Trace these and his other uses of simile and metaphor. Which ones are most or least effective? Why?

3. Bourdain categorizes some of the different types of people who eat in restaurants: "People who order their meat well-done" (paragraph 9), "People Who Brunch" (para-graph 10), vegetarians and vegans (paragraph 11). Write about a job you have had, showing through the use of categories some of the people with whom you interacted.

CHRIS WIEWIORA
This Is Tossing

I T'S 10 A.M. An hour before Lazy Moon Pizzeria opens. You have an hour—this hour—to toss. You're supposed to have 11 pies by 11 A.M. One hour.
  You have always failed to have 11 by 11. Sometimes you fail because you went to bed after midnight or didn't have a bowl of cereal in the morning or you tear a pie and then you're already down one and you don't believe you can ever be anywhere near perfect. On those days, the store manager comes over and inspects your not-yet-full pie rack and shakes his head. More often, you fail because the manager didn't turn on the doughpress, so you have to wait for it to warm up; or he didn't pull a tray of dough from the fridge, so all the doughballs are still frozen; or one of the two ovens wasn't turned on, so you'll be slower without being able to cook two pies at once. On those days you shake your head and maybe swear a bit, cursing the situation

Published in MAKE (2013), *a Chicago-based literary magazine that is "chock full of fiction, poetry, essays, art, and review." Chris Wiewiora's essay appeared in an issue devoted to architecture.*

more than the manager, because you already feel like a failure before you've even started. Either way, this everyday failure to meet a near impossible expectation weighs down on you. If you could do 11 by 11—just once—you feel like you would truly be a professional, albeit a professional pizza tosser, and it would prove that what you do in this restaurant matters.

But instead of focusing on all that, focus on what you can do: try to go to bed early the night before, in the morning eat a bowl of cereal with your coffee, and on the way to work take it easy, drive nice and easy—not slow or fast, but easy—because 11 by 11 is hard, almost impossible, and you don't need to think about that when you open the door to the restaurant's *err-err* electronic buzzer.

And today when you walk in, in between the *err-err*, the music blasting through the restaurant's sound system is good; some simple drum beats, a bass line thumping in your throat, and guitar riffs with a hook. Bluesy rock 'n' roll. You bounce your foot as you put on your apron and clock in a few minutes early.

You wash your hands humming the Happy Birthday song to yourself. It's not your birthday, or anyone's birthday that you know of, but you're supposed to wash your hands for approximately 20 seconds. There's a laminated paper above all the hand-washing sinks that says to sing the ABCs, but you don't want to feel like some kid who doesn't know how to do his job.

Today, and all days that you toss, you're tucked behind the counter by the door, where you will welcome customers when they come in. But for now you should focus on tossing. You take a look at the clock. It blinks 9:59 a.m. You have an hour.

You check that the doughpress is on; it ticks like a coffeemaker's hotplate. The temperature knob is set right. And (yes!) there's a tray of dough already out. You're ready. Here goes.

The dough has risen a little, each bag forming a sliced-off cone, a plateau. You take the spray bottle of extra virgin olive oil and squirt twice on a hubcap-size round plate that you call the swivel plate because it's set on a swivel arm attached to the dough press. You spread the oil on the swivel plate with your bare hands, glossing the surface as well as your skin.

You pick up a bag of dough, feeling its weight settle in your palm. You know it's at least three point five pounds, no more than three point seven five. And out of the plastic, the dough feels like condensed flesh, like a too-heavy breast. You can't help that that's what you think of when you take the mound of dough in your hands and place it nippleside up on the swivel plate.

You push the cone down into itself to form a thick circle. You keep pushing with the palm of your hand around and around the circle to even it out, so the circle of dough will fit in the space the swivel plate will swivel under. Above is a heated plate that will come down and sandwich the dough.

You swivel the swivel plate, lining it up with the hotplate, and take hold of a lever in front of you and pull down with both hands. You don't press down so hard that the dough spills out of the circumference, but also not so lightly that the dough only warms on the outside while the core is still cold. You count six "Mississippi's" as the dough flattens and warms and expands into a bigger and bigger and bigger and bigger and bigger and bigger circle.

You pull up the handle, swivel out that swivel plate, take the edge of the dough in your hand, flip it over like a pancake, swivel the swivel plate back into its space and pull down on the handle, letting the hotplate press down again. You repeat until the fourth flip, when you *really* press down, spilling the dough out the sides. You lift up the handle and again swivel out the swivel plate, but now you lift the dough up and off the swivel plate altogether, placing it onto a tray called a sheetpan.

This circle of dough is called a patout, because before the dough press—and you can imagine how hard it was to do this—tossers would have to physically push down on the cold dough and shape it with force. No more than six patouts stack each tray, because more than that squishes them with their own weight. When you have filled two trays they go one above the other on a rack-cart that you wheel under a stainless steel counter.

At the counter, you burrito-roll each patout off the tray and unfurl it. There are two plastic containers: one with bright yellow grains like sand (but it's cornmeal), and another filled with fluffy flour. For now, it's only flour you need. You take a handful and spread it on the stainless steel counter, powdering the olive-oil-slick dough. Along the edge of the floured patout, you press into the dough with your fingers in a 180-degree arc, forming a crust on half of one side and then the other. And so, one by one, your stack of patouts is floured up.

15   Behind you is the pie rack where large wooden paddles called peels rest after they've pulled pies out of the oven to cool. On top of the pie rack is a square peel without a handle. Next to the floury counter is another counter where this particular peel goes. On it, you will sprinkle—just sprinkle—a little bit of cornmeal so that when the big thirty-inch "skin" of the pie is laid on top and the sauce is ladled onto the skin—when that is all done you can easily shake the pie off the peel, leaving it in the oven to bake.

Now, you set your stance. Lower body: legs under your shoulders and knees bent, with your weight up on your forefoot, your heels hardly touching the linoleum floor. Upper body: torso taut but elastic, because you know that you will be twisting back and forth. Then with your hands straight out, fingers together like you're about to go swimming and thumbs tucked in so they don't pierce the dough, you're ready.

You lightly pinch the first patout. The flour makes taking the patout off the stack feel like a silky turn of a page. You lay the patout over your other hand and, it's odd, but initially you slap the dough back and forth with your hands. It begins in your wrists, the dough not only slapping but also rotating between your palms in a figure eight, an infinity symbol, an hourglass.

If someone looked closely they would see that in front of your chest, your right middle finger briefly touches your left middle finger. Then your right hand slides from your left middle finger toward your left inner elbow, while your left forearm remains straight. From above, when your two middle fingers touch, your arms will look like an equilateral triangle with one side always collapsing toward its opposite corner, pivoting back and forth, back and forth.

It's confusing. But you've done this so much by now that you just feel it. As you go on, your hands slap the dough in a curvy crisscross motion, making it turn, making it stretch into a larger circle. A circle big enough now to toss.

And this is what a tosser does. (Yes, you will sauce the skin of dough, and   20
put the pie in the oven, and set the timer for 3 minutes, maybe 30 seconds more
or less depending on how cool or hot the ovens are that day. And after the pies
have cooled, you'll cut some of them into halves and quarters, while leaving a
few pies whole.) But what really defines you as a tosser is not the patouts or the
flouring or the cutting, but the tossing. It sounds so simple, but you're a tosser
because you toss. And this, this is it:

You drape the dough over your left forearm like a dishrag. No, not a dishrag. That's too much like a waiter. And you're so much more than that. You
think, How many people in the world know how to do something so particular?

You're not even in the restaurant when you toss. You're elsewhere. It's you
and the dough, like matador and bull. You can imagine that flap of dough like
a cape. And since you imagine the dough to be a cape, you can imagine the
rest of it all as sport, too. And the dough hangs down, slung low, where your
right hand cups the heaviest, lowest edge. Your left hand will spring up and
out, and your entire left arm will straighten as your shoulder locks, then your
elbow, then your wrist, so that your arm shoots out like a discus thrower's.

But before that, your body winds up by corkscrewing down: your left arm
lurches to your hips and curls behind your back, your torso twists, and you're
crunched down with so much potential energy that when you come up, it all
goes into your right hand, which whisks the dough off your wrist like it's a Fris-
bee. And if you snapped a picture of this moment, your left hand would be turning over, palm-side up, opening. That same swimming hand that slapped the
dough now ready to receive it when it comes back like a boomerang. That dough
spinning, spinning, spinning in the air, its beauty summed up by little kids who
come to the counter to watch. You know they want to ask you how you do it, but
instead of asking, maybe because you're an adult, they point and then explain to
you, or the parent holding them up, or especially a younger sibling: "It's magic!"

You know exactly what these kids mean, because every time you are here
under the dough, you remember back—way back—to kindergarten. When you
were out on the playground for recess, away from the dull pounding of the fluo-
rescent lights. The best days of recess were when you all played parachute with
the extraordinarily large multicolored nylon circle. You and all the rest of the
kids got hold of a spot and, together, lifted the parachute up and then down,
trapping air under it, like catching a big empty cloud. But what you really loved
was when everyone lifted the parachute up again, releasing the air, and before
the parachute floated down, one by one, you all got a turn to run under its
stained-glass canopy.

You come out of the zone. You glance at the clock. Its red block numbers   25
blink 10:55. You're on your last pie. The others are on the rack, cut, and logged
in. And this one will only take 3 minutes in the oven. It doesn't take you longer
than 2 minutes and change to toss and sauce a pie. You've almost played a perfect game. 11 by 11. One hour. Just one more.

And you take this last circle of dough, slap it back and forth, and wind up
and toss it so that the dough nearly brushes one bulb of the draped Christmas
tree lights strung from the ceiling tiles. And as you're under the dough—for
a second you feel trapped, because you realize after this you can't ever be

better—you wish you could be back in school, having fun like a kid again with no expectation of something perfect never being better. But you're here, on this last pie, with your left arm open and ready and waiting as it spins and spins and spins above you, about to come down.

MLA CITATION

Wiewiora, Chris. "This Is Tossing." *The Norton Reader: An Anthology of Nonfiction*, edited by Melissa A. Goldthwaite et al., 15th ed., W. W. Norton, 2020, pp. 236–40.

QUESTIONS

1. Chris Wiewiora uses sensory language—specifically sight, sound, touch, and visual cues—to help readers imaginatively experience the process of tossing a pizza crust. Locate places in the essay where his use of sensory language helps you imagine this process clearly.

2. Wiewiora uses the second-person point of view ("you") and present tense. Why do you think he uses that perspective and verb tense? How do these choices affect your reading of the essay?

3. Write an essay in which you guide readers through a process, teaching them to do something that may be unfamiliar to them. Like Wiewiora, use sensory language, the second-person point of view, and present tense.

JJ GOODE
Single-Handed Cooking

MY BACK ACHES. My eyes burn. I've been peeling and chopping for an hour, but I'm still being taunted by a pile of untouched vegetables. My problem is not the quantity. It's that the task of steadying each item falls to an almost useless appendage: the short, goofy arm, inexplicably bent into an L-shape and graced by just three fingers, that dangles from my right shoulder.

No one knows why I was born like this. My mom wasn't exposed to any radiation while she was pregnant, nor did she, say, have one too many sips of wine. Yet I do occasionally wonder whether my dad's Ph.D. dissertation subject—a pre-PETA endeavor for which he plucked the legs from frogs and studied their regeneration—sparked some sort of cosmic payback.

Whatever the reason, I occupy a sort of upper middle class of the handicapped. Sure, there's plenty to complain about, but all in all, things aren't so bad. While the wheelchair-bound struggle to reach their stoves, it feels a bit "Princess and the Pea" of me to grumble that peeling potatoes is as grueling

Published in Gourmet (2009), *a monthly magazine devoted to food and wine, which was in print from 1941 to 2009.*

as making *mole*.[1] ("Vegetables are distressingly round," said a commiserating friend.) Or to lament that day last winter when my girlfriend took a trip to Philadelphia, leaving me at home in Brooklyn with a dozen oysters and not enough hands to shuck them with. Disability is relative: I'd rather be incapable of prying open shellfish than allergic to them. Still, I see jimmying an oyster, which otters manage without much difficulty, as an ability that's not too much to ask for.

I happily live without most of the things I can't do. The kitchen, however, is where what I love butts up against what can be so discouragingly difficult. Forget shucking an oyster; even a mundane task such as draining a pot of pasta can be death-defying. After swathing my right arm in towels to prevent it from searing (the last thing I need is for it to be less useful), I lodge it beneath the pot's handle with the same care that I imagine a window washer uses to secure his harness to a skyscraper. Then I inch toward the sink, the whole time bracing for scalding disaster and indulging in an equally scalding torrent of self-pity. Some people say the kitchen is where they clear their heads; for me, it's where I face my demons.

Every meal is a proving ground, and I suffer mistakes as though they were   5 failures, even when they have nothing to do with my arm. "It's really good," friends insist, as I sulk over hanger steak that doesn't have a perfectly rosy center or a gratin whose top has barely browned, forever fighting the feeling that somehow it all would have gone right had I been born a little more symmetrical. I can even find fault with the faultless because what I'm truly after is unreachable: two normal arms.

When I first started to cook, I developed a crush on any ingredient that leveled the playing field. I adored canned anchovies, since the fillets simply melted in hot oil. I loved beets because after I roasted them in foil, their skins would slip right off. But soon my attraction to convenience gave way to a relishing of the arduous.

Having previously avoided anything that required peeling, I now dove into recipes that called for celery root and butternut squash. I embraced Thai stir-fries, which had me meticulously slicing raw pork into matching strips so they'd all finish cooking at the same time. I can't count the times friends have watched me tackle an overly complicated prep job—always girding themselves for a bloodbath—and anxiously urged me to try using a food processor. I refuse for the same reason I insist on balancing a pan on my raised right knee when I sauce tableside instead of asking anyone for help. (It's the same reason I refused to sit out in baseball when it came time for me to bat.) I appreciate the thought, I sniff, but I can handle it.

This masochistic streak is why I'm still chopping. I'm having some friends over for dinner and I'm making braised chicken, a dish that's a breeze for most cooks but presents, for me, just the right level of hardship for a dinner party. The only way to get what I casually call my right arm to act like one is to hunch awkwardly over my cutting board, so it can reach the food that needs to be sta-

---

1. Spanish word for a variety of sauces used in Mexican cuisine, the most common being *mole poblano*, which includes chili peppers and chocolate.

bilized. For an hour, that was celery, onions, and carrots. A rough chop would surely suffice, but I'm attempting to dice, chasing the satisfaction of seeing perfect cubes conjured by a blur of hand and knife.

My back is bent again. This time, I'm close enough to a chicken to kiss it—unfortunate no matter how comfortable you are with raw poultry. As I try to detach a leg, it slips from my right hand's feeble grasp, spattering my cheek with cold chicken liquid. I seethe but rinse off and continue. I could, of course, have bought chicken parts. But a whole chicken is always cheaper by the pound, and why shouldn't I have access? I like to think of the price discrepancy as a one-arm tax.

10   Half an hour later, I've successfully dismantled the thing and begun the rewarding task of browning it, savoring the knowledge that any cook would, at this point in the process, be upright at the stove and wielding tongs in exactly the same manner as I am. After setting the chicken aside and spooning some of the golden fat from the pot, I take a seat, sweep the vegetables from my cutting board into a big bowl supported by my knees, and ferry the bowl to the stove. The vegetables sizzle when I dump them in. Now, to add the wine.

The wine! I forgot I'd have to open a bottle, a potential catastrophe. I should turn off the burner, just in case I take as long to open this bottle as I did the last one. Instead, I bet my hard-won diced vegetables that I won't scorch them. Springing into action, I wedge the bottle between my thighs, wrap my right arm around the neck (its effect is almost purely symbolic), and struggle to work the screw through the cork. I already detect a faint acridity wafting from the pot, a whiff of defeat. I quickly adjust my technique, somehow wrenching the cork out in one piece, and rush back to the stove. The vegetables have more color than I wanted, but they're fine. In goes some wine, a few sprigs of thyme, and the chicken. I cover the pot and shove it into the oven.

I know there are more compelling examples of fortitude than me braising chicken. Like a paraplegic racing uphill in a tricked-out wheelchair on marathon day, or my late grandfather, who at 90 walked down and up 20-odd flights in the pitch darkness of New York City's 2003 blackout to get groceries for his wife. But turn a spotlight on any accomplishment, however minor, and it seems like a triumph. Away from that glare, though, there's only the struggle.

My right arm swathed again, my back contorted, I stoop down and heave the pot out of the oven without incident (once I dipped so low to retrieve a casserole dish perched on the bottom rack that I singed my forehead on the top one). I call in my friends, and we sit down to a dinner that, I have to admit, is pretty good. Someone even admires my fastidious touch, the precise little cubes of carrots and celery scattered beneath the burnished chicken. "Thanks," I say. "It was nothing."

MLA CITATION

Goode, JJ. "Single-Handed Cooking." *The Norton Reader: An Anthology of Nonfiction*,
      edited by Melissa A. Goldthwaite et al., 15th ed., W. W. Norton, 2020,
      pp. 240–42.

QUESTIONS

1. How would you characterize JJ Goode's attitude toward his disability? What parts of the essay reveal his attitude?

2. Goode presents cooking as an adventure, writing, for example, that when he adds wine to a dish he springs into action and wedges the wine bottle between his thighs (paragraph 11). Two strategies he uses to heighten this sense of adventure are present tense and strong verbs. Which verb choices do you find especially effective? Why?

3. Goode writes, "[T]urn a spotlight on any accomplishment, however minor, and it seems like a triumph" (paragraph 12). Write an essay about a minor accomplishment you've had. Use present tense, strong verbs, and detail to make that accomplishment seem like a triumph.

TERESA LUST
The Same Old Stuffing

BEFORE YOU SET OUT to revamp your Thanksgiving meal, it pays to consider all the repercussions. Just because the editors of the glossy food magazines have grown weary of the same old turkey and fixings, and even though they are absolutely giddy with excitement over the smoked quail, the spicy black bean stuffing, and the sun-dried tomato and arugula gratin they have in store for this year's feast, it does not mean that everyone will welcome innovation at the Thanksgiving table. Quite the contrary. All some people really want is the tried and true. Some people have grown quite fond of their annual mix of turkey and trimmings, each and every dish, and they do not consider it an onerous task to repeat the meal from one year to the next. They gain comfort from the familiarity and the ritual of it all; any tampering with the menu, no matter how minor or well intentioned, only serves to make them feel shortchanged.

This fact my mother discovered to her dismay when she tried out a little something at our own Thanksgiving meal. For years before anyone realized it had become a tradition, she roasted our holiday turkey with two types of stuffing inside it. She filled the bird's main cavity with my paternal grandmother's sage-and-onion dressing. This quintessential American farmhouse preparation was a genuine family heirloom, as Nana had learned to make it at her own mother's side. And for the bird's neck cavity, my mom fixed what you could call an Italian-American hybrid stuffing. Although this filling was not authentically Italian, it was a recipe from my mother's family, and it bespoke her immigrant heritage with its classic Mediterranean combination of sausage, spinach, raisins and nuts.

Published in Pass the Polenta: And Other Writings from the Kitchen *(1998), a collection of essays about food and family.*

Then one autumn as the holiday loomed near, my mom found herself contemplating our annual Thanksgiving spread. She saw it suddenly in a new and somewhat bothersome light. What had seemed a skillful act of diplomacy all these years, this bringing together of two family traditions inside one bird, why, it now smacked to her of excess. How the fact had escaped her for so long, she did not know, for she did not go for over-indulgence when it came to family meals. My mother was accommodating, don't misunderstand me. She was a mom who once finished up a marathon session of Dr. Seuss[1] books with a breakfast of green eggs and ham at the behest of her four daughters. Still, she made us eat our peas, and she said things like, "The day your papa starts raising cows that don't come with livers is the day I'll quit serving liver and onions for dinner. Now eat up." Yes, she knew where to draw the line.

What suddenly struck my mother as disturbing was not a matter of gluttony or expense or grams of fat, but of balance. What with the mashed potatoes, the baked yams, the penny rolls, and two types of stuffing, there was altogether too much starch on the plate. Starch, starch, starch. The redundancy of it became an offense that the English teacher in her could no longer abide. Of an instant, the solution became clear: two stuffings were one stuffing too many. One of them would have to go.

5   So she said to my father, "Jim, which stuffing do you prefer at Thanksgiving?"

He replied, "My mother's sage-and-onion dressing, of course. It's the stuffing of my youth. It's the heart of the Thanksgiving meal. By God, it's a national tradition, that stuffing, and I can't even imagine the holiday without it."

This was not the response my mother had in mind. Nana's sage-and-onion dressing had been her candidate for dismissal, because naturally, she preferred her family's stuffing, the one with the Italian touch of sausage, spinach, and raisins. She saw my father's point, though. We celebrated the holiday with his side of the family, and she had them to bear in mind. The children would be too preoccupied with the mashed potatoes to care a whit one way or the other about the stuffing, but her in-laws would feel deprived, no doubt, if Nana's dish didn't grace the table. And she had to admit that the sage-and-onion version was more in keeping with the all-American spirit of the holiday. It was more faithful, she assumed, to history. Good heavens, even schoolchildren knew that sage-and-onion dressing appeared on the Pilgrims' rough-hewn banquet table, right alongside the spit-roasted wild turkey, the hearth-braised sweet potatoes, the cranberry sauce, and the pumpkin pie.

I must admit I envisioned such a meal, just as I pictured Miles Standish[2] brandishing a kitchen knife and gallantly carving the turkey roast while he gazed deep into the limpid eyes of Priscilla Mullens.[3] But there is no record of

1. Pseudonym of Theodor Seuss Geisel (1904–1991), who wrote children's books such as *Green Eggs and Ham* (1960) and *The Cat in the Hat* (1957).

2. English military officer (c. 1584–1656), and later captain hired by the Pilgrims.

3. In the poem *The Courtship of Miles Standish* (1858) by Henry Wadsworth Longfellow, Miles Standish and John Alden vie for the love and attention of Priscilla Mullens.

stuffing—sage-and-onion or otherwise—bedecking the table at the Pilgrims'
first thanksgiving, which it turns out was not a somber meal, but a frolicsome
affair of hunting, games, and wine which lasted three days. For that matter,
there isn't even any specific mention of turkeys having been served, though one
colonist wrote of an abundance of fowl at the event, and most scholars feel safe
in assuming this bounty included a few turkeys. All anyone knows for certain
is that the Mayflower folks cooked up five deer, oysters, cod, eel, corn bread,
goose, watercress, leeks, berries, and plums. Pumpkins made an appearance,
too, but no one bothered to record just how they were cooked. They certainly
were not baked in a pie crust, though, for the wheat crop had failed and the
ship's supply of flour had long since run out.

The traditional meal as we know it dates back not to the solemn, high-
collared Pilgrims, nor even to Colonial times, but to home cooks of the nineteenth century. Not until this era did the idea of an annual day of thanksgiving
first take hold. The driving force behind the holiday was New Englander Sarah
Josepha Hale (whose legacy also includes the nursery rhyme "Mary Had a Little
Lamb"). As editor of the popular magazine *Godey's Lady's Book,* she promoted
the holiday for nearly twenty years within the periodical's pages. She wrote letters annually to the state governors and to the president, and one by one the
states gradually took up the idea. Finally, Abraham Lincoln, desperate for any
means to promote unity in the war-ravaged country, declared the first national
Thanksgiving in 1863.

And what did the mistress of the house serve up at this new holiday meal?   10
Her standard company fare for autumn, of course: roast turkey with cranberry
sauce, scalloped and mashed potatoes, candied sweet potatoes, braised turnips,
creamed onions, cranberry sauce, mince pie, pumpkin pie—the menu has
endured remarkably unchanged. And yes, it was standard procedure then to
roast the turkey with a stuffing.

The actual practice of filling up a bird's cavity dates back to antiquity; the
space made a handy cooking vessel for families who all too often owned only
one pot. Recipes have varied over the millennia. The cookbook attributed to
the Roman gastronome Apicius gives a formula that includes ground meat,
chopped brains, couscous, pine nuts, lovage, and ginger; other than the brains,
it sounds like something right out of a trendy contemporary cookbook. English
cooks during the Middle Ages favored heavily spiced and honeyed productions
based on pieces of offal that today would make our rarefied stomachs churn.
Nineteenth-century American cooks went on stuffing birds, no matter how
many pots and pans they had on hand in the kitchen, and recipes much like
Nana's sage-and-onion dressing were a beloved part of many an early Thanksgiving repast.

No less dear, though, or popular, or traditional, were a number of other
variations. Homemakers in the corn-growing south who went to stuff a turkey
favored cornbread in their recipes. Along the eastern seaboard, they tucked in
dozens of nectar-sweet shucked oysters, while across the country as far north
as the chestnut tree once grew, they featured loads of tender chestnuts in their
fillings. And many cooks treasured recipes that called for ground meat, dried

fruits, autumn greens, and shelled nuts—the very products of the fall harvest upon which my mother's family recipe was based, so she need not have dismissed her version as unconventional so hastily.

The genteel ladies of the last century would have viewed my mother's dilemma not as a surplus of starch at the meal, but as a paucity of meats. They were impassioned carnivores, these American predecessors of ours, and one meager turkey would have seemed woefully inadequate at a meal showcasing the prodigious bounty of the land. Pull out the stops, Darlene, I can all but hear them tell her. Along with the requisite turkey, they decorated their tables with a chicken pie, a joint of beef, a roast goose, if the budget would allow. Certainly these additional viands would serve to put my mother's menu back on kilter.

I'm sure, too, that at least one of these women would have felt bound by duty to draw my mother aside and whisper that she really ought to call her preparation *dressing* and not *stuffing*. The word "stuffing" has been in use for centuries. Sir Thomas Elyot's *Dictionary* of 1538 uses it as a synonym for "forcemeat," defined as "that wherewith any foule is crammed." Sir Thomas obviously wasn't much of a cook, or he would have known that cramming a fowl isn't such a great idea, for the filling expands during the roasting, and it can burst out at the seams if it is packed too tightly. At any rate, all this stuffing and forcing and cramming proved simply too much for the delicate sensibilities of the Victorian age, and the more discreet term "dressing" came into fashion. Today, schoolmarmish cookbooks often wag a finger and insist that when it is on the inside of the bird it is stuffing, and when it is baked in a separate dish, it's dressing. In reality, this does not play out. If Grandma calls her dish stuffing, then stuffing it is, regardless of its location inside or alongside the bird. Same goes for Aunt Pearl's dressing, no matter where she puts it.

15   Had my mother sought the counsel of Mrs. Sarah Josepha Hale or her contemporaries, then, she might have spared herself some anxiety. For although she had resolved herself to her decision, the idea of forgoing her family recipe did not rest easy with her. The days wore on and she grew positively disgruntled. Then one brisk, gray morning with two weeks yet to go before Thanksgiving, she found herself pushing her cart down the butcher's aisle at the supermarket when inspiration struck. Who ever said holiday recipes were for holidays, and holidays only? Who? She need not go without her annual dose of her family's stuffing after all. So she hoisted a fresh turkey into the cart, made a few other spur-of-the-moment additions to her shopping list, and went home and set to work.

She pulled her big frying pan out of the cupboard, set it over a low flame on the stove-top, melted half a stick of butter in it, then crumbled in three-quarters of a pound of bulk pork sausage. After the meat began to brown, she stirred in a diced onion, a couple of cloves of pressed garlic, a few stalks of cut-up celery, and a cup or so of sliced button mushrooms. These she let simmer gently until the onions were translucent. She added a large container of the chopped garden spinach she had blanched and frozen last spring, heated it through, then scraped the contents of the pan into a large ceramic bowl. When the mixture cooled to room temperature she sliced a stale loaf of French bread into cubes—enough to make about four cups—then added the bread to the bowl along with a couple of ample handfuls of raisins, sliced almonds, and freshly grated Parmesan cheese—a good half cup of each. She seasoned the stuffing with salt, black pepper, and generous pinches of oregano and rosemary, then drizzled in a glass of white wine. Using her hands, she combined all the ingredients thoroughly, then put a finger to her tongue. A pinch more salt and that would do it. Finally, she spooned the stuffing into the bird, trussed it up, and put it in the oven to roast for the rest of the afternoon.

Incidentally, my mother is quite an accomplished seamstress. She could sew bound buttonholes on a turkey if she wanted to. But she agrees with me that trussing need not be the intricate knit-one-purl-two operation that many cookbooks describe. Such elaborate needlework lingers from the days of the kitchen hearth-fire, when trussing was done to keep the drumsticks and wings from dangling in the flames as the bird turned on a spit. It now functions as a stuffy, old guard test of a cook's dexterity—yes, but can she truss a turkey? By the turn of this century, the massive iron kitchen range had become a standard feature in the American home, and oven roasting rendered unnecessary all the knotting and stitching and battening down. Trussing now primarily serves to keep the stuffing in place, and to give the bird a demure appearance, its ankles politely crossed, when it arrives at the table. Folding back the wings and tying the drumsticks together with kitchen twine usually make for ample treatment.

As my mom put the neck and giblets into a stock-pot on the stove for gravy, she decided a side dish of mashed potatoes would be just the accompaniment to round out the meal. Then she discovered she had a few sweet potatoes in the bin under the kitchen sink, and she thought, now wouldn't those be nice, too, roasted with a little butter, ginger, and brown sugar? And when she remembered the tiny boiling onions that had been rolling around in the refrigerator's bottom drawer, she decided she might as well bake them up au gratin with some bread crumbs and cream.

The turkey spittered and spattered away in the oven, filling every nook in the house with its buttery, winter-holiday scent, and the next thing my mom knew, she was rolling out the crust for a pumpkin pie. My father arrived home from work, draped his overcoat across the banister, and walked into the kitchen just in time to see her plopping the cranberry sauce out of the can. She placed it on the table in a sterling silver dish, its ridged imprints still intact and its jellied body quivering gloriously—God bless those folks at Ocean Spray, they were always a part of our turkey dinners, too. She turned to my father and said, "Dinner's almost ready."

My mom watched as her family gathered around the table and enjoyed a complete turkey feast on that evening in early November. After the meal, my father stretched back in his chair and folded his hands behind his head. He'd always thought it a shame, he said, a needless deprivation, that Americans ate roast turkey only once a year at Thanksgiving. This fine dinner just proved his point. What a treat, yes, what a treat. But the family's pleasure that night was merely an added perk for my mother, as she had prepared the meal for herself, only for herself, and she was feeling deeply satisfied.

20

When the official holiday finally arrived, my mother made good on her vow and let Nana's sage-and-onion dressing preside at the evening meal. Out came the frying pan, and she started to sauté two chopped onions and four thinly sliced stalks of celery, including the leaves, in a stick of butter. After a moment's thought, she added two plump cloves of minced garlic to the simmering pan. She couldn't resist. She knew Nana thought her a bit heavy-handed in the garlic department, but so what, it was her kitchen.

When the vegetables were limp and fragrant, she pulled the pan from the heat and set it aside to cool. She put the mixture into a bowl along with eight cups of firm, stale bread cubes, a generous spoonful of dried sage, a healthy handful of chopped fresh parsley, some salt and pepper, and a pinch of nutmeg. She gave these ingredients a light mixing, drizzled in enough broth to make the filling hold together when she squeezed a handful of it between her fingers—three-quarters of a cup, maybe a bit more—then tossed the dressing together again lightly before she spooned it into the Thanksgiving bird.

That evening Nana arrived with her sweet pickles and her three pies—apple, pumpkin, mincemeat. Cousins poured into the house toting covered casserole dishes, an uncle walked through the door, then an aunt. We soon sat down around two tables to dine, our plates heaped to the angle of repose. Amid the clanking of cutlery and the giggling and guffawing, and the festive bustle, my father paused. His fork pierced a juicy slice of dark thigh meat and his knife was poised in midstroke. He looked down intently and his eyes circled clockwise, studying the contents of his plate. He craned his neck and took an inventory of the platters and bowls laid out on the buffet counter across the room. "Darlene," he said, "this is some spread we have here, don't get me wrong. But you know what's missing is that other stuffing you make. The one we had the other day with the cornucopia of raisins and nuts and such."

My mom nearly dropped her fork. "But you told me you preferred your mother's dressing."

25   He looked back down at the turkey and trimmings before him. "Well, yes, but that doesn't mean I don't prefer yours, too. It just doesn't seem like a proper Thanksgiving without that second stuffing on the table. Don't you agree?"

What he meant, of course, was that my mom's dish had to turn up missing before he understood just what a part of the celebration it had become. So the year the turkey had only one stuffing was the year that both recipes became permanent fixtures on my mother's Thanksgiving menu. When time-honored traditions get their start while you're not looking, it seems, they need not concern themselves with balance, or daily nutritional requirements, or even historical accuracy. For such rituals rise up out of memories, and memories are not subject to hard facts. They are not interested in making room for change.

MLA CITATION

Lust, Teresa. "The Same Old Stuffing." *The Norton Reader: An Anthology of Nonfiction*, edited by Melissa A. Goldthwaite et al., 15th ed., W. W. Norton, 2020, pp. 243–48.

QUESTIONS

1. Teresa Lust includes both family anecdotes and historical research in her essay. Was there anything about her description of the development of Thanksgiving as a holiday that surprised you?

2. In different ways, both Lust and Diana Abu-Jaber (pp. 249–52) show how families whose members come from different cultural backgrounds either accommodate or resist change, and that change is often represented by food. What similarities and differences do you see between Lust's and Abu-Jaber's essays?

3. Write an essay about a holiday tradition in your family. Use both family anecdotes and historical research. If your essay includes a recipe, consider incorporating it—as Lust does—in narrative form.

DIANA ABU-JABER
Lamb Two Ways

EVERY YEAR BETWEEN Halloween and Christmas, my grandmother Grace transforms her apartment into a bakery. Tables and chairs are covered with racks of cooling cookies, eight baking sheets slip in and out of the oven—as tiny as something in a troll's house. The Mixmaster drones. A universe of cookies: chocolate-planted peanut butter; sinus-kicking bourbon balls; leaping reindeer and sugar bells; German press-form cookies from her grandparents' Bavarian village—*Springerle—green wreaths, candy berries; and a challenging, grown-uppy variety named for the uncut dough's sausage shape: Wurstcakes. All part of Grace's arsenal: she's engaged in an internecine war with my father, Bud, over the loyalties of the children. Her Wurstcakes are slim as Communion wafers. Bud dunks them in his demitasse of ahweh[1] and calls them "Catholic cookies."* Her eyes tighten as she watches him eat.

"Only higher civilizations bake cookies," she says to me, raking fingers through the shrubbery of my hair. "I don't know how you people would celebrate Christmas if I wasn't around. Run wild like savages."

My parents were married in Gram's church. When the priest presented Dad with a contract to raise his children within the Catholic faith, Dad signed in Arabic. He nudged Gram in the ribs, as if she were in on the joke, and, instead of his name, wrote: *I make no promises.* In my parents' satiny wedding photographs, Grace stared at Bud. *I'm on to you, friend.*

First published in the New Yorker *(2015). An extended version of this essay, titled "Crack," appears as the first chapter of Abu-Jaber's memoir* Life without a Recipe *(2016).*

1. Lebanese and Turkish coffee made with sugar using a traditional Lebanese Rakweh coffeepot.

"Never learn how to sew, cook, type, or iron." She bends over the board, passes the hissing iron back and forth, slave rowing a galley ship. "That's how they get you." She pauses long enough to turn that shrewd gaze on me and after a moment I look away. There's cooking, sure, but then there's baking. I learn from Grace that sugar represents a special kind of freedom. It charms almost everyone; it brings love and luck and good favor. Cakes and cookies are exalted—a gift of both labor and sweetness—so good a smart woman is willing to give herself to them.

5   Adversaries, even enemies, can rely on each other. My father and my grandmother teach me this by accident. They don't get along and they agree on everything. Especially the two essentials:

    1. Men are terrible.
    2. Save your money (Gram: in bra. Bud: somewhere, preferably not at
       the horse races).

Also, they both want all the love. As if there is a limited supply and never enough to go around. They wrangle over the children's souls and both set out food for us, bait inside a trap. Bud cooks—earthy, meaty dishes with lemon and oil and onion. Gram is more ruthless—she pries open those foil-lined tins, cookies covered with sugar crystals like crushed rubies, the beckoning finger of vanilla. I think about the story of the witch in her gingerbread house, how she schemed to push Hansel and Gretel into her oven. Gram reads me the story; I sit, rapt, watching her, her sky-blue eyes glittering. *I will fight anyone for you*, she seems to say. Even if it means cooking you and gobbling you up.

Bud doesn't quite grasp the concept of this fight; his wrath is more episodic. Anything that strikes him as American-disrespectful—say, one of us kids gives him the old eye-roll, or an "oh, yuh"—and he'll be shouting the cupboards off the walls. Then he'll storm into the kitchen and fill it with the scent of cauliflower seething in olive oil and garlic, the bitter, sulfurous ingredients he hacks up when he's in a mood. Stuff that tastes like punishment to an eight-year-old. Most of the time, though, when Grace is around he forgets there's a war on. He argues casually, conversationally, segues into offhanded, cheerful observations and questions: "Why do cookies always come in circles?" Etc. This deepens her rage and despair—he can't even be bothered to remember that they're fighting. So disrespectful!

Grace is vigilant, tallying all those casual betrayals between men and women, as if she were jotting them in a notebook. It's not just Bud, it's all of them. Men as a general category are disappointing and traitorous—in money and family and work and power. Romantic love is another of their snares. "They tell you to wait, wait, wait," she says. "True love will come. True love will make everything so much better. So you wait and wait and wait, and true love turns out to be a nincompoop with a venereal disease."

The insults, the sharp little arrows seem to be everywhere, even in places and moments that seem the most innocent. Gram will take me to see Snow White of the limpid flesh and cretinous voice—and the Prince with the powerful shoulders who must save her from another woman—an old lady!—and raise the helpless thing, literally, from the dead. After the movie, Gram scowls and mutters, "Flibbertigibbet." Afterward, we go to a café, where they bring us crepes with cherries and whipped cream. "Did you see," she grouses. "Those dwarves, they only wanted her to stay *after* she offered to cook for them."

Only a few of us in the family understand how those crisply divided feelings, love and complaint, float together, united. All grudges are softened by the approach of dinner. Those who labor with Bud in the kitchen are joined in a confederacy—cooking restores us to our senses. During the week, my father works two or more jobs. But Saturday breakfast is a profusion: the sizzling morsels of lamb on the fava beans; diced tomato, celery, and onion on the hummus; tidy, half-fried eggs bundled around their yolks. We hurry to sit and then spend half the meal begging Bud, "Come to the table! Sit down. *Sit.*" Always, he wants to slice one more cucumber.

Throughout my childhood, I hear Americans joke about Bud and his   10
harem—his wife and three daughters. He laughs, strong white teeth; he says, "Don't forget my mother-in-law."

Before they'd met, neither Grace nor Bud could have imagined each other, not once in a million years. They came with their ingredients like particles of lost and opposing worlds, the dying old divisions—East and West.

Among my father's library of made-up true stories is a favorite, about meeting his mother-in-law:

Grace was not pleased about her only child falling in with this questionable young man with a mustache. But that was a separate issue from good manners and laying out a nice table for company. At the time, the fanciest dish Grace knew of was shrimp poached in a wine and butter sauce. My father, most recently of the semi-arid village of Yahdoudeh,[2] studied the pale, curling bodies on the plate and saw a combination of cockroach and scorpion; he also deduced that the older lady with the stiff blonde hair and see-through eyes was some sort of *bruja*.[3] He ate only the sweet dinner rolls—which were quite good—and left the rest untouched. Bud somehow had himself a marvelous time, even with the *bruja*'s blue eye fixed on him. Maybe because of it. Afterward, mortally offended and stiff-backed, Grace scraped shrimp into the garbage, her throat filled with a dark will for revenge.

A few months later, my poor mother, Patty, barely twenty years old, eternal optimist, proposed a do-over: this time in honor of their engagement. Grace decided to pull out all the stops. Telling her version, my grandmother had said, "You know how that is—the more you hate someone the nicer you are to them?" To her, there was nothing better than a glistening, pink ham. In anguish, she slathered it with brown sugar and pineapple slices, voodoo-piercing it with cloves—each a tiny dart.

2. Town in Jordan.
3. Witch.

15   Dizzy with dismay, my Muslim father stood at the table, staring at the ham—forbidden, "unclean" meat. As soon as Gram saw his expression, she went to the phone book and jotted down the address of the White Castle. She swore she'd had no idea of this dietary restriction. "Who doesn't eat *ham?*" she'd cried twenty years later, still in disbelief. "I was so angry, I was almost laughing."

Bud brought back fries for the table.

You want most what you can't have. Gram would fight him for her daughter, long after the fight was over.

When I am nine, I cook a leg of lamb for my grandmother. A whole leg, just the two of us, but it's important because, in my mind, it's a possible culinary meeting place for him and her. When I suggest it, Gram says *Oh!* She *adores* leg of lamb. She hasn't had it in for_ever_. This is the first dinner I've ever cooked for her. All day I fan away her questions and suggestions. I'm as bossy and kitchen-difficult as my dad. For hours, the big joint burbles in wine and vinegar on top of the stove and fills her apartment with a round, heady scent that makes you weak-kneed. I set the table carefully, with napkins and water glasses. I carve and plate the lamb on top of the stove, then carry it out and place it before her.

She lowers her fork after a few bites, her mouth wilting. "What's wrong?" I'd crushed each garlic clove—a whole head—with salt, pepper, snips of rosemary, and had slipped the paste into slits in the meat, just the way I'd seen my father do. The tender meat breaks into fragments beneath the fork; I could drink the braising sauce with a spoon. "What did I do?"

20   Gram takes off her glasses and knuckles the corners of her eyes. Finally she says, "I like my lamb *rare*. With mint *jelly*." Her voice is pure pout. She sounds like my four-year-old sister, parked on the top step shouting, "Nobody loves me! You're not the boss of me!" Rummaging through accusations until she finds whatever lines up with the way she feels inside, abandoned in the hard world.

At nine, it's only just beginning to occur to me that I'm on my own here. The adults give you what they can, richer or poorer. Mint jelly! It is accusation and insult. She has detected my father's hand in the sauce. Affronted, I want to slap the table, bluster away, just like my dad does. But how do you argue with mint jelly? I took a risk and failed. It had never occurred to me that tastes and preferences could be so embedded in personality and history.

To me, deliciousness is still a simple matter—I don't have enough experience yet to understand how personal such things are. How you must choose the ingredients and tools slowly, putting together a palate, just as you build a life. Taste is desire, permitted or not, encouraged or not. There is no arguing it away, there is no winner in this fight, no recipe to follow. There is only blind faith and improvisation.

MLA CITATION

Abu-Jaber, Diana. "Lamb Two Ways." *The Norton Reader: An Anthology of Nonfiction,* edited by Melissa A. Goldthwaite et al., 15th ed., W. W. Norton, 2020, pp. 249–52.

QUESTIONS

1. Diana Abu-Jaber shows the "war" between her grandmother Grace and her father Bud "over the loyalties of the children" (paragraph 1). Although Grace and Bud come from different cultures, they also have some similar personality traits. What similarities and differences between these two characters figure most prominently in the essay?

2. When telling anecdotes about her relationship with her grandmother, Abu-Jaber references children's stories and fairytales, such as Hansel and Gretel (paragraph 5) and Snow White (paragraph 8). What lessons does Grace impart to her granddaughter through her response to these stories?

3. After recounting a failed attempt to please her grandmother by cooking lamb, Abu-Jaber writes, "It had never occurred to me that tastes and preferences could be so embedded in personality and history" (paragraph 21). Have you ever tried to please someone with food that person could not appreciate? Write about the elements of personality and history that shaped that person's preferences.

KATE HOLBROOK

Good to Eat: Culinary Priorities in the Nation of Islam and the Church of Jesus Christ of Latter-day Saints

W HEN IT COMES to diet, two religious groups considered outsiders by mainstream Americans have more in common than perhaps anyone imagined. Members of the Nation of Islam (Nation) have been marginalized as much for their perceived militancy and racism as for abstaining from sweet potatoes and pork, and members of the Church of Jesus Christ of Latter-day Saints (Mormons) are as infamous for a past that included plural marriage as for prohibitions against coffee and alcohol. Yet both religious groups choose what to eat by hallmarks as similar and American as apple pie: the attainment of self-sufficiency and the pursuit of good health.

As historian R. Laurence Moore has persuasively argued, religious outsiders in the United States are, in many respects, true insiders.[1] To rebel, to create one's own movement—these acts are consummately American. Through their rebellion on issues of food and drink, both the Nation and the Latter-day Saints have proved themselves to be American religious insiders. In fact, recipes for the marginalized Mormons and members of the Nation flesh out Moore's account of American religious identities. Close readings of recipes and favorite dishes show that the

Published in Religion, Food, and Eating in North America *(2014), an anthology of academic essays about the relationships between food, religion, and identity. All notes in this piece were written by the author.*

1. R. Laurence Moore, *Religious Outsiders and the Making of Americans* (New York: Oxford University Press, 1986).

American values of self-sufficiency, economy, and health have influenced the cuisine of the Nation and the Latter-day Saints at least as much as the specifics of their religious dietary codes have. What this means is that even when groups purport to reject American culture, or when popular culture rejects them, religious groups born in America are deeply influenced by American sensibilities.

WHAT THE OUTSIDERS FOUND BAD TO EAT

For Nation of Islam members, a series of articles in the official Nation newspaper, *Muhammad Speaks*, set the dietary code, which was eventually published in 1967 as two slim volumes entitled *How to Eat to Live*. Nation leader Elijah Muhammad taught that he had received these guidelines from his mentor W. D. Fard, who was also God incarnate, and thus they were revelation. Like Mormons, Nation members were instructed to abstain from alcohol and tobacco, and like Muslims and Jews they were to abstain from pork. Also forbidden were sweet potatoes, quick breads (like biscuits, cornbread, and pancakes), leafy greens, and most legumes (particularly lima beans and black-eyed peas), although Elijah Muhammad encouraged eating small pink navy beans. Those who would follow the diet were promised increased spiritual strength, freedom from disease, and longevity.

For Latter-day Saints, the dietary code is the Word of Wisdom, a short passage of just thirty-nine verses in the *Doctrine and Covenants*, a book of scripture based primarily on God's revelations to founding prophet Joseph Smith. Recorded on February 27, 1833, these verses recommended a diet of fruits, vegetables, herbs, and grains in season, with limited meat intake.[2] Prohibitions against "hot drinks," "strong drinks," and tobacco were familiar among dietary reformers of the day such as Sylvester Graham but set Mormons apart from mainstream Americans. Mormons spent the next one hundred years grappling with what it meant to obey the Word of Wisdom. (Should they be vegetarian? Were beer and wine permissible?) Church president Heber J. Grant spelled out the details in the 1920s, making obedience to the principle a firm requirement for temple attendance, hence full church membership, and defined the minimum standard of compliance as abstinence from tea, coffee, alcohol, and tobacco. Church members believed obedience to these guidelines and God's law would bring spiritual blessings, as well as physical blessings such as increased health and strength.

5   The uniqueness and stringency of these dietary codes set Nation members and Mormons apart from mainstream Americans. But concurrently, leaders and members justified them by making links with inherently American values of the period, particularly health and self-sufficiency.[3]

2. "And again, verily I say unto you, all wholesome herbs God hath ordained for the constitution, nature, and use of man—Every herb in the season thereof, and every fruit in the season thereof; all these to be used with prudence and thanksgiving. . . . All grain is good for the food of man; as also the fruit of the vine; that which yieldeth fruit, whether in the ground or above the ground." *Doctrine and Covenants*, section 89.

3. For a description of the transition in American Protestantism from a notion of physical suffering as evidence of God's love to God's love as a means to physical healing, see Heather D. Curtis, *Faith in the Great Physician: Suffering and Divine Healing in American Culture, 1860–1900* (Baltimore: Johns Hopkins University Press, 2007).

How Different Religious Creeds Led to Common Responses at the Table

Bringing these two groups into apparent conversation may seem counterintuitive. There are obvious and important differences between the Church of Jesus Christ of Latter-day Saints and the Nation of Islam. Formed one hundred years apart (Mormons in 1830, the Nation of Islam in 1930), these groups were distanced by geographical roots, membership profile, and theology. Where Mormons were predominantly white in their beginning,[4] the Nation was almost exclusively African American. Where Mormonism saw itself as reforming Christianity, the Nation explicitly rejected it. Mormons defined eternal life as eternity spent in God's presence, the Nation taught that there was no afterlife.

On the other hand, each group actively set itself apart from the mainstream. The Nation read mainstream culture as racist and corrupt, citing the horrible legacy of American slavery and the bitter present of Jim Crow laws and discrimination. Mormons also saw mainstream America as corrupt, citing what they saw as Protestant heresies and persecution. Both groups, not unlike mainstream Protestants and Catholics, took to heart the Christian New Testament teaching (Romans 12:2) to be "in the world but not of the world," believing they were called to keep themselves more pure than the status quo.

As a result, both Nation members and Mormons held a common wariness about mainstream behavior and influences. Both saw peril in government financial assistance, for example. Both Mormons and Nation members believed their lives should demonstrate a spiritually higher way of living than mainstream Americans. Their pursuits of good health and self-sufficiency were not to make them *like* the mainstream, but *better* than the mainstream. Their priority, albeit practiced differently at their marginalized tables, was to please God and create their own mode of living for God's sake, not to impress their American neighbors.

As both groups worked out what this meant in everyday patterns of eating, each developed a cuisine that represented its deeply held religious priorities. Until now, the Nation's interpretation of black American racial identity has been seen as the primary influence on its cuisine, and bystanders have assumed that the Word of Wisdom most strongly influenced what Mormons ate. Yet a closer look at recipes and favorite foods of the Nation and Mormons shows that each group's cooking was deeply influenced by mainstream American values, rather than religious mandates. For the Nation, the American value of physical health was prioritized; for Mormons, the American value of self-sufficiency most strongly influenced their foodways.

The Nation's Pursuit of Health

The Nation's regulations prohibited many foods that were typically identified   10
as "southern" and that were historically prepared by enslaved African Americans, including collard greens, black-eyed peas, pork, and corn bread. As a

4. Newell G. Bringhurst, *Saints, Slaves, and Blacks: The Changing Place of Black People within Mormonism* (Westport, Conn: Greenwood, 1981), appendix C.

result, most observers have viewed the Nation's food habits as a rejection of "slave food" and a deliberate embrace of foreign foods that crafted a new non-American identity. In contrast, evaluating Nation practices more broadly, historian Edward E. Curtis IV contends that rather than adopting non-American habits (African or Middle Eastern), Elijah Muhammad incorporated middle-class Protestant values into a new Islamic framework as a method of empowerment.[5] I argue that one of those middle-class values was an emphasis on cuisine as crucial to *health*; the Nation sought to make familiar dishes healthier. The changes were not necessarily healthier by today's standards of nutrition science, but Elijah Muhammad taught that they were scientifically better for health. A close reading of favorite dishes and recipes illustrates the rhetoric of health that attended the substitutions of nonslave for slave foods. For example, mashed sweet potatoes became carrot fluff, because Elijah Muhammad taught that carrots were healthier than sweet potatoes. Similarly, sweet potato pie turned into higher-protein bean pie. Barbecued ribs were made from beef instead of harmful pork. These substitutions were about keeping to the Nation's dietary code because it was healthy.

The Nation's genesis and evolution make it harder to see the connection between its new foodways and health. Nation of Islam founder Elijah Muhammad became acquainted in 1931 with a mysterious man named W. D. Fard. For three years Fard took Muhammad under his wing, teaching him truths about the black man's real identity. Fard explained that black people in the United States descended from an honorable tribe; their true nature was noble, and they were Muslim; and that he, Fard, was the incarnation of Allah himself. Fard's teachings were to be trusted as more thoroughly true than traditions that relied on less-explicit inspiration, prophecy, or centuries of scriptural interpretation.[6] Elijah Muhammad founded the Nation of Islam to help black people in America relearn and acquire their birthright. Elijah Muhammad knew that centuries of mistreatment by oppressors—slavery in the American South in particular—had left a toll on black people in America. From his perspective, they had no understanding of their worthy origins, they were largely unexposed to the correct Islamic faith of their ancestors, and whites had encouraged addiction and vice to keep blacks from realizing their splendid destiny. Worship and praxis therefore focused on the rehabilitation of and provision for the black race—in other words, the construction of a Nation of Islam. Culinary ideals, particularly proscription of particular foods, were central to realizing this goal of racial rehabilitation.

Scholars have downplayed the significance of Elijah Muhammad's rhetoric about health to reveal the "real" reason for food habits, which they have seen as

5. Edward E. Curtis IV, *Black Muslim Religion in the Nation of Islam, 1960–1975* (Chapel Hill: University of North Carolina Press, 2006), 127–30.
6. Karl Evanzz, *The Messenger: The Rise and Fall of Elijah Muhammad* (New York: Pantheon, 1999).

the construction of non-American identity.[7] Elijah Muhammad did write in *How to Eat to Live* that the slave diet hurt both body and spirit, and that slaves had been forced to eat certain foods by masters with two main motives: a desire to economize (by finding a use for foods that were inexpensive and that the wealthy were not willing to eat), and the "devilish" aim to undermine slaves' well-being (through the consumption of polluted food). There were clearly strong racial themes in Muhammad's culinary directions, but he did not tell his followers to eat small navy beans in search of a new, postslave, post-American identity. He taught them to eat small navy beans because they were healthy. Muhammad's significant emphasis on health has been underinvestigated. But the health emphasis is important, not least because the attainment of good physical health was a priority of mainstream American culture.

Elijah Muhammad did not believe in life after death. There would be no blissful eternity in Heaven. "We only have one life," he taught, "and, if this life is destroyed, we would have a hard time trying to get more life; it is impossible. So try to keep this life that you have as long as possible."[8] In Elijah Muhammad's view, proper nutrition was essential, and members internalized this emphasis.[9] For example, Sister Pattie X testified: "Messenger Muhammad has taught me how to eat, when to eat, and what to eat; therefore, my life has been prolonged."[10] Those who adhered to the Nation's creeds for diet could also ameliorate already existing medical conditions, like diabetes, and be free of additional complaints. "If you eat the proper food—which I have given to you from Allah (in the Person of Master Fard Muhammad to Whom be praise forever) in this book—you will hardly ever have a headache."[11]

In Sonsyrea Tate's autobiography about growing up in the Nation during the 1960s and 1970s, she confirmed that the idea of eating well for health was deeply ingrained. She recalled eating at a Nation-run school as a child, with "wholesome smells" emanating from the cafeteria as workers prepared nutritious beef burgers and wheat doughnuts. After Elijah Muhammad's death,

7. Algernon Austin, *Achieving Blackness: Race, Black Nationalism, and Afrocentrism in the Twentieth Century* (New York: New York University Press, 2006), 35; Richard Brent Turner, *Islam in the African-American Experience*, 2nd ed. (Bloomington: Indiana University Press, 2003), 159; Edward E. Curtis IV, "Islamizing the Black Body: Ritual and Power in Elijah Muhammad's Nation of Islam," *Religion and American Culture* 12, no. 2 (Summer 2002): 167–96; Curtis, *Black Muslim Religion in the Nation of Islam, 1960–1975*; and C. Eric Lincoln, *The Black Muslims in America*, 3rd ed. (Grand Rapids, Mich: Eerdmans, 1994), 22, 25, 47.

8. Elijah Muhammad, *How to Eat to Live, Book No. 1* (Phoenix: Secretarius, 1997), 19. Original edition: Fard Muhammad and Elijah Muhammad, *How to Eat to Live, Book One* (Atlanta: Messenger Elijah Muhammad Propagation Society, 1967).

9. Martha Lee has argued convincingly that the Nation's fixation with this-worldly reform qualifies it as a millenarian movement: "At its core was millenarianism, the belief in an imminent, ultimate, collective, this-worldly, and total salvation." *The Nation of Islam, An American Millenarian Movement* (Lewiston: Edwin Mellen, 1988).

10. Pattie X, "Original Black Woman Is Proud of Natural Heritage," *Muhammad Speaks*, July 28, 1967.

11. Muhammad, *How to Eat to Live, Book No. 1*, 22.

when Nation schools (called the University of Islam) closed, Tate transferred to a public school, where she came to dread the stench escaping cafeteria doors.[12] She said that the priority of good nutrition was so ingrained in members that even after her mother left the Nation to practice an alternate form of Islam, she continued to prioritize nutrition.[13]

15   Similarly, Betty Shabbaz, wife of Malcolm X, focused on the health aspects of diet both before and after her husband's martyrdom. Her daughter recalled, "My mother, as a rule, did not allow us to have much candy. Being a nurse and a Muslim she was extremely health-conscious and carefully monitored what we ate."[14]

Elijah Muhammad also stressed that healthy eating led to achieving another American value: physical beauty. He wrote: "Eating the proper food also brings about a better surface appearance. Our features are beautified by the health that the body now enjoys from the eating of proper food and also eating at the proper time."[15] For the Nation, the healthy appearance a Muslim derived from eating well was even seen as God's blessing. The Nation had held this value in common with some Evangelical Christians, who viewed slim bodies as evidence of personal righteousness, but the Nation took things a step further.[16] Elijah Muhammad taught that slenderness was more than a blessing—it was a priority.

One former member of the Nation described a penny tax implemented at temple meetings under Elijah Muhammad's leadership. Brothers had to demonstrate specific, scientifically determined standards of appropriate weight according to their height. They would weigh in at meetings, standing on a scale, and pay one penny for each pound that exceeded the standard.[17] In that odd and stern encounter stands a potent reminder of just how thoroughly the Nation of Islam had implemented, in its own distinctive way, the American emphasis on physical health and beauty as markers of success.

MODIFYING SOUL

Nation practices and mainstream American traditions began to intersect in another way too. Recipes show that popular Nation foods were derived mainly from southern tradition, instead of looking extensively to the Muslim world for culinary guidance.[18] Recipes are a reliable source for understanding praxis in the

12. Sonsyrea Tate [Montgomery], *Little X: Growing Up in the Nation of Islam* (San Francisco: HarperSanFrancisco, 1997), 120.

13. Interview with Sonsyrea Tate Montgomery, telephone, September 19, 2010.

14. Ilyasah Shabazz, *Growing Up X* (New York: One World/Ballantine, 2003), 44.

15. Muhammad, *How to Eat to Live, Book No. 1*, 32.

16. R. Marie Griffith, *Born Again Bodies: Flesh and Spirit in American Christianity* (Berkeley: University of California Press, 2004).

17. Interview with Sonsyrea Tate Montgomery.

18. Women in the Nation did circulate some recipes that nodded toward Muslim tradition, such as kebabs or carrot halwa. But the bulk of the recipes, including the most popular dishes, closely resembled the foods their female ancestors had prepared.

Nation because they had hierarchical support and were prescriptive. Sisters in the temple developed recipes intended to fulfill Elijah Muhammad's culinary standards, then taught them to new-comers in their own kitchens with the expectation that they would then feed their families in the same way. Thus women in the Nation learned to cook from one another, under the shaping influence of Elijah Muhammad. Tate, for example, confirmed that this is how her grandmother learned to cook according to Nation standards in the 1950s.[19] Eventually this training became more formally organized at the temples in courses called Muslim Girls Training (MGT). Women and girls attended this gender-specific training once a week, often on Saturdays, and learned how to cook as "Muslims."

The original MGT classes dissolved along with the University of Islam not long after Elijah Muhammad's death in 1975. One former student, Reda Faard Khalifah, saved her MGT recipes and published them in 1995 as *The Muslim Recipe Book: Recipes for Muslim Girls Training and General Civilization Class (MGT/GCC) of the Honorable Elijah Muhammad*—a hallmark work containing recipes used by the Nation's women throughout the movement. Because Khalifah felt she was only reporting recipes taught to her, and that they were based on Elijah Muhammad's teachings, she listed Elijah Muhammad as her coauthor.

The brief introduction to *The Muslim Recipe Book* reinforces the fact that the American value of pursuing good health was more central to the Nation's food habits than idealized racial identity. Khalifah highlights how recipes should facilitate health when she says, in the spirit of Elijah Muhammad's priorities, that even healthier cooking options have developed since the recipes were created. For example, she explains that the old technique of browning rice to improve its nutritive value was outdated since "wholesome naturally brown rice" was now readily available. She also makes a disclaimer about the book's high proportion of meat recipes—that people are now catching up to what Elijah Muhammad already knew: "that meat is one of the major causes of sickness and disease." Her introduction calls attention to vegetable and vegetarian recipes in the book because they "build radiant health."[20]

However, the most revealing aspect of these recipes is how Nation menus incorporated what came to be known in the 1960s as "soul food." Soul food is a fluid category, overlapping with the idea of southern food. When the Black Power movement brought the phrase to popular awareness in the 1960s, restaurants began serving soul food that others deemed simply southern. For example, in an essay for the November 3, 1968, issue of the *New York Times Magazine*, Craig Claiborne reported that displaced southern devotees of soul food found the offerings in New York soul-food restaurants were "more Southern than soul. The menus mostly feature such typical Southern dishes as fried chicken, spareribs, candied yams and mustard or collard greens. One rarely

---

19. Interview with Sonsyrea Tate Montgomery; Tate, *Little X*, 15–21.

20. Reda Faard Khalifah, *The Muslim Recipe Book: Recipes for Muslim Girls Training & General Civilization Class (MGT/GCC) of the Honorable Elijah Muhammad* (Charlotte: United Brothers Communication Systems, 1995), 6–7.

finds trotters, neckbones, pigs' tails and chitterlings."[21] Others did not care to differentiate between southern and soul. And many argued that the essence of soul food was about emotion—the care that went into the food.[22] For people in the mainstream, then, soul food became a more positive term for typical slave fare of chitterlings, mustard greens, black-eyed peas, and cornbread. Soul food improved perceptions of African American identity, celebrating heritage rather than shaming through the derogatory association with slavery.

Elijah Muhammad denounced both categories—southern and soul—at once, deeming all of it "slave food." Sisters in the Nation then took familiar soul dishes and modified the recipes, substituting acceptable ingredients for forbidden ones, believing these substitutions would safeguard health. These substitutions were viewed as not just safeguards but as transformations of soul food into soul-made-wholesome food. For instance, MGT courses taught that sweet potatoes were unhealthy, full of too much starch and causing gas. So carrots were substituted for sweet potatoes in many soul food dishes. The Muslim Recipe Book was filled with similar ingredient swaps: barbequed meats and barbeque short ribs, similar to recipes for barbequed pork, but with beef substituted for pork.[23]

In A Pinch of Soul, a quintessential soul food cookbook, a recipe for barbecue sauce calls for chutney, catsup or tomato sauce, brown sugar, dry mustard, hot sauce, cayenne pepper, garlic powder, and onion to be used with pork.[24] The barbecue sauce recipe in The Muslim Recipe Book has a similar flavor base: vinegar (which would add the piquancy of the chutney, above), green pepper (like vinegar, often in chutney), tomato paste, dry mustard, red pepper, garlic, and onion. There is little distinction between the two sauces. The barbecue instructions are also similar, calling for the technique of cooking on top of the stove, then browning in the oven or broiler. The barbecue section of A Pinch of Soul instructs: "Out-door barbecuing for simple enjoyment has not traditionally been a 'soul' thing . . . few of our grandparents indulged in a whole pig or side of beef cooked on an open fire. Soul barbecuing took place mainly in the oven of a wood-burning stove."[25] Like the A Pinch of Soul recipes, The Muslim Recipe Book calls for initial cooking on top of the stove, to be finished in the oven. Cooking time marks the main difference in technique. The soul recipe for "Mrs. Shorey's Ribs" requires thirty-five to forty minutes in the oven, while the Muslim "Barbecue Short Ribs of Beef" not only cooks in the oven for two hours, "or until the meat is well done," but specifies the meat as beef.[26] Thus the only

21. Craig Claiborne, "Cooking with Soul," New York Times Magazine, November 3, 1968, 109; Doris Witt, Black Hunger: Food and the Politics of U.S. Identity (New York: Oxford University Press, 1999), 80–82.

22. Frederick Douglass Opie, Hog & Hominy: Soul Food from Africa to America (New York: Columbia University Press, 2008), 130–31.

23. Khalifah, The Muslim Recipe Book, 31, 34.

24. Pearl Bowser and Joan Eckstein, A Pinch of Soul (New York: Avon, 1970), 201.

25. Ibid., 197–98.

26. Khalifah, The Muslim Recipe Book, 30.

substantive differences between the *A Pinch of Soul* recipe and the Nation sauce are abstinence from pork and cooking time, both of which were seen by the Nation as healthy changes. Elijah Muhammad taught that, for health, meat should be cooked until very well done. In practice, many of the Nation recipes are soul-made-wholesome.[27]

Some soul food recipes contain substitutions for proper ingredients and do not include a title change. For example, *A Pinch of Soul* includes a recipe for navy bean soup, one of Elijah Muhammad's favorite dishes and a classic Nation recipe. *A Pinch of Soul's* navy bean soup included streak o' lean (a pork product, sometimes made into lard) and cubed salt pork, but otherwise closely resembled the MGT's recipe.[28] Because its soup is vegetarian, the Nation recipe calls for tomato paste instead of canned tomatoes and pork; tomato paste imparts a deeper flavor to compensate for the lack of meat.

Of all recipes, though, one stands out most of all: bean pie, the dish emblematic of the Nation of Islam. Often bean pie is all people know about the Nation, because they have seen well-dressed men selling individual pies on street corners in major metropolitan areas. Unlike the overlapping representative dishes of other religious groups (for example, Mormons, Methodists, and Presbyterians might each claim green Jell-O salad), bean pie is unique to the Nation of Islam. Members of the Nation believed bean pie was healthier than sweet potato pie. Comparing the two pies was inevitable as even Nation members described bean pie as sweet potato pie made with mashed up navy beans instead of sweet potatoes (though, technically, bean pie had a custard base and sweet potato pie did not). Elijah Muhammad's son, Jabir, explained bean pie in these terms on YouTube in 2010.[29] Jabir Muhammad worked for years as Nation member and famed boxer Muhammad Ali's manager and reported that Ali's personal cook, Lana Shabazz, first developed bean pie to safeguard the champ's health.[30]

THE MORMON PURSUIT OF SELF-SUFFICIENCY

Mormons, too, have used American values to inform their food habits. In fact, the church's welfare program, adopted in 1936, has shaped Mormon cuisine even more than has the Word of Wisdom, which is a canonized part of scripture. Established during the height of the Great Depression, the welfare program's goal was to help Mormons be financially self-sufficient both as individuals and as a church. Its major tenets included frugality, hard work, food storage, and

27. Muhammad, *How to Eat to Live, Book No. 1*, 64–65.

28. Bowser and Eckstein, *A Pinch of Soul*, 80; Khalifah, *The Muslim Recipe Book*, 14.

29. Katharine Shilcutt, "Bean Pie, My Brother?" December 29, 2010, https://www. houstonpress.com/restaurants/houstons-new-summer-menus-11305903.

30. Richard Goldstein, "Jabir Herbert Muhammad, Who Managed Muhammad Ali, Dies at 79," *New York Times*, August 27, 2008 https://www.nytimes.com/2008/08/28 /sports/othersports/28muhammad.html. For recipes, see Lana Shabazz, *Cooking for the Champ* (New York: Jones-McMillon, 1979).

work on behalf of others.[31] In practice, Mormons were instructed to maintain a one- to two-year supply of emergency food. In daily life this meant rotating food storage staples into everyday cooking, and avoiding luxury items. Members made inexpensive meals from food storage staples like whole wheat and pow- dered milk, using inexpensive ingredients like peanut butter, canned garden produce, and seasoning mixes. It also meant working hard to cater their own parties (including weddings and funerals) instead of hiring help. In effect, then, Mormons shaped their cuisine with two of America's most intrinsic and related values: self-sufficiency and frugality.

When one woman yearned for the Mormon food of her past, she requested a dish that exemplified the welfare program's standards. Trish had not attended church for decades. Her home was big, in a fashionable section of Brookline, Massachusetts. As befits the owner of such a home, she structured her culinary calendar around traditional New England fare like Yorkshire pudding, fruitcake with hard sauce, and corned beef and cabbage. But during the final weeks of her life, these held no appeal.[32] Days before liver cancer finally took her life on August 17, 1990, she asked for a dish from her past: tuna noodle casserole. Her family called a church member, Shelley Hammond, who brought the casserole in time for dinner that night. Trish's sister recalled, "It was exactly as Trish remembered, and she ate with pleasure. . . . My mother and I took turns feeding it to her."[33] But why was tuna noodle casserole quintessentially Mormon?

Tuna noodle casserole could have been found at just about any middle American potluck. But often specific dishes distinguish a particular tradition only because they are *believed* to be distinctive, not because they actually are; tuna noodle casserole represented Mormon religious priorities, and they appro- priated it as their own. It promoted the Mormon goal of self-sufficiency because it was made from items in food storage, economy because it used inexpensive ingredients, and self-sufficiency (within their religious community) because it fulfilled an ideal of food as service—easy to make in large quantities and trans- port. Tuna noodle casserole was a staple of the Mormon culinary lexicon.

Similarly, Mormons famously ate Jell-O and "funeral potatoes."[34] But Protestants throughout the country also brought Jell-O salads to potlucks, and funeral potatoes were simply a version of cheesy scalloped potatoes that had

---

31. For some members, food storage was a crucial component of preparing for Armagge- don, when stores would be needed during the chaos that would precede Christ's Second Coming. Heber J. Grant, *Gospel Standards: Selections from the Sermons and Writings of Heber J. Grant, Seventh President of the Church of Jesus Christ of Latter-Day Saints* (Salt Lake City: Bookcraft, 1998), 111; Marion G. Romney, "Living Welfare Principles—Ensign Nov. 1981," https://www.churchofjesuschrist.org/study/ensign/1981/11/living-welfare -principles?lang=eng; and Garth L. Mangum, *The Mormons' War on Poverty: A History of LDS Welfare, 1830–1990* (Salt Lake City: University of Utah Press, 1993).

32. Judith Dushku, *Saints Well-Seasoned: Musings on How Food Nourishes Us—Body, Heart, and Soul* (Salt Lake City: Deseret, 1998), 72.

33. Ibid., 73–74.

34. Funeral potatoes were not known as such until the 1980s, but the recipe, calling for potatoes, cheese, sour cream, onion, and cream of mushroom soup, was in circula- tion before then.

been assigned a particular name by Mormons. In and of themselves, these dishes were not unique to Mormons—they were, in fact, American, and Mormons helped to create that American identity by applying deeply held Mormon kitchen values that promoted the treasured American quality of self-sufficiency. As Mormons recontextualized and slightly modified these American staples, they were able to reimagine them as outside the mainstream and particular to their own religion.

Just as the Nation's cookbooks made soul food into Nation food, Latter-day Saints cookbooks interpreted middle American foods, adapting them for rotation of food storage staples and economy, and made them Mormon. A prime example is the collection in Winnifred Jardine's *Mormon Country Cooking* (1980), which called for ingredients accessible through much of the Mormon corridor (apricots, peaches, rhubarb, zucchini), and maintained the Mormon ideal of drawing upon a year's food supply.[35] Jardine's recipes actually came from multiple Mormon sources and represented a shared culinary consciousness. In 1948 Jardine became food editor of the *Deseret News,* a church-owned newspaper and one of Salt Lake City's two major dailies, and wrote food columns until her retirement in 1984. Readers submitted many of the recipes to her column and later voted on which *Deseret News* recipes to include in the cookbook. Jardine even dedicated the book "to our *Deseret News* readers who contributed many of these recipes."[36]

These recipes are not only exemplary because they were gathered from the community; Jardine herself belonged to Mormonism's inner circle. As her editor wrote: "Winnifred Cannon Jardine's food-fixing background is as Mormon as the great turtle-shaped Tabernacle on Salt Lake City's Temple Square."[37] She descended from early Mormon leaders Brigham Young and George Q. Cannon, served on the church general boards, wrote homemaking lessons for Relief Society Manuals, and sang in the Mormon Tabernacle Choir. With these qualifications, she maintained a sense of spiritual responsibility for the book, working to present an ideal Mormon cuisine; and she included recipes representative of what Mormons actually prepared and enjoyed.

Just as Khalifah made notes in *The Muslim Recipe Book* when community recipes did not fully meet Elijah Muhammad's ideal for health, so Jardine tried to address similar inconsistencies in *Mormon Country Cooking* recipes. For example, when the book failed to represent the Word of Wisdom standard of limited meat intake, Jardine still looked to the ideal. The introduction to "Eggs and Cheese" reminded readers, "Eggs and cheese together make a nutritious, delicious combination that is grand for a people who have been counseled to use meat 'sparingly.'"[38] In her introductory section on "Meat, Fish and Poultry," she

35. The book's preface reinforces this fact: "Many of Winnifred's dishes start right on the Bing cherry tree, peach trees, raspberry bushes, or tomato or zucchini plants in the Jardine home garden." Winnifred C. Jardine, *Mormon Country Cooking* (Salt Lake City: Deseret, 1980), 9.

36. Ibid., 15.

37. Ibid., 7.

38. *Mormon Country Cooking,* 65.

wrote, "Although counseled to eat meat and poultry 'sparingly,' Mormons still build many of the main meals around them. But they do not seem to eat large quantities."[39] Jardine's assessment about the quantity of meat consumption likely reflected her wishes more than actual fact, as well as her discomfort when practice failed to match ideal.

THE MORMON PURSUITS OF ECONOMY AND INDEPENDENCE

Jardine's recipes stemmed directly from Mormon practices informed by American values: using food storage staples and inexpensive ingredients to promote self-sufficiency. Mormon recipes relied greatly on wheat—more than recipes in other twentieth-century American cookbooks, which used all-purpose flour instead. Wheat was especially important to Mormons both because it was perceived as providing superior nutrition and because it was a popular component of food storage owing to its long shelf-life.[40] Jardine theorized that the penchant for bread making and baking with wheat may have come to Mormons from their pioneer ancestry. More likely the reliance on wheat came from the church's welfare program, which encouraged hundreds of pounds of wheat to be stored in the cool basements of Mormon homes. Such provision was intended to sustain families not only during natural disasters but also during personal crises like unemployment, disability, and financial reverses. Wheat was a source of security for Mormons, a convenience, and an economic advantage, since quantity buying generally meant lower prices and buying ahead slowed down the bite of inflation.[41]

Food storage practices inevitably shaped Mormon cuisine. For example, a recipe for carrot cake included no all-purpose flour and incorporated a number of items with long shelf lives: vegetable oil instead of butter, canned pineapple, preserved stock like raisins, and coconut. Mormons could store these items with staggering amounts of wheat, testifying to their commitment to self-sufficiency and economy. Other food recipes demonstrated the deliberate Mormon food choices for independence and frugality too: bread recipes from more typical middle American cook-books called for fresh milk, whereas Mormon recipes were just as likely to use powdered or evaporated milk.

Aside from the stored foods, growing your own food was an essential element of the Welfare Program, and some recipes emphasized the use of garden

35

---

39. Ibid., 93.

40. The Relief Society had a long tradition of storing wheat for use in emergency. Brigham Young encouraged Mormons to store wheat against famine since they first put down roots in Utah. When Young gave up on the men following his orders, he put women in charge of this task, which they pursued from 1877 to 1941. Because of this history, wheat is prominent on the Relief Society emblem. Jessie L. Embry, "Relief Society Grain Storage Program, 1876–1940," Master's thesis, Brigham Young University, 1974; and E. Cecil McGavin, "Grain Storage among the Latter-day Saints," *The Improvement Era*, March 1941.

41. *Mormon Country Cooking*, 39.

produce. "Rhubarb Iced Cocktail," for instance, which involved rhubarb, sugar, and ginger ale, apparently existed solely as a means for keeping stalks of rhubarb, a fixture in Utah gardens, from going to waste. Parenthetical recipe instructions to use the extra drained rhubarb in pie or cobbler was a declaration against waste. Since drained rhubarb would not have much flavor, adding it to another dish would not improve flavor, which shows economy trumping pleasure. The "Rhubarb Iced Cocktail" recipe took a vegetable that flourished in the Utah climate and made of it a nonalcoholic party beverage. A recipe for Italian seasoning also invoked cooking with garden produce and focused on the value of frugality, since making your own Italian seasoning was supposed to save money. In her cookbook Jardine told readers in a chapter heading that this recipe, along with others for dried onion soup and French herbs, "can be made in quantity for a fraction of the supermarket price and are excellent for seasoning food storage dinners."[42]

Why not just buy Lipton onion soup mix or Italian seasoning and keep those in one's food storage? Because exercising frugality was as much a priority to Mormons as food storage, and making one's own mix or seasoning was less expensive. What is interesting here is how these values were combined with the Word of Wisdom instruction to use vegetables and herbs in season. Making one's own seasonings and mixes meant using fresh herbs from the garden but also using products like lemon pepper and garlic powder, which were obtained through the workings of a factory. Making one's own seasoning was not, therefore, about purity but about frugality. Many a well-stocked Mormon pantry prioritized self-sufficiency over other values. In some respects the Word of Wisdom was marginalized to better attain American values like economy, independence, and self-sufficiency over other values.

Mormon eating habits did reflect Word of Wisdom standards to some extent—Mormon cookbooks contained recipes neither for tiramisu (lady-fingers soaked in cappuccino) nor boeuf bourguignon with its reliance on red wine. But whereas the Word of Wisdom text itself emphasized eating foods in season, Mormon cookbooks contained recipes for preserves and pickles, so that food could be eaten out of season.[43] The Word of Wisdom urged restrained meat eating, but cookbooks were replete with ideas for dressing viands, which fed large groups and were easily purchased when on sale and stored in the chest freezer.[44] Instead of a strict implementation of Word of Wisdom ideals, Mormon cuisine reflected practicality, frugality, and the need to assemble food stores for an ever-uncertain future.

---

42. Ibid., 209.

43. *Doctrine and Covenants* 89:11: "Every herb in the season thereof, and every fruit in the season thereof; all these to be used with prudence and thanksgiving."

44. *Doctrine and Covenants* 89:12: "Yea, flesh also of beasts and of the fowls of the air, I, the Lord, have ordained for the use of man with thanksgiving; nevertheless they are to be used sparingly."

Just as with the Nation, the Mormon diet—a complex merger of slightly modified American cuisine recontextualized within the religious community's values—served as a simultaneous emblem for a distinctive, outsider subculture and the broader American culture.

MORE AMERICAN THAN APPLE PIE

In the kitchens and dining rooms of mid-twentieth-century America, members of two outsider groups negotiated relationships with America's mainstream in creative ways. Even as they explicitly savored their outsider status, Nation of Islam Muslims and Latter-day Saints subtly bought in to mainstream American values. The ways they altered familiar American staples like sweet potato pie or tuna casseroles reflected their endorsement of broader American ideals. Two main processes were taking place in the kitchens and dining tables of these groups: the construction of difference, and a striving to be better than the mainstream according to the rules of the mainstream.

40

The space these outsiders created for themselves within twentieth-century America speaks to just how complex and subtle are the differences between insider and outsider groups, and how dependent they can be on the assertion that they are indeed different. Carrot fluff and funeral potatoes look and taste much the same as the American staples they are meant to replace, but in the deliberate appropriation of these and other dishes, Nation of Islam and Mormon people assert their distinctiveness. Simultaneous with their assertions of difference, Mormons and Nation members brought a fervent commitment to excellence to the mainstream. At times outsiders seem to incorporate a hypertrophied version of the insider culture. If good Americans value physical health, Nation Muslims will bring health to bear on every dish they consider at the table. If good Americans value self-sufficiency, then Mormons will build a cuisine around inexpensive, durable goods.

Watching Nation Muslims and Mormons cook and eat provides important new insights into the ways participants in American society negotiate the paradoxes of fitting in and intentionally failing to fit in, a potent reminder of the importance the perception and practice of otherness plays in the construction of American society.

RECOMMENDED READING

Bowman, Matthew. *The Mormon People: The Making of an American Faith*. New York: Random House, 2012.

Curtis, Edward E., IV. *Black Muslim Religion in the Nation of Islam, 1960–1975*. Chapel Hill: University of North Carolina Press, 2006.

Derr, Jill Mulvay, Janath Russell Cannon, and Maureen Ursenbach Beecher. *Women of Covenant: The Story of Relief Society*. Salt Lake City: Deseret, 1992.

Tate, Sonsyrea. *Little X: Growing Up in the Nation of Islam*. San Francisco: HarperSanFrancisco, 1997.

MLA CITATION

Holbrook, Kate. "Good to Eat." *The Norton Reader: An Anthology of Nonfiction*, edited
    by Melissa A. Goldthwaite et al., 15th ed., W. W. Norton, 2020, pp. 253–66.

QUESTIONS

1. Kate Holbrook examines the culinary practices of two different religious
groups—the Nation of Islam and the Church of Jesus Christ of Latter-day Saints.
What similarities does she find between these two religious groups and their
approaches to food? What examples does she provide to support her argument?

2. Holbrook's "Good to Eat" is an example of an academic argument. What conventions of academic writing do you recognize in this piece? Which conventions
help her make and support her argument most clearly?

3. Research the food practices (restrictions and favored foods) of a particular religious group. What are the stated reasons for the restrictions? Are there recipes or
practices endorsed by that group that suggest other values—beyond religious
tenets—shaped the approach to food? Write an argument in which you make and
support a specific claim about the food practices of your chosen group.

DAN BARBER
What Farm-to-Table Got Wrong

T'S SPRING AGAIN. Hip deep in asparagus—and, soon enough, tomatoes
and zucchini—farm-to-table advocates finally have something from the
farm to put on the table.

The crowds clamoring for just-dug produce at the farmers' market
and the local food co-op suggest that this movement is no longer just a
foodie fad. Today, almost 80 percent of Americans say sustainability is a priority when purchasing food. The promise of this kind of majority is that eating
local can reshape landscapes and drive lasting change.

Except it hasn't. More than a decade into the movement, the promise has
fallen short. For all its successes, farm-to-table has not, in any fundamental way,
reworked the economic and political forces that dictate how our food is grown
and raised. Big Food is getting bigger, not smaller. In the last five years, we've
lost nearly 100,000 farms (mostly midsize ones). Today, 1.1 percent of farms in
the United States account for nearly 45 percent of farm revenues. Despite being
farm-to-table's favorite targets, corn and soy account for more than 50 percent

Published as an op-ed in the New York Times *(2014) by the chef and co-owner of the Blue
Hill and Blue Hill at Stone Barns restaurants. Dan Barber also wrote* The Third Plate: Field
Notes on the Future of Food *(2014), which offers a history of cuisine in the United States
and proposes ways of eating that are both delicious and environmentally responsible.*

of our harvested acres for the first time ever. Between 2006 and 2011, over a million acres of native prairie were plowed up in the so-called Western Corn Belt to make way for these two crops, the most rapid loss of grasslands since we started using tractors to bust sod on the Great Plains in the 1920s.

How do we make sense of this odd duality: a food revolution on one hand, an entrenched status quo on the other?

5   I got a hint of the answer a few years ago, while standing in a field in upstate New York. I was there because, many years before, I'd decided I wanted local flour for my restaurants. I chose Lakeview Organic, a grain farm operated by Klaas and Mary-Howell Martens. Klaas was growing a rare variety of emmer wheat (also known as farro), nearly extinct but for the efforts of a few farmers.

Milled and baked into whole wheat bread, the emmer was a revelation— intensely sweet and nutty. I spoke routinely about the importance of local grain and the resurrection of lost flavors. I was waving the farm-to-table flag and feeling pretty good about it, too.

Visiting Klaas those years later, hoping to learn what made the emmer so delicious, I realized I was missing the point entirely. The secret to great-tasting wheat, Klaas told me, is that it's not about the wheat. It's about the soil.

In fact, on a tour of his farm, there was surprisingly little wheat to see. Instead, Klaas showed me fields of less-coveted grains and legumes like millet, barley and kidney beans, as well as cover crops like mustard and clover, all of which he plants in meticulously planned rotations. The rotations dictate the quality of the soil, which means they dictate the flavor of the harvests as well. They are the recipe for his delicious emmer.

Each planting in the sequence has a specific function. Klaas likes his field rotations to begin with a cover crop like the mustard plant. Cover crops are often grown to restore nutrients depleted from a previous harvest. Plowed into the soil after maturity, mustard offers the added benefit of reducing pest and disease problems for subsequent crops.

10   Next Klaas will plant a legume, which does the neat trick of fixing nitrogen: grabbing it from the atmosphere and storing it in the plant's roots. Soybeans are a good choice; or kidney beans, if the local processor is paying enough to make it worth his while; or cowpeas, which he harvests for animal feed. If there's a dry spell, he'll forgo beans altogether and pop in some hardy millet. Oats or rye is next; rye builds soil structure and suppresses weeds. Only then is Klaas's soil locked and loaded with the requisite fertility needed for his wheat.

As much as I cling to tried and true recipes, Klaas doesn't. Depending on what the soil is telling him, he may roll out an entirely different rotation. If there's a buildup of fungal disease in the field, the next season he'll plant a brassica like cabbage or broccoli, followed by buckwheat, and then barley. Barley is among Klaas's favorite crops. In addition to cleansing the soil of pathogens, it can be planted along with a nitrogen fixer like clover, further benefiting the soil. Once again, the soil is ready for wheat.

Standing in Klaas's fields, I saw how single-minded I had been. Yes, I was creating a market for local emmer wheat, but I wasn't doing anything to sup-

Lakeview Organic Grain Farm, owned by Klaas and Mary-Howell Martens.

port the recipe behind it. Championing Klaas's wheat and only his wheat was tantamount to treating his farm like a grocery store. I was cherry-picking what I most wanted for my menu without supporting the whole farm.

I am not the only one. In celebrating the All-Stars of the farmers' market—asparagus, heirloom tomatoes, emmer wheat—farm-to-table advocates are often guilty of ignoring a whole class of humbler crops that are required to produce the most delicious food.

With limited American demand for local millet, rye and barley, 70 percent of Klaas's harvest was going into livestock feed for chickens, pigs and dairy cattle. In general, Klaas earned pennies on the dollar compared with what he'd make selling his crops for human consumption. And we were missing out as well, on nutritious foods that are staples of the best cuisines in the world.

Diversifying our diet to include more local grains and legumes is a delicious first step to improving our food system. Millet and rye are an easy substitute for rice or pasta. But that addresses only the low-hanging fruit of Klaas's farm. More challenging is to think about how to honor the other underutilized parts of his rotations—classic cover crops like cowpeas and mustard, which fertilize the soil to ensure healthy harvests in the future.

Today, the best farmers are tying up valuable real estate for long periods of time (in an agonizingly short growing season) simply to benefit their soil. Imagine if Macy's reserved half of its shelf space at Christmas for charitable donations. A noble idea. But profitable? Not so much. By creating a market for these crops, we can provide more value for the farmer and for our own diets, while supporting the long-term health of the land.

In Klaas's field, I bent down and ripped off a green shoot of Austrian winter peas. I took a bite. Inedible? No, delicious! Thirty acres of the most tender and sweet pea shoots I'd ever tasted. (Harvesting the leaves would somewhat reduce the amount plowed back into the soil, but the plant's soil benefits would remain.) In the distance I could make out a field of mustards. Klaas plants Tilney mustard, similar to the spicy green you find in a mesclun mix. I realized I wasn't just looking at a cover crop. I was looking at a salad bowl.

Back at the restaurant, I created a new dish called "Rotation Risotto," a collection of all of Klaas's lowly, soil-supporting grains and legumes, cooked and presented in the manner of a classic risotto. I used a purée of cowpea shoots and mustard greens to thicken the grains and replace the starchiness of rice. As one waiter described the idea, it was a "nose-to-tail approach to the farm"—an edible version of Klaas's farming strategy.

It's one thing for chefs to advocate cooking with the whole farm; it's another thing to make these uncelebrated crops staples in ordinary kitchens. Bridging that divide will require a new network of regional processors and distributors.

20   Take beer, for example. The explosion in local microbreweries has meant a demand for local barley malt. A new malting facility near Klaas's farm recently opened in response. He now earns 30 percent more selling barley for malt than he did selling it for animal feed. For other farmers, it's a convincing incentive to diversify their grain crops.

Investing in the right infrastructure means the difference between a farmer's growing crops for cows or for cafeterias. It will take the shape of more local mills (for grains), canneries (for beans) and processors (for greens). As heretical as this may sound, farm-to-table needs to embrace a few more middlemen.

Perhaps the problem with the farm-to-table movement is implicit in its name. Imagining the food chain as a field on one end and a plate of food at the other is not only reductive, it also puts us in the position of end users. It's a passive system—a grocery-aisle mentality—when really, as cooks and eaters, we need to engage in the nuts and bolts of true agricultural sustainability. Flavor can be our guide to reshaping our diets, and our landscapes, from the ground up.

MLA CITATION

Barber, Dan. "What Farm-to-Table Got Wrong." *The Norton Reader: An Anthology of Nonfiction*, edited by Melissa A. Goldthwaite et al., 15th ed., W. W. Norton, 2020, pp. 267–70.

QUESTIONS

1. The phrase "farm-to-table" suggests a simple process of transferring locally grown produce to nearby homes and restaurants. How does Dan Barber complicate our understanding of this process? Why is this complication important to his argument?

2. Barber suggests ways that he, as a chef, can aid local organic farmers by utilizing grains and vegetables essential to crop rotation—as in paragraph 18 where he describes "Rotation Risotto." Can you infer from his argument how consumers who read his op-ed might also aid the cause?

3. Visit a farmers' market, restaurant, or organic grocery store that sells locally grown produce. Choose a grain or vegetable you haven't eaten or don't know well, research it, and write a short account of its cultivation and uses.

MARION NESTLE
Superfoods Are a Marketing Ploy

REGARDLESS OF WHO ISSUES THEM, guidelines for health promotion and disease prevention universally recommend diets that are largely plant-based, meaning those that include plenty of fruits, vegetables, grains, beans, and nuts. The U.S. dietary guidelines also recommend foods in the "protein" category. Grains, beans, and nuts are good sources of protein, but the guidelines use "protein" to mean low-fat dairy, lean meats, and fish. Recommended eating patterns include all these foods, relatively unprocessed, but with minimal addition of salt and sugars. Such patterns provide nutrients and energy in proportions that meet physiological needs but also minimize the risk of obesity, type 2 diabetes, and other chronic diseases. One more definition: "Patterns" refer to diets as a whole, not to single foods. No one food makes a diet healthful. The healthiest diets include a wide variety of foods in each of the recommended categories in amounts that balance calories.

In their largely unprocessed forms, foods from the earth, trees, or animals are healthful by definition. So why, you might ask, would the producers of foods such as cranberries, pears, avocados, or walnuts fund research aimed at proving that these particular foods—rather than fruits, vegetables, or nuts in general—have special health benefits? Marketing, of course. Every food producer wants to expand sales. Health claims sell. The FDA[1] requires research to support health claims and greatly prefers studies that involve human subjects rather than animals.

All of this explains why Royal Hawaiian Macadamia Nut petitioned the FDA in 2015 to allow it to say in advertisements that daily consumption of macadamias—along with eating a healthy diet—may reduce the risk of heart disease. The 81-page petition cited several studies done in humans, one of them

Published in the Atlantic *(2018), this article was adapted from Nestle's* Unsavory Truth: How Food Companies Skew the Science of What We Eat *(2018), in which she argues that funded food studies are more about marketing than science.*

1. Food and Drug Administration.

funded by the Hershey Company, which sells chocolate-covered macadamias. The FDA ruled that it would permit a qualified health claim for macadamia nuts with this precise wording: "Supportive but not conclusive research shows that eating 1.5 ounces per day of macadamia nuts, as part of a diet low in saturated fat and cholesterol and not resulting in increased intake of saturated fat or calories, may reduce the risk of coronary heart disease." Can a statement this cumbersome help sell macadamia nuts? Definitely, with a little help from the press: "Go nuts, folks! FDA declares macadamia nuts heart healthy."

Legitimate scientific questions can be asked about specific foods—their nutrient content or digestibility, for example—but most such issues were addressed ages ago. Foods are not drugs. To ask whether one single food has special health benefits defies common sense. We do not eat just one food. We eat many different foods in combinations that differ from day to day; varying our food intake takes care of nutrient needs. But when marketing imperatives are at work, sellers want research to claim that their products are "superfoods," a nutritionally meaningless term. "Superfoods" is an advertising concept.

5   But what is wrong with promoting the benefits of healthful foods? Wouldn't we be better off eating more of them? Yes, we would, but many industry-funded studies are misleading, which is why the FDA requires so many qualifications in the claims it allows. This kind of research is designed to produce results implying that people who eat this one food will be healthier and can forget about everything else in their diets. Research aimed at marketing raises questions about biases in design and interpretation, may create reputational risks for investigators, and reflects poorly on the integrity of nutrition science. It also raises questions about the role of government agencies in promoting single-food

research and about their failure to do a better job of regulating marketers' claims about health benefits based on that research. To illustrate why such concerns matter, consider some of the marketing issues related to a well-known healthy food: blueberries.

The trade association Wild Blueberries of North America wants you to understand that frozen, fresh Wild Blueberries (always capitalized) are better for you than unfrozen, fresh supermarket highbush berries: "Jam-packed with a variety of natural phytochemicals such as anthocyanin, Wild Blueberries have twice the antioxidant capacity per serving of regular blueberries. A growing body of research is establishing Wild Blueberries as a potential ally to protect against diseases such as cancer, heart disease, diabetes and Alzheimer's." This is an impressive range of health benefits for a tiny fruit consumed in small amounts, but selling them as an antioxidant powerhouse has done wonders for the Maine wild-blueberry industry.

For years, I have had a potted highbush-blueberry plant on my 12th-floor Manhattan terrace, satisfyingly productive in years when I can manage to fend off the hordes of voracious finches. Unlike the easy-to-get-at highbush varieties, the wild ones grow close to the ground on sandy soils left behind by receding glaciers and are more difficult to harvest. In Maine, these blueberries are an important agricultural commodity. Since 1945, Maine blueberry growers have supported research—then and now focused on production practices—at the state's university. As techniques improved, blueberry growers produced more berries. These needed to be sold.

The Maine Wild Blueberry Commission consulted with marketing specialists. In 1992, a consultant advised focusing on taste as a means of differentiating wild blueberries from cultivated blueberries. But the consultant then read an article in a USDA[2] magazine extolling the virtues of plant antioxidant pigments in "boosting the immune system, reducing inflammation and allergies, [and] detoxifying contaminants and pollutants." The article said that USDA investigators had invented an assay for antioxidants demonstrating that blueberries have the highest levels of any fruit tested (kale was highest among vegetables). The consultant advised the commission to focus on antioxidants. From 1997 to 2000, half of the Maine Wild Blueberry Commission's marketing resources went into repositioning blueberries as a health icon. The strategy worked. Maine's wild-blueberry industry flourished—at least for a while. Recent overproduction and competition from Canadian fruit have dropped prices below profitability.

I love blueberries, wild and cultivated, but they are a fruit like any other. Their antioxidants may counteract the damaging actions of oxidizing agents (free radicals) in the body, but studies of how well antioxidants protect against disease yield results that are annoyingly inconsistent. When tested, antioxidant supplements have not been shown to reduce disease risk and sometimes have been shown to cause harm. The USDA no longer publishes data on food antioxidant levels "due to mounting evidence that the values indicating anti-

2. United States Department of Agriculture.

oxidant capacity have no relevance to the effects of specific bioactive compounds, including polyphenols, on human health." The U.S. National Center for Complementary and Integrative Health at the NIH[3] judges antioxidants as having no special benefits. People who eat more fruits and vegetables have less risk of chronic disease, but nobody really knows whether this is because of antioxidants, other food components, or other lifestyle choices.

10   Blueberries, like every other fruit and vegetable, have a unique combination of antioxidants. So what? It is best not to expect miracles—like this especially wishful-thinking headline: "Blueberries associated with reduced risk of erectile dysfunction." Two of the authors of this study reported receiving funding from the U.S. Blueberry Highbush Council "for a separate project unrelated to this publication."

A more critical question is what to make of all this. If I may overgeneralize, the quality of single-food marketing studies does not always hold up to scrutiny. For example, a nutritional biochemist criticized a 2015 raisin study connected to funding from the California Marketing Raisin Board for its misuse of statistics and for comparing raisins to processed snack foods: "With the design used you can't really say that raisins were 'good' for the participants, just not as bad as the junk snacks."

Even when done well, studies so clearly aimed at marketing skew the research agenda. If food companies were not funding marketing studies, investigators might be working on more important biological problems. All these foods are highly nutritious and well worth eating for their taste and texture—as well as for their health benefits. Is one fruit, vegetable, or nut better for you than another? The answer, as I keep saying, depends on everything else you eat or do. People who habitually eat largely plant-based diets are healthier. Variety in food intake and calorie balance are fundamental principles of healthful diets.

Again, to be fair, not all studies funded by plant trade associations come out the way they are supposed to. The California Strawberry Commission, for example, sponsored a study to see whether eating 40 grams of dried strawberry powder a day—equivalent to a pound of strawberries—would counteract the effects on blood lipids of eating a high-fat diet. It did not. I do not want to even think about strawberry powder. But does this result mean we should not be eating strawberries? Of course not. All fruits, vegetables, and nuts have vitamins, minerals, fiber, antioxidants, and other components that collectively promote health. If we are fortunate enough to have choices, we can eat the ones we like.

MLA CITATION

Nestle, Marion. "Superfoods Are a Marketing Ploy." *The Norton Reader: An Anthology of Nonfiction*, edited by Melissa A. Goldthwaite et al., 15th ed., W. W. Norton, 2020, pp. 271–74.

---

3. National Institutes of Health.

QUESTIONS

1. Why does Marion Nestle argue against promoting the health benefits of a single food?

2. What problems with food industry–funded studies does Nestle identify? What examples does she provide to support her concerns?

3. Look carefully at the packaging of a food you eat. Does it make any claims about the health benefits of that product? To what extent does advertising about health benefits influence your purchases? Write a short argument in which you make a claim about what kinds of health information should or should not be included on food packaging.

6 SPORTS

You may write me down in history
With your bitter, twisted lies,
You may trod me in the very dirt
But still, like dust, I'll rise.
—MAYA ANGELOU, "Still I Rise"

During its broadcast of the 2016 Wimbledon championships, at which Serena Williams won an unprecedented twenty-second Grand Slam title, the BBC aired a video montage in which Williams recites Maya Angelou's iconic celebration of African American female strength over highlights from her athletic career. This montage was not merely a tribute to Williams, arguably the greatest athlete of all time; it also gestures toward the power of sports to inspire us, to elevate us, to reveal the greatness and the complexity of the human spirit. Viewed in this way, sports are much more than mere entertainment; they become a lens through which we can consider the struggles and successes of our ordinary lives, so that we can live those lives better.

The selections in this chapter are diverse in genre—they include personal essays, long-form reporting, an op-ed, and even a selection from a book-length "lyric"—but they share a thematic breadth: all of them are about sports, of course, but none of them are *only* about sports. As a group, they address several interwoven themes, including history, memory, and nostalgia; race, ethnicity, community, and identity; spectatorship and performance; and the meaning of athletic excellence.

Five of the chapter's nine readings—those by Roger Angell, Michael Lewis, A. Bartlett Giamatti, Maya Angelou, and Claudia Rankine—treat professional sports. The excerpt from Lewis's *The Blind Side* shows how the rules and strategies of professional football changed in response to the transformative play of the linebacker Lawrence Taylor. Angell's "The Interior Stadium" and Giamatti's "The Green Fields of the Mind" explore professional baseball's unique pull on our memories, as well as the game's mythic appeal and importance as a counterpoise to the frenetic quality of modern life. The selections from Angelou's biography *I Know Why the Caged Bird Sings* and Rankine's *Citizen: An American Lyric* are more explicitly political, reading the performances of two extraordinary African American athletes—the boxer Joe Louis for Angelou, the tennis player Serena Williams for Rankine—in relation to broader racial dynamics.

Three of the chapter's readings—those by Aimee Nezhukumatathil, David Epstein, and David Joy—concern participation in sports. Nezhukumatathil's "This Landshark Is Your Landshark," a personal essay about her decision as the daughter of South Asian immigrants to perform as her high school's mascot, offers important insights about the power of such symbols to nurture or damage communities. Although she writes in a different register, Nezhukumatathil, like Angelou and Rankine, pushes us to confront sports' uncomfortable racial politics. Epstein's op-ed "Sports Should Be Child's Play," an argument against premature "hyperspecialization" in children's sports, invites us to consider what children's or amateur sports are for. Joy's nostalgic "Hunting Camp" is a tender and richly detailed evocation of a way of life that is fast disappearing. Like Angell, Giamatti, and Angelou, Joy invites us to reflect on the organizing role sports can play in our personal memories and communal histories.

The chapter closes with David Shields's "Words Can't Begin to Describe What I'm Feeling," a humorously exhaustive montage of sports clichés. Although quite different from everything else in the chapter, it nevertheless illuminates a particular rhetorical challenge that anyone writing about sports must face: how to communicate one's meaning accurately and specifically, without devolving into tired phrasings, empty generalizations, or easy platitudes.

As you read the selections in this chapter, consider how they each use sports to broach fundamental human themes. What do sports tell us about ourselves and our communities? Why do sports seem to exert such a powerful pull on memory? What does it mean—or take—to be truly excellent? How should we respond to the inevitability of change? How should we respond to the palpable injustices afflicting our world? Consider also the different ways in which the chapter's authors write about their subjects: through personal memory and reflection, through exposition and analysis, through detailed narration and description, even through humor. Why might an author have adopted one or another of these modes? How might you use them in your own writing?

AIMEE NEZHUKUMATATHIL

This Landshark Is Your Landshark

I WAS QUITE THE ACTRESS as I stalled at my high school locker, pretending to look for my lunch or search for a notebook. I knew exactly how much time I had to waste before I could grab my sack lunch and—without anyone seeing me—run to the nearest bathroom and eat its contents while hiding in a stall. My younger sister never knew. Neither did my parents. Day after day I kept up the act that everything was fine.

As the new girl in my junior year at Beavercreek High—in a large suburb of Dayton, Ohio—I simply couldn't bear to sit alone in the boisterous school cafeteria, where people who knew one another since kindergarten laughed and traded jokes and snacks. If I wasn't hiding in a bathroom during the lunch hour, I was eating in our school elevator, conveniently hidden near the library, the place I loved to scurry into, so at least I could get lost in books afterward. This went on for almost an entire academic year.

Besides my studies, the only thing at Beavercreek I knew I loved was football. Coming from a rural region in western New York where the Buffalo Bills

First published in the 2018 Thanksgiving issue of ESPN The Magazine.

dominated the news cycle and homeroom talk, and where I was a "manager" for my junior varsity football team, I was attracted to Beavercreek High's football games: giddy for the grind and crunch of a play, for the smell of popcorn in waxy paper sacks and hot cocoa in white Styrofoam cups; how strangers in wooden bleachers, regardless of race and class, could become high-fiving friends in less than an hour.

I wanted to be part of that. So I found a new way to hide. I knew if I could hide in this particular way—with a new face, a new body—I would finally feel at home in this giant suburban school.

A few weeks before my senior year began at Beavercreek, I told Coach   5
Woods, the cheerleading coach, that I wanted to be the mascot for the football team. *I can dance*, I said, *and I make people laugh when I tell them stories with exaggerated hand gestures!*

Coach Woods was sold.

When I came home from school and told my immigrant parents—my Filipino mom and South Asian dad—that Coach Woods had agreed to let me be the football mascot, they looked at me with a mixture of confusion and anger and incredulity: *We did not sacrifice and leave our countries for our eldest daughter to become Mickey Mouse!*

But becoming Bucky Beaver brought me closer to the people who ultimately befriended me and made me more outgoing toward those who hadn't. Every Friday night, I slapped hands, hugged and danced with everyone and anyone in the stands. On Mondays, I began participating more often in class discussions. I joined the student council and offered up opinions in meetings.

Finally, I felt seen. I felt heard.

I now teach at the University of Mississippi. The school is in the process of   10
rebranding and distancing itself from its Confederate past, in particular its most famous mascot: Colonel Reb.[1]

The university introduced him to the sidelines in 1979. He bore the image of an elderly white plantation owner leaning on a cane and wearing a wide-brimmed gray hat. After years of complaints that Colonel Reb was a racist symbol and, furthermore, a direct insult to a student body in which more than one in 10 students are African-American, the mascot was removed from on-field duties in 2003. It was a point of pride—and no small feat—that the student body led the way in making this change.

Alex McDaniel, a local journalist who was a student when the mascot vote took place, says that "removing Colonel Reb was a firm statement that the school was heading in a direction that wouldn't be determined by angry alumni and their donations."

In 2010, Ole Miss[2] settled on Rebel the Black Bear as a replacement, but Rebel never quite caught on with fans. During my first year in Oxford, in 2017,

1. Abbreviation for "Rebel," a term for a Confederate soldier during the American Civil War.
2. Nickname for the University of Mississippi.

the student government initiated a move to adopt a new mascot. Dion Kevin III, the student body president that year, calls the process "an organic result of school spirit" that accomplished something I knew well: "It objectively unified students, athletes and alumni alike." The result was Tony the Landshark, a half-human/half-shark with arms and legs and a shark's anvil-shaped head featuring a signature grinning, toothy smile. The Landshark is a tribute to Tony Fein, an Army veteran and star linebacker for the 2008 team that upset Tim Tebow's[3] Florida Gators on the road. After a successful defensive play, Fein would hold his hand up to his helmet to imitate a shark fin.[4] Now "Fins up" is a battle cry for the team's defensive unit. "We have a mascot inspired by and named for an African-American football player," McDaniel says. "Anyone who doesn't understand the significance of that doesn't understand history and why it matters."

I watched the Landshark work before the Alabama game earlier this season. So many children and teens were drawn to him, and the feeling—as best as Tony could mime back—seemed to be mutual, with Tony often forming his gloved hands into a heart shape after a kid asked for a hug. These kids who dotted The Grove[5]—black, white, Latino, even my own half-Asian kids—all wore giant smiles and clamored to take a selfie with Tony or just high-five him. It's impossible, grotesque even, to imagine such a scene centered on Colonel Reb.

15   It is easy to think of a mascot as a clown or distraction, a buffoon with over-the-top dance moves, trying to score an easy laugh between plays. But the point of a mascot isn't just humor. With each hug for a child or photograph with a fan, our Landshark ties a group of people together, helps make them a community.

Tony has given that new community traditions we call our own: He does an elaborate halftime routine with the dance team, and the band now plays a hilarious rendition of the *Jaws*[6] theme during pregame. The Landshark is a symbol that angles and swims in a new direction, propelling a whole school toward the light.

During football season my senior year at Beavercreek High, I begged my parents to attend just one game so they could see me "work." They led busy lives but managed to make it for homecoming, their first high school football game ever. They sat in the stands, huddled close in the October chill. I could see through my beaver mask that no one talked to them, and they didn't make an effort to chat up anyone either. My family moved six times before my senior year in high school, and we were often one of the only Asian American families in town. Sometimes people made fun of my parents' accents. We all learned to smile through gritted teeth. We were always the outsiders.

3. Quarterback (b. 1987) who received the Heisman Trophy in 2007 and later played in the National Football League.

4. The original "Land Shark" was a recurring bit in the first season (1975) of the NBC comedy show, *Saturday Night Live*.

5. Area on the Ole Miss campus used for tailgating.

6. Popular 1975 film about a marauding great white shark, based on the novel by Peter Benchley and directed by Steven Spielberg.

After I finished clapping out a set of cheers, I climbed to their section in the stands, high-fiving kids on my way. I had described the beaver costume to my parents—its two giant protruding teeth were bigger than half my face—and yet they still didn't recognize me through the mesh netting of my mouth until I scream-whispered their names (a big no-no in the mascot trade). I saw their stoic faces suddenly brighten in recognition, and they started clapping to the halftime music. That only made me want to shake my tail even more, and the crowd began to clap in time to my giant rodent steps: first everyone around my parents, then my parents too.

I felt audacious in that costume. I felt joyous. I danced so hard to Prince's[7] "1999," my mascot tail fell off. (It was reattached with safety pins for the rest of the game.) My mother suddenly couldn't help herself and told anyone within shouting distance that I was her daughter. *Yes, yes, the beaver is my daughter! Isn't she so funny? Yes, I think she gets that from me!*

MLA CITATION

Nezhukumatathil, Aimee. "This Landshark Is Your Landshark." *The Norton Reader: An Anthology of Nonfiction,* edited by Melissa A. Goldthwaite et al., 15th ed., W. W. Norton, 2020, pp. 278–81.

QUESTIONS

1. Aimee Nezhukumatathil considers four mascots in her essay: Bucky Beaver, Colonel Reb, Rebel the Black Bear, and the Landshark. What does she celebrate or criticize about each of them?

2. Nezhukumatathil's title refers to the mascot of the University of Mississippi football team, but she begins and ends her essay by recounting her experience performing as a mascot in high school. Why do you think Nezhukumatathil chose to frame her essay this way?

3. Nezhukumatathil tries to join her high school community by masking her identity: "I knew if I could hide in this particular way—with a new face, a new body—I would finally feel at home in this giant suburban school" (paragraph 4). What does performing as a mascot teach her about herself, her community, her family?

4. Controversies over mascots for high school, college, and professional sports teams are frequently in the news. Using Nezhukumatathil's essay as a model, research and write about one such controversy.

7. Influential American pop, funk, and rock musician (1958–2016) who had numerous hits in the late 1970s, 1980s, and after.

ROGER ANGELL
The Interior Stadium

SPORTS ARE TOO MUCH WITH US.[1] Late and soon, sitting and watching—mostly watching on television—we lay waste our powers of identification and enthusiasm and, in time, attention as more and more closing rallies and crucial putts and late field goals and final playoffs and sudden deaths and world records and world championships unreel themselves ceaselessly before our half-lidded eyes. Professional leagues expand like bubble gum, ever larger and thinner, and the extended sporting seasons, now bunching and overlapping at the ends, conclude in exhaustion and the wrong weather. So, too, goes the secondary business of sports—the news or non-news off the field. Sports announcers (ex-halfbacks in Mod hairdos) bring us another live, exclusive interview in depth with the twitchy coach of some as yet undefeated basketball team, or with a weeping (for joy) fourteen-year-old champion female backstroker, and the sports pages, now almost the largest single part of the newspaper, brim with salary disputes, medical bulletins, franchise maneuverings, all-star ballots, drug scandals, close-up biogs, after-dinner tributes, union tactics, weekend wrap-ups, wire-service polls, draft-choice trades, clubhouse gossip, and the latest odds. The American obsession with sports is not a new phenomenon, of course, except in its current dimensions, its excessive excessiveness. What *is* new, and what must at times unsettle even the most devout and unselective fan, is a curious sense of loss. In the midst of all these successive spectacles and instant replays and endless reportings and recapitulations, we seem to have forgotten what we came for. More and more, each sport resembles all sports; the flavor, the special joys of place and season, the unique displays of courage and strength and style that once isolated each game and fixed it in our affections have disappeared somewhere in the noise and crush.

Of all sports, none has been so buffeted about by this unselective proliferation, so maligned by contemporary cant, or so indifferently defended as baseball. Yet the game somehow remains the same, obdurately unaltered and comparable only with itself. Baseball has one saving grace that distinguishes it—for me, at any rate—from every other sport. Because of its pace, and thus the perfectly observed balance, both physical and psychological, between opposing forces, its clean lines can be restored in retrospect. This inner game—baseball in the mind—has no season, but it is best played in the winter, without the distraction of other baseball news. At first, it is a game of recollections, recapturing, and visions. Figures and occasions return, enormous sounds rise and swell, and the interior stadium fills with light and yields up the sight of a young ballplayer—

Originally published in the New Yorker *(1971), this essay also appeared in* The Summer Game *(1978), Roger Angell's book about baseball in the United States.*

1. Allusion to "The World Is Too Much with Us" (1808), a poem by William Wordsworth.

some hero perfectly memorized—just completing his own unique swing and now racing toward first. See the way he runs? Yes, that's him! Unmistakable, he leans in, still following the distant flight of the ball with his eyes, and takes his big turn at the base. Yet this is only the beginning, for baseball in the mind is not a mere returning. In time, this easy summoning up of restored players, winning hits, and famous rallies gives way to reconsiderations and reflections about the sport itself. By thinking about baseball like this—by playing it over, keeping it warm in a cold season—we begin to make discoveries. With luck, we may even penetrate some of its mysteries. One of those mysteries is its vividness—the absolutely distinct inner vision we retain of that hitter, that eager base-runner, of however long ago. My father was talking the other day about some of the ballplayers he remembered. He grew up in Cleveland, and the Indians were his team. Still are. "We had Nap Lajoie at second," he said. "You've heard of him. A great big broad-shouldered fellow, but a beautiful fielder. He was a rough customer. If he didn't like an umpire's call, he'd give him a faceful of tobacco juice. The shortstop was Terry Turner—a smaller man, and blond. I can still see Lajoie picking up a grounder and wheeling and floating the ball over to Turner. Oh, he was quick on his feet! In right field we had Elmer Flick, now in the Hall of Fame. I liked the center fielder, too. His name was Harry Bay, and he wasn't a heavy hitter, but he was very fast and covered a lot of ground. They said he could circle the bases in twelve seconds flat. I saw him get a home run inside the park—the ball hit on the infield and went right past the second baseman and out to the wall, and Bay beat the relay. I remember Addie Joss, our great right-hander. Tall, and an elegant pitcher. I once saw him pitch a perfect game. He died young."[2]

My father has been a fan all his life, and he has pretty well seen them all. He has told me about the famous last game of the 1912 World Series, in Boston, and seeing Fred Snodgrass[3] drop that fly ball in the tenth inning, when the Red Sox scored twice and beat the Giants. I looked up Harry Bay and those other Indians in the *Baseball Encyclopedia,* and I think my father must have seen that inside-the-park homer in the summer of 1904. Lajoie batted .376 that year, and Addie Joss led the American League with an earned-run average of 1.59, but the Indians finished in fourth place. 1904. . . . Sixty-seven years have gone by, yet Nap Lajoie is in plain view, and the ball still floats over to Terry Turner. Well, my father is eighty-one now, and old men are great rememberers of the distant past. But I am fifty, and I can also bring things back: Lefty Gomez, skinny-necked and frighteningly wild, pitching his first game at Yankee Stadium, against the White Sox and Red Faber in 1930. Old John McGraw,[4] in a business suit and a white fedora, sitting lumpily in a dark corner of the dugout at the Polo Grounds[5] and glowering out at the field. Babe Ruth,[6] wearing

2. Ballplayers mentioned in this paragraph played for the Cleveland Indians in the early twentieth century.

3. New York Giants outfielder (1887–1974).

4. New York Giants manager (1873–1934).

5. Home of the New York Giants until 1957; demolished in 1964.

6. Boston pitcher and New York Yankee outfielder (1895–1948).

a new, bright yellow glove, trotting out to right field—a swollen ballet dancer, with those delicate, almost feminine feet and ankles. Ruth at the plate, upper-cutting and missing, staggering with the force of his swing. Ruth and Gehrig,[7] hitting back-to-back homers. Gehrig, in the summer of 1933, running bases with a bad leg in a key game against the Senators; hobbling, he rounds third, closely followed by young Dixie Walker, then a Yankee. The throw comes in to the plate, and the Washington catcher—it must have been Luke Sewell—tags out the sliding Gehrig and, in the same motion, the sliding Dixie Walker. A double play at the plate. The Yankees lose the game; the Senators go on to a pennant.[8] And, back across the river again, Carl Hubbell. My own great pitcher, a southpaw, tall and elegant. Hub pitching: the loose motion; two slow, formal bows from the waist, glove and hands held almost in front of his face as he pivots, the long right leg (in long, peculiar pants) striding; and the ball, angling oddly, shooting past the batter. Hubbell walks gravely back to the bench, his pitching arm, as always, turned the wrong way round, with the palm out. Screwballer.

Any fan, as I say, can play this private game, extending it to extraordinary varieties and possibilities in his mind. Ruth bats against Sandy Koufax or Sam McDowell.[9] . . . Hubbell pitches to Ted Williams,[10] and the Kid, grinding the bat in his fists, twitches and blocks his hips with the pitch; he holds off but still follows the ball, leaning over and studying it like some curator as it leaps in just under his hands. Why this vividness, even from an imaginary confrontation? I have watched many other sports, and I have followed some—football, hockey, tennis—with eagerness, but none of them yields these permanent interior pictures, these ancient and precise excitements. Baseball, I must conclude, is intensely remembered because only baseball is so intensely watched. The game forces intensity upon us. In the ballpark, scattered across an immense green, each player is isolated in our attention, utterly visible. Watch that fielder just below us. Little seems to be expected of him. He waits in easy composure, his hands on his knees; when the ball at last soars or bounces out to him, he seizes it and dispatches it with swift, haughty ease. It all looks easy, slow, and, above all, safe. Yet we know better, for what is certain in baseball is that someone, perhaps several people, will fail. They will be searched out, caught in the open, and defeated, and there will be no confusion about it or sharing of the blame. This is sure to happen, because what baseball requires of its athletes, of course, is nothing less than perfection, and perfection cannot be eased or divided. Every movement of every game, from first pitch to last out, is measured and recorded against an absolute standard, and thus each success is also a fail-ure. Credit that strikeout to the pitcher, but also count it against the batter's

7. Lou Gehrig (1903–1941), New York Yankees first baseman.

8. Triangular flag flown by the Major League Baseball's American League and National League champions.

9. Koufax (b. 1935), pitcher for the Brooklyn and Los Angeles Dodgers; McDowell (b. 1942), pitcher, most notably with the Cleveland Indians.

10. Boston Red Sox outfielder (1918–2002); "the Kid" was one of his nicknames.

average; mark his run unearned, because the left fielder bobbled the ball for an instant and a runner moved up. Yet, faced with this sudden and repeated presence of danger, the big-league player defends himself with such courage and skill that the illusion of safety is sustained. Tension is screwed tighter and tighter as the certain downfall is postponed again and again, so that when disaster does come—a half-topped infield hit, a walk on a close three-and-two call, a low drive up the middle that just eludes the diving shortstop—we rise and cry out. It is a spontaneous, inevitable, irresistible reaction.

Televised baseball, I must add, does not seem capable of transmitting this   5
emotion. Most baseball is seen on the tube now, and it is presented faithfully and with great technical skill. But the medium is irrevocably two-dimensional; even with several cameras, television cannot bring us the essential distances of the game—the simultaneous flight of a batted ball and its pursuit by the racing, straining outfielders, the swift convergence of runner and ball at a base. Foreshortened on our screen, the players on the field appear to be squashed together, almost touching each other, and, watching them, we lose the sense of their separateness and lonesome waiting.

This is a difficult game. It is so demanding that the best teams and the weakest teams can meet on almost even terms, with no assurance about the result of any one game. In March 1962, in St. Petersburg, the World Champion Yankees played for the first time against the newborn New York Mets—one of the worst teams of all time—in a game that each badly wanted to win; the winner, to nobody's real surprise, was the Mets. In 1970, the World Champion Orioles won a hundred and eight games and lost fifty-four; the lowest cellar team, the White Sox, won fifty-six games and lost a hundred and six. This looks like an enormous disparity, but what it truly means is that the Orioles managed to win two out of every three games they played, while the White Sox won one out of every three. That third game made the difference—and a kind of difference that can be appreciated when one notes that the winning margin given up by the White Sox to all their opponents during the season averaged 1.1 runs per game. Team form is harder to establish in baseball than in any other sport, and the hundred-and-sixty-two-game season not uncommonly comes down to October with two or three teams locked together at the top of the standings on the final weekend. Each inning of baseball's slow, searching time span, each game of its long season is essential to the disclosure of its truths.

Form is the imposition of a regular pattern upon varying and unpredictable circumstances, but the patterns of baseball, for all the game's tautness and neatness, are never regular. Who can predict the winner and shape of today's game? Will it be a brisk, neat two-hour shutout? A languid, error-filled 12-3 laugher? A riveting three-hour, fourteen-inning deadlock? What other sport produces these manic swings? For the players, too, form often undergoes terrible reversals; in no other sport is a champion athlete so often humiliated or a journeyman so easily exalted. The surprise, the upset, the total turnabout of expectations and reputations—these are delightful commonplaces of baseball. Al Gionfriddo, a part-time Dodger outfielder, stole second base in the ninth inning of the fourth game of the 1947 World Series to help set up Lavagetto's game-winning double (and the only Dodger hit of the game) off the Yankees' Bill Bevens. Two days later, Gionfriddo robbed Joe DiMaggio[11] with a famous game-saving catch of a four-hundred-and-fifteen-foot drive in deepest left field at Yankee Stadium. Gionfriddo never made it back to the big leagues after that season. Another irregular, the Mets' Al Weis, homered in the fifth and last game of the 1969 World Series, tying up the game that the Mets won in the next inning; it was Weis's third homer of the year and his first ever at Shea Stadium.[12] And so forth. Who remembers the second game of the 1956 World Series— an appallingly bad afternoon of baseball in which the Yankees' starter, Don Larsen, was yanked after giving up a single and four walks in less than two innings? It was Larsen's *next* start, the fifth game, when he pitched his perfect game.

There is always a heavy splash of luck in these reversals. Luck, indeed, plays an almost predictable part in the game; we have all seen the enormous enemy clout into the bleachers that just hooks foul at the last instant, and the half-checked swing that produces a game-winning blooper over second. Everyone complains about baseball luck, but I think it adds something to the game that is nearly essential. Without it, such a rigorous and unforgiving pastime would be almost too painful to enjoy.

No one, it becomes clear, can conquer this impossible and unpredictable game. Yet every player tries, and now and again—very rarely—we see a man who seems to have met all the demands, challenged all the implacable averages, spurned the mere luck. He has defied baseball, even altered it, and for a time at least the game is truly his. One thinks of Willie Mays,[13] in the best of his youth, batting at the Polo Grounds, his whole body seeming to leap at the ball as he swings in an explosion of exuberance. Or Mays in center field, play-ing in so close that he appears at times to be watching the game from over the second baseman's shoulder, and then that same joyful leap as he takes off after a long, deep drive and runs it down, running so hard and so far that the ball itself seems to stop in the air and wait for him. One thinks of Jackie Robin-son[14] in a close game—any close game—playing the infield and glaring in at the enemy hitter, hating him and daring him, refusing to be beaten. And Sandy Koufax pitching in the last summers before he was disabled, in that time when he pitched a no-hitter every year for four years. Kicking swiftly, hiding the ball until the last instant, Koufax throws in a blur of motion, coming over the top, and the fast ball, appearing suddenly in the strike zone, sometimes jumps up so immoderately that his catcher has to take it with his glove shooting upward, like an infielder stabbing at a bad-hop grounder. I remember some batter tak-ing a strike like that and then stepping out of the box and staring back at the

11. New York Yankees center fielder (1914–1999).

12. Home of the New York Mets from 1964 to 2008; demolished in 2009.

13. Outfielder for New York Giants, San Francisco Giants, and New York Mets (b. 1931).

14. Player for the Brooklyn Dodgers and the first African American to play in Major League Baseball (1919–1972).

pitcher with a look of utter incredulity—as if Koufax had just thrown an Easter egg past him.

Joe DiMaggio batting sometimes gave the same impression—the suggestion that the old rules and dimensions of baseball no longer applied to him, and that the game had at last grown unfairly easy. I saw DiMaggio once during his famous hitting streak in 1941; I'm not sure of the other team or the pitcher—perhaps it was the Tigers and Bobo Newsom—but I'm sure of DiMaggio pulling a line shot to left that collided preposterously with the bag at third base and ricocheted halfway out to center field. That record of hitting safely in fifty-six straight games seems as secure as any in baseball, but it does not awe me as much as the fact that DiMadge's old teammates claim they *never* saw him commit an error of judgment in a ball game. Thirteen years, and never a wrong throw, a cutoff man missed, an extra base passed up. Well, there was one time when he stretched a single against the Red Sox and was called out at second, but the umpire is said to have admitted later that he blew the call.

And one more for the pantheon: Carl Yastrzemski. To be precise, Yaz in September of the 1967 season, as his team, the Red Sox, fought and clawed against the White Sox and the Twins and the Tigers in the last two weeks of the closest and most vivid pennant race of our time. The presiding memory of that late summer is of Yastrzemski approaching the plate, once again in a situation where all hope rests on him, and settling himself in the batter's box—touching his helmet, tugging at his belt, and just touching the tip of the bat to the ground, in precisely the same set of gestures—and then, in a storm of noise and pleading, swinging violently and perfectly . . . and hitting. In the last two weeks of that season, Yaz batted .522—twenty-three hits for forty-four appearances: four doubles, five home runs, sixteen runs batted in. In the final two games, against the Twins, both of which the Red Sox *had* to win for the pennant, he went seven for eight, won the first game with a homer, and saved the second with a brilliant, rally-killing throw to second base from deep left field. (He cooled off a little in the World Series, batting only .400 for seven games and hitting three homers.) Since then, the game and the averages have caught up with Yastrzemski, and he has never again approached that kind of performance. But then, of course, neither has anyone else.

Only baseball, with its statistics and isolated fragments of time, permits so precise a reconstruction from box score and memory. Take another date—October 7, 1968, at Detroit, the fifth game of the World Series. The fans are here, and an immense noise—a cheerful, 53,634-man vociferosity—utterly fills the green, steep, high-walled box of Tiger Stadium. This is a good baseball town, and the cries have an anxious edge, for the Tigers are facing almost sure extinction. They trail the Cardinals by three games to one, and never for a moment have they looked the equal of these defending World Champions. Denny McLain, the Tigers' thirty-one-game winner, was humiliated in the opener by the Cardinals' Bob Gibson, who set an all-time Series record by striking out seventeen Detroit batters. The Tigers came back the next day, winning rather easily behind their capable left-hander Mickey Lolich, but the Cardinals demolished them in the next two games, scoring a total of seventeen runs and again brushing McLain aside; Gibson has now struck out twenty-seven Tigers, and he will be ready to pitch again in the Series if needed. Even more disheartening is Lou Brock, the Cards' left fielder, who has already lashed out eight hits in the first four games and has stolen seven bases in eight tries; Bill Freehan, the Tigers' catcher, has a sore arm. And here, in the very top of the first, Brock leads off against Lolich and doubles to left; a moment later, Curt Flood singles, and Orlando Cepeda homers into the left-field stands. The Tigers are down, 3-0, and the fans are wholly stilled.

In the third inning, Brock leads off with another hit—a single—and there is a bitter overtone to the home-town cheers when Freehan, on a pitchout, at last throws him out, stealing, at second. There is no way for anyone to know, of course, that this is a profound omen; Brock has done his last damage to the Tigers in this Series. Now it is the fourth, and hope and shouting return. Mickey Stanley leads off the Detroit half with a triple that lands, two inches fair, in the right-field corner. He scores on a fly. Willie Horton also triples. With two out, Jim Northrup smashes a hard grounder directly at the Cardinal second baseman, Javier, and at the last instant the ball strikes something on the infield and leaps up and over Javier's head, and Horton scores. Luck! Luck twice over, if you remember how close Stanley's drive came to falling foul. But never mind; it's 3-2 now, and a game again.

But Brock is up, leading off once again, and an instant later he has driven a Lolich pitch off the left-field wall for a double. Now Javier singles to left, and Brock streaks around third base toward home. Bill Freehan braces himself in front of the plate, waiting for the throw; he has had a miserable Series, going hitless in fourteen at-bats so far, and undergoing those repeated humiliations by the man who is now racing at him full speed—the man who must surely be counted, along with Gibson, as the Series hero. The throw comes in chest-high on the fly from Willie Horton in left; ball and base-runner arrive together; Brock does not slide. Brock does not slide, and his left foot, just descending on the plate, is banged away as he collides with Freehan. Umpire Doug Harvey shoots up his fist: Out! It is a great play. Nothing has changed, the score is still 3-2, but everything has changed; something has shifted irrevocably in this game.

15   In the seventh inning, with one out and the Tigers still one run shy, Tiger manager Mayo Smith allows Lolich to bat for himself. Mickey Lolich has hit .114 for the season, and Smith has a pinch-hitter on the bench named Gates Brown, who hit .370. But Lolich got two hits in his other Series start, including the first homer of his ten years in baseball. Mayo, sensing something that he will not be able to defend later if he is wrong, lets Lolich bat for himself, and Mickey pops a foolish little fly to right that falls in for a single. Now there is another single. A walk loads the bases, and Al Kaline comes to the plate. The noise in the stadium is insupportable. Kaline singles, and the Tigers go ahead by a run. Norm Cash drives in another. The Tigers win this searching, turned-about, lucky, marvelous game by 5-3.

Two days later, back in St. Louis, form shows its other face as the Tigers rack up ten runs in the third inning and win by 13-1. McLain at last has his

Series win. So it is Lolich against Gibson in the finale, of course. Nothing happens. Inning after inning goes by, zeros accumulate on the scoreboard, and anxiety and silence lengthen like shadows. In the sixth, Lou Brock singles. Daring Lolich, daring the Tiger infielders' nerves, openly forcing his luck, hoping perhaps to settle these enormous tensions and difficulties with one more act of bravado, he takes an excessive lead off first, draws the throw from Lolich, breaks for second, and is erased, just barely, by Cash's throw. A bit later, Curt Flood singles, and, weirdly, he too is picked off first and caught in a rundown. Still no score. Gibson and Lolich, both exhausted, pitch on. With two out in the seventh, Cash singles for the Tigers' second hit of the day. Horton is safe on a slow bouncer that *just* gets through the left side of the infield. Jim Northrup hits the next pitch deep and high but straight at Flood, who is the best center fielder in the National League. Flood starts in and then halts, stopping so quickly that his spikes churn up a green flap of turf; he turns and races back madly, but the ball sails over his head for a triple. Disaster. Suddenly, irreversibly, it has happened. Two runs are in, Freehan doubles in another, and, two innings later, the Tigers are Champions of the World.

I think I will always remember those two games—the fifth and the seventh—perfectly. And I remember something else about the 1968 Series when it was over—a feeling that almost everyone seemed to share: that Bob Gibson had not lost that last game, and the Cardinals had not lost the Series. Certainly no one wanted to say that the Tigers had not won it, but there seemed to be something more that remained to be said. It was something about the levels and demands of the sport we had seen—as if the baseball itself had somehow surpassed the players and the results. It was the baseball that won.

Always, it seems, there is something more to be discovered about this game. Sit quietly in the upper stand and look at the field. Half close your eyes against the sun, so that the players recede a little, and watch the movements of baseball. The pitcher, immobile on the mound, holds the inert white ball, his little lump of physics. Now, with abrupt gestures, he gives it enormous speed and direction, converting it suddenly into a line, a moving line. The batter, wielding a plane, attempts to intercept the line and acutely alter it, but he fails; the ball, a line again, is redrawn to the pitcher, in the center of this square, the diamond. Again the pitcher studies his task—the projection of his next line through the smallest possible segment of an invisible seven-sided solid (the strike zone has depth as well as height and width) sixty feet and six inches away; again the batter considers his even more difficult proposition, which is to reverse this imminent white speck, to redirect its energy not in a soft parabola or a series of diminishing squiggles but into a beautiful and dangerous new force, of perfect straightness and immense distance. In time, these and other lines are drawn on the field; the batter and the fielders are also transformed into fluidity, moving and converging, and we see now that all movement in baseball is a convergence toward fixed points—the pitched ball toward the plate, the thrown ball toward the right angles of the bases, the batted ball toward the as yet undrawn but already visible point of congruence with either the ground or a glove. Simultaneously, the fielders hasten toward that same point of meeting with the ball, and both the base-runner and the ball, now redirected, toward their encounter at the base. From our perch, we can sometimes see three or four or more such geometries appearing at the same instant on the green board below us, and, mathematicians that we are, can sense their solution even before they are fully drawn. It is neat, it is pretty, it is satisfying. Scientists speak of the profoundly moving aesthetic beauty of mathematics, and perhaps the baseball field is one of the few places where the rest of us can glimpse this mystery.

The last dimension is time. Within the ballpark, time moves differently, marked by no clock except the events of the game. This is the unique, unchangeable feature of baseball, and perhaps explains why this sport, for all the enormous changes it has undergone in the past decade or two, remains somehow rustic, unviolent, and introspective. Baseball's time is seamless and invisible, a bubble within which players move at exactly the same pace and rhythms as all their predecessors. This is the way the game was played in our youth and in our fathers' youth, and even back then—back in the country days—there must have been the same feeling that time could be stopped. Since baseball time is measured only in outs, all you have to do is succeed utterly; keep hitting, keep the rally alive, and you have defeated time. You remain forever young. Sitting in the stands, we sense this, if only dimly. The players below us—Mays, DiMaggio, Ruth, Snodgrass—swim and blur in memory, the ball floats over to Terry Turner, and the end of this game may never come.

MLA CITATION

Angell, Roger. "The Interior Stadium." *The Norton Reader: An Anthology of Nonfiction*, edited by Melissa A. Goldthwaite et al., 15th ed., W. W. Norton, 2020, pp. 282–90.

QUESTIONS

1. Roger Angell wrote, "Sports are too much with us" (paragraph 1) in the early 1970s. Think about sports today: the endless speculation about signings and contracts, gossip about players' salaries and behavior, and twenty-four-hour sports channels. Are sports even more "with us" today? What does "too much with us" mean to you?

2. Gerald Graff writes of his youthful obsession with baseball with its "challenging arguments, debates, problems for analysis, and intricate statistics" (paragraph 11) in "Hidden Intellectualism" (pp. 360–63). What signs do you see of a not-so-hidden intellectualism in Angell's essay?

3. In paragraph 1, Angell writes "More and more, each sport resembles all sports; the flavor, the special joys of place and season, the unique displays of courage and strength and style that once isolated each game and fixed it in our affections have disappeared somewhere in the noise and crush." But his essay refutes this statement, singling out baseball as an example of a sport that retains its distinctiveness. Pick a different sport you know well and in an essay (as a spectator, like Angell, or as a participant), describe that sport, showing how it does or does not resemble "all sports."

MICHAEL LEWIS
from *The Blind Side*

ROM THE SNAP of the ball to the snap of the first bone is closer to four seconds than to five. One Mississippi: The quarterback of the Washington Redskins, Joe Theismann, turns and hands the ball to running back John Riggins. He watches Riggins run two steps forward, turn, and flip the ball back to him. It's what most people know as a "flea-flicker," but the Redskins call it a "throw back special." Two Mississippi: Theismann searches for a receiver but instead sees Harry Carson coming straight at him. It's a running down—the start of the second quarter, first and 10 at midfield, with the score tied 7–7—and the New York Giants' linebacker has been so completely suckered by the fake that he's deep in the Redskins' backfield. Carson thinks he's come to tackle Riggins but Riggins is long gone, so Carson just keeps running, toward Theismann. Three Mississippi: Carson now sees that Theismann has the ball. Theismann notices Carson coming straight at him, and so he has time to avoid him. He steps up and to the side and Carson flies right on by and out of the play. The play is now 3.5 seconds old. Until this moment it has been defined by what the quarterback can see. Now it—and he—is at the mercy of what he can't see.

You don't think of fear as a factor in professional football. You assume that the sort of people who make it to the NFL are immune to the emotion. Perhaps they don't mind being hit, or maybe they just don't get scared; but the idea of pro football players sweating and shaking and staring at the ceiling at night worrying about the next day's violence seems preposterous. The head coach of the Giants, Bill Parcells, didn't think it preposterous, however. Parcells, whose passion is the football defense, believed that fear played a big role in the game. So did his players. They'd witnessed up close the response of opposing players to their own Lawrence Taylor.

The tackle who had just quit the Philadelphia Eagles, for instance. Jerry Sisemore had played tackle in the NFL for eight years when, in 1981, Taylor arrived. Sisemore played on the right side of the offensive line and Taylor usually came off the other end, but Sisemore still had to worry about the few times Taylor lined up across from him. Their teams were in the same NFL division and met twice each regular season. The week leading up to those games, Sisemore confessed, unnerved him. "Towards the middle of the week something would come over you and you'd just start sweating," he told the *New York Times*. "My last year in the league, opening day, he immediately got past me. . . . He just looked at me and laughed. Right there I thought I had to get out of this game." And after that season, 1984, he did.

From The Blind Side: Evolution of a Game *(2006), which analyzes the game of football and details the life and career of football player Michael Oher. In the last twenty years Michael Lewis has written numerous books on sports and business.*

The feelings of those assigned to prevent Taylor from hurting quarterbacks were trivial compared to those of the quarterbacks he wanted to hurt. In Taylor's first season in the NFL, no official records were kept of quarterback sacks. In 1982, after Taylor had transformed the quarterback sack into the turning point of a football game, a new official NFL statistic was born. The record books defined the sack as tackling the quarterback behind the line of scrimmage as he attempts to pass. Taylor offered his own definition: "A sack is when you run up behind somebody who's not watching, he doesn't see you, and you really put your helmet into him. The ball goes fluttering everywhere and the coach comes out and asks the quarterback, 'Are you all right?' That's a sack." After his first NFL season Taylor became the only rookie ever named the league's most valuable defensive player, and he published a treatise on his art. "I don't like to just wrap the quarterback," he explained. "I really try to make him see seven fingers when they hold up three. I'll drive my helmet into him, or, if I can, I'll bring my arm up over my head and try to axe the sonuvabitch in two. So long as the guy is holding the ball, I intend to hurt him. . . . If I hit the guy right, I'll hit a nerve and he'll feel electrocuted, he'll forget for a few seconds that he's on a football field."

5   The game of football evolved and here was one cause of its evolution, a new kind of athlete doing a new kind of thing. All by himself, Lawrence Taylor altered the environment and forced opposing coaches and players to adapt. After Taylor joined the team, the Giants went from the second worst defense in the NFL to the third best. The year before his debut they gave up 425 points; his first year they gave up 257 points. They had been one of the weakest teams in the NFL and were now, overnight, a contender. Of course, Taylor wasn't the only change in the New York Giants between 1980 and 1981. There was one other important newcomer, Bill Parcells, hired first to coach the Giants' defense and then the entire team. Parcells became a connoisseur of the central nervous system of opposing quarterbacks. The symptoms induced by his sack-happy linebacker included, but were not restricted to: "intimidation, lack of confidence, quick throws, nervous feet, concentration lapses, wanting to know where Lawrence is all the time." The players on the Giants' defense picked up the same signals. As defensive back Beasley Reece told the New York Times, "I've seen quarterbacks look at Lawrence and forget the snap count." One opposing quarterback, finding himself under the center before the snap and unable to locate Taylor, called a time-out rather than run the play—only to find Taylor standing on the sidelines. "I think I saw it more with the quarterbacks in our division," says Giants linebacker Harry Carson. "They knew enough to be afraid. But every quarterback had a certain amount of fear when he played us."

By his fourth pro season Taylor was not just feeding these fears but feeding off them. "They come to the line of scrimmage and the first thing they do is start looking for me," he said. "I know, and they know. When they'd find me they'd start screaming: 56 left! 56 left! [Taylor wore No. 56.] So there's this thing I did. After the play was over I'd come up behind them and whisper: don't worry where I am. I'll tell you when I get there."

A new force in pro football, Taylor demanded not just a tactical response but an explanation. Many people pointed to his unusual combination of size and speed. As one of the Redskins' linemen put it, "No human being should be six four, two forty-five, and run a four-five forty." Bill Parcells thought Taylor's size and speed were closer to the beginning than to the end of the explanation. New York Giants' scouts were scouring the country for young men six three or taller, 240 pounds or heavier, with speed. They could be found. In that pool of physical specimens what was precious—far more precious than an inch, or ten pounds, or one tenth of a second—was Taylor's peculiar energy and mind: relentless, manic, with grandiose ambitions and private standards of performance. Parcells believed that even in the NFL a lot of players were more concerned with seeming to want to win than with actually winning, and that many of them did not know the difference. What they wanted, deep down, was to keep their jobs, make their money, and go home. Lawrence Taylor wanted to win. He expected more of himself on the field than a coach would dare to ask of any player.

Parcells accumulated lots of anecdotal evidence in support of his view of Taylor's football character. One of his favorites involved these very same Washington Redskins. "Joe Gibbs in a game in Giants Stadium basically decided that Taylor wasn't going to make any plays," said Parcells. "He put two tight ends on Taylor's side—along with the left tackle—and two wide receivers in the slot away from Taylor." This was extreme. An NFL football field is a tightly strung economy. Everything on it comes at a price. Take away from one place and you give to another. Three men blocking Taylor meant two Giants with no one to block them. Taylor's effect on the game, which the Giants won, was not obvious but it was nonetheless great. "But after the game," Parcells continued:

> The press sees that Lawrence doesn't have a sack and hasn't made a tackle and they're all asking me "what's the matter with Taylor?" The next week we go out to San Diego to play the Chargers. Dan Henning is the coach. He sees the strategy. They do the same thing. Two tight ends on Lawrence, two wide receivers in the slot. Lawrence doesn't get a sack. We win again. But after the game everyone is asking me all over again: "what's the matter with Taylor?" I grab Lawrence in the locker room and say to him, "I'm going to change your first name from Lawrence to What's The Matter With?" At practice that next week he was What's The Matter With? "What you doin' over there What's The Matter With?" "Hey, What's The Matter With?, how come you aren't making plays?" By Thursday it's not funny to him. And I mean it is really *not* funny.
>
> The next game we have is against the Vikings on Monday Night Football. Tommy Kramer is the quarterback. They don't employ the strategy. He knocks Kramer out of the game, causes two fumbles and recovers one of them. I'm leaving the field, walking down the tunnel towards the locker room for the press conference. And out of nowhere this . . . *thing* comes and jumps on my back. I didn't know he was coming. He basically knocks me over. He's still got his helmet on. Sweat's still pouring down his face. He comes right up into my face and hollers, "I tell you what Coachy, they aren't going to ask you What's The Matter With?!!"

Parcells believed Taylor's greatness was an act of will, a refusal to allow the world to understand him as anything less than great. "That's why I loved him so much," he said. "He responded to *anything* that threatened his status."

When in the middle of his career Taylor became addicted to cocaine, Parcells interpreted the problem as a simple extension of the man's character. Lawrence Taylor trusted in one thing, the power of his own will. He assumed that his will could control NFL football games, and that it could also control his own chemical desires.

10   He was right about the NFL games. By November 18, 1985, when the Giants went into Robert F. Kennedy Stadium in Washington, DC, to play the Redskins, opposing teams have taken to lining up their players in new and creative ways simply to deal with him. The Redskins are a case in point. Early in the very first game in which his Redskins had faced this new force, back in 1981, Joe Gibbs had watched Taylor sprint past the blocker as if he wasn't there and clobber Joe Theismann from behind. "I was standing there," said Gibbs, "and I said, 'What? Did you see that? Oh Lord.'" Gibbs had flopped about looking for a solution to this new problem, and had come up with the "one back offense"—a formation, widely imitated in the NFL, that uses one running back instead of two. Until that moment, football offenses had typically used running backs to block linebackers who came charging after quarterbacks. But running backs were smaller, weaker, and, surprisingly often, given their job description, slower than Lawrence Taylor. Lynn Cain, a running back for the Atlanta Falcons, was the first to dramatize the problem. The first time Cain went to block Taylor he went in very low, got up underneath him, and sent Taylor flying head over heels. The next play Cain tried it again—and was carried off the field on a stretcher. "People figured out *very* quickly that they couldn't block Lawrence with a running back," Parcells said. "Then the question became: who do you block him with?" Hence Joe Gibbs's first solution: to remove the running back from the game and insert, across the line from Lawrence Taylor, a bigger, stronger tight end. The one back offense.

That will be the strategy tonight, but Joe Theismann knows too well its imperfections. Having that extra blocker to help the tackle addressed the problem, Theismann thought, without solving it. Too often Taylor came free. The week of practice leading up to the game had been a seminar on Lawrence Taylor. "If you looked at our overhead projector or our chalkboard," said Theismann, "all the other Giants players were X's or O's. Lawrence was the only one who had a number: fifty-six. He was a little red fifty-six and the number was always highlighted and circled. The goal was: let's identify where Lawrence is on every play." Taylor moved around a lot, to confuse the defense, but he and his coach were happiest when he came from his own right side and the quarterback's left. "The big reason I put him over there," said Bill Parcells, "is the right side is the quarterback's blind side, since most quarterbacks are right-handed. And no one wants to get his ass knocked off from the back side." Lawrence Taylor was more succinct: "Why the hell would I want to come from where he can see me?" But then he added: "It wasn't really called the blind side when I came into the league. It was called the right side. It *became* the blind side after I started knocking people's heads off."

Where Taylor is at the start of the play, of course, isn't the problem. It's where he ends up. "When I dropped back," says Theismann, "the first thing I still did was to glance over my shoulder to see if he was coming. If he was dropping back in coverage, a sense of calm came over me. If he was coming, I had a sense of urgency."

Four Mississippi: Taylor is coming. From the snap of the ball Theismann has lost sight of him. He doesn't see Taylor carving a wide circle behind his back; he doesn't see Taylor outrun his blocker upfield and then turn back down; and he doesn't see the blocker diving, frantically, at Taylor's ankles. He doesn't see Taylor leap, both arms over his head, and fill the sky behind him. Theismann prides himself on his ability to stand in the pocket and disregard his fear. He thinks this quality is a prerequisite in a successful NFL quarterback. "When a quarterback looks at the rush," he says, "his career is over." Theismann has played in 163 straight games, a record for the Washington Redskins. He's led his team to two Super Bowls, and won one. He's thirty-six years old. He's certain he still has a few good years left in him. He's wrong. He has less than half a second.

The game is on ABC's *Monday Night Football,* and 17.6 million people have tuned in. Frank Gifford[1] is in the booth, flanked by O. J. Simpson and Joe Namath. "Theismann's in a lot of trouble," the audience hears Gifford say, just before Taylor's arms jackknife Theismann's head to his knees and Taylor's torso pins Theismann's right leg to the ground. Four other players, including, oddly, the Redskins' John Riggins, pile on. They're good for dramatic effect but practically irrelevant. The damage is done by Taylor alone. One hundred and ninety-six pounds of quarterback come to rest beneath a thousand or so pounds of other things. Then Lawrence Taylor pops to his feet and begins to scream and wave and clutch his helmet with both hands, as if in agony.

His reaction is a mystery until ABC Sports clarifies the event, by replaying it over and again, in slow motion. "Again, we'll look at it with the reverse angle one more time," says Frank Gifford. "And I suggest if your stomach is weak, you just don't watch." People watched; the replay was almost surely better attended than the original play. Doug Flutie was probably a representative viewer. Flutie had just finished a glorious college quarterbacking career at Boston College and started a professional one in the USFL. On the evening of November 18, 1985, he was at home with his mother. She had the football game on; he had other things to do. "I heard my mother scream," he told a reporter. "And then I saw the replay. It puts fear in your heart and makes you wonder what the heck you're doing playing football."

15

There's an instant before it collapses into some generally agreed-upon fact when a football play, like a traffic accident, is all conjecture and fragments and partial views. Everyone wants to know the whole truth but no one possesses it. Not the coach on the sidelines, not the coach in the press box, and certainly not the quarterback—no one can see the whole field and take in the movement of twenty-two bodies, each with his own job assignment. In baseball or basketball all the players see, more or less, the same events. Points of view vary, but slightly.

1. Gifford (1930–2015), Simpson (b. 1947), and Namath (b. 1943), all members of football's Hall of Fame, served as ABC broadcasters in 1985.

In football many of the players on the field have no idea what happened—much less why it happened—until after the play is done. Even then, most of them will need to watch a videotape to be sure. The fans, naturally more interested in effect than cause, follow the ball, and come away thinking they know perfectly well what just happened. But what happened to the ball, and to the person holding the ball, was just the final link in a chain of events that began well before the ball was snapped. At the beginning of the chain that ended Joe Theismann's career was an obvious question: who was meant to block Lawrence Taylor?

Two players will be treated above all others as the authorities on the play: Joe Theismann and Lawrence Taylor. The victim didn't have a view of the action; the perpetrator was so intent on what he was doing that he didn't stop to look. "The play was a blur," said Taylor. "I had taken the outside. I was thinking: keep him in the pocket and squeeze him. Then I broke free." Why he broke free he couldn't say, as he didn't actually notice who was trying to block him. Theismann, when asked who was blocking Taylor on that play, will reply, "Joe Jacoby, our left tackle." He won't *blame* Jacoby, as the guy was one of the two or three finest left tackles of his era, and was obviously just doing his best. That's why it made no sense, in Joe Theismann's opinion, for an NFL team to blow big bucks on an offensive lineman: there was only so much a lineman could do. Even when his name was Joe Jacoby.

That was one point of view. Another was Jacoby's who, on that night, was standing on the sidelines, in street clothes. He'd strained ligaments in his knee and was forced to sit out. When Joe Jacoby played, he was indeed a splendid left tackle. Six seven and 315 pounds, he was shaped differently from most left tackles of his time, and more like the left tackle of the future. "A freak of nature ahead of his time," his position coach, Joe Bugel, called him, two decades later. Jacoby wasn't some lump of cement; he was an athlete. In high school he'd been a star basketball player. He could run, he could jump, he had big, quick hands. "We put him at left tackle for one reason," said Bugel, "to match up against Lawrence Taylor." The first time they'd met, Jacoby had given Lawrence Taylor fits—he was a 300-pounder before the era of 300-pounders, with hands so big they felt like hooks. Taylor had been forced to create a move just for Jacoby. "Geritol," Taylor called it, "because after the snap I tried to look like an old man running up to him." Unable to overwhelm him physically, Taylor sought to lull Jacoby into a tactical mistake. He'd come off the ball at a trot to lure Jacoby into putting his hands up before he reached him. The moment he did— *Wham!*—he'd try to knock away Jacoby's hands before he latched on. A burst of violence and he was off to the races.

Still, Jacoby was one of the linemen that always gave Taylor trouble, because he was so big and so quick and so long. "The hardest thing for me to deal with," said Taylor, "was that big, agile left tackle."

20   Offensive linemen were the stay-at-home mothers of the NFL: everyone paid lip service to the importance of their contribution yet hardly anyone could tell you exactly what that was. In 1985 the left tackle had no real distinction. He was still expected to believe himself more or less interchangeable with the other linemen. The Washington Redskins' offensive line was perhaps the most famous in NFL history. It had its own nickname: the Hogs. Fans dressed as

pigs in their honor. And yet they weren't understood, even by their own team-mates, in the way running backs or quarterbacks were understood, as individual players with particular skills. "Even people who said they were fans of the Hogs had no idea who we were," said Jacoby. "They couldn't even tell the black ones from the white ones. I had people see me and scream, 'Hey May!'" (Right tackle Mark May was black; Jacoby was not.)

That night, with Jacoby out, the Redskins moved Russ Grimm from his position at left guard to left tackle. Grimm was four inches shorter, 30 pounds lighter, and far less agile than Jacoby. "Little Porky Grimm," line coach Joe Bugel called him. As a result, he needed help, and got it, in the form of the extra tight end, a fellow named Don Warren. If Taylor made his move to the inside, Grimm was expected to deal with him; if Taylor went on a wide loop outside, Grimm was meant, at most, to punch him, to slow him down, and give Warren the time to stay with him. From his spot on the sidelines, Jacoby watched as Taylor went outside. Grimm couldn't lay a hand on him and so Warren was left alone with Taylor. "They weren't used to his speed," said Jacoby. He watched Taylor race upfield and leave Warren in the dust, then double back on the quarterback.

Jacoby then heard what sounded like a gunshot—the tibia and fibula in Joe Theismann's right leg snapping beneath Taylor. He watched as Grimm and Warren removed their helmets and walked quickly toward the sidelines, like men fleeing the scene of a crime. He listened as Grimm told him that Theismann's bone lay exposed, and his blood was spurting straight up in the air. "Russ was a hunter," said Jacoby. "He'd gutted deer. And he said, 'That's the most disgusting thing I've ever seen.'" And Jacoby thought: *It happened because I'm standing over here.* Years later he wouldn't be surprised that Theismann did not realize his great left tackle was standing on the sidelines. "But that's why his leg got broken," he said.

A few minutes later, six men bore Theismann on a stretcher to an ambulance. In ABC's booth, Joe Namath said, "I just hope it's not his last play in football." But it was. Nearly a year later Joe Theismann would be wandering around the Redskins locker room unable to feel his big toe, or to push off his right leg. He'd become a statistic: the *American Journal of Sports Medicine* article on the injuries to NFL quarterbacks between 1980 and 2001 would count Theismann's two broken bones as just one of a sample of 1,534—77.4 percent of which occur, just as this one had, during games, on passing plays. The game continued and the Redskins, surprisingly, won, 28–23. And most people who did not earn their living in the NFL trying to figure out how to protect their increasingly expensive quarterbacks shoved the incident to the back of their minds. Not ten minutes after Theismann was hauled off the field, Lawrence Taylor himself pounced on a fumble and ran to the bench, jubilant. Frank Gifford sought to persuade his audience that Taylor was still obviously feeling upset about what he had done to Joe Theismann. But the truth is that he didn't look at all upset. He looked as if he'd already gotten over it.

What didn't make sense on that night was Taylor's initial reaction. He leapt out of the pile like a man on fire. Those who had watched Taylor's career closely might have expected a bit more sangfroid in the presence of an injured quarterback. The destruction of Joe Theismann may have been classified an accident, but it wasn't an aberration. It was an extension of what Lawrence Taylor had been doing to NFL quarterbacks for four and a half years. It wasn't even the first time Taylor had broken a quarterback's leg, or ended a quarterback's career. In college, in the Gator Bowl, he had taken out the University of Michigan's quarterback, John Wangler. Before Taylor hit him, Wangler had been a legitimate NFL prospect. ("I was invited to try out for the Lions and the Cowboys," Wangler said later. "But everyone was kind of afraid of the severity of my injury.")

25   As it turned out, there was a simple explanation: Taylor was claustrophobic. His claustrophobia revealed itself in the way he played the game: standing up looking for the best view, refusing to bend over and get down in the dirt with the other players, preferring the long and open outside route to the quarterback over the short, tight inside one. It revealed itself, also, in the specific fear of being trapped at the bottom of a pile and not being able to escape. "That's what made me so frantic," he said. "I've already dreamed it—if I get on the bottom of a pile and I'm really hurt. And I can't get out." Now he lay at, or near, the bottom of a pile, on top of a man whose leg he'd broken so violently that the sound was heard by Joe Jacoby on the sidelines. And he just had to get out. He leapt to his feet screaming, hands clutching the sides of his helmet, and—the TV cameras didn't pick this up—lifting one foot unconsciously and rubbing his leg with it. It was the only known instance of Lawrence Taylor imagining himself into the skin of a quarterback he had knocked from a game. "We all have fears," he said. "We all have fears."

MLA CITATION

Lewis, Michael. "From *The Blind Side*." *The Norton Reader: An Anthology of Nonfiction*, edited by Melissa A. Goldthwaite et al., 15th ed., W. W. Norton, 2020, pp. 291–98.

QUESTIONS

1. Examine the way Michael Lewis tells the story of Joe Theismann's career-ending leg injury, interspersing narrative with analysis. What effect does this manner of writing have on your reading experience? Does his approach have anything in common with other writers in this chapter on sports?

2. Football-related injuries are frequently covered in the news, and the personal consequences of these injuries for the athletes are often discussed. Has your attitude toward the game been affected by reports of injuries? Why or why not? Brainstorm a list of ways such injuries might be prevented.

3. Lewis describes a significant change in football tactics in response to the threat of Lawrence Taylor. Do some research on the invention of a new tactic in a sport and then describe it in an essay (for example, the T formation in football, the zone defense in basketball, the designated hitter in baseball, improved safety in race cars, or the invention of free climbing). If you wish, tie the change to the presence of a single player or a distinct group of players.

A. BARTLETT GIAMATTI
The Green Fields of the Mind

I T BREAKS YOUR HEART. It is designed to break your heart. The game begins in the spring, when everything else begins again, and it blossoms in the summer, filling the afternoons and evenings, and then as soon as the chill rains come, it stops and leaves you to face the fall alone. You count on it, rely on it to buffer the passage of time, to keep the memory of sunshine and high skies alive, and then just when the days are all twilight, when you need it most, it stops. Today, October 2, a Sunday of rain and broken branches and leaf-clogged drains and slick streets, it stopped, and summer was gone.

Somehow, the summer seemed to slip by faster this time. Maybe it wasn't this summer, but all the summers that, in this my 40th summer, slipped by so fast. There comes a time when every summer will have something of autumn about it. Whatever the reason, it seemed to me that I was investing more and more in baseball, making the game do more of the work that keeps time fat and slow and lazy. I was counting on the game's deep patterns, three strikes, three outs, three times three innings, and its deepest impulse, to go out and back, to leave and to return home, to set the order of the day and to organize the daylight. I wrote a few things this last summer, this summer that did not last, nothing grand but some things, and yet that work was just camouflage. The real activity was done with the radio—not the all-seeing, all-falsifying television—and was the playing of the game in the only place it will last, the enclosed green field of the mind. There, in that warm, bright place, what the old poet called Mutability[1] does not so quickly come.

But out here, on Sunday, October 2, where it rains all day, Dame Mutability never loses. She was in the crowd at Fenway[2] yesterday, a grey day full of bluster and contradiction, when the Red Sox came up in the last of the ninth trailing Baltimore 8–5, while the Yankees, rain-delayed against Detroit, only needing to win one or have Boston lose one to win it all, sat in New York washing down cold cuts with beer and watching the Boston game. Boston had won two, the Yankees had lost two, and suddenly it seemed as if the whole season might go to the last day, or beyond, except here was Boston losing 8–5, while New York sat in its family room and put its feet up. Lynn,[3] both ankles hurting now as they had in July, hits a single down the right-field line. The crowd stirs. It is on its feet. Hobson, third baseman, former Bear Bryant quarterback, strong,

First published in the Yale Alumni Magazine and Journal (1977) and on the Yale Alumni Magazine website (2012); it was also included in A Great and Glorious Game: Baseball Writings of A. Bartlett Giamatti (1998). In this essay, A. Bartlett Giamatti describes a game played by the Boston Red Sox and the Baltimore Orioles on October 1, 1977.

1. Dame Mutability, character created by the poet Edmund Spenser and representative of change in one's fortune.
2. Fenway Park, home stadium of the Boston Red Sox.
3. Fred Lynn (b. 1952), outfielder, most notably with the Red Sox.

quiet, over 100 RBIs, goes for three breaking balls and is out.[4] The goddess smiles and encourages her agent, a canny journeyman named Nelson Briles.[5]

Now comes a pinch hitter, Bernie Carbo, onetime Rookie of the Year, erratic, quick, a shade too handsome, so laid-back he is always, in his soul, stretched out in the tall grass, one arm under his head, watching the clouds and laughing; now he looks over some low stuff unworthy of him and then, uncoiling, sends one out, straight on a rising line, over the center-field wall, no cheap Fenway shot, but all of it, the physics as elegant as the arc the ball describes.

5   New England is on its feet, roaring. The summer will not pass. Roaring, they recall the evening, late and cold, in 1975, the sixth game of the World Series, perhaps the greatest baseball game played in the last fifty years, when Carbo, loose and easy, had uncoiled to tie the game that Fisk[6] would win. It is 8–7, one out, and school will never start, rain will never come, sun will warm the back of your neck forever. Now Bailey,[7] picked up from the National League recently, big arms, heavy gut, experienced, new to the league and the club; he fouls off two and then, checking, tentative, a big man off balance, he pops a soft liner to the first baseman. It is suddenly darker and later, and the announcer doing the game coast to coast, a New Yorker who works for a New York television station, sounds relieved. His little world, well-lit, hot-combed, split-second-timed, had no capacity to absorb this much gritty, grainy, contrary reality.

Cox[8] swings a bat, stretches his long arms, bends his back, the rookie from Pawtucket[9] who broke in two weeks earlier with a record six straight hits, the kid drafted ahead of Fred Lynn, rangy, smooth, cool. The count runs two and two, Briles is cagey, nothing too good, and Cox swings, the ball beginning toward the mound and then, in a jaunty, wayward dance, skipping past Briles, feinting to the right, skimming the last of the grass, finding the dirt, moving now like some small, purposeful marine creature negotiating the green deep, easily avoiding the jagged rock of second base, traveling steady and straight now out into the dark, silent recesses of center field.

The aisles are jammed, the place is on its feet, the wrappers, the programs, the Coke cups and peanut shells, the detritus of an afternoon; the anxieties, the things that have to be done tomorrow, the regrets about yesterday, the accumulation of a summer: all forgotten, while hope, the anchor, bites and takes hold where a moment before it seemed we would be swept out with the tide. Rice[10] is up. Rice whom Aaron[11] had said was the only one he'd seen with the

4. Butch Hobson (b. 1951), Red Sox third baseman; Bear Bryant (1913–1983), University of Alabama football coach.

5. Veteran Baltimore Orioles pitcher (1943–2005) in the 1977 game Giamatti describes.

6. Carlton Fisk (b. 1947), catcher for the Red Sox and the Chicago White Sox.

7. Bob Bailey (1942–2018), third baseman for the Red Sox.

8. Ted Cox (b. 1955), shortstop for the Red Sox.

9. Red Sox minor league team.

10. Jim Rice (b. 1953), Red Sox left fielder.

11. Hank Aaron (b. 1934), right fielder, mostly with the Milwaukee and Atlanta Braves.

ability to break his records. Rice the best clutch hitter on the club, with the best slugging percentage in the league. Rice, so quick and strong he once checked his swing halfway through and snapped the bat in two. Rice the Hammer of God sent to scourge the Yankees, the sound was overwhelming, fathers pounded their sons on the back, cars pulled off the road, households froze, New England exulted in its blessedness, and roared its thanks for all good things, for Rice and for a summer stretching halfway through October. Briles threw, Rice swung, and it was over. One pitch, a fly to center, and it stopped. Summer died in New England and like rain sliding off a roof, the crowd slipped out of Fenway, quickly, with only a steady murmur of concern for the drive ahead remaining of the roar. Mutability had turned the seasons and translated hope to memory once again. And, once again, she had used baseball, our best invention to stay change, to bring change on. That is why it breaks my heart, that game—not because in New York they could win because Boston lost; in that, there is a rough justice, and a reminder to the Yankees of how slight and fragile are the circumstances that exalt one group of human beings over another. It breaks my heart because it was meant to, because it was meant to foster in me again the illusion that there was something abiding, some pattern and some impulse that could come together to make a reality that would resist the corrosion; and because, after it had fostered again that most hungered-for illusion, the game was meant to stop, and betray precisely what it promised.

Of course, there are those who learn after the first few times. They grow out of sports. And there are others who were born with the wisdom to know that nothing lasts. These are the truly tough among us, the ones who can live without illusion, or without even the hope of illusion. I am not that grown-up or up-to-date. I am a simpler creature, tied to more primitive patterns and cycles. I need to think something lasts forever, and it might as well be that state of being that is a game; it might as well be that, in a green field, in the sun.

MLA CITATION

Giamatti, A. Bartlett. "The Green Fields of the Mind." *The Norton Reader: An Anthology of Nonfiction*, edited by Melissa A. Goldthwaite et al., 15th ed., W. W. Norton, 2020, pp. 299–301.

QUESTIONS

1. Throughout his essay A. Bartlett Giamatti uses both the present tense and the past tense even though he is describing a game that took place the previous day. Why do you think he made this choice? How would the essay be different if he had chosen to write only in the past tense?

2. Both Giamatti and Maya Angelou (in "Champion of the World," pp. 302–04) describe a particular game or match. How are their essays similar? How are they different?

3. In framing his essay, Giamatti reflects on "Mutability" (paragraph 2), how the only thing that is certain is change. How does he connect the themes of baseball,

seasons, and change? How does his description of a particular game support or illustrate those themes?

4. Using Giamatti's essay as a model, write about a particular moment from a sports event that you have witnessed. Try altering your verb tense to capture different aspects of the event, as Giamatti does.

MAYA ANGELOU
Champion of the World

HE LAST INCH of space was filled, yet people continued to wedge themselves along the walls of the Store. Uncle Willie had turned the radio up to its last notch so that youngsters on the porch wouldn't miss a word. Women sat on kitchen chairs, dining-room chairs, stools, and upturned wooden boxes. Small children and babies perched on every lap available and men leaned on the shelves or on each other.

The apprehensive mood was shot through with shafts of gaiety, as a black sky is streaked with lightning.

"I ain't worried 'bout this fight. Joe's gonna whip that cracker like it's open season."

"He gone whip him till that white boy call him Momma."

5   At last the talking finished and the string-along songs about razor blades[1] were over and the fight began.

"A quick jab to the head." In the Store the crowd grunted. "A left to the head and a right and another left." One of the listeners cackled like a hen and was quieted.

"They're in a clinch, Louis is trying to fight his way out."

Some bitter comedian on the porch said, "That white man don't mind hugging that niggah now, I betcha."

"The referee is moving in to break them up, but Louis finally pushed the contender away and it's an uppercut to the chin. The contender is hanging on, now he's backing away. Louis catches him with a short left to the jaw."

10   A tide of murmuring assent poured out the door and into the yard.

"Another left and another left. Louis is saving that mighty right. . . ." The mutter in the Store had grown into a baby roar and it was pierced by the clang of a bell and the announcer's "That's the bell for round three, ladies and gentlemen."

From Maya Angelou's autobiography I Know Why the Caged Bird Sings *(1969), in which she recounts her experiences growing up in Stamps, Arkansas. In this part of her story, she remembers watching the June 25, 1935, boxing match between Joe Louis and Primo Carnera.*

1. Gillette, a major brand of shaving products, was a main sponsor of fight broadcasts.

As I pushed my way into the Store I wondered if the announcer gave any thought to the fact that he was addressing as "ladies and gentlemen" all the Negroes around the world who sat sweating and praying, glued to their "Master's voice."[2]

There were only a few calls for RC Colas, Dr Peppers, and Hires root beer. The real festivities would begin after the fight. Then even the old Christian ladies who taught their children and tried themselves to practice turning the other cheek would buy soft drinks, and if the Brown Bomber's[3] victory was a particularly bloody one they would order peanut patties and Baby Ruths also.

Bailey and I laid the coins on top of the cash register. Uncle Willie didn't allow us to ring up sales during a fight. It was too noisy and might shake up the atmosphere. When the gong rang for the next round we pushed through the near-sacred quiet to the herd of children outside.

"He's got Louis against the ropes and now it's a left to the body and a right to the ribs. Another right to the body, it looks like it was low. . . . Yes, ladies and gentlemen, the referee is signaling but the contender keeps raining the blows on Louis. It's another to the body, and it looks like Louis is going down."

My race groaned. It was our people falling. It was another lynching, yet another Black man hanging on a tree. One more woman ambushed and raped. A Black boy whipped and maimed. It was hounds on the trail of a man running through slimy swamps. It was a white woman slapping her maid for being forgetful.

The men in the Store stood away from the walls and at attention. Women greedily clutched the babes on their laps while on the porch the shufflings and smiles, flirting and pinchings of a few minutes before were gone. This might be the end of the world. If Joe lost we were back in slavery and beyond help. It would all be true; the accusations that we were lower types of human beings. Only a little higher than apes. True that we were stupid and ugly and lazy and dirty and unlucky and worst of all, that God himself hated us and ordained us to be hewers of wood and drawers of water, forever and ever, world without end.

We didn't breathe. We didn't hope. We waited.

"He's off the ropes, ladies and gentlemen. He's moving towards the corner of the ring." There was no time to be relieved. The worst might still happen.

"And now it looks like Joe is mad. He's caught Carnera with a left hook to the head and a right to the head. It's a left jab to the body and another left to the head. There's a left cross and a right to the head. The contender's right eye is bleeding and he can't seem to keep his block up. Louis is penetrating every block. The referee is moving in, but Louis sends a left to the body and it's an uppercut to the chin and the contender is dropping. He's on the canvas, ladies and gentlemen."

Babies slid to the floor as women stood up and men leaned toward the radio.

15

20

2. Reference to RCA's advertising campaign featuring a dog listening to a phonograph.
3. Joe Louis's nickname.

"Here's the referee. He's counting. One, two, three, four, five, six, seven. . . . Is the contender trying to get up again?"

All the men in the store shouted, "NO."

"—eight, nine, ten." There were a few sounds from the audience, but they seemed to be holding themselves in against tremendous pressure.

25   "The fight is all over, ladies and gentlemen. Let's get the microphone over to the referee. . . . Here he is. He's got the Brown Bomber's hand, he's holding it up. . . . Here he is. . . ."

Then the voice, husky and familiar, came to wash over us—"The winnah, and still heavyweight champeen of the world . . . Joe Louis."

Champion of the world. A Black boy. Some Black mother's son. He was the strongest man in the world. People drank Coca-Colas like ambrosia and ate candy bars like Christmas. Some of the men went behind the Store and poured white lightning in their soft-drink bottles, and a few of the bigger boys followed them. Those who were not chased away came back blowing their breath in front of themselves like proud smokers.

It would take an hour or more before the people would leave the Store and head for home. Those who lived too far had made arrangements to stay in town. It wouldn't be fit for a Black man and his family to be caught on a lonely country road on a night when Joe Louis had proved that we were the strongest people in the world.

MLA CITATION

Angelou, Maya. "Champion of the World." *The Norton Reader: An Anthology of Nonfiction*, edited by Melissa A. Goldthwaite et al., 15th ed., W. W. Norton, 2020, pp. 302–04.

QUESTIONS

1. Some athletic contests have larger things at stake than just the win of one opponent against another, like the racial pride in the fight Maya Angelou recounts. Can you recall a match you witnessed in which the stakes were greater than the contest itself?

2. Angelou uses hyperbole, or deliberate overstatement, in her writing. For example, she writes, "It was another lynching" (paragraph 16) and "women greedily clutched the babes on their laps" (paragraph 17). Pick out some other examples in the text. How do these overstatements work to make Angelou's point about the fight and the position of blacks in America in the 1930s?

3. Look closely at Angelou's use of dialogue, as she tries to capture the exact sounds and grammar of her fellow listeners as well as the voices on the radio. How does she manage it? How would her piece read if she didn't use dialogue?

4. Note that much more than half of Angelou's account is about the spectators, not the fight. Using Angelou's essay as a model, write about a crowd's appearance and reaction during an athletic contest. Give plenty of detail about the action both on and off the field.

DAVID EPSTEIN
Sports Should Be Child's Play

THE NATIONAL FUROR over concussions misses the primary scourge that is harming kids and damaging youth sports in America.

The heightened pressure on child athletes to be, essentially, adult athletes has fostered an epidemic of hyperspecialization that is both dangerous and counterproductive.

One New York City soccer club proudly advertises its development pipeline for kids under age 6, known as U6. The coach-picked stars, "poised for elite level soccer," graduate to the U7 "pre-travel" program. Parents, visions of scholarships dancing in their heads, enable this by paying for private coaching and year-round travel.

Children are playing sports in too structured a manner too early in life on adult-size fields—i.e., too large for optimal skill development—and spending too much time in one sport. It can lead to serious injuries and, a growing body of sports science shows, a lesser ultimate level of athletic success.

We should urge kids to avoid hyperspecialization and instead sample a variety of sports through at least age 12.   5

Nearly a third of youth athletes in a three-year longitudinal study led by Neeru Jayanthi, director of primary care sports medicine at Loyola University in Chicago, were highly specialized—they had quit multiple sports in order to focus on one for more than eight months a year—and another third weren't far behind. Even controlling for age and the total number of weekly hours in sports, kids in the study who were highly specialized had a 36 percent increased risk of suffering a serious overuse injury. Dr. Jayanthi saw kids with stress fractures in their backs, arms or legs; damage to elbow ligaments; and cracks in the cartilage in their joints.

Because families with greater financial resources were better able to facilitate the travel and private coaching that specialization requires, socioeconomic status turned up as a positive predictor of serious injury. Some young athletes now face surgeries befitting their grandparents. Young hockey goaltenders repeatedly practice butterfly style—which stresses the developing hip joint when the legs are splayed to block the bottom of the goal. The sports surgeon Marc Philippon, based in Vail, Colo., saw a 25-year-old goalie who already needed a hip replacement.

In the Loyola study, sport diversification had a protective effect. But in case health risks alone aren't reason enough for parents to ignore the siren call of specialization, diversification also provides performance benefits.

Kids who play multiple "attacking" sports, like basketball or field hockey, transfer learned motor and anticipatory skills—the unconscious ability to read

Published in the New York Times *(2014) shortly after the appearance of David Epstein's book,* The Sports Gene: Inside the Science of Extraordinary Athletic Performance *(2013).*

bodies and game situations—to other sports. They take less time to master the
sport they ultimately choose.

10   Several studies on skill acquisition now show that elite athletes generally
practiced their sport less through their early teenage years and specialized only
in the mid-to-late teenage years, while so-called sub-elites—those who never
quite cracked the highest ranks—homed in on a single sport much sooner.

Data presented at the April meeting of the American Medical Society for
Sports Medicine showed that varsity athletes at U.C.L.A.—many with full
scholarships—specialized on average at age 15.4, whereas U.C.L.A. undergrads
who played sports in high school, but did not make the intercollegiate level,
specialized at 14.2.

We may prize the story of Tiger Woods, who demonstrated his swing at age 2 for Bob Hope. But the path of the two-time N.B.A. M.V.P. Steve Nash (who grew up playing soccer and didn't own a basketball until age 13) or the tennis star Roger Federer (whose parents encouraged him to play badminton, basketball and soccer) is actually the norm.

A Swedish study of sub-elite and elite tennis players—including five who ranked among the top 15 in the world—found that those who topped out as sub-elites dropped all other sports by age 11. Eventual elites developed in a "harmonious club environment without greater demands for success," and played multiple sports until age 14.

The sports science data support a "sampling period" through at least age 12. Mike Joyner, a Mayo Clinic physician and human performance expert, would add general physical literacy-building to the youth sports menu: perhaps using padded gymnastics gyms for parkour, which is essentially running, climbing or vaulting on any obstacle one can find.

In addition to athletic diversity, kids' sports should be kid-size.   15

In Brazil, host of this month's World Cup, kids are weaned on "futsal," a lightly structured and miniaturized form of soccer. Futsal is played on tiny patches of grass or concrete or on indoor courts and typically by teams of five players.

Players touch the ball up to five times as frequently as they do in traditional soccer, and the tighter playing area forces children to develop foot and decision-making skills under pressure.

A futsalization of youth sports generally would serve engagement, skill development and health.

USA Hockey (which has barred checking in youth games) recently invited adults to play on a 310-by-130-foot ice rink to show them what it's like for an 8-year-old to play on a regulation rink. The grown-ups' assessments: "too much time between the action"; "it's hard to communicate because everyone is spread out so far"; "you end up spending a lot of time in open space."

Futsal, basketball and . . . padded parkour? Sounds like a strange three-sport athlete, and a perfect model for kids.   20

MLA CITATION

Epstein, David. "Sports Should Be Child's Play." *The Norton Reader: An Anthology of Nonfiction*, edited by Melissa A. Goldthwaite et al., 15th ed., W. W. Norton, 2020, pp. 305–07.

QUESTIONS

1. David Epstein makes two arguments against what he calls children's "hyperspecialization" in sports (paragraph 2). Identify these two arguments. Do you find one more convincing than the other? Why?

2. Consider Epstein's use of evidence. What types of evidence does he use to support his arguments? Where is that support most effective? Where is it least effective? Why?

3. Among Epstein's solutions to the problem of children specializing too early is "futsalization" (paragraph 18), based on the game of futsal played in Brazil. What features of futsal does Epstein praise and believe should be modeled in other children's sports?

4. Interview three or four campus athletes, asking them when they started their sport, what other sports they played, and what their goals might be in participating in collegiate sports. Write an essay in which you respond to Epstein's argument, incorporating the testimony of the athletes you interviewed.

DAVID JOY
Hunting Camp

I N SOUTH CAROLINA, season opens the first week of October. A few diehards at camp come at the start and stay till the end, but most of us filter in and out whenever time allows. We drive down, go home, work jobs and sneak back on weekends. For three months, life is governed by deer hunting.

Our camp is located in McCormick County. More specifically Plum Branch, a town that is little more than a crossroads. A rutted gravel road cuts between pines to a series of flat-tired, pull-behind campers tarped and covered with tin, a bathhouse, a picnic shelter and a fire pit.

Spread over a few acres, there's Burt and Carole, Zeno and Diana, Billy and Nancy, Florida Joe, Son in Law, Ted, Shady Grady, Jackie, Randall, Jason, Lewis and me. Sometimes Son in Law's son-in-law comes with his son. It's a tongue-twisting maze of names and connections that would be hard to keep straight even if you were there from the beginning.

Most of these men have been coming here since before I was born. They're in their 60s, a few mid-70s, one inching fast for 80. After 45 seasons wandering the same woods, they've come to know the land intimately. They throw around names—the Owl Boxes, the UFO Hole, the Refrigerator Stand—places where they've killed deer for decades. At 34, I'm the youngest one here.

5   Sometimes at night the train goes by, and as the whistle blows the coyotes get to crying and it's about as lonesome a sound as any of us have ever heard. For a few seconds the stories stop, and we turn our ears away from the campfire to listen. The wood crackles and pops, and Florida Joe pokes at the coals with his walking stick.

Sometimes Zeno Ponder passes around a gallon jug of muscadine cordial. The bottle always stops a little longer when it reaches Son in Law. He takes one sip, glances around, sneaks another. Someone gives him hell and everyone

Originally published in Time Magazine *(2018), in a special issue on the American South.*

gets to laughing, and, though none of us air a breath of sentimentality, I know it's been a year since any of us felt this good.

Sometimes the South Carolina boys come to visit—Jim, Gary, Mark, Spike and Ugly Buck. Once a season, Jim brings a giant pot of chicken and rice. It's a dish we look forward to same as Florida Joe's cornbread, Son In Law's potatoes and onions or Nancy's cheesecake. We scrape the pot clean and lick our plates knowing every time may be the last because Jim's beat cancer once and has cancer again. Even the toughest men don't last forever.

Two years ago we spread Larry's ashes under the rocks circling the fire. Larry lost one of his legs to a landmine near Ben Luc, pulling patrols along the Mekong River.[1] He had a prosthetic, but that never stopped him from working a climbing stand 20 feet up a pine. It was his liver and heart that failed him. Agent Orange.[2] A large portion of camp served in Vietnam.

Aside from Florida Joe and Billy from Texas, everyone at camp comes from the Blue Ridge Mountains. Jackie's the one first brought me here. He and I ride together from Jackson County, North Carolina. The pine flats of South Carolina are a different landscape altogether from the mountains where we live. This is where the piedmont transitions to sand hills. The sun is relentless and there is seldom a drop of rain. But there are deer here, more than we could ever hope to find back home.

I come from a family of small-game hunters, so it was the men and women at camp who taught me to hunt deer. Jackie Medford showed me how to read sign, scrapes, rubs and licking branches. Last November, Burt Hogsed gave me the tree where I would later kill my biggest deer to date. Zeno Ponder was the one who first handed me a knife and told me where to cut. Any gap that may exist in age is bridged by a deep belief that there is something greater than mere subsistence gained from time afield.

For the most part, ours is a culture on the brink of extinction. Fewer are finding their way into the sport, and every year there is less land to roam. More than just the hunting, though, what we hold on to is a microcosm of what the growing urban-rural divide has erased across much of the rural South. It's that old-time communion that used to be commonplace.

The meals we share are no different than what used to be Sunday suppers. The storytelling around the fire used to be front-porch affairs. The large, extended families that filled church pews, the kinds of families with tongue-twisting mazes of names and connections, don't hold together like they did in the past. Kids move away and seldom return. The fellowship halls where people gathered for reunions are empty. The family graves are grown over with weeds. But there are holdout pockets where story still matters and people are still tied to the land.

At camp we hold on to tradition, and as the moon rises behind the pines, the old men talk and I listen. Deep down I know it won't last, that it can't, so I linger

1. Ben Luc, Mekong River, locations of battles and transit routes during the Vietnam War (1954–75).
2. Herbicide used by the American military to clear foliage during the Vietnam War.

on every word. If time favors us all the same, there will come a season when I am alone. Sooner or later, there will come a night when the last of the fire burns out.

MLA CITATION

Joy, David. "Hunting Camp." *The Norton Reader: An Anthology of Nonfiction*, edited by Melissa A. Goldthwaite et al., 15th ed., W. W. Norton, 2020, pp. 308–10.

QUESTIONS

1. Toward the end of his essay, David Joy calls hunting "a culture on the brink of extinction," and then adds: "More than just the hunting, though, what we hold on to is a microcosm of what the growing urban-rural divide has erased across much of the rural South. It's that old-time communion that used to be commonplace" (paragraph 11). What, exactly, is being erased, and what is Joy's attitude toward it? Why does Joy wait until nearly the end of his essay to deliver this observation?

2. Joy's essay is rich with descriptions, histories, stories. How do these details contribute to his essay?

3. Memory is a theme that run through several of the essays in this chapter: Angell's "The Interior Stadium," Giamatti's "The Green Fields of the Mind," Angelou's "Champion of the World," Joy's "Hunting Camp." Why do sports exert such a powerful pull on our memories? What memories do you have that are related to playing or watching sports?

4. Using Joy's essay as a model, write an essay about a place that is meaningful to you. Like Joy, try to evoke the feel of your place through concrete description, recollection, and reflection.

CLAUDIA RANKINE
from *Citizen*

Hennessy Youngman aka Jayson Musson,[1] whose *Art Thoughtz* take the form of tutorials on YouTube, educates viewers on contemporary art issues. In one of his many videos, he addresses how to become a successful black artist, wryly suggesting black people's anger is marketable. He advises black artists to cultivate

From Claudia Rankine's Citizen: An American Lyric (2014), *a genre-challenging book of poetry and prose that powerfully interrogates the contours of race in contemporary America.*

1. Artist, performer, and YouTuber (b. 1977); Hennessy Youngman is a persona Musson adopts in his internet videos.

"an angry nigger exterior" by watching, among other things, the Rodney King video[2] while working.

Youngman's suggestions are meant to expose expectations for blackness as well as to underscore the difficulty inherent in any attempt by black artists to metabolize real rage. The commodified anger his video advocates rests lightly on the surface for spectacle's sake. It can be engaged or played like the race card and is tied solely to the performance of blackness and not to the emotional state of particular individuals in particular situations.

On the bridge between this sellable anger and "the artist" resides, at times, an actual anger. Youngman in his video doesn't address this type of anger: the anger built up through experience and the quotidian struggles against dehumanization every brown or black person lives simply because of skin color. This other kind of anger in time can prevent, rather than sponsor, the production of anything except loneliness.

You begin to think, maybe erroneously, that this other kind of anger is really a type of knowledge: the type that both clarifies and disappoints. It responds to insult and attempted erasure simply by asserting presence, and the energy required to present, to react, to assert is accompanied by visceral disappointment: a disappointment in the sense that no amount of visibility will alter the ways in which one is perceived.

Recognition of this lack might break you apart. Or recognition might illuminate the erasure the attempted erasure triggers. Whether such discerning creates a healthier, if more isolated, self, you can't know. In any case, Youngman doesn't speak to this kind of anger. He doesn't say that witnessing the expression of this more ordinary and daily anger might make the witness believe that a person is "insane."   5

And insane is what you think, one Sunday afternoon, drinking an Arnold Palmer,[3] watching the 2009 Women's US Open semifinal,[4] when brought to full attention by the suddenly explosive behavior of Serena Williams. Serena in HD before your eyes becomes overcome by a rage you recognize and have been taught to hold at a distance for your own good. Serena's behavior, on this particular Sunday afternoon, suggests that all the injustice she has played through all the years of her illustrious career flashes before her and she decides finally to respond to all of it with a string of invectives. Nothing, not even the repetition of negations ("no, no, no") she employed in a similar situation years before as a younger player at the 2004 US Open, prepares you for this. Oh my God, she's gone crazy, you say to no one.

2. In 1991, four Los Angeles police officers were videoed beating Rodney King, an African American, during his arrest. The officers were charged with using excessive force, but the lack of any guilty verdicts precipitated the 1992 Los Angeles riots.
3. Beverage that is half iced tea and half lemonade, named for the professional golfer.
4. One of the four "Grand Slam" professional tennis tournaments.

What does a victorious or defeated black woman's body in a historically white space look like? Serena and her big sister Venus Williams brought to mind Zora Neale Hurston's[5] "I feel most colored when I am thrown against a sharp white background." This appropriated line, stenciled on canvas by Glenn Ligon,[6] who used plastic letter stencils, smudging oil sticks, and graphite to transform the words into abstractions, seemed to be ad copy for some aspect of life for all black bodies.

Hurston's statement has been played out on the big screen by Serena and Venus: they win sometimes, they lose sometimes, they've been injured, they've been happy, they've been sad, ignored, booed mightily, they've been cheered, and through it all and evident to all were those people who are enraged they are there at all—graphite against a sharp white background.

For years you attribute to Serena Williams a kind of resilience appropriate only for those who exist in celluloid. Neither her father nor her mother nor her sister nor Jehovah her God nor NIKE camp could shield her ultimately from people who felt her black body didn't belong on their court, in their world.[7] From the start many made it clear Serena would have done better struggling to survive in the two-dimensionality of a Millet painting,[8] rather than on their tennis court—better to put all that strength to work in their fantasy of her working the land, rather than be caught up in the turbulence of our ancient dramas, like a ship fighting a storm in a Turner seascape.[9]

10   The most notorious of Serena's detractors takes the form of Mariana Alves, the distinguished tennis chair umpire. In 2004 Alves was excused from officiating any more matches on the final day of the US Open after she made five bad calls against Serena in her quarterfinal matchup against fellow American Jennifer Capriati. The serves and returns Alves called out were landing, stunningly unreturned by Capriati, inside the lines, no discerning eyesight needed. Commentators, spectators, television viewers, line judges, everyone could see the balls were good, everyone, apparently, except Alves. No one could understand what was happening. Serena, in her denim skirt, black sneaker boots, and dark mascara, began wagging her finger and saying "no, no, no," as if by negating the moment she could propel us back into a legible world. Tennis superstar John McEnroe,[10] given his own keen eye for injustice during

5. Major African American novelist, folklorist, and anthropologist (1891–1960).

6. American painter, sculptor, and visual artist (b. 1960) who often integrates references to other artists, writers, and cultural figures into his work.

7. Richard Williams (b. 1942), Serena and Venus's father, also served as their coach; he and their mother Oracene (b. 1952) raised their daughters as Jehovah's Witnesses; the NIKE shoe and apparel company sponsors camps for a variety of sports.

8. Jean-François Millet (1814–1875), French realist painter.

9. J. M. W. Turner (1775–1851), English Romantic painter; the reference is to his 1840 painting The Slave Ship.

10. American tennis player (b. 1959) with the most combined singles and doubles championships, known for his heated arguments with referees.

his professional career, was shocked that Serena was able to hold it together after losing the match.

Though no one was saying anything explicitly about Serena's black body, you are not the only viewer who thought it was getting in the way of Alves's sight line. One commentator said he hoped he wasn't being unkind when he stated, "Capriati wins it with the help of the umpires and the lines judges." A year later that match would be credited for demonstrating the need for the speedy installation of Hawk-Eye, the line-calling technology that took the seeing away from the beholder. Now the umpire's call can be challenged by a replay; however, back then after the match Serena said, "I'm very angry and bitter right now. I felt cheated. Shall I go on? I just feel robbed."

And though you felt outrage for Serena after that 2004 US Open, as the years go by, she seems to put Alves, and a lengthening list of other curious calls and oversights, against both her and her sister, behind her as they happen.

Yes, and the body has memory. The physical carriage hauls more than its weight. The body is the threshold across which each objectionable call passes into consciousness—all the unintimidated, unblinking, and unflappable resilience does not erase the moments lived through, even as we are eternally stupid or everlastingly optimistic, so ready to be inside, among, a part of the games.

And here Serena is, five years after Alves, back at the US Open, again in a semifinal match, this time against Belgium's Kim Clijsters. Serena is not playing well and loses the first set. In response she smashes her racket on the court. Now McEnroe isn't stunned by her ability to hold herself together and is moved to say, "That's as angry as I've ever seen her." The umpire gives her a warning; another violation will mean a point penalty.

She is in the second set at the critical moment of 5–6 in Clijsters's favor, serving to stay in the match, at match point. The line judge employed by the US Open to watch Serena's body, its every move, says Serena stepped on the line while serving. What? (The Hawk-Eye cameras don't cover the feet, only the ball, apparently.) What! Are you serious? She is serious; she has seen a foot fault, one no one else is able to locate despite the numerous replays. "No foot fault, you definitely do not see a foot fault there," says McEnroe. "That's overofficiating for certain," says another commentator. Even the ESPN tennis commentator, who seems predictable in her readiness to find fault with the Williams sisters, says, "Her foot fault call was way off." Yes, and even if there had been a foot fault, despite the rule, they are rarely ever called at critical moments in a Grand Slam match because "You don't make a call," tennis official Carol Cox says, "that can decide a match unless it's flagrant."

As you look at the affable Kim Clijsters, you try to entertain the thought that this scenario could have played itself out the other way. And as Serena turns to the lineswoman and says, "I swear to God I'm fucking going to take this fucking ball and shove it down your fucking throat, you hear that? I swear to God!" As offensive as her outburst is, it is difficult not to applaud her for reacting immediately to being thrown against a sharp white background. It is difficult not to applaud her for existing in the moment, for fighting crazily against the so-called wrongness of her body's positioning at the service line.

She says in 2009, belatedly, the words that should have been said to the umpire in 2004, the words that might have snapped Alves back into focus, a focus that would have acknowledged what actually was happening on the court. Now Serena's reaction is read as insane. And her punishment for this moment of manumission is the threatened point penalty resulting in the loss of the match, an $82,500 fine, plus a two-year probationary period by the Grand Slam Committee.

Perhaps the committee's decision is only about context, though context is not meaning. It is a public event being watched in homes across the world. In any case, it is difficult not to think that if Serena lost context by abandoning all rules of civility, it could be because her body, trapped in a racial imaginary, trapped in disbelief—code for being black in America—is being governed not by the tennis match she is participating in but by a collapsed relationship that had promised to play by the rules. Perhaps this is how racism feels no matter the context—randomly the rules everyone else gets to play by no longer apply to you, and to call this out by calling out "I swear to God!" is to be called insane, crass, crazy. Bad sportsmanship.

Two years later, September 11, 2011, Serena is playing the Australian Sam Stosur in the US Open final. She is expected to win, having just beaten the number-one player, the Dane Caroline Wozniacki, in the semifinal the night before. Some speculate Serena especially wants to win this Grand Slam because it is the tenth anniversary of the attack on the Twin Towers. It's believed that by winning she will prove her red-blooded American patriotism and will once and for all become beloved by the tennis world (think Arthur Ashe[11] after his death). All the bad calls, the boos, the criticisms that she has made ugly the game of tennis—through her looks as well as her behavior—that entire cluster of betrayals will be wiped clean with this win.

20   One imagines her wanting to say what her sister would say a year later after being diagnosed with Sjögren's syndrome[12] and losing her match to shouts of "Let's go, Venus!" in Arthur Ashe Stadium: "I know this is not proper tennis etiquette, but this is the first time I've ever played here that the crowd has been behind me like that. Today I felt American, you know, for the first time at the US Open. So I've waited my whole career to have this moment and here it is."

It is all too exhausting and Serena's exhaustion shows in her playing: she is losing, a set and a game down. Yes, and finally she hits a great shot, a big forehand, and before the ball is safely past Sam Stosur's hitting zone, Serena yells, "Come on!" thinking she has hit an irretrievable winner. The umpire, Eva Asderaki, rules correctly that Serena, by shouting, interfered with Stosur's concentration. Subsequently, a ball that Stosur seemingly would not have been able to return becomes Stosur's point. Serena's reply is to ask the umpire if she is trying to screw her again. She remembers the umpire doing this to her before.

11. African American professional tennis player (1943–1993) who became a public-health advocate after contracting HIV; awarded the Presidential Medal of Freedom shortly after his death.
12. Autoimmune disorder.

As a viewer, you too, along with John McEnroe, begin to wonder if this is the same umpire from 2004 or 2009. It isn't—in 2004 it was Mariana Alves and in 2009 it was Sharon Wright; however, the use of the word "again" by Serena returns her viewers to other times calling her body out.

Again Serena's frustrations, her disappointments, exist within a system you understand not to try to understand in any fair-minded way because to do so is to understand the erasure of the self as systemic, as ordinary. For Serena, the daily diminishment is a low flame, a constant drip. Every look, every comment, every bad call blossoms out of history, through her, onto you. To understand is to see Serena as hemmed in as any other black body thrown against our American background. "Aren't you the one that screwed me over last time here?" she asks umpire Asderaki. "Yeah, you are. Don't look at me. Really, don't even look at me. Don't look my way. Don't look my way," she repeats, because it is that simple.

Yes, and who can turn away? Serena is not running out of breath. Despite all her understanding, she continues to serve up aces while smashing rackets and fraying hems. In the 2012 Olympics she brought home two of the three gold medals the Americans would win in tennis. After her three-second celebratory dance on center court at the All England Club,[13] the American media reported, "And there was Serena . . . Crip-Walking[14] all over the most lily-white place in the world. . . . You couldn't help but shake your head. . . . What Serena did was akin to cracking a tasteless, X-rated joke inside a church. . . . What she did was immature and classless."

Before making the video *How to Be a Successful Black Artist*, Hennessy Youngman uploaded to YouTube *How to Be a Successful Artist*. While putting forward the argument that one needs to be white to be truly successful, he adds, in an aside, that this might not work for blacks because if "a nigger paints a flower it becomes a slavery flower, flower de *Amistad*,"[15] thereby intimating that any relationship between the white viewer and the black artist immediately becomes one between white persons and black property, which was the legal state of things once upon a time, as Patricia Williams[16] has pointed out in *The Alchemy of Race and Rights*: "The cold game of equality staring makes me feel like a thin sheet of glass. . . . I could force my presence, the real me contained in those eyes, upon them, but I would be smashed in the process."

Interviewed by the Brit Piers Morgan after her 2012 Olympic victory, Serena is informed by Morgan that he was planning on calling her victory dance "the Serena Shuffle"; however, he has learned from the American press that it is a Crip Walk, a gangster dance. Serena responds incredulously by asking if she looks like a gangster to him. Yes, he answers. All in a day's fun, perhaps, and in

25

13. Located in London, home of the Wimbledon Championships, a Grand Slam tournament.

14. Dance style originally associated with the Crips, a predominantly African American gang based in southern California.

15. American slave ship whose human cargo mutinied on July 2, 1839.

16. American legal scholar (b. 1951) known for her writings on race and the law.

spite and despite it all, Serena Williams blossoms again into Serena Williams. When asked if she is confident she can win her upcoming matches, her answer remains, "At the end of the day, I am very happy with me and I'm very happy with my results."

Serena would go on to win every match she played between the US Open and the year-end 2012 championship tournament, and because tennis is a game of adjustments, she would do this without any reaction to a number of questionable calls. More than one commentator would remark on her ability to hold it together during these matches. She is a woman in love, one suggests. She has grown up, another decides, as if responding to the injustice of racism is childish and her previous demonstration of emotion was free-floating and detached from any external actions by others. Some others theorize she is developing the admirable "calm and measured logic" of an Arthur Ashe, who the sportswriter Bruce Jenkins felt was "dignified" and "courageous" in his ability to confront injustice without making a scene. Jenkins, perhaps inspired by Serena's new comportment, felt moved to argue that her continued boycott of Indian Wells[17] in 2013, where she felt traumatized by the aggression of racist slurs hurled at her in 2001, was lacking in "dignity" and "integrity" and demonstrated "only stubbornness and a grudge." (Serena lifted her boycott in 2015, and Venus lifted hers in 2016.)

Watching this newly contained Serena, you begin to wonder if she finally has given up wanting better from her peers or if she too has come across Hennessy's *Art Thoughtz* and is channeling his assertion that the less that is communicated the better. Be ambiguous. This type of ambiguity could also be diagnosed as dissociation and would support Serena's claim that she has had to split herself off from herself and create different personae.

Now that there is no calling out of injustice, no yelling, no cursing, no finger wagging or head shaking, the media decides to take up the mantle when on December 12, 2012, two weeks after Serena is named WTA Player of the Year, the Dane Caroline Wozniacki, a former number-one player, imitates Serena by stuffing towels in her top and shorts, all in good fun, at an exhibition match. Racist? CNN wants to know if outrage is the proper response.

It's then that Hennessy's suggestions about "how to be a successful artist" return to you: be ambiguous, be white. Wozniacki, it becomes clear, has finally enacted what was desired by many of Serena's detractors, consciously or unconsciously, the moment the Compton[18] girl first stepped on court. Wozniacki (though there are a number of ways to interpret her actions—playful mocking of a peer, imitation of the mimicking antics of the tennis player known as the joker, Novak Djokovic) finally gives the people what they have wanted all along by embodying Serena's attributes while leaving Serena's "angry nigger exterior" behind. At last, in this real, and unreal, moment, we

17. Held in Indian Wells, California, a "Premier Mandatory" tournament on the women's professional tennis tour.
18. Serena Williams's birthplace, a city south of Los Angeles, California.

have Wozniacki's image of smiling blond goodness posing as the best female tennis player of all time.

MLA CITATION

Rankine, Claudia. "From *Citizen*." *The Norton Reader: An Anthology of Nonfiction*, edited by Melissa A. Goldthwaite et al., 15th ed., W. W. Norton, 2020, pp. 310–17.

QUESTIONS

1. Claudia Rankine asks, "What does a victorious or defeated black woman's body in a historically white space look like?" (paragraph 7). Her answer is Serena (and Venus) Williams. How, according to Rankine, has Serena Williams's race affected the way she has been treated as a professional athlete in a traditionally "white" sport?

2. Although Serena Williams is Claudia Rankine's main subject, she frames her essay by beginning and ending with the YouTube persona Hennessy Youngman, whose videos "are meant to expose expectations for blackness as well as to underscore the difficulty inherent in any attempt by black artists to metabolize real rage" (paragraph 2). How is this framing important to Rankine's discussion of Williams? How would the essay read differently if it began at paragraph 6 (as does a version excerpted in the online magazine *Slate*)?

3. Throughout her essay, Rankine deliberately and prominently uses the second-person pronouns "you" and "yours." What is the effect of this choice of style?

4. Write an essay about a time you were treated unfairly. What was the situation? How did you react? If you could go back and do things differently, would you? If so, how? If not, why not?

5. Many others in addition to Rankine have written about Serena Williams. Rankine herself has also written about Williams elsewhere. Find some of these other articles and essays, and write an essay of your own comparing one or more of them with Rankine's.

DAVID SHIELDS

Words Can't Begin to Describe What I'm Feeling

I'LL BE HONEST WITH YOU: I'm here to tell you: The big key is: The bottom line is:

There's no question about it. There's no doubt about it. You got that right. I couldn't agree with you more. Obviously, the statistics speak for themselves.

He's a highly touted freshman. Last week was his coming-out party. He has all the makings of a great one. He has unlimited potential. He's a can't-miss prospect. You'll be hearing a lot from him. He can play at the next level. He can play on Sundays. He's got his whole future ahead of him. He's a youngster who bears watching. He's being groomed for a future starting job. The team is really high on him. He's going to set the world on fire. He's a rookie phenom.

He moves well for a big man. He's sneaky-fast. He has lightning-fast reflexes. He has great lateral mobility. He can pick 'em up and put 'em down. He has speed *and* quickness. He's a cutter and a slasher. He has speed to burn. He's fleet-footed. He's a speed merchant. He can fly. You can't teach speed.

5   He's a unique physical specimen. He has a low center of gravity. He plays bigger than his size. He's built like a brick outhouse. He's a stud. He's a warrior. He's a bulldog. He has a linebacker mentality. He's fearless. He's a physical player. He's an impact player.

He's a tough, hard-nosed player. He's their spark plug. He's their role player. He understands his role on this team. He lets the game come to him. He's the consummate team player. He's an unselfish player. He's a real throwback. He plays with a lot of emotion. He has a passion for the game. He always gives 110 percent. He plays for the name on the front of the jersey, not the name on the back of it.

He's their playmaker. He's their field general. He's their floor general. He's a good table-setter. He's the glue that holds this team together. He makes the players around him better. He's a stand-up guy. The team looks to him for leadership. He's a leader on this team. He's a leader on and off the field.

He's a true professional. He's a professional hitter. He just goes out there and gets the job done. I was just doing my job. I was just hoping I could make a contribution in whatever way they needed me.

10   He's some kind of player. He's the real deal. He's legit. He can flat-out play. He's as good a player as there is in this league. He's one of the best in the business. He's a franchise player. Players like that don't come along very often. He's in a league of his own. He's a future Hall of Famer. He's a first-ballot lock. You can't say enough about him.

Originally published in Verbatim: The Language Quarterly (2003) *and reprinted in David Shields's book* Other People: Takes and Mistakes (2017), *this piece is as much about language as it is about sports.*

He's got ice water running through his veins. He's got the guts of a burglar. He thrives under pressure. He always comes through in the clutch. He always comes through at crunch time. He's their go-to guy when the game's on the line. He's money. He can carry the team on his shoulders. He can take them to the promised land.

He's shooting well from downtown. He's making a living behind the arc. He's getting some good open looks. He's shooting the lights out. He's in a zone. He's feeling it. He's in a groove. He's lighting it up. He's on fire. He's hot. He's locked in. He's unconscious.

He blew 'em away.

They pay him to make those catches. That pass was very catchable. He's usually a sure-handed receiver. He usually makes that catch. He heard footsteps. He's become a little gun-shy. He's got all the skills—he just needs to put them together. He needs to bulk up in the off-season. He needs to elevate his game. He's playing out of position. He lacks the killer instinct.

He's only played sparingly this season. He's the subject of trade rumors. He's being shopped around. He's on the trading block. He's bounced around a lot. He's a journeyman. He's the player to be named later. He's lost a step. He's their elder statesman. He has a new lease on life. I just want to give something back to the community. He's a great role model. He's a winner in the bigger game of life. I just want to be able to take care of myself and my family.

He doesn't have that good fastball today. He's getting by with breaking stuff. He took something off that pitch. He's getting shelled. He's getting rocked. They're teeing off on him. Stick a fork in him—he's done. They need to pull the plug. He hits the showers. Today I didn't have my plus-stuff. Regardless of what kind of stuff you have on a given day, you just try to go out there and pitch to the best of your ability and give your team an opportunity to win.

He got hung out to dry on that play. That was blown coverage. That was a missed assignment. They're playing in the shadow of their goalposts. He couldn't turn the corner. They're looking at third down and forever. They have to establish the running game. They have to air it out more. They have to take care of the football. That missed extra point could come back to haunt them. You gotta hit the holes they make for you. You gotta follow your blockers out there. He's been quiet so far—they need to get him some more carries in the second half. This is their deepest penetration of the half. They've got to punch it in from here. They can't cough it up here. They need to just go out and make football plays.

He has all the time in the world. He has all day back there. He has all kinds of time. He has an eternity. He threw into double coverage. He threw up a prayer. He'd like to have that one back.

We just couldn't execute. We weren't able to sustain anything. They got us out of our game plan early. They took us completely out of our rhythm.

We got beat like a gong. They beat us like a drum. They outplayed us. We ran into a buzz saw. Turnovers absolutely killed us. We didn't get any calls. Sometimes this game just comes down to the way the ball bounces. We didn't get any breaks. They were the better team today. Give them credit. We just didn't get the job done. We weren't mentally prepared. For some reason they've

15

just got our number. We didn't come to play. They stepped up and made football plays. Football players make football plays. They wanted it more than we
did. This was a wake-up call. I tip my hat to them. We beat ourselves. We only
have to look in the mirror. I don't want to point any fingers. We came up a little
short. We had our chances. They outplayed us in every phase of the game.
They just made the big plays and we didn't. We dug ourselves a deep hole. We
have to put this loss behind us. It's going to be a long plane ride home.

20   The coach is on the hot seat. His head is on the chopping block. Unfortunately, there are days like this. We're in the business of winning. It's the nature
of this business. It's time to move on. We have to look forward. We need a
change of direction. We need a clean slate. We need someone who can take us
to the next level.

I feel the time has come for new leadership of this ball club. Everyone has
to be held accountable. It's all about winning and losing. I take the blame. I'm
not going to stand up here and make excuses. Obviously, I'm disappointed things
didn't work out. This is my responsibility and I feel badly I haven't been able to
get us where we should be. I want to thank our great fans. I'm looking forward
to the next chapter in my life. First I'm going to spend more time with my family.

I'm excited about this opportunity. I'm looking forward to the challenge. I
have high expectations for this team. This franchise has a great winning tradition. We've got a good solid foundation to build on. We're going to right the
ship. We're going to get things turned around. This is a great sports town.

They stumbled coming out of the gate. They got off on the wrong foot.
They're finally showing signs of life. They need a late surge. It's been an up-
and-down season. It's a marathon, not a sprint.

This team is starting to make some noise. They've finally gotten off the
schneid. The players have bought into the system. He's got them headed in the
right direction. He's a players' coach. He's more of a people person than an X's
and O's guy. These guys have been busting their tails for him. He gets the most
out of his players. They've turned the corner. They've raised the bar. They've
gotten over the hump. They're loaded this year. They're stacked. They have a
strong supporting cast. There's no *I* in "team." They've added a new wrinkle to
their offense. They're finally getting the respect they deserve. They're for real.
They're here to stay. They're playing with newfound confidence. They've got
great team chemistry. This team is like a family. Everything's clicking. We're
starting to gel. Everybody's on the same page. We're hitting on all cylinders
now. Everybody's contributing.

25   We've got the league's best offense against the league's best defense—
something's gotta give. We've got an intriguing matchup. This is a pivotal
game. This game is for the bragging rights. These teams flat don't like each
other. There's no love lost between these two teams. There's bad blood between
these two teams. It's gonna be a war out there. When these two teams get
together, you really *can* throw out their records.

You have to respect their athleticism. You have to respect their quickness.
They have tremendous leaping ability. They can put up big numbers. They do
a great job defensively. They play tough D.

They're feeling each other out. Here's the payoff pitch. He chased a bad pitch. Tough to lay off that pitch. Three up, three down. This is shaping up to be a real pitchers' duel. That ball should be playable. It's a can of corn. The ball took a bad hop. Strike-'im-out, throw-'im-out double play. Inning over. He got a good jump. That brings the tying run to the plate. He hits 'em where they ain't. He's a long-ball threat. He hit a solo shot back in the fifth. He's seeing the ball real well. He wears them out. He made good contact. He hit that ball squarely. He hit that ball on the sweet spot. He knocked the cover off the ball. In any other ballpark, that's a home run. Chicks dig the long ball. He's sitting dead red. He got all of it. He went yard. He hit it into the cheap seats. He flat jacked it. He went deep. He went downtown. Going, going, gone. It's outta here. See ya later. Goodbye, baseball. Kiss it goodbye. Aloha means goodbye.

It's been all theirs to this point. It's theirs to lose. They're not playing to win—they're playing not to lose. They're putting the ball in the deep freeze. They've gone four corners. Now's the time to run some clock.

Looks like we've got some extracurricular activity going on out there. Let's hope cooler heads prevail. They're mucking it up in the corner. He stood him up on the blue line. That's gotta hurt. He was mugged. He's gonna feel that one on Monday. Looks like we've got a player shaken up. Looks like he got his bell rung. That hit really cleaned his clock. He ran into a brick wall. He was literally run over by a freight train. He was blindsided. He's slow getting up. He was really clotheslined. They can ill afford to lose him. Their locker room must look like a MASH unit. X-rays are inconclusive. He left the field under his own power. We hate to speculate on the nature of the injury.

There's a flag on the play. It depends on where they spot it. Terrible call, terrible call. We got hosed. We got jobbed. We got robbed. Highway robbery. We knew it was going to be tough going up against the other team—I didn't know we were going to have to play the guys in the striped shirts as well. They're the best refs money can buy. The refs should just let them play. Bad calls even out over the course of a season. 30

It ain't over till it's over. As Yogi said, it ain't over till it's over. It ain't over till the fat lady sings. They won't go quietly. We've still got plenty of football left. No need to panic—there's plenty of time left.

You can feel the momentum shifting. Big Mo. They're going for the jugular. They can smell blood in the water. They're within striking distance. *Now* we've got a football game. It's a whole new ball game. This team shows a lot of character. This team shows a lot of poise. This team shows a lot of resiliency. This team shows a lot of heart.

It all started out with good field position. They've marched down the field. That was a goal-scorer's goal. He lit the lamp. He went high to the top shelf. He put the biscuit in the basket. He found the twine. He went upstairs. He nailed the buzzer-beater. She really stuck the landing. He hit pay dirt. Nothing but net. This should be a chip shot for him. The kick splits the uprights.

What an incredible turnaround.

We found a way to win. A win is a win. It wasn't pretty, but we'll take it. 35 I'm really proud of the way our guys hung in there. This is always a tough place to play. We're just glad to get out of here with a W. We're happy we could pull this one out at the end. They're tough competitors. They gave us all we could handle. They're a class act. Give them a lot of credit. I tip my hat to them. There are no easy games in this league. The game was a lot closer than the final score indicates. They weren't going to come in here and just lie down for us. We're going to use this as a building block. We'll use this win as a stepping-stone to the next level.

What a difference a week makes.

We were really on our game. We took them out of their game. We really came to play. We brought our A game. We knew what we had to do and went out and did it. We answered the call. This team has finally learned how to win. It was a total team effort. Obviously, this was a great win for us. It was a big win for us. We came to play. We stuck to the game plan. We wanted to make a statement. We sent a message. We came through when it counted. We're going to savor the victory tonight, then tomorrow morning we'll start looking at film.

The only thing that matters in the Stanley Cup playoffs is the man between the pipes. You can't win an NBA championship without a dominant big man. You can't win in the NFL without establishing the run. Offense puts fannies in the seats—defense wins championships. You've got to have pitching if you're going to make it through the postseason.

We just need to go out there and take care of business. It all just comes down to execution. You can't leave anything on the table. We have to go out and leave it all on the ice. We need to bring it. We need to dig deeper than we've ever dug before. We just gotta go out tomorrow and have fun.

40   They've battled back from the brink of elimination. They're down but not out. They're in a must-win situation. They need a win to stave off elimination. Lose and go home. Go big or go home. There's no tomorrow. I know it's a cliché, but we just have to take it one game at a time.

We gotta stick to the basics. We need to remember what got us here. You gotta dance with who brung you. This is it. This is for all the marbles.

They need to keep up their intensity. They have to stay focused. They have to get after it. They have to rise to the occasion. They've got tremendous mental toughness. They're a blue-collar team. They're overachievers. They've come out of nowhere. They're a real Cinderella story. They have to stay hungry. They're loaded for bear.

The city has rallied around this team. We've got die-hard fans. We feed off the energy of our fans. Our fans are our twelfth man. We've got the greatest fans in the world.

We're happy to be in the postseason and now we want to go out there and do some damage. We're capable of going deep in the postseason. We're not just happy to be here. This team has a chance to do something special. Hopefully, we can steal one on the road. In the playoffs, anything can happen.

45   Game time.

The fans are on their feet. This crowd is going wild. This place is a madhouse. This place is pandemonium. You can feel the electricity. Ya gotta love these fans. Ya gotta love this game.

MLA CITATION

Shields, David. "Words Can't Begin to Describe What I'm Feeling." *The Norton Reader: An Anthology of Nonfiction*, edited by Melissa A. Goldthwaite et al., 15th ed., W. W. Norton, 2020, pp. 318–22.

QUESTIONS

1. The journal in which this piece of writing originally appeared, *Verbatim: The Language Quarterly*, is subtitled "Language and linguistics for the layperson since 1974." What is David Shields showing us about the nature of language with this montage of sports clichés? What makes a cliché a cliché?

2. Consider the piece as a whole: How is it organized paragraph by paragraph? What, in terms of genre, would you call it? An essay? A short story? Something else? Why would you characterize it in this way?

3. Listen carefully to a conversation about a subject that interests you and note when the speakers use clichés. Do they help or hinder the speakers in communicating their meaning?

4. Swap papers with another student. Mark any sentences in your partner's paper that contain clichés. Swap back and revise to eliminate the clichés in your own paper that your partner marked.

7 EDUCATION

Intelligence plus character—that is the goal of true education.
The complete education gives one not only power of concentration, but worthy objectives upon which to concentrate.
—MARTIN LUTHER KING JR.

What is the goal of true education? Is it, as Martin Luther King Jr. asserts, "intelligence plus character"? If it is, what is the best way to achieve that goal? What kinds of schools, activities, technologies, content, and pedagogies enhance true education? What pressures and challenges threaten it? Is there more than one kind of intelligence? Who defines "character"? The readings in this chapter will help you explore these questions and others.

Some of the readings in this chapter examine specific pedagogies and technologies used in education. The chapter begins with two essays that argue for the importance of engaging one's whole body in activities rather than a move toward more screen learning. In "Look Up from Your Screen," Nicholas Tampio grounds his argument in experience as well as philosophical and neuroscientific research. Taking a different approach, journalist Florence Williams investigates the benefits of adventure-based education for a specific group of students: those diagnosed with ADHD; further, she considers the historically important role of exploration and adventure in benefiting humanity.

Such arguments for the benefits of particular pedagogies, though, assume an availability of resources, parental attention, and access to education, access that is not always available to everyone. In "The Sanctuary of School," Lynda Barry describes being neglected at home but finding a true sanctuary at school; she argues for more public school funding, especially for after-school programs and arts programs. Tara Westover, who never attended school until she enrolled in college, shows the inadequacy of the limited home schooling she had, how it resulted in gaps in her knowledge and understanding of history. Frederick Douglass, a former slave, helps readers think even more deeply about history and access to education. He shows how others—because of their beliefs—both aided and sought to prevent his literacy. Douglass's narrative illustrates how some individuals have thrived even under the strain of cruelty and systemic racism. Yet his narrative also encourages readers to think about history and its effects on who has access to what kind of education. Maya Angelou, in "Graduation," shows the disparity between the resources provided and the expectations for schools and students during a time when schools were segregated; she writes, "The white kids were going to have a chance to become Galileos and Madame Curies and Gauguins, and our boys (the girls weren't even in on it) would try to be Jesse Owenses and Joe Louises." Although a 1954 law makes segregation illegal in America, are there ways in which resources for and expectations of different groups of people still differ? What disparities still exist in our educational system?

Despite various privileges and disparities, all students face challenges. In "College Pressures," William Zinsser considers the anxieties and fears expressed by students at Yale in the 1970s. He categorizes four kinds of pressures—economic, parental, peer, and self-induced—college students face. Although his essay was published more than 40 years ago, you might recognize and experience similar problems. In what ways have the pressures he describes changed, intensified, or resolved?

In the opening epigraph, Martin Luther King Jr. defines education as "intelligence plus character." At least two of the readings in this chapter help readers think directly about what counts as intelligence. In "Hidden Intellectualism," Gerald Graff argues that schools should recognize "street smarts" as a form of intellect. He uses his own experience of loving sports to show how street smarts "satisfy an intellectual thirst more thoroughly than school culture, which seems pale and unreal." In "Blue-Collar Brilliance," Mike Rose questions generalizations about work, social class, and intelligence, and he details the knowledge and problem-solving skills required to succeed in many blue-collar jobs. Like Tampio, whose essay begins this chapter, Rose critiques the Cartesian separation of body and mind; he argues that intelligence is social, interactive, embodied, and diverse.

As you read and then turn to writing about education, consider your own definition. What does it mean, to you, to be educated? What technologies and pedagogies have aided your learning? Which educational experiences were positive? Which ones were negative? What pressures do you face as a student? Do you see any potential solutions that might ease those pressures? What form and sources will allow you to get across your points about education most effectively? You might draw from your personal experience yet also make a critique as Maya Angelou does in "Graduation." Or perhaps you'll take a more journalistic approach, as Florence Williams does, to feature a non-mainstream educational approach. Or, like Mike Rose, you might write a "cognitive biography" of someone who demonstrates a kind of intelligence you value.

Nicholas Tampio
Look Up from Your Screen

A ROOSTER CROWS and awakens my family at the farm where we are staying for a long weekend. The air is crisp, and stars twinkle in the sky as the Sun rises over the hill. We walk to the barn, where horses, cows, chickens, pigs, dogs and cats vie for our attention. We wash and replenish water bowls, and carry hay to the cows and horses. The kids collect eggs for breakfast.

Published in Aeon (2018), a digital magazine "committed to big ideas, serious enquiry and a humane worldview." All notes were written by the author unless indicated otherwise.

The wind carries the smells of winter turning to spring. The mud wraps around our boots as we step in puddles. When we enter a stall, the pigs bump into us; when we look at the sheep, they cower together in a corner. We are learning about the urban watershed, where eggs and beef come from, and how barns were built in the 19th century with wood cauls rather than metal nails. We experience the smells of the barn, the texture of the ladder, the feel of the shovels, the vibration when the pigs grunt, the taste of fresh eggs, and the camaraderie with the farmers.

As a parent, it is obvious that children learn more when they engage their entire body in a meaningful experience than when they sit at a computer. If you doubt this, just observe children watching an activity on a screen and then doing the same activity for themselves. They are much more engaged riding a horse than watching a video about it, playing a sport with their whole bodies rather than a simulated version of it in an online game.

Today, however, many powerful people are pushing for children to spend more time in front of computer screens, not less. Philanthropists such as Bill Gates and Mark Zuckerberg have contributed millions of dollars to "personal learning," a term that describes children working by themselves on computers, and Laurene Powell Jobs has bankrolled the XQ Super School project to use technology to "transcend the confines of traditional teaching methodologies."[1] Policymakers such as the US Secretary of Education Betsy DeVos call personalized learning "one of the most promising developments in K-12 education,"[2] and Rhode Island has announced a statewide personalized learning push for all public school students.[3] Think tanks such as the Brookings Institution recommend that Latin-American countries build "massive e-learning hubs that reach millions."[4] School administrators tout the advantages of giving all students, including those at kindergarten, personal computers.

5   Many adults appreciate the power of computers and the internet, and think that children should have access to them as soon as possible. Yet screen learning displaces other, more tactile ways to discover the world. Human beings learn with their eyes, yes, but also their ears, nose, mouth, skin, heart, hands, feet. The more time kids spend on computers, the less time they have to go on field

1. "XQ: The Super School Project," Emerson Collective, accessed June 25, 2019, https://www.emersoncollective.com/xq-the-super-school-project/.

2. Alyson Klein, "Betsy DeVos: Many Students Aren't Being Prepared for the Careers of Tomorrow," *Education Week - Politics K-12*, accessed June 25, 2019, http://blogs.edweek.org/edweek/campaign-k-12/2017/11/betsy_devos_jobs_future_choice_florida.html?cmp=SOC-SHR-FB.

3. Benjamin Herold, "Rhode Island Announces Statewide K-12 Personalized Learning Push," *Education Week - Digital Education*, accessed June 25, 2019, https://blogs.edweek.org/edweek/DigitalEducation/2017/02/rhode_island_personalized_learning.html?cmp=SOC-SHR-FB.

4. Rebecca Winthrop and Adam Barton, "Innovation to Leapfrog Educational Progress in Latin America," *Brookings* (blog), March 22, 2018, https://www.brookings.edu/research/innovation-to-leapfrog-educational-progress-in-latin-america/.

trips, build model airplanes, have recess, hold a book in their hands, or talk with teachers and friends. In the 21st century, schools should not get with the times, as it were, and place children on computers for even more of their days. Instead, schools should provide children with rich experiences that engage their entire bodies.

To better understand why so many people embrace screen learning, we can turn to a classic of 20th-century French philosophy: Maurice Merleau-Ponty's *Phenomenology of Perception* (1945).[5]

According to Merleau-Ponty, European philosophy has long prioritized "seeing" over "doing" as a path to understanding. Plato, René Descartes, John Locke, David Hume, Immanuel Kant: each, in different ways, posits a gap between the mind and the world, the subject and the object, the thinking self and physical things. Philosophers take for granted that the mind sees things from a distance. When Descartes announced "I think therefore I am," he was positing a fundamental gulf between the thinking self and the physical body. Despite the novelty of digital media, Merleau-Ponty would contend that Western thought has long assumed that the mind, not the body, is the site of thinking and learning.

According to Merleau-Ponty, however, "consciousness is originally not an 'I think that,' but rather an 'I can.'"[6] In other words, human thinking emerges out of lived experience, and what we can do with our bodies profoundly shapes what philosophers think or scientists discover. "The entire universe of science is constructed upon the lived world," he wrote.[7] *Phenomenology of Perception* aimed to help readers better appreciate the connection between the lived world and consciousness.

Philosophers are in the habit of saying that we "have" a body. But as Merleau-Ponty points out: "I am not in front of my body, I am in my body, or rather I am my body."[8] This simple correction carries important implications about learning. What does it mean to say that I am my body?

The mind is not somehow outside of time and space. Instead, the body thinks, feels, desires, hurts, has a history, and looks ahead. Merleau-Ponty invented the term "intentional arc" to describe how consciousness connects "our past, our future, our human milieu, our physical situation, our ideological situation, and our moral situation."[9] He makes readers attend to the countless aspects of the world that permeate our thinking.   10

Merleau-Ponty challenges us to stop believing that the human mind transcends the rest of nature. Humans are thinking animals whose thinking is

5. Phenomenology: a branch of philosophy devoted to the study of consciousness and experience [Editor's Note]. Maurice Merleau-Ponty, *Phenomenology of Perception*, trans. Donald Landes (New York: Routledge, 2013).

6. Merleau-Ponty, 139.

7. Merleau-Ponty, lxxii.

8. Merleau-Ponty, 151.

9. Merleau-Ponty, xli.

always infused with our animality. As the cognitive scientist Alan Jasanoff explains in a recent *Aeon* essay, it is even misleading to idealize the brain independent of the rest of the viscera.[10] The learning process happens when an embodied mind "gears" into the world.

Take the example of dancing. From a Cartesian perspective, the mind moves the body like a puppeteer pulls strings to move a puppet. To learn to dance, in this paradigm, a person needs to memorize a sequence of steps. For Merleau-Ponty, on the contrary, the way to learn to dance is to move one's physical body in space: "in order for the new dance to integrate particular elements of general motricity, it must first have received, so to speak, a motor consecration."[11] The mind does not reflect and make a conscious decision before the body moves; the body "catches" the movement.

Philosophers have long attributed a spectatorial stance to the mind, when in fact the body participates in the world. It is common sense that the head is the "seat of thought," but "the principal regions of my body are consecrated to actions," and the "parts of my body participate in their value."[12] People learn, think and value with every part of their bodies, and our bodies know things that we can never fully articulate in words.

Surely, one could reply, this might be true for physical activities such as dancing but does not apply to all intellectual pursuits. Merleau-Ponty would respond: "The body is our general means of having a world."[13] Everything we learn, think or know emanates from our body. It is by walking through a meadow, hiking beside a river, and boating down a lake that we are able to appreciate the science of geography.[14] It is by talking with other people and learning their stories that we can appreciate literature. Buying food for our family infuses us with a conviction that we need to learn mathematics. We cannot always trace the route from experience to knowledge, from a childhood activity to adult insight. But there is no way for us to learn that bypasses the body: "the body is our anchorage in a world."[15]

15   Merleau-Ponty would not be surprised if people showed him students learning on a screen. Students can project themselves into the world that they see on a screen, just as many people are capable of thinking abstractly. As long as children have had some exposure to the world and other people, they should be able to make some sense of what they see on screens.[16]

Still, Merleau-Ponty gives us reasons to resist the trend towards computer-based education. Proponents of personalized learning point to the advantages

10. "We Are More than Our Brains: On Neuroscience and Being Human—Alan Jasanoff | Aeon Essays," *Aeon*, accessed June 25, 2019, https://aeon.co/essays/we-are -more-than-our-brains-on-neuroscience-and-being-human.

11. Merleau-Ponty, 144.

12. Merleau-Ponty, 147.

13. Merleau-Ponty, 147.

14. Merleau-Ponty, lxxii.

15. Merleau-Ponty, 146.

16. On the word "projection," see Merleau-Ponty, 115.

of having kids on computers for much of the school day, including students working at their own pace to meet learning objectives. However, from a phenomenological perspective, it is not clear why students will want to do this for very long when the experience is so removed from their flesh-and-blood lives. Teachers and parents will have to use incentives, threats and medication to make children sit at computers for long stretches of time when children want to run, play, paint, eat, sing, compete and laugh. To put it bluntly: advocates of screen learning sometimes seem to forget that children are young animals that want to move in the world, not watch it from a distance.

At the farm, my children learned from being around the animals, trees, pastures, streams, stars and other physical objects. Things became more real, more immediate, than they would have been if a screen had mediated them. However, the experience was as deep as it was because of the relationships we formed with our hosts. The farmers would hold my children when placing them on horses or look them in the eye when explaining how to move sheep from one stall to the next. Our children had fun with their children while playing by the stream at dusk before dinner. When we drove away from the farm, my young son had tears in his eyes; he didn't want to leave his new friends.

For proponents such as DeVos, computer-based education empowers students to work independently at their own pace, including at home rather than in brick-and-mortar public schools. Based on my experience at the farm, however, I would argue that this highlights one of the problems of screen learning: it does not easily enable children to form human relationships that are crucial to a satisfying educational experience.

In his important book *Face-to-Face Diplomacy: Social Neuroscience and International Relations* (2018), Marcus Holmes explains the science that justifies this intuition.[17] Drawing upon research in philosophy of mind, cognitive science and social neuroscience, Holmes argues that physical copresence is essential to generate trust and empathy among human beings. Though his research addresses the puzzle of why diplomats insist on meeting face-to-face for important discussions, his work also explains the science of why people find it more satisfying to meet in person than to communicate by screens.

According to Holmes, diplomats insist on meeting in person with their colleagues. Good negotiators have a "feel for the game" that works only when they share drinks, go on walks, shake hands, or have private conversations with their peers.[18] Diplomats know that they need to embrace, breathe the same air, and look each other in the eye if they are going to arrive at optimal outcomes.

Holmes draws upon neuroscience to explain why face-to-face meetings, as a rule, achieve better results. Researchers such as the neuroscientist Marco Lacoboni at the University of California, Los Angeles have diagrammed the

20

---

17. Marcus Holmes, *Face-to-Face Diplomacy: Social Neuroscience and International Relations* (Cambridge, United Kingdom; New York: Cambridge University Press, 2018).

18. Holmes, 8.

"mirroring system" that enables human beings to understand each other's intentions. Within the brain, there are mirror neurons that fire when we do an action or when we see another person doing the action. Folk psychology holds that when we see another person, we think for a moment before deciding how to react. According to the new "simulation theory," we actually feel what the other person feels as mirror neurons fire in just the same manner as if the experience was happening to us. The mirroring system "enables advanced neural synchronization between individuals."[19]

Communicating in person enables people to "pick up micro-changes in facial expressions" and detect other people's sincerity.[20] Neuroscience shows that humans do a good job of reading other people's minds. People often deceive one another, but meeting face-to-face aids the detection of deceit. In games, people are more likely to trust one another when they play in person rather than when they play online. Likewise, there is greater rapport and "coupling" when people get together in the flesh:[21] "Put simply, face-to-face interaction is an unrivaled mechanism for intention understanding."[22]

To what extent can new technology replicate face-to-face interactions? Holmes acknowledges that writing, calling or video-chatting often works fine for many forms of communication but insists that people must meet in the flesh to achieve a high degree of trust or social bonding. Citing the sociologist Randall Collins at the University of Pennsylvania, Holmes explains that people want to be in the physical presence of other people to generate emotional energy, "a feeling of confidence, elation, strength, enthusiasm, and initiative in taking action."[23] Communicating via email or the internet makes it harder to read another's body language or perceive what is happening in the background as the other person talks into the computer's camera. Communicating from a distance does "not provide the same physical and emotional connection" as bodily co-participation.[24]

We can transfer insights about social neuroscience from international relations theory to education theory. Placing children in front of screens enables them to access information, meet people around the world, play games, read things, purchase things and so forth that would otherwise be inaccessible. But as an "interaction ritual," screen learning generates less emotional energy than sharing a physical space with other teachers and students. Students looking at a screen will not trust, or care about, their teachers or students to the same degree. People might speak their mind more freely when there aren't the same visual cues to hold their tongues, but this also means that people are more likely to be uninhibited and antagonistic.[25] People will not have the same investment in an online education community.

19. Holmes, 6.
20. Holmes, 6.
21. Holmes, 40.
22. Holmes, 5.
23. Holmes, 263.
24. Holmes, 264.
25. Lynne Wainfan and Paul K. Davis, *Challenges in Virtual Collaboration*, Product Page, 2004, https://www.rand.org/pubs/monographs/MG273.html.

A screen cannot provide the same emotional resonance as staying at a   25
farm, participating in its rhythms, and forming bonds with the other people.
Educators should be considering how to provide such opportunities to more
students, including those whose parents do not have the time and resources to
plan such trips themselves.

For many young people, digital media, even when used appropriately, can
make education and community life worse. Digital media is a mixed blessing,
at best, and many young people would prefer to spend less time on screens. At
some level, most of us already know this. When private schools advertise, the
images are often of kids doing physical activities or hanging out with a group
of friends. People are fighting common sense, philosophy and science when
they argue for children to spend more time on screens.

One could reasonably reply that many young people enjoy being on screens,
and gain efficacy by being on the internet. This is the claim of the report
"Children's Rights in the Digital Age" (2014), made by a team of Australian
researchers partnering with the United Nations Children's Fund (UNICEF).[26]
The researchers interviewed children around the world and used their words
and examples to conclude: "Hearing the sentiments of children in eight different
languages allows one truth to sound loud and clear: we need to take the necessary
steps to ensure that all children can reap the opportunities of digital access."

The report describes the real benefits that children accrue from spending
time on digital media. Children can gain access to information, get faster service delivery, express themselves artistically and politically, have fun, and make
and maintain friendships with others around the world. The report acknowledges the dangers of digital media, including exposure to violent and porno-
graphic images, excessive use, and data-privacy concerns. But it argues that the
"risk narrative" is overstated. If children and their caregivers are responsible, it
maintains, then they will likely reap the benefits of online access.

In a remarkable epilogue, however, the report quotes young people from
around the world answering the question of what would happen if digital media
disappeared. Here are a few of the responses from teenagers in different counties:
"I'd spend more time doing things outside, not watching TV or my phone or anything, I'd find more productive things to do" (Australia). "If I don't have any digital
media then I would read story books" (Thailand). "It would not do any harm. In
the end we are not hard-wired to digital media. We are not controlled by digital
media" (Turkey). "It would make other people more confident to be able to talk to
other people face to face, not over the internet, actually be able to have conversations with them" (Australia). "People would learn to live with other things, using
other ways" (Brazil). "At first it would be very hard just to get used to it, but since
everyone would not have it, everyone would get over it. It'd be better as well 'cause
everyone would be able to talk more, to work harder for friendship" (Australia).[27]

26. Amanda Third et al., "Children's Rights in the Digital Age: A Download from
Children around the World" (Young and Well Cooperative Research Centre, 2014),
https://www.unicef.org/publications/index_76268.html.
27. Third et al., 76–77.

30   If the move to digital learning continues, children will spend much, if not most, of their waking hours in front of screens. They will use apps before they go to school, spend their days in front of computers, do their homework online, and then entertain themselves with digital media. Children are losing opportunities to experience the world in all its richness. The gestalt of a farm transcends what pixels and speakers can convey. Screens drain the vitality from many educational experiences that could be better done in the flesh. This drift toward screen learning is only inevitable if people do nothing to stop it. So let's stop it.

BIBLIOGRAPHY

Herold, Benjamin. "Rhode Island Announces Statewide K-12 Personalized Learning Push." *Education Week - Digital Education*. Accessed June 25, 2019.
  https://blogs.edweek.org/edweek/DigitalEducation/2017/02/rhode_island_personalized_learning.html?cmp=SOC-SHR-FB.

Holmes, Marcus. *Face-to-Face Diplomacy: Social Neuroscience and International Relations*. Cambridge, United Kingdom; New York: Cambridge University Press, 2018.

Klein, Alyson. "Betsy DeVos: Many Students Aren't Being Prepared for the Careers of Tomorrow." *Education Week - Politics K-12*. Accessed June 25, 2019.
  http://blogs.edweek.org/edweek/campaign-k-12/2017/11/betsy_devos_jobs_future_choice_florida.html?cmp=SOC-SHR-FB.

Merleau-Ponty, Maurice. *Phenomenology of Perception*. Translated by Donald Landes. New York: Routledge, 2013.

Third, Amanda, et al. "Children's Rights in the Digital Age: A Download from Children around the World." Young and Well Cooperative Research Centre, 2014.
  https://www.unicef.org/publications/index_76268.html.

Wainfan, Lynne, and Paul K. Davis. *Challenges in Virtual Collaboration: Videoconferencing, Audioconferencing, and Computer-Mediated Communications*. Product Page. Santa Monica, CA: RAND Corporation, 2004.
  https://www.rand.org/pubs/monographs/MG273.html.

"We Are More than Our Brains: On Neuroscience and Being Human—Alan Jasanoff | Aeon Essays." *Aeon*. Accessed April 2, 2019.
  https://aeon.co/essays/we-are-more-than-our-brains-on-neuroscience-and-being-human.

Winthrop, Rebecca, and Adam Barton. "Innovation to Leapfrog Educational Progress in Latin America." *Brookings* (blog), March 22, 2018.
  https://www.brookings.edu/research/innovation-to-leapfrog-educational-progress-in-latin-america/.

"XQ: The Super School Project." Emerson Collective. Accessed June 25, 2019.
  https://www.emersoncollective.com/xq-the-super-school-project/.

MLA CITATION

Tampio, Nicholas. "Look Up from Your Screen." *The Norton Reader: An Anthology of Nonfiction*, edited by Melissa A. Goldthwaite et al., 15th ed., W. W. Norton, 2020, pp. 325–32.

QUESTIONS

1. Nicholas Tampio quotes philosophers, scientists, and proponents of education to make the argument that education is better suited to in-the-flesh interactions than screen learning. He also draws from his own experience of spending time on a farm with his children. Which sources helped you understand his argument best? Why?

2. Tampio and Florence Williams (pp. 333–42) both make an argument for more physical, in-person, and outdoor education. How are their arguments similar? How are they different?

3. Consider the place of both "screen learning" and "more tactile ways to discover the world" (paragraph 5) in your own educational experience. Write about a valuable educational experience you've had—whether it involves screens or field trips or sports—and why it was successful.

FLORENCE WILLIAMS
ADHD Is Fuel for Adventure

BY SECOND GRADE, it was clear that while Zack Smith could sit in a chair, he had no intention of staying in it. He was disruptive in class, spoke in a loud voice, and had a hard time taking turns with others. His parents fed him a series of medications for attention-deficit hyperactivity disorder, or ADHD, many of which didn't work. Zack, who attended school in West Hartford, Connecticut, was placed in special classrooms where he showed a propensity for lashing out. Twice suspended, he was miserable. He didn't seem to care about anything at school. When his parents realized that his path would likely lead to worse trouble, they pulled the ripcord on eighth grade.

Where Zack eventually landed is clinging spread-eagle to an east-facing slab of quartzite in the West Virginia panhandle. His chin-length, strawberry blond hair curls out beneath a Minion-yellow helmet. A harness cinches his T-shirt—the sleeves of which have been ripped off—obscuring the *Call of Duty: Advanced Warfare* lettering.

"I have a wedgie!" he bellows out from 20 feet up.

Belaying him is another 14-year-old—pale, earnest Daniel. Earlier in the day, Daniel asked, "Do I have to belay? I'm only 95 pounds." Both kids still look a little apprehensive, but there's no question that they are paying full attention to the wall of rock and to the rope that unites them. Yesterday beneath a picnic awning in a campground near Seneca Rocks, they and 12 other scrappy teens from the Academy at SOAR learned how to tie figure-eights and Prusiks, the knots that would safeguard their lives, under the tutelage of trip leader Joseph

Originally published in Outside *(2016), a revised and extended version of this piece is included in Florence Williams's book* The Nature Fix: Why Nature Makes Us Happier, Healthier, and More Creative *(2017).*

Geier, the academy's director, and seven other energetic field instructors mostly in their twenties. The students' ages span five years, but in the spectrum of puberty, the younger kids look like they could be the square roots of the biggest ones. Zack occupies an awkward middle ground, lanky and knock-kneed, with a surprisingly deep voice and a crooked smile.

5   He gradually moves his right foot to a new nub and pulls himself higher. He scrabbles upward, finally victoriously slapping a carabiner on the top rope before rappelling down. "Oh man, my arms hurt," he says at the bottom, his pale cheeks flushed from sun and exertion. Daniel accidentally steps on the climbing rope and, per the rules, has to kiss it. This happens so often that no one remarks on it. For a moment both boys cheer on Tim, a small boy from the D.C. area with bright eyes behind eyeglasses so thick they look like safety gear. The aspirational name tape on the back of his helmet reads T Bone Sizzler. A group chant begins: "Go, Tim, go—oh, go Tim!"

Before enrolling in this adventure-based boarding school for grades seven through twelve, Zack, like a lot of these students, had already spent some summers at SOAR's Balsam, North Carolina, camp or its programs in California, Florida, and Wyoming for kids of both sexes with ADHD, dyslexia, and other learning disabilities. SOAR's founding principle—radical several decades ago and still surprisingly underappreciated—was that kids with attention deficits thrive in the outdoors. Since then ADHD diagnoses have exploded—11 percent of American kids are now said to have it—while recess, PE, and access to nature have shriveled miserably.

Zack's first SOAR summer involved a three-week stint of horse-packing in the Wind River Range. Before the trip, he says, he would have preferred to stay home and play video games. "I hated nature," as he puts it. But something clicked under the wide Wyoming skies. He found he was able to focus on tasks; he was making friends and feeling less terrible about himself. Zack turned his restlessness into a craving for adventure—which is perhaps what it was meant to be all along.

It's one thing to let kids unplug and run loose in the woods in summer, but shifting the whole academic year outside—SOAR students alternate two weeks on the forested campus in North Carolina and two weeks in the field—reflects either parental desperation, intrepid educational insight, or a combination of the two. Zack's backstory is a common one, especially among boys, who are diagnosed at more than twice the rate of girls. History is full of examples of restless youths who went on to become celebrated iconoclasts, like wilderness advocate John Muir, who spent his early childhood sneaking out at night, dangling from the windowsill by his fingertips, and scaling treacherous seaside cliffs in Dunbar, Scotland. Frederick Law Olmsted, who would later change the torso of Manhattan and influence scores of other cities with his park designs, hated school. His tolerant headmaster would let him roam the countryside instead. Ansel Adams's parents plucked their fidgety boy out of class, gave him a Brownie box camera, and took him on a grand tour of Yosemite. It was unschooling, California style.

Olmsted, looking back on his life, identified the problem as the stifling classroom, not troublesome boys. "A boy," he wrote, "who would not in any weather & under all ordinary circumstances, rather take a walk of ten to twelve miles some time in the course of every day than stay quietly about a house all day, must be suffering from disease or a defective education."

The Academy at SOAR—which became accredited three years ago—is determined to find a better way. The school has just 32 students, 26 of them boys, divided into four mixed-age houses. Each kid has an individualized curriculum, and the student-teacher ratio is five to one. Tuition is a steep $49,500 per year, on par with other boarding schools, although you won't find a Hogwartsian dining hall or stacks of leather-bound books. The school still covers the required academics, as well as basic life skills like cooking, but finds that the kids pay more attention to a history lesson while standing in the middle of a battlefield or a geology lecture while camping on a monocline.

"We started from scratch," says SOAR's executive director John Willson, who began working there as a camp counselor in 1991. "We're not reinventing the wheel—we threw out the wheel." The school's founders didn't have any particular allegiance to adventure sports; they just found that climbing, backpacking, and canoeing were a magic fit for these kids, at these ages, when their neurons are exploding in a million directions. "When you're on a rock ledge," Willson says, "there's a sweet spot of arousal and stress that opens you up for adaptive learning. You find new ways of solving problems."

Some of the teens who arrive at SOAR are still putting their clothes on backward, not uncommon among kids with ADHD. They forget to eat or they can't stop. They lash out in anger, and they're easily frustrated. Symptoms tend to express themselves differently in boys and girls. The classic symptoms in boys, which are better understood, are hyperactivity, impulsivity, and distractibility; girls tend to show less of the hyperactivity, which makes the condition harder to spot. We all fall somewhere on the continuum of these traits, but people with more-extreme symptoms appear to have different chemistry in the parts of their brains that govern reward, movement, and attention. They may have trouble listening or sitting still, and they get distracted by external stimuli. They can be hyper-focused, but they also get bored easily, so they tend to be risk takers, looking for charged activities that help flood their brains with feel-good neurotransmitters like dopamine and norepinephrine, which otherwise get gummed up in the ADHD brain. Kids with the condition are more likely to suffer head injuries, accidentally ingest poisons, and take street drugs.

With all these liabilities, you might think such heritable traits would diminish in humans over time; that's the way Darwin awards work. The fact that they remain so common, though, means that these same characteristics must have once conferred tremendous advantages on individuals and ultimately on the human race.

It's worth taking a look into the brains of kids like Zack, because not only do kids with ADHD need exploration, but exploration needs them. Zack and his tethered band of misfits might look like merry miscreants, but they hold clues to the adventure impulses lurking in all of us, impulses that are increasingly at risk in a world moving indoors—onto screens and away from nature. Attentional mutants everywhere have saved the human species, and they may yet spare us the death of adventure.

15   The human brain evolved outside, in a world filled with interesting things, but not an overwhelming number of interesting things. Everything in a child's world was nameable: foods, creatures, the stars. We were supposed to notice passing distractions; if we didn't, we could get eaten. But we also needed a certain amount of stick-to-itiveness so that we could build tools, stalk game, raise babies, and plan big. Evolution favored early humans who could both stay on task and switch tasks when needed, and our prefrontal cortex evolved to let us master the ability. In fact, how nimbly we allocate our attention may be one of humanity's greatest and most distinctive skills, argues neuroscientist Daniel Levitin of McGill University.

Most humans had brains that craved novelty and wanted to explore—to a degree. This worked out for us. As Levitin writes in *The Organized Mind*, our species expanded into more habitats than any creature the earth had ever seen, to the point where humans plus our livestock and pets now account for 98 percent of the planet's terrestrial vertebrates. But evolution also favored variability, and some of us pushed exploration more than others.

Wondering if we have a specific adventure gene, researchers have looked at the DNA of humans in the farthest reaches of the globe—the descendants of people who kept moving until there was no place else to go. One mutation kept popping up: a variant called 7R on the DRD4 gene that helps regulate how signals from dopamine are processed. People with 7R are more likely to take financial risks and to travel and try new things, probably as a way to juice up their stingy dopamine delivery. Long story short, this gene mutation, which affects roughly 20 percent of today's global population, does indeed cluster in places like Siberia, Tierra del Fuego, and Australia, where humans had migrated over the longest routes.

It turns out that the gene also clusters in people who have ADHD. It would be too easy to say that any one gene or set of genes explains the human capacity to explore or explains ADHD, since both are determined by numerous genetic and environmental factors. And not all kids with ADHD like risk taking. But to Dale Archer, a Lake Charles, Louisiana, psychiatrist and author of The ADHD Advantage, the link makes sense. Once upon a time, the dominant traits of ADHD were highly adaptive. They were—and still can be—gifts that enable rapid interpretation of sensory data, thinking on your feet, curiosity, and creative restlessness. "The thing with the ADHDer is that we get bored easily but we do great in a crisis, we can function really well," says Archer, a surf kayaker, solo sailor, and cyclist who shares the diagnosis with his adult son. According to him and others in the learning-differences community, Napoleon probably had ADHD (along with some other issues) and so did Captain James Cook, Ernest Shackleton, Thomas Edison, and Eleanor Roosevelt.

If you take a typical ADHD kid, layer on some experience and maturity, tamp down the impulsive bits, and add some goal aspirations and a keen ability to plan and dream, you end up with a high-adrenaline achiever like alpinist Conrad Anker or adventurer Sir Richard Branson, both of whom believe they have the condition. They are comfortable in extreme environments, enlivened by risk, able to thrive on the unknown. When Branson dropped out of school at age 16 to start his first company, he says, "The headmaster told me that I would either end up in prison or become a millionaire." Since then he has scored two first-ever transoceanic ballooning records, received eight helicopter rescues, and founded the Virgin Group.

20   "I am hyper situationally aware," says Anker. "It was a trainwreck in second grade—every input received my attention. When I'm alpine climbing, that keeps me alive." Anker can nimbly process snow conditions, incoming weather, and rope integrity to make quick decisions. His brain likes intense environments, he says, but too much pointless stimulation, like on a busy city street, drives him bananas. Precision wingsuit flier Jeb Corliss was diagnosed with ADHD when he was ten. "My sisters are normal people. I'm hyper, yeah, big deal," he says. "I believe that a lot of people are like that, and they use it to their advantage." Corliss says flying through the air is when he feels calm and peaceful.

As a laconic, impulsive, and depressed teen in northeast Ohio, Matt Rutherford landed in juvenile detention five times for petty crimes and in rehab twice. Some 15 years later, he became the first sailor to circumnavigate the Americas alone. During his 308 days at sea, his secondhand 27-foot boat started falling apart under him. It caught on fire, he lost his water supply, his fuel bladder sprang a leak, and, just past French Guiana, he nearly smacked into a freighter. "The more challenging it is," he says, "the happier I am. The more rocks, the more ice, the better."

In fact, ADHD traits are so common among modern-day alpinists, rock climbers, BASE jumpers, snowboarders, and other extreme athletes that the observation raises several important questions: If adventure sports are such a great fit for people with ADHD, why aren't more doctors, schools, and families boosting participation? And, as kids are asked to sit still for longer periods of time indoors and given more medications to help them do it, what is the fate of the next generation of adventurers? Does the mass medicalization of ADHD mean the human species has reached peak exploration?

If you're the sort of person who eats chaos for breakfast, sitting in school all day may well suck out your soul. But with the rise of industrialism, educators thought all kids should be in standardized classrooms. "ADHD got its start 150 years ago when compulsory education got started," says Stephen Hinshaw, a psychologist at the University of California at Berkeley. "In that sense, you could say it's partially a social construct. If you look at the symptoms of ADHD, maybe they're not really symptoms anymore if you get in the right profession or the right ecological niche. We've learned some of this by looking at extreme athletes, who have found that niche."

But school often isn't it. To oversimplify, it's like taking kids who are genetically meant to be hunters and gatherers and making them tend crops instead. Not only will they feel bored and inadequate, but the constrained setting will actually make their symptoms worse. For kids like Zack, school feels stifling and rule bound. They act up. They may get moved into even more restrictive environments, sometimes with chain-link fences, guards, and neurotropic meds that go beyond ADHD to deal with the ensuing anxiety, depression, and aggression. Sometimes they end up in trouble or, as Zack feared might happen to him, get "gooned" in the middle of the night by burly strangers intent on packing him off to a residential therapeutic program that looks like Outward Bound in the brochure but ends up feeling like a gulag.

Interestingly, researchers have observed similar patterns in lab rats—who, let's face it, suffer the ultimate cosmic gooning. When Jaak Panksepp, a neuroscientist at Washington State University, restricted the play of young rats, their frontal lobes (which control executive function) failed to grow normally. "We had the insight that if animals don't play, if there are not sufficient spaces for them to engage, they develop play hunger," says Panksepp. "They have impulse-control problems and eventually problems with social interactions."

Panksepp points out that while common stimulant medications for ADHD like Ritalin and Adderall may improve attention skills and academic performance in many kids, they do so at the cost of reducing the playfulness urge— at least temporarily. "We know these are anti-play drugs in animals," he says.

"That is clear and unambiguous." The bigger question is whether the drugs—and all the enforced sedentary behavior—squeeze the adventure impulse out of kids in the longer term. Psychologists tend to disagree on this point, but the truth is, no one really knows. It's not a boutique question. Of the 6.4 million diagnosed kids in America, about half are taking prescription stimulants, an increase of 28 percent since 2007.

For athletes like Corliss and swimmer Michael Phelps, who has also been diagnosed with ADHD, the sport itself becomes their medication, filling their brains with endorphins and endocannabinoids. But for every hour that a drug is supplying a kid's fix, that's an hour a potential explorer is not looking longingly out the window plotting escape. Of course, some kids, Hinshaw points out, need medication even to make big plans, not to mention learn algebra. Other families, he notes, are seeing the value in medication holidays, allowing kids to come off their drugs on weekends and during summers.

At SOAR, many students arrive on meds, and many stay on them. At all times, the instructors have locked and sealed messenger bags full of pharmaceuticals strapped to their torsos like baby marsupials. Though Willson emphasizes that SOAR is not a way to get kids off ADHD meds, some do find that they can taper off. Zack's parents said they're planning to toss his during his holiday break, and they expect to lower the dose of his stimulant as well. "The changes in him have been nothing short of miraculous," says his mother, Marlene De Pecol. "Now he's just happy."

Taking meds didn't seem to alter the daring trajectory of solo sailor Rutherford. He took multiple pills for six years until he was 16, when, like Zack, he managed to find a place more compatible with his brain's wiring—the Eagle Rock School in Estes Park, Colorado, an adventure-based boarding school funded by the American Honda Education Corporation. Anker, meanwhile, says it's possible he wouldn't be making first ascents today if he'd taken Ritalin through his teenage years. His parents encouraged him to go outside instead. Climbing developed his technical mastery while helping him sit still when he needed to. It also likely helped his prefrontal cortex mature.

30   The senior Ankers were ahead of the curve, or perhaps about 10,000 years behind the curve, depending on how you look at it.

The fact is, all human children learn by exploration, and we are tying their shoelaces together—not just with medication, but through over-structured, over-managed classrooms and sports teams, less freedom to roam, and ever more dazzling indoor seductions. Modern life has made all of us distractible and overwhelmed. As McGill's Levitin explains, the average American owns and must keep track of thousands of times more possessions than the average hunter-gatherer. Each of us, one 2013 study projected, consumes 74 gigabytes daily. Teens now interact with screens more than six and a half hours per day, and that's not including time at school, according to Common Sense Media, a non-profit that helps parents make smart technology choices. "The digital age is profoundly narrowing our horizons and our creativity, not to mention our bodies and physiological capabilities," says environmental photographer James Balog, even as his hard-won chronicles of a changing planet are delivered to millions digitally. Yet Balog, who says he has mild ADHD, can hardly get his eighth-grade daughter off her phone. "These are hours not being spent outside," he says. "It kills me."

The news isn't all bad. While per capita visits to natural areas are down, participation by young people in a number of adventure sports like snowboarding and rock climbing is up. Solid research continues to make the case that kids benefit from time outside and regular exercise, and some schools are getting the message by instituting early-morning programs. More psychiatrists are also prescribing exercise for kids with ADHD. But the National Institute of Mental Health makes no mention of physical activity as a treatment option on its extensive website.

The radio silence on exercise is surprising, because studies consistently show that aerobic activity targets the same attentional networks that ADHD medication does. While fitness improves learning in both kids and adults, it's adolescents like Zack—whose prefrontal cortex is in the very midst of laying down a lifetime of hardware—who seem to benefit the most. John Green, a biobehavioral psychologist at the University of Vermont, and graduate student Meghan Eddy exercised some adult and juvenile rats and then tasked them with learning how to find food in a maze. The young rats who exercised bested the non-exercisers and did as well as rats on Ritalin. It seemed the playful and exploratory adolescent years exist to boost learning in mammals, just as SOAR's Willson intuited. Or, as Green more formally puts it, "The adolescent prefrontal cortex is ready to be molded by environmental experience."

So there you have it: the time is now. There's a limited window to best launch these kids and, perhaps in so doing, safeguard a future of innovative exploration by the very young people who are wired to do it better than anybody else.

The ADHD population is an advance guard. If they can recognize how to better adapt their environments for their brains, there's hope for the rest of us.

35

After many years languishing in the Formica-filled classrooms of West Hartford, Zack Smith is ready. He and his pals gather around the fire pit back at camp, bellies full of hamburgers and pickles. It's very dark out. Tomorrow all 14 boys will make the four pitches up the South Peak at Seneca Rocks. A couple of days after that, they'll backpack across the Dolly Sods Wilderness Area, and then they'll visit Stonewall Jackson's grave and read poetry written by the general's sister-in-law. For now, they're tired if not exactly mellow.

Zack's job for the day is Captain Planet, meaning he's the mighty taker-out of trash. Another kid named Max is Scribe. At 16, Max is an expeller of colossal farts, and proud of it. "I don't do anything halfway in the outdoors," he says. He shared with me on the trail that he is also an expert squirrel hunter, climber, and river runner. When he is done with school, he intends to find a job guiding. Now, beturbaned in a purple bandana, he opens the group journal and prepares to record notes on the day's events under the narrow red beam of a headlamp.

Zack is lying on his back and looking up at the stars. He is impressed. "We don't have these at home," he says.

MLA CITATION

Williams, Florence. "ADHD Is Fuel for Adventure." *The Norton Reader: An Anthology of Nonfiction*, edited by Melissa A. Goldthwaite et al., 15th ed., W. W. Norton, 2020, pp. 333–42.

QUESTIONS

1. Florence Williams argues that there may be an advantage to attention-deficit/hyperactivity disorder (ADHD). What positive qualities does she associate with ADHD?

2. What aspects of the Academy at SOAR seem most educationally sound to you? Are there any downsides you see to this type of education? Are there aspects of outdoor education that should be incorporated into more traditional classrooms?

3. Research a diagnosed learning disability—such as dyscalculia, dysgraphia, or dyslexia. What kinds of activities and educational settings would be most beneficial to those with the learning disability you researched? Make a list of specific activities that could be beneficial. Be creative, thinking beyond activities usually done in traditional classroom spaces.

LYNDA BARRY

The Sanctuary of School

I WAS 7 YEARS OLD the first time I snuck out of the house in the dark. It was winter and my parents had been fighting all night. They were short on money and long on relatives who kept "temporarily" moving into our house because they had nowhere else to go.

My brother and I were used to giving up our bedroom. We slept on the couch, something we actually liked because it put us that much closer to the light of our lives, our television.

At night when everyone was asleep, we lay on our pillows watching it with the sound off. We watched Steve Allen's[1] mouth moving. We watched Johnny Carson's[2] mouth moving. We watched movies filled with gangsters shooting machine guns into packed rooms, dying soldiers hurling a last grenade and beautiful women crying at windows. Then the sign-off finally came and we tried to sleep.

Published in the New York Times *(1992). Lynda Barry is a cartoonist and author.*

1. Host of *The Tonight Show*, 1954–1956.
2. Host of *The Tonight Show Starring Johnny Carson*, 1962–1992.

The morning I snuck out, I woke up filled with a panic about needing to get to school. The sun wasn't quite up yet but my anxiety was so fierce that I just got dressed, walked quietly across the kitchen and let myself out the back door.

It was quiet outside. Stars were still out. Nothing moved and no one was in the street. It was as if someone had turned the sound off on the world.   5

I walked the alley, breaking thin ice over the puddles with my shoes. I didn't know why I was walking to school in the dark. I didn't think about it. All I knew was a feeling of panic, like the panic that strikes kids when they realize they are lost.

A DARK OUTLINE

That feeling eased the moment I turned the corner and saw the dark outline of my school at the top of the hill. My school was made up of about 15 nondescript portable classrooms set down on a fenced concrete lot in a rundown Seattle neighborhood, but it had the most beautiful view of the Cascade Mountains. You could see them from anywhere on the playfield and you could see them from the windows of my classroom—Room 2.

I walked over to the monkey bars and hooked my arms around the cold metal. I stood for a long time just looking across Rainier Valley. The sky was beginning to whiten and I could hear a few birds.

EASY TO SLIP AWAY

In a perfect world my absence at home would not have gone unnoticed. I would have had two parents in a panic to locate me, instead of two parents in a panic to locate an answer to the hard question of survival during a deep financial and emotional crisis.

But in an overcrowded and unhappy home, it's incredibly easy for any child to slip away. The high levels of frustration, depression and anger in my house made my brother and me invisible. We were children with the sound turned off. And for us, as for the steadily increasing number of neglected children in this country, the only place where we could count on being noticed was at school.   10

"Hey there, young lady. Did you forget to go home last night?" It was Mr. Gunderson, our janitor, whom we all loved. He was nice and he was funny and he was old with white hair, thick glasses and an unbelievable number of keys. I could hear them jingling as he walked across the playfield. I felt incredibly happy to see him.

He let me push his wheeled garbage can between the different portables as he unlocked each room. He let me turn on the lights and raise the window shades and I saw my school slowly come to life. I saw Mrs. Holman, our school secretary, walk into the office without her orange lipstick on yet. She waved.

I saw the fifth-grade teacher, Mr. Cunningham, walking under the breezeway eating a hard roll. He waved.

And I saw my teacher, Mrs. Claire LeSane, walking toward us in a red coat and calling my name in a very happy and surprised way, and suddenly my throat got tight and my eyes stung and I ran toward her crying. It was something that surprised us both.

15   It's only thinking about it now, 28 years later, that I realize I was crying from relief. I was with my teacher, and in a while I was going to sit at my desk, with my crayons and pencils and books and classmates all around me, and for the next six hours I was going to enjoy a thoroughly secure, warm and stable world. It was a world I absolutely relied on. Without it, I don't know where I would have gone that morning.

Mrs. LeSane asked me what was wrong and when I said "Nothing," she seemingly left it at that. But she asked me if I would carry her purse for her, an honor above all honors, and she asked if I wanted to come into Room 2 early and paint.

PAINTING'S POWER

She believed in the natural healing power of painting and drawing for troubled children. In the back of her room there was always a drawing table and an easel with plenty of supplies, and sometimes during the day she would come up to you for what seemed like no good reason and quietly ask if you wanted to go to the back table and "make some pictures for Mrs. LeSane." We all had a chance at it—to sit apart from the class for a while to paint, draw and silently work out impossible problems on 11 × 17 sheets of newsprint.

Drawing came to mean everything to me. At the back table in Room 2, I learned to build myself a life preserver that I could carry into my home.

We all know that a good education system saves lives, but the people of this country are still told that cutting the budget for public schools is necessary, that poor salaries for teachers are all we can manage and that art, music and all creative activities must be the first to go when times are lean.

NO BABY-SITTING

20   Before- and after-school programs are cut and we are told that public schools are not made for baby-sitting children. If parents are neglectful temporarily or permanently, for whatever reason, it's certainly sad, but their unlucky children must fend for themselves. Or slip through the cracks. Or wander in a dark night alone.

We are told in a thousand ways that not only are public schools not important, but that the children who attend them, the children who need them most, are not important either. We leave them to learn from the blind eye of a television, or to the mercy of "a thousand points of light"[3] that can be as far away as stars.

---

3. Metaphor for private philanthropy and volunteer service, implicitly in contrast to government-run social programs; popularized by former U.S. president George H. W. Bush.

I was lucky. I had Mrs. LeSane. I had Mr. Gunderson. I had an abundance of art supplies. And I had a particular brand of neglect in my home that allowed me to slip away and get to them. But what about the rest of the kids who weren't as lucky? What happened to them?

By the time the bell rang that morning I had finished my drawing and Mrs. LeSane pinned it up on the special bulletin board she reserved for drawings from the back table. It was the same picture I always drew—a sun in the corner of a blue sky over a nice house with flowers all around it.

Mrs. LeSane asked us to please stand, face the flag, place our right hands over our hearts and say the Pledge of Allegiance. Children across the country do it faithfully. I wonder now when the country will face its children and say a pledge right back.

MLA CITATION

Barry, Lynda. "The Sanctuary of School." *The Norton Reader: An Anthology of Nonfiction,* edited by Melissa A. Goldthwaite et al., 15th ed., W. W. Norton, 2020, pp. 342–46.

QUESTIONS

1. How does Lynda Barry's school experience contrast with her home life? What specifically makes school a "sanctuary"?

2. In paragraphs 19–21, Barry calls for better funding for public schools. Imagine that Barry has received an unrestricted $100,000 grant to improve her elementary school. How do you think she would spend it?

3. Compare Barry's view of school to Gerald Graff's (pp. 360–63). What aspects of school does each author emphasize? Where do they agree? Where might they disagree?

4. Drawing on your own experience, write an argument about how we might improve our schools.

FREDERICK DOUGLASS
Learning to Read

I LIVED IN MASTER HUGH'S FAMILY about seven years.[1] During this time, I succeeded in learning to read and write. In accomplishing this, I was compelled to resort to various stratagems. I had no regular teacher. My mistress, who had kindly commenced to instruct me, had, in compliance with the advice and direction of her husband, not only ceased to instruct, but had set her face against my being instructed by any one else. It is due, however, to my mistress to say of her, that she did not adopt this course of treatment immediately. She at first lacked the depravity indispensable to shutting me up in mental darkness. It was at least necessary for her to have some training in the exercise of irresponsible power, to make her equal to the task of treating me as though I were a brute.

From Frederick Douglass's autobiography, Narrative of the Life of Frederick Douglass, an American Slave, Written by Himself *(1845).*

1. In Baltimore, Maryland.

My mistress was, as I have said, a kind and tender-hearted woman; and in the simplicity of her soul she commenced, when I first went to live with her, to treat me as she supposed one human being ought to treat another. In entering upon the duties of a slaveholder, she did not seem to perceive that I sustained to her the relation of a mere chattel, and that for her to treat me as a human being was not only wrong, but dangerously so. Slavery proved as injurious to her as it did to me. When I went there, she was a pious, warm, and tender-hearted woman. There was no sorrow or suffering for which she had not a tear. She had bread for the hungry, clothes for the naked, and comfort for every mourner that came within her reach. Slavery soon proved its ability to divest her of these heavenly qualities. Under its influence, the tender heart became stone, and the lamblike disposition gave way to one of tigerlike fierceness. The first step in her downward course was in her ceasing to instruct me. She now commenced to practise her husband's precepts. She finally became even more violent in her opposition than her husband himself. She was not satisfied with simply doing as well as he had commanded; she seemed anxious to do better. Nothing seemed to make her more angry than to see me with a newspaper. She seemed to think that here lay the danger. I have had her rush at me with a face made all up of fury, and snatch from me a newspaper, in a manner that fully revealed her apprehension. She was an apt woman; and a little experience soon demonstrated, to her satisfaction, that education and slavery were incompatible with each other.

From this time I was most narrowly watched. If I was in a separate room any considerable length of time, I was sure to be suspected of having a book, and was at once called to give an account of myself. All this, however, was too late. The first step had been taken. Mistress, in teaching me the alphabet, had given me the *inch*, and no precaution could prevent me from taking the *ell*.[2]

The plan which I adopted, and the one by which I was most successful, was that of making friends of all the little white boys whom I met in the street. As many of these as I could, I converted into teachers. With their kindly aid, obtained at different times and in different places, I finally succeeded in learning to read. When I was sent of errands, I always took my book with me, and by going one part of my errand quickly, I found time to get a lesson before my return. I used also to carry bread with me, enough of which was always in the house, and to which I was always welcome; for I was much better off in this regard than many of the poor white children in our neighborhood. This bread I used to bestow upon the hungry little urchins, who, in return, would give me that more valuable bread of knowledge. I am strongly tempted to give the names of two or three of those little boys, as a testimonial of the gratitude and affection I bear them; but prudence forbids;—not that it would injure me, but it might embarrass them; for it is almost an unpardonable offence to teach slaves to read in this Christian country. It is enough to say of the dear little fellows, that they lived on Philpot Street, very near Durgin and Bailey's ship-yard. I used to talk this matter of slavery over with them. I would sometimes say to them, I wished I could be as free as they would be when they got to be men.

2. Once a unit of measurement equal to forty-five inches; the saying is proverbial.

"You will be free as soon as you are twenty-one, *but I am a slave for life!* Have not I as good a right to be free as you have?" These words used to trouble them; they would express for me the liveliest sympathy, and console me with the hope that something would occur by which I might be free.

5   I was now about twelve years old, and the thought of being *a slave for life* began to bear heavily upon my heart. Just about this time, I got hold of a book entitled "The Columbian Orator."[3] Every opportunity I got, I used to read this book. Among much of other interesting matter, I found in it a dialogue between a master and his slave. The slave was represented as having run away from his master three times. The dialogue represented the conversation which took place between them, when the slave was retaken the third time. In this dialogue, the whole argument in behalf of slavery was brought forward by the master, all of which was disposed of by the slave. The slave was made to say some very smart as well as impressive things in reply to his master—things which had the desired though unexpected effect; for the conversation resulted in the voluntary emancipation of the slave on the part of the master.

In the same book, I met with one of Sheridan's mighty speeches on and in behalf of Catholic emancipation.[4] These were choice documents to me. I read them over and over again with unabated interest. They gave tongue to interesting thoughts of my own soul, which had frequently flashed through my mind, and died away for want of utterance. The moral which I gained from the dialogue was the power of truth over the conscience of even a slaveholder. What I got from Sheridan was a bold denunciation of slavery, and a powerful vindication of human rights. The reading of these documents enabled me to utter my thoughts, and to meet the arguments brought forward to sustain slavery; but while they relieved me of one difficulty, they brought on another even more painful than the one of which I was relieved. The more I read, the more I was led to abhor and detest my enslavers. I could regard them in no other light than a band of successful robbers, who had left their homes, and gone to Africa, and stolen us from our homes, and in a strange land reduced us to slavery. I loathed them as being the meanest as well as the most wicked of men. As I read and contemplated the subject, behold! that very discontentment which Master Hugh had predicted would follow my learning to read had already come, to torment and sting my soul to unutterable anguish. As I writhed under it, I would at times feel that learning to read had been a curse rather than a blessing. It had given me a view of my wretched condition, without the remedy. It opened my eyes to the horrible pit, but to no ladder upon which to get out. In moments of agony, I envied my fellow-slaves for their stupidity. I have often wished myself a beast. I preferred the condition of the meanest reptile to my own. Any thing, no matter what, to get rid of thinking! It was this everlasting

---

3. Popular collection of poems, dialogues, plays, and speeches.
4. Richard Brinsley Sheridan (1751–1816), Irish dramatist and political leader. The speech, arguing for the abolition of laws denying Roman Catholics in Great Britain and Ireland civil and political liberties, was actually made by the Irish patriot Arthur O'Connor.

thinking of my condition that tormented me. There was no getting rid of it. It was pressed upon me by every object within sight or hearing, animate or inanimate. The silver trump of freedom had roused my soul to eternal wakefulness. Freedom now appeared, to disappear no more forever. It was heard in every sound, and seen in every thing. It was ever present to torment me with a sense of my wretched condition. I saw nothing without seeing it, I heard nothing without hearing it, and felt nothing without feeling it. It looked from every star, it smiled in every calm, breathed in every wind, and moved in every storm.

I often found myself regretting my own existence, and wishing myself dead; and but for the hope of being free, I have no doubt but that I should have killed myself, or done something for which I should have been killed. While in this state of mind, I was eager to hear any one speak of slavery. I was a ready listener. Every little while, I could hear something about the abolitionists. It was some time before I found what the word meant. It was always used in such connections as to make it an interesting word to me. If a slave ran away and succeeded in getting clear, or if a slave killed his master, set fire to a barn, or did any thing very wrong in the mind of a slaveholder, it was spoken of as the fruit of *abolition*. Hearing the word in this connection very often, I set about learning what it meant. The dictionary afforded me little or no help. I found it was "the act of abolishing"; but then I did not know what was to be abolished. Here I was perplexed. I did not dare to ask any one about its meaning, for I was satisfied that it was something they wanted me to know very little about. After a patient waiting, I got one of our city papers, containing an account of the number of petitions from the north, praying for the abolition of slavery in the District of Columbia, and of the slave trade between the States. From this time I understood the words *abolition* and *abolitionist*, and always drew near when that word was spoken, expecting to hear something of importance to myself and fellow-slaves. The light broke in upon me by degrees. I went one day down on the wharf of Mr. Waters; and seeing two Irishmen unloading a scow of stone, I went, unasked, and helped them. When we had finished, one of them came to me and asked me if I were a slave. I told him I was. He asked, "Are ye a slave for life?" I told him that I was. The good Irishman seemed to be deeply affected by the statement. He said to the other that it was a pity so fine a little fellow as myself should be a slave for life. He said it was a shame to hold me. They both advised me to run away to the north; that I should find friends there, and that I should be free. I pretended not to be interested in what they said, and treated them as if I did not understand them; for I feared they might be treacherous. White men have been known to encourage slaves to escape, and then, to get the reward, catch them and return them to their masters. I was afraid that these seemingly good men might use me so; but I nevertheless remembered their advice, and from that time I resolved to run away. I looked forward to a time at which it would be safe for me to escape. I was too young to think of doing so immediately; besides, I wished to learn how to write, as I might have occasion to write my own pass. I consoled myself with the hope that I should one day find a good chance. Meanwhile, I would learn to write.

The idea as to how I might learn to write was suggested to me by being in Durgin and Bailey's ship-yard, and frequently seeing the ship carpenters, after hewing, and getting a piece of timber ready for use, write on the timber the name of that part of the ship for which it was intended. When a piece of timber was intended for the larboard side, it would be marked thus—"L." When a piece was for the starboard side, it would be marked thus—"S." A piece for the larboard side forward, would be marked thus—"L. F." When a piece was for starboard side forward, it would be marked thus—"S. F." For larboard aft, it would be marked thus—"L. A." For starboard aft, it would be marked thus—"S. A." I soon learned the names of these letters, and for what they were intended when placed upon a piece of timber in the shipyard. I immediately commenced copying them, and in a short time was able to make the four letters named. After that, when I met with any boy who I knew could write, I would tell him I could write as well as he. The next word would be, "I don't believe you. Let me see you try it." I would then make the letters which I had been so fortunate as to learn, and ask him to beat that. In this way I got a good many lessons in writing, which it is quite possible I should never have gotten in any other way. During this time, my copy-book was the board fence, brick wall, and pavement; my pen and ink was a lump of chalk. With these, I learned mainly how to write. I then commenced and continued copying the Italics in Webster's Spelling Book,[5] until I could make them all without looking on the book. By this time, my little Master Thomas had gone to school, and learned how to write, and had written over a number of copy-books. These had been brought home, and shown to some of our near neighbors, and then laid aside. My mistress used to go to class meeting at the Wilk Street meetinghouse every Monday afternoon, and leave me to take care of the house. When left thus, I used to spend the time in writing in the spaces left in Master Thomas's copy-book, copying what he had written. I continued to do this until I could write a hand very similar to that of Master Thomas. Thus, after a long, tedious effort for years, I finally succeeded in learning how to write.

MLA CITATION

Douglass, Frederick. "Learning to Read." *The Norton Reader: An Anthology of Nonfiction,* edited by Melissa A. Goldthwaite et al., 15th ed., W. W. Norton, 2020, pp. 346–50.

QUESTIONS

1. Frederick Douglass's story might today be called a "literacy narrative"—an account of how someone learns to read and write. What are the key features of this narrative? What obstacles did Douglass face? How did he overcome them?

2. Many literacy narratives include an enabling figure, someone who helps the young learner along his or her way. Is there such a figure in Douglass's narrative? Why or why not?

5. *The American Spelling Book* (1783) by Noah Webster, American lexicographer.

3. At the end of this narrative, Douglass mentions that he wrote "in the spaces left in Master Thomas's copy-book, copying what he had written" (paragraph 8). To what extent is imitation (copying) part of learning? To what extent does this narrative show originality?

4. Write your own literacy narrative—an account of how you learned to read and write.

TARA WESTOVER
from *Educated*

AMERICAN HISTORY was held in an auditorium named for the prophet Joseph Smith.[1] I'd thought American history would be easy because Dad had taught us about the Founding Fathers—I knew all about Washington, Jefferson, Madison. But the professor barely mentioned them at all, and instead talked about "philosophical underpinnings" and the writings of Cicero and Hume,[2] names I'd never heard.

In the first lecture, we were told that the next class would begin with a quiz on the readings. For two days I tried to wrestle meaning from the textbook's dense passages, but terms like "civic humanism" and "the Scottish Enlightenment" dotted the page like black holes, sucking all the other words into them. I took the quiz and missed every question.

That failure sat uneasily in my mind. It was the first indication of whether I would be okay, whether whatever I had in my head by way of *education* was enough. After the quiz, the answer seemed clear: it was not enough. On realizing this, I might have resented my upbringing but I didn't. My loyalty to my father had increased in proportion to the miles between us. On the mountain, I could rebel. But here, in this loud, bright place, surrounded by gentiles disguised as saints, I clung to every truth, every doctrine he had given me. Doctors were Sons of Perdition. Homeschooling was a commandment from the Lord.

Failing a quiz did nothing to undermine my new devotion to an old creed, but a lecture on Western art did.

The classroom was bright when I arrived, the morning sun pouring in   5
warmly through a high wall of windows. I chose a seat next to a girl in a high-

Excerpted from Educated *(2018), Tara Westover's memoir about growing up in a Mormon survivalist family, having her first classroom experience when she enrolled at Brigham Young University at the age of 17, and going on to earn a Ph.D. from Cambridge University.*

1. Founder of Mormonism (1805–1844).
2. Marcus Tullius Cicero (106–43 B.C.E.), Roman orator, philosopher, politician, and lawyer; David Hume (1711–1776), Scottish Enlightenment philosopher and historian, author of *A Treatise of Human Nature*.

necked blouse. Her name was Vanessa. "We should stick together," she said. "I think we're the only freshmen in the whole class."

The lecture began when an old man with small eyes and a sharp nose shuttered the windows. He flipped a switch and a slide projector filled the room with white light. The image was of a painting. The professor discussed the composition, the brushstrokes, the history. Then he moved to the next painting, and the next and the next.

Then the projector showed a peculiar image, of a man in a faded hat and overcoat. Behind him loomed a concrete wall. He held a small paper near his face but he wasn't looking at it. He was looking at us.

I opened the picture book I'd purchased for the class so I could take a closer look. Something was written under the image in italics but I couldn't understand it. It had one of those black-hole words, right in the middle, devouring the rest. I'd seen other students ask questions, so I raised my hand.

The professor called on me, and I read the sentence aloud. When I came to the word, I paused. "I don't know this word," I said. "What does it mean?"

10   There was silence. Not a hush, not a muting of the noise, but utter, almost violent silence. No papers shuffled, no pencils scratched.

The professor's lips tightened. "Thanks for *that*," he said, then returned to his notes.

I scarcely moved for the rest of the lecture. I stared at my shoes, wondering what had happened, and why, whenever I looked up, there was always someone staring at me as if I was a freak. Of course I *was* a freak, and I knew it, but I didn't understand how *they* knew it.

When the bell rang, Vanessa shoved her notebook into her pack. Then she paused and said, "You shouldn't make fun of that. It's not a joke." She walked away before I could reply.

I stayed in my seat until everyone had gone, pretending the zipper on my coat was stuck so I could avoid looking anyone in the eye. Then I went straight to the computer lab to look up the word "Holocaust."

15   I don't know how long I sat there reading about it, but at some point I'd read enough. I leaned back and stared at the ceiling. I suppose I was in shock, but whether it was the shock of learning about something horrific, or the shock of learning about my own ignorance, I'm not sure. I do remember imagining for a moment, not the camps, not the pits or chambers of gas, but my mother's face. A wave of emotion took me, a feeling so intense, so unfamiliar, I wasn't sure what it was. It made me want to shout at her, at my own mother, and that frightened me.

I searched my memories. In some ways the word "Holocaust" wasn't wholly unfamiliar. Perhaps Mother *had* taught me about it, when we were picking rosehips or tincturing hawthorn. I did seem to have a vague knowledge that Jews had been killed somewhere, long ago. But I'd thought it was a small conflict, like the Boston Massacre, which Dad talked about a lot, in which half a dozen people had been martyred by a tyrannical government. To have misunderstood it on this scale—five versus six million—seemed impossible.

I found Vanessa before the next lecture and apologized for the joke. I didn't explain, because I couldn't explain. I just said I was sorry and that I wouldn't do it again. To keep that promise, I didn't raise my hand for the rest of the semester.

MLA CITATION

Westover, Tara. "From *Educated*." *The Norton Reader: An Anthology of Nonfiction*, edited by Melissa A. Goldthwaite et al., 15th ed., W. W. Norton, 2020, pp. 351–53.

QUESTIONS

1. Tara Westover recounts an experience that revealed her lack of knowledge about history. How did her professor respond to her question about the Holocaust? What other ways might he have responded?

2. Westover describes reading terms that seem like "black holes, sucking all the other words into them" (paragraph 2). Have there been any "black hole" words for you in reading for your classes? What do you do when you encounter a word or term you don't understand?

3. Most people have had the experience of being confused or realizing they don't know something that others seem to know or understand. Write about an experience you or someone you know has had in recognizing the limits of personal knowledge.

WILLIAM ZINSSER
College Pressures

> Dear Carlos: I desperately need a dean's excuse for my chem midterm which will begin in about 1 hour. All I can say is that I totally blew it this week. I've fallen incredibly, inconceivably behind.

> Carlos: Help! I'm anxious to hear from you. I'll be in my room and won't leave it until I hear from you. Tomorrow is the last day for . . .

> Carlos: I left town because I started bugging out again. I stayed up all night to finish a take-home make-up exam & am typing it to hand in on the 10th. It was due on the 5th. P.S. I'm going to the dentist. Pain is pretty bad.

> Carlos: Probably by Friday I'll be able to get back to my studies. Right now I'm going to take a long walk. This whole thing has taken a lot out of me.

> Carlos: I'm really up the proverbial creek. The problem is I really *bombed* the history final. Since I need that course for my major I . . .

Written when William Zinsser was head of a residential college at Yale University and published in a small-circulation bimonthly magazine about rural life, Blair and Ketchum's Country Journal *(1979), which has since ceased publication.*

Carlos: Here follows a tale of woe. I went home this weekend, had to help my Mom, & caught a fever so didn't have much time to study. My professor . . .

Carlos: Aargh! Trouble. Nothing original but everything's piling up at once. To be brief, my job interview . . .

Hey Carlos, good news! I've got mononucleosis.

Who are these wretched supplicants, scribbling notes so laden with anxiety, seeking such miracles of postponement and balm? They are men and women who belong to Branford College, one of the twelve residential colleges at Yale University, and the messages are just a few of the hundreds that they left for their dean, Carlos Hortas—often slipped under his door at 4 A.M.— last year.

But students like the ones who wrote those notes can also be found on campuses from coast to coast—especially in New England and at many other private colleges across the country that have high academic standards and highly motivated students. Nobody could doubt that the notes are real. In their urgency and their gallows humor they are authentic voices of a generation that is panicky to succeed.

My own connection with the message writers is that I am master of Branford College. I live in its Gothic quadrangle and know the students well. (We have 485 of them.) I am privy to their hopes and fears—and also to their stereo music and their piercing cries in the dead of night ("Does anybody ca-a-are?"). If they went to Carlos to ask how to get through tomorrow, they come to me to ask how to get through the rest of their lives.

Mainly I try to remind them that the road ahead is a long one and that it will have more unexpected turns than they think. There will be plenty of time to change jobs, change careers, change whole attitudes and approaches. They don't want to hear such liberating news. They want a map—right now—that they can follow unswervingly to career security, financial security, Social Security and, presumably, a prepaid grave.

5   What I wish for all students is some release from the clammy grip of the future. I wish them a chance to savor each segment of their education as an experience in itself and not as a grim preparation for the next step. I wish them the right to experiment, to trip and fall, to learn that defeat is as instructive as victory and is not the end of the world.

My wish, of course, is naive. One of the few rights that America does not proclaim is the right to fail. Achievement is the national god, venerated in our media—the million-dollar athlete, the wealthy executive—and glorified in our praise of possessions. In the presence of such a potent state religion, the young are growing up old.

I see four kinds of pressure working on college students today: economic pressure, parental pressure, peer pressure, and self-induced pressure. It is easy to look around for villains—to blame the colleges for charging too much money, the professors for assigning too much work, the parents for pushing their children too far, the students for driving themselves too hard. But there are no villains; only victims.

"In the late 1960s," one dean told me, "the typical question that I got from students was 'Why is there so much suffering in the world?' or 'How can I make a contribution?' Today it's 'Do you think it would look better for getting into law school if I did a double major in history and political science, or just majored in one of them?'" Many other deans confirmed this pattern. One said: "They're trying to find an edge—the intangible something that will look better on paper if two students are about equal."

Note the emphasis on looking better. The transcript has become a sacred document, the passport to security. How one appears on paper is more important than how one appears in person. A is for Admirable and B is for Borderline, even though, in Yale's official system of grading, A means "excellent" and B means "very good." Today, looking very good is no longer good enough, especially for students who hope to go on to law school or medical school. They know that entrance into the better schools will be an entrance into the better law firms and better medical practices where they will make a lot of money. They also know that the odds are harsh. Yale Law School, for instance, matriculates 170 students from an applicant pool of 3,700; Harvard enrolls 550 from a pool of 7,000.

It's all very well for those of us who write letters of recommendation for   10
our students to stress the qualities of humanity that will make them good lawyers or doctors. And it's nice to think that admission officers are really reading our letters and looking for the extra dimension of commitment or concern. Still, it would be hard for a student not to visualize these officers shuffling so many transcripts studded with As that they regard a B as positively shameful.

The pressure is almost as heavy on students who just want to graduate and get a job. Long gone are the days of the "gentleman's C," when students journeyed through college with a certain relaxation, sampling a wide variety of courses—music, art, philosophy, classics, anthropology, poetry, religion—that would send them out as liberally educated men and women. If I were an employer I would rather employ graduates who have this range and curiosity than those who narrowly pursued safe subjects and high grades. I know countless students whose inquiring minds exhilarate me. I like to hear the play of their ideas. I don't know if they are getting As or Cs, and I don't care. I also like them as people. The country needs them, and they will find satisfying jobs. I tell them to relax. They can't.

Nor can I blame them. They live in a brutal economy. Tuition, room, and board at most private colleges now comes to at least $7,000, not counting books and fees. This might seem to suggest that the colleges are getting rich. But they are equally battered by inflation. Tuition covers only 60 percent of what it costs to educate a student, and ordinarily the remainder comes from what colleges receive in endowments, grants, and gifts. Now the remainder keeps being swallowed by the cruel costs—higher every year—of just opening the doors. Heating oil is up. Insurance is up. Postage is up. Health-premium costs are up.

Everything is up. Deficits are up. We are witnessing in America the creation of a brotherhood of paupers—colleges, parents, and students, joined by the common bond of debt.

Today it is not unusual for a student, even if he works part time at college and full time during the summer, to accrue $5,000 in loans after four years—loans that he must start to repay within one year after graduation. Exhorted at commencement to go forth into the world, he is already behind as he goes forth. How could he not feel under pressure throughout college to prepare for this day of reckoning? I have used "he," incidentally, only for brevity. Women at Yale are under no less pressure to justify their expensive education to themselves, their parents, and society. In fact, they are probably under more pressure. For although they leave college superbly equipped to bring fresh leadership to traditionally male jobs, society hasn't yet caught up with this fact.

Along with economic pressure goes parental pressure. Inevitably, the two are deeply intertwined.

15   I see many students taking pre-medical courses with joyless tenacity. They go off to their labs as if they were going to the dentist. It saddens me because I know them in other corners of their life as cheerful people.

"Do you want to go to medical school?" I ask them.

"I guess so," they say, without conviction, or "Not really."

"Then why are you going?"

"Well, my parents want me to be a doctor. They're paying all this money and . . ."

20   Poor students, poor parents. They are caught in one of the oldest webs of love and duty and guilt. The parents mean well; they are trying to steer their sons and daughters toward a secure future. But the sons and daughters want to major in history or classics or philosophy—subjects with no "practical" value. Where's the payoff on the humanities? It's not easy to persuade such loving parents that the humanities do indeed pay off. The intellectual faculties developed by studying subjects like history and classics—an ability to synthesize and relate, to weigh cause and effect, to see events in perspective—are just the faculties that make creative leaders in business or almost any general field. Still, many fathers would rather put their money on courses that point toward a specific profession—courses that are pre-law, pre-medical, pre-business, or, as I sometimes heard it put, "pre-rich."

But the pressure on students is severe. They are truly torn. One part of them feels obligated to fulfill their parents' expectations; after all, their parents are older and presumably wiser. Another part tells them that the expectations that are right for their parents are not right for them.

I know a student who wants to be an artist. She is very obviously an artist and will be a good one—she has already had several modest local exhibits. Meanwhile she is growing as a well-rounded person and taking humanistic subjects that will enrich the inner resources out of which her art will grow. But her father is strongly opposed. He thinks that an artist is a "dumb" thing to be. The student vacillates and tries to please everybody. She keeps up with her art somewhat furtively and takes some of the "dumb" courses her father wants her to take—at least they are dumb courses for her. She is a free spirit on a campus of tense students—no small achievement in itself—and she deserves to follow her muse.

Peer pressure and self-induced pressure are also intertwined, and they begin almost at the beginning of freshman year.

"I had a freshman student I'll call Linda," one dean told me, "who came in and said she was under terrible pressure because her roommate, Barbara, was much brighter and studied all the time. I couldn't tell her that Barbara had come in two hours earlier to say the same thing about Linda."

The story is almost funny—except that it's not. It's symptomatic of all the   25
pressures put together. When every student thinks every other student is working harder and doing better, the only solution is to study harder still. I see students going off to the library every night after dinner and coming back when it closes at midnight. I wish they would sometimes forget about their peers and go to a movie. I hear the clacking of typewriters in the hours before dawn. I see the tension in their eyes when exams are approaching and papers are due: *"Will I get everything done?"*

Probably they won't. They will get sick. They will get "blocked." They will sleep. They will oversleep. They will bug out. *Hey Carlos, help!*

Part of the problem is that they do more than they are expected to do. A professor will assign five-page papers. Several students will start writing ten-page papers to impress him. Then more students will write ten-page papers, and a few will raise the ante to fifteen. Pity the poor student who is still just doing the assignment.

"Once you have twenty or thirty percent of the student population deliberately overexerting," one dean points out, "it's bad for everybody. When a teacher gets more and more effort from his class, the student who is doing normal work can be perceived as not doing well. The tactic works, psychologically."

Why can't the professor just cut back and not accept longer papers? He can, and he probably will. But by then the term will be half over and the damage done. Grade fever is highly contagious and not easily reversed. Besides, the professor's main concern is with his course. He knows his students only in relation to the course and doesn't know that they are also overexerting in their other courses. Nor is it really his business. He didn't sign up for dealing with the student as a whole person and with all the emotional baggage the student brought along from home. That's what deans, masters, chaplains, and psychiatrists are for.

To some extent this is nothing new: a certain number of professors have   30
always been self-contained islands of scholarship and shyness, more comfortable with books than with people. But the new pauperism has widened the gap still further, for professors who actually like to spend time with students don't have as much time to spend. They also are overexerting. If they are young, they are busy trying to publish in order not to perish, hanging by their finger nails onto a shrinking profession. If they are old and tenured, they are buried under the duties of administering departments—as departmental chairmen or members of committees—that have been thinned out by the budgetary axe.

Ultimately it will be the students' own business to break the circles in which they are trapped. They are too young to be prisoners of their parents' dreams and their classmates' fears. They must be jolted into believing in themselves as unique men and women who have the power to shape their own future.

"Violence is being done to the undergraduate experience," says Carlos Hortas. "College should be open-ended: at the end it should open many, many roads. Instead, students are choosing their goal in advance, and their choices narrow as they go along. It's almost as if they think that the country has been codified in the type of jobs that exist—that they've got to fit into certain slots. Therefore, fit into the best-paying slot.

"They ought to take chances. Not taking chances will lead to a life of colorless mediocrity. They'll be comfortable. But something in the spirit will be missing."

I have painted too drab a portrait of today's students, making them seem a solemn lot. That is only half of their story; if they were so dreary I wouldn't so thoroughly enjoy their company. The other half is that they are easy to like. They are quick to laugh and to offer friendship. They are not introverts. They are unusually kind and are more considerate of one another than any student generation I have known.

35   Nor are they so obsessed with their studies that they avoid sports and extracurricular activities. On the contrary, they juggle their crowded hours to play on a variety of teams, perform with musical and dramatic groups, and write for campus publications. But this in turn is one more cause of anxiety. There are too many choices. Academically, they have 1,300 courses to select from; outside class they have to decide how much spare time they can spare and how to spend it.

This means that they engage in fewer extracurricular pursuits than their predecessors did. If they want to row on the crew and play in the symphony they will eliminate one; in the '60s they would have done both. They also tend to choose activities that are self-limiting. Drama, for instance, is flourishing in all twelve of Yale's residential colleges as it never has before. Students hurl themselves into these productions—as actors, directors, carpenters, and technicians—with a dedication to create the best possible play, knowing that the day will come when the run will end and they can get back to their studies.

They also can't afford to be the willing slave of organizations like the *Yale Daily News*. Last spring at the one-hundredth anniversary banquet of that paper—whose past chairmen include such once and future kings as Potter Stewart, Kingman Brewster, and William F. Buckley, Jr.—much was made of the fact that the editorial staff used to be small and totally committed and that "newsies" routinely worked fifty hours a week. In effect they belonged to a club; Newsies is how they defined themselves at Yale. Today's student will write one or two articles a week, when he can, and he defines himself as a student. I've never heard the word Newsie except at the banquet.

If I have described the modern undergraduate primarily as a driven creature who is largely ignoring the blithe spirit inside who keeps trying to come out and play, it's because that's where the crunch is, not only at Yale but through-out American education. It's why I think we should all be worried about the values that are nurturing a generation so fearful of risk and so goal-obsessed at such an early age.

I tell students that there is no one "right" way to get ahead—that each of them is a different person, starting from a different point and bound for a different destination. I tell them that change is a tonic and that all the slots are not codified nor the frontiers closed. One of my ways of telling them is to invite men and women who have achieved success outside the academic world to come and talk informally with my students during the year. They are heads of compa-nies or ad agencies, editors of magazines, politicians, public officials, television magnates, labor leaders, business executives, Broadway producers, artists, writ-ers, economists, photographers, scientists, historians—a mixed bag of achievers.

I ask them to say a few words about how they got started. The students   40
assume that they started in their present profession and knew all along that it was what they wanted to do. Luckily for me, most of them got into their field by a circuitous route, to their surprise, after many detours. The students are startled. They can hardly conceive of a career that was not pre-planned. They can hardly imagine allowing the hand of God or chance to nudge them down some unforeseen trail.

MLA CITATION

Zinsser, William. "College Pressures." *The Norton Reader: An Anthology of Nonfiction*, edited by Melissa A. Goldthwaite et al., 15th ed., W. W. Norton, 2020, pp. 353–59.

QUESTIONS

1. What are the four kinds of pressure William Zinsser describes for the 1970s? Are they the same kinds of pressure that trouble students today, or have new ones taken their place?

2. Compare Zinsser's description of college with Tara Westover's account of her experience (pp. 351–53). What pressure might Westover add to Zinsser's list?

3. Write an essay in which you explain how you have experienced and handled the pressures of college.

GERALD GRAFF
Hidden Intellectualism

EVERYONE KNOWS SOME YOUNG PERSON who is impressively "street smart" but does poorly in school. What a waste, we think, that one who is so intelligent about so many things in life seems unable to apply that intelligence to academic work. What doesn't occur to us, though, is that schools and colleges might be at fault for missing the opportunity to tap into such street smarts and channel them into good academic work.

Nor do we consider one of the major reasons why schools and colleges overlook the intellectual potential of street smarts: the fact that we associate those street smarts with anti-intellectual concerns. We associate the educated life, the life of the mind, too narrowly and exclusively with subjects and texts that we consider inherently weighty and academic. We assume that it's possible to wax intellectual about Plato, Shakespeare, the French Revolution, and nuclear fission, but not about cars, dating, fashion, sports, TV, or video games.

The trouble with this assumption is that no necessary connection has ever been established between any text or subject and the educational depth and weight of the discussion it can generate. Real intellectuals turn any subject, however lightweight it may seem, into grist for their mill through the thoughtful questions they bring to it, whereas a dullard will find a way to drain the interest out of the richest subject. That's why a George Orwell[1] writing on the cultural meanings of penny postcards is infinitely more substantial than the cogitations of many professors on Shakespeare or globalization.

Students do need to read models of intellectually challenging writing—and Orwell is a great one—if they are to become intellectuals themselves. But they would be more prone to take on intellectual identities if we encouraged them to do so at first on subjects that interest them rather than ones that interest us.

5   I offer my own adolescent experience as a case in point. Until I entered college, I hated books and cared only for sports. The only reading I cared to do or could do was sports magazines, on which I became hooked, becoming a regular reader of *Sport* magazine in the late forties, *Sports Illustrated* when it began publishing in 1954, and the annual magazine guides to professional baseball, football, and basketball. I also loved the sports novels for boys of John R. Tunis and Clair Bee and autobiographies of sports stars like Joe DiMaggio's *Lucky to Be a Yankee* and Bob Feller's *Strikeout Story*. In short, I was your typical teenage

This essay is adapted from Gerald Graff's book Clueless in Academe: How Schooling Obscures the Life of the Mind *(2003).*

1. Pen name of Eric Blair (1903–1950), English writer and public intellectual. See p. 415 and p. 728 for his essays.

anti-intellectual—or so I believed for a long time. I have recently come to think, however, that my preference for sports over schoolwork was not anti-intellectualism so much as intellectualism by other means.

In the Chicago neighborhood I grew up in, which had become a melting pot after World War II, our block was solidly middle class, but just a block away—doubtless concentrated there by the real estate companies—were African Americans, Native Americans, and "hillbilly" whites who had recently fled postwar joblessness in the South and Appalachia. Negotiating this class boundary was a tricky matter. On the one hand, it was necessary to maintain the boundary between "clean-cut" boys like me and working-class "hoods," as we called them, which meant that it was good to be openly smart in a bookish sort of way. On the other hand, I was desperate for the approval of the hoods, whom I encountered daily on the playing field and in the neighborhood, and for this purpose it was not at all good to be book-smart. The hoods would turn on you if they sensed you were putting on airs over them: "Who you lookin' at, smart ass?" as a leather-jacketed youth once said to me as he relieved me of my pocket change along with my self-respect.

I grew up torn, then, between the need to prove I was smart and the fear of a beating if I proved it too well; between the need not to jeopardize my respectable future and the need to impress the hoods. As I lived it, the conflict came down to a choice between being physically tough and being verbal. For a boy in my neighborhood and elementary school, only being "tough" earned you complete legitimacy. I still recall endless, complicated debates in this period with my closest pals over who was "the toughest guy in the school." If you were less than negligible as a fighter, as I was, you settled for the next best thing, which was to be inarticulate, carefully hiding telltale marks of literacy like correct grammar and pronunciation.

In one way, then, it would be hard to imagine an adolescence more thoroughly anti-intellectual than mine. Yet in retrospect, I see that it's more complicated, that I and the 1950s themselves were not simply hostile toward intellectualism, but divided and ambivalent. When Marilyn Monroe[2] married the playwright Arthur Miller in 1956 after divorcing the retired baseball star Joe DiMaggio, the symbolic triumph of geek over jock suggested the way the wind was blowing. Even Elvis, according to his biographer Peter Guralnick, turns out to have supported Adlai over Ike in the presidential election of 1956.[3] "I don't dig the intellectual bit," he told reporters. "But I'm telling you, man, he knows the most."

Though I too thought I did not "dig the intellectual bit," I see now that I was unwittingly in training for it. The germs had actually been planted in the seemingly philistine debates about which boys were the toughest. I see now that in the interminable analysis of sports teams, movies, and toughness that my friends and

2. American movie star and celebrity (1926–1962).

3. Elvis Presley (1935–1977), American rock-and-roll star and movie actor; Republican Dwight D. "Ike" Eisenhower defeated Adlai Stevenson in 1952 to become the thirty-fourth president of the United States (1953–1961).

I engaged in—a type of analysis, needless to say, that the real toughs would never have stooped to—I was already betraying an allegiance to the egghead world. I was practicing being an intellectual before I knew that was what I wanted to be.

10   It was in these discussions with friends about toughness and sports, I think, and in my reading of sports books and magazines, that I began to learn the rudiments of the intellectual life: how to make an argument, weigh different kinds of evidence, move between particulars and generalizations, summarize the views of others, and enter a conversation about ideas. It was in reading and arguing about sports and toughness that I experienced what it felt like to propose a generalization, restate and respond to a counterargument, and perform other intellectualizing operations, including composing the kind of sentences I am writing now.

Only much later did it dawn on me that the sports world was more compelling than school because it was *more intellectual than school*, not less. Sports after all was full of challenging arguments, debates, problems for analysis, and intricate statistics that you could care about, as school conspicuously was not. I believe that street smarts beat out book smarts in our culture not because street smarts are nonintellectual, as we generally suppose, but because they satisfy an intellectual thirst more thoroughly than school culture, which seems pale and unreal.

They also satisfy the thirst for community. When you entered sports debates, you became part of a community that was not limited to your family and friends, but was national and public. Whereas schoolwork isolated you from others, the pennant race or Ted Williams's .400 batting average was something you could talk about with people you had never met. Sports introduced you not only to a culture steeped in argument, but to a public argument culture that transcended the personal. I can't blame my schools for failing to make intellectual culture resemble the Super Bowl, but I do fault them for failing to learn anything from the sports and entertainment worlds about how to organize and represent intellectual culture, how to exploit its gamelike element and turn it into arresting public spectacle that might have competed more successfully for my youthful attention.

For here is another thing that never dawned on me and is still kept hidden from students, with tragic results: that the real intellectual world, the one that existed in the big world beyond school, is organized very much like the world of team sports, with rival texts, rival interpretations and evaluations of texts, rival theories of why they should be read and taught, and elaborate team competitions in which "fans" of writers, intellectual systems, methodologies, and -isms contend against each other.

To be sure, school contained plenty of competition, which became more invidious as one moved up the ladder (and has become even more so today with the advent of high-stakes testing). In this competition, points were scored not by making arguments, but by a show of information or vast reading, by gradegrubbing, or other forms of one-upmanship. School competition, in short, reproduced the less attractive features of sports culture without those that create close bonds and community.

15   And in distancing themselves from anything as enjoyable and absorbing as sports, my schools missed the opportunity to capitalize on an element of drama

and conflict that the intellectual world shares with sports. Consequently, I failed to see the parallels between the sports and academic worlds that could have helped me cross more readily from one argument culture to the other.

Sports is only one of the domains whose potential for literacy training (and not only for males) is seriously underestimated by educators, who see sports as competing with academic development rather than a route to it. But if this argument suggests why it is a good idea to assign readings and topics that are close to students' existing interests, it also suggests the limits of this tactic. For students who get excited about the chance to write about their passion for cars will often write as poorly and unreflectively on that topic as on Shakespeare or Plato. Here is the flip side of what I pointed out before: that there's no necessary relation between the degree of interest a student shows in a text or subject and the quality of thought or expression such a student manifests in writing or talking about it. The challenge, as college professor Ned Laff has put it, "is not simply to exploit students' nonacademic interests, but to get them to see those interests through academic eyes."

To say that students need to see their interests "through academic eyes" is to say that street smarts are not enough. Making students' nonacademic interests an object of academic study is useful, then, for getting students' attention and overcoming their boredom and alienation, but this tactic won't in itself necessarily move them closer to an academically rigorous treatment of those interests. On the other hand, inviting students to write about cars, sports, or clothing fashions does not have to be a pedagogical cop-out as long as students are required to see these interests "through academic eyes," that is, to think and write about cars, sports, and fashions in a reflective, analytical way, one that sees them as microcosms of what is going on in the wider culture.

If I am right, then schools and colleges are missing an opportunity when they do not encourage students to take their nonacademic interests as objects of academic study. It is self-defeating to decline to introduce any text or subject that figures to engage students who will otherwise tune out academic work entirely. If a student cannot get interested in Mill's *On Liberty*[4] but will read *Sports Illustrated* or *Vogue* or the hip-hop magazine *Source* with absorption, this is a strong argument for assigning the magazines over the classic. It's a good bet that if students get hooked on reading and writing by doing term papers on *Source*, they will eventually get to *On Liberty*. But even if they don't, the magazine reading will make them more literate and reflective than they would be otherwise. So it makes pedagogical sense to develop classroom units on sports, cars, fashions, rap music, and other such topics. Give me the student anytime who writes a sharply argued, sociologically acute analysis of an issue in *Source* over the student who writes a lifeless explication of *Hamlet* or Socrates' *Apology*.[5]

4. John Stuart Mill (1806–1873), British political economist and philosopher.

5. *Hamlet* (1603), a tragedy by William Shakespeare; Socrates (c. 469–399 B.C.E.), ancient Greek philosopher; the *Apology* was written by his student Plato.

WORKS CITED

Cramer, Richard Ben. *Joe DiMaggio: The Hero's Life*. Simon & Schuster, 2000.

DiMaggio, Joe. *Lucky to Be a Yankee*. Bantam, 1949.

Feller, Bob. *Bob Feller's Strikeout Story*. Bantam, 1948.

Guralnick, Peter. *Last Train to Memphis: The Rise of Elvis Presley*. Little, Brown, 1994.

Orwell, George. *A Collection of Essays*. Harcourt, 1953.

MLA CITATION

Graff, Gerald. "Hidden Intellectualism." *The Norton Reader: An Anthology of Nonfiction*, edited by Melissa A. Goldthwaite et al., 15th ed., W. W. Norton, 2020, pp. 360–63.

QUESTIONS

1. Gerald Graff observes that through sports, he "experienced what it felt like to propose a generalization, restate and respond to a counterargument, and perform other intellectualizing operations" (paragraph 10). Where and how does Graff offer generalizations in this essay? Where and how does he restate and respond to the arguments of others or develop counterarguments? What other kinds of "intellectualizing operations" does he perform?

2. Graff and Roger Angell (pp. 282–90) both write about baseball. How are their perspectives similar? How are they different?

3. Frederick Douglass's "Learning to Read" (pp. 346–50) is also a literacy narrative: an account of how someone learned to read and write. Compare Graff's essay with this essay. Would you characterize Graff's essay as a literacy narrative? Why or why not?

4. In an essay of your own, summarize and respond to Graff's argument about intellectualism and what he calls "school culture" (paragraph 11). Consider writing about an activity or experience that fits the definition of what Graff might call "hidden intellectualism."

MIKE ROSE
Blue-Collar Brilliance

Y MOTHER, ROSE MERAGLIO ROSE (Rosie), shaped her adult identity as a waitress in coffee shops and family restaurants. When I was growing up in Los Angeles during the 1950s, my father and I would occasionally hang out at the restaurant until her shift ended, and then we'd ride the bus

Published in the American Scholar *(2009), the magazine of the Phi Beta Kappa society. In this essay, as in much of his other work, Mike Rose approaches his arguments about class, education, and literacy through his personal experience and family history.*

home with her. Sometimes she worked the register and the counter, and we sat there; when she waited booths and tables, we found a booth in the back where the waitresses took their breaks.

There wasn't much for a child to do at the restaurant, and so as the hours stretched out, I watched the cooks and waitresses and listened to what they said. At mealtimes, the pace of the kitchen staff and the din from customers picked up. Weaving in and out around the room, waitresses warned *behind you* in impassive but urgent voices. Standing at the service window facing the kitchen, they called out abbreviated orders. *Fry four on two,* my mother would say as she clipped a check onto the metal wheel. Her tables were *deuces, four-tops,* or *six-tops* according to their size; seating areas also were nicknamed. The *racetrack,* for instance, was the fast-turnover front section. Lingo conferred authority and signaled know-how.

Rosie took customers' orders, pencil poised over pad, while fielding questions about the food. She walked full tilt through the room with plates stretching up her left arm and two cups of coffee somehow cradled in her right hand. She stood at a table or booth and removed a plate for this person, another for that person, then another, remembering who had the hamburger, who had the fried shrimp, almost always getting it right. She would haggle with the cook about a returned order and rush by us, saying. *He gave me lip, but I got him.* She'd take a minute to flop down in the booth next to my father. *I'm all in,* she'd say, and whisper something about a customer. Gripping the outer edge of the table with one hand, she'd watch the room and note, in the flow of our conversation, who needed a refill, whose order was taking longer to prepare than it should, who was finishing up.

I couldn't have put it in words when I was growing up, but what I observed in my mother's restaurant defined the world of adults, a place where competence was synonymous with physical work. I've since studied the working habits of blue-collar workers and have come to understand how much my mother's kind of work demands of both body and brain. A waitress acquires knowledge and intuition about the ways and the rhythms of the restaurant business. Waiting on seven to nine tables, each with two to six customers, Rosie devised memory strategies so that she could remember who ordered what. And because she knew the average time it took to prepare different dishes, she could monitor an order that was taking too long at the service station.

Like anyone who is effective at physical work, my mother learned *to*   5
work smart, as she put it, *to make every move count.* She'd sequence and group tasks: What could she do first, then second, then third as she circled through her station? What tasks could be clustered? She did everything on the fly, and when problems arose—technical or human—she solved them within the flow of work, while taking into account the emotional state of her co-workers. Was the manager in a good mood? Did the cook wake up on the wrong side of the bed? If so, how could she make an extra request or effectively return an order?

And then, of course, there were the customers who entered the restaurant with all sorts of needs, from physiological ones, including the emotions

Rosie solved technical and human problems on the fly.

that accompany hunger, to a sometimes complicated desire for human contact. Her tip depended on how well she responded to these needs, and so she became adept at reading social cues and managing feelings, both the customers' and her own. No wonder, then, that Rosie was intrigued by psychology. The restaurant became the place where she studied human behavior, puzzling over the problems of her regular customers and refining her ability to deal with people in a difficult world. She took pride in *being among the public*, she'd say. *There isn't a day that goes by in the restaurant that you don't learn something.*

My mother quit school in the seventh grade to help raise her brothers and sisters. Some of those siblings made it through high school, and some dropped out to find work in railroad yards, factories, or restaurants. My father finished a grade or two in primary school in Italy and never darkened the schoolhouse door again. I didn't do well in school either. By high school I had accumulated a spotty academic record and many hours of hazy disaffection. I spent a few years on the vocational track, but in my senior year I was inspired by my English teacher and managed to squeak into a small college on probation.

My freshman year was academically bumpy, but gradually I began to see formal education as a means of fulfillment and as a road toward making a living. I studied the humanities and later the social and psychological sciences and taught for 10 years in a range of situations—elementary school, adult education courses, tutoring centers, a program for Vietnam veterans[1] who wanted to go to college. Those students had socioeconomic and educational backgrounds similar to mine. Then I went back to graduate school to study education and cognitive psychology[2] and eventually became a faculty member in a school of education.

Intelligence is closely associated with formal education—the type of schooling a person has, how much and how long—and most people seem to move comfortably from that notion to a belief that work requiring less schooling requires less intelligence. These assumptions run through our cultural history, from the post–Revolutionary War period, when mechanics were characterized by political rivals as illiterate and therefore incapable of participating in government, until today. More than once I've heard a manager label his workers as "a bunch of dummies." Generalizations about intelligence, work, and social class deeply affect our assumptions about ourselves and each other, guiding the ways we use our minds to learn, build knowledge, solve problems, and make our way through the world.

Although writers and scholars have often looked at the working class, they have generally focused on the values such workers exhibit rather than on the thought their work requires—a subtle but pervasive omission. Our cultural iconography promotes the muscled arm, sleeve rolled tight against biceps, but no brightness behind the eye, no image that links hand and brain.   10

One of my mother's brothers, Joe Meraglio, left school in the ninth grade to work for the Pennsylvania Railroad.[3] From there he joined the Navy, returned to the railroad, which was already in decline, and eventually joined his older brother at General Motors[4] where, over a 33-year career, he moved from working on the assembly line to supervising the paint-and-body department. When I was a young man, Joe took me on a tour of the factory. The floor was loud—in some places deafening—and when I turned a corner or opened a door, the smell of chemicals knocked my head back. The work was repetitive and taxing, and the pace was inhumane.

1. American veterans of a twenty-year (1954–75) conflict between South Vietnam, which was allied with the United States, and communist North Vietnam.
2. Branch of psychology concerned with such subjects as perception, memory, thinking, and learning.
3. Railroad (1846–1968) that extended from the mid-Atlantic region of the United States to the Midwest.
4. American company that for much of the twentieth century was the world's largest automaker.

Still, for Joe the shop floor provided what school did not; it was *like school-ing*, he said, a place where *you're constantly learning*. Joe learned the most effi-cient way to use his body by acquiring a set of routines that were quick and preserved energy. Otherwise he would never have survived on the line.

As a foreman, Joe constantly faced new problems and became a consum-mate multi-tasker, evaluating a flurry of demands quickly, parceling out physical and mental resources, keeping a number of ongoing events in his mind, returning to whatever task had been interrupted, and maintaining a cool head under the pressure of grueling production schedules. In the midst of all this, Joe learned more and more about the auto industry, the technological and social dynamics of the shop floor, the machinery and production processes, and the basics of paint chemistry and of plating and baking. With further promotions, he not only solved problems but also began to find problems to solve: Joe initi-ated the redesign of the nozzle on a paint sprayer, thereby eliminating costly and unhealthy overspray. And he found a way to reduce energy costs on the baking ovens without affecting the quality of the paint. He lacked formal knowl-edge of how the machines under his supervision worked, but he had direct experience with them, hands-on knowledge, and was savvy about their quirks and operational capabilities. He could experiment with them.

In addition, Joe learned about budgets and management. Coming off the line as he did, he had a perspective of workers' needs and management's demands, and this led him to think of ways to improve efficiency on the line while relieving some of the stress on the assemblers. He had each worker in a unit learn his or her co-workers' jobs so they could rotate across stations to relieve some of the monotony. He believed that rotation would allow assem-blers to get longer and more frequent breaks. It was an easy sell to the people on the line. The union, however, had to approve any modification in job duties, and the managers were wary of the change. Joe had to argue his case on a num-ber of fronts, providing him a kind of rhetorical education.

15   Eight years ago I began a study of the thought processes involved in work like that of my mother and uncle. I catalogued the cognitive demands of a range of blue-collar and service jobs, from waitressing and hair styling to plumbing and welding. To gain a sense of how knowledge and skill develop, I observed experts as well as novices. From the details of this close examination, I tried to fashion what I called "cognitive biographies" of blue-collar workers. Biographi-cal accounts of the lives of scientists, lawyers, entrepreneurs, and other pro-fessionals are rich with detail about the intellectual dimension of their work. But the life stories of working-class people are few and are typically accounts of hardship and courage or the achievements wrought by hard work.

Our culture—in Cartesian[5] fashion—separates the body from the mind, so that, for example, we assume that the use of a tool does not involve abstrac-tion. We reinforce this notion by defining intelligence solely on grades in school

5. Recalling the dualist philosophy of René Descartes (1596–1650), French scientist, mathematician, and philosopher.

With an eighth-grade education, Joe (hands together) advanced to
supervisor of a G.M. paint-and-body department.

and numbers on IQ tests.[6] And we employ social biases pertaining to a person's place on the occupational ladder. The distinctions among blue, pink, and
white collars carry with them attributions of character, motivation, and intelligence. Although we rightly acknowledge and amply compensate the play of mind
in white-collar and professional work, we diminish or erase it in considerations
about other endeavors—physical and service work particularly. We also often
ignore the experience of everyday work in administrative deliberations and
policymaking.

But here's what we find when we get in close. The plumber seeking leverage in order to work in tight quarters and the hair stylist adroitly handling scissors and comb manage their bodies strategically. Though work-related actions
become routine with experience, they were learned at some point through
observation, trial and error, and, often, physical or verbal assistance from a co-
worker or trainer. I've frequently observed novices talking to themselves as
they take on a task, or shaking their head or hand as if to erase an attempt
before trying again. In fact, our traditional notions of routine performance
could keep us from appreciating the many instances within routine where quick
decisions and adjustments are made. I'm struck by the thinking-in-motion that
some work requires, by all the mental activity that can be involved in simply

6. Tests that give a numerical measure of intelligence, the "Intelligence Quotient."

getting from one place to another: the waitress rushing back through her station to the kitchen or the foreman walking the line.

The use of tools requires the studied refinement of stance, grip, balance, and fine-motor skills. But manipulating tools is intimately tied to knowledge of what a particular instrument can do in a particular situation and do better than other similar tools. A worker must also know the characteristics of the material one is engaging—how it reacts to various cutting or compressing devices, to degrees of heat, or to lines of force. Some of these things demand judgment, the weighing of options, the consideration of multiple variables, and, occasionally, the creative use of a tool in an unexpected way.

In manipulating material, the worker becomes attuned to aspects of the environment, a training or disciplining of perception that both enhances knowledge and informs perception. Carpenters have an eye for length, line, and angle; mechanics troubleshoot by listening; hair stylists are attuned to shape, texture, and motion. Sensory data merge with concept, as when an auto mechanic relies on sound, vibration, and even smell to understand what cannot be observed.

20   Planning and problem solving have been studied since the earliest days of modern cognitive psychology and are considered core elements in Western definitions of intelligence. To work is to solve problems. The big difference between the psychologist's laboratory and the workplace is that in the former the problems are isolated and in the latter they are embedded in the real-time flow of work with all its messiness and social complexity.

Much of physical work is social and interactive. Movers determining how to get an electric range down a flight of stairs require coordination, negotiation, planning, and the establishing of incremental goals. Words, gestures, and sometimes a quick pencil sketch are involved, if only to get the rhythm right. How important it is, then, to consider the social and communicative dimension of physical work, for it provides the medium for so much of work's intelligence.

Given the ridicule heaped on blue-collar speech, it might seem odd to value its cognitive content. Yet, the flow of talk at work provides the channel for organizing and distributing tasks, for troubleshooting and problem solving, for learning new information and revising old. A significant amount of teaching, often informal and indirect, takes place at work. Joe Meraglio saw that much of his job as a supervisor involved instruction. In some service occupations, language and communication are central: observing and interpreting behavior and expression, inferring mood and motive, taking on the perspective of others, responding appropriately to social cues, and knowing when you're understood. A good hair stylist, for instance, has the ability to convert vague requests (*I want something light and summery*) into an appropriate cut through questions, pictures, and hand gestures.

Verbal and mathematical skills drive measures of intelligence in the Western Hemisphere, and many of the kinds of work I studied are thought to require relatively little proficiency in either. Compared to certain kinds of white-collar occupations, that's true. But written symbols flow through physical work.

Numbers are rife in most workplaces: on tools and gauges, as measurements, as indicators of pressure or concentration or temperature, as guides to
sequence, on ingredient labels, on lists and spreadsheets, as markers of quantity and price. Certain jobs require workers to make, check, and verify calculations, and to collect and interpret data. Basic math can be involved, and some
workers develop a good sense of numbers and patterns. Consider, as well, what
might be called material mathematics: mathematical functions embodied in
materials and actions, as when a carpenter builds a cabinet or a flight of stairs.
A simple mathematical act can extend quickly beyond itself. Measuring, for
example, can involve more than recording the dimensions of an object. As I
watched a cabinetmaker measure a long strip of wood, he read a number off the
tape out loud, looked back over his shoulder to the kitchen wall, turned back to
his task, took another measurement, and paused for a moment in thought. He
was solving a problem involving the molding, and the measurement was important
to his deliberation about structure and appearance.

In the blue-collar workplace, directions, plans, and reference books rely   25
on illustrations, some representational and others, like blueprints, that require
training to interpret. Esoteric symbols—visual jargon—depict switches and
receptacles, pipe fittings, or types of welds. Workers themselves often make
sketches on the job. I frequently observed them grab a pencil to sketch something on a scrap of paper or on a piece of the material they were installing.

Though many kinds of physical work don't require a high literacy level,
more reading occurs in the blue-collar workplace than is generally thought,
from manuals and catalogues to work orders and invoices, to lists, labels, and
forms. With routine tasks, for example, reading is integral to understanding
production quotas, learning how to use an instrument, or applying a product.
Written notes can initiate action, as in restaurant orders or reports of machine
malfunction, or they can serve as memory aids.

True, many uses of writing are abbreviated, routine, and repetitive, and
they infrequently require interpretation or analysis. But analytic moments can
be part of routine activities, and seemingly basic reading and writing can be
cognitively rich. Because workplace language is used in the flow of other activities, we can overlook the remarkable coordination of words, numbers, and
drawings required to initiate and direct action.

If we believe everyday work to be mindless, then that will affect the work we
create in the future. When we devalue the full range of everyday cognition, we
offer limited educational opportunities and fail to make fresh and meaningful
instructional connections among disparate kinds of skill and knowledge. If we
think that whole categories of people—identified by class or occupation—are
not that bright, then we reinforce social separations and cripple our ability to
talk across cultural divides.

Affirmation of diverse intelligence is not a retreat to a softhearted definition of the mind. To acknowledge a broader range of intellectual capacity is to
take seriously the concept of cognitive variability, to appreciate in all the Ros-
ies and Joes the thought that drives their accomplishments and defines who
they are. This is a model of the mind that is worthy of a democratic society.

MLA CITATION

Rose, Mike. "Blue-Collar Brilliance." *The Norton Reader: An Anthology of Nonfiction*, edited by Melissa A. Goldthwaite et al., 15th ed., W. W. Norton, 2020, pp. 364–71.

QUESTIONS

1. In his closing paragraph, Mike Rose asserts that the expanded understanding of intelligence for which he is arguing suggests "a model of the mind that is worthy of a democratic society." What are the social or political implications of this connection between mind and democracy?

2. Rose's essay was originally subtitled "Questioning Assumptions about Intelligence, Work, and Social Class." What assumptions is Rose questioning, either directly or indirectly?

3. Rose introduces his general argument with detailed accounts of the work-lives of two family members: his mother and his uncle. Why do you think he makes this choice?

4. Rose describes himself as writing "'cognitive biographies' of blue-collar workers" (paragraph 15). Drawing as Rose does on interviews and careful observation, write a cognitive biography of your own.

MAYA ANGELOU
Graduation

THE CHILDREN IN STAMPS[1] trembled visibly with anticipation. Some adults were excited too, but to be certain the whole young population had come down with graduation epidemic. Large classes were graduating from both the grammar school and the high school. Even those who were years removed from their own day of glorious release were anxious to help with preparations as a kind of dry run. The junior students who were moving into the vacating classes' chairs were tradition-bound to show their talents for leadership and management. They strutted through the school and around the campus exerting pressure on the lower grades. Their authority was so new that occasionally if they pressed a little too hard it had to be overlooked. After all, next term was com-

From I Know Why the Caged Bird Sings *(1969), the first volume of Maya Angelou's autobiography of growing up in a segregated southern town. After its success, Angelou continued her life story in seven sequential volumes, ending with* Mom & Me & Mom *(2013).*

1. Town in Arkansas.

ing, and it never hurt a sixth grader to have a play sister in the eighth grade, or a tenth-year student to be able to call a twelfth grader Bubba. So all was endured in a spirit of shared understanding. But the graduating classes themselves were the nobility. Like travelers with exotic destinations on their minds, the graduates were remarkably forgetful. They came to school without their books or tablets or even pencils. Volunteers fell over themselves to secure replacements for the missing equipment. When accepted, the willing workers might or might not be thanked, and it was of no importance to the pregraduation rites. Even teachers were respectful of the now quiet and aging seniors, and tended to speak to them, if not as equals, as beings only slightly lower than themselves. After tests were returned and grades given, the student body, which acted like an extended family, knew who did well, who excelled, and what piteous ones had failed.

Unlike the white high school, Lafayette County Training School distinguished itself by having neither lawn, nor hedges, nor tennis court, nor climbing ivy. Its two buildings (main classrooms, the grade school and home economics) were set on a dirt hill with no fence to limit either its boundaries or those of bordering farms. There was a large expanse to the left of the school which was used alternately as a baseball diamond or basketball court. Rusty hoops on swaying poles represented the permanent recreational equipment, although bats and balls could be borrowed from the P.E. teacher if the borrower was qualified and if the diamond wasn't occupied.

Over this rocky area relieved by a few shady tall persimmon trees the graduating class walked. The girls often held hands and no longer bothered to speak to the lower students. There was a sadness about them, as if this old world was not their home and they were bound for higher ground. The boys, on the other hand, had become more friendly, more outgoing. A decided change from the closed attitude they projected while studying for finals. Now they seemed not ready to give up the old school, the familiar paths and classrooms. Only a small percentage would be continuing on to college—one of the South's A & M (agricultural and mechanical) schools, which trained Negro youths to be carpenters, farmers, handymen, masons, maids, cooks and baby nurses. Their future rode heavily on their shoulders, and blinded them to the collective joy that had pervaded the lives of the boys and girls in the grammar school graduating class.

Parents who could afford it had ordered new shoes and readymade clothes for themselves from Sears and Roebuck or Montgomery Ward. They also engaged the best seamstresses to make the floating graduating dresses and to cut down secondhand pants which would be pressed to a military slickness for the important event.

Oh, it was important, all right. Whitefolks would attend the ceremony, and   5
two or three would speak of God and home, and the Southern way of life, and Mrs. Parsons, the principal's wife, would play the graduation march while the lower-grade graduates paraded down the aisles and took their seats below the platform. The high school seniors would wait in empty classrooms to make their dramatic entrance.

In the Store[2] I was the person of the moment. The birthday girl. The center.
Bailey[3] had graduated the year before, although to do so he had had to forfeit
all pleasures to make up for his time lost in Baton Rouge.

My class was wearing butter-yellow piqué dresses, and Momma launched
out on mine. She smocked the yoke into tiny crisscrossing puckers, then shirred
the rest of the bodice. Her dark fingers ducked in and out of the lemony cloth
as she embroidered raised daisies around the hem. Before she considered herself finished she had added a crocheted cuff on the puff sleeves, and a pointy
crocheted collar.

I was going to be lovely. A walking model of all the various styles of fine
hand sewing and it didn't worry me that I was only twelve years old and merely
graduating from the eighth grade. Besides, many teachers in Arkansas Negro
schools had only that diploma and were licensed to impart wisdom.

The days had become longer and more noticeable. The faded beige of former times had been replaced with strong and sure colors. I began to see my
classmates' clothes, their skin tones, and the dust that waved off pussy willows.
Clouds that lazed across the sky were objects of great concern to me. Their
shiftier shapes might have held a message that in my new happiness and with
a little bit of time I'd soon decipher. During that period I looked at the arch of
heaven so religiously my neck kept a steady ache. I had taken to smiling more
often, and my jaws hurt from the unaccustomed activity. Between the two physical sore spots, I suppose I could have been uncomfortable, but that was not
the case. As a member of the winning team (the graduating class of 1940) I
had outdistanced unpleasant sensations by miles. I was headed for the freedom of open fields.

10   Youth and social approval allied themselves with me and we trammeled
memories of slights and insults. The wind of our swift passage remodeled my
features. Lost tears were pounded to mud and then to dust. Years of withdrawal
were brushed aside and left behind, as hanging ropes of parasitic moss.

My work alone had awarded me a top place and I was going to be one of
the first called in the graduating ceremonies. On the classroom blackboard, as
well as on the bulletin board in the auditorium, there were blue stars and white
stars and red stars. No absences, no tardinesses, and my academic work was
among the best of the year. I could say the preamble to the Constitution even
faster than Bailey. We timed ourselves often: "We the people of the United
States in order to form a more perfect union . . ." I had memorized the Presidents of the United States from Washington to Roosevelt in chronological as
well as alphabetical order.

My hair pleased me too. Gradually the black mass had lengthened and
thickened, so that it kept at last to its braided pattern, and I didn't have to yank
my scalp off when I tried to comb it.

Louise and I had rehearsed the exercises until we tired out ourselves.
Henry Reed was class valedictorian. He was a small, very black boy with

2. Owned by the author's grandmother, whom she and her brother called "Momma."
3. Author's brother.

hooded eyes, a long, broad nose and an oddly shaped head. I had admired him for years because each term he and I vied for the best grades in our class. Most often he bested me, but instead of being disappointed I was pleased that we shared top places between us. Like many Southern Black children, he lived with his grandmother, who was as strict as Momma and as kind as she knew how to be. He was courteous, respectful and soft-spoken to elders, but on the playground he chose to play the roughest games. I admired him. Anyone, I reckoned, sufficiently afraid or sufficiently dull could be polite. But to be able to operate at a top level with both adults and children was admirable.

His valedictory speech was entitled "To Be or Not to Be." The rigid tenth-grade teacher had helped him write it. He'd been working on the dramatic stresses for months.

The weeks until graduation were filled with heady activities. A group of small children were to be presented in a play about buttercups and daisies and bunny rabbits. They could be heard throughout the building practicing their hops and their little songs that sounded like silver bells. The older girls (non-graduates, of course) were assigned the task of making refreshments for the night's festivities. A tangy scent of ginger, cinnamon, nutmeg and chocolate wafted around the home economics building as the budding cooks made samples for themselves and their teachers. 15

In every corner of the workshop, axes and saws split fresh timber as the woodshop boys made sets and stage scenery. Only the graduates were left out of the general bustle. We were free to sit in the library at the back of the building or look in quite detachedly, naturally, on the measures being taken for our event.

Even the minister preached on graduation the Sunday before. His subject was, "Let your light so shine that men will see your good works and praise your Father, Who is in Heaven." Although the sermon was purported to be addressed to us, he used the occasion to speak to backsliders, gamblers and general ne'er-do-wells. But since he had called our names at the beginning of the service we were mollified.

Among Negroes the tradition was to give presents to children going only from one grade to another. How much more important this was when the person was graduating at the top of the class. Uncle Willie and Momma had sent away for a Mickey Mouse watch like Bailey's. Louise gave me four embroidered handkerchiefs. (I gave her crocheted doilies.) Mrs. Sneed, the minister's wife, made me an undershirt to wear for graduation, and nearly every customer gave me a nickel or maybe even a dime with the instruction "Keep on moving to higher ground," or some such encouragement.

Amazingly the great day finally dawned and I was out of bed before I knew it. I threw open the back door to see it more clearly, but Momma said, "Sister, come away from that door and put your robe on."

I hoped the memory of that morning would never leave me. Sunlight was itself young, and the day had none of the insistence maturity would bring it in a few hours. In my robe and barefoot in the backyard, under cover of going to see 20 about my new beans, I gave myself up to the gentle warmth and thanked God that no matter what evil I had done in my life He had allowed me to live to see this day. Somewhere in my fatalism I had expected to die, accidentally, and never have the chance to walk up the stairs in the auditorium and gracefully receive my hard-earned diploma. Out of God's merciful bosom I had won reprieve.

Bailey came out in his robe and gave me a box wrapped in Christmas paper. He said he had saved his money for months to pay for it. It felt like a box of chocolates, but I knew Bailey wouldn't save money to buy candy when we had all we could want under our noses.

He was as proud of the gift as I. It was a soft-leather-bound copy of a collection of poems by Edgar Allan Poe, or, as Bailey and I called him, "Eap." I turned to "Annabel Lee" and we walked up and down the garden rows, the cool dirt between our toes, reciting the beautifully sad lines.

Momma made a Sunday breakfast although it was only Friday. After we finished the blessing, I opened my eyes to find the watch on my plate. It was a dream of a day. Everything went smoothly and to my credit, I didn't have to be reminded or scolded for anything. Near evening I was too jittery to attend to chores, so Bailey volunteered to do all before his bath.

Days before, we had made a sign for the Store, and as we turned out the lights Momma hung the cardboard over the doorknob. It read clearly: CLOSED. GRADUATION.

25   My dress fitted perfectly and everyone said that I looked like a sunbeam in it. On the hill, going toward the school, Bailey walked behind with Uncle Willie, who muttered, "Go on, Ju." He wanted him to walk ahead with us because it embarrassed him to have to walk so slowly. Bailey said he'd let the ladies walk together, and the men would bring up the rear. We all laughed, nicely.

Little children dashed by out of the dark like fireflies. Their crepe-paper dresses and butterfly wings were not made for running and we heard more than one rip, dryly, and the regretful "uh uh" that followed.

The school blazed without gaiety. The windows seemed cold and unfriendly from the lower hill. A sense of ill-fated timing crept over me, and if Momma hadn't reached for my hand I would have drifted back to Bailey and Uncle Willie, and possibly beyond. She made a few slow jokes about my feet getting cold, and tugged me along to the now-strange building.

Around the front steps, assurance came back. There were my fellow "greats," the graduating class. Hair brushed back, legs oiled, new dresses and pressed pleats, fresh pocket handkerchiefs and little handbags, all homesewn. Oh, we were up to snuff, all right. I joined my comrades and didn't even see my family go in to find seats in the crowded auditorium.

The school band struck up a march and all classes filed in as had been rehearsed. We stood in front of our seats, as assigned, and on a signal from the choir director, we sat. No sooner had this been accomplished than the band started to play the national anthem. We rose again and sang the song, after which we recited the pledge of allegiance. We remained standing for a brief minute before the choir director and the principal signaled to us, rather desperately I thought, to take our seats. The command was so unusual that our carefully rehearsed and smooth-running machine was thrown off. For a full minute we fumbled for our chairs and bumped into each other awkwardly. Habits change or solidify under pressure, so in our state of nervous tension we had been ready to follow our usual assembly pattern: the American national anthem, then the pledge of allegiance, then the song every Black person I knew called the Negro National Anthem. All done in the same key, with the same passion and most often standing on the same foot.

Finding my seat at last, I was overcome with a presentiment of worse things to come. Something unrehearsed, unplanned, was going to happen, and we were going to be made to look bad. I distinctly remember being explicit in the choice of pronoun. It was "we," the graduating class, the unit, that concerned me then.

The principal welcomed "parents and friends" and asked the Baptist minister to lead us in prayer. His invocation was brief and punchy, and for a second I thought we were getting on the high road to right action. When the principal came back to the dais, however, his voice had changed. Sounds always affected me profoundly and the principal's voice was one of my favorites. During assembly it melted and lowed weakly into the audience. It had not been in my plan to listen to him, but my curiosity was piqued and I straightened up to give him my attention.

He was talking about Booker T. Washington, our "late great leader," who said we can be as close as the fingers on the hand, etc. . . . Then he said a few vague things about friendship and the friendship of kindly people to those less fortunate than themselves. With that his voice nearly faded, thin, away. Like a river diminishing to a stream and then to a trickle. But he cleared his throat and said, "Our speaker tonight, who is also our friend, came from Texarkana to deliver the commencement address, but due to the irregularity of the train schedule, he's going to, as they say, 'speak and run.'" He said that we understood and wanted the man to know that we were most grateful for the time he was able to give us and then something about how we were willing always to adjust to another's program, and without more ado—"I give you Mr. Edward Donleavy."

Not one but two white men came through the door off-stage. The shorter one walked to the speaker's platform, and the tall one moved to the center seat and sat down. But that was our principal's seat, and already occupied. The dislodged gentleman bounced around for a long breath or two before the Baptist minister gave him his chair, then with more dignity than the situation deserved, the minister walked off the stage.

Donleavy looked at the audience once (on reflection, I'm sure that he wanted only to reassure himself that we were really there), adjusted his glasses and began to read from a sheaf of papers.

He was glad "to be here and to see the work going on just as it was in the other schools."

At the first "Amen" from the audience I willed the offender to immediate death by choking on the word. But Amens and Yes, sirs began to fall around the room like rain through a ragged umbrella.

30

35

He told us of the wonderful changes we children in Stamps had in store. The Central School (naturally, the white school was Central) had already been granted improvements that would be in use in the fall. A well-known artist was coming from Little Rock to teach art to them. They were going to have the newest microscopes and chemistry equipment for their laboratory. Mr. Donleavy didn't leave us long in the dark over who made these improvements available to Central High. Nor were we to be ignored in the general betterment scheme he had in mind.

He said that he had pointed out to people at a very high level that one of the first-line football tacklers at Arkansas Agricultural and Mechanical College had graduated from good old Lafayette County Training School. Here fewer Amens were heard. Those few that did break through lay dully in the air with the heaviness of habit.

He went on to praise us. He went on to say how he had bragged that "one of the best basketball players at Fisk sank his first ball right here at Lafayette County Training School."

40   The white kids were going to have a chance to become Galileos and Madame Curies and Edisons and Gauguins, and our boys (the girls weren't even in on it) would try to be Jesse Owenses and Joe Louises.

Owens and the Brown Bomber were great heroes in our world, but what school official in the white-goddom of Little Rock had the right to decide that those two men must be our only heroes? Who decided that for Henry Reed to become a scientist he had to work like George Washington Carver, as a boot-black, to buy a lousy microscope? Bailey was obviously always going to be too small to be an athlete, so which concrete angel glued to what country seat had decided that if my brother wanted to become a lawyer he had to first pay penance for his skin by picking cotton and hoeing corn and studying correspondence books at night for twenty years?

The man's dead words fell like bricks around the auditorium and too many settled in my belly. Constrained by hard-learned manners I couldn't look behind me, but to my left and right the proud graduating class of 1940 had dropped their heads. Every girl in my row had found something new to do with her handkerchief. Some folded the tiny squares into love knots, some into triangles, but most were wadding them, then pressing them flat on their yellow laps.

On the dais, the ancient tragedy was being replayed. Professor Parsons sat, a sculptor's reject, rigid. His large, heavy body seemed devoid of will or willingness, and his eyes said he was no longer with us. The other teachers examined the flag (which was draped stage right) or their notes, or the windows which opened on our now-famous playing diamond.

Graduation, the hush-hush magic time of frills and gifts and congratulations and diplomas, was finished for me before my name was called. The accomplishment was nothing. The meticulous maps, drawn in three colors of ink, learning and spelling decasyllabic words, memorizing the whole of *The Rape of Lucrece*[4]—it was for nothing. Donleavy had exposed us.

---

4. A 1,855-line narrative poem (1594) by the playwright William Shakespeare, which recounts the story of the daughter of a Roman prefect. When she was defiled, she stabbed herself in the presence of her father and her husband.

We were maids and farmers, handymen and washerwomen, and anything   45
higher that we aspired to was farcical and presumptuous.

Then I wished that Gabriel Prosser and Nat Turner[5] had killed all whitefolks in their beds and that Abraham Lincoln had been assassinated before the
signing of the Emancipation Proclamation, and that Harriet Tubman[6] had
been killed by that blow on her head and Christopher Columbus had drowned
in the *Santa Maria*.

It was awful to be a Negro and have no control over my life. It was brutal
to be young and already trained to sit quietly and listen to charges brought
against my color with no chance of defense. We should all be dead. I thought
I should like to see us all dead, one on top of the other. A pyramid of flesh with
the whitefolks on the bottom, as the broad base, then the Indians with their silly
tomahawks and teepees and wigwams and treaties, the Negroes with their
mops and recipes and cotton sacks and spirituals sticking out of their mouths.
The Dutch children should all stumble in their wooden shoes and break their
necks. The French should choke to death on the Louisiana Purchase (1803)
while silkworms ate all the Chinese with their stupid pigtails. As a species, we
were an abomination. All of us.

Donleavy was running for election, and assured our parents that if he won
we could count on having the only colored paved playing field in that part of
Arkansas. Also—he never looked up to acknowledge the grunts of acceptance—
also, we were bound to get some new equipment for the home economics
building and the workshop.

He finished, and since there was no need to give any more than the most
perfunctory thank-you's, he nodded to the men on the stage, and the tall
white man who was never introduced joined him at the door. They left with
the attitude that now they were off to something really important. (The graduation ceremonies at Lafayette County Training School had been a mere
preliminary.)

The ugliness they left was palpable. An uninvited guest who wouldn't leave.   50
The choir was summoned and sang a modern arrangement of "Onward, Christian Soldiers," with new words pertaining to graduates seeking their place in the
world. But it didn't work. Elouise, the daughter of the Baptist minister,
recited "Invictus,"[7] and I could have cried at the impertinence of "I am the
master of my fate, I am the captain of my soul."

My name had lost its ring of familiarity and I had to be nudged to go and
receive my diploma. All my preparations had fled. I neither marched up to the
stage like a conquering Amazon, nor did I look in the audience for Bailey's nod
of approval. Marguerite Johnson, I heard the name again, my honors were read,

---

5. Gabriel Prosser (c. 1776–1800) and Nat Turner (1800–1831), executed leaders of
slave rebellions in Virginia.
6. Black abolitionist (c. 1822–1913), known for her work on the Underground Railroad, which brought slaves to free states through a network of secret paths and routes.
7. Inspirational poem (1888) by William Ernest Henley, once very popular for occasions such as this one.

there were noises in the audience of appreciation, and I took my place on the stage as rehearsed.

I thought about colors I hated: ecru, puce, lavender, beige and black.

There was shuffling and rustling around me, then Henry Reed was giving his valedictory address, "To Be or Not to Be." Hadn't he heard the whitefolks? We couldn't *be,* so the question was a waste of time. Henry's voice came out clear and strong. I feared to look at him. Hadn't he got the message? There was no "nobler in the mind" for Negroes because the world didn't think we had minds, and they let us know it. "Outrageous fortune"? Now, that was a joke. When the ceremony was over I had to tell Henry Reed some things. That is, if I still cared. Not "rub," Henry, "erase." "Ah, there's the erase." Us.

Henry had been a good student in elocution. His voice rose on tides of promise and fell on waves of warnings. The English teacher had helped him to create a sermon winging through Hamlet's soliloquy. To be a man, a doer, a builder, a leader, or to be a tool, an unfunny joke, a crusher of funky toad-stools. I marveled that Henry could go through with the speech as if we had a choice.

55   I had been listening and silently rebutting each sentence with my eyes closed; then there was a hush, which in an audience warns that something unplanned is happening. I looked up and saw Henry Reed, the conservative, the proper, the A student, turn his back to the audience and turn to us (the proud graduating class of 1940) and sing, nearly speaking,

> "Lift ev'ry voice and sing
> Till earth and heaven ring
> Ring with the harmonies of Liberty . . ."

It was the poem written by James Weldon Johnson. It was the music composed by J. Rosamond Johnson. It was the Negro national anthem. Out of habit we were singing it.

Our mothers and fathers stood in the dark hall and joined the hymn of encouragement. A kindergarten teacher led the small children onto the stage and the buttercups and daisies and bunny rabbits marked time and tried to follow:

> "Stony the road we trod
> Bitter the chastening rod
> Felt in the days when hope, unborn, had died.
> Yet with a steady beat
> Have not our weary feet
> Come to the place for which our fathers sighed?"

Each child I knew had learned that song with his ABC's and along with "Jesus Loves Me This I Know." But I personally had never heard it before. Never heard the words, despite the thousands of times I had sung them. Never thought they had anything to do with me.

On the other hand, the words of Patrick Henry had made such an impression on me that I had been able to stretch myself tall and trembling and say, "I know not what course others may take, but as for me, give me liberty or give me death."

And now I heard, really for the first time:

> "We have come over a way that with tears
>   has been watered,
> We have come, treading our path through
>   the blood of the slaughtered."

While echoes of the song shivered in the air, Henry Reed bowed his head, 60 said "Thank you," and returned to his place in the line. The tears that slipped down many faces were not wiped away in shame.

We were on top again. As always, again. We survived. The depths had been icy and dark, but now a bright sun spoke to our souls. I was no longer simply a member of the proud graduating class of 1940; I was a proud member of the wonderful, beautiful Negro race.

Oh, Black known and unknown poets, how often have your auctioned pains sustained us? Who will compute the lonely nights made less lonely by your songs, or the empty pots made less tragic by your tales?

If we were a people much given to revealing secrets, we might raise monuments and sacrifice to the memories of our poets, but slavery cured us of that weakness. It may be enough, however, to have it said that we survive in exact relationship to the dedication of our poets (include preachers, musicians and blues singers).

MLA CITATION

Angelou, Maya. "Graduation." *The Norton Reader: An Anthology of Nonfiction*, edited by Melissa A. Goldthwaite et al., 15th ed., W. W. Norton, 2020, pp. 372–81.

QUESTIONS

1. Presumably, all of Maya Angelou's readers would have witnessed a graduation ceremony and brought their memories to her essay. How does she fulfill the reader's expectations for what graduation includes? How does she surprise us with details we may not expect?

2. In paragraph 43 Angelou writes that "the ancient tragedy was being replayed." What does she mean? How does her essay help to resist the tragic script?

3. Write a personal essay about an event you anticipated hopefully but that did not fulfill your expectations, incorporating an explanation of your disappointment into your account, as Angelou does.

8 Words and Writing

Show up, show up, show up, and after a while the muse shows up, too.

—ISABEL ALLENDE

There is great pleasure in watching someone practice a craft. The more intricate and complex the process, the more wonder we experience watching someone engage in it. Museums and festivals draw us to the sight of people blowing glass, weaving cloth, shaping wood to make a fiddle. The internet boasts of such wonders: time-lapse photography of miniatures coming together, origami animals coming to life, and huge spirals of dominoes tumbling with satisfying precision. Writing is no less intricate and precise, but the craft of writing, the process by which an idea turns into words and those words get written, re-written, and edited into art, is notoriously difficult to show. An actor scowling at a laptop or crossing out a phrase on a piece of paper doesn't come close to conveying the process of weighing how best to express an idea.

Writing is a skill, a craft, and an art. Each of the essays in this chapter explains and celebrates the process of writing. None of them pretends that writing is easy. But each one explains what for the author makes the struggle worthwhile: the pleasure of watching an editor improve something we've written, of remembering a moment from jottings in an old notebook, of learning when to stop reading and go for a walk, of learning how to say what it is that we really think. When we write a good sentence—not to mention a great one—we may even get a little jolt of joy, a joy that, with luck, is passed on to our readers. Each of these essays, in their own way, offers a window into why writing matters to its author, into the reasons for taking care to get it right.

This chapter opens with essays about coming to take words seriously, coming to understand and love how very much words can matter: Stephen King describes watching his writing be edited by a professional when he was just starting out; Leslie Jamison recalls her deepening recognition of how people were reading the motto she chose for her tattoo; Benjamin Franklin and Joan Didion reflect on the exercises and assignments they gave themselves as they were striving to become better writers; and Rebecca Solnit shares advice. From there, this chapter moves to essays on the politics of words: how words do and don't identify us, how using words carelessly causes us to misunderstand our world, and how being able to use words capably can set us free: Amy Sequenzia, a non-speaking Autistic activist and writer, details the long struggle she had communicating before she learned how to type; Jaswinder Bolina, using his immigrant father's advice as a catalyst, explores his own ambivalent attitude toward how his ethnically marked name may affect his chances to succeed; and George Orwell offers his time-tested advice on using language to combat totalitarianism, groupthink, and generally sloppy thoughts. This chapter ends with two essays, both about words taken one at a time: Kathy Fish's essay on collective nouns and Kory Stamper's on the project of defining the word "take." They remind us, if we have not already gotten it, that every word we choose has the power of dynamite.

As you sit down to write, you might think about what parts of the process are hardest for you and which come easiest: it's different for everyone. Watch yourself as you go from receiving an assignment to making it your own, and try to describe your own thought processes. How do you approach the practice of writing? What inspires you when your energy runs low? Do you have rules for writing that you'd like to share with others? Or ideas about how best to take notes and keep a notebook? What parts of the writing craft are you still working on? And what are the things that you've come closer to figuring out?

STEPHEN KING
On Writing

HARDLY A WEEK after being sprung from detention hall, I was once more invited to step down to the principal's office. I went with a sinking heart, wondering what new shit I'd stepped in.

It wasn't Mr. Higgins who wanted to see me, at least; this time the school guidance counselor had issued the summons. There had been discussions about me, he said, and how to turn my "restless pen" into more constructive channels. He had enquired of John Gould, editor of Lisbon's weekly newspaper, and had discovered Gould had an opening for a sports reporter. While the school couldn't *insist* that I take this job, everyone in the front office felt it would be a good idea. *Do it or die,* the G.C.'s eyes suggested. Maybe that was just paranoia, but even now, almost forty years later, I don't think so.

I groaned inside. I was shut of *Dave's Rag,* almost shut of *The Drum,* and now here was the Lisbon *Weekly Enterprise.* Instead of being haunted by waters, like Norman Maclean in *A River Runs through It,*[1] I was as a teenager haunted by newspapers. Still, what could I do? I rechecked the look in the guidance counselor's eyes and said I would be delighted to interview for the job.

Gould—not the well-known New England humorist or the novelist who wrote *The Greenleaf Fires* but a relation of both, I think—greeted me warily but with some interest. We would try each other out, he said, if that suited me.

Now that I was away from the administrative offices of Lisbon High, I felt   5
able to muster a little honesty. I told Mr. Gould that I didn't know much about sports. Gould said, "These are games people understand when they're watching them drunk in bars. You'll learn if you try."

From On Writing: A Memoir of the Craft *(2000). Stephen King is primarily known for his horror and suspense novels and stories.*

1. Story collection (1976) by Maclean, which includes the often-quoted words, "I am haunted by waters."

He gave me a huge roll of yellow paper on which to type my copy—I think I still have it somewhere—and promised me a wage of half a cent a word. It was the first time someone had promised me wages for writing.

The first two pieces I turned in had to do with a basketball game in which an LHS player broke the school scoring record. One was a straight piece of reporting. The other was a sidebar about Robert Ransom's record-breaking performance. I brought both to Gould the day after the game so he'd have them for Friday, which was when the paper came out. He read the game piece, made two minor corrections, and spiked it.[2] Then he started in on the feature piece with a large black pen.

I took my fair share of English Lit classes in my two remaining years at Lisbon, and my fair share of composition, fiction, and poetry classes in college, but John Gould taught me more than any of them, and in no more than ten minutes. I wish I still had the piece—it deserves to be framed, editorial corrections and all—but I can remember pretty well how it went and how it looked after Gould had combed through it with that black pen of his. Here's an example:

> Last night, in the ~~well-loved~~ gymnasium of Lisbon
> High School, partisans and Jay Hills fans alike were
> stunned by an athletic performance unequalled in
> school history. Bob Ransom, ~~known as "Bullet" Bob~~
> ~~for both his size and accuracy,~~ scored thirty-seven
> points. Yes, you heard me right. ~~Plus~~ he did it with
> grace, speed . . . and with an odd courtesy as well,
> committing only two personal fouls in his ~~knight-like~~
> quest for a record which has eluded Lisbon ~~thinclads~~ *players*
> since the ~~years of Korea~~ . . . *1953.*

Gould stopped at "the years of Korea" and looked up at me. "What year was the last record made?" he asked.

10   Luckily, I had my notes. "1953," I said. Gould grunted and went back to work. When he finished marking my copy in the manner indicated above, he looked up and saw something on my face. I think he must have mistaken it for horror. It wasn't; it was pure revelation. Why, I wondered, didn't English teachers ever do this? It was like the Visible Man Old Raw Diehl had on his desk in the biology room.

"I only took out the bad parts, you know," Gould said. "Most of it's pretty good."

"I know," I said, meaning both things: yes, most of it was good—okay anyway, serviceable—and yes, he had only taken out the bad parts. "I won't do it again."

---

2. Journalistic slang for withholding publication, often out of fear that the story cannot be sufficiently verified.

He laughed. "If that's true, you'll never have to work for a living. You can do *this* instead. Do I have to explain any of these marks?"

"No," I said.

"When you write a story, you're telling yourself the story," he said. "When you rewrite, your main job is taking out all the things that are *not* the story." 15

Gould said something else that was interesting on the day I turned in my first two pieces: write with the door closed, rewrite with the door open. Your stuff starts out being just for you, in other words, but then it goes out. Once you know what the story is and get it right—as right as you can, anyway—it belongs to anyone who wants to read it. Or criticize it. If you're very lucky (this is my idea, not John Gould's, but I believe he would have subscribed to the notion), more will want to do the former than the latter.

MLA CITATION

King, Stephen. "On Writing." *The Norton Reader: An Anthology of Nonfiction*, edited by Melissa A. Goldthwaite et al., 15th ed., W. W. Norton, 2020, pp. 383–85.

QUESTIONS

1. Stephen King provides an example of the way his editor marked up his work. What rationale can you provide for the edits? Would you have made different choices if you were the editor? Why?

2. King uses dialogue and description to help characterize his editor. In which parts of the text do you get the best sense of who Gould is? Why are those parts effective?

3. King writes about learning from an editor. In "Learning to Write" (pp. 389–92), Benjamin Franklin writes about learning from his reading, while, in "On Keeping a Notebook" (pp. 392–98), Joan Didion writes about her notebook. Which of these techniques, if any, has helped you as a writer? How?

4. Write about a time someone responded to your writing in a way that helped you learn to be a better writer. What kinds of comments and edits did that person make? Why was that response helpful to you?

LESLIE JAMISON
Mark My Words. Maybe.

M Y TATTOO KEPT GETTING DELAYED by other people's weddings: a bachelorette party in Vegas, cliff-top vows in Zion, a ceremony in Westchester. I wasn't just attending the ceremony in Westchester, I was officiating at the ceremony in Westchester. I couldn't picture giving my blessing in front of 200

Published in the New York Times *(2014). Leslie Jamison is the author of* The Empathy Exams *(2014), a collection of essays.*

people while my left arm glistened under Saran Wrap. I felt the slightest twinge of resentment. My life seemed perpetually tucked into the pockets of time created between the milestones of other lives.

I was getting the tattoo, in part, to mark a break from the man with whom I'd spent four years building and then dismantling a life. I was branding myself to mark a new era: my body was no longer entwined with someone else's. It was mine alone again. I was moving to a new city and I had a new book coming out, and the tattoo would be its epigraph: "I am human: nothing human is alien to me."

The quotation belongs to Terence, the Roman playwright. In the original Latin, it reads: homo sum: humani nil a me alienum puto. When I first came upon it, I felt its force beyond rational explanation. I knew it was something I needed to keep saying.

I got the job done by an artist who worked in a converted fire station. His walls were lined with giant beetles in jars of formaldehyde, taxidermied birds and bright oil paintings full of wizards and dragons. "Sure you don't want anything drawn?" he asked, gesturing to his art. I pictured a dragon with a thought bubble: "nothing human is alien to me. . . ." I said I was fine with just words. He wrote them in a cursive line from elbow to wrist. "I'm going to do this so we miss your veins," he said. I said that sounded great.

5   It hurt just enough to make me feel like something was happening. There was a sense of deserving—that I'd earned this by hurting for it. It was an old logic I hadn't felt in a while: Pain justifies ownership. It scared me, a bit. It also thrilled me. I left with Very Serious Aftercare Instructions and an arm encased like a pale sausage in plastic wrap.

The woman at the drugstore where I bought my Very Serious Aftercare supplies immediately wanted to know what the tattoo said. When I told her, she looked at me for a long time. "I think there is so much evil in this world," she said, "and so much good."

From now on, I realized, my body would basically be asking every stranger, "What do you think about the possibilities of human understanding?" During the months that followed, I found myself explaining the tattoo to a parade of strangers and acquaintances. It's about empathy and camaraderie, I would say. Or else, it's a denial of this lifelong obsession I've had with singularity and exceptionality.

We often think of tattoos as declarations of selfhood: this is what I am, love, believe. But there are other things we might inscribe on ourselves: what we fear, what we hate, what we hope to be but can't yet manage.

"I am human; nothing human is alien to me"—my tattoo wasn't true for me, not yet. But it was what I most needed to hear, an asymptote, a horizon.

10   On a hot day near the end of summer, another drugstore clerk reached for my arm with a searching look on his face. He was a large man, imposing.

When I told him what the tattoo meant, he shook his head. "There are people going through things in this world that are really bad," he said. "Do you understand that?"

I tried to explain about aspiration, asymptote, attempt.

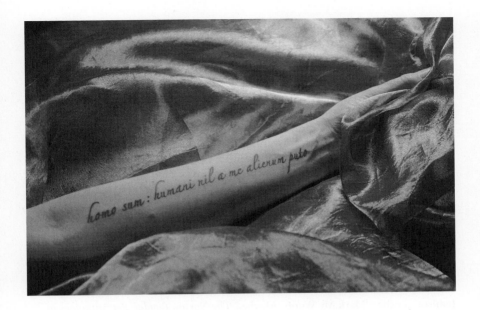

"You will leave a little piece of yourself with everyone you imagine," he said. "You will get exhausted trying to give yourself away."

I didn't know what to say to this. I felt exhausted by *him*. I felt how much I needed, from him and everyone, a certain kind of response: to feel inspired by the tat, and tell me so.

"You tried to give me something," he said, pointing at my arm. "But I blocked it. I blocked what you were giving me."

15

He was interrupting the ticktock rhythm of my righteousness, saying something about the easy aphorism on my arm: how it didn't go down easy for him and shouldn't go down easy for me, either.

He wasn't the only one with questions. My father wrote from the Rwanda Genocide Memorial: Did I really believe what my tattoo said, even about perpetrators of genocide? And on a first date, a man asked me whether my tattoo could even apply to evil? We never went out again. But there were other dates, other men wanting translations, running their fingers along the script. It started to feel uncomfortably like philosophy as accessory, something to match a certain kind of intellectual posture.

Before these men, there was a moment with the original man, the one from whom the tattoo marked my liberation. I ran into him on an ordinary afternoon, about a week after I got the tattoo and a week before I moved away from the city we shared. He was surprised to see my arm holding something it hadn't held before.

I realized how different things were now. Something could happen to my body and it would be weeks or months before he knew about it. The tattoo was supposed to represent a new freedom but in that moment it felt like a shackle.

It showed me how much it still hurt to feel the new distance between us. I felt that loss of proximity like a flesh wound.

20   It's like being pregnant, people would tell me. Your body is a conversation-starter. Eventually I started drawing the comparison myself. But the truth was it didn't feel like being pregnant at all. I was alone; my body was my own. It was a deep privacy, an autonomy tinged with sadness. It was the opposite of pregnancy, the residue of intimacy.

I'd always insisted I didn't get the tattoo so that people would talk to me about it. In fact, I told myself I wanted nothing less. But at a certain point I've had to admit to a desire for contact I couldn't own at first: It's there and it isn't.

The script is full of vectors pointing in opposite directions, a statement both aspirational and self-scolding, a desire to be seen and a desire to be left alone; a desire to have my body admired and a desire for my body to need nothing but itself, to need no affirmation from anyone. The tattoo holds an idea and its refutation, a man and his absence, a vote of confidence from the world and—in that downtown drugstore, on that humid day in summer—something more like the opposite.

MLA CITATION

Jamison, Leslie. "Mark My Words. Maybe." *The Norton Reader: An Anthology of Nonfiction*, edited by Melissa A. Goldthwaite et al., 15th ed., W. W. Norton, 2020, pp. 385–88.

QUESTIONS

1. Leslie Jamison initially thinks her tattoo will help her get over a breakup, but it comes to mean several different things. What do you think the tattoo ends up meaning to her? Point to passages in the text that support your answer.

2. Jamison titles her essay "Mark My Words. Maybe." Whom might she be addressing with this title? Consider the reactions of the drugstore clerk (paragraphs 10–16) and Jamison's father (paragraph 17) as you think about how this title relates to the broader points she makes in her essay.

3. Jamison writes about the power bodies have to communicate messages that would otherwise be expressed through speaking and writing. Write an essay discussing the power and the limitation of tattoos as a mode of communication. If you have a tattoo, consider incorporating your personal experience.

BENJAMIN FRANKLIN

Learning to Write

ABOUT THIS TIME I met with an odd Volume of the *Spectator*.[1] I had never before seen any of them. I bought it, read it over and over, and was much delighted with it. I thought the Writing excellent, and wish'd if possible to imitate it. With that View, I took some of the Papers, and making short Hints of the Sentiment in each Sentence, laid them by a few Days, and then without looking at the Book, tried to complete the Papers again, by expressing each hinted Sentiment at length and as fully as it had been express'd before in any suitable Words that should come to hand.

Then I compar'd my *Spectator* with the Original, discover'd some of my Faults and corrected them. But I found I wanted a Stock of Words or a Readiness in recollecting and using them which I thought I should have acquir'd before that time, if I had gone on making Verses, since the continual Occasion for Words of the same Import but of different Length, to suit the Measure,[2] or of different Sound for the Rhyme, would have laid me under a constant Necessity of searching for Variety, and also have tended to fix that Variety in my Mind, and make me Master of it. Therefore I took some of the Tales and turn'd them into Verse: And after a time, when I had pretty well forgotten the Prose, turn'd them back again. I also sometimes jumbled my Collections of Hints into Confusion, and after some Weeks, endeavor'd to reduce them into the best Order, before I began to form the full Sentences, and complete the Paper. This was to teach me Method in the Arrangement of Thoughts. By comparing my Work afterwards with the original, I discover'd many faults and amended them; but I sometimes had the Pleasure of Fancying that in certain Particulars of small Import, I had been lucky enough to improve the Method or the Language and this encourag'd me to think I might possibly in time come to be a tolerable English Writer, of which I was extremely ambitious.

My Time for these Exercises and for Reading, was at Night after Work, or before Work began in the Morning; or on Sundays, when I contrived to be in the Printing-House alone, evading as much as I could the common Attendance on public Worship, which my Father used to exact of me when I was under his Care: And which indeed I still thought a Duty; tho' I could not, as it seemed to me, afford the Time to practice it.

When about 16 Years of Age, I happen'd to meet with a Book written by one Tryon,[3] recommending a Vegetable Diet. I determined to go into it. My Brother being yet unmarried, did not keep House, but boarded himself and his

Drawn from Benjamin Franklin's Autobiography, *first published in 1791.*

1. Daily English periodical noted for its excellence in prose.
2. Meter.
3. Thomas Tryon (1634–1703), author of *Way to Health and Happiness* (1682).

Apprentices in another Family. My refusing to eat Flesh occasioned an Inconveniency, and I was frequently chid for my singularity. I made myself acquainted with Tryon's Manner of preparing some of his Dishes, such as Boiling Potatoes or Rice, making Hasty Pudding,[4] and a few others, and then propos'd to my Brother, that if he would give me Weekly half the Money he paid for my Board, I would board myself. He instantly agreed to it, and I presently found that I could save half what he paid me. This was an additional Fund for buying Books: But I had another Advantage in it. My Brother and the rest going from the Printing-House to their Meals, I remain'd there alone, and dispatching presently my light Repast, (which often was no more than a Biscuit or a Slice of Bread, a Handful of Raisins or a Tart from the Pastry Cook's, and a Glass of Water) had the rest of the Time till their Return, for Study, in which I made the greater Progress from that greater Clearness of Head and quicker Apprehension which usually attend Temperance in Eating and Drinking. And now it was that being on some Occasion made asham'd of my Ignorance in Figures; which I had twice fail'd in learning when at School, I took Cocker's Book of Arithmetic,[5] and went thro' the whole by myself with great Ease. I also read Seller's and Sturmy's[6] Books of Navigation, and became acquainted with the little Geometry they contain, but never proceeded far in that Science. And I read about this Time Locke on Human Understanding and the Art of Thinking by Messrs. du Port Royal.[7]

5   While I was intent on improving my Language, I met with an English Grammar (I think it was Greenwood's[8]) at the End of which there were two little Sketches of the Arts of Rhetoric and Logic, the latter finishing with a Specimen of a Dispute in the Socratic Method. And soon after I procur'd Xenophon's Memorable Things of Socrates,[9] wherein there are many Instances of the same Method. I was charm'd with it, adopted it, dropped my abrupt Contradiction and positive Argumentation, and put on the humble Enquirer and Doubter. And being then, from reading Shaftesbury and Collins,[10] became a real Doubter in many Points of our Religious Doctrine. I found this Method safest for myself and very embarrassing to those against whom I used it, there-

4. Porridge.

5. Well-known textbook, first published in 1677.

6. John Seller (bap. 1632, d. 1697), author of *Practical Navigation* (1694); Samuel Sturmy (1633–1669), author of *The Mariner's Magazine* (1699).

7. John Locke (1632–1704), British philosopher and author of *An Essay Concerning Human Understanding* (1690); Pierre Nicole (1625–1695) of Port Royal published his book in 1662; it was translated into English as *Logic: Or the Art of Thinking* in 1687.

8. James Greenwood (d. 1737), author of *An Essay towards a Practical English Grammar* (1711).

9. Xenophon's (c. 430–355 B.C.E.) *The Memorable Things of Socrates* was published in English translation by Edward Bysshe in 1712.

10. Anthony Ashley Cooper, 3rd earl of Shaftesbury (1671–1713), famous for his *Characteristics of Men, Manners, Opinions, Times* (1711); Anthony Collins (1676–1729), a friend of Locke; author of *A Discourse of Free Thinking* (1713).

fore I took a Delight in it, practic'd it continually and grew very artful and expert in drawing People even of superior Knowledge into Concessions the Consequences of which they did not foresee, entangling them in Difficulties out of which they could not extricate themselves, and so obtaining Victories that neither myself nor my Cause always deserved. I continu'd this Method some few Years, but gradually left it, retaining only the Habit of expressing myself in Terms of modest Diffidence, never using when I advance any thing that may possibly be disputed, the Words, *Certainly, undoubtedly,* or any others that give the Air of Positiveness to an Opinion; but rather say, *I conceive,* or I *apprehend* a Thing to be so or so. *It appears to me,* or I *should think it so or so for such and such Reasons,* or *I imagine* it to be so, or *it is so if I am not mistaken.* This Habit I believe has been of great Advantage to me, when I have had occasion to inculcate my Opinions and persuade Men into Measures that I have been from time to time engag'd in promoting. And as the chief Ends of Conversation are to *inform,* or to be *informed,* to *please* or to *persuade,* I wish well-meaning sensible Men would not lessen their Power of doing Good by a Positive assuming Manner that seldom fails to disgust, tends to create Opposition, and to defeat every one of those Purposes for which Speech was given us, to wit, giving or receiving Information, or Pleasure: For if you would *inform,* a positive dogmatical Manner in advancing your Sentiments, may provoke Contradiction and prevent a candid Attention. If you wish Information and Improvement from the Knowledge of others and yet at the same time express yourself as firmly fix'd in your present Opinions, modest sensible Men, who do not love Disputation, will probably leave you undisturb'd in the Possession of your Error; and by such a Manner you can seldom hope to recommend yourself in *pleasing* your Hearers, or to persuade those whose Concurrence you desire. Pope says, judiciously,

> Men should be taught as if you taught them not,
> And things unknown propos'd as things forgot,

farther recommending it to us,

> To speak tho' sure, with seeming Diffidence.[11]

And he might have coupled with this Line that which he has coupled with another, I think less properly,

> For want of Modesty is want of Sense.

If you ask why *less properly,* I must repeat the Lines;

> "Immodest Words admit of *no* Defence;
> For Want of Modesty is Want of Sense."[12]

11. Adapted from *An Essay on Criticism* (1711), by Alexander Pope.

12. Franklin wrongly attributes these two lines to Pope. They are from *Essay on Translated Verse* (1684) by Wentworth Dillon. The second line should read "For Want of Decency is Want of Sense."

Now is not *Want of Sense*, (where a Man is so unfortunate as to want it) some Apology for his *Want of Modesty*? and would not the Lines stand more justly thus?

> Immodest Words admit *but this* Defence.
> That Want of Modesty is Want of Sense.

This however I should submit to better Judgments.

MLA CITATION

Franklin, Benjamin. "Learning to Write." *The Norton Reader: An Anthology of Nonfiction*, edited by Melissa A. Goldthwaite et al., 15th ed., W. W. Norton, 2020, pp. 389–92.

QUESTIONS

1. Benjamin Franklin describes his youthful practice of imitating successful writers' sentences. Have you ever done this? If so, how was it helpful or unhelpful? What might writers likely learn from such a practice?

2. Franklin has been called an autodidact, a self-teacher. Recount what Franklin learned in this manner, and note what he failed to teach himself. What kinds of knowledge did Franklin seek to acquire? Was his learning broad or narrow? What kinds of endeavors was this knowledge most suited for?

3. When he was sixteen, Franklin read a book about vegetarian diets and immediately was converted. Write about how you or someone you know was converted to following a distinct path, either religious, ethical, or physical. Did the conversion happen suddenly, as it did with Franklin, or did it take place slowly, over time? In your essay you might consider imitating Franklin's style, or that of a writer you admire.

JOAN DIDION

On Keeping a Notebook

T HAT WOMAN ESTELLE,'" the note reads, "'is partly the reason why George Sharp and I are separated today.' *Dirty crepe-de-Chine wrapper, hotel bar, Wilmington RR, 9:45 a.m. August Monday morning.*"

Since the note is in my notebook, it presumably has some meaning to me. I study it for a long while. At first I have only the most general notion of what I was doing on an August Monday morning in the bar of the hotel across from the Pennsylvania Railroad station in Wilmington, Delaware (waiting for a train? missing one? 1960? 1961? why Wilmington?), but

From Slouching towards Bethlehem (1968), Joan Didion's first work of nonfiction, which includes essays analyzing American culture in the 1960s.

I do remember being there. The woman in the dirty crepe-de-Chine wrapper had come down from her room for a beer, and the bartender had heard before the reason why George Sharp and she were separated today. "Sure," he said, and went on mopping the floor. "You told me." At the other end of the bar is a girl. She is talking, pointedly, not to the man beside her but to a cat lying in the triangle of sunlight cast through the open door. She is wearing a plaid silk dress from Peck & Peck, and the hem is coming down.

Here is what it is: the girl has been on the Eastern Shore, and now she is going back to the city, leaving the man beside her, and all she can see ahead are the viscous summer sidewalks and the 3 a.m. long-distance calls that will make her lie awake and then sleep drugged through all the steaming mornings left in August (1960? 1961?). Because she must go directly from the train to lunch in New York, she wishes that she had a safety pin for the hem of the plaid silk dress, and she also wishes that she could forget about the hem and the lunch and stay in the cool bar that smells of disinfectant and malt and make friends with the woman in the crepe-de-Chine wrapper. She is afflicted by a little self-pity, and she wants to compare Estelles. That is what that was all about.

Why did I write it down? In order to remember, of course, but exactly what was it I wanted to remember? How much of it actually happened? Did any of it? Why do I keep a notebook at all? It is easy to deceive oneself on all those scores. The impulse to write things down is a peculiarly compulsive one, inexplicable to those who do not share it, useful only accidentally, only secondarily, in the way that any compulsion tries to justify itself. I suppose that it begins or does not begin in the cradle. Although I have felt compelled to write things down since I was five years old, I doubt that my daughter ever will, for she is a singularly blessed and accepting child, delighted with life exactly as life presents itself to her, unafraid to go to sleep and unafraid to wake up. Keepers of private notebooks are a different breed altogether, lonely and resistant rearrangers of things, anxious malcontents, children afflicted apparently at birth with some presentiment of loss.

My first notebook was a Big Five tablet, given to me by my mother with the sensible suggestion that I stop whining and learn to amuse myself by writing down my thoughts. She returned the tablet to me a few years ago; the first entry is an account of a woman who believed herself to be freezing to death in the Arctic night, only to find, when day broke, that she had stumbled onto the Sahara Desert, where she would die of the heat before lunch. I have no idea what turn of a five-year-old's mind could have prompted so insistently "ironic" and exotic a story, but it does reveal a certain predilection for the extreme which has dogged me into adult life; perhaps if I were analytically inclined I would find it a truer story than any I might have told about Donald Johnson's birthday party or the day my cousin Brenda put Kitty Litter in the aquarium.

So the point of my keeping a notebook has never been, nor is it now, to have an accurate factual record of what I have been doing or thinking. That would be a different impulse entirely, an instinct for reality which I sometimes envy but do not possess. At no point have I ever been able successfully to keep a diary; my approach to daily life ranges from the grossly negligent to the merely absent, and on those few occasions when I have tried dutifully to record a day's events, boredom has so overcome me that the results are mysterious at best. What is this business about "shopping, typing piece, dinner with E, depressed"? Shopping for what? Typing what piece? Who is E? Was this "E" depressed, or was I depressed? Who cares?

In fact I have abandoned altogether that kind of pointless entry; instead I tell what some would call lies. "That's simply not true," the members of my family frequently tell me when they come up against my memory of a shared event. "The party was *not* for you, the spider was *not* a black widow, *it wasn't that way at all.*" Very likely they are right, for not only have I always had trouble distinguishing between what happened and what merely might have happened, but I remain unconvinced that the distinction, for my purposes, matters. The cracked crab that I recall having for lunch the day my father came home from Detroit in 1945 must certainly be embroidery, worked into the day's pattern to lend verisimilitude; I was ten years old and would not now remember the cracked crab. The day's events did not turn on cracked crab. And yet it is precisely that fictitious crab that makes me see the afternoon all over again, a home movie run all too often, the father bearing gifts, the child weeping, an exercise in family love and guilt. Or that is what it was to me. Similarly, perhaps it never did snow that August in Vermont; perhaps there never were flurries in the night wind, and maybe no one else felt the ground hardening and summer already dead even as we pretended to bask in it, but that was how it felt to me, and it might as well have snowed, could have snowed, did snow.

How it felt to me: that is getting closer to the truth about a notebook. I sometimes delude myself about why I keep a notebook, imagine that some thrifty virtue derives from preserving everything observed. See enough and write it down, I tell myself, and then some morning when the world seems drained of wonder, some day when I am only going through the motions of doing what I am supposed to do, which is write—on that bankrupt morning I will simply open my notebook and there it will all be, a forgotten account with accumulated interest, paid passage back to the world out there: dialogue overheard in hotels and elevators and at the hat-check counter in Pavillon (one middle-aged man shows his hat check to another and says, "That's my old football number"); impressions of Bettina Aptheker and Benjamin Sonnenberg and Teddy ("Mr. Acapulco") Stauffer; careful *aperçus* about tennis bums and failed fashion models and Greek shipping heiresses, one of whom taught me a significant lesson (a lesson I could have learned from F. Scott Fitzgerald, but perhaps we all must meet the very rich for ourselves) by asking, when I arrived to interview her in her orchid-filled sitting room on the second day of a paralyzing New York blizzard, whether it was snowing outside.

I imagine, in other words, that the notebook is about other people. But of course it is not. I have no real business with what one stranger said to another at the hat-check counter in Pavillon; in fact I suspect that the line "That's my old football number" touched not my own imagination at all, but merely some memory of something once read, probably "The Eighty-Yard Run."[1] Nor is my

1. Short story by Irwin Shaw (1914–1984).

concern with a woman in a dirty crepe-de-Chine wrapper in a Wilmington bar. My stake is always, of course, in the unmentioned girl in the plaid silk dress. *Remember what it was to be me*: that is always the point.

It is a difficult point to admit. We are brought up in the ethic that others, any   10
others, all others, are by definition more interesting than ourselves; taught to be diffident, just this side of self-effacing. ("You're the least important person in the room and don't forget it," Jessica Mitford's[2] governess would hiss in her ear on the advent of any social occasion; I copied that into my notebook because it is only recently that I have been able to enter a room without hearing some such phrase in my inner ear.) Only the very young and the very old may recount their dreams at breakfast, dwell upon self, interrupt with memories of beach picnics and favorite Liberty lawn dresses and the rainbow trout in a creek near Colorado Springs. The rest of us are expected, rightly, to affect absorption in other people's favorite dresses, other people's trout.

And so we do. But our notebooks give us away, for however dutifully we record what we see around us, the common denominator of all we see is always, transparently, shamelessly, the implacable "I." We are not talking here about the kind of notebook that is patently for public consumption, a structural conceit for binding together a series of graceful *pensées*;[3] we are talking about something private, about bits of the mind's string too short to use, an indiscriminate and erratic assemblage with meaning only for its maker.

And sometimes even the maker has difficulty with the meaning. There does not seem to be, for example, any point in my knowing for the rest of my life that, during 1964, 720 tons of soot fell on every square mile of New York City, yet there it is in my notebook, labeled "FACT." Nor do I really need to remember that Ambrose Bierce liked to spell Leland Stanford's[4] name "£eland $tanford" or that "smart women almost always wear black in Cuba," a fashion hint without much potential for practical application. And does not the relevance of these notes seem marginal at best?:

> In the basement museum of the Inyo County Courthouse in Independence, California, sign pinned to a mandarin coat: "This MANDARIN COAT was often worn by Mrs. Minnie S. Brooks when giving lectures on her TEAPOT COLLECTION."
> Redhead getting out of car in front of Beverly Wilshire Hotel, chinchilla stole, Vuitton bags with tags reading:
>
> MRS LOU FOX
> HOTEL SAHARA
> VEGAS

2. British essayist and social critic (1917–1996).
3. French for "thoughts."
4. Bierce (1842–1914), American journalist and fiction writer, known for such ironic writing as *The Devil's Dictionary*; Stanford (1824–1893), railroad magnate, governor of California, and founder of Stanford University.

Well, perhaps not entirely marginal. As a matter of fact, Mrs. Minnie S. Brooks and her MANDARIN COAT pull me back into my own childhood, for although I never knew Mrs. Brooks and did not visit Inyo County until I was thirty, I grew up in just such a world, in houses cluttered with Indian relics and bits of gold ore and ambergris and the souvenirs my Aunt Mercy Farnsworth brought back from the Orient. It is a long way from that world to Mrs. Lou Fox's world, where we all live now, and is it not just as well to remember that? Might not Mrs. Minnie S. Brooks help me to remember what I am? Might not Mrs. Lou Fox help me to remember what I am not?

But sometimes the point is harder to discern. What exactly did I have in mind when I noted down that it cost the father of someone I know $650 a month to light the place on the Hudson in which he lived before the Crash?[5] What use was I planning to make of this line by Jimmy Hoffa:[6] "I may have my faults, but being wrong ain't one of them"? And although I think it interesting to know where the girls who travel with the Syndicate have their hair done when they find themselves on the West Coast, will I ever make suitable use of it? Might I not be better off just passing it on to John O'Hara?[7] What is a recipe for sauerkraut doing in my notebook? What kind of magpie keeps this notebook? *"He was born the night the Titanic went down."* That seems a nice enough line, and I even recall who said it, but is it not really a better line in life than it could ever be in fiction?

15   But of course that is exactly it: not that I should ever use the line, but that I should remember the woman who said it and the afternoon I heard it. We were on her terrace by the sea, and we were finishing the wine left from lunch, trying to get what sun there was, a California winter sun. The woman whose husband was born the night the *Titanic* went down wanted to rent her house, wanted to go back to her children in Paris. I remember wishing that I could afford the house, which cost $1,000 a month. "Someday you will," she said lazily. "Someday it all comes." There in the sun on her terrace it seemed easy to believe in someday, but later I had a low-grade afternoon hangover and ran over a black snake on the way to the supermarket and was flooded with inexplicable fear when I heard the checkout clerk explaining to the man ahead of me why she was finally divorcing her husband. "He left me no choice," she said over and over as she punched the register. "He has a little seven-month-old baby by her, he left me no choice." I would like to believe that my dread then was for the human condition, but of course it was for me, because I wanted a baby and did not then have one and because I wanted to own the house that cost $1,000 a month to rent and because I had a hangover.

It all comes back. Perhaps it is difficult to see the value in having one's self back in that kind of mood, but I do see it; I think we are well advised to keep on nodding terms with the people we used to be whether we find them

5. Stock market crash of 1929.

6. Head of the Teamsters Union who disappeared in 1975 and is presumed dead (1932–1982).

7. American novelist (1905–1970).

attractive company or not. Otherwise they turn up unannounced and surprise us, come hammering on the mind's door at 4 a.m. of a bad night and demand to know who deserted them, who betrayed them, who is going to make amends. We forget all too soon the things we thought we could never forget. We forget the loves and the betrayals alike, forget what we whispered and what we screamed, forget who we were. I have already lost touch with a couple of people I used to be; one of them, a seventeen-year-old, presents little threat, although it would be of some interest to me to know again what it feels like to sit on a river levee drinking vodka-and-orange-juice and listening to Les Paul and Mary Ford[8] and their echoes sing "How High the Moon" on the car radio. (You see I still have the scenes, but I no longer perceive myself among those present, no longer could even improvise the dialogue.) The other one, a twenty-three-year-old, bothers me more. She was always a good deal of trouble, and I suspect she will reappear when I least want to see her, skirts too long, shy to the point of aggravation, always the injured party, full of recriminations and little hurts and stories I do not want to hear again, at once saddening me and angering me with her vulnerability and ignorance, an apparition all the more insistent for being so long banished.

It is a good idea, then, to keep in touch, and I suppose that keeping in touch is what notebooks are all about. And we are all on our own when it comes to keeping those lines open to ourselves: your notebook will never help me, nor mine you. *"So what's new in the whiskey business?"* What could that possibly mean to you? To me it means a blonde in a Pucci bathing suit sitting with a couple of fat men by the pool at the Beverly Hills Hotel. Another man approaches, and they all regard one another in silence for a while. "So what's new in the whiskey business?" one of the fat men finally says by way of welcome, and the blonde stands up, arches one foot and dips it in the pool, looking all the while at the cabaña where Baby Pignatari[9] is talking on the telephone. That is all there is to that, except that several years later I saw the blonde coming out of Saks Fifth Avenue in New York with her California complexion and a voluminous mink coat. In the harsh wind that day she looked old and irrevocably tired to me, and even the skins in the mink coat were not worked the way they were doing them that year, not the way she would have wanted them done, and there is the point of the story. For a while after that I did not like to look in the mirror, and my eyes would skim the newspapers and pick out only the deaths, the cancer victims, the premature coronaries, the suicides, and I stopped riding the Lexington Avenue IRT[10] because I noticed for the first time that all the strangers I had seen for years—the man with the seeing-eye dog, the spinster who read the classified pages every day, the fat girl who always got off with me at Grand Central—looked older than they once had.

It all comes back. Even that recipe for sauerkraut: even that brings it back. I was on Fire Island when I first made that sauerkraut, and it was raining, and we

8. Husband-and-wife musical team of the 1940s and 1950s.
9. Brazilian playboy (1916–1977).
10. New York City subway line; one of its stops was the Grand Central railway terminal.

drank a lot of bourbon and ate the sauerkraut and went to bed at ten, and I listened to the rain and the Atlantic and felt safe. I made the sauerkraut again last night and it did not make me feel any safer, but that is, as they say, another story.

MLA CITATION

Didion, Joan. "On Keeping a Notebook." *The Norton Reader: An Anthology of Nonfiction,* edited by Melissa A. Goldthwaite et al., 15th ed., W. W. Norton, 2020, pp. 392–98.

QUESTIONS

1. What distinction does Joan Didion make between a diary and a notebook? What uses does a notebook have for Didion?

2. Didion says she uses her notebook to "tell what some would call lies" (paragraph 7). Why does she do this? Would some people call these things truths? Why?

3. Didion says, *"How it felt to me:* that is getting closer to the truth about a notebook" (paragraph 8). What writing strategies does she use to convey "how it felt"?

4. Try keeping a notebook for a week, jotting down the sorts of things that Didion does. At the end of the week, take one or two of your entries and expand on them, as Didion does with the entries on Mrs. Minnie S. Brooks and Mrs. Lou Fox (paragraphs 12 and 13).

AMY SEQUENZIA
Loud Hands

I HAVE LOUD HANDS. I must, since I use my hands to communicate. I type what I want to say.

But that's not the only reason why I have loud hands. It is because I finally learned that I cannot be silenced, I will not be silenced.

Being a non-speaking autistic once meant, to me, accepting what people decided I wanted, felt, thought.

It is the way many autistic people are treated. In my case, it got to a point where people said I did not feel pain. After a burning accident, with second-degree burns on my arm, some people decided that I wasn't feeling anything, that I should go on with my day as they had planned it. The same thing happened after I broke my nose. Nobody thought or bothered to ask me how I felt. They silenced my hands, and because my face doesn't always show my emotions, they silenced my voice.

5   I am autistic. For too long this statement, so real and true, was something I was told to be sorry about. I was expected to be grateful that people pitied me;

Originally published in the anthology Loud Hands: Autistic People, Speaking *(2012). The author is a nonspeaking Autistic activist, writer, and poet.*

that they were forgiving of the "weird" ways I behaved; that they would make decisions for me because I did "not understand anything." The word "proud" was not expected to accompany the word "autistic." So I kept my hands quiet.

I use my very loud hands today to say: I am a proud autistic woman.

Loud hands can have many meanings. It has, in my life. It meant, when I was young, to learn how to type. I had not been successful in using sign language. Typing helped me be able to choose my favorite food, my favorite color. It also allowed me to tell my parents things that, up to that point, I could only get out through crying, smiling, or screaming.

I had found a voice but it wasn't my voice. My parents believed in me but they were alone. I looked, and still do, very disabled. I also have other disabilities. The things I was typing then were not what I felt. Instead I was trying to apologize for being me. I was accepting the assumptions about myself that were the assumptions of many, if not most, neurotypical people. I was typing what I thought to be the truth about myself. I was ashamed of being autistic, like most people believed autistic kids, and all autistics, should be. I was seen, and saw myself, as a burden and an "unfortunate event."

Because of my other disabilities I was not able to communicate for a long time. I was having too many seizures and spent many days in hospitals. After that I was numb from the medication. Between the terror in my brain and all the medications trials I lost some years of learning how to speak up. I wasn't strong enough. It took a long while for me to relearn too many lost skills. When I started typing again I began to feel like I deserved to be heard.

It has been a long and slow process. My self-esteem has been severely   10
damaged by years of listening to people talking about me in front of me, calling me names, labeling me "severe" and "retarded," even saying I did not have human dignity (I heard about that later, not as it was said).

Despite this sad reality, I would no longer have "quiet hands." It all started with small poems. I was speaking up about my life and some people started to pay attention.

Typing about my life was not easy. Through poems, I began to show how similar in our dreams and expectations of being heard and respected we all are, autistic and neurotypical alike. I will call this phase the second step in my loud hands process. At this time, I also became aware of other autistics who were also speaking up for the right to be respected, the right to be heard. They were, and still are, an inspiration.

I like to think that my coming out with autistic pride helped me gather the support from some neurotypical friends. This is very important to me because I need a lot of help with everything I do. They respect me, understand my difficulties and allow me to be myself. Having these friends' support allows me to continue to type my thoughts. Their help with my safety and general care allows me to focus on speaking out. If I had to focus on things like, for example, eating without making a mess, this would take a lot of energy from me (besides, the cerebral palsy interferes with my coordination). I prefer to use my energy on things I believe are more important to my life, and things that I can try to change and have a greater impact.

But my process wasn't finished. To have really loud hands I needed to speak out and state it clear that I am autistic and proud of it. I had to overcome the anxiety of exposing myself and the echo of old voices in my head, the voices of teachers and "experts" who said so many times that I was nothing.

15   So I started by typing letters on disabilities advocacy; I went places and challenged people's misconceptions about me; I wrote an essay. The final phase of my process: I now have loud hands.

But being proud of being autistic is not enough to end stereotypes. We are part of a large spectrum and each one of us has very specific challenges. The many labels given to us by neurotypical "experts" make our struggles towards inclusion more difficult.

Autistics with a "high functioning" label might also have hidden disabilities that make others deny the accommodations necessary for them to thrive. They are expected to overcome their autistic related anxieties and fit in, "get over it."

Autistics with the label "low functioning" are not expected to succeed, ever. Unless, maybe, after many years, they can look and act a little more like a "normal" person. They are the "hopeless" ones, the ones who need to be "fixed." Their stories become "tragedies" and their real self, ignored. Most neurotypical people refuse or never think about trying to understand their language or allow them to express themselves. They are segregated, bullied, pitied but never heard, never listened to. There is still very little interest in trying new approaches to address the usually extreme anxiety and sensory issues that are manifested in what is, again, labeled "odd behavior." The favorite approach still is to "fix" the autistic, children and adults. The children might be lucky with a sensible early intervention that values who they are and make sure their abilities are valued too. The adults are usually ignored, isolated from community living or, almost always, treated like children, chastised for their "wrong behavior."

Non-speaking autistics are also labeled "low functioning." That's me. There still is a misconception that if you don't speak you can't understand, think or even hear. People talk about you, not to you; they ask questions not to you, but direct the conversation towards a third person, even when you can communicate through signs or other augmentative communication devices; or they talk to you by yelling, as if a loud voice will make us "understand better."

20   Despite many non-speaking autistics coming out as self-advocates, there still is great bias and suspicion about their abilities. In some cases, these autistic individuals communicate through facilitated communication (FC)—I am one of them. Because of many years of being labeled "low functioning," "severe," "difficult," and despite a very complete set of guidelines intended to assure the FC user authorship, we are often looked at with suspicion, as frauds. The fact that many have been validated in several studies and others now type independently is conveniently ignored.

Is it because of the way we look? Is it because some of us need breaks to recharge, calm down or just do a little flapping between lines? We still want to be respected as we are, with the whole set of things we do to manage better our responses to outside stimuli. Even though we might have found a way to communicate and show expressive intelligence, we still have to fight for the right to be ourselves.

I personally can tell that it is very frustrating when I am so misunderstood. When I decide to type, it can take days or even weeks for me to finish an essay. Then I have to review it, line by line. I need breaks, my arms get stiff. If I have a bad seizure, I might need more than a day to recover. But sometimes I type quickly and without breaks. Every time, I get very tired from the brainwork, trying to organize thoughts in an intelligible way. And then, when I meet people, I might be completely overwhelmed and unable to type or focus on anything. That's when I most need to do the things I do to be able to focus again. Or I need to be left alone. It is also when I am dismissed as "too severe." It is as if I am only worthy if I behave in a certain way that the neurotypicals find acceptable.

Hidden abilities created the myth of "low functioning" autistics, like hidden disabilities created the myth of "high functioning" autistics. It doesn't really matter to our lives and how we live what label we are given. We still fight misconceptions, from all sides. It seems that the great majority of neurotypicals want us to be more like them, talk like them, and not do things, when we speak, that they don't do when they speak. That's one important reason for the neurodiversity movement. That's why having loud hands is so imperative. We are who we are and we are not ashamed of it.

When I started typing essays and reading articles by other autistic self-advocates, I saw that we all want the same things, no matter where in the spectrum or where in our personal lives we find ourselves. We want to be respected for who we are, autistics that flap, spin, twirl, fidget; autistics that communicate not only by talking but by any other way; we want to be included for the things we can do, the way we can do these things; we want to be supported so we can be ourselves and reach our potential, at our own time and in our own terms.

We have loud hands and we want to be heard.   25

MLA CITATION

Sequenzia, Amy. "Loud Hands." *The Norton Reader: An Anthology of Nonfiction*, edited by Melissa A. Goldthwaite et al., 15th ed., W. W. Norton, 2020, pp. 398–401.

QUESTIONS

1. Amy Sequenzia tells an empowering story of having been silenced and then learning how to speak for herself. Describe a time when you felt silenced. How did you learn to find your voice?

2. Describe some of the challenges Sequenzia faced—and still faces—in expressing herself. How do these challenges—and her pride in communicating despite them—affect your sense of the importance of writing?

3. Although we use our hands to make noise, we do not usually think of hands as "loud." List all of the reasons Sequenzia offers for calling her hands "loud."

4. Sequenzia writes about those who understand and believe in her and those who misunderstand her. Write an essay in which you explain the difference that friends and allies make in your life, especially around something you find challenging.

REBECCA SOLNIT
How to Be a Writer

1) WRITE. THERE IS NO SUBSTITUTE. Write what you most passionately want to write, not blogs, posts, tweets or all the disposable bubblewrap in which modern life is cushioned. But start small: write a good sentence, then a good paragraph, and don't be dreaming about writing the great American novel or what you'll wear at the awards ceremony because that's not what writing's about or how you get there from here. The road is made entirely out of words. Write a lot. Maybe at the outset you'll be like a toddler—the terrible twos are partly about being frustrated because you're smarter than your motor skills or your mouth, you want to color the picture, ask for the toy, and you're bumbling, incoherent and no one gets it, but it's not only time that gets the kid onward to more sophistication and skill, it's effort and practice. Write bad stuff because the road to good writing is made out of words and not all of them are well-arranged words.

2) **Remember that writing is not typing.** Thinking, researching, contemplating, outlining, composing in your head and in sketches, maybe some typing, with revisions as you go, and then more revisions, deletions, emendations, additions, reflections, setting aside and returning afresh, because a good writer is always a good editor of his or her own work. Typing is this little transaction in the middle of two vast thoughtful processes. There is such a thing as too much revision—I've seen things that were amazing in the 17th version get flattened out in the 23rd—but nothing is born perfect. Well, some things almost are, but they're freaks. And you might get those magical perfect passages if you write a lot, including all the stuff that isn't magic that has to be cut, rethought, revised, fact-checked, and cleaned up.

3) **Read. And don't read.** Read good writing, and don't live in the present. Live in the deep past, with the language of the Koran or the Mabinogion or Mother Goose or Dickens or Dickinson or Baldwin or whatever speaks to you deeply. Literature is not high school and it's not actually necessary to know what everyone around you is wearing, in terms of style, and being influenced by people who are being published in this very moment is going to make you look just like them, which is probably not a good long-term goal for being yourself or making a meaningful contribution. At any point in history there is a great tide of writers of similar tone, they wash in, they wash out, the strange starfish stay behind, and the conches. Check out the bestseller list for April 1935 or August 1978 if you don't believe me. Originality is partly a matter of having your own influences: read evolutionary biology textbooks or the Old Testament, find your metaphors where no one's looking, don't belong. Or belong to the other world that is not quite this one, the world from which you send back your messages. Imagine Herman Melville in workshop in 1849 being told by all his peers that he needed to cut all those informative digressions and really his big whale book was kind of dull and

Originally published at Literary Hub (lithub.com) *in 2016. Rebecca Solnit is a San Francisco–based writer, historian, and activist.*

why did it take him so long to get to the point. And actually it was a quiet failure at the time. So was pretty much everything Thoreau published, and Emily Dickinson published only a handful of poems in her lifetime but wrote thousands.

4) Listen. Don't listen. Feedback is great, from your editor, your agent, your readers, your friends, your classmates, but there are times when you know exactly what you're doing and why and obeying them means being out of tune with yourself. Listen to your own feedback and remember that you move forward through mistakes and stumbles and flawed but aspiring work, not perfect pirouettes performed in the small space in which you initially stood. Listen to what makes your hair stand on end, your heart melt, and your eyes go wide, what stops you in your tracks and makes you want to live, wherever it comes from, and hope that your writing can do all those things for other people. Write for other people, but don't listen to them too much.

5) Find a vocation. Talent is overrated, and it is usually conflated with nice style.   5
Passion, vocation, vision, and dedication are rarer, and they will get you through the rough spots in your style when your style won't give you a reason to get up in the morning and stare at the manuscript for the hundredth day in a row or even give you a compelling subject to write about. If you're not passionate about writing and about the world and the things in it you're writing about, then why are you writing? It starts with passion even before it starts with words. You want to read people who are wise, deep, wild, kind, committed, insightful, attentive; you want to be those people. I am all for style, but only in service of vision.

6) Time. It takes time. This means that you need to find that time. Don't be too social. Live below your means and keep the means modest (people with trust funds and other cushions: I'm not talking to you, though money makes many, many things easy, and often, vocation and passion harder). You probably have to do something else for a living at the outset or all along, but don't develop expensive habits or consuming hobbies. I knew a waitress once who thought fate was keeping her from her painting but taste was: if she'd given up always being the person who turned going out for a burrito into ordering the expensive wine at the bistro she would've had one more free day a week for art.

7) Facts. Always get them right. The wrong information about a bumblebee in a poem is annoying enough, but inaccuracy in nonfiction is a cardinal sin. No one will trust you if you get your facts wrong, and if you're writing about living or recently alive people or politics you absolutely must not misrepresent. (Ask yourself this: do I like it when people lie about me?) No matter what you're writing about, you have an obligation to get it right, for the people you're writing about, for the readers, and for the record. It's why I always tell students that it's a slippery slope from the things your stepfather didn't actually do to the weapons of mass destruction Iraq didn't actually have.[1] If you want to

---

1. President George W. Bush justified starting the Second Iraq War in 2003 on the claim that Iraq was developing these weapons. This claim turned out to be false.

write about a stepfather who did things your stepfather didn't, or repeat conversations you don't actually remember with any detail, at least label your product accurately. Fiction operates under different rules but it often has facts in it too, and your credibility rests on their accuracy. (If you want to make up facts, like that Emily Brontë was nine feet tall and had wings but everyone in that Victorian era was too proper to mention it, remember to get the details about her cobbler and the kind of hat in fashion at the time right, and maybe put a little cameo at her throat seven and a half feet above the earth.)

8) **Joy.** Writing is facing your deepest fears and all your failures, including how hard it is to write a lot of the time and how much you loathe what you've just written and that you're the person who just committed those flawed sentences (many a writer, and God, I know I'm one, has worried about dying before the really crappy version is revised so that posterity will never know how awful it was). When it totally sucks, pause, look out the window (there should always be a window) and say, I'm doing exactly what I want to be doing. I am hanging out with the English language (or the Spanish or the Korean). I get to use the word turquoise or melting or supernova right now if I want. I'm with Shelley, who says that poets are the unacknowledged legislators of the universe, and I am not fracking or selling useless things to lonely seniors or otherwise abusing my humanity. Find pleasure and joy. Maybe even make lists of joys for emergencies. When all else fails, put on the gospel song "Steal My Joy"—refrain is "Ain't gonna let nobody steal my joy." Nobody, not even yourself.

But it's not about the joy, it's about the work, and there has to be some kind of joy in the work, some kind from among the many kinds, including the joy of hard truths told honestly. Carpenters don't say, I'm just not feeling it today, or I don't give a damn about this staircase and whether people fall through it; how you feel is something that you cannot take too seriously on your way to doing something, and doing something is a means of not being stuck in how you feel. That is, there's a kind of introspection that's wallowing and being stuck, and there's a kind that gets beyond that into something more interesting and then maybe takes you out into the world or into the place where deepest interior and cosmological phenomena are at last talking to each other. I've written stuff amidst hideous suffering, and it was a way not to be so stuck in the hideous suffering, though it was hard, but also, hard is not impossible, and I didn't sign up with the expectation that it would be easy.

10   9) **What we call success is very nice and comes with useful byproducts, but success is not love**, or at least it is at best the result of love of the work and not of you, so don't confuse the two. Cultivating love for others and maybe receiving some for yourself is another job and an important one. The process of making art is the process of becoming a person with agency, with independent thought, a producer of meaning rather than a consumer of meanings that may be at odds with your soul, your destiny, your humanity, so there's another kind of success in becoming conscious that matters and that is up to you and nobody else and within your reach.

10) It's all really up to you, but you already knew that and knew everything else you need to know somewhere underneath the noise and the bustle and the anxiety and the outside instructions, including these ones.

MLA CITATION

Solnit, Rebecca. "How to Be a Writer." *The Norton Reader: An Anthology of Nonfiction*, edited by Melissa A. Goldthwaite et al., 15th ed., W. W. Norton, 2020, pp. 402–05.

QUESTIONS

1. Rebecca Solnit's first rule for writing is "Write": a clue that this how-to essay is a little offbeat. Which of her rules took you most by surprise? Which are you going to try out for yourself?

2. Study the numbered items in Solnit's list. What internal organization and logic stands behind this list?

3. In paragraph 3, Solnit recommends reading things that are old, unpopular, and out of the way. Do you have cultural texts (books, movies, or music) that you love that most people have not heard of or don't much listen to now? How do those items shape your outlook? Why are the statements in this order?

4. Write your own "How to Be a Writer," complete with numbered paragraphs. Following Solnit's example, experiment with mixing seriousness and humor.

JASWINDER BOLINA
Writing Like a White Guy: On Language, Race, and Poetry

M Y FATHER SAYS I should use a pseudonym. "They won't publish you if they see your name. They'll know you're not one of them. They'll know you're one of us." This has never occurred to me, at least not in a serious way. "No publisher in America's going to reject my poems because I have a foreign name," I reply. "Not in 2002." I argue, "These are educated people. My name won't be any impediment." Yet in spite of my faith in the egalitarian attitude of editors and the anonymity of book contests, I understand my father's angle on the issue.

With his beard shaved and his hair shorn, his turban undone and left behind in Bolina Doaba, Punjab—the town whose name we take as our own—

Originally appeared on the website of The Poetry Foundation *(2011), "an independent literary organization committed to a vigorous presence for poetry in our culture."*

he lands at Heathrow in 1965, a brown boy of 18 become a Londoner. His circumstance then must seem at once exhilarating and also like drifting in a lifeboat: necessary, interminable. I imagine the English of the era sporting an especially muted and disdainful brand of racism toward my alien father, his brother and sister-in-law, toward his brother-in-law and sister, his nieces and nephews, and the other Indians they befriend on Nadine Street, Charlton, just east of Greenwich. The sense of exclusion arrives over every channel, dull and constant.

At least one realtor, a couple of bankers, and a few foremen must have a different attitude. One white supervisor at the industrial bakery my father labors in invites him home for dinner. The Brit wants to offer an introduction to his single daughters. He knows my father's a hard worker, a trait so commonly attributed to the immigrant it seems sometimes a nationality unto itself, and maybe the quietude of the nonnative speaker appeals to the man's sense of civility. As a result he finds my father humble, upstanding, his complexion a light beach sand indicative of a vigor exceeding that of the pale English suitors who come calling. In my imagination, my father's embarrassed and placid demeanor, his awkward formality in that setting, is charming to the bashful, giggly daughters, and this impresses the supervisor even further. But nothing much comes of that evening. My father never visits again. He marries my mother, another Sikh Punjabi also, a few years later, but that event is evidence that one Englishman considered my father the man, not my father the "paki."

When he moves to hodgepodge Chicago nine years after arriving in England, he becomes another denizen of the immigrant nation, the huddled masses. He might be forgiven for thinking he will not be excluded here, but he isn't so naïve. America in 1974 is its own version of the UK's insular empire, though the nature of its exclusion is different, is what we call institutional. He knows that in America nobody should be rejected, not unabashedly and without some counterfeit of a reason, but all my father's nearly three decades as a machinist at the hydraulics plant near the airport teach him is that economies boom and economies bust, and if your name isn't "Bill" or "Earl" or "Frank Malone," you don't get promoted. You mind the machines. "Bills" and "Earls" supervise. "Frank" is the name the bosses go by, all of them hired after my dad but raised higher. So when my father suggests I use a pseudonym, he's only steadying my two-wheeler, only buying me a popsicle from the cart at Foster Avenue Beach. This is only an extension of covering my tuition, of paying my room and board.

5   At the time, I'm only a year or so into an MFA. I stop by the office of a friend, an older white poet in my department. Publication to me feels impossible then, and the friend means to be encouraging when he says, "With a name like Jaswinder Bolina, you could publish plenty of poems right now if you wrote about the first-generation, minority stuff. What I admire is that you don't write that kind of poetry." He's right. I don't write "that kind" of poetry. To him, this is upstanding, correct, what a poet ought to do. It's indicative of a vigor exceeding that of other minority poets come calling. It turns out I'm a hard worker too. I

should be offended—if not for myself, then on behalf of writers who do take on the difficult subject of minority experience in their poetry—but I understand that my friend means no ill by it. To his mind, embracing my difference would open editorial inboxes, but knowing that I tend to eschew/exclude/deny "that kind" of subject in my poetry, he adds, "This'll make it harder for you." When, only a few months later, my father—who's never read my poems, whose fine but mostly functional knowledge of English makes the diction and syntax of my work difficult to follow, who doesn't know anything of the themes or subjects of my poetry—tells me to use another name, he's encouraging also. He means: Let them think you're a white guy. This will make it easier for you.

The one thing I least believe about race in America is that we can disregard it. I'm nowhere close to alone in this, but the person I encounter far more often than the racist—closeted or proud—is the one who believes race isn't an active factor in her thinking, isn't an influence on his interaction with the racial Other. Such blindness to race seems unlikely, but I suspect few of us entirely understand why it's so improbable. I'm not certain either, but I've been given some idea. At a panel discussion in 2004, a professor of political philosophy, Caribbean-born with a doctorate from the University of Toronto, explains that he never understood why the question in America is so often a question of race. A scholar of Marxist thinking, he says in nearly every other industrialized nation on Earth, the first question is a question of class, and accordingly class is the first conflict. He says it wasn't until he moved to the United States in the early '70s—about the same time my father arrived—that he intellectually and viscerally understood that America is a place where class historically coincides with race. This, he says, is the heaviest legacy of slavery and segregation.

To many immigrants, the professor and my father included, this conflation between success and skin color is a foreign one. In their native lands, where there exists a relative homogeneity in the racial makeup of the population or a pervasive mingling of races, the "minorities" of America are classed based on socioeconomic status derived from any number of factors, and race is rarely, if ever, principal in these. You can look down on anybody even though they share your skin color if you have land enough, wealth enough, caste and education enough. It's only arriving in England that the Indian—who might not even recognize the descriptor "Indian," preferring instead a regional or religious identity to a national one—realizes anyone resembling him is subject to the derision "coolie." It's only in America that such an immigrant discovers any brown-skinned body can have a "camel fucker" or a "sand nigger" hurled at him from a passing car—a bit of cognitive dissonance that's been directed at me on more than one occasion. The racially African but ethnically Other philosophy professor understands the oddness of this as well as anyone. He explains that in the United States, as anywhere, the first question remains a question of class, but the coincidence between class and color makes the first American social conflict a conflict of race. As such, for the racial immigrant and his offspring, racial difference need be mitigated whenever possible, if only to lubricate the cogs of class mobility: nearer to whiteness, nearer to wealth.

If the racial Other aspires to equal footing on the socioeconomic playing field, he is tasked with forcing his way out of the categorical cul-de-sac that his name and appearance otherwise squeeze him into. We call the process by which he does this "assimilation." Though the Latin root here—shared with the other word "similar"—implies that the process is one of becoming absorbed or incorporated, it is a process that relies first on the negation of one identity in order to adopt another. In this sense, assimilation is a destructive rather than constructive process. It isn't a come-as-you-are proposition, a simple matter of being integrated into the American milieu because there exists a standing invitation to do so. Rather, assimilation first requires refuting assumptions the culture makes about the immigrant based on race, and in this sense assimilation requires the erasure of one's preexisting cultural identity even though that identity wasn't contingent upon race in the first place.

The first and perhaps essential step in assimilating into any culture is the successful adoption of the host country's language. What's unusual in America is that this is no different for the immigrant than for the native-born non-white. This is most obvious when I consider African Americans, whose language is variously described as "urban" (as in "of the slums of the inner city"), "street" (as in "of the gutter"), and "Ebonic" (as in "of ebony, of blackness"). These descriptors imply that whatever it is, black vernacular isn't English. Rather, it's "broken English," which is of course what we also call the English of the nonnative speaker. I'm tempted to categorize so-called "countrified" or "redneck" dialects similarly, except I remember that any number of recent U.S. presidents and presidential candidates capable in that vernacular are regarded as more down-to-earth and likable rather than less well-spoken or intelligent. It seems

that such white dialect serves as evidence of charisma, charm, and folksiness
rather than of ignorance.

In 2007, the eventual vice president campaigning in the primary election   10
against the eventual president says, "I mean, you got the first mainstream African American who is *articulate* and bright and *clean* and a nice-looking guy.
I mean, that's a storybook, man." The ensuing kerfuffle is almost entirely
unsurprising. Though the white candidate believes he's merely describing the
candidate of color and doing so with ample objectivity and perhaps even with
generosity, the description implies that the black man's appearance and eloquence constitute an exception to his blackness, which is a function of genetics, which only further suggests that the black candidate is an exception to
his basic nature. The implication is that he is being praised for his approximate
whiteness. Not shockingly, this very conflation of his eloquence with white
racial identity leads pundits in another context to ask the obnoxious question,
"But is he black enough?" The conundrum the candidate faces is that he need
be an exceptional speaker and writer, but part of the "exceptional" here is the
idea that he's an "exception" to his race. He has co-opted the language of whiteness. If he then neglects to take on the subject of race with that language, with
the fierce urgency of now, he might further be accused of rejecting his own
racial identity. Is he a candidate or a black candidate? If it's the former, he might
not be "black enough." If it's the latter, he can't win.

In a country where class and race structurally overlap, what we call "standard" English reflexively becomes the English of whiteness rather than simply
the English of the educated or privileged classes. When I adopt the language I'm
taught in prep school, in university, and in graduate school, I'm adopting the
English language, but in the States, that language is intrinsically associated with
one race over any another. By contrast, in the England of history, the one prior to
the more recent influx of immigrants from its imperial colonies, Oxford English
is spoken by subjects as white as those who bandy about in Cockney. Adeptness
of language usage isn't a function then of melanin but of socioeconomic location.
Color isn't the question; class is. Unlike the Cockney of England or the dialects
of India, none of which are contingent upon racial difference, alternate dialects
in American English are inherently racialized. Assimilation in America then
comes to mean the appropriation of a specific racial identity by way of language.
The conundrum for the poet of color becomes no different than the one that
faces the candidate of color: Am I a writer or a minority writer?

The day I'm born, my father engages in the American custom of handing out
cigars to the "Bills" and "Earls" and "Franks" of the factory floor, even though
he has never smoked in his life. Smoking is anathema to his Sikh Punjabi identity. Drinking, on the other hand, is most certainly not, and he gets gleefully
and mercilessly drunk with his brothers at home. He boasts everywhere, "My
son will be president." He believes it. Twenty-four years later, in 2002, when
he counsels me to use a pseudonym, he knows I'm already adept in the language.
I've been educated in it, and in spite of all his diligence and intelligence, this is
a key he's never been given. I talk like them. I write like them. I'm an agile agent
in the empire so long as nobody grows wise. He no longer expects a presidency,

but he sees no limit to potential success in my chosen field, except for the limits placed on me by my racial difference from the dominant culture. He doesn't consider the possibility that I write about race in my work, that I might want to embrace the subject, because he knows, like the candidate of black Kenyan and white Kansan bloodlines, I've been conditioned to resist making race the essential issue.

And it's true. The manner with which I avoid the subject of race in my first book is nearly dogmatic. Race is a subject I don't offer any attention to. To do so would seem only to underscore my Otherness, which would only result in the same sorts of requisite exclusions I experienced growing up in mostly white schools and neighborhoods. Assimilation in those circumstances isn't a choice so much political as it is necessary. Some remnant of a survival instinct kicks in, and one's best efforts are directed at joining rather than resisting the herd. To be racialized is to be marginalized. When another Asian kid joins the playground, we unwittingly vie to out-white each other. This tactic I learned from practice but also from my immigrant family. When your numbers are few, assimilation is the pragmatic gambit.

It's not something that we engage in without a queasy feeling. When my father suggests I Wite-Out my name, he's entirely aware that he's suggesting I relinquish the name he and my mother gave me. This isn't an easy thing, but growing up, I've never been kept from doing what the "American" kids do— though I'm born here and though my parents have long been citizens, "American" remains a descriptor my family uses to signify whiteness. Like the white kids, I join the Cub Scouts and play football at recess, I attend birthday parties at my American classmates' houses and go to junior high socials. In high school, after years of elementary school mockery, I attempt—not unlike the young Barry Obama—to anglicize my name, going by "Jason" instead, a stratagem that those who become my friends quickly reject after only a few weeks. I go to the homecoming dance. I go to the prom. I stay out past curfew and grow my hair long. I insist that my mother close all the bedroom doors when she cooks so my clothes don't reek of cumin and turmeric. I resist any suggestion that I study the sciences in order to prepare for a career in medicine or engineering. I never meet an Indian girl; there aren't any in the philosophy and English departments I'm a member of anyway. My parents know I'm bereft of their culture. They must at times feel a lucid resentment, a sense of rejection and exclusion. Their son has become one of the English-speakers, as "Frank" or "Bill" to them as any American. But this, they know, is necessary. If the first generation is to succeed here, it's by resisting the ingrained cultural identity and mores of its immigrant forebears. If their son is to become president, my parents know it won't happen while he's wearing a turban. This is why they never keep me from engaging American culture, though it quickly comes to supplant their own. Assimilation is pragmatic, but pragmatism calls for concessions that compound and come to feel like a chronic ache.

15   It's because of the historical convergence of race and class in America that we conflate the language of the educated, ruling classes with the language of a

particular racial identity. If I decouple the two, as I might be able to do in another nation, I realize that what's being described isn't the language of whiteness so much as the language of privilege. When I say "privilege" here, I mean the condition of not needing to consider what others are forced to consider. The privilege of whiteness in America—particularly male, heteronormative whiteness—is the privilege to speak from a blank slate, to not need to address questions of race, gender, sexuality, or class except by choice, to not need to acknowledge wherefrom one speaks. It's the position of no position, the voice from nowhere or from everywhere. In this, it is Godlike, and if nothing else, that's saying something.

To the poet, though, the first question isn't one of class or color. The first question is a question of language. Poetry—as Stéphane Mallarmé famously tells the painter and hapless would-be poet Edgar Degas—is made of words, not ideas. However, to the poet of color or the female poet, to the gay or transgendered writer in America, and even to the white male writer born outside of socioeconomic privilege, a difficult question arises: "Whose language is it?" Where the history of academic and cultural institutions is so dominated by white men of means, "high" language necessarily comes to mean the language of whiteness and a largely wealthy, heteronormative maleness at that. The minority poet seeking entry into the academy and its canon finds that her language is deracialized/sexualized/gendered/classed at the outset. In trafficking in "high" English, writers other than educated, straight, white, male ones of privilege choose to become versed in a language that doesn't intrinsically or historically coincide with perceptions of their identities. It's true that minority poets are permitted to bring alternative vernaculars into our work. Poets from William Wordsworth in the preface to *Lyrical Ballads* to Frank O'Hara in his "Personism: A Manifesto" demand as much by insisting that poetry incorporate language nearer to conversational speech than anything overly elevated. Such calls for expansions of literary language in conjunction with continuing experiments by recent generations of American poets are transforming the canon for sure, but this leaves me and perhaps others like me in a slightly awkward position. I don't possess a vernacular English that's significantly different from that of plain old Midwestern English. As such, it seems I'm able to write from a perspective that doesn't address certain realities about myself, and this makes me queasy as anything. The voice in my head is annoyed with the voice in my writing. The voice in my head says I'm disregarding difference, and this feels like a denial of self, of reality, of a basic truth.

It isn't exactly intentional. It's a product of being privileged. In the 46 years since my father left Punjab, the 40 or so years since my mother left also, my parents clambered the socioeconomic ladder with a fair amount of middle-class success. We're not exactly wealthy, but I do wind up in prep school instead of the public high school, which only isolates me further from those with a shared racial identity. Later I attend university, where I'm permitted by my parents' successes to study the subjects I want to study rather than those that might guarantee future wealth. I don't need to become a doctor or a lawyer to support the clan. I get to major in philosophy and later attend graduate school in creative writing. Through all of this, though I experience occasional instances of bigotry while walking down streets or in bars, and though I study in programs where I'm often one of only two or three students of color, my racial identity is generally overlooked or disregarded by those around me. I've become so adept in the language and culture of the academy that on more than one occasion when I bring up the fact of my race, colleagues reply with some variation of "I don't think of you as a minority." Or, as a cousin who's known me since infancy jokes, "You're not a minority. You're just a white guy with a tan." What she means is that my assimilation is complete. But she can't be correct. Race is simply too essential to the American experience to ever be entirely overlooked. As such, I can't actually write like a white guy any more than I can revise my skin color. This, however, doesn't change the fact that if a reader were to encounter much of my work not knowing my name or having seen a photograph of me, she might not be faulted for incorrectly assigning the poems a white racial identity. This is a product of my language, which is a product of my education, which is a product of the socioeconomic privilege afforded by my parents' successes. The product of all those factors together is that the writing—this essay included—can't seem to help sounding *white*.

Recently, I was invited to give a few poetry readings as part of a literary festival taking place in a rural part of the country. I borrow my father's compact SUV and let its GPS guide me for a few days on the road. I spend afternoons and evenings reading poems with local and visiting writers in front of small audiences at community centers and public libraries. The audiences are largely made up of kind, white-haired, white-skinned locals enthusiastic to hear us read from and speak about our work, even when they've never heard of most of us. They at least appreciate poetry, a rarity I'm grateful for. During the introductions that preface each event, even the organizers who've invited me have difficulty getting my name right, and in one school library, I enunciate it over and over again. I say, "*Jas* as in the first part of *justice*; *win* as in the opposite of defeat; *der*, which rhymes with *err*, meaning to be mistaken." I say, "JasWINder," lilting the second syllable, and smile as about a dozen audience members mouth each syllable along with me until they feel they have it right. When they do, they grin broadly. After each event, I chat with them one or two at a time, and I do my best to reflect their warmth. They're complimentary about the work, and though I don't expect they're a demographic that'll especially like my poems—even when you write poems like a white guy, you might not be writing poems everyone will like—the compliments are earnest.

Still, in all this pleasantness, the awkward moment occurs more than once. It's some variation on a recurring question I get in town after town. The question usually comes up as a matter of small talk while I'm signing a book or shaking someone's hand. No one delivers it better, with so much beaming warmth and unwitting irony, than the woman who says she enjoyed my poems very much and follows this quickly with an admiring "You're so Americanized, what nationality are you?" She doesn't pick up on the oxymoron in her question. She doesn't hear the hint of tiredness in my reply. "I was born and raised in Chicago, but my parents are from northern India." Once more, I ought to be offended, but I'm not really. Hers is an expression of curiosity that's born of genuine interest rather than of sideshow spectacle. I'm the only nonwhite writer at the events I participate in. I'm the only one who gets this question. It makes me bristle, but I understand where it comes from.

After my brief tour is over, I make the 500-mile trip to suburban Chicago to return the Toyota to my parents. I eat dinner at home, and after, my father drops me back in the city. Invariably, the trip down the Kennedy Expressway toward the skyline makes him nostalgic for his early, underpaid days in small apartments on the North Side, his city long before it became my city. He tells a story or two, and we talk as usual about the news, politics, the latest way my uncle annoys him. He goes on a while before his attention returns to the moment, and he asks how my trip went. I tell him it went well. I say the audiences were kind and the drives were long. I say, out there, the country looks like a painting of itself. I don't mention what the woman asked, the recurring question echoed by others. "You're so Americanized, what nationality are you?" It won't matter that she asked it while eagerly shaking my hand. It won't matter that she asked while asking me also to sign a copy of my book for her. It won't matter that she offered her gratitude that I'd come all that way to read in her hamlet on the outskirts of America. Though she might have meant the opposite, he'll hear the question as the old door closing again. The doorway, then, is both welcome and departure, is border guard and border crossing, and though I'm not on the woman's side of it, I'm not entirely on my father's side either.

Perhaps for this reason, there's the continuing sense that I *ought* to write about race even as I resent that I need be troubled by the subject in the first place. After all, I should permit myself to be a poet first and a minority second, same as any male, white writer. But even as I attempt to ignore the issue altogether, I find myself thinking about it, and I realize now that this fact more than any other makes it so that I can't write like a white poet. Writing is as much the process of arriving at the point of composition as it is the act of composition itself. That my awareness of racial identity so often plays a part in my thinking about my writing makes it so that I can't engage in that writing without race being a live wire. Even one's evasions are born of one's fixations. More to the point, what appears to be an evasion might not be exactly that at all. John Ashbery doesn't make a subject matter of his sexuality, but this doesn't mean he's unable to inhabit the identity of a gay writer. Similarly, even though Mary Ruefle might not take on gender identity overtly in a given poem, it doesn't make that poem an adversary to the cause of feminism. I don't bring all this up to absolve myself exactly, though it's true I'm trying to figure out a way to alleviate a guilt I'm annoyed to feel in the first place. I imagine male, white poets will recognize this feeling. I bet any poet of conscience who doesn't actively write about sociopolitical subjects knows this feeling, but the poet is trying to write the original thing, and that originality might not take up orbit around a more obvious facet of a poet's identity. When any of us doesn't take on such a

20

subject in our writing, it might not be because we neglected to do so. Rather, it might be that the subject informed every bit of our deciding to write about something else.

More importantly, when it comes to writing about difficult issues of identity, especially those with far-reaching political and cultural implications, maybe the choice needn't be a dichotomous one. Maybe I don't need to choose between being the brown guy writing like a white guy or the brown guy writing about being Othered. Instead, maybe I need only be a brown guy writing out his study of language and the self—the same as the Paterson doctor, the Hartford insurance executive, the lesbian expat in Paris, the gay Jew from New Jersey, the male white poet teaching at the University of Houston, or the straight black female professor reading her poem at the American president's inauguration. Though "high" English might be born of a culture once dominated by straight white men of privilege, each of us wields our English in ways those men might not have imagined. This is okay. Language, like a hammer, belongs to whoever picks it up to build or demolish. Whether we take language in hand to deconstruct itself, to confess a real experience or an imagined one, or to meditate upon the relationship between the individual and the political, social, historical, or cosmological, ownership of our language need not be bound up with the history of that language. Whether I choose to pound on the crooked nail of race or gender, self or Other, whether I decide on some obscure subject while forgoing the other obvious one, when I write, the hammer belongs to me.

MLA CITATION

Bolina, Jaswinder. "Writing Like a White Guy: On Language, Race, and Poetry." *The Norton Reader: An Anthology of Nonfiction*, edited by Melissa A. Goldthwaite et al., 15th ed., W. W. Norton, 2020, pp. 405–14.

QUESTIONS

1. Throughout this essay, Jaswinder Bolina compares the role of race in his life with the role of race in his poetry. List some of his ambivalent feelings, explore their sources, and discuss where he seems to land in the end with regard to the relationship between his poetry and his race.

2. What, according to Bolina, is the relationship between language and race in the United States? How is this relationship different from other countries he discusses?

3. Bolina writes that, as a child, he tried to "out-white" (paragraph 13) other Asian kids on the playground. The essays by Chang-Rae Lee, Durga-Chew Bose, and Chimamanda Adichie each describe the feeling of being one of the only members of a minority group within a larger, mostly white group. Based on Bolina's account and others (including, perhaps, your own experience), what are the hazards of encountering another person who shares the same minority status in a predominantly white space?

4. Using Bolina's essay as a starting point, write about how an artist should balance artistic ambitions with the need or desire to speak for a group to which she or he belongs (e.g., racial or ethnic minority, religion, sexual orientation, and so on).

GEORGE ORWELL
Politics and the English Language

M OST PEOPLE WHO BOTHER with the matter at all would admit that the English language is in a bad way, but it is generally assumed that we cannot by conscious action do anything about it. Our civilization is decadent and our language—so the argument runs—must inevitably share in the general collapse. It follows that any struggle against the abuse of language is a sentimental archaism, like preferring candles to electric light or hansom cabs to aeroplanes. Underneath this lies the half-conscious belief that language is a natural growth and not an instrument which we shape for our own purposes.

Now, it is clear that the decline of a language must ultimately have political and economic causes: it is not due simply to the bad influence of this or that individual writer. But an effect can become a cause, reinforcing the original cause and producing the same effect in an intensified form, and so on indefinitely. A man may take to drink because he feels himself to be a failure, and then fail all the more completely because he drinks. It is rather the same thing that is happening to the English language. It becomes ugly and inaccurate because our thoughts are foolish, but the slovenliness of our language makes it easier for us to have foolish thoughts. The point is that the process is reversible. Modern English, especially written English, is full of bad habits which spread by imitation and which can be avoided if one is willing to take the necessary trouble. If one gets rid of these habits one can think more clearly, and to think clearly is a necessary first step towards political regeneration: so that the fight against bad English is not frivolous and is not the exclusive concern of professional writers. I will come back to this presently, and I hope that by that time the meaning of what I have said here will have become clearer. Meanwhile, here are five specimens of the English language as it is now habitually written.

These five passages have not been picked out because they are especially bad—I could have quoted far worse if I had chosen—but because they illustrate various of the mental vices from which we now suffer. They are a little below the average, but are fairly representative samples. I number them so that I can refer back to them when necessary:

From Shooting an Elephant, and Other Essays (1950), *a collection of George Orwell's best-known essays. "Politics and the English Language" is one of the most famous modern arguments for a clear, unadorned writing style.*

"(1) I am not, indeed, sure whether it is not true to say that the Milton who once seemed not unlike a seventeenth-century Shelley had not become, out of an experience ever more bitter in each year, more alien [sic] to the founder of that Jesuit sect which nothing could induce him to tolerate."

—PROFESSOR HAROLD LASKI (*ESSAY IN FREEDOM OF EXPRESSION*).

"(2) Above all, we cannot play ducks and drakes with a native battery of idioms which prescribes such egregious collocations of vocables as the Basic *put up with* for *tolerate* or *put at a loss* for *bewilder*."

—PROFESSOR LANCELOT HOGBEN (*INTERGLOSSA*).

"(3) On the one side we have the free personality: by definition it is not neurotic, for it has neither conflict nor dream. Its desires, such as they are, are transparent, for they are just what institutional approval keeps in the forefront of consciousness; another institutional pattern would alter their number and intensity; there is little in them that is natural, irreducible, or culturally dangerous. But *on the other side,* the social bond itself is nothing but the mutual reflection of these self-secure integrities. Recall the definition of love. Is not this the very picture of a small academic? Where is there a place in this hall of mirrors for either personality or fraternity?"

—ESSAY ON PSYCHOLOGY IN *POLITICS* (NEW YORK).

"(4) All the 'best people' from the gentlemen's clubs, and all the frantic fascist captains, united in common hatred of Socialism and bestial horror of the rising tide of the mass revolutionary movement, have turned to acts of provocation, to foul incendiarism, to medieval legends of poisoned wells, to legalize their own destruction of proletarian organizations, and rouse the agitated petty-bourgeoisie to chauvinistic fervour on behalf of the fight against the revolutionary way out of the crisis."

—COMMUNIST PAMPHLET.

"(5) If a new spirit *is* to be infused into this old country, there is one thorny and contentious reform which must be tackled, and that is the humanization and galvanization of the B.B.C. Timidity here will bespeak cancer and atrophy of the soul. The heart of Britain may be sound and of strong beat, for instance, but the British lion's roar at present is like that of Bottom in Shakespeare's *Midsummer Night's Dream*—as gentle as any sucking dove. A virile new Britain cannot continue indefinitely to be traduced in the eyes or rather ears, of the world by the effete languors of Langham Place, brazenly masquerading as 'standard English.' When the Voice of Britain is heard at nine o'clock, better far and infinitely less ludicrous to hear aitches honestly dropped than the present priggish, inflated, inhibited, school-ma'amish arch braying of blameless bashful mewing maidens!"

—LETTER IN *TRIBUNE*.

Each of these passages has faults of its own, but, quite apart from avoidable ugliness, two qualities are common to all of them. The first is staleness of imagery; the other is lack of precision. The writer either has a meaning and cannot express it, or he inadvertently says something else, or he is almost indifferent as to whether his words mean anything or not. This mixture of vagueness and sheer incompetence is the most marked characteristic of modern English prose, and especially of any kind of political writing. As soon as certain topics are raised, the concrete melts into the abstract and no one seems able to think of turns of speech that are not hackneyed: prose consists less and less of *words* chosen for the sake of their meaning, and more and more of *phrases* tacked together like the sections of a prefabricated henhouse. I list below, with notes and examples, various of the tricks by means of which the work of prose-construction is habitually dodged:

DYING METAPHORS

A newly invented metaphor assists thought by evoking a visual image, while on the other hand a metaphor which is technically "dead" (e.g. *iron resolution*) has in effect reverted to being an ordinary word and can generally be used without loss of vividness. But in between these two classes there is a huge dump of worn-out metaphors which have lost all evocative power and are merely used because they save people the trouble of inventing phrases for themselves. Examples are: *Ring the changes on, take up the cudgels for, toe the line, ride roughshod over, stand shoulder to shoulder with, play into the hands of, no axe to grind, grist to the mill, fishing in troubled waters, on the order of the day, Achilles' heel, swan song, hotbed.* Many of these are used without knowledge of their meaning (what is a "rift," for instance?), and incompatible metaphors are frequently mixed, a sure sign that the writer is not interested in what he is saying. Some metaphors now current have been twisted out of their original meaning without those who use them even being aware of the fact. For example, *toe the line* is sometimes written *tow the line*. Another example is *the hammer and the anvil*, now always used with the implication that the anvil gets the worst of it. In real life it is always the anvil that breaks the hammer, never the other way about: a writer who stopped to think what he was saying would be aware of this, and would avoid perverting the original phrase.

OPERATORS OR VERBAL FALSE LIMBS

These save the trouble of picking out appropriate verbs and nouns, and at the same time pad each sentence with extra syllables which give it an appearance of symmetry. Characteristic phrases are: *render inoperative, militate against, make contact with, be subjected to, give rise to, give grounds for, have the effect of, play a leading part (role) in, make itself felt, take effect, exhibit a tendency to, serve the purpose of, etc., etc.* The keynote is the elimination of simple verbs. Instead of being a single word, such as *break, stop, spoil, mend, kill*, a verb becomes a *phrase*, made up of a noun or adjective tacked on to some general-purposes verb such as *prove, serve, form, play, render*. In addition, the passive voice is wherever possible used in preference to the active, and noun constructions are used instead of gerunds (*by examination of* instead of *by examining*). The range of verbs is further cut down by means of the *-ize* and *de-* formation, and the banal statements are given an appearance of profundity by means of the *not un-* formation. Simple conjunctions and prepositions are replaced by such phrases as *with respect to, having regard to, the fact that, by dint of, in view of, in the interests of, on the hypothesis that*; and the ends of sentences are saved from anticlimax by such resounding commonplaces as *greatly to be desired, can-*

not be left out of account, a development to be expected in the near future, deserving of serious consideration, brought to a satisfactory conclusion, and so on and so forth.

PRETENTIOUS DICTION

Words like *phenomenon, element, individual* (as noun), *objective, categorical, effective, virtual, basic, primary, promote, constitute, exhibit, exploit, utilize, eliminate, liquidate,* are used to dress up simple statements and give an air of scientific impartiality to biased judgments. Adjectives like *epoch-making, epic, historic, unforgettable, triumphant, age-old, inevitable, inexorable, veritable,* are used to dignify the sordid processes of international politics, while writing that aims at glorifying war usually takes on an archaic colour, its characteristic words being: *realm, throne, chariot, mailed fist, trident, sword, shield, buckler, banner, jackboot, clarion.* Foreign words and expressions such as *cul de sac, ancien régime, deus ex machina, mutatis mutandis, status quo, gleichschaltung, weltanschauung,* are used to give an air of culture and elegance. Except for the useful abbreviations *i.e., e.g.,* and *etc.,* there is no real need for any of the hundreds of foreign phrases now current in English. Bad writers, and especially scientific, political and sociological writers, are nearly always haunted by the notion that Latin or Greek words are grander than Saxon ones, and unnecessary words like *expedite, ameliorate, predict, extraneous, deracinated, clandestine, subaqueous* and hundreds of others constantly gain ground from their Anglo-Saxon opposite numbers.[1] The jargon peculiar to Marxist writing (*hyena, hangman, cannibal, petty bourgeois, these gentry, lackey, flunkey, mad dog, White Guard,* etc.) consists largely of words and phrases translated from Russian, German or French; but the normal way of coining a new word is to use a Latin or Greek root with the appropriate affix and, where necessary, the *-ize* formation. It is often easier to make up words of this kind (*deregionalize, impermissible, extramarital, nonfragmentatory* and so forth) than to think up the English words that will cover one's meaning. The result, in general, is an increase in slovenliness and vagueness.

MEANINGLESS WORDS

In certain kinds of writing, particularly in art criticism and literary criticism, it is normal to come across long passages which are almost completely lacking in meaning.[2] Words like *romantic, plastic, values, human, dead, sentimental, natu-*

---

1. An interesting illustration of this is the way in which the English flower names which were in use till very recently are being ousted by Greek ones, *snapdragon* becoming *antirrhinum, forget-me-not* becoming *myosotis,* etc. It is hard to see any practical reason for this change of fashion: it is probably due to an instinctive turning-away from the more homely word and a vague feeling that the Greek word is scientific [Orwell's note].

2. Example: "Comfort's catholicity of perception and image, strangely Whitmanesque in range, almost the exact opposite in aesthetic compulsion, continues to evoke that trembling atmospheric accumulative hinting at a cruel, an inexorably serene timelessness. . . . Wrey Gardiner scores by aiming at simple bull's-eyes with precision. Only they are not so simple, and through this contented sadness runs more than the surface bittersweet of resignation" (*Poetry Quarterly*) [Orwell's note].

ral, vitality, as used in art criticism, are strictly meaningless in the sense that they not only do not point to any discoverable object, but are hardly ever expected to do so by the reader. When one critic writes, "The outstanding feature of Mr. X's work is its living quality," while another writes, "The immediately striking thing about Mr. X's work is its peculiar deadness," the reader accepts this as a simple difference of opinion. If words like *black* and *white* were involved, instead of the jargon words *dead* and *living,* he would see at once that language was being used in an improper way. Many political words are similarly abused. The word *Fascism* has now no meaning except in so far as it signifies "something not desirable." The words *democracy, socialism, freedom, patriotic, realistic, justice,* have each of them several different meanings which cannot be reconciled with one another. In the case of a word like *democracy,* not only is there no agreed definition, but the attempt to make one is resisted from all sides. It is almost universally felt that when we call a country democratic we are praising it: consequently the defenders of every kind of régime claim that it is a democracy, and fear that they might have to stop using the word if it were tied down to any one meaning. Words of this kind are often used in a consciously dishonest way. That is, the person who uses them has his own private definition, but allows his hearer to think he means something quite different. Statements like *Marshal Pétain was a true patriot, The Soviet Press is the freest in the world, The Catholic Church is opposed to persecution,* are almost always made with intent to deceive. Other words used in variable meanings, in most cases more or less dishonestly, are: *class, totalitarian, science, progressive, reactionary, bourgeois, equality.*

Now that I have made this catalogue of swindles and perversions, let me give another example of the kind of writing that they lead to. This time it must of its nature be an imaginary one. I am going to translate a passage of good English into modern English of the worst sort. Here is a well-known verse from *Ecclesiastes:*

> "I returned and saw under the sun, that the race is not to the swift, nor the battle to the strong, neither yet bread to the wise, nor yet riches to men of understanding, nor yet favour to men of skill; but time and chance happeneth to them all."

Here it is in modern English: 10

> "Objective consideration of contemporary phenomena compels the conclusion that success or failure in competitive activities exhibits no tendency to be commensurate with innate capacity, but that a considerable element of the unpredictable must invariably be taken into account."

This is a parody, but not a very gross one. Exhibit (3), above, for instance, contains several patches of the same kind of English. It will be seen that I have not made a full translation. The beginning and ending of the sentence follow the original meaning fairly closely, but in the middle the concrete illustrations—race, battle, bread—dissolve into the vague phrase "success or failure in competitive activities." This had to be so, because no modern writer of the kind I am discussing—no one capable of using phrases like "objective consideration of contemporary phenomena"—would ever tabulate his thoughts in that precise

and detailed way. The whole tendency of modern prose is away from concrete-
ness. Now analyse these two sentences a little more closely. The first contains forty-nine words but only sixty syllables, and all its words are those of
everyday life. The second contains thirty-eight words of ninety syllables: eighteen of its words are from Latin roots, and one from Greek. The first sentence
contains six vivid images, and only one phrase ("time and chance") that could
be called vague. The second contains not a single fresh, arresting phrase, and in
spite of its ninety syllables it gives only a shortened version of the meaning
contained in the first. Yet without a doubt it is the second kind of sentence that
is gaining ground in modern English. I do not want to exaggerate. This kind of
writing is not yet universal, and outcrops of simplicity will occur here and there
in the worst-written page. Still, if you or I were told to write a few lines on the
uncertainty of human fortunes, we should probably come much nearer to my
imaginary sentence than to the one from *Ecclesiastes*.

As I have tried to show, modern writing at its worst does not consist in picking out words for the sake of their meaning and inventing images in order to
make the meaning clearer. It consists in gumming together long strips of words
which have already been set in order by someone else, and making the results
presentable by sheer humbug. The attraction of this way of writing is that it is
easy. It is easier—even quicker, once you have the habit—to say *In my opinion
it is a not unjustifiable assumption that* than to say *I think*. If you use ready-made
phrases, you not only don't have to hunt about for words; you also don't have to
bother with the rhythms of your sentences, since these phrases are generally so
arranged as to be more or less euphonious. When you are composing in a
hurry—when you are dictating to a stenographer, for instance, or making a
public speech—it is natural to fall into a pretentious, Latinized style. Tags like
a consideration which we should do well to bear in mind or *a conclusion to
which all of us would readily assent* will save many a sentence from coming down
with a bump. By using stale metaphors, similes and idioms, you save much mental effort, at the cost of leaving your meaning vague, not only for your reader
but for yourself. This is the significance of mixed metaphors. The sole aim of a
metaphor is to call up a visual image. When these images clash—as in *The
Fascist octopus has sung its swan song, the jackboot is thrown into the melting
pot*—it can be taken as certain that the writer is not seeing a mental image of
the objects he is naming; in other words he is not really thinking. Look again
at the examples I gave at the beginning of this essay. Professor Laski (1) uses
five negatives in fifty-three words. One of these is superfluous, making nonsense of the whole passage, and in addition there is the slip *alien* for akin, making further nonsense, and several avoidable pieces of clumsiness which increase
the general vagueness. Professor Hogben (2) plays ducks and drakes with a
battery which is able to write prescriptions, and, while disapproving of the
everyday phrase *put up with,* is unwilling to look *egregious* up in the dictionary
and see what it means. (3), if one takes an uncharitable attitude towards it, is
simply meaningless: probably one could work out its intended meaning by
reading the whole of the article in which it occurs. In (4), the writer knows more
or less what he wants to say, but an accumulation of stale phrases chokes him

like tea leaves blocking a sink. In (5), words and meaning have almost parted company. People who write in this manner usually have a general emotional meaning—they dislike one thing and want to express solidarity with another— but they are not interested in the detail of what they are saying. A scrupulous writer, in every sentence that he writes, will ask himself at least four questions, thus: What am I trying to say? What words will express it? What image or idiom will make it clearer? Is this image fresh enough to have an effect? And he will probably ask himself two more: Could I put it more shortly? Have I said anything that is avoidably ugly? But you are not obliged to go to all this trouble. You can shirk it by simply throwing your mind open and letting the ready-made phrases come crowding in. They will construct your sentences for you—even think your thoughts for you, to a certain extent—and at need they will perform the important service of partially concealing your meaning even from yourself. It is at this point that the special connection between politics and the debasement of language becomes clear.

In our time it is broadly true that political writing is bad writing. Where it is not true, it will generally be found that the writer is some kind of rebel, expressing his private opinions and not a "party line." Orthodoxy, of whatever colour, seems to demand a lifeless, imitative style. The political dialects to be found in pamphlets, leading articles, manifestos, White Papers and the speeches of under-secretaries do, of course, vary from party to party, but they are all alike in that one almost never finds in them a fresh, vivid, homemade turn of speech. When one watches some tired hack on the platform mechanically repeating the familiar phrases—*bestial atrocities, iron heel, blood-stained tyranny, free peoples of the world, stand shoulder to shoulder*—one often has a curious feeling that one is not watching a live human being but some kind of dummy: a feeling which suddenly becomes stronger at moments when the light catches the speaker's spectacles and turns them into blank discs which seem to have no eyes behind them. And this is not altogether fanciful. A speaker who uses that kind of phraseology has gone some distance towards turning himself into a machine. The appropriate noises are coming out of his larynx, but his brain is not involved as it would be if he were choosing his words for himself. If the speech he is making is one that he is accustomed to make over and over again, he may be almost unconscious of what he is saying, as one is when one utters the responses in church. And this reduced state of consciousness, if not indispensable, is at any rate favourable to political conformity.

In our time, political speech and writing are largely the defence of the indefensible. Things like the continuance of British rule in India, the Russian purges and deportations, the dropping of the atom bombs on Japan, can indeed be defended, but only by arguments which are too brutal for most people to face, and which do not square with the professed aims of political parties. Thus political language has to consist largely of euphemism, question-begging and sheer cloudy vagueness. Defenceless villages are bombarded from the air, the inhabitants driven out into the countryside, the cattle machine-gunned, the huts set on fire with incendiary bullets: this is called *pacification*. Millions of peasants are robbed of their farms and sent trudging along the roads with no more than they can carry: this is called *transfer of population* or *rectification of frontiers*. People are imprisoned for years without trial, or shot in the back of the neck or sent to die of scurvy in Arctic lumber camps: this is called *elimination of unreliable elements*. Such phraseology is needed if one wants to name things without calling up mental pictures of them. Consider for instance some comfortable English professor defending Russian totalitarianism. He cannot say outright, "I believe in killing off your opponents when you can get good results by doing so." Probably, therefore, he will say something like this:

15   "While freely conceding that the Soviet régime exhibits certain features which the humanitarian may be inclined to deplore, we must, I think, agree that a certain curtailment of the right to political opposition is an unavoidable concomitant of transitional periods, and that the rigors which the Russian people have been called upon to undergo have been amply justified in the sphere of concrete achievement."

The inflated style is itself a kind of euphemism. A mass of Latin words falls upon the facts like soft snow, blurring the outlines and covering up all the details. The great enemy of clear language is insincerity. When there is a gap between one's real and one's declared aims, one turns as it were instinctively to long words and exhausted idioms, like a cuttlefish squirting out ink. In our age there is no such thing as "keeping out of politics." All issues are political issues, and politics itself is a mass of lies, evasions, folly, hatred and schizophrenia. When the general atmosphere is bad, language must suffer. I should expect to find—this is a guess which I have not sufficient knowledge to verify—that the German, Russian and Italian languages have all deteriorated in the last ten or fifteen years, as a result of dictatorship.

But if thought corrupts language, language can also corrupt thought. A bad usage can spread by tradition and imitation, even among people who should and do know better. The debased language that I have been discussing is in some ways very convenient. Phrases like *a not unjustifiable assumption, leaves much to be desired, would serve no good purpose, a consideration which we should do well to bear in mind,* are a continuous temptation, a packet of aspirins always at one's elbow. Look back through this essay, and for certain you will find that I have again and again committed the very faults I am protesting against. By this morning's post I have received a pamphlet dealing with conditions in Germany. The author tells me that he "felt impelled" to write it. I open it at random, and here is almost the first sentence that I see: "(The Allies) have an opportunity not only of achieving a radical transformation of Germany's social and political structure in such a way as to avoid a nationalistic reaction in Germany itself, but at the same time of laying the foundations of a co-operative and unified Europe." You see, he "feels impelled" to write—feels, presumably, that he has something new to say—and yet his words, like cavalry horses answering the bugle, group themselves automatically into the familiar dreary pattern. This invasion of one's mind by ready-made phrases (*lay the foundations, achieve a radical transformation*) can only be prevented if one is constantly on guard against them, and every such phrase anaesthetizes a portion of one's brain.

I said earlier that the decadence of our language is probably curable. Those who deny this would argue, if they produced an argument at all, that language merely reflects existing social conditions, and that we cannot influence its development by any direct tinkering with words and constructions. So far as the general tone or spirit of a language goes, this may be true, but it is not true in detail. Silly words and expressions have often disappeared, not through any evolutionary process but owing to the conscious action of a minority. Two recent examples were *explore every avenue* and *leave no stone unturned,* which were killed by the jeers of a few journalists. There is a long list of fly-blown metaphors which could similarly be got rid of if enough people would interest themselves in the job; and it should also be possible to laugh the *not un-* formation out of existence,[3] to reduce the amount of Latin and Greek in the average sentence, to drive out foreign phrases and strayed scientific words, and, in general, to make pretentiousness unfashionable. But all these are minor points. The defence of the English language implies more than this, and perhaps it is best to start by saying what it does *not* imply.

To begin with it has nothing to do with archaism, with the salvaging of obsolete words and turns of speech, or with the setting up of a "standard English" which must never be departed from. On the contrary, it is especially concerned with the scrapping of every word or idiom which has outworn its usefulness. It has nothing to do with correct grammar and syntax, which are of no importance so long as one makes one's meaning clear, or with the avoidance of Americanisms, or with having what is called a "good prose style." On the other hand it is not concerned with fake simplicity and the attempt to make written English colloquial. Nor does it even imply in every case preferring the Saxon word to the Latin one, though it does imply using the fewest and shortest words that will cover one's meaning. What is above all needed is to let the meaning choose the word, and not the other way about. In prose, the worst thing one can do with words is to surrender to them. When you think of a concrete object, you think wordlessly, and then, if you want to describe the thing you have been visualizing you probably hunt about till you find the exact words that seem to fit. When you think of something abstract you are more inclined to use words from the start, and unless you make a conscious effort to prevent it, the existing dialect will come rushing in and do the job for you, at the expense of blurring or even changing your meaning. Probably it is better to put off using words as long as possible and get one's meaning as clear as one can through pictures or sensations. Afterwards one can choose—not simply *accept*—the phrases that will best cover the meaning, and then switch round and decide what impression one's words are likely to make on another person. This last effort of the mind cuts out all stale or mixed images, all prefabricated phrases, needless repetitions, and humbug and vagueness generally. But one can often be in doubt about the effect of a word or a phrase, and one needs rules that one can rely on when instinct fails. I think the following rules will cover most cases:

3. One can cure oneself of the *not un-* formation by memorizing this sentence: *A not unblack dog was chasing a not unsmall rabbit across a not ungreen field* [Orwell's note].

(i)   Never use a metaphor, simile or other figure of speech which you are used to seeing in print.

(ii) Never use a long word where a short one will do.

(iii) If it is possible to cut a word out, always cut it out.

(iv) Never use the passive where you can use the active.

(v)   Never use a foreign phrase, a scientific word or a jargon word if you can think of an everyday English equivalent.

(vi) Break any of these rules sooner than say anything outright barbarous.

These rules sound elementary, and so they are, but they demand a deep change of attitude in anyone who has grown used to writing in the style now fashionable. One could keep all of them and still write bad English, but one could not write the kind of stuff that I quoted in those five specimens at the beginning of this article.

20   I have not here been considering the literary use of language, but merely language as an instrument for expressing and not for concealing or preventing thought. Stuart Chase[4] and others have come near to claiming that all abstract words are meaningless, and have used this as a pretext for advocating a kind of political quietism. Since you don't know what Fascism is, how can you struggle against Fascism? One need not swallow such absurdities as this, but one ought to recognize that the present political chaos is connected with the decay of language, and that one can probably bring about some improvement by starting at the verbal end. If you simplify your English, you are freed from the worst follies of orthodoxy. You cannot speak any of the necessary dialects, and when you make a stupid remark its stupidity will be obvious, even to yourself. Political language—and with variations this is true of all political parties, from Conservatives to Anarchists—is designed to make lies sound truthful and murder respectable, and to give an appearance of solidity to pure wind. One cannot change this all in a moment, but one can at least change one's own habits, and from time to time one can even, if one jeers loudly enough, send some worn-out and useless phrase—some *jackboot, Achilles' heel, hotbed, melting pot, acid test, veritable inferno* or other lump of verbal refuse—into the dustbin where it belongs.

MLA CITATION

Orwell, George. "Politics and the English Language." *The Norton Reader: An Anthology of Nonfiction*, edited by Melissa A. Goldthwaite et al., 15th ed., W. W. Norton, 2020, pp. 415–24.

---

4. Chase (in *The Tyranny of Words* [1938] and *The Power of Words* [1954]) and S. I. Hayakawa (in *Language in Action* [1939]) popularized the semantic theories of Alfred Koryzbski.

QUESTIONS

1. State George Orwell's main point as precisely as possible.

2. What kinds of prose does Orwell analyze in this essay? Look, in particular, at the passages he quotes in paragraph 3. Where would you find their contemporary equivalents?

3. Apply Orwell's rule iv, "Never use the passive where you can use the active" (paragraph 19), to paragraph 14 of his essay. What happens when you change his passive constructions to active? Has Orwell forgotten rule iv or is he covered by rule vi, "Break any of these rules sooner than say anything outright barbarous"?

4. Orwell wrote this essay in 1946. Choose at least two examples of political discourse from current media and discuss, in an essay, the extent to which Orwell's analysis of the language of politics still applies today. Which features that he singles out for criticism appear most frequently in the examples you chose?

KATHY FISH
Collective Nouns for Humans in the Wild

 GROUP OF GRANDMOTHERS is a *tapestry*. A group of toddlers, a *jubilance* (see also: a *bewailing*). A group of librarians is an *enlightenment*. A group of visual artists is a *bioluminescence*. A group of short story writers is a *Flannery*. A group of musicians is—a *band*.

A *resplendence* of poets.

A *beacon* of scientists.

A *raft* of social workers.

A group of first responders is a *valiance*. A group of peaceful protestors is   5
a *dream*. A group of special education teachers is a *transcendence*. A group of neonatal ICU nurses is a *divinity*. A group of hospice workers, a *grace*.

Originally published in the Jellyfish Review *(2017), an online journal that publishes "beautiful things with stings."*

Humans in the wild, gathered and feeling good, previously an *exhilaration*, now: *a target.*

A *target* of concert-goers.

A *target* of movie-goers.

A *target* of dancers.

10   A group of schoolchildren is a *target.*

MLA CITATION

Fish, Kathy. "Collective Nouns for Humans in the Wild." *The Norton Reader: An Anthology of Nonfiction,* edited by Melissa A. Goldthwaite et al., 15th ed., W. W. Norton, 2020, pp. 425–26.

QUESTIONS

1. In this essay Kathy Fish takes the oddity of collective nouns and plays with them for dramatic effect. Now that you know the impact of the conclusion, look back at the essay itself: are there other places where the author helps prepare you for the seriousness with which she ends?

2. Find a list of collective nouns online. Look at them and discuss which ones are the most interesting, apt, poetic, and surprising.

3. Choose a linguistic phenomenon of your own—collective nouns or, perhaps, texting abbreviations, phrasal verbs, or clichés—and following Fish's model, write a very brief essay that starts off as a catalogue, then takes a more serious turn.

KORY STAMPER
Capturing "Take" for the Dictionary

I T WAS 2001, three years into my tenure as a writer and editor of dictionaries at Merriam-Webster. There were about 20 of us lexicographers working on revising the *Collegiate Dictionary* for its eleventh edition. We had just finished the letter S.

By the time that last batch of defining and its citations—snippets of words used in context—for S had been signed back in on the production spreadsheet, the editors were not just pleased; we were giddy. You'd go to the sign-out sheet, see that we're into *T,* and make some little ritual obeisance to the moment:

This essay was first published in Slate, *an online magazine that covers culture, politics, and current affairs, in 2017.*

a fist pump, a sigh of relief and a heavenward glance, a little "oh yeah" and a tiny dance restricted to your shoulders (you *are* at work, after all). Sadly, lexicographers are not suited to survive extended periods of giddiness. In the face of such woozy delight, the chances are good that you will do something rash and brainless.

Unfortunately, my rash brainlessness was obscured from me. I signed out the next batch in *T* and grabbed the printouts of the entries I'd be revising for that batch along with the boxes—*two boxes!*—of citations for the batch. While flipping through the galley pages, I realized that my batch—the entire thing—was just one word: "take." *Hmm,* I thought, *that's curious.*

Lexicography, like most professions, offers its devotees some benchmarks by which you can measure your sad little existence, and one is the size of the words you are allowed to handle. Most people assume that long words or rare words are the hardest to define because they are often the hardest to spell, say, and remember. The truth is, those are usually a snap. "Schadenfreude" may be difficult to spell, but it's a cinch to define, because all the uses of it are very, very semantically and syntactically clear. It's always a noun, and it's often glossed, because even though it's now an English word, it's one of those delectable German compounds we love to slurp into English.

Generally speaking, the smaller and more commonly used the word is, the more difficult it is to define. Words like "but," "as," and "for" have plenty of uses that are syntactically similar but not identical. Verbs like "go" and "do" and "make" (and, yes, "take") don't just have semantically oozy uses that require careful definition but semantically drippy uses as well. "Let's do dinner" and "let's do laundry" are identical syntactically but feature very different semantic meanings of "do." And how do you describe what the word "how" is doing in this sentence?

It's not just semantic fiddliness that causes lexicographical pain. Some words, like "the" and "a," are so small that we barely think of them as words. Most of the publicly available databases that we use for citational spackling don't even index some of these words, let alone let you search for them—for entirely practical reasons. A search for "the" in our in-house citation database returns over 1 million hits, which sends the lexicographer into fits of audible swearing, then weeping.

To keep the lexicographers from crying and disturbing the people around them, sometimes these small words are pulled from the regular batches and are given to more senior editors for handling. They require the balance of concision, grammatical prowess, speed, and fortitude usually found in wiser and more experienced editors.

I didn't know any of that at the time, of course, because I was not a wise or more experienced editor. I was hapless and dumb, but dutifully so: grabbing a fistful of index cards from one of the two boxes, I began sorting the cards into piles by part of speech. This is the first job you must do as a lexicographer dealing with paper, because those citations aren't sorted for you. I figured that "take" wasn't going to be too terrible in this respect: there's just a verb and a noun to contend with. When those piles were two-and-a-half inches high and began cascading onto my desk, I decided to dump the rest of the citations into my pencil drawer and stack my citations in the now-empty boxes.

Sorting citations by their part of speech is usually simple. Most words entered in the dictionary only have one part of speech, and if they have more than one, the parts of speech are usually easy to distinguish between—the noun "blemish" and the verb "blemish," for example, or the noun "courtesy" and the adjective "courtesy." By the time you've hit *T* on a major dictionary overhaul like a new edition of the *Collegiate,* you can sort citations by part of speech in your sleep. For a normal-sized word like "blemish," it's a matter of minutes.

10   Five hours in, I had finished sorting the first box of citations for "take."

It is unfortunate that the entries that take up most of the lexicographer's time are often the entries that no one looks at. We used to be able to kid ourselves while tromping through "get" that someone, somewhere, at some point in time, was going to look up the word, read sense 11c ("hear"), and say to themselves, "Yes, *finally,* now I understand what 'Did you get that?' means. Thanks, Merriam-Webster!" Sometimes, in the delirium that sets in at the end of a project when you are proofreading pronunciations in 6-point type for eight hours a day, a little corner of your mind wanders off to daydream about how perhaps your careful revision of "get" will somehow end with your winning the lottery, bringing about world peace, and finally becoming the best dancer in the room.

But nowadays, thanks to the marvels of the internet, we know exactly what sorts of words people look up regularly. They generally don't look up long, hard-to-spell words—no "rhadamanthine" or "vecturist" unless the Scripps National Spelling Bee is on TV. They tend to look up words in the middle of the road. Some of the all-time top lookups at Merriam-Webster are "paradigm," "disposition," "ubiquitous," and "esoteric," words that are used fairly regularly but also in contexts that don't tell the reader much about what they mean.

This also means that the smallest words, like "but" and "as" and "make," are not looked up either. Most native English speakers know how to navigate the collocative waters of "make" or don't need to figure out what exactly "as" means in the sentence "You are as dull as a mud turtle." They recognize that it marks comparison, somehow, and that's it. But that's not good enough for lexicography.

It is also a perverse irony that the entries that end up taking the most lexicographical time are usually fairly fixed. Steve Kleinedler, the executive editor of *The American Heritage Dictionary,* notes that one of his editors overhauled 50 or 60 of the most basic English verbs back in the first decade of the 21st century. "Because he did that, they don't really need to be done again anytime soon. That was probably the first time they'd been done in 40 years." This isn't dereliction on *The American Heritage Dictionary*'s part: These words don't make quick semantic shifts. "Adding new idioms to these entries: easy-peasy," Steve says. "But in terms of overhauling 'take' or 'bring' or 'go,' if you do it once every 50 years, you're probably set."

15   The citations sorted, I decided to tackle the verb first. The entry for the verb is far longer than the entry for the noun: 107 distinct senses, subsenses, and defined phrases. And, perhaps hidden in all those cards, a few senses or idioms to add.

When one works with paper citations, the unit of work measurement is the pile. Every citation gets sorted into a pile that represents the current definitions for the word, and new piles for potential new definitions. I looked at the galleys, then my desk, and began methodically moving everything on my desk that I could—date stamp, desk calendar, coffee—to the bookshelf behind me.

My first citation read, "She was taken aback." I exhaled in relief: This is simple. I scanned the galley and found the appropriate definition—"to catch or come upon in a particular situation or action" (sense 3b)—and began my pile. The next handful of citations were similarly dispatched—a pile for sense 2, a pile for sense 1a, a pile for sense 7d—and I began to relax. In spite of its size, this is no different from any other batch, I reasoned. I am going to whip through this, and then I am going to take a two-week vacation, visit my local library, and *go outside*.

Fate, now duly tempted, intervened. My next cit read, "Reason has taken a back seat to sentiment." I confidently flipped it onto the pile with "taken aback" and then reconsidered. This use of "take" didn't really mean "to catch or come upon in a particular situation or action," did it? I tried substitution: Reason did not catch or come upon a backseat. No: Reason was made secondary to sentiment. I scanned the galleys and saw nothing that matched, then put the citation in a "new sense" pile. But before I could grab the next citation, I thought, "Unless . . ."

When a lexicographer says "unless . . ." in the middle of defining, you should turn out the lights and go home, first making sure you've left them a supply of water and enough nonperishable food to last several days. "Unless . . ." almost always marks the beginning of a wild lexical goose chase.

There is a reality to what words mean that is amplified when you're dealing with the little words. The meaning of a word depends on its context, but if the context changes, so does the meaning of the word. The meaning of "take" in "take a back seat" changes depending on the whole context: "There's no room up front, so you have to take a back seat" has a different meaning from "reason takes a back seat to sentiment." This second use is an idiom, which means it gets defined as a phrase at the end of the entry. I started a new pile.

My rhythm had been thrown off, but upon reading the next citation, I was confident I'd regain momentum: ". . . take a shit." Profanity and a clear, fixed idiom that will need its own definition at the end of the entry—yes, I can do this.

Only "take a shit" is not a fixed idiom like "take a back seat" is. You can also take a crap. Or a walk, or a breather, or a nap, or a break. I scanned the galleys, flipping from page to page. "To undertake and make, do, or perform," sense 17a. I considered. I tried substitution with hysterical results: "to undertake and make a shit," "to undertake a shit," "to undertake and do a shit," "to undertake and perform a shit." This got me thinking, which is always dangerous. Can one "perform" or "do" a nap? Does one "undertake and make" a breather? Maybe that's 17b, "to participate in." But my sprachgefühl, my internal feeling for English and how it worked, screeched: "participate" implies that the thing being participated in has an originating point outside the speaker.

So you take (participate in) a meeting, or you take (participate in) a class on French philosophy. I tentatively placed the citation in the pile for 17a, then spent the next five minutes writing each sense number and definition down on a sticky note and affixing it to the top citation of each pile. My note for sense 17a included the parenthetical "(Refine/revise def? Make/do/perform?)."

I sat back and berated myself a bit. I have redefined "Monophysite" and "Nestorianism"; I can swear in a dozen languages; I am not a moron. This should be easy. My next citation read, ". . . arrived 20 minutes late, give or take."

What? This isn't a verbal use! How did this get in here? I took a pinched-lip look around my cubicle for the guilty party—someone has been in here futzing with my citations!—then realized I was the guilty party. Clearly, I needed to refile this. But where? After five minutes of staring at the citation, I took the well-trod path of least resistance and decided that maybe it's adverbial ("eh, close enough"). Yes, I'll just put this citation . . . in the nonexistent spot for adverbial uses of "take," because there are no adverbial uses of "take." My teeth began to hurt.

25   I placed the citation in a far corner of my desk, which I mentally labeled "Which Will Be Dealt With in Two or Three Days."

Next: ". . . this will only take about a week." My brain saw "take about" and spat out "phrasal verb." Phrasal verbs are two- or three-word phrases that are made up of a verb and a preposition or adverb (or both), that function like a verb, and whose meaning cannot be figured out from the meanings of each individual constituent. "Look down on" in "He looked down on lexicography as a career" is a phrasal verb. The whole phrase functions as a verb, and "look down on" here does not mean that the anonymous He was physically towering over lexicography as a career and staring down at it, but rather that he thought lexicography as a career was unimportant or not worth his respect. Phrasal verbs tend to be completely invisible to a native speaker of English, which is why I was so very proud of spotting one at first glance. I created a new pile for the phrasal verb "take about," and then my sprachgefühl found its voice: "That's not a phrasal verb."

I squeezed my eyes shut and silently asked the cosmos to send the office up in a fireball right now. After a moment, I realized that my sprachgefühl had picked loose a bit of information that fell neatly to the bottom of my brainpan: The "about" is entirely optional. Try it: "This will only take a week" and "this will only take about a week" mean almost the same thing. The pivot point for meaning is not "take" but "about," which means that this use of "take" is a straightforward transitive use. I flipped the card onto the pile for sense 10e(2), "to use up (as space or time)."

It had been an hour, and I had gotten through perhaps 20 citations. I sifted all my "Done" piles into one and grabbed a ruler. The pile of handled citations was a quarter-inch thick. Then I measured the cit boxes. Each was full. Each was 16 inches long.

Over the next two weeks, the tensile strength of my last nerve was tested by "take." My working definition of "desk" expanded as I ran out of flat spaces to stack citations. Piles appeared on the top of my monitor, in my pencil drawer, filed between rows on my keyboard, teetering on the top of the cubicle wall, shuffled onto the top of the CPU under my desk. Still I didn't have enough space: I began to carefully, carefully put piles of citations on the floor. My cubicle looked as if it had hosted the world's neatest ticker-tape parade.

When dealing with entries of this size, you will inevitably hit the Wall. If you run, or have tried to run, then you are familiar with the Wall. It's the point in a run when you are pushed (or pushing) beyond your physical endurance. Your focus pulls inward on your searing lungs, your aching calves, that hitch in your right hip that is probably because you didn't stretch but might just be a precursor to your lower body literally (sense 2: figuratively) exploding from the effort you are putting forth. The ground has tilted upward; your feet are made of concrete and are 50 times bigger than you thought; your neck begins to bow because even the effort of holding your fat melon upright is too much. You are not euphoric, or Zen, or any of the other things that *Runner's World* magazine makes running look like. You are at the Wall, where you are nothing but a loose collection of human limits.

I hit my human limits about three-quarters of the way through the verb "take." As I looked at a citation for "took first things first," I felt myself slowly unspooling into idiocy. I knew the glyphs before me had to be words, because my job was all about words, and I knew they had to be English, because my job was all about English. But knowing something doesn't make it true. *This was all garbage*, I thought, and as I felt my brain slip sideways, and the yawing ache open up in my gut, one thought flitted across my mind before I slammed headlong into the lexicographer's equivalent of the Wall: "Oh my God, I'm going to die at my desk like in that urban legend, and they will find my body under an avalanche of 'take.'"

That night over dinner, my husband asked if I was OK. I looked up at him, utterly lost. "I don't think I speak English anymore." He looked mildly alarmed; he only speaks English. "You're probably just stressed," he said. "But what does that even mean?" I whined. "Just thinking about what it means makes my brain itch!" He went back to looking mildly alarmed.

It took me three more days to finish sorting the citations for the verb "take." I was ecstatic—yes, I had done it!—and then immediately depressed: Shit, I still had to actually do the defining work on "take," and I still had the noun to go! Lucky for me, I had decided to use the sticky notes to make changes to existing entries. "Make, do, or undertake" didn't end up getting a revision in the end, but a rough handful of senses needed expanding or fixing; one definition meant to cover uses like "she took the sea air for her health" had been unfortunately phrased "to expose oneself to (as sun or air) for pleasure or physical benefit," which I hurriedly changed to "to put oneself into (as sun, air, or water) for pleasure or physical benefit" so as not to encourage medicinal flashing.

On the floor were my piles for citations that I needed to mentally squint at a bit more and piles of citations for new senses of "take." It was late in the afternoon, the sun slicing gold along the wall. Before I took care of those, I decided to reward myself by answering the email correspondence I had let accumulate while I had been ears-deep in "take." I'd start afresh in the morning.

The next morning, I came into work and discovered that the overnight cleaning crew had decided to move all the piles I had left on the floor, dumping them into a cascade of paper on my chair. It was a cinematic moment: I dropped my bag and stared open-mouthed at the blank spaces where 20 or so piles of citations used to sit. As my sinuses prickled, I realized, almost too late, that I was about to cry, and if I cried, I would most certainly make noise. I left my bag in the middle of the floor and went to the ladies', where I leaned against the paper towel dispenser and wondered if it was too late to go back to the bakery where I had once worked and have indignant people throw cakes at my head again.

Lexicography is a steady plod in one direction: onward. I was doing no good standing there with my head on the cool plastic. Besides, a few of my colleagues were waiting for me to move so they could dry their hands. I re-sorted the tidy stack the cleaning crew left and papered every flat surface within five feet of my cubicle with "DO NOT MOVE MY PAPERS!!! KLS!!!!" I sat grimly in my chair and decided that a little fun was in order: It was time to stamp the covered citations and file them away.

When you're done working on an entry, the paper citations get put in one of three places: the "Used" group, which are the citations used as evidence for every existing definition in the entry; the "New" group, which holds the citations for each new sense you draft; and the "Rejected" group, which holds the citations for any use whose meaning isn't covered by the existing entry or by a newly proposed definition. Used and new citations are stamped by the editor who worked on the entry to mark that they were used for a particular book. When the whole floor was consumed with a defining project, you'd occasionally hear a sudden rhythmic thumping, like someone tapping their toe in miniature. It was an editor stamping citations.

I took out my customized date stamp and began marking the covered cits, pile by pile, as used. After the first handful, I stamped a little more exuberantly, and my cubemate hemmed in irritation. No matter. I had no punching bag to pummel; I had no nuclear device to detonate. But I had a date stamp, and by the power vested in me by Samuel Johnson and Noah Webster,[1] I was going to put this goddamned verb to bed.

MLA CITATION

Stamper, Kory. "Capturing 'Take' for the Dictionary." *The Norton Reader: An Anthology of Nonfiction*, edited by Melissa A. Goldthwaite et al., 15th ed., W. W. Norton, 2020, pp. 426–32.

---

1. Johnson (1709–1784), British writer and lexicographer, whose *Dictionary of the English Language* (1755) was the first English dictionary; Webster (1758–1843), American lexicographer and spelling reformer, wrote the first American dictionary of the English language in 1828.

Questions

1. Kory Stamper writes about the ups and downs of finally getting to the letter "T" in the dictionary. Describe a time when you experienced a similar roller coaster of accomplishment and recognition of how far you had yet to go.

2. Look up the word "take" in the Merriam-Webster dictionary. Read the whole definition. Knowing what you know now about how a lexicographer works, what surprises you most about this definition?

3. Look at the moments in which Stamper writes about procrastinating (see, for example, paragraph 25). What kind of procrastinator is she? How do her habits of procrastination compare with yours?

4. Look up one of the unusual words Stamper uses in this essay, such as *sprachegefül* or *monophysite* and write a short essay about that word and its uses. Spend enough time with the word that it becomes part of your vocabulary.

9 Nature and the Environment

> All things are connected. Whatever befalls the earth befalls the sons of earth.
>
> —Chief Seattle

In his "Letter to President Pierce, 1855," Chief Seattle affirms the connection between humans and the earth and its creatures, and he warns of the consequences of not respecting the land. Although some of the selections in "Nature and the Environment" consider environmental consequences, many of the pieces show the sheer pleasure of being connected to particular places and wildlife. Through different genres and taking different tones, the authors included in this chapter explore connections, helping readers glimpse different places and different ways of writing about nature, the environment, and humans.

Some of the essays focus on particular animals, yet these pieces often reveal as much about human nature as they do about animals. The chapter begins with hummingbirds, opening with Brian Doyle's lyric essay "Joyas Voladoras," which poetically shows a common feature of humans and animals: hearts—from the tiny, fast-beating hearts of hummingbirds to the room-sized hearts of whales to the torn and repaired hearts of humans. Doyle's tone is elevated, marked by long lists, similes, and metaphors. David Sedaris in "Untamed" takes a more conversational tone and humorously anthropomorphizes the animals—especially a fox he calls Carol—with whom he feels a relationship. Although John McPhee in "Under the Snow" takes a more serious tone as he tells of his experience working with wildlife biologists studying bears, he too shows the deep affection he feels for the bear cubs, comparing them to his daughters when they were infants.

It's not difficult to imagine why many humans feel connected to cute baby animals or beautiful places. Other connections, though, might surprise some readers. John Muir, instead of taking shelter during a violent wind-storm in the forest, goes outside; he describes the sound of the wind in the trees as music and even climbs a tall tree as it "flapped and swished in the passionate torrent." Although Edward Abbey in "The Great American Desert" proclaims his love for the Utah desert, he uses a hyperbolic and acerbic tone to warn others away by listing the hazards they might encounter, such as kissing bugs as "quiet as an assassin" and "like Dracula." And in her lyric essay "The Soils I Have Eaten," Aimee Nezhukumatathil shows her unique connection to various places by poetically describing the state soils of New York, Florida, Arizona, Kansas, Illinois, and Ohio.

As these nature essays illustrate, not all places worth writing about are full of colorful wildflowers, towering mountains, and glorious sunsets. Nature isn't just the idealized and filtered images that appear on Nature Conservancy calendars and Instagram feeds. In "The Trouble with Wilderness," William Cronon argues that wilderness is "a human creation," not a "pristine sanctuary" apart from the "contaminating taint of civilization." That is, nature, culture, history, and humans are intricately connected.

In the epigraph to this chapter opening, Chief Seattle warns that what "befalls the earth befalls the sons of earth," pointing to the dangers of failing to care for the earth and its creatures, an argument he develops in his "Letter to President Pierce, 1855." We end this chapter with two essays that feature daughters—Terry Tempest Williams, who claims her place in "The Clan of One-Breasted Women" along with her mother and other women in her family whose cancer may have been caused by nuclear testing, and Sandra Steingraber, who researches the environmental effects of pollutants on fetuses and children and writes about her daughter Faith. In "Tune of the Tuna Fish," Steingraber shows the literal connection between humans and nature, writing, "bodies are entirely made up of rearranged molecules of air, food, and water."

As you write about nature and the environment, consider the places you feel most connected to: a backyard, a city park, a garden, a stream. You may need to visit that place to write about it, describing the sights, sounds, smells, and other sensory features. What kind of wildlife inhabits that place? Look up the names of trees and birds and flowers and weeds. Why do you feel connected to that place? What memories of it do you have? How have humans shaped that place? Is there anything that threatens that place or its inhabitants? Is there someone or a group seeking to protect that place? What happened there in the past? What hopes do you have for that place for the future?

BRIAN DOYLE

Joyas Voladoras

CONSIDER THE HUMMINGBIRD for a long moment. A hummingbird's heart beats ten times a second. A hummingbird's heart is the size of a pencil eraser. A hummingbird's heart is a lot of the hummingbird. *Joyas voladoras,* flying jewels, the first white explorers in the Americas called them, and the white men had never seen such creatures, for hummingbirds came into the world only in the Americas, nowhere else in the universe, more than three hundred species of them whirring and zooming and nectaring in hummer time zones nine times removed from ours, their hearts hammering faster than we could clearly hear if we pressed our elephantine ears to their infinitesimal chests.

Each one visits a thousand flowers a day. They can dive at sixty miles an hour. They can fly backward. They can fly more than five hundred miles without pausing to rest. But when they rest they come close to death: on frigid nights, or when they are starving, they retreat into torpor, their metabolic rate slowing to a fifteenth of their normal sleep rate, their hearts sludging nearly to a halt, barely beating, and if they are not soon warmed, if they do not soon find that which

First published in the American Scholar *(2004), a "quirky magazine of public affairs, literature, science, history, and culture," and later chosen for inclusion in* The Best American Essays *(2005).*

is sweet, their hearts grow cold, and they cease to be. Consider for a moment those hummingbirds who did not open their eyes again today, this very day, in the Americas: bearded helmetcrests and booted racket-tails, violet-tailed sylphs and violet-capped woodnymphs, crimson topazes and purple-crowned fairies, red-tailed comets and amethyst woodstars, rain-bow-bearded thornbills and glittering-bellied emeralds, velvet-purple coronets and golden-bellied star-frontlets, fiery-tailed awlbills and Andean hillstars, spatuletails and pufflegs, each the most amazing thing you have never seen, each thunderous wild heart the size of an infant's fingernail, each mad heart silent, a brilliant music stilled.

Hummingbirds, like all flying birds but more so, have incredible enormous immense ferocious metabolisms. To drive those metabolisms they have race-car hearts that eat oxygen at an eye-popping rate. Their hearts are built of thinner, leaner fibers than ours. Their arteries are stiffer and more taut. They have more mitochondria in their heart muscles—anything to gulp more oxygen. Their hearts are stripped to the skin for the war against gravity and inertia, the mad search for food, the insane idea of flight. The price of their ambition is a life closer to death; they suffer more heart attacks and aneurysms and ruptures than any other living creature. It's expensive to fly. You burn out. You fry the machine. You melt the engine. Every creature on earth has approximately two billion heartbeats to spend in a lifetime. You can spend them slowly, like a tortoise, and live to be two hundred years old, or you can spend them fast, like a hummingbird, and live to be two years old.

The biggest heart in the world is inside the blue whale. It weighs more than seven tons. It's as big as a room. It *is* a room, with four chambers. A child could walk around in it, head high, bending only to step through the valves. The valves are as big as the swinging doors in a saloon. This house of a heart drives a creature a hundred feet long. When this creature is born it is twenty feet long and weighs four tons. It is waaaaay bigger than your car. It drinks a hundred gallons of milk from its mama every day and gains two hundred pounds a day, and when it is seven or eight years old it endures an unimaginable puberty and then it essentially disappears from human ken, for next to nothing is known of the mating habits, travel patterns, diet, social life, language, social structure, diseases, spirituality, wars, stories, despairs, and arts of the blue whale. There are perhaps ten thousand blue whales in the world, living in every ocean on earth, and of the largest mammal who ever lived we know nearly nothing. But we know this: the animals with the largest hearts in the world generally travel in pairs, and their penetrating moaning cries, their piercing yearning tongue, can be heard underwater for miles and miles.

5   Mammals and birds have hearts with four chambers. Reptiles and turtles have hearts with three chambers. Fish have hearts with two chambers. Insects and mollusks have hearts with one chamber. Worms have hearts with one chamber, although they may have as many as eleven single-chambered hearts. Unicellular bacteria have no hearts at all; but even they have fluid eternally in motion, washing from one side of the cell to the other, swirling and whirling. No living being is without interior liquid motion. We all churn inside.

So much held in a heart in a lifetime. So much held in a heart in a day, an hour, a moment. We are utterly open with no one, in the end—not mother and father, not wife or husband, not lover, not child, not friend. We open windows to each but we live alone in the house of the heart. Perhaps we must. Perhaps we could not bear to be so naked, for fear of a constantly harrowed heart. When young we think there will come one person who will savor and sustain us always; when we are older we know this is the dream of a child, that all hearts finally are bruised and scarred, scored and torn, repaired by time and will, patched by force of character, yet fragile and rickety forevermore, no matter how ferocious the defense and how many bricks you bring to the wall. You can brick up your heart as stout and tight and hard and cold and impregnable as you possibly can and down it comes in an instant, felled by a woman's second glance, a child's apple breath, the shatter of glass in the road, the words "I have something to tell you," a cat with a broken spine dragging itself into the forest to die, the brush of your mother's papery ancient hand in the thicket of your hair, the memory of your father's voice early in the morning echoing from the kitchen where he is making pancakes for his children.

MLA CITATION

Doyle, Brian. "Joyas Voladoras." *The Norton Reader: An Anthology of Nonfiction*, edited by Melissa A. Goldthwaite et al., 15th ed., W. W. Norton, 2020, pp. 435–37.

QUESTIONS

1. Brian Doyle considers the hearts of hummingbirds (paragraphs 1–3), blue whales (paragraph 4), and humans (paragraph 6) in this lyric essay, which uses poetic features such as metaphor, contrast, and repetition. What is his purpose in doing so? How does he make a transition from a focus on animals to a focus on humans?

2. Doyle incorporates several lists into this essay. Trace his use of lists throughout the essay. Which list do you find most effective? Why?

3. Write a lyric essay in which you closely consider some element of human and animal nature. Consider using some of the poetic features identified in the first question.

DAVID SEDARIS
Untamed

A SIDE FROM PETER, who supposedly guards the gates of heaven and is a pivotal figure in any number of jokes, the only saint who's ever remotely interested me is Francis of Assisi, who was friends with the animals. I recall pictures of him, birds perched on his shoulders and his outstretched hands, deer at his feet, maybe a cougar in the background looking on and thinking, *There are some birds*

First published, with a different ending, in the New Yorker *(2016). This revised version of "Untamed" appears in David Sedaris's essay collection* Calypso *(2018).*

and deer I can kill, but wait . . . who's he? Creatures gravitated to St. Francis because they recognized something in him, a quality that normal men lacked. *Let that be me,* I used to wish when I was ten and felt so desperately alone. There'd usually be a hamster clutched tight in my fist, trying with all his might to escape instead of resting companionably in my palm the way he was supposed to.

Skip ahead fifty years. It's late summer in West Sussex and I'm seated on the patio outside the converted stable I use as my office. It might be midnight or two a.m. I've brought out a lamp and set it on the table in front of me. To a casual observer, I'm tabulating receipts or writing letters, but what I'm really doing is waiting, almost breathlessly, for Carol.

I grew up in the suburbs of Raleigh, North Carolina, so didn't see a fox until I moved to France in 1998. There were plenty of them in Normandy, and every so often I'd come upon one, usually at dusk. It was hard to get a good look at them, since they'd run the moment they saw me, not as if they were frightened but as if they were guilty. This had to do with their heads, the way they were hanging, and their eyes, which were watchful but at the same time averted.

In Sussex too, foxes are common, though most of the ones I come upon are dead—hit by cars and rotting by the side of the road. The first time Hugh[1] and I visited the area in 2010, we stayed with our friends Viv and Gretchen, who live in the village of Sutton. They'd roasted a chicken for dinner, and when we finished eating Viv threw the carcass into the yard. "For whoever wants it," he said.

5   When we got our own house, not far from theirs, we started doing the same thing: tossing our bones into the meadow our backyard opens onto. Whatever we put out vanishes by morning, but who or what took it is anyone's guess. We have badgers, but, as with foxes, you're more apt to come across them dead than alive. Occasionally I'll see a hedgehog on our property—Galveston, his name is—and there's no shortage of deer and partridge. We have pheasant and stoats and so many rabbits that in the spring and summer it looks as if our house is the backdrop for an Easter commercial.

One of the reasons I don't want a cat is that it will kill our wildlife. My brother has to change his doormat every two months—that's how much his savages drag home—and my sister Gretchen's are just as bad. She's forever returning from work to find a chipmunk on her sofa, its head chewed to a paste, or a bird that's not quite dead flapping the stump that used to be a wing against her blood-spattered kitchen floor.

Another argument against pets—at least for Hugh and me—are the fights they lead to. In the midnineties we got two cats, the last of thirty owned by the actress Sandy Dennis, who had recently died of ovarian cancer and who had lived in a house in Connecticut that, on a summer day, you could smell from our apartment in SoHo. Angel and Barratos were black with white spots, both short-haired. We changed their names to Sandy and Dennis, and from the day they

1. Hugh Hamrick, Sedaris's partner.

entered our lives until the day they died, Hugh and I fought over how to feed and care for them.

I'm of the "Let's-fatten-you-up-until-you're-too-obese-to-do-much-of-anything" school, while he's more practical, or "mean," as I'm apt to call it. "You don't know what it's like, living in a small apartment day and night with nothing to look forward to," I used to say. "All they live for is food, so why not give it to them?"

This "healthy pet" nonsense—I just don't buy it. I can't tell you how many times I've gone to a neighbor with a bag of leftovers, only to be told that their dog doesn't "do" table scraps. And bones—no way. "He could choke!"

These are the same people who avoid canned food in favor of dry nuggets   10
that remain in the bowl, ignored, for days at a time but are, I'm told, "so-o-o-o-o much better for him than that other stuff."

I once knew someone in New York who insisted that his black Lab was a vegetarian.

"Just like you," I said. "Gosh, what a coincidence!"

When the dog charged after a hamburger someone had dropped on the sidewalk outside a McDonald's on Eighth Avenue, he was, I guess, just going after the pickle.

Then there are all the behavioral arguments that joint pet ownership leads to: "Don't let her jump up on the table/countertop/stereo," etc. As if you can stop a cat from going where she likes. That's why you want them fifteen pounds overweight. It keeps them lower to the ground.

Sandy was old and died a year after we got her. We brought Dennis to France   15
when we left New York and shuttled him between the house in Normandy and the apartment in Paris. This led to regular fights over how to get him into his cat carrier, and how often to let him outside. When he died, we fought over where to bury him, and how deep.

All I can say is: Thank God we never had children.

We even fight about the creatures I drag home—things I find, most often, on my walks and wrap up in a handkerchief. They're usually mice or shrews, already doomed, though not by anything obvious: They haven't been run over. There are never any teeth marks on them. Perhaps they're diseased or just too old to run away from me.

"You're not giving it *croutons*, are you?" Hugh will say.

"'It' is named Canfield, and I'm not forcing him to eat anything," I'll answer, dropping what will look like a fistful of dice into the terrarium or, if that's already in use as a hospice for some dying toad or vole, my backup bucket. "They're just there if he wants them."

Onto this battleground, Carol arrived. "It's the funniest thing," Hugh said one   20
evening in mid-July. "I had the kitchen door open earlier and this little fox walked by, looked in at me, and continued on her way. Not running, not in any hurry. She looks to me like she might be named Carol."

The next afternoon I threw a steak bone into the pasture, and at dusk I glanced out and saw a fox with it in her mouth. "Hugh," I called, "come look."

At the sound of my voice, the fox—most certainly the Carol I'd been hearing about—returned the bone to the ground, the way you might if you were caught trying to shoplift something. "I was just . . . seeing how . . . heavy this was," she seemed to say, before taking off.

The following night we ate chicken at the table on the patio outside my office. It was dusk, and just as we finished there was Carol. One of the things I've come to appreciate is that you never see her coming. Rather, she simply appears. When she reached a distance of six feet or so, I threw her the bones off my plate. "What are you *doing*?" Hugh hissed as she commenced eating them.

Here we go, I thought.

25   Once a week during this past summer I'd stay awake all night, tying up loose ends. I liked the way I was left feeling at dawn—not tired but just the opposite: speedy, almost, and brilliant. Not long after the chicken dinner, I was working at my outdoor table when, at around four a.m., Carol showed up. We had no meat in the refrigerator, but she waited while I found some cheese and opened a tin of sardines.

Foxes often bury their food, saving it for later. I thought that meant a day or two, but apparently there's nothing they consider too spoiled. Rotten is acceptable, as is putrid. Since we met Carol, our backyard has become a graveyard for pork chops and beef jerky and raw chicken legs. "What's *this*?" Hugh demanded not long ago. He was on his knees in a flower bed, a trowel in one hand and what looked like a desiccated thumb in the other.

I squinted in his direction. "Um, half a hot dog?"

He was furious. "What are you *doing*? Foxes don't want junk like this. Hot dogs are disgusting."

"Not to someone who eats *maggots*," I said.

30   He claims that I'm manipulating Carol. "That's you, the puppet master. It's the same way you are with people—constantly trying to buy them."

He's under the impression that the occasional chicken carcass is enough, that anything else will "spoil" Carol—will, in fact, endanger her. "Believe me, she was just fine before you came along."

But was she? Really? It's a hard life out there for a fox. Yes, there are rabbits and birds around, but they don't surrender easily. According to the websites I've visited, Carol's diet consists mainly of beetles and worms. There's an occasional mouse, and insect larvae, maybe some roadkill—just awful-tasting stuff.

"And I'm willing to bet that all those same websites advise against feeding wild animals," Hugh said.

"Well, not *all* of them," I told him.

35   They do discourage hand-feeding, not because you'll be bitten but because, once tame, the fox is likely to approach your neighbor, who may not be as receptive to his or her company as you are. I can see how that might be a problem in America, where everyone has a gun, but in England, what are you going to do, stab Carol to death? Good luck getting that close, because the only person she really trusts is *me*.

You should see the way she follows me to the garden bench, almost as if she were a dog but at the same time catlike, nimble, her tail straight out and bobbing slightly as she walks. Then she'll lie on the grass at my feet, her paws crossed, and look at me for a second before turning away. Carol's uncomfortable making eye contact—a shame, as hers have the brilliance of freshly minted pennies. From nose to tail her coloring is remarkable: the burnt orange fading to what looks like a white bib protecting her chest, then darkening from rust to black on her front legs, which resemble spent matchsticks. Because I give her only the best ground beef and free-range chicken, her coat is full, not mangy like those other foxes'. Carol has come as close as two inches from my hand, but I have to look away as she approaches. Again, it's the eye-contact thing.

In pictures she looks like a stuffed animal. And, oh, I show them to everyone. "Have you seen my fox? No? Hold on while I get my phone . . ." In my favorite photograph she's outside the kitchen door. It's around seven in the evening, still light, and you can see her perfectly, just sitting there. It's actually Hugh who took the picture, so the expression on her face says, "Yes, but where's *David*?"

The response to my photos is wonderment tinged with envy: "How come *I* don't have a Carol?" Unless, of course, the person I'm speaking to is small-minded. A lot of small-minded people out where we live raise chickens.

"Horrible, brutal things, foxes," they say. "Once one gets into the hen-house it'll kill everything in sight, just for the hell of it."

The charge was repeated in the comments section of a YouTube video I watched one night about a vixen named Tammy that was hit by a car and healed by a veterinarian, who later released her back into the wild. "I know how much people love to save wildlife, but how would you feel if a fox killed your chickens or turkey?" someone named Pat Stokes asked.

To this a man responded, "My chickens are cunts."

I don't know if this made him pro-fox or if he was just stating the facts.

If I had to bad-mouth Carol, my one complaint would be her sense of humor. "You are so-o-o-o-o serious," I often tell her. I'd add that she never grows any more comfortable in my presence. She seems to me very English in her awkwardness.

"Then stop making her uncomfortable," Hugh says. He thinks that, instead of feeding her on the patio outside my office, I should leave her food in the field and let her eat it on her own time.

The first problem with that suggestion is slugs. I thought I knew them from my youth in Raleigh, but the slugs of North America are nothing compared to their British cousins. They're like walruses in Sussex—long and fat from eating everything Hugh tries to grow that the rabbits and deer happen to miss. I've seen them feast on the viscous bodies of their stepped-on relatives, so when something decent is presented, pork shoulder, say, or a fresh lamb kidney, they go wild. And we must have—no exaggeration—at least twelve million slugs on our two-acre property. Galveston the hedgehog keeps their numbers down, as do two toads, Lane and Courtney, but it's a losing battle.

The second problem with throwing food into the pasture is one of perception. It would allow Carol to feel, if not like a huntress, then at least like a successful scavenger—*Look what I found*, she'd think. This as opposed to, *Look what David gave me*.

I insist that Carol eat in my presence for the same reason I wait for the coffee shop employee to turn back in my direction before putting a tip in his basket. I want to be acknowledged as a generous provider. This is about *me*, not them.

I don't need Hugh to point out how ridiculous this is. Wild animals do not give a damn about our little feelings. They're incapable of it. "I love you, I love you, I love you," we say.

What they hear is senseless noise. It's like us trying to discern emotion in the hum of a hair dryer or the chortle of an engine as it fails to turn over. That's the drawback but also the glory of creatures that were never domesticated. Nothing feels better than being singled out by something that at best should fear you and at worst would like to eat you. I think of the people I've known over the years who've found a baby raccoon or possum and brought it home to raise it. When young, the animals were sweet. Then one day they became moody and violent, like human teenagers but with claws and sharp, pointy teeth. It was their wildness reclaiming them. After the change it was back into their cages, their heartsick owners—jailers now—watching as they tore at the bars, never tiring of it, thinking only of escape.

50   *But wait*, we tell ourselves, always wanting to project, to anthropomorphize, to turn the story in our favor. *But what about this:* One night in late September, as I was walking home in the dark from the neighboring village, I felt a presence next to me. *A dog?* I wondered. But the footsteps I heard were daintier, and I wasn't near any houses. I keep a flashlight in my backpack, so I turned it on, and there was Carol. "Is this where you are when I call for you at two in the morning?" I asked.

There was a canopy of leaves over my head. Once I moved beyond it, the moon lit my path, so I turned off the flashlight. I'd expected Carol to be gone by that point, but for the next half mile, all the way home, she walked with me, sometimes by my side and sometimes a few steps ahead, leading the way. No cars approached or passed. The road was ours, and we marched right down the center of it, all the way to the front of the house and through the garden gate to the kitchen door.

I didn't know it then, but this would be the last time I would see Carol. Foxes are like gang members. They can't go wherever they like. That next patch of land is someone else's territory, so chances are she was killed somehow. If she'd been hit by a car I'd have seen her body by the side of the road, but maybe she dragged herself off into the woods and died there. She could have been poisoned, which happens. Hunters pay good money to bag the pheasant that are released here every fall. These are birds that, honestly, you have to work *not to* kill. The landowners want to protect their investments, which means keeping down the predators. "That's likely what happened to Carol," Hugh says. I know this makes sense, but I refuse to hear it.

She's just taking a little break, I think. *Trying to establish her independence, which is normal for someone her age.* I still call for her when I step into the yard at night. Still look into the shadows for some hint of movement, waiting to change my tone from the voice you use when summoning someone, to the less plaintive and much more preferable one you use to welcome them back home.

MLA CITATION

Sedaris, David. "Untamed." *The Norton Reader: An Anthology of Nonfiction,* edited by Melissa A. Goldthwaite et al., 15th ed., W. W. Norton, 2020, pp. 437–43.

QUESTIONS

1. Many writers try to avoid anthropomorphizing animals, refusing to attribute human characteristics to wildlife. David Sedaris's "Untamed," however, is full of anthropomorphism. Mark some examples. What does the author's use of anthropomorphism show about humans—and about wildlife?

2. Sedaris is known as a humorist. What parts of his essay do you find funny? What makes those parts humorous?

3. Have you ever had an encounter with an undomesticated animal? If so, write a narrative about that experience.

JOHN MCPHEE
Under the Snow

WHEN MY THIRD DAUGHTER WAS AN INFANT, I could place her against my shoulder and she would stick there like velvet. Only her eyes jumped from place to place. In a breeze, her bright-red hair might stir, but she would not. Even then, there was profundity in her repose.

When my fourth daughter was an infant, I wondered if her veins were full of ants. Placing her against a shoulder was a risk both to her and to the shoulder. Impulsively, constantly, everything about her moved. Her head seemed about to revolve as it followed the bestirring world.

These memories became very much alive some months ago when—one after another—I had bear cubs under my vest. Weighing three, four, 5.6 pounds, they were wild bears, and for an hour or so had been taken from their dens in Pennsylvania. They were about two months old, with fine short brown hair. When they were made to stand alone, to be photographed in the mouth of a den, they shivered. Instinctively, a person would be moved to hold them. Picked up

Originally published in the New Yorker *(1983) and included in John McPhee's essay collection* Table of Contents *(1985).*

by the scruff of the neck, they splayed their paws like kittens and screamed like baby bears. The cry of a baby bear is muted, like a human infant's heard from her crib down the hall. The first cub I placed on my shoulder stayed there like a piece of velvet. The shivering stopped. Her bright-blue eyes looked about, not seeing much of anything. My hand, cupped against her back, all but encompassed her rib cage, which was warm and calm. I covered her to the shoulders with a flap of down vest and zipped up my parka to hold her in place.

I was there by invitation, an indirect result of work I had been doing nearby. Would I be busy on March 14th? If there had been a conflict—if, say, I had been invited to lunch on that day with the Queen of Scotland and the King of Spain—I would have gone to the cubs. The first den was a rock cavity in a lichen-covered sandstone outcrop near the top of a slope, a couple of hundred yards from a road in Hawley. It was on posted property of the Scrub Oak Hunting Club—dry hardwood forest underlain by laurel and patches of snow—in the northern Pocono woods. Up in the sky was Buck Alt. Not long ago, he was a dairy farmer, and now he was working for the Keystone State, with directional antennae on his wing struts angled in the direction of bears. Many bears in Pennsylvania have radios around their necks as a result of the summer trapping work of Alt's son Gary, who is a wildlife biologist. In winter, Buck Alt flies the country listening to the radio, crissing and crossing until the bears come on. They come on stronger the closer to them he flies. The transmitters are not omnidirectional. Suddenly, the sound cuts out. Buck looks down, chooses a landmark, approaches it again, on another vector. Gradually, he works his way in, until he is flying in ever tighter circles above the bear. He marks a map. He is accurate within two acres. The plane he flies is a Super Cub.

5   The den could have served as a set for a Passion play. It was a small chamber, open on one side, with a rock across its entrance. Between the freestanding rock and the back of the cave was room for one large bear, and she was curled in a corner on a bed of leaves, her broad head plainly visible from the outside, her cubs invisible between the rock and a soft place, chuckling, suckling, in the wintertime tropics of their own mammalian heaven. Invisible they were, yes, but by no means inaudible. What biologists call chuckling sounded like starlings in a tree.

People walking in woods sometimes come close enough to a den to cause the mother to get up and run off, unmindful of her reputation as a fearless defender of cubs. The cubs stop chuckling and begin to cry: possibly three, four cubs—a ward of mewling bears. The people hear the crying. They find the den and see the cubs. Sometimes they pick them up and carry them away, reporting to the state that they have saved the lives of bear cubs abandoned by their mother. Wherever and whenever this occurs, Gary Alt collects the cubs. After ten years of bear trapping and biological study, Alt has equipped so many sows with radios that he has been able to conduct a foster-mother program with an amazingly high rate of success. A mother in hibernation will readily accept a foster cub. If the need to place an orphan arises somewhat later, when mothers and their cubs are out and around, a sow will kill an alien cub as soon as she smells it. Alt has overcome this problem by stuffing sows' noses with Vicks

VapoRub. One way or another, he has found new families for forty-seven orphaned cubs. Forty-six have survived. The other, which had become accustomed over three weeks to feedings and caresses by human hands, was not content in a foster den, crawled outside, and died in the snow.

With a hypodermic jab stick, Alt now drugged the mother, putting her to sleep for the duration of the visit. From deeps of shining fur, he fished out cubs. One. Two. A third. A fourth. Five! The fifth was a foster daughter brought earlier in the winter from two hundred miles away. Three of the four others were male—a ratio consistent with the heavy preponderance of males that Alt's studies have shown through the years. To various onlookers he handed the cubs for safekeeping while he and several assistants carried the mother into the open and weighed her with block and tackle. To protect her eyes, Alt had blindfolded her with a red bandanna. They carried her upside down, being extremely careful lest they scrape and damage her nipples. She weighed two hundred and nineteen pounds. Alt had caught her and weighed her some months before. In the den, she had lost ninety pounds. When she was four years old, she had had four cubs; two years later, four more cubs; and now, after two more years, four cubs. He knew all that about her, he had caught her so many times. He referred to her as Daisy. Daisy was as nothing compared with Vanessa, who was sleeping off the winter somewhere else. In ten seasons, Vanessa had given birth to twenty-three cubs and had lost none. The growth and reproductive rates of black bears are greater in Pennsylvania than anywhere else. Black bears in Pennsylvania grow more rapidly than grizzlies in Montana. Eastern black bears are generally much larger than Western ones. A seven-hundred-pound bear is unusual but not rare in Pennsylvania. Alt once caught a big boar like that who had a thirty-seven-inch neck and was a hair under seven feet long.

This bear, nose to tail, measured five feet five. Alt said, "That's a nice long sow." For weighing the cubs, he had a small nylon stuff sack. He stuffed it with bear and hung it on a scale. Two months before, when the cubs were born, each would have weighed approximately half a pound—less than a newborn porcupine. Now the cubs weighed 3.4, 4.1, 4.4, 4.6, 5.6—cute little numbers with soft tan noses and erectile pyramid ears. Bears have sex in June and July, but the mother's system holds the fertilized egg away from the uterus until November, when implantation occurs. Fetal development lasts scarcely six weeks. Therefore, the creatures who live upon the hibernating mother are so small that everyone survives.

The orphan, less winsome than the others, looked like a chocolate-covered possum. I kept her under my vest. She seemed content there and scarcely moved. In time, I exchanged her for 5.6—the big boy in the litter. Lifted by the scruff and held in the air, he bawled, flashed his claws, and curled his lips like a woofing boar. I stuffed him under the vest, where he shut up and nuzzled. His claws were already more than half an inch long. Alt said that the family would come out of the den in a few weeks but that much of the spring would go by before the cubs gained weight. The difference would be that they were no longer malleable and ductile. They would become pugnacious and scratchy, not to say vicious, and would chew up the hand that caressed them. He said, "If you have an enemy, give him a bear cub."

10   Six men carried the mother back to the den, the red bandanna still tied around her eyes. Alt repacked her into the rock. "We like to return her to the den as close as possible to the way we found her," he said. Someone remarked that one biologist can work a coon, while an army is needed to deal with a bear. An army seemed to be present. Twelve people had followed Alt to the den. Some days, the group around him is four times as large. Alt, who is in his thirties, was wearing a visored khaki cap with a blue-and-gold keystone on the forehead, and a khaki cardigan under a khaki jump suit. A lithe and light-bodied man with tinted glasses and a blond mustache, he looked like a lieutenant in the Ardennes Forest.[1] Included in the retinue were two reporters and a news photographer. Alt encourages media attention, the better to soften the image of the bears. He says, "People fear bears more than they need to, and respect them not enough." Over the next twenty days, he had scheduled four hundred visitors—state senators, representatives, commissioners, television reporters, word processors, biologists, friends—to go along on his rounds of dens. Days before, he and the denned bears had been hosts to the BBC.[2] The Brits wanted snow. God was having none of it. The BBC brought in the snow.

In the course of the day, we made a brief tour of dens that for the time being stood vacant. Most were rock cavities. They had been used before, and in all likelihood would be used again. Bears in winter in the Pocono Plateau are like chocolate chips in a cookie. The bears seldom go back to the same den two years running, and they often change dens in the course of a winter. In a forty-five-hundred-acre housing development called Hemlock Farms are twenty-three dens known to be in current use and countless others awaiting new tenants. Alt showed one that was within fifteen feet of the intersection of East Spur Court and Pommel Drive. He said that when a sow with two cubs was in there he had seen deer browsing by the outcrop and ignorant dogs stopping off to lift a leg. Hemlock Farms is expensive, and full of cantilevered cypress and unencumbered glass. Houses perch on high flat rock. Now and again, there are bears in the rock—in, say, a floor-through cavity just under the porch. The owners are from New York. Alt does not always tell them that their property is zoned for bears. Once, when he did so, a "For Sale" sign went up within two weeks.

Not far away is Interstate 84. Flying over it one day, Buck Alt heard an oddly intermittent signal. Instead of breaking off once and cleanly, it broke off many times. Crossing back over, he heard it again. Soon he was in a tight turn, now hearing something, now nothing, in a pattern that did not suggest anything he had heard before. It did, however, suggest the interstate. Where a big green sign says, "Milford 11, Port Jervis 20," Gary hunted around and found the bear. He took us now to see the den. We went down a steep slope at the side of the highway and, crouching, peered into a culvert. It was about fifty yards

1. Area of Belgium, Luxembourg, and France where the 1944–45 Battle of the Bulge took place.
2. British Broadcasting Corporation.

long. There was a disc of daylight at the opposite end. Thirty inches in diameter, it was a perfect place to stash a body, and that is what the bear thought, too. On Gary's first visit, the disc of daylight had not been visible. The bear had denned under the eastbound lanes. She had given birth to three cubs. Soon after he found her, heavy rains were predicted. He hauled the family out and off to a vacant den. The cubs weighed less than a pound. Two days later, water a foot deep was racing through the culvert.

Under High Knob, in remote undeveloped forest about six hundred metres above sea level, a slope falling away in an easterly direction contained a classic excavated den: a small entrance leading into an intimate ovate cavern, with a depression in the center for a bed—in all, about twenty-four cubic feet, the size of a refrigerator-freezer. The den had not been occupied in several seasons, but Rob Buss, a district game protector who works regularly with Gary Alt, had been around to check it three days before and had shined his flashlight into a darkness stuffed with fur. Meanwhile, six inches of fresh snow had fallen on High Knob, and now Alt and his team, making preparations a short distance from the den, scooped up snow in their arms and filled a big sack. They had nets of nylon mesh. There was a fifty-fifty likelihood of yearling bears in the den. Mothers keep cubs until their second spring. When a biologist comes along and provokes the occupants to emerge, there is no way to predict how many will appear. Sometimes they keep coming and coming, like clowns from a compact car. As a bear emerges, it walks into the nylon mesh. A drawstring closes. At the same time, the den entrance is stuffed with a bag of snow. That stops the others. After the first bear has been dealt with, Alt removes the sack of snow. Out comes another bear. A yearling weighs about eighty pounds, and may move so fast that it runs over someone on the biological team and stands on top of him sniffing at his ears. Or her ears. Janice Gruttadauria, a research assistant, is a part of the team. Bear after bear, the procedure is repeated until the bag of snow is pulled away and nothing comes out. That is when Alt asks Rob Buss to go inside and see if anything is there.

Now, moving close to the entrance, Alt spread a tarp on the snow, lay down on it, turned on a five-cell flashlight, and put his head inside the den. The beam played over thick black fur and came to rest on a tiny foot. The sack of snow would not be needed. After drugging the mother with a jab stick, he joined her in the den. The entrance was so narrow he had to shrug his shoulders to get in. He shoved the sleeping mother, head first, out of the darkness and into the light.

While she was away, I shrugged my own shoulders and had a look inside. 15 The den smelled of earth but not of bear. The walls were dripping with roots. The water and protein metabolism of hibernating black bears has been explored by the Mayo Clinic as a research model for, among other things, human endurance on long flights through space and medical situations closer to home, such as the maintenance of anephric human beings who are awaiting kidney transplants.

Outside, each in turn, the cubs were put in the stuff sack—a male and a female. The female weighed four pounds. Greedily, I reached for her when Alt took her out of the bag. I planted her on my shoulder while I wrote down facts about her mother: weight, a hundred and ninety-two pounds; length, fifty-eight inches; some toes missing; severe frostbite from a bygone winter evidenced along the edges of the ears.

Eventually, with all weighing and tagging complete, it was time to go. Alt went into the den. Soon he called out that he was ready for the mother. It would be a tight fit. Feet first, she was shoved in, like a safe-deposit box. Inside, Alt tugged at her in close embrace, and the two of them gradually revolved until she was at the back and their positions had reversed. He shaped her like a doughnut—her accustomed den position. The cubs go in the center. The male was handed in to him. Now he was asking for the female. For a moment, I glanced around as if looking to see who had her. The thought crossed my mind that if I bolted and ran far enough and fast enough I could flag a passing car and keep her. Then I pulled her from under the flap of my vest and handed her away.

Alt and others covered the entrance with laurel boughs, and covered the boughs with snow. They camouflaged the den, but that was not the purpose. Practicing wildlife management to a fare-thee-well, Alt wanted the den to be even darker than it had been before; this would cause the family to stay longer inside and improve the cubs' chances when at last they faced the world.

In the evening, I drove down off the Pocono Plateau and over the folded mountains and across the Great Valley and up the New Jersey Highlands and down into the basin and home. No amount of intervening terrain, though— and no amount of distance—could remove from my mind the picture of the covered entrance in the Pennsylvania hillside, or the thought of what was up there under the snow.

MLA CITATION

McPhee, John. "Under the Snow." *The Norton Reader: An Anthology of Nonfiction*, edited by Melissa A. Goldthwaite et al., 15th ed., W. W. Norton, 2020, pp. 443–48.

QUESTIONS

1. John McPhee opens with a memory of holding his daughter when she was an infant, saying she would stick to his shoulder "like velvet" (paragraph 1). Two paragraphs later, he writes about holding a bear cub that stayed on his shoulder "like a piece of velvet" (paragraph 3). Why do you think McPhee makes this comparison? What purpose does it serve in this essay?

2. Trace McPhee's use of simile throughout the essay. For example, he compares bears to chocolate chips (paragraph 11), likens their movement to "clowns from a compact car" (paragraph 13), and describes a researcher positioning a bear "like a doughnut" (paragraph 17). What is the effect of such comparisons? What other similes are significant in this essay?

3. What is the purpose of the kind of bear trapping and biological study McPhee describes? What is your position on this interaction between humans and wildlife? Write an argument in which you either defend the kind of research McPhee describes or make a case for leaving wildlife alone. Consider using a specific animal (as McPhee uses bears) in making your claim.

JOHN MUIR
A Wind-Storm in the Forests

THE MOUNTAIN WINDS, like the dew and rain, sunshine and snow, are measured and bestowed with love on the forests to develop their strength and beauty. However restricted the scope of other forest influences, that of the winds is universal. The snow bends and trims the upper forests every winter, the lightning strikes a single tree here and there, while avalanches mow down thousands at a swoop as a gardener trims out a bed of flowers. But the winds go to every tree, fingering every leaf and branch and furrowed bole; not one is forgotten; the Mountain Pine towering with outstretched arms on the rugged buttresses of the icy peaks, the lowliest and most retiring tenant of the dells; they seek and find them all, caressing them tenderly, bending them in lusty exercise, stimulating their growth, plucking off a leaf or limb as required, or removing an entire tree or grove, now whispering and cooing through the branches like a sleepy child, now roaring like the ocean; the winds blessing the forests, the forests the winds, with ineffable beauty and harmony as the sure result.

After one has seen pines six feet in diameter bending like grasses before a mountain gale, and ever and anon some giant falling with a crash that shakes the hills, it seems astonishing that any, save the lowest thickset trees, could ever have found a period sufficiently stormless to establish themselves; or, once established, that they should not, sooner or later, have been blown down. But when the storm is over, and we behold the same forests tranquil again, towering fresh and unscathed in erect majesty, and consider what centuries of storms have fallen upon them since they were first planted,—hail, to break the tender seedlings; lightning, to scorch and shatter; snow, winds, and avalanches, to crush and overwhelm,—while the manifest result of all this wild storm-culture is the glorious perfection we behold; then faith in Nature's forestry is established, and we cease to deplore the violence of her most destructive gales, or of any other storm-implement whatsoever.

There are two trees in the Sierra forests that are never blown down, so long as they continue in sound health. These are the Juniper and the Dwarf Pine of the summit peaks. Their stiff, crooked roots grip the storm-beaten ledges like eagles' claws, while their lithe, cord-like branches bend round compliantly, offering but slight holds for winds, however violent. The other alpine conifers— the Needle Pine, Mountain Pine, Two-leaved Pine, and Hemlock Spruce—are never thinned out by this agent to any destructive extent, on account of their admirable toughness and the closeness of their growth. In general the same is true of the giants of the lower zones. The kingly Sugar Pine, towering aloft to a height of more than 200 feet, offers a fine mark to storm-winds: but it is not densely foliaged, and its long, horizontal arms swing round compliantly in the

From John Muir's The Mountains of California *(1894), a book of scientific observation and personal memoir.*

A wind-storm in the California forests (after a sketch by the author).

blast, like tresses of green, fluent algæ in a brook; while the Silver Firs in most places keep their ranks well together in united strength. The Yellow or Silver Pine is more frequently overturned than any other tree on the Sierra, because its leaves and branches form a larger mass in proportion to its height, while in many places it is planted sparsely, leaving open lanes through which storms may enter with full force. Furthermore, because it is distributed along the lower portion of the range, which was the first to be left bare on the breaking up of the ice-sheet at the close of the glacial winter, the soil it is growing upon has been longer exposed to post-glacial weathering, and consequently is in a more crumbling, decayed condition than the fresher soils farther up the range, and therefore offers a less secure anchorage for the roots.

While exploring the forest zones of Mount Shasta, I discovered the path of a hurricane strewn with thousands of pines of this species. Great and small had been uprooted or wrenched off by sheer force, making a clean gap, like that made by a snow avalanche. But hurricanes capable of doing this class of work are rare in the Sierra, and when we have explored the forests from one extremity of the range to the other, we are compelled to believe that they are the most beautiful on the face of the earth, however we may regard the agents that have made them so.

5   There is always something deeply exciting, not only in the sounds of winds in the woods, which exert more or less influence over every mind, but in their varied waterlike flow as manifested by the movements of the trees, especially those of the conifers. By no other trees are they rendered so extensively and impressively visible, not even by the lordly tropic palms or tree-ferns responsive to the gentlest breeze. The waving of a forest of the giant Sequoias is indescribably impressive and sublime, but the pines seem to me the best interpreters of winds. They are mighty waving goldenrods, ever in tune, singing and writing wind-music all their long century lives. Little, however, of this noble tree-waving and tree-music will you see or hear in the strictly alpine portion of the forests. The burly Juniper, whose girth sometimes more than equals its height, is about as rigid as the rocks on which it grows. The slender lash-like sprays of the Dwarf Pine stream out in wavering ripples, but the tallest and slenderest

are far too unyielding to wave even in the heaviest gales. They only shake in quick, short vibrations. The Hemlock Spruce, however, and the Mountain Pine, and some of the tallest thickets of the Two-leaved species bow in storms with considerable scope and gracefulness. But it is only in the lower and middle zones that the meeting of winds and woods is to be seen in all its grandeur.

One of the most beautiful and exhilarating storms I ever enjoyed in the Sierra occurred in December, 1874, when I happened to be exploring one of the tributary valleys of the Yuba River. The sky and the ground and the trees had been thoroughly rain-washed and were dry again. The day was intensely pure, one of those incomparable bits of California winter, warm and balmy and full of white sparkling sunshine, redolent of all the purest influences of the spring, and at the same time enlivened with one of the most bracing wind-storms conceivable. Instead of camping out, as I usually do, I then chanced to be stopping at the house of a friend. But when the storm began to sound, I lost no time in pushing out into the woods to enjoy it. For on such occasions Nature has always something rare to show us, and the danger to life and limb is hardly greater than one would experience crouching deprecatingly beneath a roof.

It was still early morning when I found myself fairly adrift. Delicious sunshine came pouring over the hills, lighting the tops of the pines, and setting free a stream of summery fragrance that contrasted strangely with the wild tones of the storm. The air was mottled with pine-tassels and bright green plumes, that went flashing past in the sunlight like birds pursued. But there was not the slightest dustiness, nothing less pure than leaves, and ripe pollen, and flecks of withered bracken and moss. I heard trees falling for hours at the rate of one every two or three minutes; some uprooted, partly on account of the loose, water-soaked condition of the ground; others broken straight across, where some weakness caused by fire had determined the spot. The gestures of the various trees made a delightful study. Young Sugar Pines, light and feathery as squirrel-tails, were bowing almost to the ground; while the grand old patriarchs, whose massive boles had been tried in a hundred storms, waved solemnly above them, their long, arching branches streaming fluently on the gale, and every needle thrilling and ringing and shedding off keen lances of light like a diamond. The Douglas Spruces,[1] with long sprays drawn out in level tresses, and needles massed in a gray, shimmering glow, presented a most striking appearance as they stood in bold relief along the hilltops. The madroños[2] in the dells, with their red bark and large glossy leaves tilted every way, reflected the sunshine in throbbing spangles like those one so often sees on the rippled surface of a glacier lake. But the Silver Pines were now the most impressively beautiful of all. Colossal spires 200 feet in height waved like supple goldenrods chanting and bowing low as if in worship, while the whole mass of their long, tremulous foliage was kindled into one continuous blaze of white sun-fire. The force of the gale was such that the most steadfast monarch of them all rocked down to its roots with a motion plainly perceptible when one leaned

1. Another name for Douglas fir.
2. Type of evergreen tree.

against it. Nature was holding high festival, and every fiber of the most rigid giants thrilled with glad excitement.

I drifted on through the midst of this passionate music and motion, across many a glen, from ridge to ridge; often halting in the lee of a rock for shelter, or to gaze and listen. Even when the grand anthem had swelled to its highest pitch, I could distinctly hear the varying tones of individual trees,—Spruce, and Fir, and Pine, and leafless Oak—and even the infinitely gentle rustle of the withered grasses at my feet. Each was expressing itself in its own way,— singing its own song, and making its own peculiar gestures,—manifesting a richness of variety to be found in no other forest I have yet seen. The conifer- ous woods of Canada, and the Carolinas, and Florida, are made up of trees that resemble one another about as nearly as blades of grass, and grow close together in much the same way. Coniferous trees, in general, seldom possess individual character, such as is manifest among Oaks and Elms. But the Cali- fornia forests are made up of a greater number of distinct species than any other in the world. And in them we find, not only a marked differentiation into spe- cial groups, but also a marked individuality in almost every tree, giving rise to storm effects indescribably glorious.

Toward midday, after a long, tingling scramble through copses of hazel and ceanothus,[3] I gained the summit of the highest ridge in the neighborhood; and then it occurred to me that it would be a fine thing to climb one of the trees to obtain a wider outlook and get my ear close to the Æolian music[4] of its topmost needles. But under the circumstances the choice of a tree was a serious mat- ter. One whose instep was not very strong seemed in danger of being blown down, or of being struck by others in case they should fall; another was branch- less to a considerable height above the ground, and at the same time too large to be grasped with arms and legs in climbing; while others were not favorably situated for clear views. After cautiously casting about, I made choice of the tallest of a group of Douglas Spruces that were growing close together like a tuft of grass, no one of which seemed likely to fall unless all the rest fell with it. Though comparatively young, they were about 100 feet high, and their lithe, brushy tops were rocking and swirling in wild ecstasy. Being accustomed to climb trees in making botanical studies, I experienced no difficulty in reach- ing the top of this one, and never before did I enjoy so noble an exhilaration of motion. The slender tops fairly flapped and swished in the passionate torrent, bending and swirling backward and forward, round and round, tracing inde- scribable combinations of vertical and horizontal curves, while I clung with muscles firm braced, like a bobolink on a reed.

10   In its widest sweeps my tree-top described an arc of from twenty to thirty degrees, but I felt sure of its elastic temper, having seen others of the same spe- cies still more severely tried—bent almost to the ground indeed, in heavy snows—without breaking a fiber. I was therefore safe, and free to take the wind into my pulses and enjoy the excited forest from my superb outlook. The view

3. Type of evergreen shrub.
4. Music made by the wind; from Aeolus, the Greek god of the winds, the strings of whose harp were sounded by the wind.

from here must be extremely beautiful in any weather. Now my eye roved over the piny hills and dales as over fields of waving grain, and felt the light running in ripples and broad swelling undulations across the valleys from ridge to ridge, as the shining foliage was stirred by corresponding waves of air. Oftentimes these waves of reflected light would break up suddenly into a kind of beaten foam, and again, after chasing one another in regular order, they would seem to bend forward in concentric curves, and disappear on some hillside, like sea-waves on a shelving shore. The quantity of light reflected from the bent needles was so great as to make whole groves appear as if covered with snow, while the black shadows beneath the trees greatly enhanced the effect of the silvery splendor.

Excepting only the shadows there was nothing somber in all this wild sea of pines. On the contrary, notwithstanding this was the winter season, the colors were remarkably beautiful. The shafts of the pine and libocedrus[5] were brown and purple, and most of the foliage was well tinged with yellow; the laurel groves, with the pale undersides of their leaves turned upward, made masses of gray; and then there was many a dash of chocolate color from clumps of manzanita,[6] and jet of vivid crimson from the bark of the madroños, while the ground on the hillsides, appearing here and there through openings between the groves, displayed masses of pale purple and brown.

The sounds of the storm corresponded gloriously with this wild exuberance of light and motion. The profound bass of the naked branches and boles booming like waterfalls; the quick, tense vibrations of the pine-needles, now rising to a shrill, whistling hiss, now falling to a silky murmur; the rustling of laurel groves in the dells, and the keen metallic click of leaf on leaf—all this was heard in easy analysis when the attention was calmly bent.

The varied gestures of the multitude were seen to fine advantage, so that one could recognize the different species at a distance of several miles by this means alone, as well as by their forms and colors, and the way they reflected the light. All seemed strong and comfortable, as if really enjoying the storm, while responding to its most enthusiastic greetings. We hear much nowadays concerning the universal struggle for existence, but no struggle in the common meaning of the word was manifest here; no recognition of danger by any tree; no deprecation; but rather an invincible gladness as remote from exultation as from fear.

I kept my lofty perch for hours, frequently closing my eyes to enjoy the music by itself, or to feast quietly on the delicious fragrance that was streaming past. The fragrance of the woods was less marked than that produced during warm rain, when so many balsamic buds and leaves are steeped like tea; but, from the chafing of resiny branches against each other, and the incessant attrition of myriads of needles, the gale was spiced to a very tonic degree. And besides the fragrance from these local sources there were traces of scents brought from afar. For this wind came first from the sea, rubbing against its fresh, briny waves, then distilled through the redwoods, threading rich ferny

5. Genus of cedar trees. In the Sierra Nevada, *Libocedrus decurrens* often reaches a height of 150 feet.
6. Type of evergreen shrub.

gulches, and spreading itself in broad undulating currents over many a flower-enameled ridge of the coast mountains, then across the golden plains, up the purple foot-hills, and into these piny woods with the varied incense gathered by the way.

15   Winds are advertisements of all they touch, however much or little we may be able to read them; telling their wanderings even by their scents alone. Mariners detect the flowery perfume of land-winds far at sea, and sea-winds carry the fragrance of dulse and tangle far inland, where it is quickly recognized, though mingled with the scents of a thousand land-flowers. As an illustration of this, I may tell here that I breathed sea-air on the Firth of Forth, in Scotland, while a boy; then was taken to Wisconsin, where I remained nineteen years; then, without in all this time having breathed one breath of the sea, I walked quietly, alone, from the middle of the Mississippi Valley to the Gulf of Mexico, on a botanical excursion, and while in Florida, far from the coast, my attention wholly bent on the splendid tropical vegetation about me, I suddenly recognized a sea-breeze, as it came sifting through the palmettos and blooming vine-tangles, which at once awakened and set free a thousand dormant associations, and made me a boy again in Scotland, as if all the intervening years had been annihilated.

Most people like to look at mountain rivers, and bear them in mind; but few care to look at the winds, though far more beautiful and sublime, and though they become at times about as visible as flowing water. When the north winds in winter are making upward sweeps over the curving summits of the High Sierra, the fact is sometimes published with flying snow-banners a mile long. Those portions of the winds thus embodied can scarce be wholly invisible, even to the darkest imagination. And when we look around over an agitated forest, we may see something of the wind that stirs it, by its effects upon the trees. Yonder it descends in a rush of water-like ripples, and sweeps over the bending pines from hill to hill. Nearer, we see detached plumes and leaves, now speeding by on level currents, now whirling in eddies, or, escaping over the edges of the whirls, soaring aloft on grand, upswelling domes of air, or tossing on flame-like crests. Smooth, deep currents, cascades, falls, and swirling eddies, sing around every tree and leaf, and over all the varied topography of the region with telling changes of form, like mountain rivers conforming to the features of their channels.

After tracing the Sierra streams from their fountains to the plains, marking where they bloom white in falls, glide in crystal plumes, surge gray and foam-filled in boulder-choked gorges, and slip through the woods in long, tranquil reaches—after thus learning their language and forms in detail, we may at length hear them chanting all together in one grand anthem, and comprehend them all in clear inner vision, covering the range like lace. But even this spectacle is far less sublime and not a whit more substantial than what we may behold of these storm-streams of air in the mountain woods.

We all travel the milky way together, trees and men; but it never occurred to me until this stormday, while swinging in the wind, that trees are travelers, in the ordinary sense. They make many journeys, not extensive ones, it is true;

but our own little journeys, away and back again, are only little more than tree-wavings—many of them not so much.

When the storm began to abate, I dismounted and sauntered down through the calming woods. The storm-tones died away, and, turning toward the east, I beheld the countless hosts of the forests hushed and tranquil, towering above one another on the slopes of the hills like a devout audience. The setting sun filled them with amber light, and seemed to say, while they listened, "My peace I give unto you."

As I gazed on the impressive scene, all the so-called ruin of the storm was   20
forgotten, and never before did these noble woods appear so fresh, so joyous, so immortal.

MLA CITATION

Muir, John. "A Wind-Storm in the Forests." *The Norton Reader: An Anthology of Nonfiction*, edited by Melissa A. Goldthwaite et al., 15th ed., W. W. Norton, 2020, pp. 449–55.

QUESTIONS

1. What preconceptions might a reader bring to John Muir's title, "A Wind-Storm in the Forests"? Does the opening sentence—indeed, the entire opening paragraph—suggest a different perspective? How so?

2. The central adventure in this essay occurs when Muir climbs a Douglas Spruce (paragraph 9). Why does Muir undertake this climb? What does he wish to experience?

3. Write about an experience you have had in nature, whether dramatic, as in Muir's essay, or more quiet.

EDWARD ABBEY
The Great American Desert

I N MY CASE IT WAS LOVE AT FIRST SIGHT. This desert, all deserts, any desert. No matter where my head and feet may go, my heart and my entrails stay behind, here on the clean, true, comfortable rock, under the black sun of God's forsaken country. When I take on my next incarnation, my bones will remain bleaching nicely in a stone gulch under the rim of some faraway plateau, way out there in the back of beyond. An unrequited and excessive love, inhuman no doubt but painful anyhow, especially when I see my desert under attack. "The one death I cannot bear," said the Sonoran-

Solicited in 1973 for the hiking book Sierra Club Naturalist's Guide to the Deserts of the Southwest *(1977), this essay was, in revised form, also collected in Edward Abbey's* The Journey Home: Some Words in Defense of the American West *(1977).*

Arizonan poet Richard Shelton. The kind of love that makes a man selfish, possessive, irritable. If you're thinking of a visit, my natural reaction is like a rattlesnake's—to warn you off. What I want to say goes something like this.

Survival Hint #1: Stay out of there. Don't go. Stay home and read a good book, this one for example. The Great American Desert is an awful place. People get hurt, get sick, get lost out there. Even if you survive, which is not certain, you will have a miserable time. The desert is for movies and God-intoxicated mystics, not for family recreation.

Let me enumerate the hazards. First the Walapai tiger, also known as cone-nose kissing bug. *Triatoma protracta* is a true bug, black as sin, and it flies through the night quiet as an assassin. It does not attack directly like a mosquito or deerfly, but alights at a discreet distance, undetected, and creeps upon you, its hairy little feet making not the slightest noise. The kissing bug is fond of warmth and like Dracula requires mammalian blood for sustenance. When it reaches you the bug crawls onto your skin so gently, so softly that unless your senses are hyperacute you feel nothing. Selecting a tender point, the bug slips its conical proboscis into your flesh, injecting a poisonous anesthetic. If you are asleep you will feel nothing. If you happen to be awake you may notice the faintest of pinpricks, hardly more than a brief ticklish sensation, which you will probably disregard. But the bug is already at work. Having numbed the nerves near the point of entry the bug proceeds (with a sigh of satisfaction, no doubt) to withdraw blood. When its belly is filled, it pulls out, backs off, and waddles away, so drunk and gorged it cannot fly.

At about this time the victim awakes, scratching at a furious itch. If you recognize the symptoms at once, you can sometimes find the bug in your vicinity and destroy it. But revenge will be your only satisfaction. Your night is ruined. If you are of average sensitivity to a kissing bug's poison, your entire body breaks out in hives, skin aflame from head to toe. Some people become seriously ill, in many cases requiring hospitalization. Others recover fully after five or six hours except for a hard and itchy swelling, which may endure for a week.

5   After the kissing bug, you should beware of rattlesnakes; we have half a dozen species, all offensive and dangerous, plus centipedes, millipedes, tarantulas, black widows, brown recluses, Gila monsters, the deadly poisonous coral snakes, and giant hairy desert scorpions. Plus an immense variety and near-infinite number of ants, midges, gnats, bloodsucking flies, and blood-guzzling mosquitoes. (You might think the desert would be spared at least mosquitoes? Not so. Peer in any water hole by day: swarming with mosquito larvae. Venture out on a summer's eve: The air vibrates with their mournful keening.) Finally, where the desert meets the sea, as on the coasts of Sonora and Baja California, we have the usual assortment of obnoxious marine life: sandflies, ghost crabs, stingrays, electric jellyfish, spiny sea urchins, man-eating sharks, and other creatures so distasteful one prefers not even to name them.

It has been said, and truly, that everything in the desert either stings, stabs, stinks, or sticks. You will find the flora here as venomous, hooked, barbed, thorny, prickly, needled, saw-toothed, hairy, stickered, mean, bitter, sharp, wiry, and fierce as the animals. Something about the desert inclines all living things to harshness and acerbity. The soft evolve out. Except for sleek and oily growths like the poison ivy—oh yes, indeed—that flourish in sinister profusion on the dank walls above the quicksand down in those corridors of gloom and labyrinthine monotony that men call canyons.

We come now to the third major hazard, which is sunshine. Too much of a good thing can be fatal. Sunstroke, heatstroke, and dehydration are common misfortunes in the bright American Southwest. If you can avoid the insects, reptiles, and arachnids, the cactus and the ivy, the smog of the southwestern cities, and the lung fungus of the desert valleys (carried by dust in the air), you cannot escape the desert sun. Too much exposure to it eventually causes, quite literally, not merely sunburn but skin cancer.

Much sun, little rain also means an arid climate. Compared with the high humidity of more hospitable regions, the dry heat of the desert seems at first not terribly uncomfortable—sometimes even pleasant. But that sensation of comfort is false, a deception, and therefore all the more dangerous, for it induces overexertion and an insufficient consumption of water, even when water is available. This leads to various internal complications, some immediate—sunstroke, for example—and some not apparent until much later. Mild but prolonged dehydration, continued over a span of months or years, leads to the crystallization of mineral solutions in the urinary tract, that is, to what urologists call urinary calculi or kidney stones. A disability common in all the world's arid regions. Kidney stones, in case you haven't met one, come in many shapes and sizes, from pellets smooth as BB shot to highly irregular calcifications resembling asteroids, Vietcong shrapnel, and crown-of-thorns starfish. Some of these objects may be "passed" naturally; others can be removed only by means of the Davis stone basket or by surgery. Me—I was lucky; I passed mine with only a groan, my forehead pressed against the wall of a pissoir in the rear of a Tucson bar that I cannot recommend.

You may be getting the impression by now that the desert is not the most suitable of environments for human habitation. Correct. Of all the Earth's climatic zones, excepting only the Antarctic, the deserts are the least inhabited, the least "developed," for reasons that should now be clear.

You may wish to ask, Yes, okay, but among North American deserts which is the *worst*? A good question—and I am happy to attempt an answer.

Geographers generally divide the North American desert—what was once termed "the Great American Desert"—into four distinct regions or subdeserts. These are the Sonoran Desert, which comprises southern Arizona, Baja California, and the state of Sonora in Mexico; the Chihuahuan Desert, which includes west Texas, southern New Mexico, and the states of Chihuahua and Coahuila in Mexico; the Mojave Desert, which includes southeastern California and small portions of Nevada, Utah, and Arizona; and the Great Basin Desert, which includes most of Utah and Nevada, northern Arizona, northwestern New Mexico, and much of Idaho and eastern Oregon.

Privately, I prefer my own categories. Up north in Utah somewhere is the canyon country—places like Zeke's Hole, Death Hollow, Pucker Pass, Buckskin Gulch, Nausea Crick, Wolf Hole, Mollie's Nipple, Dirty Devil River, Horse

Canyon, Horseshoe Canyon, Lost Horse Canyon, Horsethief Canyon, and Horseshit Canyon, to name only the more classic places. Down in Arizona and Sonora there's the cactus country; if you have nothing better to do, you might take a look at High Tanks, Salome Creek, Tortilla Flat, Esperero ("Hoper") Canyon, Holy Joe Peak, Depression Canyon, Painted Cave, Hell Hole Canyon, Hell's Half Acre, Iceberg Canyon, Tiburon (Shark) Island, Pinacate Peak, Infernal Valley, Sykes Crater, Montezuma's Head, Gu Oidak, Kuakatch, Pisinimo, and Baboquivari Mountain, for example.

Then there's The Canyon. *The* Canyon. The Grand. That's one world. And North Rim—that's another. And Death Valley, still another, where I lived one winter near Furnace Creek and climbed the Funeral Mountains, tasted Badwater, looked into the Devil's Hole, hollered up Echo Canyon, searched for and never did find Seldom Seen Slim.[1] Looked for *satori*[2] near Vana, Nevada, and found a ghost town named Bonnie Claire. Never made it to Winnemucca. Drove through the Smoke Creek Desert and down through Big Pine and Lone Pine and home across the Panamints to Death Valley[3] again—home sweet home that winter.

And which of these deserts is the worst? I find it hard to judge. They're all bad—not half bad but all bad. In the Sonoran Desert, Phoenix will get you if the sun, snakes, bugs, and arthropods don't. In the Mojave Desert, it's Las Vegas, more sickening by far than the Glauber's salt in the Death Valley sinkholes. Go to Chihuahua and you're liable to get busted in El Paso and sandbagged in Ciudad Juárez—where all old whores go to die. Up north in the Great Basin Desert, on the Plateau Province, in the canyon country, your heart will break, seeing the strip mines open up and the power plants rise where only cowboys and Indians and J. Wesley Powell ever roamed before.

15   Nevertheless, all is not lost; much remains, and I welcome the prospect of an army of lug-soled hiker's boots on the desert trails. To save what wilderness is left in the American Southwest—and in the American Southwest only the wilderness is worth saving—we are going to need all the recruits we can get. All the hands, heads, bodies, time, money, effort we can find. Presumably—and the Sierra Club, the Wilderness Society, the Friends of the Earth, the Audubon Society, the Defenders of Wildlife[4] operate on this theory—those who learn to love what is spare, rough, wild, undeveloped, and unbroken will be willing to fight for it, will help resist the strip miners, highway builders, land developers, weapons testers, power producers, tree chainers, clear cutters, oil drillers, dam beavers, subdividers—the list goes on and on—before that zinc-

1. Nickname for Charles Ferge (1889–1968), prospector and sole resident of Ballarat ghost town.

2. Buddhist term for understanding or enlightenment.

3. "Winnemucca . . . Death Valley," desert towns in Nevada and California. Throughout the essay Abbey uses local as well as official names to convey a feel for desert places.

4. "Sierra Club . . . Defenders of Wildlife," organizations founded—from 1892 to 1969—to protect wilderness habitat and its plants and animals.

hearted, termite-brained, squint-eyed, near-sighted, greedy crew succeeds in completely californicating what still survives of the Great American Desert.

So much for the Good Cause. Now what about desert hiking itself, you may ask. I'm glad you asked that question. I firmly believe that one should never—I repeat *never*—go out into that formidable wasteland of cactus, heat, serpents, rock, scrub, and thorn without careful planning, thorough and cautious preparation, and complete—never mind the expense!—*complete* equipment. My motto is: Be Prepared.

That is my belief and that is my motto. My practice, however, is a little different. I tend to go off in a more or less random direction myself, half-baked, half-assed, half-cocked, and half-ripped. Why? Well, because I have an indolent and melancholy nature and don't care to be bothered getting all those *things* together—all that bloody *gear*—maps, compass, binoculars, poncho, pup tent, shoes, first-aid kit, rope, flashlight, inspirational poetry, water, food—and because anyhow I approach nature with a certain surly ill-will, daring Her to make trouble. Later when I'm deep into Natural Bridges Natural Moneymint or Zion National Parkinglot or say General Shithead National Forest Land of Many Abuses why then, of course, when it's a bit late, then I may wish I had packed that something extra: matches perhaps, to mention one useful item, or maybe a spoon to eat my gruel with.

If I hike with another person it's usually the same; most of my friends have indolent and melancholy natures too. A cursed lot, all of them. I think of my comrade John De Puy,[5] for example, sloping along for mile after mile like a goddamned camel—indefatigable—with those J. C. Penny [*sic*] hightops on his feet and that plastic pack on his back he got with five books of Green Stamps and nothing inside it but a sketchbook, some homemade jerky and a few cans of green chiles. Or Douglas Peacock,[6] ex–Green Beret, just the opposite. Built like a buffalo, he loads a ninety-pound canvas pannier on his back at trailhead, loaded with guns, ammunition, bayonet, pitons and carabiners, cameras, field books, a 150-foot rope, geologist's sledge, rock samples, assay kit,[7] field glasses, two gallons of water in steel canteens, jungle boots, a case of C-rations, rope hammock, pharmaceuticals in a pig-iron box, raincoat, overcoat, two-man mountain tent, Dutch oven, hibachi, shovel, ax, inflatable boat, and near the top of the load and distributed through side and back pockets, easily accessible, a case of beer. Not because he enjoys or needs all that weight—he may never get to the bottom of that cargo on a ten-day outing—but simply because Douglas uses his packbag for general storage both at home and on the trail and prefers not to have to rearrange everything from time to time merely for the purposes of a hike. Thus my friends De Puy and Peacock; you may wish to avoid such extremes.

A few tips on desert etiquette:

5. Painter (b. 1927) living in Taos, New Mexico, who met Abbey when Abbey was editing the Taos newspaper *El Crepusculo*.
6. Vietnam veteran (b. 1942) and author.
7. Used to test water purity.

1. Carry a cooking stove, if you must cook. Do not burn desert wood, which is rare and beautiful and required ages for its creation (an ironwood tree lives for over 1,000 years and juniper almost as long).

2. If you must, out of need, build a fire, then for God's sake allow it to burn itself out before you leave—do not bury it, as Boy Scouts and Campfire Girls do, under a heap of mud or sand. Scatter the ashes; replace any rocks you may have used in constructing a fireplace; do all you can to obliterate the evidence that you camped here. (The Search & Rescue Team may be looking for you.)

3. Do not bury garbage—the wildlife will only dig it up again. Burn what will burn and pack out the rest. The same goes for toilet paper: Don't bury it, *burn it.*

4. Do not bathe in desert pools, natural tanks, *tinajas*, potholes. Drink what water you need, take what you need, and leave the rest for the next hiker and more important for the bees, birds, and animals—bighorn sheep, coyotes, lions, foxes, badgers, deer, wild pigs, wild horses—whose *lives* depend on that water.

5. Always remove and destroy survey stakes, flagging, advertising signboards, mining claim markers, animal traps, poisoned bait, seismic exploration geophones, and other such artifacts of industrialism. The men who put those things there are up to no good and it is our duty to confound them. Keep America Beautiful. Grow a Beard. Take a Bath. Burn a Billboard.

20   Anyway—why go into the desert? Really, why do it? That sun, roaring at you all day long. The fetid, tepid, vapid little water holes slowly evaporating under a scum of grease, full of cannibal beetles, spotted toads, horsehair worms, liver flukes, and down at the bottom, inevitably, the pale cadaver of a ten-inch centipede. Those pink rattlesnakes down in The Canyon, those diamondback monsters thick as a truck driver's wrist that lurk in shady places along the trail, those unpleasant solpugids and unnecessary Jerusalem crickets that scurry on dirty claws across your face at night. Why? The rain that comes down like lead shot and wrecks the trail, those sudden rockfalls of obscure origin that crash like thunder ten feet behind you in the heart of a dead-still afternoon. The ubiquitous buzzard, so patient—but only so patient. The sullen and hostile Indians, all on welfare. The ragweed, the tumbleweed, the Jimson weed, the snakeweed. The scorpion in your shoe at dawn. The dreary wind that blows all spring, the psychedelic Joshua trees waving their arms at you on moonlight nights. Sand in the soup du jour. Halazone tablets in your canteen. The barren hills that always go up, which is bad, or down, which is worse. Those canyons like catacombs with quicksand lapping at your crotch. Hollow, mummified horses with forelegs casually crossed, dead for ten years, leaning against the corner of a barbed-wire fence. Packhorses at night, iron-shod, clattering over the slickrock through your camp. The last tin of tuna, two flat tires, not enough water and a forty-mile trek to Tule Well. An osprey on a cardón cactus, snatching the

head off a living fish—always the best part first. The hawk sailing by at 200 feet, a squirming snake in its talons. Salt in the drinking water. Salt, selenium, arsenic, radon and radium in the water, in the gravel, in your bones. Water so hard it bends light, drills holes in rock and chokes up your radiator. Why go there? Those places with the hardcase names: Starvation Creek, Poverty Knoll, Hungry Valley, Bitter Springs, Last Chance Canyon, Dungeon Canyon, Whipsaw Flat, Dead Horse Point, Scorpion Flat, Dead Man Draw, Stinking Spring, Camino del Diablo, Jornado del Muerto . . . Death Valley.

Well then, why indeed go walking into the desert, that grim ground, that bleak and lonesome land where, as Genghis Khan[8] said of India, "the heat is bad and the water makes men sick"?

Why the desert, when you could be strolling along the golden beaches of California? Camping by a stream of pure Rocky Mountain spring water in colorful Colorado? Loafing through a laurel slick in the misty hills of North Carolina? Or getting your head mashed in the greasy alley behind the Elysium Bar and Grill in Hoboken, New Jersey? Why the desert, given a world of such splendor and variety?

A friend and I took a walk around the base of a mountain up beyond Coconino County, Arizona. This was a mountain we'd been planning to circumambulate for years. Finally we put on our walking shoes and did it. About halfway around this mountain, on the third or fourth day, we paused for a while—two days—by the side of a stream, which the Navajos call Nasja because of the amber color of the water. (Caused perhaps by juniper roots—the water seems safe enough to drink.) On our second day there I walked down the stream, alone, to look at the canyon beyond. I entered the canyon and followed it for half the afternoon, for three or four miles, maybe, until it became a gorge so deep, narrow and dark, full of water and the inevitable quagmires of quicksand, that I turned around and looked for a way out. A route other than the way I'd come, which was crooked and uncomfortable and buried—I wanted to see what was up on top of this world. I found a sort of chimney flue on the east wall, which looked plausible, and sweated and cursed my way up through that until I reached a point where I could walk upright, like a human being. Another 300 feet of scrambling brought me to the rim of the canyon. No one, I felt certain, had ever before departed Nasja Canyon by that route.

But someone had. Near the summit I found an arrow sign, three feet long, formed of stones and pointing off into the north toward those same old purple vistas, so grand, immense, and mysterious, of more canyons, more mesas and plateaus, more mountains, more cloud-dappled sun-spangled leagues of desert sand and desert rock, under the same old wide and aching sky.

The arrow pointed into the north. But what was it pointing *at*? I looked at   25
the sign closely and saw that those dark, desert-varnished stones had been in place for a long, long time; they rested in compacted dust. They must have been there for a century at least. I followed the direction indicated and came promptly to the rim of another canyon and a drop-off straight down of a good 500 feet. Not that way, surely. Across this canyon was nothing of any unusual interest

8. Founder and ruler of the Mongol empire (c. 1162–1227).

that I could see—only the familiar sun-blasted sandstone, a few scrubby clumps of blackbrush and prickly pear, a few acres of nothing where only a lizard could graze, surrounded by a few square miles of more nothingness interesting chiefly to horned toads. I returned to the arrow and checked again, this time with field glasses, looking away for as far as my aided eyes could see toward the north, for ten, twenty, forty miles into the distance. I studied the scene with care, looking for an ancient Indian ruin, a significant cairn, perhaps an abandoned mine, a hidden treasure of some inconceivable wealth, the mother of all mother lodes. . . .

But there was nothing out there. Nothing at all. Nothing but the desert. Nothing but the silent world.

That's why.

MLA CITATION

Abbey, Edward. "The Great American Desert." *The Norton Reader: An Anthology of Nonfiction*, edited by Melissa A. Goldthwaite et al., 15th ed., W. W. Norton, 2020, pp. 455–62.

QUESTIONS

1. Edward Abbey loves the desert, as he states in the first sentence. Why, then, does he enumerate all of its negative features? What is his strategy?

2. Many paragraphs in this essay use lists. Choose one list, analyze its structure (if there is one), and explain what the arrangement of details achieves.

3. How do you explain the ending of this essay—both what Abbey discovers and how he uses it to convey his point?

4. Write an essay about a place you love, detailing its negative features as Abbey does.

AIMEE NEZHUKUMATATHIL
The Soils I Have Eaten

T HE STATE SOIL OF NEW YORK is named for the place[1] where a man lost his finger to a rattlesnake. The finger lays quiet in the ground. The snake's great-great-grandsnakes still chitter through this soil. Sometimes one snake gets the idea he can blink his eye. He concentrates on this single violet thought. A slick frog crunches a maple seed, and the snake immediately forgets what he was thinking.

*

Published in the online magazine Brevity: A Journal of Concise Literary Nonfiction, *which publishes essays of 750 words or fewer.*

1. Honeoye, a hamlet in northwest New York State.

Each bend of cypress root drinks a soft fen mud. Each beard dangling from a branch says: I am a dirty man who had soup for lunch. The state soil of Florida is Myakka—a fancy way of saying, S*and, sand, sand,* and if you dig further still? *Watery sand.*

*

Casa Grande is, of course, Arizona's state soil—salty and robin-red enough to make even the bottom of your pant legs blush. Dust devils whip against a flat house set against the side of Camelback Mountain. The camel's legs tuck up around palm tree and strip mall. He longs to eat a salad of thorn and dates. He longs to eat the leather of a saddle. If you squint, you can see the tongue clean his eye of gnats at night.

*

Harney sounds like a friend who will help you in a pinch: silty, loamy, good enough to feed your family, and mine too. In Kansas, we sit around the table and break bread with Harney soil. Good guy, that Harney.

*

In Illinois, I ate dark Drummer soil—mottled loam and gray clay. A little bit of city grit and soybean. A little light and dark. Street corner and silo.   5

*

Ohio's Miamian soil is like coffee at a dive bar: medium roast, hickory ash, a tiny dash of guitar and smoke. Where is the waitress with red stain on her cheeks, old phone numbers tucked into the ticket book at her hip? That used to be me. Where is the torn and pilled-up pool table, the dart board, the wall behind it pimpled with holes?

MLA CITATION

Nezhukumatathil, Aimee. "The Soils I Have Eaten." *The Norton Reader: An Anthology of Nonfiction*, edited by Melissa A. Goldthwaite et al., 15th ed., W. W. Norton, 2020, pp. 462–63.

QUESTIONS

1. Lyric essays often feature poetic elements such as imagery, metaphor, simile, and personification. What poetic conventions do you recognize in Aimee Nezhukumatathil's essay?

2. Both "The Soils I Have Eaten" and Brian Doyle's "Joyas Voladoras" (pp. 435–37) are lyric essays about nature and the environment. How are these essays similar? How do they differ?

3. Most U.S. states have state soils, birds, trees, flowers, and animals. Research the state names of natural features from a place you have lived. Write a lyric essay in which you use poetic elements to describe that place.

WILLIAM CRONON
The Trouble with Wilderness

P RESERVING WILDERNESS has for decades been a fundamental
tenet—indeed, a passion—of the environmental movement, especially in the United States. For many Americans, wilderness stands
as the last place where civilization, that all-too-human disease, has
not fully infected the earth. It is an island in the polluted sea of
urban-industrial modernity, a refuge we must somehow recover to save the
planet. As Henry David Thoreau famously declared, "In Wildness is the preservation of the World."

But is it? The more one knows of its peculiar history, the more one realizes that wilderness is not quite what it seems. Far from being the one place
on earth that stands apart from humanity, it is quite profoundly a human
creation—indeed, the creation of very particular human cultures at very particular moments in human history. It is not a pristine sanctuary where the last
remnant of an endangered but still transcendent nature can be encountered
without the contaminating taint of civilization. Instead, it is a product of that
civilization. As we gaze into the mirror it holds up for us, we too easily imagine
that what we behold is nature when in fact we see the reflection of our own
longings and desires. Wilderness can hardly be the solution to our culture's
problematic relationship with the nonhuman world, for wilderness is itself a
part of the problem.

To assert the unnaturalness of so natural a place may seem perverse: we
can all conjure up images and sensations that seem all the more hauntingly
real for having engraved themselves so indelibly on our memories. Remember
this? The torrents of mist shooting out from the base of a great waterfall in the
depths of a Sierra Nevada canyon, the droplets cooling your face as you listen
to the roar of the water and gaze toward the sky through a rainbow that hovers
just out of reach. Or this: Looking out across a desert canyon in the evening
air, the only sound a lone raven calling in the distance, the rock walls dropping
away into a chasm so deep that its bottom all but vanishes as you squint into
the amber light of the setting sun. Remember the feelings of such moments,
and you will know as well as I do that you were in the presence of something
irreducibly nonhuman, something profoundly Other than yourself. Wilderness
is made of that too.

And yet: what brought each of us to the places where such memories
became possible is entirely a cultural invention.

5   For the Americans who first celebrated it, wilderness was tied to the myth
of the frontier. The historian Frederick Jackson Turner wrote the classic academic statement of this myth in 1893, but it had been part of American thought

*William Cronon published a number of versions of this essay, each aimed at a different
audience. This version comes from the* New York Times *(1995); another version appears as
the introduction to a book Cronon edited,* Uncommon Ground: Toward Reinventing
Nature *(1995), a collection of essays on the environment.*

for well over a century. As Turner described the process, Easterners and European immigrants, in moving to the wild lands of the frontier, shed the trappings of civilization and thereby gained an energy, an independence and a creativity that were the sources of American democracy and national character. Seen this way, wilderness became a place of religious redemption and national renewal, the quintessential location for experiencing what it meant to be an American.

Those who celebrate the frontier almost always look backward, mourning an older, simpler world that has disappeared forever. That world and all its attractions, Turner said, depended on free land—on wilderness. It is no accident that the movement to set aside national parks and wilderness areas gained real momentum just as laments about the vanishing frontier reached their peak. To protect wilderness was to protect the nation's most sacred myth of origin.

The decades following the Civil War saw more and more of the nation's wealthiest citizens seeking out wilderness for themselves. The passion for wild land took many forms: enormous estates in the Adirondacks and elsewhere (disingenuously called "camps" despite their many servants and amenities); cattle ranches for would-be roughriders on the Great Plains; guided big-game hunting trips in the Rockies. Wilderness suddenly emerged as the landscape of choice for elite tourists. For them, it was a place of recreation.

In just this way, wilderness came to embody the frontier myth, standing for the wild freedom of America's past and seeming to represent a highly attractive natural alternative to the ugly artificiality of modern civilization. The irony, of course, was that in the process wilderness came to reflect the very civilization its devotees sought to escape. Ever since the nineteenth century, celebrating wilderness has been an activity mainly for well-to-do city folks. Country people generally know far too much about working the land to regard unworked land as their ideal.

There were other ironies as well. The movement to set aside national parks and wilderness areas followed hard on the heels of the final Indian wars, in which the prior human inhabitants of these regions were rounded up and moved onto reservations so that tourists could safely enjoy the illusion that they were seeing their nation in its pristine, original state—in the new morning of God's own creation. Meanwhile, its original inhabitants were kept out by dint of force, their earlier uses of the land redefined as inappropriate or even illegal. To this day, for instance, the Blackfeet continue to be accused of "poaching" on the lands of Glacier National Park, in Montana, that originally belonged to them and that were ceded by treaty only with the proviso that they be permitted to hunt there.

The removal of Indians to create an "uninhabited wilderness" reminds us 10
just how invented and how constructed the American wilderness really is. One of the most striking proofs of the cultural invention of wilderness is its thoroughgoing erasure of the history from which it sprang. In virtually all its manifestations, wilderness represents a flight from history. Seen as the original garden, it is a place outside time, from which human beings had to be ejected before

the fallen world of history could properly begin.[1] Seen as the frontier, it is a savage world at the dawn of civilization, whose transformation represents the very beginning of the national historical epic. Seen as sacred nature, it is the home of a God who transcends history, untouched by time's arrow. No matter what the angle from which we regard it, wilderness offers us the illusion that we can escape the cares and troubles of the world in which our past has ensnared us. It is the natural, unfallen antithesis of an unnatural civilization that has lost its soul, the place where we can see the world as it really is, and so know ourselves as we really are—or ought to be.

The trouble with wilderness is that it reproduces the very values its devotees seek to reject. It offers the illusion that we can somehow wipe clean the slate of our past and return to the tabula rasa[2] that supposedly existed before we began to leave our marks on the world. The dream of an unworked natural landscape is very much the fantasy of people who have never themselves had to work the land to make a living—urban folk for whom food comes from a supermarket or a restaurant instead of a field, and for whom the wooden houses in which they live and work apparently have no meaningful connection to the forests in which trees grow and die. Only people whose relation to the land was already alienated could hold up wilderness as a model for human life in nature, for the romantic ideology of wilderness leaves no place in which human beings can actually make their living from the land.

We live in an urban-industrial civilization, but too often pretend to ourselves that our real home is in the wilderness. We work our nine-to-five jobs, we drive our cars (not least to reach the wilderness), we benefit from the intricate and all too invisible networks with which society shelters us, all the while pretending that these things are not an essential part of who we are. By imagining that our true home is in the wilderness, we forgive ourselves for the homes we actually inhabit. In its flight from history, in its siren song[3] of escape, in its reproduction of the dangerous dualism that sets human beings somehow outside nature—in all these ways, wilderness poses a threat to responsible environmentalism at the end of the twentieth century.

Do not misunderstand me. What I criticize here is not wild nature, but the alienated way we often think of ourselves in relation to it. Wilderness can still teach lessons that are hard to learn anywhere else. When we visit wild places, we find ourselves surrounded by plants and animals and landscapes whose otherness compels our attention. In forcing us to acknowledge that they are not of our making, that they have little or no need for humanity, they recall for us a creation far greater than our own. In wilderness, we need no reminder that a tree has its own reasons for being, quite apart from us—proof that ours is not the only presence in the universe.

1. Reference to the biblical story of Adam and Eve, who were ejected from the Garden of Eden for disobeying God's command.
2. Latin for "clean slate."
3. In Homer's *Odyssey*, the Sirens use irresistible songs to tempt Odysseus and his crew to steer their ship toward destruction; so a siren song is an alluring but deceptive appeal.

We get into trouble only if we see the tree in the garden as wholly artificial and the tree in the wilderness as wholly natural. Both trees in some ultimate sense are wild; both in a practical sense now require our care. We need to reconcile them, to see a natural landscape that is also cultural, in which city, suburb, countryside and wilderness each has its own place. We need to discover a middle ground in which all these things, from city to wilderness, can somehow be encompassed in the word "home." Home, after all, is the place where we live. It is the place for which we take responsibility, the place we try to sustain so we can pass on what is best in it (and in ourselves) to our children.

Learning to honor the wild—learning to acknowledge the autonomy of the   15
other—means striving for critical self-consciousness in all our actions. It means that reflection and respect must accompany each act of use, and means we must always consider the possibility of nonuse. It means looking at the part of nature we intend to turn toward our own ends and asking whether we can use it again and again and again—sustainably—without diminishing it in the process. Most of all, it means practicing remembrance and gratitude for the nature, culture and history that have come together to make the world as we know it. If wildness can stop being (just) out there and start being (also) in here, if it can start being as humane as it is natural, then perhaps we can get on with the unending task of struggling to live rightly in the world—not just in the garden, not just in the wilderness, but in the home that encompasses them both.

MLA CITATION

Cronon, William. "The Trouble with Wilderness." *The Norton Reader: An Anthology of Nonfiction*, edited by Melissa A. Goldthwaite et al., 15th ed., W. W. Norton, 2020, pp. 464–67.

QUESTIONS

1. In paragraph 12 William Cronon writes, "We live in an urban-industrial civilization, but too often pretend to ourselves that our real home is in the wilderness." Cronon gives no examples. What examples might back up Cronon's statement? Can you think of counterexamples as well?

2. Who is Cronon's "we" throughout his essay? Why does he use "we" so frequently?

3. Paragraph 2 raises the issue of whether wilderness provides us with a "mirror." Look through the essay for similar visual imagery; then explain the role that such imagery plays.

4. If you found significant counterexamples in response to Question 1, write an essay in which you question or object to one or more aspects of Cronon's argument.

CHIEF SEATTLE
Letter to President Pierce, 1855

W E KNOW THAT the white man does not understand our ways. One portion of the land is the same to him as the next, for he is a stranger who comes in the night and takes from the land whatever he needs. The earth is not his brother, but his enemy, and when he has conquered it, he moves on. He leaves his fathers' graves, and his children's birthright is forgotten. The sight of your cities pains the eyes of the red man. But perhaps it is because the red man is a savage and does not understand.

There is no quiet place in the white man's cities. No place to hear the leaves of spring or the rustle of insects' wings. But perhaps because I am a savage and do not understand, the clatter only seems to insult the ears. The Indian prefers the soft sound of the wind darting over the face of the pond, the smell of the wind itself cleansed by a mid-day rain, or scented with the piñon pine. The air is precious to the red man. For all things share the same breath—the beasts, the trees, the man. The white man does not seem to notice the air he breathes. Like a man dying for many days, he is numb to the stench.

What is man without the beasts? If all the beasts were gone, men would die from great loneliness of spirit, for whatever happens to the beasts also happens to man. All things are connected. Whatever befalls the earth befalls the sons of the earth.

It matters little where we pass the rest of our days; they are not many. A few more hours, a few more winters, and none of the children of the great tribes that once lived on this earth, or that roamed in small bands in the woods, will be left to mourn the graves of a people once as powerful and hopeful as yours.

5   The whites, too, shall pass—perhaps sooner than other tribes. Continue to contaminate your bed, and you will one night suffocate in your own waste. When the buffalo are all slaughtered, the wild horses all tamed, the secret corners of the forest heavy with the scent of many men, and the view of the ripe hills blotted by talking wires,[1] where is the thicket? Gone. Where is the eagle? Gone. And what is it to say goodby to the swift and the hunt, the end of living and the beginning of survival? We might understand if we knew what it was that the white man dreams, what he describes to his children on the long winter nights, what visions he burns into their minds, so they will wish for tomorrow. But we are savages. The white man's dreams are hidden from us.

Because of its origin as an oration given in Salish, a language spoken in the Pacific Northwest, there are many different versions of Chief Seattle's speech; this one comes from Native American Testimony: An Anthology of Indian and White Relations, *edited by Peter Nabokov (1977).*

1. Telegraph.

MLA CITATION

Chief Seattle. "Letter to President Pierce, 1855." *The Norton Reader: An Anthology of Nonfiction*, edited by Melissa A. Goldthwaite et al., 15th ed., W. W. Norton, 2020, p. 468.

QUESTIONS

1. Chief Seattle repeatedly refers to the red man as "a savage" who "does not understand," yet he gives evidence of a great deal of understanding. What is the purpose of such ironic comments and apparently self-disparaging remarks?

2. Scholars have suggested that Chief Seattle's "Letter" is in fact the creation of a white man, based on Seattle's public oratory. If so, what rhetorical techniques does the white editor associate with Indian speech? Why might he have done so?

3. Chief Seattle demonstrates an awareness of ecology—the study of relationships among organisms, and between organisms and their environment—when he says, "whatever happens to the beasts also happens to man. All things are connected" (paragraph 3). Locate two or three similar observations, and explain their effectiveness.

4. Chief Seattle says that the red man might understand the white man better "if we knew what it was that the white man dreams, what he describes to his children on the long winter nights, what visions he burns into their minds, so they will wish for tomorrow" (paragraph 5). Write a short essay explaining—using irony if you'd like—how "the white man" might reply. If you prefer, write the reply itself.

TERRY TEMPEST WILLIAMS
The Clan of One-Breasted Women

I BELONG TO a Clan of One-Breasted Women. My mother, my grandmothers, and six aunts have all had mastectomies. Seven are dead. The two who survive have just completed rounds of chemotherapy and radiation.

I've had my own problems: two biopsies for breast cancer and a small tumor between my ribs diagnosed as "a border-line malignancy."

This is my family history.

Most statistics tell us breast cancer is genetic, hereditary, with rising percentages attached to fatty diets, childlessness, or becoming pregnant after thirty. What they don't say is living in Utah may be the greatest hazard of all.

We are a Mormon family with roots in Utah since 1847. The word-of- 5 wisdom, a religious doctrine of health, kept the women in my family aligned with

From The Witness *(1989), a small-circulation journal that called itself "a feisty, independent, provocative, intelligent, feminist voice of Christian social conscience"; later included in* Refuge: An Unnatural History of Family and Place *(1991). All notes are the author's unless indicated otherwise.*

good foods: no coffee, no tea, tobacco, or alcohol. For the most part, these
women were finished having their babies by the time they were thirty. And only
one faced breast cancer prior to 1960. Traditionally, as a group of people, Mormons have a low rate of cancer.

Is our family a cultural anomaly? The truth is we didn't think about it.
Those who did, usually the men, simply said, "bad genes." The women's attitude
was stoic. Cancer was part of life. On February 16, 1971, the eve before my
mother's surgery, I accidently picked up the telephone and overheard her ask
my grandmother what she could expect.

"Diane, it is one of the most spiritual experiences you will ever encounter."
I quietly put down the receiver.

Two days later, my father took my three brothers and me to the hospital to
visit her. She met us in the lobby in a wheelchair. No bandages were visible. I'll
never forget her radiance, the way she held herself in a purple velour robe and
how she gathered us around her.

"Children, I am fine. I want you to know I felt the arms of God around me."

We believed her. My father cried. Our mother, his wife, was thirty-eight
years old.

Two years ago, after my mother's death from cancer, my father and I were
having dinner together. He had just returned from St. George where his con-
struction company was putting in natural gas lines for towns in southern Utah.
He spoke of his love for the country: the sandstoned landscape, bare-boned and
beautiful. He had just finished hiking the Kolob trail in Zion National Park.
We got caught up in reminiscing, recalling with fondness our walk up Angel's
Landing on his fiftieth birthday and the years our family had vacationed there.
This was a remembered landscape where we had been raised.

Over dessert, I shared a recurring dream of mine. I told my father that for
years, as long as I could remember, I saw this flash of light in the night in the
desert. That this image had so permeated my being, I could not venture south
without seeing it again, on the horizon, illuminating buttes and mesas.

"You did see it," he said.

"Saw what?" I asked, a bit tentative.

"The bomb. The cloud. We were driving home from Riverside, California.
You were sitting on your mother's lap. She was pregnant. In fact, I remember
the date, September 7, 1957. We had just gotten out of the Service. We were
driving north, past Las Vegas. It was an hour or so before dawn, when this
explosion went off. We not only heard it, but felt it. I thought the oil tanker in
front of us had blown up. We pulled over and suddenly, rising from the desert
floor, we saw it, clearly, this golden-stemmed cloud, the mushroom. The sky
seemed to vibrate with an eerie pink glow. Within a few minutes, a light ash was
raining on the car."

I stared at my father. This was new information to me.

"I thought you knew that," my father said. "It was a common occurrence
in the fifties."

It was at this moment I realized the deceit I had been living under. Children growing up in the American Southwest, drinking contaminated milk from

contaminated cows, even from the contaminated breasts of their mother, my
mother—members, years later, of the Clan of One-breasted Women.

It is a well-known story in the Desert West, "The Day We Bombed Utah," or
perhaps, "The Years We Bombed Utah."[1] Above ground atomic testing in
Nevada took place from January 27, 1951, through July 11, 1962. Not only were
the winds blowing north, covering "low use segments of the population" with
fallout and leaving sheep dead in their tracks, but the climate was right.[2] The
United States of the 1950s was red, white, and blue. The Korean War was raging. McCarthyism was rampant. Ike was it and the Cold War was hot.[3] If you
were against nuclear testing, you were for a Communist regime.

Much has been written about this "American nuclear tragedy." Public
health was secondary to national security. The Atomic Energy Commissioner,
Thomas Murray, said, "Gentlemen, we must not let anything interfere with this
series of tests, nothing."[4]

Again and again, the American public was told by its government, in spite
of burns, blisters, and nausea, "It has been found that the tests may be conducted with adequate assurance of safety under conditions prevailing at the
bombing reservations."[5] Assuaging public fears was simply a matter of public
relations. "Your best action," an Atomic Energy Commission booklet read, "is
not to be worried about fallout." A news release typical of the times stated, "We
find no basis for concluding that harm to any individual has resulted from radioactive fallout."[6]

On August 30, 1979, during Jimmy Carter's presidency, a suit was filed entitled "Irene Allen vs. the United States of America." Mrs. Allen was the first to
be alphabetically listed with twenty-four test cases, representative of nearly
1200 plaintiffs seeking compensation from the United States government for
cancers caused from nuclear testing in Nevada.

Irene Allen lived in Hurricane, Utah. She was the mother of five children
and had been widowed twice. Her first husband with their two oldest boys had

20

---

1. Fuller, John G., *The Day We Bombed Utah* (New York: New American Library, 1984).

2. Discussion on March 14, 1988, with Carole Gallagher, photographer and author,
American Ground Zero: The Secret Nuclear War, published by Random House, 1994.

3. Events and figures of the 1950s: the Korean War (1950–53) pitted the combined
forces of the Republic of Korea and the United Nations (primarily the United States)
against the invading armies of Communist North Korea; McCarthyism, after Republican senator Joseph S. McCarthy, the Communist "witch-hunt" led by the senator; Ike
is the nickname of Dwight D. Eisenhower, president from 1953 to 1961; the Cold War,
the power struggle between the Western powers and the Communist bloc that began
at the end of World War II [Editor's note].

4. Szasz, Ferenc M., "Downwind from the Bomb," *Nevada Historical Society Quarterly*,
Fall 1987, Vol. XXX, No. 3, p. 185.

5. Fradkin, Philip L., *Fallout* (Tucson: University of Arizona Press, 1989), 98.

6. Ibid., 109.

watched the tests from the roof of the local high school. He died of leukemia in 1956. Her second husband died of pancreatic cancer in 1978.

25   In a town meeting conducted by Utah Senator Orrin Hatch, shortly before the suit was filed, Mrs. Allen said, "I am not blaming the government, I want you to know that, Senator Hatch. But I thought if my testimony could help in any way so this wouldn't happen again to any of the generations coming up after us . . . I am really happy to be here this day to bear testimony of this."[7]

God-fearing people. This is just one story in an anthology of thousands.

On May 10, 1984, Judge Bruce S. Jenkins handed down his opinion. Ten of the plaintiffs were awarded damages. It was the first time a federal court had determined that nuclear tests had been the cause of cancers. For the remaining fourteen test cases, the proof of causation was not sufficient. In spite of the split decision, it was considered a landmark ruling.[8] It was not to remain so for long.

In April, 1987, the 10th Circuit Court of Appeals overturned Judge Jenkins' ruling on the basis that the United States was protected from suit by the legal doctrine of sovereign immunity, the centuries-old idea from England in the days of absolute monarchs.[9]

In January, 1988, the Supreme Court refused to review the Appeals Court decision. To our court system, it does not matter whether the United States Government was irresponsible, whether it lied to its citizens or even that citizens died from the fallout of nuclear testing. What matters is that our government is immune. "The King can do no wrong."

30   In Mormon culture, authority is respected, obedience is revered, and independent thinking is not. I was taught as a young girl not to "make waves" or "rock the boat."

"Just let it go—" my mother would say. "You know how you feel, that's what counts."

For many years, I did just that—listened, observed, and quietly formed my own opinions within a culture that rarely asked questions because they had all the answers. But one by one, I watched the women in my family die common, heroic deaths. We sat in waiting rooms hoping for good news, always receiving the bad. I cared for them, bathed their scarred bodies and kept their secrets. I watched beautiful women become bald as cytoxan, cisplatin and adriamycin were injected into their veins. I held their foreheads as they vomited green-black bile and I shot them with morphine when the pain became inhuman. In the end, I witnessed their last peaceful breaths, becoming a midwife to the rebirth of their souls. But the price of obedience became too high.

The fear and inability to question authority that ultimately killed rural communities in Utah during atmospheric testing of atomic weapons was the same

7. Town meeting held by Senator Orrin Hatch in St. George, Utah, April 17, 1979, transcript, 26–28.

8. Fradkin, *Fallout*, 228.

9. U.S. v. Allen, 816 Federal Reporter, 2d/1417 (10th Circuit Court 1987), cert. denied, 108 S. Ct. 694 (1988).

fear I saw being held in my mother's body. Sheep. Dead sheep. The evidence is buried.

I cannot prove that my mother, Diane Dixon Tempest, or my grandmothers, Lettie Romney Dixon and Kathryn Blackett Tempest, along with my aunts contracted cancer from nuclear fallout in Utah. But I can't prove they didn't.

My father's memory was correct, the September blast we drove through in 1957 was part of Operation Plumbbob, one of the most intensive series of bomb tests to be initiated. The flash of light in the night in the desert I had always thought was a dream developed into a family nightmare. It took fourteen years, from 1957 to 1971, for cancer to show up in my mother—the same time, Howard L. Andrews, an authority on radioactive fallout at the National Institutes of Health, says radiation cancer requires to become evident.[10] The more I learn about what it means to be a "downwinder," the more questions I drown in.

What I do know, however, is that as a Mormon woman of the fifth generation of "Latter-Day-Saints," I must question everything, even if it means losing my faith, even if it means becoming a member of a border tribe among my own people. Tolerating blind obedience in the name of patriotism or religion ultimately takes our lives.

When the Atomic Energy Commission described the country north of the Nevada Test Site as "virtually uninhabited desert terrain," my family members were some of the "virtual uninhabitants."

One night, I dreamed women from all over the world circling a blazing fire in the desert. They spoke of change, of how they hold the moon in their bellies and wax and wane with its phases. They mocked at the presumption of even-tempered beings and made promises that they would never fear the witch inside themselves. The women danced wildly as sparks broke away from the flames and entered the night sky as stars.

And they sang a song given to them by Shoshoni grandmothers:

> *Ah ne nah, nah*
> *nin nah nah—*
> *Ah ne nah, nah*
> *nin nah nah—*
> *Nyaga mutzi*
> *oh ne nay—*
> *Nyaga mutzi*
> *oh ne nay—*[11]

10. Fradkin, Op. cit., 116.

11. This song was sung by the Western Shoshone women as they crossed the line at the Nevada Test Site on March 18, 1988, as part of their "Reclaim the Land" action. The translation they gave was: "Consider the rabbits how gently they walk on the earth. Consider the rabbits how gently they walk on the earth. We remember them. We can walk gently also. We remember them. We can walk gently also."

35

40   The women danced and drummed and sang for weeks, preparing themselves for what was to come. They would reclaim the desert for the sake of their
children, for the sake of the land.

A few miles downwind from the fire circle, bombs were being tested. Rabbits felt the tremors. Their soft leather pads on paws and feet recognized the
shaking sands while the roots of mesquite and sage were smoldering. Rocks
were hot from the inside out and dust devils hummed unnaturally. And each
time there was another nuclear test, ravens watched the desert heave. Stretch
marks appeared. The land was losing its muscle.

The women couldn't bear it any longer. They were mothers. They had suffered labor pains but always under the promise of birth. The red hot pains
beneath the desert promised death only as each bomb became a stillborn. A
contract had been broken between human beings and the land. A new contract was being drawn by the women who understood the fate of the earth as
their own.

Under the cover of darkness, ten women slipped under the barbed wire
fence and entered the contaminated country. They were trespassing. They
walked toward the town of Mercury in moonlight, taking their cues from coyote, kit fox, antelope squirrel, and quail. They moved quietly and deliberately
through the maze of Joshua trees. When a hint of daylight appeared they rested,
drinking tea and sharing their rations of food. The women closed their eyes.
The time had come to protest with the heart, that to deny one's genealogy with
the earth was to commit treason against one's soul.

At dawn, the women draped themselves in mylar, wrapping long streamers
of silver plastic around their arms to blow in the breeze. They wore clear masks
that became the faces of humanity. And when they arrived on the edge of Mercury, they carried all the butterflies of a summer day in their wombs. They
paused to allow their courage to settle.

45   The town which forbids pregnant women and children to enter because of
radiation risks to their health was asleep. The women moved through the streets
as winged messengers, twirling around each other in slow motion, peeking
inside homes and watching the easy sleep of men and women. They were astonished by such stillness and periodically would utter a shrill note or low cry just
to verify life.

The residents finally awoke to what appeared as strange apparitions. Some
simply stared. Others called authorities, and in time, the women were appre-
hended by wary soldiers dressed in desert fatigues. They were taken to a white,
square building on the other edge of Mercury. When asked who they were and
why they were there, the women replied, "We are mothers and we have come
to reclaim the desert for our children."

The soldiers arrested them. As the ten women were blindfolded and hand-
cuffed, they began singing:

> *You can't forbid us everything*
> *You can't forbid us to think—*
> *You can't forbid our tears to flow*
> *And you can't stop the songs that we sing.*

The women continued to sing louder and louder, until they heard the voices of their sisters moving across the mesa.

> *Ah ne nah, nah*
> *nin nah nah—*
> *Ah ne nah, nah*
> *nin nah nah—*
> *Nyaga mutzi*
> *oh ne nay—*
> *Nyaga mutzi*
> *oh ne nay—*

"Call for re-enforcement," one soldier said.

"We have," interrupted one woman. "We have—and you have no idea of   50
our numbers."

On March 18, 1988, I crossed the line at the Nevada Test Site and was arrested with nine other Utahns for trespassing on military lands. They are still conducting nuclear tests in the desert. Ours was an act of civil disobedience. But as I walked toward the town of Mercury, it was more than a gesture of peace. It was a gesture on behalf of the Clan of One-Breasted Women.

As one officer cinched the handcuffs around my wrists, another frisked my body. She found a pen and a pad of paper tucked inside my left boot.

"And these?" she asked sternly.

"Weapons," I replied.

Our eyes met. I smiled. She pulled the leg of my trousers back over my boot.   55

"Step forward, please," she said as she took my arm.

We were booked under an afternoon sun and bussed to Tonapah, Nevada. It was a two-hour ride. This was familiar country to me. The Joshua trees standing their ground had been named by my ancestors who believed they looked like prophets pointing west to the promised land. These were the same trees that bloomed each spring, flowers appearing like white flames in the Mojave. And I recalled a full moon in May when my mother and I had walked among them, flushing out mourning doves and owls.

The bus stopped short of town. We were released. The officials thought it was a cruel joke to leave us stranded in the desert with no way to get home. What they didn't realize is that we were home, soul-centered and strong, women who recognized the sweet smell of sage as fuel for our spirits.

MLA CITATION

Williams, Terry Tempest. "The Clan of One-Breasted Women." *The Norton Reader: An Anthology of Nonfiction*, edited by Melissa A. Goldthwaite et al., 15th ed., W. W. Norton, 2020, pp. 469–75.

QUESTIONS

1. Terry Tempest Williams uses a variety of evidence in this essay, including personal memory, family history, government documents, and other sources. List the

evidence and the order in which she uses it. Why might Williams present her material in this order?

2. The essay begins with a description of what Williams later calls a "family nightmare" (paragraph 35) and ends with a dream vision. What is the rhetorical effect of
this interactive opening and closing?

3. What do you think Williams means by the statement "I must question everything"
(paragraph 36)?

4. Conduct some research on an environmental issue that affects you, your friends,
or your family, and, using Williams as a model, write an essay that combines both
your personal experience and research.

SANDRA STEINGRABER
Tune of the Tuna Fish

T O COMMEMORATE my daughter's first piano recital last spring, my
mother sent a package of old songbooks and sheet music that
she had scooped from the bench of my own childhood piano,
where they had undoubtedly sat for more than thirty years. Faith
immediately seized on *The Red Book,* one of my very first lesson
books, and began to sight-read some of the pieces. Her favorite
was "Tune of the Tuna Fish" (copyright 1945), which introduces the key of F
major. The cartoon drawing accompanying the song depicts a yodeling fish.
The lyrics are as follows:

> Tuna fish! Tuna fish! Sing a tune of tuna fish!
> Tuna fish! Tuna fish! It's a favorite dish.
> Everybody likes it so. From New York to Kokomo.
> Tuna fish! Tuna fish! It's a favorite dish.

After we belted the song out a few times together, Faith asked, "Mama, what is
a tuna fish? Have I ever eaten one?" In fact, she hadn't. Although tuna salad
sandwiches were a mainstay of my own childhood diet, tuna has, during the time
period between my childhood and my daughter's, become so contaminated with
mercury that I choose not to buy it.

A few weeks later, at a potluck picnic, an elderly woman offered Faith a
tuna salad sandwich. She loved it. On the ride home, she announced that she
would like tuna sandwiches for her school lunches. She wants to eat one *every*

Published in Orion *(2006), a magazine founded in 1982 to explore "an emerging alternative
worldview informed by a growing ecological awareness and the need for cultural change";
the magazine includes photos and paintings as well as essays. A revised version of this essay
also appeared in Sandra Steingraber's book* Raising Elijah: Protecting Our Children in an
Age of Environmental Crisis *(2011).*

day. I smiled that noncommittal motherly smile and said, "We'll see." She broke into song, "Everybody likes it so. From New York to Kokomo . . ."

A month after that, Faith walked up to me with an alarmed look. Is it true, she wanted to know, that tuna fish have mercury in them? And mercury poisons children? Will she die from eating that sandwich at the picnic? I was able to reassure her that she was fine, but I was left wondering where she'd heard all this. Then I noticed that I'd left out on my office desk a copy of an article about the impact of mercury on fetal brain growth and development. It was one that I myself had authored. Could she have seen it? At age six, can she read well enough to have figured it out?

Other than the twenty-three chromosomes that each of us parents contributes to our offspring during the moment of conception, their growing bodies are entirely made up of rearranged molecules of air, food, and water. Our children are the jet stream, the food web, and the water cycle. Whatever is in the environment is also in them. We know that this now includes hundreds of industrial pollutants. A recent study of umbilical cord blood, collected by the Red Cross from ten newborns and analyzed in two different laboratories, revealed the presence of pesticides, stain removers, wood preservatives, heavy metals, and industrial lubricants, as well as the wastes from burning coal, garbage, and gasoline. Of the 287 chemicals detected, 180 were suspected carcinogens, 217 were toxic to the brain and nervous system, and 208 have been linked to abnormal development and birth defects in lab animals.

One of these chemicals was methylmercury, the form of mercury found in   5
fish. Its presence in umbilical cord blood is especially troubling because methylmercury has been shown to paralyze migrating fetal brain cells and halt their cell division. As a result, the architecture of the brain is subtly altered in ways that can lead to learning disabilities, delayed mental development, and shortened attention spans in later childhood. Moreover, the placenta actively pumps methylmercury into the umbilical cord, raising the concentration of mercury in fetal blood above that of the mother's own blood. Most pregnant mothers probably don't realize that when they eat tuna, the mercury within is transferred to and concentrated in the blood of their unborn babies.

Recently, I've been talking with my children about why we buy organically grown food. I've explained to Faith and her younger brother, Elijah, that I like to give my food dollars to farmers who sustain the soil, are kind to their animals, and don't use chemicals that poison birds, fish, and toads. I add that I like to buy food that is grown right here in our own county. It tastes better and doesn't require lots of gasoline to get to our house. I haven't shared with them the results of the 2003 Seattle study, which revealed that children with conventional diets had, on average, nine times more insecticide residues in their urine than those who ate organic produce.

But there is no "organic" option for buying tuna. No mercury-free tuna exists. When mercury from coal-burning power plants rains down from the atmosphere into the world's oceans, ancient anaerobic bacteria found in marine sediments transform this heavy metal into methylmercury, which is quickly siphoned up the food chain. Because tuna is a top-of-the-food chain predator, methylmercury inexorably concentrates in the flesh of its muscle tissue. There is no special way of cleaning or cooking tuna that would lower its body burden. Nor is there any way of keeping mercury from trespassing into a child's brain, once he or she consumes the tuna. Nor is there a way of preventing those molecules of mercury from interfering with brain cell functioning. In that sense, the problem of tuna fish is more akin to the problem of air and water pollution: it is not a problem we can shop our way out of.

Recognizing the potential for methylmercury to create neurological problems in children, the U.S. Food and Drug Administration has now promulgated advisories and guidelines on how much tuna is safe for pregnant women and children—as well as nursing mothers and women who might become pregnant—to eat in a month's time. There is debate about whether these current restrictions are protective enough. But even if they are sufficient, I find them highly impractical. Children do not want to eat a food they like once a month, or even once a week. In my experience, when children discover a new food item to their liking, they want it all the time. They want it for breakfast, lunch, and dinner from here to Sunday. Children's dining habits are, for mysterious reasons, highly ritualized. Elijah, for example, consumed two avocados a day for the better part of his second year. I vaguely recall one summer when I, at about age seven, ate liver sausage on Saltines as part of every meal.

How, then, do you explain to a young child with a tuna jones that she'll have to wait until next month before she can have her favorite dish again? Do you tell her that she's already consumed her monthly quota of a known brain poison, as determined by the federal government? Or do you make up some other excuse?

10   I eventually sat down with Faith and showed her the article I had written. I said that I was working hard to stop the mercury contamination of seafood so that she could someday enjoy tuna without needing to worry. I said that keeping mercury out of tuna required generating electricity in some way other than burning coal, which is why her father and I support solar energy and wind power.

Soon after, we went hiking in the woods near the day camp she had attended earlier in the summer. Faith summarized for me the history of the old stone building where snakes and turtles are housed in one wing and bunk beds fill the other. It was originally built, she explained, as a *pre-ven-tor-i-um*. Children whose parents were sick with tuberculosis were brought there to live so they wouldn't get sick, too. In fact, I already knew the history of the Cayuga Nature Center but was, nonetheless, amazed at my daughter's ability to recount this information. I tried to gauge whether she was worried about the idea of children being separated from their families because of disease. "You know," I said, "we don't have to worry about tuberculosis anymore. We fixed that problem." She said she knew that. That's why the building had been turned into a camp for everyone.

The top of the hill offered a view across Cayuga Lake. On the far bank floated the vaporous emissions from New York State Electric and Gas Corporation's Cayuga Plant, whose coal-burning stacks were plainly visible against an otherwise cloudless sky. It's one of the state's biggest emitters of mercury. In the year my daughter was born, the Cayuga facility released 323 pounds of mercury into the environment. Pointing it out to Faith, I said that's where the mercury comes from that gets inside the fish. I said that I hoped one day we could fix that problem, too. She thought about it a minute and said, then they can do something else with the building.

MLA CITATION

Steingraber, Sandra. "Tune of the Tuna Fish." *The Norton Reader: An Anthology of Nonfiction*, edited by Melissa A. Goldthwaite et al., 15th ed., W. W. Norton, 2020, pp. 476–79.

QUESTIONS

1. Sandra Steingraber's essay informs readers of the high levels of mercury in fish and the dangers of eating a tuna fish sandwich. Why, then, does she begin with her daughter's piano playing? What roles do her daughter, Faith, and later her son, Elijah, play in this essay?

2. What facts about industrial pollutants, including methylmercury, does Steingraber provide? Where do they appear in the essay? How do they relate—structurally and conceptually—to the episodes with her daughter?

3. Does Steingraber suggest a solution to the problem of industrial pollutants? In terms of the environment, does the essay end on a hopeful or despairing note?

4. Write an essay about another kind of environmental problem, ideally one with personal or local significance. Interweave facts with examples or short narratives.

10 WHERE WE LIVE, WHAT WE LIVE FOR

> I went to the woods because I wished to live deliberately, to front only the essential facts of life, and see if I could not learn what it had to teach, and not, when I came to die, discover that I had not lived.
>
> —HENRY DAVID THOREAU

What is the relationship between where and how we live? How might we live in personally fulfilling ways with the least amount of harm to others and to the environment? What can individuals, communities, and governments do when faced with differing predictions of the complex challenges caused by climate change? Can we help others and the environment? Whether you retreat to a cabin in the woods for a couple of years, as Thoreau did, or move to a large city like Miami, your life will be affected not only by your personal choices but also by realities beyond an individual's control. The selections in this chapter show—on both a large and small scale—how where we live and what we live for are shaped by a complex mix of personal, cultural, economic, scientific, governmental, ecological, and legal dimensions.

Some of the selections in this chapter ask readers to think in terms of scale—to consider our place in the larger universe. Although Thoreau lived for a time in a tiny cabin in Massachusetts just a mile and a half outside of Concord, he felt his perspective enlarged by his simplified life, writing, "Both place and time were changed, and I dwelt nearer to those parts of the universe and to those eras of history which had most attracted me. Where I lived was as far off as many a region viewed nightly by astronomers." Alan Lightman in "Our Place in the Universe: Face to Face with the Infinite" asks the reader to think even more expansively, asking, "[T]o what extent are we human beings, living on a small planet orbiting one star among billions of stars," part of the "nature" of the universe? Amanda Petrusich, like Lightman, considers the awe-inspiring night sky, yet this sight brings her thinking back to earth; she writes about light pollution, as well as fear of the dark, and considers its effects on the environment, on science, and on humans' understanding of the world and themselves.

What happens when the place where you live is threatened? While Petrusich brings up several environmental concerns, Elizabeth Kolbert and David Wallace-Wells show the urgency of the situation, providing extensive journalistic reports: Kolbert reports on the rising sea levels in South Florida, and Wallace-Wells provides a more expansive report on possible devastating effects of global climate change.

One problem with learning about serious threats to the planet and its inhabitants is that some people feel helpless or despairing; others throw up their hands or ignore or deny the problems. The women Taté Walker profiles in "The (Native) American Dream" have a different response. Monycka Snowbird, even while living in an urban environment, raises animals for meat and grows indigenous plants, feeding and educating people in her community. Karen Ducheneaux and her community are "building a series of ecodomes and straw bale buildings powered by solar, wind, and water." Like the women Walker profiles, Robin Wall Kimmerer—in "Goldenrod and Asters: My Life with Plants"—draws from her indigenous culture, combining this knowledge with her scientific training to "produce a new species of knowledge, a new way of being in the world. After all, there aren't two worlds, there is just this one good green earth." These women take important individual actions and share their knowledge with their communities. Cormac Cullinan, though, offers a different solution in "If Nature Had Rights," arguing that elements of nature should have legal standing as persons; he advocates for restorative justice and a legal system that protects all members of an ecosystem.

The authors in this chapter all agree that where we live affects how we live, yet they get across their differing messages and ideas through various genres, from personal essays to arguments, journalistic reports to profiles. As you consider the issues and ideas presented in this chapter, think about what you can contribute to the evolving conversation and what genre will help you best communicate those ideas. You might write a personal essay about a place where you've lived and how that place shaped your thinking and actions. Or perhaps you could interview and write a profile of someone who is doing interesting work in sustainable living. Who are the people you admire in your school or community? What kinds of knowledge do they have to share?

HENRY DAVID THOREAU
Where I Lived, and What I Lived For

WHEN I FIRST took up my abode in the woods, that is, began to spend my nights as well as days there, which, by accident, was on Independence day, or the fourth of July, 1845, my house was not finished for winter, but was merely a defence against the rain, without plastering or chimney, the walls being of rough weather-stained boards, with wide chinks, which made it cool at night. The upright white hewn studs and freshly planed door and window casings gave it a clean and airy look, especially in the morning, when its timbers were saturated with dew, so that I fancied that by noon some sweet gum would exude from them. To my imagination it retained throughout the day more or less of this auroral character, reminding me of a certain house on a mountain which I had visited the year before. This was an airy and unplastered cabin, fit to entertain a travelling god, and where a goddess might trail her garments. The winds which passed over my dwelling were such as sweep over the ridges of mountains, bearing the broken strains, or celestial parts

From Henry David Thoreau's book Walden (1854), *an account of his life in a small cabin on Walden Pond, outside the village of Concord, Massachusetts; in* Walden, *Thoreau not only describes his life in the woods but also develops a philosophy for living.*

only, of terrestrial music. The morning wind forever blows, the poem of creation is uninterrupted; but few are the ears that hear it. Olympus[1] is but the outside of the earth every where.

The only house I had been the owner of before, if I except a boat, was a tent, which I used occasionally when making excursions in the summer, and this is still rolled up in my garret; but the boat, after passing from hand to hand, has gone down the stream of time. With this more substantial shelter about me, I had made some progress toward settling in the world. This frame, so slightly clad, was a sort of crystallization around me, and reacted on the builder. It was suggestive somewhat as a picture in outlines. I did not need to go out doors to take the air, for the atmosphere within had lost none of its freshness. It was not so much within doors as behind a door where I sat, even in the rainiest weather. The Harivansa[2] says, "An abode without birds is like a meat without seasoning." Such was not my abode, for I found myself suddenly neighbor to the birds; not by having imprisoned one, but having caged myself near them. I was not only nearer to some of those which commonly frequent the garden and the orchard, but to those wilder and more thrilling songsters of the forest which never, or rarely, serenade a villager,—the wood-thrush, the veery, the scarlet tanager, the field-sparrow, the whippoorwill, and many others.

I was seated by the shore of a small pond, about a mile and a half south of the village of Concord and somewhat higher than it, in the midst of an extensive wood between that town and Lincoln, and about two miles south of that our only field known to fame, Concord Battle Ground;[3] but I was so low in the woods that the opposite shore, half a mile off, like the rest, covered with wood, was my most distant horizon. For the first week, whenever I looked out on the pond it impressed me like a tarn high up on the side of a mountain, its bottom far above the surface of other lakes, and, as the sun arose, I saw it throwing off its nightly clothing of mist, and here and there, by degrees, its soft ripples or its smooth reflecting surface was revealed, while the mists, like ghosts, were stealthily withdrawing in every direction into the woods, as at the breaking up of some nocturnal conventicle. The very dew seemed to hang upon the trees later into the day than usual, as on the sides of mountains.

This small lake was of most value as a neighbor in the intervals of a gentle rain storm in August, when, both air and water being perfectly still, but the sky overcast, mid-afternoon had all the serenity of evening, and the wood-thrush sang around, and was heard from shore to shore. A lake like this is never smoother than at such a time; and the clear portion of the air above it being shallow and darkened by clouds, the water, full of light and reflections, becomes a lower heaven itself so much the more important. From a hill top near by, where the wood had been recently cut off, there was a pleasing vista southward across the pond, through a wide indentation in the hills which form the shore there, where their opposite sides sloping toward each other suggested a stream flow-

1. Mountain where the Greek gods dwell.
2. Fifth-century epic poem about the Hindu god Krishna.
3. Site of the famous Battle of Concord, April 19, 1775, considered the start of the American Revolution.

ing out in that direction through a wooded valley, but stream there was none. That way I looked between and over the near green hills to some distant and higher ones in the horizon, tinged with blue. Indeed, by standing on tiptoe I could catch a glimpse of some of the peaks of the still bluer and more distant mountain ranges in the north-west, those true-blue coins from heaven's own mint, and also of some portion of the village. But in other directions, even from this point, I could not see over or beyond the woods which surrounded me. It is well to have some water in your neighborhood, to give buoyancy to and float the earth. One value even of the smallest well is, that when you look into it you see that earth is not continent but insular. This is as important as that it keeps butter cool. When I looked across the pond from this peak toward the Sudbury meadows, which in time of flood I distinguished elevated perhaps by a mirage in their seething valley, like a coin in a basin, all the earth beyond the pond appeared like a thin crust insulated and floated even by this small sheet of intervening water, and I was reminded that this on which I dwelt was but *dry land*.

Though the view from my door was still more contracted, I did not feel   5
crowded or confined in the least. There was pasture enough for my imagination. The low shrub-oak plateau to which the opposite shore arose, stretched away toward the prairies of the West and the steppes of Tartary,[4] affording ample room for all the roving families of men. "There are none happy in the world but beings who enjoy freely a vast horizon,"—said Damodara,[5] when his herds required new and larger pastures.

Both place and time were changed, and I dwelt nearer to those parts of the universe and to those eras in history which had most attracted me. Where I lived was as far off as many a region viewed nightly by astronomers. We are wont to imagine rare and delectable places in some remote and more celestial corner of the system, behind the constellation of Cassiopeia's Chair, far from noise and disturbance. I discovered that my house actually had its site in such a withdrawn, but forever new and unprofaned, part of the universe. If it were worth the while to settle in those parts near to the Pleiades or the Hyades, to Aldebaran or Altair,[6] then I was really there, or at an equal remoteness from the life which I had left behind, dwindled and twinkling with as fine a ray to my nearest neighbor, and to be seen only in moonless nights by him. Such was that part of creation where I had squatted;—

> "There was a shepherd that did live,
>   And held his thoughts as high
> As were the mounts whereon his flocks
>   Did hourly feed him by."[7]

4. Region that includes what is today northern Pakistan.
5. One of the many names of Krishna, the Hindu god.
6. Cassiopeia's Chair, the Pleiades, and the Hyades are constellations; Aldebaran and Altair are stars.
7. Lines from "The Shepherd's Love for Philladay," from Thomas Evans's *Old Ballads* (1810).

What should we think of the shepherd's life if his flocks always wandered to higher pastures than his thoughts?

Every morning was a cheerful invitation to make my life of equal simplicity, and I may say innocence, with Nature herself. I have been as sincere a worshipper of Aurora[8] as the Greeks. I got up early and bathed in the pond; that was a religious exercise, and one of the best things which I did. They say that characters were engraven on the bathing tub of king Tching-thang[9] to this effect: "Renew thyself completely each day; do it again, and again, and forever again." I can understand that. Morning brings back the heroic ages. I was as much affected by the faint hum of a mosquito making its invisible and unimaginable tour through my apartment at earliest dawn, when I was sitting with door and windows open, as I could be by any trumpet that ever sang of fame. It was Homer's[10] requiem; itself an Iliad and Odyssey in the air, singing its own wrath and wanderings. There was something cosmical about it; a standing advertisement, till forbidden, of the everlasting vigor and fertility of the world. The morning, which is the most memorable season of the day, is the awakening hour. Then there is least somnolence in us; and for an hour, at least, some part of us awakes which slumbers all the rest of the day and night. Little is to be expected of that day, if it can be called a day, to which we are not awakened by our Genius, but by the mechanical nudgings of some servitor, are not awakened by our own newly-acquired force and aspirations from within, accompanied by the undulations of celestial music, instead of factory bells, and a fragrance filling the air—to a higher life than we fell asleep from; and thus the darkness bear its fruit, and prove itself to be good, no less than the light. That man who does not believe that each day contains an earlier, more sacred, and auroral hour than he has yet profaned, has despaired of life, and is pursuing a descending and darkening way. After a partial cessation of his sensuous life, the soul of man, or its organs rather, are reinvigorated each day, and his Genius tries again what noble life it can make. All memorable events, I should say, transpire in morning time and in a morning atmosphere. The Vedas[11] say, "All intelligences awake with the morning." Poetry and art, and the fairest and most memorable of the actions of men, date from such an hour. All poets and heroes, like Memnon,[12] are the children of Aurora, and emit their music at sunrise. To him whose elastic and vigorous thought keeps pace with the sun, the day is a perpetual morning. It matters not what the clocks say or the attitudes and labors of men. Morning is when I am awake and there is a dawn in me. Moral reform is the effort to throw off sleep. Why is it that men give so poor an account of their day if they have not been slumbering? They

---

8. Goddess of dawn.

9. Confucius (551–479 B.C.E.), Chinese philosopher.

10. Greek epic poet (eighth century B.C.E.), author of the *Odyssey* and the *Iliad*.

11. Sacred texts that contain hymns, incantations, and rituals from ancient India.

12. Son of Aurora, the goddess of dawn, and a mortal, Memnon was king of the Ethiopians; he was slain by Achilles while fighting the Greeks in Troy. When he died, his mother's tears formed the morning dew.

are not such poor calculators. If they had not been overcome with drowsiness they would have performed something. The millions are awake enough for physical labor; but only one in a million is awake enough for effective intellectual exertion, only one in a hundred millions to a poetic or divine life. To be awake is to be alive. I have never yet met a man who was quite awake. How could I have looked him in the face?

We must learn to reawaken and keep ourselves awake, not by mechanical aids, but by an infinite expectation of the dawn, which does not forsake us in our soundest sleep. I know of no more encouraging fact than the unquestionable ability of man to elevate his life by a conscious endeavor. It is something to be able to paint a particular picture, or to carve a statue, and so to make a few objects beautiful; but it is far more glorious to carve and paint the very atmosphere and medium through which we look, which morally we can do. To affect the quality of the day, that is the highest of arts. Every man is tasked to make his life, even in its details, worthy of the contemplation of his most elevated and critical hour. If we refused, or rather used up, such paltry information as we get, the oracles would distinctly inform us how this might be done.

I went to the woods because I wished to live deliberately, to front only the essential facts of life, and see if I could not learn what it had to teach, and not, when I came to die, discover that I had not lived. I did not wish to live what was not life, living is so dear, nor did I wish to practise resignation, unless it was quite necessary. I wanted to live deep and suck out all the marrow of life, to live so sturdily and Spartan-like as to put to rout all that was not life, to cut a broad swath and shave close, to drive life into a corner, and reduce it to its lowest terms, and, if it proved to be mean, why then to get the whole and genuine meanness of it, and publish its meanness to the world; or if it were sublime, to know it by experience, and be able to give a true account of it in my next excursion. For most men, it appears to me, are in a strange uncertainty about it, whether it is of the devil or of God, and have *somewhat hastily* concluded that it is the chief end of man here to "glorify God and enjoy him forever."

Still we live meanly, like ants; though the fable tells us that we were long ago changed into men;[13] like pygmies we fight with cranes;[14] it is error upon error, and clout upon clout, and our best virtue has for its occasion a superfluous and evitable wretchedness. Our life is frittered away by detail. An honest man has hardly need to count more than his ten fingers, or in extreme cases he may add his ten toes, and lump the rest. Simplicity, simplicity, simplicity! I say, let your affairs be as two or three, and not a hundred or a thousand; instead of a million count half a dozen, and keep your accounts on your thumb nail. In the midst of this chopping sea of civilized life, such are the clouds and storms and quicksands and thousand-and-one items to be allowed for, that a man has to live, if he would not founder and go to the bottom and not make his port at all, by dead reckoning, and he must be a great calculator indeed who succeeds.

10

13. In a Greek fable Aeacus asks Zeus to increase a scanty population by turning ants into men.
14. From the *Iliad* by Homer, in which the Trojans are represented as the cranes.

Simplify, simplify. Instead of three meals a day, if it be necessary eat but one; instead of a hundred dishes, five; and reduce other things in proportion. Our life is like a German Confederacy, made up of petty states, with its boundary forever fluctuating, so that even a German cannot tell you how it is bounded at any moment. The nation itself, with all its so called internal improvements, which, by the way, are all external and superficial, is just such an unwieldy and overgrown establishment, cluttered with furniture and tripped up by its own traps, ruined by luxury and heedless expense, by want of calculation and a worthy aim, as the million households in the land; and the only cure for it as for them is in a rigid economy, a stern and more than Spartan simplicity of life and elevation of purpose. It lives too fast. Men think that it is essential that the *Nation* have commerce, and export ice, and talk through a telegraph, and ride thirty miles an hour, without a doubt, whether *they* do or not; but whether we should live like baboons or like men, is a little uncertain. If we do not get our sleepers, and forge rails, and devote days and nights to the work, but go to tinkering upon our *lives* to improve *them*, who will build railroads? And if railroads are not built, how shall we get to heaven in season? But if we stay at home and mind our business, who will want railroads? We do not ride on the railroad; it rides upon us. Did you ever think what those sleepers are that underlie the railroad? Each one is a man, an Irishman, or a Yankee man. The rails are laid on them, and they are covered with sand, and the cars run smoothly over them. They are sound sleepers, I assure you. And every few years a new lot is laid down and run over; so that, if some have the pleasure of riding on a rail, others have the misfortune to be ridden upon. And when they run over a man that is walking in his sleep, a supernumerary sleeper in the wrong position, and wake him up, they suddenly stop the cars, and make a hue and cry about it, as if this were an exception. I am glad to know that it takes a gang of men for every five miles to keep the sleepers down and level in their beds as it is, for this is a sign that they may sometime get up again.

Why should we live with such hurry and waste of life? We are determined to be starved before we are hungry. Men say that a stitch in time saves nine, and so they take a thousand stitches to-day to save nine to-morrow. As for *work*, we haven't any of any consequence. We have the Saint Vitus' dance,[15] and cannot possibly keep our heads still. If I should only give a few pulls at the parish bell-rope, as for a fire, that is, without setting the bell, there is hardly a man on his farm in the outskirts of Concord, notwithstanding that press of engagements which was his excuse so many times this morning, nor a boy, nor a woman, I might almost say, but would forsake all and follow that sound, not mainly to save property from the flames, but, if we will confess the truth, much more to see it burn, since burn it must, and we, be it known, did not set it on fire,—or to see it put out, and have a hand in it, if that is done as handsomely; yes, even if it were the parish church itself. Hardly a man takes a half hour's nap after dinner, but when he wakes he holds up his head and asks, "What's

15. Nervous disorder marked by jerky, spasmodic movements that occurs in cases of rheumatic fever involving the connective tissue of the brain.

the news?" as if the rest of mankind had stood his sentinels. Some give directions to be waked every half hour, doubtless for no other purpose; and then, to pay for it, they tell what they have dreamed. After a night's sleep the news is as indispensable as the breakfast. "Pray tell me any thing new that has happened to a man any where on this globe,"—and he reads it over his coffee and rolls, that a man has had his eyes gouged out this morning on the Wachito River;[16] never dreaming the while that he lives in the dark unfathomed mammoth cave of this world, and has but the rudiment of an eye himself.

For my part, I could easily do without the post-office. I think that there are very few important communications made through it. To speak critically, I never received more than one or two letters in my life—I wrote this some years ago—that were worth the postage. The penny-post is, commonly, an institution through which you seriously offer a man that penny for his thoughts which is so often safely offered in jest. And I am sure that I never read any memorable news in a newspaper. If we read of one man robbed, or murdered, or killed by accident, or one house burned, or one vessel wrecked, or one steamboat blown up, or one cow run over on the Western Railroad, or one mad dog killed, or one lot of grasshoppers in the winter,—we never need read of another. One is enough. If you are acquainted with the principle, what do you care for a myriad instances and applications? To a philosopher all *news*, as it is called, is gossip, and they who edit and read it are old women over their tea. Yet not a few are greedy after this gossip. There was such a rush, as I hear, the other day at one of the offices to learn the foreign news by the last arrival, that several large squares of plate glass belonging to the establishment were broken by the pressure,—news which I seriously think a ready wit might write a twelvemonth or twelve years beforehand with sufficient accuracy. As for Spain, for instance, if you know how to throw in Don Carlos and the Infanta, and Don Pedro and Seville and Granada, from time to time in the right proportions,—they may have changed the names a little since I saw the papers,—and serve up a bullfight when other entertainments fail, it will be true to the letter, and give us as good an idea of the exact state of ruin of things in Spain as the most succinct and lucid reports under this head in the newspapers: and as for England, almost the last significant scrap of news from that quarter was the revolution of 1649; and if you have learned the history of her crops for an average year, you never need attend to that thing again, unless your speculations are of a merely pecuniary character. If one may judge who rarely looks into the newspapers, nothing new does ever happen in foreign parts, a French revolution not excepted.

What news! how much more important to know what that is which was never old! "Kieou-he-yu (great dignitary of the state of Wei) sent a man to Khoung-tseu to know his news. Khoung-tseu caused the messenger to be seated near him, and questioned him in these terms: What is your master doing? The messenger answered with respect: My master desires to diminish the number of his faults, but he cannot come to the end of them. The messenger being gone, the philosopher remarked: What a worthy messenger! What a worthy messen-

16. In southern Arkansas.

ger!" The preacher, instead of vexing the ears of drowsy farmers on their day of rest at the end of the week,—for Sunday is the fit conclusion of an ill-spent week, and not the fresh and brave beginning of a new one,—with this one other draggle-tail of a sermon, should shout with thundering voice,—"Pause! Avast! Why so seeming fast, but deadly slow?"

Shams and delusions are esteemed for soundest truths, while reality is fabulous. If men would steadily observe realities only, and not allow themselves to be deluded, life, to compare it with such things as we know, would be like a fairy tale and the Arabian Nights' Entertainments. If we respected only what is inevitable and has a right to be, music and poetry would resound along the streets. When we are unhurried and wise, we perceive that only great and worthy things have any permanent and absolute existence,—that petty fears and petty pleasures are but the shadow of the reality. This is always exhilarating and sublime. By closing the eyes and slumbering, and consenting to be deceived by shows, men establish and confirm their daily life of routine and habit every where, which still is built on purely illusory foundations. Children, who play life, discern its true law and relations more clearly than men, who fail to live it worthily, but who think that they are wiser by experience, that is, by failure. I have read in a Hindoo book, that "There was a king's son, who, being expelled in infancy from his native city, was brought up by a forester, and, growing up to maturity in that state, imagined himself to belong to the barbarous race with which he lived. One of his father's ministers having discovered him, revealed to him what he was, and the misconception of his character was removed, and he knew himself to be a prince. So soul," continues the Hindoo philosopher, "from the circumstances in which it is placed, mistakes its own character, until the truth is revealed to it by some holy teacher, and then it knows itself to be *Brahme*."[17] I perceive that we inhabitants of New England live this mean life that we do because our vision does not penetrate the surface of things. We think that that *is* which *appears* to be. If a man should walk through this town and see only the reality, where, think you, would the "Mill-dam"[18] go to? If he should give us an account of the realities he beheld there, we should not recognize the place in his description. Look at a meeting-house, or a court-house, or a jail, or a shop, or a dwelling-house, and say what that thing really is before a true gaze, and they would all go to pieces in your account of them. Men esteem truth remote, in the outskirts of the system, behind the farthest star, before Adam and after the last man. In eternity there is indeed something true and sublime. But all these times and places and occasions are now and here. God himself culminates in the present moment, and will never be more divine in the lapse of all the ages. And we are enabled to apprehend at all what is sublime and noble only by the perpetual instilling and drenching of the reality that surrounds us. The universe constantly and obediently answers to our conceptions; whether we travel fast or slow, the track is laid for us. Let us spend our

17. Supreme soul, the essence of all being, in Hinduism.
18. Dam built in 1635 in the town of Concord on the site of an Indian fishing weir.

lives in conceiving then. The poet or the artist never yet had so fair and noble a design but some of his posterity at least could accomplish it.

Let us spend one day as deliberately as Nature, and not be thrown off the track by every nutshell and mosquito's wing that falls on the rails. Let us rise early and fast, or break fast, gently and without perturbation; let company come and let company go, let the bells ring and the children cry,—determined to make a day of it. Why should we knock under and go with the stream? Let us not be upset and overwhelmed in that terrible rapid and whirlpool called a dinner, situated in the meridian shallows. Weather this danger and you are safe, for the rest of the way is down hill. With unrelaxed nerves, with morning vigor, sail by it, looking another way, tied to the mast like Ulysses. If the engine whistles, let it whistle till it is hoarse for its pains. If the bell rings, why should we run? We will consider what kind of music they are like. Let us settle ourselves, and work and wedge our feet downward through the mud and slush of opinion, and prejudice, and tradition, and delusion, and appearance, that alluvion which covers the globe, through Paris and London, through New York and Boston and Concord, through church and state, through poetry and philosophy and religion, till we come to a hard bottom and rocks in place, which we can call *reality*, and say, This is, and no mistake; and then begin, having a *point d'appui*,[19] below freshet and frost and fire, a place where you might found a wall or a state, or set a lamp-post safely, or perhaps a gauge, not a Nilometer,[20] but a Realometer, that future ages might know how deep a freshet of shams and appearances had gathered from time to time. If you stand right fronting and face to face to a fact, you will see the sun glimmer on both its surfaces, as if it were a cimeter,[21] and feel its sweet edge dividing you through the heart and marrow, and so you will happily conclude your mortal career. Be it life or death, we crave only reality. If we are really dying, let us hear the rattle in our throats and feel cold in the extremities; if we are alive, let us go about our business.

Time is but the stream I go a-fishing in. I drink at it; but while I drink I see the sandy bottom and detect how shallow it is. Its thin current slides away, but eternity remains. I would drink deeper; fish in the sky, whose bottom is pebbly with stars. I cannot count one. I know not the first letter of the alphabet. I have always been regretting that I was not as wise as the day I was born. The intellect is a cleaver; it discerns and rifts its way into the secret of things. I do not wish to be any more busy with my hands than is necessary. My head is hands and feet. I feel all my best faculties concentrated in it. My instinct tells me that my head is an organ for burrowing, as some creatures use their snout and fore-paws, and with it I would mine and burrow my way through these hills. I think that the richest vein is somewhere hereabouts; so by the divining rod and thin rising vapors I judge; and here I will begin to mine.

19. Reference point.
20. Gauge placed in the Nile River in ancient times to measure the rise of the water.
21. Saber with a curved blade, usually spelled "scimitar."

MLA CITATION

Thoreau, Henry David. "Where I Lived, and What I Lived For." *The Norton Reader: An Anthology of Nonfiction*, edited by Melissa A. Goldthwaite et al., 15th ed., W. W. Norton, 2020, pp. 481–89.

QUESTIONS

1. Henry David Thoreau's title might be rephrased as two questions: "Where did I live?" and "What did I live for?" What answers does Thoreau give to each?

2. Throughout this essay Thoreau poses questions—for example, "Why is it that men give so poor an account of their day if they have not been slumbering?" (paragraph 7) or "Why should we live with such hurry and waste of life?" (paragraph 11). To what extent does he answer these questions? Why might he leave some unanswered or only partially answered?

3. Thoreau is known for his aphorisms (short, witty nuggets of wisdom). Find one you like and explain its relevance for living today.

4. If you have ever chosen to live unconventionally at some point in your life, write about your decision, including the reasons and the consequences.

ALAN LIGHTMAN

Our Place in the Universe: Face to Face with the Infinite

MY MOST VIVID ENCOUNTER with the vastness of nature occurred years ago on the Aegean Sea.[1] My wife and I had chartered a sailboat for a two-week holiday in the Greek islands. After setting out from Piraeus, we headed south and hugged the coast, which we held three or four miles to our port. In the thick summer air, the distant shore appeared as a hazy beige ribbon—not entirely solid, but a reassuring line of reference. With binoculars, we could just make out the glinting of houses, fragments of buildings.

Then we passed the tip of Cape Sounion and turned west toward Hydra. Within a couple of hours, both the land and all other boats had disappeared. Looking around in a full circle, all we could see was water, extending out and out in all directions until it joined with the sky. I felt insignificant, misplaced, a tiny odd trinket in a cavern of ocean and air.

Naturalists, biologists, philosophers, painters, and poets have labored to express the qualities of this strange world that we find ourselves in. Some things are prickly, others are smooth. Some are round, some jagged. Lumines-

Published in Harper's Magazine *(2012), an American monthly covering politics, society, culture, and the environment.*

1. Sea bounded by Greece, Turkey, and Crete.

Rocky Mountains, Falling Star by Peter de Lory.

cent or dim. Mauve colored. Pitter-patter in rhythm. Of all these aspects of things, none seems more immediate or vital than *size*. Large versus small. Consciously and unconsciously, we measure our physical size against the dimensions of other people, against animals, trees, oceans, mountains. As brainy as we think ourselves to be, our bodily size, our bigness, our simple volume and bulk are what we first present to the world. Somewhere in our fathoming of the cosmos, we must keep a mental inventory of plain size and scale, going from atoms to microbes to humans to oceans to planets to stars. And some of the most impressive additions to that inventory have occurred at the high end. Simply put, the cosmos has gotten larger and larger. At each new level of distance and scale, we have had to contend with a different conception of the world that we live in.

The prize for exploring the greatest distance in space goes to a man named Garth Illingworth, who works in a ten-by-fifteen-foot office at the University of California, Santa Cruz. Illingworth studies galaxies so distant that their light has traveled through space for more than 13 billion years to get here. His office is packed with tables and chairs, bookshelves, computers, scattered papers, issues of *Nature,*[2] and a small refrigerator and a microwave to fuel research that can extend into the wee hours of the morning.

    Like most professional astronomers these days, Illingworth does not look 5
directly through a telescope. He gets his images by remote control—in his case, quite remote. He uses the Hubble Space Telescope, which orbits Earth once every ninety-seven minutes, high above the distorting effects of Earth's atmosphere. Hubble takes digital photographs of galaxies and sends the images to other orbiting satellites, which relay them to a network of earthbound anten-

2. Science journal, founded in 1869.

nae; these, in turn, pass the signals on to the Goddard Space Flight Center in Greenbelt, Maryland. From there the data is uploaded to a secure website that Illingworth can access from a computer in his office.

The most distant galaxy Illingworth has seen so far goes by the name UDFj-39546284 and was documented in early 2011. This galaxy is about 100,000,000,000,000,000,000,000 miles away from Earth, give or take. It appears as a faint red blob against the speckled night of the distant universe— red because the light has been stretched to longer and longer wavelengths as the galaxy has made its lonely journey through space for billions of years. The actual color of the galaxy is blue, the color of young, hot stars, and it is twenty times smaller than our galaxy, the Milky Way. UDFj-39546284 was one of the first galaxies to form in the universe.

"That little red dot is hellishly far away," Illingworth told me recently. At sixty-five, he is a friendly bear of a man, with a ruddy complexion, thick strawberry-blond hair, wire-rimmed glasses, and a broad smile. "I sometimes think to myself: What would it be like to be out there, looking around?"

One measure of the progress of human civilization is the increasing scale of our maps. A clay tablet dating from about the twenty-fifth century B.C. found near what is now the Iraqi city of Kirkuk depicts a river valley with a plot of land labeled as being 354 *iku* (about thirty acres) in size. In the earliest recorded cosmologies, such as the Babylonian *Enuma Elish*,[3] from around 1500 B.C., the oceans, the continents, and the heavens were considered finite, but there were no scientific estimates of their dimensions. The early Greeks, including Homer,[4] viewed Earth as a circular plane with the ocean enveloping it and Greece at the center, but there was no understanding of scale. In the early sixth century B.C., the Greek philosopher Anaximander, whom historians consider the first mapmaker, and his student Anaximenes proposed that the stars were attached to a giant crystalline sphere. But again there was no estimate of its size.

The first large object ever accurately measured was Earth, accomplished in the third century B.C. by Eratosthenes, a geographer who ran the Library of Alexandria.[5] From travelers, Eratosthenes had heard the intriguing report that at noon on the summer solstice, in the town of Syene, due south of Alexandria, the sun casts no shadow at the bottom of a deep well. Evidently the sun is directly overhead at that time and place. (Before the invention of the clock, noon could be defined at each place as the moment when the sun was highest in the sky, whether that was exactly vertical or not.) Eratosthenes knew that the sun was not overhead at noon in Alexandria. In fact, it was tipped 7.2 degrees from the vertical, or about one fiftieth of a circle—a fact he could determine by measuring the length of the shadow cast by a stick planted in the ground. That the sun could be directly overhead in one place and not another

3. Epic telling of the creation of the world.
4. Greek epic poet (eighth century B.C.E.).
5. Founded in the third century B.C.E., the greatest library of antiquity, accidentally burned by Julius Caesar in 48 B.C.E.

was due to the curvature of Earth. Eratosthenes reasoned that if he knew the distance from Alexandria to Syene, the full circumference of the planet must be about fifty times that distance. Traders passing through Alexandria told him that camels could make the trip to Syene in about fifty days, and it was known that a camel could cover one hundred stadia (almost eleven and a half miles) in a day. So the ancient geographer estimated that Syene and Alexandria were about 570 miles apart. Consequently, the complete circumference of Earth he figured to be about 50×570 miles, or 28,500 miles. This number was within 15 percent of the modern measurement, amazingly accurate considering the imprecision of using camels as odometers.

As ingenious as they were, the ancient Greeks were not able to calculate the size of our solar system. That discovery had to wait for the invention of the telescope, nearly two thousand years later. In 1672, the French astronomer Jean Richer determined the distance from Earth to Mars by measuring how much the position of the latter shifted against the background of stars from two different observation points on Earth. The two points were Paris (of course) and Cayenne, French Guiana. Using the distance to Mars, astronomers were also able to compute the distance from Earth to the sun, approximately 100 million miles. 10

A few years later, Isaac Newton[6] managed to estimate the distance to the nearest stars. (Only someone as accomplished as Newton could have been the first to perform such a calculation and have it go almost unnoticed among his other achievements.) If one assumes that the stars are similar objects to our sun, equal in intrinsic luminosity, Newton asked, how far away would our sun have to be in order to appear as faint as nearby stars? Writing his computations in a spidery script, with a quill dipped in the ink of oak galls, Newton correctly concluded that the nearest stars are about 100,000 times the distance from Earth to the sun, about 10 trillion miles away. Newton's calculation is contained in a short section of his *Principia* titled simply "On the distance of the stars."

Newton's estimate of the distance to nearby stars was larger than any distance imagined before in human history. Even today, nothing in our experience allows us to relate to it. The fastest most of us have traveled is about 500 miles per hour, the cruising speed of a jet. If we set out for the nearest star beyond our solar system at that speed, it would take us about 5 million years to reach our destination. If we traveled in the fastest rocket ship ever manufactured on Earth, the trip would last 100,000 years, at least a thousand human life spans.

But even the distance to the nearest star is dwarfed by the measurements made in the early twentieth century by Henrietta Leavitt, an astronomer at the Harvard College Observatory. In 1912, she devised a new method for determining the distances to faraway stars. Certain stars, called Cepheid variables, were known to oscillate in brightness. Leavitt discovered that the cycle times of such stars are closely related to their intrinsic luminosities. More luminous stars have longer cycles. Measure the cycle time of such a star and you know

6. English mathematician and physicist (1642–1727).

its intrinsic luminosity. Then, by comparing its intrinsic luminosity with how bright it appears in the sky, you can infer its distance, just as you could gauge the distance to an approaching car at night if you knew the wattage of its headlights. Cepheid variables are scattered throughout the cosmos. They serve as cosmic distance signs in the highway of space.

Using Leavitt's method, astronomers were able to determine the size of the Milky Way, a giant congregation of about 200 billion stars. To express such mind-boggling sizes and distances, twentieth-century astronomers adopted a new unit called the light-year, the distance that light travels in a year—about 6 trillion miles. The nearest stars are several light-years away. The diameter of the Milky Way has been measured at about 100,000 light-years. In other words, it takes a ray of light 100,000 years to travel from one side of the Milky Way to the other.

15   There are galaxies beyond our own. They have names like Andromeda (one of the nearest), Sculptor, Messier 87, Malin 1, IC 1101. The average distance between galaxies, again determined by Leavitt's method, is about twenty galactic diameters, or 2 million light-years. To a giant cosmic being leisurely strolling through the universe and not limited by distance or time, galaxies would appear as illuminated mansions scattered about the dark countryside of space. As far as we know, galaxies are the largest objects in the cosmos. If we sorted the long inventory of material objects in nature by size, we would start with subatomic particles like electrons and end up with galaxies.

Over the past century, astronomers have been able to probe deeper and deeper into space, looking out to distances of hundreds of millions of light-years and farther. A question naturally arises: Could the physical universe be unending in size? That is, as we build bigger and bigger telescopes sensitive to fainter and fainter light, will we continue to see objects farther and farther away—like the third emperor of the Ming Dynasty, Yongle, who surveyed his new palace in the Forbidden City and walked from room to room to room, never reaching the end?

Here we must take into account a curious relationship between distance and time. Because light travels at a fast (186,000 miles per second) but not infinite speed, when we look at a distant object in space we must remember that a significant amount of time has passed between the emission of the light and the reception at our end. The image we see is what the object looked like when it emitted that light. If we look at an object 186,000 miles away, we see it as it appeared one second earlier; at 1,860,000 miles away, we see it as it appeared ten seconds earlier; and so on. For extremely distant objects, we see them as they were millions or billions of years in the past.

Now the second curiosity. Since the late 1920s we have known that the universe is expanding, and that as it does so it is thinning out and cooling. By measuring the current rate of expansion, we can make good estimates of the moment in the past when the expansion began—the Big Bang—which was about 13.7 billion years ago, a time when no planets or stars or galaxies existed and the entire universe consisted of a fantastically dense nugget of pure energy. No matter how big our telescopes, we cannot see beyond the distance light has traveled since the Big Bang. Farther than that, and there simply hasn't been enough time since the birth of the universe for light to get from there to here. This giant sphere, the maximum distance we can see, is only the *observable* universe. But the universe could extend far beyond that.

In his office in Santa Cruz, Garth Illingworth and his colleagues have mapped out and measured the cosmos to the edge of the observable universe. They have reached out almost as far as the laws of physics allow. All that exists in the knowable universe—oceans and sky; planets and stars; pulsars, quasars, and dark matter; distant galaxies and clusters of galaxies; and great clouds of star-forming gas—has been gathered within the cosmic sensorium gauged and observed by human beings.

"Every once in a while," says Illingworth, "I think: By God, we are studying things that we can never physically touch. We sit on this miserable little planet in a midsize galaxy and we can characterize most of the universe. It is astonishing to me, the immensity of the situation, and how to relate to it in terms we can understand."

The idea of Mother Nature has been represented in every culture on Earth. But to what extent is the new universe, vastly larger than anything conceived of in the past, part of *nature*? One wonders how connected Illingworth feels to this astoundingly large cosmic terrain, to the galaxies and stars so distant that their images have taken billions of years to reach our eyes. Are the little red dots on his maps part of the same landscape that Wordsworth and Thoreau[7] described, part of the same environment of mountains and trees, part of the same cycle of birth and death that orders our lives, part of our physical and emotional conception of the world we live in? Or are such things instead digitized abstractions, silent and untouchable, akin to us only in their (hypothesized) makeup of atoms and molecules? And to what extent are we human beings, living on a small planet orbiting one star among billions of stars, part of that same nature?

The heavenly bodies were once considered divine, made of entirely different stuff than objects on Earth. Aristotle[8] argued that all matter was constituted from four elements: earth, fire, water, and air. A fifth element, ether, he reserved for the heavenly bodies, which he considered immortal, perfect, and indestructible. It wasn't until the birth of modern science, in the seventeenth century, that we began to understand the similarity of heaven and Earth. In 1610, using his new telescope, Galileo[9] noted that the sun had dark patches and blemishes, suggesting that the heavenly bodies are not perfect. In 1687, Newton proposed a universal law of gravity that would apply equally to the fall of an apple from a tree and to the orbits of planets around the sun. Newton then went further, suggesting that all the laws of nature apply to phenomena

7. William Wordsworth (1770–1850), English Romantic poet; Henry David Thoreau (1817–1862), American writer and naturalist.

8. Greek philosopher (384–322 B.C.E.).

9. Galileo Galilei (1564–1642), Italian astronomer and mathematician.

Tallulah Falls by George Cooke.

in the heavens as well as on Earth. In later centuries, scientists used our understanding of terrestrial chemistry and physics to estimate how long the sun could continue shining before depleting its resources of energy; to determine the chemical composition of stars; to map out the formation of galaxies.

Yet even after Galileo and Newton, there remained another question: Were living things somehow different from rocks and water and stars? Did animate and inanimate matter differ in some fundamental way? The "vitalists" claimed that animate matter had some special essence, an intangible spirit or soul, while the "mechanists" argued that living things were elaborate machines and obeyed precisely the same laws of physics and chemistry as did inanimate material. In the late nineteenth century, two German physiologists, Adolf Eugen Fick and Max Rubner, each began testing the mechanistic hypothesis by painstakingly tabulating the energies required for muscle contraction, body heat, and other physical activities and comparing these energies against the chemical energy stored in food. Each gram of fat, carbohydrate, and protein had its energy equivalent. Rubner concluded that the amount of energy used by a living creature was exactly equal to the energy it consumed in its food. Living things were to be viewed as complex arrangements of biological pulleys and levers, electric currents, and chemical impulses. Our bodies are made of the same atoms and molecules as stones, water, and air.

And yet many had a lingering feeling that human beings were somehow separate from the rest of nature. Such a view is nowhere better illustrated than in the painting *Tallulah Falls* (1841), by George Cooke, an artist associated with the Hudson River School. Although this group of painters celebrated nature, they also believed that human beings were set apart from the natural world. Cooke's painting depicts tiny human figures standing on a small promontory above a deep canyon. The people are dwarfed by tree-covered mountains, massive rocky ledges, and a waterfall pouring down to the canyon below. Not only insignificant in size compared with their surroundings, the human beings are mere witnesses to a scene they are not part of and never could be. Just a few years earlier, Ralph Waldo Emerson[10] had published his famous essay "Nature," an appreciation of the natural world that nonetheless held humans separate from nature, at the very least in the moral and spiritual domain: "Man is fallen; nature is erect."

Today, with various back-to-nature movements attempting to resist the dislocations brought about by modernity, and with our awareness of Earth's precarious environmental state ever increasing, many people feel a new sympathy with the natural world on this planet. But the gargantuan cosmos beyond remains remote. We might understand at some level that those tiny points of light in the night sky are similar to our sun, made of atoms identical to those in our bodies, and that the cavern of outer space extends from our galaxy of stars to other galaxies of stars, to distances that would take light billions of years to traverse. We might understand these discoveries in intellectual terms, but they are baffling abstractions, even disturbing, like the notion that each of us once was the size of a dot, without mind or thought. Science has vastly expanded the scale of our cosmos, but our emotional reality is still limited by what we can touch with our bodies in the time span of our lives. George Berkeley, the eighteenth-century Irish philosopher, argued that the entire cosmos is a construct of our minds, that there is no material reality outside our thoughts. As a scientist, I cannot accept that belief. At the emotional and psychological level, however, I can have some sympathy with Berkeley's views. Modern science

25

10. American author and philosopher (1803–1882).

has revealed a world as far removed from our bodies as colors are from the blind.

Very recent scientific findings have added yet another dimension to the question of our place in the cosmos. For the first time in the history of science, we are able to make plausible estimates of the rate of occurrence of life in the universe. In March 2009, NASA launched a spacecraft called *Kepler*[11] whose mission was to search for planets orbiting in the "habitable zone" of other stars. The habitable zone is the region in which a planet's surface temperature is not so cold as to freeze water and not so hot as to boil it. For many reasons, biologists and chemists believe that liquid water is required for the emergence of life, even if that life may be very different from life on Earth. Dozens of candidates for such planets have been found, and we can make a rough preliminary calculation that something like 3 percent of all stars are accompanied by a potentially life-sustaining planet. The totality of living matter on Earth—humans and animals, plants, bacteria, and pond scum—makes up 0.00000001 percent of the mass of the planet. Combining this figure with the results from the *Kepler* mission, and assuming that all potentially life-sustaining planets do indeed have life, we can estimate that the fraction of stuff in the visible universe that exists in living form is something like 0.000000000000001 percent, or one millionth of one billionth of 1 percent. If some cosmic intelligence created the universe, life would seem to have been only an afterthought. And if life emerges by random processes, vast amounts of lifeless material are needed for each particle of life. Such numbers cannot help but bear upon the question of our significance in the universe.

Decades ago, when I was sailing with my wife in the Aegean Sea, in the midst of unending water and sky, I had a slight inkling of infinity. It was a sensation I had not experienced before, accompanied by feelings of awe, fear, sublimity, disorientation, alienation, and disbelief. I set a course for 255°, trusting in my compass—a tiny disk of painted numbers with a sliver of rotating metal—and hoped for the best. In a few hours, as if by magic, a pale ocher smidgen of land appeared dead ahead, a thing that drew closer and closer, a place with houses and beds and other human beings.

MLA CITATION

Lightman, Alan. "Our Place in the Universe: Face to Face with the Infinite." *The Norton Reader: An Anthology of Nonfiction*, edited by Melissa A. Goldthwaite et al., 15th ed., W. W. Norton, 2020, pp. 490–98.

QUESTIONS

1. What, according to Alan Lightman, is "our place in the universe"?

2. Lightman recognizes that the study of nature is not the purview of science alone: "Naturalists, biologists, philosophers, painters, and poets," he writes, "have labored

11. Named after the German astronomer Johannes Kepler (1571–1630).

to express the qualities of this strange world that we find ourselves in" (paragraph 3). How does this sensibility inform his essay?

3. What does Lightman do as a writer to get his readers to experience (not just acknowledge) nature's vastness?

4. Lightman begins and ends his essay by recalling his sailing trip on the Aegean, which he describes as his "most vivid encounter with the vastness of nature" (paragraph 1). Write an essay in which you describe and reflect on a transformative experience of your own.

AMANDA PETRUSICH

Night Moves: Preserving the Sublime at One of the Darkest Places in America

EVERY CIVILIZATION WE KNOW OF has devised a system—scientific, religious, numinous, what have you—to make sense of the night sky. The mystery of what's up there, where it came from, and what it means has long transcended geographic and cultural barriers. It has been inherited and puzzled over for generations. Questioning the universe's origins and its contents feels innate to our humanity; those questions might be the most human ones we have.

Due to pervasive light pollution—glare from excessive, misaimed, and unshielded night lighting—80 percent of Europe and North America no longer experience real darkness. By extension, these populations possess a compromised understanding of the night sky as vista, a shifting landscape of constellations and planets, as multitudinous and astounding as any Earthly terrain. For anyone living near a major metropolis, a satellite image of the Milky Way is even more abstract and antipodal than a Brontosaurus skeleton posed in a museum: We understand it to be a document of something true, but that understanding remains purely theoretical. In 1994, after a predawn earthquake cut power to most of Los Angeles, the Griffith Observatory received phone calls from spooked residents asking about "the strange sky." What those callers were seeing were stars.

I grew up in a small town in the Hudson River valley, about an hour north of New York City. Like most children, I regarded the night sky (or what I could see of it) with extraordinary wonder. I understood that nobody could say for sure what was out there. Little kids are often frustrated by the smallness of their lives, in part because the imagination-to-agency ratio of the average toddler is roughly infinity to one. As a child, you can conjure complex, unbound, spooling worlds, but in your own life, you are largely powerless to make significant moves. Looking up, the tininess I felt was validated, confirmed, but it no

Published in Virginia Quarterly Review (2016), "a national journal of literature and discussion."

longer felt like a liability. If the night sky offers us one thing, continuously, it is a deeply liberating sense of ourselves in perspective, and of the many things we can neither comprehend nor control.

"I wish to know an entire heaven and an entire earth," Thoreau wrote in 1856. He understood heaven and Earth as separate, but still in some essential conversation with each other—as if to receive one without the other was to misunderstand both. But how can we know a heaven if we can barely see it? What happens when mankind divorces itself from a true experience of the cosmos, separating from the vastness above, taming it by erasing it? If you keep distilling the problem—boiling and straining—it becomes wholly spiritual. Thoreau's wanting feels important, imperative. Humans have lived and evolved under the stars for millennia. It isn't unreasonable to think that some part of us is designed to orient around them, to learn from them, and that we are right now failing this part of ourselves.

5   In 2001, the amateur astronomer John Bortle devised a scale to measure relative darkness. His classifications range from "Inner-City Sky" (Class 9), in which the only "pleasing telescopic views are the Moon, the planets, and a few of the brightest star clusters (if you can find them)," to a sky so dark "the Milky Way casts obvious diffuse shadows on the ground" (Class 1). Most North Americans and Europeans live under Class 6 or 7 skies, in which the Milky Way is undetectable and the sky has been smudged by "a vague, grayish white hue." In that kind of night, a person can wander outside, unfold a lawn chair, open a newspaper, and recite the headlines, if not the stories.

Darkness is a complicated thing to quantify, defined as it is by deficiency. In addition to the Bortle scale, scientists often use photodiode light sensors to measure and compare base levels of darkness by calculating the illuminance of the night sky as perceived by the human eye. Unihedron's Sky Quality Meter is the most popular instrument for this kind of measurement, in part because of its portability (about the size of a garage-door opener) and also because it connects to an online global database of user-submitted data. According to that database, Cherry Springs State Park—an eighty-two-acre park in a remote swath of rural, north-central Pennsylvania, built by the Civilian Conservation Corps during the Great Depression—presently has the second darkest score listed (23.27, reported in 2007; 23.69, the highest ever recorded, was taken on a ranch in Big Smoky Valley, Nevada, in 2011). On the Bortle scale, Cherry Springs usually registers between 1 and 2. The International Dark-Sky Association (IDA), a nonprofit organization that recognizes, supports, and protects dark-sky preserves around the world, designated it a Gold-tier International Dark Sky Park in 2008, only the second in the United States at the time, following Natural Bridges National Monument in San Juan County, Utah.

Earlier this year, I drove the six hours to Cherry Springs from New York City to meet Chip Harrison, the park's manager, his wife, Maxine, and a park volunteer named Pam for a 4:30 P.M. dinner of baked fish. Afterward, Chip had promised, we'd go see stars.

"Most children, right now, growing up in the US, will never see the Milky Way," Chip said while we waited for our entrees.

"Their parents never saw it either," Maxine added.

"You come to a place like Cherry Springs, you're gonna see four or five   10
thousand stars, maybe more," he continued. "I've seen people who are fairly
serious amateur astronomers, and they can't find their way around this night
sky—there are too many stars."

After supper, we drove to the park, arriving around sunset and unloading
several bags of equipment from the trunk before setting out, together, into the
blackness. White light isn't permitted on the astronomy grounds, but red-
filtered light, which won't cause the rods of the eye to become overexposed and
less efficient, is allowed if not quite encouraged.

"If you hear crunching, you're on the right path," Maxine announced over
her shoulder. I only presumed she said it over her shoulder. The dark around
us was compact, bottomless, sonorous. I was echolocating poorly. I blinked
city eyes. We crunched along a gravel path toward the astronomy field, where
Chip was assembling an Orion SkyQuest telescope. The SkyQuest is a large-
aperture, reflecting scope—a design actualized by Isaac Newton in 1668 and
adapted, three hundred years later, by an amateur astronomer and Vedanta monk
named John Dobson. It's stout but sizable, about eight inches in diameter, and
is ideal for locating deep-sky objects like dim star clusters, nebulae, and galaxies.
Chip was piecing it together on top of a small concrete slab.

At the edge of the field, a former airstrip, killdeer cheeped eagerly, constantly; a woodcock sounded a burp-like call. It was four days after the new
moon, and the sky was so black that even the tiny slice of visible moon—a dainty,
waxing crescent—felt like a bare bulb screwed into the ceiling of an interrogation
chamber.

On a clear night, from the proper vantage, watching constellations emerge
over Cherry Springs is like watching a freshly exposed photograph sink into a
bath of developer, slowly becoming known to the eye: a single crumb of light,
then another, until the entire tableau is realized. Pam pointed the telescope
toward Jupiter, which had risen over the east end of the field. The four Galilean
moons—Io, Europa, Ganymede, and Callisto—were clearly visible through
the lens. Galileo discovered these moons in 1610, in the skies above Padua.
They were the first celestial bodies proven to be orbiting something other than
Earth, thus thwarting Ptolemy's geocentric world system. With my face still
pressed into the telescope, I gasped.

Pam laughed. "Usually when people look through the telescope, I point   15
out the big 'wow' items, like the planets, Saturn and Jupiter, some of the clusters," she said. "Everybody looks at them and goes, 'Oh, my God.' They go, 'Is
that real?'"

Cherry Springs is singular in that it is located less than 300 miles inland
from the Eastern Seaboard, in a region—the East Coast—that contains
36 percent of the country's total population and is lit up like one of those back-
stage makeup mirrors every night of the year. When pinpointed on a satellite
image, Cherry Springs is in the middle of an uncharacteristically dark patch—
insulated, on all sides, by protected land (262,000 acres of Susquehannock
State Forest, an impenetrable thicket of eastern hemlock and white pine), and
perched atop the Allegheny Plateau, 2,300 feet above sea level. Most of the

small towns surrounding the park are situated in valleys where outdoor light is already sparse (the 2014 census estimate puts Potter County at just over 17,000 residents). This unusual combination of factors explains, to a certain degree, how Cherry Springs became one of the darkest places in America.

Which isn't to say the sanctity of the sky here is not being encroached upon. In the last decade, a handful of energy companies (the Chesapeake Energy Company, the Seneca Resources Corp., Pennsylvania General Energy, and others) have begun extracting natural gas from the Marcellus and Utica Shales underneath Pennsylvania via hydraulic fracturing, or fracking, a much-reviled practice that involves the release of gas or petroleum via a high-pressure injection of fluid through a narrow shaft bored into the ground. In Potter County—GOD'S COUNTRY, the signs promise—there are presently forty active fracking sites. The work cycle in a gas field is nonstop; energy companies not only rig up colossal, stadium-style spotlights, they also burn off excess gas in open pits or through steel pipes, in a process known as flaring.

From afar, a flare resembles a giant blowtorch; clusters of flares are clearly visible on satellite images from space. One of the wells closest to the Cherry Springs astronomy field—Ken Ton 902 3H, operated by Swepi LP, a Houston-based subsidiary of Shell—has accumulated twelve violations since it opened in 2009, including "discharge of pollutional material to waters of Commonwealth."

The Utica Shale, which underlies much of the northeastern United States and parts of Canada, is already a source of so-called "tight gas"—gas contained in rocks so impermeable it can only be accessed via fracking—in Quebec, but energy companies in Pennsylvania have recently begun experimenting with mining it (a 2012 report by the US Geological Survey suggests the Utica Shale might hold up to 38.2 trillion cubic feet of "technically recoverable" gas; in parts of Pennsylvania, it's extraordinarily deep, reaching to almost two miles below sea level, and several thousand feet deeper than the Marcellus Shale).

20   Chip—who is exceedingly kind and mild-mannered, possessing the sort of preternatural calm seemingly required of park rangers—has worked out an informal agreement with representatives from nearby wells, in which workers abstain from flaring at night during Star Parties, when amateur astronomers gather in Cherry Springs to observe and record astral phenomena, or when the park is hosting astronomy-related public programs. But it's chiefly a gentleman's agreement, reliant on neighborly goodwill. At present, there are no light-pollution restrictions placed on energy companies by the state of Pennsylvania.

Chip puttered around the perimeter of the field. He mentioned something about elk. "Most recently, JKLM Energy, which is drilling locally here—they elected last summer not to flare," Chip said. Pam adjusted the telescope.

"The flare from a Utica well is serious," Maxine said, in a voice that had taken on a heavier timbre.

"A flare can essentially put out as much light as a town of four thousand people," Chip said. "It is very bright. [JKLM] elected to do daytime flaring only, so that they would not impact the dark skies here. But at the same time, I believe it's a two-way street. During the dark of the moon, and if it's going to be raining, I find it amazing that I'm e-mailing back and forth saying the forecast is this, there's no reason you can't flare tonight."

Chip hadn't anticipated becoming a dark-sky steward. Maxine tells me he used to go to bed at 9 P.M. every night. "It's been a very neat journey, the development of this," he said. "In this day and age, it's not often that someone like me, a resource manager, gets to be involved in a brand new resource. You get to thinking you know everything."

Gary Honis, an electrical engineer and astrophotographer based in Sugarloaf, Pennsylvania, has been visiting Cherry Springs for twenty-five years, since long before it was recognized internationally for its dark skies. Feeling disheartened by the bright skies in their area, his local astronomy group had "pulled out an old Air Force map, a satellite map, that showed a dark area in Potter County. We compared that to a Pennsylvania road map, and it was Cherry Springs State Park. That's how we found it, by looking at light-pollution maps. My first view was through a friend's six-inch Dobsonian telescope, and it was of M51, the twin galaxies in Ursa Major," Honis said when we spoke on the telephone. "It looked photographic. We never saw that back home."   25

Chip eventually came upon Honis, tented by foil, peering up at the heavens. The park had been closed for hours, but Honis convinced Chip to let him stick around and take some pictures. Their meeting was serendipitous. With Chip's advocacy, the park's hours eventually changed to allow for visiting stargazers, who, with the proper permit, can now camp overnight on the astronomy field.

Since then, Honis has been outspoken about the effect fracking is having on the skies above Cherry Springs. He's posted videos to YouTube—often accompanied by ominous music he performs himself on his Moog Theremini—linking fracking to declining sky-quality readings. The videos are convincing, showing, via time-lapse photography, how gas flares and unshielded drill-site lights are compromising the park for astronomers (his entire video page is worth perusing; in one clip, a mangy brown bear, "Mohawk Moe," wanders onto the astronomy field and ambles toward Honis's friend Tony, who is eating pepperoni). "We started doing sky-quality meter readings of the night sky brightness in 2006, and since then, the skies over Cherry Springs have been getting much brighter," Honis said. "Ten years ago, the only sky glow we had was in the Coudersport area, in the northwest direction, and it was very minor. If you're truly dark-adapted, now you can see sky glow [close to the horizon] across the north, the east, the south, and even the west. It's all around now, on a moonless night. We didn't have that years ago. When the fracking started, sky-quality readings went very bad."

The nocturnal world, of course, also generates its own light, and those deviations can affect dark-sky conditions. The National Park Service cites moonlight, starlight from individual stars and planets, the Milky Way (also called galactic light, or integrated starlight), zodiacal light (sunlight reflected off dust particles in the solar system), airglow (a faint aurora caused by radiation striking air molecules in the upper atmosphere), wildfire, lightning strikes, and meteors as organic sources of evening light. Atmospheric moisture or dust particles can refract or reflect that light, amplifying glow (deserts, for example, are low in moisture but high in dust; forests are the inverse). Air pollution makes it all worse.

In Cherry Springs, Maxine—a former game warden, one of just a few women to hold that position in Pennsylvania—had fixed her gaze toward the sky. We were quiet. The night wasn't perfectly cloudless—it had rained earlier; ambient moisture lingered—but the viewing conditions were favorable. Everyone agreed we'd gotten lucky. Maxine was wearing a pair of dangly moon-and-stars earrings, which glinted in the starlight. "This is where the word awesome comes from," she whispered.

30   In the seventeenth century, under the reign of the self-described Sun King, Louis XIV, tallow candles fashioned from rendered beef or mutton fat were placed in iron-framed glass boxes and strung above the streets of Paris. Lamplighters wandered the districts of the city at dusk, unlocking the boxes and igniting the wicks (mischievous vagrants and the over-served often yanked down and smashed the boxes, a wilding tradition that endures today in cities where inconveniently placed streetlights are often shot dark, presumably to facilitate illegal transactions).

Other places followed Paris's model, and candles eventually gave way to oil and then gas lamps. By 1890, more than 175,000 electric streetlights had been installed in the US; there are now somewhere around 26 million, which collectively cost American taxpayers about $6 billion in annual energy costs. The idea at its inception—an idea that has endured—was that street lighting would help officials of the state more effectively survey and control city streets after dark. Whether streetlights actually make anyone safer remains a contentious topic. Most studies fail to indicate a clear or inarguable correlation between street lighting and decreases in traffic accidents or crime, although it feels willfully obtuse to suggest that taking the dark way home is always just as safe.

Street lighting is undeniably pervasive, but it isn't the only culprit of our perpetually bright skies. Light pollution is aggravated by any kind of irresponsibly aimed outdoor lighting: stadium floodlights, the beams dissecting superstore parking lots, illuminated billboards, futuristic Exxon stations beckoning tired drivers toward off-ramps with neat rows of pumps, roofs pocked with glowing bulbs—any umbrella of safe, welcoming, antiseptic light. Proper shielding and direction can mitigate the glare of these often blinding emanations, and the IDA publishes guidelines for easily modifying outdoor lighting to be more dark-sky friendly. But in most places, following the IDA's suggestions is optional. The right to light isn't easily denied.

In recent years, Chicago, Seattle, Boston, Philadelphia, Detroit, and Los Angeles have been swapping out the high-pressure sodium bulbs in their streetlights—which produced puddles of gassy, orange-hued light, that grittily romantic, archetypal streetlight glow—for comparably cost-effective LED bulbs. Sodium bulbs are usually around 2,200 kelvin, a temperature that registers to the eye as warm. LED bulbs burn closer to 4,000 kelvin and emit an intrusive, bluish glare. If you live in a major American city, it is virtually impossible to spend any time at all in the dark.

The new LED streetlights are almost universally described as unpleasant. New York City is presently in the midst of its own retrofit, a colossal overhaul scheduled to be completed by the end of 2017. The bulbs last longer and will ultimately reduce energy use by up to 75 percent, according to the US Department of Energy. But after the new bulbs were installed in Windsor Terrace, a residential neighborhood in Brooklyn, citizens reacted with disbelief. In an opinion piece for the *New York Times* Sunday Review, the novelist and Windsor Terrace local Lionel Shriver wrote: "Although going half-blind at 58, I can read by the beam that the new lamp blasts into our front room without tapping our own Con Ed service. Once the LEDs went in, our next-door neighbor began walking her dog at night in sunglasses . . . These lights are ugly. They're invasive. They're depressing. New York deserves better." On the local news, a woman from nearby Kensington announced, "My seventy-four-year-old mother, her glasses go dark when she goes outside, because her glasses think it's daylight outside." The woman added that the lights were raising her own blood pressure and giving her anxiety.

Susan Harder, the New York State representative of the IDA and a board member of the Montauk Observatory in East Hampton, has been rallying aggressively against the installation of LED streetlights in New York. "We still think that God lives in the heavens, in part because the sky was so dynamic to ancient cultures," she explained when I asked her to expand the problem beyond the bulbs themselves. "How could you ignore a changing, moving night sky? It struck them with awe. They attributed all sorts of things to the night sky. We're going to lose that if towns and cities keep installing these LED streetlights."

Harder previously had a career as an art dealer (she was the associate director of the LIGHT gallery, once one of only two galleries in New York City dedicated entirely to photography), but now works full time as a dark-sky activist; in 2010, she was named the Long Island Sierra Club's Environmentalist of the Year. Harder has the kind of fast-talking, no-nonsense comportment that recalls Rosalind Russell in *His Girl Friday*,[1] and is, by all accounts, a formidable opponent. In 2006, a *New York Times* reporter described her as "a virtual one-woman dark-sky mover and shaker," and characterized her particular approach to advocacy as a "combination of sweet talk, cajoling and bullying."

"The New York City Department of Transportation [DOT] absolutely, positively refuses to listen to any common sense about LED streetlights," she told me. "We shouldn't be using any LEDs outside until they improve the technology and bring down the blue light, which they can do. But DOT won't listen to us, so we're trying to get legislation passed in the city council."

The bill Harder was referring to, sponsored by city council member Donovan Richards Jr., is clear in its expectations: "This bill would require that any lamp installed as part of the lighting of streets, highways, parks, or any other public place have a correlated color temperature no higher than 3,000 kelvin. All new and replacement outdoor lamps would be required to meet this standard." It

35

---

1. Rosalind Russell (1907–1976) played reporter Hildy Johnson in the screwball comedy *His Girl Friday* (1940), which also starred Cary Grant (1904–1986).

was introduced to the council last summer [June 2015], and is still under consideration.

When I mention that there's not a lot of reliable data proving streetlights actually prevent highway accidents, she sounds immediately exasperated. "It sounds counterintuitive, but we don't need them anymore. The majority of the roadway lighting we have in our country is unnecessary," she said. "Cars have headlights. The whole Long Island Expressway is lit up, and it doesn't need to be."

40   Of course, electric lighting, employed judiciously at night, can be terrifically beautiful. Large-scale light artists like James Turrell, who deliberately seek out areas unmarred by light pollution, manipulate and re-contextualize light in astonishing ways. And sometimes light at night is unquestionably necessary, like the lights that land airplanes, or the ones that warn passing ships away from outcroppings of rock.

But a wanton insistence upon light can also be very dumb. Consider the colossal beam shooting into space from the top of the Luxor Resort & Casino in Las Vegas. The beam is described, in press materials, as being visible from 275 miles away by an aircraft at cruising altitude, and as "the brightest single visible light on Earth." There is something nearly petulant about it: light for light's sake, a perfectly erect middle finger to the natural world.

The single biggest challenge facing dark-sky advocates is working out a way to change our fundamental understanding of darkness as a nefarious force, a thing that needs to be avoided or controlled if not vanquished entirely. This is an obvious vestige of an evolutionary process: For millions of years, our most aggressive natural predators hunted us nocturnally. Early man didn't stand a chance against a pride of lions slinking across the African plains in the dark; it was clearly to his advantage to stay curled up in a cave. There were other dangers at night, too: walking directly into a tree branch at an unkind angle and inadvertently kebab-ing an eyeball, stepping on a coiled snake, wandering through the wrong spider web, and so on.

But there's a significant gulf between fearing death by lion and fearing darkness itself. What might seem like a logical and instinctive aversion—our vision is impaired at night—has been socially reinforced via so many disparate avenues that it's exhausting to even try to tally them up. From a very young age, we are taught that nighttime is when dubious things transpire: nothing but trouble out there in the blackness. At best, night is considered a middling expanse ("No occupation but sleepe, feed, and fart," is how the Jacobean poet Thomas Middleton put it). At worst, it is terrifying.

In his book At Day's Close: Night in Times Past, A. Roger Ekirch historicizes this anxiety, detailing the ways in which nearly every known civilization figured darkness as a source of evil: "Everywhere one looks in the ancient world, demons filled the night air," he writes. Even in our earliest folklore, night is put forth as a proxy for wickedness, worthy of trepidation. According to the Iliad, Nyx, the Greek goddess of night, was a foreboding enough force she made even Zeus quiver and recede; Nyx eventually birthed a delightful crew, including Moros (Doom), Thanatos (Death), Momus (Blame), Oizys (Pain), Nemesis (Retribution), Apate (Deceit), and Eris (Strife).

Christianity positioned God as a source of eternal and unblinking light, a 45
corrective to spiritual darkness and chaos. The narrator of St. John of the
Cross's "Dark Night of the Soul"—still a foundational text for Catholic mystics, recounting, as it does, an intimate union with the Divinity—traverses the
night to achieve a final, ecstatic communion with God in which "All ceased
and I abandoned myself."

Torches, candles, oil lamps, gas lamps, the light bulb—facilitators of productivity and examples of the extraordinary ingenuity of man, sure, but also sacred
talismans to ward off ever-encroaching night and the malevolence it supposedly
enables. In "Nightfall," from 1941, Isaac Asimov describes a fictional planet called
Lagash, which is continually illuminated by six suns. When darkness finally comes
to Lagash via a series of eclipses, its population goes completely insane. A Cultist
finds a prophecy redeemed: "And in this blackness there appeared the Stars, in
countless numbers, and to the strains of music of such beauty that the very leaves
of the trees cried out in wonder. And in that moment the souls of men departed
from them, and their abandoned bodies became even as beasts."

Most historical reasons to fear darkness are now moot, easily recognizable
as hysterical. Our unease at night is more transcendental than pragmatic. It's
true that a lot of American crime transpires at night, although not as much as
one might presume: Per the Bureau of Justice Statistics, 67.5 percent of violent
crimes actually occur during the daytime, between 6 A.M. and 6 P.M.

Still, a kind of basic, axiomatic discomfort with darkness persists. Anyone
who has stayed up until dawn fretting about the future, suffering through the
gloaming, hungrily watching the sunrise, cherishing the relief it entails
("People are buying newspapers!"), understands the weirdness of night in her
bones. Awake in the dark, we are scared, vulnerable, and existentially afloat.
Reconfiguring deeply engrained cultural ideas about darkness is a complicated
task. It's not just darkness we fear, it's the vastness and loneliness of the universe, spreading out from here to God-knows-where. The relative size and
emptiness of the universe is a lot to hold in mind: "The eternal silence of these
infinite spaces terrifies me," Pascal admits in his *Pensées*.

I wrote to Ekirch to see how he understood the stakes. His research on
"segmented sleep"—the revelation that Western civilizations once practiced a
biphasic sleep pattern, wherein two periods of nighttime sleep were punctuated by a brief, intervening period of wakefulness in which they prayed, wrote,
had sex, or committed petty crimes—is still considered revelatory, seminal. He
is a person who knows from night, understands the ways in which a true experience of darkness is fundamental to our humanity and our interpersonal relations. "At the least, we stand to forfeit age-old opportunities for human
intimacy of the sort that darkness alone enhances—not just by affording privacy but by drawing couples closer together physically and emotionally," he
replied in an e-mail. Then he quoted an anonymous early Italian essayist, who
positioned darkness as its own lubricant for human communion: "Darkness
made it easy to tell all."

Ekirch also evoked the idea that, centuries ago, the night sky itself was 50
powerful enough—irrefutable enough—to trump even the most pervasive cul-

tural institutions. That's nearly impossible to conceive of now, when the night sky barely registers to most Americans. "Prior to the Industrial Revolution, night as a source of inspiration knew no bounds, all the more as vestiges of church and state, to name but two powerful institutions, receded in the darkness," he wrote. "On a moonlit evening in Naples, Goethe felt 'overwhelmed' by 'a feeling of infinite space.' Exclaimed an English laborer in the eighteenth century as he treaded home from an alehouse: 'Would I had but as many fat bullocks as there are stars.' To which, replied his companion, 'With all my heart, if I had but a meadow as large as the sky.' Today, few modern critics of light pollution, I suspect, could put the case more passionately."

When I asked James Karl Fischer, an architect and the executive director for the Zoological Lighting Institute—a nonprofit lighting design practice that combines Fischer's interests and expertise in physics, conservation, and art— how he thought dark-sky advocates could ever begin to overcome humanity's frenetic insistence upon light, he acknowledged the enormity of the mission, all the ways in which ideas about light, reinforced by folklore, have permeated the collective unconscious. We found shapes in the cosmos, and told tales to make sense of them. Now, those fictions have lost relevance, or have been replaced.

"I think when we start hearing that people want their light, or that they have anxiety about changing it—it's really a question of language and stories, of how people build up their understanding of the world, their desires and wishes," he said. "There's a wonderful figure in Japanese culture, this character called Oiwa. She's from a ghost story, 'Yotsuya Kaidan.' Without being too obscure, the remarkable thing about the story is that Oiwa, the ghost, always comes out of the light. It's very different from the way current Western movies would portray it."

He paused, then added: "[In the West], light is always this positive thing. I see this in architecture and lighting quite often. People hang their self-worth on this idea that light is a positive force in the universe without really understanding what light is. I think that's where the physical model gets to be so important. The physical fact is that light only breaks things down. It's about destroying chemical bonds. It's not about creating them." Light is often as damaging as it is nourishing.

Besides being costly and inefficient, too much artificial light at night is also supremely unhealthy for humans. In 2001, two epidemiologic studies published in the *Journal of the National Cancer Institute* found that exposure to visible light at night was a potential risk factor for breast cancer. Other studies link the reduced generation of melatonin, a hormone stimulated by darkness and inhibited by light, to mood disorders; one, from The Ohio State University, found that chronic exposure to a relatively low level of artificial light at night increased signs of depression in hamsters. Comparable studies have established links between melatonin deficiencies and diabetes, even obesity.

55   Artificial light is equally threatening to flora and fauna, and can destabilize various ecosystems. It's been particularly hazardous for sea turtle hatchlings, which, after emerging from their nests, instinctively begin waddling toward the brightest horizon. Historically, that's always been the ocean, lit up

by moon or starlight reflecting off the surface of the water. Now, in nesting grounds in Florida, rare loggerhead, leatherback, and green turtle hatchlings are becoming confused by inland light and crawling away from the water, where they become dehydrated, are hunted by predators, run over by cars, or drown in swimming pools. Meanwhile, seabirds that feed on bioluminescent plankton are being fatally drawn to offshore drilling platforms and the lamps strung up by fishermen to lure squid to the surface, while migratory birds, which instinctively orient around the moon and stars, are becoming confused when moving through major cities at night, colliding into buildings or flying off course. The Chicago Audubon Society presently oversees the Chicago Bird Collision Monitors, a team that protects and recovers migratory birds that have been injured or killed in downtown Chicago. It also advocates for "bird-safe lighting and building design" to reduce collision hazards, and has successfully pushed its Lights Out! program, which asks buildings taller than forty stories to switch off decorative lighting on the upper floors after 11 P.M. and to leave nighttime lights off entirely from 4 A.M. until daylight during both the spring and fall migration seasons.

Light pollution is generally considered a minor predicament even by otherwise ardent conservationists—particularly when compared with more broadly worrisome issues such as climate change. But Fischer believes it's a deeply urgent concern. He acknowledged that bird corpses (the Chicago Bird Collision Monitoring Team helps feed an extensive avian morgue, drawers upon drawers of stiff little bird bodies, held by the Field Museum) and squished newborn turtles elicit more sympathetic reactions. But mass insect deaths, he said, are just as significant—if not more so.

Entomologists haven't quite worked out why so many insects practice transverse navigation—engaging in a never-ending series of wild, kamikaze dives toward your porch light, or, in the absence of artificial light, flying at a constant angle relative to a light source like the moon. In the 1970s, Dr. Philip Callahan, an entomologist working for the US Department of Agriculture, floated a theory that the infrared light spectrum emitted by a candle flame is perhaps a strange simulacrum of the light given off by female moths' pheromones (he'd previously discovered that moth pheromones are luminescent). If Callahan is right, male moths are attracted to candles because they believe a flame is actually a female sending out a sex signal. Whatever the precise cause, artificial night lighting disrupts insects' normal flight patterns (thereby dramatically altering their migrations), and attracts many that wouldn't otherwise emerge from their habitats. Once they've been hypnotized—a full psychic capture by the light—they're either zapped on contact, or preyed upon by enterprising predators while they careen about blindly. Occasionally, an insect will exhaust itself and simply drop out of the air.

"It's a disaster," Fischer said. "It seems like a very simple thing, but a streetlight—on the coast, in particular—has a cascading effect. And I have yet to hear how it has been beneficial. A bug zapper, we used to joke, was good old country entertainment. But it highlights an incredible problem: If you think of insects as the food for many of the animal classes, for birds and fish, if the insects are removed because of the artificial light, there's less food for whoever's there, and the habitat is degraded."

When I asked what species he thought was presently the most threatened by light pollution, he neither paused nor equivocated. "Humans," he said.

60   "Stability is biodiversity," he went on. "How do you maintain life on the planet? It's not about fuel. It's not about a way of life. It's not about making sure we're economically feasible. All of those things might be important, but the fact of the matter is, if you're interested in human life, wildlife is the most important—you really can't lose that. You can lose fossil fuels. But you can't lose wildlife. If you lose wildlife, nothing matters, everything goes. Fossil fuels? We'll say, 'Okay, we have to change the way we do things.' Wildlife, though, is the most critical thing. It has to be saved."

A few weeks before I visited Cherry Springs, I went with a couple of buddies to a sensory deprivation chamber in Brooklyn. Formerly a hallmark of psychological experiments (and, on occasion, deployed as an interrogation technique), sensory deprivation was now being reconfigured as a kind of bourgeois meditation aid: For $99, you could float for an hour in a foot or so of heavily salted mineral water (roughly 1,000 pounds of Epsom salt per tub), calibrated precisely to your body temperature, inside a sealed, soundproof, lightproof, womb-like chamber. The idea was to disappear a little. The stresses and expectations of an accelerated modern life seemed to demand an antidote of, well, nothingness.

I was not a natural inhabitant of the tank. I spent the first fifteen minutes karate-kicking the door open and then pulling it closed again—mostly to make sure it would, in fact, still open and close. I pressed the button that turns the lights on and off approximately fifty times. I decided to stretch one hand out—ostensibly to see if I could still see it in the dark; I could not—and accidentally dribbled warm, salty water into my open eyes, which felt sort of like squeezing a whole lemon deep into the bloodied crevices of a festering wound.

Eventually, once I had tired myself out, I was able to consider the experience of pure darkness, unbroken even by starlight. I understood how people found it curative: There's a dissembling that occurs, a loosening of certain grips. But darkness, without the galactic punctuations of the night sky—without stars and planets and moons—feels more finite than infinite. It feels claustrophobic.

On my third night in Pennsylvania, I went back to the park by myself, after midnight. I stumbled onto the astronomy field, wearing a pair of pajamas underneath my coat. My rental was the only car in the lot. It had been raining earlier that afternoon, and thick, heavy clouds now hung low in the atmosphere, obscuring the moon and almost all of the stars. It was as dark a place as I'd ever been. There, shivering, I again felt something akin to genuine panic. When the brain is deprived of visual information—when all external stimuli are washed out—we are alone in new ways. I wondered, then, if the dark acted as a kind of Rorschach test: if our perception of it wasn't also a manifestation of our biggest, most profound fears. Whatever you conjure there, in the blackness, speaks to your innermost terrors: a man with a gun, a bear, a goblin, a ghost. Your own inveterate isolation.

When I got back to New York, I visited with Matt Stanley, a beloved col-   65
league at the university where I teach. Stanley holds degrees in astronomy,
religion, physics, and the history of science, and has a particular interest in
how science has changed from a theistic practice to a naturalistic one. He
leads a seminar called "Achilles' Shield: Mapping the Ancient Cosmos," and
another called "Understanding the Universe."

"I've found that probably 95 percent of my students come from either an
urban or suburban environment, which means they can only see a dozen stars
at night, and no planets," Stanley said. "When you say the Milky Way to them,
they imagine a spiral galaxy, which is fine, but that's not what the Milky Way
looks like—it's a big, whitish smear across the sky. I have to do a lot of work to
orient them to what human beings actually saw when they looked at the sky.
They don't know that stars rise and set. Their minds explode."

An alarmist might wonder if light pollution is effectively ending astronomy—
if the skies will eventually become so impossibly illuminated that we'll no longer
be able to identify new celestial objects, given that we can barely see the ones we
already know are there. Stanley tells me there's always been an active debate raging about whether science as we know it could, in fact, be over one day. "This is a
trope, going back to Newton—that science is always almost finished," he laughed.
"The historian of science Thomas Kuhn said we have to think that about science,
because we need assurance that the science we are doing is correct—that we're
just filling in the gaps. But actually, every now and then, we discover there's a
whole new puzzle." He continued: "The best astronomy nowadays is being done
from space. When I did my astronomy degree, I never looked through a telescope. Now, you can imagine a world—almost a dystopia—where no human
being has ever seen a celestial body with the naked eye, but we have fantastically
sophisticated astronomy, because we do it all above the atmosphere. It's efficient,
but it breaks with those initial questions: Why does the sky behave like that?"

In many ways, the whole of science was derived from early man's fascination with the stars. The sky told us what kinds of things to ask. "Science, as we
understand it, comes from this very old tradition of trying to understand what
we saw in the night sky," Stanley said.

That inescapable curiosity was the lone catalyst for centuries of intellectual
and spiritual growth. Babylonian astronomy gave us time, later mathematics;
astronomy is, in one way or another, central to every foundational philosophy
we know. Our instinctive preoccupation with the content of the sky seems
tangled up, somehow, with all those other inborn human desires: to know and
be known. To feel cowed, sublimated. To wonder and to worship.

An optimist might presume that, in its absence, we'll find new reasons to   70
ask questions of the natural world and of ourselves, and to continually enlarge
and revise our understanding of the universe. That we will not, instead, drift
further toward a detached, solipsistic worldview that wants for little beyond
itself. Still, it's hard not to do the mental arithmetic—to worry that our disinter-
est in preserving darkness and our present detachment from it might suggest
something troubling about the insularity of the modern condition. What other
romantic fascinations will we lock ourselves out of, and at what cost?

"The experience of looking up at the sky—that's what Kant uses to explain the sublime," Stanley said. "In 1788, he said, 'There are two things that fill my heart with wonder. One is the moral sense within me, and the other is the order in the heavens above me.' That's an extraordinary feeling, and ineffable. You can't describe it, but once you've experienced it, you never forget it."

It almost sounded, to me, like Stanley was talking about love. The experience of oneself in relation to an other—the miracle of it, the magnificence.

MLA CITATION

Petrusich, Amanda. "Night Moves: Preserving the Sublime at One of the Darkest Places in America." *The Norton Reader: An Anthology of Nonfiction*, edited by Melissa A. Goldthwaite et al., 15th ed., W. W. Norton, 2020, pp. 499–512.

QUESTIONS

1. Amanda Petrusich details several challenges that dark-sky advocates face. What are those challenges? Which one seems most significant?

2. Petrusich often uses similes. For example, she describes a slice of moon as "like a bare bulb" (paragraph 13) and watching constellations emerge as "like watching a freshly exposed photograph sink into a bath of developer" (paragraph 14). Look for other similes in the article. Which ones are especially effective in helping you understand the phenomena Petrusich describes?

3. Write an essay about an experience you've had with darkness, the night sky, or light pollution. Consider using similes to describe that experience.

ELIZABETH KOLBERT
The Siege of Miami

THE CITY OF MIAMI BEACH floods on such a predictable basis that if, out of curiosity or sheer perversity, a person wants to she can plan a visit to coincide with an inundation. Knowing the tides would be high around the time of the "super blood moon," in late September, I arranged to meet up with Hal Wanless, the chairman of the University of Miami's geological-sciences department. Wanless, who is seventy-three, has spent nearly half a century studying how South Florida came into being. From this, he's concluded that much of the region may have less than half a century more to go.

We had breakfast at a greasy spoon not far from Wanless's office, then set off across the MacArthur Causeway. (Out-of-towners often assume that Miami

Published in the New Yorker (2015), a weekly magazine of "reportage, commentary, criticism, essays, fiction, satire, cartoons, and poetry," for which Kolbert has been a staff writer since 1999.

Beach is part of Miami, but it's situated on a separate island, a few miles off the coast.) It was a hot, breathless day, with a brilliant blue sky. Wanless turned onto a side street, and soon we were confronting a pond-sized puddle. Water gushed down the road and into an underground garage. We stopped in front of a four-story apartment building, which was surrounded by a groomed lawn. Water seemed to be bubbling out of the turf. Wanless took off his shoes and socks and pulled on a pair of polypropylene booties. As he stepped out of the car, a woman rushed over. She asked if he worked for the city. He said he did not, an answer that seemed to disappoint but not deter her. She gestured at a palm tree that was sticking out of the drowned grass.

"Look at our yard, at the landscaping," she said. "That palm tree was super-expensive." She went on, "It's crazy—this is saltwater."

"Welcome to rising sea levels," Wanless told her.

According to the Intergovernmental Panel on Climate Change, sea levels could rise by more than three feet by the end of this century. The United States Army Corps of Engineers projects that they could rise by as much as five feet; the National Oceanic and Atmospheric Administration predicts up to six and a half feet. According to Wanless, all these projections are probably low. In his office, Wanless keeps a jar of meltwater he collected from the Greenland ice sheet. He likes to point out that there is plenty more where that came from.

"Many geologists, we're looking at the possibility of a ten-to-thirty-foot range by the end of the century," he told me.

We got back into the car. Driving with one hand, Wanless shot pictures out the window with the other. "Look at that," he said. "Oh, my gosh!" We'd come to a neighborhood of multimillion-dollar homes where the water was creeping under the security gates and up the driveways. Porsches and Mercedeses sat flooded up to their chassis.

"This is today, you know," Wanless said. "This isn't with two feet of sea-level rise." He wanted to get better photos, and pulled over onto another side street. He handed me the camera so that I could take a picture of him standing in the middle of the submerged road. Wanless stretched out his arms, like a magician who'd just conjured a rabbit. Some workmen came bouncing along in the back of a pickup. Every few feet, they stuck a depth gauge into the water. A truck from the Miami Beach Public Works Department pulled up. The driver asked if we had called City Hall. Apparently, one of the residents of the street had mistaken the high tide for a water-main break. As we were chatting with him, an elderly woman leaning on a walker rounded the corner. She looked at the lake the street had become and wailed, "What am I supposed to do?" The men in the pickup truck agreed to take her home. They folded up her walker and hoisted her into the cab.

To cope with its recurrent flooding, Miami Beach has already spent something like a hundred million dollars. It is planning on spending several hundred million more. Such efforts are, in Wanless's view, so much money down the drain. Sooner or later—and probably sooner—the city will have too much water to deal with. Even before that happens, Wanless believes, insurers will stop selling policies on the luxury condos that line Biscayne Bay. Banks will stop writing mortgages.

10   "If we don't plan for this," he told me, once we were in the car again, driving toward the Fontainebleau hotel, "these are the new Okies." I tried to imagine Ma and Pa Joad[1] heading north, their golf bags and espresso machine strapped to the Range Rover.

The amount of water on the planet is fixed (and has been for billions of years). Its distribution, however, is subject to all sorts of rearrangements. In the coldest part of the last ice age, about twenty thousand years ago, so much water was tied up in ice sheets that sea levels were almost four hundred feet lower than they are today. At that point, Miami Beach, instead of being an island, was fifteen miles from the Atlantic Coast. Sarasota was a hundred miles inland from the Gulf of Mexico, and the outline of the Sunshine State looked less like a skinny finger than like a plump heel.

As the ice age ended and the planet warmed, the world's coastlines assumed their present configuration. There's a good deal of evidence—much of it now submerged—that this process did not take place slowly and steadily but, rather, in fits and starts. Beginning around 12,500 B.C., during an event known as meltwater pulse 1A, sea levels rose by roughly fifty feet in three or four centuries, a rate of more than a foot per decade. Meltwater pulse 1A, along with pulses 1B, 1C, and 1D, was, most probably, the result of ice-sheet collapse. One after another, the enormous glaciers disintegrated and dumped their contents into the oceans. It's been speculated—though the evidence is sketchy—that a sudden flooding of the Black Sea toward the end of meltwater pulse 1C, around seventy-five hundred years ago, inspired the deluge story in Genesis.

As temperatures climb again, so, too, will sea levels. One reason for this is that water, as it heats up, expands. The process of thermal expansion follows well-known physical laws, and its impact is relatively easy to calculate. It is more difficult to predict how the earth's remaining ice sheets will behave, and this difficulty accounts for the wide range in projections.

Low-end forecasts, like the I.P.C.C.'s, assume that the contribution from the ice sheets will remain relatively stable through the end of the century. High-end projections, like NOAA's, assume that ice-melt will accelerate as the earth warms (as, under any remotely plausible scenario, the planet will continue to do at least through the end of this century, and probably beyond). Recent observations, meanwhile, tend to support the most worrisome scenarios.

15   The latest data from the Arctic [2015], gathered by a pair of exquisitely sensitive satellites, show that in the past decade Greenland has been losing more ice each year. In August, NASA announced that, to supplement the satellites, it was launching a new monitoring program called—provocatively—Oceans Melting Greenland, or O.M.G. In November, researchers reported that, owing to the loss of an ice shelf off northeastern Greenland, a new "floodgate" on the ice sheet had opened. All told, Greenland's ice holds enough water to raise global sea levels by twenty feet.

1. Characters in John Steinbeck's novel *The Grapes of Wrath* (1939) who, due to the Dust Bowl and inability to pay bank loans, lose their crops and farm in Oklahoma and travel west, seeking work in California.

At the opposite end of the earth, two groups of researchers—one from NASA's Jet Propulsion Lab and the other from the University of Washington—concluded last year that a segment of the West Antarctic ice sheet has gone into "irreversible decline." The segment, known as the Amundsen Sea sector, contains enough water to raise global sea levels by four feet, and its melting could destabilize other parts of the ice sheet, which hold enough ice to add ten more feet. While the "decline" could take centuries, it's also possible that it could be accomplished a lot sooner. NASA is already planning for the day when parts of the Kennedy Space Center, on Florida's Cape Canaveral, will be underwater.

The day I toured Miami Beach with Hal Wanless, I also attended a panel discussion at the city's Convention Center titled "Eyes on the Rise." The discussion was hosted by the French government, as part of the lead-up to the climate convention in Paris, at that point two months away. Among the members of the panel was a French scientist named Eric Rignot, a professor at the University of California, Irvine. Rignot is one of the researchers on O.M.G., and in a conference call with reporters during the summer he said he was "in awe" of how fast the Greenland ice sheet was changing. I ran into him just as he was about to go onstage.

"I'm going to scare people out of this room," he told me. His fellow-panelists were a French geophysicist, a climate scientist from the University of Miami, and Miami Beach's mayor, Philip Levine. Levine was elected in 2013, after airing a commercial that tapped into voters' frustration with the continual flooding. It showed him preparing to paddle home from work in a kayak.

"Some people get swept into office," Levine joked when it was his turn at the mike. "I always say I got floated in." He described the steps his administration was taking to combat the effects of rising seas. These include installing enormous underground pumps that will suck water off the streets and dump it into Biscayne Bay. Six pumps have been completed, and fifty-four more are planned. "We had to raise people's storm-water fees to be able to pay for the first hundred-million-dollar tranche," Levine said. "So picture this: you get elected to office and the first thing you tell people is 'By the way, I'm going to raise your rates.'"

He went on, "When you are doing this, there's no textbooks, there's no 'How to Protect Your City from Sea Level Rise,' go to Chapter 4." So the city would have to write its own. "We have a team that's going to get it done, that's going to protect this city," the Mayor said. "We can't let investor confidence, resident confidence, confidence in our economy start to fall away."

John Morales, the chief meteorologist at NBC's South Florida affiliate, was moderating the discussion. He challenged the Mayor, offering a version of the argument I'd heard from Wanless—that today's pumps will be submerged by the seas of tomorrow.

"Down the road, this is just a Band-Aid," Morales said.

"I believe in human innovation," Levine responded. "If, thirty or forty years ago, I'd told you that you were going to be able to communicate with your friends around the world by looking at your watch or with an iPad or an iPhone, you would think I was out of my mind." Thirty or forty years from now, he said, "We're going to have innovative solutions to fight back against sea-level rise that we cannot even imagine today."

Many of the world's largest cities sit along a coast, and all of them are, to one degree or another, threatened by rising seas. Entire countries are endangered—the Maldives, for instance, and the Marshall Islands. Globally, it's estimated that a hundred million people live within three feet of mean high tide and another hundred million or so live within six feet of it. Hundreds of millions more live in areas likely to be affected by increasingly destructive storm surges.

Against this backdrop, South Florida still stands out. The region has been called "ground zero when it comes to sea-level rise." It has also been described as "the poster child for the impacts of climate change," the "epicenter for studying the effects of sea-level rise," a "disaster scenario," and "the New Atlantis." Of all the world's cities, Miami ranks second in terms of assets vulnerable to rising seas—No. 1 is Guangzhou—and in terms of population it ranks fourth, after Guangzhou, Mumbai, and Shanghai. A recent report on storm surges in the United States listed four Florida cities among the eight most at risk. (On that list, Tampa came in at No. 1.) For the past several years, the daily high-water mark in the Miami area has been racing up at the rate of almost an inch a year, nearly ten times the rate of average global sea-level rise. It's unclear exactly why this is happening, but it's been speculated that it has to do with changes in ocean currents which are causing water to pile up along the coast. Talking about climate change in the Everglades this past Earth Day [2015], President Obama said, "Nowhere is it going to have a bigger impact than here in South Florida."

The region's troubles start with its topography. Driving across South Florida is like driving across central Kansas, except that South Florida is greener and a whole lot lower. In Miami-Dade County, the average elevation is just six feet above sea level. The county's highest point, aside from man-made structures, is only about twenty-five feet, and no one seems entirely sure where it is. (The humorist Dave Barry once set out to climb Miami-Dade's tallest mountain, and ended up atop a local garbage dump nicknamed Mt. Trashmore.) Broward County, which includes Fort Lauderdale, is equally flat and low, and Monroe County, which includes the Florida Keys, is even more so.

But South Florida's problems also run deeper. The whole region—indeed, most of the state—consists of limestone that was laid down over the millions of years Florida sat at the bottom of a shallow sea. The limestone is filled with holes, and the holes are, for the most part, filled with water. (Near the surface, this is generally freshwater, which has a lower density than saltwater.)

Until the eighteen-eighties, when the first channels were cut through the region by steam-powered dredges, South Florida was one continuous wetland—the Everglades. Early efforts to drain the area were only half successful; Northerners lured by turn-of-the-century real-estate scams found the supposedly rich farmland they'd purchased was more suitable for swimming.

"I have bought land by the acre, and I have bought land by the foot; but, by God, I have never before bought land by the gallon," one arrival from Iowa complained.

Even today, with the Everglades reduced to half its former size, water in
the region is constantly being shunted around. The South Florida Water Management District, a state agency, claims that it operates the "world's largest
water control system," which includes twenty-three hundred miles of canals,
sixty-one pump stations, and more than two thousand "water control structures." Floridians south of Orlando depend on this system to prevent their
lawns from drowning and their front steps from becoming docks. (Basement
flooding isn't an issue in South Florida, because no one has a basement—the
water table is too high.)

When the system was designed—redesigned, really—in the nineteen-
fifties, the water level in the canals could be maintained at least a foot and a
half higher than the level of high tide. Thanks to this difference in elevation,
water flowed off the land toward the sea. At the same time, there was enough
freshwater pushing out to prevent saltwater from pressing in. Owing in part to
sea-level rise, the gap has since been cut by about eight inches, and the region
faces the discomfiting prospect that, during storms, it will be inundated not
just along the coasts but also inland, by rainwater that has nowhere to go.
Researchers at Florida Atlantic University have found that with just six more
inches of sea-level rise the district will lose almost half its flood-control capacity. Meanwhile, what's known as the saltwater front is advancing. One city—
Hallandale Beach, just north of Miami—has already had to close most of its
drinking wells, because the water is too salty. Many other cities are worried
that they will have to do the same.

Jayantha Obeysekera is the Water Management District's chief modeller,
which means it's his job to foresee South Florida's future. One morning, I
caught up with him at a flood-control structure known as S13, which sits on a
canal known as C11, west of Fort Lauderdale.

"We have a triple whammy," he said. "One whammy is sea-level rise.
Another whammy is the water table comes up higher, too. And in this area the
higher the water table, the less space you have to absorb storm water. The
third whammy is if the rainfall extremes change, and become more extreme.
There are other whammies probably that I haven't mentioned. Someone said
the other day, 'The water comes from six sides in Florida.'"

A month after the super blood moon, South Florida experienced another series
of very high tides—"king tides," as Miamians call them. This time, I went out
to see the effects with Nicole Hernandez Hammer, an environmental-studies
researcher who works for the Union of Concerned Scientists. Hammer had
looked over elevation maps and decided that Shorecrest, about five miles north
of downtown Miami, was a neighborhood where we were likely to find flooding. It was another hot, blue morning, and as we drove along, in Hammer's
Honda, at first it seemed that she'd miscalculated. Then, all of a sudden, we
arrived at a major intersection that was submerged. We parked and made our
way onto a side street, also submerged. We were standing in front of a low-
slung apartment building, debating what to do next, when one of the residents
came by.

35   "I've been trying to figure out: Where is the water coming from?" he said. "It'll be drying up and then it'll be just like this again." He had complained to the building's superintendent. "I told him, 'Something needs to be done about this water, man.' He says he'll try to do something." A cable-repair truck trailing a large wake rolled by and then stalled out.

The water on the street was so deep that it was, indeed, hard to tell where it was coming from. Hammer explained that it was emerging from the storm drains. Instead of funnelling rainwater into the bay, as they were designed to do, the drains were directing water from the bay onto the streets. "The infrastructure we have is built for a world that doesn't exist anymore," she said.

Neither of us was wearing boots, a fact that, as we picked our way along, we agreed we regretted. I couldn't help recalling stories I'd heard about Miami's antiquated sewer system, which leaks so much raw waste that it's the subject of frequent lawsuits. (To settle a suit brought by the federal government, the county recently agreed to spend $1.6 billion to upgrade the system, though many question whether the planned repairs adequately account for sea-level rise.) Across the soaked intersection, in front of a single-family home, a middle-aged man was unloading groceries from his car. He, too, told us he didn't know where the water was coming from.

"I heard on the news it's because the moon turned red," he said. "I don't have that much detail about it." During the past month, he added, "it's happened very often." (In an ominous development, Miami this past fall experienced several very high tides at times of the month when, astronomically speaking, it shouldn't have.)

"Honestly, sometimes, when I'm talking to people, I think, Oh, I wish I had taken more psychology courses," Hammer told me. A lot of her job involves visiting low-lying neighborhoods like Shorecrest, helping people understand what they're seeing. She shows them elevation maps and climate-change projections, and explains that the situation is only going to get worse. Often, Hammer said, she feels like a doctor: "You hear that they're trying to teach these skills in medical schools, to encourage them to have a better bedside manner. I think I might try to get that kind of training, because it's really hard to break bad news."

40   It was garbage-collection day, and in front of one house county-issued trash bins bobbed in a stretch of water streaked with oil. Two young women were surveying the scene from the driveway, as if from a pier.

"It's horrible," one of them said to us. "Sometimes the water actually smells." They were sisters, originally from Colombia. They wanted to sell the house, but, as the other sister observed, "No one's going to want to buy it like this."

"I have called the city of Miami," the first sister said. "And they said it's just the moon. But I don't think it's the moon anymore."

After a couple of minutes, their mother came out. Hammer, who was born in Guatemala, began chatting with her in Spanish. "Oh," I heard the mother exclaim. "*Dios mío! El cambio climático!*"[2]

---

2. Spanish for "Oh my God! Climate change!"

Marco Rubio, Florida's junior senator, who has been running third in Republican primary polls, grew up not far from Shorecrest, in West Miami, which sounds like it's a neighborhood but is actually its own city. For several years, he served in Florida's House of Representatives, and his district included Miami's flood-vulnerable airport. Appearing this past spring on "Face the Nation," Rubio was asked to explain a statement he had made about climate change. He offered the following: "What I said is, humans are not responsible for climate change in the way some of these people out there are trying to make us believe, for the following reason: I believe that climate is changing because there's never been a moment where the climate is not changing."

Around the same time, it was revealed that aides to Florida's governor, Rick Scott, also a Republican, had instructed state workers not to discuss climate change, or even to use the term. The Scott administration, according to the Florida Center for Investigative Reporting, also tried to ban talk of sea-level rise; state employees were supposed to speak, instead, of "nuisance flooding." Scott denied having imposed any such Orwellian restrictions, but I met several people who told me they'd bumped up against them. One was Hammer, who, a few years ago, worked on a report to the state about threats to Florida's transportation system. She said that she was instructed to remove all climate-change references from it. "In some places, it was impossible," she recalled. "Like when we talked about the Intergovernmental Panel on Climate Change, which has 'climate change' in the title." 45

Scientists who study climate change (and the reporters who cover them) often speculate about when the partisan debate on the issue will end. If Florida is a guide, the answer seems to be never. During September's series of king tides, former Vice-President Al Gore spent a morning sloshing through the flooded streets of Miami Beach with Mayor Levine, a Democrat. I met up with Gore the following day, and he told me that the boots he'd worn had turned out to be too low; the water had poured in over the top.

"When the governor of the state is a full-out climate denier, the irony is just excruciatingly painful," Gore observed. He said that he thought Florida ought to "join with the Maldives and some of the small island states that are urging the world to adopt stronger restrictions on global-warming pollution."

Instead, the state is doing the opposite. In October, Florida filed suit against the Environmental Protection Agency, seeking to block new rules aimed at limiting warming by reducing power-plant emissions. (Two dozen states are participating in the lawsuit.)

"The level of disconnect from reality is pretty profound," Jeff Goodell, a journalist who's working on a book on the impacts of sea-level rise, told me. "We're sort of used to that in the climate world. But in Florida there are real consequences. The water is rising right now."

Meanwhile, people continue to flock to South Florida. Miami's metropolitan area, which includes Fort Lauderdale, has been one of the fastest growing in the country; from 2013 to 2014, in absolute terms it added more residents than San Francisco and, proportionally speaking, it outdid Los Angeles and New York. Currently, in downtown Miami there are more than twenty-five 50 thousand new condominium units either proposed or under construction. Much of the boom is being financed by "flight capital" from countries like Argentina and Venezuela; something like half of recent home sales in Miami were paid for in cash.

And just about everyone who can afford to buys near the water. Not long ago, Kenneth Griffin, a hedge-fund billionaire, bought a penthouse in Miami Beach for sixty million dollars, the highest amount ever paid for a single-family residence in Miami-Dade County (and ten million dollars more than the original asking price). The penthouse, in a new building called Faena House, offers eight bedrooms and a seventy-foot rooftop pool. When I read about the sale, I plugged the building's address into a handy program called the Sea Level Rise Toolbox, created by students and professors at Florida International University. According to the program, with a little more than one foot of rise the roads around the building will frequently flood. With two feet, most of the streets will be underwater, and with three it seems that, if Faena House is still habitable, it will be accessible only by boat.

I asked everyone I met in South Florida who seemed at all concerned about sea-level rise the same question: What could be done? More than a quarter of the Netherlands is below sea level and those areas are home to millions of people, so low-elevation living is certainly possible. But the geology of South Florida is peculiarly intractable. Building a dike on porous limestone is like putting a fence on top of a tunnel: it alters the route of travel, but not necessarily the amount.

"You can't build levees on the coast and stop the water" is the way Jayantha Obeysekera put it. "The water would just come underground."

Some people told me that they thought the only realistic response for South Florida was retreat.

55   "I live opposite a park," Philip Stoddard, the mayor of South Miami—also a city in its own right—told me. "And there's a low area in it that fills up when it rains. I was out there this morning walking my dog, and I saw fish in it. Where the heck did the fish come from? They came from underground. We have fish that travel underground!

"What that means is, there's no keeping the water out," he went on. "So ultimately this area has to depopulate. What I want to work toward is a slow and graceful depopulation, rather than a sudden and catastrophic one."

More often, I heard echoes of Mayor Levine's Apple Watch line. Who knows what amazing breakthroughs the future will bring?

"I think people are underestimating the incredible innovative imagination in the world of adaptive design," Harvey Ruvin, the Clerk of the Courts of Miami-Dade County and the chairman of the county's Sea Level Rise Task Force, said when I went to visit him in his office. A quote from Buckminster Fuller hung on the wall: "We are all passengers on Spaceship Earth." Ruvin became friendly with Fuller in the nineteen-sixties, after reading about a plan Fuller had drawn up for a floating city in Tokyo Bay.

"I would agree that things can't continue exactly the way they are today," Ruvin told me. "But what we will evolve to may be better."

"I keep telling people, 'This is my patient,'" Bruce Mowry, Miami Beach's 60
city engineer, was saying. "I can't lose my patient. If I don't do anything, Miami
Beach may not be here." It was yet another day of bright-blue skies and "nuisance flooding," and I was walking with Mowry through one of Miami Beach's
lowest neighborhoods, Sunset Harbour.

If Miami Beach is on a gurney, then Mowry might be said to be thumping
its chest. It's his job to keep the city viable, and since no one has yet come up
with a smart-watch-like breakthrough, he's been forced to rely on more primitive means, like pumps and asphalt. We rounded a corner and came to a set of
stairs, which led down to some restaurants and shops. Until recently, Mowry
explained, the shops and the street had been at the same level. But the street
had recently been raised. It was now almost a yard higher than the sidewalk.

"I call this my five-step program," he said. "What are the five steps?" He
counted off the stairs as we descended: "One, two, three, four, five." Some
restaurants had set up tables at the bottom, next to what used to be a curb but
now, with the elevation of the road, is a three-foot wall. Cars whizzed by at the
diners' eye level. I found the arrangement disconcerting, as if I'd suddenly
shrunk. Mowry told me that some of the business owners, who had been unhappy
when the street flooded, now were unhappy because they had no direct access to
the road: "It's, like, can you win?"

Several nearby streets had also been raised, by about a foot. The elevated
roadbeds were higher than the driveways, which now all sloped down. The
parking lot of a car-rental agency sat in a kind of hollow.

I asked about the limestone problem. "That is the one that scares us more
than anything," Mowry said. "New Orleans, the Netherlands—everybody understands putting in barriers, perimeter levees, pumps. Very few people understand:
What do you do when the water's coming up through the ground?

"What I'd really like to do is pick the whole city up, spray on a membrane, 65
and drop it back down," he went on. I thought of Calvino's "Invisible Cities,"[3]
where such fantastical engineering schemes are the norm.

Mowry said he was intrigued by the possibility of finding some kind of
resin that could be injected into the limestone. The resin would fill the holes,
then set to form a seal. Or, he suggested, perhaps one day the city would
require that builders, before constructing a house, lay a waterproof shield
underneath it, the way a camper spreads a tarp under a tent. Or maybe some
sort of clay could be pumped into the ground that would ooze out and fill the
interstices.

"Will it hold?" Mowry said of the clay. "I doubt it. But these are things
we're exploring." It was hard to tell how seriously he took any of these ideas;
even if one of them turned out to be workable, the effort required to, in effect,
caulk the entire island seemed staggering. At one point, Mowry declared, "If
we can put a man on the moon, then we can figure out a way to keep Miami

---

3. Italo Calvino's novel *Le Città Invisibili*—dialogues and prose poems that describe
fifty-five fictitious cities—was published in Italian in 1972 and in English, *Invisible Cities*, in 1974.

Beach dry." At another, he mused about the city's reverting to "what it came from," which was largely mangrove swamp: "I'm sure if we had poets, they'd be writing about the swallowing of Miami Beach by the sea."

We headed back toward Mowry's office around the time of maximum high tide. The elevated streets were still dry, but on the way to City Hall we came to an unreconstructed stretch of road that was flooding. Evidently, this situation had been anticipated, because two mobile pumps, the size and shape of ice-cream trucks, were parked near the quickly expanding pool. Neither was oper-ating. After making a couple of phone calls, Mowry decided that he would try to switch them on himself. As he fiddled with the controls, I realized that we were standing not far from the drowned palm tree I'd seen on my first day in Miami Beach, and that it was once again underwater.

About a dozen miles due west of Miami, the land gives out, and what's left of the Everglades begins. The best way to get around in this part of Florida is by airboat, and on a gray morning I set out in one with a hydrologist named Christopher McVoy. We rented the boat from a concession run by members of the Miccosukee tribe, which, before the Europeans arrived, occupied large swaths of Georgia and Tennessee. The colonists hounded the Miccosukee ever farther south, until, eventually, they ended up with a few hundred mostly flooded square miles between Miami and Naples. On a fence in front of the dock, a sign read, "Beware: Wild alligators are dangerous. Do not feed or tease." Our guide, Betty Osceola, handed out headsets to block the noise of the rotors, and we zipped off.

70   The Everglades is often referred to as a "river of grass," but it might just as accurately be described as a prairie of water. Where the airboats had made a track, the water was open, but mostly it was patchy—interrupted by clumps of sawgrass and an occasional tree island. We hadn't been out very long when it started to pour. As the boat sped into the rain, it felt as if we were driving through a sandstorm.

The same features that now make South Florida so vulnerable—its flat-ness, its high water table, its heavy rains—are the features that brought the Everglades into being. Before the drainage canals were dug, water flowed from Lake Okeechobee, about seventy miles north of Miami, to Florida Bay, about forty miles to the south of the city, in one wide, slow-moving sheet. Now much of the water is diverted, and the water that does make it to the wetlands gets impounded, so the once continuous "sheet flow" is no more. There's a comprehensive Everglades restoration plan, which goes by the acro-nym *cerp*, but this has got hung up on one political snag after another, and climate change adds yet one more obstacle. The Everglades is a freshwater ecosystem; already, at the southern margin of Everglades National Park, the water is becoming salty. The sawgrass is in retreat, and mangroves are mov-ing in. In coming decades, there's likely to be more and more demand for the freshwater that remains. As McVoy put it, "You've got a big chunk of agricul-ture, a big chunk of people, and a big chunk of nature reserve all competing for the same resources."

The best that can be hoped for with the restoration project is that it will prolong the life of the wetland and, with that, of Miami's drinking-water system. But you can't get around geophysics. Send the ice sheets into "irreversible decline," as it seems increasingly likely we have done, and there's no going back. Eventually, the Everglades, along with Shorecrest and Miami Beach and much of the rest of South Florida, will be inundated. And, if Hal Wanless is right, eventually isn't very far off.

To me, the gunmetal expanse of water and grass appeared utterly without markers, but Osceola, who could read the subtlest of ridges, knew exactly where we were at every moment. We stopped to have sandwiches on an island with enough dry land for a tiny farm, and stopped again at a research site that McVoy had set up in the muck. There was a box of electrical equipment on stilts, and a solar panel to provide power. McVoy dropped out of the boat to collect some samples in empty water-cooler bottles. The rain let up, and then started again.

MLA CITATION

Kolbert, Elizabeth. "The Siege of Miami." *The Norton Reader: An Anthology of Nonfiction*, edited by Melissa A. Goldthwaite et al., 15th ed., W. W. Norton, 2020, pp. 512–23.

QUESTIONS

1. Elizabeth Kolbert provides different predictions for how much sea levels could rise by the end of this century (paragraph 5). What explanation does she provide for why these predictions vary?

2. Kolbert discusses the potential effects of rising sea levels globally, but she focuses specifically on South Florida. Why do you think she chose this area? Point to passages that support your answer.

3. Kolbert reports on several possible responses to rising sea levels in South Florida. Write an argument for or against one of these possible responses.

DAVID WALLACE-WELLS
The Uninhabitable Earth

I. "DOOMSDAY"

Peering beyond scientific reticence.

IT IS, I PROMISE, worse than you think. If your anxiety about global warming is dominated by fears of sea-level rise, you are barely scratching the surface of what terrors are possible, even within the lifetime of a teenager today. And yet the swelling seas—and the cities they will drown—have so dominated the picture of global warming, and so overwhelmed our capacity for climate panic, that they have occluded our perception of other threats, many much closer at hand. Rising oceans are bad, in fact very bad; but fleeing the coastline will not be enough.

Indeed, absent a significant adjustment to how billions of humans conduct their lives, parts of the Earth will likely become close to uninhabitable, and other parts horrifically inhospitable, as soon as the end of this century.

Even when we train our eyes on climate change, we are unable to comprehend its scope. This past winter, a string of days 60 and 70 degrees warmer than normal baked the North Pole, melting the permafrost that encased Norway's Svalbard seed vault—a global food bank nicknamed "Doomsday," designed to ensure that our agriculture survives any catastrophe, and which appeared to have been flooded by climate change less than ten years after being built.

The Doomsday vault is fine, for now: The structure has been secured and the seeds are safe. But treating the episode as a parable of impending flooding missed the more important news. Until recently, permafrost was not a major concern of climate scientists, because, as the name suggests, it was soil that stayed permanently frozen. But Arctic permafrost contains 1.8 trillion tons of carbon, more than twice as much as is currently suspended in the Earth's atmosphere. When it thaws and is released, that carbon may evaporate as methane, which is 34 times as powerful a greenhouse-gas warming blanket as carbon dioxide when judged on the timescale of a century; when judged on the timescale of two decades, it is 86 times as powerful. In other words, we have, trapped in Arctic permafrost, twice as much carbon as is currently wrecking the atmosphere of the planet, all of it scheduled to be released at a date that keeps getting moved up, partially in the form of a gas that multiplies its warming power 86 times over.

5   Maybe you know that already—there are alarming stories in the news every day, like those, last month, that seemed to suggest satellite data showed the

First published in New York *magazine (2017), parts of the article—revised and expanded—appear in David Wallace-Wells's book,* The Uninhabitable Earth: Life after Warming *(2019). After its initial publication,* New York *magazine published an annotated version of the article with sources and responses to readers. All notes are the editor's unless indicated otherwise.*

globe warming since 1998 more than twice as fast as scientists had thought (in fact, the underlying story was considerably less alarming than the headlines). Or the news from Antarctica this past May [2017], when a crack in an ice shelf grew 11 miles in six days, then kept going; the break now has just three miles to go— by the time you read this, it may already have met the open water, where it will drop into the sea one of the biggest icebergs ever, a process known poetically as "calving."

But no matter how well-informed you are, you are surely not alarmed enough. Over the past decades, our culture has gone apocalyptic with zombie movies and *Mad Max*[1] dystopias, perhaps the collective result of displaced climate anxiety, and yet when it comes to contemplating real-world warming dangers, we suffer from an incredible failure of imagination. The reasons for that are many: the timid language of scientific probabilities, which the climatologist James Hansen once called "scientific reticence" in a paper chastising scientists for editing their own observations so conscientiously that they failed to communicate how dire the threat really was; the fact that the country is dominated by a group of technocrats who believe any problem can be solved and an opposing culture that doesn't even see warming as a problem worth addressing; the way that climate denialism has made scientists even more cautious in offering speculative warnings; the simple speed of change and, also, its slowness, such that we are only seeing effects now of warming from decades past; our uncertainty about uncertainty, which the climate writer Naomi Oreskes in particular has suggested stops us from preparing as though anything worse than a median outcome were even possible; the way we assume climate change will hit hardest elsewhere, not everywhere; the smallness (two degrees) and largeness (1.8 trillion tons) and abstractness (400 parts per million) of the numbers; the discomfort of considering a problem that is very difficult, if not impossible, to solve; the altogether incomprehensible scale of that problem, which amounts to the prospect of our own annihilation; simple fear. But aversion arising from fear is a form of denial, too.

In between scientific reticence and science fiction is science itself. This article is the result of dozens of interviews and exchanges with climatologists and researchers in related fields and reflects hundreds of scientific papers on the subject of climate change. What follows is not a series of predictions of what will happen—that will be determined in large part by the much-less-certain science of human response. Instead, it is a portrait of our best understanding of where the planet is heading absent aggressive action. It is unlikely that all of these warming scenarios will be fully realized, largely because the devastation along the way will shake our complacency. But those scenarios, and not the present climate, are the baseline. In fact, they are our schedule.

The present tense of climate change—the destruction we've already baked into our future—is horrifying enough. Most people talk as if Miami and Bangladesh still have a chance of surviving; most of the scientists I spoke with assume

---

1. Dystopian action-film series that includes *Mad Max* (1979), *Mad Max 2* (1981), *Mad Max: Beyond Thunderdome* (1985), and *Mad Max: Fury Road* (2015).

we'll lose them within the century, even if we stop burning fossil fuel in the next decade. Two degrees of warming used to be considered the threshold of catastrophe: tens of millions of climate refugees unleashed upon an unprepared world. Now two degrees is our goal, per the Paris climate accords, and experts give us only slim odds of hitting it. The UN Intergovernmental Panel on Climate Change issues serial reports, often called the "gold standard" of climate research; the most recent one projects us to hit four degrees of warming by the beginning of the next century, should we stay the present course. But that's just a median projection. The upper end of the probability curve runs as high as eight degrees— and the authors still haven't figured out how to deal with that permafrost melt. The IPCC reports also don't fully account for the albedo effect (less ice means less reflected and more absorbed sunlight, hence more warming); more cloud cover (which traps heat); or the dieback of forests and other flora (which extract carbon from the atmosphere). Each of these promises to accelerate warming, and the history of the planet shows that temperature can shift as much as five degrees Celsius within thirteen years. The last time the planet was even four degrees warmer, Peter Brannen points out in *The Ends of the World*, his new history of the planet's major extinction events, the oceans were hundreds of feet higher.[2]

The Earth has experienced five mass extinctions before the one we are living through now, each so complete a slate-wiping of the evolutionary record it functioned as a resetting of the planetary clock, and many climate scientists will tell you they are the best analog for the ecological future we are diving headlong into. Unless you are a teenager, you probably read in your high-school textbooks that these extinctions were the result of asteroids. In fact, all but the one that killed the dinosaurs were caused by climate change produced by greenhouse gas. The most notorious was 252 million years ago; it began when carbon warmed the planet by five degrees, accelerated when that warming triggered the release of methane in the Arctic, and ended with 97 percent of all life on Earth dead. We are currently adding carbon to the atmosphere at a considerably faster rate; by most estimates, at least ten times faster. The rate is accelerating. This is what Stephen Hawking had in mind when he said, this spring [2017], that the species needs to colonize other planets in the next century to survive, and what drove Elon Musk, last month, to unveil his plans to build a Mars habitat in 40 to 100 years. These are nonspecialists, of course, and probably as inclined to irrational panic as you or I. But the many sober-minded scientists I interviewed over the past several months—the most credentialed and tenured in the field, few of them inclined to alarmism and many advisers to the IPCC who nevertheless criticize its conservatism—have quietly reached an apocalyptic conclusion, too: No plausible program of emissions reductions alone can prevent climate disaster.

---

2. This article has been updated to provide context for the recent news reports about revisions to a satellite data set, to more accurately reflect the rate of warming during the Paleocene–Eocene Thermal Maximum, to clarify a reference to Peter Brannen's *The Ends of the World*, and to make clear that James Hansen still supports a carbon-tax based approach to emissions [Author's note].

10   Over the past few decades, the term "Anthropocene" has climbed out of
academic discourse and into the popular imagination—a name given to the geo-
logic era we live in now, and a way to signal that it is a new era, defined on the
wall chart of deep history by human intervention. One problem with the term is
that it implies a conquest of nature (and even echoes the biblical "dominion").
And however sanguine you might be about the proposition that we have already
ravaged the natural world, which we surely have, it is another thing entirely to
consider the possibility that we have only provoked it, engineering first in ignorance and then in denial a climate system that will now go to war with us for
many centuries, perhaps until it destroys us. That is what Wallace Smith
Broecker, the avuncular oceanographer who coined the term "global warming,"
means when he calls the planet an "angry beast." You could also go with "war
machine." Each day we arm it more.

II. HEAT DEATH

The bahraining of New York.

Humans, like all mammals, are heat engines; surviving means having to continually cool off, like panting dogs. For that, the temperature needs to be low
enough for the air to act as a kind of refrigerant, drawing heat off the skin so the
engine can keep pumping. At seven degrees of warming, that would become
impossible for large portions of the planet's equatorial band, and especially the
tropics, where humidity adds to the problem; in the jungles of Costa Rica, for
instance, where humidity routinely tops 90 percent, simply moving around outside when it's over 105 degrees Fahrenheit would be lethal. And the effect would
be fast: Within a few hours, a human body would be cooked to death from both
inside and out.

Climate-change skeptics point out that the planet has warmed and cooled
many times before, but the climate window that has allowed for human life is
very narrow, even by the standards of planetary history. At 11 or 12 degrees of
warming, more than half the world's population, as distributed today, would die
of direct heat. Things almost certainly won't get that hot this century, though
models of unabated emissions do bring us that far eventually. This century, and
especially in the tropics, the pain points will pinch much more quickly even
than an increase of seven degrees. The key factor is something called wet-bulb
temperature, which is a term of measurement as home-laboratory-kit as it sounds:
the heat registered on a thermometer wrapped in a damp sock as it's swung
around in the air (since the moisture evaporates from a sock more quickly in dry
air, this single number reflects both heat and humidity). At present, most regions
reach a wet-bulb maximum of 26 or 27 degrees Celsius; the true red line for
habitability is 35 degrees. What is called heat stress comes much sooner.

Actually, we're about there already. Since 1980, the planet has experienced
a 50-fold increase in the number of places experiencing dangerous or extreme
heat; a bigger increase is to come. The five warmest summers in Europe since
1500 have all occurred since 2002, and soon, the IPCC warns, simply being
outdoors that time of year will be unhealthy for much of the globe. Even if we

meet the Paris goals of two degrees warming, cities like Karachi and Kolkata will become close to uninhabitable, annually encountering deadly heat waves like those that crippled them in 2015. At four degrees, the deadly European heat wave of 2003, which killed as many as 2,000 people a day, will be a normal summer. At six, according to an assessment focused only on effects within the U.S. from the National Oceanic and Atmospheric Administration, summer labor of any kind would become impossible in the lower Mississippi Valley, and everybody in the country east of the Rockies would be under more heat stress than anyone, anywhere, in the world today. As Joseph Romm has put it in his authoritative primer *Climate Change: What Everyone Needs to Know*, heat stress in New York City would exceed that of present-day Bahrain, one of the planet's hottest spots, and the temperature in Bahrain "would induce hyperthermia in even sleeping humans." The high-end IPCC estimate, remember, is two degrees warmer still. By the end of the century, the World Bank has estimated, the coolest months in tropical South America, Africa, and the Pacific are likely to be warmer than the warmest months at the end of the 20th century. Air-conditioning can help but will ultimately only add to the carbon problem; plus, the climate-controlled malls of the Arab emirates aside, it is not remotely plausible to wholesale air-condition all the hottest parts of the world, many of them also the poorest. And indeed, the crisis will be most dramatic across the Middle East and Persian Gulf, where in 2015 the heat index registered temperatures as high as 163 degrees Fahrenheit. As soon as several decades from now, the hajj will become physically impossible for the 2 million Muslims who make the pilgrimage each year.

It is not just the hajj, and it is not just Mecca; heat is already killing us. In the sugarcane region of El Salvador, as much as one-fifth of the population has chronic kidney disease, including over a quarter of the men, the presumed result of dehydration from working the fields they were able to comfortably harvest as recently as two decades ago. With dialysis, which is expensive, those with kidney failure can expect to live five years; without it, life expectancy is in the weeks. Of course, heat stress promises to pummel us in places other than our kidneys, too. As I type that sentence, in the California desert in mid-June, it is 121 degrees outside my door. It is not a record high.

III. THE END OF FOOD
Praying for cornfields in the tundra.

15   Climates differ and plants vary, but the basic rule for staple cereal crops grown at optimal temperature is that for every degree of warming, yields decline by 10 percent. Some estimates run as high as 15 or even 17 percent. Which means that if the planet is five degrees warmer at the end of the century, we may have as many as 50 percent more people to feed and 50 percent less grain to give them. And proteins are worse: It takes 16 calories of grain to produce just a single calorie of hamburger meat, butchered from a cow that spent its life polluting the climate with methane farts.

Pollyannaish plant physiologists will point out that the cereal-crop math applies only to those regions already at peak growing temperature, and they are right—theoretically, a warmer climate will make it easier to grow corn in Greenland. But as the pathbreaking work by Rosamond Naylor and David Battisti has shown, the tropics are already too hot to efficiently grow grain, and those places where grain is produced today are already at optimal growing temperature—which means even a small warming will push them down the slope of declining productivity. And you can't easily move croplands north a few hundred miles, because yields in places like remote Canada and Russia are limited by the quality of soil there; it takes many centuries for the planet to produce optimally fertile dirt.

Drought might be an even bigger problem than heat, with some of the world's most arable land turning quickly to desert. Precipitation is notoriously hard to model, yet predictions for later this century are basically unanimous: unprecedented droughts nearly everywhere food is today produced. By 2080, without dramatic reductions in emissions, southern Europe will be in permanent extreme drought, much worse than the American dust bowl ever was. The same will be true in Iraq and Syria and much of the rest of the Middle East; some of the most densely populated parts of Australia, Africa, and South America; and the breadbasket regions of China. None of these places, which today supply much of the world's food, will be reliable sources of any. As for the original dust bowl: The droughts in the American plains and Southwest would not just be worse than in the 1930s, a 2015 NASA study predicted, but worse than any droughts in a thousand years—and that includes those that struck between 1100 and 1300, which "dried up all the rivers East of the Sierra Nevada mountains"[3] and may have been responsible for the death of the Anasazi civilization.

Remember, we do not live in a world without hunger as it is. Far from it: Most estimates put the number of undernourished at 800 million globally. In case you haven't heard, this spring has already brought an unprecedented quadruple famine to Africa and the Middle East; the UN has warned that separate starvation events in Somalia, South Sudan, Nigeria, and Yemen could kill 20 million this year alone.

IV. CLIMATE PLAGUES

What happens when the bubonic ice melts?

Rock, in the right spot, is a record of planetary history, eras as long as millions of years flattened by the forces of geological time into strata with amplitudes of just inches, or just an inch, or even less. Ice works that way, too, as a climate ledger, but it is also frozen history, some of which can be reanimated when unfrozen. There are now, trapped in Arctic ice, diseases that have not circulated in the air for millions of years—in some cases, since before humans were around to encounter them. Which means our immune systems would

3. Quotation from Joseph Romm's *Climate Change: What Everyone Needs to Know* (2016).

have no idea how to fight back when those prehistoric plagues emerge from the ice.

The Arctic also stores terrifying bugs from more recent times. In Alaska,   20
already, researchers have discovered remnants of the 1918 flu that infected as many as 500 million and killed as many as 100 million—about 5 percent of the world's population and almost six times as many as had died in the world war for which the pandemic served as a kind of gruesome capstone. As the BBC reported in May, scientists suspect smallpox and the bubonic plague are trapped in Siberian ice, too—an abridged history of devastating human sickness, left out like egg salad in the Arctic sun.

Experts caution that many of these organisms won't actually survive the thaw and point to the fastidious lab conditions under which they have already reanimated several of them—the 32,000-year-old "extremophile" bacteria revived in 2005, an 8 million-year-old bug brought back to life in 2007, the 3.5 million–year–old one a Russian scientist self-injected just out of curiosity—to suggest that those are necessary conditions for the return of such ancient plagues. But already last year, a boy was killed and 20 others infected by anthrax released when retreating permafrost exposed the frozen carcass of a reindeer killed by the bacteria at least 75 years earlier; 2,000 present-day reindeer were infected, too, carrying and spreading the disease beyond the tundra.

What concerns epidemiologists more than ancient diseases are existing scourges relocated, rewired, or even re-evolved by warming. The first effect is geographical. Before the early modern period, when adventuring sailboats accelerated the mixing of peoples and their bugs, human provinciality was a guard against pandemic. Today, even with globalization and the enormous intermingling of human populations, our ecosystems are mostly stable, and this functions as another limit, but global warming will scramble those ecosystems and help disease trespass those limits as surely as Cortés[4] did. You don't worry much about dengue or malaria if you are living in Maine or France. But as the tropics creep northward and mosquitoes migrate with them, you will. You didn't much worry about Zika a couple of years ago, either.

As it happens, Zika may also be a good model of the second worrying effect—disease mutation. One reason you hadn't heard about Zika until recently is that it had been trapped in Uganda; another is that it did not, until recently, appear to cause birth defects. Scientists still don't entirely understand what happened, or what they missed. But there are things we do know for sure about how climate affects some diseases: Malaria, for instance, thrives in hotter regions not just because the mosquitoes that carry it do, too, but because for every degree increase in temperature, the parasite reproduces ten times faster. Which is one reason that the World Bank estimates that by 2050, 5.2 billion people will be reckoning with it.

4. Hernán Cortés (1485–1547), Spanish Conquistador and colonizer who was a key figure in the Spanish conquest of the Aztec Empire.

V. Unbreathable Air

A rolling death smog that suffocates millions.

Our lungs need oxygen, but that is only a fraction of what we breathe. The fraction of carbon dioxide is growing: It just crossed 400 parts per million, and high-end estimates extrapolating from current trends suggest it will hit 1,000 ppm by 2100. At that concentration, compared to the air we breathe now, human cognitive ability declines by 21 percent.

Other stuff in the hotter air is even scarier, with small increases in pollution capable of shortening life spans by ten years. The warmer the planet gets, the more ozone forms, and by mid-century, Americans will likely suffer a 70 percent increase in unhealthy ozone smog, the National Center for Atmospheric Research has projected. By 2090, as many as 2 billion people globally will be breathing air above the WHO "safe" level; one paper last month showed that, among other effects, a pregnant mother's exposure to ozone raises the child's risk of autism (as much as tenfold, combined with other environmental factors). Which does make you think again about the autism epidemic in West Hollywood.

Already, more than 10,000 people die each day from the small particles emitted from fossil-fuel burning; each year, 339,000 people die from wildfire smoke, in part because climate change has extended forest-fire season (in the U.S., it's increased by 78 days since 1970). By 2050, according to the U.S. Forest Service, wildfires will be twice as destructive as they are today; in some places, the area burned could grow fivefold. What worries people even more is the effect that would have on emissions, especially when the fires ravage forests arising out of peat. Peatland fires in Indonesia in 1997, for instance, added to the global CO_2 release by up to 40 percent, and more burning only means more warming only means more burning. There is also the terrifying possibility that rain forests like the Amazon, which in 2010 suffered its second "hundred-year drought" in the space of five years, could dry out enough to become vulnerable to these kinds of devastating, rolling forest fires—which would not only expel enormous amounts of carbon into the atmosphere but also shrink the size of the forest. That is especially bad because the Amazon alone provides 20 percent of our oxygen.

Then there are the more familiar forms of pollution. In 2013, melting Arctic ice remodeled Asian weather patterns, depriving industrial China of the natural ventilation systems it had come to depend on, which blanketed much of the country's north in an unbreathable smog. Literally unbreathable. A metric called the Air Quality Index categorizes the risks and tops out at the 301-to-500 range, warning of "serious aggravation of heart or lung disease and premature mortality in persons with cardiopulmonary disease and the elderly" and, for all others, "serious risk of respiratory effects"; at that level, "everyone should avoid all outdoor exertion." The Chinese "airpocalypse" of 2013 peaked at what would have been an Air Quality Index of over 800. That year, smog was responsible for a third of all deaths in the country.

VI. PERPETUAL WAR
The violence baked into heat.

Climatologists are very careful when talking about Syria. They want you to know that while climate change did produce a drought that contributed to civil war, it is not exactly fair to say that the conflict is the result of warming; next door, for instance, Lebanon suffered the same crop failures. But researchers like Marshall Burke and Solomon Hsiang have managed to quantify some of the non-obvious relationships between temperature and violence: For every half-degree of warming, they say, societies will see between a 10 and 20 percent increase in the likelihood of armed conflict. In climate science, nothing is simple, but the arithmetic is harrowing: A planet five degrees warmer would have at least half again as many wars as we do today. Overall, social conflict could more than double this century.

This is one reason that, as nearly every climate scientist I spoke to pointed out, the U.S. military is obsessed with climate change: The drowning of all American Navy bases by sea-level rise is trouble enough, but being the world's policeman is quite a bit harder when the crime rate doubles. Of course, it's not just Syria where climate has contributed to conflict. Some speculate that the elevated level of strife across the Middle East over the past generation reflects the pressures of global warming—a hypothesis all the more cruel considering that warming began accelerating when the industrialized world extracted and then burned the region's oil.

30
What accounts for the relationship between climate and conflict? Some of it comes down to agriculture and economics; a lot has to do with forced migration, already at a record high, with at least 65 million displaced people wandering the planet right now. But there is also the simple fact of individual irritability. Heat increases municipal crime rates, and swearing on social media, and the likelihood that a major-league pitcher, coming to the mound after his teammate has been hit by a pitch, will hit an opposing batter in retaliation. And the arrival of air-conditioning in the developed world, in the middle of the past century, did little to solve the problem of the summer crime wave.

VII. PERMANENT ECONOMIC COLLAPSE
Dismal capitalism in a half-poorer world.

The murmuring mantra of global neoliberalism, which prevailed between the end of the Cold War and the onset of the Great Recession, is that economic growth would save us from anything and everything.

But in the aftermath of the 2008 crash, a growing number of historians studying what they call "fossil capitalism" have begun to suggest that the entire history of swift economic growth, which began somewhat suddenly in the 18th century, is not the result of innovation or trade or the dynamics of global capitalism but simply our discovery of fossil fuels and all their raw power—a onetime injection of new "value" into a system that had previously been characterized by global subsistence living. Before fossil fuels, nobody lived better than their parents or grandparents or ancestors from 500 years before, except in the immediate aftermath of a great plague like the Black Death, which allowed the lucky survivors to gobble up the resources liberated by mass graves. After we've burned all the fossil fuels, these scholars suggest, perhaps we will return to a "steady state" global economy. Of course, that onetime injection has a devastating long-term cost: climate change.

The most exciting research on the economics of warming has also come from Hsiang and his colleagues, who are not historians of fossil capitalism but who offer some very bleak analysis of their own: Every degree Celsius of warming costs, on average, 1.2 percent of GDP (an enormous number, considering we count growth in the low single digits as "strong"). This is the sterling work in the field, and their median projection is for a 23 percent loss in per capita earning globally by the end of this century (resulting from changes in agriculture, crime, storms, energy, mortality, and labor).

Tracing the shape of the probability curve is even scarier: There is a 12 percent chance that climate change will reduce global output by more than 50 percent by 2100, they say, and a 51 percent chance that it lowers per capita GDP by 20 percent or more by then, unless emissions decline. By comparison, the Great Recession lowered global GDP by about 6 percent, in a onetime shock; Hsiang and his colleagues estimate a one-in-eight chance of an ongoing and irreversible effect by the end of the century that is eight times worse.

The scale of that economic devastation is hard to comprehend, but you can start by imagining what the world would look like today with an economy half as big, which would produce only half as much value, generating only half as much to offer the workers of the world. It makes the grounding of flights out of heat-stricken Phoenix last month seem like pathetically small economic potatoes. And, among other things, it makes the idea of postponing government action on reducing emissions and relying solely on growth and technology to solve the problem an absurd business calculation.

Every round-trip ticket on flights from New York to London, keep in mind, costs the Arctic three more square meters of ice.

VIII. POISONED OCEANS
Sulfide burps off the skeleton coast.

That the sea will become a killer is a given. Barring a radical reduction of emissions, we will see at least four feet of sea-level rise and possibly ten by the end of the century. A third of the world's major cities are on the coast, not to mention its power plants, ports, navy bases, farmlands, fisheries, river deltas, marshlands, and rice-paddy empires, and even those above ten feet will flood much more easily, and much more regularly, if the water gets that high. At least 600 million people live within ten meters of sea level today.

But the drowning of those homelands is just the start. At present, more than a third of the world's carbon is sucked up by the oceans—thank God, or else we'd have that much more warming already. But the result is what's called "ocean acidification," which, on its own, may add a half a degree to warming this century. It is also already burning through the planet's water basins—you may remember these as the place where life arose in the first place. You have probably heard of "coral bleaching"—that is, coral dying—which is very bad news, because reefs support as much as a quarter of all marine life and supply food for half a billion people. Ocean acidification will fry fish populations directly, too, though scientists aren't yet sure how to predict the effects on the stuff we haul out of the ocean to eat; they do know that in acid waters, oysters and mussels will struggle to grow their shells, and that when the pH of human blood drops as much as the oceans' pH has over the past generation, it induces seizures, comas, and sudden death.

That isn't all that ocean acidification can do. Carbon absorption can initiate a feedback loop in which underoxygenated waters breed different kinds of microbes that turn the water still more "anoxic," first in deep ocean "dead zones," then gradually up toward the surface. There, the small fish die out, unable to breathe, which means oxygen-eating bacteria thrive, and the feedback loop doubles back. This process, in which dead zones grow like cancers, choking off marine life and wiping out fisheries, is already quite advanced in parts of the Gulf of Mexico and just off Namibia, where hydrogen sulfide is bubbling out of the sea along a thousand-mile stretch of land known as the "Skeleton Coast." The name originally referred to the detritus of the whaling industry, but today it's more apt than ever. Hydrogen sulfide is so toxic that evolution has trained us to recognize the tiniest, safest traces of it, which is why our noses are so exquisitely skilled at registering flatulence. Hydrogen sulfide is also the thing that finally did us in that time 97 percent of all life on Earth died, once all the feedback loops had been triggered and the circulating jet streams of a warmed ocean ground to a halt—it's the planet's preferred gas for a natural holocaust. Gradually, the ocean's dead zones spread, killing off marine species that had dominated the oceans for hundreds of millions of years, and the gas the inert waters gave off into the atmosphere poisoned everything on land. Plants, too. It was millions of years before the oceans recovered.

IX. THE GREAT FILTER

Our present eeriness cannot last.

40   So why can't we see it? In his recent book-length essay *The Great Derangement*, the Indian novelist Amitav Ghosh wonders why global warming and natural disaster haven't become major subjects of contemporary fiction—why we don't seem able to imagine climate catastrophe, and why we haven't yet had a spate of novels in the genre he basically imagines into half-existence and names "the environmental uncanny." "Consider, for example, the stories that congeal around questions like, 'Where were you when the Berlin Wall fell?' or 'Where were you on 9/11?'" he writes. "Will it ever be possible to ask, in the same vein, 'Where were you at 400 ppm?' or 'Where were you when the Larsen B ice shelf broke up?'" His answer: Probably not, because the dilemmas and dramas of climate change are simply incompatible with the kinds of stories we tell ourselves

about ourselves, especially in novels, which tend to emphasize the journey of an individual conscience rather than the poisonous miasma of social fate.

Surely this blindness will not last—the world we are about to inhabit will not permit it. In a six-degree-warmer world, the Earth's ecosystem will boil with so many natural disasters that we will just start calling them "weather": a constant swarm of out-of-control typhoons and tornadoes and floods and droughts, the planet assaulted regularly with climate events that not so long ago destroyed whole civilizations. The strongest hurricanes will come more often, and we'll have to invent new categories with which to describe them; tornadoes will grow longer and wider and strike much more frequently, and hail rocks will quadruple in size. Humans used to watch the weather to prophesy the future; going forward, we will see in its wrath the vengeance of the past. Early naturalists talked often about "deep time"—the perception they had, contemplating the grandeur of this valley or that rock basin, of the profound slowness of nature. What lies in store for us is more like what the Victorian anthropologists identified as "dreamtime," or "everywhen": the semi-mythical experience, described by Aboriginal Australians, of encountering, in the present moment, an out-of-time past, when ancestors, heroes, and demigods crowded an epic stage. You can find it already watching footage of an iceberg collapsing into the sea—a feeling of history happening all at once.

It is. Many people perceive climate change as a sort of moral and economic debt, accumulated since the beginning of the Industrial Revolution and now come due after several centuries—a helpful perspective, in a way, since it is the carbon-burning processes that began in 18th-century England that lit the fuse of everything that followed. But more than half of the carbon humanity has exhaled into the atmosphere in its entire history has been emitted in just the past three decades; since the end of World War II, the figure is 85 percent. Which means that, in the length of a single generation, global warming has brought us to the brink of planetary catastrophe, and that the story of the industrial world's kamikaze mission is also the story of a single lifetime. My father's, for instance: born in 1938, among his first memories the news of Pearl Harbor and the mythic Air Force of the propaganda films that followed, films that doubled as advertisements for imperial-American industrial might; and among his last memories the coverage of the desperate signing of the Paris climate accords on cable news, ten weeks before he died of lung cancer last July. Or my mother's: born in 1945, to German Jews fleeing the smokestacks through which their relatives were incinerated, now enjoying her 72nd year in an American commodity paradise, a paradise supported by the supply chains of an industrialized developing world. She has been smoking for 57 of those years, unfiltered.

Or the scientists'. Some of the men who first identified a changing climate (and given the generation, those who became famous were men) are still alive; a few are even still working. Wally Broecker is 84 years old and drives to work at the Lamont-Doherty Earth Observatory across the Hudson every day from the Upper West Side. Like most of those who first raised the alarm, he believes that no amount of emissions reduction alone can meaningfully help avoid disaster. Instead, he puts his faith in carbon capture—untested technology to extract carbon dioxide from the atmosphere, which Broecker estimates will cost at least several trillion dollars—and various forms of "geoengineering," the catchall name for a variety of moon-shot technologies far-fetched enough that many climate scientists prefer to regard them as dreams, or nightmares, from science fiction. He is especially focused on what's called the aerosol approach—dispersing so much sulfur dioxide into the atmosphere that when it converts to sulfuric acid, it will cloud a fifth of the horizon and reflect back 2 percent of the sun's rays, buying the planet at least a little wiggle room, heat-wise. "Of course, that would make our sunsets very red, would bleach the sky, would make more acid rain," he says. "But you have to look at the magnitude of the problem. You got to watch that you don't say the giant problem shouldn't be solved because the solution causes some smaller problems." He won't be around to see that, he told me. "But in your lifetime . . ."

Jim Hansen is another member of this godfather generation. Born in 1941, he became a climatologist at the University of Iowa, developed the groundbreaking "Zero Model" for projecting climate change, and later became the head of climate research at NASA, only to leave under pressure when, while still a federal employee, he filed a lawsuit against the federal government charging inaction on warming (along the way he got arrested a few times for protesting, too). The lawsuit, which is brought by a collective called Our Children's Trust and is often described as "kids versus climate change," is built on an appeal to the equal-protection clause, namely, that in failing to take action on warming, the government is violating it by imposing massive costs on future generations; it is scheduled to be heard this winter in Oregon district court. Hansen has recently given up on solving the climate problem with a carbon tax alone, which had been his preferred approach, and has set about calculating the total cost of the additional measure of extracting carbon from the atmosphere.

45   Hansen began his career studying Venus, which was once a very Earth-like planet with plenty of life-supporting water before runaway climate change rapidly transformed it into an arid and uninhabitable sphere enveloped in an unbreathable gas; he switched to studying our planet by 30, wondering why he should be squinting across the solar system to explore rapid environmental change when he could see it all around him on the planet he was standing on. "When we wrote our first paper on this, in 1981," he told me, "I remember saying to one of my co-authors, 'This is going to be very interesting. Sometime during our careers, we're going to see these things beginning to happen.'"

Several of the scientists I spoke with proposed global warming as the solution to Fermi's famous paradox, which asks, If the universe is so big, then why haven't we encountered any other intelligent life in it? The answer, they suggested, is that the natural life span of a civilization may be only several thousand years, and the life span of an industrial civilization perhaps only several hundred. In a universe that is many billions of years old, with star systems separated as much by time as by space, civilizations might emerge and develop and burn themselves up simply too fast to ever find one another. Peter Ward, a charismatic paleontologist among those responsible for discovering that the planet's mass extinctions were caused by greenhouse gas, calls this the "Great Filter": "Civilizations rise, but there's an environmental filter that causes them to die off again and disappear fairly quickly," he told me. "If you look at planet Earth, the filtering we've had in the past has been in these mass extinctions." The mass extinction we are now living through has only just begun; so much more dying is coming.

And yet, improbably, Ward is an optimist. So are Broecker and Hansen and many of the other scientists I spoke to. We have not developed much of a religion of meaning around climate change that might comfort us, or give us purpose, in the face of possible annihilation. But climate scientists have a strange kind of faith: We will find a way to forestall radical warming, they say, because we must.

It is not easy to know how much to be reassured by that bleak certainty, and how much to wonder whether it is another form of delusion; for global warming to work as parable, of course, someone needs to survive to tell the story. The scientists know that to even meet the Paris goals, by 2050, carbon emissions from energy and industry, which are still rising, will have to fall by half each decade; emissions from land use (deforestation, cow farts, etc.) will have to zero out; and we will need to have invented technologies to extract, annually, twice as much carbon from the atmosphere as the entire planet's plants now do. Nevertheless, by and large, the scientists have an enormous confidence in the ingenuity of humans—a confidence perhaps bolstered by their appreciation for climate change, which is, after all, a human invention, too. They point to the Apollo project, the hole in the ozone we patched in the 1980s, the passing of the fear of mutually assured destruction. Now we've found a way to engineer our own doomsday, and surely we will find a way to engineer our way out of it, one way or another. The planet is not used to being provoked like this, and climate systems designed to give feedback over centuries or millennia prevent us—even those who may be watching closely—from fully imagining the damage done already to the planet. But when we do truly see the world we've made, they say, we will also find a way to make it livable. For them, the alternative is simply unimaginable.

MLA CITATION

Wallace-Wells, David. "The Uninhabitable Earth." *The Norton Reader: An Anthology of Nonfiction*, edited by Melissa A. Goldthwaite et al., 15th ed., W. W. Norton, 2020, pp. 524–37.

QUESTIONS

1. What is the organizing principle for how David Wallace-Wells structures this article? How effective do you find his use of sections? Why?

2. How would you characterize Wallace-Wells's tone? What words or phrases does the author use that support your answer?

3. Wallace-Wells wants his readers to be alarmed. Which sections did you find most alarming? Why?

4. The last two paragraphs of Wallace-Wells's article show the optimism and hope of some climate scientists. Write an essay in which you take a position on—and provide reasons for—whether we should have confidence in the ingenuity of humans to deal effectively with climate change.

TATÉ WALKER

The (Native) American Dream

I N THE MIDST of Colorado Springs' urban sprawl, Monycka Snowbird (Ojibwe) raises fowl, goats, rabbits, and indigenous plants to feed and make household products for her family and neighbors.

About 650 miles north in a sprawling rural landscape on the Cheyenne River reservation in South Dakota, Karen Ducheneaux (Lakota) and her tiospaye[1] are slowly building a series of ecodomes and straw bale buildings powered by solar, wind, and water in an effort to disconnect from pollutants of mind, body, and earth.

The two women represent a growing number of Native people and organizations in the United States both on and off tribal land committed to leading clean, sustainable, and culturally competent lives.

The efforts of individuals like these women, in addition to the prevalence of companies specializing in mainstreaming indigenous foods and non-profits committed to building energy efficient and sustainable housing in tribal communities, highlight the popularity and return of such lifestyles.

Published in Native Peoples *(2015), a magazine edited by Taté Walker and devoted to "American Indian history, contemporary arts, Native film, theatre, music, culture, Native American recipes, pow-wows & events in North & South America," which was published from 1987 to 2016.*

1. Lakota for "extended family."

"Our people had this tiospaye system, where you really made a life with the   5
people you felt close to, and had skills that complemented each other," says
Ducheneaux. "We've spent generations at this point getting away from that
beautiful system, and we're taught the only way to be successful is to follow the
American dream, which is one of autonomy and being paid for your skills."

The American dream, Ducheneaux says, doesn't work on the reservation.

"It's not in our nature to turn our back on people who need us," she continues. "Our people without even realizing it sometimes are still living in a
tiospaye system, because any success we've had as a people—success in material wealth—is because we can depend on each other."

Studies show food stability, affordability, and access is severely limited
for Native communities. According to a report from the USDA's Economic
Research Service released in December [2014], just 25.6 percent of all tribal areas
were within a mile's distance from a supermarket, compared with 58.8 percent
of the total U.S. population.

The latest USDA data also shows 23.5 million people nationwide live in a
food desert—that is to say, their access to a grocery store and healthy, affordable food is limited—and more than half of those people are low-income.
Many tribal communities and urban areas with high populations of Native
people are considered food deserts.

Given the staggering rates of poverty, diseases like diabetes, and unemploy-   10
ment for Natives nationwide—higher for those living on reservations—both
Snowbird and Ducheneaux point to the many economic and health benefits of
individuals creating their own energies, whether it's food, fuel and power, or
social capital.

Returning to traditional roots in a literal sense is also what drives Snowbird, who has lived in Colorado Springs for more than 20 years.

"We as indigenous people have gotten farther away from our traditional food sources than anyone else in this country, and I think that's why we have this sort of swelling epidemic of diabetes and obesity in Indian Country, because we're losing the knowledge of our traditional foods," says Snowbird, 40.

Some 440,000 people live in the Colorado Springs area, and Snowbird works with both Native and non-Native organizations throughout her region to educate and promote the benefits of urban food production, known in some places as backyard or micro farming. She leads educational classes for children and adults, including seed cultivation, plant recognition, harvesting, livestock butchering, and more.

"You can't be sovereign if you can't feed yourself," says Snowbird, borrowing a line from Winona LaDuke (Anishinaabe), an environmental activist and founder of Honor the Earth. "One of the ways colonizers controlled Indian people was to take our food sources away. Let's reclaim our food.

15   "We have to teach our kids it's not just about preserving our cultures and language; it's about restorative stewardship and about knowing where food comes from, who tribally it comes from," Snowbird says. "Indigenous food is medicine. And food brings everyone together."

• • •

Snowbird learned to appreciate indigenous food systems from her father, who hunted wild game and imparted an appreciation for knowing where your dinner comes from and how to prepare it beyond simply opening a box and heating up the contents.

But being known throughout Colorado Springs as "the Goat Lady" and earning a reputation as a knowledgeable indigenous educator didn't happen until a few years ago, when Snowbird spearheaded a city-wide movement to change and educate people on the local laws of urban food production.

Now Snowbird manages the Colorado Springs Urban Homesteading support group, which boasts roughly 1,200 members. Through that group, Snowbird leads several classes per season on animal husbandry, butchering, and more with her fiery brand of wit and know-how.

Perhaps closer to her heart, however, are the lessons she imparts on the city's urban Native youth. Colorado Springs School District 11, in which Snowbird's two daughters, ages 11 and 13, are enrolled, has the only Title VII Indian Education Program in the city.

20   "I talk to Title VII kids about what indigenous food is—that it's not just buffalo or corn," she explains. "I try to break it down for them in terms of what they ate at lunch that day, even if it was junk food."

Thanks in large part to Snowbird's efforts, the program has several garden beds and a greenhouse growing traditional Native edibles, including Apache brown-striped sunflower seeds, Navajo robin's egg, Pueblo chiles, and more.

"I come in sometimes and kids are bouncing off all the walls," Snowbird says. "But the moment you get their hands in the dirt, it's like all that contact with the earth just calms them."

The children also learn to grow, harvest and cook with chokecherries, prickly pears, beans, and other local vegetation.

"Starting the kids off with food let's us also discuss Indian issues without putting people on the defensive," Snowbird explains. "It's hard to get mad when you're talking about food."

Re-introducing and re-popularizing indigenous foods and traditional cooking, especially among Native youth, will help strengthen Native people and the communities they live in, Snowbird insists.

25

Snowbird admits maintaining a lifestyle committed to food sovereignty can be hard on her tight budget. However, she says it helps her save and earn money in the long run. Snowbird is able to collect, grow, use and sell or barter with the milk, eggs, meat, vegetables, cleaning and toiletry items, and other useful goods produced on her property.

"I'm not completely self-sufficient by any means. But urban homesteading—or whatever you want to call it—is about as traditional as you can get," she insists. "It's living off the land within the radius of where you live and knowing the Creator has put what you need right where you are."

• • •

For outsiders following along on Facebook as Ducheneaux and her family transition to living efficiently and sustainably, the process of building an ecodome and maintaining a traditional garden may have seemed as easy as digging a hole.

Except that the hole in question—12 feet across and 4 to 6 feet deep in which the ecodome sits—took three months to dig out back in 2012, thanks to heavy rains and a landscape of gumbo.

30

"It was so much work," Ducheneaux recalls. "We had to move the gumbo out one wheelbarrow at a time."

But the effort, shared by about seven members of Ducheneaux's tiospaye—including her mom, siblings, and their spouses, as well as volunteers—has been well worth it.

On 10 acres of family land on the Cheyenne River reservation, Ducheneaux and her family are creating the Tatanka Wakpala Model Sustainable Community. The family has funded the project with help from Honor the Earth and Bread of Life Church, which donated $4,000 and $2,500 respectively toward the electric power system.

The shell of the small, ecodome home—which the family learned to build via video and trial-by-error— is complete, and a garden featuring plants indigenous to the area produces hundreds of pounds of produce each year.

Considering hers is a reservation located within counties consistently listed as some of the poorest in the nation, and recognizing the tribe suffers from insufficient and inefficient housing where utility bills can reach into the high hundreds or more during the winter months. Ducheneaux hopes her family's model sparks a trend for other tribal members.

35 "We really believe that even people who aren't eco-friendly will be inspired by our use of wind and solar energy. We put up our own electric system and we'll never have to pay another utility bill," Ducheneaux says.

"We were waiting for the blueprint to drop in our laps. Then we realized no one was going to do it for us, so we said we'd do it ourselves. We'll make mistakes and figure it out."

This year, the goal is to build a round, communal use center out of straw bale and/or tires where things like cooking, bathing, learning, ceremony, or business can be conducted. Ducheneaux hopes the latest building will be complete within the next two years.

"What we have going on out there is a desire to be more self-sufficient. When we sat around talking about this, we asked ourselves, 'What do we need?'" Ducheneaux explains. "We needed to start feeding ourselves and taking responsibility for our own food needs . . . Not just growing food and raising animals, but going back to our Lakota traditions and treating the Earth respectfully by using what it gives us."

•••

Living in an urban or reservation setting provides those who want to live sustainably unique challenges, both Snowbird and Ducheneaux say.

"One of the challenges is being so far away from everything," Ducheneaux   40
says of rural reservation life. "For a lot of our volunteers, it's eye-opening for them that the hardware store is a one-hour trip just in one direction."

Planning far ahead is key, Ducheneaux says.

Infrastructure, including a severe lack of Internet connectivity, weather, and a disinterested tribal government can also be setbacks, although Ducheneaux notes the latter can benefit sustainability projects due to few, if any, restrictions on things like harvesting rainwater or land use.

For urban Natives, being disconnected from tribal knowledge—for instance, the indigenous names and uses of plants—is a major disadvantage, Snowbird said.

When someone in the community comes forward with that knowledge, it's often exploited for profit, and the people who would benefit most—namely Native youth—are left out.

"I always find it surprising how removed from the whole food process   45
people are; they don't know or care where their food comes from," says Snowbird, who harvests edibles on hikes through the mountains or on strolls through downtown. She tries to combat this by giving eggs and other food produced on her property to those who wouldn't—or couldn't—normally buy organic in a supermarket.

"Pretty soon those people are asking me for more eggs and then we're talking about how they can get started with chickens in their backyard or growing

herbs on their window sills," Snowbird says, adding those conversations eventually lead to discussions on indigenous issues, regardless of whether the person is
Native or not. "We're trying to put the culture back in agriculture."

MLA CITATION

Walker, Taté. "The (Native) American Dream." *The Norton Reader: An Anthology of
Nonfiction*, edited by Melissa A. Goldthwaite et al., 15th ed., W. W. Norton,
2020, pp. 538–44.

QUESTIONS

1. Many writers of profiles limit themselves to one subject. Why do you think Taté
Walker chose to profile two people who live in different locations?

2. Monycka Snowbird and Karen Ducheneaux draw knowledge from their Native
cultures. Describe the practices that reflect Native knowledge and how these
women apply that knowledge in their communities. Do you think this knowledge
could benefit other communities? How so?

3. Ducheneaux often mentions a "tiospaye system," a cooperative way of living
with those one feels close to and who have complementary skills; she contrasts this
way of living with following "the American dream, which is one of autonomy and
being paid for your skills" (paragraph 5). Write an essay in which you compare and/
or contrast these different approaches to living.

ROBIN WALL KIMMERER
Goldenrod and Asters: My Life with Plants

I LIKE TO IMAGINE that they were the first flowers I saw, over my mother's
shoulder, as the pink blanket slipped away from my face and their colors flooded my consciousness. I've heard that early experience can
attune the brain to certain stimuli, so that they are processed with
greater speed and certainty, so that they can be used again and again,
so that we remember. Love at first sight. Through cloudy newborn eyes their
radiance formed the first botanical synapses in my wide-awake brain, which
until then had encountered only the blurry gentleness of pink faces. I'm guess-
ing all eyes were on me, a little round baby all swaddled in bunting, but mine
were on goldenrod and asters. I was born to these flowers and they came back
for my birthday every year, weaving me into our mutual celebration.

Published in its current form in Commons: A Gathering of Stories & Culture, *a publication
of Blue Mountain Center, which offers residencies and retreats for writers, artists, and those
working for social justice. This piece, in a slightly different form, also appears in the chapter
"Asters and Goldenrod" from Robin Wall Kimmerer's* Braiding Sweetgrass: Indigenous Wisdom, Scientific Knowledge, and the Teachings of Plants *(2013).*

People flock to our hills for the fiery suite of October but they often miss the sublime prelude of September fields. As if harvest time were not enough— peaches, grapes, sweet corn, squash—the fields are also embroidered with drifts of golden yellow and pools of deepest purple, a masterpiece.

I wanted to make a good first impression. There were hardly any women at the forestry school in those days and certainly none who looked like me. For the freshman intake interview, I wore my new red plaid shirt, a hallmark of foresters, so I'd fit right in. My new faculty adviser peered at me over his glasses and said, "So, Miss Wall, why do you want to major in botany?" His pencil was poised over the registrar's form, twitching, while portraits of Linnaeus and Asa Gray[1] looked on from his walls.

How could I answer, how could I tell him that I was born a botanist, that I had shoeboxes of seeds and piles of pressed leaves under my bed, that plants colored my dreams, that the plants had chosen me?

So I told him the truth. I was proud of my well-planned answer, its fresh-man sophistication apparent to anyone, revealing what I hoped was a deep knowledge of plants. I told him that I chose botany because I wanted to learn about why asters and goldenrod looked so beautiful together. I'm sure I was smiling then, in my new red plaid shirt.   5

But he was not. He laid down his pencil as if there was no need to record what I had said. "Miss Wall," he said, fixing me with a disappointed smile, "I must tell you that that is not science. Beauty is not the sort of thing with which botanists concern themselves." I tried again: I'd like to learn why plants make medicines, why willow bends for baskets and why strawberries are sweeter in the shade. "Also not science," he said and he ought to know, sitting in his laboratory, a learned professor of botany. "And if you want to study beauty, you should go to art school."

I had no rejoinder; I had made a mistake. I did not have the words for resistance, only embarrassment at my error. But he promised to put me right. "I'll enroll you in General Botany so you can learn what it is." And so it began.

I didn't think about it at the time, the echo of my grandfather's first day at the Carlisle Indian school, when he was ordered to leave everything—language, culture, family—behind. But they did not cut my hair.

If a fountain could jet bouquets of chrome yellow in dazzling arches of chrysanthemum fireworks, that would be Canada goldenrod. Each three-foot stem is a geyser of tiny gold daisies, ladylike in miniature, exuberant en masse. Where the soil is damp enough, they stand side by side with their perfect counterpart, New England asters. Not the pale domesticates of the perennial border, the weak sauce of lavender or sky blue, but full-on royal purple that would make a violet shrink. The daisy-like fringe of purple petals surrounds a disc as bright as the sun at high noon, a golden-orange pool, just a tantalizing

1. Carl Linnaeus (1717–1778), Swedish botanist known as the "father of modern tax-onomy"; Asa Gray (1810–1888), American botanist and author of *Manual of the Botany of the Northern United States, from New England to Wisconsin and South to Ohio and Pennsylvania Inclusive* (1848), which is now referred to as *Gray's Manual*.

shade darker than the surrounding goldenrod. Alone, each is a botanical superlative. Together, the visual effect is stunning. Purple and gold, the heraldic colors of the king and queen of the meadow, a regal procession in complementary colors. I just wanted to know why.

10   Why do they stand beside each other when they could grow alone? There are plenty of pinks and whites and blues dotting the fields, so is it only happenstance that the magnificence of purple and gold end up side by side? Einstein himself said that "God doesn't play dice with the universe." Why is the world so beautiful? It seemed like a good question to me.

In moving from a childhood in the woods to the university I had unknowingly shifted between worldviews, from a natural history of experience, in which I knew plants as teachers and companions into the realm of science. The questions scientists raised were not "Who are you?" but "What is it?" No one asked plants "What can you tell us?" The primary question was "How does it work?" The botany I was taught was reductionist, mechanistic. Plants were reduced to objects; they were no longer subjects. The way botany was conceived and taught didn't seem to leave much room for a person who thought the way I did. The only way I could make sense of it was to conclude that the things I had always believed about plants must not be true after all.

That first plant science class was almost a disaster. I barely scraped by with a C and could not muster much enthusiasm for memorizing the concentrations of essential plant nutrients. There were times when I wanted to quit, but the more I learned, the more fascinated I became with the intricate structures that made up a leaf and the alchemy of photosynthesis. Companionship between asters and goldenrod was never mentioned, but I memorized botanical Latin as if it was poetry, eagerly tossing aside the name "goldenrod" for *Solidago canadensis*.

I scarcely doubted the primacy of scientific thought. Following the path of science trained me to separate, to distinguish perception from physical reality, to atomize complexity into its smallest components, to honor the chain of evidence and logic, to discern one thing from another, to savor the pleasure of precision. The more I did this, the better I got at it. A master's degree, a PhD followed. No doubt on the strength of the letter of recommendation from that freshman adviser, which read, "She's done remarkably well for an Indian girl."

I am grateful for the knowledge that was shared with me and deeply privileged to carry the powerful tools of science as a way of engaging the world. I remember feeling, as a new professor, as if I finally understood plants. I too began to teach the mechanics of botany, emulating the approach that I had been taught. And yet there was always something tapping at my shoulder, willing me to turn around.

15   To walk the science path I had stepped off the path of indigenous knowledge. But the world has a way of guiding your steps. Seemingly out of the blue came an invitation to a small gathering of Native elders, to talk about traditional knowledge of plants. One teacher I will never forget—a Navajo woman without a day of university botany training—spoke for hours and I hung on every word. One by one, name by name, she told of the plants in her valley. Where each one lived, when it bloomed, who it liked to live near and all its relationships, who ate

it, who lined their nests with its fibers, what kind of medicine it offered. She also shared the stories held by those plants, their origin myths, how they got their names, and what they have to tell us. She spoke of beauty.

Her words were like smelling salts for me—I was suddenly newborn wide awake—and profoundly humbled in the shallowness of my own understanding. Her knowledge was so much deeper and wider and engaged all the human ways of knowing. She could have explained asters and goldenrod. It was the beginning of my reclaiming that other way of knowing that I had helplessly let science supplant. I felt like a malnourished refugee invited to a feast, the dishes scented with the herbs of home.

I circled right back to where I had begun, to the question of beauty. Back to the questions that science does not ask, not because they aren't important, but because science as a way of knowing is too narrow for the task. Had my adviser been a better scholar, he would have celebrated my questions, not dismissed them. He offered me only the cliché that beauty is in the eye of the beholder, and since science separates the observer and the observed, by definition beauty could not be a valid scientific question. I should have been told that my questions were bigger than science could touch.

He was right about beauty being in the eye of the beholder, especially when it comes to purple and yellow. Color perception in humans relies on banks of specialized receptor cells, the rods and cones in the retina. The job of the cone cells is to absorb light of different wavelengths and pass it on to the brain's visual cortex, where it can be interpreted. The visible light spectrum, the rainbow of colors, is broad, so the most effective means of discerning color is not one generalized jack-of-all-trades cone cell, but rather an array of specialists, each perfectly tuned to absorb certain wavelengths. The human eye has three kinds. One type excels at detecting red and associated wavelengths. There is one for blue and the last one optimally perceives light of two colors: purple and yellow.

The human eye is superbly equipped to detect these colors and send a signal pulsing to the brain. This doesn't explain why I perceive them as beautiful, but it does explain why that combination gets my undivided attention. I asked my artist friends about the power of purple and gold, and they sent me right to the color wheel: these two are complementary colors, as different in nature as could be. In composing a palette, putting them together makes each more vivid; just a touch of one will bring out the other. Purple and yellow are a reciprocal pair.

Our eyes are so sensitive to these wavelengths that the cones can get oversaturated and the stimulus pours over onto the other cells. A printmaker I know showed me that if you stare for a long time at a block of yellow and then shift your gaze to a white sheet of paper, you will see it, for a moment, as violet. This phenomenon—the colored afterimage—occurs because there is energetic reciprocity between purple and yellow pigments, which goldenrod and asters knew well before we did.

The real beholder whose eye they hope to catch is a bee bent on pollination. As it turns out, goldenrod and asters appear very similarly to bee eyes and human eyes. Their striking contrast when they grow together makes them the

20

most attractive target in the whole meadow. Growing together, both receive more pollinator visits than they would if they were growing alone.

It's a testable hypothesis; it's a question of science, a question of art, and a question of beauty. Why are they beautiful together? It is a phenomenon simultaneously material and spiritual, for which we need all wavelengths of knowledge. When I stare too long at the world with science eyes, I see an afterimage of indigenous knowledge. Might science and traditional knowledge be purple and yellow to one another? We see the world more fully when we use both.

The question of goldenrod and asters was of course just emblematic of what I really wanted to know. It was an architecture of relationships that I yearned to understand. I wanted to see the shimmering threads that hold it all together and why the most ordinary scrap of meadow can rock us back on our heels in awe. And I wanted to know why we love the world.

There was a time when I teetered precariously with an awkward foot in each of two worlds: the scientific and the indigenous. But then I learned to fly. It was the bees that showed me how to move between different flowers—to drink the nectar and gather pollen from both. It is this dance of cross-pollination that can produce a new species of knowledge, a new way of being in the world. After all, there aren't two worlds, there is just this one good green earth.

25   That September pairing of purple and gold is lived reciprocity; its wisdom is that the beauty of one is illuminated by the radiance of the other. Science and art, matter and spirit, indigenous knowledge and Western science—can they be goldenrod and asters for each other? When I am in their presence, their beauty asks me for reciprocity, to be the complementary color, to make something beautiful in response.

MLA CITATION

Kimmerer, Robin Wall. "Goldenrod and Asters: My Life with Plants." *The Norton Reader: An Anthology of Nonfiction*, edited by Melissa A. Goldthwaite et al., 15th ed., W. W. Norton, 2020, pp. 544–48.

QUESTIONS

1. Robin Wall Kimmerer describes a time when she "teetered precariously with an awkward foot in each of two worlds" (paragraph 24), but she learned to bring scientific and indigenous knowledge together. What does she value from each of those worlds? How do those areas of knowledge complement each other?

2. Beauty is a theme in Kimmerer's essay. What disciplines does she draw from to discuss beauty?

3. Choose two disciplines or areas of knowledge that interest you. What distinguishes these disciplines? How might you bring these areas of knowledge together? Write a proposal for an interdisciplinary project that looks at a specific question through the lenses of two disciplines.

CORMAC CULLINAN
If Nature Had Rights

I T WAS THE SUDDEN RUSH of the goats' bodies against the side of the *boma*[1] that woke him. Picking up a spear and stick, the Kenyan farmer slipped out into the warm night and crept toward the pen. All he could see was the spotted, sloping hindquarters of the animal trying to force itself between the poles to get at the goats—but it was enough. He drove his spear deep into the hyena.

The elders who gathered under the meeting tree to deliberate on the matter were clearly unhappy with the farmer's explanation. A man appointed by the traditional court to represent the interests of the hyena had testified that his careful examination of the body had revealed that the deceased was a female who was still suckling pups. He argued that given the prevailing drought and the hyena's need to nourish her young, her behavior in attempting to scavenge food from human settlements was reasonable and that it was wrong to have killed her. The elders then cross-examined the farmer carefully. Did he appreciate, they asked, that such killings were contrary to customary law? Had he considered the hyena's situation and whether or not she had caused harm? Could he not have simply driven her away? Eventually the elders ordered the man's clan to pay compensation for the harm done by driving more than one hundred of their goats (a fortune in that community) into the bush, where they could be eaten by the hyenas and other wild carnivores.

The story, told to me by a Kenyan friend, illustrates African customary law's concern with restorative justice rather than retribution. Wrongdoing is seen as a symptom of a breakdown in relationships within the wider community, and the elders seek to restore the damaged relationship rather than focusing on identifying and punishing the wrongdoer.

The verdict of a traditional African court regarding hyenacide may seem of mere anthropological interest to contemporary Americans. In most of today's legal systems, decisions that harm ecological communities have to be challenged primarily on the basis of whether or not the correct procedures have been followed. Yet consider how much greater the prospects of survival would be for most of life on Earth if mechanisms existed for imposing collective responsibility and liability on human communities and for restoring damaged relations with the larger natural community. Imagine if we had elders with a deep understanding of the lore of the wild who spoke for the Earth as well as for humans. If we did, how might they order us to compensate for, say, the anticipated destruction of the entire Arctic ecosystem because of global climate change, to

Published in Orion (2008), *a magazine founded in 1982 to explore "an emerging alternative worldview informed by a growing ecological awareness and the need for cultural change."*

1. Swahili for a hut or enclosure.

restore relations with the polar bears and other people and creatures who depend on that ecosystem? How many polluting power plants and vehicles would it be fair to sacrifice to make amends?

5   "So what would a radically different law-driven consciousness look like?" The question was posed over three decades ago by a University of Southern California law professor as his lecture drew to a close. "One in which Nature had rights," he continued. "Yes, rivers, lakes, trees. . . . How could such a posture in law affect a community's view of itself?" Professor Christopher Stone may as well have announced that he was an alien life form. Rivers and trees are objects, not subjects, in the eyes of the law and are by definition incapable of holding rights. His speculations created an uproar.

Stone stepped away from that lecture a little dazed by the response from the class but determined to back up his argument. He realized that for nature to have rights the law would have to be changed so that, first, a suit could be brought in the name of an aspect of nature, such as a river; second, a polluter could be held liable for harming a river; and third, judgments could be made that would benefit a river. Stone quickly identified a pending appeal to the United States Supreme Court against a decision of the Ninth Circuit that raised these issues. The Ninth Circuit Court of Appeals had found that the Sierra Club Legal Defense Fund was not "aggrieved" or "adversely affected" by the proposed development of the Mineral King Valley in the Sierra Nevada Mountains by Walt Disney Enterprises, Inc. This decision meant that the Sierra Club did not have "standing" so the court didn't need to consider the merits of the matter. Clearly, if the Mineral King Valley itself had been recognized as having rights, it would have been an adversely affected party and would have had the necessary standing.

Fortuitously, Supreme Court Justice William O. Douglas was writing a preface to the next edition of the *Southern California Law Review*. Stone's seminal "Should Trees Have Standing? Toward Legal Rights for Natural Objects" ("Trees") was hurriedly squeezed into the journal and read by Justice Douglas before the Court issued its judgment. In "Trees," Stone argued that courts should grant legal standing to guardians to represent the rights of nature, in much the same way as guardians are appointed to represent the rights of infants. In order to do so, the law would have to recognize that nature was not just a conglomeration of objects that could be owned, but was a subject that itself had legal rights and the standing to be represented in the courts to enforce those rights. The article eventually formed the basis for a famous dissenting judgment by Justice Douglas in the 1972 case of *Sierra Club v. Morton* in which he expressed the opinion that "contemporary public concern for protecting nature's ecological equilibrium should lead to the conferral of standing upon environmental objects to sue for their own preservation."

Perhaps one of the most important things about "Trees" is that it ventured beyond the accepted boundaries of law as we know it and argued that the conceptual framework for law in the United States (and by analogy, elsewhere) required further evolution and expansion. Stone began by addressing the initial reaction that such ideas are outlandish. Throughout legal history, as he pointed out, each extension of legal rights had previously been unthinkable. The emancipation of slaves and the extension of civil rights to African Americans, women, and children were once rejected as absurd or dangerous by authorities. The Founding Fathers, after all, were hardly conscious of the hypocrisy inherent in proclaiming the inalienable rights of all men while simultaneously denying basic rights to children, women, and to African and Native Americans.

"Trees" has since become a classic for students of environmental law, but after three decades its impact on law in the United States has been limited. After it was written, the courts made it somewhat easier for citizens to litigate on behalf of other species and the environment by expanding the powers and responsibilities of authorities to act as trustees of areas used by the public (e.g., navigable waters, beaches, and parks). Unfortunately, these gains have been followed in more recent years by judicial attempts to restrict the legal standing of environmental groups. Damages for harm to the environment are now recoverable in some cases and are sometimes applied for the benefit of the environment. However, these changes fall far short of what Stone advocated for in "Trees." The courts still have not recognized that nature has directly enforceable rights.

Communities have always used laws to express the ideals to which they aspire and to regulate how power is exercised. Law is also a social tool that is usually shaped and wielded most effectively by the powerful. Consequently, law tends to entrench a society's fundamental idea of itself and of how the world works. So, for example, even when American society began to regard slavery as morally abhorrent, it was not able to peaceably end the practice because the fundamental concept that slaves were property had been hard-wired into the legal system. The abolition of slavery required not only that the enfranchised recognize that slaves were entitled to the same rights as other humans, but also a political effort to change the laws that denied those rights. It took both the Civil War and the Thirteenth Amendment to outlaw slavery. The Thirteenth Amendment, in turn, played a role in changing American society's idea of what was acceptable, thereby providing the bedrock for the subsequent civil rights movement.

In the eyes of American law today, most of the community of life on Earth remains mere property, natural "resources" to be exploited, bought, and sold just as slaves were. This means that environmentalists are seldom seen as activists fighting to uphold fundamental rights, but rather as criminals who infringe upon the property rights of others. It also means that actions that damage the ecosystems and the natural processes on which life depends, such as Earth's climate, are poorly regulated. Climate change is an obvious and dramatic symptom of the failure of human government to regulate human behavior in a manner that takes account of the fact that human welfare is directly dependent on the health of our planet and cannot be achieved at its expense.

In the scientific world there has been more progress. It's been almost forty years since James Lovelock first proposed the "Gaia hypothesis": a theory that

Earth regulates itself in a manner that keeps the composition of the atmosphere and average temperatures within a range conducive to life. Derided or dismissed by most people at the time, the Gaia hypothesis is now accepted by many as scientific theory. In 2001, more than a thousand scientists signed a declaration that begins "The Earth is a self-regulating system made up from all life, including humans, and from the oceans, the atmosphere and the surface rocks," a statement that would have been unthinkable for most scientists when "Trees" was written.

The acceptance of Lovelock's hypothesis can be understood as part of a drift in the scientific world away from a mechanistic understanding of the universe toward the realization that no aspect of nature can be understood without looking at it within the context of the systems of which it forms a part. Unfortunately, this insight has been slow to penetrate the world of law and politics.

But what if we were to imagine a society in which our purpose was to act as good citizens of the Earth as a whole?

15   What might a governance system look like if it were established to protect the rights of all members of a particular biological community, instead of only humans? Cicero[2] pointed out that each of our rights and freedoms must be limited in order that others may be free. It is far past time that we should consider limiting the rights of humans so they cannot unjustifiably prevent nonhuman members of a community from playing their part. Any legal system designed to give effect to modern scientific understandings (or, indeed, to many cultures' ancient understandings) of how the universe functions would have to prohibit humans from driving other species to extinction or deliberately destroying the functioning of major ecosystems. In the absence of such regulatory mechanisms, an oppressive and self-destructive regime will inevitably emerge. As indeed it has.

In particular, we should examine the fact that, in the eyes of the law, corporations are considered people and entitled to civil rights. We often forget that corporations are only a few centuries old and have been continually evolving since their inception. Imagine what could be done if we changed the fiduciary responsibilities of directors to include obligations not only to profitability but also to the whole natural world, and if we imposed collective personal liability on corporate managers and stockholders to restore any damage that they cause to natural communities. Imagine if landowners who abused and degraded land lost the right to use it. In an Earth-centered community, all institutions through which humans act collectively would be designed to require behavior that is socially responsible from the perspective of the whole community. A society whose concern is to maintain the integrity or wholeness of the Earth must also refine its ideas about what is "right" and "wrong." We may find it more useful to condone or disapprove of human conduct by considering the extent to which an action increases or decreases the health of the whole community and the quality or intimacy of the relationships between its members. As Aldo Leopold's famous land ethic states, "a thing is right when it tends to preserve the integrity, stability, and beauty of the biotic community. It is wrong

2. Roman orator and lawyer (106–43 B.C.E.).

when it tends otherwise."[3] From this perspective, individual and collective human rights must be contextualized within, and balanced against, the rights of the other members and communities of Earth.

On September 19, 2006, the Tamaqua Borough of Schuylkill County, Pennsylvania, passed a sewage sludge ordinance that recognizes natural communities and ecosystems within the borough as legal persons for the purposes of enforcing civil rights. It also strips corporations that engage in the land application of sludge of their rights to be treated as "persons" and consequently of their civil rights. One of its effects is that the borough or any of its residents may file a lawsuit on behalf of an ecosystem to recover compensatory and punitive damages for any harm done by the land application of sewage sludge. Damages recovered in this way must be paid to the borough and used to restore those ecosystems and natural communities.

According to Thomas Linzey, the lawyer from the Community Environmental Legal Defense Fund who assisted Tamaqua Borough, this ordinance marks the first time in the history of municipalities in the United States that something like this has happened. Coming after more than 150 years of judicially sanctioned expansion of the legal powers of corporations in the U.S., this ordinance is more than extraordinary—it is revolutionary. In a world where the corporation is king and all forms of life other than humans are objects in the eyes of the law, this is a small community's Boston tea party.[4]

In Africa, nongovernmental organizations in eleven countries are also asserting local community rights in order to promote the conservation of biodiversity and sustainable development. Members of the African Biodiversity Network (ABN) have coined the term "cultural biodiversity" to emphasize that knowledge and practices that support biodiversity are embedded in cultural tradition. The ABN works with rural communities and schools to recover and spread traditional knowledge and practices.

This is part of a wider effort to build local communities, protect the environment by encouraging those communities to value, retain, and build on traditional African cosmologies, and to govern themselves as part of a wider Earth community.

These small examples, emerging shoots of what might be termed "Earth democracy," are pressing upward despite the odds. It may well be that Earth-centered legal systems will have to grow organically out of human-scale communities, and communities of communities, that understand that they must function as integrated parts of wider natural communities. In the face of climate change and other enormous environmental challenges, our future as a species depends on those people who are creating the legal and political spaces within which our connection to the rest of our community here on Earth is recognized. The day will come when the failure of our laws to recognize the

20

3. Aldo Leopold (1887–1948), author of *A Sand County Almanac* (1949), which includes his essay "The Land Ethic."
4. American colonist protest (1773) against the British-imposed Tea Act.

right of a river to flow, to prohibit acts that destabilize Earth's climate, or to impose a duty to respect the intrinsic value and right to exist of all life will be as reprehensible as allowing people to be bought and sold. We will only flourish by changing these systems and claiming our identity, as well as assuming our responsibilities, as members of the Earth community.

MLA CITATION

Cullinan, Cormac. "If Nature Had Rights." *The Norton Reader: An Anthology of Nonfiction*, edited by Melissa A. Goldthwaite et al., 15th ed., W. W. Norton, 2020, pp. 549–54.

QUESTIONS

1. Cormac Cullinan asks, "What might a governance system look like if it were established to protect the rights of all members of a particular biological community, instead of only humans?" (paragraph 15). What are the features of that system for Cullinan? Point to passages that support your answer.

2. Cullinan often references slavery in his argument. Explain the comparisons he makes. Do you find these comparisons compelling? Why or why not?

3. Write an argument either for or against giving legal rights to elements of nature. If you argue for such rights, use evidence beyond what Cullinan provides.

11 MEDIA AND COMMUNICATION

> The specific which you have discovered is an aid not to memory, but to reminiscence, and you give your disciples not truth, but only the semblance of truth; they will be hearers of many things and will have learned nothing; they will appear to be omniscient and will generally know nothing; they will be tiresome company, having the show of wisdom without the reality.
>
> —PLATO

In Plato's *Phaedrus*, Socrates recounts an Egyptian myth in which the god Theuth presents a series of inventions to Thamus, the king of Egypt. The last of these inventions is writing. Thamus responds in the words of our epigraph, not by thanking Theuth for his innovation but by predicting its unintended harmful effects. In modern terms, he worries that writing will cause reality (memory, knowledge, truth) to be supplanted by mere simulation (reminiscence, the semblance of truth, the appearance of knowledge); he recognizes that writing is not simply a tool that people can use as they will but a technology that through its use will change the nature of people.

The authors in this chapter similarly consider modern media and communication technologies, from the first telephone through the latest smartphone. Like Plato, they are concerned less with the technologies themselves than with how they change our inherent human capacities, our connection to the world, and our relationships to one another. As you read the chapter's selections, attend not just to what their authors are saying but also to how they say it, to their style and form. Some of the chapter's authors—Nicholas Carr in "Is Google Making Us Stupid?," Sherry Turkle in "The End of Forgetting," and Jean M. Twenge in "Have Smartphones Destroyed a Generation?"—express ambivalences akin to those voiced by Plato's Thamus. Drawing on personal report, historical examples, and references to experts, Carr argues that the internet has eroded our ability to give sustained attention to ordinary printed texts; Turkle interprets stories of people interacting with talking machines to show how such interactions are altering the nature and meaning of relationships and conversation; Twenge relies on statistical evidence leavened by anecdote to document the ways in which smartphones are defining today's generation of teenagers, which she dubs "iGen." In the eyes of each of these writers, our new media and communication technologies threaten to alter what it is to be human. Eula Biss, in her lyric essay "Time and Distance Overcome," expresses an ambivalence of a different sort. By juxtaposing historical exposition and stark description, she illuminates an unsettling correlation between the proliferation of telephone poles, which were being rapidly erected in the decades after Alexander Graham Bell invented the telephone in 1876, and the frequency of their use in lynchings. The telephone's link to these atrocities forces us to consider a challenging truth: a new technology is not *apart from* but *a part of* the society that creates it. As such, in the uses to which it is put, it can reflect the best and worst of a society's character.

Other of the chapter's authors are more enthusiastic. In his article "Harnessing the Power of Feedback Loops," Thomas Goetz extols the potential of cheap, ubiquitous sensors to provide us with real-time information that we can use to improve every aspect of our lives. In "Be a Gamer, Save the World," Jane McGonigal touts the virtues of video games, contending that far from being a waste of time or even dangerous, they can be sources of community and innovation. Tom Bissell is likewise a champion of video games, but his personal essay "Extra Lives: Why Video Games Matter" focuses not on their practical utility but on the unique aesthetic pleasures video games can deliver. Lauren Michele Jackson, in "A Unified Theory of Meme Death," acknowledges memes as a cultural form worthy of serious critical attention and develops a powerful framework for understanding them. Culinary historian Laura Shapiro, in her op-ed "Instagram Your Leftovers: History Depends on It," suggests that social media can capture for the historical record aspects of ordinary life that would otherwise be lost.

As you read the selections in this chapter, think about the place of media and communication technologies in your own life. How do the internet, video games, and your smartphone affect the way you relate to others? How do they affect your sense of self, of purpose, of happiness? Consider too the ways in which media and communication technologies both shape and are shaped by the broader society and culture, a society and culture that have given rise to them and of which they are a part. What new potentials have they created, and at what costs? You might also step back from the present to research an older technology: paper, the printing press, the telegraph, the ball-point pen. What developments or disruptions did it enable or encourage? Then, in light of what you learned, think again about our own time. Ours is certainly an age of profound change, but change is not exclusive to our age. What has precedent, and what seems truly new?

NICHOLAS CARR

Is Google Making Us Stupid?

AVE, STOP. STOP, WILL YOU? Stop, Dave. Will you stop, Dave?" So the supercomputer HAL pleads with the implacable astronaut Dave Bowman in a famous and weirdly poignant scene toward the end of Stanley Kubrick's *2001: A Space Odyssey*.[1] Bowman, having nearly been sent to a deep-space death by the malfunc-

Published in the Atlantic *(2008), a magazine covering literature, culture, and politics, and expanded into a book,* The Shallows: What the Internet Is Doing to Our Brains *(2010). Nicholas Carr has written widely on the impact of technology; he blogs at roughtype.com.*

1. Science fiction film (1968) about artificial intelligence in which HAL, a computer, threatens to take control of a human space mission.

tioning machine, is calmly, coldly disconnecting the memory circuits that control its artificial "brain." "Dave, my mind is going," HAL says, forlornly. "I can feel it. I can feel it."

I can feel it, too. Over the past few years I've had an uncomfortable sense that someone, or something, has been tinkering with my brain, remapping the neural circuitry, reprogramming the memory. My mind isn't going—so far as I can tell—but it's changing. I'm not thinking the way I used to think. I can feel it most strongly when I'm reading. Immersing myself in a book or a lengthy article used to be easy. My mind would get caught up in the narrative or the turns of the argument, and I'd spend hours strolling through long stretches of prose. That's rarely the case anymore. Now my concentration often starts to drift after two or three pages. I get fidgety, lose the thread, begin looking for something else to do. I feel as if I'm always dragging my wayward brain back to the text. The deep reading that used to come naturally has become a struggle.

I think I know what's going on. For more than a decade now, I've been spending a lot of time online, searching and surfing and sometimes adding to the great databases of the Internet. The Web has been a godsend to me as a writer. Research that once required days in the stacks or periodical rooms of libraries can now be done in minutes. A few Google searches, some quick clicks on hyperlinks, and I've got the telltale fact or pithy quote I was after. Even when I'm not working, I'm as likely as not to be foraging in the Web's info-thickets— reading and writing e-mails, scanning headlines and blog posts, watching videos and listening to podcasts, or just tripping from link to link to link. (Unlike footnotes, to which they're sometimes likened, hyperlinks don't merely point to related works; they propel you toward them.)

For me, as for others, the Net is becoming a universal medium, the conduit for most of the information that flows through my eyes and ears and into my mind. The advantages of having immediate access to such an incredibly rich store of information are many, and they've been widely described and duly applauded. "The perfect recall of silicon memory," *Wired*'s Clive Thompson has written, "can be an enormous boon to thinking." But that boon comes at a price. As the media theorist Marshall McLuhan[2] pointed out in the 1960s, media are not just passive channels of information. They supply the stuff of thought, but they also shape the process of thought. And what the Net seems to be doing is chipping away my capacity for concentration and contemplation. My mind now expects to take in information the way the Net distributes it: in a swiftly moving stream of particles. Once I was a scuba diver in the sea of words. Now I zip along the surface like a guy on a Jet Ski.

5   I'm not the only one. When I mention my troubles with reading to friends and acquaintances—literary types, most of them—many say they're having similar experiences. The more they use the Web, the more they have to fight to stay focused on long pieces of writing. Some of the bloggers I follow have also begun mentioning the phenomenon. Scott Karp, who writes a blog about online media, recently confessed that he has stopped reading books altogether. "I was a lit major in college, and used to be [a] voracious book reader," he wrote. "What happened?" He speculates on the answer: "What if I do all my reading on the web not so much because the way I read has changed, i.e. I'm just seeking convenience, but because the way I THINK has changed?"

Bruce Friedman, who blogs regularly about the use of computers in medicine, also has described how the Internet has altered his mental habits. "I now have almost totally lost the ability to read and absorb a longish article on the web or in print," he wrote earlier this year. A pathologist who has long been on the faculty of the University of Michigan Medical School, Friedman elaborated on his comment in a telephone conversation with me. His thinking, he said, has taken on a "staccato" quality, reflecting the way he quickly scans short passages of text from many sources online. "I can't read *War and Peace*[3] anymore," he admitted. "I've lost the ability to do that. Even a blog post of more than three or four paragraphs is too much to absorb. I skim it."

Anecdotes alone don't prove much. And we still await the long-term neurological and psychological experiments that will provide a definitive picture of how Internet use affects cognition. But a recently published study of online research habits, conducted by scholars from University College London, suggests that we may well be in the midst of a sea change in the way we read and think. As part of the five-year research program, the scholars examined computer logs documenting the behavior of visitors to two popular research sites, one operated by the British Library and one by a U.K. educational consortium, that provide access to journal articles, e-books, and other sources of written

---

2. Canadian media critic (1911–1980) known for his phrase "the medium is the message."

3. Five-volume novel (1869) by Leo Tolstoy depicting five Russian families' experiences during the Napoleonic Wars (1803–14).

information. They found that people using the sites exhibited "a form of skimming activity," hopping from one source to another and rarely returning to any source they'd already visited. They typically read no more than one or two pages of an article or book before they would "bounce" out to another site. Sometimes they'd save a long article, but there's no evidence that they ever went back and actually read it. The authors of the study report:

> It is clear that users are not reading online in the traditional sense; indeed there are signs that new forms of "reading" are emerging as users "power browse" horizontally through titles, contents pages and abstracts going for quick wins. It almost seems that they go online to avoid reading in the traditional sense.

Thanks to the ubiquity of text on the Internet, not to mention the popularity of text-messaging on cell phones, we may well be reading more today than we did in the 1970s or 1980s, when television was our medium of choice. But it's a different kind of reading, and behind it lies a different kind of thinking—perhaps even a new sense of the self. "We are not only *what* we read," says Maryanne Wolf, a developmental psychologist at Tufts University and the author of *Proust and the Squid: The Story and Science of the Reading Brain*. "We are *how* we read." Wolf worries that the style of reading promoted by the Net, a style that puts "efficiency" and "immediacy" above all else, may be weakening our capacity for the kind of deep reading that emerged when an earlier technology, the printing press, made long and complex works of prose commonplace. When we read online, she says, we tend to become "mere decoders of information." Our ability to interpret text, to make the rich mental connections that form when we read deeply and without distraction, remains largely disengaged.

Reading, explains Wolf, is not an instinctive skill for human beings. It's not etched into our genes the way speech is. We have to teach our minds how to translate the symbolic characters we see into the language we understand. And the media or other technologies we use in learning and practicing the craft of reading play an important part in shaping the neural circuits inside our brains. Experiments demonstrate that readers of ideograms, such as the Chinese, develop a mental circuitry for reading that is very different from the circuitry found in those of us whose written language employs an alphabet. The variations extend across many regions of the brain, including those that govern such essential cognitive functions as memory and the interpretation of visual and auditory stimuli. We can expect as well that the circuits woven by our use of the Net will be different from those woven by our reading of books and other printed works.

Sometime in 1882, Friedrich Nietzsche[4] bought a typewriter—a Malling-Hansen   10
Writing Ball, to be precise. His vision was failing, and keeping his eyes focused on a page had become exhausting and painful, often bringing on crushing headaches. He had been forced to curtail his writing, and he feared that he would soon have to give it up. The typewriter rescued him, at least for a time. Once he

---

4. German critic and philosopher (1844–1900).

had mastered touch-typing, he was able to write with his eyes closed, using only the tips of his fingers. Words could once again flow from his mind to the page.

But the machine had a subtler effect on his work. One of Nietzsche's friends, a composer, noticed a change in the style of his writing. His already terse prose had become even tighter, more telegraphic. "Perhaps you will through this instrument even take to a new idiom," the friend wrote in a letter, noting that, in his own work, his "thoughts in music and language often depend on the quality of pen and paper."

"You are right," Nietzsche replied, "our writing equipment takes part in the forming of our thoughts." Under the sway of the machine, writes the German media scholar Friedrich A. Kittler, Nietzsche's prose "changed from arguments to aphorisms, from thoughts to puns, from rhetoric to telegram style."

The human brain is almost infinitely malleable. People used to think that our mental meshwork, the dense connections formed among the 100 billion or so neurons inside our skulls, was largely fixed by the time we reached adulthood. But brain researchers have discovered that that's not the case. James Olds, a professor of neuroscience who directs the Krasnow Institute for Advanced Study at George Mason University, says that even the adult mind "is very plastic." Nerve cells routinely break old connections and form new ones. "The brain," according to Olds, "has the ability to reprogram itself on the fly, altering the way it functions."

As we use what the sociologist Daniel Bell has called our "intellectual technologies"—the tools that extend our mental rather than our physical capacities—we inevitably begin to take on the qualities of those technologies. The mechanical clock, which came into common use in the 14th century, provides a compelling example. In *Technics and Civilization*, the historian and cultural critic Lewis Mumford described how the clock "disassociated time from human events and helped create the belief in an independent world of mathematically measurable sequences." The "abstract framework of divided time" became "the point of reference for both action and thought."

15   The clock's methodical ticking helped bring into being the scientific mind and the scientific man. But it also took something away. As the late MIT computer scientist Joseph Weizenbaum observed in his 1976 book, *Computer Power and Human Reason: From Judgment to Calculation*, the conception of the world that emerged from the widespread use of timekeeping instruments "remains an impoverished version of the older one, for it rests on a rejection of those direct experiences that formed the basis for, and indeed constituted, the old reality." In deciding when to eat, to work, to sleep, to rise, we stopped listening to our senses and started obeying the clock.

The process of adapting to new intellectual technologies is reflected in the changing metaphors we use to explain ourselves to ourselves. When the mechanical clock arrived, people began thinking of their brains as operating "like clockwork." Today, in the age of software, we have come to think of them as operating "like computers." But the changes, neuroscience tells us, go much deeper than metaphor. Thanks to our brain's plasticity, the adaptation occurs also at a biological level.

The Internet promises to have particularly far-reaching effects on cognition. In a paper published in 1936, the British mathematician Alan Turing proved that a digital computer, which at the time existed only as a theoretical machine, could be programmed to perform the function of any other information-processing device. And that's what we're seeing today. The Internet, an immeasurably powerful computing system, is subsuming most of our other intellectual technologies. It's becoming our map and our clock, our printing press and our typewriter, our calculator and our telephone, and our radio and TV.

When the Net absorbs a medium, that medium is re-created in the Net's image. It injects the medium's content with hyperlinks, blinking ads, and other digital gewgaws, and it surrounds the content with the content of all the other media it has absorbed. A new e-mail message, for instance, may announce its arrival as we're glancing over the latest headlines at a newspaper's site. The result is to scatter our attention and diffuse our concentration.

The Net's influence doesn't end at the edges of a computer screen, either. As people's minds become attuned to the crazy quilt of Internet media, traditional media have to adapt to the audience's new expectations. Television programs add text crawls and pop-up ads, and magazines and newspapers shorten their articles, introduce capsule summaries, and crowd their pages with easy-to-browse info-snippets. When, in March of this year, *The New York Times* decided to devote the second and third pages of every edition to article abstracts, its design director, Tom Bodkin, explained that the "shortcuts" would give harried readers a quick "taste" of the day's news, sparing them the "less efficient" method of actually turning the pages and reading the articles. Old media have little choice but to play by the new-media rules.

Never has a communications system played so many roles in our lives—or exerted such broad influence over our thoughts—as the Internet does today. Yet, for all that's been written about the Net, there's been little consideration of how, exactly, it's reprogramming us. The Net's intellectual ethic remains obscure. 20

About the same time that Nietzsche started using his typewriter, an earnest young man named Frederick Winslow Taylor carried a stopwatch into the Midvale Steel plant in Philadelphia and began a historic series of experiments aimed at improving the efficiency of the plant's machinists. With the approval of Midvale's owners, he recruited a group of factory hands, set them to work on various metalworking machines, and recorded and timed their every movement as well as the operations of the machines. By breaking down every job into a sequence of small, discrete steps and then testing different ways of performing each one, Taylor created a set of precise instructions—an "algorithm," we might say today—for how each worker should work. Midvale's employees grumbled about the strict new regime, claiming that it turned them into little more than automatons, but the factory's productivity soared.

More than a hundred years after the invention of the steam engine, the Industrial Revolution had at last found its philosophy and its philosopher. Taylor's tight industrial choreography—his "system," as he liked to call it—was embraced by manufacturers throughout the country and, in time, around the world. Seeking maximum speed, maximum efficiency, and maximum output, factory owners used time-and-motion studies to organize their work and configure the jobs of their workers. The goal, as Taylor defined it in his celebrated

1911 treatise, *The Principles of Scientific Management*, was to identify and adopt, for every job, the "one best method" of work and thereby to effect "the gradual substitution of science for rule of thumb throughout the mechanic arts." Once his system was applied to all acts of manual labor, Taylor assured his followers, it would bring about a restructuring not only of industry but of society, creating a utopia of perfect efficiency. "In the past the man has been first," he declared; "in the future the system must be first."

Taylor's system is still very much with us; it remains the ethic of industrial manufacturing. And now, thanks to the growing power that computer engineers and software coders wield over our intellectual lives, Taylor's ethic is beginning to govern the realm of the mind as well. The Internet is a machine designed for the efficient and automated collection, transmission, and manipulation of information, and its legions of programmers are intent on finding the "one best method"—the perfect algorithm—to carry out every mental movement of what we've come to describe as "knowledge work."

Google's headquarters, in Mountain View, California—the Googleplex—is the Internet's high church, and the religion practiced inside its walls is Taylorism. Google, says its chief executive, Eric Schmidt, is "a company that's founded around the science of measurement," and it is striving to "systematize everything" it does. Drawing on the terabytes of behavioral data it collects through its search engine and other sites, it carries out thousands of experiments a day, according to the *Harvard Business Review*, and it uses the results to refine the algorithms that increasingly control how people find information and extract meaning from it. What Taylor did for the work of the hand, Google is doing for the work of the mind.

25   The company has declared that its mission is "to organize the world's information and make it universally accessible and useful." It seeks to develop "the perfect search engine," which it defines as something that "understands exactly what you mean and gives you back exactly what you want." In Google's view, information is a kind of commodity, a utilitarian resource that can be mined and processed with industrial efficiency. The more pieces of information we can "access" and the faster we can extract their gist, the more productive we become as thinkers.

Where does it end? Sergey Brin and Larry Page, the gifted young men who founded Google while pursuing doctoral degrees in computer science at Stanford, speak frequently of their desire to turn their search engine into an artificial intelligence, a HAL-like machine that might be connected directly to our brains. "The ultimate search engine is something as smart as people—or smarter," Page said in a speech a few years back. "For us, working on search is a way to work on artificial intelligence." In a 2004 interview with *Newsweek*, Brin said, "Certainly if you had all the world's information directly attached to your brain, or an artificial brain that was smarter than your brain, you'd be better off." Last year, Page told a convention of scientists that Google is "really trying to build artificial intelligence and to do it on a large scale."

Such an ambition is a natural one, even an admirable one, for a pair of math whizzes with vast quantities of cash at their disposal and a small army of computer scientists in their employ. A fundamentally scientific enterprise, Google is motivated by a desire to use technology, in Eric Schmidt's words, "to solve problems that have never been solved before," and artificial intelligence is the hardest problem out there. Why wouldn't Brin and Page want to be the ones to crack it?

Still, their easy assumption that we'd all "be better off" if our brains were supplemented, or even replaced, by an artificial intelligence is unsettling. It suggests a belief that intelligence is the output of a mechanical process, a series of discrete steps that can be isolated, measured, and optimized. In Google's world, the world we enter when we go online, there's little place for the fuzziness of contemplation. Ambiguity is not an opening for insight but a bug to be fixed. The human brain is just an outdated computer that needs a faster processor and a bigger hard drive.

The idea that our minds should operate as high-speed data-processing machines is not only built into the workings of the Internet, it is the network's reigning business model as well. The faster we surf across the Web—the more links we click and pages we view—the more opportunities Google and other companies gain to collect information about us and to feed us advertisements. Most of the proprietors of the commercial Internet have a financial stake in collecting the crumbs of data we leave behind as we flit from link to link—the more crumbs, the better. The last thing these companies want is to encourage leisurely reading or slow, concentrated thought. It's in their economic interest to drive us to distraction.

Maybe I'm just a worrywart. Just as there's a tendency to glorify technological progress, there's a countertendency to expect the worst of every new tool or machine. In Plato's *Phaedrus*,[5] Socrates bemoaned the development of writing. He feared that, as people came to rely on the written word as a substitute for the knowledge they used to carry inside their heads, they would, in the words of one of the dialogue's characters, "cease to exercise their memory and become forgetful." And because they would be able to "receive a quantity of information without proper instruction," they would "be thought very knowledgeable when they are for the most part quite ignorant." They would be "filled with the conceit of wisdom instead of real wisdom." Socrates wasn't wrong— the new technology did often have the effects he feared—but he was shortsighted. He couldn't foresee the many ways that writing and reading would serve to spread information, spur fresh ideas, and expand human knowledge (if not wisdom).

The arrival of Gutenberg's printing press, in the 15th century, set off another round of teeth gnashing. The Italian humanist Hieronimo Squarciafico worried that the easy availability of books would lead to intellectual laziness, making men "less studious" and weakening their minds. Others argued that cheaply printed books and broadsheets would undermine religious authority, demean the work of scholars and scribes, and spread sedition and debauchery. As New York University professor Clay Shirky notes, "Most of the arguments made against the printing

30

5. As noted in the chapter introduction, the *Phaedrus*, a philosophical dialogue by the Greek philosopher Plato (c. 429–347 B.C.E.), contains an extended discussion of the relative merits of speech and writing.

press were correct, even prescient." But, again, the doomsayers were unable to imagine the myriad blessings that the printed word would deliver.

So, yes, you should be skeptical of my skepticism. Perhaps those who dismiss critics of the Internet as Luddites[6] or nostalgists will be proved correct, and from our hyperactive, data-stoked minds will spring a golden age of intellectual discovery and universal wisdom. Then again, the Net isn't the alphabet, and although it may replace the printing press, it produces something altogether different. The kind of deep reading that a sequence of printed pages promotes is valuable not just for the knowledge we acquire from the author's words but for the intellectual vibrations those words set off within our own minds. In the quiet spaces opened up by the sustained, undistracted reading of a book, or by any other act of contemplation, for that matter, we make our own associations, draw our own inferences and analogies, foster our own ideas. Deep reading, as Maryanne Wolf argues, is indistinguishable from deep thinking.

If we lose those quiet spaces, or fill them up with "content," we will sacrifice something important not only in our selves but in our culture. In a recent essay, the playwright Richard Foreman eloquently described what's at stake:

> I come from a tradition of Western culture, in which the ideal (my ideal) was the complex, dense and "cathedral-like" structure of the highly educated and articulate personality—a man or woman who carried inside themselves a personally constructed and unique version of the entire heritage of the West. [But now] I see within us all (myself included) the replacement of complex inner density with a new kind of self—evolving under the pressure of information overload and the technology of the "instantly available."

As we are drained of our "inner repertory of dense cultural inheritance," Foreman concluded, we risk turning into "pancake people—spread wide and thin as we connect with that vast network of information accessed by the mere touch of a button."

I'm haunted by that scene in *2001*. What makes it so poignant, and so weird, is the computer's emotional response to the disassembly of its mind: its despair as one circuit after another goes dark, its childlike pleading with the astronaut—"I can feel it. I can feel it. I'm afraid"—and its final reversion to what can only be called a state of innocence. HAL's outpouring of feeling contrasts with the emotionlessness that characterizes the human figures in the film, who go about their business with an almost robotic efficiency. Their thoughts and actions feel scripted, as if they're following the steps of an algorithm. In the world of *2001*, people have become so machinelike that the most human character turns out to be a machine. That's the essence of Kubrick's dark prophecy: as we come to rely on computers to mediate our understanding of the world, it is our own intelligence that flattens into artificial intelligence.

6. Originally nineteenth-century textile workers who opposed industrial automation; the term now refers to anyone who opposes new technologies.

MLA CITATION

Carr, Nicholas. "Is Google Making Us Stupid?" *The Norton Reader: An Anthology of Nonfiction*, edited by Melissa A. Goldthwaite et al., 15th ed., W. W. Norton, 2020, pp. 556–65.

QUESTIONS

1. Nicholas Carr poses a question with the title of this essay. How would you answer it? What examples does he offer to illustrate how Google is making us stupid? What counterexamples does he offer? What examples, on either side, would you add?

2. What are the most important advantages of "Taylorism" (paragraphs 21–24), or the application of scientific methods to human behavior? Are there aspects of human behavior that cannot be improved by such methods?

3. Carr is ambivalent about our reliance on technology, but Thomas Goetz (pp. 591–603) is more enthusiastic. Compare Carr's attitude about a new technology with Goetz's. What is your stance on these authors' relationships to technology, and why?

4. Interview a few people, including some who grew up using the internet and some who remember doing research mainly using books. Write your own analysis of the impact of the internet on our ability to think, reason, and research, building on Carr's essay and the anecdotes you collect.

SHERRY TURKLE
The End of Forgetting

> There are some people who have tried to make friends . . . but
> they've fallen through so badly that they give up. So when they
> hear this idea about robots being made to be companions, well,
> it's not going to be like a human and have its own mind to walk
> away or ever leave you or anything like that.
> —A SIXTEEN-YEAR-OLD GIRL, CONSIDERING
> THE IDEA OF A MORE SOPHISTICATED SIRI

THOREAU TALKS OF THREE CHAIRS and I think about a fourth.[1] Thoreau says that for the most expansive conversations, the deepest ones, he brought his guests out into nature—he calls it his withdrawing room, his "best room." For me, the fourth chair defines a philosophical space. Thoreau could go into nature, but now, we

From Sherry Turkle's book Reclaiming Conversation: The Power of Talk in a Digital Age *(2015). Turkle is a renowned authority on the psychological, interpersonal, and social effects of computers and communication technologies.*

1. Reference to *Walden* (1854), by American transcendentalist Henry David Thoreau, from which Turkle takes the epigraph of her book: "I had three chairs in my house; one for solitude, two for friendship, three for society."

contemplate both nature and a second nature of our own making, the world of the artificial and virtual. There, we meet machines that present themselves as open for conversation. The fourth chair raises the question: Who do we become when we talk to machines?

Some talking machines have modest ambitions—such as putting you through the paces of a job interview. But others aspire to far more. Most of these are just now coming on the scene: "caring robots" that will tend to our children and elders if we ourselves don't have the time, patience, or resources; automated psychotherapy programs that will substitute for humans in conversation. These present us with something new.

It may not feel new. All day every day, we connect with witty apps, we type our information into dialogue programs, and we get information from personal digital assistants. We are comfortable talking at machines and through machines. Now we are asked to join a new kind of conversation, one that promises "empathic" connections.

Machines have none to offer, and yet we persist in the desire for companionship and even communion with the inanimate. Has the simulation of empathy become empathy enough? The simulation of communion, communion enough?

5   The fourth chair defines a space that Thoreau could not have seen. It is our nick of time.

What do we forget when we talk to machines—and what can we remember?

"A COMPUTER BEAUTIFUL ENOUGH THAT A SOUL WOULD WANT TO LIVE IN IT"

In the early 1980s, I interviewed one of Marvin Minsky's young students who told me that, as he saw it, his hero, Minsky, one of the founders of artificial intelligence (AI), was "trying to create a computer beautiful enough that a soul would want to live in it."

That image has stayed with me for more than thirty years.

In the AI world, things have gone from mythic to prosaic. Today, children grow up with robotic pets and digital dolls. They think it natural to chat with their phones. We are at what I have called a "robotic moment," not because of the merits of the machines we've built but because of our eagerness for their company. Even before we make the robots, we remake ourselves as people ready to be their companions.

10   For a long time, putting hope in robots has expressed an enduring technological optimism, a belief that as things go wrong, science will go right. In a complicated world, what robots promise has always seemed like calling in the cavalry. Robots save lives in war zones; they can function in space and in the sea—indeed, anywhere that humans would be in danger. They perform medical procedures that humans cannot do; they have revolutionized design and manufacturing.

But robots get us to hope for more. Not only for the feats of the cavalry, but for simple salvations. What are the simple salvations? These are the hopes that robots will be our companions. That taking care of us will be their jobs. That we will take comfort in their company and conversation. This is a station on our voyage of forgetting.

What do we forget when we talk to machines? We forget what is special about being human. We forget what it means to have authentic conversation. Machines are programmed to have conversations "as if" they understood what the conversation is about. So when we talk to them, we, too, are reduced and confined to the "as if."

SIMPLE SALVATIONS

Over the decades, I have heard the hopes for robot companionship grow stronger, even though most people don't have experience with an embodied robot companion at all but rather with something like Siri, Apple's digital assistant, where the conversation is most likely to be "locate a restaurant" or "locate a friend."

But even telling Siri to "locate a friend" moves quickly to the fantasy of finding a friend in Siri. People tell me that they look forward to the time, not too far down the road, when Siri or one of her near cousins will be something like a best friend, but in some ways better: one you can always talk to, one that will never be angry, one you can never disappoint.

And, indeed, Apple's first television advertising campaign for Siri introduced "her" not as a feature, a convenient way of getting information, but as a companion. It featured a group of movie stars—Zooey Deschanel, Samuel L. Jackson, John Malkovich—who put Siri in the role of confidante. Deschanel, playing the ditzy ingénue, discusses the weather, and how she doesn't want to wear shoes or clean house on a rainy day. She just wants to dance and have tomato soup. Siri plays the role of the best friend who "gets her." Jackson has a conversation with Siri that is laced with double meanings about a hot date: A lady friend is coming over and Jackson is cooking gazpacho and risotto. It's fun to joke with his sidekick Siri about his plans for seduction. Malkovich, sitting in a deep leather chair in a room with heavy wall moldings and drapes—it might be an apartment in Paris or Barcelona—talks seriously with Siri about the meaning of life. He likes it that Siri has a sense of humor.

In all of this, we are being schooled in how to have conversations with a machine that may approximate banter but doesn't understand our meaning at all; in these conversations, we're doing all the work but we don't mind.

I was on a radio show about Siri with a panel of engineers and social scientists. The topic turned to how much people like to talk to Siri, part of the general phenomenon that people feel uninhibited when they talk to a machine. They like the feeling of no judgment. One of the social scientists on the program suggested that soon a souped-up and somewhat smoothed-out Siri could serve as a psychiatrist.

It didn't seem to bother him that Siri, in the role of psychiatrist, would be counseling people about their lives without having lived one. If Siri could *behave* like a psychiatrist, he said, it could be a psychiatrist. If no one minded

15

the difference between the as if and the real thing, let the machine take the place of the person. This is the pragmatism of the robotic moment.

But the suggestions of a robotic friend or therapist—the simple salvations of the robotic moment—are not so simple at all.

20   Because for all that they are programmed to pretend, machines that talk to us as though they care about us don't know the arc of a human life. When we speak to them of our human problems of love and loss, or the pleasures of tomato soup and dancing barefoot on a rainy day, they can deliver only performances of empathy and connection.

What an artificial intelligence *can* know is your schedule, the literal content of your email, your preferences in film, TV, and food. If you wear body-sensing technologies, an AI can know what emotionally activates you because it may infer this from physiological markers. But it won't understand what any of these things *mean* to you.

But the meaning of things is just what we want our machines to understand. And we are willing to fuel the fantasy that they do.

VULNERABILITY GAMES

We have been playing vulnerability games with artificial intelligence for a very long time, since before programs were anywhere near as sophisticated as they are now. In the 1960s, a computer program called ELIZA, written by MIT's Joseph Weizenbaum, adopted the "mirroring" style of a Rogerian psychotherapist. So, if you typed, "Why do I hate my mother?" ELIZA might respond, "I hear you saying that you hate your mother." This program was effective—at least for a short while—in creating the illusion of intelligent listening. And there is this: *We want to talk to machines even when we know they do not deserve our confidences. I call this the "ELIZA effect."*

Weizenbaum was shocked that people (for example, his secretary and graduate students) who knew the limits of ELIZA's ability to know and understand nevertheless wanted to be alone with the program in order to confide in it. ELIZA demonstrated that almost universally, people project human attributes onto programs that present as humanlike, an effect that is magnified when they are with robots called "sociable" machines—machines that do such things as track your motion, make eye contact, and remember your name. Then people feel in the presence of a knowing other that cares about them. A young man, twenty-six, talks with a robot named Kismet that makes eye contact, reads facial expressions, and vocalizes with the cadences of human speech. The man finds Kismet so supportive that he speaks with it about the ups and downs of his day.

25   Machines with voices have particular power to make us feel understood. Children first learn to know their mothers by recognizing their voices, even while still in the womb. During our evolution, the only speech we heard was the speech of other humans. Now, with the development of sophisticated artificial speech, we are the first humans asked to distinguish human from non-human speech. Neurologically, we are not set up to do this job. Since human

beings have for so long—say, 200,000 years—heard only human voices, it takes serious mental effort to distinguish human speech from the machine-generated kind. To our brains, speaking is something that people do.

And machines with humanlike faces have particular power as well.

In humans, the shape of a smile or a frown releases chemicals that affect our mental state. Our mirror neurons fire both when we act and when we observe others acting. *We feel what we see on the face of another.* An expressive robot face can have this impact on us. The philosopher Emmanuel Lévinas writes that the presence of a face initiates the human ethical compact. The face communicates, "Thou shalt not kill me." We are bound by the face even before we know what stands behind it, even before we might learn it is the face of a machine that cannot be killed. And the robot's face certainly announces, for Lévinas, "Thou shalt not abandon me"—again, an ethical and emotional compact that captures us but has no meaning when we feel it for a machine.

An expressive machine face—on a robot or on a screen-based computer program—puts us on a landscape where we seek recognition and feel we can get it. We are in fact triggered to seek empathy from an object that has none to give.

I worked at the MIT Artificial Intelligence Laboratory as people met the sociable, emotive robot Kismet for the first time. What Kismet actually said had no meaning, but the sound came out warm or inquiring or concerned.

Sometimes Kismet's visitors felt the robot had recognized them and had "heard" their story. When things worked perfectly from a technical stand-point, they experienced what felt like an empathic connection. This convincing imitation of understanding is impressive and can be a lot of fun if you think of these encounters as theater. But I saw children look to Kismet for a friend in the real. I saw children hope for the robot's recognition, and some-times become bereft when there was nothing nourishing on offer.

Estelle, twelve, comes to Kismet wanting a conversation. She is lonely, her parents are divorced; her time with Kismet makes her feel special. Here is a robot who will listen just to her. On the day of Estelle's visit, she is engaged by Kismet's changing facial expressions, but Kismet is not at its vocal best. At the end of a disappointing session, Estelle and the small team of researchers who have been working with her go back to the room where we interview children before and after they meet the robots. Estelle begins to eat the juice, crackers, and cookies we have left out as snacks. And she does not stop, not until we ask her to please leave some food for the other children. Then she stops, but only briefly. She begins to eat again, hurriedly, as we wait for the car service that will take her back to her after-school program.

Estelle tells us why she is upset: Kismet does not like her. The robot began to talk with her and then turned away. We explain that this is not the case. The problem had been technical. Estelle is not convinced. From her point of view, she has failed on her most important day. As Estelle leaves, she takes four boxes of cookies from the supply closet and stuffs them into her back-pack. We do not stop her. Exhausted, my team reconvenes at a nearby coffee shop to ask ourselves a hard question: Can a broken robot break a child?

We would not be concerned with the ethics of having a child play with a buggy copy of Microsoft Word or a torn Raggedy Ann doll. A word-processing program is there to do an instrumental thing. If it does worse than usual on a particular day, well, that leads to frustration but no more. But a program that encourages you to connect with it—this is a different matter.

How is a broken Kismet different from a broken doll? A doll encourages children to project their own stories and their own agendas onto a passive object. But children see sociable robots as "alive enough" to have their own agendas. Children attach to them not with the psychology of projection but with the psychology of relational engagement, more in the way they attach to people.

35   If a little girl is feeling guilty for breaking her mother's crystal, she may punish a row of Barbie dolls, putting the dolls into detention as a way of working through her own feelings. The dolls are material for what the child needs to accomplish emotionally. That is how the psychology of projection works: It enables the working through of the child's feelings. But the sociable robot presents itself as having a mind of its own. As the child sees it, if this robot turns away, it wanted to. That's why children consider winning the heart of a sociable robot to be a personal achievement. You've gotten something lovable to love you. Again, children interact with sociable robots, not with the psychology of projection but with engagement. They react as though they face another person. There is room for new hurt.

Estelle responded to this emotionally charged situation with depression and a search for comfort food. Other children who faced a disappointing conversation with Kismet responded with aggression. When Kismet began an animated conversation that Edward, six, could not understand, he shoved objects into Kismet's mouth—a metal pin, a pencil, a toy caterpillar—things Edward found in the robotics laboratory. But at no point did Edward disengage from Kismet. He would not give up his chance for Kismet's recognition.

The important question here is not about the risks of broken robots. Rather, we should ask, "Emotionally, what positive thing would we have given to these children if the robots had been in top form?" Why do we propose machine companionship to children in the first place? For a lonely child, a conversational robot is a guarantee against rejection, a place to entrust confidences. But what children really need is not the guarantee that an inanimate object will simulate acceptance. They need relationships that will teach them real mutuality, caring, and empathy.

So, the problem doesn't start when the machine breaks down. Children are not well served even when the robots are working perfectly. In the case of a robot babysitter, you already have a problem when you have to explain to a child why there isn't a person available for the job.

TREATING MACHINES AS PEOPLE;
TREATING PEOPLE AS MACHINES

In all of this, an irony emerges: Even as we treat machines as if they were almost human, we develop habits that have us treating human beings as almost-machines. To take a simple example, we regularly put people "on pause" in the middle of a conversation in order to check our phones. And when we talk to people who are not paying attention to us, it is a kind of preparation for talking to uncomprehending machines. When people give us less, talking to machines doesn't seem as much of a downgrade.

At a panel on "cyberetiquette," I was onstage with a technology reporter and two "advice and manners" columnists. There was general agreement among the panelists on most matters: No texting at family dinners. No texting at restaurants. Don't bring your laptop to your children's sporting events, no matter how tempting.   40

And then came this question from the audience: A woman said that as a working mother she had very little time to talk to her friends, to email, to text, to keep up. "Actually," she confessed, "the only time I have is at night, after I'm off work and before I go home, when I go family shopping at Trader Joe's. But the cashier, the guy at the checkout counter, he wants to talk. I just want to be on my phone, into my texts and Facebook. Do I have the right to just ignore him?" The two manners experts went first. Each said a version of the same thing: The man who does the checkout has a job to do. The woman who asked the question has a right to privacy and to her texting as he provides his service.

I listened uncomfortably. I thought of all the years I went shopping with my grandmother as I grew up and all the relationships she had with tradespeople at every store: the baker, the fishmonger, the fruit man, the grocery man (for this is what we called them). These days, we all know that the job the man at the checkout counter does could be done by a machine. In fact, down the street at another supermarket, it is done by a machine that automatically scans your groceries. And so I shared this thought: Until a machine replaces the man, surely he summons in us the recognition and respect you show a person. Sharing a few words at the checkout may make this man feel that in his job, this job that *could* be done by a machine, he is still seen as a human being.

This was not what the audience and my fellow panelists wanted to hear. As I took stock of their cool reaction to what I said, I saw a new symmetry: We want more from technology and less from each other. What once would have seemed like "friendly service" at a community market had become an inconvenience that keeps us from our phones.

It used to be that we imagined our mobile phones were there so that we could talk to each other. Now we want our mobile phones to talk to us. That's what the new commercials for Siri are really about: fantasies of these new conversations and a kind of tutelage in what they might sound like. We are at a moment of temptation, ready to turn to machines for companionship even as we seem pained or inconvenienced to engage with each other in settings as simple as a grocery store. We want technology to step up as we ask people to step back.

People are lonely and fear intimacy, and robots seem ready to hand. *And   45 we are ready for their company if we forget what intimacy is.* And having nothing to forget, our children learn new rules for when it is appropriate to talk to a machine.

Stephanie is forty, a real estate agent in Rhode Island. Her ten-year-old daughter, Tara, is a perfectionist, always the "good girl," sensitive to any suggestion of criticism. Recently, she has begun to talk to Siri. It is not surprising that children like to talk to Siri. There is just enough inventiveness in Siri's responses to make children feel that someone might be listening. And if children are afraid of judgment, Siri is safe. So Tara expresses anger to Siri that she doesn't show to her parents or friends—with them she plays the part of a "perfect child." Stephanie overhears her daughter yelling at Siri and says, "She vents to Siri. She starts to talk but then becomes enraged."

Stephanie wonders if this is "perhaps a good thing, certainly a more honest conversation" than Tara is having with others in her life. It's a thought worth looking at more closely. It is surely positive for Tara to discover feelings that she censors for other audiences. But talking to Siri leaves Tara vulnerable. She may get the idea that her feelings are something that people cannot handle. She may persist in her current idea that pretend perfection is all other people want from her or can accept from her. Instead of learning that people can value how she really feels, Tara is learning that it is easier not to deal with people at all.

If Tara can "be herself" only with a robot, she may grow up believing that only an object can tolerate her truth. What Tara is doing is not "training" for relating to people. For that, Tara needs to learn that you can attach to people with trust, make some mistakes, and risk open conversations. Her talks with the inanimate are taking her in another direction: to a world without risk and without caring.

● ● ●

From Better than Nothing to Better than Anything

The bonds of attachment and the expression of emotion are one for the child. When children talk with people, they come to recognize, over time, how vocal inflection, facial expression, and bodily movement flow together. Seamlessly. Fluidly. And they learn how human emotions play in layers, again seamlessly and fluidly.

50   Children need to learn what complex human feelings and human ambivalence look like. And they need other people to respond to their own expressions of that complexity. These are the most precious things that people give to children in conversation as they grow up. No robot has these things to teach.

These are the things that we forget when we think about children spending any significant amount of time talking with machines, looking into robotic faces, trusting in their care. Why would we play with fire when it comes to such delicate matters?

But we do. It's part of a general progression that I've called "from better than nothing to better than anything." We begin with resignation, with the idea that machine companionship is better than nothing, as in "there are no people for these jobs." From there, we exalt the possibilities of what simulation can offer until, in time, we start to talk as though what we will get from the artificial may actually be better than what life could ever provide. Child-care workers might be abusive. Nurses or well-meaning mothers might make mistakes. Children say that a robotic dog like the AIBO pet will never get sick, and can be turned off when you want to put your attention elsewhere. And, crucially, it will never die. Grown-ups have similar feelings. A robot dog, says an older woman, "won't die suddenly, abandon you, and make you very sad."

In our new culture of connection, we are lonely but afraid of intimacy. Fantasies of "conversation" with artificial beings solve a dilemma. They propose the illusion of companionship without the demands of friendship. They allow us to imagine a friction-free version of friendship. One whose demands are in our control, perhaps literally.

I've said that part of what makes our new technologies of connection so seductive is that they respond to our fantasies, our wishes, that we will always be heard, that we can put our attention wherever we want it to be, and that we will never have to be alone. And, of course, they respond to an implied fourth fantasy: that we will never have to be bored.

When people voice these fantasies, they are also describing, often without realizing it, a relationship with a robot. The robot would always be at attention, and it would be tolerant of wherever your attention might take you. It certainly wouldn't mind if you interrupted your conversation to answer a text or take a call. And it would never abandon you, although there is the question of whether it was ever really there in the first place. As for boredom, well, it would do its best to make boredom, for you, a thing of the past.

If, like Tara, we choose to share our frustrations with robot friends because we don't want to upset our human friends with who we really are and what we're really feeling, the meaning of human friendship will change. It may become the place you go for small talk. You'd be afraid that people would be tired out by big talk. This means that there won't be any more big talk because robots won't understand it.

Yet so many people talk to me about their hope that someday, not too far down the road, an advanced version of Siri will be like a best friend. One who will listen when others won't. I believe this wish reflects a painful truth I've learned in my years of research: The feeling that "no one is listening to me" plays a large part in our relationships with technology. That's why it is so appealing to have a Facebook page or a Twitter feed—so many automatic listeners. And that feeling that "no one is listening to me" makes us want to spend time with machines that seem to care about us. We are willing to take their performances of caring and conversation at "interface value."

When roboticists show videos of people happy to engage with sociable robots, the tendency is to show them off as moments of exalted play. It is as though a small triumph is presented: We did it! We got a person to talk happily with a machine! *But this is an experiment in which people are the "reengineered" experimental subjects.* We are learning how to take as-if conversations with a machine seriously. Our "performative" conversations begin to change what we think of as conversation.

55

We practice something new. But we are the ones who are changing. Do we like what we are changing into? Do we want to get better at it?

TURNING OURSELVES INTO SPECTATORS

60   In the course of my research, there was one robotic moment that I have never forgotten because it changed my mind.

I had been bringing robots designed as companions for the elderly into nursing homes and to elderly people living on their own. I wanted to explore the possibilities. One day I saw an older woman who had lost a child talking to a robot in the shape of a baby seal. It seemed to be looking in her eyes. It seemed to be following the conversation. It comforted her. Many people on my research team and who worked at the nursing home thought this was amazing.

This woman was trying to make sense of her loss with a machine that put on a good show. And we're vulnerable: People experience even pretend empathy as the real thing. But robots can't empathize. They don't face death or know life. So when this woman took comfort in her robot companion, I didn't find it amazing. I felt we had abandoned this woman. Being part of this scene was one of the most wrenching moments in my then fifteen years of research on sociable robotics.

For me, it was a turning point: I felt the enthusiasm of my team and of the staff and the attendants. There were so many people there to help, but we all stood back, a room of spectators now, only there to hope that an elder would bond with a machine. It seemed that we all had a stake in outsourcing the thing we do best—understanding each other, taking care of each other.

That day in the nursing home, I was troubled by how we allowed ourselves to be sidelined, turned into spectators by a robot that understood nothing. That day didn't reflect poorly on the robot. It reflected poorly on us and how we think about older people when they try to tell the stories of their lives. Over the past decades, when the idea of older people and robots has come up, the emphasis has been on whether the older person will talk to the robot. Will the robot facilitate their talking? Will the robot be persuasive enough to do that?

65   But when you think about the moment of life we are considering, it is not just that older people are supposed to be talking. *Younger people are supposed to be listening.* This is the compact between generations. I was once told that some older cultures have a saying: When a young person misbehaves, it means that "they had no one to tell them the old stories." When we celebrate robot listeners that cannot listen, we show too little interest in what our elders have to say. We build machines that guarantee that human stories will fall upon deaf ears.

There are so many wonderful things that robots can do to help the elderly—all those things that put the robot in the role of the cavalry. Robots can help older people (or the ill or homebound) feel greater independence by reaching for cans of soup or articles of clothing on high shelves; robots can help shaky hands cook. Robots can help to lower an unsteady body onto a bed. Robots can help locate a mislaid pair of glasses. All of these things seem so much for the good. Some argue that a robot chatting with an older person is also unequivocally for the good. But here, I think we need to carefully consider the human specificity of conversation and emotional care.

Sociable robots act as evocative objects—objects that cause us to reflect on ourselves and our deepest values. We are in the domain of that fourth chair where we consider nature—our natures and the second natures we have built. Here, talking with machines forces the question: What is the value of an interaction that contains no shared experience of life and contributes nothing to a shared store of human meaning—and indeed may devalue it? This is not a question with a ready answer. But this is a question worth asking and returning to.

It is not easy to have this kind of conversation once we start to take the idea of robotic companionship seriously. Once we assume it as the new normal, this conversation begins to disappear.

Right now we work on the premise that putting in a robot to do a job is always better than nothing. The premise is flawed. If you have a problem with care and companionship and you try to solve it with a robot, you may not try to solve it with your friends, your family, and your community.

The as-if self of a robot calling forth the as-if self of a person performing for it—this is not helpful for children as they grow up. It is not helpful for adults as they try to live authentically.   70

And to say that it is just the thing for older people who are at that point where they are often trying to make sense of their lives is demeaning. They, of all people, should be given occasions to talk about their real lives, filled with real losses and real loves, to someone who knows what those things are.

MLA CITATION

Turkle, Sherry. "The End of Forgetting." *The Norton Reader: An Anthology of Nonfiction*, edited by Melissa A. Goldthwaite et al., 15th ed., W. W. Norton, 2020, pp. 565–75.

Questions

1. This essay, excerpted from Sherry Turkle's book *Reclaiming Conversation*, considers the ways in which the advent of "talking machines" is changing the nature and meaning of "conversation." What do we traditionally understand conversation to be? How, according to Turkle, is that understanding changing? What is her attitude toward these changes? What is yours?

2. Turkle breaks her essay into short sections, each organized around a story of individual people's interactions with a computer program, talking machine, or robot. Why do you think Turkle uses this structure? How does it contribute to the essay's argument and effect?

3. At the beginning of the section called "Turning Ourselves into Spectators," Turkle writes, "In the course of my research, there was one robotic moment that I

have never forgotten because it changed my mind" (paragraph 60). Specifically, Turkle shifts from wanting to "explore the possibilities" of communicative or emotive robots to being deeply ambivalent about them. What were those "possibilities" and what provoked her change of mind?

4. For one day, document all the times you talk to a machine: programs, apps, devices, terminals, computers, robots, and so on. Note the time, duration, and nature of each interaction. Drawing on these notes, write an essay about your own "conversations" with machines.

EULA BISS
Time and Distance Overcome

F WHAT USE is such an invention?" the *New York World* asked shortly after Alexander Graham Bell first demonstrated his telephone in 1876. The world was not waiting for the telephone.

Bell's financial backers asked him not to work on his new invention because it seemed too dubious an investment. The idea on which the telephone depended—the idea that every home in the country could be connected by a vast network of wires suspended from poles set an average of one hundred feet apart—seemed far more unlikely than the idea that the human voice could be transmitted through a wire.

Even now it is an impossible idea, that we are all connected, all of us.

"At the present time we have a perfect network of gas pipes and water pipes throughout our large cities," Bell wrote to his business partners in defense of his idea. "We have main pipes laid under the streets communicating by side pipes with the various dwellings. . . . In a similar manner it is conceivable that cables of telephone wires could be laid under ground, or suspended overhead, communicating by branch wires with private dwellings, counting houses, shops, manufactories, etc., uniting them through the main cable."

5   Imagine the mind that could imagine this. That could see us joined by one branching cable. This was the mind of a man who wanted to invent, more than the telephone, a machine that would allow the deaf to hear.

For a short time the telephone was little more than a novelty. For twenty-five cents you could see it demonstrated by Bell himself, in a church, along with singing and recitations by local talent. From some distance away, Bell would

From Notes from No Man's Land: American Essays *(2009), Eula Biss's collection of writings on contemporary race relations in America.*

receive a call from "the invisible Mr. Watson."[1] Then the telephone became a plaything of the rich. A Boston banker paid for a private line between his office and his home so that he could let his family know exactly when he would be home for dinner.

Mark Twain was among the first Americans to own a telephone, but he wasn't completely taken with the device. "The human voice carries entirely too far as it is," he remarked.

By 1889, the *New York Times* was reporting a "War on Telephone Poles." Wherever telephone companies were erecting poles, home owners and business owners were sawing them down or defending their sidewalks with rifles.

Property owners in Red Bank, New Jersey, threatened to tar and feather the workers putting up telephone poles. A judge granted a group of home owners an injunction to prevent the telephone company from erecting any new poles. Another judge found that a man who had cut down a pole because it was "obnoxious" was not guilty of malicious mischief.

Telephone poles, newspaper editorials complained, were an urban blight. The poles carried a wire for each telephone—sometimes hundreds of wires. And in some places there were also telegraph wires, power lines, and trolley cables. The sky was netted with wires.

The war on telephone poles was fueled, in part, by that terribly American concern for private property, and a reluctance to surrender it for a shared utility. And then there was a fierce sense of aesthetics, an obsession with purity, a dislike for the way the poles and wires marred a landscape that those other new inventions, skyscrapers and barbed wire, were just beginning to complicate. And then perhaps there was also a fear that distance, as it had always been known and measured, was collapsing.

The city council in Sioux Falls, South Dakota, ordered policemen to cut down all the telephone poles in town. And the mayor of Oshkosh, Wisconsin, ordered the police chief and the fire department to chop down the telephone poles there. Only one pole was chopped down before the telephone men climbed all the poles along the line, preventing any more chopping. Soon, Bell Telephone Company began stationing a man at the top of each pole as soon as it had been set, until enough poles had been set to string a wire between them, at which point it became a misdemeanor to interfere with the poles. Even so, a constable cut down two poles holding forty or fifty wires. And a home owner sawed down a recently wired pole, then fled from police. The owner of a cannery ordered his workers to throw dirt back into the hole the telephone company was digging in

10

1. Thomas Watson (1854–1934), engineer and assistant to Bell. His name became the first words ever spoken on a telephone: "Mr. Watson, come here—I want to see you."

front of his building. His men threw the dirt back in as fast as the telephone workers could dig it out. Then he sent out a team with a load of stones to dump into the hole. Eventually, the pole was erected on the other side of the street.

Despite the war on telephone poles, it would take only four years after Bell's first public demonstration of the telephone for every town of more than ten thousand people to be wired, although many towns were wired only to themselves. By the turn of the century, there were more telephones than bathtubs in America.

"Time and dist. overcome," read an early advertisement for the telephone. Rutherford B. Hayes pronounced the installation of a telephone in the White House "one of the greatest events since creation." The telephone, Thomas Edison declared, "annihilated time and space, and brought the human family in closer touch."

15   In 1898, in Lake Cormorant, Mississippi, a black man was hanged from a telephone pole. And in Weir City, Kansas. And in Brookhaven, Mississippi. And in Tulsa, Oklahoma, where the hanged man was riddled with bullets. In Danville, Illinois, a black man's throat was slit, and his dead body was strung up on a telephone pole. Two black men were hanged from a telephone pole in Lewisburg, West Virginia. And two in Hempstead, Texas, where one man was dragged out of the courtroom by a mob, and another was dragged out of jail.

A black man was hanged from a telephone pole in Belleville, Illinois, where a fire was set at the base of the pole and the man was cut down half-alive, covered in coal oil, and burned. While his body was burning the mob beat it with clubs and cut it to pieces.

Lynching, the first scholar of the subject determined, is an American invention. Lynching from bridges, from arches, from trees standing alone in fields, from trees in front of the county courthouse, from trees used as public billboards, from trees barely able to support the weight of a man, from telephone poles, from streetlamps, and from poles erected solely for that purpose. From the middle of the nineteenth century to the middle of the twentieth century, black men were lynched for crimes real and imagined, for whistles, for rumors, for "disputing with a white man," for "unpopularity," for "asking a white woman in marriage," for "peeping in a window."

The children's game of telephone depends on the fact that a message passed quietly from one ear to another to another will get distorted at some point along the line.

More than two hundred antilynching bills were introduced to the U.S. Congress during the twentieth century, but none were passed. Seven presidents lobbied for antilynching legislation, and the House of Representatives passed three separate measures, each of which was blocked by the Senate.

In Pine Bluff, Arkansas, a black man charged with kicking a white girl was
hanged from a telephone pole. In Longview, Texas, a black man accused of
attacking a white woman was hanged from a telephone pole. In Greenville, Mississippi, a black man accused of attacking a white telephone operator was
hanged from a telephone pole. "The negro only asked time to pray." In Purcell,
Oklahoma, a black man accused of attacking a white woman was tied to a telephone pole and burned. "Men and women in automobiles stood up to watch
him die."

The poles, of course, were not to blame. It was only coincidence that they
became convenient as gallows, because they were tall and straight, with a cross-
bar, and because they stood in public places. And it was only coincidence that
the telephone poles so closely resembled crucifixes.

Early telephone calls were full of noise. "Such a jangle of meaningless noises
had never been heard by human ears," Herbert Casson wrote in his 1910 *History of the Telephone*. "There were spluttering and bubbling, jerking and rasp-
ing, whistling and screaming."

In Shreveport, Lousiana, a black man charged with attacking a white girl was
hanged from a telephone pole. "A knife was left sticking in the body." In Cum-
ming, Georgia, a black man accused of assaulting a white girl was shot repeatedly, then hanged from a telephone pole. In Waco, Texas, a black man convicted
of killing a white woman was taken from the courtroom by a mob and burned,
then his charred body was hanged from a telephone pole.

A postcard was made from the photo of a burned man hanging from a telephone pole in Texas, his legs broken off below the knee and his arms curled up
and blackened. Postcards of lynchings were sent out as greetings and warnings
until 1908, when the postmaster general declared them unmailable. "This is
the barbecue we had last night," reads one.

"If we are to die," W. E. B. DuBois[2] wrote in 1911, "in God's name let us perish
like men and not like bales of hay." And "if we must die," Claude McKay[3] wrote
ten years later, "let it not be like hogs."

In Pittsburg, Kansas, a black man was hanged from a telephone pole, cut down,
burned, shot, and stoned with bricks. "At first the negro was defiant," the *New
York Times* reported, "but just before he was hanged he begged hard for his life."

In the photographs, the bodies of the men lynched from telephone poles are
silhouetted against the sky. Sometimes two men to a pole, hanging above the
buildings of a town. Sometimes three. They hang like flags in still air.

2. American historian and writer (1868–1963).
3. Jamaican American writer (1889–1948).

In Cumberland, Maryland, a mob used a telephone pole as a battering ram to break into the jail where a black man charged with the murder of a policeman was being held. They kicked him to death, then fired twenty shots into his head. They wanted to burn his body, but a minister asked them not to.

The lynchings happened everywhere, in all but four states. From shortly before the invention of the telephone to long after the first transatlantic call. More in the South, and more in rural areas. In the cities and in the North, there were race riots.

30   Riots in Cincinnati, New Orleans, Memphis, New York, Atlanta, Philadelphia, Houston . . .

During the race riots that destroyed the black section of Springfield, Ohio, a black man was shot and hanged from a telephone pole.

During the race riots that set fire to East St. Louis and forced five hundred black people to flee their homes, a black man was hanged from a telephone pole. The rope broke and his body fell into the gutter. "Negros are lying in the gutters every few feet in some places," read the newspaper account.

In 1921, the year before Bell died, four companies of the National Guard were called out to end a race war in Tulsa that began when a white woman accused a black man of rape. Bell had lived to complete the first call from New York to San Francisco, which required 14,000 miles of copper wire and 130,000 telephone poles.

My grandfather was a lineman. He broke his back when a telephone pole fell. "Smashed him onto the road," my father says.

35   When I was young, I believed that the arc and swoop of telephone wires along the roadways was beautiful. I believed that the telephone poles, with their transformers catching the evening sun, were glorious. I believed my father when he said, "My dad could raise a pole by himself." And I believed that the telephone itself was a miracle.

Now, I tell my sister, these poles, these wires, do not look the same to me. Nothing is innocent, my sister reminds me. But nothing, I would like to think, remains unrepentant.

One summer, heavy rains fell in Nebraska and some green telephone poles grew small leafy branches.

On "Time and Distance Overcome"[4]

I began my research for this essay by searching for every instance of the phrase "telephone pole" in the *New York Times* from 1880 to 1920, which resulted in 370 articles. I was planning to write an essay about telephone poles and telephones, not lynchings, but after reading an article headlined "Colored Scoundrel Lynched," and then another headlined "Mississippi Negro Lynched," and then another headlined "Texas Negro Lynched," I searched for every instance of the word "lynched" in the *New York Times* from 1880 to 1920, which resulted in 2,354 articles.

I refer, in this essay, to the first scholar of lynching, meaning James E. Cutler, author of the 1905 book *Lynch-Law,* in which he writes, on the first page, "Lynching is a criminal practice which is peculiar to the United States." This is debatable, of course, and very possibly not true, but there is good evidence that the Italian Antonio Meucci invented a telephone years before Bell began working on his device, so as long as we are going to lay claim to one invention, we might as well take responsibility for the other.

Bell would say, late in his life: "Recognition for my work with the deaf has   40
always been more pleasing than the recognition of my work with the telephone." His own hearing was failing by the time he placed the first cross-country call, from New York to his old friend Thomas Watson in San Francisco, and what he said to Watson then was an echo of the first sentence he ever spoke into his invention, a famous and possibly mythical sentence that is now remembered in several slightly different versions, one being, "Mr. Watson, come here—I want you," and another being, "Mr. Watson, come here—I need you!"

MLA CITATION

Biss, Eula. "Time and Distance Overcome." *The Norton Reader: An Anthology of Nonfiction,* edited by Melissa A. Goldthwaite et al., 15th ed., W. W. Norton, 2020, pp. 576–81.

QUESTIONS

1. Eula Biss focuses on the historical coincidence of the installation of telephone poles and the lynching of African Americans. List all the ways that Biss connects these topics and discuss the merits of the juxtaposition. How does she make the coincidence into something meaningful?

2. Consider Biss's style and form. How would you describe her sentences? Biss notes that even into the early twentieth century, postcards of lynchings were sent through the mail (paragraph 24). How are her paragraphs like postcards? How is her essay organized? What is its arc?

3. Following Biss's model (paragraphs 38–40), write an author's note for an old research paper. In your note, describe how the paper changed as you did your research.

---

4. At the end of her book, Biss provides background information for each of her essays, including how she arrived at the topic and the research involved.

4. Every new technology brings benefits and problems, as Biss explores. Choose a different medium or technology (e.g., TV, smartphones, texting) and write an essay discussing its benefits and problems, using Biss's essay as a model.

JEAN M. TWENGE
Have Smartphones Destroyed a Generation?

ONE DAY LAST SUMMER, around noon, I called Athena, a 13-year-old who lives in Houston, Texas. She answered her phone—she's had an iPhone since she was 11—sounding as if she'd just woken up. We chatted about her favorite songs and TV shows, and I asked her what she likes to do with her friends. "We go to the mall," she said. "Do your parents drop you off?," I asked, recalling my own middle-school days, in the 1980s, when I'd enjoy a few parent-free hours shopping with my friends. "No—I go with my family," she replied. "We'll go with my mom and brothers and walk a little behind them. I just have to tell my mom where we're going. I have to check in every hour or every 30 minutes."

Those mall trips are infrequent—about once a month. More often, Athena and her friends spend time together on their phones, unchaperoned. Unlike the teens of my generation, who might have spent an evening tying up the family landline with gossip, they talk on Snapchat, the smartphone app that allows users to send pictures and videos that quickly disappear. They make sure to keep up their Snapstreaks, which show how many days in a row they have Snapchatted with each other. Sometimes they save screenshots of particularly ridiculous pictures of friends. "It's good blackmail," Athena said. (Because she's a minor, I'm not using her real name.) She told me she'd spent most of the summer hanging out alone in her room with her phone. That's just the way her generation is, she said. "We didn't have a choice to know any life without iPads or iPhones. I think we like our phones more than we like actual people."

I've been researching generational differences for 25 years, starting when I was a 22-year-old doctoral student in psychology. Typically, the characteristics that come to define a generation appear gradually, and along a continuum. Beliefs and behaviors that were already rising simply continue to do so. Millennials,[1] for instance, are a highly individualistic generation, but individualism had been increasing since the Baby Boomers[2] turned on, tuned in, and dropped

---

Published in the Atlantic *(2017), this essay is taken from a chapter in Jean M. Twenge's book* iGen: Why Today's Super-Connected Kids Are Growing Up Less Rebellious, More Tolerant, Less Happy—and Completely Unprepared for Adulthood—and What That Means for the Rest of Us *(2017).*

1. Generation born from the early 1980s through the mid-1990s, conventionally 1981 through 1996.
2. Generation born in the two decades following World War II, conventionally 1946 through 1964.

out.[3] I had grown accustomed to line graphs of trends that looked like modest hills and valleys. Then I began studying Athena's generation.

Around 2012, I noticed abrupt shifts in teen behaviors and emotional states. The gentle slopes of the line graphs became steep mountains and sheer cliffs, and many of the distinctive characteristics of the Millennial generation began to disappear. In all my analyses of generational data—some reaching back to the 1930s—I had never seen anything like it.

At first I presumed these might be blips, but the trends persisted, across   5
several years and a series of national surveys. The changes weren't just in degree, but in kind. The biggest difference between the Millennials and their predecessors was in how they viewed the world; teens today differ from the Millennials not just in their views but in how they spend their time. The experiences they have every day are radically different from those of the generation that came of age just a few years before them.

What happened in 2012 to cause such dramatic shifts in behavior? It was after the Great Recession, which officially lasted from 2007 to 2009 and had a starker effect on Millennials trying to find a place in a sputtering economy. But it was exactly the moment when the proportion of Americans who owned a smartphone surpassed 50 percent.

The more I pored over yearly surveys of teen attitudes and behaviors, and the more I talked with young people like Athena, the clearer it became that theirs is a generation shaped by the smartphone and by the concomitant rise of social media. I call them iGen. Born between 1995 and 2012, members of this generation are growing up with smartphones, have an Instagram account before they start high school, and do not remember a time before the internet. The Millennials grew up with the web as well, but it wasn't ever-present in their lives, at hand at all times, day and night. iGen's oldest members were early adolescents when the iPhone was introduced, in 2007, and high-school students when the iPad entered the scene, in 2010. A 2017 survey of more than 5,000 American teens found that three out of four owned an iPhone.

The advent of the smartphone and its cousin the tablet was followed quickly by hand-wringing about the deleterious effects of "screen time." But the impact of these devices has not been fully appreciated, and goes far beyond the usual concerns about curtailed attention spans. The arrival of the smartphone has radically changed every aspect of teenagers' lives, from the nature of their social interactions to their mental health. These changes have affected young people in every corner of the nation and in every type of household. The trends appear among teens poor and rich; of every ethnic background; in cities, suburbs, and small towns. Where there are cell towers, there are teens living their lives on their smartphone.

To those of us who fondly recall a more analog adolescence, this may seem foreign and troubling. The aim of generational study, however, is not to succumb

---

3. Slogan coined in 1966 by psychologist Timothy Leary (1920–1996), a countercultural icon who advocated the use of psychedelic drugs.

to nostalgia for the way things used to be; it's to understand how they are now. Some generational changes are positive, some are negative, and many are both. More comfortable in their bedrooms than in a car or at a party, today's teens are physically safer than teens have ever been. They're markedly less likely to get into a car accident and, having less of a taste for alcohol than their predecessors, are less susceptible to drinking's attendant ills.

10   Psychologically, however, they are more vulnerable than Millennials were: Rates of teen depression and suicide have skyrocketed since 2011. It's not an exaggeration to describe iGen as being on the brink of the worst mental-health crisis in decades. Much of this deterioration can be traced to their phones.

Even when a seismic event—a war, a technological leap, a free concert in the mud—plays an outsize role in shaping a group of young people, no single factor ever defines a generation. Parenting styles continue to change, as do school curricula and culture, and these things matter. But the twin rise of the smartphone and social media has caused an earthquake of a magnitude we've not seen in a very long time, if ever. There is compelling evidence that the devices we've placed in young people's hands are having profound effects on their lives—and making them seriously unhappy.

In the early 1970s, the photographer Bill Yates shot a series of portraits at the Sweetheart Roller Skating Rink in Tampa, Florida. In one, a shirtless teen stands with a large bottle of peppermint schnapps stuck in the waistband of his jeans. In another, a boy who looks no older than 12 poses with a cigarette in his mouth. The rink was a place where kids could get away from their parents and inhabit a world of their own, a world where they could drink, smoke, and make out in the backs of their cars. In stark black-and-white, the adolescent Boomers gaze at Yates's camera with the self-confidence born of making your own choices—even if, perhaps especially if, your parents wouldn't think they were the right ones.

Fifteen years later, during my own teenage years as a member of Generation X,[4] smoking had lost some of its romance, but independence was definitely still in. My friends and I plotted to get our driver's license as soon as we could, making DMV appointments for the day we turned 16 and using our newfound freedom to escape the confines of our suburban neighborhood. Asked by our parents, "When will you be home?," we replied, "When do I have to be?"

But the allure of independence, so powerful to previous generations, holds less sway over today's teens, who are less likely to leave the house without their parents. The shift is stunning: 12th-graders in 2015 were going out less often than *eighth-graders* did as recently as 2009.

15   Today's teens are also less likely to date. The initial stage of courtship, which Gen Xers called "liking" (as in "Ooh, he likes you!"), kids now call "talking"—an ironic choice for a generation that prefers texting to actual conversation. After two teens have "talked" for a while, they might start dating. But only about 56 percent of high-school seniors in 2015 went out on dates; for Boomers and Gen Xers, the number was about 85 percent.

4. Generation born from the mid-1960s through the early 1980s, conventionally 1965 through 1980.

The decline in dating tracks with a decline in sexual activity. The drop is the sharpest for ninth-graders, among whom the number of sexually active teens has been cut by almost 40 percent since 1991. The average teen now has had sex for the first time by the spring of 11th grade, a full year later than the average Gen Xer. Fewer teens having sex has contributed to what many see as one of the most positive youth trends in recent years: The teen birth rate hit an all-time low in 2016, down 67 percent since its modern peak, in 1991.

Even driving, a symbol of adolescent freedom inscribed in American popular culture, from *Rebel Without a Cause* to *Ferris Bueller's Day Off*,[5] has lost its appeal for today's teens. Nearly all Boomer high-school students had their driver's license by the spring of their senior year; more than one in four teens today still lack one at the end of high school. For some, Mom and Dad are such good chauffeurs that there's no urgent need to drive. "My parents drove me everywhere and never complained, so I always had rides," a 21-year-old student in San Diego told me. "I didn't get my license until my mom told me I had to because she could not keep driving me to school." She finally got her license six months after her 18th birthday. In conversation after conversation, teens described getting their license as something to be nagged into by their parents—a notion that would have been unthinkable to previous generations.

Independence isn't free—you need some money in your pocket to pay for gas, or for that bottle of schnapps. In earlier eras, kids worked in great numbers, eager to finance their freedom or prodded by their parents to learn the value of a dollar. But iGen teens aren't working (or managing their own money) as much. In the late 1970s, 77 percent of high-school seniors worked for pay during the school year; by the mid-2010s, only 55 percent did. The number of eighth-graders who work for pay has been cut in half. These declines accelerated during the Great Recession, but teen employment has not bounced back, even though job availability has.

Of course, putting off the responsibilities of adulthood is not an iGen innovation. Gen Xers, in the 1990s, were the first to postpone the traditional markers of adulthood. Young Gen Xers were just about as likely to drive, drink alcohol, and date as young Boomers had been, and more likely to have sex and get pregnant as teens. But as they left their teenage years behind, Gen Xers married and started careers later than their Boomer predecessors had.

Gen X managed to stretch adolescence beyond all previous limits: Its   20
members started becoming adults earlier and finished becoming adults later. Beginning with Millennials and continuing with iGen, adolescence is contracting again—but only because its onset is being delayed. Across a range of behaviors—drinking, dating, spending time unsupervised—18-year-olds now act more like 15-year-olds used to, and 15-year-olds more like 13-year-olds. Childhood now stretches well into high school.

Why are today's teens waiting longer to take on both the responsibilities and the pleasures of adulthood? Shifts in the economy, and parenting, certainly play a role. In an information economy that rewards higher education more than

5. *Rebel Without a Cause* (1955), *Ferris Bueller's Day Off* (1986), popular movies about teenage rebellion that feature iconic driving scenes.

early work history, parents may be inclined to encourage their kids to stay home and study rather than to get a part-time job. Teens, in turn, seem to be content with this homebody arrangement—not because they're so studious, but because their social life is lived on their phone. They don't need to leave home to spend time with their friends.

If today's teens were a generation of grinds, we'd see that in the data. But eighth-, 10th-, and 12th-graders in the 2010s actually spend less time on homework than Gen X teens did in the early 1990s. (High-school seniors headed for four-year colleges spend about the same amount of time on homework as their predecessors did.) The time that seniors spend on activities such as student clubs and sports and exercise has changed little in recent years. Combined with the decline in working for pay, this means iGen teens have more leisure time than Gen X teens did, not less.

So what are they doing with all that time? They are on their phone, in their room, alone and often distressed.

One of the ironies of iGen life is that despite spending far more time under the same roof as their parents, today's teens can hardly be said to be closer to their mothers and fathers than their predecessors were. "I've seen my friends with their families—they don't talk to them," Athena told me. "They just say 'Okay, okay, whatever' while they're on their phones. They don't pay attention to their family." Like her peers, Athena is an expert at tuning out her parents so she can focus on her phone. She spent much of her summer keeping up with friends, but nearly all of it was over text or Snapchat. "I've been on my phone more than I've been with actual people," she said. "My bed has, like, an imprint of my body."

25   In this, too, she is typical. The number of teens who get together with their friends nearly every day dropped by more than 40 percent from 2000 to 2015; the decline has been especially steep recently. It's not only a matter of fewer kids partying; fewer kids are spending time simply hanging out. That's something most teens used to do: nerds and jocks, poor kids and rich kids, C students and A students. The roller rink, the basketball court, the town pool, the local necking spot—they've all been replaced by virtual spaces accessed through apps and the web.

You might expect that teens spend so much time in these new spaces because it makes them happy, but most data suggest that it does not. The Monitoring the Future survey, funded by the National Institute on Drug Abuse and designed to be nationally representative, has asked 12th-graders more than 1,000 questions every year since 1975 and queried eighth- and 10th-graders since 1991. The survey asks teens how happy they are and also how much of their leisure time they spend on various activities, including nonscreen activities such as in-person social interaction and exercise, and, in recent years, screen activities such as using social media, texting, and browsing the web. The results could not be clearer: Teens who spend more time than average on screen activities are more likely to be unhappy, and those who spend more time than average on nonscreen activities are more likely to be happy.

There's not a single exception. All screen activities are linked to less happiness, and all nonscreen activities are linked to more happiness. Eighth-graders who spend 10 or more hours a week on social media are 56 percent more likely to say they're unhappy than those who devote less time to social media. Admittedly, 10 hours a week is a lot. But those who spend six to nine hours a week on social media are still 47 percent more likely to say they are unhappy than those who use social media even less. The opposite is true of in-person interactions. Those who spend an above-average amount of time with their friends in person are 20 percent less likely to say they're unhappy than those who hang out for a below-average amount of time.

If you were going to give advice for a happy adolescence based on this survey, it would be straightforward: Put down the phone, turn off the laptop, and do something—anything—that does not involve a screen. Of course, these analyses don't unequivocally prove that screen time *causes* unhappiness; it's possible that unhappy teens spend more time online. But recent research suggests that screen time, in particular social-media use, does indeed cause unhappiness. One study asked college students with a Facebook page to complete short surveys on their phone over the course of two weeks. They'd get a text message with a link five times a day, and report on their mood and how much they'd used Facebook. The more they'd used Facebook, the unhappier they felt, but feeling unhappy did not subsequently lead to more Facebook use.

Social-networking sites like Facebook promise to connect us to friends. But the portrait of iGen teens emerging from the data is one of a lonely, dislocated generation. Teens who visit social-networking sites every day but see their friends in person less frequently are the most likely to agree with the statements "A lot of times I feel lonely," "I often feel left out of things," and "I often wish I had more good friends." Teens' feelings of loneliness spiked in 2013 and have remained high since.

This doesn't always mean that, on an individual level, kids who spend more time online are lonelier than kids who spend less time online. Teens who spend more time on social media also spend more time with their friends in person, on average—highly social teens are more social in both venues, and less social teens are less so. But at the generational level, when teens spend more time on smartphones and less time on in-person social interactions, loneliness is more common.

So is depression. Once again, the effect of screen activities is unmistakable: The more time teens spend looking at screens, the more likely they are to report symptoms of depression. Eighth-graders who are heavy users of social media increase their risk of depression by 27 percent, while those who play sports, go to religious services, or even do homework more than the average teen cut their risk significantly.

Teens who spend three hours a day or more on electronic devices are 35 percent more likely to have a risk factor for suicide, such as making a suicide plan. (That's much more than the risk related to, say, watching TV.) One piece of data that indirectly but stunningly captures kids' growing isolation, for good and for bad: Since 2007, the homicide rate among teens has declined, but the suicide rate has increased. As teens have started spending less time together, they have become less likely to kill one another, and more likely to kill themselves. In 2011, for the first time in 24 years, the teen suicide rate was higher than the teen homicide rate.

30

Depression and suicide have many causes; too much technology is clearly not the only one. And the teen suicide rate was even higher in the 1990s, long before smartphones existed. Then again, about four times as many Americans now take antidepressants, which are often effective in treating severe depression, the type most strongly linked to suicide.

What's the connection between smartphones and the apparent psychological distress this generation is experiencing? For all their power to link kids day and night, social media also exacerbate the age-old teen concern about being left out. Today's teens may go to fewer parties and spend less time together in person, but when they do congregate, they document their hangouts relentlessly—on Snapchat, Instagram, Facebook. Those not invited to come along are keenly aware of it. Accordingly, the number of teens who feel left out has reached all-time highs across age groups. Like the increase in loneliness, the upswing in feeling left out has been swift and significant.

35   This trend has been especially steep among girls. Forty-eight percent more girls said they often felt left out in 2015 than in 2010, compared with 27 percent more boys. Girls use social media more often, giving them additional opportunities to feel excluded and lonely when they see their friends or classmates getting together without them. Social media levy a psychic tax on the teen doing the posting as well, as she anxiously awaits the affirmation of comments and likes. When Athena posts pictures to Instagram, she told me, "I'm nervous about what people think and are going to say. It sometimes bugs me when I don't get a certain amount of likes on a picture."

Girls have also borne the brunt of the rise in depressive symptoms among today's teens. Boys' depressive symptoms increased by 21 percent from 2012 to 2015, while girls' increased by 50 percent—more than twice as much. The rise in suicide, too, is more pronounced among girls. Although the rate increased for both sexes, three times as many 12-to-14-year-old girls killed themselves in 2015 as in 2007, compared with twice as many boys. The suicide rate is still higher for boys, in part because they use more-lethal methods, but girls are beginning to close the gap.

These more dire consequences for teenage girls could also be rooted in the fact that they're more likely to experience cyberbullying. Boys tend to bully one another physically, while girls are more likely to do so by undermining a victim's social status or relationships. Social media give middle- and high-school girls a platform on which to carry out the style of aggression they favor, ostracizing and excluding other girls around the clock.

Social-media companies are of course aware of these problems, and to one degree or another have endeavored to prevent cyberbullying. But their various motivations are, to say the least, complex. A recently leaked Facebook document indicated that the company had been touting to advertisers its ability to determine teens' emotional state based on their on-site behavior, and even to pinpoint "moments when young people need a confidence boost." Facebook acknowledged that the document was real, but denied that it offers "tools to target people based on their emotional state."

In July 2014, a 13-year-old girl in North Texas woke to the smell of something burning. Her phone had overheated and melted into the sheets. National news outlets picked up the story, stoking readers' fears that their cellphone might spontaneously combust. To me, however, the flaming cellphone wasn't the only surprising aspect of the story. *Why*, I wondered, *would anyone sleep with her phone beside her in bed?* It's not as though you can surf the web while you're sleeping. And who could slumber deeply inches from a buzzing phone?

Curious, I asked my undergraduate students at San Diego State University   40 what they do with their phone while they sleep. Their answers were a profile in obsession. Nearly all slept with their phone, putting it under their pillow, on the mattress, or at the very least within arm's reach of the bed. They checked social media right before they went to sleep, and reached for their phone as soon as they woke up in the morning (they had to—all of them used it as their alarm clock). Their phone was the last thing they saw before they went to sleep and the first thing they saw when they woke up. If they woke in the middle of the night, they often ended up looking at their phone. Some used the language of addiction. "I know I shouldn't, but I just can't help it," one said about looking at her phone while in bed. Others saw their phone as an extension of their body—or even like a lover: "Having my phone closer to me while I'm sleeping is a comfort."

It may be a comfort, but the smartphone is cutting into teens' sleep: Many now sleep less than seven hours most nights. Sleep experts say that teens should get about nine hours of sleep a night; a teen who is getting less than seven hours a night is significantly sleep deprived. Fifty-seven percent more teens were sleep deprived in 2015 than in 1991. In just the four years from 2012 to 2015, 22 percent more teens failed to get seven hours of sleep.

The increase is suspiciously timed, once again starting around when most teens got a smartphone. Two national surveys show that teens who spend three or more hours a day on electronic devices are 28 percent more likely to get less than seven hours of sleep than those who spend fewer than three hours, and teens who visit social-media sites every day are 19 percent more likely to be sleep deprived. A meta-analysis of studies on electronic-device use among children found similar results: Children who use a media device right before bed are more likely to sleep less than they should, more likely to sleep poorly, and more than twice as likely to be sleepy during the day.

Electronic devices and social media seem to have an especially strong ability to disrupt sleep. Teens who read books and magazines more often than the average are actually slightly less likely to be sleep deprived—either reading lulls them to sleep, or they can put the book down at bedtime. Watching TV for several hours a day is only weakly linked to sleeping less. But the allure of the smartphone is often too much to resist.

Sleep deprivation is linked to myriad issues, including compromised thinking and reasoning, susceptibility to illness, weight gain, and high blood pressure. It also affects mood: People who don't sleep enough are prone to depression and anxiety. Again, it's difficult to trace the precise paths of causation. Smartphones could be causing lack of sleep, which leads to depression, or the phones could be causing depression, which leads to lack of sleep. Or some other factor could be causing both depression and sleep deprivation to rise. But the smartphone, its blue light glowing in the dark, is likely playing a nefarious role.

45   The correlations between depression and smartphone use are strong enough to suggest that more parents should be telling their kids to put down their phone. As the technology writer Nick Bilton has reported, it's a policy some Silicon Valley executives follow. Even Steve Jobs limited his kids' use of the devices he brought into the world.

What's at stake isn't just how kids experience adolescence. The constant presence of smartphones is likely to affect them well into adulthood. Among people who suffer an episode of depression, at least half become depressed again later in life. Adolescence is a key time for developing social skills; as teens spend less time with their friends face-to-face, they have fewer opportunities to practice them. In the next decade, we may see more adults who know just the right emoji for a situation, but not the right facial expression.

I realize that restricting technology might be an unrealistic demand to impose on a generation of kids so accustomed to being wired at all times. My three daughters were born in 2006, 2009, and 2012. They're not yet old enough to display the traits of iGen teens, but I have already witnessed firsthand just how ingrained new media are in their young lives. I've observed my toddler, barely old enough to walk, confidently swiping her way through an iPad. I've experienced my 6-year-old asking for her own cellphone. I've overheard my 9-year-old discussing the latest app to sweep the fourth grade. Prying the phone out of our kids' hands will be difficult, even more so than the quixotic efforts of my parents' generation to get their kids to turn off MTV and get some fresh air. But more seems to be at stake in urging teens to use their phone responsibly, and there are benefits to be gained even if all we instill in our children is the importance of moderation. Significant effects on both mental health and sleep time appear after two or more hours a day on electronic devices. The average teen spends about two and a half hours a day on electronic devices. Some mild boundary-setting could keep kids from falling into harmful habits.

In my conversations with teens, I saw hopeful signs that kids themselves are beginning to link some of their troubles to their ever-present phone. Athena told me that when she does spend time with her friends in person, they are often looking at their device instead of at her. "I'm trying to talk to them about something, and they don't actually look at my face," she said. "They're looking at their phone, or they're looking at their Apple Watch." "What does that feel like, when you're trying to talk to somebody face-to-face and they're not looking at you?," I asked. "It kind of hurts," she said. "It hurts. I know my parents' generation didn't do that. I could be talking about something super important to me, and they wouldn't even be listening."

Once, she told me, she was hanging out with a friend who was texting her boyfriend. "I was trying to talk to her about my family, and what was going on, and she was like, 'Uh-huh, yeah, whatever.' So I took her phone out of her hands and I threw it at my wall."

I couldn't help laughing. "You play volleyball," I said. "Do you have a pretty   50
good arm?" "Yep," she replied.

MLA CITATION

Twenge, Jean M. "Have Smartphones Destroyed a Generation?" *The Norton Reader:
An Anthology of Nonfiction*, edited by Melissa A. Goldthwaite et al., 15th ed.,
W. W. Norton, 2020, pp. 582–91.

QUESTIONS

1. In the title of her essay, Jean M. Twenge poses a question: "Have Smartphones
Destroyed a Generation?" What is her answer? What is yours? Why?

2. What, according to Twenge, are the defining characteristics of iGen, her term
for the generation born between 1995 and 2012? Why in her view is this generation so unhappy?

3. To support her claims, Twenge relies on at least two kinds of evidence: reports
of her own experiences and statistics. Why does she choose to use both? How do
they complement one another?

4. Write an essay in which you respond to Twenge by explaining and reflecting on
what your smartphone means to you.

THOMAS GOETZ
Harnessing the Power of Feedback Loops

I N 2003, officials in Garden Grove, California, a community of 170,000
people wedged amid the suburban sprawl of Orange County, set out
to confront a problem that afflicts most every town in America: drivers speeding through school zones.

Local authorities had tried many tactics to get people to slow
down. They replaced old speed limit signs with bright new ones to remind drivers of the 25-mile-an-hour limit during school hours. Police began ticketing
speeding motorists during drop-off and pickup times. But these efforts had
only limited success, and speeding cars continued to hit bicyclists and pedes-
trians in the school zones with depressing regularity.

So city engineers decided to take another approach. In five Garden Grove
school zones, they put up what are known as dynamic speed displays, or driver
feedback signs: a speed limit posting coupled with a radar sensor attached to a
huge digital readout announcing "Your Speed."

The signs were curious in a few ways. For one thing, they didn't tell drivers anything they didn't already know—there is, after all, a speedometer in every

First published in Wired *(2011), a magazine that covers technology and its influence on politics and culture.*

car. If a motorist wanted to know their speed, a glance at the dashboard would do it. For another thing, the signs used radar, which decades earlier had appeared on American roads as a talisman technology, reserved for police officers only. Now Garden Grove had scattered radar sensors along the side of the road like traffic cones. And the Your Speed signs came with no punitive follow-up—no police officer standing by ready to write a ticket. This defied decades of law-enforcement dogma, which held that most people obey speed limits only if they face some clear negative consequence for exceeding them.

5   In other words, officials in Garden Grove were betting that giving speed-ers redundant information with no consequence would somehow compel them to do something few of us are inclined to do: slow down.

The results fascinated and delighted the city officials. In the vicinity of the schools where the dynamic displays were installed, drivers slowed an average of 14 percent. Not only that, at three schools the average speed dipped below the posted speed limit. Since this experiment, Garden Grove has installed 10 more driver feedback signs. "Frankly, it's hard to get people to slow down," says Dan Candelaria, Garden Grove's traffic engineer. "But these encourage people to do the right thing."

In the years since the Garden Grove project began, radar technology has dropped steadily in price and Your Speed signs have proliferated on American roadways. Yet despite their ubiquity, the signs haven't faded into the landscape like so many other motorist warnings. Instead, they've proven to be consistently effective at getting drivers to slow down—reducing speeds, on average, by about 10 percent, an effect that lasts for several miles down the road. Indeed, traffic engineers and safety experts consider them to be more effective at changing driving habits than a cop with a radar gun. Despite their redundancy, despite their lack of repercussions, the signs have accomplished what seemed impossible: They get us to let up on the gas.

The signs leverage what's called a feedback loop, a profoundly effective tool for changing behavior. The basic premise is simple. Provide people with infor-mation about their actions in real time (or something close to it), then give them an opportunity to change those actions, pushing them toward better behaviors. Action, information, reaction. It's the operating principle behind a home ther-mostat, which fires the furnace to maintain a specific temperature, or the con-sumption display in a Toyota Prius, which tends to turn drivers into so-called hypermilers trying to wring every last mile from the gas tank. But the simplic-ity of feedback loops is deceptive. They are in fact powerful tools that can help people change bad behavior patterns, even those that seem intractable. Just as important, they can be used to encourage good habits, turning progress itself into a reward. In other words, feedback loops change human behavior. And thanks to an explosion of new technology, the opportunity to put them into action in nearly every part of our lives is quickly becoming a reality.

A feedback loop involves four distinct stages. First comes the data: A behavior must be measured, captured, and stored. This is the evidence stage. Second, the information must be relayed to the individual, not in the raw-data form in

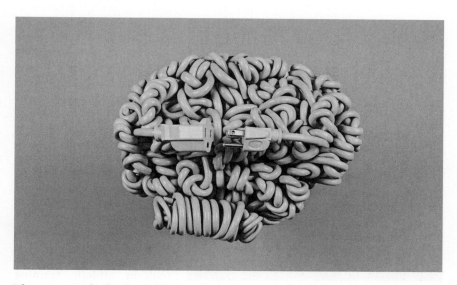

The premise of a feedback loop is simple: Provide people with information about their actions in real time, then give them a chance to change those actions, pushing them toward better behaviors.

which it was captured but in a context that makes it emotionally resonant. This is the relevance stage. But even compelling information is useless if we don't know what to make of it, so we need a third stage: consequence. The information must illuminate one or more paths ahead. And finally, the fourth stage: action. There must be a clear moment when the individual can recalibrate a behavior, make a choice, and act. Then that action is measured, and the feedback loop can run once more, every action stimulating new behaviors that inch us closer to our goals.

This basic framework has been shaped and refined by thinkers and research- 10 ers for ages. In the 18th century, engineers developed regulators and governors to modulate steam engines and other mechanical systems, an early application of feedback loops that later became codified into control theory, the engineering discipline behind everything from aerospace to robotics. The mathematician Norbert Wiener expanded on this work in the 1940s, devising the field of cybernetics, which analyzed how feedback loops operate in machinery and electronics and explored how those principles might be broadened to human systems.

The potential of the feedback loop to affect behavior was explored in the 1960s, most notably in the work of Albert Bandura, a Stanford University psychologist and pioneer in the study of behavior change and motivation. Drawing on several education experiments involving children, Bandura observed that giving individuals a clear goal and a means to evaluate their progress toward that goal greatly increased the likelihood that they would achieve it. He later expanded this notion into the concept of self-efficacy, which holds

Over the past 40 years, feedback loops have been thoroughly researched and validated in psychology, epidemiology, military strategy, environmental studies, engineering, and economics.

that the more we believe we can meet a goal, the more likely we will do so. In the 40 years since Bandura's early work, feedback loops have been thoroughly researched and validated in psychology, epidemiology, military strategy, environmental studies, engineering, and economics. (In typical academic fashion, each discipline tends to reinvent the methodology and rephrase the terminology, but the basic framework remains the same.) Feedback loops are a common tool in athletic training plans, executive coaching strategies, and a multitude of other self-improvement programs (though some are more true to the science than others).

Despite the volume of research and a proven capacity to affect human behavior, we don't often use feedback loops in everyday life. Blame this on two factors: Until now, the necessary catalyst—personalized data—has been an expensive commodity. Health spas, athletic training centers, and self-improvement workshops all traffic in fastidiously culled data at premium rates. Outside of those rare realms, the cornerstone information has been just too expensive to come by. As a technologist might put it, personalized data hasn't really scaled.

Second, collecting data on the cheap is cumbersome. Although the basic idea of self-tracking has been available to anyone willing to put in the effort, few people stick with the routine of toting around a notebook, writing down every Hostess cupcake they consume or every flight of stairs they climb. It's just too much bother. The technologist would say that capturing that data involves too much friction. As a result, feedback loops are niche tools, for the most part, rewarding for those with the money, willpower, or geeky inclination to obsessively track their own behavior, but impractical for the rest of us.

That's quickly changing because of one essential technology: sensors. Adding sensors to the feedback equation helps solve problems of friction and scale. They automate the capture of behavioral data, digitizing it so it can be readily crunched and transformed as necessary. And they allow passive measurement, eliminating the need for tedious active monitoring.

15   In the past two or three years, the plunging price of sensors has begun to foster a feedback-loop revolution. Just as Your Speed signs have been adopted

worldwide because the cost of radar technology keeps dropping, other feed-back loops are popping up everywhere because sensors keep getting cheaper and better at monitoring behavior and capturing data in all sorts of environ-ments. These new, less expensive devices include accelerometers (which mea-sure motion), GPS sensors (which track location), and inductance sensors (which measure electric current). Accelerometers have dropped to less than $1 each—down from as much as $20 a decade ago—which means they can now be built into tennis shoes, MP3 players, and even toothbrushes. Radio-frequency ID chips are being added to prescription pill bottles, student ID cards, and casino chips. And inductance sensors that were once deployed only in heavy industry are now cheap and tiny enough to be connected to residen-tial breaker boxes, letting consumers track their home's entire energy diet.

Of course, technology has been tracking what people do for years. Call-center agents have been monitored closely since the 1990s, and the nation's tractor-trailer fleets have long been equipped with GPS and other location sensors—not just to allow drivers to follow their routes but so that companies can track their cargo and the drivers. But those are top-down, Big Brother[1] techniques. The true power of feedback loops is not to control people but to give them control. It's like the difference between a speed trap and a speed feed-back sign—one is a game of gotcha, the other is a gentle reminder of the rules of the road. The ideal feedback loop gives us an emotional connection to a ratio-nal goal.

And today, their promise couldn't be greater. The intransigence of human behavior has emerged as the root of most of the world's biggest challenges. Wit-ness the rise in obesity, the persistence of smoking, the soaring number of people who have one or more chronic diseases. Consider our problems with carbon emissions, where managing personal energy consumption could be the differ-ence between a climate under control and one beyond help. And feedback loops aren't just about solving problems. They could create opportunities. Feedback loops can improve how companies motivate and empower their employees, allowing workers to monitor their own productivity and set their own sched-ules. They could lead to lower consumption of precious resources and more productive use of what we do consume. They could allow people to set and achieve better-defined, more ambitious goals and curb destructive behaviors, replacing them with positive actions. Used in organizations or communities, they can help groups work together to take on more daunting challenges. In short, the feedback loop is an age-old strategy revitalized by state-of-the-art technology. As such, it is perhaps the most promising tool for behavioral change to have come along in decades.

In 2006, Shwetak Patel, then a graduate student in computer science at Geor-gia Tech, was working on a problem: How could technology help provide remote care for the elderly? The obvious approach would be to install cameras and

---

1. Allusion to the authoritarian government in George Orwell's dystopian novel *Nine-teen Eighty-Four* (1949).

motion detectors throughout a home, so that observers could see when somebody fell or became sick. Patel found those methods unsophisticated and impractical. "Installing cameras or motion sensors everywhere is unreasonably expensive," he says. "It might work in theory, but it just won't happen in practice. So I wondered what would give us the same information and be reasonably priced and easy to deploy. I found those really interesting constraints."

The answer, Patel realized, is that every home emits something called voltage noise. Think of it as a steady hum in the electrical wires that varies depending on what systems are drawing power. If there were some way to disaggregate this noise, it might be possible to deliver much the same information as cameras and motion sensors. Lights going on and off, for instance, would mean that someone had moved from room to room. If a blender were left on, that might signal that someone had fallen—or had forgotten about the blender, perhaps indicating dementia. If we could hear electricity usage, Patel thought, we could know what was happening inside the house.

20   A nifty idea, but how to make it happen? The problem wasn't measuring the voltage noise; that's easily tracked with a few sensors. The challenge was translating the cacophony of electromagnetic interference into the symphony of signals given off by specific appliances and devices and lights. Finding that pattern amid the noise became the focus of Patel's PhD work, and in a few years he had both his degree and his answer: a stack of algorithms that could discern a blender from a light switch from a television set and so on. All this data could be captured not by sensors in every electrical outlet throughout the house but through a single device plugged into a single outlet.

This, Patel soon realized, went way beyond elder care. His approach could inform ordinary consumers, in real time, about where the energy they paid for every month was going. "We kind of stumbled across this stuff," Patel says. "But we realized that, combined with data on the house's overall draw on power"—which can be measured through a second sensor easily installed at the circuit box—"we were getting really great information about resource consumption in the home. And that could be more than interesting information. It could encourage behavior change."

By 2008, Patel had started a new job in the computer science and engineering departments at the University of Washington, and his idea had been turned into the startup Zensi. At Washington, he focused on devising similar techniques to monitor home consumption of water and gas. The solutions were even more elegant, perhaps, than the one for monitoring electricity. A transducer affixed to an outdoor spigot can detect changes in water pressure that correspond to the resident's water usage. That data can then be disaggregated to distinguish a leaky toilet from an over-indulgent bather. And a microphone sensor on a gas meter listens to changes in the regulator to determine how much gas is consumed.

Last year, consumer electronics company Belkin acquired Zensi and made energy conservation a centerpiece of its corporate strategy, with feedback loops as the guiding principle. Belkin has begun modestly, with a device called the Conserve Insight. It's an outlet adapter that gives consumers a close read of

HOW A FEEDBACK LOOP WORKS

A modified traffic sign can have a profound effect on drivers' behavior. Here's what happens.

1. Evidence

The radar-equipped sign flashes a car's current speed.

First comes the data—quantifying a behavior and presenting that data back to the individual so they know where they stand. After all, you can't change what you don't measure.

2. Relevance

The sign also displays the legal speed limit—most people don't want to be seen as bad drivers.

Data is just digits unless it hits home. Through information design, social context, or some other proxy for meaning, the right incentive will transform rational information into an emotional imperative.

3. Consequences

People are reminded of the downside of speeding, including traffic tickets and the risk of accidents.

Even compelling information is useless unless it ties into some larger goal or purpose. People must have a sense of what to do with the information and any opportunities they will have to act on it.

4. Action

Drivers slow an average of 10 percent—usually for several miles.

The individual has to engage with all of the above and act—thus closing the loop and allowing that new action to be measured.

---

the power used by one select appliance: Plug it into a wall socket and then plug an appliance or gadget into it and a small display shows how much energy the device is consuming, in both watts and dollars. It's a window into how energy is actually used, but it's only a proof-of-concept prototype of the more ambitious product, based on Patel's PhD work, that Belkin will begin beta-testing in Chicago later this year with an eye toward commercial release in 2013. The company calls it Zorro.[2]

At first glance, the Zorro is just another so-called smart meter, not that different from the boxes that many power companies have been installing in consumers' homes, with a vague promise that the meters will educate citizens and provide better data to the utility. To the surprise of the utility companies, though, these smart meters have been greeted with hostility in some commu-

---

2. Allusion to the fictional character Zorro, a masked swordsman who defends the poor and oppressed in California while it was under Spanish rule (1769–1821).

nities. A small but vocal number of customers object to being monitored, while others worry that the radiation from RFID transmitters is unhealthy (though this has been measured at infinitesimal levels).

25   Politics aside, in pure feedback terms smart meters fail on at least two levels. For one, the information goes to the utility first, rather than directly to the consumer. For another, most smart meters aren't very smart; they typically measure overall household consumption, not how much power is being consumed by which specific device or appliance. In other words, they are a broken feedback loop.

Belkin's device avoids these pitfalls by giving the data directly to consumers and delivering it promptly and continuously. "Real-time feedback is key to conservation," says Kevin Ashton, Zensi's former CEO who took over Belkin's Conserve division after the acquisition. "There's a visceral impact when you see for yourself how much your toaster is costing you."

The Zorro is just the first of several Belkin products that Ashton believes will put feedback loops into effect throughout the home. Ashton worked on RFID chips at MIT in the late 1990s and lays claim to coining the phrase "Internet of Things," meaning a world of interconnected, sensor-laden devices and objects. He predicts that home sensors will one day inform choices in all aspects of our lives. "We're consuming so many things without thinking about them—energy, plastic, paper, calories. I can envision a ubiquitous sensor network, a platform for real-time feedback that will enhance the comfort, security, and control of our lives."

As a starting point for a consumer products company, that's not half bad.

If there is one problem in medicine that confounds doctors, insurers, and pharmaceutical companies alike, it's noncompliance, the unfriendly term for patients who don't follow doctors' orders. Most vexing are those who don't take their medications as prescribed—which, it turns out, is pretty much most of us. Studies have shown that about half of patients who are prescribed medication take their pills as directed. For drugs like statins, which must be used for years, the rate is even worse, dropping to around 30 percent after a year. (Since the effect of these drugs can be invisible, the thinking goes, patients don't detect any benefit.) Research has found that noncompliance adds $100 billion annually to US health care costs and leads to 125,000 unnecessary deaths from cardiovascular diseases alone every year. And it can be blamed almost entirely on human foibles—people failing to do what they know they should.

30   David Rose is a perfect example of this. He has a family history of heart disease. Now 44, he began taking medication for high blood pressure a few years ago, making him not so different from the nearly one-third of Americans with hypertension. Where Rose is exceptional is in his capacity to do something about noncompliance. He has a knack for inventing beautiful, engaging, alluring objects that get people to do things like take their pills.

A decade ago, Rose, whose stylish glasses and soft-spoken manner bring to mind a college music teacher, started a company called Ambient Devices. His most famous product is the Orb, a translucent sphere that turns different colors to reflect different information inputs. If your stocks go down, it might glow red; if it snows, it might glow white, and so on, depending on what information you tell the Orb you are interested in. It's a whimsical product and is still available for purchase online. But as far as Rose is concerned, the Orb was merely a prelude to his next company, Vitality, and its marquee product: the GlowCap.

A FEEDBACK LOOP FOR EVERY GOAL

Rypple
Work Better Rypple's online platform helps workers give and receive feedback. Picture it as Facebook for the office: Users can set up private projects, post comments, make their goals public, and even assign badges to one another's profiles. Supervisors can use it to track the progress of their employees, and there's a tool for coaching workers and managers.

Zeo
Sleep Better Zeo's headband measures the brainwaves that are correlated with sleep quality, and a bedside monitor presents users with a score in the morning. The display also shows the amount of time spent in various sleep cycles and how long it took you to fall asleep. If you're sleeping poorly, Zeo's online tools will ask you questions—Do your kids sleep in your bed? Do you have pets? Do you exercise?—then offer up strategies for better sleep.

Belkin Conserve Insight
Conserve Better Belkin makes a simple plug-in device that measures the power consumed by any appliance. It then translates that into cash burned and carbon emitted. The idea is to help consumers budget their energy use by showing them how much their electronics cost.

GreenRoad
Drive Better GreenRoad's in-vehicle display uses GPS and accelerometers to let drivers spot and correct risky or fuel-inefficient driving habits in real time. Red, yellow, and green lights on the dash warn drivers when they're making too many dangerous moves—like accelerating into turns or stopping suddenly. (The data is also posted online so supervisors can review employees' driving and see if certain routes or shifts are more hazardous for their drivers.)

GreenGoose
Live Better GreenGoose uses wireless sensors and simple game mechanics to encourage behaviors like brushing your teeth, riding your bike, and walking your dog. Users get points as rewards for their everyday actions and bonus points for consistency. Starting this fall, people will be able to use those points in simple online games.

The device is simple. When a patient is prescribed a medication, a physician or pharmacy provides a GlowCap to go on top of the pill bottle, replacing the standard childproof cap. The GlowCap, which comes with a plug-in unit that Rose calls a night-light, connects to a database that knows the patient's particular dosage directions—say, two pills twice a day, at 8 am and 8 pm. When 8 am rolls around, the GlowCap and the night-light start to pulse with a gentle orange light. A few minutes later, if the pill bottle isn't opened, the light pulses a little more urgently. A few minutes more and the device begins to play a melody—not an annoying buzz or alarm. Finally, if more time elapses (the intervals are adjustable), the patient receives a text message or a recorded phone call reminding them to pop the GlowCap. The overall effect is a persistent feedback loop urging patients to take their meds.

These nudges have proven to be remarkably effective. In 2010, Partners HealthCare and Harvard Medical School conducted a study that gave Glow-Caps to 140 patients on hypertension medications; a control group received nonactivated GlowCap bottles. After three months, adherence in the control group had declined to less than 50 percent, the same dismal rate observed in countless other studies. But patients using GlowCaps did remarkably better: More than 80 percent of them took their pills, a rate that lasted for the duration of the six-month study.

The power of the device can perhaps be explained by the fact that the GlowCap incorporates several schools of behavioral change. Vitality has experimented with charging consumers for the product, drawing on the behavioral-economics theory that people are more willing to use something they've paid for. But in other circumstances the company has given users a financial reward for taking their medication, using a carrot-and-stick methodology. Different models work for different people, Rose says. "We use reminders and social incentives and financial incentives—whatever we can," he says. "We want to provide enough feedback so that it's complementary to people's lives, but not so much that you can't handle the onslaught."

35   Here Rose grapples with an essential challenge of feedback loops: Make them too passive and you'll lose your audience as the data blurs into the background of everyday life. Make them too intrusive and the data turns into noise, which is easily ignored. Borrowing a concept from cognitive psychology called pre-attentive processing, Rose aims for a sweet spot between these extremes, where the information is delivered unobtrusively but noticeably. The best sort of delivery device "isn't cognitively loading at all," he says. "It uses colors, patterns, angles, speed—visual cues that don't distract us but remind us." This creates what Rose calls "enchantment." Enchanted objects, he says, don't register as gadgets or even as technology at all, but rather as friendly tools that beguile us into action. In short, they're magical.

This approach to information delivery is a radical departure from how our health care system usually works. Conventional wisdom holds that medical information won't be heeded unless it sets off alarms. Instead of glowing orbs, we're pummeled with FDA cautions and Surgeon General warnings and front-page reports, all of which serve to heighten our anxiety about our health. This fear-based approach can work—for a while. But fear, it turns out, is a poor cata-lyst for sustained behavioral change. After all, biologically our fear response girds us for short-term threats. If nothing threatening actually happens, the fear dissipates. If this happens too many times, we end up simply dismissing the alarms.

It's worth noting here how profoundly difficult it is for most people to improve their health. Consider: Self-directed smoking-cessation programs typ-ically work for perhaps 5 percent of participants, and weight-loss programs are considered effective if people lose as little as 5 percent of their body weight. Part of the problem is that so much in our lives—the foods we eat, the ads we see, the things our culture celebrates—is driven by feedback loops that sustain bad behaviors. But we can counterprogram this onslaught with another feed-back loop, increasing our odds of changing course.

Though GlowCaps improved compliance by an astonishing 40 percent, feedback loops more typically improve outcomes by about 10 percent compared to traditional methods. That 10 percent figure is surprisingly persistent; it turns up in everything from home energy monitors to smoking cessation programs to those Your Speed signs. At first glance, 10 percent may not seem like a lot. After all, if you're 250 pounds and obese, losing 25 pounds is a start, but your BMI is likely still in the red zone. But it turns out that 10 percent does matter. A lot. An obese 40-year-old man would spare himself three years of hypertension and nearly two years of diabetes by losing 10 percent of his weight. A 10 percent reduction in home energy consumption could reduce carbon emissions by as much as 20 percent (generating energy during peak demand periods creates more pollution than off-peak generation). And those Your Speed signs? It turns out that reducing speeds by 10 percent from 40 to 35 mph would cut fatal inju-ries by about half.

In other words, 10 percent is something of an inflection point, where lots of great things happen. The results are measurable, the economics calculable. "The value of behavior change is incredibly large: nearly $5,000 a year," says David Rose, citing a CVS pharmacy white paper. "At that rate, we can afford to give every diabetic a connected glucometer. We can give the morbidly obese a Wi-Fi-enabled scale and a pedometer. The value is there; the savings are there. The cost of the sensors is negligible."

So feedback loops work. Why? Why does putting our own data in front of us somehow compel us to act? In part, it's that feedback taps into something core to the human experience, even to our biological origins. Like any organism, humans are self-regulating creatures, with a multitude of systems working to achieve homeostasis. Evolution itself, after all, is a feedback loop, albeit one so elongated as to be imperceptible by an individual. Feedback loops are how we learn, whether we call it trial and error or course correction. In so many areas of life, we succeed when we have some sense of where we stand and some evaluation of our progress. Indeed, we tend to crave this sort of information; it's something we viscerally want to know, good or bad. As Stanford's Bandura put it, "People are proactive, aspiring organisms." Feedback taps into those aspirations.

The visceral satisfaction and even pleasure we get from feedback loops is the organizing principle behind GreenGoose, a startup being hatched by Brian Krejcarek, a Minnesota native who wears a near-constant smile, so enthusiastic is he about the power of cheap sensors. His mission is to stitch feedback loops into the fabric of our daily lives, one sensor at a time.

As Krejcarek describes it, GreenGoose started with a goal not too different from Shwetak Patel's: to measure household consumption of energy. But the company's mission took a turn in 2009, when he experimented with putting one of those ever-cheaper accelerometers on a bicycle wheel. As the wheel rotated, the sensor picked up the movement, and before long Krejcarek had a vision of a grander plan. "I wondered what else we could measure. Where else could we stick these things?" The answer he came up with: everywhere. The GreenGoose concept starts with a sheet of stickers, each containing an accelerometer labeled with a cartoon icon of a familiar household object—a refrigerator handle, a water bottle, a toothbrush, a yard rake. But the secret to GreenGoose isn't the accelerometer; that's a less-than-a-dollar commodity. The key is the algorithm that Krejcarek's team has coded into the chip next to the accelerometer that recognizes a particular pattern of movement. For a toothbrush, it's a rapid back-and-forth that indicates somebody is brushing their teeth. For a water bottle, it's a simple up-and-down that correlates with somebody taking a sip. And so on. In essence, GreenGoose uses sensors to spray feedback loops like atomized perfume throughout our daily life—in our homes, our vehicles, our backyards. "Sensors are these little eyes and ears on whatever we do and how we do it," Krejcarek says. "If a behavior has a pattern, if we can calculate a desired duration and intensity, we can create a system that rewards that behavior and encourages more of it." Thus the first component of a feedback loop: data gathering.

Then comes the second step: relevance. GreenGoose converts the data into points, with a certain amount of action translating into a certain number of points, say 30 seconds of teeth brushing for two points. And here Krejcarek gets noticeably excited. "The points can be used in games on our website," he says. "Think FarmVille but with live data." Krejcarek plans to open the platform to game developers, who he hopes will create games that are simple, easy, and sticky. A few hours of raking leaves might build up points that can be used in a gardening game. And the games induce people to earn more points, which means repeating good behaviors. The idea, Krejcarek says, is to "create a bridge between the real world and the virtual world. This has all got to be fun."

As powerful as the idea appears now, just a few months ago it seemed like a fading pipe dream. Then based in Cambridge, Massachusetts, Krejcarek had nearly run out of cash—not just for his company, but for himself. During the day, he was working on GreenGoose in an office building near the MIT campus—and each night, he'd sneak into the building's air shaft, where he'd stashed an air mattress and some clothes. Then, in late February, he went to the Launch conference in San Francisco, a two-day event where select entrepreneurs get a chance to demo their company to potential funders. Krejcarek hadn't been selected for an onstage demo, but when the conference organizers saw a crowd eyeing his product on the exhibit floor, he was given four minutes to make a presentation. It was one of those only-in-Silicon Valley moments. The crowd "just got it," he recalls. Within days, he had nearly $600,000 in new funding. He moved to San Francisco, rented an apartment—and bought a bed. Green-Goose will release its first product, a kit of sensors that encourages pet owners to play and interact with their dogs, with sensors for dog collar, pet toys, and dog doors, sometime this fall.

Part of the excitement around GreenGoose is that the company is so good at "gamification," the much-blogged-about notion that game elements like points or levels can be applied to various aspects of our lives. Gamification is exciting because it promises to make the hard stuff in life fun—just sprinkle a little videogame magic and suddenly a burden turns into bliss. But as happens with fads, gamification is both overhyped and misunderstood. It is too often just a shorthand for badges or points, like so many gold stars on a spelling test. But just as no number of gold stars can trick children into thinking that yesterday's quiz was fun, game mechanics, to work, must be an informing principle, not a veneer.

With its savvy application of feedback loops, though, GreenGoose is onto more than just the latest fad. The company represents the fruition of a long-promised technological event horizon: the Internet of Things, in which a sensor-rich world measures our every action. This vision, championed by Kevin Ashton at Belkin, Sandy Pentland at MIT, and Bruce Sterling . . . has long had the whiff of vaporware, something promised by futurists but never realized. But as GreenGoose, Belkin, and other companies begin to use sensors to deploy feedback loops throughout our lives, we can finally see the potential of a sensor-rich environment. The Internet of Things isn't about the things; it's about us.

For now, the reality still isn't as sexy as the visions. Stickers on toothbrushes and plugs in wall sockets aren't exactly disappearing technology. But maybe requiring people to do a little work—to stick accelerometers around their house or plug a device into a wall socket—is just enough of a nudge to get our brains engaged in the prospect for change. Perhaps it's good to have the infrastructure of feedback loops just a bit visible now, before they disappear into our environments altogether, so that they can serve as a subtle reminder that we have something to change, that we can do better—and that the tools for doing better are rapidly, finally, turning up all around us.

MLA CITATION

Goetz, Thomas. "Harnessing the Power of Feedback Loops." *The Norton Reader: An Anthology of Nonfiction*, edited by Melissa A. Goldthwaite et al., 15th ed., W. W. Norton, 2020, pp. 591–603.

QUESTIONS

1. In paragraph 9, Thomas Goetz describes the four stages of a feedback loop. Look again at his definition and then find how those stages work in several of the inventions he describes here. How does the repetition of the loop several times across the essay affect your understanding of the process?

2. Goetz looks forward to a future in which ubiquitous sensors enable feedback loops to enhance every aspect of our lives (paragraph 46). Can you imagine any negative consequences of this development? Why, for example, does Goetz disparage monitors that send information to companies rather than to individuals as "top-down, Big Brother techniques" (paragraph 16)?

3. Think of a behavior or habit that you would like to change and write an essay in which you describe an invention to encourage that change based on the principle of the feedback loop.

Jane McGonigal
Be a Gamer, Save the World

Videogames make players feel like their best selves. Why not give them real problems to solve?

WE OFTEN THINK of immersive computer and videogames—like *FarmVille*, *Guitar Hero* and *World of Warcraft*—as "escapist," a kind of passive retreat from reality. Many critics consider such games a mind-numbing waste of time, if not a corrupting influence. But the truth about games is very nearly the opposite. In today's society, they consistently fulfill genuine human needs that the real world fails to satisfy. More than that, they may prove to be a key resource for solving some of our most pressing real-world problems.

Hundreds of millions of people around the globe are already devoting larger and larger chunks of time to this alternate reality. Collectively, we spend three billion hours a week gaming. In the United States, where there are 183 million active gamers, videogames took in about $15.5 billion last year. And though a typical gamer plays for just an hour or two a day, there are now more than five million "extreme" gamers in the United States who play an average of 45 hours a week. To put this in perspective, the number of hours that gamers world-wide have spent playing *World of Warcraft* alone adds up to 5.93 million years.

These gamers aren't rejecting reality entirely, of course. They have careers, goals, schoolwork, families and real lives that they care about. But as they devote more of their free time to game worlds, they often feel that the real world is missing something.

Published in the "Life and Culture" section of the Wall Street Journal *(2011), a daily newspaper covering international and national news with an emphasis on business and economics. Jane McGonigal is the director of game research and development at the Institute for the Future, cofounder of SuperBetter, a website and online game designed to boost physical and emotional well-being, and author of* SuperBetter: The Power of Living Gamefully *(2016).*

Gamers want to know: Where in the real world is the gamer's sense of being fully alive, focused and engaged in every moment? The real world just doesn't offer up the same sort of carefully designed pleasures, thrilling challenges and powerful social bonding that the gamer finds in virtual environments. Reality doesn't motivate us as effectively. Reality isn't engineered to maximize our potential or to make us happy.

Those who continue to dismiss games as merely escapist entertainment will   5
find themselves at a major disadvantage in the years ahead, as more gamers start to harness this power for real good. My research over the past decade at the University of California, Berkeley, and the Institute for the Future has shown that games consistently provide us with the four ingredients that make for a happy and meaningful life: satisfying work, real hope for success, strong social connections and the chance to become a part of something bigger than ourselves.

We get these benefits from our real lives sometimes, but we get them almost every time we play a good game. These benefits are what positive psychologists call intrinsic rewards—we don't play games to make money, improve our social status, or achieve any external signposts of success. And these intrinsic rewards, studies at the University of Pennsylvania, Harvard and U.C. Berkeley have shown, provide the foundation for optimal human experience.

In a good game, we feel blissfully productive. We have clear goals and a sense of heroic purpose. More important, we're constantly able to see and feel the impact of our efforts on the virtual world around us. As a result, we have a stronger sense of our own agency—and we are more likely to set ambitious

Could games like *Guitar Hero* help cure cancer and end poverty?

real-life goals. One recent study found, for example, that players of *Guitar Hero* are more likely to pick up a real guitar and learn how to play it.

When we play, we also have a sense of urgent optimism. We believe whole-heartedly that we are up to any challenge, and we become remarkably resilient in the face of failure. Research shows that gamers spend on average 80% of their time failing in game worlds, but instead of giving up, they stick with the diffi-cult challenge and use the feedback of the game to get better. With some effort, we can learn to apply this resilience to the real-world challenges we face.

Games make it easy to build stronger social bonds with our friends and family. Studies show that we like and trust someone better after we play a game with them—even if they beat us. And we're more likely to help someone in real life after we've helped them in an online game. It's no wonder that 40% of all user time on Facebook is spent playing social games. They're a fast and reli-able way to strengthen our connection with people we care about.

10   Today's videogames are increasingly created on an epic scale, with com-pelling stories, sweeping mythologies and massive multiplayer environments that produce feelings of awe and wonder. Researchers on positive emotion have found that whenever we feel awe or wonder, we become more likely to serve a larger cause and to collaborate selflessly with others.

With so much blissful productivity and urgent optimism, stronger social bonds and extreme cooperation, it's not surprising that so many players feel that they become the best version of themselves in games. That's one of the

Videogames make players feel like their best selves. Why not give them real problems to solve?

reasons I believe we can take the benefits of games a step further. We can harness the power of game design to tackle real-world problems. We can empower gamers to use their virtual-world strengths to accomplish real feats. Indeed, when game communities have been matched with challenging real-world problems, they have already proven themselves capable of producing tangible, potentially world-changing results.

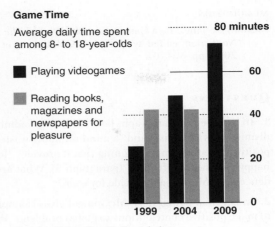

Game Time

Average daily time spent among 8- to 18-year-olds

■ Playing videogames

▨ Reading books, magazines and newspapers for pleasure

80 minutes
60
40
20
0

1999   2004   2009

Source: Kaiser Family Foundation.

In 2010, more than 57,000 gamers were listed as co-authors for a research paper in the prestigious scientific journal *Nature*. The gamers—with no previous background in biochemistry—had worked in a 3D game environment called *Foldit*, folding virtual proteins in new ways that could help cure cancer or prevent Alzheimer's. The game was developed by scientists at the University of Washington who believed that gamers could outperform supercomputers at this creative task— and the players proved them right, beating the supercomputers at more than half of the game's challenges.

More recently, more than 19,000 players of *EVOKE*, an online game that I created for the World Bank Institute, undertook real-world missions to improve food security, increase access to clean energy and end poverty in more than 130 countries. The game focused on building up players' abilities to design and launch their own social enterprises.

After 10 weeks, they had founded more than 50 new companies—real businesses working today from South Africa and India to Buffalo, N.Y. My favorite is Libraries Across Africa, a new franchise system that empowers local entrepreneurs to set up free community libraries. It also creates complementary business opportunities for selling patrons refreshments, WiFi access and cellphone time. The first is currently being tested in Gabon.

These examples are just the beginning of what is possible if we take advantage of the power of games to make us better and change the world. Those who understand this power will be the people who invent our future. We can create rewarding, transformative games for ourselves and our families; for our schools, businesses and neighborhoods; for an entire industry or an entirely new movement.

We can play any games we want. We can create any future we can imagine. Let the games begin.

15

MLA CITATION

McGonigal, Jane. "Be a Gamer, Save the World." *The Norton Reader: An Anthology of Nonfiction*, edited by Melissa A. Goldthwaite et al., 15th ed., W. W. Norton, 2020, pp. 604–07.

QUESTIONS

1. In her opening paragraph, Jane McGonigal admits that video games are usually dismissed as "escapist" and "a mind-numbing waste of time." She presents a more positive case for gaming, arguing that it provides "four ingredients that make for a happy and meaningful life" (paragraph 5). What are those ingredients? What evidence does McGonigal provide for each?

2. In her final paragraphs, McGonigal gives examples of games that allow gamers to make positive contributions to global problems. What evidence does McGonigal provide that these games "make us better and change the world" (paragraph 15)?

3. Given the word limitations, op-ed writers often have little space to acknowledge counterarguments. What negative aspects of gaming does McGonigal not acknowledge? How could including other viewpoints have strengthened her own argument?

4. Play or research one of the games McGonigal mentions in her op-ed. Write an essay evaluating the positive and negative aspects of the game.

TOM BISSELL

Extra Lives: Why Video Games Matter

SOMEDAY MY CHILDREN WILL ASK ME where I was and what I was doing when the United States elected its first black president. I could tell my children—who are entirely hypothetical; call them Kermit and Hussein[1]—that I was home at the time and, like hundreds of millions of other Americans, watching television. This would be a politician's answer, which is to say, factual but inaccurate in every important detail. Because Kermit and Hussein deserve an honestly itemized answer, I will tell them that, on November 4, 2008, their father was living in

This essay is taken from a chapter of Tom Bissell's book Extra Lives: Why Video Games Matter *(2010). In addition to being an author and journalist, Bissell is an avid gamer who has written scripts for several video games.*

1. Kermit, name of a son, grandson, and great-grandson of President Theodore Roosevelt (1858–1919), now associated with Kermit the Frog, a puppet created by Jim Henson (1936–1990); Hussein, name that recalls Saddam Hussein (1937–2006), the president of Iraq who was deposed near the beginning of the Iraq War (2003–11) and subsequently executed; also the middle name of Barack Hussein Obama (b. 1961), forty-fourth president of the United States.

Tallinn, Estonia, where the American Election Day's waning hours were a cold, salmon-skied November 5 morning. My intention that day was to watch CNN International until the race was called. I will then be forced to tell Kermit and Hussein about what else happened on November 4, 2008.

The postapocalyptic video game *Fallout 3* had been officially released to the European market on October 30, but in Estonia it was nowhere to be found. For several weeks, Bethesda Softworks, *Fallout 3*'s developer, had been posting online a series of promotional gameplay videos, which I had been watching and rewatching with fetish-porn avidity. I left word with Tallinn's best game store: *Call me the moment* Fallout 3 *arrives.* In the late afternoon of November 4, they finally rang. When I slipped the game into the tray of my Xbox 360, the first polls were due to close in America in two hours. One hour of *Fallout 3,* I told myself. Maybe two. Absolutely no more than three. Seven hours later, blinking and dazed, I turned off my Xbox 360, checked in with CNN, and discovered that the acceptance speech had already been given.

And so, my beloved Kermit, my dear little Hussein, at the moment America changed forever, your father was wandering an ICBM^2-denuded wasteland, nervously monitoring his radiation level, armed only with a baseball bat, a 10mm pistol, and six rounds of ammunition, in search of a vicious gang of mohawked marauders who were 100 percent bad news and totally had to be dealt with. Trust Daddy on this one.

Fallout 3 was Bethesda's first release since 2006's *The Elder Scrolls IV: Oblivion.* Both games fall within a genre known by various names: the open-world or sandbox or free-roaming game. This genre is superintended by a few general conventions, which include the sensation of being inside a large and disinterestedly functioning world, a main story line that can be abandoned for subordinate story lines (or for no purpose at all), large numbers of supporting characters with whom meaningful interaction is possible, and the ability to customize (or pimp, in the parlance of our time) the game's player-controlled central character. The pleasures of the open-world game are ample, complicated, and intensely private; their potency is difficult to explain, sort of like religion, of which these games become, for many, an aspartame form. Because of the freedom they grant gamers, the narrative- and mission-generating manner in which they reward exploration, and their convincing illusion of endlessness, the best open-world games tend to become leisure-time-eating viruses. As incomprehensible as it may seem, I have somehow spent more than two hundred hours playing *Oblivion.* I know this because the game keeps a running tally of the total time one has spent with it.

It is difficult to describe *Oblivion* without atavistic fears of being savaged   5
by the same jean-jacketed dullards who in 1985 threw my *Advanced Dungeons & Dragons Monster Manual II* into Lake Michigan (That I did not even play D&D, and only had the book because I liked to look at the pictures, left my assailants

2. Intercontinental ballistic missile.

Fallout 3 poster promoting the game's release.

unmoved.) As to what *Oblivion* is about, I note the involvement of orcs and a "summon skeleton" spell and leave it at that. So: two hundred hours playing *Oblivion*? How is that even possible? I am not actually sure. Completing the game's narrative missions took a fraction of that time, but in the world of *Oblivion* you can also pick flowers, explore caves, dive for treasure, buy houses, bet on gladiatorial arena fights, hunt bear, and read books. *Oblivion* is less a game than a world that best rewards full citizenship, and for a while I lived there and claimed it. At the time I was residing in Rome on a highly coveted literary fellowship, surrounded by interesting and brilliant people, and quite naturally mired in a lagoon of depression more dreadfully lush than any before or since. I would be lying if I said *Oblivion* did not, in some ways, aggravate my depression, but it also gave me something with which to fill my days other than piranhic self-hatred. It was an extra life; I am grateful to have had it.

When Bethesda announced that it had purchased the rights to develop *Fallout 3* from the defunct studio Interplay, the creators of the first two *Fallout* games, many were doubtful. How would the elvish imaginations behind *Oblivion* manage with the rather different milieu of an annihilated twenty-third-century America? The first *Fallout* games, which were exclusive to the personal computer, were celebrated for their clever satire and often freakishly exaggerated violence. *Oblivion* is about as satirical as a colonoscopy, and the fighting in the game, while not unviolent, is often weirdly inert.

Bethesda released *Fallout 3*'s first gameplay video in the summer of 2008. In it, Todd Howard, the game's producer, guides the player-controlled character into a disorientingly nuked Washington, D.C., graced with just enough ravaged familiarities—among which a pummeled Washington Monument stands out—to be powerfully unsettling. Based on these few minutes, *Fallout 3* appeared guaranteed to take its place among the most visually impressive games ever made. When Bethesda posted a video showcasing *Fallout 3*'s in-game combat—a brilliant synthesis of trigger-happy first-person-style shooting and the more deliberative, turn-based tactics of the traditional role-playing video game, wherein you attack, suffer your enemy's counterattack, counterattack yourself, and so on, until one of you is dead—many could not believe the audacity of its cartoon-Peckinpah[3] violence. Much of it was rendered in a slo-mo as disgusting as it was oddly beautiful: skulls exploding into the distinct flotsam of eyeballs, gray matter, and upper vertebrae; limbs liquefying into constellations of red pearls; torsos somersaulting through the air. The consensus was a bonfire of the skepticisms:[4] *Fallout 3* was going to be fucking awesome.

Needless to say, the first seven hours I spent with the game were distinguished by a bounty of salutary things. Foremost among them was how the world of *Fallout 3* looked. The art direction in a good number of contemporary big-budget video games has the cheerful parasitism of a tribute band. Visual inspirations are perilously few: Forests will be Tolkienishly[5] enchanted; futuristic industrial zones will be mazes of predictably grated metal catwalks; gunfights will erupt amid rubble- and car-strewn boulevards on loan from a thousand war-movie sieges. Once video games shed their distinctive vector-graphic and primary-color 8-bit origins, a commercially ascendant subset of game slowly but surely matured into what might well be the most visually derivative popular art form in history. *Fallout 3* is the rare big-budget game to begin rather than end with its derivativeness.

It opens in 2277, two centuries after a nuclear conflagration between the United States and China. Chronologically speaking, the world this Sino-American war destroyed was of late-twenty-first-century vintage, and yet its ruins are those of the gee-whiz futurism popular during the Cold War. *Fallout 3*'s Slinky-armed sentry Protectrons, for instance, are knowing plagiarisms of *Forbidden Planet*'s Robby the Robot,[6] and the game's many specimens of faded prewar advertising mimic the nascent slickness of 1950s-era graphic design. *Fallout 3* bravely takes as its aesthetic foundation a future that is both six decades old and one of the least convincing ever conceptualized. The result is a fascinating past-future never-never-land weirdness that infects the game's every corner: *George Jetson Beyond Thunderdome*.[7]

---

3. Sam Peckinpah (1925–1984), American film director and screenwriter known for his violent Westerns.

4. Allusion to "bonfire of the vanities," a term for the burning of items deemed sinful by religious authorities.

5. Allusion to J. R. R. Tolkien (1892–1973), British philologist and fantasy writer.

6. Multilingual robotic hero first introduced in the science-fiction film *Forbidden Planet* (1956).

7. Never-never-land, allusion to Neverland, island home of the fictional character Peter Pan; George Jetson, father of a futuristic family in the cartoon *The Jetsons* (1962–63); *Mad Max: Beyond Thunderdome* (1985), sequel to the postapocalyptic Australian film *Mad Max* (1979).

The player-controlled character of *Fallout* 3 in a futuristic Washington, D.C.

10   What also impressed me about *Fallout* 3 was the buffet of choices set out by its early stages. The first settlement one happens upon, Megaton, has been built around an undetonated nuclear warhead, which a strange religious cult native to the town actually worships. Megaton can serve as base of operations or be wiped off the face of the map shortly after one's arrival there by detonating its nuke in exchange for a handsome payment. I spent quite a while poking around Megaton and getting to know its many citizens. What this means is that the first several hours I spent inside *Fallout* 3 were, in essence, optional. Even for an open-world game, this suggests an awesome range of narrative variability. (Eventually, of course, I made the time to go back and nuke the place.)

 Fallout 3, finally, looks beautiful. Most modern games—even shitty ones—look beautiful. Taking note of this is akin to telling the chef of a Michelin-starred restaurant that the tablecloths were lovely. Nonetheless, at one point in *Fallout* 3 I was running up the stairs of what used to be the Dupont Circle Metro station and, as I turned to bash in the brainpan of a radioactive ghoul, noticed the playful, lifelike way in which the high-noon sunlight streaked along the grain of my sledgehammer's wooden handle. During such moments, it is hard not to be startled—even moved—by the care poured into the game's smallest atmospheric details.

 Despite all this, I had problems with *Fallout* 3, and a number of these problems seem to me emblematic of the intersection at which games in general currently find themselves stalled. Take, for instance, *Fallout* 3's tutorial. One feels for game designers: It would be hard to imagine a formal convention more inherently bizarre than the video-game tutorial. Imagine that, every time you open a novel, you are forced to suffer through a chapter in which the characters do nothing but talk to one another about the physical mechanics of how one goes about reading a book. Unfortunately, game designers do not really have a choice. Controller schemas change, sometimes drastically, from game to game, and designers cannot simply banish a game's relevant instructions to a directional booklet: That would be a violation of the interactive pact between game and gamer. Many games thus have to come up with a narratively plausible way in which one's controlled character engages in activity comprehensive enough to be instructive but not so intense as to involve a lot of failure. Games with a strong element of combat almost always solve this dilemma by opening with some sort of indifferently conceived boot-camp exercise or training round.

Fallout 3's tutorial opens, rather more ambitiously, with your character's birth, during which you pick your race and gender (if given the choice, I always opt for a woman, for whatever reason) and design your eventual appearance (probably this is the reason). The character who pulls you from your mother's birth canal is your father, whose voice is provided by Liam Neeson.[8] (Many games attempt to class themselves up with early appearances by accomplished actors; Patrick Stewart's[9] platinum larynx served this purpose in *Oblivion*.) Now, aspects of *Fallout 3*'s tutorial are brilliant: When you learn to walk as a baby, you are actually learning how to move within the game; you decide whether you want your character to be primarily strong, intelligent, or charismatic by reading a children's book; and, when the tutorial flashes forward to your tenth birthday party, you learn to fire weapons when you receive a BB gun as a gift. The tutorial flashes forward again, this time to a high school classroom, where you further define your character by answering ten aptitude-test-style questions. What is interesting about this is that it allows you to customize your character *indirectly* rather than directly, and many of the questions (one asks what you would do if your grandmother ordered you to kill someone) are morbidly amusing. While using an in-game aptitude test as a character-design aid is not exactly a new innovation, *Fallout 3* provides the most streamlined, narratively economical, and interactively inventive go at it yet.

By the time I was taking this aptitude test, however, I was a dissident citizen of Vault 101, the isolated underground society in which *Fallout 3* proper begins. My revolt was directed at a few things. The first was *Fallout 3*'s dialogue, some of it so appalling ("Oh, James, we did it. A daughter. Our beautiful daughter") as to make Stephenie Meyer look like Ibsen.[10] The second was *Fall-*

8. Irish film actor (b. 1952).

9. English stage, TV, and film actor (b. 1940).

10. Meyer (b. 1973), young-adult fiction writer and author of the *Twilight* series of vampire romance novels (2005–08); Henrik Ibsen (1828–1906), Norwegian playwright, considered by many to have revolutionized modern drama.

out 3's addiction to trust-shattering storytelling redundancy, such as when your father announces, "I can't believe you're already ten," at what is clearly established as your tenth birthday party. The third, and least forgivable, was *Fallout* 3's Jell-O-mold characterization: In the game's first ten minutes you exchange gossip with the spunky best friend, cower beneath the megalomaniacal leader, and gain the trust of the goodhearted cop. Vault 101 even has a resident cadre of hoodlums, the Tunnel Snakes, whose capo resembles a malevolent Fonz.[11] Even with its backdrop of realized Cold War futurism, a greaser-style youth gang in an underground vault society in the year 2277 is the working definition of a dumb idea. During the tutorial's final sequence, the Tunnel Snakes' leader, your tormentor since childhood, requests your help in saving his mother from radioactive cockroaches (long story), a reversal of such tofu drama that, in my annoyance, I killed him, his mother, and then everyone else I could find in Vault 101, with the most perversely satisfying weapon I had on hand: a baseball bat. Allowing your decisions to establish for your character an in-game identity as a skull-crushing monster, a saint of patience, or some mixture thereof is another attractive feature of *Fallout* 3. These pretensions to morality, though, suddenly bored me, because they were occurring in a universe that had been designed by geniuses and written by Ed Wood Jr.[12]

15   Had I really waited a year for this? And was I really missing a cardinal event in American history to keep playing it? I had, and I was, and I could not really explain why.

What I know is this: If I were reading a book or watching a film that, every ten minutes, had me gulping a gallon of aesthetic Pepto, I would stop reading or watching. Games, for some reason, do not have this problem. Or rather, their problem is not having this problem. I routinely tolerate in games crudities I would never tolerate in any other form of art or entertainment. For a long time my rationalization was that, provided a game was fun to play, certain failures could be overlooked. I came to accept that games were generally incompetent with almost every aspect of what I would call traditional narrative. In the last few years, however, a dilemma has become obvious. Games have grown immensely sophisticated in any number of ways while at the same time remaining stubbornly attached to aspects of traditional narrative for which they have shown little feeling. Too many games insist on telling stories in a manner in which some facility with plot and character is fundamental to—and often even determinative of—successful storytelling.

The counterargument to all this is that games such as *Fallout* 3 are more about the world in which the game takes place than the story concocted to govern one's progress through it. It is a fair point, especially given how beautifully devastated and hypnotically lonely the world of *Fallout* 3 is. But if the world is paramount, why bother with a story at all? Why not simply cut the ribbon on

11. Nickname of Arthur Fonzarelli, a character in the TV sitcom *Happy Days* (1974–84).
12. American director (1924–1978) of "B" movies such as *Plan 9 from Outer Space* (1958) and known among his cult following as the "worst director of all time."

the invented world and let gamers explore it? The answer is that such a game would probably not be very involving. Traps, after all, need bait. In a narrative game, story and world combine to create an experience. As the game designer Jesse Schell writes in *The Art of Game Design*, "The game is not the experience. The game enables the experience, but it *is not the experience*." In a world as large as that of *Fallout 3*, which allows for an experience framed in terms of wandering and lonesomeness, story provides, if nothing else, badly needed direction and purpose. Unless some narrative game comes along that radically changes gamer expectation, stories, with or without Super Mutants, will continue to be what many games will use to harness their uniquely extravagant brand of fictional absorption.

I say this in full disclosure: The games that interest me the most are the games that choose to tell stories. Yes, video games have always told some form of story. PLUMBER'S GIRLFRIEND CAPTURED BY APE![13] is a story, but it is a rudimentary fairytale story without any of the proper fairytale's evocative nuances and dreads. Games are often compared to films, which would seem to make sense, given their many apparent similarities (both are scored, both have actors, both are cinematographical, and so on). Upon close inspection comparison falls leprously apart. In terms of storytelling, they could not be more different. Films favor a compressed type of storytelling and are able to do this because they have someone deciding where to point the camera. Games, on the other hand, contain more than most gamers can ever hope to see, and the person deciding where to point the camera is, in many cases, you—and you might never even see the "best part." The best part of looking up at a night sky, after all, is not any one star but the infinite possibility of what is between stars. Games often provide an approximation of this feeling, with the difference that you can find out what is out there. Teeming with secrets, hidden areas, and surprises that may pounce only on the second or third (or fourth) playthrough—I still laugh to think of the time I made it to an isolated, hard-to-find corner of *Fallout 3*'s Wasteland and was greeted by the words FUCK YOU spray-painted on a rock—video games favor a form of storytelling that is, in many ways, completely unprecedented. The conventions of this form of storytelling are only a few decades old and were created in a formal vacuum by men and women who still walk among us. There are not many mediums whose Dantes and Homers one can ring up and talk to.[14] With games, one can.

I am uninterested in whether games are better or worse than movies or novels or any other form of entertainment. More interesting to me is what games *can* do and how they make me feel while they are doing it. Comparing games to other forms of entertainment only serves as a reminder of what games are not. Storytelling, however, does not belong to film any more than it belongs to

13. Allusion to *Donkey Kong*, an arcade game introduced in 1981 that is credited with introducing storytelling to video games.
14. Dante Alighieri (1265–1321), Italian poet who wrote the *Divine Comedy*; Homer (unknown), ancient Greek poet to whom the epics the *Iliad* and the *Odyssey* are traditionally attributed.

the novel. Film, novels, and video games are separate economies in which storytelling is the currency. The problem is that video-game storytelling, across a wide spectrum of games, too often feels counterfeit, and it is easy to tire of laundering the bills.

20   It should be said that *Fallout 3* gets much better as you play through it. A few of its set pieces (such as stealing the Declaration of Independence from a ruined National Archives, which is protected by a bewigged robot programmed to believe itself to be Button Gwinnett,[15] the Declaration's second signatory) are as gripping as any fiction I have come across. But it cannot be a coincidence that every scene involving human emotion (confronting a mind-wiped android who believes he is human, watching as a character close to you suffocates and dies) is at best unaffecting and at worst risible. Can it really be a surprise that deeper human motivations remain beyond the reach of something that regards character as the assignation of numerical values to hypothetical abilities and characteristics?

Viewed as a whole, *Fallout 3* is a game of profound stylishness, sophistication, and intelligence—so much so that every example of Etch A Sketch[16] characterization, every stone-shoed narrative pivot, pains me. When we say a game is sophisticated, are we grading on a distressingly steep curve? Or do we need a new curve altogether? Might we really mean that the game in question only occasionally insults one's intelligence? Or is this kind of intelligence, at least when it comes to playing games, beside the point? How is it, finally, that I keep returning to a form of entertainment that I find so uniquely frustrating? To what part of me do games speak, and on which frequency?

MLA CITATION

Bissell, Tom. "Extra Lives: Why Video Games Matter." *The Norton Reader: An Anthology of Nonfiction*, edited by Melissa A. Goldthwaite et al., 15th ed., W. W. Norton, 2020, pp. 608–16.

QUESTIONS

1. A common objection to video games is that they encourage violence. How do you think Tom Bissell would respond to this objection? How does he treat violence in his essay?

2. Bissell asserts, "The pleasures of the open-world game are ample, complicated, and intensely private; their potency is difficult to explain" (paragraph 4). What sorts of pleasures does Bissell find in games? How are these pleasures connected or in tension with each other? How, in his prose style and manner of arguing, does Bissell wrestle with the difficulty of explaining these pleasures?

3. As he nears the end of his essay, Bissell declares, "The games that interest me most are the games that choose to tell stories" (paragraph 18). What, according to

15. Georgia delegate (1735–1777) to the Second Continental Congress in Philadelphia.
16. Iconic drawing toy.

Bissell, are the special challenges and opportunities of what he calls "video-game storytelling" (paragraph 19)? (As you reread the essay to answer this question, pay attention not just to what Bissell *says* in his final paragraphs but also to what he *suggests* in his earlier assessment of *Fallout 3*.)

4. Bissell concludes his essay with a series of questions. What is the effect of this gesture? Write an essay that responds to these questions. If you are a gamer, consider relating your own experiences to Bissell's. If not, consider interviewing a gamer or writing about an activity that is important to you.

LAUREN MICHELE JACKSON
A Unified Theory of Meme Death

MEMES AREN'T BUILT TO LAST. This is an accepted fact of online life. Some of our most beloved cultural objects are not only ephemeral but transmitted around the world at high speed before the close of business. Memes sprout from the ether (or so it seems). They charm and amuse us. They sicken and annoy us. They bore us. They linger for a while on Facebook and then they die—or rather retreat back into the cybernetic ooze unless called upon again.

The constancy of this narrative may be observed in any number of internet memes in recent memory, from the incredibly short-lived (Damn Daniel, Dat Boi, Salt Bae, queer Babadook) to the ones seemingly too perfect to ever perish like Harambe the gorilla[1] and Crying Jordan. The recent "Disloyal Man Walking With His Girlfriend and Looking Amazed at Another Seductive Girl," the title of the stock image shot by photographer Antonio Guillem, just made the rounds a few months ago.

At a glance—even from a digital native—meme death seems like a much less mysterious phenomenon than meme birth. While tracing the origin of any individual meme requires a separate trip down the rabbit hole, it makes sense to assume that memes die because people get tired of them. Even as a concept such as "average attention span" is not incredibly useful to psychologists who study attention (different tasks require different attention strategies), there's a general assumption that this number is shrinking. "Everybody knows" a generation raised on feeds and apps must have focus issues, and that assessment isn't totally false. Our devices are "engineered to chip away at [our] concentration" in what's called the "attention economy," writes Bianca Bosker in *The Atlantic*, and apps such as Twitter keep us anxious for the next big thing in news, pop culture, or memes. Our overextended attention leads to an obvious

Published in the Atlantic *(2017). Lauren Michele Jackson writes widely about issues of race, culture, and technology.*

1. Gorilla at the Cincinnati Zoo who in 2016 was shot and killed after a child fell into his enclosure.

explanation for meme death: We are so overstimulated that what brings us joy cannot even hold our focus for long. But is that really why memes die?

In 2012, the third and final meeting of ROFLCon, a biennial convention on internet memes hosted by the Massachusetts Institute of Technology, anticipated a shift in the formal qualities of meme culture, ushered in by social-media sites like Facebook and Twitter. Indeed, this was the tail end of an era, one defined by the once-ubiquitous image-macro template as applied to subgenres like Advice Animals, LOLcats, and Doge. At the conference, 4chan[2] founder Christopher "moot" Poole was "wistfully nostalgic for the slower-speed good ol' days," *Wired*'s Brian Barrett reported, fearful that memes gone "mainstream" would betray the niche communities that considered memes a kind of intellectual property all their own.

5   "These days, memes spread faster and wider than ever, with social networks acting as the fuel for mass distribution," *Wired*'s Andy Baio wrote that same year. "As internet usage shifts from desktops and laptops to mobile devices and tablets, the ability to mutate memes in a meaningful way becomes harder." Both Poole and Baio suggest that memes lose something essential—whether a close-knit humor or the opportunity to add a unique, creative contribution—when they are enjoyed by a larger community. Social networks, some feared, would drive memes to extinction. But Chris Torres, the creator of Nyan cat, antici-pated that the break from the old-school would be a good thing. "The internet doesn't really need to have its hand held anymore with websites that choose memes for them," he told *The Daily Dot*'s Fernando Alfonso III in 2014. "As long as there is creativity in this world then they are never going away. This may just be the calm before the storm of amazing new material."

And in 2017, it's clear that the doomsday crew vastly underestimated inter-net users' creativity. Increased mobility and access across platforms and com-munities has brought to the surface some of the funniest and weirdest content the web has ever known. Contrary to what Poole and Baio implied, weird humor and memes are hardly the exclusive domain of Redditors[3] or the mostly white tech bros who populated ROFLCon. Today, many of the internet's favorite memes come from fringe or ostracized communities—often from black com-munities, for whom oddball humor has long been an art form.

While internet memes categorically remain alive and well, individual memes *do* seem to die off faster than in Poole's "good ol' days." They just don't last like they used to: Compare the lifespans of say, Bad Luck Brian to Arthur's clenched fist or confused Mr. Krabs. But if overexposure is partially to blame for their demise, it certainly doesn't tell the whole story. Nor can it alone account for the varied lifespans amongst concurrent memes. Crying Jordan lasted years; did Damn Daniel even last two weeks? Salt Bae took over social media in January 2017, but was quickly overshadowed by gifs of Drew Scanlon

2. Website for sharing anonymously posted images.
3. Users of the popular thread-based website, Reddit.com.

("white guy blinking") and rapper Conceited ("black guy duck face"), which lasted throughout the spring.

Why do some memes last longer than others? Are they just funnier? *Better*? And if so, what makes a meme better? The answer lies not in traditional memetics, but in the study of jokes.

Though he has yet to return to the subject in earnest since 1976's *The Selfish Gene*, Richard Dawkins[4] remains a specter over discussions of internet memes. The study, in which Dawkins extends evolutionary theory to cultural development, has been elaborated upon as well as critiqued in the three decades since its publication, spawning the field of memetics and drawing ire from neurologists and anthropologists alike. In *The Selfish Gene* and in memetics at large, "memes" are components of culture that survive, propagate, and/or die off just like genes do. Memetics in general is uninterested in *why* these components survive, or the contexts that allow them to do so—and much as individual persons are considered unwitting actors within the gene pool at large, so too are our intentions deemed irrelevant when it comes to the transmission of culture.

On the scientific side, researchers such as the behavioral scientists Carsta Simon and William M. Baum worry that the scientific rigor implied by "memes as genes" has yet to be met by actual memetics research. Anthropologists and sociologists "charge that memetics sees 'culture' as a series of discrete individual units, and that it blurs the lines between metaphor and biology," wrote the Fordham University researcher Alice Marwick in 2013. And, as I've written, thinking of memes solely in this way tends to "relegate agency to the memes themselves" as if they are not subject to human innovation, creation, and responses. Memetics, more interested in the movement of memes than their content, may be helpful in tracking or predicting meme lifespans, but cannot fully account for how human participation factors in.

The weakness of the memes-as-genes theory becomes more apparent in an online context. By Dawkins's deliberately capacious definition, the word "meme" may apply to sayings, bass lines, accents, clothing, myths, and body modification. In this vein, a meme in terms of digital culture could mean a viral hashtag like #tbt, tweet threading as a form of storytelling, or netspeak. However, memes as they're popularly discussed nowadays often index something much more specific—a phrase or set of text, often coupled with an image, that follows a certain format within which user adjustments can be made before being redistributed to amuse others. Also known as: a joke.

Jokes are more than funny business and, in fact, laughter (even in acronym form) is not the standard for defining what is or is not a joke. We often laugh at things that are not jokes (like wipeouts); and jokes do not always elicit laughter (like a bad wedding toast). That memes employ humorous devices does not de facto render them jokes. But as it so happens, memes and jokes do

---

4. English evolutionary biologist and writer (b. 1941) known for championing atheism.

share several formal qualities. And looking at memes as jokes may also help answer why some memes dry up, and why and when others return.

"Only when it comes to jokes is the idea of 'meaning' so often vehemently denied," Elise Kramer, an anthropologist currently at the University of Illinois, wrote in a 2011 study of online rape jokes. "Poems, paintings, photographs, songs, and so on are all seen as having meaning 'beneath' the aesthetic surface, and the relationship between the message and the medium is often the focus of appreciation." Kramer's point is not that jokes cannot be explicated or unpacked, but rather that jokes—and memes, I'll add—uniquely and deliberately make depth inconsequential to their appreciation. As displayed by recent gaffes like Bill Maher's "house nigger" joke[5] and Tina Fey's "let them eat cake" sketch,[6] comedy remains the most resilient place for ethically dodgy art. Reading "too much" into jokes is frowned upon and offended audiences are often told "it's not that deep."

Memes are viewed the same way, even by those who write about them. There's an obligatory defense embedded in most meme coverage, as if writers sense they must keep the analysis at a minimum lest they spoil the fun. In a love letter to Doge, Adrian Chen[7] wondered if "by writing it I played a crucial role" in guiding the meme toward obsolescence, "proving once again that writing about internet culture is basically inseparable from ruining internet culture." Last summer, while declaring Harambe too dark to be corporatized and therefore too weird to die, *New York Magazine*'s Brian Feldman admitted "there are other ways to end the Harambe meme. Like writing a think piece about it." A month later *The Guardian*'s Elena Cresci repeated the line like gospel: "When it comes to memes, there's a rule: It is dead as soon as the think pieces come out." She even likens memes to jokes directly, asserting that "when memes go mainstream it means they're not funny anymore. Memes are just in-jokes between people on the internet, and everyone knows jokes are much less funny one you've explained them."

15   This evaluation shows another way memes and jokes are similar: Both are, returning to Kramer, "aesthetic forms where felicity (i.e., 'getting' it) is seen as an instantaneous process." Unlike a painting, novel, or even a rousing Twitter thread which one is expected to "savor" like "a good meal," the person who does not get the joke or meme immediately is considered a lost cause. "The person who spends too much time mulling over a joke is accused of ruining it," Kramer writes. Tech reporters included, apparently.

But a commonly held accusation doesn't equal truth. We might observe a correlation between a summer of Harambe think pieces and its decline not long

---

5. In 2017, while interviewing Senator Ben Sasse of Nebraska, Maher (b. 1956), a comedian and talk-show host known for his provocative political commentary, ironically referred to himself with this epithet. He later apologized.

6. Fey (b. 1970), American comedian, writer, and actress, appeared on *Saturday Night Live*'s comedic news broadcast *Weekend Update* to offer a controversial response to white nationalist demonstrations in Charlottesville, Virginia, in 2017.

7. American journalist (b. 1984) and writer for the *New Yorker*.

after, or blame *The New Yorker* for making Crying Jordan uncool, but it's worth noting that such pieces exist *because* their subject matter has reached a certain critical mass that makes them worth writing about. (With all due respect, I don't believe *New York Magazine*, *The New Yorker*, or even *The Atlantic* is propelling memes into zeitgeist.) "Mainstream" doesn't exactly signal the death knell, either. The "white guy blinking" gif continues to make the rounds when called upon—following the season finale of *Game of Thrones*, for example—and the line "ain't nobody got time for that," from a popular 2012 meme, met hearty laughter and applause when I attended Disney's *Aladdin*, the musical, this fall. Some memes "die" and come back again, some surge and then are all but obsolete. Applying theories on the joke might help explain why.

Because of the shared attributes between jokes and memes, research on jokes can provide a template for how to study memes as both creative and formulaic. That includes finally finding a satisfactory answer to how and why memes "die." In a 2015 thesis, Ashley Dainas argues that what folklorists call the "joke cycle" is "the best analogue to internet memes." The joke cycle describes the kinds of commonplace, well-circulated jokes that become known to mass culture at large, such as lightbulb jokes or dead-baby jokes. Unlike other jokes that are highly specific—an inside joke between two friends, for example—these jokes have a mass appeal that compels them to be shared and adjusted enough to stay fresh without losing the source frame. These jokes evolve in stages, from joke to anti-joke, and will retreat over time only to resurge again later, even a whole generation later.

Viewing jokes as cultural artifacts, researchers aren't just concerned with plotting a joke's life cycle but also the social contexts that make the public latch onto a specific joke during a certain time. Lightbulb jokes, for example, arose as a type of ethnic joke in the '60s and "had swept the country" by the late '70s, wrote the late folklorist Alan Dundes. The joke, with its theme of sexual impotence (something/one is inevitably getting screwed), was "a metaphor which lends itself easily to minority groups seeking power." It was one means to thinly veil prejudices, using the joke as an outlet for anxieties about the civil-rights legislation achieved in the '60s, and carried out in the '70s and beyond. Hence most lightbulb jokes, even when they don't cross ethnic or racial lines, tend to be a comment on some social, cultural, or economic position—"How many sorority girls does it take to change a lightbulb?" et al.

Dead-baby jokes became popular in around the same period, a time marked not only by racial upheaval but gendered, domestic changes alongside second-wave feminism: increased access to contraception, sex education in school, women forestalling or even forfeiting motherhood in favor of financial independence. While determining exact causal relationships is a sticky matter, Dundes advised, "folklore is always a reflection of the age in which it flourishes . . . . whether we like it or not."

And so too memes. Like jokes, memes are often asserted to be hollow, devoid of depth, but it would be foolish to believe that. Memes capture and maintain people's attention in a given moment because something about that 20 moment provides a context that makes that meme attractive. This might provide a more satisfying, but also more expansive, answer than simple boredom for why memes fall out of immediate favor. The context that makes a meme, once gone, breaks it. New contexts warrant new memes.

The 2016 U.S. election season and aftermath brought into focus how memes become political symbols, from Pepe the Frog to protest signs. In Pepe's case, the otherwise chill and harmless character created by artist Matt Furie in the early 2000s was on the decline until he got a new context when the alt-right reappropriated him leading into the election. Pepe was resurrected from obscurity when internet culture found a new need for the cartoon's special brand of male millennial grotesquerie.

Memes don't just arise out of atmospheric necessity but disappear as well. The same election season effectively killed off Crying Jordan, when perhaps the idea of loss suddenly became too poignant, too meaningful for the disembodied head of a crying black figure to read as playful. Memes catch on when we need them most and retreat when they are no longer attuned to public sentiment.

Ultimately, fans and founders of the old-school meme-distribution methods aren't entirely wrong. Flash-in-the-pan memes like Dat Boi are limited by a format that restricts the meme's ability to evolve to the next creative iteration of itself. Dat Boi—which didn't have much going on beneath the surface weirdness of a unicycling frog—could mutate no further, got stale, and trailed off without the chance to become cyclical (the irony) in a way that would allow it to last beyond its moment. Harambe, for all its weirdness, could not survive much beyond the life of the news story that spawned it. (In the meantime, as a friend points out, the Cincinnati Zoo has been working overtime with PR for nine-month-old hippo Fiona,[8] who's since become something of an internet sensation herself.)

The "expanding brain" meme, however, continues to chug along for the greater portion of 2017. The meme, which mocks the infinite levels of intellectual one-upmanship common to any and all online discussions, is exactly what's called for in this post-truth moment where everyone is a pundit. I foresee this one sticking around for a long while yet. Meanwhile, it's easy to see why a festive meme like "couples costume idea," would come and go in accordance with the month of October.

25   As Dundes cautioned with jokes, we should not be too confident in claiming cause and effect between memes and their present contexts. Time and distance can assist us in evaluating why some memes ignited our feed, why some burned out quickly, and why others stuck around. The answers to these questions are not so random, but suggestive of the cultural, political, and economic times we live in. Provided we actually remember the memes.

"The World Wide Web has become the international barometer of current events," the music librarian Carl Rahkonen wrote back in 2000. "The life of a joke cycle will never be the same as it was before the internet." No kidding. The

8. Nile hippopotamus born at the Cincinnati Zoo on January 24, 2017, six weeks prematurely.

pace of life online tests the durability of culture like nothing else before, but it is still ultimately *culture*. The memes we forget say as much about us as the memes that hold our attention—for however long that is. We create and pass on the things that call to our current experiences and situations. Memes are us.

MLA CITATION

Jackson, Lauren Michele. "A Unified Theory of Meme Death." *The Norton Reader: An Anthology of Nonfiction*, edited by Melissa A. Goldthwaite et al., 15th ed., W. W. Norton, 2020, pp. 617–23.

QUESTIONS

1. Consider Lauren Michele Jackson's title: "A Unified Theory of Meme Death." It plays on a term from physics, "unified field theory," first used by Albert Einstein to refer to a single theory that would reconcile the theories of relativity and electromagnetism. Why might Jackson have chosen a title that invokes the hard sciences? What is "meme death" and why does she choose it as her topic? What does she mean by "theory," and what specifically is she endeavoring to "unify"?

2. Jackson rejects Richard Dawkins's notion that cultural "memes" are like biological "genes" and argues instead that memes are more like jokes. What are her objections to Dawkins's metaphor, and why does she think memes are better understood by analogy to jokes?

3. In addition to writing about technology, Jackson is also a scholar of black culture. How does race or ethnicity play into her understanding of memes?

4. In an essay of your own, apply Jackson's "theory" to analyze the birth, life, and death of a particular meme with which you are familiar.

LAURA SHAPIRO

Instagram Your Leftovers: History Depends on It

I AM A CULINARY HISTORIAN, and scrolling through the endless food on Instagram makes me hungry. No, not for the fresh-baked sourdough rolls nestled so prettily in a linen napkin or that jaunty tumbler of strawberry mousse sporting its shiny green sprigs of mint. They look delicious, but what really makes my mouth water is the thought of all the stories behind them—everything that happened in the kitchen before you picked up your phone and clicked.

I'm hungry for a look at the messy, bulging envelope where you keep the recipe. I want to see the toddler plunging a dirty fist into the strawberries, and the scenes from your schlep through four markets as you searched for some decent-looking mint. Add a caption and tell me who came to dinner but refused

Published as an op-ed in the New York Times *on September 2, 2017.*

to taste the rolls—"No, thanks, I'm gluten-free"—and who turned out to be allergic to strawberries, and whether you went to bed swearing never to cook again.

Both by instinct and by profession, I've always been curious about people's eating habits. So I've tried to latch onto the astonishing culinary kaleidoscope that is Instagram, poring over the images of avocado toast and seafood paella in search of whatever they can tell me about taste and cultural identity and the secrets of appetite. After all, that's what food does—it talks to us.

President Harry Truman, for instance, once hosted a dinner for Prime Minister Jawaharlal Nehru of India, hoping to encourage his young democracy to tilt toward the United States in the Cold War.[1] The menu featured roast turkey, cranberry sauce and a molded ginger-ale fruit salad with toasted Triscuits—a short course in the history of American cuisine and a remarkable example of patriotism made edible. This meal was practically singing the national anthem. (Nehru was unmoved and remained skeptical about America for years. Was it the Triscuits?)

5   But no matter how hard I scrutinize the pictures on Instagram, they don't speak up. Or rather, they all say the same thing—"Look at this amazing food!" To be fair, that's what high-style food photography was invented to do: It has always been far more interested in our dreams than in our actual meals. The best-selling "Betty Crocker's Picture Cook Book" set the tone for food photography back in 1950, with page after page of lurid baked hams and frosted cookies. Later came gigantic coffee-table cookbooks, with sumptuous photographs of laughing families gathered for summer lunches in Provence, or sari-clad Indian home cooks sitting on the floor crushing spices.

Today we have Instagram, overflowing with glamorous images created not by professional photographers but by home cooks in kitchens around the world. What an opportunity! With its vast reach and the technological savvy of its users, Instagram could go beyond mere glamour and open up a domestic world that has always been elusive. I'm talking about ordinary meals at home— the great unknown in the study of food.

Sure, we have agricultural statistics and marketing surveys; we have household records from 18th-century castles and charts showing the average consumption of Popsicles in the United States from 1953 to 1982. But there's nothing to tell us what a schoolteacher in Connecticut served to her family on a Thursday in 1895. Or what she was thinking when she boiled the string beans for 45 minutes, put ketchup in the salad dressing and decided to try her neighbor's recipe for rice pudding, the one with a little cinnamon.

Could Instagram capture today's version of that story? Could it zero in on the third consecutive night of frozen tacos or the mug of milky Sanka[2] that makes you feel like somebody's grandfather but has become an unexpected

---

1. Global rivalry between the United States and the former Soviet Union that extended from the end of World War II to the collapse of the Soviet Union in 1991.
2. Brand of instant, decaffeinated coffee.

nighttime addiction? Next time you eat a meal that's certain to be forgettable, that's the very moment to pull out your phone and hit "share."

Start with the refrigerator—anything good in there? And who's standing next to you, stuffing himself with handfuls of cereal because he can't wait another minute? Hand him an apple, figure out whether there's enough cheese for a grilled cheese sandwich, check the bread for mold and click. Add a hashtag admitting that you found a few green spots. When he's finished, don't forget to take a picture of the plate with most of the sandwich still on it. Make it your own lunch, and take a selfie.

There will always be room for adorable cupcakes and whole roast pigs, but   10
if you're a food lover with a smartphone, don't limit yourself to these social media classics. Do a huge favor for culinary historians and offer us a glimpse of the ordinary.

If there's nothing on the breakfast table except a slice of cold pizza—click. If you've just returned from the farmers market with bags of fresh produce but you're ordering Chinese anyway—assemble a picture. Show the mess, show the kitchen flops, show the dumb choices we all make when we're standing alone at the refrigerator. You can even skip the filter. A hundred years from now (assuming somebody has figured out how to archive this stuff) scholars will be riveted to your images of the everyday, and you—or at least your Instagram handle—will be immortal.

MLA CITATION

Shapiro, Laura. "Instagram Your Leftovers: History Depends on It." *The Norton Reader: An Anthology of Nonfiction*, edited by Melissa A. Goldthwaite et al., 15th ed., W. W. Norton, 2020, pp. 623–25.

QUESTIONS

1. What is Laura Shapiro's complaint about the pictures of food she finds on Instagram? Why, as a historian, do these pictures trouble her?

2. Shapiro exhorts her readers to post pictures of what they actually eat on Instagram. Would you be willing to do as she asks? Why or why not?

3. What do Shapiro's observations about pictures of food on Instagram suggest about social media generally?

4. For one day, take a picture of everything you eat or drink. Then write an essay inspired by those images.

12 PHILOSOPHY AND ETHICS

> It is well for our vanity that we slay the criminal, for if we
> suffered him to live he might show us what we had gained by
> his crime. It is well for his peace that the saint goes to his
> martyrdom. He is spared the sight of the horror of his harvest.
> —OSCAR WILDE

What does it mean to be "good"? This is the central question of moral philosophy and ethical inquiry, but it is also, as Wilde suggests, notoriously slippery. We judge people to be good or bad, saints or criminals, almost habitually, and most of us strive to be good people ourselves. But how can we be sure of those judgments or of the "goodness" of our own choices and actions? We might trust to our virtue or character, allowing ourselves to be guided by a sense of honor or by feelings of empathy, conscience, or friendship. But how do we know these will not lead us astray? We might adhere to our societies' rules, principles, and laws. But how can we tell which are expressions of genuine moral truths and which are merely reflections of a particular time and place? We might assess our actions according to their consequences. But who could possibly predict them with sufficient confidence?

Together, the readings in this chapter invite you to consider complex questions of ethics and ethical judgment, both abstractly and as they manifest in specific situations and circumstances. The first three approach the chapter's topic in general terms. In his lecture "Advice to Youth," humorist Mark Twain delivers a comic send-up of the commonplaces—bits of conventional wisdom about good behavior—we share with children, thus encouraging his audience to examine and question them. As you read this piece, imagine Twain delivering it orally, and consider how its style contributes to its humor. In his essay "Be Nice," Matt Dinan, a professor of politics, philosophy, and religion, recruits Aristotle to intervene in a contemporary discussion of the politics of civility. You might notice how Dinan's authorial persona complements his thesis: he challenges a position with which he disagrees, but he's nice about it. In "Trying Out One's New Sword," philosopher Mary Midgley offers a different sort of essay, a philosophical argument refuting "moral isolationism," or the view that it is impossible to make valid moral judgments about cultures other than one's own. Her rebuttal is forceful, but the essay is also brisk and lively, even witty, demonstrating that rigorous argument need not be plodding.

The chapter's remaining selections address specific ethical questions or consider the ethics of particular situations. Although they vary in form and style, they all explore the complexity of real-world choices and stakes they involve. The three essays in the middle of the chapter, Atul Gawande's "When Doctors Make Mistakes," Rebecca Skloot's

"The Woman in the Photograph," and Michael Pollan's "An Animal's Place," show their authors wrestling with such choices at a personal level. Gawande, a practicing surgeon, draws on his own experiences to illuminate and humanize the problem of medical error even as he identifies systemic improvements that might mitigate it. Skloot, a science journalist, considers the case of Henrietta Lacks, an African American woman whose cancer cells have been cultivated and used in medical research for decades but also tells the story of her own captivation with that case, raising questions not only about the ethics of medical research but also about her own practice as a journalist and writer. Pollan refuses the stark binaries that too often characterize arguments about the ethics of meat consumption and works his way toward a principled justification for it. His tone is not strident or defensive, but ruminative and questioning, and he supports his views not just abstractly and intellectually but also by offering concrete examples of what ethical meat production and consumption look like.

The chapter closes with two journalistic essays: Michelle Nijhuis's "Which Species Will Live?" and Nora Ephron's "The Boston Photographs." Nijhuis examines the procedures, principles, and criteria by which scientists, conservationists, and policymakers decide how to allocate their efforts and resources; Ephron explains how several newspapers decided to publish explicit photographs of a woman and child falling from a burning building. These essays draw less explicitly on their authors' personal experiences and reflections than do those that preceded them, but they still challenge their readers to form ethical judgments.

As you read the chapter, consider how its selections approach the matter of moral and ethical argument and judgment. Don't expect simple judgments of right and wrong. Attend not just to the authors' points and positions but also to how they develop and defend them: What forms of evidence do they offer? What sorts of reasoning do they employ? What other kinds of appeals do they make? Push back: Where do you find yourself resisting or questioning a train of thought or line of inquiry? Finally, reflect on your own beliefs and commitments: How would you respond to the questions and situations the chapter's readings broach, and why?

MARK TWAIN
Advice to Youth

BEING TOLD I WOULD BE expected to talk here, I inquired what sort of a talk I ought to make. They said it should be something suitable to youth—something didactic, instructive, or something in the nature of good advice. Very well. I have a few things in my mind which I have often longed to say for the instruction of the young; for it is in one's tender early years that such things will best take root

Text of a lecture given by Mark Twain (the pen name of Samuel Clemens) in 1882. The original audience and occasion for this lecture remain unknown.

and be most enduring and most valuable. First, then, I will say to you, my young friends—and I say it beseechingly, urgingly—

Always obey your parents, when they are present. This is the best policy in the long run, because if you don't they will make you. Most parents think they know better than you do, and you can generally make more by humoring that superstition than you can by acting on your own better judgment.

Be respectful to your superiors, if you have any, also to strangers, and sometimes to others. If a person offend you, and you are in doubt as to whether it was intentional or not, do not resort to extreme measures; simply watch your chance and hit him with a brick. That will be sufficient. If you shall find that he had not intended any offense, come out frankly and confess yourself in the wrong when you struck him; acknowledge it like a man and say you didn't mean to. Yes, always avoid violence; in this age of charity and kindliness, the time has gone by for such things. Leave dynamite to the low and unrefined.

Go to bed early, get up early—this is wise. Some authorities say get up with the sun; some others say get up with one thing, some with another. But a lark is really the best thing to get up with. It gives you a splendid reputation with everybody to know that you get up with the lark; and if you get the right kind of a lark, and work at him right, you can easily train him to get up at half past nine, every time—it is no trick at all.

5   Now as to the matter of lying. You want to be very careful about lying; otherwise you are nearly sure to get caught. Once caught, you can never again be, in the eyes of the good and the pure, what you were before. Many a young person has injured himself permanently through a single clumsy and illfinished lie, the result of carelessness born of incomplete training. Some authorities hold that the young ought not to lie at all. That, of course, is putting it rather stronger than necessary; still, while I cannot go quite so far as that, I do maintain, and I believe I am right, that the young ought to be temperate in the use of this great art until practice and experience shall give them that confidence, elegance, and precision which alone can make the accomplishment graceful and profitable. Patience, diligence, painstaking attention to detail—these are the requirements; these, in time, will make the student perfect; upon these, and upon these only, may he rely as the sure foundation for future eminence. Think what tedious years of study, thought, practice, experience, went to the equipment of that peerless old master who was able to impose upon the whole world the lofty and sounding maxim that "truth is mighty and will prevail"—the most majestic compound fracture of fact which any of woman born has yet achieved. For the history of our race, and each individual's experience, are sown thick with evidence that a truth is not hard to kill and that a lie told well is immortal. There is in Boston a monument of the man who discovered anaesthesia; many people are aware, in these latter days, that that man didn't discover it at all, but stole the discovery from another man. Is this truth mighty, and will it prevail? Ah no, my hearers, the monument is made of hardy material, but the lie it tells will outlast it a million years. An awkward, feeble, leaky lie is a thing which you ought to make it your unceasing study to

avoid; such a lie as that has no more real permanence than an average truth. Why, you might as well tell the truth at once and be done with it. A feeble, stupid, preposterous lie will not live two years—except it be a slander upon somebody. It is indestructible, then, of course, but that is no merit of yours. A final word: begin your practice of this gracious and beautiful art early—begin now. If I had begun earlier, I could have learned how.

Never handle firearms carelessly. The sorrow and suffering that have been caused through the innocent but heedless handling of firearms by the young! Only four days ago, right in the next farmhouse to the one where I am spending the summer, a grandmother, old and gray and sweet, one of the loveliest spirits in the land, was sitting at her work, when her young grandson crept in and got down an old, battered, rusty gun which had not been touched for many years and was supposed not to be loaded, and pointed it at her, laughing and threatening to shoot. In her fright she ran screaming and pleading toward the door on the other side of the room; but as she passed him he placed the gun almost against her very breast and pulled the trigger! He had supposed it was not loaded. And he was right—it wasn't. So there wasn't any harm done. It is the only case of that kind I ever heard of. Therefore, just the same, don't you meddle with old unloaded firearms; they are the most deadly and unerring things that have ever been created by man. You don't have to take any pains at all with them; you don't have to have a rest, you don't have to have any sights on the gun, you don't have to take aim, even. No, you just pick out a relative and bang away, and you are sure to get him. A youth who can't hit a cathedral at thirty yards with a Gatling gun in three-quarters of an hour, can take up an old empty musket and bag his grandmother every time, at a hundred. Think what Waterloo[1] would have been if one of the armies had been boys armed with old muskets supposed not to be loaded, and the other army had been composed of their female relations. The very thought of it makes one shudder.

There are many sorts of books; but good ones are the sort for the young to read. Remember that. They are a great, an inestimable, an unspeakable means of improvement. Therefore be careful in your selection, my young friends; be very careful; confine yourselves exclusively to Robertson's Sermons, Baxter's *Saint's Rest, The Innocents Abroad,* and works of that kind.[2]

But I have said enough. I hope you will treasure up the instructions which I have given you, and make them a guide to your feet and a light to your understanding. Build your character thoughtfully and painstakingly upon these precepts, and by and by, when you have got it built, you will be surprised and gratified to see how nicely and sharply it resembles everybody else's.

---

1. Bloody battle (1815) in which Napoleon suffered his final defeat at the hands of English and German troops under the Duke of Wellington.
2. Five volumes of sermons by Frederick William Robertson (1816–1853), an English clergyman, and Richard Baxter's *Saints' Everlasting Rest* (1650), well-known religious works; *The Innocents Abroad,* Twain's own collection of humorous travel sketches.

MLA CITATION

Twain, Mark. "Advice to Youth." *The Norton Reader: An Anthology of Nonfiction*,
    edited by Melissa A. Goldthwaite et al., 15th ed., W. W. Norton, 2020,
    pp. 627–29.

QUESTIONS

1. Underline the various pieces of "serious" advice that Mark Twain offers and notice where and how he begins to turn each one upside down.

2. Twain was already known as a comic author when he delivered "Advice to Youth" as a lecture in 1882; it was not published until 1923. We do not know the circumstances under which he delivered it or to whom. Using evidence from the text, imagine both the circumstances and the audience.

3. Rewrite "Advice to Youth" for a modern audience, perhaps as a lecture for a school assembly or a commencement address.

MATT DINAN
Be Nice

GROWING UP, I NEVER CONSIDERED MYSELF to be particularly nice, perhaps because I'm from a rural part of New Brunswick, one of Canada's Maritime Provinces—the conspicuously "nicest" region in a self-consciously nice country. My parents are nice in a way that almost beggars belief—my mother's tact is such that the strongest condemnation in her arsenal is "Well, I wouldn't say I don't like it, per se . . ." As for me, teenage eye-rolls gave way to undergraduate seriousness, which gave way to graduate-student irony. I thought of Atlantic Canadian nice as a convenient way to avoid telling the truth about the way things are—a disingenuous evasion of the nasty truth about the world. Even the word *nice* seems the moral equivalent of "uninteresting"—anodyne, tedious, otiose.

That's why I remember being a bit shocked when my colleagues at my first job in Massachusetts kept informing me that I was "too nice" to share my opinion about something or someone. Didn't they know they were speaking to a percipient and courageous truth-teller? Maybe it was my harrowing stint as a commuter in Worcester—why won't these people on the MassPike in fact *use* their "blinkahs"?[1]—or maybe becoming a dad softened me up, but I have,

This essay first appeared in The Hedgehog Review *(2018), a journal of cultural studies published by the University of Virginia's Institute for Advanced Studies in Culture.*

1. The Mass Pike, Interstate 90, runs across Massachusetts; "blinkahs" mimicks a stereotypical Boston accent, in which "er" is pronounced "ah."

initially with some dismay, found myself increasingly enjoying trying to be nice.

But my newfound appreciation for niceness may have come too late: Niceness has fallen on hard times. Even bare civility has become the target of a serious theoretical critique. As Tavia Nyong'o and Kyla Wazana Tompkins[2] bracingly put it in a recent online article, "Eleven Theses on Civility," "Civility is not care, but it pretends to be." By masking the violence of unjust social systems with complaints about discursive violence, "calls for civility seek to evade . . . calls for change."

Doubtless, these and other criticisms are partly, even mostly, true about the way civility is often deployed in political argument. But as Teresa Bejan[3] shows so well in her book *Mere Civility*, civility doesn't necessarily mean being nice or polite, and it's more than a set of procedural rules for public argument. Civility, rather, means engaging with those with whom one fundamentally disagrees, and so a curious feature of these latest skirmishes in the civility war is the basic civility of civility's critics. In observing that the entire civility game—usually identified as "tone policing"—is often marshaled to constrain political discussion within certain parameters, civility's critics are doing the heavy lifting of civil discourse.

One strength of *Mere Civility* is Bejan's insistence that civility is actually   5
a sort of conversational virtue, though not a particularly nice one. So one defense of civility would consist of contrasting it with a milquetoast quality like "niceness." But can we push things just a little further and actually defend being, for lack of a better word, *nice*? Even *online*? Could being nice be a virtue, and can it be a virtue even in the struggle for social justice?

When it comes to virtue, it's difficult to find a better guide than Aristotle.[4] While there is no description of the virtue of civility or niceness in his most famous account of the good life, the *Nicomachean Ethics*,[5] he *does* present an array of seemingly minor virtues pertaining to common life that cover similar ground. Ranging from gentleness and honesty to wit or tact, the social virtues seem like a decided step down after the memorable peak of his discussion of moral virtue in greatness of soul. But it is precisely in contrast to greatness of soul that the social virtues emerge as so important.

Aristotle initially presents greatness of soul as the ordered whole of moral virtue—an ornament for the *megalopsychos*, the person with complete virtue, that makes the rest of the virtues shine that much brighter. This person is truly great, and knows it. Greatness of soul is presented as virtue that governs one's relationship to the greatest honors and thus to the esteem of the community,

2. Nyong'o (b. 1974), cultural critic and professor of American studies at Yale University; Wazana Tompkins (b. 1968), cultural critic and professor of English and gender and women's studies at Pomona College.

3. Professor of political theory (b. 1984), Oriel College, Oxford. See her essay "The Two Clashing Meanings of 'Free Speech,'" pp. 897–902.

4. Greek philosopher (c. 384–322 B.C.E.).

5. Aristotle's principal treatise on ethics, written in 350 B.C.E.

but it turns out that the only person whose judgment the *megalopsychos* ultimately consults is himself. The great-souled one cares little for the world outside himself, even to the point of lacking wonder (*thaumastikos*), which in the *Metaphysics*[6] Aristotle says comes naturally to human beings. It perhaps goes without saying that the person with greatness of soul is not a great party guest: He is unusually direct in his evaluations of others, and "disposed to feeling contempt for others." He refuses most honors and requests for aid, fails to remember boons or evils done him by others, and is incapable of living with consideration of another (unless it is a friend). Aristotle's description of the *megalopsychos* culminates in an almost comic portrayal of a man (of course it's a man) with a low voice and a slow gait, who can hardly be bothered to interact with those around him. The great-souled person is thus the image of perfect self-sufficiency. As a result, he isn't very civil and definitely isn't nice.

From a certain vantage point, Aristotle at first blush seems to condone the apparent haughtiness of the great-souled person, since it's justified. But since greatness of soul seems to abstract so completely from human dependence on others, the inclusion of such attributes as gentleness, friendliness, and wit in his catalogue of virtues directly after his characterization of the *megalopsychos* seems like an invitation to consider what it might mean to flourish alongside others. Since the great-souled individual cares little for the affairs of others, it's impossible to imagine him possessing a virtue like friendliness. Friendliness, we learn, differs from friendship per se because it arises not from passion but "as a result of being the sort of person one is" in order to give pleasure to others. A friendly person therefore acts similarly toward people she knows and people she doesn't—she is discriminately indiscriminate in her pleasantness.

Aristotle enumerates yet another similar virtue at the very end of his description of the moral virtues, variously called wit or tact. Wit or tact is what the friendly person displays in times of relaxation—not only being funny, but doing so in the right way and listening to others. It's not clear what precisely makes one tactful from Aristotle's perspective, although it's necessarily situational (and what could be worse than defining what it means to be funny?). But the comparison here seems not just to what might be amusing, but to the ways in which wit differs from the other major image of excellence in the *Ethics*. When Aristotle emphasizes the lightness and motion of the character of the tactful or witty person, we cannot help but see it as a counterpoint to the inactivity of greatness of soul. Aristotle even makes an Aristotle joke in his account of wit, saying that the *eutrapelos* (witty person) is etymologically related to *eutropos*, a word meaning dexterity, versatility, or being "good at turning." Wit may not be as grand as greatness of soul, but its seeming motion and life are themselves winsome.

10   Aristotle bestows unusually high praise on this humble virtue, noting that the tactful person is "a sort of law unto [himself]"; in thinking of the other, we learn how to most fully govern ourselves. But the irruptive character of laughter—the fact that it is always surprising and unbidden (which is probably

---

6. Treatise by Aristotle on what he termed "first philosophy."

why "lol" is the preeminent surviving Internet shorthand from the AOL Messenger[7] days)—demonstrates our lack of self-sufficiency. Wit and tact thereby allow for a certain independence or self-governance by helping us say the right things so as not to offend, while also reminding us that we are limited, relational beings.

So "being nice" can be more than cynically smoothing over differences. Niceness's concern for pleasing others, *and* its affirmation of our dependence and limitation, paints a fuller picture of what it means to be human. The great-souled person, who is both right and good, is in danger of losing this insight, and perhaps those who would jettison civility in the interest of justice run a parallel risk in a way that might be inimical to solidarity. If the goal of social justice is in part to help us understand the full extent to which solidarity is an ethical necessity, then cultivating the virtue of being nice is not a barrier to justice, but a path toward it.

MLA CITATION

Dinan, Matt. "Be Nice." *The Norton Reader: An Anthology of Nonfiction*, edited by Melissa A. Goldthwaite et al., 15th ed., W. W. Norton, 2020, pp. 630–33.

QUESTIONS

1. Matt Dinan's essay is an argument for the imperative in its title: "Be Nice." What is Dinan's thesis or main point, and where in his essay does he state it most fully and directly? How does the structure of Dinan's essay reflect his thesis?

2. Dinan cites several sources in his essay: Tavia Nyong'o and Kyla Wazana Tompkins's "Eleven Theses on Civility," Teresa Bejan's *Mere Civility*, and Aristotle's *Nicomachean Ethics* and *Metaphysics*. How does he use each of these to further his argument? What do you imagine the authors of these other sources might say back to Dinan?

3. Using Dinan's essay as a model, write an essay of your own that recuperates a virtue that, like niceness, "has fallen on hard times" (paragraph 3).

7. One of the first Internet messaging applications, developed in the late 1990s.

MARY MIDGLEY

Trying Out One's New Sword

ALL OF US ARE, MORE OR LESS, in trouble today about trying to understand cultures strange to us. We hear constantly of alien customs. We see changes in our lifetime which would have astonished our parents. I want to discuss here one very short way of dealing with this difficulty, a drastic way which many people now theoretically favour. It consists in simply denying that we can ever understand any culture except our own well enough to make judgements about it. Those who recommend this hold that the world is sharply divided into separate societies, sealed units, each with its own system of thought. They feel that the respect and tolerance due from one system to another forbids us ever to take up a critical position to any other culture. Moral judgement, they suggest, is a kind of coinage valid only in its country of origin.

I shall call this position 'moral isolationism'. I shall suggest that it is certainly not forced upon us, and indeed that it makes no sense at all. People usually take it up because they think it is a respectful attitude to other cultures. In fact, however, it is not respectful. Nobody can respect what is entirely unintelligible to them. To respect someone, we have to know enough about him to make a *favourable* judgement, however general and tentative. And we do understand people in other cultures to this extent. Otherwise a great mass of our most valuable thinking would be paralysed.

To show this, I shall take a remote example, because we shall probably find it easier to think calmly about it than we should with a contemporary one, such as female circumcision in Africa or the Chinese Cultural Revolution.[1] The principles involved will still be the same. My example is this. There is, it seems, a verb in classical Japanese which means 'to try out one's new sword on a chance wayfarer'. (The word is *tsujigiri*, literally 'crossroads-cut'.) A Samurai[2] sword had to be tried out because, if it was to work properly, it had to slice through someone at a single blow, from the shoulder to the opposite flank. Otherwise, the warrior bungled his stroke. This could injure his honour, offend his ancestors, and even let down his emperor. So tests were needed, and wayfarers had to be expended. Any wayfarer would do—provided, of course, that he was not another Samurai. Scientists will recognize a familiar problem about the rights of experimental subjects.

Originally a radio broadcast, this essay was first published in Mary Midgley's book Heart and Mind: The Varieties of Moral Experience *(1981). This version is from the 2003 edition.*

1. Female circumcision, also known as female genital mutilation, is regarded by the World Health Organization as a human rights violation; the Chinese Cultural Revolution (1966–76), initiated by Communist Party Chairman Mao Zedong (1893–1976) to purge Chinese society of "bourgeois" influences, involved mass persecutions and the destruction of traditional cultural artifacts.

2. Japanese warrior class that rose to power in the twelfth century.

Now when we hear of a custom like this, we may well reflect that we simply do not understand it; and therefore are not qualified to criticize it at all, because we are not members of that culture. But we are not members of any other culture either, except our own. So we extend the principle to cover all extraneous cultures, and we seem therefore to be moral isolationists. But this is, as we shall see, an impossible position. Let us ask what it would involve.

We must ask first: Does the isolating barrier work both ways? Are people   5
in other cultures equally unable to criticize us? This question struck me sharply when I read a remark in *The Guardian* by an anthropologist about a South American Indian who had been taken into a Brazilian town for an operation, which saved his life. When he came back to his village, he made several highly critical remarks about the white Brazilians' way of life. They may very well have been justified. But the interesting point was that the anthropologist called these remarks 'a damning indictment of Western civilization'. Now the Indian had been in that town about two weeks. Was he in a position to deliver a damning indictment? Would we ourselves be qualified to deliver such an indictment on the Samurai, provided we could spend two weeks in ancient Japan? What do we really think about this?

My own impression is that we believe that outsiders can, in principle, deliver perfectly good indictments—only, it usually takes more than two weeks to make them damning. Understanding has degrees. It is not a slapdash yes-or-no matter. Intelligent outsiders can progress in it, and in some ways will be at an advantage over the locals. But if this is so, it must clearly apply to ourselves as much as anybody else.

Our next question is this: Does the isolating barrier between cultures block praise as well as blame? If I want to say that the Samurai culture has many virtues, or to praise the South American Indians, am I prevented from doing *that* by my outside status? Now, we certainly do need to praise other societies in this way. But it is hardly possible that we could praise them effectively if we could not, in principle, criticize them. Our praise would be worthless if it rested on no definite grounds, if it did not flow from some understanding. Certainly we may need to praise things which we do not *fully* understand. We say 'there's something very good here, but I can't quite make out what it is yet'. This happens when we want to learn from strangers. And we can learn from strangers. But to do this we have to distinguish between those strangers who are worth learning from and those who are not. Can we then judge which is which?

This brings us to our third question: What is involved in judging? Now plainly there is no question here of sitting on a bench in a red robe and sentencing people. Judging simply means forming an opinion, and expressing it if it is called for. Is there anything wrong about this? Naturally, we ought to avoid forming—and expressing—*crude* opinions, like that of a simple-minded missionary, who might dismiss the whole Samurai culture as entirely bad, because non-Christian. But this is a different objection. The trouble with crude opinions is that they are crude, whoever forms them, not that they are formed by the wrong people.

Anthropologists, after all, are outsiders quite as much as missionaries. Moral isolationism forbids us to form *any* opinions on these matters. Its ground for doing so is that we don't understand them. But there is much that we don't understand in our own culture too. This brings us to our last question: If we can't judge other cultures, can we really judge our own? Our efforts to do so will be much damaged if we are really deprived of our opinions about other societies, because these provide the range of comparison, the spectrum of alternatives against which we set what we want to understand. We would have to stop using the mirror which anthropology so helpfully holds up to us.

10   In short, moral isolationism would lay down a general ban on moral reasoning. Essentially, this is the programme of immoralism, and it carries a distressing logical difficulty. Immoralists like Nietzsche[3] are actually just a rather specialized sect of moralists. They can no more afford to put moralizing out of business than smugglers can afford to abolish customs regulations. The power of moral judgement is, in fact, not a luxury, not a perverse indulgence of the self-righteous. It is a necessity. When we judge something to be bad or good, better or worse than something else, we are taking it as an example to aim at or avoid. Without opinions of this sort, we would have no framework of comparison for our own policy, no chance of profiting by other people's insights or mistakes. In this vacuum, we could form no judgements on our own actions.

Now it would be odd if *Homo sapiens* had really got himself into a position as bad as this—a position where his main evolutionary asset, his brain, was so little use to him. None of us is going to accept this sceptical diagnosis. We cannot do so, because our involvement in moral isolationism does not flow from apathy, but from a rather acute concern about human hypocrisy and other forms of wickedness. But we polarize that concern around a few selected moral truths. We are rightly angry with those who despise, oppress or steamroll other cultures. We think that doing these things is actually *wrong*. But this is itself a moral judgement. We could not condemn oppression and insolence if we thought that all our condemnations were just a trivial local quirk of our own culture. We could still less do it if we tried to stop judging altogether.

Real moral scepticism, in fact, could lead only to inaction, to our losing all interest in moral questions, most of all in those which concern other societies. When we discuss these things, it becomes instantly clear how far we are from doing this.

Suppose, for instance, that I criticize the bisecting Samurai, that I say his behaviour is brutal. What will usually happen next is that someone will protest, will say that I have no right to make criticisms like that of another culture. But it is most unlikely that he will use this move to end the discussion of the subject. Instead, he will justify the Samurai. He will try to fill in the background, to make me understand the custom, by explaining the exalted ideals of discipline and devotion which produced it. He will probably talk of the lower value which the ancient Japanese placed on individual life generally. He may well suggest

3. Friedrich Wilhelm Nietzsche (1844–1900), German scholar, critic, and philosopher who was critical of traditional Christian morality.

that this is a healthier attitude than our own obsession with security. He may add, too, that the wayfarers did not seriously mind being bisected, that in principle they accepted the whole arrangement.

Now an objector who talks like this is implying that it is possible to understand alien customs. That is just what he is trying to make me do. And he implies, too, that if I do succeed in understanding them, I shall do something better than giving up judging them. He expects me to change my present judgement to a truer one—namely, one that is favourable. And the standards I must use to do this cannot just be Samurai standards. They have to be ones current in my own culture. Ideals like discipline and devotion will not move anybody unless he himself accepts them. As it happens, neither discipline nor devotion is very popular in the West at present. Anyone who appeals to them may well have to do some more arguing to make them acceptable, before he can use them to explain the Samurai. But if he does succeed here, he will have persuaded us, not just that there was something to be said for them in ancient Japan, but that there would be here as well.

Isolating barriers simply cannot arise here. If we accept something as a   15
serious moral truth about one culture, we can't refuse to apply it—in however different an outward form—to other cultures as well, wherever circumstances admit it. If we refuse to do this, we just are not taking the other culture seriously.

This becomes clear if we look at the last argument used by my objector— that of justification by consent of the victim. It is suggested that sudden bisection is quite in order, *provided* that it takes place between consenting adults. I cannot now discuss how conclusive this justification is. What I am pointing out is simply that it can only work if we believe that *consent* can make such a transaction respectable—and this is a thoroughly modern and Western idea. It would probably never occur to a Samurai: if it did, it would surprise him very much. It is *our* standard.

In applying it, too, we are likely to make another typically Western demand. We shall ask for good factual evidence that the wayfarers actually do have this rather surprising taste—that they are really willing to be bisected. In applying Western standards in this way, we are not being confused or irrelevant. We are asking the questions which arise *from where we stand,* questions which we can see the sense of. We do this because asking questions which you can't see the sense of is humbug. Certainly we can extend our questioning by imaginative effort. We can come to understand other societies better. By doing so, we may make their questions our own, or we may see that they are really forms of the questions which we are asking already. This is not impossible. It is just very hard work. The obstacles which often prevent it are simply those of ordinary ignorance, laziness and prejudice.

If there were really an isolating barrier, of course, our own culture could never have been formed. It is no sealed box, but a fertile jungle of different influences—Greek, Jewish, Roman, Norse, Celtic and so forth, into which further influences are still pouring—American, Indian, Japanese, Jamaican, you name it. The moral isolationist's picture of separate, unmixable cultures is quite unreal. People who talk about British history usually stress the value of this fertilizing mix, no doubt rightly. But this is not just an odd fact about Britain. Except for the very smallest and most remote, all cultures are formed out of many streams. All have the problem of digesting and assimilating things which, at the start, they do not understand. All have the choice of learning something from this challenge, or, alternatively, of refusing to learn, and fighting it mind-lessly instead.

This universal predicament has been obscured by the fact that anthropolo-gists used to concentrate largely on very small and remote cultures, which did not seem to have this problem. These tiny societies, which had often forgotten their own history, made neat, self-contained subjects for study.

20   No doubt it was valuable to emphasize their remoteness, their extreme strangeness, their independence of our cultural tradition. This emphasis was, I think, the root of moral isolationism. But, as the tribal studies themselves showed, even there the anthropologists were able to interpret what they saw and make judgements—often favourable—about the tribesmen. And the tribesmen, too, were quite equal to making judgements about the anthropologists—and about the tourists and Coca-Cola salesmen who followed them. Both sets of judgements, no doubt, were somewhat hasty, both have been refined in the light of further experience. A similar transaction between us and the Samurai might take even longer. But that is no reason at all for deeming it impossible. Morally as well as physically, there is only one world, and we all have to live in it.

MLA CITATION

Midgley, Mary. "Trying Out One's New Sword." *The Norton Reader: An Anthology of Nonfiction*, edited by Melissa A. Goldthwaite et al., 15th ed., W. W. Norton, 2020, pp. 634–38.

Questions

1. Mary Midgley challenges a philosophical position she labels "moral isolationism" (paragraph 2). What is "moral isolationism," and what are Midgley's main objec-tions to it? What responses to her argument can you imagine?

2. This essay was revised from a radio broadcast. How does its style reflect this origin?

3. To support her argument against "moral isolationism," Midgley invokes several human capacities, including reason, the imagination, and the ability to learn from experience. How do each of these figure into her argument?

4. This essay was first published in 1981. Write a response assessing its relevance to the present day. In what ways has it remained relevant, and in what ways does it need to be updated?

ATUL GAWANDE
When Doctors Make Mistakes

I—CRASH VICTIM

A T 2 A.M. ON A CRISP FRIDAY IN WINTER, I was in sterile gloves and gown, pulling a teenage knifing victim's abdomen open, when my pager sounded. "Code Trauma, three minutes," the operating-room nurse said, reading aloud from my pager display. This meant that an ambulance would be bringing another trauma patient to the hospital momentarily, and, as the surgical resident on duty for emergencies, I would have to be present for the patient's arrival. I stepped back from the table and took off my gown. Two other surgeons were working on the knifing victim: Michael Ball, the attending (the staff surgeon in charge of the case), and David Hernandez, the chief resident (a general surgeon in his last of five years of training). Ordinarily, these two would have come later to help with the trauma, but they were stuck here. Ball, a dry, imperturbable forty-two-year-old Texan, looked over to me as I headed for the door. "If you run into any trouble, you call, and one of us will peel away," he said.

I did run into trouble. In telling this story, I have had to change significant details about what happened (including the names of the participants and aspects of my role), but I have tried to stay as close to the actual events as I could while protecting the patient, myself, and the rest of the staff. The way that things go wrong in medicine is normally unseen and, consequently, often misunderstood. Mistakes do happen. We think of them as aberrant; they are anything but.

The emergency room was one floor up, and, taking the stairs two at a time, I arrived just as the emergency medical technicians wheeled in a woman who appeared to be in her thirties and to weigh more than two hundred pounds. She lay motionless on a hard orange plastic spinal board—eyes closed, skin pale, blood running out of her nose. A nurse directed the crew into Trauma Bay 1, an examination room outfitted like an O.R., with green tiles on the wall, monitoring devices, and space for portable X-ray equipment. We lifted her onto the bed and then went to work. One nurse began cutting off the woman's clothes. Another took vital signs. A third inserted a large-bore intravenous line into her right arm. A surgical intern put a Foley catheter[1] into her bladder. The emergency-medicine attending was Samuel Johns, a gaunt, Ichabod

First published in the New Yorker *(1999) and then in Atul Gawande's first book,* Complications: A Surgeon's Notes on an Imperfect Science *(2002). Gawande has continued to write books on medicine; his latest is* Being Mortal: Medicine and What Matters in the End *(2014). He is a surgeon at Boston's Brigham and Women's Hospital.*

1. Thin tube inserted into the bladder to drain urine.

Crane–like[2] man in his fifties. He was standing to one side with his arms crossed, observing, which was a sign that I could go ahead and take charge.

If you're in a hospital, most of the "moment to moment" doctoring you get is from residents—physicians receiving specialty training and a small income in exchange for their labor. Our responsibilities depend on our level of training, but we're never entirely on our own: there's always an attending, who oversees our decisions. That night, since Johns was the attending and was responsible for the patient's immediate management, I took my lead from him. But he wasn't a surgeon, and so he relied on me for surgical expertise.

5   "What's the story?" I asked.

An E.M.T. rattled off the details: "Unidentified white female unrestrained driver in high-speed rollover. Ejected from the car. Found unresponsive to pain. Pulse a hundred, B.P. a hundred over sixty, breathing at thirty on her own . . ."

As he spoke, I began examining her. The first step in caring for a trauma patient is always the same. It doesn't matter if a person has been shot eleven times or crushed by a truck or burned in a kitchen fire. The first thing you do is make sure that the patient can breathe without difficulty. This woman's breaths were shallow and rapid. An oximeter, by means of a sensor placed on her finger, measured the oxygen saturation of her blood. The "O_2 sat"[3] is normally more than ninety-five percent for a patient breathing room air. The woman was wearing a face mask with oxygen turned up full blast, and her sat was only ninety percent.

"She's not oxygenating well," I announced in the flattened-out, wake-me-up-when-something-interesting-happens tone that all surgeons have acquired by about three months into residency. With my fingers, I verified that there wasn't any object in her mouth that would obstruct her airway; with a stethoscope, I confirmed that neither lung had collapsed. I got hold of a bag mask, pressed its clear facepiece over her nose and mouth, and squeezed the bellows, a kind of balloon with a one-way valve, shooting a litre of air into her with each compression. After a minute or so, her oxygen came up to a comfortable ninety-eight percent. She obviously needed our help with breathing. "Let's tube her," I said. That meant putting a tube down through her vocal cords and into her trachea, which would insure a clear airway and allow for mechanical ventilation.

Johns, the attending, wanted to do the intubation. He picked up a Mac 3 laryngoscope, a standard but fairly primitive-looking L-shaped metal instrument for prying open the mouth and throat, and slipped the shoehornlike blade deep into her mouth and down to her larynx. Then he yanked the handle up toward the ceiling to pull her tongue out of the way, open her mouth and throat, and reveal the vocal cords, which sit like fleshy tent flaps at the entrance to the trachea. The patient didn't wince or gag: she was still out cold.

10   "Suction!" he called. "I can't see a thing."

2. Fictional hero of Washington Irving's "Legend of Sleepy Hollow" (1802), who was described as having a lanky frame.

3. "Sat" is an abbreviation for saturation.

He sucked out about a cup of blood and clot. Then he picked up the endotracheal tube—a clear rubber pipe about the diameter of an index finger and three times as long—and tried to guide it between her cords. After a minute, her sat started to fall.

"You're down to seventy percent," a nurse announced.

Johns kept struggling with the tube, trying to push it in, but it banged vainly against the cords. The patient's lips began to turn blue.

"Sixty percent," the nurse said.

Johns pulled everything out of the patient's mouth and fitted the bag mask   15
back on. The oximeter's luminescent-green readout hovered at sixty for a moment and then rose steadily, to ninety-seven percent. After a few minutes, he took the mask off and again tried to get the tube in. There was more blood, and there may have been some swelling, too: all the poking down the throat was probably not helping. The sat fell to sixty percent. He pulled out and bagged her until she returned to ninety-five percent.

When you're having trouble getting the tube in, the next step is to get specialized expertise. "Let's call anesthesia," I said, and Johns agreed. In the meantime, I continued to follow the standard trauma protocol: completing the examination and ordering fluids, lab tests, and X-rays. Maybe five minutes passed as I worked.

The patient's sats drifted down to ninety-two percent—not a dramatic change but definitely not normal for a patient who is being manually ventilated. I checked to see if the sensor had slipped off her finger. It hadn't. "Is the oxygen up full blast?" I asked a nurse.

"It's up all the way," she said.

I listened again to the patient's lungs—no collapse. "We've got to get her tubed," Johns said. He took off the oxygen mask and tried again.

Somewhere in my mind, I must have been aware of the possibility that her   20
airway was shutting down because of vocal-cord swelling or blood. If it was, and we were unable to get a tube in, then the only chance she'd have to survive would be an emergency tracheostomy: cutting a hole in her neck and inserting a breathing tube into her trachea. Another attempt to intubate her might even trigger a spasm of the cords and a sudden closure of the airway—which is exactly what did happen.

If I had actually thought this far along, I would have recognized how ill-prepared I was to do an emergency "trache." Of the people in the room, it's true, I had the most experience doing tracheostomies, but that wasn't saying much. I had been the assistant surgeon in only about half a dozen, and all but one of them had been non-emergency cases, employing techniques that were not designed for speed. The exception was a practice emergency trache I had done on a goat. I should have immediately called Dr. Ball for backup. I should have got the trache equipment out—lighting, suction, sterile instruments—just in case. Instead of hurrying the effort to get the patient intubated because of a mild drop in saturation, I should have asked Johns to wait until I had help nearby. I might even have recognized that she was already losing her airway. Then I could have grabbed a knife and started cutting her a tracheostomy while things were still relatively stable and I had time to proceed slowly. But for whatever reasons—hubris, inattention, wishful thinking, hesitation, or the uncertainty of the moment—I let the opportunity pass.

Johns hunched over the patient, intently trying to insert the tube through her vocal cords. When her sat once again dropped into the sixties, he stopped and put the mask back on. We stared at the monitor. The numbers weren't coming up. Her lips were still blue. Johns squeezed the bellows harder to blow more oxygen in.

"I'm getting resistance," he said.

The realization crept over me: this was a disaster. "Damn it, we've lost her airway," I said. "Trache kit! Light! Somebody call down to O.R. 25 and get Ball up here!"

25   People were suddenly scurrying everywhere. I tried to proceed deliberately, and not let panic take hold. I told the surgical intern to get a sterile gown and gloves on. I took a bactericidal solution off a shelf and dumped a whole bottle of yellow-brown liquid on the patient's neck. A nurse unwrapped the tracheostomy kit—a sterilized set of drapes and instruments. I pulled on a gown and a new pair of gloves while trying to think through the steps. This is simple, really, I tried to tell myself. At the base of the thyroid cartilage, the Adam's apple, is a little gap in which you find a thin, fibrous covering called the cricothyroid membrane. Cut through that and—voilà! You're in the trachea. You slip through the hole a four-inch plastic tube shaped like a plumber's elbow joint, hook it up to oxygen and a ventilator, and she's all set. Anyway, that was the theory.

I threw some drapes over her body, leaving the neck exposed. It looked as thick as a tree. I felt for the bony prominence of the thyroid cartilage. But I couldn't feel anything through the rolls of fat. I was beset by uncertainty— where should I cut? should I make a horizontal or a vertical incision?—and I hated myself for it. Surgeons never dithered, and I was dithering.

"I need better light," I said.

Someone was sent out to look for one.

"Did anyone get Ball?" I asked. It wasn't exactly an inspiring question.

30   "He's on his way," a nurse said.

There wasn't time to wait. Four minutes without oxygen would lead to permanent brain damage, if not death. Finally, I took the scalpel and cut. I just cut. I made a three-inch left-to-right swipe across the middle of the neck, following the procedure I'd learned for elective cases. I figured that if I worked through the fat I might be able to find the membrane in the wound. Dissecting down with scissors while the intern held the wound open with retractors, I hit a vein. It didn't let loose a lot of blood, but there was enough to fill the wound: I couldn't see anything. The intern put a finger on the bleeder. I called for suction. But the suction wasn't working; the tube was clogged with the clot from the intubation efforts.

"Somebody get some new tubing," I said. "And where's the light?"

Finally, an orderly wheeled in a tall overhead light, plugged it in, and flipped on the switch. It was still too dim; I could have done better with a flashlight.

I wiped up the blood with gauze, then felt around in the wound with my fingertips. This time, I thought I could feel the hard ridges of the thyroid cartilage and, below it, the slight gap of the cricothyroid membrane, though I couldn't be sure. I held my place with my left hand.

James O'Connor, a silver-haired, seen-it-all anesthesiologist, came into the room. Johns gave him a quick rundown on the patient and let him take over bagging her.

Holding the scalpel in my right hand like a pen, I stuck the blade down into the wound at the spot where I thought the thyroid cartilage was. With small, sharp strokes—working blindly, because of the blood and the poor light—I cut down through the overlying fat and tissue until I felt the blade scrape against the almost bony cartilage. I searched with the tip of the knife, walking it along until I felt it reach a gap. I hoped it was the cricothyroid membrane, and pressed down firmly. Then I felt the tissue suddenly give, and I cut an inch-long opening.

When I put my index finger into it, it felt as if I were prying open the jaws of a stiff clothespin. Inside, I thought I felt open space. But where were the sounds of moving air that I expected? Was this deep enough? Was I even in the right place?

"I think I'm in," I said, to reassure myself as much as anyone else.

"I hope so," O'Connor said. "She doesn't have much longer."

I took the tracheostomy tube and tried to fit it in, but something seemed to be blocking it. I twisted it and turned it, and finally jammed it in. Just then, Ball, the surgical attending, arrived. He rushed up to the bed and leaned over for a look. "Did you get it?" he asked. I said that I thought so. The bag mask was plugged onto the open end of the trache tube. But when the bellows were compressed the air just gurgled out of the wound. Ball quickly put on gloves and a gown.

"How long has she been without an airway?" he asked.

"I don't know. Three minutes."

Ball's face hardened as he registered that he had about a minute in which to turn things around. He took my place and summarily pulled out the trache tube. "God, what a mess," he said. "I can't see a thing in this wound. I don't even know if you're in the right place. Can we get better light and suction?" New suction tubing was found and handed to him. He quickly cleaned up the wound and went to work.

The patient's sat had dropped so low that the oximeter couldn't detect it anymore. Her heart rate began slowing down—first to the sixties and then to the forties. Then she lost her pulse entirely. I put my hands together on her chest, locked my elbows, leaned over her, and started doing chest compressions.

Ball looked up from the patient and turned to O'Connor. "I'm not going to get her an airway in time," he said. "You're going to have to try from above." Essentially, he was admitting my failure. Trying an oral intubation again was pointless—just something to do instead of watching her die. I was stricken, and concentrated on doing chest compressions, not looking at anyone. It was over, I thought.

And then, amazingly, O'Connor: "I'm in." He had managed to slip a pediatric-size endotracheal tube through the vocal cords. In thirty seconds, with oxygen being manually ventilated through the tube, her heart was back, racing at a hundred and twenty beats a minute. Her sat registered at sixty and then climbed. Another thirty seconds and it was at ninety-seven percent. All the people in the room exhaled, as if they, too, had been denied their breath. Ball and I said little except to confer about the next steps for her. Then he went back downstairs to finish working on the stab-wound patient still in the O.R.

We eventually identified the woman, whom I'll call Louise Williams; she was thirty-four years old and lived alone in a nearby suburb. Her alcohol level on arrival had been three times the legal limit, and had probably contributed to her unconsciousness. She had a concussion, several lacerations, and significant soft-tissue damage. But X-rays and scans revealed no other injuries from the crash. That night, Ball and Hernandez brought her to the O.R. to fit her with a proper tracheostomy. When Ball came out and talked to family members, he told them of the dire condition she was in when she arrived, the difficulties "we" had had getting access to her airway, the disturbingly long period of time that she had gone without oxygen, and thus his uncertainty about how much brain function she still possessed. They listened without protest; there was nothing for them to do but wait.

II—THE BANALITY OF ERROR

To much of the public—and certainly to lawyers and the media—medical error is a problem of bad physicians. Consider some other surgical mishaps. In one, a general surgeon left a large metal instrument in a patient's abdomen, where it tore through the bowel and the wall of the bladder. In another, a cancer surgeon biopsied the wrong part of a woman's breast and thereby delayed her diagnosis of cancer for months. A cardiac surgeon skipped a small but key step during a heart-valve operation, thereby killing the patient. A surgeon saw a man racked with abdominal pain in the emergency room and, without taking a C.T. scan, assumed that the man had a kidney stone; eighteen hours later, a scan showed a rupturing abdominal aortic aneurysm, and the patient died not long afterward.

How could anyone who makes a mistake of that magnitude be allowed to practice medicine? We call such doctors "incompetent," "unethical," and "negligent." We want to see them punished. And so we've wound up with the public system we have for dealing with error: malpractice lawsuits, media scandal, suspensions, firings.

50   There is, however, a central truth in medicine that complicates this tidy vision of misdeeds and misdoers: *All* doctors make terrible mistakes. Consider the cases I've just described. I gathered them simply by asking respected surgeons I know—surgeons at top medical schools—to tell me about mistakes they had made just in the past year. Every one of them had a story to tell.

In 1991, *The New England Journal of Medicine* published a series of landmark papers from a project known as the Harvard Medical Practice Study—a review of more than thirty thousand hospital admissions in New York State.

The study found that nearly four percent of hospital patients suffered complications from treatment which prolonged their hospital stay or resulted in disability or death, and that two-thirds of such complications were due to errors in care. One in four, or one percent of admissions, involved actual negligence. It was estimated that, nationwide, a hundred and twenty thousand patients die each year at least partly as a result of errors in care. And subsequent investigations around the country have confirmed the ubiquity of error. In one small study of how clinicians perform when patients have a sudden cardiac arrest, twenty-seven of thirty clinicians made an error in using the defibrillator; they may have charged it incorrectly or lost valuable time trying to figure out how to work a particular model. According to a 1995 study, mistakes in administering drugs—giving the wrong drug or the wrong dose, say—occur, on the average, about once for every hospital admission, mostly without ill effects, but one percent of the time with serious consequences.

If error were due to a subset of dangerous doctors, you might expect malpractice cases to be concentrated among a small group, but in fact they follow a uniform, bell-shaped distribution. Most surgeons are sued at least once in the course of their careers. Studies of specific types of error, too, have found that repeat offenders are not the problem. The fact is that virtually everyone who cares for hospital patients will make serious mistakes, and even commit acts of negligence, every year. For this reason, doctors are seldom outraged when the press reports yet another medical horror story. They usually have a different reaction: *That could be me.* The important question isn't how to keep bad physicians from harming patients; it's how to keep good physicians from harming patients.

Medical-malpractice suits are a remarkably ineffective remedy. Troyen Brennan, a Harvard professor of law and public health, points out that research has consistently failed to find evidence that litigation reduces medical-error rates. In part, this may be because the weapon is so imprecise. Brennan led several studies following up on the patients in the Harvard Medical Practice Study. He found that fewer than two percent of the patients who had received substandard care ever filed suit. Conversely, only a small minority among the patients who did sue had in fact been the victims of negligent care. And a patient's likelihood of winning a suit depended primarily on how poor his or her outcome was, regardless of whether that outcome was caused by disease or unavoidable risks of care.

The deeper problem with medical-malpractice suits, however, is that by demonizing errors they prevent doctors from acknowledging and discussing them publicly. The tort system makes adversaries of patient and physician, and pushes each to offer a heavily slanted version of events. When things go wrong, it's almost impossible for a physician to talk to a patient honestly about mistakes. Hospital lawyers warn doctors that, although they must, of course, tell patients about complications that occur, they are never to intimate that they were at fault, lest the "confession" wind up in court as damning evidence in a black-and-white morality tale. At most, a doctor might say, "I'm sorry that things didn't go as well as we had hoped."

55   There is one place, however, where doctors can talk candidly about their mistakes, if not with patients, then at least with one another. It is called the Morbidity and Mortality Conference—or, more simply, M. & M.—and it takes place, usually once a week, at nearly every academic hospital in the country. This institution survives because laws protecting its proceedings from legal discovery have stayed on the books in most states, despite frequent challenges. Surgeons, in particular, take the M. & M. seriously. Here they can gather behind closed doors to review the mistakes, complications, and deaths that occurred on their watch, determine responsibility, and figure out what to do differently next time.

III—SHOW AND TELL

At my hospital, we convene every Tuesday at five o'clock in a steep, plush amphitheatre lined with oil portraits of the great doctors whose achievements we're meant to live up to. All surgeons are expected to attend, from the interns to the chairman of surgery; we're also joined by medical students doing their surgery "rotation." An M. & M. can include almost a hundred people. We file in, pick up a photocopied list of cases to be discussed, and take our seats. The front row is occupied by the most senior surgeons: terse, serious men, now out of their scrubs and in dark suits, lined up like a panel of senators at a hearing. The chairman is a leonine presence in the seat closest to the plain wooden podium from which each case is presented. In the next few rows are the remaining surgical attendings; these tend to be younger, and several of them are women. The chief residents have put on long white coats and usually sit in the side rows. I join the mass of other residents, all of us in short white coats and green scrub pants, occupying the back rows.

     For each case, the chief resident from the relevant service—cardiac, vascular, trauma, and so on—gathers the information, takes the podium, and tells the story. Here's a partial list of cases from a typical week (with a few changes to protect confidentiality): a sixty-eight-year-old man who bled to death after heart-valve surgery; a forty-seven-year-old woman who had to have a reoperation because of infection following an arterial bypass done in her left leg; a forty-four-year-old woman who had to have bile drained from her abdomen after gall-bladder surgery; three patients who had to have reoperations for bleeding following surgery; a sixty-three-year-old man who had a cardiac arrest following heart-bypass surgery; a sixty-six-year-old woman whose sutures suddenly gave way in an abdominal wound and nearly allowed her intestines to spill out. Ms. Williams's case, my failed tracheostomy, was just one case on a list like this. David Hernandez, the chief trauma resident, had subsequently reviewed the records and spoken to me and others involved. When the time came, it was he who stood up front and described what had happened.

     Hernandez is a tall, rollicking, good old boy who can tell a yarn, but M. & M. presentations are bloodless and compact. He said something like: "This was a thirty-four-year-old female unrestrained driver in a high-speed rollover. The patient apparently had stable vitals at the scene but was unresponsive, and brought in by ambulance unintubated. She was G.C.S. 7 on arrival." G.C.S. stands for the Glasgow Coma Scale, which rates the severity of head injuries, from three to fifteen. G.C.S. 7 is in the comatose range. "Attempts to intubate were made without success in the E.R. and may have contributed to airway closure. A cricothyroidotomy[4] was attempted without success."

These presentations can be awkward. The chief residents, not the attendings, determine which cases to report. That keeps the attendings honest—no one can cover up mistakes—but it puts the chief residents, who are, after all, underlings, in a delicate position. The successful M. & M. presentation inevitably involves a certain elision of detail and a lot of passive verbs. No one screws up a cricothyroidotomy. Instead, "a cricothyroidotomy was attempted without success." The message, however, was not lost on anyone.

Hernandez continued, "The patient arrested and required cardiac compressions. Anesthesia was then able to place a pediatric E.T. tube and the patient recovered stable vitals. The tracheostomy was then completed in the O.R."

So Louise Williams had been deprived of oxygen long enough to go into cardiac arrest, and everyone knew that meant she could easily have suffered a disabling stroke or been left a vegetable. Hernandez concluded with the fortunate aftermath: "Her workup was negative for permanent cerebral damage or other major injuries. The tracheostomy was removed on Day 2. She was discharged to home in good condition on Day 3." To the family's great relief, and mine, she had woken up in the morning a bit woozy but hungry, alert, and mentally intact. In a few weeks, the episode would heal to a scar.

But not before someone was called to account. A front-row voice immediately thundered, "What do you mean, 'A cricothyroidotomy was attempted without success?'" I sank into my seat, my face hot.

"This was my case," Dr. Ball volunteered from the front row. It is how every attending begins, and that little phrase contains a world of surgical culture. For all the talk in business schools and in corporate America about the virtues of "flat organizations," surgeons maintain an old-fashioned sense of hierarchy. When things go wrong, the attending is expected to take full responsibility. It makes no difference whether it was the resident's hand that slipped and lacerated an aorta; it doesn't matter whether the attending was at home in bed when a nurse gave a wrong dose of medication. At the M. & M., the burden of responsibility falls on the attending.

Ball went on to describe the emergency attending's failure to intubate Williams and his own failure to be at her bedside when things got out of control. He described the bad lighting and her extremely thick neck, and was careful to make those sound not like excuses but merely like complicating factors. Some attendings shook their heads in sympathy. A couple of them asked questions to clarify certain details. Throughout, Ball's tone was objective, detached. He had the air of a CNN newscaster describing unrest in Kuala Lumpur.[5]

60

4. Emergency incision through the cricothyroid membrane to secure a patient's airway during an emergency, described in paragraphs 31–46.
5. Capital of Malaysia hit by economic crisis and political unrest in the late 1990s.

65   As always, the chairman, responsible for the over-all quality of our surgery
service, asked the final question. What, he wanted to know, would Ball have
done differently? Well, Ball replied, it didn't take long to get the stab-wound
patient under control in the O.R., so he probably should have sent Hernandez
up to the E.R. at that point or let Hernandez close the abdomen while he himself came up. People nodded. Lesson learned. Next case.

At no point during the M. & M. did anyone question why I had not called
for help sooner or why I had not had the skill and knowledge that Williams
needed. This is not to say that my actions were seen as acceptable. Rather, in
the hierarchy, addressing my errors was Ball's role. The day after the disaster,
Ball had caught me in the hall and taken me aside. His voice was more wounded
than angry as he went through my specific failures. First, he explained, in an
emergency tracheostomy it might have been better to do a vertical neck incision; that would have kept me out of the blood vessels, which run up and down—
something I should have known at least from my reading. I might have had a
much easier time getting her an airway then, he said. Second, and worse to him
than mere ignorance, he didn't understand why I hadn't called him when there
were clear signs of airway trouble developing. I offered no excuses. I promised to
be better prepared for such cases and to be quicker to ask for help.

Even after Ball had gone down the fluorescent-lit hallway, I felt a sense of
shame like a burning ulcer. This was not guilt: guilt is what you feel when you
have done something wrong. What I felt was shame: *I* was what was wrong. And
yet I also knew that a surgeon can take such feelings too far. It is one thing to
be aware of one's limitations. It is another to be plagued by self-doubt. One
surgeon with a national reputation told me about an abdominal operation in
which he had lost control of bleeding while he was removing what turned out
to be a benign tumor and the patient had died. "It was a clean kill," he said.
Afterward, he could barely bring himself to operate. When he did operate, he
became tentative and indecisive. The case affected his performance for months.

Even worse than losing self-confidence, though, is reacting defensively.
There are surgeons who will see faults everywhere except in themselves. They
have no questions and no fears about their abilities. As a result, they learn nothing from their mistakes and know nothing of their limitations. As one surgeon
told me, it is a rare but alarming thing to meet a surgeon without fear. "If you're
not a little afraid when you operate," he said, "you're bound to do a patient a
grave disservice."

The atmosphere at the M. & M. is meant to discourage both attitudes—
self-doubt and denial—for the M. & M. is a cultural ritual that inculcates in
surgeons a "correct" view of mistakes. "What would you do differently?" a chairman asks concerning cases of avoidable complications. "Nothing" is seldom an
acceptable answer.

70   In its way, the M. & M. is an impressively sophisticated and human institution. Unlike the courts or the media, it recognizes that human error is generally not something that can be deterred by punishment. The M. & M. sees
avoiding error as largely a matter of will—of staying sufficiently informed and
alert to anticipate the myriad ways that things can go wrong and then trying to

head off each potential problem before it happens. Why do things go wrong? Because, doctors say, making them go right is hard stuff. It isn't damnable that an error occurs, but there is some shame to it. In fact, the M. & M.'s ethos can seem paradoxical. On the one hand, it reinforces the very American idea that error is intolerable. On the other hand, the very existence of the M. & M., its place on the weekly schedule, amounts to an acknowledgment that mistakes are an inevitable part of medicine.

But why do they happen so often? Lucian Leape, medicine's leading expert on error, points out that many other industries—whether the task is manufacturing semiconductors or serving customers at the Ritz-Carlton—simply wouldn't countenance error rates like those in hospitals. The aviation industry has reduced the frequency of operational errors to one in a hundred thousand flights, and most of those errors have no harmful consequences. The buzzword at General Electric these days is "Six Sigma," meaning that its goal is to make product defects so rare that in statistical terms they are more than six standard deviations away from being a matter of chance—almost a one-in-a-million occurrence.

Of course, patients are far more complicated and idiosyncratic than airplanes, and medicine isn't a matter of delivering a fixed product or even a catalogue of products; it may well be more complex than just about any other field of human endeavor. Yet everything we've learned in the past two decades—from cognitive psychology, from "human factors" engineering, from studies of disasters like Three Mile Island and Bhopal[6]—has yielded the same insights: not only do all human beings err but they err frequently and in predictable, patterned ways. And systems that do not adjust for these realities can end up exacerbating rather than eliminating error.

The British psychologist James Reason argues, in his book *Human Error,* that our propensity for certain types of error is the price we pay for the brain's remarkable ability to think and act intuitively—to sift quickly through the sensory information that constantly bombards us without wasting time trying to work through every situation anew. Thus systems that rely on human perfection present what Reason calls "latent errors"—errors waiting to happen. Medicine teems with examples. Take writing out a prescription, a rote procedure that relies on memory and attention, which we know are unreliable. Inevitably, a physician will sometimes specify the wrong dose or the wrong drug. Even when the prescription is written correctly, there's a risk that it will be misread. (Computerized ordering systems can almost eliminate errors of this kind, but only a small minority of hospitals have adopted them.) Medical equipment, which manufacturers often build without human operators in mind, is another area rife with latent errors: one reason physicians are bound to have problems

6. In 1979 there was a partial meltdown of a pressurized water reactor at Three Mile Island Nuclear Generating Station near Harrisburg, Pennsylvania; the Bhopal gas disaster occurred in December 1984 at the Union Carbide pesticide plant in Bhopal, Madhya Pradesh, India, exposing 500,000 people to dangerous chemicals.

when they use cardiac defibrillators is that the devices have no standard design. You can also make the case that onerous workloads, chaotic environments, and inadequate team communication all represent latent errors in the system.

James Reason makes another important observation: disasters do not simply occur; they evolve. In complex systems, a single failure rarely leads to harm. Human beings are impressively good at adjusting when an error becomes apparent, and systems often have built-in defenses. For example, pharmacists and nurses routinely check and counter-check physicians' orders. But errors do not always become apparent, and backup systems themselves often fail as a result of latent errors. A pharmacist forgets to check one of a thousand prescriptions. A machine's alarm bell malfunctions. The one attending trauma surgeon available gets stuck in the operating room. When things go wrong, it is usually because a series of failures conspire to produce disaster.

75   The M. & M. takes none of this into account. For that reason, many experts see it as a rather shabby approach to analyzing error and improving performance in medicine. It isn't enough to ask what a clinician could or should have done differently so that he and others may learn for next time. The doctor is often only the final actor in a chain of events that set him or her up to fail. Error experts, therefore, believe that it's the process, not the individuals in it, which requires closer examination and correction. In a sense, they want to industrialize medicine. And they can already claim one success story: the specialty of anesthesiology, which has adopted their precepts and seen extraordinary results.

IV—NEARLY PERFECT

At the center of the emblem of the American Society of Anesthesiologists is a single word: "Vigilance." When you put a patient to sleep under general anesthesia, you assume almost complete control of the patient's body. The body is paralyzed, the brain rendered unconscious, and machines are hooked up to control breathing, heart rate, blood pressure—all the vital functions. Given the complexity of the machinery and of the human body, there are a seemingly infinite number of ways in which things can go wrong, even in minor surgery. And yet anesthesiologists have found that if problems are detected they can usually be solved. In the nineteen-forties, there was only one death resulting from anesthesia in every twenty-five hundred operations, and between the nineteen-sixties and the nineteen-eighties the rate had stabilized at one or two in every ten thousand operations.

But Ellison (Jeep) Pierce had always regarded even that rate as unconscionable. From the time he began practicing, in 1960, as a young anesthesiologist out of North Carolina and the University of Pennsylvania, he had maintained a case file of details from all the deadly anesthetic accidents he had come across or participated in. But it was one case in particular that galvanized him. Friends of his had taken their eighteen-year-old daughter to the hospital to have her wisdom teeth pulled, under general anesthesia. The anesthesiologist inserted the breathing tube into her esophagus instead of her trachea, which is a relatively common mishap, and then failed to spot the error, which is not. Deprived of oxygen, she died within minutes. Pierce knew that a one-in-ten-thousand death rate, given that anesthesia was administered in the United States an estimated thirty-five million times each year, meant thirty-five hundred avoidable deaths like that one.

In 1982, Pierce was elected vice-president of the American Society of Anesthesiologists and got an opportunity to do something about the death rate. The same year, ABC's *20/20* aired an exposé that caused a considerable stir in his profession. The segment began, "If you are going to go into anesthesia, you are going on a long trip, and you should not do it if you can avoid it in any way. General anesthesia [is] safe most of the time, but there are dangers from human error, carelessness, and a critical shortage of anesthesiologists. This year, six thousand patients will die or suffer brain damage." The program presented several terrifying cases from around the country. Between the small crisis that the show created and the sharp increases in physicians' malpractice-insurance premiums at that time, Pierce was able to mobilize the Society of Anesthesiologists around the problem of error.

He turned for ideas not to a physician but to an engineer named Jeffrey Cooper, the lead author of a ground-breaking 1978 paper entitled "Preventable Anesthesia Mishaps: A Study of Human Factors." An unassuming, fastidious man, Cooper had been hired in 1972, when he was twenty-six years old, by the Massachusetts General Hospital bioengineering unit, to work on developing machines for anesthesiology researchers. He gravitated toward the operating room, however, and spent hours there observing the anesthesiologists, and one of the first things he noticed was how poorly the anesthesia machines were designed. For example, a clockwise turn of a dial decreased the concentration of potent anesthetics in about half the machines but increased the concentration in the other half. He decided to borrow a technique called "critical incident analysis"—which had been used since the nineteen-fifties to analyze mishaps in aviation—in an effort to learn how equipment might be contributing to errors in anesthesia. The technique is built around carefully conducted interviews, designed to capture as much detail as possible about dangerous incidents: how specific accidents evolved and what factors contributed to them. This information is then used to look for patterns among different cases.

Getting open, honest reporting is crucial. The Federal Aviation Administration has a formalized system for analyzing and reporting dangerous aviation incidents, and its enormous success in improving airline safety rests on two cornerstones. Pilots who report an incident within ten days have automatic immunity from punishment, and the reports go to a neutral, outside agency, NASA, which has no interest in using the information against individual pilots. For Jeffrey Cooper, it was probably an advantage that he was an engineer, and not a physician, so that anesthesiologists regarded him as a discreet, unthreatening interviewer.

The result was the first in-depth, scientific look at errors in medicine. His detailed analysis of three hundred and fifty-nine errors provided a view of the

80

profession unlike anything that had been seen before. Contrary to the prevailing assumption that the start of anesthesia ("takeoff") was the most dangerous part, anesthesiologists learned that incidents tended to occur in the middle of anesthesia, when vigilance waned. The most common kind of incident involved errors in maintaining the patient's breathing, and these were usually the result of an undetected disconnection or misconnection of the breathing tubing, mistakes in managing the airway, or mistakes in using the anesthesia machine. Just as important, Cooper enumerated a list of contributory factors, including inadequate experience, inadequate familiarity with equipment, poor communication among team members, haste, inattention, and fatigue.

The study provoked widespread debate among anesthesiologists, but there was no concerted effort to solve the problems until Jeep Pierce came along. Through the anesthesiology society at first, and then through a foundation that he started, Pierce directed funding into research on how to reduce the problems Cooper had identified, sponsored an international conference to gather ideas from around the world, and brought anesthesia-machine designers into safety discussions.

It all worked. Hours for anesthesiology residents were shortened. Manufacturers began redesigning their machines with fallible human beings in mind. Dials were standardized to turn in a uniform direction; locks were put in to prevent accidental administration of more than one anesthetic gas; controls were changed so that oxygen delivery could not be turned down to zero.

Where errors could not be eliminated directly, anesthesiologists began looking for reliable means of detecting them earlier. For example, because the trachea and the esophagus are so close together, it is almost inevitable that an anesthesiologist will sometimes put the breathing tube down the wrong pipe. Anesthesiologists had always checked for this by listening with a stethoscope for breath sounds over both lungs. But Cooper had turned up a surprising number of mishaps—like the one that befell the daughter of Pierce's friends—involving undetected esophageal intubations. Something more effective was needed. In fact, monitors that could detect this kind of error had been available for years, but, in part because of their expense, relatively few anesthesiologists used them. One type of monitor could verify that the tube was in the trachea by detecting carbon dioxide being exhaled from the lungs. Another type, the pulse oximeter, tracked blood-oxygen levels, thereby providing an early warning that something was wrong with the patient's breathing system. Prodded by Pierce and others, the anesthesiology society made the use of both types of monitor for every patient receiving general anesthesia an official standard. Today, anesthesia deaths from misconnecting the breathing system or intubating the esophagus rather than the trachea are virtually unknown. In a decade, the over-all death rate dropped to just one in more than two hundred thousand cases—less than a twentieth of what it had been.

85   And the reformers have not stopped there. David Gaba, a professor of anesthesiology at Stanford, has focused on improving human performance. In aviation, he points out, pilot experience is recognized to be invaluable but

insufficient: pilots seldom have direct experience with serious plane malfunction anymore. They are therefore required to undergo yearly training in crisis simulators. Why not doctors, too?

Gaba, a physician with training in engineering, led in the design of an anesthesia-simulation system known as the Eagle Patient Simulator. It is a life-size, computer-driven mannequin that is capable of amazingly realistic behavior. It has a circulation, a heartbeat, and lungs that take in oxygen and expire carbon dioxide. If you inject drugs into it or administer inhaled anesthetics, it will detect the type and amount, and its heart rate, its blood pressure, and its oxygen levels will respond appropriately. The "patient" can be made to develop airway swelling, bleeding, and heart disturbances. The mannequin is laid on an operating table in a simulation room equipped exactly like the real thing. Here both residents and experienced attending physicians learn to perform effectively in all kinds of dangerous, and sometimes freak, scenarios: an anesthesia-machine malfunction, a power outage, a patient who goes into cardiac arrest during surgery, and even a cesarean-section patient whose airway shuts down and who requires an emergency tracheostomy.

Though anesthesiology has unquestionably taken the lead in analyzing and trying to remedy "systems" failures, there are signs of change in other quarters. The American Medical Association, for example, set up its National Patient Safety Foundation in 1997 and asked Cooper and Pierce to serve on the board of directors. The foundation is funding research, sponsoring conferences, and attempting to develop new standards for hospital drug-ordering systems that could substantially reduce medication mistakes—the single most common type of medical error.

Even in surgery there have been some encouraging developments. For instance, operating on the wrong knee or foot or other body part of a patient has been a recurrent, if rare, mistake. A typical response has been to fire the surgeon. Recently, however, hospitals and surgeons have begun to recognize that the body's bilateral symmetry makes these errors predictable. Last year, the American Academy of Orthopedic Surgeons endorsed a simple way of preventing them: make it standard practice for surgeons to initial, with a marker, the body part to be cut before the patient comes to surgery.

The Northern New England Cardiovascular Disease Study Group, based at Dartmouth, is another success story. Though the group doesn't conduct the sort of in-depth investigation of mishaps that Jeffrey Cooper pioneered, it has shown what can be done simply through statistical monitoring. Six hospitals belong to this consortium, which tracks deaths and complications (such as wound infections, uncontrolled bleeding, and stroke) arising from heart surgery and tries to identify various risk factors. Its researchers found, for example, that there were relatively high death rates among patients who developed anemia after bypass surgery, and that anemia developed most often in small patients. The fluid used to "prime" the heart-lung machine caused the anemia, because it diluted a patient's blood, so the smaller the patient (and his or her blood supply) the greater the effect. Members of the consortium now have several promising solutions to the problem. Another study found that a group at one hospital had made mistakes in "handoffs"—say, in passing preoperative lab results to the people in the operating room. The study group solved the problem by developing a pilot's checklist for all patients coming to the O.R. These efforts have introduced a greater degree of standardization, and so reduced the death rate in those six hospitals from four percent to three percent between 1991 and 1996. That meant two hundred and ninety-three fewer deaths. But the Northern New England cardiac group, even with its narrow focus and techniques, remains an exception; hard information about how things go wrong is still scarce. There is a hodgepodge of evidence that latent errors and systemic factors may contribute to surgical errors: the lack of standardized protocols, the surgeon's inexperience, the hospital's inexperience, inadequately designed technology and techniques, thin staffing, poor teamwork, time of day, the effects of managed care and corporate medicine, and so on and so on. But which are the major risk factors? We still don't know. Surgery, like most of medicine, awaits its Jeff Cooper.

V—GETTING IT RIGHT

90   It was a routine gallbladder operation, on a routine day: on the operating table was a mother in her forties, her body covered by blue paper drapes except for her round, antiseptic-coated belly. The gallbladder is a floppy, finger-length sac of bile like a deflated olive-green balloon tucked under the liver, and when gallstones form, as this patient had learned, they can cause excruciating bouts of pain. Once we removed her gallbladder, the pain would stop.

There are risks to this surgery, but they used to be much greater. Just a decade ago, surgeons had to make a six-inch abdominal incision that left patients in the hospital for the better part of a week just recovering from the wound. Today, we've learned to take out gallbladders with a minute camera and instruments that we manipulate through tiny incisions. The operation, often done as day surgery, is known as laparoscopic cholecystectomy, or "lap chole." Half a million Americans a year now have their gallbladders removed this way; at my hospital alone, we do several hundred lap choles annually.

When the attending gave me the go-ahead, I cut a discreet inch-long semicircle in the wink of skin just above the belly button. I dissected through fat and fascia until I was inside the abdomen, and dropped into place a "port," a half-inch-wide sheath for slipping instruments in and out. We hooked gas tubing up to a side vent on the port, and carbon dioxide poured in, inflating the abdomen until it was distended like a tire. I inserted the miniature camera. On a video monitor a few feet away, the woman's intestines blinked into view. With the abdomen inflated, I had room to move the camera, and I swung it around to look at the liver. The gallbladder could be seen poking out from under the edge.

We put in three more ports through even tinier incisions, spaced apart to complete the four corners of a square. Through the ports on his side, the attending put in two long "graspers," like small-scale versions of the device that a department-store clerk might use to get a hat off the top shelf. Watching the screen as he maneuvered them, he reached under the edge of the liver, clamped onto the gallbladder, and pulled it up into view. We were set to proceed.

Removing the gallbladder is fairly straightforward. You sever it from its stalk and from its blood supply, and pull the rubbery sac out of the abdomen through the incision near the belly button. You let the carbon dioxide out of the belly, pull out the ports, put a few stitches in the tiny incisions, slap some Band-Aids on top, and you're done. There's one looming danger, though: the stalk of the gallbladder is a branch off the liver's only conduit for sending bile to the intestines for the digestion of fats. And if you accidentally injure this main bile duct, the bile backs up and starts to destroy the liver. Between ten and twenty percent of the patients to whom this happens will die. Those who survive often have permanent liver damage and can go on to require liver transplantation. According to a standard textbook, "injuries to the main bile duct are nearly always the result of misadventure during operation and are therefore a serious reproach to the surgical profession." It is a true surgical error, and, like any surgical team doing a lap chole, we were intent on avoiding this mistake.

Using a dissecting instrument, I carefully stripped off the fibrous white   95
tissue and yellow fat overlying and concealing the base of the gallbladder. Now we could see its broad neck and the short stretch where it narrowed down to a duct—a tube no thicker than a strand of spaghetti peeking out from the surrounding tissue, but magnified on the screen to the size of major plumbing. Then, just to be absolutely sure we were looking at the gallbladder duct and not the main bile duct, I stripped away some more of the surrounding tissue. The attending and I stopped at this point, as we always do, and discussed the anatomy. The neck of the gallbladder led straight into the tube we were eying. So it had to be the right duct. We had exposed a good length of it without a sign of the main bile duct. Everything looked perfect, we agreed. "Go for it," the attending said.

I slipped in the clip applier, an instrument that squeezes V-shaped metal clips onto whatever you put in its jaws. I got the jaws around the duct and was about to fire when my eye caught, on the screen, a little globule of fat lying on top of the duct. That wasn't necessarily anything unusual, but somehow it didn't look right. With the tip of the clip applier, I tried to flick it aside, but, instead of a little globule, a whole layer of thin unseen tissue came up, and, underneath, we saw that the duct had a fork in it. My stomach dropped. If not for that little extra fastidiousness, I would have clipped off the main bile duct.

Here was the paradox of error in medicine. With meticulous technique and assiduous effort to insure that they have correctly identified the anatomy, surgeons need never cut the main bile duct. It is a paradigm of an avoidable error. At the same time, studies show that even highly experienced surgeons inflict this terrible injury about once in every two hundred lap choles. To put it another way, I may have averted disaster this time, but a statistician would say that, no matter how hard I tried, I was almost certain to make this error at least once in the course of my career.

But the story doesn't have to end here, as the cognitive psychologists and industrial-error experts have demonstrated. Given the results they've achieved in anesthesiology, it's clear that we can make dramatic improvements by going after the process, not the people. But there are distinct limitations to the industrial cure, however necessary its emphasis on systems and structures. It would be deadly for us, the individual actors, to give up our belief in human perfectibility. The statistics may say that someday I will sever someone's main bile duct, but each time I go into a gallbladder operation I believe that with enough will and effort I can beat the odds. This isn't just professional vanity. It's a necessary part of good medicine, even in superbly "optimized" systems. Operations like that lap chole have taught me how easily error can occur, but they've also showed me something else: effort does matter; diligence and attention to the minutest details can save you.

This may explain why many doctors take exception to talk of "systems problems," "continuous quality improvement," and "process reëngineering." It is the dry language of structures, not people. I'm no exception: something in me, too, demands an acknowledgment of my autonomy, which is also to say my ultimate culpability. Go back to that Friday night in the E.R., to the moment when I stood, knife in hand, over Louise Williams, her lips blue, her throat a swollen, bloody, and suddenly closed passage. A systems engineer might have proposed some useful changes. Perhaps a backup suction device should always be at hand, and better light more easily available. Perhaps the institution could have trained me better for such crises, could have required me to have operated on a few more goats. Perhaps emergency tracheostomies are so difficult under any circumstances that an automated device could have been designed to do a better job. But the could-haves are infinite, aren't they? Maybe Williams could have worn her seat belt, or had one less beer that night. We could call any or all of these factors latent errors, accidents waiting to happen.

100   But although they put the odds against me, it wasn't as if I had no chance of succeeding. Good doctoring is all about making the most of the hand you're dealt, and I failed to do so. The indisputable fact was that I hadn't called for help when I could have, and when I plunged the knife into her neck and made my horizontal slash my best was not good enough. It was just luck, hers and mine, that Dr. O'Connor somehow got a breathing tube into her in time.

There are all sorts of reasons that it would be wrong to take my license away or to take me to court. These reasons do not absolve me. Whatever the limits of the M. & M., its fierce ethic of personal responsibility for errors is a formidable virtue. No matter what measures are taken, medicine will sometimes falter, and it isn't reasonable to ask that it achieve perfection. What's reasonable is to ask that medicine never cease to aim for it.

MLA CITATION

Gawande, Atul. "When Doctors Make Mistakes." *The Norton Reader: An Anthology of Nonfiction*, edited by Melissa A. Goldthwaite et al., 15th ed., W. W. Norton, 2020, pp. 639–56.

QUESTIONS

1. Atul Gawande states flatly: "*All* doctors make terrible mistakes" (paragraph 50). He proceeds to analyze why. What are the main reasons he offers?

2. In section IV, "Nearly Perfect," Gawande discusses attempts by different medical groups to eliminate or reduce error. What approaches have been effective? What are the limits of these approaches?

3. Although it incorporates significant research, this essay is also a personal narrative. Gawande both begins and ends his essay by narrating a specific experience of his in the operating room. How are these examples similar? How are they different? How does the rhetorical purpose of these anecdotes change as Gawande moves through his discussion of medical error? Explain.

4. Write an essay about a time when you made a serious error. Try, like Gawande, to incorporate the research or advice of others who might help you understand the reasons for your error.

REBECCA SKLOOT

The Woman in the Photograph

THERE'S A PHOTO ON MY WALL of a woman I've never met, its left corner torn and patched together with tape. She looks straight into the camera and smiles, hands on hips, dress suit neatly pressed, lips painted deep red. It's the late 1940s and she hasn't yet reached the age of thirty. Her light brown skin is smooth, her eyes still young and playful, oblivious to the tumor growing inside her—a tumor that would leave her five children motherless and change the future of medicine. Beneath the photo, a caption says her name is "Henrietta Lacks, Helen Lane or Helen Larson."

No one knows who took that picture, but it's appeared hundreds of times in magazines and science textbooks, on blogs and laboratory walls. She's usually identified as Helen Lane, but often she has no name at all. She's simply called HeLa, the code name given to the world's first immortal human cells—*her* cells, cut from her cervix just months before she died.

Her real name is Henrietta Lacks.

I've spent years staring at that photo, wondering what kind of life she led, what happened to her children, and what she'd think about cells from her cervix living on forever—bought, sold, packaged, and shipped by the trillions to laboratories around the world. I've tried to imagine how she'd feel knowing that her cells went up in the first space missions to see what would happen to human cells in zero gravity,[1] or that they helped with some of the most important

From The Immortal Life of Henrietta Lacks (2010), *which tells the story of how the cells of one woman—taken without her consent when she died—contributed to numerous scientific discoveries in the fields of genetics, cancer treatment, and vaccination, among others. The book raises questions about science, race, and medical ethics.*

1. In 1960, a year before Yuri Gagarin became the first person to enter outer space, a sample of HeLa cells was placed on the Russian *Korabl-Sputnik 2* satellite.

advances in medicine: the polio vaccine, chemotherapy, cloning, gene mapping, in vitro fertilization. I'm pretty sure that she—like most of us—would be shocked to hear that there are trillions more of her cells growing in laboratories now than there ever were in her body.

5   There's no way of knowing exactly how many of Henrietta's cells are alive today. One scientist estimates that if you could pile all HeLa cells ever grown onto a scale, they'd weigh more than 50 million metric tons—an inconceivable number, given that an individual cell weighs almost nothing. Another scientist calculated that if you could lay all HeLa cells ever grown end-to-end, they'd wrap around the Earth at least three times, spanning more than 350 million feet. In her prime, Henrietta herself stood only a bit over five feet tall.

I first learned about HeLa cells and the woman behind them in 1988, thirty-seven years after her death, when I was sixteen and sitting in a community college biology class. My instructor, Donald Defler, a gnomish balding man, paced at the front of the lecture hall and flipped on an overhead projector. He pointed to two diagrams that appeared on the wall behind him. They were schematics of the cell reproduction cycle, but to me they just looked like a neon-colored mess of arrows, squares, and circles with words I didn't understand, like "MPF Triggering a Chain Reaction of Protein Activations."

I was a kid who'd failed freshman year at the regular public high school because she never showed up. I'd transferred to an alternative school that offered dream studies instead of biology, so I was taking Defler's class for high-school credit, which meant that I was sitting in a college lecture hall at sixteen with words like *mitosis* and *kinase inhibitors* flying around. I was completely lost.

"Do we have to memorize everything on those diagrams?" one student yelled.

Yes, Defler said, we had to memorize the diagrams, and yes, they'd be on the test, but that didn't matter right then. What he wanted us to understand was that cells are amazing things: There are about one hundred trillion of them in our bodies, each so small that several thousand could fit on the period at the end of this sentence. They make up all our tissues—muscle, bone, blood—which in turn make up our organs.

10   Under the microscope, a cell looks a lot like a fried egg: It has a white (the *cytoplasm*) that's full of water and proteins to keep it fed, and a yolk (the *nucleus*) that holds all the genetic information that makes you you. The cytoplasm buzzes like a New York City street. It's crammed full of molecules and vessels endlessly shuttling enzymes and sugars from one part of the cell to another, pumping water, nutrients, and oxygen in and out of the cell. All the while, little cytoplasmic factories work 24/7, cranking out sugars, fats, proteins, and energy to keep the whole thing running and feed the nucleus—the brains of the operation. Inside every nucleus within each cell in your body, there's an identical copy of your entire genome. That genome tells cells when to grow and divide and makes sure they do their jobs, whether that's controlling your heartbeat or helping your brain understand the words on this page.

Defler paced the front of the classroom telling us how mitosis—the process of cell division—makes it possible for embryos to grow into babies, and for our bodies to create new cells for healing wounds or replenishing blood we've lost. It was beautiful, he said, like a perfectly choreographed dance.

All it takes is one small mistake anywhere in the division process for cells to start growing out of control, he told us. Just *one* enzyme misfiring, just one wrong protein activation, and you could have cancer. Mitosis goes haywire, which is how it spreads.

"We learned that by studying cancer cells in culture," Defler said. He grinned and spun to face the board, where he wrote two words in enormous print: HENRIETTA LACKS.

Henrietta died in 1951 from a vicious case of cervical cancer, he told us. But before she died, a surgeon took samples of her tumor and put them in a petri dish. Scientists had been trying to keep human cells alive in culture for decades, but they all eventually died. Henrietta's were different: they reproduced an entire generation every twenty-four hours, and they never stopped. They became the first immortal human cells ever grown in a laboratory.

"Henrietta's cells have now been living outside her body far longer than   15
they ever lived inside it," Defler said. If we went to almost any cell culture lab in the world and opened its freezers, he told us, we'd probably find millions—if not billions—of Henrietta's cells in small vials on ice.

Her cells were part of research into the genes that cause cancer and those that suppress it; they helped develop drugs for treating herpes, leukemia, influenza, hemophilia, and Parkinson's disease; and they've been used to study lactose digestion, sexually transmitted diseases, appendicitis, human longevity, mosquito mating, and the negative cellular effects of working in sewers. Their chromosomes and proteins have been studied with such detail and precision that scientists know their every quirk. Like guinea pigs and mice, Henrietta's cells have become the standard laboratory workhorse.

"HeLa cells were one of the most important things that happened to medicine in the last hundred years," Defler said.

Then, matter-of-factly, almost as an afterthought, he said, "She was a black woman." He erased her name in one fast swipe and blew the chalk from his hands. Class was over.

As the other students filed out of the room, I sat thinking, *That's it? That's all we get? There has to be more to the story.*

I followed Defler to his office.   20

"Where was she from?" I asked. "Did she know how important her cells were? Did she have any children?"

"I wish I could tell you," he said, "but no one knows anything about her."

After class, I ran home and threw myself onto my bed with my biology textbook. I looked up "cell culture" in the index, and there she was, a small parenthetical:

> In culture, cancer cells can go on dividing indefinitely, if they have a con-
> tinual supply of nutrients, and thus are said to be "immortal." A striking
> example is a cell line that has been reproducing in culture since 1951.
> (Cells of this line are called HeLa cells because their original source was a
> tumor removed from a woman named Henrietta Lacks.)

That was it. I looked up HeLa in my parents' encyclopedia, then my dictionary:
No Henrietta.

As I graduated from high school and worked my way through college
toward a biology degree, HeLa cells were omnipresent. I heard about them in
histology, neurology, pathology; I used them in experiments on how neighboring cells communicate. But after Mr. Defler, no one mentioned Henrietta.

25   When I got my first computer in the mid-nineties and started using the
Internet, I searched for information about her, but found only confused snippets: most sites said her name was Helen Lane; some said she died in the thirties; others said the forties, fifties, or even sixties. Some said ovarian cancer
killed her, others said breast or cervical cancer.

Eventually I tracked down a few magazine articles about her from the seventies. *Ebony* quoted Henrietta's husband saying, "All I remember is that she
had this disease, and right after she died they called me in the office wanting to
get my permission to take a sample of some kind. I decided not to let them." *Jet*
said the family was angry—angry that Henrietta's cells were being sold for
twenty-five dollars a vial, and angry that articles had been published about the
cells without their knowledge. It said, "Pounding in the back of their heads was
a gnawing feeling that science and the press had taken advantage of them."

The articles all ran photos of Henrietta's family: her oldest son sitting at
his dining room table in Baltimore, looking at a genetics textbook. Her middle
son in military uniform, smiling and holding a baby. But one picture stood out
more than any other: in it, Henrietta's daughter, Deborah Lacks, is surrounded
by family, everyone smiling, arms around each other, eyes bright and excited.
Except Deborah. She stands in the foreground looking alone, almost as if someone pasted her into the photo after the fact. She's twenty-six years old and
beautiful, with short brown hair and catlike eyes. But those eyes glare at the
camera, hard and serious. The caption said the family had found out just a few
months earlier that Henrietta's cells were still alive, yet at that point she'd been
dead for twenty-five years.

All of the stories mentioned that scientists had begun doing research on
Henrietta's children, but the Lackses didn't seem to know what that research
was for. They said they were being tested to see if they had the cancer that killed
Henrietta, but according to the reporters, scientists were studying the Lacks
family to learn more about Henrietta's cells. The stories quoted her son Lawrence, who wanted to know if the immortality of his mother's cells meant that
he might live forever too. But one member of the family remained voiceless:
Henrietta's daughter, Deborah.

As I worked my way through graduate school studying writing, I became
fixated on the idea of someday telling Henrietta's story. At one point I even

called directory assistance in Baltimore looking for Henrietta's husband, David
Lacks, but he wasn't listed. I had the idea that I'd write a book that was a biography of both the cells and the woman they came from—someone's daughter,
wife, and mother.

I couldn't have imagined it then, but that phone call would mark the begin-   30
ning of a decadelong adventure through scientific laboratories, hospitals, and
mental institutions, with a cast of characters that would include Nobel laure-
ates, grocery store clerks, convicted felons, and a professional con artist. While
trying to make sense of the history of cell culture and the complicated ethical
debate surrounding the use of human tissues in research, I'd be accused of con-
spiracy and slammed into a wall both physically and metaphorically, and I'd
eventually find myself on the receiving end of something that looked a lot like
an exorcism. I did eventually meet Deborah, who would turn out to be one of
the strongest and most resilient women I'd ever known. We'd form a deep personal bond, and slowly, without realizing it, I'd become a character in her story,
and she in mine.

Deborah and I came from very different cultures: I grew up white and agnos-
tic in the Pacific Northwest, my roots half New York Jew and half Midwestern
Protestant; Deborah was a deeply religious black Christian from the South. I
tended to leave the room when religion came up in conversation because it
made me uncomfortable; Deborah's family tended toward preaching, faith heal-
ings, and sometimes voodoo. She grew up in a black neighborhood that was one
of the poorest and most dangerous in the country; I grew up in a safe, quiet
middle-class neighborhood in a predominantly white city and went to high school
with a total of two black students. I was a science journalist who referred to all
things supernatural as "woo-woo stuff"; Deborah believed Henrietta's spirit
lived on in her cells, controlling the life of anyone who crossed its path. Including me.

"How else do you explain why your science teacher knew her real name
when everyone else called her Helen Lane?" Deborah would say. "She was trying to get your attention." This thinking would apply to everything in my life:
when I married while writing this book, it was because Henrietta wanted someone to take care of me while I worked. When I divorced, it was because she'd
decided he was getting in the way of the book. When an editor who insisted I
take the Lacks family out of the book was injured in a mysterious accident,
Deborah said that's what happens when you piss Henrietta off.

The Lackses challenged everything I thought I knew about faith, science,
journalism, and race. Ultimately, this [story] is the result. It's not only the story
of HeLa cells and Henrietta Lacks, but of Henrietta's family—particularly
Deborah—and their lifelong struggle to make peace with the existence of those
cells, and the science that made them possible.

MLA CITATION

Skloot, Rebecca. "The Woman in the Photograph." *The Norton Reader: An Anthology
of Nonfiction*, edited by Melissa A. Goldthwaite et al., 15th ed., W. W. Norton,
2020, pp. 657–661.

QUESTIONS

1. Was the surgeon who first cultivated Henrietta Lacks's cells for research justified in doing so? Why or why not?

2. Rebecca Skloot writes, "As I worked my way through graduate school studying writing, I became fixated on the idea of someday telling Henrietta's story" (paragraph 29). Why does Skloot find Lacks's story so compelling?

3. This essay is the prologue to Skloot's book *The Immortal Life of Henrietta Lacks*. Why does Skloot dwell so extensively on her own story in the essay?

4. Write the story of a research project of your own. What or who motivated you to undertake the project? How did you go about your research? What obstacles did you encounter? What discoveries did you make? Looking back on the process, what did you learn about yourself as a researcher or as a person?

MICHAEL POLLAN
An Animal's Place

THE FIRST TIME I opened Peter Singer's *Animal Liberation,* I was dining alone at the Palm, trying to enjoy a rib-eye steak cooked medium-rare.[1] If this sounds like a good recipe for cognitive dissonance (if not indigestion), that was sort of the idea. Preposterous as it might seem, to supporters of animal rights, what I was doing was tantamount to reading *Uncle Tom's Cabin*[2] on a plantation in the Deep South in 1852.

Singer and the swelling ranks of his followers ask us to imagine a future in which people will look back on my meal, and this steakhouse, as relics of an equally backward age. Eating animals, wearing animals, experimenting on animals, killing animals for sport: all these practices, so resolutely normal to us, will be seen as the barbarities they are, and we will come to view "speciesism"—a neologism I had encountered before only in jokes—as a form of discrimination as indefensible as racism or anti-Semitism.

Even in 1975, when *Animal Liberation* was first published, Singer, an Australian philosopher now teaching at Princeton, was confident that he had the wind of history at his back. The recent civil rights past was prologue, as one liberation movement followed on the heels of another. Slowly but surely, the white man's circle of moral consideration was expanded to admit first blacks, then women, then homosexuals. In each case, a group once thought to be so differ-

Published in the New York Times Magazine *(2002), a Sunday supplement of the daily newspaper.*

1. Singer (b. 1946), Australian philosopher and ethicist; *Animal Liberation* (1975) makes an influential argument for animal rights; the Palm, a famous New York City steakhouse.
2. Novel (1852) critical of slavery by abolitionist Harriet Beecher Stowe.

ent from the prevailing "we" as to be undeserving of civil rights was, after a struggle, admitted to the club. Now it was animals' turn.

That animal liberation is the logical next step in the forward march of moral progress is no longer the fringe idea it was back in 1975. A growing and increasingly influential group of philosophers, ethicists, law professors and activists are convinced that the great moral struggle of our time will be for the rights of animals.

So far the movement has scored some of its biggest victories in Europe.   5
Earlier this year, Germany became the first nation to grant animals a constitutional right: the words "and animals" were added to a provision obliging the state to respect and protect the dignity of human beings. The farming of animals for fur was recently banned in England. In several European nations, sows may no longer be confined to crates nor laying hens to "battery cages"—stacked wired cages so small the birds cannot stretch their wings. The Swiss are amending their laws to change the status of animals from "things" to "beings."

Though animals are still very much "things" in the eyes of American law, change is in the air. Thirty-seven states have recently passed laws making some forms of animal cruelty a crime, twenty-one of them by ballot initiative. Following protests by activists, McDonald's and Burger King forced significant improvements in the way the U.S. meat industry slaughters animals. Agribusiness and the cosmetics and apparel industries are all struggling to defuse mounting public concerns over animal welfare.

Once thought of as a left-wing concern, the movement now cuts across ideological lines. Perhaps the most eloquent recent plea on behalf of animals, a new book called *Dominion*, was written by a former speechwriter for President Bush. And once outlandish ideas are finding their way into mainstream opinion. A recent Zogby poll found that fifty-one percent of Americans believe that primates are entitled to the same rights as human children.

What is going on here? A certain amount of cultural confusion, for one thing. For at the same time many people seem eager to extend the circle of our moral consideration to animals, in our factory farms and laboratories we are inflicting more suffering on more animals than at any time in history. One by one, science is dismantling our claims to uniqueness as a species, discovering that such things as culture, toolmaking, language and even possibly self-consciousness are not the exclusive domain of *Homo sapiens*. Yet most of the animals we kill lead lives organized very much in the spirit of Descartes,[3] who famously claimed that animals were mere machines, incapable of thought or feeling. There's a schizoid quality to our relationship with animals, in which sentiment and brutality exist side by side. Half the dogs in America will receive Christmas presents this year, yet few of us pause to consider the miserable life of the pig—an animal easily as intelligent as a dog—that becomes the Christmas ham.

We tolerate this disconnect because the life of the pig has moved out of view. When's the last time you saw a pig? (Babe doesn't count.) Except for our pets, real animals—animals living and dying—no longer figure in our everyday

3. René Descartes (1596–1650), French philosopher.

lives. Meat comes from the grocery store, where it is cut and packaged to look as little like parts of animals as possible. The disappearance of animals from our lives has opened a space in which there's no reality check, either on the sentiment or the brutality. This is pretty much where we live now, with respect to animals, and it is a space in which the Peter Singers and Frank Perdues[4] of the world can evidently thrive equally well.

10   Several years ago, the English critic John Berger wrote an essay, "Why Look at Animals?," in which he suggested that the loss of everyday contact between ourselves and animals—and specifically the loss of eye contact—has left us deeply confused about the terms of our relationship to other species. That eye contact, always slightly uncanny, had provided a vivid daily reminder that animals were at once crucially like and unlike us; in their eyes we glimpsed something unmistakably familiar (pain, fear, tenderness) and something irretrievably alien. Upon this paradox people built a relationship in which they felt they could both honor and eat animals without looking away. But that accommodation has pretty much broken down; nowadays, it seems, we either look away or become vegetarians. For my own part, neither option seemed especially appetizing. Which might explain how I found myself reading *Animal Liberation* in a steakhouse.

This is not something I'd recommend if you're determined to continue eating meat. Combining rigorous philosophical argument with journalistic description, *Animal Liberation* is one of those rare books that demand that you either defend the way you live or change it. Because Singer is so skilled in argument, for many readers it is easier to change. His book has converted countless thousands to vegetarianism, and it didn't take long for me to see why: within a few pages, he had succeeded in throwing me on the defensive.

Singer's argument is disarmingly simple and, if you accept its premises, difficult to refute. Take the premise of equality, which most people readily accept. Yet what do we really mean by it? People are not, as a matter of fact, equal at all—some are smarter than others, better looking, more gifted. "Equality is a moral idea," Singer points out, "not an assertion of fact." The moral idea is that everyone's interests ought to receive equal consideration, regardless of "what abilities they may possess." Fair enough; many philosophers have gone this far. But fewer have taken the next logical step. "If possessing a higher degree of intelligence does not entitle one human to use another for his or her own ends, how can it entitle humans to exploit nonhumans for the same purpose?"

This is the nub of Singer's argument, and right around here I began scribbling objections in the margin. *But humans differ from animals in morally significant ways.* Yes they do, Singer acknowledges, which is why we shouldn't treat pigs and children alike. Equal consideration of interests is not the same as equal treatment, he points out: children have an interest in being educated; pigs, in rooting around in the dirt. But where their interests are the same, the princi-

4. Perdue (1920–2005) was president and CEO of Perdue Farms, one of the largest poultry processors in the United States.

ple of equality demands they receive the same consideration. And the one all-important interest that we share with pigs, as with all sentient creatures, is an interest in avoiding pain.

Here Singer quotes a famous passage from Jeremy Bentham, the eighteenth-century utilitarian philosopher, that is the wellspring of the animal rights movement. Bentham was writing in 1789, soon after the French colonies freed black slaves, granting them fundamental rights. "The day *may* come," he speculates, "when the rest of the animal creation may acquire those rights." Bentham then asks what characteristic entitles any being to moral consideration. "Is it the faculty of reason or perhaps the faculty of discourse?" Obviously not, since "a full-grown horse or dog is beyond comparison a more rational, as well as a more conversable animal, than an infant." He concludes: "The question is not, Can they *reason*? nor, Can they *talk*? but, Can they *suffer*?"

Bentham here is playing a powerful card philosophers call the "argument   15 from marginal cases," or AMC for short. It goes like this: There are humans—infants, the severely retarded, the demented—whose mental function cannot match that of a chimpanzee. Even though these people cannot reciprocate our moral attentions, we nevertheless include them in the circle of our moral consideration. So on what basis do we exclude the chimpanzee?

Because he's a chimp, I furiously scribbled in the margin, *and they're human!* For Singer that's not good enough. To exclude the chimp from moral consideration simply because he's not human is no different from excluding the slave simply because he's not white. In the same way we'd call that exclusion racist, the animal rightist contends that it is speciesist to discriminate against the chimpanzee solely because he's not human.

But the differences between blacks and whites are trivial compared with the differences between my son and a chimp. Singer counters by asking us to imagine a hypothetical society that discriminates against people on the basis of something nontrivial—say, intelligence. If that scheme offends our sense of equality, then why is the fact that animals lack certain human characteristics any more just as a basis for discrimination? Either we do not owe any justice to the severely retarded, he concludes, or we do owe it to animals with higher capabilities.

This is where I put down my fork. If I believe in equality, and equality is based on interests rather than characteristics, then I have to either take the interests of the steer I'm eating into account or concede that I am a speciesist. For the time being, I decided to plead guilty as charged. I finished my steak.

But Singer had planted a troubling notion, and in the days afterward, it grew and grew, watered by the other animal rights thinkers I began reading: the philosophers Tom Regan and James Rachels; the legal theorist Steven M. Wise; the writers Joy Williams and Matthew Scully. I didn't *think* I minded being a speciesist, but could it be, as several of these writers suggest, that we will someday come to regard speciesism as an evil comparable to racism? Will history someday judge us as harshly as it judges the Germans who went about their ordinary lives in the shadow of Treblinka? Precisely that question was recently posed by J. M. Coetzee, the South African novelist, in a lecture delivered at Princeton; he answered it in the affirmative. If animal rightists are right, "a crime of stupefying proportions" (in Coetzee's words) is going on all around us every day, just beneath our notice.

20   It's an idea almost impossible to entertain seriously, much less to accept, and in the weeks following my restaurant face-off between Singer and the steak, I found myself marshaling whatever mental power I could muster to try to refute it. Yet Singer and his allies managed to trump almost all my objections.

My first line of defense was obvious. *Animals kill one another all the time. Why treat animals more ethically than they treat one another?* (Ben Franklin tried this one long before me: during a fishing trip, he wondered, "If you eat one another, I don't see why we may not eat you." He admits, however, that the rationale didn't occur to him until the fish were in the frying pan, smelling "admirably well." The advantage of being a "reasonable creature," Franklin remarks, is that you can find a reason for whatever you want to do.) To the "they do it too" defense, the animal rightist has a devastating reply: Do you really want to base your morality on the natural order? Murder and rape are natural too. Besides, humans don't need to kill other creatures in order to survive; animals do. (Though if my cat, Otis, is any guide, animals sometimes kill for sheer pleasure.)

This suggests another defense. *Wouldn't life in the wild be worse for these farm animals?* "Defenders of slavery imposed on black Africans often made a similar point," Singer retorts. "The life of freedom is to be preferred."

But domesticated animals can't survive in the wild; in fact, without us they wouldn't exist at all. Or as one nineteenth-century political philosopher put it, "The pig has a stronger interest than anyone in the demand for bacon. If all the world were Jewish, there would be no pigs at all." But it turns out that this would be fine by the animal rightists: for if pigs don't exist, they can't be wronged.

Animals on factory farms have never known any other life. Singer replies that "animals feel a need to exercise, stretch their limbs or wings, groom themselves and turn around, whether or not they have ever lived in conditions that permit this." The measure of their suffering is not their prior experiences but the unremitting daily frustration of their instincts.

25   *OK, the suffering of animals is a legitimate problem, but the world is full of problems, and surely human problems must come first!* Sounds good, and yet all the animal people are asking me to do is to stop eating meat and wearing animal furs and hides. There's no reason I can't devote myself to solving humankind's problems while being a vegetarian who wears synthetics.

But doesn't the fact that we could choose to forgo meat for moral reasons point to a crucial moral difference between animals and humans? As Kant pointed out, the human being is the only moral animal, the only one even capable of entertaining a concept of "rights." What's wrong with reserving moral consideration for those able to reciprocate it? Right here is where you run smack into the AMC: the moral status of the retarded, the insane, the infant and the Alzheimer's patient. Such "marginal cases," in the detestable argot of modern moral philosophy, cannot participate in moral decision-making any more than a monkey can, yet we nevertheless grant them rights.

That's right, I respond, for the simple reason that they're one of us. And all of us have been, and will probably once again be, marginal cases ourselves.

What's more, these people have fathers and mothers, daughters and sons, which makes our interest in their welfare deeper than our interest in the welfare of even the most brilliant ape.

Alas, none of these arguments evade the charge of speciesism; the racist, too, claims that it's natural to give special consideration to one's own kind. A utilitarian like Singer would agree, however, that the feelings of relatives do count for something. Yet the principle of equal consideration of interests demands that, given the choice between performing a painful medical experiment on a severely retarded orphan and on a normal ape, we must sacrifice the child. Why? Because the ape has a greater capacity for pain.

Here in a nutshell is the problem with the AMC: it can be used to help the animals, but just as often it winds up hurting the marginal cases. Giving up our speciesism will bring us to a moral cliff from which we may not be prepared to jump, even when logic is pushing us.

And yet this isn't the moral choice I am being asked to make. (Too bad; it would be so much easier!) In everyday life, the choice is not between babies and chimps but between the pork and the tofu. Even if we reject the "hard utilitarianism" of a Peter Singer, there remains the question of whether we owe animals that can feel pain *any* moral consideration, and this seems impossible to deny. And if we do owe them moral consideration, how can we justify eating them? 30

This is why killing animals for meat (and clothing) poses the most difficult animal rights challenge. In the case of animal testing, all but the most radical animal rightists are willing to balance the human benefit against the cost to the animals. That's because the unique qualities of human consciousness carry weight in the utilitarian calculus: human pain counts for more than that of a mouse, since our pain is amplified by emotions like dread; similarly, our deaths are worse than an animal's because we understand what death is in a way they don't. So the argument over animal testing is really in the details: Is this particular procedure or test *really* necessary to save human lives? (Very often it's not, in which case we probably shouldn't do it.) But if humans no longer need to eat meat or wear skins, then what exactly are we putting on the human side of the scale to outweigh the interests of the animal?

I suspect that this is finally why the animal people managed to throw me on the defensive. It's one thing to choose between the chimp and the retarded child or to accept the sacrifice of all those pigs surgeons practiced on to develop heart-bypass surgery. But what happens when the choice is between "a lifetime of suffering for a nonhuman animal and the gastronomic preference of a human being?" You look away—or you stop eating animals. And if you don't want to do either? Then you have to try to determine if the animals you're eating have really endured "a lifetime of suffering."

Whether our interest in eating animals outweighs their interest in not being eaten (assuming for the moment that is their interest) turns on the vexed question of animal suffering. Vexed, because it is impossible to know what really goes on in the mind of a cow or a pig or even an ape. Strictly speaking, this is true of other humans, too, but since humans are all basically wired the same way, we have excellent reason to assume that other people's experience of pain feels much like our own. Can we say that about animals? Yes and no.

I have yet to find anyone who still subscribes to Descartes's belief that animals cannot feel pain because they lack a soul. The general consensus among scientists and philosophers is that when it comes to pain, the higher animals are wired much the way we are for the same evolutionary reasons, so we should take the writhings of the kicked dog at face value. Indeed, the very premise of a great deal of animal testing—the reason it has value—is that animals' experience of physical and even some psychological pain closely resembles our own. Otherwise, why would cosmetics testers drip chemicals into the eyes of rabbits to see if they sting? Why would researchers study head trauma by traumatizing chimpanzee heads? Why would psychologists attempt to induce depression and "learned helplessness" in dogs by exposing them to ceaseless random patterns of electrical shock?

35   That said, it can be argued that human pain differs from animal pain by an order of magnitude. This qualitative difference is largely the result of our possession of language and, by virtue of language, an ability to have thoughts about thoughts and to imagine alternatives to our current reality. The philosopher Daniel C. Dennett suggests that we would do well to draw a distinction between pain, which a great many animals experience, and suffering, which depends on a degree of self-consciousness only a few animals appear to command. Suffering, in this view, is not just lots of pain but pain intensified by human emotions like loss, sadness, worry, regret, self-pity, shame, humiliation and dread.

Consider castration. No one would deny the procedure is painful to animals, yet animals appear to get over it in a way humans do not. (Some rhesus monkeys competing for mates will bite off a rival's testicle; the very next day the victim may be observed mating, seemingly little the worse for wear.) Surely the suffering of a man able to comprehend the full implications of castration, to anticipate the event and contemplate its aftermath, represents an agony of another order.

By the same token, however, language and all that comes with it can also make certain kinds of pain *more* bearable. A trip to the dentist would be a torment for an ape that couldn't be made to understand the purpose and duration of the procedure.

As humans contemplating the pain and suffering of animals, we do need to guard against projecting onto them what the same experience would feel like to us. Watching a steer force-marched up the ramp to the kill-floor door, as I have done, I need to remind myself that this is not Sean Penn in *Dead Man Walking*, that in a bovine brain the concept of nonexistence is blissfully absent. "If we fail to find suffering in the [animal] lives we can see," Dennett writes in *Kinds of Minds*, "we can rest assured there is no invisible suffering somewhere in their brains. If we find suffering, we will recognize it without difficulty."

Which brings us—reluctantly, necessarily—to the American factory farm, the place where all such distinctions turn to dust. It's not easy to draw lines between pain and suffering in a modern egg or confinement hog operation. These are places where the subtleties of moral philosophy and animal cognition mean less than nothing, where everything we've learned about animals at least since Darwin has been simply . . . set aside. To visit a modern CAFO (Confined Animal Feeding Operation) is to enter a world that, for all its technological sophistication, is still designed according to Cartesian principles: animals are machines incapable of feeling pain. Since no thinking person can possibly believe this anymore, industrial animal agriculture depends on a suspension of disbelief on the part of the people who operate it and a willingness to avert your eyes on the part of everyone else.

From everything I've read, egg and hog operations are the worst. Beef cat- 40 tle in America at least still live outdoors, albeit standing ankle deep in their own waste, eating a diet that makes them sick. And broiler chickens, although they do get their beaks snipped off with a hot knife to keep them from cannibalizing one another under the stress of their confinement, at least don't spend their eight-week lives in cages too small to ever stretch a wing. That fate is reserved for the American laying hen, who passes her brief span piled together with a half-dozen other hens in a wire cage whose floor a single page of this magazine could carpet. Every natural instinct of this animal is thwarted, leading to a range of behavioral "vices" that can include cannibalizing her cagemates and rubbing her body against the wire mesh until it is featherless and bleeding. Pain? Suffering? Madness? The operative suspension of disbelief depends on more neutral descriptors, like "vices" and "stress." Whatever you want to call what's going on in those cages, the ten percent or so of hens that can't bear it and simply die is built into the cost of production. And when the output of the others begins to ebb, the hens will be "force-molted"—starved of food and water and light for several days in order to stimulate a final bout of egg-laying before their life's work is done.

Simply reciting these facts, most of which are drawn from poultry-trade magazines, makes me sound like one of those animal people, doesn't it? I don't mean to, but this is what can happen when . . . you look. It certainly wasn't my intention to ruin anyone's breakfast. But now that I probably have spoiled the eggs, I do want to say one thing about the bacon, mention a single practice (by no means the worst) in modern hog production that points to the compound madness of an impeccable industrial logic.

Piglets in confinement operations are weaned from their mothers ten days after birth (compared with thirteen weeks in nature) because they gain weight faster on their hormone- and antibiotic-fortified feed. This premature weaning leaves the pigs with a life-long craving to suck and chew, a desire they gratify in confinement by biting the tail of the animal in front of them. A normal pig would fight off his molester, but a demoralized pig has stopped caring. "Learned helplessness" is the psychological term, and it's not uncommon in confinement operations, where tens of thousands of hogs spend their entire lives ignorant of sunshine or earth or straw, crowded together beneath a metal roof upon metal slats suspended over a manure pit. So it's not surprising that an animal as sensitive and intelligent as a pig would get depressed, and a depressed pig will allow his tail to be chewed on to the point of infection. Sick pigs, being underperforming "production units," are clubbed to death on the spot. The USDA's recommended solution to the problem is called "tail docking." Using a pair of pliers (and no anesthetic), most but not all of the tail is snipped off. Why the little stump? Because the whole point of the exercise is not to remove the object of tail-biting so much as to render it *more* sensitive. Now, a bite on the tail is so painful that even the most demoralized pig will mount a struggle to avoid it.

Much of this description is drawn from *Dominion*, Matthew Scully's recent book in which he offers a harrowing description of a North Carolina hog operation. Scully, a Christian conservative, has no patience for lefty rights talk, arguing instead that while God did give man "dominion" over animals ("Every moving thing that liveth shall be meat for you"), he also admonished us to show them mercy. "We are called to treat them with kindness, not because they have rights or power or some claim to equality but . . . because they stand unequal and powerless before us."

Scully calls the contemporary factory farm "our own worst nightmare" and, to his credit, doesn't shrink from naming the root cause of this evil: unfettered capitalism. (Perhaps this explains why he resigned from the Bush administration just before his book's publication.) A tension has always existed between the capitalist imperative to maximize efficiency and the moral imperatives of religion or community which have historically served as a counterweight to the moral blindness of the market. This is one of "the cultural contradictions of capitalism"—the tendency of the economic impulse to erode the moral underpinnings of society. Mercy toward animals is one such casualty.

45   More than any other institution, the American industrial animal farm offers a nightmarish glimpse of what capitalism can look like in the absence of moral or regulatory constraint. In these places life itself is redefined—as protein production—and with it suffering. *That* venerable word becomes "stress," an economic problem in search of a cost-effective solution, like tail-docking or beak-clipping or, in the industry's latest plan, by simply engineering the "stress gene" out of pigs and chickens. "Our own worst nightmare" such a place may well be; it is also real life for the billions of animals unlucky enough to have been born beneath these grim steel roofs, into the brief, pitiless life of a "production unit" in the days before the suffering gene was found.

Vegetarianism doesn't seem an unreasonable response to such an evil. Who would want to be made complicit in the agony of these animals by eating them? You want to throw *something* against the walls of those infernal sheds, whether it's the Bible, a new constitutional right or a whole platoon of animal rightists bent on breaking in and liberating the inmates. In the shadow of these factory farms, Coetzee's notion of a "stupefying crime" doesn't seem far-fetched at all.

But before you swear off meat entirely, let me describe a very different sort of animal farm. It is typical of nothing, and yet its very existence puts the whole moral question of animal agriculture in a different light. Polyface Farm occupies 550 acres of rolling grassland and forest in the Shenandoah Valley of Virginia. Here, Joel Salatin and his family raise six different food animals—cattle, pigs, chickens, rabbits, turkeys and sheep—in an intricate dance of symbiosis designed to allow each species, in Salatin's words, "to fully express its physiological distinctiveness."

What this means in practice is that Salatin's chickens live like chickens; his cows, like cows; pigs, pigs. As in nature, where birds tend to follow herbivores, once Salatin's cows have finished grazing a pasture, he moves them out and tows in his "eggmobile," a portable chicken coop that houses several hundred laying hens—roughly the natural size of a flock. The hens fan out over the pasture, eating the short grass and picking insect larvae out of the cowpats—all the while spreading the cow manure and eliminating the farm's parasite problem. A diet of grubs and grass makes for exceptionally tasty eggs and contented chickens, and their nitrogenous manure feeds the pasture. A few weeks later, the chickens move out and the sheep come in, dining on the lush new growth as well as on the weed species (nettles, nightshade) that the cattle and chickens won't touch.

Meanwhile, the pigs are in the barn turning the compost. All winter long, while the cattle were indoors, Salatin layered their manure with straw, wood chips—and corn. By March, this steaming compost layer cake stands three feet high, and the pigs, whose powerful snouts can sniff out and retrieve the fermented corn at the bottom, get to spend a few happy weeks rooting through the pile, aerating it as they work. All you can see of these pigs, intently nosing out the tasty alcoholic morsels, are their upturned pink hams and corkscrew tails churning the air. The finished compost will go to feed the grass; the grass, the cattle; the cattle, the chickens; and eventually all of these animals will feed us.

I thought a lot about vegetarianism and animal rights during the day I spent 50 on Joel Salatin's extraordinary farm. So much of what I'd read, so much of what I'd accepted, looked very different from here. To many animal rightists, even Polyface Farm is a death camp. But to look at these animals is to see this for the sentimental conceit it is. In the same way that we can probably recognize animal suffering when we see it, animal happiness is unmistakable, too, and here I was seeing it in abundance.

For any animal, happiness seems to consist in the opportunity to express its creaturely character—its essential pigness or wolfness or chickenness. Aristotle speaks of each creature's "characteristic form of life." For domesticated species, the good life, if we can call it that, cannot be achieved apart from humans—apart from our farms and, therefore, our meat-eating. This, it seems to me, is where animal rightists betray a profound ignorance about the workings of nature. To think of domestication as a form of enslavement or even exploitation is to misconstrue the whole relationship, to project a human idea of power onto what is, in fact, an instance of mutualism between species. Domestication is an evolutionary, rather than a political, development. It is certainly not a regime humans imposed on animals some ten thousand years ago.

Rather, domestication happened when a small handful of especially opportunistic species discovered through Darwinian trial and error that they were more likely to survive and prosper in an alliance with humans than on their own. Humans provided the animals with food and protection, in exchange for which the animals provided the humans their milk and eggs and—yes—their flesh. Both parties were transformed by the relationship: animals grew tame and lost their ability to fend for themselves (evolution tends to edit out unneeded traits), and humans gave up their hunter-gatherer ways for the settled life of agriculturists. (Humans changed biologically too, evolving such new traits as a tolerance for lactose as adults.)

From the animals' point of view, the bargain with humanity has been a great success, at least until our own time. Cows, pigs, dogs, cats and chickens have thrived, while their wild ancestors have languished. (There are ten thousand wolves in North America, fifty million dogs.) Nor does their loss of autonomy seem to trouble these creatures. It is wrong, the rightists say, to treat animals as "means" rather than "ends," yet the happiness of a working animal like the dog consists precisely in serving as a "means." Liberation is the last thing such a creature wants. To say of one of Joel Salatin's caged chickens that "the life of freedom is to be preferred" betrays an ignorance about chicken preferences—which on this farm are heavily focused on not getting their heads bitten off by weasels.

But haven't these chickens simply traded one predator for another—weasels for humans? True enough, and for the chickens this is probably not a bad deal. For brief as it is, the life expectancy of a farm animal would be considerably briefer in the world beyond the pasture fence or chicken coop. A sheep farmer told me that a bear will eat a lactating ewe alive, starting with her udders. "As a rule," he explained, "animals don't get 'good deaths' surrounded by their loved ones."

55   The very existence of predation—animals eating animals—is the cause of much anguished hand-wringing in animal rights circles. "It must be admitted," Singer writes, "that the existence of carnivorous animals does pose one problem for the ethics of Animal Liberation, and that is whether we should do anything about it." Some animal rightists train their dogs and cats to become vegetarians. (Note: cats will require nutritional supplements to stay healthy.) Matthew Scully calls predation "the intrinsic evil in nature's design. . . . among the hardest of all things to fathom." *Really?* A deep Puritan streak pervades animal rights activists, an abiding discomfort not only with our animality but with the animals' animality too.

However it may appear to us, predation is not a matter of morality or politics; it, also, is a matter of symbiosis. Hard as the wolf may be on the deer he eats, the herd depends on him for its well-being; without predators to cull the herd, deer overrun their habitat and starve. In many places, human hunters have taken over the predator's ecological role. Chickens also depend for their continued well-being on their human predators—not individual chickens, but chickens as a species. The surest way to achieve the extinction of the chicken would be to grant chickens a "right to life."

Yet here's the rub: the animal rightist is not concerned with species, only individuals. Tom Regan, author of *The Case for Animal Rights*, bluntly asserts that because "species are not individuals . . . the rights view does not recognize the moral rights of species to anything, including survival." Singer concurs, insisting that only sentient individuals have interests. But surely a species can have interests—in its survival, say—just as a nation or community or a corporation can. The animal rights movement's exclusive concern with individual animals makes perfect sense given its roots in a culture of liberal individualism, but does it make any sense in nature?

Consider this hypothetical episode: In 1611 Juan da Goma (a.k.a. Juan the Disoriented) made accidental landfall on Wrightson Island, a six-square-mile rock in the Indian Ocean. The island's sole distinction is as the only known home of the Arcania tree and the bird that nests in it, the Wrightson giant sea sparrow. Da Goma and his crew stayed a week, much of that time spent in a failed bid to recapture the ship's escaped goat—who happened to be pregnant. Nearly four centuries later, Wrightson Island is home to 380 goats that have consumed virtually every scrap of vegetation in their reach. The youngest Arcania tree on the island is more than three hundred years old, and only fifty-two sea sparrows remain. In the animal rights view, any one of those goats have at least as much right to life as the last Wrightson sparrow on earth, and the trees, because they are not sentient, warrant no moral consideration whatsoever. (In the mid-1980s a British environmental group set out to shoot the goats, but was forced to cancel the expedition after the Mammal Liberation Front bombed its offices.)

The story of Wrightson Island (invented by the biologist David Ehrenfeld in *Beginning Again*) suggests at the very least that a human morality based on individual rights makes for an awkward fit when applied to the natural world. This should come as no surprise: morality is an artifact of human culture, devised to help us negotiate social relations. It's very good for that. But just as we recognize that nature doesn't provide an adequate guide for human social conduct, isn't it anthropocentric to assume that our moral system offers an adequate guide for nature? We may require a different set of ethics to guide our dealings with the natural world, one as well suited to the particular needs of plants and animals and habitats (where sentience counts for little) as rights suit us humans today.

To contemplate such questions from the vantage of a farm is to appreciate just   60
how parochial and urban an ideology animal rights really is. It could thrive only in a world where people have lost contact with the natural world, where animals no longer pose a threat to us and human mastery of nature seems absolute. "In our normal life," Singer writes, "there is no serious clash of interests between human and nonhuman animals." Such a statement assumes a decidedly urbanized "normal life," one that certainly no farmer would recognize.

The farmer would point out that even vegans have a "serious clash of interests" with other animals. The grain that the vegan eats is harvested with a combine that shreds field mice, while the farmer's tractor crushes woodchucks in their burrows, and his pesticides drop songbirds from the sky. Steve Davis, an animal scientist at Oregon State University, has estimated that if America were to adopt a strictly vegetarian diet, the total number of animals killed every year would actually *increase*, as animal pasture gave way to row crops. Davis contends that if our goal is to kill as few animals as possible, then people should eat the largest possible animal that can live on the least intensively cultivated land: grass-fed beef for everybody. It would appear that killing animals is unavoidable no matter what we choose to eat.

When I talked to Joel Salatin about the vegetarian utopia, he pointed out that it would also condemn him and his neighbors to importing their food from distant places, since the Shenandoah Valley receives too little rainfall to grow many row crops. Much the same would hold true where I live, in New England. We get plenty of rain, but the hilliness of the land has dictated an agriculture based on animals since the time of the Pilgrims. The world is full of places where the best, if not the only, way to obtain food from the land is by grazing animals on it—especially ruminants, which alone can transform grass into protein and whose presence can actually improve the health of the land.

The vegetarian utopia would make us even more dependent than we already are on an industrialized national food chain. That food chain would in turn be even more dependent than it already is on fossil fuels and chemical fertilizer, since food would need to travel farther and manure would be in short supply. Indeed, it is doubtful that you can build a more sustainable agriculture without animals to cycle nutrients and support local food production. If our concern is for the health of nature—rather than, say, the internal consistency of our moral code or the condition of our souls—then eating animals may sometimes be the most ethical thing to do.

There is, too, the fact that we humans have been eating animals as long as we have lived on this earth. Humans may not need to eat meat in order to survive, yet doing so is part of our evolutionary heritage, reflected in the design of our teeth and the structure of our digestion. Eating meat helped make us what we are, in a social and biological sense. Under the pressure of the hunt, the human brain grew in size and complexity, and around the fire where the meat was cooked, human culture first flourished. Granting rights to animals may lift us up from the brutal world of predation, but it will entail the sacrifice of part of our identity—our own animality.

65   Surely this is one of the odder paradoxes of animal rights doctrine. It asks us to recognize all that we share with animals and then demands that we act toward them in a most unanimalistic way. Whether or not this is a good idea, we should at least acknowledge that our desire to eat meat is not a trivial matter, no mere "gastronomic preference." We might as well call sex—also now technically unnecessary—a mere "recreational preference." Whatever else it is, our meat-eating is something very deep indeed.

Are any of these good enough reasons to eat animals? I'm mindful of Ben Franklin's definition of the reasonable creature as one who can come up with reasons for whatever he wants to do. So I decided I would track down Peter Singer and ask him what he thought. In an e-mail message, I described Polyface and asked him about the implications for his position of the Good Farm—one where animals got to live according to their nature and to all appearances did not suffer.

"I agree with you that it is better for these animals to have lived and died than not to have lived at all," Singer wrote back. Since the utilitarian is concerned exclusively with the sum of happiness and suffering and the slaughter of an animal that doesn't comprehend that death need not involve suffering, the Good Farm adds to the total of animal happiness, provided you replace the slaughtered animal with a new one. However, he added, this line of thinking doesn't obviate the wrongness of killing an animal that "has a sense of its own existence over time and can have preferences for its own future." In other words, it's OK to eat the chicken, but he's not so sure about the pig. Yet, he wrote, "I would not be sufficiently confident of my arguments to condemn someone who purchased meat from one of these farms."

Singer went on to express serious doubts that such farms could be practical on a large scale, since the pressures of the marketplace will lead their owners to cut costs and corners at the expense of the animals. He suggested, too, that killing animals is not conducive to treating them with respect. Also, since humanely raised food will be more expensive, only the well-to-do can afford morally defensible animal protein. These are important considerations, but they don't alter my essential point: what's wrong with animal agriculture—with eating animals—is the practice, not the principle.

What this suggests to me is that people who care should be working not for animal rights but animal welfare—to ensure that farm animals don't suffer and that their deaths are swift and painless. In fact, the decent-life-merciful-death line is how Jeremy Bentham justified his own meat-eating. Yes, the philosophical father of animal rights was himself a carnivore. In a passage rather less frequently quoted by animal rightists, Bentham defended eating animals on the grounds that "we are the better for it, and they are never the worse. . . . The death they suffer in our hands commonly is, and always may be, a speedier and, by that means, a less painful one than that which would await them in the inevitable course of nature."

My guess is that Bentham never looked too closely at what happens in a   70
slaughterhouse, but the argument suggests that, in theory at least, a utilitarian can justify the killing of humanely treated animals—for meat or, presumably, for clothing. (Though leather and fur pose distinct moral problems. Leather is a byproduct of raising domestic animals for food, which can be done humanely. However, furs are usually made from wild animals that die brutal deaths—usually in leg-hold traps—and since most fur species aren't domesticated, raising them on farms isn't necessarily more humane.) But whether the issue is food or fur or hunting, what should concern us is the suffering, not the killing. All of which I was feeling pretty good about—until I remembered that utilitarians can also justify killing retarded orphans. Killing just isn't the problem for them that it is for other people, including me.

During my visit to Polyface Farm, I asked Salatin where his animals were slaughtered. He does the chickens and rabbits right on the farm, and would do the cattle, pigs and sheep there too if only the USDA would let him. Salatin showed me the open-air abattoir he built behind the farmhouse—a sort of outdoor kitchen on a concrete slab, with stainless-steel sinks, scalding tanks, a feather-plucking machine and metal cones to hold the birds upside down while they're being bled. Processing chickens is not a pleasant job, but Salatin insists on doing it himself because he's convinced he can do it more humanely and cleanly than any processing plant. He slaughters every other Saturday through the summer. Anyone's welcome to watch.

I asked Salatin how he could bring himself to kill a chicken.

"People have a soul; animals don't," he said. "It's a bedrock belief of mine." Salatin is a devout Christian. "Unlike us, animals are not created in God's image, so when they die, they just die."

The notion that only in modern times have people grown uneasy about killing animals is a flattering conceit. Taking a life is momentous, and people have been working to justify the slaughter of animals for thousands of years. Religion and especially ritual has played a crucial part in helping us reckon the moral costs. Native Americans and other hunter-gatherers would give thanks to their prey for giving up its life so the eater might live (sort of like saying grace). Many cultures have offered sacrificial animals to the gods, perhaps as a way to convince themselves that it was the gods' desires that demanded the slaughter, not their own. In ancient Greece, the priests responsible for the slaughter (priests!—now we entrust the job to minimum-wage workers) would sprinkle holy water on the sacrificial animal's brow. The beast would promptly shake its head, and this was taken as a sign of assent. Slaughter doesn't necessarily preclude respect. For all these people, it was the ceremony that allowed them to look, then to eat.

75   Apart from a few surviving religious practices, we no longer have any rituals governing the slaughter or eating of animals, which perhaps helps to explain why we find ourselves where we do, feeling that our only choice is to either look away or give up meat. Frank Perdue is happy to serve the first customer; Peter Singer, the second.

Until my visit to Polyface Farm, I had assumed these were the only two options. But on Salatin's farm, the eye contact between people and animals whose loss John Berger mourned is still a fact of life—and of death, for neither the lives nor the deaths of these animals have been secreted behind steel walls. "Food with a face," Salatin likes to call what he's selling, a slogan that probably scares off some customers. People see very different things when they look into the eyes of a pig or a chicken or a steer—a being without a soul, a "subject of a life" entitled to rights, a link in a food chain, a vessel for pain and pleasure, a tasty lunch. But figuring out what we do think, and what we can eat, might begin with the looking.

We certainly won't philosophize our way to an answer. Salatin told me the story of a man who showed up at the farm one Saturday morning. When Salatin noticed a PETA bumper sticker on the man's car, he figured he was in for it. But the man had a different agenda. He explained that after sixteen years as a vegetarian, he had decided that the only way he could ever eat meat again was if he killed the animal himself. He had come to *look*.

"Ten minutes later we were in the processing shed with a chicken," Salatin recalled. "He slit the bird's throat and watched it die. He saw that the animal did not look at him accusingly, didn't do a Disney double take. The animal had been treated with respect when it was alive, and he saw that it could also have a respectful death—that it wasn't being treated as a pile of protoplasm."

Salatin's open-air abattoir is a morally powerful idea. Someone slaughtering a chicken in a place where he can be watched is apt to do it scrupulously, with consideration for the animal as well as for the eater. This is going to sound quixotic, but maybe all we need to do to redeem industrial animal agriculture in this country is to pass a law requiring that the steel and concrete walls of the CAFOs and slaughterhouses be replaced with . . . glass. If there's any new "right" we need to establish, maybe it's this one: the right to look.

No doubt the sight of some of these places would turn many people into vegetarians. Many others would look elsewhere for their meat, to farmers like Salatin. There are more of them than I would have imagined. Despite the relentless consolidation of the American meat industry, there has been a revival of small farms where animals still live their "characteristic form of life." I'm thinking of the ranches where cattle still spend their lives on grass, the poultry farms where chickens still go outside and the hog farms where pigs live as they did fifty years ago—in contact with the sun, the earth and the gaze of a farmer.

For my own part, I've discovered that if you're willing to make the effort, it's entirely possible to limit the meat you eat to nonindustrial animals. I'm tempted to think that we need a new dietary category, to go with the vegan and lactovegetarian and piscatorian. I don't have a catchy name for it yet (humano-carnivore?), but this is the only sort of meat-eating I feel comfortable with these days. I've become the sort of shopper who looks for labels indicating that his meat and eggs have been humanely grown (the American Humane Association's new "Free Farmed" label seems to be catching on), who visits the farms where his chicken and pork come from and who asks kinky-sounding questions about touring slaughterhouses. I've actually found a couple of small processing plants willing to let a customer onto the kill floor, including one, in Cannon Falls, Minnesota, with a glass abattoir.

The industrialization—and dehumanization—of American animal farming is a relatively new, evitable and local phenomenon: no other country raises and slaughters its food animals quite as intensively or as brutally as we do. Were the walls of our meat industry to become transparent, literally or even figuratively, we would not long continue to do it this way. Tail-docking and sow crates and beak-clipping would disappear overnight, and the days of slaughtering four hundred head of cattle an hour would come to an end. For who could stand the sight? Yes, meat would get more expensive. We'd probably eat less of it, too, but maybe when we did eat animals, we'd eat them with the consciousness, ceremony and respect they deserve.

MLA CITATION

Pollan, Michael. "An Animal's Place." *The Norton Reader: An Anthology of Nonfiction,* edited by Melissa A. Goldthwaite et al., 15th ed., W. W. Norton, 2020, pp. 662–77.

QUESTIONS

1. Precisely how much of the position represented by Peter Singer's *Animal Liberation* does Michael Pollan accept? How can you tell?

2. Things change when Pollan visits Polyface Farm, the humane operation run by Joel Salatin. What about the farm convinces Pollan that it represents an alternative to Singer's approach?

3. Describe the structure of Pollan's essay. How does he introduce animal liberation and how does he argue against it?

4. Write your own argument about the ethical treatment of animals. It can be about animal cruelty, whether (and how) animals should be used in experiments or product testing, under what (if any) circumstances humans should eat animals, or another issue raising questions about "an animal's place."

MICHELLE NIJHUIS

Which Species Will Live?

THE ASHY STORM-PETREL, a tiny, dark-gray seabird, nests on 11 rocky, isolated islands in the Pacific Ocean off the coasts of California and Mexico. Weighing little more than a hefty greeting card and forced to contend with invasive rats, mice and cats, aggressive seagulls, oil spills and sea-level rise, it faces an outsize fight for survival. At last count, only 10,000 remained. Several other species of storm-petrels are similarly endangered.

Yet at least one conservation group has decided to ignore the petrel. In the winter of 2008 the Wildlife Conservation Society was focusing its far-flung efforts on a small number of animals. The society's researchers had spent months analyzing thousands of declining bird and mammal species around the world and had chosen several hundred that could serve as cornerstones for the organization's work. They then turned to people with decades of experience studying wildlife to further narrow the possibilities.

Dozens of these experts gathered in small conference rooms in New York City, southwestern Montana and Buenos Aires to make their choices. They judged each species for its importance to its ecosystem, its economic and cultural value, and its potential to serve as a conservation emblem. They voted on each animal publicly, holding up red, yellow or green cards. When significant disagreement occurred, the experts backed up their reasoning with citations, and the panels voted again. By the middle of the first day most panels had eliminated more than half the species from their lists.

Published in Scientific American *(2012), a monthly science magazine written for a general audience.*

At some point in the afternoon, however, in every meeting, the reality of the process would hit. As entire groups of species, including storm-petrels, were deemed valuable but not valuable enough, a scientist would quietly shut down, shoulders slumped and eyes glazed. "I'm just overwhelmed," he or she might say. Panel members would encourage their colleague, reminding him or her that these choices were necessary and that the science behind them was solid. John Fraser, a conservation psychologist who moderated the panels, would suggest a coffee break. "I'd say, 'I'm sorry, but we have to stop. This is a very important part of the process,'" he remembers. "It was important to recognize the enormity of what we were doing—that we were confronting loss on a huge scale."

The experts knew that all conservation groups and government agencies were coping with similar choices in tacit ways, but the Wildlife Conservation Society process made those decisions more explicit and more painful. As budgets shrink, environmental stresses grow, and politicians and regulators increasingly favor helping the economy over helping the planet, many scientists have come to acknowledge the need for triage. It is time, they say, to hold up their cards.

TRIAGE: A FOUR-LETTER WORD

The concept of conservation triage is based loosely on medical triage, a decision-making system used by battlefield medics since the Napoleonic Wars.[1] Medical triage has several variations, but all of them involve sorting patients for treatment in difficult situations where time, expertise or supplies, or all three, are scarce. The decisions are agonizing but are considered essential for the greater good.

In 1973, however, when the U.S. Congress passed the Endangered Species Act, the mood was not one of scarcity but of generosity. The act, still considered the most powerful environmental law in the world, stipulated eligibility for protection for all nonpest species, from bald eagles to beetles. Later court decisions confirmed its broad reach. In their book *Noah's Choice,* journalist Charles C. Mann and economist Mark L. Plummer describe the act's reasoning as the Noah Principle: all species are fundamentally equal, and everything can and should be saved, regardless of its importance to humans.

Trouble arose in the late 1980s, when proposed endangered-species listings of the northern spotted owl and some salmon varieties threatened the economic interests of powerful timber and fishing industries, setting off a series of political and legal attempts to weaken the law. Environmentalists fought off the attacks, but the bitter struggle made many supporters suspicious of any proposed changes to the law, even those intended to increase its effectiveness. In particular, proponents feared that any overt attempt to prioritize endangered

---

1. Series of military campaigns (1803–15) initiated by French emperor Napoleon Bonaparte against other European nations.

species—to apply the general principle of triage—would only strengthen opponents' efforts to try to cut species from the list. If such decisions had to happen, better that they be made quietly, out of political reach.

"The environmental community was always unwilling to talk about triage," says Holly Doremus, a law professor at the University of California, Berkeley. "Even though they knew it was going on, they were unwilling to talk about it."

10   Today triage is one of the most provocative ideas in conservation. To many, it invokes not only political threats to laws such as the Endangered Species Act but an abandonment of the moral responsibility for nature implied in the Noah Principle. "Triage is a four-letter word," conservation biologist Stuart Pimm recently told Slate's Green Lantern blog. "And I know how to count."

PINE TREES OR CAMELS

Conservationists who are pushing for explicit triage say they are bringing more systematic thinking and transparency to practices that have been carried out implicitly for a long time. "The way we're doing it right now in the United States is the worst of all possible choices," says Tim Male, a vice president at Defenders of Wildlife. "It essentially reflects completely ad hoc prioritization." Politically controversial species attract more funding, he says, as do species in heavily studied places: "We live in a world of unconscious triage."

In recent years researchers have proposed several ways to make triage decisions, with the aim of providing maximum benefit for nature as a whole. Some scientists argue for weighting species according to their role in the ecosystem, an approach we might call "function first." Threatened species with a unique job, they say, or "umbrella" species whose own survival ensures the survival of many others, should be protected before those with a so-called redundant role. One example is the campaign to protect the Rocky Mountains' high-elevation whitebark pines, trees stressed by warming temperatures and associated beetle outbreaks. Because high-fat whitebark pine nuts are an important food source for grizzly bears in the fall and spring, many conservation groups view the pine as a priority species.

The advantage of this function-first approach is that it focuses on specific ecological roles rather than raw numbers of species, giving conservationists a better chance at protecting functioning ecosystems. The approach, however, is useful only in well-understood systems, and the number of those is small. An exclusively function-first analysis would almost certainly leave many ecologically important species behind.

As an alternative, the EDGE (Evolutionarily Distinct and Globally Endangered) of Existence program run by the Zoological Society of London argues for prioritizing species at the genomic level, an approach we might call "evolution first." Rather than focusing on well-known species with many near relatives, the EDGE program favors the most genetically unusual threatened species. Examples include the two-humped Bactrian camel; the long-beaked echidna, a short, spiny mammal that lays eggs; and the Chinese giant salamander, which can grow to six feet in length.

The evolution-first approach emphasizes the preservation of genetic diver-   15
sity, which can help all the world's species survive and adapt in fast-changing
environmental conditions by providing a robust gene pool. But as University of
Washington ecologist Martha Groom points out, exclusive use of the approach
could miss broader threats that affect entire taxa, leaving groups of species vulnerable to wholesale extinction. "What if a whole branch of the evolutionary
tree is endangered?" she asks. "What do we do then?"

Of course, species are valuable for many different reasons. Some play a
vital role in the ecosystem, some have unique genes, some provide extensive
services to humans. No single criterion can capture all these qualities. The
Wildlife Conservation Society combined different triage approaches in its analyses: it gave priority to threatened species that have larger body size and wider
geographic range, reasoning that protection of these creatures would likely benefit many other plants and animals. It also gave higher rankings to species
with greater genetic distinctiveness. The expert panels then considered more
subjective qualities, such as cultural importance and charisma, which, like it
or not, are important to fund-raising.

Groom, who helped to lead the society's analysis, says it opted for the
combined approach because much of the information she and her colleagues
needed was unknown or unquantifiable. "There's an awful lot of uncertainty
and ignorance about all species," she says. But with a combination of available
data and expert opinions, the analysis identified a small group of "global priority" species that the organization can focus on.

ECOSYSTEMS OVER SPECIES

Given the importance of protecting not simply individual animals but also the
relations among them, some researchers say that triage approaches should select
among ecosystems instead of species. In the late 1980s British environmentalist
Norman Meyers proposed that his global colleagues try to protect the maximum
number of species by focusing on land areas that were full of plants found nowhere
else on the planet and that were also under pressing environmental threats.

Meyers called such places hotspots. He and his partners at Conservation
International eventually identified 25 hotspots worldwide, from coastal California
to Madagascar, that they thought should top priority lists. In a sense, the approach
combines the function-first and evolution-first processes: it protects ecological
relations by focusing on entire ecosystems, and it protects genetic diversity by
prioritizing endemic species. The idea caught on and influences decisions by
many philanthropists, environmental organizations and governments today.

Nevertheless, in recent years researchers have criticized hotspots for over-   20
simplifying a global problem and for giving short shrift to human needs. . . .
"It was brilliant for its time," says Hugh Possingham of the University of
Queensland in Australia. "But it used just two criteria."

In an effort to refine the concept, Possingham and his colleagues developed Marxan, a software program that is now in wide use. It aims to maximize
the effectiveness of conservation reserves by considering not only the presence

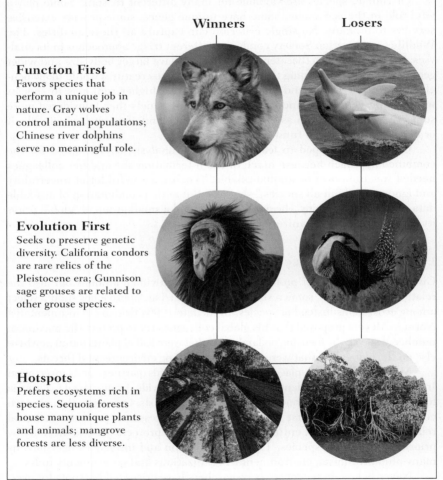

———— POSTER CHILDREN ————
Winners and Losers

Conservationists are trying different forms of triage to help them decide which species to save and not to save. Each method favors certain priorities, such as an animal's role in preserving a food chain or in maintaining genetic diversity. Serving those priorities ultimately deems species winners or losers; some samples are shown below.

Winners   **Losers**

Function First
Favors species that perform a unique job in nature. Gray wolves control animal populations; Chinese river dolphins serve no meaningful role.

Evolution First
Seeks to preserve genetic diversity. California condors are rare relics of the Pleistocene era; Gunnison sage grouses are related to other grouse species.

Hotspots
Prefers ecosystems rich in species. Sequoia forests house many unique plants and animals; mangrove forests are less diverse.

of endemic species and the level of conservation threats but also factors such as the cost of protection and "complementarity"—the contribution of each new reserve to existing biodiversity protections. Mangrove forests, for instance, are not particularly rich in species and might never be selected by a traditional hotspot analysis; Possingham's program, however, might recommend protection of mangrove forests in an area where representative swaths of other, more diverse forest types had already been preserved, resulting in a higher total number of species protected.

Protected areas and parks, however, can be difficult to establish and police, and because climate change is already shifting species ranges, static boundaries may not offer the best long-term protection for some species. In response, Possingham has created a resource-allocation process that goes well beyond the selection of hotspots, allowing decision makers to weigh costs, benefits and the likelihood of success as they decide among different conservation tactics. "You do actions—you don't do species," Possingham says. "All prioritizations should be about actions, not least because in many cases actions help multiple species."

The New Zealand Department of Conservation has used the resource-allocation process to analyze protection strategies for about 710 declining native species. It concluded that by focusing on the actions that were cheapest and most likely to succeed, it could save roughly half again as many plants and animals from extinction with the same amount of money. Although some scientists worry that the process places too much emphasis on preserving sheer numbers of threatened species and too little on preserving ecosystem function, resource-allocation analysis is now under way in Australia, and Possingham has spoken with U.S. Fish and Wildlife Service officials about the process.

"People think triage is about abandoning species or admitting defeat," says Madeleine Bottrill of Conservation International, who is a colleague of Possingham. To the contrary, she argues: by quantifying the costs and payoffs of particular actions, the trade-offs become explicit. Agencies and organizations can identify what is being saved, what is being lost and what could be saved with a bigger budget, giving them a much stronger case for more funding.

SUCCESS BREEDS SUCCESS

It is possible that the very act of setting priorities more overtly could inspire   25
societies to spend more money on conservation efforts. Defenders of Wildlife's Male says prioritization schemes, far from exposing nature to political risks, offer practical and political advantages. "If we focus more effort on the things we know how to help, we're going to produce more successes," he says. "More successes are a really compelling argument—not just to politicians but to ordinary people—for why [conservation programs] should continue."

Trailing behind such successes, however, are undeniable losses, and true triage must acknowledge them. "We're very good as humans, aren't we, at justifying any amount of work on anything based on undeclared values," says Richard Maloney of the New Zealand Department of Conservation. "We're not very good at saying, 'Because I'm working on this species, I'm not going to fund or work on these seven or eight species, and they're going to go extinct.'" And yet Maloney himself is reluctant to name the species likely to lose out in his agency's resource-allocation analysis. Rockhopper penguins—whose vital supply of krill has declined because of shrinking sea ice driven by climate change—fall to the bottom of the department's list because of the costly, long-shot measures needed to protect them. Yet the species' low priority, Maloney argues, should be seen not as a death sentence but as a call to action by other groups.

Sooner or later, though, a vulnerable species or habitat—the rockhopper penguin, the whitebark pine ecosystem—will require measures too expensive for any government or group to shoulder. What then? Do societies continue to pour money into a doomed cause or allow a species to die out, one by one, in plain sight? Even though the conversation about triage has come a long way, many conservationists remain uncomfortable taking responsibility for the final, fateful decisions that triage requires.

The central difficulty is that, just as with battlefield triage, the line between opportunity and lost cause is almost never clear. In the 1980s, when the population of California condors stood at just 22, even some environmentalists argued that the species should be permitted to "die with dignity." Yet others made an evolution-first argument, calling for heroic measures to save the rare Pleistocene relic.[2] With heavy investments of money, time and expertise, condors were bred in captivity and eventually returned to the wild, where 217 fly today, still endangered but very much alive.

"We can prevent extinction; we've demonstrated that," says John Nagle, a law professor at the University of Notre Dame who has written extensively about environmental issues. But "knowing that an extinction was something we could have stopped and chose not to—I think that's where people kind of gulp and don't want to go down that road," he adds.

30   Similarly, by creating what prominent restoration ecologist Richard Hobbs calls a "too-hard basket" for species that would cost too much to save, a triage system could allow societies to prematurely jettison tough cases, choosing short-term economic rewards over long-term conservation goals. The Endangered Species Act itself has one provision for such a too-hard basket—it allows for a panel of experts that can, in unusual circumstances, permit a federal agency to violate the act's protections. But the so-called God Squad is deliberately difficult to convene and has so far made only one meaningful exemption to the act: letting the Forest Service approve some timber sales in habitats of the struggling northern spotted owl.

As climate change, population expansion and other global pressures on biodiversity continue, however, more and more species are likely to require heroic measures for survival. Prioritizing species by ecological function, evolutionary history or other criteria will help shape conservation strategies, but for the greater good of many other species, societies will almost certainly have to consciously forgo some of the most expensive and least promising rescue efforts.

In the U.S., legal scholars have suggested ways of reforming the Endangered Species Act to reckon with this reality—to help the law bend instead of break under political pressure. Yet Nagle says that the essence of the law, the Noah Principle, remains acutely relevant. Given the temptations that accompany triage, he says, the exhortation to save all species remains a worthy, and

2. Geological epoch lasting from 1,800,000 to approximately 10,000 years ago.

perhaps even necessary, goal. Just as a battlefield medic works unstintingly to save lives, even while knowing that he or she cannot save them all, societies should still aspire to the Noah Principle—and stuff the ark to the brim.

MLA CITATION

Nijhuis, Michelle. "Which Species Will Live?" *The Norton Reader: An Anthology of Nonfiction,* edited by Melissa A. Goldthwaite et al., 15th ed., W. W. Norton, 2020, pp. 678–85.

QUESTIONS

1. Michelle Nijhuis explains several ways scientists and policy makers "triage" species threatened with extinction. What are these ways? Which do you favor and why?

2. Compare the attitudes toward animals and nature that inform the debate over "conservation triage" (paragraph 6) with those expressed by Chief Seattle (p. 468), Michael Pollan (pp. 662–77), or William Cronon (pp. 464–67). Would these writers embrace or reject conservation triage? Why?

3. Although Nijhuis acknowledges the need for conservation triage, she also holds up the "Noah Principle" (paragraph 7) as an ideal. What is this principle, and why does Nijhuis consider it so important?

4. Write an essay explaining a difficult decision you've made. How did you balance competing goals, values, and principles?

NORA EPHRON
The Boston Photographs

I MADE ALL KINDS OF PICTURES because I thought it would be a good rescue shot over the ladder . . . never dreamed it would be anything else. . . . I kept having to move around because of the light set. The sky was bright and they were in deep shadow. I was making pictures with a motor drive and he, the fire fighter, was reaching up and, I don't know, everything started falling. I followed the girl down taking pictures . . . I made three or four frames. I realized what was going on and I completely turned around, because I didn't want to see her hit."

You probably saw the photographs. In most newspapers, there were three of them. The first showed some people on a fire escape—a fireman, a woman and a child. The fireman had a nice strong jaw and looked very brave. The woman was holding the child. Smoke was pouring from the building behind them. A rescue ladder was approaching, just a few feet away, and the fireman

Nora Ephron wrote this essay as a columnist on media for Esquire *magazine (1975). It later appeared in her collection* Scribble, Scribble: Notes on the Media *(1978).*

had one arm around the woman and one arm reaching out toward the ladder. The second picture showed the fire escape slipping off the building. The child had fallen on the escape and seemed about to slide off the edge. The woman was grasping desperately at the legs of the fireman, who had managed to grab the ladder. The third picture showed the woman and child in midair, falling to the ground. Their arms and legs were outstretched, horribly distended. A potted plant was falling too. The caption said that the woman, Diana Bryant, nineteen, died in the fall. The child landed on the woman's body and lived.

The pictures were taken by Stanley Forman, thirty, of the *Boston Herald American*. He used a motor-driven Nikon F set at 1/250, f 5.6—8. Because of the motor, the camera can click off three frames a second. More than four hundred newspapers in the United States alone carried the photographs; the tear sheets from overseas are still coming in. The *New York Times* ran them on the first page of its second section; a paper in south Georgia gave them nineteen columns; the *Chicago Tribune*, the *Washington Post* and the *Washington Star* filled almost half their front pages, the *Star* under a somewhat redundant headline that read: SENSATIONAL PHOTOS OF RESCUE ATTEMPT THAT FAILED.

The photographs are indeed sensational. They are pictures of death in action, of that split second when luck runs out, and it is impossible to look at them without feeling their extraordinary impact and remembering, in an almost subconscious way, the morbid fantasy of falling, falling off a building, falling to one's death. Beyond that, the pictures are classics, old-fashioned but perfect examples of photojournalism at its most spectacular. They're throwbacks, really, fire pictures, 1930s tabloid shots; at the same time they're technically superb and thoroughly modern—the sequence could not have been taken at all until the development of the motor-driven camera some sixteen years ago.

5   Most newspaper editors anticipate some reader reaction to photographs like Forman's; even so, the response around the country was enormous, and almost all of it was negative. I have read hundreds of the letters that were printed in letters-to-the-editor sections, and they repeat the same points. "Invading the privacy of death." "Cheap sensationalism." "I thought I was reading the *National Enquirer*." "Assigning the agony of a human being in terror of imminent death to the status of a side-show act." "A tawdry way to sell newspapers." The *Seattle Times* received sixty letters and calls; its managing editor even got a couple of them at home. A reader wrote the *Philadelphia Inquirer*: "*Jaws* and *Towering Inferno* are playing downtown; don't take business away from people who pay good money to advertise in your own paper." Another reader wrote the *Chicago Sun-Times:* "I shall try to hide my disappointment that Miss Bryant wasn't wearing a skirt when she fell to her death. You could have had some award-winning photographs of her underpants as her skirt billowed over her head, you voyeurs." Several newspaper editors wrote columns defending the pictures: Thomas Keevil of the *Costa Mesa* (California) *Daily Pilot* printed a ballot for readers to vote on whether they would have printed the pictures; Marshall L. Stone of Maine's *Bangor Daily News*, which refused to print the famous assassination picture of the Vietcong prisoner in Saigon, claimed that the Boston pictures

showed the dangers of fire escapes and raised questions about slumlords. (The burning building was a five-story brick apartment house on Marlborough Street in the Back Bay section of Boston.)

For the last five years, the *Washington Post* has employed various journalists as ombudsmen, whose job is to monitor the paper on behalf of the public. The *Post*'s current ombudsman is Charles Seib, former managing editor of the *Washington Star*; the day the Boston photographs appeared, the paper received over seventy calls in protest. As Seib later wrote in a column about the pictures, it was "the largest reaction to a published item that I have experienced in eight months as the *Post*'s ombudsman. . . .

"In the *Post*'s newsroom, on the other hand, I found no doubts, no second thoughts . . . the question was not whether they should be printed but how they should be displayed. When I talked to editors . . . they used words like 'interesting' and 'riveting' and 'gripping' to describe them. The pictures told something about life in the ghetto, they said (although the neighborhood where the tragedy occurred is not a ghetto, I am told). They dramatized the need to check on the safety of fire escapes. They dramatically conveyed something that had happened, and that is the business we're in. They were news. . . .

"Was publication of that [third] picture a bow to the same taste for the morbidly sensational that makes gold mines of disaster movies? Most papers will

not print the picture of a dead body except in the most unusual circumstances. Does the fact that the final picture was taken a millisecond before the young woman died make a difference? Most papers will not print a picture of a bare female breast. Is that a more inappropriate subject for display than the picture of a human being's last agonized instant of life?" Seib offered no answers to the questions he raised, but he went on to say that although as an editor he would probably have run the pictures, as a reader he was "revolted by them."

In conclusion, Seib wrote: "Any editor who decided to print those pictures without giving at least a moment's thought to what purpose they served and what their effect was likely to be on the reader should ask another question: Have I become so preoccupied with manufacturing a product according to professional traditions and standards that I have forgotten about the consumer, the reader?"

10   It should be clear that the phone calls and letters and Seib's own reaction were occasioned by one factor alone: the death of the woman. Obviously, had she survived the fall, no one would have protested; the pictures would have had a completely different impact. Equally obviously, had the child died as well—or instead—Seib would undoubtedly have received ten times the phone calls he did. In each case, the pictures would have been exactly the same—only the captions, and thus the responses, would have been different.

But the questions Seib raises are worth discussing—though not exactly for the reasons he mentions. For it may be that the real lesson of the Boston photographs is not the danger that editors will be forgetful of reader reaction, but that they will continue to censor pictures of death precisely because of that reaction. The protests Seib fielded were really a variation on an old theme—and we saw plenty of it during the Nixon-Agnew years—the "Why doesn't the press print the good news?" argument. In this case, of course, the objections were all dressed up and cleverly disguised as righteous indignation about the privacy of death. This is a form of puritanism that is often justifiable; just as often it is merely puritanical.

Seib takes it for granted that the widespread though fairly recent newspaper policy against printing pictures of dead bodies is a sound one; I don't know that it makes any sense at all. I recognize that printing pictures of corpses raises all sorts of problems about taste and titillation and sensationalism; the fact is, however, that people die. Death happens to be one of life's main events. And it is irresponsible—and more than that, inaccurate—for newspapers to fail to show it, or to show it only when an astonishing set of photos comes in over the Associated Press wire. Most papers covering fatal automobile accidents will print pictures of mangled cars. But the significance of fatal automobile accidents is not that a great deal of steel is twisted but that people die. Why not show it? That's what accidents are about. Throughout the Vietnam war, editors were reluctant to print atrocity pictures. Why *not* print them? That's what that war was about. Murder victims are almost never photographed; they are granted their privacy. But their relatives are relentlessly pictured on their way in and out of hospitals and morgues and funerals.

I'm not advocating that newspapers print these things in order to teach their readers a lesson. The *Post* editors justified their printing of the Boston pictures with several arguments in that direction; every one of them is irrelevant. The pictures don't show anything about slum life; the incident could have happened anywhere, and it did. It is extremely unlikely that anyone who saw them rushed out and had his fire escape strengthened. And the pictures were not news—at least they were not national news. It is not news in Washington, or New York, or Los Angeles that a woman was killed in a Boston fire. The only newsworthy thing about the pictures is that they were taken. They deserve to be printed because they are great pictures, breathtaking pictures of something that happened. That they disturb readers is exactly as it should be: that's why photojournalism is often more powerful than written journalism.

MLA CITATION

Ephron, Nora. "The Boston Photographs." *The Norton Reader: An Anthology of Nonfiction*, edited by Melissa A. Goldthwaite et al., 15th ed., W. W. Norton, 2020, pp. 685–91.

QUESTIONS

1. Why does Nora Ephron begin with the words of the photographer Stanley Forman? What information—as well as perspective—does her opening paragraph convey?

2. What was the public reaction to the publication of the Boston photographs? What reasons did newspeople give for printing them? How does Ephron arrange these responses?

3. Does Ephron suggest any limits to what can be published in print or online? Do you think there should be limits? How would you go about deciding what those limits should be?

4. Find a startling photographic image that recently appeared in print or online, and write an argument for or against its publication.

13 History and Politics

> It is a fair summary of history to say that the safeguards of liberty have been forged in controversies involving not very nice people.
>
> —Felix Frankfurter

Supreme Court Justice Felix Frankfurter wrote the above in his 1950 dissenting opinion in the case of *United States v. Rabinowitz*. In that case, a forger's office was raided without a proper warrant, but Frankfurter's words were intended to have a further reach than just the one case. Instead, Frankfurter speaks on behalf of a challenging truth: lawyers often have to defend "not very nice people" in the name of a broader principle; at the same time, principles sometimes act as cover for not very nice people doing not very nice things. How do we decide what principles are worth fighting for? How do we know when to violate a principle in order to protect (or punish) a person? History helps us make sense of how individuals come into contact with principles. Politics is the means through which those of us who live in a democracy decide on the principles that will guide us.

The chapter begins with "The Question Stated," historian Jill Lepore's introduction to her history of the United States, *These Truths*: in it, she invites us into her thinking on what belongs in a history book and what gets left out. From there, we move back in time, first to the *Declaration of Independence*, and then to Elizabeth Cady Stanton's *Declaration of Sentiments and Resolutions*, which emulates Jefferson's style as a strategy to make her plea on behalf of women's rights. Reaching even further back in time, Jonathan Swift's satire and Niccolò Machiavelli's treatise explore some blunt political truths that remain relevant centuries later. We have inaugural addresses from two of our greatest presidents, Lincoln and Kennedy, and a powerful condemnation of gradualism in civil rights in Martin Luther King's "Letter from Birmingham Jail." Thoreau, Orwell, Danticat, and Solnit each draw upon a personal experience to identify and analyze a broader political phenomenon. These four texts are the most like the other essays in this volume and comparing them with the other texts in the chapter can help reveal the breadth of possible strategies for writing on history and politics.

This chapter includes some of the United States' core documents. It also includes challenges to those ideas, precursors, satire, revisions, and case studies of how principles, when in conflict, affect individual lives. As you read through these essays, a mix of the classic and the new, you might want to think about the context in which each piece was published. (The introductory source note and the biographical note in the back of the book will help you figure that out.) Is the author writing from a position of power—as a founder of a nation, an advisor to a prince, or a president? Or is the author writing to persuade those in power to change—from a prison cell, a library carrel, or a journalist's desk? Are you reading a speech, designed to persuade a large group of listeners, or a quieter text, addressed from one individual to another, meant for solitary reflection? How do these different stances and imagined audiences affect the authors' approach to the topic?

Writing about these topics can be intimidating, so it may help to start by thinking about how the more essayistic writers worked: you might, like Thoreau, think about how a natural phenomenon makes a good analogy for a political one; or, following Danticat, compare your experience of something to how it was covered on the news. Alternatively, you might think about a principle that really matters to you and then explore a time when that principle was tested. Write an essay about something you once believed about which you are no longer sure. Has your understanding of history deepened your belief or cast it into doubt? How do your politics affect your sense of your place in the world? Is there a principle you once held dear that has been tested? And on what basis are you now placing your convictions? Whatever you choose to write, think about how what you are writing fits into a larger pattern, what principles it challenges and what it upholds.

JILL LEPORE
The Question Stated

THE COURSE OF HISTORY IS UNPREDICTABLE, as irregular as the weather, as errant as affection, nations rising and falling by whim and chance, battered by violence, corrupted by greed, seized by tyrants, raided by rogues, addled by demagogues. This was all true until one day, Tuesday, October 30, 1787, when readers of a newspaper called the *New-York Packet* found on the front page an advertisement for an almanac that came bound with tables predicting the "Rising and Setting of the Sun," the "Judgment of the Weather," the "Length of Days and Nights," and, as a bonus, something entirely new: the Constitution of the United States, forty-four hundred words that attempted to chart the motions of the branches of government and the separation of their powers as if these were matters of physics, like the transit of the sun and moon and the comings and goings of the tides.[1] It was meant to mark the start of a new era, in which the course of history might be made predictable and a government established that would be ruled not by accident and force but by reason and choice. The origins of that idea, and its fate, are the story of American history.

The Constitution entailed both toil and argument. Knee-breeched, sweat-drenched delegates to the constitutional convention had met all summer in

This essay is the Introduction to Jill Lepore's one-volume history of the United States, These Truths (2018). All notes in this piece were written by the author.

1. *New-York Packet*, October 30, 1787.

Philadelphia in a swelter of secrecy, the windows of their debating hall nailed shut against eavesdroppers. By the middle of September, they'd drafted a proposal written on four pages of parchment. They sent that draft to printers who set the type of its soaring preamble with a giant W, as sharp as a bird's claw:

> We the People of the United States, in Order to form a more perfect Union, establish Justice, insure domestic Tranquility, provide for the common defence, promote the general Welfare, and secure the Blessings of Liberty to ourselves and our Posterity, do ordain and establish this Constitution for the United States of America.

As summer faded to fall, the free people of the United States, finding the Constitution folded into their newspapers and almanacs, were asked to decide whether or not to ratify it, even as they went about baling hay, milling corn, tanning leather, singing hymns, and letting out the seams on last year's winter coats, for mothers and fathers grown fatter, and letting down the hems, for children grown taller.

They read this strange, intricate document, and they debated its plan. Some feared that the new system granted too much power to the federal government—to the president, or to Congress, or to the Supreme Court, or to all three. Many, like sixty-one-year-old George Mason of Virginia, a delegate who'd refused to sign it, wanted the Constitution to include a bill of rights. ("A bill might be prepared in a few hours," Mason had begged at the convention, to no avail.)[2] Others complained about this clause or that, down to commas. It was not an easy thing to read. A few suggested scrapping it and starting all over again. "Cannot the same power which called the late convention, call another?" one citizen wondered. "Are not the people still their own masters?"[3]

Much of what they said is a matter of record. "The infant periods of most nations are buried in silence, or veiled in fable," James Madison once remarked.[4] Not the United States. Its infancy is preserved, like baby teeth kept in a glass jar, in the four parchment sheets of the Constitution, in the pages of almanacs that chart the weather of a long-ago climate, and in hundreds of newspapers, where essays for and against the new system of government appeared alongside the shipping news, auction notices, and advertisements for the return of people who never were their own masters—women and children, slaves and servants—and who had run away, hoping to ordain and establish, for themselves and their posterity, the blessings of liberty.

5   The season of ratification was an autumn of ordinary bustle and business. In that October 30, 1787, issue of the *New-York Packet*, a school-master

---

2. September 12, 1787, *The Records of the Federal Convention of 1787*, ed. Max Farrand, 3 vols. (New Haven, CT: Yale University Press, 1911), 2:588.

3. "An Old Whig IV," [Philadelphia] *Independent Gazetteer*, October 27, 1787.

4. James Madison to William Eustis, July 6, 1819, in *The Papers of James Madison*, Retirement Series, ed. David B. Mattern, J. C. A. Stagg, Mary Parke Johnson, and Anne Mandeville Colony, 12 vols. (Charlottesville: University of Virginia Press, 2009), 1:478–80.

announced that he was offering lessons in "reading, writing, arithmetic, and merchants' accounts" in rooms near city hall. The estate of Gearey, Champion, and Co., consisting chiefly of "a large and general Assortment of Drugs and Medicines," was to be auctioned. Many-masted sailing ships from London and Liverpool and trim schooners from St. Croix, Baltimore, and Norfolk had dropped anchor in the depths of the harbor; sloops from Charleston and Savannah had tied their painters to the docks. A Scotsman offered a reward for the return of his stolen chestnut-colored mare, fourteen hands high, "lofty carriage, trots and canters very handsome." A merchant with a warehouse on Peck Slip wanted readers to know that he had for sale dry codfish, a quantity of molasses, ground ginger in barrels, York rum, pickled codfish, writing paper, and men's shoes. And the *Columbian Almanack* was for sale, with or without the Constitution as an appendix, at the printers' shop, where New Yorkers might also inquire after two people, for a price:

> TO BE SOLD. A LIKELY young NEGRO WENCH, 20 years of age, she is healthy and had the small pox, she has a young male child.

The mother was said to be "remarkably handy at housework"; her baby was "about 6 months old," still nursing. Their names were not mentioned.[5] They were not ruled by reason and choice. They were ruled by violence and force.

Between the everyday atrocity of slavery and the latest news from the apothecary there appeared on page 2 of that day's *New-York Packet* an essay titled THE FEDERALIST No. 1. It had been written, anonymously, by a brash thirty-year-old lawyer named Alexander Hamilton. "You are called upon to deliberate on a new Constitution for the United States of America," he told his readers. But more was at stake, too, he insisted; the wrong decision would result in "the general misfortune of mankind." The United States, he argued, was an experiment in the science of politics, marking a new era in the history of government:

> It seems to have been reserved to the people of this country, by their conduct and example, to decide the important question, whether societies of men are really capable or not of establishing good government from reflection and choice, or whether they are forever destined to depend for their political constitutions on accident and force.[6]

This was the question of that autumn. And, in a way, it has been the question of every season since, the question of every rising and setting of the sun, on rainy days and snowy days, on clear days and cloudy days, at the clap of every thunderstorm. Can a political society really be governed by reflection and election, by reason and truth, rather than by accident and violence, by prejudice and deceit? Is there any arrangement of government—any constitution—by which it's possible for a people to rule themselves, justly and fairly, and as

5. *New-York Packet*, October 30, 1787.
6. Ibid.

equals, through the exercise of judgment and care? Or are their efforts, no matter their constitutions, fated to be corrupted, their judgment muddled by demagoguery, their reason abandoned for fury?

This question in every kind of weather is the question of American history. It is also the question of this book, an account of the origins, course, and consequences of the American experiment over more than four centuries. It is not a simple question. I once came across a book called *The Constitution Made Easy*.[7] The Constitution cannot be made easy. It was never meant to be easy.

The American experiment rests on three political ideas—"these truths," Thomas Jefferson called them—political equality, natural rights, and the sovereignty of the people. "We hold these truths to be sacred & undeniable," Jefferson wrote in 1776, in a draft of the Declaration of Independence:

> that all men are created equal & independent, that from that equal creation they derive rights inherent & inalienable, among which are the preservation of life, & liberty, & the pursuit of happiness; that to secure these ends, governments are instituted among men, deriving their just powers from the consent of the governed.

10   The roots of these ideas are as ancient as Aristotle and as old as Genesis and their branches spread as wide as the limbs of an oak. But they are this nation's founding principles: it was by declaring them that the nation came to be. In the centuries since, these principles have been cherished, decried, and contested, fought for, fought over, and fought against. After Benjamin Franklin read Jefferson's draft, he picked up his quill, scratched out the words "sacred & undeniable," and suggested that "these truths" were, instead, "self-evident." This was more than a quibble. Truths that are sacred and undeniable are God-given and divine, the stuff of religion. Truths that are self-evident are laws of nature, empirical and observable, the stuff of science. This divide has nearly rent the Republic apart.

Still, this divide is nearly always overstated and it's easy to exaggerate the difference between Jefferson and Franklin, which, in those lines, came down, too, to style: Franklin's revision is more forceful. The real dispute isn't between Jefferson and Franklin, each attempting, in his way, to reconcile faith and reason, as many have tried both before and since. The real dispute is between "these truths" and the course of events: Does American history prove these truths, or does it belie them?

Before the experiment began, the men who wrote the Declaration of Independence and the Constitution made an extraordinarily careful study of history. They'd been studying history all their lives. Benjamin Franklin was eighty-one years old, hunched and crooked, when he signed the Constitution in 1787, with his gnarled and speckled hand. In 1731, when he was twenty-

7. Michael Holler, *The Constitution Made Easy* (n.p.: The Friends of Freedom, 2008).

five, straight as a sapling, he'd written an essay called "Observations on Reading History," on a "little Paper, accidentally preserv'd."[8] And he'd kept on
reading history, and taking notes, asking himself, year after year: What does
the past teach?

The United States rests on a dedication to equality, which is chiefly a moral
idea, rooted in Christianity, but it rests, too, on a dedication to inquiry, fearless and unflinching. Its founders agreed with the Scottish philosopher and
historian David Hume, who wrote, in 1748, that "Records of Wars, Intrigues,
Factions, and Revolutions are so many Collections of Experiments."[9] They
believed that truth is to be found in ideas about morality but also in the study
of history.

It has often been said, in the twenty-first century and in earlier centuries,
too, that Americans lack a shared past and that, built on a cracked foundation,
the Republic is crumbling.[10] Part of this argument has to do with ancestry:
Americans are descended from conquerors and from the conquered, from
people held as slaves and from the people who held them, from the Union and
from the Confederacy, from Protestants and from Jews, from Muslims and
from Catholics, and from immigrants and from people who have fought to end
immigration. Sometimes, in American history—in nearly all national histories—
one person's villain is another's hero. But part of this argument has to do with
ideology: the United States is founded on a set of ideas, but Americans have
become so divided that they no longer agree, if they ever did, about what those
ideas are, or were.

I wrote this book because writing an American history from beginning to   15
end and across that divide hasn't been attempted in a long time, and it's important, and it seemed worth a try. One reason it's important is that understanding history as a form of inquiry—not as something easy or comforting but as
something demanding and exhausting—was central to the nation's founding.
This, too, was new. In the West, the oldest stories, the *Iliad* and the *Odyssey*,
are odes and tales of wars and kings, of men and gods, sung and told. These
stories were memorials, and so were the histories of antiquity: they were meant
as monuments. "I have written my work, not as an essay which is to win the
applause of the moment," Thucydides wrote, "but as a possession for all time."
Herodotus believed that the purpose of writing history was "so that time not
erase what man has brought into being." A new kind of historical writing, less
memorial and more unsettling, only first emerged in the fourteenth century.
"History is a philosophical science," the North African Muslim scholar Ibn

---

8. Benjamin Franklin, "Observations on Reading History," May 9, 1731, in *The Papers
of Benjamin Franklin* (hereafter *PBF*), online edition at Franklinpapers.org.

9. David Hume, "An Enquiry Concerning Human Understanding [1748]," *Essays and
Treatises on Various Subjects* (Boston: J. P. Mendum, 1868), 54.

10. For example, Ross Douthat, "Who Are We?," *New York Times* [hereafter *NYT*],
February 4, 2017.

Khaldun wrote in 1377, in the prologue to his history of the world, in which he defined history as the study "of the causes and origins of existing things."[11]

Only by fits and starts did history become not merely a form of memory but also a form of investigation, to be disputed, like philosophy, its premises questioned, its evidence examined, its arguments countered. Early in the seventeenth century, Sir Walter Ralegh began writing his own *History of the World*, from a prison in the Tower of London where he was allowed to keep a library of five hundred books. The past, Ralegh explained, "hath made us acquainted with our dead ancestors," but it also casts light on the present, "by the comparison and application of other men's fore-passed miseries with our own like errors and ill deservings."[12] To study the past is to unlock the prison of the present.

This new understanding of the past attempted to divide history from faith. The books of world religions—the Hebrew Bible, the New Testament, and the Quran—are pregnant with mysteries, truths known only by God, taken on faith. In the new history books, historians aimed to solve mysteries and to discover their own truths. The turn from reverence to inquiry, from mystery to history, was crucial to the founding of the United States. It didn't require abdicating faith in the truths of revealed religion and it relieved no one of the obligation to judge right from wrong. But it did require subjecting the past to skepticism, to look to beginnings not to justify ends, but to question them—with evidence.

"I offer nothing more than simple facts, plain arguments, and common sense," Thomas Paine, the spitfire son of an English grocer, wrote in *Common Sense*, in 1776. Kings have no right to reign, Paine argued, because, if we could trace hereditary monarchy back to its beginnings—"could we take off the dark covering of antiquity, and trace them to their first rise"—we'd find "the first of them nothing better than the principal ruffian of some restless gang." James Madison explained Americans' historical skepticism, this deep empiricism, this way: "Is it not the glory of the people of America, that, whilst they have paid a decent regard to the opinions of former times and other nations, they have not suffered a blind veneration for antiquity, for custom, or for names, to overrule the suggestions of their own good sense, the knowledge of their own situation, and the lessons of their own experience?"[13] Evidence, for Madison, was everything.

"A new era for politics is struck," Paine wrote, his pen aflame, and "a new method of thinking hath arisen."[14] Declaring independence was itself an argu-

11. Thucydides, *History of the Peloponnesian War*, Book I, ch. 1; Herodotus, *The Essential Herodotus*, translation, introduction, and annotations by William A. Johnson (New York: Oxford University Press, 2017), 2; Ibn Khaldûn, *The Muqaddimah: An Introduction to History*, trans. Franz Rosenthal (1967; Princeton, NJ: Princeton University Press, 2005), 5.

12. Sir Walter Ralegh, *The Historie of the World* (London: Walter Burre, 1614), 4.

13. Thomas Paine, *Common Sense* (Philadelphia: R. Bell, 1776), 17, 12. James Madison, Federalist No. 14 (1787).

14. Paine, *Common Sense*, 18.

ment about the relationship between the present and the past, an argument that required evidence of a very particular kind: historical evidence. That's why most of the Declaration of Independence is a list of historical claims. "To prove this," Jefferson wrote, "let facts be submitted to a candid world."

Facts, knowledge, experience, proof. These words come from the law.   20
Around the seventeenth century, they moved into what was then called "natural history": astronomy, physics, chemistry, geology. By the eighteenth century they were applied to history and to politics, too. *These truths:* this was the language of reason, of enlightenment, of inquiry, and of history. In 1787, then, when Alexander Hamilton asked "whether societies of men are really capable or not of establishing good government from reflection and choice, or whether they are forever destined to depend for their political constitutions on accident and force," that was the kind of question a scientist asks before beginning an experiment. Time alone would tell. But time has passed. The beginning has come to an end. What, then, is the verdict of history?

This book attempts to answer that question by telling the story of American history, beginning in 1492, with Columbus's voyage, which tied together continents, and ending in a world not merely tied together but tangled, knotted, and bound. It chronicles the settlement of American colonies; the nation's founding and its expansion through migration, immigration, war, and invention; its descent into civil war; its entrance into wars in Europe; its rise as a world power and its role, after the Second World War, in the establishment of the modern liberal world order: the rule of law, individual rights, democratic government, open borders, and free markets. It recounts the nation's confrontations with communism abroad and discrimination at home; its fractures and divisions, and the wars it has waged since 2001, when two airplanes crashed into the two towers of the World Trade Center eight blocks from the site of a long-gone shop where the printers of the *New-York Packet* had once offered for sale a young mother and her six-month old baby and the *Columbian Almanack,* bound with the Constitution, or without.

With this history, I've told a story; I've tried to tell it fairly. I have written a beginning and I have written an ending and I have tried to cross a divide, but I haven't attempted to tell the whole story. No one could. Much is missing in these pages. In the 1950s, the historian Carl Degler explained the rule he'd used in deciding what to leave in and what to leave out of his own history of the United States, a lovely book called *Out of Our Past.* "Readers should be warned that they will find nothing here on the Presidential administrations between 1868 and 1901, no mention of the American Indians or the settlement of the seventeenth-century colonies," Degler advised. "The War of 1812 is touched on only in a footnote."[15] I, too, have had to skip over an awful lot. Some very important events haven't even made it into the footnotes, which I've kept clipped and short, like a baby's fingernails.

---

15. Carl Degler, *Out of Our Past: The Forces That Shaped Modern America* (New York: Harper & Brothers, 1959), xi.

In deciding what to leave in and what to leave out, I've confined myself to what, in my view, a people constituted as a nation in the early twenty-first century need to know about their own past, mainly because this book is meant to double as an old-fashioned civics book, an explanation of the origins and ends of democratic institutions, from the town meeting to the party system, from the nominating convention to the secret ballot, from talk radio to Internet polls. This book is chiefly a political history. It pays very little attention to military and diplomatic history or to social and cultural history. But it does include episodes in the history of American law and religion, journalism and technology, chiefly because these are places where what is true, and what's not, have sometimes gotten sorted out.

Aside from being a brief history of the United States and a civics primer, this book aims to be something else, too: it's an explanation of the nature of the past. History isn't only a subject; it's also a method. My method is, generally, to let the dead speak for themselves. I've pressed their words between these pages, like flowers, for their beauty, or like insects, for their hideousness. The work of the historian is not the work of the critic or of the moralist; it is the work of the sleuth and the storyteller, the philosopher and the scientist, the keeper of tales, the sayer of sooth, the teller of truth.

25   What, then, of the American past? There is, to be sure, a great deal of anguish in American history and more hypocrisy. No nation and no people are relieved of these. But there is also, in the American past, an extraordinary amount of decency and hope, of prosperity and ambition, and much, especially, of invention and beauty. Some American history books fail to criticize the United States; others do nothing but. This book is neither kind. The truths on which the nation was founded are not mysteries, articles of faith, never to be questioned, as if the founding were an act of God, but neither are they lies, all facts fictions, as if nothing can be known, in a world without truth. Between reverence and worship, on the one side, and irreverence and contempt, on the other, lies an uneasy path, away from false pieties and petty triumphs over people who lived and died and committed both their acts of courage and their sins and errors long before we committed ours. "We cannot hallow this ground," Lincoln said at Gettysburg. We are obliged, instead, to walk this ground, dedicating ourselves to both the living and the dead.

A last word, then, about storytelling, and truth. "I have begun this letter five times and torn it up," James Baldwin wrote, in a letter to his nephew begun in 1962. "I keep seeing your face, which is also the face of your father and my brother." His brother was dead; he meant to tell his nephew about being a black man, about the struggle for equality, and about the towering importance and gripping urgency of studying the past and reckoning with origins. He went on,

> I have known both of you all your lives, have carried your Daddy in my arms and on my shoulders, kissed and spanked him and watched him learn to walk. I don't know if you've known anybody from that far back; if you've loved anybody that long, first as an infant, then as a child, then as a man, you gain a strange perspective on time and human pain and effort. Other

people cannot see what I see whenever I look into your father's face, for behind your father's face as it is today are all those faces which were his.[16]

No one can know a nation that far back, from its infancy, with or without baby teeth kept in a jar. But studying history is like that, looking into one face and seeing, behind it, another, face after face after face. "Know whence you came," Baldwin told his nephew.[17] The past is an inheritance, a gift and a burden. It can't be shirked. You carry it everywhere. There's nothing for it but to get to know it.

MLA CITATION

Lepore, Jill. "The Question Stated." *The Norton Reader: An Anthology of Nonfiction*, edited by Melissa A. Goldthwaite et al., 15th ed., W. W. Norton, 2020, pp. 693–701.

QUESTIONS

1. Jill Lepore notes that, at twenty-five, Benjamin Franklin was not only reading, but writing short papers on history (paragraph 12). What justifications for reading history do you think Franklin found in his study of it? What does Lepore propose as her reasons for reading history today? What, for you, are the most compelling reasons to study history?

2. According to Lepore, what was the connotation of the phrase "these truths" for the Founders? How has that phrase shifted meaning, if at all, today?

3. What does Lepore select as important to include in a one-volume history of the United States? What does she leave out? In what ways might your choices differ and why?

4. Look at a newspaper's front page, online or on paper, and list all the information on that page as Lepore does with the October 30, 1787, *New-York Packet*. Imagine that you're a historian and write about what seems most—and least—important among the top stories of the day.

16. The letter was originally published as James Baldwin, "A Letter to My Nephew," *The Progressive*, January 1, 1962; a revision appears in James Baldwin, *The Fire Next Time* (1963; New York: Vintage International, 1993), 3–5.
17. Ibid.

THOMAS JEFFERSON AND OTHERS

The Declaration of Independence

ORIGINAL DRAFT

A Declaration of the Representatives of the UNITED STATES
OF AMERICA, in General Congress Assembled.

W HEN IN THE COURSE OF HUMAN EVENTS it becomes necessary for a people to advance from that subordination in which they have hitherto remained, & to assume among the powers of the earth the equal & independant station to which the laws of nature & of nature's god entitle them, a decent respect to the opinions of mankind requires that they should declare the causes which impel them to the change.

We hold these truths to be sacred & undeniable; that all men are created equal & independant, that from that equal creation they derive rights inherent & inalienable, among which are the preservation of life, & liberty, & the pursuit of happiness; that to secure these ends, governments are instituted among men, deriving their just powers from the consent of the governed; that whenever any form of government shall become destructive of these ends, it is the right of the people to alter or to abolish it, & to institute new government, laying it's foundation on such principles & organising its powers in such form, as to them shall seem most likely to effect their safety & happiness. Prudence indeed will dictate that governments long established should not be changed for light & transient causes: and accordingly all experience hath shewn that mankind are more disposed to suffer while evils are sufferable, than to right themselves by abolishing the forms to which they are accustomed. but when a long train of abuses & usurpations, begun at a distinguished period, & pursuing invariably the same object, evinces a design to subject them to arbitrary power, it is their right, it is their duty, to throw off such government & to provide new guards for their future security. such has been the patient sufferance of these colonies; & such is now the necessity which constrains them to expunge their former systems of government. The history of his present majesty, is a history of unremitting injuries and usurpations, among which no one fact stands single or solitary to contradict the uniform tenor of the rest, all of which have in direct object the establishment of an absolute tyranny over these states. to prove this, let facts be submitted to a candid world, for the truth of which we pledge a faith yet unsullied by falsehood.

On June 11, 1776, Thomas Jefferson was elected by the Second Continental Congress to join John Adams, Benjamin Franklin, Roger Sherman, and Robert Livingston in drafting a declaration of independence. The draft presented to Congress on June 28 was primarily the work of Jefferson. The final version resulted from revisions made to Jefferson's original draft by members of the committee, including Adams and Franklin, and by members of the Continental Congress.

he has refused his assent to laws the most wholesome and necessary for the public good:

he has forbidden his governors to pass laws of immediate & pressing importance, unless suspended in their operation till his assent should be obtained; and when so suspended, he has neglected utterly to attend to them.

he has refused to pass other laws for the accommodation of large districts of people unless those people would relinquish the right of representation, a right inestimable to them, & formidable to tyrants alone:[1]

he has dissolved Representative houses repeatedly & continually, for opposing with manly firmness his invasions on the rights of the people:

he has refused for a long space of time to cause others to be elected, whereby the legislative powers, incapable of annihilation, have returned to the people at large for their exercise, the state remaining in the mean time exposed to all the dangers of invasion from without, &, convulsions within:

he has suffered the administration of justice totally to cease in some of these colonies, refusing his assent to laws for establishing judiciary powers:

he has made our judges dependant on his will alone, for the tenure of their offices, and amount of their salaries:

he has erected a multitude of new offices by a self-assumed power, & sent hither swarms of officers to harrass our people & eat out their substance: he has kept among us in times of peace standing armies & ships of war:

he has affected[2] to render the military, independent of & superior to the civil power:

he has combined with others to subject us to a jurisdiction foreign to our constitutions and unacknowledged by our laws; giving his assent to their pretended acts of legislation, for quartering large bodies of armed troops among us;

for protecting them by a mock-trial from punishment for any murders they should commit on the inhabitants of these states;

for cutting off our trade with all parts of the world;

for imposing taxes on us without our consent;

for depriving us of the benefits of trial by jury

he has endeavored to prevent the population of these states; for that purpose obstructing the laws for naturalization of foreigners; refusing to pass others to encourage their migrations hither; & raising the conditions of new appropriations of lands;

for transporting us beyond seas to be tried for pretended offences:

for taking away our charters & altering fundamentally the forms of our governments;

for suspending our own legislatures & declaring themselves invested with power to legislate for us in all cases whatsoever:

he has abdicated government here, withdrawing his governors, & declaring us out of his allegiance & protection:

he has plundered our seas, ravaged our coasts, burnt our towns & destroyed the lives of our people:

---

1. At this point in the manuscript, a strip containing the following clause is inserted: "he called together legislative bodies at places unusual, unco[mfortable, & distant from] the depository of their public records for the sole purpose of fatiguing [them into compliance] with his measures." Missing parts in the Library of Congress text are supplied from the copy made by Jefferson for George Wythe. This copy is in the New York Public Library. The fact that this passage was omitted from John Adams's transcript suggests that it was not a part of Jefferson's original rough draft.

2. Tried.

he is at this time transporting large armies of foreign mercenaries to compleat
the works of death, desolation & tyranny, already begun with circumstances
of cruelty & perfidy unworthy the head of a civilized nation:

he has endeavored to bring on the inhabitants of our frontiers the merciless
Indian savages, whose known rule of warfare is an undistinguished destruction of all ages, sexes, & conditions of existence:

he has incited treasonable insurrections of our fellow-citizens, with the allure-
ments of forfeiture & confiscation of our property:

he has waged cruel war against human nature itself, violating it's most sacred
rights of life & liberty in the persons of a distant people who never offended
him, captivating & carrying them into slavery in another hemisphere, or to
incur miserable death in their transportation thither. this piratical warfare,
the opprobrium of *infidel* powers, is the warfare of the CHRISTIAN king
of Great Britain. determined to keep open a market where MEN should be
bought & sold; he has prostituted his negative for suppressing every legislative attempt to prohibit or to restrain this execrable commerce: and that this
assemblage of horrors might want no fact of distinguished die, he is now exciting those very people to rise in arms among us, and to purchase that liberty of
which *he* has deprived them, by murdering the people upon whom *he* also
obtruded them; thus paying off former crimes committed against the *liberties*
of one people, with crimes which he urges them to commit against the *lives* of
another.

20   in every stage of these oppressions we have petitioned for redress in the most
humble terms; our repeated petitions have been answered by repeated injury.
a prince whose character is thus marked by every act which may define a tyrant,
is unfit to be the ruler of a people who mean to be free. future ages will scarce
believe that the hardiness of one man, adventured within the short compass
of twelve years only, on so many acts of tyranny without a mask, over a people
fostered & fixed in principles of liberty.

Nor have we been wanting in attentions to our British brethren. we have
warned them from time to time of attempts by their legislature to extend a jurisdiction over these our states. we have reminded them of the circumstances of
our emigration & settlement here, no one of which could warrant so strange a
pretension: that these were effected at the expence of our own blood & treasure, unassisted by the wealth or the strength of Great Britain: that in consti-
tuting indeed our several forms of government, we had adopted one common
king, thereby laying a foundation for perpetual league & amity with them; but
that submission to their [Parliament, was no Part of our Constitution, nor ever
in Idea, if History may be][3] credited: and we appealed to their native justice &
magnanimity, as to the ties of our common kindred to disavow these usurpations which were likely to interrupt our correspondence & connection. they too
have been deaf to the voice of justice & of consanguinity, & when occasions have
been given them, by the regular course of their laws, of removing from their
councils the disturbers of our harmony, they have by their free election re-
established them in power. at this very time too they are permitting their chief
magistrate to send over not only soldiers of our common blood, but Scotch

---

3. Passage illegible in the original; supplied here from John Adams's transcription.

& foreign mercenaries to invade & deluge us in blood. these facts have given the last stab to agonizing affection, and manly spirit bids us to renounce for ever these unfeeling brethren. we must endeavor to forget our former love for them, and to hold them as we hold the rest of mankind, enemies in war, in peace friends. we might have been a free & a great people together; but a communication of grandeur & of freedom it seems is below their dignity. be it so, since they will have it: the road to glory & happiness is open to us too; we will climb it in a separate state, and acquiesce in the necessity which pronounces our everlasting Adieu!

We therefore the representatives of the United States of America in General Congress assembled do, in the name & by authority of the good people of these states, reject and renounce all allegiance & subjection to the kings of Great Britain & all others who may hereafter claim by, through, or under them; we utterly dissolve & break off all political connection which may have heretofore subsisted between us & the people or parliament of Great Britain; and finally we do assert and declare these colonies to be free and independant states, and that as free & independant states they shall hereafter have power to levy war, conclude peace, contract alliances, establish commerce, & to do all other acts and things which independant states may of right do. And for the support of this declaration we mutually pledge to each other our lives, our fortunes, & our sacred honour.

FINAL DRAFT

In Congress, July 4, 1776
The unanimous Declaration of the
Thirteen United States of America

WHEN IN THE COURSE OF HUMAN EVENTS it becomes necessary for one people to dissolve the political bands which have connected them with another, and to assume among the powers of the earth, the separate and equal station to which the Laws of Nature and of Nature's God entitle them, a decent respect to the opinions of mankind requires that they should declare the causes which impel them to the separation.

We hold these truths to be self-evident, that all men are created equal, that they are endowed by their Creator with certain unalienable Rights, that among these are Life, Liberty and the pursuit of Happiness. That to secure these rights, Governments are instituted among Men, deriving their just powers from the consent of the governed. That whenever any Form of Government becomes destructive of these ends, it is the Right of the People to alter or to abolish it, and to institute new Government, laying its foundation on such principles and organizing its powers in such form, as to them shall seem most likely to effect their Safety and Happiness. Prudence, indeed, will dictate that Governments long established should not be changed for light and transient causes; and accordingly all experience hath shewn that mankind are more disposed to suffer, while evils are sufferable, than to right themselves by abolishing the forms

to which they are accustomed. But when a long train of abuses and usurpations, pursuing invariably the same Object evinces a design to reduce them
under absolute Despotism, it is their right, it is their duty, to throw off such
Government, and to provide new Guards for their future security. Such has
been the patient sufferance of these Colonies; and such is now the necessity
which constrains them to alter their former Systems of Government. The history of the present King of Great Britain is a history of repeated injuries and
usurpations, all having in direct object the establishment of an absolute Tyranny
over these States. To prove this, let Facts be submitted to a candid world.

He has refused his Assent to Laws, the most wholesome and necessary for
the public good.

He has forbidden his Government to pass laws of immediate and pressing
importance, unless suspended in their operation till his Assent should be
obtained; and when so suspended, he has utterly neglected to attend to them.

5   He has refused to pass other Laws for the accommodation of large districts
of people, unless those people would relinquish the right of Representation in
the Legislature, a right inestimable to them and formidable to tyrants only.

He has called together legislative bodies at places unusual, uncomfortable,
and distant from the depository of their Public Records, for the sole purpose of
fatiguing them into compliance with his measures.

He has dissolved Representative Houses repeatedly, for opposing with
manly firmness his invasions on the rights of the people.

He has refused for a long time, after such dissolutions, to cause others to be
elected; whereby the Legislative Powers, incapable of Annihilation, have
returned to the People at large for their exercise; the State remaining in the mean
time exposed to all the dangers of invasion from without, and convulsions within.

He has endeavored to prevent the population of these States; for that purpose obstructing the Laws for Naturalization of Foreigners; refusing to pass
others to encourage their migration hither, and raising the conditions of new
Appropriations of Lands.

10   He has obstructed the Administration of Justice, by refusing his Assent to
Laws for establishing Judiciary Powers.

He has made Judges dependent on his Will alone, for the tenure of their
offices, and the amount and payment of their salaries.

He has erected a multitude of New Offices, and sent hither swarms of Officers to harass our people, and eat out their substance.

He has kept among us, in times of peace, Standing Armies without the
Consent of our legislatures.

He has affected to render the Military independent of and superior to the
Civil Power.

15   He has combined with others to subject us to a jurisdiction foreign to our
constitution, and unacknowledged by our laws; giving his Assent to their Acts
of pretended Legislation: For quartering large bodies of armed troops among
us: For protecting them, by a mock Trial, from punishment for any Murders
which they should commit on the Inhabitants of these States: For cutting off
our Trade with all parts of the world: For imposing Taxes on us without our

Consent: For depriving us in many cases, of the benefits of Trial by Jury: For transporting us beyond Seas to be tried for pretended offenses: For abolishing the free System of English Laws in a neighboring Province, establishing therein an Arbitrary government, and enlarging its Boundaries so as to render it at once an example and fit instrument for introducing the same absolute rule into these Colonies: For taking away our Charters, abolishing our most valuable Laws, and altering fundamentally the Forms of our Governments: For suspending our own Legislatures, and declaring themselves invested with power to legislate for us in all cases whatsoever.

He has abdicated Government here, by declaring us out of his Protection and waging War against us.

He has plundered our seas, ravaged our Coasts, burnt our towns, and destroyed the lives of our people.

He is at this time transporting large Armies of foreign Mercenaries to complete the works of death, desolation and tyranny, already begun with circumstances of Cruelty & Perfidy scarcely paralleled in the most barbarous ages, and totally unworthy the Head of a civilized nation.

He has constrained our fellow Citizens taken Captive on the high Seas to bear Arms against their Country, to become the executioners of their friends and Brethren, or to fall themselves by their Hands.

He has excited domestic insurrections amongst us, and has endeavored to 20 bring on the inhabitants of our frontiers, the merciless Indian Savages, whose known rule of warfare, is an undistinguished destruction of all ages, sexes, and conditions.

In every stage of these Oppressions We have Petitioned for Redress in the most humble terms: Our repeated Petitions have been answered only by repeated injury. A Prince, whose character is thus marked by every act which may define a Tyrant, is unfit to be the ruler of a free people.

Nor have We been wanting in attention to our British brethren. We have warned them from time to time of attempts by their legislature to extend an unwarrantable jurisdiction over us. We have reminded them of the circumstances of our emigration and settlement here. We have appealed to their native justice and magnanimity, and we have conjured them by the ties of our common kindred to disavow these usurpations, which would inevitably interrupt our connections and correspondence. They too have been deaf to the voice of justice and of consanguinity. We must, therefore, acquiesce in the necessity, which denounces our Separation, and hold them, as we hold the rest of mankind, Enemies in War, in Peace Friends.

We, THEREFORE the Representatives of the UNITED STATES OF AMERICA, in General Congress, Assembled, appealing to the Supreme Judge of the world for the rectitude of our intentions, do, in the Name, and by Authority of the good People of these Colonies, solemnly publish and declare, That these United Colonies are, and of Right ought to be FREE AND INDEPENDENT STATES; that they are Absolved from all Allegiance to the British Crown, and that all political connection between them and the State of Great Britain, is and ought to be totally dissolved; and that as Free and Independent States, they have full Power to levy War, conclude Peace, contract Alliances, establish Commerce, and to do all other Acts and Things which Independent States may of right do. And for the support of this Declaration, with a firm reliance on the protection of Divine Providence, we mutually pledge to each other our Lives, our Fortunes, and our sacred Honor.

MLA CITATION

Jefferson, Thomas, et al. "The Declaration of Independence." *The Norton Reader: An Anthology of Nonfiction*, edited by Melissa A. Goldthwaite et al., 15th ed., W. W. Norton, 2020, pp. 702–08.

QUESTIONS

1. The Declaration of Independence is an example of deductive argument: Thomas Jefferson sets up general principles, details particular instances, and then draws conclusions. In both the original and final drafts, locate the three sections of the Declaration that use deduction. Explain how they work as arguments.

2. Locate the general principles (or "truths") that Jefferson sets up in the first section of both the original and final drafts. Mark the language he uses to describe them: for example, he calls them "sacred & undeniable" in the original draft and "self-evident" (paragraph 2) in the final draft. What kinds of authority does his language appeal to in each draft? Why might he or others have revised the language?

3. Note the stylistic differences (including choices of grammar and punctuation) between the original and final drafts of the Declaration of Independence. What effect do those differences have?

4. In an essay, choose one or two significant revisions that Thomas Jefferson made between the original draft and the final draft of the Declaration, and explain why they are significant.

ELIZABETH CADY STANTON
Declaration of Sentiments and Resolutions

W HEN, IN THE COURSE OF HUMAN EVENTS, it becomes necessary for one portion of the family of man to assume among the people of the earth a position different from that which they have hitherto occupied, but one to which the laws of nature and of nature's God entitle them, a decent respect

Written and presented at the first U.S. women's rights convention in Seneca Falls, New York, in 1848. Elizabeth Cady Stanton published this version in A History of Woman Suffrage *(1881), edited by herself, Susan B. Anthony, and Matilda Joslyn Gage, all prominent leaders of the American women's movement.*

to the opinions of mankind requires that they should declare the causes that impel them to such a course.

We hold these truths to be self-evident: that all men and women are created equal; that they are endowed by their Creator with certain inalienable rights; that among these are life, liberty, and the pursuit of happiness; that to secure these rights governments are instituted, deriving their just powers from the consent of the governed. Whenever any form of government becomes destructive of these ends, it is the right of those who suffer from it to refuse allegiance to it, and to insist upon the institution of a new government, laying its foundation on such principles, and organizing its powers in such form, as to them shall seem most likely to effect their safety and happiness. Prudence indeed, will dictate that governments long established should not be changed for light and transient causes; and accordingly all experience hath shown that mankind are more disposed to suffer, while evils are sufferable, than to right themselves by abolishing the forms to which they were accustomed. But when a long train of abuses and usurpations, pursuing invariably the same object evinces a design to reduce them under absolute despotism, it is their duty to throw off such government, and to provide new guards for their future security. Such has been the patient sufferance of the women under this government, and such is now the necessity which constrains them to demand the equal station to which they are entitled.

The history of mankind is a history of repeated injuries and usurpations on the part of man toward woman, having in direct object the establishment of an absolute tyranny over her. To prove this, let facts be submitted to a candid world.

He has never permitted her to exercise her inalienable right to the elective franchise.

He has compelled her to submit to laws, in the formation of which she had 5 no voice.

He has withheld from her rights which are given to the most ignorant and degraded men—both natives and foreigners.

Having deprived her of this first right of a citizen, the elective franchise, thereby leaving her without representation in the halls of legislation, he has oppressed her on all sides.

He has made her, if married, in the eye of the law, civilly dead.

He has taken from her all right in property, even to the wages she earns.

He has made her, morally, an irresponsible being, as she can commit many 10 crimes with impunity, provided they be done in the presence of her husband. In the covenant of marriage, she is compelled to promise obedience to her husband, he becoming, to all intents and purposes, her master—the law giving him power to deprive her of her liberty, and to administer chastisement.

He has so framed the laws of divorce, as to what shall be the proper causes, and in case of separation, to whom the guardianship of the children shall be given, as to be wholly regardless of the happiness of women—the law, in all cases, going upon a false supposition of the supremacy of man, and giving all power into his hands.

After depriving her of all rights as a married woman, if single, and the owner of property, he has taxed her to support a government which recognizes her only when her property can be made profitable to it.

He has monopolized nearly all the profitable employments, and from those she is permitted to follow, she receives but a scanty remuneration. He closes against her all the avenues to wealth and distinction which he considers most honorable to himself. As a teacher of theology, medicine, or law, she is not known.

He has denied her the facilities for obtaining a thorough education, all colleges being closed against her.

15   He allows her in Church, as well as State, but a subordinate position, claiming Apostolic authority for her exclusion from the ministry, and, with some exceptions, from any public participation in the affairs of the Church.

He has created a false public sentiment by giving to the world a different code of morals for men and women, by which moral delinquencies which exclude women from society, are not only tolerated, but deemed of little account in man.

He has usurped the prerogative of Jehovah himself, claiming it as his right to assign for her a sphere of action, when that belongs to her conscience and to her God.

He has endeavored, in every way that he could, to destroy her confidence in her own powers, to lessen her self-respect, and to make her willing to lead a dependent and abject life.

Now, in view of this entire disfranchisement of one-half the people of this country, their social and religious degradation—in view of the unjust laws above mentioned, and because women do feel themselves aggrieved, oppressed, and fraudulently deprived of their most sacred rights, we insist that they have immediate admission to all the rights and privileges which belong to them as citizens of the United States.

20   In entering upon the great work before us, we anticipate no small amount of misconception, misrepresentation, and ridicule; but we shall use every instrumentality within our power to effect our object. We shall employ agents, circulate tracts, petition the State and National legislatures, and endeavor to enlist the pulpit and the press in our behalf. We hope this Convention will be followed by a series of Conventions embracing every part of the country.

MLA CITATION

Stanton, Elizabeth Cady. "Declaration of Sentiments and Resolutions." *The Norton Reader: An Anthology of Nonfiction*, edited by Melissa A. Goldthwaite et al., 15th ed., W. W. Norton, 2020, pp. 708–10.

QUESTIONS

1. Elizabeth Cady Stanton imitates both the argument and the style of the Declaration of Independence. Where does her declaration diverge from Thomas Jefferson's? For what purpose?

2. Stanton's declaration was presented at the first conference on women's rights in Seneca Falls, New York, in 1848. Using books or web resources, do research on this conference; then use your research to explain the political aims of one of the resolutions.

3. Write your own "declaration" of political, educational, or social rights, using the declarations of Jefferson and Stanton as models.

JONATHAN SWIFT
A Modest Proposal

FOR PREVENTING THE CHILDREN OF POOR PEOPLE IN IRELAND FROM BEING A BURDEN TO THEIR PARENTS OR COUNTRY, AND FOR MAKING THEM BENEFICIAL TO THE PUBLIC

I T IS A MELANCHOLY OBJECT to those who walk through this great town[1] or travel in the country, when they see the streets, the roads, and cabin doors, crowded with beggars of the female-sex, followed by three, four, or six children, all in rags and importuning every passenger for an alms. These mothers, instead of being able to work for their honest livelihood, are forced to employ all their time in strolling to beg sustenance for their helpless infants, who, as they grow up, either turn thieves for want of work, or leave their dear native country to fight for the Pretender in Spain, or sell themselves to the Barbadoes.[2]

I think it is agreed by all parties that this prodigious number of children in the arms, or on the backs, or at the heels of their mothers, and frequently of their fathers, is in the present deplorable state of the kingdom a very great additional grievance; and therefore whoever could find out a fair, cheap, and easy method of making these children sound, useful members of the commonwealth would deserve so well of the public as to have his statue set up for a preserver of the nation.

But my intention is very far from being confined to provide only for the children of professed beggars; it is of a much greater extent, and shall take in the whole number of infants at a certain age who are born of parents in effect as little able to support them as those who demand our charity in the streets.

Printed in 1729 as a pamphlet, a form commonly used for political debate in the eighteenth century.

1. Dublin.
2. Many poor Irish sought to escape poverty by emigrating to the Barbados and other western English colonies, paying for transport by binding themselves to work for a landowner there for a period of years. The Pretender, James Francis Edward Stuart (1688–1766), was a claimant to the English throne. He was barred from succession after his father, King James II, was deposed in a Protestant revolution; thereafter, many Irish Catholics joined the Pretender in his exile in France and Spain and in his unsuccessful attempts at counterrevolution.

As to my own part, having turned my thoughts for many years upon this important subject, and maturely weighed the several schemes of other projectors,[3] I have always found them grossly mistaken in their computation. It is true, a child just dropped from its dam may be supported by her milk for a solar year, with little other nourishment; at most not above the value of two shillings,[4] which the mother may certainly get, or the value in scraps, by her lawful occupation of begging; and it is exactly at one year old that I propose to provide for them in such a manner as instead of being a charge upon their parents or the parish, or wanting food and raiment for the rest of their lives, they shall on the contrary contribute to the feeding, and partly to the clothing, of many thousands.

5   There is likewise another great advantage in my scheme, that it will prevent those voluntary abortions, and that horrid practice of women murdering their bastard children, alas, too frequent among us, sacrificing the poor innocent babes, I doubt, more to avoid the expense than the shame, which would move tears and pity in the most savage and inhuman breast.

The number of souls in this kingdom being usually reckoned one million and a half, of these I calculate there may be about two hundred thousand couple whose wives are breeders; from which number I subtract thirty thousand couples who are able to maintain their own children, although I apprehend there cannot be so many under the present distresses of the kingdom; but this being granted, there will remain an hundred and seventy thousand breeders. I again subtract fifty thousand for those women who miscarry, or whose children die by accident or disease within the year. There only remain an hundred and twenty thousand children of poor parents annually born. The question therefore is, how this number shall be reared and provided for, which, as I have already said, under the present situation of affairs, is utterly impossible by all the methods hitherto proposed. For we can neither employ them in handicraft or agriculture; we neither build houses (I mean in the country) nor cultivate land. They can very seldom pick up a livelihood by stealing till they arrive at six years old, except where they are of towardly parts;[5] although I confess they learn the rudiments much earlier, during which time they can however be looked upon only as probationers, as I have been informed by a principal gentleman in the county of Cavan, who protested to me that he never knew above one or two instances under the age of six, even in a part of the kingdom so renowned for the quickest proficiency in that art.

I am assured by our merchants that a boy or a girl before twelve years old is no salable commodity; and even when they come to this age they will not yield above three pounds, or three pounds and half a crown[6] at most on the Exchange; which cannot turn to account either to the parents or the kingdom, the charge of nutriment and rags having been at least four times that value.

3. People with projects; schemers.
4. One shilling used to be worth about twenty-five cents.
5. Promising abilities.
6. One crown was worth one quarter of a pound.

I shall now therefore humbly propose my own thoughts, which I hope will not be liable to the least objection.

I have been assured by a very knowing American of my acquaintance in London, that a young healthy child well nursed is at a year old a most delicious, nourishing, and wholesome food, whether stewed, roasted, baked, or boiled; and I make no doubt that it will equally serve in a fricassee or a ragout.

I do therefore humbly offer it to public consideration that of the hundred   10
and twenty thousand children, already computed, twenty thousand may be reserved for breed, whereof only one fourth part to be males, which is more than we allow to sheep, black cattle, or swine; and my reason is that these children are seldom the fruits of marriage, a circumstance not much regarded by our savages, therefore one male will be sufficient to serve four females. That the remaining hundred thousand may at a year old be offered in sale to the persons of quality and fortune through the kingdom, always advising the mother to let them suck plentifully in the last month, so as to render them plump and fat for a good table. A child will make two dishes at an entertainment for friends; and when the family dines alone, the fore or hind quarter will make a reasonable dish, and seasoned with a little pepper or salt will be very good boiled on the fourth day, especially in winter.

I have reckoned upon a medium that a child just born will weigh twelve pounds, and in a solar year if tolerably nursed increaseth to twenty-eight pounds.

I grant this food will be somewhat dear, and therefore very proper for landlords, who, as they have already devoured most of the parents, seem to have the best title to the children.

Infant's flesh will be in season throughout the year, but more plentiful in March, and a little before and after. For we are told by a grave author, an eminent French physician,[7] that fish being a prolific diet, there are more children born in Roman Catholic countries about nine months after Lent than at any other season; therefore, reckoning a year after Lent, the markets will be more glutted than usual, because the number of popish infants is at least three to one in this kingdom; and therefore it will have one other collateral advantage, by lessening the number of Papists among us.[8]

I have already computed the charge of nursing a beggar's child (in which list I reckon all cottagers, laborers, and four fifths of the farmers) to be about two shillings per annum, rags included; and I believe no gentleman would repine to give ten shillings for the carcass of a good fat child, which, as I have said, will make four dishes of excellent nutritive meat, when he hath only some particular friend or his own family to dine with him. Thus the squire will learn to be a good landlord, and grow popular among the tenants; the mother will have eight shillings net profit, and be fit for work till she produces another child.

7. Comic writer François Rabelais (1483–1553).
8. The speaker is addressing Protestant Anglo-Irish, who were the chief landowners and administrators, and his views of Catholicism in Ireland and abroad echo theirs.

15   Those who are more thrifty (as I must confess the times require) may flay the carcass; the skin of which artificially[9] dressed will make admirable gloves for ladies, and summer boots for fine gentlemen.

As to our city of Dublin, shambles[10] may be appointed for this purpose in the most convenient parts of it, and butchers we may be assured will not be wanting; although I rather recommend buying the children alive, and dressing them hot from the knife as we do roasting pigs.

A very worthy person, a true lover of his country, and whose virtues I highly esteem, was lately pleased in discoursing on this matter to offer a refinement upon my scheme. He said that many gentlemen of this kingdom, having of late destroyed their deer, he conceived that the want of venison might be well supplied by the bodies of young lads and maidens, not exceeding fourteen years of age nor under twelve, so great a number of both sexes in every county being now ready to starve for want of work and service; and these to be disposed of by their parents, if alive, or otherwise by their nearest relations. But with due deference to so excellent a friend and so deserving a patriot, I cannot be altogether in his sentiments; for as to the males, my American acquaintance assured me from frequent experience that their flesh was generally tough and lean, like that of our schoolboys, by continual exercise, and their taste disagreeable; and to fatten them would not answer the charge. Then as to the females, it would, I think with humble submission, be a loss to the public, because they soon would become breeders themselves: and besides, it is not improbable that some scrupulous people might be apt to censure such a practice (although indeed very unjustly) as a little bordering upon cruelty; which, I confess, hath always been with me the strongest objection against any project, how well soever intended.

But in order to justify my friend, he confessed that this expedient was put into his head by the famous Psalmanazar, a native of the island Formosa,[11] who came from thence to London above twenty years ago, and in conversation told my friend that in his country when any young person happened to be put to death, the executioner sold the carcass to persons of quality as a prime dainty; and that in his time the body of a plump girl of fifteen, who was crucified for an attempt to poison the emperor, was sold to his Imperial Majesty's prime minister of state, and other great mandarins of the court, in joints from the gibbet, at four hundred crowns. Neither indeed can I deny that if the same use were made of several plump young girls in this town, who without one single groat[12] to their fortunes cannot stir abroad without a chair,[13] and appear at the playhouse and assemblies in foreign fineries which they never will pay for, the kingdom would not be the worse.

9. Skillfully.

10. Slaughterhouses.

11. Actually a Frenchman, George Psalmanazar had passed himself off as from Formosa (now Taiwan) and had written a fictitious book about his "homeland," with descriptions of human sacrifice and cannibalism.

12. Coin worth about four English pennies.

13. Sedan chair.

Some persons of a desponding spirit are in great concern about that vast number of poor people who are aged, diseased, or maimed, and I have been desired to employ my thoughts what course may be taken to ease the nation of so grievous an encumbrance. But I am not in the least pain upon that matter, because it is very well known that they are every day dying and rotting by cold and famine, and filth and vermin, as fast as can be reasonably expected. And as to the younger laborers, they are now in almost as hopeful a condition. They cannot get work, and consequently pine away for want of nourishment to a degree that if at any time they are accidentally hired to common labor, they have not strength to perform it; and thus the country and themselves are happily delivered from the evils to come.

I have too long digressed, and therefore shall return to my subject. I think the advantages by the proposal which I have made are obvious and many, as well as of the highest importance.

For first, as I have already observed, it would greatly lessen the number of Papists, with whom we are yearly overrun, being the principal breeders of the nation as well as our most dangerous enemies; and who stay at home on purpose to deliver the kingdom to the Pretender, hoping to take their advantage by the absence of so many good Protestants, who have chosen rather to leave their country than to stay at home and pay tithes against their conscience to an Episcopal curate.

Secondly, the poorer tenants will have something valuable of their own, which by law may be made liable to distress,[14] and help to pay their landlord's rent, their corn and cattle being already seized and money a thing unknown.

Thirdly, whereas the maintenance of an hundred thousand children, from two years old and upwards, cannot be computed at less than ten shillings a piece per annum, the nation's stock will be thereby increased fifty thousand pounds per annum, besides the profit of a new dish introduced to the tables of all gentlemen of fortune in the kingdom who have any refinement in taste. And the money will circulate among ourselves, the goods being entirely of our own growth and manufacture.

Fourthly, the constant breeders, besides the gain of eight shillings sterling per annum by the sale of their children, will be rid of the charge of maintaining them after the first year.

Fifthly, this food would likewise bring great custom to taverns, where the vintners will certainly be so prudent as to procure the best receipts for dressing it to perfection, and consequently have their houses frequented by all the fine gentlemen, who justly value themselves upon their knowledge in good eating; and a skillful cook, who understands how to oblige his guests, will contrive to make it as expensive as they please.

Sixthly, this would be a great inducement to marriage, which all wise nations have either encouraged by rewards or enforced by laws and penalties. It would increase the care and tenderness of mothers toward their children, when they were sure of a settlement for life to the poor babes, provided in some

14. Seizure for the payment of debts.

sort by the public, to their annual profit instead of expense. We should see an honest emulation among the married women, which of them could bring the fattest child to the market. Men would become as fond of their wives during the time of their pregnancy as they are now of their mares in foal, their cows in calf, or sows when they are ready to farrow; nor offer to beat or kick them (as is too frequent a practice) for fear of a miscarriage.

Many other advantages might be enumerated. For instance, the addition of some thousand carcasses in our exportation of barreled beef, the propagation of swine's flesh, and improvement in the art of making good bacon, so much wanted among us by the great destruction of pigs, too frequent at our tables, which are no way comparable in taste or magnificence to a well-grown, fat, yearling child, which roasted whole will make a considerable figure at a lord mayor's feast or any other public entertainment. But this and many others I omit, being studious of brevity.

Supposing that one thousand families in this city would be constant customers for infants' flesh, besides others who might have it at merry meetings, particularly weddings and christenings, I compute that Dublin would take off annually about twenty thousand carcasses, and the rest of the kingdom (where probably they will be sold somewhat cheaper) the remaining eighty thousand.

I can think of no one objection that will possibly be raised against this proposal, unless it should be urged that the number of people will be thereby much lessened in the kingdom. This I freely own, and it was indeed one principal design in offering it to the world. I desire the reader will observe, that I calculate my remedy for this one individual kingdom of Ireland and for no other that ever was, is, or I think ever can be upon earth. Therefore let no man talk to me of other expedients: of taxing our absentees at five shillings a pound: of using neither clothes nor household furniture except what is of our own growth and manufacture: of utterly rejecting the materials and instruments that promote foreign luxury: of curing the expensiveness of pride, vanity, idleness, and gaming in our women: of introducing a vein of parsimony, prudence, and temperance: of learning to love our country, in the want of which we differ even from Laplanders and the inhabitants of Topinamboo:[15] of quitting our animosities and factions, nor acting any longer like the Jews, who were murdering one another at the very moment their city was taken: of being a little cautious not to sell our country and conscience for nothing: of teaching landlords to have at least one degree of mercy toward their tenants: lastly, of putting a spirit of honesty, industry, and skill into our shopkeepers; who, if a resolution could now be taken to buy only our native goods, would immediately unite to cheat and exact upon us in the price, the measure, and the goodness, nor could ever yet be brought to make one fair proposal of just dealing, though often and earnestly invited to it.[16]

---

15. District in Brazil.

16. Swift himself had made these proposals seriously in various previous works, but to no avail.

Therefore I repeat, let no man talk to me of these and the like expedients,   30
till he hath at least some glimpse of hope that there will ever be some hearty
and sincere attempt to put them in practice.

But as to myself, having been wearied out for many years with offering vain,
idle, visionary thoughts, and at length utterly despairing of success, I fortunately
fell upon this proposal, which, as it is wholly new, so it hath something solid
and real, of no expense and little trouble, full in our own power, and whereby
we can incur no danger in disobliging England. For this kind of commodity
will not bear exportation, the flesh being of too tender a consistence to admit a
long continuance in salt, although perhaps I could name a country[17] which would
be glad to eat up our whole nation without it.

After all, I am not so violently bent upon my own opinion as to reject any
offer proposed by wise men, which shall be found equally innocent, cheap,
easy, and effectual. But before something of that kind shall be advanced in
contradiction to my scheme, and offering a better, I desire the author or authors
will be pleased maturely to consider two points. First, as things now stand, how
they will be able to find food and raiment for an hundred thousand useless
mouths and backs. And secondly, there being a round million of creatures in
human figure throughout this kingdom, whose sole subsistence put into a
common stock would leave them in debt two millions of pounds sterling, adding
those who are beggars by profession to the bulk of farmers, cottagers, and laborers, with their wives and children who are beggars in effect; I desire those
politicians who dislike my overture, and may perhaps be so bold to attempt an
answer, that they will first ask the parents of these mortals whether they would
not at this day think it a great happiness to have been sold for food at a year old
in the manner I prescribe, and thereby have avoided such a perpetual scene of
misfortunes as they have since gone through by the oppression of landlords,
the impossibility of paying rent without money or trade, the want of common
sustenance, with neither house nor clothes to cover them from the inclemen-
cies of the weather, and the most inevitable prospect of entailing the like or
greater miseries upon their breed forever.

I profess, in the sincerity of my heart, that I have not the least personal
interest in endeavoring to promote this necessary work, having no other motive
than the public good of my country, by advancing our trade, providing for
infants, relieving the poor, and giving some pleasure to the rich. I have no children by which I can propose to get a single penny; the youngest being nine
years old, and my wife past childbearing.

MLA CITATION

Swift, Jonathan. "A Modest Proposal." *The Norton Reader: An Anthology of
Nonfiction*, edited by Melissa A. Goldthwaite et al., 15th ed., W. W. Norton,
2020, pp. 711–17.

17. England.

QUESTIONS

1. Identify examples of the reasonable voice of Jonathan Swift's authorial persona, such as the title of the essay itself.

2. Look, in particular, at instances in which Swift's authorial persona proposes shocking things. How does the style of "A Modest Proposal" affect its content?

3. Verbal irony consists of saying one thing and meaning another. At what point in this essay do you begin to suspect that Swift is using irony? What additional evidence of irony can you find?

4. Write a "modest proposal" of your own in the manner of Swift to remedy a real problem; that is, propose an outrageous remedy in a reasonable voice.

NICCOLÒ MACHIAVELLI
The Morals of the Prince

ON THE REASONS WHY MEN ARE PRAISED OR BLAMED—ESPECIALLY PRINCES

IT REMAINS NOW to be seen what style and principles a prince ought to adopt in dealing with his subjects and friends. I know the subject has been treated frequently before, and I'm afraid people will think me rash for trying to do so again, especially since I intend to differ in this discussion from what others have said. But since I intend to write something useful to an understanding reader, it seemed better to go after the real truth of the matter than to repeat what people have imagined. A great many men have imagined states and princedoms such as nobody ever saw or knew in the real world, for there's such a difference between the way we really live and the way we ought to live that the man who neglects the real to study the ideal will learn how to accomplish his ruin, not his salvation. Any man who tries to be good all the time is bound to come to ruin among the great number who are not good. Hence a prince who wants to keep his post must learn how not to be good, and use that knowledge, or refrain from using it, as necessity requires.

Putting aside, then, all the imaginary things that are said about princes, and getting down to the truth, let me say that whenever men are discussed (and especially princes because they are prominent), there are certain qualities that bring them either praise or blame. Thus some are considered generous, others stingy (I use a Tuscan term, since "greedy" in our speech means a man who wants to take other people's goods. We call a man "stingy" who clings to his own); some are givers, others grabbers; some cruel, others merciful; one man

From The Prince *(1532), a book on statecraft written for Giuliano de' Medici (1479–1516), a member of one of the most famous and powerful families of Renaissance Italy. This selection is from an edition translated and edited by Robert M. Adams (1977).*

is treacherous, another faithful; one is feeble and effeminate, another fierce and spirited; one humane, another proud; one lustful, another chaste; one straightforward, another sly; one harsh, another gentle; one serious, another playful; one religious, another skeptical, and so on. I know everyone will agree that among these many qualities a prince certainly ought to have all those that are considered good. But since it is impossible to have and exercise them all, because the conditions of human life simply do not allow it, a prince must be shrewd enough to avoid the public disgrace of those vices that would lose him his state. If he possibly can, he should also guard against vices that will not lose him his state; but if he cannot prevent them, he should not be too worried about indulging them. And furthermore, he should not be too worried about incurring blame for any vice without which he would find it hard to save his state. For if you look at matters carefully, you will see that something resembling virtue, if you follow it, may be your ruin, while something else resembling vice will lead, if you follow it, to your security and well-being.

On Liberality and Stinginess

Let me begin, then, with the first of the qualities mentioned above, by saying that a reputation for liberality is doubtless very fine; but the generosity that earns you that reputation can do you great harm. For if you exercise your generosity in a really virtuous way, as you should, nobody will know of it, and you cannot escape the odium of the opposite vice. Hence if you wish to be widely known as a generous man, you must seize every opportunity to make a big display of your giving. A prince of this character is bound to use up his entire revenue in works of ostentation. Thus, in the end, if he wants to keep a name for generosity, he will have to load his people with exorbitant taxes and squeeze money out of them in every way he can. This is the first step in making him odious to his subjects; for when he is poor, nobody will respect him. Then, when his generosity has angered many and brought rewards to a few, the slightest difficulty will trouble him, and at the first approach of danger, down he goes. If by chance he foresees this, and tries to change his ways, he will immediately be labeled a miser.

Since a prince cannot use this virtue of liberality in such a way as to become known for it unless he harms his own security, he won't mind, if he judges prudently of things, being known as a miser. In due course he will be thought the more liberal man, when people see that his parsimony enables him to live on his income, to defend himself against his enemies, and to undertake major projects without burdening his people with taxes. Thus he will be acting liberally toward all those people from whom he takes nothing (and there are an immense number of them), and in a stingy way toward those people on whom he bestows nothing (and they are very few). In our times, we have seen great things being accomplished only by men who have had the name of misers; all the others have gone under. Pope Julius II, though he used his reputation as a generous man to gain the papacy, sacrificed it in order to be able to make war; the present king of France has waged many wars without levying a single extra tax on his

people, simply because he could take care of the extra expenses out of the savings from his long parsimony. If the present king of Spain had a reputation for
generosity, he would never have been able to undertake so many campaigns, or
win so many of them.

5   Hence a prince who prefers not to rob his subjects, who wants to be able
to defend himself, who wants to avoid poverty and contempt, and who doesn't
want to become a plunderer, should not mind in the least if people consider
him a miser; this is simply one of the vices that enable him to reign. Someone
may object that Caesar used a reputation for generosity to become emperor,
and many other people have also risen in the world, because they were generous
or were supposed to be so. Well, I answer, either you are a prince already, or
you are in the process of becoming one; in the first case, this reputation for
generosity is harmful to you, in the second case it is very necessary. Caesar
was one of those who wanted to become ruler in Rome; but after he had reached
his goal, if he had lived, and had not cut down on his expenses, he would have
ruined the empire itself. Someone may say: there have been plenty of princes,
very successful in warfare, who have had a reputation for generosity. But I
answer: either the prince is spending his own money and that of his subjects,
or he is spending someone else's. In the first case, he ought to be sparing; in
the second case, he ought to spend money like water. Any prince at the head of
his army, which lives on loot, extortion, and plunder, disposes of other people's
property, and is bound to be very generous; otherwise, his soldiers would desert him. You can always be a more generous giver when what you give is not
yours or your subjects'; Cyrus, Caesar, and Alexander[1] were generous in this
way. Spending what belongs to other people does no harm to your reputation,
rather it enhances it; only spending your own substance harms you. And there
is nothing that wears out faster than generosity; even as you practice it, you
lose the means of practicing it, and you become either poor and contemptible
or (in the course of escaping poverty) rapacious and hateful. The thing above all
against which a prince must protect himself is being contemptible and hateful;
generosity leads to both. Thus, it's much wiser to put up with the reputation
of being a miser, which brings you shame without hate, than to be forced—just
because you want to appear generous—into a reputation for rapacity, which
brings shame on you and hate along with it.

ON CRUELTY AND CLEMENCY: WHETHER IT IS BETTER TO BE LOVED OR FEARED

Continuing now with our list of qualities, let me say that every prince should
prefer to be considered merciful rather than cruel, yet he should be careful not
to mismanage this clemency of his. People thought Cesare Borgia[2] was cruel,
but that cruelty of his reorganized the Romagna, united it, and established it

---

1. Persian, Roman, and Macedonian conquerors and rulers, respectively, in ancient times.
2. Son of Pope Alexander VI; he was duke of Romagna, which he subjugated from
1499 to 1502.

in peace and loyalty. Anyone who views the matter realistically will see that this prince was much more merciful than the people of Florence, who, to avoid the reputation of cruelty, allowed Pistoia to be destroyed.[3] Thus, no prince should mind being called cruel for what he does to keep his subjects united and loyal; he may make examples of a very few, but he will be more merciful in reality than those who, in their tenderheartedness, allow disorders to occur, with their attendant murders and lootings. Such turbulence brings harm to an entire community, while the executions ordered by a prince affect only one individual at a time. A new prince, above all others, cannot possibly avoid a name for cruelty, since new states are always in danger. And Virgil, speaking through the mouth of Dido,[4] says:

> My cruel fate
> And doubts attending an unsettled state
> Force me to guard my coast from foreign foes.

Yet a prince should be slow to believe rumors and to commit himself to action on the basis of them. He should not be afraid of his own thoughts; he ought to proceed cautiously, moderating his conduct with prudence and humanity, allowing neither overconfidence to make him careless, nor overtimidity to make him intolerable.

Here the question arises: is it better to be loved than feared, or vice versa? I don't doubt that every prince would like to be both; but since it is hard to accommodate these qualities, if you have to make a choice, to be feared is much safer than to be loved. For it is a good general rule about men, that they are ungrateful, fickle, liars and deceivers, fearful of danger and greedy for gain. While you serve their welfare, they are all yours, offering their blood, their belongings, their lives, and their children's lives, as we noted above—so long as the danger is remote. But when the danger is close at hand, they turn against you. Then, any prince who has relied on their words and has made no other preparations will come to grief; because friendships that are bought at a price, and not with greatness and nobility of soul, may be paid for but they are not acquired, and they cannot be used in time of need. People are less concerned with offending a man who makes himself loved than one who makes himself feared: the reason is that love is a link of obligation which men, because they are rotten, will break any time they think doing so serves their advantage; but fear involves dread of punishment, from which they can never escape.

Still, a prince should make himself feared in such a way that, even if he gets no love, he gets no hate either; because it is perfectly possible to be feared and not hated, and this will be the result if only the prince will keep his hands off the property of his subjects or citizens, and off their women. When he does have to shed blood, he should be sure to have a strong justification and manifest cause; but above all, he should not confiscate people's property, because

3. By unchecked rioting between opposing factions in 1502.
4. Queen of Carthage and tragic heroine of Virgil's epic, the *Aeneid*.

men are quicker to forget the death of a father than the loss of a patrimony. Besides, pretexts for confiscation are always plentiful, it never fails that a prince who starts living by plunder can find reasons to rob someone else. Excuses for proceeding against someone's life are much rarer and more quickly exhausted.

But a prince at the head of his armies and commanding a multitude of soldiers should not care a bit if he is considered cruel; without such a reputation, he could never hold his army together and ready for action. Among the marvelous deeds of Hannibal,[5] this was prime: that, having an immense army, which included men of many different races and nations, and which he led to battle in distant countries, he never allowed them to fight among themselves or to rise against him, whether his fortune was good or bad. The reason for this could only be his inhuman cruelty, which, along with his countless other talents, made him an object of awe and terror to his soldiers; and without the cruelty, his other qualities would never have sufficed. The historians who pass snap judgments on these matters admire his accomplishments and at the same time condemn the cruelty which was their main cause.

10   When I say, "His other qualities would never have sufficed," we can see that this is true from the example of Scipio,[6] an outstanding man not only among those of his own time, but in all recorded history; yet his armies revolted in Spain, for no other reason than his excessive leniency in allowing his soldiers more freedom than military discipline permits. Fabius Maximus rebuked him in the senate for this failing, calling him the corrupter of the Roman armies. When a lieutenant of Scipio's plundered the Locrians,[7] he took no action in behalf of the people, and did nothing to discipline that insolent lieutenant; again, this was the result of his easygoing nature. Indeed, when someone in the senate wanted to excuse him on this occasion, he said there are many men who knew better how to avoid error themselves than how to correct error in others. Such a soft temper would in time have tarnished the fame and glory of Scipio, had he brought it to the office of emperor; but as he lived under the control of the senate, this harmful quality of his not only remained hidden but was considered creditable.

Returning to the question of being feared or loved, I conclude that since men love at their own inclination but can be made to fear at the inclination of the prince, a shrewd prince will lay his foundations on what is under his own control, not on what is controlled by others. He should simply take pains not to be hated, as I said.

---

5. Carthaginian general who led a massive but unsuccessful invasion of Rome in 218–203 B.C.E.

6. Roman general whose successful invasion of Carthage in 203 B.C.E. caused Hannibal's army to be recalled from Italy. The episode described here occurred in 206 B.C.E.

7. Fabius Maximus, not only a senator but also a high public official and general who had fought against Hannibal in Italy; Locrians, people of Sicily defeated by Scipio in 205 B.C.E. and placed under Q. Pleminius.

THE WAY PRINCES SHOULD KEEP THEIR WORD

How praiseworthy it is for a prince to keep his word and live with integrity rather than by craftiness, everyone understands; yet we see from recent experience that those princes have accomplished most who paid little heed to keeping their promises, but who knew how craftily to manipulate the minds of men. In the end, they won out over those who tried to act honestly.

You should consider then, that there are two ways of fighting, one with laws and the other with force. The first is properly a human method, the second belongs to beasts. But as the first method does not always suffice, you sometimes have to turn to the second. Thus a prince must know how to make good use of both the beast and the man. Ancient writers made subtle note of this fact when they wrote that Achilles and many other princes of antiquity were sent to be reared by Chiron the centaur, who trained them in his discipline.[8] Having a teacher who is half man and half beast can only mean that a prince must know how to use both these two natures, and that one without the other has no lasting effect.

Since a prince must know how to use the character of beasts, he should pick for imitation the fox and the lion. As the lion cannot protect himself from traps, and the fox cannot defend himself from wolves, you have to be a fox in order to be wary of traps, and a lion to overawe the wolves. Those who try to live by the lion alone are badly mistaken. Thus a prudent prince cannot and should not keep his word when to do so would go against his interest, or when the reasons that made him pledge it no longer apply. Doubtless if all men were good, this rule would be bad; but since they are a sad lot, and keep no faith with you, you in your turn are under no obligation to keep it with them.

Besides, a prince will never lack for legitimate excuses to explain away his breaches of faith. Modern history will furnish innumerable examples of this behavior, showing how many treaties and promises have been made null and void by the faithlessness of princes, and how the man succeeded best who knew best how to play the fox. But it is a necessary part of this nature that you must conceal it carefully; you must be a great liar and hypocrite. Men are so simple of mind, and so much dominated by their immediate needs, that a deceitful man will always find plenty who are ready to be deceived. One of many recent examples calls for mention. Alexander VI[9] never did anything else, never had another thought, except to deceive men, and he always found fresh material to work on. Never was there a man more convincing in his assertions, who sealed his promises with more solemn oaths, and who observed them less. Yet his deceptions were always successful, because he knew exactly how to manage this sort of business.

In actual fact, a prince may not have all the admirable qualities we listed, but it is very necessary that he should seem to have them. Indeed, I will venture to say that when you have them and exercise them all the time, they are harm-

15

---

8. Achilles, foremost among the Greek heroes in the Trojan War; Chiron, mythical half man and half horse, said to have taught the arts of war and peace, including hunting, medicine, music, and prophecy.

9. Pope from 1492 to 1503.

ful to you; when you just seem to have them, they are useful. It is good to appear merciful, truthful, humane, sincere, and religious; it is good to be so in reality. But you must keep your mind so disposed that, in case of need, you can turn to the exact contrary. This has to be understood: a prince, and especially a new prince, cannot possibly exercise all those virtues for which men are called "good." To preserve the state, he often has to do things against his word, against charity, against humanity, against religion. Thus he has to have a mind ready to shift as the winds of fortune and the varying circumstances of life may dictate. And as I said above, he should not depart from the good if he can hold to it, but he should be ready to enter on evil if he has to.

Hence a prince should take great care never to drop a word that does not seem imbued with the five good qualities noted above; to anyone who sees or hears him, he should appear all compassion, all honor, all humanity, all integrity, all religion. Nothing is more necessary than to seem to have this last virtue. Men in general judge more by the sense of sight than by the sense of touch, because everyone can see but only a few can test by feeling. Everyone sees what you seem to be, few know what you really are; and those few do not dare take a stand against the general opinion, supported by the majesty of the government. In the actions of all men, and especially of princes who are not subject to a court of appeal, we must always look to the end. Let a prince, therefore, win victories and uphold his state; his methods will always be considered worthy, and everyone will praise them, because the masses are always impressed by the superficial appearance of things, and by the outcome of an enterprise. And the world consists of nothing but the masses; the few who have no influence when the many feel secure. A certain prince of our own time, whom it's just as well not to name,[10] preaches nothing but peace and mutual trust, yet he is the determined enemy of both; and if on several different occasions he had observed either, he would have lost both his reputation and his throne.

MLA CITATION

Machiavelli, Niccolò. "The Morals of the Prince." *The Norton Reader: An Anthology of Nonfiction*, edited by Melissa A. Goldthwaite et al., 15th ed., W. W. Norton, 2020, pp. 718–24.

QUESTIONS

1. This selection contains four sections of *The Prince*: "On the Reasons Why Men Are Praised or Blamed—Especially Princes"; "On Liberality and Stinginess"; "On Cruelty and Clemency: Whether It Is Better to Be Loved or Feared"; and "The Way Princes Should Keep Their Word." How, in each section, does Niccolò Machiavelli contrast the real and the ideal, what he calls "the way we really live and the way we ought to live" (paragraph 1)? Mark some of the sentences in which he expresses these contrasts.

10. Probably Ferdinand of Spain, then allied with the house of Medici.

2. Rewrite some of Machiavelli's advice to princes less forcibly and shockingly, and more palatably. For example, "Any man who tries to be good all the time is bound to come to ruin among the great number who are not good" (paragraph 1) might be rewritten as "Good men are often taken advantage of and harmed by men who are not good."

3. Describe Machiavelli's view of human nature. How do his views of government follow from it?

4. Machiavelli might be described as a sixteenth-century spin doctor teaching a ruler how to package himself. Adapt his advice to a current figure in national, state, or local politics, and write about that figure in a brief essay.

HENRY DAVID THOREAU
The Battle of the Ants

ONE DAY WHEN I went out to my wood-pile, or rather my pile of stumps, I observed two large ants, the one red, the other much larger, nearly half an inch long, and black, fiercely contending with one another. Having once got hold they never let go, but struggled and wrestled and rolled on the chips incessantly. Looking farther, I was surprised to find that the chips were covered with such combatants, that it was not a *duellum*, but a *bellum*, a war between two races of ants, the red always pitted against the black, and frequently two red ones to one black. The legions of these Myrmidons[1] covered all the hills and vales in my wood-yard, and the ground was already strewn with the dead and dying, both red and black. It was the only battle which I have ever witnessed, the only battle-field I ever trod while the battle was raging; internecine war; the red republicans on the one hand, and the black imperialists on the other. On every side they were engaged in deadly combat, yet without any noise that I could hear, and human soldiers never fought so resolutely. I watched a couple that were fast locked in each other's embraces, in a little sunny valley amid the chips, now at noonday prepared to fight till the sun went down, or life went out. The smaller red champion had fastened himself like a vice to his adversary's front, and through all the tumblings on that field never for an instant ceased to gnaw at one of his feelers near the root, having already caused the other to go by the board; while the stronger black one dashed him from side to side, and, as I saw on looking nearer, had already divested him of several of his members. They fought with more pertinacity than bulldogs. Neither manifested the least disposition to retreat. It was evident that their battle-cry was "Conquer or die." In the meanwhile there came along a single red ant

From Henry David Thoreau's book, Walden (1854), *an account of his life in a small cabin on Walden Pond, outside the village of Concord, Massachusetts.*

1. Achilles's powerful soldiers in Homer's *Iliad.*

on the hillside of this valley, evidently full of excitement, who either had des-
patched his foe, or had not yet taken part in the battle; probably the latter, for
he had lost none of his limbs; whose mother had charged him to return with
his shield or upon it. Or perchance he was some Achilles, who had nourished
his wrath apart, and had now come to avenge or rescue his Patroclus.[2] He saw
this unequal combat from afar—for the blacks were nearly twice the size of
the red—he drew near with rapid pace till he stood on his guard within half an
inch of the combatants; then, watching his opportunity, he sprang upon the
black warrior, and commenced his operations near the root of his right fore leg,
leaving the foe to select among his own members; and so there were three
united for life, as if a new kind of attraction had been invented which put all
other locks and cements to shame. I should not have wondered by this time to
find that they had their respective musical bands stationed on some eminent
chip, and playing their national airs the while, to excite the slow and cheer the
dying combatants. I was myself excited somewhat even as if they had been
men. The more you think of it, the less the difference. And certainly there is
not the fight recorded in Concord history, at least, if in the history of America,
that will bear a moment's comparison with this, whether for the numbers
engaged in it, or for the patriotism and heroism displayed. For numbers and
for carnage it was an Austerlitz or Dresden.[3] Concord Fight! Two killed on
the patriots' side, and Luther Blanchard wounded! Why here every ant was a
Buttrick—"Fire! for God's sake fire!"—and thousands shared the fate of Davis
and Hosmer. There was not one hireling there. I have no doubt that it was a
principle they fought for, as much as our ancestors, and not to avoid a three-
penny tax on their tea; and the results of this battle will be as important and
memorable to those whom it concerns as those of the battle of Bunker Hill, at
least.

I took up the chip on which the three I have particularly described were
struggling, carried into my house, and placed it under a tumbler on my windowsill, in order to see the issue. Holding a microscope to the first-mentioned
red ant, I saw that, though he was assiduously gnawing at the near fore leg of
his enemy, having severed his remaining feeler, his own breast was all torn away,
exposing what vitals he had there to the jaws of the black warrior, whose breast-
plate was apparently too thick for him to pierce; and the dark carbuncles of the
sufferer's eyes shone with ferocity such as war only could excite. They struggled half an hour longer under the tumbler, and when I looked again the black
soldier had severed the heads of his foes from their bodies, and the still living
heads were hanging on either side of him like ghastly trophies at his saddle-
bow, still apparently as firmly fastened as ever, and he was endeavoring with

2. Greek warrior and friend whose death Achilles avenges in the *Iliad*. Achilles had previously refused to fight after a falling-out with Agamemnon, the leader of the Greek army.
3. Austerlitz and Dresden were bloody Napoleonic victories. The battles at Lexington
and Concord, opening the American Revolution, took place on April 19, 1775; the names
that follow are those of men who took part, and the words "Fire! for God's sake fire!"
were those that, by popular account, started the war.

feeble struggles, being without feelers, and with only the remnant of a leg, and I know not how many other wounds, to divest himself of them; which at length, after half an hour more, he accomplished. I raised the glass, and he went off over the window-sill in that crippled state. Whether he finally survived that combat, and spent the remainder of his days in some Hôtel des Invalides,[4] I do not know; but I thought that his industry would not be worth much thereafter. I never learned which party was victorious, nor the cause of the war, but I felt for the rest of that day as if I had my feelings excited and harrowed by witnessing the struggle, the ferocity and carnage, of a human battle before my door.

Kirby and Spence tell us that the battles of ants have long been celebrated and the date of them recorded, though they say that Huber[5] is the only modern author who appears to have witnessed them. "Aeneas Sylvius," say they, "after giving a very circumstantial account of one contested with great obstinacy by a great and small species on the trunk of a pear tree," adds that "'this action was fought in the pontificate of Eugenius the Fourth, in the presence of Nicholas Pistoriensis, an eminent lawyer, who related the whole history of the battle with the greatest fidelity.' A similar engagement between great and small ants is recorded by Olaus Magnus, in which the small ones, being victorious, are said to have buried the bodies of their own soldiers, but left those of their giant enemies a prey to the birds. This event happened previous to the expulsion of the tyrant Christiern the Second from Sweden." The battle which I witnessed took place in the Presidency of Polk, five years before the passage of Webster's Fugitive-Slave Bill.[6]

MLA CITATION

Thoreau, Henry David. "The Battle of the Ants." *The Norton Reader: An Anthology of Nonfiction*, edited by Melissa A. Goldthwaite et al., 15th ed., W. W. Norton, 2020, pp. 725–27.

QUESTIONS

1. Henry David Thoreau uses the Latin word *bellum* to describe the battle of the ants and follows it with a reference to the Myrmidons, the soldiers of Achilles in Homer's *Iliad* (paragraph 1). Locate additional examples of this kind of allusion. How does it work? Why does Thoreau compare the ants to Greek soldiers?

2. Ordinarily we speak of accounts of natural events as "natural history" and accounts of human events as "history." How does Thoreau, in this selection, blur the distinction? For what purpose?

---

4. French hospital for wounded soldiers and sailors.

5. Kirby and Spence, nineteenth-century American entomologists; François Huber (1750–1831), a great Swiss entomologist.

6. Passed in 1851.

3. Look up a description of the behavior of ants in a book by one of the entomologists Thoreau refers to or in another scientific text. Compare the scientist's style with Thoreau's. Take another event in nature and describe it twice, once in scientific and once in allusive language. Or write an essay in which you describe and analyze the differences between the scientist's style and Thoreau's.

GEORGE ORWELL
Shooting an Elephant

I N MOULMEIN, in Lower Burma, I was hated by large numbers of people— the only time in my life that I have been important enough for this to happen to me. I was sub-divisional police officer of the town, and in an aimless, petty kind of way anti-European feeling was very bitter. No one had the guts to raise a riot, but if a European woman went through the bazaars alone somebody would probably spit betel juice over her dress. As a police officer I was an obvious target and was baited whenever it seemed safe to do so. When a nimble Burman tripped me up on the football field and the referee (another Burman) looked the other way, the crowd yelled with hideous laughter. This happened more than once. In the end the sneering yellow faces of young men that met me everywhere, the insults hooted after me when I was at a safe distance, got badly on my nerves. The young Buddhist priests were the worst of all. There were several thousands of them in the town and none of them seemed to have anything to do except stand on street corners and jeer at Europeans.

All this was perplexing and upsetting. For at that time I had already made up my mind that imperialism was an evil thing and the sooner I chucked up my job and got out of it the better. Theoretically—and secretly, of course—I was all for the Burmese and all against their oppressors, the British. As for the job I was doing, I hated it more bitterly than I can perhaps make clear. In a job like that you see the dirty work of Empire at close quarters. The wretched prisoners huddling in the stinking cages of the lock-ups, the grey, cowed faces of the long-term convicts, the scarred buttocks of the men who had been flogged with bamboos—all these oppressed me with an intolerable sense of guilt. But I could get nothing into perspective. I was young and ill-educated and I had had to think out my problems in the utter silence that is imposed on every Englishman in the East. I did not even know that the British Empire is dying, still less did I know that it is a great deal better than the younger empires that are going to supplant it. All I knew was that I was stuck between my hatred of the empire I served and my rage against the evil-spirited little beasts who tried to make my job impossible. With one part of my mind I thought of the

Published in the periodical New Writing *(1936), at the beginning of George Orwell's writing career and soon after his novel* Burmese Days *(1934) appeared. The essay later became the title piece in the collection* Shooting an Elephant, and Other Essays *(1950).*

British Raj[1] as an unbreakable tyranny, as something clamped down, in *saecula saeculorum*,[2] upon the will of prostrate peoples; with another part I thought that the greatest joy in the world would be to drive a bayonet into a Buddhist priest's guts. Feelings like these are the normal by-products of imperialism; ask any Anglo-Indian official, if you can catch him off duty.

One day something happened which in a roundabout way was enlightening. It was a tiny incident in itself, but it gave me a better glimpse than I had had before of the real nature of imperialism—the real motives for which despotic governments act. Early one morning the sub-inspector at a police station the other end of the town rang me up on the 'phone and said that an elephant was ravaging the bazaar. Would I please come and do something about it? I did not know what I could do, but I wanted to see what was happening and I got on to a pony and started out. I took my rifle, an old .44 Winchester and much too small to kill an elephant, but I thought the noise might be useful *in terrorem*. Various Burmans stopped me on the way and told me about the elephant's doings. It was not, of course, a wild elephant, but a tame one which had gone "must."[3] It had been chained up, as tame elephants always are when their attack of "must" is due, but on the previous night it had broken its chain and escaped. Its mahout, the only person who could manage it when it was in that state, had set out in pursuit, but had taken the wrong direction and was now twelve hours' journey away, and in the morning the elephant had suddenly reappeared in the town. The Burmese population had no weapons and were quite helpless against it. It had already destroyed somebody's bamboo hut, killed a cow and raided some fruit-stalls and devoured the stock; also it had met the municipal rubbish van and, when the driver jumped out and took to his heels, had turned the van over and inflicted violences upon it.

The Burmese sub-inspector and some Indian constables were waiting for me in the quarter where the elephant had been seen. It was a very poor quarter, a labyrinth of squalid bamboo huts, thatched with palm-leaf, winding all over a steep hillside. I remember that it was a cloudy, stuffy morning at the beginning of the rains. We began questioning the people as to where the elephant had gone and, as usual, failed to get any definite information. That is invariably the case in the East; a story always sounds clear enough at a distance, but the nearer you get to the scene of events the vaguer it becomes. Some of the people said that the elephant had gone in one direction, some said that he had gone in another, some professed not even to have heard of any elephant. I had almost made up my mind that the whole story was a pack of lies, when we heard yells a little distance away. There was a loud, scandalized cry of "Go away, child! Go away this instant!" and an old woman with a switch in her hand came round the corner of a hut, violently shooing away a crowd of naked children. Some more women followed, clicking their tongues and exclaiming; evidently there was something that the children ought not to have seen. I rounded the

1. Imperial government of British India and Burma.
2. Forever and ever.
3. Gone into sexual heat.

hut and saw a man's dead body sprawling in the mud. He was an Indian, a black Dravidian coolie,[4] almost naked, and he could not have been dead many minutes. The people said that the elephant had come suddenly upon him round the corner of the hut, caught him with its trunk, put its foot on his back and ground him into the earth. This was the rainy season and the ground was soft, and his face had scored a trench a foot deep and a couple of yards long. He was lying on his belly with arms crucified and head sharply twisted to one side. His face was coated with mud, the eyes wide open, the teeth bared and grinning with an expression of unendurable agony. (Never tell me, by the way, that the dead look peaceful. Most of the corpses I have seen looked devilish.) The friction of the great beast's foot had stripped the skin from his back as neatly as one skins a rabbit. As soon as I saw the dead man I sent an orderly to a friend's house nearby to borrow an elephant rifle. I had already sent back the pony, not wanting it to go mad with fright and throw me if it smelt the elephant.

5   The orderly came back in a few minutes with a rifle and five cartridges, and meanwhile some Burmans had arrived and told us that the elephant was in the paddy fields below, only a few hundred yards away. As I started forward practically the whole population of the quarter flocked out of the houses and followed me. They had seen the rifle and were all shouting excitedly that I was going to shoot the elephant. They had not shown much interest in the elephant when he was merely ravaging their homes, but it was different now that he was going to be shot. It was a bit of fun to them, as it would be to an English crowd; besides they wanted the meat. It made me vaguely uneasy. I had no intention of shooting the elephant—I had merely sent for the rifle to defend myself if necessary—and it is always unnerving to have a crowd following you. I marched down the hill, looking and feeling a fool, with the rifle over my shoulder and an ever-growing army of people jostling at my heels. At the bottom, when you got away from the huts, there was a metalled road and beyond that a miry waste of paddy fields a thousand yards across, not yet ploughed but soggy from the first rains and dotted with coarse grass. The elephant was standing eight yards from the road, his left side towards us. He took not the slightest notice of the crowd's approach. He was tearing up bunches of grass, beating them against his knees to clean them and stuffing them into his mouth.

I had halted on the road. As soon as I saw the elephant I knew with perfect certainty that I ought not to shoot him. It is a serious matter to shoot a working elephant—it is comparable to destroying a huge and costly piece of machinery—and obviously one ought not to do it if it can possibly be avoided. And at that distance, peacefully eating, the elephant looked no more dangerous than a cow. I thought then and I think now that his attack of "must" was already passing off; in which case he would merely wander harmlessly about until the mahout came back and caught him. Moreover, I did not in the least

4. When Orwell wrote this essay, the word "coolie" referred to a hired worker from southern India. The word became a slur against immigrant workers in the United States, India, and the Caribbean, and is considered to be an offensive term today.

want to shoot him. I decided that I would watch him for a little while to make sure that he did not turn savage again, and then go home.

But at that moment I glanced round at the crowd that had followed me. It was an immense crowd, two thousand at the least and growing every minute. It blocked the road for a long distance on either side. I looked at the sea of yellow faces above the garish clothes—faces all happy and excited over this bit of fun, all certain that the elephant was going to be shot. They were watching me as they would watch a conjurer about to perform a trick. They did not like me, but with the magical rifle in my hands I was momentarily worth watching. And suddenly I realized that I should have to shoot the elephant after all. The people expected it of me and I had got to do it; I could feel their two thousand wills pressing me forward, irresistibly. And it was at this moment, as I stood there with the rifle in my hands, that I first grasped the hollowness, the futility of the white man's dominion in the East. Here was I, the white man with his gun, standing in front of the unarmed native crowd—seemingly the leading actor of the piece; but in reality I was only an absurd puppet pushed to and fro by the will of those yellow faces behind. I perceived in this moment that when the white man turns tyrant it is his own freedom that he destroys. He becomes a sort of hollow, posing dummy, the conventionalized figure of a sahib. For it is the condition of his rule that he shall spend his life in trying to impress the "natives," and so in every crisis he has got to do what the "natives" expect of him. He wears a mask, and his face grows to fit it. I had got to shoot the elephant. I had committed myself to doing it when I sent for the rifle. A sahib has got to act like a sahib; he has got to appear resolute, to know his own mind and do definite things. To come all that way, rifle in hand, with two thousand people marching at my heels, and then to trail feebly away, having done nothing—no, that was impossible. The crowd would laugh at me. And my whole life, every white man's life in the East, was one long struggle not to be laughed at.

But I did not want to shoot the elephant. I watched him beating his bunch of grass against his knees, with that preoccupied grandmotherly air that elephants have. It seemed to me that it would be murder to shoot him. At that age I was not squeamish about killing animals, but I had never shot an elephant and never wanted to. (Somehow it always seems worse to kill a *large* animal.) Besides, there was the beast's owner to be considered. Alive, the elephant was worth at least a hundred pounds; dead, he would only be worth the value of his tusks, five pounds, possibly. But I had got to act quickly. I turned to some experienced-looking Burmans who had been there when we arrived, and asked them how the elephant had been behaving. They all said the same thing: he took no notice of you if you left him alone, but he might charge if you went too close to him.

It was perfectly clear to me what I ought to do. I ought to walk up to within, say, twenty-five yards of the elephant and test his behavior. If he charged, I could shoot; if he took no notice of me, it would be safe to leave him until the mahout came back. But also I knew that I was going to do no such thing. I was a poor shot with a rifle and the ground was soft mud into which one would sink at every step. If the elephant charged and I missed him, I should have about as much chance as a toad under a steam-roller. But even then I was not thinking

particularly of my own skin, only of the watchful yellow faces behind. For at that
moment, with the crowd watching me, I was not afraid in the ordinary sense, as
I would have been if I had been alone. A white man mustn't be frightened in
front of "natives"; and so, in general, he isn't frightened. The sole thought in my
mind was that if anything went wrong those two thousand Burmans would see
me pursued, caught, trampled on and reduced to a grinning corpse like that
Indian up the hill. And if that happened it was quite probable that some of them
would laugh. That would never do. There was only one alternative. I shoved the
cartridges into the magazine and lay down on the road to get a better aim.

10   The crowd grew very still, and a deep, low, happy sigh, as of people who see
the theatre curtain go up at last, breathed from innumerable throats. They were
going to have their bit of fun after all. The rifle was a beautiful German thing
with cross-hair sights. I did not then know that in shooting an elephant one
would shoot to cut an imaginary bar running from ear-hole to ear-hole. I ought,
therefore, as the elephant was sideways on, to have aimed straight at his ear-
hole; actually I aimed several inches in front of this, thinking the brain would
be further forward.

When I pulled the trigger I did not hear the bang or feel the kick—one
never does when a shot goes home—but I heard the devilish roar of glee that
went up from the crowd. In that instant, in too short a time, one would have
thought, even for the bullet to get there, a mysterious, terrible change had come
over the elephant. He neither stirred nor fell, but every line of his body had
altered. He looked suddenly stricken, shrunken, immensely old, as though the
frightful impact of the bullet had paralysed him without knocking him down.
At last, after what seemed a long time—it might have been five seconds, I dare
say—he sagged flabbily to his knees. His mouth slobbered. An enormous senil-
ity seemed to have settled upon him. One could have imagined him thousands
of years old. I fired again into the same spot. At the second shot he did not
collapse but climbed with desperate slowness to his feet and stood weakly
upright, with legs sagging and head drooping. I fired a third time. That was
the shot that did for him. You could see the agony of it jolt his whole body and
knock the last remnant of strength from his legs. But in falling he seemed for
a moment to rise, for as his hind legs collapsed beneath him he seemed to tower
upward like a huge rock toppling, his trunk reaching skywards like a tree. He
trumpeted, for the first and only time. And then down he came, his belly towards
me, with a crash that seemed to shake the ground even where I lay.

I got up. The Burmans were already racing past me across the mud. It was
obvious that the elephant would never rise again, but he was not dead. He was
breathing very rhythmically with long rattling gasps, his great mound of a side
painfully rising and falling. His mouth was wide open—I could see far down
into caverns of pale pink throat. I waited a long time for him to die, but his
breathing did not weaken. Finally I fired my two remaining shots into the spot
where I thought his heart must be. The thick blood welled out of him like red
velvet, but still he did not die. His body did not even jerk when the shots hit
him, the tortured breathing continued without a pause. He was dying, very
slowly and in great agony, but in some world remote from me where not even a

bullet could damage him further. I felt that I had got to put an end to that dreadful noise. It seemed dreadful to see the great beast lying there, powerless to move and yet powerless to die, and not even to be able to finish him. I sent back for my small rifle and poured shot after shot into his heart and down his throat. They seemed to make no impression. The tortured gasps continued as steadily as the ticking of a clock.

In the end I could not stand it any longer and went away. I heard later that it took him half an hour to die. Burmans were bringing dahs[5] and baskets even before I left, and I was told they had stripped his body almost to the bones by the afternoon.

Afterwards, of course, there were endless discussions about the shooting of the elephant. The owner was furious, but he was only an Indian and could do nothing. Besides, legally I had done the right thing, for a mad elephant has to be killed, like a mad dog, if its owner fails to control it. Among the Europeans opinion was divided. The older men said I was right, the younger men said it was a damn shame to shoot an elephant for killing a coolie, because an elephant was worth more than any damn Coringhee coolie.[6] And afterwards I was very glad that the coolie had been killed; it put me legally in the right and it gave me a sufficient pretext for shooting the elephant. I often wondered whether any of the others grasped that I had done it solely to avoid looking a fool.

MLA CITATION

Orwell, George. "Shooting an Elephant." *The Norton Reader: An Anthology of Nonfiction*, edited by Melissa A. Goldthwaite et al., 15th ed., W. W. Norton, 2020, pp. 728–33.

QUESTIONS

1. Why did George Orwell shoot the elephant? Account for the motives that led him to shoot, and then categorize them as personal motives, circumstantial motives, social motives, or political motives. Is it easy to assign his motives to categories? Why or why not?

2. In this essay the proportion of narrative to analysis is high. Mark each paragraph as narrative or analytic, and note, in particular, how much analysis Orwell places in the middle of the essay. What are the advantages and disadvantages of having it there rather than at the beginning or the end of the essay?

3. Facts ordinarily do not speak for themselves. How does Orwell present his facts to make them speak in support of his analytic points? Look, for example, at the death of the elephant (paragraphs 11 to 13).

4. Write an essay in which you present a personal experience that illuminates a larger issue: schooling, affirmative action, homelessness, law enforcement, taxes, or some other local or national issue.

---

5. Butcher knives.
6. Hired worker from the seaport of Coringa, in Madras, India.

ABRAHAM LINCOLN
Second Inaugural Address

A T THIS SECOND appearing to take the oath of the presidential office, there is less occasion for an extended address than there was at the first. Then a statement, somewhat in detail, of a course to be pursued, seemed fitting and proper. Now, at the expiration of four years, during which public declarations have been constantly called forth on every point and phase of the great contest which still absorbs the attention, and engrosses the energies of the nation, little that is new could be presented. The progress of our arms, upon which all else chiefly depends, is as well known to the public as to myself; and it is, I trust, reasonably satisfactory and encouraging to all. With high hope for the future, no prediction in regard to it is ventured.

On the occasion corresponding to this four years ago, all thoughts were anxiously directed to an impending civil war. All dreaded it—all sought to avert it. While the inaugural address was being delivered from this place, devoted altogether to *saving* the Union without war, insurgent agents were in the city seeking to *destroy* it without war—seeking to dissolve the Union, and divide effects, by negotiation. Both parties deprecated war; but one of them would *make* war rather than let the nation survive; and the other would *accept* war rather than let it perish. And the war came.

One-eighth of the whole population were colored slaves, not distributed generally over the Union, but localized in the Southern part of it. These slaves constituted a peculiar and powerful interest. All knew that this interest was, somehow, the cause of the war. To strengthen, perpetuate, and extend this interest was the object for which the insurgents would rend the Union, even by war; while the government claimed no right to do more than to restrict the territorial enlargement of it. Neither party expected for the war, the magnitude, or the duration, which it has already attained. Neither anticipated that the *cause* of the conflict might cease with, or even before, the conflict itself should cease. Each looked for an easier triumph, and a result less fundamental and astounding. Both read the same Bible, and pray to the same God; and each invokes His aid against the other. It may seem strange that any men should dare to ask a just God's assistance in wringing their bread from the sweat of other men's faces; but let us judge not that we be not judged.[1] The prayers of both could not be answered; that of neither has been answered fully. The Almighty has His own purposes. "Woe unto the world because of offenses! for it must needs

---

Delivered on March 4, 1865, as Abraham Lincoln took office for a second term as America's sixteenth president. In the nineteenth century U.S. presidents took office in March, not in January as they do today.

1. Lincoln alludes to Jesus's statement in the Sermon on the Mount—"Judge not, that ye be not judged" (Matthew 7:1)—and to God's curse on Adam—"In the sweat of thy face shalt thou eat bread, till thou return unto the ground" (Genesis 3:19).

be that offenses come; but woe to that man by whom the offense cometh!"[2] If we shall suppose that American slavery is one of those offenses which, in the providence of God, must needs come, but which, having continued through His appointed time, He now wills to remove, and that He gives to both North and South, this terrible war, as the woe due to those by whom the offense came, shall we discern therein any departure from those divine attributes which the believers in a Living God always ascribe to Him? Fondly do we hope—fervently do we pray—that this mighty scourge of war may speedily pass away. Yet, if God wills that it continue, until all the wealth piled by the bondman's two hundred and fifty years of unrequited toil shall be sunk, and until every drop of blood drawn with the lash, shall be paid by another drawn with the sword, as was said three thousand years ago, so still it must be said "the judgments of the Lord are true and righteous altogether."[3]

With malice toward none; with charity for all; with firmness in the right, as God gives us to see the right, let us strive on to finish the work we are in; to bind up the nation's wounds; to care for him who shall have borne the battle, and for his widow, and his orphan—to do all which may achieve and cherish a just, and a lasting peace, among ourselves, and with all nations.

MLA CITATION

Lincoln, Abraham. "Second Inaugural Address." *The Norton Reader: An Anthology of Nonfiction*, edited by Melissa A. Goldthwaite et al., 15th ed., W. W. Norton, 2020, pp. 734–35.

QUESTIONS

1. Abraham Lincoln's speech includes both allusions to and direct quotations from the Bible. What argument do these references support? Why might biblical references be important as a persuasive technique for Lincoln's audience?

2. In paragraphs 1 and 2, Lincoln reflects on his first inaugural speech in order to set the stage for his present speech. Find a copy of the first inaugural speech online or in the library. In what ways does that thirty-five-paragraph speech help inform this four-paragraph speech? What aspects of the "Second Inaugural Address" does it clarify?

3. Read the text of a more recent presidential address and compare or contrast it to Lincoln's address. (John F. Kennedy's inaugural address follows this selection; others can be found online.) Does the more recent address use a similar style, language, or set of allusions? How does it differ?

2. From Jesus's speech to his disciples (Matthew 18:7).
3. Psalms 19:9.

JOHN F. KENNEDY
Inaugural Address

W E OBSERVE TODAY not a victory of a party but a celebration of freedom—symbolizing an end as well as a beginning—signifying renewal as well as change. For I have sworn before you and Almighty God the same solemn oath our forebears prescribed nearly a century and three quarters ago.

The world is very different now. For man holds in his mortal hands the power to abolish all forms of human poverty and all forms of human life. And yet the same revolutionary beliefs for which our forebears fought are still at issue around the globe—the belief that the rights of man come not from the generosity of the state but from the hand of God.

We dare not forget today that we are the heirs of that first revolution. Let the word go forth from this time and place, to friend and foe alike, that the torch has been passed to a new generation of Americans—born in this century, tempered by war, disciplined by a hard and bitter peace, proud of our ancient heritage—and unwilling to witness or permit the slow undoing of those human rights to which this nation has always been committed, and to which we are committed today at home and around the world.

Let every nation know, whether it wishes us well or ill, that we shall pay any price, bear any burden, meet any hardship, support any friend, oppose any foe to assure the survival and success of liberty.

5   This much we pledge—and more.

To those old allies whose cultural and spiritual origins we share, we pledge the loyalty of faithful friends. United, there is little we cannot do in a host of cooperative ventures. Divided, there is little we can do—for we dare not meet a powerful challenge at odds and split asunder.

To those new states whom we welcome to the ranks of the free, we pledge our word that one form of colonial control shall not have passed away merely to be replaced by a far more iron tyranny. We shall not always expect to find them supporting our view. But we shall always hope to find them strongly supporting their own freedom—and to remember that, in the past, those who foolishly sought power by riding the back of the tiger ended up inside.

To those peoples in the huts and villages of half the globe struggling to break the bonds of mass misery, we pledge our best efforts to help them help themselves, for whatever period is required—not because the Communists may be doing it, not because we seek their votes, but because it is right. If a free society cannot help the many who are poor, it cannot save the few who are rich.

To our sister republics south of our border,[1] we offer a special pledge—to convert our good words into good deeds—in a new alliance for progress—to

---

Inaugural address of John F. Kennedy (1917–1963), America's thirty-fifth president, delivered on January 20, 1961.

1. In this paragraph, Kennedy makes many references to Cuba, which by 1961 had turned to communism under Fidel Castro and had allied itself with the Soviet Union.

assist free men and free governments in casting off the chains of poverty. But this peaceful revolution of hope cannot become the prey of hostile powers. Let all our neighbors know that we shall join with them to oppose aggression or subversion anywhere in the Americas. And let every other power know that this hemisphere intends to remain the master of its own house.

To that world assembly of sovereign states, the United Nations, our last best hope in an age where the instruments of war have far outpaced the instruments of peace, we renew our pledge of support—to prevent it from becoming merely a forum for invective—to strengthen its shield of the new and the weak—and to enlarge the area in which its writ may run.

Finally, to those nations who would make themselves our adversary, we offer not a pledge but a request: that both sides begin anew the quest for peace, before the dark powers of destruction unleashed by science[2] engulf all humanity in planned or accidental self-destruction.

We dare not tempt them with weakness. For only when our arms are sufficient beyond doubt can we be certain beyond doubt that they will never be employed.

But neither can two great and powerful groups of nations take comfort from our present course—both sides overburdened by the cost of modern weapons, both rightly alarmed by the steady spread of the deadly atom, yet both racing to alter that uncertain balance of terror that stays the hand of mankind's final war.

So let us begin anew—remembering on both sides that civility is not a sign of weakness, and sincerity is always subject to proof. Let us never negotiate out of fear. But let us never fear to negotiate.

Let both sides explore what problems unite us instead of belaboring those problems which divide us. Let both sides, for the first time, formulate serious and precise proposals for the inspection and control of arms—and bring the absolute power to destroy other nations under the absolute control of all nations.

Let both sides seek to invoke the wonders of science instead of its terrors. Together let us explore the stars, conquer the deserts, eradicate disease, tap the ocean depths, and encourage the arts and commerce.

Let both sides unite to heed in all corners of the earth the command of Isaiah—to "undo the heavy burdens and to let the oppressed go free."[3]

And if a beachhead of cooperation may push back the jungle of suspicion, let both sides join in creating a new endeavor—not a new balance of power but a new world of law, where the strong are just and the weak secure and the peace preserved.

All this will not be finished in the first one hundred days. Nor will it be finished in the first one thousand days, nor in the life of this administration, nor even perhaps in our lifetime on this planet. But let us begin.

2. Reference to atomic weapons.
3. Isaiah 58:6.

20   In your hands, my fellow citizens, more than mine, will rest the final success or failure of our course. Since this country was founded, each generation of Americans has been summoned to give testimony to its national loyalty. The graves of young Americans who answered the call to service surround the globe.

Now the trumpet summons us again—not as a call to bear arms, though arms we need—not as a call to battle, though embattled we are—but a call to bear the burden of a long twilight struggle, year in and year out, "rejoicing in hope, patient in tribulation"[4]—a struggle against the common enemies of man: tyranny, poverty, disease, and war itself.

Can we forge against these enemies a grand and global alliance, North and South, East and West, that can assure a more fruitful life for all mankind? Will you join in that historic effort?

In the long history of the world, only a few generations have been granted the role of defending freedom in its hour of maximum danger. I do not shrink from this responsibility—I welcome it. I do not believe that any of us would exchange places with any other people or any other generation. The energy, the faith, the devotion which we bring to this endeavor will light our country and all who serve it—and the glow from that fire can truly light the world.

And so, my fellow Americans, ask not what your country can do for you—ask what you can do for your country.

25   My fellow citizens of the world, ask not what America will do for you, but what together we can do for the freedom of man.

Finally, whether you are citizens of America or citizens of the world, ask of us here the same high standards of strength and sacrifice which we ask of you. With a good conscience our only sure reward, with history the final judge of our deeds, let us go forth to lead the land we love, asking His blessing and His help, but knowing that here on earth God's work must truly be our own.

MLA CITATION

Kennedy, John F. "Inaugural Address." *The Norton Reader: An Anthology of Nonfiction*, edited by Melissa A. Goldthwaite et al., 15th ed., W. W. Norton, 2020, pp. 736–38.

QUESTIONS

1. Choose a prominent rhetorical device (for example: repetition, allusion, lists, or juxtaposition) that John F. Kennedy uses in his speech and identify where it occurs. For the device you have identified, read it to yourself and then out loud. Why is it effective?

2. On what level of generality is Kennedy operating? When does he get specific?

3. Consider and deepen your answer to question 1 by writing an analysis of Kennedy's speech. Make a claim about the significance of one or more rhetorical devices used in the speech; support your thesis with specific examples from the text.

---

4. Romans 12:12.

MARTIN LUTHER KING JR.
Letter from Birmingham Jail[1]

M Y DEAR FELLOW CLERGYMEN:
While confined here in the Birmingham city jail, I came across your recent statement calling my present activities "unwise and untimely." Seldom do I pause to answer criticism of my work and ideas. If I sought to answer all the criticisms that cross my desk, my secretaries would have little time for anything other than such correspondence in the course of the day, and I would have no time for constructive work. But since I feel that you are men of genuine good will and that your criticisms are sincerely set forth, I want to try to answer your statement in what I hope will be patient and reasonable terms.

I think I should indicate why I am here in Birmingham, since you have been influenced by the view which argues against "outsiders coming in." I have the honor of serving as president of the Southern Christian Leadership Conference, an organization operating in every southern state, with headquarters in Atlanta, Georgia. We have some eighty-five affiliated organizations across the South, and one of them is the Alabama Christian Movement for Human Rights. Frequently we share staff, educational, and financial resources with our affiliates. Several months ago the affiliate here in Birmingham asked us to be on call to engage in a nonviolent direct-action program if such were deemed necessary. We readily consented, and when the hour came we lived up to our promise. So I, along with several members of my staff, am here because I was invited here. I am here because I have organizational ties here.

But more basically, I am in Birmingham because injustice is here. Just as the prophets of the eighth century B.C. left their villages and carried their "thus saith the Lord" far beyond the boundaries of their home towns, and just as the Apostle Paul left his village of Tarsus and carried the gospel of Jesus Christ to the far corners of the Greco-Roman world, so am I compelled to carry the gospel of freedom beyond my own home town. Like Paul, I must constantly respond to the Macedonian call for aid.

Written on April 16, 1963, while Martin Luther King Jr. was jailed for civil disobedience; subsequently published in Why We Can't Wait *(1964), King's book on nonviolent resistance to segregation in America.*

---

1. This response to a published statement by eight fellow clergymen from Alabama (Bishop C. C. J. Carpenter, Bishop Joseph A. Durick, Rabbi Milton L. Grafman, Bishop Paul Hardin, Bishop Nolan B. Harmon, the Reverend George M. Murray, the Reverend Edward V. Ramage and the Reverend Earl Stallings) was composed under somewhat constricting circumstances. Begun on the margins of the newspaper in which the statement appeared while I was in jail, the letter was continued on scraps of writing paper supplied by a friendly Negro trusty, and concluded on a pad my attorneys were eventually permitted to leave me. Although the text remains in substance unaltered, I have indulged in the author's prerogative of polishing it for publication [King's note].

Moreover, I am cognizant of the interrelatedness of all communities and states. I cannot sit idly by in Atlanta and not be concerned about what happens in Birmingham. Injustice anywhere is a threat to justice everywhere. We are caught in an inescapable network of mutuality, tied in a single garment of destiny. Whatever affects one directly, affects all indirectly. Never again can we afford to live with the narrow, provincial "outside agitator" idea. Anyone who lives inside the United States can never be considered an outsider anywhere within its bounds.

5   You deplore the demonstrations taking place in Birmingham. But your statement, I am sorry to say, fails to express a similar concern for the conditions that brought about the demonstrations. I am sure that none of you would want to rest content with the superficial kind of social analysis that deals merely with effects and does not grapple with underlying causes. It is unfortunate that demonstrations are taking place in Birmingham, but it is even more unfortunate that the city's white power structure left the Negro community with no alternative.

In any nonviolent campaign there are four basic steps: collection of the facts to determine whether injustices exist; negotiation; self-purification; and direct action. We have gone through all these steps in Birmingham. There can be no gainsaying the fact that racial injustice engulfs this community. Birmingham is probably the most thoroughly segregated city in the United States. Its ugly record of brutality is widely known. Negroes have experienced grossly unjust treatment in the courts. There have been more unsolved bombings of Negro homes and churches in Birmingham than in any other city in the nation. These are the hard, brutal facts of the case. On the basis of these conditions, Negro leaders sought to negotiate with the city fathers. But the latter consistently refused to engage in good-faith negotiation.

Then, last September, came the opportunity to talk with leaders of Birmingham's economic community. In the course of the negotiations, certain promises were made by the merchants—for example, to remove the stores' humiliating racial signs. On the basis of these promises, the Reverend Fred Shuttlesworth and the leaders of the Alabama Christian Movement for Human Rights agreed to a moratorium on all demonstrations. As the weeks and months went by, we realized that we were the victims of a broken promise. A few signs, briefly removed, returned; the others remained.

As in so many past experiences, our hopes had been blasted, and the shadow of deep disappointment settled upon us. We had no alternative except to prepare for direct action, whereby we would present our very bodies as a means of laying our case before the conscience of the local and the national community. Mindful of the difficulties involved, we decided to undertake a process of self-purification. We began a series of workshops on nonviolence, and we repeatedly asked ourselves: "Are you able to accept blows without retaliating?" "Are you able to endure the ordeal of jail?" We decided to schedule our direct-action program for the Easter season, realizing that except for Christmas, this is the main shopping period of the year. Knowing that a strong economic-withdrawal program would be the by-product of direct action, we felt that this would be the best time to bring pressure to bear on the merchants for the needed change.

Then it occurred to us that Birmingham's mayoral election was coming up in March, and we speedily decided to postpone action until after election day. When we discovered that the Commissioner of Public Safety, Eugene "Bull" Connor, had piled up enough votes to be in the run-off, we decided again to postpone action until the day after the run-off so that the demonstrations could not be used to cloud the issues. Like many others, we wanted to see Mr. Connor defeated, and to this end we endured postponement after postponement. Having aided in this community need, we felt that our direct-action program could be delayed no longer.

You may well ask, "Why direct action? Why sit-ins, marches, and so forth? 10 Isn't negotiation a better path?" You are quite right in calling for negotiation. Indeed, this is the very purpose of direct action. Nonviolent direct action seeks to create such a crisis and foster such a tension that a community which has constantly refused to negotiate is forced to confront the issue. It seeks so to dramatize the issue that it can no longer be ignored. My citing the creation of tension as part of the work of the nonviolent-resister may sound rather shocking. But I must confess that I am not afraid of the word "tension." I have earnestly opposed violent tension, but there is a type of constructive, nonviolent tension which is necessary for growth. Just as Socrates felt that it was necessary to create a tension in the mind so that individuals could rise from the bondage of myths and half-truths to the unfettered realm of creative analysis and objective appraisal, so must we see the need for nonviolent gadflies to create the kind of tension in society that will help men rise from the dark depths of prejudice and racism to the majestic heights of understanding and brotherhood.

The purpose of our direct-action program is to create a situation so crisis-packed that it will inevitably open the door to negotiation. I therefore concur with you in your call for negotiation. Too long has our beloved Southland been bogged down in a tragic effort to live in monologue rather than dialogue.

One of the basic points in your statement is that the action that I and my associates have taken in Birmingham is untimely. Some have asked: "Why didn't you give the new city administration time to act?" The only answer that I can give to this query is that the new Birmingham administration must be prodded about as much as the outgoing one, before it will act. We are sadly mistaken if we feel that the election of Albert Boutwell as mayor will bring the millennium to Birmingham. While Mr. Boutwell is a much more gentle person than Mr. Connor, they are both segregationists, dedicated to maintenance of the status quo. I have hoped that Mr. Boutwell will be reasonable enough to see the futility of massive resistance to desegregation. But he will not see this without pressure from devotees of civil rights. My friends, I must say to you that we have not made a single gain in civil rights without determined legal and nonviolent pressure. Lamentably, it is an historical fact that privileged groups seldom give up their privileges voluntarily. Individuals may see the moral light and voluntarily give up their unjust posture; but, as Reinhold Niebuhr[2] has reminded us, groups tend to be more immoral than individuals.

We know through painful experience that freedom is never voluntarily given by the oppressor; it must be demanded by the oppressed. Frankly, I have yet to engage in a direct-action campaign that was "well timed" in the view of those who have not suffered unduly from the disease of segregation. For years now I have heard the word "Wait!" It rings in the ear of every Negro with piercing familiarity. This "Wait" has almost always meant "Never." We must come to see, with one of our distinguished jurists, that "justice too long delayed is justice denied."

We have waited for more than 340 years for our constitutional and God-given rights. The nations of Asia and Africa are moving with jetlike speed toward gaining political independence, but we still creep at horse-and-buggy pace toward gaining a cup of coffee at a lunch counter. Perhaps it is easy for those who have never felt the stinging darts of segregation to say, "Wait." But when you have seen vicious mobs lynch your mothers and fathers at will and drown your sisters and brothers at whim; when you have seen hate-filled policemen curse, kick, and even kill your black brothers and sisters; when you see the vast majority of your twenty million Negro brothers smothering in an airtight cage of poverty in the midst of an affluent society; when you suddenly find your tongue twisted and your speech stammering as you seek to explain to your six-year-old daughter why she can't go to the public amusement park that has just been advertised on television, and see tears welling up in her eyes when she is told that Funtown is closed to colored children, and see ominous clouds of inferiority beginning to form in her little mental sky, and see her beginning to distort her personality by developing an unconscious bitterness toward white people; when you have to concoct an answer for a five-year-old son who is asking, "Daddy, why do white people treat colored people so mean?"; when you take a cross-country drive and find it necessary to sleep night after night in the uncomfortable corners of your automobile because no motel will accept you; when you are humiliated day in and day out by nagging signs reading "white" and "colored"; when your first name becomes "nigger," your middle name becomes "boy" (however old you are) and your last name becomes "John," and your wife and mother are never given the respected title "Mrs."; when you are harried by day and haunted by night by the fact that you are a Negro, living constantly at tiptoe stance, never quite knowing what to expect next, and are plagued with inner fears and outer resentments; when you are forever fighting a degenerating sense of "nobodiness"—then you will understand why we find it difficult to wait. There comes a time when the cup of endurance runs over, and men are no longer willing to be plunged into the abyss of despair. I hope, sirs, you can understand our legitimate and unavoidable impatience.

15   You express a great deal of anxiety over our willingness to break laws. This is certainly a legitimate concern. Since we so diligently urge people to obey the Supreme Court's decision of 1954 outlawing segregation in the public schools,

2. American Protestant theologian (1892–1971).

at first glance it may seem rather paradoxical for us consciously to break laws. One may well ask: "How can you advocate breaking some laws and obeying others?" The answer lies in the fact that there are two types of laws: just and unjust. I would be the first to advocate obeying just laws. One has not only a legal but a moral responsibility to obey just laws. Conversely, one has a moral responsibility to disobey unjust laws. I would agree with St. Augustine[3] that "an unjust law is no law at all."

Now, what is the difference between the two? How does one determine whether a law is just or unjust? A just law is a man-made code that squares with the moral law or the law of God. An unjust law is a code that is out of harmony with the moral law. To put it in the terms of St. Thomas Aquinas:[4] An unjust law is a human law that is not rooted in eternal law and natural law. Any law that uplifts human personality is just. Any law that degrades human personality is unjust. All segregation statutes are unjust because segregation distorts the soul and damages the personality. It gives the segregator a false sense of superiority and the segregated a false sense of inferiority. Segregation, to use the terminology of the Jewish philosopher Martin Buber,[5] substitutes an "I-it" relationship for an "I-thou" relationship and ends up relegating persons to the status of things. Hence segregation is not only politically, economically, and sociologically unsound, it is morally wrong and sinful. Paul Tillich[6] has said that sin is separation. Is not segregation an existential expression of man's tragic separation, his awful estrangement, his terrible sinfulness? Thus it is that I can urge men to obey the 1954 decision of the Supreme Court, for it is morally right; and I can urge them to disobey segregation ordinances, for they are morally wrong.

Let us consider a more concrete example of just and unjust laws. An unjust law is a code that a numerical or power majority group compels a minority group to obey but does not make binding on itself. This is *difference* made legal. By the same token, a just law is a code that a majority compels a minority to follow and that it is willing to follow itself. This is *sameness* made legal.

Let me give another explanation. A law is unjust if it is inflicted on a minority that, as a result of being denied the right to vote, had no part in enacting or devising the law. Who can say that the legislature of Alabama which set up that state's segregation laws was democratically elected? Throughout Alabama all sorts of devious methods are used to prevent Negroes from becoming registered voters, and there are some counties in which, even though Negroes constitute a majority of the population, not a single Negro is registered. Can any law enacted under such circumstances be considered democratically structured?

Sometimes a law is just on its face and unjust in its application. For instance, I have been arrested on a charge of parading without a permit. Now, there is nothing wrong in having an ordinance which requires a permit for a parade.

3. Early Christian church father (354–430).
4. Christian philosopher and theologian (1225–1274).
5. Austrian-born Israeli philosopher (1878–1965).
6. German-born American Protestant theologian (1886–1965).

But such an ordinance becomes unjust when it is used to maintain segregation and to deny citizens the First-Amendment privilege of peaceful assembly and protest.

20   I hope you are able to see the distinction I am trying to point out. In no sense do I advocate evading or defying the law, as would the rabid segregationist. That would lead to anarchy. One who breaks an unjust law must do so openly, lovingly, and with a willingness to accept the penalty. I submit that an individual who breaks a law that conscience tells him is unjust, and who willingly accepts the penalty of imprisonment in order to arouse the conscience of the community over its injustice, is in reality expressing the highest respect for law.

Of course, there is nothing new about this kind of civil disobedience. It was evidenced sublimely in the refusal of Shadrach, Meshach, and Abednego to obey the laws of Nebuchadnezzar,[7] on the ground that a higher moral law was at stake. It was practiced superbly by the early Christians, who were willing to face hungry lions and the excruciating pain of chopping blocks rather than submit to certain unjust laws of the Roman Empire. To a degree, academic freedom is a reality today because Socrates practiced civil disobedience.[8] In our own nation, the Boston Tea Party represented a massive act of civil disobedience.

We should never forget that everything Adolf Hitler did in Germany was "legal" and everything the Hungarian freedom fighters[9] did in Hungary was "illegal." It was "illegal" to aid and comfort a Jew in Hitler's Germany. Even so, I am sure that, had I lived in Germany at the time, I would have aided and comforted my Jewish brothers. If today I lived in a Communist country where certain principles dear to the Christian faith are suppressed, I would openly advocate disobeying that country's anti-religious laws.

I must make two honest confessions to you, my Christian and Jewish brothers. First, I must confess that over the past few years I have been gravely disappointed with the white moderate. I have almost reached the regrettable conclusion that the Negro's great stumbling block in his stride toward freedom is not the White Citizen's Counciler or the Ku Klux Klanner, but the white moderate, who is more devoted to "order" than to justice; who prefers a negative peace which is the absence of tension to a positive peace which is the presence of justice; who constantly says, "I agree with you in the goal you seek, but I cannot agree with your methods of direct action"; who paternalistically believes he can set the timetable for another man's freedom; who lives by a mythical concept of time and who constantly advises the Negro to wait for a "more convenient season." Shallow understanding from people of good will is more frus-

7. Their story is told in Daniel 3.

8. Socrates, the ancient Greek philosopher, was tried by the Athenians for corrupting their youth through his skeptical, questioning manner of teaching. He refused to change his ways and was condemned to death.

9. In the anti-Communist revolution of 1956, which was quickly put down by the Soviet army.

trating than absolute misunderstanding from people of ill will. Lukewarm acceptance is much more bewildering than outright rejection.

I had hoped that the white moderate would understand that law and order exist for the purpose of establishing justice and that when they fail in this purpose they become the dangerously structured dams that block the flow of social progress. I had hoped that the white moderate would understand that the present tension in the South is a necessary phase of the transition from an obnoxious negative peace, in which the Negro passively accepted his unjust plight, to a substantive and positive peace, in which all men will respect the dignity and worth of human personality. Actually, we who engage in nonviolent direct action are not the creators of tension. We merely bring to the surface the hidden tension that is already alive. We bring it out in the open, where it can be seen and dealt with. Like a boil that can never be cured so long as it is covered up but must be opened with all its ugliness to the natural medicines of air and light, injustice must be exposed, with all the tension its exposure creates, to the light of human conscience and the air of national opinion, before it can be cured.

In your statement you assert that our actions, even though peaceful, must   25
be condemned because they precipitate violence. But is this a logical assertion? Isn't this like condemning a robbed man because his possession of money precipitated the evil act of robbery? Isn't this like condemning Socrates because his unswerving commitment to truth and his philosophical inquiries precipitated the act by the misguided populace in which they made him drink hemlock? Isn't this like condemning Jesus because his unique God-consciousness and never-ceasing devotion to God's will precipitated the evil act of crucifixion? We must come to see that, as the federal courts have consistently affirmed, it is wrong to urge an individual to cease his efforts to gain his basic constitutional rights because the quest may precipitate violence. Society must protect the robbed and punish the robber.

I had also hoped that the white moderate would reject the myth concerning time in relation to the struggle for freedom. I have just received a letter from a white brother in Texas. He writes: "All Christians know that the colored people will receive equal rights eventually, but it is possible that you are in too great a religious hurry. It has taken Christianity almost two thousand years to accomplish what it has. The teachings of Christ take time to come to earth." Such an attitude stems from a tragic misconception of time, from the strangely irrational notion that there is something in the very flow of time that will inevitably cure all ills. Actually, time itself is neutral; it can be used either destructively or constructively. More and more I feel that the people of ill will have used time much more effectively than have the people of good will. We will have to repent in this generation not merely for the hateful words and actions of the bad people, but for the appalling silence of the good people. Human progress never rolls in on wheels of inevitability; it comes through the tireless efforts of men willing to be co-workers with God, and without this hard work, time itself becomes an ally of the forces of social stagnation. We must use time creatively, in the knowledge that the time is always ripe to do right.

Now is the time to make real the promise of democracy and transform our pending national elegy into a creative psalm of brotherhood. Now is the time to lift our national policy from the quicksand of racial injustice to the solid rock of human dignity.

You speak of our activity in Birmingham as extreme. At first I was rather disappointed that fellow clergymen would see my nonviolent efforts as those of an extremist. I began thinking about the fact that I stand in the middle of two opposing forces in the Negro community. One is a force of complacency, made up in part of Negroes who, as a result of long years of oppression, are so drained of self-respect and a sense of "somebodiness" that they have adjusted to segregation; and in part of a few middle-class Negroes who, because of a degree of academic and economic security and because in some ways they profit by segregation, have become insensitive to the problems of the masses. The other force is one of bitterness and hatred, and it comes perilously close to advocating violence. It is expressed in the various black nationalist groups that are springing up across the nation, the largest and best-known being Elijah Muhammad's Muslim movement.[10] Nourished by the Negro's frustration over the continued existence of racial discrimination, this movement is made up of people who have lost faith in America, who have absolutely repudiated Christianity, and who have concluded that the white man is an incorrigible "devil."

I have tried to stand between these two forces, saying that we need emulate neither the "do-nothingism" of the complacent nor the hatred and despair of the black nationalist. For there is the more excellent way of love and nonviolent protest. I am grateful to God that, through the influence of the Negro church, the way of nonviolence became an integral part of our struggle.

If this philosophy had not emerged, by now many streets of the South would, I am convinced, be flowing with blood. And I am further convinced that if our white brothers dismiss as "rabblerousers" and "outside agitators" those of us who employ nonviolent direct action, and if they refuse to support our nonviolent efforts, millions of Negroes will, out of frustration and despair, seek solace and security in black-nationalist ideologies—a development that would inevitably lead to a frightening racial nightmare.

30   Oppressed people cannot remain oppressed forever. The yearning for freedom eventually manifests itself, and that is what has happened to the American Negro. Something within has reminded him of his birthright of freedom, and something without has reminded him that it can be gained. Consciously or unconsciously, he has been caught up by the *Zeitgeist*,[11] and with his black brothers of Africa and his brown and yellow brothers of Asia, South America, and the Caribbean, the United States Negro is moving with a sense of great urgency toward the promised land of racial justice. If one recognizes this vital urge that has engulfed the Negro community, one should readily understand why public demonstrations are taking place. The Negro has many pent-up resentments and latent frustrations, and he must release them. So let him

10. Muhammad (1897–1975) succeeded to the leadership of the Nation of Islam in 1934.
11. Spirit of the times.

march; let him make prayer pilgrimages to the city hall; let him go on freedom rides—and try to understand why he must do so. If his repressed emotions are not released in nonviolent ways, they will seek expression through violence; this is not a threat but a fact of history. So I have not said to my people, "Get rid of your discontent." Rather, I have tried to say that this normal and healthy discontent can be channeled into the creative outlet of nonviolent direct action. And now this approach is being termed extremist.

But though I was initially disappointed at being categorized as an extremist, as I continued to think about the matter I gradually gained a measure of satisfaction from the label. Was not Jesus an extremist for love: "Love your enemies, bless them that curse you, do good to them that hate you, and pray for them which despitefully use you, and persecute you." Was not Amos an extremist for justice: "Let justice roll down like waters and righteousness like an everflowing stream." Was not Paul an extremist for the Christian gospel: "I bear in my body the marks of the Lord Jesus." Was not Martin Luther an extremist: "Here I stand; I cannot do otherwise, so help me God." And John Bunyan:[12] "I will stay in jail to the end of my days before I make a butchery of my conscience." And Abraham Lincoln: "This nation cannot survive half slave and half free." And Thomas Jefferson: "We hold these truths to be self-evident, that all men are created equal. . . ." So the question is not whether we will be extremists, but what kind of extremists we will be. Will we be extremists for hate or for love? Will we be extremists for the preservation of injustice or for the extension of justice? In that dramatic scene on Calvary's hill three men were crucified. We must never forget that all three were crucified for the same crime—the crime of extremism. Two were extremists for immorality, and thus fell below their environment. The other, Jesus Christ, was an extremist for love, truth, and goodness, and thereby rose above his environment. Perhaps the South, the nation, and the world are in dire need of creative extremists.

I had hoped that the white moderate would see this need. Perhaps I was too optimistic; perhaps I expected too much. I suppose I should have realized that few members of the oppressor race can understand the deep groans and passionate yearnings of the oppressed race, and still fewer have the vision to see that injustice must be rooted out by strong, persistent, and determined action. I am thankful, however, that some of our white brothers in the South have grasped the meaning of this social revolution and committed themselves to it. They are still all too few in quantity, but they are big in quality. Some—such as Ralph McGill, Lillian Smith, Harry Golden, James McBride Dabbs, Ann Braden, and Sarah Patton Boyle—have written about our struggle in eloquent and prophetic terms. Others have marched with us down nameless streets of the South. They have languished in filthy, roach-infested jails, suffering the abuse and brutality of policemen who view them as "dirty nigger-lovers." Unlike so many of their moderate brothers and sisters, they have recognized the urgency

12. Amos, Old Testament prophet; Paul, New Testament apostle; Luther (1483–1546), German Protestant reformer; Bunyan (1628–1688), English preacher and author.

of the moment and sensed the need for powerful "action" antidotes to combat the disease of segregation.

Let me take note of my other major disappointment. I have been so greatly disappointed with the white church and its leadership. Of course, there are some notable exceptions. I am not unmindful of the fact that each of you has taken some significant stands on this issue. I commend you, Reverend Stallings, for your Christian stand on this past Sunday, in welcoming Negroes to your worship service on a nonsegregated basis. I commend the Catholic leaders of this state for integrating Spring Hill College several years ago.

But despite these notable exceptions, I must honestly reiterate that I have been disappointed with the church. I do not say this as one of those negative critics who can always find something wrong with the church. I say this as a minister of the gospel, who loves the church; who was nurtured in its bosom; who has been sustained by its spiritual blessings and who will remain true to it as long as the cord of life shall lengthen.

35   When I was suddenly catapulted into the leadership of the bus protest in Montgomery, Alabama, a few years ago,[13] I felt we would be supported by the white church. I felt that the white ministers, priests, and rabbis of the South would be among our strongest allies. Instead, some have been outright opponents, refusing to understand the freedom movement and misrepresenting its leaders; all too many others have been more cautious than courageous and have remained silent behind the anesthetizing security of stained-glass windows.

In spite of my shattered dreams, I came to Birmingham with the hope that the white religious leadership of this community would see the justice of our cause and, with deep moral concern, would serve as the channel through which our just grievances could reach the power structure. I had hoped that each of you would understand. But again I have been disappointed.

I have heard numerous southern religious leaders admonish their worshipers to comply with a desegregation decision because it is the law, but I have longed to hear white ministers declare: "Follow this decree because integration is morally right and because the Negro is your brother." In the midst of blatant injustices inflicted upon the Negro, I have watched white churchmen stand on the sideline and mouth pious irrelevancies and sanctimonious trivialities. In the midst of a mighty struggle to rid our nation of racial and economic injustice, I have heard many ministers say: "Those are social issues, with which the gospel has no real concern." And I have watched many churches commit themselves to a completely otherworldly religion which makes a strange, un-Biblical distinction between body and soul, between the sacred and the secular.

I have traveled the length and breadth of Alabama, Mississippi, and all the other southern states. On sweltering summer days and crisp autumn mornings I have looked at the South's beautiful churches with their lofty spires pointing heavenward. I have beheld the impressive outlines of her massive religious-education buildings. Over and over I have found myself asking: "What kind of

---

13. In December 1955, when Rosa Parks refused to move to the back of a bus.

people worship here? Who is their God? Where were their voices when the lips of Governor Barnett dripped with words of interposition and nullification? Where were they when Governor Wallace gave a clarion call for defiance and hatred?[14] Where were their voices of support when bruised and weary Negro men and women decided to rise from the dark dungeons of complacency to the bright hills of creative protest?"

Yes, these questions are still in my mind. In deep disappointment I have wept over the laxity of the church. But be assured that my tears have been tears of love. There can be no deep disappointment where there is not deep love. Yes, I love the church. How could I do otherwise? I am in the rather unique position of being the son, the grandson, and the great-grandson of preachers. Yes, I see the church as the body of Christ. But, oh! How we have blemished and scarred that body through social neglect and through fear of being nonconformists.

There was a time when the church was very powerful—in the time when the early Christians rejoiced at being deemed worthy to suffer for what they believed. In those days the church was not merely a thermometer that recorded the ideas and principles of popular opinion; it was a thermostat that transformed the mores of society. Whenever the early Christians entered a town, the people in power became disturbed and immediately sought to convict the Christians for being "disturbers of the peace" and "outside agitators." But the Christians pressed on, in the conviction that they were "a colony of heaven," called to obey God rather than man. Small in number, they were big in commitment. They were too God-intoxicated to be "astronomically intimidated." By their effort and example they brought an end to such ancient evils as infanticide and gladiatorial contests.

Things are different now. So often the contemporary church is a weak, ineffectual voice with an uncertain sound. So often it is an archdefender of the status quo. Far from being disturbed by the presence of the church, the power structure of the average community is consoled by the church's silent—and often even vocal—sanction of things as they are.

But the judgment of God is upon the church as never before. If today's church does not recapture the sacrificial spirit of the early church, it will lose its authenticity, forfeit the loyalty of millions, and be dismissed as an irrelevant social club with no meaning for the twentieth century. Every day I meet young people whose disappointment with the church has turned into outright disgust.

Perhaps I have once again been too optimistic. Is organized religion too inextricably bound to the status quo to save our nation and the world? Perhaps I must turn my faith to the inner spiritual church, the church within the church, as the true *ekklesia*[15] and the hope of the world. But again I am thankful to God that some noble souls from the ranks of organized religion have broken loose from the paralyzing chains of conformity and joined us as active part-

40

---

14. Ross Barnett (1898–1987), governor of Mississippi, opposed James Meredith's admission to the University of Mississippi; George Wallace (1919–1998), governor of Alabama, opposed admission of several black students to the University of Alabama.

15. Greek New Testament word for the early Christian church.

ners in the struggle for freedom. They have left their secure congregations and walked the streets of Albany, Georgia, with us. They have gone down the highways of the South on tortuous rides for freedom. Yes, they have gone to jail with us. Some have been dismissed from their churches, have lost the support of their bishops and fellow ministers. But they have acted in the faith that right defeated is stronger than evil triumphant. Their witness has been the spiritual salt that has preserved the true meaning of the gospel in these troubled times. They have carved a tunnel of hope through the dark mountain of disappointment.

I hope the church as a whole will meet the challenge of this decisive hour. But even if the church does not come to the aid of justice, I have no despair about the future. I have no fear about the outcome of our struggle in Birmingham, even if our motives are at present misunderstood. We will reach the goal of freedom in Birmingham and all over the nation, because the goal of America is freedom. Abused and scorned though we may be, our destiny is tied up with America's destiny. Before the pilgrims landed at Plymouth, we were here. Before the pen of Jefferson etched the majestic words of the Declaration of Independence across the pages of history, we were here. For more than two centuries our forebears labored in this country without wages; they made cotton king; they built the homes of their masters while suffering gross injustice and shameful humiliation—and yet out of a bottomless vitality they continued to thrive and develop. If the inexpressible cruelties of slavery could not stop us, the opposition we now face will surely fail. We will win our freedom because the sacred heritage of our nation and the eternal will of God are embodied in our echoing demands.

45   Before closing I feel impelled to mention one other point in your statement that has troubled me profoundly. You warmly commended the Birmingham police force for keeping "order" and "preventing violence." I doubt that you would have so warmly commended the police force if you had seen its dogs sinking their teeth into unarmed, nonviolent Negroes. I doubt that you would so quickly commend the policemen if you were to observe their ugly and inhumane treatment of Negroes here in the city jail; if you were to watch them push and curse old Negro women and young Negro girls; if you were to see them slap and kick old Negro men and young boys; if you were to observe them, as they did on two occasions, refuse to give us food because we wanted to sing our grace together. I cannot join you in your praise of the Birmingham police department.

It is true that the police have exercised a degree of discipline in handling the demonstrators. In this sense they have conducted themselves rather "nonviolently" in public. But for what purpose? To preserve the evil system of segregation. Over the past few years I have consistently preached that nonviolence demands that the means we use must be as pure as the ends we seek. I have tried to make clear that it is wrong to use immoral means to attain moral ends. But now I must affirm that it is just as wrong, or perhaps even more so, to use moral means to preserve immoral ends. Perhaps Mr. Connor and his policemen have been rather nonviolent in public, as was Chief Pritchett in Albany, Georgia, but they have used the moral means of nonviolence to maintain the immoral end of racial injustice. As T. S. Eliot has said, "The last temptation is the greatest treason: To do the right deed for the wrong reason."[16]

I wish you had commended the Negro sit-inners and demonstrators of Birmingham for their sublime courage, their willingness to suffer, and their amazing discipline in the midst of great provocation. One day the South will recognize its real heroes. They will be the James Merediths,[17] with the noble sense of purpose that enables them to face jeering and hostile mobs, and with the agonizing loneliness that characterizes the life of the pioneer. They will be old, oppressed, battered Negro women, symbolized in a seventy-two-year-old woman in Montgomery, Alabama, who rose up with a sense of dignity and with her people decided not to ride segregated buses, and who responded with ungrammatical profundity to one who inquired about her weariness: "My feets is tired, but my soul is at rest." They will be the young high school and college students, the young ministers of the gospel and a host of their elders, courageously and nonviolently sitting in at lunch counters and willingly going to jail for conscience' sake. One day the South will know that when these disinherited children of God sat down at lunch counters, they were in reality standing up for what is best in the American dream and for the most sacred values in our Judaeo-Christian heritage, thereby bringing our nation back to those great wells of democracy which were dug deep by the founding fathers in their formulation of the Constitution and the Declaration of Independence.

Never before have I written so long a letter. I'm afraid it is much too long to take your precious time. I can assure you that it would have been much shorter if I had been writing from a comfortable desk, but what else can one do when he is alone in a narrow jail cell, other than write long letters, think long thoughts, and pray long prayers?

If I have said anything in this letter that overstates the truth and indicates an unreasonable impatience, I beg you to forgive me. If I have said anything that understates the truth and indicates my having a patience that allows me to settle for anything less than brotherhood, I beg God to forgive me.

I hope this letter finds you strong in the faith. I also hope that circumstances will soon make it possible for me to meet each of you, not as an integrationist or a civil-rights leader but as a fellow clergyman and a Christian brother. Let us all hope that the dark clouds of racial prejudice will soon pass away and the deep fog of misunderstanding will be lifted from our fear-drenched communities, and in some not too distant tomorrow the radiant stars of love and brotherhood will shine over our great nation with all their scintillating beauty.

> Yours for the cause of Peace and Brotherhood,
> MARTIN LUTHER KING JR.

50

16. American-born English poet (1888–1965); the lines are from his play *Murder in the Cathedral*.
17. Meredith (b. 1933) was the first black student to enroll at the University of Mississippi.

MLA CITATION

King, Martin Luther, Jr. "Letter from Birmingham Jail." *The Norton Reader: An Anthology of Nonfiction,* edited by Melissa A. Goldthwaite et al., 15th ed., W. W. Norton, 2020, pp. 739–51.

QUESTIONS

1. Martin Luther King Jr. addressed "Letter from Birmingham Jail" to eight fellow clergy members who had written a statement criticizing his activities (see note 1). Where and how, in the course of the "Letter," does he attempt to make common cause with them?

2. King was trained in oral composition, that is, in composing and delivering sermons. One device he uses is prediction: he announces, in advance, the organization of what he is about to say. Locate examples of prediction in the "Letter."

3. Summarize the theory of nonviolent resistance that King presents in this essay.

4. Imagine an unjust law that, to you, would justify civil disobedience. In an essay describe the law, the form your resistance would take, and the penalties you would expect to incur.

EDWIDGE DANTICAT
Another Country

> The sea was walking the earth with a heavy heel. . . . The folks in the quarters and the people in the big houses further around the shore heard the big lake and wondered. The people felt uncomfortable but safe because there were the seawalls to chain the senseless monster in his bed. The folks let the people do the thinking. If the castles thought themselves secure, the cabins needn't worry.
> —ZORA NEALE HURSTON,
> *Their Eyes Were Watching God*

IN ZORA NEALE HURSTON'S VISIONARY 1937 NOVEL, Janie Crawford and her boyfriend, Tea Cake, a day laborer, refuse to evacuate their small, unsteady house before a deadly hurricane batters the Florida Everglades, near where I currently live.

"Everybody was talking about it that night. But nobody was worried," wrote Hurston. "You couldn't have a hurricane when you're making seven and eight dollars a day."

Originally published in The Progressive (2005), *"a monthly magazine of investigative reporting, political commentary, cultural coverage, activism, interviews, poetry, and humor"; later included, with additions, in Edwidge Danticat's essay collection* Create Dangerously: The Immigrant Artist at Work *(2010).*

It turns out you could have a hurricane, and other disasters too, even if you're making considerably less than that. And if you manage to survive that hurricane, you might end up with nothing at all. No home. No food or water. No medical care for your sick and wounded. Not even body bags or coffins for your dead.

Americans have experienced this scenario before. Not just in prophetic literature or apocalyptic blockbuster movies, but through the very real natural disasters that have plagued other countries. Catastrophes that are eventually reduced to single, shorthand images that, if necessary, can later be evoked. Take, for example, visions of skyscraper-size waves washing away entire crowds in Thailand and other Asian countries devastated by the December 2004 tsunamis. Or remember Sophia Pedro, the Mozambican woman who in March 2000 was plucked by a South African military helicopter from the tree where she had clung for three days and then given birth as the floodwaters swirled beneath her? And let's not forget Haiti's September 2004 encounter with Tropical Storm Jeanne, which left three thousand people dead and a quarter million homeless. In that disaster, patients drowned in hospital beds. Children watched as parents were washed away. Survivors sought shelter in trees and on rooftops while corpses floated in the muddy, contaminated waters around them.

As I watched all this unfold again on my television set, this time in the streets of New Orleans in the summer of 2005, I couldn't help but think of the Bush administration's initial response to the Haitian victims of Tropical Storm Jeanne the year before Hurricane Katrina struck New Orleans: sixty thousand dollars in aid and the repatriation of Haitian refugees from the United States back to the devastated region even before the waters had subsided. New Orleans' horrific tragedy had been foreshadowed in America's so-called backyard, and the initial response had been: "Po' man ain't got no business at de show," as Zora Neale Hurston's Tea Cake might have put it.

In the weeks that followed Hurricane Katrina's landing, I, immigrant writer and southern coastal city resident, heard many Americans of all geographical persuasions, pundits and citizens alike, make the case that the types of horrors that plagued Katrina-ravaged New Orleans—the desperation of ordinary citizens, some of whom resorted to raiding stores to feed themselves and their families; the forgotten public hospitals where nurses pumped oxygen into dying patients by hand; the makeshift triage wards on bridges and airports; the roaming armed gangs—are more in line with our expectations of the "third world" than the first.

Turning to the Kenyan CNN correspondent Jeff Koinange on *American Morning* a week after Hurricane Katrina struck New Orleans, the anchorwoman Soledad O'Brien said, "You know, to some degree, when you were watching the original pictures . . . if you turned the sound down on your television, if you didn't know where you were, you might think it was Haiti or maybe one of those African countries, many of which you cover."

"Watching helpless New Orleans suffering day by day left people everywhere stunned and angry and in ever greater pain," echoed *Time* magazine's Nancy Gibbs. "These things happened in Haiti, they said, but not here."

5

Not to be outdone, even the Canadians got in on the act. Chiding her fellow citizens for their self-righteous attitude toward American poverty, Kate Heartfield of the *Ottawa Citizen* nevertheless added, "Ottawa is not New Orleans. And it is definitely not Freetown or Port-au-Prince."

10   It's hard for those of us who are from places like Freetown or Port-au-Prince, and those of us who are immigrants who still have relatives living in places like Freetown or Port-au-Prince, not to wonder why the so-called developed world needs so desperately to distance itself from us, especially at times when an unimaginable disaster shows exactly how much alike we are. The rest of the world's poor do not expect much from their governments and they're usually not disappointed. The poor in the richest country in the world, however, should not be poor at all. They should not even exist. Maybe that's why both their leaders and a large number of their fellow citizens don't even realize that they actually do exist.

This is not the America we know, chimed many field reporters who, haunted by the faces and voices of the dying, the stench of bloated corpses on city streets during the day and screams for help rising from attics at night, recorded the early absence of first responders with both sorrow and rage. Their fury could only magnify ours, for if they could make it to New Orleans, Mississippi, and Alabama and give us minute-by-minute accounts of the storm and its aftermath, why couldn't the government agencies find their way there? Indeed, what these early charged news reports offered was a passport to an America where one does not always have bus fare, much less an automobile, where health insurance is as distant a dream as a college education, where poverty is a birthright, not an accident of fortune. This is the America that continues to startle, the America of the needy and never-have-enoughs, the America of the undocumented, the unemployed and underemployed, the elderly, and the infirm. An America that remains invisible until a rebellion breaks out, gunshots ring out, or a flood rages through. Perhaps this America does have more in common with the developing world than with the one it inhabits. For the poor and outcast everywhere dwell within their own country, where more often than not they must fend for themselves. That's why one can so easily become a refugee within one's own borders—because one's perceived usefulness and precarious citizenship are always in question, whether in Haiti or in that other America, the one where people have no flood insurance.

I don't know why it seems always to surprise some Americans that many of their fellow citizens are vulnerable to horrors that routinely plague much of the world's population. After all, we do share a planet whose climate is gradually being altered by unbalanced exploration and dismal environmental policies that may one day render us all, first world and third world residents alike, helpless in the face of more disasters like Tropical Storm Jeanne and Hurricane Katrina. Let us also not forget the ever-looming menace of 9/11-like terrorism, which can potentially have the same effect, landing thousands on street corners and in Astrodomes asking themselves how they came to be there.

The poor and displaced are indeed sometimes better off in places far from their impoverished homes. But in the end, must poverty also force us to live deprived of homestead, birthplace, history, memory? In the case of Hurricane Katrina, was it really a flood that washed away that nuanced privilege of deciding where one should build one's life, or was this right slowly being stripped away while we were already too horrified to watch?

One of the advantages of being an immigrant is that two very different countries are forced to merge within you. The language you were born speaking and the one you will probably die speaking have no choice but to find a common place in your brain and regularly merge there. So too with catastrophes and disasters, which inevitably force you to rethink facile allegiances.

Shortly after the terrorist attacks of September 11, 2001, Masood Farivar, a former Afghan mujahideen who received part of his education in a madrassa in Pakistan, wrote, "As an Afghan, I'd never carried the black, red, and green flag of my own country. Suddenly though, I wanted to feel what it was like to proudly hold a flag, wave it at passing ambulances, police cars, and fire trucks. It would be a good way to show my solidarity with Americans. It was my way of saying, we're in this together. I'm with you, I share your pain."

"I come from the so-called Third World," wrote the Chilean novelist and memoirist Isabel Allende after September 11, 2001, a day that also marked the twenty-eighth anniversary of a U.S.-sponsored coup d'ètat against her uncle, Salvador Allende. Still, she writes,

> Until only a short time ago, if someone had asked me where I'm from, I would have answered, without much thought, Nowhere; or, Latin America; or, maybe, In my heart I'm Chilean. Today, however, I say I'm an American, not simply because that's what my passport verifies, or because that word includes all of America from north to south, or because my husband, my son, my grandchildren, most of my friends, my books, and my home are in northern California; but because a terrorist attack destroyed the twin towers of the World Trade Center, and starting with that instant, many things have changed. We can't be neutral in moments of crisis. . . . I no longer feel that I am an alien in the United States.

After the horrible carnage of September 11th, hadn't the world echoed Farivar's and Allende's sentiments and also declared, through many headlines in newspapers across the globe, that we were all Americans?

At least for a while.

Among the many realities brought to light by Hurricane Katrina was that never again could we justifiably deny the existence of this country within a country, that other America, which America's immigrants and the rest of the world may know much more intimately than many Americans do, the America that is always on the brink of humanitarian and ecological disaster. No, it is not Haiti or Mozambique or Bangladesh, but it might as well be.

MLA CITATION

Danticat, Edwidge. "Another Country." *The Norton Reader: An Anthology of Nonfiction*, edited by Melissa A. Goldthwaite et al., 15th ed., W. W. Norton, 2020, pp. 752–55.

QUESTIONS

1. Throughout this essay Edwidge Danticat draws parallels between New Orleans, where Hurricane Katrina hit in 2005, and countries such as Thailand and Haiti, where similar disasters have struck. What is the point of these comparisons? What argument does Danticat make from them?

2. In paragraph 5 Danticat criticizes then U.S. president George W. Bush for initially offering "sixty thousand dollars in aid" to Haitian victims of Hurricane Jeanne. Using online resources, find out how much aid was eventually sent to Haiti and how that amount compares with aid to American victims of Hurricane Katrina.

3. Why do you think Danticat named this essay "Another Country"? Consider paragraph 11 as you formulate your answer.

4. Write an essay in which you present principles for how the federal government should respond to natural disasters. Give examples, positive and negative, from the past decade.

REBECCA SOLNIT
Bird in a Cage

THERE ARE TWO THINGS I think about nearly every time I row out into San Francisco Bay. One is a passage from Shankar Vedantam's *The Hidden Brain,* in which he talks about a swim he once took. A decent swimmer in his own estimate, Vedantam went out into the sea one day and discovered that he had become superb and powerful; he was instantly proud of his new abilities. Far from shore, he realized he had been riding a current and was going to have to fight it all the way back to shore. "Unconscious bias influences our lives in exactly the same manner as that undercurrent," Vedantam writes. "Those who travel with the current will always feel they are good swimmers; those who swim against the current may never realize they are better swimmers than they imagine."

Most mornings I row out against the current, and the moment when I turn around is exhilarating. Strokes that felt choppy and ineffectual are suddenly graceful and powerful. I feel very good at what I do, even though I know that the tide is going my way.

Rowing is the closest I will ever come to flying. On calm, flat days my battered old oars make twin circles of ripples that spread out until they intersect behind the stern of the boat. I'm forever retreating from that gentle disturbance, the water smoothing itself into glass again as I go. On the calmest days,

Published in Harper's Magazine *(2016), an American magazine covering politics, society, culture, and the environment.*

when the bay is a mirror, these oars pull me and my scull through reflected clouds in long glides, the two nine-foot oars moving together like wings in that untrammeled space.

The birds are one of the great joys, the terns and pelicans and gulls, the coots and stilts and cormorants, who dive and fly and float, living in the air and the water and the plane between them. The freedom of rowing is enlarged by the freedom of the birds. I set out from the estuary of Corte Madera Creek as it pours into San Francisco Bay. En route I pass Point San Quentin, and San Quentin Prison. When I row past the prison I think about currents and I think about Jarvis Jay Masters, who's been on my mind for a long time. We were born eight months apart and are both children of coastal California. We're both storytellers. But he has been in San Quentin since he was nineteen, more than a third of a century ago, and has swum against the current all his life. For the past twenty-five years, he's been on death row, though the evidence is on the side of his innocence.

Until he turned twenty-three, Masters's story could have been that of any number of poor inner-city boys: his father missing in action; his mother drawn into the vortex of heroin; his early neglect; and a ride through the best and worst of the foster-care system, which dropped him straight into the juvenile-prison system. At nineteen, he was sent to San Quentin for armed robbery. Four years later, on June 8, 1985, Howell Burchfield, a prison guard and father of five, was murdered. Two members of a black prison gang were convicted of planning and carrying out the crime. They were given life sentences. Masters was accused of conspiring in the murder and of sharpening the weapon that was used to stab Burchfield in the heart. He received the death penalty.

In books and movies, resourceful lawyers or investigators find a subtle detail, possibly two, to undermine an otherwise credible case. But in Masters's case there aren't merely one or two weak links. So far as I can tell, the whole chain is rotten.

Major witnesses changed their testimony, and several of the prisoners who testified against Masters recanted. Some testified that they had been offered incentives to incriminate him. One star witness was so unreliable and so widely used as an informant that dozens of cases in the state had to be thrown out because of his involvement. He has recanted his testimony about Masters. The man convicted of carrying out the murder said in 2004 that Masters was innocent and that all three men on trial were "under orders from [gang] commanders that, under threat of death, none of us could discuss the [gang] in any way." Meaning that Masters faced two death penalties, and one set him up for the other.

I first read about Masters in *Altars in the Street*, a 1997 book by Melody Ermachild Chavis, who was the defense investigator for his murder trial. They have remained close for thirty years. Chavis and I later became friends ourselves. "It was obvious working on it even way back then, between 1985 and 1990, that they had a lot of suspects and a lot of theories," she told me earlier this year. "The big mistake they made was: they destroyed the crime scene. They bagged it all up and threw it in the Marin County dump."

5

She described the way prisoners and prison officials got rid of hundreds of notes that had been exchanged between prisoners, as well as a large collection of prison-made knives, which had been thrown out of the cells when the prisoners realized that they were going to be searched. According to one account in Masters's mountain of legal documents, guards collected two different potential murder weapons, which they say they put into envelopes as evidence. Both disappeared before the trial.

10   Masters was a gang member at the time of the killing, but the gang's leaders eventually gave many reasons why it was impossible that he had sharpened the missing weapon. One was that he had voted against killing Burchfield, an act of insubordination for which he had been stripped of responsibilities. Another was geography; he was on the fourth tier of a cell block, and the murder took place on the second tier. Moving a weapon back and forth would have been difficult and dangerous, and a witness testified that the weapon never left the second tier. Most critically, someone else admitted to making it.

Masters's attorneys filed the opening brief of his appeal in 2001, after which his case progressed slowly. It was not until November of last year that the California Supreme Court heard oral arguments on the appeal. Even by the standards of California's glacial appeals process, this is an unusually long time.

Though only 6.5 percent of Californians are black, African Americans make up 29 percent of the state's incarcerated and 36 percent of those condemned to death. They are more likely than others convicted of similar crimes to receive the death penalty, and assailants of any race who kill a white person are far more likely to be sentenced to death than killers of other victims. There are those who swim with the current and those who swim against it, and then there are those who have firehoses turned on them.

The first time I saw Masters was at a session of a 2011 evidentiary hearing. There, in the small courtroom, stood a tall, gracious man in shackles and an orange jumpsuit. A dozen or so friends and supporters were present, most of them from the Buddhist community. Since his sentencing, Masters had become a devoted Buddhist practitioner. He told me that he meditates daily and tries to incorporate teachings about compassion into his daily life among prisoners and guards. In 1989, he took vows from Chagdud Tulku Rinpoche, an exiled Tibetan lama and distinguished teacher who died in 2002. (The first vow was "From this day forward I will not hurt or harm other people even if it costs my life.") Pema Chödrön, a writer and abbess who is perhaps the best-known Buddhist in the West after the Dalai Lama, speaks of Masters with admiration, and she visits him every year.

When we began talking on the phone, a few months ago, Masters told me how much prisoners crave connection with the outside world. Buddhism allowed him to join a community of ethical and idealistic people with practical ideas about how to respond to suffering and rage. It took him outward and inward. "Meditation has become something I cannot do without. I see and hear more clearly, feel more relaxed and calm, and I actually find my experiences slowing down," he wrote in 1997. "I'm more appreciative of each day as I observe how things constantly change and dissolve. I've realized that everything is in a continual process of coming and going. I don't hold happiness or anger for a long time. It just comes and goes."

He's also connected to the outside world through his writing. He's the author of two books and many magazine essays. He told me that his essays "go out on their own wings and some of them fly back to me." It's not the first time he's used flight as a metaphor for his own reach; the title of his memoir comes from an incident when he stopped another prisoner from nailing a seagull with a basketball in the prison yard. Asked why, he said off the top of his head, "That bird has my wings," and so the gripping, moving narrative of his early years is titled *That Bird Has My Wings*.

"You know, it's really hard to get in," I told Masters about my attempts to figure out how to move through the prison system. "It was easy for me," he replied, and we laughed. From the time I first wrote him, it took me approximately two months of bureaucratic wrangling to be able to visit him. Finally, on a cold Sunday in January, I showed up at the visitors' entrance wearing the permitted clothing and carrying what few articles I was allowed: a key, a state-issued I.D., some coins and bills for the vending machines, and a few pages of fact-checker's questions and quotes to verify, sealed inside a clear Ziploc bag. I passed through something much like airport security, and on the other side, I stepped out to face a shabby jumble of sinister architectural styles. I was suddenly left alone to find my way to the visiting rooms a couple hundred yards away.

There were more doors to go through, operated by a young woman in the guard booth who let me in and took my license and pass. I entered a room in which everything except the vending machines was painted a pale buttery yellow. There were fifteen cages in which prisoners were locked with their visitors, a U-shaped arrangement with guards on the inside (where prisoners entered) and outside (where the visitors entered). Each cage was about four by eight feet, just slightly smaller than the cells the prisoners live in, and was furnished with two plastic chairs and a tiny table.

A guard wearing a heavy belt with keys dangling on steel chains locked me in the cage closest to the door through which the prisoners entered and exited. Masters arrived with his hands cuffed behind him. Once inside the cage he offered them up to the guard to be unlocked, a gesture both had apparently engaged in so many times that it appeared utterly routine. Thus began my first face-to-face meeting with Masters. Soon afterward a stocky white man with gray hair passed by on his way out of the visiting room, and he and Masters shouted something at each other. It was a little unclear whether this was animosity or friendship, but Masters said it was the latter. The two men had known each other since being in foster care together. It was as though they'd been groomed for death row since they were little boys.

Another prisoner passed by and said that his daughter was on break from college and coming to see him. After a brief discussion with the man, Masters told me that he'd become a confidant, someone who, because of his writings

15

and the way he conducted himself, was trusted with things that prisoners might not ordinarily share. He reminded me that he's been in prison since before some of the younger inmates and guards were born.

20   "I have been so blessed because I was thinking about all that could have gone wrong, that could've affected me," he told me. "All the things that didn't go wrong. I have seen a lot of tragedy, and all of those things could've been me. I've seen the violent heart, and I count my blessings that I haven't had that kind of hatred. Being on death row, I have a front-row seat on what suffering is. I'm not damaged, not had this place tear me up like I've seen a hundred times. I'm probably crazy for not being crazy. I count my blessings every day."

When I started rowing, I thought it would be a meditation practice of sorts, because so much concentration goes into the single gesture that moves you across the water. That repetitive movement requires the orchestration of the whole body, and it contains a host of subtleties in timing and positioning and force. You could spend a lifetime learning to do it right, but even as you're learning you can go miles across the water. Gradually the gestures became second nature, and I could think about other things.

        Though I don't get lost in thought much. It's too beautiful.

        I want to keep rowing, to keep relishing that freedom on the open water under the changing weather, going with and against the tides, but I don't need so much freedom that I can't go inside a prison on occasion. Buddhism calls for the liberation of all beings, and it's a useful set of tools for thinking about prisons and what we do with our freedoms.

        We are all rowing past one another, and it behooves us to know how the tides move and who's being floated along and who's being dragged down and who might not even be allowed in the water. I bought Masters some things from the vending machines just outside the cages, which I could access and he couldn't. He asked whether I was going to eat, and I said maybe I'd get a taco after. He said, "That's freedom." He was right. Freedom to eat tacos on my own schedule, to pursue the maximum freedom of rowing, to enter the labyrinth of San Quentin and leave a couple of hours later, to listen to stories and to tell them, to try to figure out which stories might free us.

25   It was stories, written down by Melody Ermachild Chavis; by Alan Senauke, a Zen priest; and by Jarvis Masters himself that made me care about him and think about him and talk to him and visit him. And it was these stories that made me hope to see him leave that cage on his own wings. Meanwhile, there is a way Jarvis is already free; as a storyteller he's escaped the narratives about himself he's been given and he's made his own version of what a life means.

        "Whatever the outcome, I want to be in a position to deal with that," he told me. "There are a lot of people who say, 'Jarvis, you gonna win this case.' It's the same way the other way," meaning people who say he won't win. "I'm scared both ways; I'm scared to think this way and scared that way. Do I lose sleep? Of course I lose sleep. I do have some faith in this system, I just have to. The possibility of them coming to the right decision is there. I do have faith in the outcome of this system. History doesn't give you a lot of good reasons for it. That's just my bottom line."

MLA CITATION

Solnit, Rebecca. "Bird in a Cage." *The Norton Reader: An Anthology of Nonfiction*, edited by Melissa A. Goldthwaite et al., 15th ed., W. W. Norton, 2020, pp. 756–61.

QUESTIONS

1. This essay begins and ends with a description of rowing. How does the metaphor of rowing relate to the essay's main idea?

2. Both Rebecca Solnit and her friend, Jarvis Jay Masters, are fond of birds and use the metaphor of a bird's flight to connect to a feeling. Look at the moments where birds come up in the essay. How do birds work as symbols for each person and for the essay overall?

3. Solnit connects the political problem of death row and wrongful incarceration to the spiritual idea of freedom. How does the principle of freedom help us understand Masters's incarceration?

4. Many people every year are wrongfully incarcerated. Solnit tells the story of one such person. How does this individual story help you understand the history and politics of the issue?

14 LITERATURE AND THE ARTS

> The illusion of art is to make one believe that great literature is very close to life, but exactly the opposite is true. Life is amorphous, literature is formal.
>
> —FRANÇOISE SAGAN

The essays in this chapter describe encounters with art—literature, music, photography, film, and painting. Collectively, they represent a wide range of ways to deepen our response to literature and the arts. The arts appeal to us in ways that language cannot entirely capture and yet, when we try to explain why a work of art moves us, we find ourselves caught with words as our tools, words that can feel inadequate to expressing what we want to share.

For some, this makes writing about art itself off-putting. There can be a moment in analysis when an emotional experience becomes so intellectual that we barely recognize it. Overanalysis like this can feel like someone has taken apart a beautiful stopwatch and now all we see is a work table littered with gears, springs, and tiny screws. But really great criticism, that is, writing that describes, analyzes, and assesses the merits of art, shows you the inner workings of that beautiful machine in a way that allows us to reassemble it with a renewed appreciation for both the piece and the artist who made it.

The chapter begins, somewhat improbably, with a data-driven essay on feelings. Specifically, Jonathan Gottschall presents research that demonstrates the power of literature to make us more empathetic people, not only while reading, but in our everyday lives. Gottschall's research offers a fitting introduction to the next two essays, Matt de la Peña's meditation on when and how children's literature should cover dark and sad themes and Kate DiCamillo's response. Both pieces are also about empathy, and they exemplify why these two writers are so beloved by young readers. The next four essays move through genres—painting, photography, music, and film—but more than that, they offer a range of ways to enhance our understanding of a work of art. Philip Kennicott offers a powerful counterpoint to our rushed world with a serious lesson in the importance of really slowing down and taking the time to look. Geoff Dyer shows how to find a pattern in the subjects an artist returns to again and again. Michael Hamad demonstrates how our own creative noodling and doodling can unlock some of the deep mysteries in the structure of a piece of music. Anna Deavere Smith articulates the power of bringing a multilayered understanding of historical context to our understanding of a movie. You might think of these four essays as a menu of possible ways to write criticism.

The chapter ends with two essays that reconsider literature and language: what happens when, after some years, what has served you well no longer fits? Scott Russell

Sanders documents his encounters with Thoreau's *Walden* over the years, tracing how his appreciation and his disagreement developed alongside each other. Ngũgĩ wa Thiong'o explains his choice to return to composing in Gĩkũyũ, his first language—and a language he was once punished for using—turning from the English he had been forced to learn in school.

As you write in response to these essays, think about the art that has shaped you. What works of art (in any genre) do you return to again and again and what impact have they had on your character? You might think, too, about how these works are constructed. Following some of the methods of analysis here, see if you can put into words what makes a work of art powerful.

JONATHAN GOTTSCHALL
Why Fiction Is Good for You

I s FICTION GOOD FOR US? We spend huge chunks of our lives immersed in novels, films, TV shows, and other forms of fiction. Some see this as a positive thing, arguing that made-up stories cultivate our mental and moral development. But others have argued that fiction is mentally and ethically corrosive. It's an ancient question: Does fiction build the morality of individuals and societies, or does it break it down?

This controversy has been flaring up—sometimes literally, in the form of book burnings—ever since Plato tried to ban fiction from his ideal republic. In 1961, FCC chairman Newton Minow famously said that television was not working in "the public interest" because its "formula comedies about totally unbelievable families, blood and thunder, mayhem, violence, sadism, murder, western bad men, western good men, private eyes, gangsters, more violence, and cartoons" amounted to a "vast wasteland." And what he said of TV programming has also been said, over the centuries, of novels, theater, comic books, and films: They are not in the public interest.

Until recently, we've only been able to guess about the actual psychological effects of fiction on individuals and society. But new research in psychology and broad-based literary analysis is finally taking questions about morality out of the realm of speculation.

This research consistently shows that fiction does mold us. The more deeply we are cast under a story's spell, the more potent its influence. In fact, fiction seems to be more effective at changing beliefs than nonfiction, which is designed to persuade through argument and evidence. Studies show that when we read nonfiction, we read with our shields up. We are critical and skeptical. But when we are absorbed in a story, we drop our intellectual guard. We are moved emotionally, and this seems to make us rubbery and easy to shape.

First published in the Boston Globe *(2012), this essay grew into Jonathan Gottschall's book* The Storytelling Animal *(2012).*

5   But perhaps the most impressive finding is just how fiction shapes us: mainly for the better, not for the worse. Fiction enhances our ability to understand other people; it promotes a deep morality that cuts across religious and political creeds. More peculiarly, fiction's happy endings seem to warp our sense of reality. They make us believe in a lie: that the world is more just than it actually is. But believing that lie has important effects for society—and it may even help explain why humans tell stories in the first place.

It's not hard to see why social critics have often been dismayed by fiction. We spend a huge amount of time lost in stories, with the average American spending four hours per day watching television alone.

And if the sheer time investment were not enough, there's the content. Since fiction's earliest beginnings, morally repulsive behavior has been a great staple of the stories we tell. From the sickening sexual violence of "The Girl with the Dragon Tattoo," to the deranged sadism of Shakespeare's Titus Andronicus, to Oedipus stabbing his eyes out in disgust, to the horrors portrayed on TV shows like "Breaking Bad" and "CSI"—throughout time, the most popular stories have often featured the most unpleasant subject matter. Fiction's obsession with filth and vice has led critics of different stripes to condemn plays, novels, comic books, and TV for corroding values and corrupting youth.

Moreover, it's clear that these stories really can change our views. As the psychologist Raymond Mar writes, "Researchers have repeatedly found that reader attitudes shift to become more congruent with the ideas expressed in a [fictional] narrative." For example, studies reliably show that when we watch a TV show that treats gay families nonjudgmentally (say, "Modern Family"), our own views on homosexuality are likely to move in the same nonjudgmental direction. History, too, reveals fiction's ability to change our values at the societal level, for better and worse. For example, Harriet Beecher Stowe's "Uncle Tom's Cabin" helped bring about the Civil War by convincing huge numbers of Americans that blacks are people, and that enslaving them is a mortal sin. On the other hand, the 1915 film "The Birth of a Nation" inflamed racist sentiments and helped resurrect an all but defunct KKK.

So those who are concerned about the messages in fiction—whether they are conservative or progressive—have a point. Fiction is dangerous because it has the power to modify the principles of individuals and whole societies.

10   But fiction is doing something that all political factions should be able to get behind. Beyond the local battles of the culture wars, virtually all storytelling, regardless of genre, increases society's fund of empathy and reinforces an ethic of decency that is deeper than politics.

For a long time literary critics and philosophers have argued, along with the novelist George Eliot, that one of fiction's main jobs is to "enlarge men's sympathies." Recent lab work suggests they are right. The psychologists Mar and Keith Oatley tested the idea that entering fiction's simulated social worlds enhances our ability to connect with actual human beings. They found that heavy fiction readers outperformed heavy nonfiction readers on tests of empathy, even after they controlled for the possibility that people who already had high empathy might naturally gravitate to fiction. As Oatley puts it, fiction serves the function of "making the world a better place by improving interpersonal understanding."

Follow-up studies have reached similar conclusions. For example, one study showed that small children (age 4–6) who were exposed to a large number of children's books and films had a significantly stronger ability to read the mental and emotional states of other people. Similarly, Washington & Lee psychologist Dan Johnson recently had people read a short story that was specifically written to induce compassion in the reader. He wanted to see not only if fiction increased empathy, but whether it would lead to actual helping behavior. Johnson found that the more absorbed subjects were in the story, the more empathy they felt, and the more empathy they felt, the more likely the subjects were to help when the experimenter "accidentally" dropped a handful of pens—highly absorbed readers were twice as likely to help out. "In conclusion," Johnson writes, "it appears that 'curling up with a good book' may do more than provide relaxation and entertainment. Reading narrative fiction allows one to learn about our social world and as a result fosters empathic growth and pro-social behavior."

Similarly, novelists such as Leo Tolstoy and John Gardner have contended that fiction is morally beneficial, and here, too, research is bearing them out. While fiction often dwells on lewdness, depravity, and simple selfishness, storytellers virtually always put us in a position to judge wrongdoing, and we do so with gusto. As the Brandeis literary scholar William Flesch argues, fiction all over the world is strongly dominated by the theme of poetic justice. Generally speaking, goodness is endorsed and rewarded and badness is condemned and punished. Stories—from modern films to ancient fairy tales—steep us all in the same powerful norms and values. True, antiheroes, from Milton's Satan to Tony Soprano, captivate us, but bad guys are almost never allowed to live happily ever after. And fiction generally teaches us that it is profitable to be good.

Take a study of television viewers by the Austrian psychologist Marcus Appel. Appel points out that, for a society to function properly, people have to believe in justice. They have to believe that there are rewards for doing right and punishments for doing wrong. And, indeed, people generally do believe that life punishes the vicious and rewards the virtuous. But one class of people appear to believe these things in particular: those who consume a lot of fiction.

In Appel's study, people who mainly watched drama and comedy on TV—as opposed to heavy viewers of news programs and documentaries—had substantially stronger "just-world" beliefs. Appel concludes that fiction, by constantly exposing us to the theme of poetic justice, may be partly responsible for the sense that the world is, on the whole, a just place.

This is despite the fact, as Appel puts it, "that this is patently not the case." As people who watch the news know very well, bad things happen to good people all the time, and most crimes go unpunished. In other words, fiction seems to teach us to see the world through rose-colored lenses. And the fact

15

that we see the world that way seems to be an important part of what makes human societies work.

All these questions about the effects of fiction lead up to one big one: Why are humans storytelling animals at all? Why are we—as a species—so hopelessly addicted to narratives about the fake struggles of pretend people? Evolution is a ruthlessly utilitarian process. How has the seeming luxury of fiction—the apparent waste in time and creative energy—not been eliminated by the evolutionary process?

One possibility is that fiction has hidden benefits that outweigh its costs. For instance, anthropologists have long argued that stories have group-level benefits. Traditional tales, from hero epics to sacred myths, perform the essential work of defining group identity and reinforcing cultural values.

Along with three colleagues, the literary scholar Joseph Carroll and the psychologists John Johnson and Dan Kruger, I wanted to explore the possibility that fiction generally—not just folk tales—may act as a kind of social glue among humans, binding fractious individuals together around common values. So we asked hundreds of literary scholars and avid readers to respond to a questionnaire about 19th-century British novels. We asked them to answer questions about the motives and personalities of characters, and to classify them as protagonists or antagonists; we also asked questions that explored how readers felt about these characters. The results showed that antagonists and protagonists had sharply differentiated personalities. Antagonists were overwhelmingly driven by motives of power, wealth, and prestige. They didn't care about winning mates, making friends, or even helping their own kin. They were loveless, emotionally isolated egomaniacs. The protagonists, meanwhile, were keen on romance and eager to help their friends and relatives.

20   These results, which will be published in a book called "Graphing Jane Austen,"[1] may seem unsurprising: In short, our heroes are heroes. But our findings were consistent with the work of the anthropologist Chris Boehm, who studies social dynamics in hunter-gatherers. Boehm notes that hunter-gatherers are egalitarian, with all members of the tribe coming together to suppress bully-boy behavior in individuals. The same kind of dynamic applies in the simulated social worlds of Victorian novels. The bad guys in these ultra-"civilized" Victorian novels were like the bullies in a hunter-gatherer band, while the good guys were self-effacing and cooperative.

Our survey respondents reacted to the characters as though they were real people: They admired the protagonists, disliked the antagonists, felt happy when the good guys succeeded, and felt sad or angry when they were threatened. By simulating a world where antisocial behavior is strongly condemned and punished, these novels were promoting ancient human values. And from these books, and from fiction more broadly, readers learn by association that if

---

1. *Graphing Jane Austen* by Joseph Carroll, Jonathan Gottschall, John A. Johnson, and Daniel Kruger was published in 2012.

they are more like the protagonists, they'll be more likely to live happily ever after.

Fiction is often treated like a mere frill in human life, if not something worse. But the emerging science of story suggests that fiction is good for more than kicks. By enhancing empathy, fiction reduces social friction. At the same time, story exerts a kind of magnetic force, drawing us together around common values. In other words, most fiction, even the trashy stuff, appears to be in the public interest after all.

MLA CITATION

Gottschall, Jonathan. "Why Fiction Is Good for You." *The Norton Reader: An Anthology of Nonfiction*, edited by Melissa A. Goldthwaite et al., 15th ed., W. W. Norton, 2020, pp. 763–67.

QUESTIONS

1. When has your reading led you to greater empathy? Has that empathy had consequences on how you act?

2. Jonathan Gottschall claims that the more time we spend reading stories, the better we will understand others. But he also admits in paragraph 8 that there have been times, notably with *The Birth of a Nation* (1915), when narrative has inflamed racist feelings. How does this counterexample affect Gottschall's argument overall?

3. Gottschall uses research, data, and stories to make his argument about the power of story. Which type of evidence is most convincing to you and why do you find it so? How do you reconcile the tension inherent in using data to explain how much stories matter?

4. According to Gottschall, even when narratives are violent or have unhappy endings, they tend to reinforce the "lie"—"that the world is more just than it actually is" (paragraph 5). Drawing on some of his examples and your own, discuss the value of our faith in this "lie."

5. Survey your friends on how they feel about characters from one of your favorite books or shows: ask them to identify protagonists, antagonists, what motivates each, and whom they admire. Then, write a short paper discussing the extent to which your findings confirm Gottschall's conclusions.

Why We Shouldn't Shield Children from Darkness

Twice this past fall I was left speechless by a child. The first time happened at an elementary school in Huntington, New York. I was standing on their auditorium stage, in front of a hundred or so students, and after talking to them about books and writing and the power of story, I fielded questions. The first five or six were the usual fare. Where do I get my ideas? How long does it take to write a book? Am I rich? (*Hahahahaha!*) But then a fifth-grade girl wearing bright green glasses stood and asked something different. "If you had the chance to meet an author *you* admire," she said, "what would *you* ask?"

For whatever reason this girl's question, on this morning, cut through any pretense that might ordinarily sneak into an author presentation. The day before, a man in Las Vegas had opened fire on concertgoers from his Mandalay Bay hotel room. Tensions between America and North Korea were reaching a boiling point. Puerto Ricans continued to suffer the nightmarish aftereffects of Hurricane Maria. I studied all the fresh-faced young people staring up at me, trying to square the light of childhood with the darkness in our current world.

All of this, of course, was wildly inappropriate for such a young audience—and had little to do with the question—so I just stood there in awkward silence, the seconds ticking by.

5   Eventually I gave the girl some pre-packaged sound bite about dealing with rejection, or the importance of revision, and then our time was up. But hours later, as I sat in a crowded airport, waiting for a delayed flight, I was still thinking about that girl's question. What *would* I ask an author I admire? Writers like Kate DiCamillo came to mind. Sandra Cisneros. Christopher Paul Curtis.[1]

Now I wanted a do-over.

A thoughtful question like that deserved a more thoughtful response.

Just as my plane reached its cruising altitude, it came to me. If I had the chance to ask Kate DiCamillo anything, it would be this: How honest can an author be with an auditorium full of elementary school kids? How honest should we be with our readers? Is the job of the writer for the very young to tell the truth or preserve innocence?

Originally published in Time Magazine *(2018).*

---

1. Kate DiCamillo (b. 1964), writer best known for her children's books, including *Because of Winn-Dixie*; Sandra Cisneros (b. 1954), author of *The House on Mango Street*; Christopher Paul Curtis (b. 1953), author of *Bud, not Buddy*.

A few weeks ago, illustrator Loren Long and I learned that a major gate-keeper would not support our forthcoming picture book, *Love*, an exploration of love in a child's life, unless we "softened" a certain illustration. In the scene, a despondent young boy hides beneath a piano with his dog, while his parents argue across the living room. There is an empty Old Fashioned glass resting on top of the piano. The feedback our publisher received was that the moment was a little too heavy for children. And it might make parents uncomfortable. This discouraging news led me to really examine, maybe for the first time in my career, the purpose of my picture book manuscripts. What was I trying to accomplish with these stories? What thoughts and feelings did I hope to evoke in children?

This particular project began innocently enough. Finding myself over-   10
whelmed by the current divisiveness in our country, I set out to write a com-forting poem about love. It was going to be something I could share with my own young daughter as well as every kid I met in every state I visited, red or blue. But when I read over one of the early drafts, something didn't ring true. It was reassuring, uplifting even, but I had failed to acknowledge any notion of adversity.

So I started over.

A few weeks into the revision process, my wife and I received some bad news, and my daughter saw my wife openly cry for the first time. This rocked her little world and she began sobbing and clinging to my wife's leg, begging to know what was happening. We settled her down and talked to her and eventually got her ready for bed. And as my wife read her a story about two turtles who stumble across a single hat, I studied my daughter's tear-stained face. I couldn't help thinking a fraction of her innocence had been lost that day. But maybe these minor episodes of loss are just as vital to the well-adjusted child's development as moments of joy. Maybe instead of anxiously trying to protect our children from every little hurt and heartache, our job is to simply support them through such experiences. To talk to them. To hold them.

And maybe this idea also applied to the manuscript I was working on.

Loren and I ultimately fought to keep the "heavy" illustration. Aside from being an essential story beat, there's also the issue of representation. In the book world, we often talk about the power of racial inclusion—and in this respect we're beginning to see a real shift in the field—but many other facets of diversity remain in the shadows. For instance, an uncomfortable number of children out there right now are crouched beneath a meta-phorical piano. There's a power to seeing this largely unspoken part of our interior lives represented, too. And for those who've yet to experience that kind of sadness, I can't think of a safer place to explore complex emotions for the first time than inside the pages of a book, while sitting in the lap of a loved one.

We are currently in a golden age of picture books, with a tremendous   15
range to choose from. Some of the best are funny. Or silly. Or informative. Or

socially aware. Or just plain reassuring. But I'd like to think there's a place for the emotionally complex picture book, too. Jacqueline Woodson's amazing *Each Kindness* comes to mind, in which the protagonist misses the opportunity to be kind to a classmate. Margaret Wise Brown's *The Dead Bird* is a beautiful exploration of mourning from the point of view of children.

Which brings me to the second child who left me speechless last fall.

I was visiting an elementary school in Rome, Georgia, where I read and discussed one of my older books, *Last Stop on Market Street*, as I usually do. But at the end of the presentation I decided, on a whim, to read *Love* to them, too, even though it wasn't out yet. I projected Loren's illustrations as I recited the poem from memory, and after I finished, something remarkable happened. A boy immediately raised his hand, and I called on him, and he told me in front of the entire group, "When you just read that to us I got this feeling. In my heart. And I thought of my ancestors. Mostly my grandma, though . . . because she always gave us so much love. And she's gone now."

And then he started quietly crying.

And a handful of the teachers started crying, too.

20   I nearly lost it myself. Right there in front of 150 third graders. It took me several minutes to compose myself and thank him for his comment.

On the way back to my hotel, I was still thinking about that boy, and his raw emotional response. I felt so lucky to have been there to witness it. I thought of all the boys growing up in working-class neighborhoods around the country who are terrified to show any emotion. Because that's how I grew up, too—terrified. Yet this young guy was brave enough to raise his hand, in front of everyone, and share how he felt after listening to me read a book. And when he began to cry a few of his classmates patted his little shoulders in a show of support. I don't know if I've ever been so moved inside the walls of a school.

I hope one day I'll have the chance to formally ask Kate DiCamillo my questions about innocence and truth. But I do know this: My experience in Rome, Georgia? *That's* why I write books. Because the little story I'm working on alone in a room, day after day, might one day give some kid out there an opportunity to "feel." And if I'm ever there to see it in person again, next time hopefully I'll be brave enough to let myself cry, too.

MLA CITATION

Peña, Matt de la. "Why We Shouldn't Shield Children from Darkness." *The Norton Reader: An Anthology of Nonfiction*, edited by Melissa A. Goldthwaite et al., 15th ed., W. W. Norton, 2020, pp. 768–70.

QUESTIONS

1. Did you ever read something that others thought was too sad or otherwise too grown-up for you to read? What was your experience? Would you ever choose to shield children in your care from dark and sad stories?

2. Matt de la Peña writes about visiting elementary schools, something children's book authors often do. Did you ever attend such an assembly? Whether or not an author came to your school, what do you think children learn from meeting writers in person?

3. Read Jonathan Gottschall's "Why Fiction Is Good for You" (pp. 763–67) and write an essay about the importance of fiction for helping us experience and express emotions, using de la Peña, Gottschall, and your own reading as evidence.

KATE DiCAMILLO
Why Children's Books Should Be a Little Sad

ARLIER THIS WEEK, *the author Matt de la Peña wrote about the importance of including the darker sides of life in stories for children. In it, after recalling a time when an elementary school student asked him what he would ask his favorite authors, he wrote that he would like to pose some questions to one he admires, Kate DiCamillo: "How honest can an author be with an auditorium full of elementary school kids? How honest should we be with our readers? Is the job of the writer for the very young to tell the truth or preserve innocence?" DiCamillo shares her response here.*

Dear Matt,

I read *Love*, and I want you to know that when I turned the page and saw that child hiding under the piano—small, worried, afraid—I felt a wave of recognition. I felt *seen*. I was a kid who hid under the literal (and metaphorical) piano. I felt isolated by the secrets and fear in my household. For me, as a kid, to see that picture would have been such a relief. I would have known that I was not alone. I would have felt less ashamed.

You asked how honest we, as writers of books for children, should be with our readers, whether it is our job to tell them the truth or preserve their innocence.

Here's a question for you: Have you ever asked an auditorium full of kids if they know and love *Charlotte's Web?*[1] In my experience, almost all of the hands go up. And if you ask them how many of them cried when they read it, most of those hands unabashedly stay aloft.

My childhood best friend read *Charlotte's Web* over and over again as a kid. She would read the last page, turn the book over, and begin again. A few years ago, I asked her why.

This response to Matt de la Peña was originally published in Time Magazine *(2018).*

1. Children's book (1952) by E. B. White about how the friendship between a spider and a pig saves the pig's life.

5   "What was it that made you read and reread that book?" I asked her. "Did
you think that if you read it again, things would turn out differently, better?
That Charlotte wouldn't die?"

"No," she said. "It wasn't that. I kept reading it not because I wanted it to
turn out differently or thought that it would turn out differently, but because I
knew for a fact that it *wasn't* going to turn out differently. I knew that a terrible
thing was going to happen, and I also knew that it was going to be okay somehow. I thought that I couldn't bear it, but then when I read it again, it was all
so beautiful. And I found out that I could bear it. That was what the story told
me. That was what I needed to hear. That I could bear it somehow."

So that's the question, I guess, for you and for me and for all of us trying
to do this sacred task of telling stories for the young: How do we tell the truth
and make that truth bearable?

When I talk to kids in schools, I tell them about how I became a writer.
I talk about myself as a child and how my father left the family when I was
very young. Four years ago, I was in South Dakota, in this massive auditorium,
talking to 900 kids, and I did what I always do: I told them about being sick all
the time as a kid and about my father leaving. And then I talked to them about
wanting to write. I talked to them about persisting.

During the Q&A, a boy asked me if I thought I would have been a writer
if I hadn't been sick all the time as a kid and if my father hadn't left. And I said
something along the lines of "I think there is a very good chance that I wouldn't
be standing in front of you today if those things hadn't happened to me." Later,
a girl raised her hand and said, "It turns out that in the end you were stronger
than you thought you were."

10   When the kids left the auditorium, I stood at the door and talked with
them as they walked past. One boy—skinny-legged and blond-haired—grabbed
my hand and said, "I'm here in South Dakota and my dad is in California." He
flung his free hand out in the direction of California. He said, "He's there and
I'm here with my mom. And I thought I might not be okay. But you said today
that you're okay. And so I think that I will be okay, too."

What could I do?

I tried not to cry. I kept hold of his hand.

I looked him in the eye.

I said, "You will be okay. You are okay. It's just like that other kid said:
you're stronger than you know."

15   I felt so connected to that child.

I think we both felt seen.

My favorite lines of *Charlotte's Web,* the lines that always make me cry,
are toward the end of the book. They go like this: "These autumn days will
shorten and grow cold. The leaves will shake loose from the trees and fall.
Christmas will come, then the snows of winter. You will live to enjoy the
beauty of the frozen world, for you mean a great deal to Zuckerman and he
will not harm you, ever. Winter will pass, the days will lengthen, the ice will
melt in the pasture pond. The song sparrow will return and sing, the frogs
will awake, the warm wind will blow again. All these sights and sounds and

smells will be yours to enjoy, Wilbur—this lovely world, these precious days . . ."

I have tried for a long time to figure out how E. B. White did what he did, how he told the truth and made it bearable.

And I think that you, with your beautiful book about love, won't be surprised to learn that the only answer I could come up with was love. E. B. White loved the world. And in loving the world, he told the truth about it—its sorrow, its heartbreak, its devastating beauty. He trusted his readers enough to tell them the truth, and with that truth came comfort and a feeling that we were not alone.

I think our job is to trust our readers.   20

I think our job is to see and to let ourselves be seen.

I think our job is to love the world.

Love,
Kate

MLA CITATION

DiCamillo, Kate. "Why Children's Books Should Be a Little Sad." *The Norton Reader: An Anthology of Nonfiction*, edited by Melissa A. Goldthwaite et al., 15th ed., W. W. Norton, 2020, pp. 771–73.

QUESTIONS

1. Think of a sad story that you love and read or watch again and again. What do you think makes that story important and powerful to you?

2. Look again at Kate DiCamillo's favorite lines from *Charlotte's Web* quoted in paragraph 17. How do they convey what she calls E. B. White's love of the world?

3. Read the essay by Matt de la Peña (pp. 768–70) that inspired this response and write a short essay discussing how these two writers are in conversation with each other. Given that they are in substantial agreement, how do they make the dialogue interesting?

4. Write about a time when you learned that you were stronger than you thought you were.

PHILIP KENNICOTT

How to View Art: Be Dead Serious about It, but Don't Expect Too Much

1. TAKE TIME

THE BIGGEST CHALLENGE when visiting an art museum is to disengage from our distracted selves. The pervasive, relentless, all-consuming power of time is the enemy. If you are thinking about where you have to be next, what you have left undone, what you could be doing instead of standing in front of art, there is no hope that anything significant will happen. But to disengage from time has become extraordinarily complicated. We are addicted to devices that remind us of the presence of time, cellphones and watches among them, but cameras too, because the camera has become a crutch to memory, and memory is our only defense against the loss of time.

The raging debate today about whether to allow the taking of pictures inside the museum usually hinges on whether the act of photographing is intrusive or disruptive to other visitors; more important, the act is fundamentally disruptive to the photographer's experience of art, which is always fleeting. So leave all your devices behind. And never, ever make plans for what to do later in a museum; if you overhear people making plans for supper, drinks or when to relieve the baby sitter, give them a sharp, baleful look.

Some practical advice: If you go an hour before closing time, you won't have to worry about what time it is. Just wait until the guards kick you out. Also: If you have only an hour, visit only one room. Anything that makes you feel rushed, or compelled to move quickly, will reengage you with the sense of busy-ness that defines ordinary life. This is another reason that entrance fees are so pernicious: They make visitors mentally "meter" the experience, straining to get the most out of it, and thus re-inscribe it in the workaday world where time is money, and money is everything.

2. SEEK SILENCE

Always avoid noise, because noise isn't just distracting, it makes us hate other people. If you're thinking about the mind-numbing banality of the person next to you, there's little hope that you will be receptive to art. In a museum, imagine that you have a magnetic repulsion to everyone else. Move toward empty space. Indulge your misanthropy.

5   That's not always easy. Too many museums have become exceptionally noisy, and in some cases that's by design. When it comes to science and history museums, noise is often equated with visitor engagement, a sign that people

Published in the Washington Post *(2014), where Philip Kennicott is an art and architecture critic.*

are enjoying the experience. In art museums, noise isn't just a question of bad manners but a result of the celebrity status of certain artworks, such as the *Mona Lisa*, which attracts vast and inevitably tumultuous throngs of visitors to the Louvre. But any picture that attracts hordes of people has long since died, a victim of its own renown, its aura dissipated, its meaning lost in heaps of platitudes and cant. Say a prayer for its soul and move on.

Seek, rather, some quiet corner of the museum full of things no one else seems to care about. Art that is generally regarded as insipid (19th-century American genre paintings) or hermetic (religious icons from the Byzantine world) is likely to feel very lonely, and its loneliness will make it generous. It may be poor, but it will offer you everything it has.

3. Study Up

One of the most deceptive promises made by our stewards of culture over the past half century is: You don't need to know anything to enjoy art. This is true only in the most limited sense. Yes, art can speak to us even in our ignorance. But there's a far more powerful truth: Our response to art is directly proportional to our knowledge of it. In this sense, art is the opposite of popular entertainment, which becomes more insipid with greater familiarity.

So study up. Even 10 minutes on Wikipedia can help orient you and fundamentally transform the experience. Better yet, read the old cranks of art history, especially the ones who knew how to write and have now become unfashionable (Kenneth Clark, Ernst Gombrich).[1] When visiting special exhibitions, always read the catalogue, or at least the main catalogue essay. If you can't afford the catalogue, read it in the gift shop.

Rules for the gift shop: Never buy anything that isn't a book; never "save time" for the gift shop because this will make you think about time; never take children, because they will associate art with commerce.

Many museums have public education programs, including tours through   10
the galleries with trained docents. Always shadow a docent tour before joining one. If the guide spends all his or her time asking questions rather than explaining art and imparting knowledge, do not waste your time. These faux-Socratic dialogues are premised on the fallacy that all opinions about art are equally valid and that learning from authority is somehow oppressive. You wouldn't learn to ski from someone who professed indifference to form and technique, so don't waste your time with educators who indulge the time-wasting sham of endless questions about what you are feeling and thinking.

4. Engage Memory

The experience of art is ephemeral, and on one level we have to accept that. But beyond the subjective experience, art is also something to be studied and

1. Clark (1903–1983), British author and former director of the National Gallery in London; Gombrich (1909–2001), art historian and author of *The Story of Art* (1950).

debated. Unfortunately, unlike most things we study and debate, art is difficult to summarize and describe. Without a verbal description of what you have seen, you may feel as if nothing happened during your visit. You may even feel you can't remember anything about it, as if it was just a wash of images with nothing to hold on to.

But even if the actual experience of art is difficult to retain and remember, the names of the artists, the countries in which they worked, the years they lived and were active, and a host of other things are easily committed to memory. Some museum educators, who know these things, will tell you this kind of detail doesn't matter; they are lying. Always try to remember the name of and at least one work by an artist whom you didn't know before walking into the museum.

When trying to remember individual art works, make an effort to give yourself a verbal description of them. Perhaps write it in a notebook. The process of giving a verbal description will make details of the work more tangible, and will force you to look more deeply and confront your own entrenched blindness toward art. If your description feels clichéd, then go back again and again until you have said something that seems more substantial. If all else fails, simply commit the visual details of the work to memory, its subject matter, or general color scheme, or surface texture. Turn away from the work and try to remember it; turn back and check your mental image against the work itself. This isn't fun. In fact, it can be exhausting. That means you're making progress in the fight against oblivion.

5. Accept Contradiction

Art must have some utopian ambition, must seek to make the world better, must engage with injustice and misery; art has no other mission than to express visual ideas in its own self-sufficient language. As one art lover supposedly said to another: Monet, Manet,[2] both are correct.

15   Susan Sontag[3] once argued "against interpretation" and in favor of a more immediate, more sensual, more purely subjective response to art; but others argue, just as validly, that art is part of culture and embodies a wide range of cultural meanings and that our job is to ferret them out. Again, both are correct.

The experience of art always enmires us in contradictions. I loathe figurative contemporary art except when I don't; ditto on abstraction. When looking at a painting, it's often useful to try believing two wildly contradictory things: That it is just an object, and an everyday sort of object; and that it is a phenomenally radical expression of human subjectivity. Both are correct.

Art is inspiring and depressing, it excites and enervates us, it makes us more generous and more selfish. A love-hate relationship with an artist, or a great

2. Oscar-Claude Monet (1840–1926), French impressionist painter; Édouard Manet (1832–1883), early modern French painter, known for bridging realist and impressionist art movements.

3. American filmmaker and author of fiction, nonfiction, and plays (1933–2004).

work of art, is often the most intense and lasting of all relationships. After years of spending time in art museums, I've come to accept that I believe wildly contradictory and incompatible things about art. The usual cliché about this realization would be that by forcing us to confront contradiction, art makes us more human. But never trust anyone who says that last part: "art makes us more human." That's meaningless.

Rather, by forcing us to confront contradiction, art makes us ridiculous, exposes our pathetic attempts to make sense of experience, reveals the fault lines of our incredibly faulty knowledge of ourselves and the world. It is nasty, dangerous stuff, and not to be trifled with.

Some practical advice: If you feel better about yourself when you leave a museum, you're probably doing it all wrong.

MLA CITATION

Kennicott, Philip. "How to View Art: Be Dead Serious about It, but Don't Expect Too Much." *The Norton Reader: An Anthology of Nonfiction,* edited by Melissa A. Goldthwaite et al., 15th ed., W. W. Norton, 2020, pp. 774–77.

QUESTIONS

1. Philip Kennicott claims, "Our response to art is directly proportional to our knowledge of it" (paragraph 7). Do you agree? Why or why not? How important is study to the appreciation of art?

2. Kennicott uses the form of a list to guide readers in how to view art. Which of his five directives do you think is most important? Least important? Is there anything you would add to his list?

3. In paragraph 3, Kennicott cautions art viewers about feeling rushed, about anything that "will reengage you with the sense of busy-ness that defines ordinary life." Tim Kreider in "The 'Busy' Trap" (pp. 209–12) also warns against busy-ness. According to each of these authors, why is busy-ness a problem?

4. Use the form of a list to write a "how to" essay on a subject about which you could be considered an expert.

GEOFF DYER

Benches

THERE IS SOMETHING INHERENTLY SAD about a bench. Benches at bus stations have taken on the resignation, the long aftermath that frustration and impatience leave in their wake, of all who have sat there, longing to be gone, forced to settle for a wait on the bench when what they wanted was a seat on the bus. Nowhere is the defining quality of the bench—its absolute immovability—felt more powerfully than at a bus or train station. Perhaps this is why people are often reluctant in these situations to sit and relax. They prefer to sit and jangle change in their pockets, to glance again and again at the timetable that conspires, somehow, to be both implacable and unreliable. To sit down on the bench means to give in, to accept the reality of the situation, to succumb, in fact, to the intolerable *benchness* of the situation. John Vachon captures this perfectly in a picture of a man from out of town sleeping beneath a NO LOAFING sign at a railroad station in Radford, Virginia, 1940. He is not just stretched out; his dark suit is so difficult to distinguish from the bench that he seems to have merged into it.

I said that benches have their seasons—and so they do. But at some level, for the bench in the park, that season is always tending towards autumn. No wonder that Kertész[1] had a special fondness for them. One of his earliest photographs was of his younger brother, Jeno, sitting on a bench in the Woods of Népliget, Budapest, in 1913. Jeno is wearing an overcoat, his hat is also sitting on the bench beside him. The floor of the forest is strewn with fallen leaves. Some way off we can see two other benches, one empty, the other . . . I was going to say that it was occupied by another solitary sitter but, looking again, I'm not so sure. The blurred outline which I had assumed to be a person looks like it might just be a trick of light and leaves. But there was somebody there; like David Hemmings in *Blow-Up*,[2] I was sure of that. It is as if, between my last looking at the picture and my looking back now, the person has got up and left. The mistake actually compounds the very thing that occasioned it: the picture's mood of lingering and precocious melancholy. Jeno is only seventeen but he surveys the vacant woods with the look of a man in the autumn of his life, mourning his lost youth while still in its midst. André was just a few years older than his brother when he took this picture but, as was also the case with his early photographs of musicians, it is like a negative from which he will continue to make variant prints for the rest of his days.

This essay is excerpted from Geoff Dyer's 2007 book, The Ongoing Moment.

1. André Kertész (1894–1985), Hungarian-born photographer known for his innovations in both photojournalism and formalist photography. He emigrated to the United States in 1936.
2. In Michaelangelo Antonioni's 1966 film *Blow-Up*, David Hemmings plays a photographer who believes he has unwittingly captured a murder on film.

It would be claiming too much to say that the silhouetted figures seen in many of Kertész's photographs seem always to be heading towards or looking forward to death, but it would be quite reasonable to suggest that they are always on the look-out for a bench. And the bench represents a kind of death. A bench is . . . on the bench: sidelined, condemned to spectate, peripheral. The man on the bench is a surrogate for Kertész's own situation, observing life but no longer participating in it. Still, at least—like the people photographed by Brassaï and Weegee—he has a bench. On 20 September 1962, in New York, after all those long years of snubs and slights, Kertész took a photograph that summarized his own situation—or his own perception of his situation—perfectly.

Near the top of the frame two women are seated on a bench; in the distance is scattered an assortment of empty chairs and benches. A third of the frame is completely dominated by the back of a man in an overcoat looking down at a broken park bench. It is quite possible that after enough knocks and disappointments your favourite bench in a park could mean almost as much to you as a pet dog or a wife once did. Pathetic? That's the point: how sad it is that there are people for whom a bench could mean the difference between melancholy and breakdown. 'Think of being them,' Larkin urged:

> Turning over their failures
> By some bed of lobelias,
> Nowhere to go but indoors,
> No friends but empty chairs . . .[3]

And now the bench is not just empty, but broken. Etymologically, it would make sense if the man with his back to the camera were a recently declared bankrupt (*banca rotta*)[4] but, equally, he could be just a passer-by, looking at it quizzically. If, to put it crudely, Kertész wanted the broken bench to reflect the observer's dilapidation, he also saw—and saw himself as—someone looking on, curious, sympathetic but detached. It is this telescoped ambiguity that contrives to save the picture from the sentimentality it courts. I say 'contrives' because the photograph was not the happy—in the Kertészian sense of '*un*happy'—accident that it appears. Kertész's wife, Elizabeth, had met and taken under her wing a mentally unstable young woman who had to be committed to a hospital. The two women in the background are Elizabeth and the patient. The man with his back to the camera is Frank Thomas, Elizabeth's partner in the cosmetics business that provided the bulk of the Kertészs' income during the long years when André's photographic vision was unwanted, wasted. By the time this photograph was taken Thomas had become totally reliant on the Kertészs because—like the accordionist André had photographed on 6th Avenue in 1959—he was blind.

5

---

3. A quotation from Philip Larkin's poem "Toads Revisited" (1962).
4. In printing the Italian, *banca rotta*, Dyer emphasizes the word's origins as a combination of the words "bank" and "broken" (*rotta* is the past participle of the verb *rompere*, to break).

Presumably Kertész and his friends happened upon the bench and Kertész then arranged things to give the picture the symbolic association he wanted.

Kertész's melancholy view of the bench is, it goes without saying, not the only one. For Winogrand[5] the bench is like a busy street in which people are sitting rather than walking. In his photograph of a bench at the World's Fair, of 1964, eight people are simultaneously connected—it is difficult to make out where one group of people ends and the next begins—and self-contained. This bench is like a dream of New York in which separate individuals are united by the simple fact of being crammed into a small place. In a Chinese whisper of gestures, every movement is echoed, elaborated, repeated, passed on and back. A photograph of a bench, it is also a photograph of legs, dresses, shoes, bags and hands. Three different conversations are going on but, just as all the different nations are part of the World's Fair, they are all part of the same conversation. It is primarily a picture of women, bookended on one side by a middle-aged white man reading a newspaper and, at the other, by a young black guy. As always in Winogrand there is a sense of other photos going on elsewhere (the two women on the right seem to be looking in the direction of one of these). This is fundamental to Winogrand's conception of working in New York: there is always something else to look at. (Kertész was accused of saying too much in his pictures; Winogrand's don't let you get a word in edgeways.) There might even be more stuff to look at on the same bench which extends beyond the frame in either direction, as if the city is in fact an infinite bench in which easy harmony and respect hold sway. This is suggested by the way that, on the far left, the black man and the white woman are talking. Nothing very remarkable about that but it is impossible not to notice that the woman next to her is whispering something—about the conversation taking place to her right?—in *her* friend's ear. As always in Winogrand there is just enough ambiguity or hesitation to make you realize—and there is something very New York about this too—how precarious such harmony is. I don't want to make too much of this, don't want anything to detract from the civic understanding and good manners of the scene. The atmosphere is entirely convivial. Convivial but not romantic. In Winogrand romance is, at best, a marginal possibility.

MLA CITATION

Dyer, Geoff. "Benches." *The Norton Reader: An Anthology of Nonfiction*, edited by Melissa A. Goldthwaite et al., 15th ed., W. W. Norton, 2020, pp. 778–80.

QUESTIONS

1. Geoff Dyer compares the mood of Kertész's photographs of benches to the mood of Winogrand's. List the primary points of comparison and then look back at the essay's opening. Which photographer is most in sync with Dyer's own sense of benches?

---

5. Garry Winogrand (1928–1984), American street photographer.

2. Dyer makes stories out of these photographs. He also makes philosophy. Locate one of his aphorisms—perhaps the one about death in paragraph 3—and discuss how it deepens your understanding of the art and Dyer's engagement with it.

3. Without looking at the essay itself again, write a description of one of the images Dyer discusses. Then, compare your description with Dyer's. What did you see that he did not? What did you miss?

4. Dyer describes an ordinary thing with tremendous patience and emotion. Look at photographs of a common object—trees or bicycles, for example—and write an essay in which you describe their usual mood and how one artist helps us see that mood more clearly.

MICHAEL HAMAD
Song Schematics

A S A KID, I saw random shapes in my head when I listened to music. They were mostly large, abstract geometric patterns, usually either blue or yellow in color, that floated around and interacted with some unseen gravitational force; other times I saw things that looked like gears or pulleys. Last year, after two decades of studying music theory, I stumbled into this weird visual language to explain what I hear. I call these drawings "schematics" because (as far as I can tell) they look like wiring diagrams.

My schematics are all drawn in real time (though I'll go back and add details, fix bad handwriting, and so on). They're also proportional. This one, of Phish playing "Chalk Dust Torture" in Camden, New Jersey, is roughly fourteen minutes long, so if you look at the exact center of the schematic, you're seeing what happens at minute seven. Creating these schematics is a form of meditation; when I'm drawing, I'm hearing the music, but I'm also thinking about other stuff: family, work, whatever. I think about my bad posture and the thickness of writing utensils. Sometimes I'll hear music that's not coming through my headphones. That's a strange feeling. Other times I'll listen to one piece of music and look at a schematic of something else, and I'll hear both. Mostly, though, I watch random ideas surface and disappear, and then I return directly to the music.

If you make music theory something fascinating to look at, will more people become interested in learning about it? I hope so. I've done more than a hundred of these in less than a year. Improvisational rock—the Grateful Dead, Phish, Umphrey's McGee—works best, but I want to see what a Katy Perry song looks like, or *Revolver*.[1] There's work to be done.

Printed in the music issue of the Believer (2014), *"a magazine of interviews, essays, and reviews" published by McSweeney's.*

1. Grateful Dead, rock band formed in 1965; Phish, rock band formed in 1983; Umphrey's McGee, rock band formed in 1997; Katy Perry (b. 1984), American singer-songwriter; *Revolver*, Beatles album released in 1966.

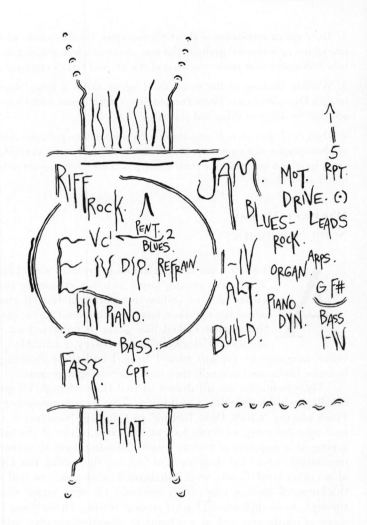

General

ARROWS = *tendencies, directions, or leanings in the music*

(.) = *major structural moments in the piece (to my ears)*

KEY = *tonal center, indicated by a capital letter (E, G, etc.)*

MODE = *the pitch collection used within a certain key*

I, II, III, ETC. = *harmonic function, or the gravity of certain chords next to each other within a certain key*

PENT = *a pentatonic (five-note) pitch collection or melody*

BLUES-ROCK = *improvisation using the blues-rock collection of pitches*

PROG = *the existence of a chord progression (it doesn't mean "progressive rock.")*

VC = *verse/chorus (1, 2, etc.); vocals are present*

ARPS = *arpeggios (instrument is usually indicated)*

MOT = *a recurring motif or melodic fragment*

^5, ^7, ETC. = *indication that a certain scale degree within the key is being emphasized melodically*

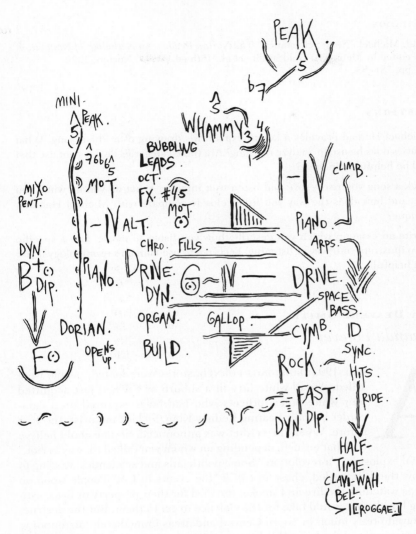

Dynamics

DYN DIP = *"dynamic dip" or a drop in volume or intensity*

BUILD = *A gradual increase in dynamics or intensity.*

DRIVE = *maintaining a pretty much full-throttle dynamics/intensity level*

GALLOP = *DRIVE on acid (you'll know it when you hear it)*

PEAK = *you'll know it when you hear it*

Percussion

FILLS = *the drummer plays outside the usual beat, adding intensity*

HITS = *two or more players lock together on a rhythmic or melodic riff*

SYNC HITS = *two or more instruments cooperate in some syncopated fashion*

Tone/Color

OCT = *the guitarist is playing in octaves*

FX = *the guitarist hits some sort of effects pedal*

MLA CITATION

Hamad, Michael. "Song Schematics." *The Norton Reader: An Anthology of Nonfiction*,
    edited by Melissa A. Goldthwaite et al., 15th ed., W. W. Norton, 2020,
    pp. 781–83.

QUESTIONS

1. Michael Hamad provides a key to explain his drawing of a Phish song. What
categories does he use to analyze the song? Are there categories he does not use that
would be helpful to include?

2. Pick a song you really love and listen to it intently. What do you do when you
listen, and how does the way you listen closely compare with Michael Hamad's
technique?

3. Write an essay in which you describe how you listen to music. Use a specific
song to illustrate your way of listening. Feel free to use Hamad's terminology if you
find it helpful.

ANNA DEAVERE SMITH

Wakanda Forever!

PRIL 1992: BUILDINGS BURNED, stores were looted, people were
killed. An all-white jury in a suburb of LA had just acquitted
four white police officers who had been captured on a cam-
corder brutally beating Rodney King, a black motorist, the year
before. When the verdict was announced, no one could believe
it. What ensued, depending on whom you talked to, was "a riot,"
a "social explosion," "a revolution." Some politicians and academics, waiting to
see how the dust settled, chose to call it "the events in LA." People stood on
rooftops watching the fire and smoke, terrified for their property or lives, esti-
mating how long it would take for the violence to get to them. But the destruction stayed pretty much in South Central and areas immediately surrounding
it—Koreatown and the lower Wilshire area. It never got to the shops in Beverly
Hills. The cry and anthem in the street was "No Justice—No Peace!"

After the news crews packed up their gear, I slipped into LA and moved
around the city and its surrounding areas, gathering stories: Simi Valley, Beverly Hills, Hollywood, Koreatown, and the epicenter of the riot, South Central. In South Central I talked with many people, including a former member
of the Black Panther Party, who was among those who fleshed out the background to what had happened. He had the demeanor of a wise man with his
graying dreadlocks, and he spoke about the war between black and brown men

Originally published in the New York Review of Books *(2018).*

and the Los Angeles Police Department, which he knew well from when he was in the BPP during the 1970s. He saw the impact that the war was having on the young brothers he worked with in the 1990s—members of gangs and ex-members of gangs.

It occurred to me in the middle of my conversation with the ex-Panther that "No Justice—No Peace" was to the Los Angeles riots and the incidents that had led up to them what "All Power to the People" had been to the rise and fall of the Black Panther Party. I asked, "Hey, has 'No Justice—No Peace' taken the place of 'All Power to the People'?" After pondering for several seconds, he burst out, "Oh no! Ain't nothin' *ever* gonna be as powerful as 'All Power to the People'!" If memory serves, I believe we finished the moment off with a rejuvenating high five and our black power fists shooting up in the air.

At the end of the 1960s and 1970s, some (but hardly enough) power got shared. Yes, blacks could sit at lunch counters and shop in department stores, but whom did that benefit? The business owners and the bankers. The color of the owners and bankers did not change enough to make it notable. There was a black arts movement in the 1960s, but that in no way changed who ran the movie studios. That is still the case today.

We moved from a desire for power to a desire for justice. "No Justice—No   5
Peace" spoke to the dismay many felt in the face of a legal system that protects power at the expense of justice. The slogan has been with us for more than twenty-five years, and it has brought us up to this moment. It is still chanted every time a police officer kills or shoots someone who appears to have been denied due process.

The megahit film *Black Panther*, released fifty years after the cultural rebellions of the 1960s, has elicited much praise. The loudest praise concerns the bottom line. It is among the ten highest-grossing films ever made. Many of its black fans praise the fact that the director, Ryan Coogler, is black and that the cast and creative team are almost entirely black. It has been difficult to get such a movie made. Coogler did it. It is only right that these fine artists were able to grab an opportunity and succeed glowingly. The movie's financial success is a kind of claim on power. Will "No Justice—No Peace" be replaced by "Wakanda Forever"?

The focus of *Black Panther* is a superhero from the Marvel Comic Universe, T'Challa, the Black Panther (played by Chadwick Boseman), who is also a king. After the sudden death of his father, T'Chaka, T'Challa has inherited the throne of the Kingdom of Wakanda, a country in Africa and a utopia in the tradition of El Dorado and Shangri-La.[1] Unmarked by the evils of colonialism, Wakanda is beautiful. It is also wealthy because it has a very valuable metal—vibranium.

Wakanda has survived by largely cutting itself off from the world, but this strategy is questioned in the course of the film. Erik Killmonger (Michael B.

---

1. El Dorado, mythical city of gold, sought by Spaniards exploring the western hemisphere; Shangri-La, fictional setting for a magical lamasery in James Hilton's *Lost Horizon* (1933).

Jordan), the cousin that King T'Challa did not know he had, shows up and disrupts utopia. He seeks to take the throne, change the values upon which Wakanda is based, and change its position in the world. In battle, he pushes T'Challa off a high cliff to his death, and that appears to be that.

Killmonger is competitive; he behaves with no decorum. He has some of the same traits as President Trump. As questionable and distressing as his behavior is to some, once he has the throne, Killmonger gains the support of many in Wakanda, including the head of the fabulously powerful all-female security guard, Okoye (Danai Gurira). In a way that people will have to see for themselves, the throne is restored in the end to T'Challa, who did not die after all.

10   The Black Panther character has a long, rich history. Seeing an opportunity to bring a black superhero into the almost entirely white comic book world, Jack Kirby, a Jewish artist, introduced the Black Panther into the world of the Fantastic Four in 1966. Stan Lee, the former publisher and chairman of Marvel Comics and who had a cameo in the movie, was cocreator. The Black Panther comic book character predated the Black Panther Party by a few months. Not wanting to carry the baggage of the controversial BPP, Marvel at one point changed the character's name to the Black Leopard, but the original name prevailed.

The Black Panther had many permutations. Christopher Priest in the late 1990s and early 2000s and Reginald Hudlin in the mid-2000s, both African-American, wrote comics in the series. They are said to have given the character a more Africa-centered, self-determining ethos. Most recently, Ta-Nehisi Coates, following the extraordinary success of his *Between the World and Me* (2015), was approached by Marvel to write a Black Panther series with the illustrator Brian Stelfreeze, and another chapter in the life of the superhero was born.

The principal artists in the film had not worked on any production of this scale before. Coogler and his core company—Michael B. Jordan, the cinematographer Rachel Morrison, the composer Ludwig Göransson, and the production designer Hannah Beachler—had worked together since Coogler's exquisite film *Fruitvale Station* (2013). To that team, Coogler added the costume designer Ruth Carter, who had worked on large productions before, Spike Lee's *Malcolm X* (1992) among them. Some of the actors are not only veterans, they are movie royalty, for example Angela Bassett and Forest Whitaker, and from South Africa, John Kani. Others are among the best of their generation: Lupita Nyong'o, Boseman, Gurira, Daniel Kaluuya, Sterling K. Brown.

The relative newcomer Letitia Wright, who plays T'Challa's sister, Shuri, is fresh-faced in every way. Early in the film, her brother is required to solidify his position as king in ritual combat following the death of his father. Breaking the intensity of the ceremony, Shuri protests about the corset she is wearing, wishing to speed things along so she can take it off. She represents a new type of young black woman—a science genius who spends her days in a lab making inventions and powering what she invents with vibranium.

Boseman, whose disciplined and often subtle performance is at the center of the wonderful acting ensemble, was asked by Brooke Anderson on *Enter-*

tainment Television to differentiate between working on the sets of *Black Panther* and *Captain America: Civil War* (2016), the film in the Avengers series in which he played the Black Panther for the first time. He replied:

> There's a certain amount of comfort with *Avengers* because it's been done before. . . . We are all comfortable with each other and we have a lot of fun. Not that we didn't have fun on the *Black Panther* set, but it was a new thing and you don't quite know what it's supposed to look like or sound like or feel like so it's a lot more pressure and angst on the *Black Panther* set.

But it was a new thing and you don't quite know what it's supposed to look like or sound like . . . There couldn't be better conditions for innovation and creativity. And yet they had to meet a high bar. They jumped with the catlike dexterity of the Panther himself, from a low-budget work to one that is mainstream and epic in scale. In an interview, Hannah Beachler spoke about having worked with smaller budgets on smaller projects. For *Black Panther* she had to manage three hundred people.

For my second viewing, I sat in the back of a theater with one of the American film industry's most accomplished production designers as she whispered to me, pointing out where computer-generated imaging was used, where it wasn't, etc. Just as Kirby and Lee brought the Black Panther into the world of comics at the right time, Coogler, Disney, and Marvel have brought the Black Panther into the world of film at the right time. Without the technological accomplishments in film that predate *Black Panther*, its captivating beauty, breathtaking views, and edge-of-your-seat moments would not be possible.

It is obvious that Disney and Marvel had Coogler's back. Filmmaking is collaborative. The producers are essential. Money needs to flow. This production must have had a squadron of veteran participants, many of whom, most likely, given the demographics of Hollywood, were not black, but supported Coogler's vision. The movie hit screens around the world following #OscarsSoWhite, #MeToo, #TimesUp, and #BlackLivesMatter, with its continuing relevance. A student of mine, a talented young black writer, believes this is a sign that doors will open for him. I hope that's true.

Black Panther was transformational to many people. Many talked about what it meant to see black folks in power. Black American males in particular talked about what it meant to "see themselves" up there on that screen. Women have commented on how thrilling it was to see powerful black women: T'Challa's ex, Nakia (Lupita Nyong'o); his sister, Shuri; and the all-female security guard, the Dora Milaje, led by Okoye. It could go without saying, but it shouldn't, that Ramonda, the queen mother, as played by Angela Bassett, reigns as only Angela can.

Ryan Coogler gave audiences over two hours of pleasure, fear, excitement, sexiness, and beauty. We have an opportunity to take the delight it has pricked and do something with it. If in fact the movie is transformative, will the transformation stop the moment we leave the theater, with the empty popcorn bucket lying on the carpet, the twisted straw from the soda under the seat? There is a conversation to be had.

20   For now, the conversations with the widest reach are the ones manufactured by the entertainment industry. Those conversations are geared toward
selling things. They evoke our desire and our fandom but they leave us in a
state of passive observance. Chadwick Boseman has forty cousins. That's
interesting. How does Michael B. Jordan get in shape? I took notes myself—he
drinks so much water he can't sleep through the night. He works out six times
a day. "How long are your workouts?," talk show hosts asked, the female ones
leaning forward and gazing at his muscles, the male ones sitting back and
grinning. He dodged the question and said it wasn't about the time—and with
a wide welcoming smile, obviously understanding that his job as a movie star
is to spread his charm. Keep it light. Swimmers say it's what's happening under
the surface of the water that gives you speed.
        An ancillary benefit of the movie could be the small but not inconsequen-
tial pockets of conversations about the condition of black people in America.
But just keeping it light won't get us there. Elaine Brown, former chairwoman
of the Black Panther Party, had this to say about buying into the drama of
transformation, of revolution:

> If you are committed—if you seriously make a commitment (and that com-
> mitment must be based not on hate but on love) . . . then you gon' have to
> realize that this may have to be a lifetime commitment. . . . So don't get
> hung up on your own ego and your own image and pumping up your mus-
> cles and putting on a black beret or some kinda Malcolm X hat or whatever
> other regalia and symbolic *vestment* you can put on your body. Think in
> terms of what are you going to do for black people. I'm saying that these are
> the long haul.

        A sense of self comes from the mirror in which you see yourself—and it
also comes from gathering information about how others see you. For eight
years, the world saw two powerful, beautiful, sexy black people: President and
Mrs. Obama. I heard as many, if not more, passing remarks about the first
lady's "guns" as I did about the work she was doing to draw attention to the
health and wellbeing of children.
        Inauguration Day 2008 was historic because we defied history and elected
an African-American president—one with an actual African father. One promise of that day was how much it would mean for little black boys and little black
girls to see themselves in the White House. I watched the redcaps at Union
Station prance with pride as they hauled luggage off the train, and the lightness of their step was not just because some of the luggage was Beyoncé's.
        There is a need among black Americans to see ourselves in power. Coogler,
Disney, Marvel, and company have tapped into that need—and they have prof-
ited from it. The need is not unique to blacks. For example, several of *Black
Panther*'s action sequences were filmed in Busan, South Korea, and a Korean
moviegoer spoke in an interview about how much he'd like to see a major
motion picture with Korean superheroes.
25   What is it about the human condition that causes us to need to see ourselves in art forms? Is it that art forms are meant to be mirrors? Have racism

and tribalism so infiltrated the manufacturers of art that distortion has prevailed? Does a project like *Black Panther*, even as it focuses on one world, help fix the mirror itself?

A. A. M. Bernstein is a physicist I talked to when I was trying to understand some things about racial identity. We wound up talking about mirrors—real mirrors, not metaphorical ones. He said:

> So a simple mirror is just a flat, reflecting substance, like, for example, it's a piece of glass which is silvered on the back. Physicists talk about distortion. It's a big subject, distortions. I'll give you an example—if you want to see the stars, you make a big reflecting mirror. That's one of the ways. You make a big telescope, so you can gather in a lot of light and then it focuses at a point. And then there's always something called the circle of confusion. So if ya don't make the thing perfectly spherical or perfectly parabolic—if there are errors in the construction which you can see, it's easy, if it's huge, then you're gonna have a circle of confusion, you see? . . . If you're counting stars, for example, and two look like one, you've blown it.

It would seem that everyone would benefit from a mirror without distortion. It would be better to see two stars than two stars that look like one. We have worked on fixing the distortion before. The original *Roots* series was one very important correction. *Roots*, however, set its heroes in frightening surroundings, and they were victims of cruelty and the capriciousness of power. *Black Panther* sets the superheroes in their own land and they are not victims, they are royals.

I am perplexed about Erik Killmonger, T'Challa's cousin, who comes to take away the throne. We learn in a flashback about his father, N'Jobu (Sterling K. Brown), who left Wakanda for the US and met an American woman there. They live in Oakland, the birthplace of the Black Panther Party. Unlike his brother, King T'Chaka, who has kept Wakanda in isolation, N'Jobu comes to believe that Wakanda should use the power and value of vibranium to start an international revolution and liberate the oppressed peoples of the world.

N'Jobu betrays T'Chaka. He reveals the presence of Wakanda to a black-market arms dealer from South Africa—one of only two white characters in the movie—who plans to infiltrate the country and steal vibranium. T'Chaka confronts N'Jobu in his Oakland apartment, kills him, and leaves his body for his son to find.

Erik grows up to be what looks like a winner. He goes to MIT. He gets a piece of the American dream. He becomes a Navy Seal, then a black-ops soldier who specializes in targeted assassinations. He takes the name Killmonger and lines his body with tattoos that stand for the many lives he has claimed.

The American dream, which would seem to be firmly in Erik's grasp, cannot cure what was taken from him when his father was killed. He is filled with rage. Does Erik's pain and brokenness suggest that even if a black male is successful in this culture, even if he climbs to the top, even if he serves the nation and is rewarded for it, he feels a loss? A loss that cannot be filled by, say, more of America? Erik is broken. The Black Panther has succeeded in giving some black viewers a feeling of being whole.

30

We won't know for a while if the effect of *Black Panther* goes beyond the box office, the proceeds of which will lie, for the most part, in the palms of the producers. We won't know how long the door will stay open for more artists of other colors to make their way through. We won't know how long it will take for a Latino superhero or an Asian superhero to have a movie, or a woman of color superhero to have her own movie, or if and when a trans superhero will walk the world stage with the grace and power of the Black Panther.

We won't know if a judge, having seen *Black Panther*, will think differently in sentencing a black man or woman standing at the bench. We won't know how *Black Panther* will affect kids in schools. We won't know if the character of Shuri will be enough to encourage a girl to become a physicist. Will Shuri have made it any easier for women heading to Silicon Valley to gain opportunity and respect? There's a lot we don't know. But anyway.

Wakanda Forever! For now.

MLA CITATION

Smith, Anna Deavere. "Wakanda Forever!" *The Norton Reader: An Anthology of Nonfiction*, edited by Melissa A. Goldthwaite et al., 15th ed., W. W. Norton, 2020, pp. 784–90.

QUESTIONS

1. How does learning some of the political context around *Black Panther* enhance your understanding of the movie?

2. This is much more than a movie review. Look at where Anna Deavere Smith included material ordinarily part of a movie review and where she includes more context, different kinds of material. How do the two work together?

3. Toward the end of the essay (paragraphs 23–26), Smith considers the importance of seeing ourselves in positions of power and in art. How is this relevant to her discussion of *Black Panther*? When have you felt yourself represented in art and in what ways did it matter to you?

4. Smith wonders if *Black Panther* will change anyone's mind about the power and wisdom of black people. Do you think the movie could have that power? How would you know if it did? What test might you devise to answer her question?

5. Watch *Black Panther* (again) and write an essay about how Smith's review changed your understanding of the movie.

SCOTT RUSSELL SANDERS
Hooks Baited with Darkness

I FIRST READ WALDEN when I was seventeen, the summer before starting college, at the urging of a high school teacher who sensed that my adolescent mind, brimming with questions, would benefit from grappling with a truly radical thinker. Much of the book baffled me. The tone shifted unpredictably from conversational to prophetic, from jokey to stern, from earthy to mystical. I was bewildered by some of the lengthy sentences, which zigzagged among ideas and images, and I was stumped by the cryptic short ones, which seemed to compress whole paragraphs of meaning into a few words. Not yet having made any big decisions about how to lead my life, I couldn't figure out what was troubling this Henry David Thoreau. So what if his neighbors thought he should use his Harvard degree to land a job and a wife, and then proceed to have kids, buy a house, get rich, and distribute alms to the poor? Couldn't he just ignore the scolds and go his own way? Not yet having lost a loved one to accident, illness, or old age, I only dimly understood his brooding about that amoral process we call nature. So what if armies of red ants and black ants slaughtered one another, herons gobbled tadpoles, a dead horse stank up the woods, or a thousand seeds perished for each one that took root? What did all that mayhem and waste have to do with us, the owners of souls aiming at heaven?

At seventeen, still a believer in souls and heaven, I didn't know which parts of the book were supposed to be wise and which parts cranky, so I read it all with an open mind. While missing much, I was sufficiently intrigued by the story of Thoreau's sojourn in the woods and sufficiently engaged by his cocky, inquisitive manner to keep reading. His brashness was evident from the opening paragraphs, where he announces that he will write in the first person, thus breaking one of the cardinal rules of composition I had learned in school, and he places himself at the center of his book without apology: "I should not talk so much about myself if there were any body else whom I knew as well. Unfortunately, I am confined to this theme by the narrowness of my experience."[1] As a boy from the back roads of Ohio, untraveled and unsophisticated, wondering what to make of my own narrow experience, I felt Thoreau was speaking to

Originally appeared in Daedalus *(2014), the quarterly journal of the American Academy of Arts and Sciences. All notes in this piece were written by the author.*

1. Henry David Thoreau, *Walden,* ed. Jeffrey S. Cramer (New Haven, Conn.: Yale University Press, 2004), 2. Originally published in 1854 under the title *Walden: or, Life in the Woods,* Thoreau's most famous book has gone through many editions. Cramer's edition, with an introduction by Denis Donoghue, is the most authoritative currently available: it has the additional virtue of being inexpensive and well suited to classroom use. All subsequent quotations from *Walden* will be taken from this edition, and the page numbers will be shown within parentheses following the quotation. All italics within quotations are in the original.

me, an impression confirmed a few lines later: "Perhaps these pages are more particularly addressed to poor students" (2). While I was a good student academically, I was a poor one financially, able to enroll in an Ivy League college that fall only thanks to a full scholarship.

Short of cash, I was long on country skills. My parents and neighbors, all of them frugal, taught me how to hunt, fish, garden, can, fence a pasture, care for livestock, fell trees, fix machines, repair a house, run electrical wiring, and sew on buttons. That summer of my first *Walden* reading I spent as an apprentice carpenter, learning to frame, hang drywall, install trim, and shingle roofs. So I took seriously Thoreau's suggestion that the students at Harvard, instead of paying rent, could have saved money and gained practical knowledge by building their own dormitories. I was fascinated by his detailed account of the cabin construction, from the digging of a cellar hole and the laying up of a chimney to the plastering of walls. Because I enjoyed such work, I understood why he would ask: "Shall we forever resign the pleasure of construction to the carpenter? What does architecture amount to in the experience of the mass of men? I never in all my walks came across a man engaged in so simple and natural an occupation as building his house" (48). Since I had cobbled together treehouses in the backyard maples, forts in the meadow, and brush huts in the woods, and since I had helped frame homes for strangers, I expected to build my own house one day.

Here was a philosopher with dirt under his fingernails and calluses on his palms. Here was a man famous for his ideas who could say, "To be a philosopher is not merely to have subtle thoughts, nor even to found a school, but so to love wisdom as to live according to its dictates, a life of simplicity, independence, magnanimity, and trust. It is to solve some of the problems of life, not only theoretically, but practically" (14). The thrifty, resourceful people among whom I grew up prepared me to admire Thoreau's effort to provide some of the necessities of life with his own hands: not only by constructing a cabin, but also by sawing and splitting fallen trees for the stove (from Emerson's woodlot), by hauling water from the pond (still safe to drink in his day), and by hoeing beans (he made it only partway through his seven miles of rows and resolved to plant fewer the following year).

5   I did not yet appreciate, however, why he took such pains to distinguish between the necessities of life and luxuries, between enough and too much. When I packed for college that summer, everything I owned—clothes, books, towel, toiletries, clock radio, slide rule—fitted into my grandfather's sea trunk, which I could carry on my shoulder. I did not feel encumbered by property. Nor did I feel, with a radio as my only electronic device and without a car, that technology was forcing me to live at a faster and faster pace, and thus I could not grasp why Thoreau fretted about the accelerating influence of railroads, factories, and telegraph. Likewise, in that limbo between high school and college, without bills to pay or appointments to keep, with no occupations aside from carpentry, reading, meals, and sleep, I felt no need to simplify my life.

While my upbringing enabled me to follow the practical side of what Thoreau called his "experiment" in simple living, my youth prevented me from fully

understanding the philosophy that accompanied it.[2] My difficulty had as much
to do with his style as with his ideas. I puzzled over his paradoxes: "We do not
ride on the railroad; it rides upon us" (98–99). I resisted his exaggerations: "I
have lived some thirty years on this planet, and I have yet to hear the first syllable of valuable or even earnest advice from my seniors" (8). Well, I found myself
asking, who had taught him to build houses, grow beans, or tie his shoes? If
people older than thirty had nothing to teach him, why did he read all those
ancient—and presumably elderly—sages from India and China and Greece?
I bridled at his boastful claims: "There is a certain class of unbelievers who
sometimes ask me such questions as, if I think that I can live on vegetable food
alone; and to strike at the root of the matter at once—for the root is faith—I am
accustomed to answer such, that I can live on board nails" (69). Really? Would
those be the nails he salvaged from the Irishman's shanty? Would he scrape
off the rust before devouring them? Such faith, as he called it, reminded me of
certain implausible beliefs I was beginning to question in church.

Thoreau often seemed to hide his meaning in riddles, like a Shakespear-
ean fool wary of offending the king. (I had read *King Lear* at the urging of the
same high school teacher.) What did he mean, for instance, by saying "I have
a great deal of company in my house; especially in the morning, when nobody
calls" (147–148)? Or what did he mean by saying of the men who came to fish
in the pond at night that "they plainly fished much more in the Walden Pond
of their own natures, and baited their hooks with darkness" (141)? It was far
from plain to me. Baiting with worms or crickets, sure. But darkness? Or when
he claims, "It is a surprising and memorable, as well as valuable experience, to
be lost in the woods any time," how does he arrive, a few lines later, at his
grand conclusion: "Not till we are lost, in other words, not till we have lost the
world, do we begin to find ourselves, and realize where we are and the infinite
extent of our relations" (186–187)? Getting lost in the woods I could imagine,
but I could not see how this might lead to finding one's place in infinity.

Time and again, *Walden* makes such dizzying leaps from the literal to the
symbolic. Consider one further example, from a passage on carpentry, a subject
I was less ignorant of than most other things:

> I would not be one of those who will foolishly drive a nail into mere lath
> and plastering; such a deed would keep me awake nights. Give me a ham-
> mer, and let me feel for the furring. Do not depend on the putty. Drive a
> nail home and clinch it so faithfully that you can wake up in the night and
> think of your work with satisfaction—a work at which you would not be
> ashamed to invoke the Muse. So will help you God, and so only. Every nail
> driven should be as another rivet in the machine of the universe, you carrying
> on the work. (358–359)

2. The words *experiment, experiments,* and *experimentalists* appear seventeen times in
Walden, a sign of Thoreau's respect for the methods and prestige of science. By calling
his stay at Walden Pond an experiment, he may also have wished to present it as a one-
man alternative to the communal experiments—most of them, like Brook Farm and
Fruitlands, short-lived—that were springing up across the United States and Europe in
the 1840s and 1850s.

I knew about lath, plaster, putty, and furring; I knew about the satisfaction of driving a nail home with two or three blows. So I followed this passage easily enough until I came to the Muse and God, and then I scratched my head, wondering how they entered the picture, and wondering even more how a well-driven nail and the person who hammered it could be useful to the universe.

10   Even where the style posed no problems, I often balked at the philosophy. Take the chapter grandly entitled "Higher Laws." In the opening lines, Thoreau confesses an urge to kill and devour a woodchuck raw, an impulse that stirs him to reflect: "I found in myself, and still find, an instinct toward a higher, or, as it is named, spiritual life, as do most men, and another toward a primitive rank and savage one, and I reverence them both" (229). Thus far I stayed with him, for I felt simultaneously the allure of science and girls, of books and basketball, and I was glad to think that both of these instincts deserved respect. But then Thoreau spends several pages elevating "purity" and denigrating everything "primitive rank and savage" about human life, from the eating of meat and the drinking of tea to "sensuality" of every kind, especially the "generative energy, which, when we are loose, dissipates and makes us unclean, when we are continent invigorates and inspires us" (239–240). Lest readers miss the allusion to sex, he goes on to insist that "Chastity is the flowering of man" (240), sounding less like a dissident thinker than like a Scoutmaster or high school nurse. Having begun by claiming to "reverence" the body's urges, Thoreau ends by declaring, "He is blessed who is assured that the animal is dying out in him day by day, and the divine being established" (240)—advice that could have come from St. Paul, the chief source of shame in my childhood.

Somewhere between hungering after a woodchuck and repudiating sex, Thoreau provoked me to say no. I could not have fully explained the grounds of my objection, neither at this point in my reading nor at any other point where I disagreed with him, but the fact of my disagreement, and the force of it, was exhilarating. I sensed that to question his philosophy, to test his ideas and opinions against my own reason and experience, was wholly in keeping with the philosophy itself.

Despite my reservations and confusions, what came through to me from *Walden*, and what most excited me, was Thoreau's desire to lead a meaningful life. The very title of the second chapter—"Where I Lived, and What I Lived For"— thrilled me. The "where" concerned me less than the "what for." At seventeen, I imagined that life must have a purpose beyond mere survival and the passing on of genes, beyond piling up money and possessions, beyond auditioning for paradise. But what might that purpose be? How could one discover it? And if life did have a purpose beyond those dictated by religion, economics, or biology, what then? How should one live in light of it?

I was haunted by such questions, yet my friends never spoke of them, and the adults I knew seemed to have resigned themselves to one or another conventional answer. So it was heartening to find Thoreau asking these very questions, in a passage I would later discover to be among the most celebrated in the book:

> I went to the woods because I wished to live deliberately, to front only the essential facts of life, and see if I could not learn what it had to teach, and not, when I came to die, discover that I had not lived. I did not wish to live what was not life, living is so dear; nor did I wish to practise resignation, unless it was quite necessary. I wanted to live deep and suck out all the marrow of life, to live so sturdily and Spartan-like as to put to rout all that was not life, to cut a broad swath and shave close, to drive life into a corner, and reduce it to its lowest terms, and, if it proved to be mean, why then to get the whole and genuine meanness of it, and publish its meanness to the world; or if it were sublime, to know it by experience, and be able to give a true account of it in my next excursion. For most men, it appears to me, are in a strange uncertainty about it, whether it is of the devil or of God, and have *somewhat hastily* concluded that it is the chief end of man here to "glorify God and enjoy him forever." (97)

Behind the bravado, I could hear his longing to find a true path, a way of spending his time and talents that would be worthy of the precious, fleeting gift of life. I shared that longing, as I shared his wariness about otherworldly philosophies. I did not recognize the source of his quotation in the last line— the Westminster Shorter Catechism, which opens with the declaration that "Man's chief end is to glorify God and to enjoy him forever"—but I had heard such pieties often, in sermons that discounted the value of life here and now except as preparation for life hereafter. What appealed to me most deeply in that first reading of *Walden* was Thoreau's determination to observe and enjoy the marvels of Earth, to be fully awake and alive, right here, right now.

Today, fifty years and many rereadings later, *Walden* is quite a different book   15 for me: less bewildering, since I have made my share of difficult choices and suffered my share of losses, and also more challenging, since I have come to recognize more clearly my own limitations as well as those of the book.

Although I have renovated the old house in which my wife and I reared our children, and in which we now entertain our grandchildren, I realize, at age sixty-seven, I will never build a house from scratch. Although I remain cautious about technology—agreeing with Thoreau that many of our inventions merely offer "improved means to an unimproved end" (55)—my life depends on electricity and petroleum and the devices they power, as well as on the global networks that supply them. I try to minimize my possessions, giving away whatever I don't use, yet I keep acquiring new ones, which must be paid for, stored, insured, cleaned, repaired, and eventually replaced, thus demonstrating the truth of Thoreau's dictum that "the cost of a thing is the amount of . . . life which is required to be exchanged for it, immediately or in the long run" (32). I would rather not think about money, yet I spend hours keeping track of its coming and going, mainly to satisfy the IRS, merchants, and banks. As a husband, father, and now a grandfather, as a teacher for the past four decades, and as a citizen engaged in numerous causes, I bear responsibilities that I could not have imagined at the age of seventeen. No matter how I strive to simplify my life, it remains stubbornly complex. In short, I have failed to become the unencumbered, self-reliant, perpetually awake person I had envisioned in my youth.

Neither, I discovered, was Thoreau as unencumbered as he appeared to be on my first reading of *Walden*. During his sojourn in the woods, he frequently visited the village, saw friends, ate meals with his family, helped in the family pencil business, earned money from surveying and other jobs, carried on correspondence, gave lectures, and took trips. He revealed only part of himself on the page, which is all that even the most personal book can do. On the other hand, he presented far more of his thoughts and observations than actually occurred during the twenty-six months he spent living in the woods. The chronicle of his experiment at Walden Pond draws on material recorded in his journal from a period beginning years before and extending years after his time at the cabin. As a result, many passages in the book seem overstuffed, as if he felt compelled to include every anecdote, aphorism, witticism, image, and insight that had ever come to him concerning a given topic. Having worked with many young writers in my classes, and having once been a young writer myself, I recognize this tendency to excess as a common sign of ambition. Better overdo it than leave out something valuable.[3] I am more tolerant now of this and other stylistic quirks in *Walden*. The bluster and bragging are more than compensated for by the vigor and candor. For every showy allusion to classical literature or mythology, there is a burst of gritty American vernacular. For every willful obscurity in the prose, there are a dozen brilliant clarities.

While I am less inclined to quarrel with the style of *Walden*, I am more inclined to question some of the postures and opinions of the brash narrator. Thoreau's portrait of a solitary, self-sufficient life in the woods now appears to me as excessively, if unconsciously, male. His radical individualism, however necessary in his day as a bulwark against demands for conformity from church and society, now appears too narrow, rejecting as it does all responsibility of the self toward others. His opposition of spirit and flesh strikes me today as an expression of the dualism at the root of our ecological crisis, a dualism that sets mind against matter, culture against wildness. Thus our patron saint of environmentalism can declare: "Nature is hard to be overcome, but she must be overcome" (241). Recognizing such misgivings does not diminish my appreciation for the book's many strengths, or my gratitude for all that it has taught me.

When I compare my current reading of *Walden* with impressions from that first reading, I am reminded of Italo Calvino's remark that books read in youth can be "formative, in the sense that they give a form to future experiences, providing models, terms of comparison, schemes for classification, scales of value, exemplars of beauty. . . . If we reread the book at a mature age, we are likely to rediscover these constants, which by this time are part of our

3. Such an encyclopedic ambition has resulted in many a bloated, shapeless tome, of course, but it also gave us *Moby-Dick* and *Leaves of Grass*, which were published, respectively, three years before and one year after *Walden*.

inner mechanisms, but whose origins we have long forgotten."[4] My experience differs from Calvino's description only in that I have not forgotten the source of those "inner mechanisms." The example of Thoreau's life and the challenge of his thought remain potent influences for me, as they have been potent influences for generations of readers.

Of all his writings, *Walden* has had the broadest impact, moving countless   20 people to seek a way of life that is close to nature, materially simple, purposeful, and reflective. His vision has been transmitted and transmuted through a lineage of American writers, from John Muir and Aldo Leopold and Rachel Carson to Wendell Berry and Terry Tempest Williams and Bill McKibben, all of them striving to harmonize human behavior with the constraints and patterns of our planetary home. We are far from achieving such a harmony—as witness climate disruption, for example, or the accelerated extinction of species—but we would be farther still without the questioning and imagining Thoreau inspired. We have him to thank, as much as anyone, for the shift in consciousness that led to the creation of America's national parks, designated wilderness areas, and laws aimed at protecting air and water and soil. We still need his cautionary, curmudgeonly voice, because in our day the craving for more—more stuff, more money, more power—no longer merely enslaves individuals; it degrades the conditions for life on Earth.

Great books read us as surely as we read them, revealing, by the aspects of our character and personal history they illuminate, who we are. Today when I revisit *Walden* it is usually in the company of my students, whose reactions remind me of my own early bafflement, resistance, and exhilaration. When they protest, as they often do, that they have no taste for Thoreau's experiment in simple living, I draw their attention to his disclaimer: "I would not have any one adopt *my* mode of living on any account; for, beside that before he has fairly learned it I may have found out another for myself, I desire that there may be as many different persons in the world as possible; but I would have each one be very careful to find out and pursue *his own* way, and not his father's or his mother's or his neighbor's instead" (75). Finding out and pursuing one's own way, while learning all one can about the ways that others have found, is the essential task not merely of education but of life.

Thoreau continued his search after moving from the cabin back into town, a search that would lead to his public denunciation of slavery, to inventions that improved the making of pencils and the refining of graphite, to meticulous natural history studies, to research on Native Americans, to essays and journals and travel accounts that would fill a shelf of books published after his death. Wanting my students to bear in mind that ongoing life, beyond the confines of *Walden*, I draw their attention to another passage, this one from the final chapter: "I left the woods for as good a reason as I went there. Perhaps it seemed to me that I had several more lives to live, and could not spare any more time for

4. Italo Calvino, *The Uses of Literature*, trans. Patrick Creagh (New York: Harcourt Brace Jovanovich, 1986), 127.

that one. It is remarkable how easily and insensibly we fall into a particular route, and make a beaten track for ourselves" (351). What he sought for himself and urged for his readers was the freedom to keep thinking, keep experimenting, keep striking out afresh.

We commonly imagine Thoreau outdoors, chasing loons on the pond, watching frozen mud thaw, identifying wild-flowers, plucking wild fruits. But those excursions were informed and interpreted during countless hours he spent indoors, reading and writing. The chapter of *Walden* called "Reading" is a hymn to books, as eloquent as any of his tributes to nature. "Books are the treasured wealth of the world and the fit inheritance of generations and nations," he declares, recommending to us not just any books, but the great ones, the classics, those "we have to stand on tip-toe to read and devote our most alert and wakeful hours to" (110, 112). Such effort, he promises, will be abundantly repaid:

> There are probably words addressed to our condition exactly, which, if we could really hear and understand, would be more salutary than the morning or the spring to our lives, and possibly put a new aspect on the face of things for us. How many a man has dated a new era in his life from the reading of a book. The book exists for us perchance which will explain our miracles and reveal new ones. The at present unutterable things we may find somewhere uttered. These same questions that disturb and puzzle and confound us have in their turn occurred to all the wise men; not one has been omitted; and each has answered them, according to his ability, by his words and his life. (115–116)

Besieged as we are by advertisements and the cult of consumerism, racing to keep up with our gadgets, rushing from one sensation to the next, we need more than ever to ask the questions posed in *Walden*: What is life for? What are the necessities of a good life? How much is enough? Do we own our devices or do they own us? What is our place in nature? How do we balance individual freedom with social responsibility? How should we spend our days? Whether or not *Walden* speaks to your condition, I tell my students, there are other books that will do so, giving voice to what you have felt but have not been able to say, asking your deepest questions, stirring you to more intense life.

MLA CITATION

Sanders, Scott Russell. "Hooks Baited with Darkness." *The Norton Reader: An Anthology of Nonfiction*, edited by Melissa A. Goldthwaite et al., 15th ed., W. W. Norton, 2020, pp. 791–98.

QUESTIONS

1. How did Scott Russell Sanders's experience working with his hands inform his reading of *Walden*?

2. What do you think are the most important changes in Sanders's understanding of Thoreau over the years?

3. Read Thoreau's "The Battle of the Ants" (pp. 725–27), an excerpt from *Walden*. How does your sense of his purpose and voice compare with Sanders's?

4. Why do you think Sanders resisted Thoreau's warnings about technology (paragraph 6)?

5. Following Sanders's model, write an honest essay in which you detail what you admire, dislike, and do not yet understand about a celebrated text.

Ngũgĩ wa Thiong'o
Decolonizing the Mind

I WAS BORN into a large peasant family: father, four wives and about twenty-eight children. I also belonged, as we all did in those days, to a wider extended family and to the community as a whole.

We spoke Gĩkũyũ[1] as we worked in the fields. We spoke Gĩkũyũ in and outside the home. I can vividly recall those evenings of storytelling around the fireside. It was mostly the grown-ups telling the children but everybody was interested and involved. We children would re-tell the stories the following day to other children who worked in the fields picking the pyrethrum[2] flowers, tea-leaves or coffee beans of our European and African landlords.

The stories, with mostly animals as the main characters, were all told in Gĩkũyũ. Hare, being small, weak but full of innovative wit and cunning, was our hero. We identified with him as he struggled against the brutes of prey like lion, leopard, hyena. His victories were our victories and we learned that the apparently weak can outwit the strong. We followed the animals in their struggle against hostile nature—drought, rain, sun, wind—a confrontation often forcing them to search for forms of co-operation. But we were also interested in their struggles amongst themselves, and particularly between the beasts and the victims of prey. These twin struggles, against nature and other animals, reflected real-life struggles in the human world.

Not that we neglected stories with human beings as the main characters. There were two types of characters in such human-centered narratives: the species of truly human beings with qualities of courage, kindness, mercy, hatred of evil, concern for others; and a man-eat-man two-mouthed species with qualities of greed, selfishness, individualism and hatred of what was good for the

Published in Decolonizing the Mind: The Politics of Language in African Literature *(1986), an essay collection that Ngũgĩ wa Thiong'o describes as his "farewell to English as a vehicle for any of [his] writings." The Kenyan novelist, playwright, and social critic has been a pioneer of African literature and a critic of colonialism. Although his first novels were composed in English, Ngũgĩ now writes in Gĩkũyũ, often translating his own work into English.*

1. Language spoken by the Gĩkũyũ (or Kikuyu) people, the majority of Kenyans.
2. Type of chrysanthemum, often used as an insecticide or for medicinal purposes.

larger co-operative community. Co-operation as the ultimate good in a community was a constant theme. It could unite human beings with animals against ogres and beasts of prey, as in the story of how dove, after being fed with castor-oil seeds, was sent to fetch a smith working far away from home and whose pregnant wife was being threatened by these man-eating two-mouthed ogres.

5   There were good and bad story-tellers. A good one could tell the same story over and over again, and it would always be fresh to us, the listeners. He or she could tell a story told by someone else and make it more alive and dramatic. The differences really were in the use of words and images and the inflection of voices to effect different tones.

We therefore learned to value words for their meaning and nuances. Language was not a mere string of words. It had a suggestive power well beyond the immediate and lexical meaning. Our appreciation of the suggestive magical power of language was reinforced by the games we played with words through riddles, proverbs, transpositions of syllables, or through nonsensical but musically arranged words. So we learned the music of our language on top of the content. The language, through images and symbols, gave us a view of the world, but it had a beauty of its own. The home and the field were then our pre-primary school but what is important, for this discussion, is that the language of our evening teach-ins, and the language of our immediate and wider community, and the language of our work in the fields were one.

And then I went to school, a colonial school, and this harmony was broken. The language of my education was no longer the language of my culture. I first went to Kamaandura, missionary run, and then to another called Maanguuū run by nationalists grouped around the Gīkūyū Independent and Karinga Schools Association. Our language of education was still Gīkūyū. The very first time I was ever given an ovation for my writing was over a composition in Gīkūyū. So for my first four years there was still harmony between the language of my formal education and that of the Limuru peasant community.

It was after the declaration of a state of emergency over Kenya in 1952 that all the schools run by patriotic nationalists were taken over by the colonial regime and were placed under District Education Boards chaired by Englishmen. English became the language of my formal education. In Kenya, English became more than a language: it was *the* language, and all the others had to bow before it in deference.

Thus one of the most humiliating experiences was to be caught speaking Gīkūyū in the vicinity of the school. The culprit was given corporal punishment—three to five strokes of the cane on bare buttocks—or was made to carry a metal plate around the neck with inscriptions such as I AM STUPID or I AM A DONKEY. Sometimes the culprits were fined money they could hardly afford. And how did the teachers catch the culprits? A button was initially given to one pupil who was supposed to hand it over to whoever was caught speaking his mother tongue. Whoever had the button at the end of the day would sing who had given it to him and the ensuing process would bring out all the culprits of the day. Thus children were turned into witch-hunters and in the process were being taught the lucrative value of being a traitor to one's immediate community.

The attitude to English was the exact opposite: any achievement in spoken 10
or written English was highly rewarded; prizes, prestige, applause; the ticket
to higher realms. English became the measure of intelligence and ability in the
arts, the sciences, and all the other branches of learning. English became *the*
main determinant of a child's progress up the ladder of formal education.

As you may know, the colonial system of education in addition to its apart-
heid racial demarcation had the structure of a pyramid: a broad primary base,
a narrowing secondary middle, and an even narrower university apex. Selections from primary into secondary were through an examination, in my time
called Kenya African Preliminary Examination, in which one had to pass six
subjects ranging from Maths to Nature Study and Kiswahili.[3] All the papers
were written in English. Nobody could pass the exam who failed the English
language paper no matter how brilliantly he had done in the other subjects. I
remember one boy in my class of 1954 who had distinctions in all subjects
except English, which he had failed. He was made to fail the entire exam. He
went on to become a turn boy[4] in a bus company. I who had only passes but a
credit in English got a place at the Alliance High School, one of the most elit-
ist institutions for Africans in colonial Kenya. The requirements for a place at
the University, Makerere University College, were broadly the same: nobody
could go on to wear the undergraduate red gown, no matter how brilliantly they
had performed in all the other subjects unless they had a credit—not even a
simple pass!—in English. Thus the most coveted place in the pyramid and in
the system was only available to the holder of an English language credit card.
English was the official vehicle and the magic formula to colonial elitedom.

Literary education was now determined by the dominant language while
also reinforcing that dominance. Orature (oral literature) in Kenyan languages
stopped. In primary school I now read simplified Dickens and Stevenson alongside Rider Haggard. Jim Hawkins, Oliver Twist, Tom Brown[5]—not Hare, Leopard
and Lion—were now my daily companions in the world of imagination. In
secondary school, Scott and G. B. Shaw vied with more Rider Haggard, John
Buchan, Alan Paton, Captain W. E. Johns.[6] At Makerere I read English: from
Chaucer to T. S. Eliot with a touch of Grahame Greene.[7]

3. Swahili, a major East African language.

4. Someone who brings in customers; a tout.

5. Charles Dickens (1812–1870), British novelist, author of *Oliver Twist*; Robert Louis
Stevenson (1850–1894), Scottish novelist, creator of Jim Hawkins in *Treasure Island*; H.
Rider Haggard (1856–1925), British adventure novelist; Brown, chief character in *Tom
Brown's Schooldays* in the novel by Thomas Hughes.

6. Sir Walter Scott (1771–1832), Scottish poet and novelist; George Bernard Shaw
(1856–1950), Irish-born playwright; Buchan (1875–1940), Scottish adventure novelist,
author of *The Thirty-Nine Steps*, and also governor general of Canada; Paton (1903–
1988), South African novelist; Johns (1893–1968), British writer, famous for the Biggles
stories for boys.

7. Geoffrey Chaucer (c. 1343–1400), English poet, author of *The Canterbury Tales*;
Eliot (1888–1965), American-born poet; Greene (1904–1991), British novelist.

Thus language and literature were taking us further and further from ourselves to other selves, from our world to other worlds.

What was the colonial system doing to us Kenyan children? What were the consequences of, on the one hand, this systematic suppression of our languages and the literature they carried, and on the other the elevation of English and the literature it carried? To answer those questions, let me first examine the relationship of language to human experience, human culture, and the human perception of reality.

15   Language, any language, has a dual character: it is both a means of communication and a carrier of culture. Take English. It is spoken in Britain and in Sweden and Denmark. But for Swedish and Danish people English is only a means of communication with non-Scandinavians. It is not a carrier of their culture. For the British, and particularly the English, it is additionally, and inseparably from its use as a tool of communication, a carrier of their culture and history. Or take Swahili in East and Central Africa. It is widely used as a means of communication across many nationalities. But it is not the carrier of a culture and history of many of those nationalities. However in parts of Kenya and Tanzania, and particularly in Zanzibar,[8] Swahili is inseparably both a means of communication and a carrier of the culture of those people to whom it is a mother-tongue.

Language as communication has three aspects or elements. There is first what Karl Marx[9] once called the language of real life, the element basic to the whole notion of language, its origins and development: that is, the relations people enter into with one another in the labor process, the links they necessarily establish among themselves in the act of a people, a community of human beings, producing wealth or means of life like food, clothing, houses. A human community really starts its historical being as a community of co-operation in production through the division of labor; the simplest is between man, woman and child within a household; the more complex divisions are between branches of production such as those who are sole hunters, sole gatherers of fruits or sole workers in metal. Then there are the most complex divisions such as those in modern factories where a single product, say a shirt or a shoe, is the result of many hands and minds. Production is co-operation, is communication, is language, is expression of a relation between human beings and it is specifically human.

The second aspect of language as communication is speech and it imitates the language of real life, that is communication in production. The verbal signposts both reflect and aid communication or the relation established between human beings in the production of their means of life. Language as a system of verbal signposts makes that production possible. The spoken word is to relations between human beings what the hand is to the relations between human beings and nature. The hand through tools mediates between human beings

8. Island off the east coast of Africa; part of Tanzania since 1964.
9. German political philosopher (1818–1883).

and nature and forms the language of real life: spoken words mediate between human beings and form the language of speech.

The third aspect is the written signs. The written word imitates the spoken. Where the first two aspects of language as communication through the hand and the spoken word historically evolved more or less simultaneously, the written aspect is a much later historical development. Writing is representation of sounds with visual symbols, from the simplest knot among shepherds to tell the number in a herd or the hieroglyphics among the Agĩkũyũ gicaandi[10] singers and poets of Kenya, to the most complicated and different letter and picture writing systems of the world today.

In most societies the written and the spoken languages are the same, in that they represent each other: what is on paper can be read to another person and be received as that language, which the recipient has grown up speaking. In such a society there is broad harmony for a child between the three aspects of language as communication. His interaction with nature and with other men is expressed in written and spoken symbols or signs which are both a result of that double interaction and a reflection of it. The association of the child's sensibility is with the language of his experience of life.

But there is more to it: communication between human beings is also the basis and process of evolving culture. In doing similar kinds of things and actions over and over again under similar circumstances, similar even in their mutability, certain patterns, moves, rhythms, habits, attitudes, experiences and knowledge emerge. Those experiences are handed over to the next generation and become the inherited basis for their further actions on nature and on themselves. There is a gradual accumulation of values which in time become almost self-evident truths governing their conception of what is right and wrong, good and bad, beautiful and ugly, courageous and cowardly, generous and mean in their internal and external relations. Over a time this becomes a way of life distinguishable from other ways of life. They develop a distinctive culture and history. Culture embodies those moral, ethical and aesthetic values, the set of spiritual eyeglasses, through which they come to view themselves and their place in the universe. Values are the basis of a people's identity, their sense of particularity as members of the human race. All this is carried by language. Language as culture is the collective memory bank of a people's experience in history. Culture is almost indistinguishable from the language that makes possible its genesis, growth, banking, articulation and indeed its transmission from one generation to the next.

Language as culture also has three important aspects. Culture is a product of the history which it in turn reflects. Culture in other words is a product and a reflection of human beings communicating with one another in the very struggle to create wealth and to control it. But culture does not merely reflect that history, or rather it does so by actually forming images or pictures of the world of nature and nurture. Thus the second aspect of language as culture is as an image-forming agent in the mind of a child. Our whole conception of

20

10. Agĩkũyũ, another term for Gĩkũyũ; gicaandi, a particular Kenyan song genre.

ourselves as a people, individually and collectively, is based on those pictures and images which may or may not correctly correspond to the actual reality of the struggles with nature and nurture which produced them in the first place. But our capacity to confront the world creatively is dependent on how those images correspond or not to that reality, how they distort or clarify the reality of our struggles. Language as culture is thus mediating between me and my own self; between my own self and other selves; between me and nature. Language is mediating in my very being. And this brings us to the third aspect of language as culture. Culture transmits or imparts those images of the world and reality through the spoken and the written language, that is through a specific language. In other words, the capacity to speak, the capacity to order sounds in a manner that makes for mutual comprehension between human beings is universal. This is the universality of language, a quality specific to human beings. It corresponds to the universality of the struggle against nature and that between human beings. But the particularity of the sounds, the words, the word order into phrases and sentences, and the specific manner, or laws, of their ordering is what distinguishes one language from another. Thus a specific culture is not transmitted through language in its universality but in its particularity as the language of a specific community with a specific history. Written literature and orature are the main means by which a particular language transmits the images of the world contained in the culture it carries.

Language as communication and as culture are then products of each other. Communication creates culture: culture is a means of communication. Language carries culture, and culture carries, particularly through orature and literature, the entire body of values by which we come to perceive ourselves and our place in the world. How people perceive themselves affects how they look at their culture, at their politics and at the social production of wealth, at their entire relationship to nature and to other beings. Language is thus inseparable from ourselves as a community of human beings with a specific form and character, a specific history, a specific relationship to the world.

So what was the colonialist imposition of a foreign language doing to us children?

The real aim of colonialism was to control the people's wealth: what they produced, how they produced it, and how it was distributed; to control, in other words, the entire realm of the language of real life. Colonialism imposed its control of the social production of wealth through military conquest and subsequent political dictatorship. But its most important area of domination was the mental universe of the colonized, the control, through culture, of how people perceived themselves and their relationship to the world. Economic and political control can never be complete or effective without mental control. To control a people's culture is to control their tools of self-definition in relationship to others.

For colonialism this involved two aspects of the same process: the destruction or the deliberate undervaluing of a people's culture, their art, dances, religions, history, geography, education, orature and literature, and the conscious elevation of the language of the colonizer. The domination of a people's language by the languages of the colonizing nations was crucial to the domination of the mental universe of the colonized.

Take language as communication. Imposing a foreign language, and suppressing the native languages as spoken and written, were already breaking the harmony previously existing between the African child and the three aspects of language. Since the new language as a means of communication was a product of and was reflecting the "real language of life" elsewhere, it could never as spoken or written properly reflect or imitate the real life of that community. This may in part explain why technology always appears to us as slightly external, *their* product and not *ours.* The word "missile" used to hold an alien faraway sound until I recently learnt its equivalent in Gĩkũyũ, *ngurukuhĩ,* and it made me apprehend it differently. Learning, for a colonial child, became a cerebral activity and not an emotionally felt experience.

But since the new, imposed languages could never completely break the native languages as spoken, their most effective area of domination was the third aspect of language as communication, the written. The language of an African child's formal education was foreign. The language of the books he read was foreign. The language of his conceptualization was foreign. Thought, in him, took the visible form of a foreign language. So the written language of a child's upbringing in the school (even his spoken language within the school compound) became divorced from his spoken language at home. There was often not the slightest relationship between the child's written world, which was also the language of his schooling, and the world of his immediate environment in the family and the community. For a colonial child, the harmony existing between the three aspects of language as communication was irrevocably broken. This resulted in the disassociation of the sensibility[11] of that child from his natural and social environment, what we might call colonial alienation. The alienation became reinforced in the teaching of history, geography, music, where bourgeois Europe was always the center of the universe.

The disassociation, divorce, or alienation from the immediate environment becomes clearer when you look at colonial language as a carrier of culture.

Since culture is a product of the history of a people which it in turn reflects, the child was now being exposed exclusively to a culture that was a product of a world external to himself. He was being made to stand outside himself to look at himself. *Catching Them Young* is the title of a book on racism, class, sex, and politics in children's literature by Bob Dixon. "Catching them young" as an aim was even more true of a colonial child. The images of his world and his place in it implanted in a child take years to eradicate, if they ever can be.

Since culture does not just reflect the world in images but actually, through those images, conditions a child to see that world a certain way, the colonial   30

11. Echo of T. S. Eliot's famous phrase "dissociation of sensibility," a break from the past, when thought and feeling were unified.

child was made to see the world and where he stands in it as seen and defined by or reflected in the culture of the language of imposition.

And since those images are mostly passed on through orature and literature it meant the child would now only see the world as seen in the literature of his language of adoption. From the point of view of alienation, that is of seeing oneself from outside oneself as if one was another self, it does not matter that the imported literature carried the great humanist tradition of the best Shakespeare, Goethe, Balzac, Tolstoy, Gorky, Brecht, Sholokhov,[12] Dickens. The location of this great mirror of imagination was necessarily Europe and its history and culture and the rest of the universe was seen from that center.

But obviously it was worse when the colonial child was exposed to images of his world as mirrored in the written languages of his colonizer. Where his own native languages were associated in his impressionable mind with low status, humiliation, corporal punishment, slow-footed intelligence and ability or downright stupidity, non-intelligibility and barbarism, this was reinforced by the world he met in the works of such geniuses of racism as a Rider Haggard or a Nicholas Monsarrat;[13] not to mention the pronouncement of some of the giants of western intellectual and political establishment, such as Hume (". . . The negro is naturally inferior to the whites. . . ."), Thomas Jefferson (". . . The blacks . . . are inferior to the whites on the endowments of both body and mind. . . ."), or Hegel[14] with his Africa comparable to a land of childhood still enveloped in the dark mantle of the night as far as the development of self-conscious history was concerned. Hegel's statement that there was nothing harmonious with humanity to be found in the African character is representative of the racist images of Africans and Africa such a colonial child was bound to encounter in the literature of the colonial languages. The results could be disastrous.

MLA CITATION

Thiong'o, Ngũgĩ wa. "Decolonizing the Mind." *The Norton Reader: An Anthology of Nonfiction*, edited by Melissa A. Goldthwaite et al., 15th ed., W. W. Norton, 2020, pp. 799–806.

12. William Shakespeare (1564–1616), English playwright; Johann Wolfgang von Goethe (1749–1832), German novelist and playwright; Honoré de Balzac (1799–1850), French novelist; Leo (Count Lev Nikolayevich) Tolstoy (1828–1910), Russian novelist; Maxim Gorky (1868–1936), Russian dramatist; Bertolt Brecht (1898–1956), German dramatist; Mikhail Aleksandrovich Sholokhov (1905–1984), Russian novelist.

13. Monsarrat's *The Tribe That Lost Its Head* (1956) was this British novelist's satirical look at British colonialism and the African independence movement.

14. David Hume (1711–1776), Scottish philosopher; Jefferson (1743–1826), third U.S. president, 1801–1809; Georg Wilhelm Friedrich Hegel (1770–1831), German philosopher.

QUESTIONS

1. The last paragraphs of Ngũgĩ wa Thiong'o's essay contain the names of many classic and contemporary European writers. Why do you think he chose to include them? Can you relate their inclusion to the way Ngũgĩ chooses to present himself in this essay?

2. What literary writers did you read in secondary school? What values were your teachers (or school) imparting in selecting those writers in particular?

3. Ngũgĩ experienced a particularly stark contrast between the values contained within the oral stories of his family and the written English of school. Discuss the different value systems. Have you noticed differences between what your extended family values and what your school seemed to want you to value?

4. Imagine an English class for a bilingual or bicultural community. Write a paper justifying the ideal balance between texts from the second language or culture (in translation or not) and English.

15 RELIGION AND SPIRITUALITY

> Is God's name *God*? Dieu? Allah? Ebbe? Waq? How do we
> approach this entity? . . . Does our practice make us perfect in
> the pursuit of knowing and honoring God? Or can God be
> found outside of ritual and structure and tradition? Can God be
> found outside the walls of our separate buildings?
> —RACHEL PIEH JONES

What do you believe? How do those beliefs affect the way you live, how you relate to others, and how you relate—if you do—to a spirit or power beyond yourself? How should we face death? Is religion destructive or helpful? What is spirituality, and how is it felt or expressed? How do individuals and groups answer these big questions? These questions and others animate the essays in this chapter on Religion and Spirituality, pieces from writers from different faith traditions, as well as some who challenge, reject, or seek to transform certain traditions.

Many of the selections in this chapter are personal essays that show different experiences with religion, allowing the authors to define and reveal their own beliefs, spiritual practices, and questions. The personal essay allows writers to illuminate specific moments when religion or spirituality shaped their lives—from Langston Hughes's description of feeling pressured to say he had "seen Jesus" to Daisy Hernández's narrative about dealing with envy through Buddhist meditation. These essays show the complexity of both cultural and personal influences—how a person's beliefs are shaped by community, circumstance, tradition, and personality. Through narration and description, the authors reveal the complexity of living out one's chosen faith—often in unorthodox ways. For example, Fariha Róisín shows how she and her sister are both Muslims, though they make different choices about the outward expression of that faith. Anita Diamant describes a symbolic act—placing an orange on the seder plate—meant to make a Jewish tradition more inclusive. And Rachel Pieh Jones shows how her friendship with a Muslim woman helped her understand that no one person, no one religion, can own either the name or the concept of God.

This chapter also includes other genres: a eulogy as well as an academic review of studies about gender and faith. Eulogies often show the good qualities of a person who has died and seek to provide comfort for the bereaved. In "Eulogy for Clementa Pinckney," Barack Obama details Reverend Pinckney's accomplishments and summons faith as comfort in hard times, yet he also makes a call for justice and social change. Orit Avishai's "Women of God," which takes a more academic tone, also considers social change—and whether conservative religions are bad or good for women.

As you read the essays in this chapter, note that not all are written from a specific religious point of view. Virginia Woolf reflects on life and death through the simple act of observing a moth, and Annie Dillard draws from philosophers, Jewish and Christian theologians, scientists, literary writers, artists, and her own experiences in nature to reflect on transcendent experiences. Many of the authors negotiate differences, reaffirming and expanding their sense of faith and belief without rejecting or vilifying others.

As you write about your own sense of religion or spirituality, you might consider childhood experiences that shaped you or a time when you questioned what someone else expected you to believe. You might write about a symbol that carries meaning in your culture or faith. Does religion give you a stronger sense of identity and link to your community? Does it exclude or harm particular groups or people? Should traditions be changed—why or why not? Feel free to think about the big questions and different ways of approaching them. You might describe an experience, make an argument, or even write a eulogy.

LANGSTON HUGHES
Salvation

I WAS SAVED FROM SIN when I was going on thirteen. But not really saved. It happened like this. There was a big revival at my Auntie Reed's church. Every night for weeks there had been much preaching, singing, praying, and shouting, and some very hardened sinners had been brought to Christ, and the membership of the church had grown by leaps and bounds. Then just before the revival ended, they held a special meeting for children, "to bring the young lambs to the fold." My aunt spoke of it for days ahead. That night I was escorted to the front row and placed on the mourners' bench[1] with all the other young sinners, who had not yet been brought to Jesus.

My aunt told me that when you were saved you saw a light, and something happened to you inside! And Jesus came into your life! And God was with you from then on! She said you could see and hear and feel Jesus in your soul. I believed her. I had heard a great many old people say the same thing and it seemed to me they ought to know. So I sat there calmly in the hot, crowded church, waiting for Jesus to come to me.

The preacher preached a wonderful rhythmical sermon, all moans and shouts and lonely cries and dire pictures of hell, and then he sang a song about the ninety and nine safe in the fold, but one little lamb was left out in the cold.[2] Then he said: "Won't you come? Won't you come to Jesus? Young lambs, won't

From The Big Sea *(1940), Langston Hughes's account of his early life.*

1. Place in the front of the church where potential converts sat during an evangelical service.
2. "The Ninety and Nine" mentioned in this paragraph and "Let the Lower Lights Be Burning," in the next, are the titles of famous evangelical hymns collected by Ira Sankey.

you come?" And he held out his arms to all us young sinners there on the mourners' bench. And the little girls cried. And some of them jumped up and went to Jesus right away. But most of us just sat there.

A great many old people came and knelt around us and prayed, old women with jet-black faces and braided hair, old men with work-gnarled hands. And the church sang a song about the lower lights are burning, some poor sinners to be saved. And the whole building rocked with prayer and song.

5   Still I kept waiting to *see* Jesus.

Finally all the young people had gone to the altar and were saved, but one boy and me. He was a rounder's[3] son named Westley. Westley and I were surrounded by sisters and deacons praying. It was very hot in the church, and getting late now. Finally Westley said to me in a whisper: "God damn! I'm tired o' sitting here. Let's get up and be saved." So he got up and was saved.

Then I was left all alone on the mourners' bench. My aunt came and knelt at my knees and cried, while prayers and songs swirled all around me in the little church. The whole congregation prayed for me alone, in a mighty wail of moans and voices. And I kept waiting serenely for Jesus, waiting, waiting—but he didn't come. I wanted to see him, but nothing happened to me. Nothing! I wanted something to happen to me, but nothing happened.

I heard the songs and the minister saying: "Why don't you come? My dear child, why don't you come to Jesus? Jesus is waiting for you. He wants you. Why don't you come? Sister Reed, what is this child's name?"

"Langston," my aunt sobbed.

10   "Langston, why don't you come? Why don't you come and be saved? Oh, Lamb of God! Why don't you come?"

Now it was really getting late. I began to be ashamed of myself, holding everything up so long. I began to wonder what God thought about Westley, who certainly hadn't seen Jesus either, but who was now sitting proudly on the platform, swinging his knickerbockered legs and grinning down at me, surrounded by deacons and old women on their knees praying. God had not struck Westley dead for taking his name in vain or for lying in the temple. So I decided that maybe to save further trouble, I'd better lie, too, and say that Jesus had come, and get up and be saved.

So I got up.

Suddenly the whole room broke into a sea of shouting, as they saw me rise. Waves of rejoicing swept the place. Women leaped in the air. My aunt threw her arms around me. The minister took me by the hand and led me to the platform.

When things quieted down, in a hushed silence, punctuated by a few ecstatic "Amens," all the new young lambs were blessed in the name of God. Then joyous singing filled the room.

15   That night, for the last time in my life but one—for I was a big boy twelve years old—I cried. I cried, in bed alone, and couldn't stop. I buried my head under the quilts, but my aunt heard me. She woke up and told my uncle I was

---

3. Loafer or someone who is frequently drunk.

crying because the Holy Ghost had come into my life, and because I had seen Jesus. But I was really crying because I couldn't bear to tell her that I had lied, that I had deceived everybody in the church, and I hadn't seen Jesus, and that now I didn't believe there was a Jesus any more, since he didn't come to help me.

MLA CITATION

Hughes, Langston. "Salvation." *The Norton Reader: An Anthology of Nonfiction,* edited by Melissa A. Goldthwaite et al., 15th ed., W. W. Norton, 2020, pp. 809–11.

QUESTIONS

1. Langston Hughes describes how he lost his faith in Jesus at the age of twelve. How did the grown-ups in his life contribute to the experience?

2. Hughes was twelve "going on thirteen" (paragraph 1) when the event he describes in first-person narration took place. How careful is he to restrict himself to the point of view of a twelve-year-old child? How does he ensure that we, as readers, understand things that the narrator does not?

3. Write a first-person narrative in which you describe a failure—yours or someone else's—to live up to the expectations of parents or other authority figures.

BARACK OBAMA
Eulogy for Clementa Pinckney

IVING ALL PRAISE AND HONOR TO GOD. (Applause.)

The Bible calls us to hope. To persevere, and have faith in things not seen.

"They were still living by faith when they died," Scripture tells us. "They did not receive the things promised; they only saw them and welcomed them from a distance, admitting that they were foreigners and strangers on Earth."

We are here today to remember a man of God who lived by faith. A man who believed in things not seen. A man who believed there were better days ahead, off in the distance. A man of service who persevered, knowing full well he would not receive all those things he was promised, because he believed his efforts would deliver a better life for those who followed.

On June 17, 2015, a twenty-one-year-old shooter entered Mother Emanuel African Methodist Episcopal Church in Charleston, South Carolina, and murdered nine people, including the senior pastor, Reverend Clementa Pinckney, also a state senator. President Barack Obama delivered this eulogy for Reverend Pinckney on June 26, 2015.

5   To Jennifer, his beloved wife; to Eliana and Malana, his beautiful, wonderful daughters; to the Mother Emanuel family and the people of Charleston,
the people of South Carolina.

        I cannot claim to have the good fortune to know Reverend Pinckney well.
But I did have the pleasure of knowing him and meeting him here in South
Carolina, back when we were both a little bit younger. (Laughter.) Back when
I didn't have visible grey hair. (Laughter.) The first thing I noticed was his gra-
ciousness, his smile, his reassuring baritone, his deceptive sense of humor—all
qualities that helped him wear so effortlessly a heavy burden of expectation.

        Friends of his remarked this week that when Clementa Pinckney entered
a room, it was like the future arrived; that even from a young age, folks knew
he was special. Anointed. He was the progeny of a long line of the faithful—a
family of preachers who spread God's word, a family of protesters who sowed
change to expand voting rights and desegregate the South. Clem heard their
instruction, and he did not forsake their teaching.

        He was in the pulpit by thirteen, pastor by eighteen, public servant by
twenty-three. He did not exhibit any of the cockiness of youth, nor youth's
insecurities; instead, he set an example worthy of his position, wise beyond his
years, in his speech, in his conduct, in his love, faith, and purity.

        As a senator, he represented a sprawling swath of the Lowcountry,[1] a place
that has long been one of the most neglected in America. A place still wracked
by poverty and inadequate schools; a place where children can still go hungry
and the sick can go without treatment. A place that needed somebody like Clem.
(Applause.)

10   His position in the minority party meant the odds of winning more resources
for his constituents were often long. His calls for greater equity were too often
unheeded, the votes he cast were sometimes lonely. But he never gave up. He
stayed true to his convictions. He would not grow discouraged. After a full day at
the capitol, he'd climb into his car and head to the church to draw sustenance
from his family, from his ministry, from the community that loved and needed
him. There he would fortify his faith, and imagine what might be.

        Reverend Pinckney embodied a politics that was neither mean, nor small.
He conducted himself quietly, and kindly, and diligently. He encouraged progress not by pushing his ideas alone, but by seeking out your ideas, partnering
with you to make things happen. He was full of empathy and fellow feeling,
able to walk in somebody else's shoes and see through their eyes. No wonder
one of his senate colleagues remembered Senator Pinckney as "the most gentle
of the forty-six of us—the best of the forty-six of us."

        Clem was often asked why he chose to be a pastor and a public servant.
But the person who asked probably didn't know the history of the AME church.
(Applause.) As our brothers and sisters in the AME church know, we don't
make those distinctions. "Our calling," Clem once said, "is not just within the

---

1. Lowcountry region of South Carolina comprises the southern coast of the state and
its islands, including the city of Charleston. Its economy was once dependent on plantations that grew rice and indigo.

walls of the congregation, but . . . the life and community in which our congregation resides." (Applause.)

He embodied the idea that our Christian faith demands deeds and not just words; that the "sweet hour of prayer"[2] actually lasts the whole week long—(applause)—that to put our faith in action is more than individual salvation, it's about our collective salvation; that to feed the hungry and clothe the naked and house the homeless is not just a call for isolated charity but the imperative of a just society.

What a good man. Sometimes I think that's the best thing to hope for when you're eulogized—after all the words and recitations and résumés are read, to just say someone was a good man. (Applause.)

You don't have to be of high station to be a good man. Preacher by thirteen. Pastor by eighteen. Public servant by twenty-three. What a life Clementa Pinckney lived. What an example he set. What a model for his faith. And then to lose him at forty-one—slain in his sanctuary with eight wonderful members of his flock, each at different stages in life but bound together by a common commitment to God.

Cynthia Hurd. Susie Jackson. Ethel Lance. DePayne Middleton-Doctor. Tywanza Sanders. Daniel L. Simmons. Sharonda Coleman-Singleton. Myra Thompson. Good people. Decent people. God-fearing people. (Applause.) People so full of life and so full of kindness. People who ran the race, who persevered. People of great faith.

To the families of the fallen, the nation shares in your grief. Our pain cuts that much deeper because it happened in a church. The church is and always has been the center of African American life—(applause)—a place to call our own in a too often hostile world, a sanctuary from so many hardships.

Over the course of centuries, black churches served as "hush harbors" where slaves could worship in safety; praise houses where their free descendants could gather and shout hallelujah—(applause)—rest stops for the weary along the Underground Railroad; bunkers for the foot soldiers of the Civil Rights Movement. They have been, and continue to be, community centers where we organize for jobs and justice; places of scholarship and network; places where children are loved and fed and kept out of harm's way, and told that they are beautiful and smart—(applause)—and taught that they matter. (Applause.) That's what happens in church.

That's what the black church means. Our beating heart. The place where our dignity as a people is inviolate. When there's no better example of this tradition than Mother Emanuel—(applause)—a church built by blacks seeking liberty, burned to the ground because its founder sought to end slavery, only to rise up again, a Phoenix from these ashes. (Applause.)

When there were laws banning all-black church gatherings, services happened here anyway, in defiance of unjust laws. When there was a righteous movement to dismantle Jim Crow, Dr. Martin Luther King Jr. preached from its pulpit, and marches began from its steps. A sacred place, this church. Not

15

20

2. "The Sweet Hour of Prayer" is a traditional hymn.

just for blacks, not just for Christians, but for every American who cares about the steady expansion—(applause)—of human rights and human dignity in this country; a foundation stone for liberty and justice for all. That's what the church meant. (Applause.)

We do not know whether the killer of Reverend Pinckney and eight others knew all of this history. But he surely sensed the meaning of his violent act. It was an act that drew on a long history of bombs and arson and shots fired at churches, not random, but as a means of control, a way to terrorize and oppress. (Applause.) An act that he imagined would incite fear and recrimination; violence and suspicion. An act that he presumed would deepen divisions that trace back to our nation's original sin.

Oh, but God works in mysterious ways. (Applause.) God has different ideas. (Applause.)

He didn't know he was being used by God. (Applause.) Blinded by hatred, the alleged killer could not see the grace surrounding Reverend Pinckney and that Bible study group—the light of love that shone as they opened the church doors and invited a stranger to join in their prayer circle. The alleged killer could have never anticipated the way the families of the fallen would respond when they saw him in court—in the midst of unspeakable grief, with words of forgiveness. He couldn't imagine that. (Applause.)

The alleged killer could not imagine how the city of Charleston, under the good and wise leadership of Mayor Riley—(applause)—how the state of South Carolina, how the United States of America would respond—not merely with revulsion at his evil act, but with big-hearted generosity and, more importantly, with a thoughtful introspection and self-examination that we so rarely see in public life.

25   Blinded by hatred, he failed to comprehend what Reverend Pinckney so well understood—the power of God's grace. (Applause.)

This whole week, I've been reflecting on this idea of grace. (Applause.) The grace of the families who lost loved ones. The grace that Reverend Pinckney would preach about in his sermons. The grace described in one of my favorite hymnals—the one we all know: Amazing grace, how sweet the sound that saved a wretch like me. (Applause.) I once was lost, but now I'm found; was blind but now I see. (Applause.)

According to the Christian tradition, grace is not earned. Grace is not merited. It's not something we deserve. Rather, grace is the free and benevolent favor of God—(applause)—as manifested in the salvation of sinners and the bestowal of blessings. Grace.

As a nation, out of this terrible tragedy, God has visited grace upon us, for he has allowed us to see where we've been blind. (Applause.) He has given us the chance, where we've been lost, to find our best selves. (Applause.) We may not have earned it, this grace, with our rancor and complacency, and short-sightedness and fear of each other—but we got it all the same. He gave it to us anyway. He's once more given us grace. But it is up to us now to make the most of it, to receive it with gratitude, and to prove ourselves worthy of this gift.

For too long, we were blind to the pain that the Confederate flag stirred in too many of our citizens. (Applause.) It's true, a flag did not cause these murders. But as people from all walks of life, Republicans and Democrats, now acknowledge—including Governor Haley,[3] whose recent eloquence on the subject is worthy of praise—(applause)—as we all have to acknowledge, the flag has always represented more than just ancestral pride. (Applause.) For many, black and white, that flag was a reminder of systemic oppression and racial subjugation. We see that now.

Removing the flag from this state's capitol would not be an act of political correctness; it would not be an insult to the valor of Confederate soldiers. It would simply be an acknowledgment that the cause for which they fought—the cause of slavery—was wrong—(applause)—the imposition of Jim Crow after the Civil War, the resistance to civil rights for all people was wrong. (Applause.) It would be one step in an honest accounting of America's history; a modest but meaningful balm for so many unhealed wounds. It would be an expression of the amazing changes that have transformed this state and this country for the better, because of the work of so many people of goodwill, people of all races striving to form a more perfect union. By taking down that flag, we express God's grace. (Applause.)

But I don't think God wants us to stop there. (Applause.) For too long, we've been blind to the way past injustices continue to shape the present. Perhaps we see that now. Perhaps this tragedy causes us to ask some tough questions about how we can permit so many of our children to languish in poverty, or attend dilapidated schools, or grow up without prospects for a job or for a career. (Applause.)

Perhaps it causes us to examine what we're doing to cause some of our children to hate. (Applause.) Perhaps it softens hearts toward those lost young men, tens and tens of thousands caught up in the criminal justice system—(applause)—and leads us to make sure that that system is not infected with bias; that we embrace changes in how we train and equip our police so that the bonds of trust between law enforcement and the communities they serve make us all safer and more secure. (Applause.)

Maybe we now realize the way racial bias can infect us even when we don't realize it, so that we're guarding against not just racial slurs, but we're also guarding against the subtle impulse to call Johnny back for a job interview but not Jamal. (Applause.) So that we search our hearts when we consider laws to make it harder for some of our fellow citizens to vote. (Applause.) By recognizing our common humanity by treating every child as important, regardless of the color of their skin or the station into which they were born, and to do what's necessary to make opportunity real for every American—by doing that, we express God's grace. (Applause.)

For too long—

AUDIENCE: For too long!

THE PRESIDENT: For too long, we've been blind to the unique mayhem that gun violence inflicts upon this nation. (Applause.) Sporadically, our eyes are open: When eight of our brothers and sisters are cut down in a church basement, twelve in a movie theater, twenty-six in an elementary school. But I hope

3. Nikki R. Haley (b. 1972), governor of South Carolina (2011–2017).

we also see the thirty precious lives cut short by gun violence in this country every single day; the countless more whose lives are forever changed—the survivors crippled, the children traumatized and fearful every day as they walk to school, the husband who will never feel his wife's warm touch, the entire communities whose grief overflows every time they have to watch what happened to them happen to some other place.

The vast majority of Americans—the majority of gun owners—want to do something about this. We see that now. (Applause.) And I'm convinced that by acknowledging the pain and loss of others, even as we respect the traditions and ways of life that make up this beloved country—by making the moral choice to change, we express God's grace. (Applause.)

We don't earn grace. We're all sinners. We don't deserve it. (Applause.) But God gives it to us anyway. (Applause.) And we choose how to receive it. It's our decision how to honor it.

None of us can or should expect a transformation in race relations overnight. Every time something like this happens, somebody says we have to have a conversation about race. We talk a lot about race. There's no shortcut. And we don't need more talk. (Applause.) None of us should believe that a handful of gun safety measures will prevent every tragedy. It will not. People of goodwill will continue to debate the merits of various policies, as our democracy requires—this is a big, raucous place, America is. And there are good people on both sides of these debates. Whatever solutions we find will necessarily be incomplete.

40   But it would be a betrayal of everything Reverend Pinckney stood for, I believe, if we allowed ourselves to slip into a comfortable silence again. (Applause.) Once the eulogies have been delivered, once the TV cameras move on, to go back to business as usual—that's what we so often do to avoid uncomfortable truths about the prejudice that still infects our society. (Applause.) To settle for symbolic gestures without following up with the hard work of more lasting change—that's how we lose our way again.

It would be a refutation of the forgiveness expressed by those families if we merely slipped into old habits, whereby those who disagree with us are not merely wrong but bad; where we shout instead of listen; where we barricade ourselves behind preconceived notions or well-practiced cynicism.

Reverend Pinckney once said, "Across the South, we have a deep appreciation of history—we haven't always had a deep appreciation of each other's history." (Applause.) What is true in the South is true for America. Clem understood that justice grows out of recognition of ourselves in each other. That my liberty depends on you being free, too. (Applause.) That history can't be a sword to justify injustice, or a shield against progress, but must be a manual for how to avoid repeating the mistakes of the past—how to break the cycle. A roadway toward a better world. He knew that the path of grace involves an open mind—but, more importantly, an open heart.

That's what I've felt this week—an open heart. That, more than any particular policy or analysis, is what's called upon right now, I think—what a friend of mine, the writer Marilynne Robinson, calls "that reservoir of goodness, beyond, and of another kind, that we are able to do each other in the ordinary cause of things."

That reservoir of goodness. If we can find that grace, anything is possible. (Applause.) If we can tap that grace, everything can change. (Applause.)

Amazing grace. Amazing grace.   45

(Begins to sing)—Amazing grace—(applause)—how sweet the sound, that saved a wretch like me; I once was lost, but now I'm found; was blind but now I see. (Applause.)

Clementa Pinckney found that grace.

Cynthia Hurd found that grace.

Susie Jackson found that grace.

Ethel Lance found that grace.   50

DePayne Middleton-Doctor found that grace.

Tywanza Sanders found that grace.

Daniel L. Simmons Sr. found that grace.

Sharonda Coleman-Singleton found that grace.

Myra Thompson found that grace.   55

Through the example of their lives, they've now passed it on to us. May we find ourselves worthy of that precious and extraordinary gift, as long as our lives endure. May grace now lead them home. May God continue to shed His grace on the United States of America. (Applause.)

MLA CITATION

Obama, Barack. "Eulogy for Clementa Pinckney." *The Norton Reader: An Anthology of Nonfiction*, edited by Melissa A. Goldthwaite et al., 15th ed., W. W. Norton, 2020, pp. 811–17.

QUESTIONS

1. Barack Obama notes that despite Reverend Pinckney's achievements, he lived without "high station" (paragraph 15). What do you think he wants to communicate to his audience with this observation, and how does it help you understand what he means by calling Pinckney "a good man"?

2. Read Martin Luther King Jr.'s "Letter from Birmingham Jail" (pp. 739–51), and compare how King and Obama speak to their audiences about the history of racism in the United States. What factors might account for the similarities and differences?

3. At several points in his eulogy, Obama calls on his audience to take action. What forms of action does he recommend? What forms of action do you think might help fight racism on your campus or in your community?

4. Look up the lyrics and listen to several recordings of one of the hymns referred to in this eulogy ("Sweet Hour of Prayer" or "Amazing Grace"), and write an essay discussing the appropriateness of the reference in this eulogy.

VIRGINIA WOOLF
The Death of the Moth

OTHS THAT FLY by day are not properly to be called moths; they do not excite that pleasant sense of dark autumn nights and ivy-blossom which the commonest yellow-underwing asleep in the shadow of the curtain never fails to rouse in us. They are hybrid creatures, neither gay like butterflies nor sombre like their own species. Nevertheless the present specimen, with his narrow hay-colored wings, fringed with a tassel of the same color, seemed to be content with life. It was a pleasant morning, mid-September, mild, benignant, yet with a keener breath than that of the summer months. The plough was already scoring the field opposite the window, and where the share had been, the earth was pressed flat and gleamed with moisture. Such vigor came rolling in from the fields and the down beyond that it was difficult to keep the eyes strictly turned upon the book. The rooks too were keeping one of their annual festivities; soaring round the tree tops until it looked as if a vast net with thousands of black knots in it had been cast up into the air; which, after a few moments sank slowly down upon the trees until every twig seemed to have a knot at the end of it. Then, suddenly, the net would be thrown into the air again in a wider circle this time, with the utmost clamor and vociferation, as though to be thrown into the air and settle slowly down upon the tree tops were a tremendously exciting experience.

The same energy which inspired the rooks, the ploughmen, the horses, and even, it seemed, the lean bare-backed downs, sent the moth fluttering from side to side of his square of the window-pane. One could not help watching him. One was, indeed, conscious of a queer feeling of pity for him. The possibilities of pleasure seemed that morning so enormous and so various that to have only a moth's part in life, and a day moth's at that, appeared a hard fate, and his zest in enjoying his meagre opportunities to the full, pathetic. He flew vigorously to one corner of his compartment, and, after waiting there a second, flew across to the other. What remained for him but to fly to a third corner and then to a fourth? That was all he could do, in spite of the size of the downs, the width of the sky, the far-off smoke of houses, and the romantic voice, now and then, of a steamer out at sea. What he could do he did. Watching him, it seemed as if a fiber, very thin but pure, of the enormous energy of the world had been thrust into his frail and diminutive body. As often as he crossed the pane, I could fancy that a thread of vital light became visible. He was little or nothing but life.

Yet, because he was so small, and so simple a form of the energy that was rolling in at the open window and driving its way through so many narrow and intricate corridors in my own brain and in those of other human beings, there

The title essay of Virginia Woolf's collection The Death of the Moth, and Other Essays *(1942), compiled after her death in 1941.*

was something marvellous as well as pathetic about him. It was as if someone had taken a tiny bead of pure life and decking it as lightly as possible with down and feathers, had set it dancing and zig-zagging to show us the true nature of life. Thus displayed one could not get over the strangeness of it. One is apt to forget all about life, seeing it humped and bossed and garnished and cumbered so that it has to move with the greatest circumspection and dignity. Again, the thought of all that life might have been had he been born in any other shape caused one to view his simple activities with a kind of pity.

After a time, tired by his dancing apparently, he settled on the window ledge in the sun, and, the queer spectacle being at an end, I forgot about him. Then, looking up, my eye was caught by him. He was trying to resume his dancing, but seemed either so stiff or so awkward that he could only flutter to the bottom of the window-pane; and when he tried to fly across it he failed. Being intent on other matters I watched these futile attempts for a time without thinking, unconsciously waiting for him to resume his flight, as one waits for a machine, that has stopped momentarily, to start again without considering the reason of its failure. After perhaps a seventh attempt he slipped from the wooden ledge and fell, fluttering his wings, on to his back on the window sill. The helplessness of his attitude roused me. It flashed upon me that he was in difficulties; he could no longer raise himself; his legs struggled vainly. But, as I stretched out a pencil, meaning to help him to right himself, it came over me that the failure and awkwardness were the approach of death. I laid the pencil down again.

The legs agitated themselves once more. I looked as if for the enemy against which he struggled. I looked out of doors. What had happened there? Presumably it was midday, and work in the fields had stopped. Stillness and quiet had replaced the previous animation. The birds had taken themselves off to feed in the brooks. The horses stood still. Yet the power was there all the same, massed outside indifferent, impersonal, not attending to anything in particular. Somehow it was opposed to the little hay-colored moth. It was useless to try to do anything. One could only watch the extraordinary efforts made by those tiny legs against an oncoming doom which could, had it chosen, have submerged an entire city, not merely a city, but masses of human beings; nothing, I knew, had any chance against death. Nevertheless after a pause of exhaustion the legs fluttered again. It was superb this last protest, and so frantic that he succeeded at last in righting himself. One's sympathies, of course, were all on the side of life. Also, when there was nobody to care or to know, this gigantic effort on the part of an insignificant little moth, against a power of such magnitude, to retain what no one else valued or desired to keep, moved one strangely. Again, somehow, one saw life, a pure bead. I lifted the pencil again, useless though I knew it to be. But even as I did so, the unmistakable tokens of death showed themselves. The body relaxed, and instantly grew stiff. The struggle was over. The insignificant little creature now knew death. As I looked at the dead moth, this minute wayside triumph of so great a force over so mean an antagonist filled me with wonder. Just as life had been strange a few minutes before, so death was now as strange. The moth having righted himself now lay most decently and uncomplainingly composed. O yes, he seemed to say, death is stronger than I am.

5

MLA CITATION

Woolf, Virginia. "The Death of the Moth." *The Norton Reader: An Anthology of Nonfiction*, edited by Melissa A. Goldthwaite et al., 15th ed., W. W. Norton, 2020, pp. 818–19.

QUESTIONS

1. Trace the sequence in which Virginia Woolf comes to identify with the moth. How does she make her identification explicit? How is it implicit in the language she uses to describe the moth?

2. Choose one of the descriptions of a small living creature or creatures in Annie Dillard's "Sight into Insight" (pp. 846–56), and compare it with Woolf's description of the moth. Does a similar identification take place in Dillard's essay? If so, how; if not, why not?

3. Henry David Thoreau, in "The Battle of the Ants" (pp. 725–27), also humanizes small living creatures. How do his strategies differ from Woolf's?

4. Write two descriptions of the same living creature, one using Woolf's strategies, the other using Thoreau's. Or, alternatively, write an essay in which you analyze the differences between them.

DAISY HERNÁNDEZ
Envidia

T HEY HAD WARNED ME about the bedsheets.
San Antonio is infamous for high temperatures in the summer, but the dorm rooms at this particular college had some kind of air-conditioning system that cranked nonstop. The combination of the refrigerated air and the windows that had been scaled for decades coated everything in a cold dampness, including the bedsheets and pillowcases and even the twin-sized mattress. I should have been prepared. I wasn't.

I was also not prepared for what would happen in that room during the week I was there to attend a writing workshop. Now that I think about it, though, it makes sense, because dorm rooms are like a monk's room. Or how I imagine a monk's room to be. There's a mattress, a pillow, and a bedsheet. There's the floor and the single light fixture and the walls stripped of color. For teenager and practitioner alike, the room is a blank canvas.

Published in Tricycle: The Buddhist Review *(2015), which seeks to provide "a unique and independent public forum for exploring Buddhism, establishing a dialogue between Buddhism and the broader culture, and introducing Buddhist thinking to Western disciplines."*

It was the second or third night of the workshop, close to midnight, when I sat on the very cold bed in that dorm room in Texas and realized that I hated at least three of my friends and a woman I knew only marginally.

"Hate" is not the right word. "Hate" is the word I want to use because everyone hates something, like the taste of root beer, for example, or mechanical pencils when the lead jams. There are also the big-world hates we can agree on: genocide, police brutality, high carbon footprints. Hate is, in public at least, accessible and acceptable.   5

I did not, however, hate three of my friends and the marginal woman. I envied them. I am trying to remember all the reasons now and even who the specific friends were at the time, but the list roughly boiled down to the fact that one friend had a spectacular book deal and another had finished her first book. A third friend was about to marry the love of her life and another had good hair. (I don't mean white folks' hair. I mean thick wavy dark hair that she didn't need to touch in the morning because she woke up looking *that good*.) I hated them all. No, I envied them. I wanted what they had.

The cold bedsheets bit into the back of my thighs while I tossed and turned that night. What makes *envidia*, or envy, so annoying is that it morphs. It looks like hate. It feels like annoyance. It turns into despair (I'll never get what I want; what's wrong with me? I love my friends, right?). And because envy is hardly ever talked about in public, it is hardly ever an isolated feeling. The moment I recognized envy that night, I felt ashamed.

In the dark, I stared at the unadorned walls, then finally sat up and doubled the flat dorm pillow. If I was going to have an envy attack, I would at least use it as fodder for practicing lovingkindness.[1] I crossed my legs and tucked the pillow-turned-cushion under me. I did a body scan first. The envy was a knob in my solar plexus. A familiar knob. My hopes rose. Maybe it was not envy I was feeling but good old-fashioned depression instead. The moment I brought up the image of one of my friends, though, the knob turned into a knife and sent a stabbing sensation through my chest. Definitely not depression. I tried another round of lovingkindness. *Nada*.

At that point, I had been sitting for a little more than a decade. I considered myself a periphery Buddhist. I had my sangha[2] and I went on silent retreats. I took copious notes at dharma talks. I saw absolutely no conflict between Buddhist teachings and my upbringing in a Cuban-Colombian home where we practiced Catholicism and the Afro-Cuban religion of *Santería*. That night in San Antonio however, I had to consider the possibility that Buddhism might not help me with envy precisely because I am a Latina, and my family and my culture had raised me to know that envy is not just bad—it's real bad. It's so bad that we have entire cultural practices set up for the sole purpose of keeping *envidia* out of our lives. Maybe this is what made that night in Texas so

---

1. Meditation practice drawn from Buddhism, also known as *Metta bhavana*, that emphasizes love and compassion for self and others.

2. Association or community of fellow spiritual practitioners.

painful. I was transgressing a cultural practice dating back hundreds of years. I was courting the demon.

For years as a child, I thought all babies were born with white wardrobes and black eyeballs dangling from their shoulders.

The whiteness was consuming. There were the undershirts, the onesies, the beanie hats, the blankets, and the diapers, and in that blinding landscape, every baby had a tiny black eyeball gleaming from her left shoulder. The eyeball—a sphere made of the semiprecious stone jet—was attached to a single red bead and pinned to the baby's onesie with a gold-plated safety pin. Sometimes the black stone had not been shaped into a perfectly round eyeball but into a fist instead, and so the baby had a black fist swaying from her shoulders or hung from a gold necklace and rucked under her onesie.

10   The babies never touched the amulets but the women did. The mothers and aunties and *comadres*.[3] In New Jersey, the Cuban women cooed at a new baby and asked about feedings, and all the while their anxious fingers pulled at the layers of white blankets and white sweaters until they found the gold-plated safety pin and the eyeball. They smiled and murmured about how good it was that the baby had her *azabache*.[4] No one spoke of the origins of this practice, but the famed Cuban anthropologist Lydia Cabrera attributed it to the religion called Regla de Ochá, or Santería. The azabache, though, is also used in Europe. It's the stone that pilgrims carried for protection on the Camino de Santiago in Spain.

My mother did not care about the origins of the eyeball. A Colombian married to a Cuban, she pinned the azabache to my baby sister because she appreciated hearing that the black eyeball protected infants from the worst evil possible: envy.

Cubans do not believe in emotion as abstraction. When Cubans talk about envy, they talk about bad eyes, or to be exact, "the" bad eye as in *el ojo malo*, the evil eye. Envy, then, is the reason babies get sick for no reason. It's the reason grown women and men lose a job or a lover or even their homes. Envy is not a feeling state; it is an eyeball no one can see. It is the look someone gives you when they want what you have. Babies, being as they are luminous, are especially vulnerable to the evil eye, and in Spanish, because we apparently do not believe that the devil comes in degrees, bad and evil are the same word: *malo*.

The irony about the evil eye is that while it lurked everywhere in my childhood, no one admitted to having it. Even now, so many decades later, when I think of asking my mother if she has ever felt envy, my tongue falters. It would be like asking her if she has had sex outside of marriage. A decent woman does not feel envidia. The evil eye is like syphilis or Ebola. It afflicts people who are not us, which is why at the age of 6, I thought envy was someone else's fault, and in my particular case, the fault of Charles Schulz.

3. Spanish for "godmothers."
4. Jet stone amulet worn to protect against "the evil eye."

In 1950, Schulz started publishing his comic strip *Peanuts*, and to be fair, he probably had no way of anticipating mass consumerism. He probably did not think, while he colored in Snoopy's black nose, that T-shirts and mugs and watches would be produced and sold at high prices based on his drawings. He probably did not think that someone would create a Snoopy telephone. But they did.

The phone, made in 1966, consisted of Snoopy standing upright, smiling   15
and holding the yellow receiver in his right paw, while his bird friend, Woodstock, grinned, a bundle of plastic yellow feathers at his side. The phone's rotary dial sat on a base painted a cherry red.

I was about 6 years old when I saw that telephone in my friend's bedroom and there the problem began. I wanted the Snoopy phone. By this, I don't mean that I hoped Santa would bring me the same phone. I mean that I *needed* to have the Snoopy phone the way my father needed his can of Budweiser and his cigars, the way the old women at the corner store needed their lotto tickets. I could not imagine going on another day of my 6-year-old life without that Snoopy telephone. But, according to my mother, that was exactly what I would have to do, because while my mother had never heard anyone say outright that craving is the root of suffering, she knew that it was and she was no fool. The craving would pass, and my 6-year-old self would get over it.

It's questionable whether I ever did move on (periodically, I eye the Snoopy phones on eBay), but I do wonder now if envy helped usher me toward Buddhism. Raised in the Catholic church and on the periphery of the Afro-Cuban religion responsible for the azabaches, I never resonated with the notion of original sin; but craving? I knew craving, and for a long time I knew it as envy. After the Snoopy phone, there were the covered stickerbooks in third grade and the Nike sneakers in high school and the things I envied that I could not name, like the girls whose parents spoke English and people whose bodies weren't pinned to the past by trauma. I wanted it all.

It is possible that Francis Bacon got it right when he said that busy people especially suffer from envy. "A man that is busy, and inquisitive, is commonly envious. . . . For envy is a gadding passion, and walketh the streets, and doth not keep home," he wrote in his essay "Of Envy." When I look back at the short course of my life, I have to admit that I have been roaming the world with a lot of curiosity about how other people live. In fact, in the last couple of years, I have learned that it is even possible to be envious of what I don't want, like a high-profile media job and being pregnant and tote bags that cost two hundred dollars. Spiritual envidia, though, might be the worst, since it's hard to acknowledge—for example, that you are envious of your Zen teacher for waking up at four in the morning to sit and never complaining (at least to you) about her knees when you are sure she is 20 years older than you.

Pema Chödrön's teacher, Chögyam Trungpa Rinpoche, used to say that we failed on the spiritual journey because if we didn't "you would get so obnoxious and uncompassionate about other people."[5] I like this idea. Maybe envy is

5. Pema Chödrön (b. 1936), American Tibetan Buddhist nun; Chögyam Trungpa Rinpoche (1939–1987), meditation master and teacher of Tibetan Buddhism.

keeping me on the spiritual journey, on the literal and metaphorical cushion. It's either that or I am the only Latina I know willing to admit that she knows where the ojo malo is located.

20   That night in San Antonio with the cold bedsheets and the envidia attack, I needed an azabache. That's why I turned to metta. If I could generate loving-kindness for the people I envied, surely it would shift my feelings and thoughts. And it worked. Actually, it began to work after about three nights. For the first two nights in that dorm room, I folded the pillow, sat on it and brought my cat to mind. The image of her owl-shaped eyes was the equivalent of turning the valve on for metta. I could practically feel the biochemical start of lovingkind-ness. I got stuck, though, when I transferred it to my friend and her new book deal. Didn't she already have enough good stuff in her life? The thought flared for the first two nights, and on the third, it flared a little less. By the time I left San Antonio, I knew I didn't have a fix for envy. But I did have a way of working with it.

    It's strange to compare metta to an amulet, but that is how I think of lov-ingkindness now. It's a black eyeball pinned to a baby's left shoulder. It's what my mother would gift me if I could ever admit to her the extent of my envidia.

MLA CITATION

Hernández, Daisy. "Envidia." *The Norton Reader: An Anthology of Nonfiction*, edited
    by Melissa A. Goldthwaite et al., 15th ed., W. W. Norton, 2020, pp. 820–24.

QUESTIONS

1. Daisy Hernández makes a distinction between "hate" and "envy." What is the difference?

2. Hernández writes that she saw no conflict between Buddhist teachings and her upbringing in Catholicism and the Afro-Cuban religion of Santería (paragraph 9). How does she bring different religious, cultural, and spiritual practices together in trying to deal with envy? Cite passages from the essay to support your answer.

3. Hernández focuses on envy as the worst evil in her culture. What was the "worst evil" in the culture in which you grew up? Were there any rituals, amulets, or icons meant to protect people from this evil? Write an essay in which you consider this evil and safeguards against it.

RACHEL PIEH JONES
A Muslim, a Christian, and a Baby Named "God"

> *And sometimes it's the very otherness of a stranger, someone who doesn't belong to our ethnic or ideological or religious group, an otherness that can repel us initially, but which can jerk us out of our habitual selfishness, and give us intonations of that sacred otherness, which is God.*
>   —KAREN ARMSTRONG, author of several books on comparative religion.

WHEN GOD AND HIS MOTHER were released from the maternity ward they came directly to my house to use the air conditioner. It was early May and the summer heat that melted lollipops and caused car tires to burst enveloped Djibouti like a wet blanket. Power outages could exceed ten hours a day. Temperatures hadn't peaked yet, 120 degrees would come in August, but the spring humidity without functioning fans during power outages turned everyone into hapless puddles. I prepared a mattress for Amaal and her newborn and prayed the electricity would stay on so she could use the air conditioner and rest, recover.

In 2004 when my family arrived in Djibouti, I needed help minimizing the constant layer of dust; Amaal needed a job. I needed a friend and Amaal, with her quick laugh and cultural insights, became my lifeline. My husband worked at the University of Djibouti and was gone most mornings and afternoons, plus some evenings. We had 4-year-old twins and without Amaal I might have packed our bags and returned to Minnesota out of loneliness and culture shock.

I hired Amaal before she had any children. She wasn't married yet and her phone often rang while she worked, boys calling to see what she was doing on Thursday evening. To see if she wanted to go for a walk down the streets without street lights where young people could clandestinely hold hands or drink beer from glass Coca-Cola bottles. She rarely said yes until Abdi Fatah[1] started calling. He didn't drink alcohol and didn't pressure her into more physical contact than she was comfortable with in this Muslim country. She felt respected. She said yes.

Djibouti is one of the hottest countries in the world, best known to Americans, if at all, as the host of the only US military base in Africa, Camp Lemonnier. Djibouti is also a former French colony, a bastion of peace in a tumultuous region with Yemen across the narrow strait, Eritrea to the west, and Somalia to the east. Djibouti is the main conduit for landlocked Ethiopia's goods, which are hauled by hundreds of trucks snaking every day from the port in Djibouti

Published in Longreads *(2017), which features and produces "in-depth investigative pieces, profiles, interviews, commentary, book reviews, audio stories, and personal essays."*

---

1. Name has been changed [Author's note].

to Ethiopia's capital, Addis Ababa. And, Djibouti is a Muslim country with a Catholic cathedral, a French Protestant church, and an Ethiopian Orthodox church. From one vantage point near the port, between two *dukaans*[2] selling fresh-squeezed orange juice and rapidly melting ice cream, you can see the white minaret and green-tinted windows of a mosque, the cross on top of the cathedral, and the golden dome of the Orthodox church.

5   The Quran says, "There is no compulsion in religion," and in Djibouti, this appears to be true. In Djibouti there is also little crossover or intermingling in religion. Djiboutians are Muslims, Ethiopian Orthodox are their specific brand of Orthodox. Other Ethiopians and European, American, and other African expatriates are Catholic or Protestant, or whatever they were when they arrived. And for the most part, they tend to remain in the religious traditions and communities of their forefathers. Each maintains their orthodoxy and orthopraxy, and each calls God by a different name.

This raises questions about the nature of God and the practice of our worship. Is God's name *God*? Dieu? Allah? Ebbe? Waq? How do we approach this entity? On our knees with our foreheads pressed to the ground, years of praying the Islamic *salat*[3] branding us with bruises? Through making the sign of the cross with our right hand, crossing over heart and chest? Through singing songs and raising our hands toward the heavens? Through ritual incense and the mediation of an Orthodox priest? Does our practice make us perfect in the pursuit of knowing and honoring God? Or can God be found outside of ritual and structure and tradition? Can God be found outside the walls of our separate buildings?

I knew Muslims before moving to Djibouti but Amaal became my first close Muslim friend. We laughed at each other's strange habits, like how she slathered her face in green paste made from crushed leaves to dye it whiter and how I brushed my teeth with a green minty paste that frothed and then spit it out. We examined each other's faith, she a Muslim and me a Christian, and how we incorporated it into our daily lives. Amaal told me I had the patience of Job while we waited for our shipped container of supplies to arrive from Dubai and spent months eating from paper plates while sitting on the floor. She told me the Islamic story of this prophet. Job, plagued by the loss of his children and livelihood and suffering from boils. He would pick the maggots that fell out of his boils to the ground and gently replace them on his skin so they wouldn't die, praising Allah for giving him life, even this life of suffering. Amaal had a conflict with a friend and I told her the story of the prophet Joseph from the Bible, how he forgave his eleven brothers who, overcome by jealousy, sold him into slavery.

Amaal taught me how to fold and fry samboosas—dough stuffed with ground beef and onions, folded into a triangle, and fried—and that it was okay to dress like a slob inside the house, but that I needed to put on perfume, makeup, and jewelry to go out in Djibouti, in what Somalis liked to call "the

2. Somali for "shops."
3. Muslim ritual prayer performed five times a day.

Paris of Somali fashion." No matter that the perfume would soon be overpowered by the sickly sweet stench of constant sweat. No matter that the makeup would melt and clump or that the jewelry would stick to my skin, cheap necklaces leaving green streaks around my neck. Amaal was patient with my languishing language skills and understood me when no one else could. She sometimes translated between me and her elderly relatives, all of us speaking Somali. Amaal had kept me in Djibouti and her friendship helped me stay sane while in Djibouti, so when she asked if she and her newborn could stay with us after the birth, I didn't hesitate.

Water was scarcer than electricity and after giving birth, Amaal wouldn't be able to push a wheelbarrow loaded with 20-liter yellow water jugs from the neighborhood water hose to her house. She could pay a neighbor to do it, she could wait for her husband to come home from work. But she didn't have cash to spare and Abdi Fatah might arrive from work at a time when the water was off, and they would miss their turn at the communal faucet. My house, with a generator and water tank, seemed like a refuge.

Her house was the second-to-last at the bottom of a steep and rocky slope.   10
Some expatriates referred to her neighborhood of Balbala as a slum but Amaal would take offense at this term. According to UN-Habitat, a slum is a run-down part of a city with substandard housing, squalor, and lacking in tenure security—inhabitants are transient, rarely staying in one location for long.

Amaal's husband had a good, secure job in the military. She refused to acquiesce to squalor and painted swooping vines and flowers and red curtains on the cement walls of her home. Amaal and her neighbors worked tirelessly against the desert dust to maintain cleanliness. She and Abdi Fatah had their own toilet, though not yet running water. They had electricity, when the electricity was on. They had two rooms and a kitchen. This was not a slum dwelling, it was Djiboutian lower-middle class. It just didn't look like what foreigners expected.

Beyond the front door that Amaal would later paint a bright blue was the cemetery. The unevenly spaced body-sized mounds with no headstones divided her quarter from Cité Barwaaqo, another section of Balbala. She only crossed the cemetery to get to her best friend's house, past goats and kids playing with cars made from milk carton boxes and tin can covers, in the middle of the day, after praying and while whispering "bismillah al-rahman al-rahiim" (In the name of Allah, the most gracious, the most merciful). If she returned alive and if no jinn[4] had possessed her, then Allah had answered the prayers made in his name, yet again proving to be gracious and merciful.

Beyond the cemetery, the lights visible on clear days, Djibouti's port towered over the Gulf of Tadjoura. Container ships to be unloaded and refueled waited further out at sea, their hulking mass a constant reminder of the world beyond Djibouti. I told Amaal the view from her house was beautiful. She said it was horrifying. I saw water and ships, commerce and travel and development. She saw the cemetery and the aluminum-sided houses, perhaps what UN-Habitat looked at when they labeled her neighborhood a slum.

---

4. Spirit or demon.

Amaal's friend in Cité Barwaaqo, Waris, had given birth to a baby girl a few months earlier. Amaal and I paced the hallway of the Dar-Al Hanan maternity hospital while Waris' mother stayed by her laboring daughter. Waris asked for Amaal to come hold her hand but Amaal started to cry from the intensity and terror of labor and retreated to the hallway. She took Waris' phone when it rang and wiped away tears while she answered Waris' husband's inquiries.

15   Yes, Waris was fine. Yes, it hurt like hell. No, there was no baby yet. No, she didn't want to talk to him.

Later Waris described the pain in vivid detail. Nurses attempting to help laboring mothers pinched their inner thighs, slapped, insulted, and sometimes sat on their bellies while they pushed and women were discouraged from crying out in pain, from revealing weakness. Amaal's takeaway was to stop taking prenatal vitamins.

"They will make the baby too big." She didn't want to push out a big baby and she didn't want to cause a C-section.

"They won't make the baby big," I said. "They will make it healthy."

"My mother-in-law won't allow it."

20   I convinced Amaal to take the vitamins but she kept them in the refrigerator at my house so her mother-in-law wouldn't discover them and toss the contraband down their hole-in-the-ground toilet. Amaal came to work every day with fresh questions. One day she called me into the bedroom and lifted her dress to show me a rash spreading over her breasts. Another day she asked which sexual positions were least cumbersome during the third trimester. She asked how to help a baby sleep through the night, how to change a diaper, whether or not to give water alongside breast milk. Her mother had died years ago and Amaal started to call me *hooyo* even though I was less than ten years older. Mother.

Three times Amaal called me after midnight and said, breathless, that labor had begun. I drove her and her husband to the French hospital, Bouffard. Because Abdi Fatah was in the military, they were allowed to use this facility. Three times the Djiboutian midwife looked at us with an unspoken question in her eyes. The nervous husband, the concerned foreign friend, and the maybe-laboring mother. Three times she sent us home and told us to come back when Amaal was unable to speak.

When Amaal's labor began in earnest, I was on an airplane returning from a conference in Kenya. My husband picked me up at the airport and drove me directly to the hospital. Soccer games raged in the parking lot over the giant white X of the helicopter landing pad. Security guards checked my passport and recognized me from my previous visits with Amaal. I knew my way to the maternity ward; I had paced outside it for hours trying to encourage my own labor a few years earlier.

There was one delivery room and if needed, the cramped exam room could be commandeered, or the floor in the hallway outside the labor room. Amaal shared the room with several other women and they all hoped they would deliver at alternating times so no one would end up on the floor. Despite the frigid air conditioning, Amaal was sweating and instead of breathing through contractions, she cried in a low voice the Djiboutian mourning cry, the sound of both grief and physical pain, "Waaaaywaaaywaaay," and clenched her teeth. Abdi Fatah looked scared and uncomfortable, the only man in the room. His eyes darted from Amaal's face to her stomach and he steadfastly refused to glance at the other women. He asked if he could wait in the hall while I stayed. We prayed for mercy, for miracles, and I wiped Amaal's forehead, whispered that she was beautiful.

Midwives said things like, *If you can't handle the pain then why did you get pregnant in the first place?* They said things like, *This is what you get for messing around.* They said things like, *If you don't hurry up you will have a C-section and then what husband will want you?* I wanted to counter these words, to speak a different reality over Amaal the same way I had needed my husband to tell me I was strong during labor. We could grasp that word, *strong*, and squeeze it dry while our babies turned us inside out.

Abdi Fatah returned with a damp towel to cool Amaal's face and kissed   25
her. Her labor progressed slowly and I had to go home to my three children, the youngest, 3 years old, the one born in Djibouti, recovering from chicken pox.

And so I missed the birth of God, hours later and by Cesarean section. In the morning I returned to the hospital to hold the baby and to assuage Amaal's guilt and anger about the vitamins, nervous that she would blame them, or me, for the C-section. Abdi Fatah met me at the gate and took me to her room. He said he didn't care about scars and surgery. He had wanted a girl but now he said he didn't care about girls either. I gave Amaal sliced watermelon and a bag of Coca-Colas and chocolate crème cookies and scooped God into my arms.

"Tell me about his name," I said. Even after five years in Somalia and Djibouti I had never heard this name before.

"God," Amaal said. She pronounced it almost like "goad" with a long *o* sound and a brisk *d*, half-way between a *t* and a *d*. "It means poisonous snake."

"Do you really spell it G-o-d?"

She nodded.   30

"Do you know what that sounds like in English?"

She nodded. "The French doctor checked on us and read his name off the chart and started laughing. He explained." She said every nurse who came to check on her and saw the chart, laughed. Some bent to kiss God.

Two-and-a-half years earlier I had given birth to the one with chicken pox, at this same hospital. She was born on 9/11 but in 2005, a baby born to a Christian family in a Muslim country with a Somali midwife on an infamous day. I named her Lucy Deeqsan. Deeqsan is a Somali name that means "gift from Allah." In its full meaning, a gift from Allah that is so sufficient I could never ask for anything else.

A few American Christians told me their opinions about this name, which boiled down into, *Anyone who would name their daughter in reference to a pagan god is a heretic.* But Arab Christians used the word Allah for God even before the prophet Mohamed was born. Arab Bibles are filled with the word Allah. If "Dios" can be translated to mean God, if "Dieu" can be translated to mean God, if "Ebbe" can be translated to mean God, these words are simply different jumbles of letters and sounds forced together in an attempt to explain the unexplainable. If "God" is who many people believe God is, neither the concept nor the word can be owned. No religious system, no language can lay claim.

Names can have multiple meanings, multiple narratives. The middle name we chose for our youngest, Deeqsan, could also euphemistically mean "that's enough." And after twins, after giving birth in Djibouti, this baby was our last. *Way noo deeqday,* she was enough for us. So sufficient I could never ask for anything else.

35   Amaal asked if she and God could stay at my house for the first week or two. Abdi Fatah had to work, he might even be called to Forêt du Day on the other side of Djibouti, in the mountainous Afar region. I had a generator that sometimes functioned, when my husband was home to pull the cord like a lawn mower, and though it never summoned enough power for an air conditioner, in theory it could motivate a ceiling fan. I also had running water.

"Of course." I promised to visit the hospital every day and on the fourth day, bundled God in a pink baby blanket my mother had shipped from Minnesota as a gift and drove them home.

Amaal and God slept on a thin foam mattress in Lucy Deeqsan's bedroom and Lucy slept with her older sister. The power cut out the first night and the generator didn't work. We lay awake in pools of sweat. In the morning I ate cereal for breakfast and Amaal sent the neighbor boy out for a baguette she could dip in her tea. Amaal invited friends and relatives and in a Djiboutian home after a baby is born, guests flood the rooms. They bring gifts and food and clean the floors and hold the baby. Her friends were shy about coming to an American's house and only Waris visited. I had to teach English at a local women's organization and no one was home to massage Amaal's shoulders or help change God's diapers.

At night, so Amaal could sleep, I rocked God in the wooden Iranian rocking chair I bought at a bazaar while pregnant with Deeqsan. I thought about God and poisonous snakes and the words that divided worlds. Strings of phonetics, scratchings of script, the human desperation to communicate, to name. Words shape the way we see the world. Or does the way we see our world shape the words we use to describe it? Somali has more words related to camels than I will ever be able to learn. English has more nuanced color vocabulary than Somalis deem reasonable. I see the world in rainbows, my Somali friends see the world in relation to camels.

When a Djiboutian asks me whether or not I worship Allah, I don't think about the spelling or the sounds or the centuries-ago and still-to-this-day conflicts and crusades. I fill that word up with what I know of our common understanding. We don't agree on all the characteristics of God but we do agree on many. Allah the creator, the ultimate, the most gracious, the giver and taker of life. Yes, when I speak Somali and answer the question, yes, *Allah baan cabuudaa*. When I speak English and then answer the question, yes, I worship God.

When people press and want to know if I am a Muslim or if I have prayed the *salat*, the five-times daily Islamic prayer, I say *no*. When they press deeper and ask if I would like to become a Muslim, I say *no, I love Jesus*. We are not the same, this isn't universalism and I'm not afraid or ashamed of my beliefs that run counter to many of the people I live around. This is acknowledging that while we disagree on concepts of God and in our convictions about things like sin, forgiveness, and the process of redemption, we are people of faith. We can still communicate.

Names tell stories, they hold histories, they convey character and belief and can be unpacked. In the unpacking of Allah or of God, different stories emerge and those stories differ depending upon who is doing the unpacking. As I rock baby God, I think of the stories of the names of my children. One named after her great-grandmother. One named, loosely, after Indiana Jones— or a long-dead Christian preacher, depending on who tells the story of that naming. One named for the country in which she was born. The baby in my arms, named for a snake. Yet none of these names conveys the fullness of that person. Each of these named children must be encountered on their own terms, in relationship, over time.

While living in a Muslim country, I have not changed in my deep convictions about God and about faith but I have witnessed the deep convictions of others about God and faith. We are not the same but that doesn't mean, in an increasingly violent and divided world, that we should join either the jihad or the drones. The differences should not be obstacles but opportunities to engage and discuss and to enter a reconciliation that doesn't insist on uniformity. When a baby is born and his name is God, I fill that word up with the shape of his eyes and the gentle curve of his cheek.

In *The Case for God*, theologian Karen Armstrong writes that God is not the exclusive property of any one tradition. Hard as I tried to make them comfortable, I could not even keep baby God exclusively in my house. I gave Amaal my battery-operated fan. After English class I made *sugo*, a greasy spaghetti sauce, and filled bowls with apple slices and chunks of banana and carried them to her room so she wouldn't have to get up. I held God and washed his white onesie with pink and blue butterflies and bounced him and sang songs.

But eventually Amaal announced that she and God could not recuperate at my home. My isolated, American-culture house was too quiet, too lonely, not any cooler than her own since our generator stubbornly refused to work, and she was taking the baby. If I wanted to hold God, I could find him in Balbala. And so, unable to rest, on the seventh day Amaal and God moved out.

MLA CITATION

Jones, Rachel Pieh. "A Muslim, a Christian, and a Baby Named 'God.'" *The Norton Reader: An Anthology of Nonfiction*, edited by Melissa A. Goldthwaite et al., 15th ed., W. W. Norton, 2020, pp. 825–32.

QUESTIONS

1. A Christian living in a primarily Muslim country, Rachel Pieh Jones shows both commonalities and differences between her own beliefs and others in Djibouti. What are some of the differences and similarities? Which seem most significant?

2. Jones reflects on the importance of names, naming, and communication. What is necessary for a name to be "unpacked" (paragraph 41), to show the fullness of its meaning?

3. Jones and her friend Amaal share stories from their different religious traditions to help guide each other. Write a letter to a friend who needs guidance or advice, using a story from your religious or cultural tradition to provide context for your advice.

FARIHA RÓISÍN
Meet a Muslim

MY SISTER PUT ON THE HIJAB when she was twenty years old. I remember the color of her first scarf—a pale blue green, maybe chiffon, crinkling at the corners of her smiling eyes, enveloping the circumference of her perfect moon-shaped face. My sister was one of the most beautiful women I knew growing up. Perhaps challenged, in beauty, only by my own mother. She had plump lips, pale and pink like the color of figs, but full like plums, always chapped like creases behind knees in the warm summer heat. She was strong, smart, and terrifying.

I was thirteen when she put on the hijab. Two years after September 11.

The day she put it on we were sitting in her cul-de-sac room. The window overlooked our pristine blue pool with leaves dredging on the surface from our overarching mango tree, shedding its leaves with a tranquil languidity. But I did not feel calm. A feeling of dread panicked through my tiny little body. My stomach lay ill with concern, plummeting through all the reasons why she shouldn't do what she was about to do. My heart, emptied out, carved only by fear, thudded against the cavity of my chest. It was like watching someone

Published in Go Home! *(2018), an anthology of memoir, poetry, and stories that deal with identity and displacement. The collection was edited by Rowan Hisayo Buchanan.*

about to take a vow, an oath—a samurai, putting on their armor. I felt scared for her.

Since then, she has explained to me that the hijab is much like armor. It acts as a shield against the world of men, meaning: by and large the patriarchy—where women are so often disposable. The hijab acts as a litmus test; it balances the playing field where men are encouraged to take women seriously not for their beauty, but for their intellect. The best explanation I've been given from my sister is that the hijab is like a second skin. It's protection from all of the earth's defenses and energetic toxicities.

The first time I realized I was Muslim, and thus different, was in grade school when I didn't know any of the words to the Christian hymns in religion class. I also knew that my religion—Islam—didn't have an assigned class dedicated to it. Back then it was considered acceptable for kids of other faiths to go to Bible Study. I used to think that this was because it bred religious tolerance, but as I got older I realized it was just out of laziness. Strangely, however, I liked going to religion class.

My sister was seven years older than me, and went to an all-girls private Catholic school in the suburbs of Brisbane. She wore a uniform that consisted of a pale yellow shirt and a forest-green checkered skirt and really ugly earth-brown socks and shoes. Every day, I would pick her up from school, my father in the front seat of the car waiting. In the interim I'd walk around the Christ-on-the-cross-laden halls and feel supremely content with my surroundings. Sometimes, if I was lucky, I'd watch the nuns mulling around the convent on campus, and even talk to Sister Catherine, my favorite sister—who was particularly zealous and enthusiastic. I developed a love of religion and spirituality in those halls, a love of the religious iconography, the gravity and significance of religious worship. It *felt* like a house of God, and I was deeply grounded by that feeling, the feeling of being embraced.

My parents weren't religious, though they weren't particularly nonreligious either. My mother is a painter and works with kids on the side, she's prayed five times a day since I've been alive. My father is a Marxist with a fondness for international development and Islamic philanthropy. He is inspired deeply by the Quran, though he never imposed it on either my sister or me. In fact, he taught me all things that I love and hold dear about Islam.

Together, we'd watch documentaries about Islamic architecture; or he would take me to exhibitions dedicated to Islamic art. I learned early on about Islamic science—and how it was responsible for so many historic findings, such as the removal of cataracts, or even the inventions of hospitals and pharmacies as we know them today. From philosophy to astronomy—from Ibn Battuta (a historic Islamic traveler) to Avicenna (the OG Renaissance man who was both a medical doctor and philosopher)—I read obsessively about Baghdad in its prime, the poet Rumi, and would listen to Nusrat Fateh Ali Khan[1] and dream of the universe and galaxies ahead of, and beyond, me.

1. Pakistani singer and musician (1948–1997).

It's a Mohsin Hamid[2] quote where he says that the day before 9/11 he was just ostensibly another American—just one with a strange name—then the day after 9/11 he was suddenly a loaded word: Muslim, a suspicion, a target.

10   I would not be able to count on my hands the amount of times my sister has been harassed on the street for wearing a hijab. I've heard so many stories of the lewd sexual harassment of Muslim women or other forms of sexual abuse, and even in some extreme cases, death. Muslim women are murdered because they represent something that the West still refuses to understand. Ironically, the misogyny that fuels a person to kill a woman is overlooked because the deaths are warranted by how a Muslim woman chooses to represent herself. Which is an offense, to some—but apparently the harassment of women isn't.

A few years ago, Richard Dawkins, your resident atheist-science bro, suggested broadcasting "loving, gentle, woman-respecting erotic videos" into Islamic theocracies, like Iran, as a means of challenging the institutionalized religion that exists in those societies. This rhetoric—one of misguided sexual and "modern" interventionism—continues to other these cultures. And of course the narrative impales Muslims as unnatural creatures who know nothing of pleasure, and only of dogma. I'm so glad that he wants to save us from our boring sexless lives. The hubris it must take to be Richard Dawkins.

To him, and his trusty band of naysayers, science—or rather the absence of religiosity—is misapprehended as a trapping of intellect. Not only that, the fetishization of Islam as a guilty male-ego-driven monolith obscures and dismisses all the powerful women making so many strides in the Muslim world. Just read Isobel Coleman's *Paradise beneath Her Feet*, which dissects feminism in the Muslim world from country to country (Pakistan and Malaysia are some case studies). This disavowal of Islam by the West pushes forward an entropic worldview that men—especially white men without religion—are not corrupted by their bravados. Which is a farce. Dawkins probably doesn't believe in God because there's nothing that he could believe in more than himself.

Men like him are so consumed by their own egos that they assume that the position of women in the Western world is not lacking in anything. That on the altar of freedom and democracy we, as women, have been given all our rights and everything is fine. That intersectional identity doesn't exist. That, in America, women no longer experience sexual harassment just by walking down the street. That women receive equal pay for equal work. That between 40 to 70 percent of female murder victims are not killed by their intimate partners. That 83 percent of girls aged twelve to sixteen do not experience some form of sexual harassment in public schools.

2. Pakistani novelist (b. 1971); his second novel, *The Reluctant Fundamentalist* (2007), is about a Pakistani man who goes to school and works in the United States and moves back to Pakistan after the 9/11 terrorist attacks.

After Charlie Hebdo in 2015, the question of freedom of speech garnered much support. #JeSuisCharlie became an international phenomenon and world leaders even marched to support a concept of freedom that some of them haven't even institutionalized in their own countries. In 2010 the Senate of France banned the wearing of the niqab and burqa. They even employed Fadela Amara, a Muslim, who served as a junior minister in the French government, to state the following: "The veil is the visible symbol of the subjugation of women, and therefore has no place in the mixed, secular spaces of France's state school system." Thing is, what the French, or the West, don't understand is that it's an act of "subjugation" to a society that has a very specific idea of what a woman should and shouldn't wear.

To me, that's not the feminism that I take solace in. To me, feminism is open   15
and brimming with diversity. I believe in a feminism for women of color, trans and queer women, nonbinary femme folk, and most definitely one for Muslim women. France's idea of secularism is based on homogeneity. The problem of that stance is that it only further negates and dismisses the identities that are more complicated than just the one prescription they have of a woman. It's a deeply limiting perspective.

I don't wear a hijab, nor do I plan on ever wearing one. But I do believe, and purport to believe, in the right of freedom for all. I, as a Muslim and a feminist, understand that feminism means comprehending that there are things outside of one's existence and frame of understanding that are just as valid as what we know for ourselves. In a post-9/11 world we have imposed so many restrictions on Muslims and yet expect dedication in return. With every drone that strikes a child in Pakistan, we refuse to comprehend the roots of Islamic terrorism; with every ban of religious freedom of expression, we tautologically debate the concept of freedom for the West; with every speech that is delivered that encourages love and compassion, we isolate a religion, and its mostly peace-loving majority because it supports our international, and national, narratives of what it means to be a nation.

Muslims are Human beings. There are over 1.5 billion of us.

It's been hard growing up in this world that has decided on what it means to be you. From every TSA checkpoint, to every nasty comment on the absurdity of the veil, Islamophobia is a very real thing. Making a concerted effort to understand Muslims is actually where it all begins.

There's something sacred about a religious experience.   20

Recently, I participated in a debate at Trinity College in Dublin where the motion was "This House Believes Religion Does More Harm Than Good." I was on the opposition side, explaining that to say something is outright bad can't be applicable when it affects so many lives in such a deeply positive way. I don't really know if it's possible to describe the nuances and folds of Islam to those who've never wanted to understand it. How do you explain what it feels like to dive into something that feels embracing, all-encompassing, how Islam, like most religions, I'm sure, has great peaks that are undefinable? That it

gives you meaning and hope in a glorious way. That it exalts you and revital-
izes your being. How can we explain what that feels like? How do we define
religion and its impact? Is it really quantifiable?

Things shift within a religious identity; since wearing the hijab my sister
has experienced rapid changes in how she feels about herself and the world.
There are times she's grappled with the weight of such a symbol, and she's
come to terms with what she needed in those times. I've experienced that in
my own way, embracing that all identities evolve and change and rupture and
blossom. I've done things to myself I'd never comprehend doing as a young
Muslim kid, like drinking or trying drugs—aiming to be honest and live with
integrity within each moment has been key. Getting older has meant understanding that the limitations of my identity are abstract, and that faith is malleable, as is desire. Everything is complex.

I think back to the day when my sister wore that hijab, a day that things
changed for her, but also inevitably for me. In many ways it was a humbling
moment, a terrifying experience of understanding what it feels like to be
openly hated, to witness others publicly disgusted. Through that, it was a day
when I realized (though it took me years to *fully* understand) that there is
something deeply powerful in subverting the norm. Pushing boundaries is
how we learn, so with each step that I change a bigoted perspective, each time
I allow someone to question and challenge their unfounded beliefs, I find
some solace. If opening up about the nuances of life is eye-opening for others,
then why not give words to your experience.

Truth is, there's no other way.

It's an act of survival to speak up, it's revolutionary to say: hey, here's my
story, please listen.

MLA CITATION

Róisín, Fariha. "Meet a Muslim." *The Norton Reader: An Anthology of Nonfiction*,
    edited by Melissa A. Goldthwaite et al., 15th ed., W. W. Norton, 2020,
    pp. 832–36.

Questions

1. Fariha Róisín opens with an anecdote of her sister putting on the hijab, and she
returns to that anecdote at the end of the essay. Why do you think this moment is
so important to her and to the essay?

2. How would you characterize Róisín's tone? Are there places where it shifts?
Why might the author shift tones where she does?

3. Róisín ends her essay by writing, "It's an act of survival to speak up, it's revolutionary to say: hey, here's my story, please listen." What is your story? Write a
personal essay that explains some aspect of your identity. Consider titling it "Meet
a _____."

ORIT AVISHAI
Women of God

I
s GOD BAD FOR WOMEN? Media consumers in North America and
Europe are probably familiar with this narrative: conservative and fundamentalist religions—those that take religion seriously and politicize
religiosity—are on the rise, and that's bad for women. In France, wearing a headscarf in public spaces is decried as an affront to French
notions of citizenship and to women's personhood. In the United States,
Afghan women's plight at the hands of the Taliban was used as a justification
for American intervention. Since the emancipation of women and the diversification of family forms and sexualities are among the hallmarks of modernity
and secularization, and since fundamentalist religious groups tend to hold traditional views on gender, sexuality, and the family, conservative religions are

typically viewed as antithetical to women's interests (not
to mention modern, demo-
cratic ideals of choice and the
freedom to chart one's own
destiny).

In a sense, conservative
religions have *earned* this
bad reputation; the historical record is full of instances
in which girls and women
have been restricted from
access to health care, educa-
tion, and employment in the name of God. Girls' and women's bodies and
mobility are regulated, their chastity is "protected," and sometimes they are
even maimed or killed as a marker of national or tribal pride, identity, unity,
or boundaries. If this is the case, how can we explain women's willingness and
motivation to participate in these religions? Some feel the Marxist explanation—
religion is the opiate of the people—and its feminist incarnation—women's
participation in conservative religions is a form of false consciousness—are
sufficient. Others believe women involved in conservative religions are simply
oppressed.

Sociologists, anthropologists, historians, and political scientists who study
women's experiences in a range of religious traditions in diverse geographical
locations have found that the "God is bad for women" formulation provides an
impoverished picture of experiences with conservative religions. These studies
show that women are simultaneously oppressed *and* empowered by their
religion, that their compliance is as much a product of active strategizing as

Published in Contexts (2010), *"a quarterly magazine about society and social behavior"*
geared toward sociologists.

passive compliance, and that religion is as much a site of negotiating traditional gender norms as it is a site of reproducing patriarchal gender relationships. If that's true, it's certainly possible that conservative religions aren't inherently and universally antithetical to women's interests (at least not *all* of the time).

Some commentators make an even more provocative claim: the "God is bad for women" formulation rests on false assumptions about religion and liberal notions of freedom and choice. That is, these scholars argue that the trope ignores the similarities between women's complicity with religious regimes and their complicity with other gendered practices like Western beauty norms.

RELIGION IS BAD FOR WOMEN

5   Religion is often viewed as a primary site for the articulation, reproduction, and institutionalization of gender inequality. The combination of male gods, institutions that encode gender inequality (think male-only clergy) and women's subordination (such as Evangelical teachings on male headship[1]), ambivalence toward the female body (think the veil across the Muslim world and a Jewish man's daily prayer with a line that thanks God for not "having made me a woman"), and the belief that gender differences are natural and essential has produced a deep-seated suspicion toward conservative religions among the reform-minded. Elizabeth Cady Stanton[2] captured this spirit in 1885 when she wrote, "History shows that the moral degradation of woman is due more to theological superstitions than to all other influences together." Such sentiments were echoed by many second wave American feminists who viewed religiously inspired ideas about women's work, reproduction, and bodies as detrimental to the women's movement's goals of gender equality and freedom.

This view of religion poses a problem, though: women *are* involved with conservative religions. They join, and they stay. Are these women opposed to equality and freedom? Do they not recognize their complicity in a regime that requires submission? Until the 1980s, the general view was that religion—as an ideology and as an institution—was nothing but a constraint on women's

1. The belief, based on the Bible verses Ephesians 5:23–24, that wives should be submissive to their husbands: "For the husband is the head of the wife, even as Christ is the head of the church: and he is the savior of the body. Therefore as the church is subject unto Christ, so let the wives be to their own husbands in every thing."
2. Suffragist and leader of women's rights movement (1815–1902).

lives, so women's active involvement with conservative religions was viewed as the product of oppression, lack of agency, or false consciousness.

Yet, when researchers turned to study women's *actual* experiences with religion (as opposed to ideologically driven assessments) in the late 1980s, their findings were startling: women—Protestant, Catholic, Jewish, Hindu, and others—are not necessarily oppressed and deprived of free choice by their religion.

MULTIPLE MEANINGS

When scholars looked past religious dogma to lived experiences, they found discrepancies between ideologies and practices. Women, they saw, don't blindly submit to religious prescriptions; instead, they adapt their religious practices (if not iterations of belief) to the realities of their lives and to dominant gender ideologies. In the process, they sometimes (consciously or unconsciously) subvert and resist official teachings without much fanfare and without explicitly resisting religious gender norms.

This subtlety, though, serves to perpetuate the myth that women are uniformly oppressed by religion. For example, when sociologists Sally Gallagher and Christian Smith interviewed Evangelical men and women in the U.S. about their family lives, their respondents professed an unwavering support for ideologies such as male headship and women's submission while rejecting egalitarian gender ideologies. Nevertheless, their *real-life* choices about work, family, and child rearing exhibited a de-facto egalitarianism that belied their ideological stance: most of the Evangelical women in their study worked outside the home and routinely participated in domestic decision making. Gallagher and Smith labeled this disjuncture "symbolic traditionalism and pragmatic egalitarianism."

In other cases, researchers have found that what looks like oppression is often a set of strategic choices made to help women navigate gender relations. In a now-classic study, sociologist Lynn Davidman explored why educated American women might embrace highly patriarchal and conservative strands of Orthodox Judaism. Rather than being duped into an anachronistic religion, these women said that they consciously turned to Orthodox Judaism as a response to problems generated by modern American culture, including its emphasis on careerism, individualism, and gender equality. Caroline Chen, a sociologist who studied the experiences of Taiwanese women who converted to conservative strands of Buddhism and Christianity after immigrating to the U.S., found women used religion to negotiate with patriarchal family structures and to carve out a space of independence and authority. Their newfound religion allowed women to undermine oppressive traditional Taiwanese practices that left them without much power within the family. Gallagher also saw similar dynamics in her study of low-income Syrian women, who use religious and cultural rationales to improve their access to income and employment while avoiding unattractive employment opportunities. The Syrian women consciously enlist religion to expand their autonomy while simultaneously maintaining a

10

semblance of deference. Defining their economic activities as "not work," for example, means they can contribute to the family economy (sometimes earning up to 40 percent of the family's income) in a society that emphasizes women's primary responsibilities as domestic. The point is: some women achieve progressive ends using traditional, but subversive, means.

So, women aren't oppressed dupes. On the contrary, women like these use religion to make choices and improve their lives; they are strategic actors who appropriate religious traditions and practices to meet the demands of contemporary life, often to further extra-religious ends such as economic opportunities, domestic relations, political ideologies, and cultural affiliation.

Other studies show how seemingly oppressive practices can serve empowering and liberating functions. This is the case with regard to the issue that best symbolizes conservative religion's purported oppression of women: the veil.

In the 1980s, when political scientist Arlene MacLeod and Turkish sociologist Nulifer Gole studied the emergent phenomenon of Muslim women's embrace of veiling in Egypt and Turkey, respectively, each found that context matters. In the Egyptian case, women's embrace of the veil came at a time when economic conditions compelled women to find gainful employment outside the home. Their movement into the workplace was at odds with traditional Egyptian notions of modesty and domesticity. These ideas had discouraged women from venturing into public spaces unaccompanied by men and frowned upon close contact between unrelated men and women. Veiling provided a solution, as it preserved women's modesty and affirmed their domesticity while also providing the mobility to work outside the home. As it opened unprecedented opportunities for women to venture beyond the domestic, the veil became liberating. Macleod terms the veil's liberating potential as "accommodating protest."

In Turkey, Gole found that, to the generation of young, educated, women who embraced the veil on college campuses, veiling symbolized resistance to Western values. Veiling, Gole argues, wasn't imposed on these women, so the act of veiling reveals them to be empowered and strategic political actors. Research on Latin American Pentecostal women reports similar dynamics of women's empowerment through the embrace of religion.

15   These studies notwithstanding, not all commentators are equally impressed by religion's liberating potential. In her award-winning study of South Korean Evangelical women, sociologist Kelly Chong writes that conversion to Evangelical Christianity helps some women navigate the forces of modernity while also reinforcing highly patriarchal and non-egalitarian gender dynamics. Further, Chong asserts that religion is *also* a site where the rules of gender relations are constantly being rewritten.

The aggregate message of these studies is that conservative religions are not necessarily oppressive, nor is religion thoroughly anti-modern. Context is extremely important but often lost in popular depictions of conservative religions and their symbols—the veil, men's headship, male-only clergy—as

uniformly oppressive. In some instances, the forces of modernity increase the appeal of conservative religion. In others, the embrace of religion helps women cope with and sometimes even challenge preexisting oppressive gender norms and social structures.

Yet, it seems that each study begins with the notion that women's involvement with conservative religions is paradoxical—only to find, time and time again, that this formula provides only a very narrow perspective on the religious experience. More recent research takes issue with the notion that women's complicity and submission are paradoxical, investigating, instead, the assumptions on which this perspective is based.

PAST THE PARADOX

Experts' bewilderment over women's embrace of conservative religions is symptomatic of the broader assumptions about religiosity and modern personhood that have shaped discussions of religion since the Enlightenment. One set of assumptions concerns the incompatibility of religion and modernity. Throughout much of the 20th century, everyone expected the significance of religion would progressively decline. Known as the "secularization thesis," the theory was that modernization and secularization (and, implicitly, westernization) are intrinsically related and that progress—including the emancipation of women from the hold of oppressive religions—follows a uniform and linear (western) trajectory. Religion, in this conception, is incompatible with rational, complex, and individualistic modern societies. When empirical reality proved this theory wrong (conservative and fundamentalist religious movements, for instance, have been on the rise around the world since the 1980s, as evidenced by the 1979 Iranian revolution, the rise of Pentecostalism in Latin America, the increased visibility of Evangelicals in American political life, and the fervor of Orthodox Jewish nationalists), the secularization thesis was replaced by explanations that recognized that *some* aspects of religion were compatible with modernity.

However, a second set of assumptions about the incompatibility of religion with liberal notions of agency, freedom, and choice persists. It is in this set of assumptions that the paradox approach is rooted. The liberal notion of freedom assumes that individuals should strive to be free of commitment and submission to a higher power—thereby precluding many forms of religious devotion. This is why explanations of women's involvement with conservative religion that revolve around strategic choice, the liberatory potential of religion, or passive resistance have been so attractive: women who realize their own economic,

20

political, or intimate interests against the weight of
custom and tradition are
redeemed.

Yet, such explanations
ultimately provide binary
explanations of religion:
either it's a site where women
are oppressed and gender
inequality is reproduced, or
it's a site of empowerment,
resistance, strategic planning
and negotiation of gender. What's missing is the possibility that women embrace
religious practices such as veiling and male headship in pursuit of religious
goals—namely, the cultivation of oneself as a pious *religious* subject.

This is the account that anthropologist Saba Mahmood provides in her
study of Islamic revival and piety among women in Cairo. Starting in the
1990s, many Egyptian women began to attend mosques to teach each other
Islamic doctrine. This trend, facilitated by women's increased mobility and
education, has subversive potential since scholarly and theological materials
had previously been the sole purview of learned men. Yet, these Muslim
women were *not* seeking to undermine existing power structures or to resist
the secular state, which discouraged their kind of learning and religious piety.
Rather, their main motivation was to learn, attain, and uphold Islamic virtues
of modesty and docility and reintegrate Islamic knowledge and practices
(including those that organize gender relationships) into everyday Egyptian
life. For Westerners, it seems impossibly paradoxical: the nature of piety that
these women promote depends on subordination to Islamic virtues of femi-
ninity that includes modesty and docility and is achieved by teaching the body
"modest disciplines" through practices such as veiling and the cultivation of
shyness.

It's easy to dismiss something like the cultivation of shyness as oppressive,
functional, or a symbol of resistance to the forces of modernity. However,
Mahmood presents a different explanation: this practice provides a pathway to
achieve piety and to make meaning in the world. Mahmood likens the achievement of piety through submission to the lengthy and painful regime of learning to which musicians or dancers subject themselves as they seek mastery in
their field. Like a dancer or musician, the religious woman submits herself to
a lifelong regime of ongoing discipline; she becomes a masterful religious
woman through daily practice. But, like the dancer or the musician, the religious woman is not oppressed by her regime; rather, her very personhood and
agency are predicated upon the ability to be instructed and transformed by
submission to her practices.

Mahmood came under fire for positing that the embrace of docility doesn't
necessarily amount to oppression and that "freedom" and "choice" aren't universal terms; most discussions of religion, it seems, still spring from the "God

is bad for women" formulation. Yet, the most important point that Mahmood makes is that the assumptions that shape discussions of women's experiences with conservative religions are flawed. A shift in perspective opens up new avenues for thinking about religion as a site of identity making. Other commentators approach this question of assumptions from a different perspective by noting the irony of anti-religious fervor among Westerners and citing the similarities between patriarchal regulations emanating from religious dogma and those hailing from cultural norms and standards like the Western beauty ideal.

CHURCH OF GOD, CHURCH OF BEAUTY

Bring up conservative religion and its symbols on any American college campus, and students will immediately point out paradoxes of complicity. With astonishing predictability, they associate compliance with conservative religions with lack of agency, choice, or freedom. Students are usually willing to concede that complicity sometimes masks strategic choices or latent resistance, but arguments such as Mahmood's—that women find meaning through docility—are a hard sell. Students like to point out—triumphantly—that *their* lives in a modern democracy that values women are free of the constraints that characterize the lives of veiled women.

Fatima Mernissi, a Moroccan sociologist who has written extensively about gender and religion in the Middle East, puts these self-satisfied indictments in perspective. In the late 1990s, Mernissi lectured extensively in Europe and the U.S. about her memoir. In it, she recounts her childhood in a typical Moroccan household: a harem. This multi-generational living arrangement housed siblings, families, and parents. The harem limited women's spatial mobility, but was also a site of ongoing power struggles. In the course of her book tour, Mernissi was inundated by questions that exposed the depth of Westerners' ignorance about gender relations in Muslim societies. Westerners, she learned, assumed that Muslims were women-haters and that Muslim women were oppressed, dependent, sex starved, and powerless.

Intrigued by the dissonance between Western perceptions and her own experiences, Mernissi set out on a complementary mission (and wrote a complementary book) to uncover how Westerners represent Muslim gender relations. In the process, Mernissi stumbled upon a revelation: Westerners, too, have their own harem, one that she titles "size 6." Mernissi criticizes Western commentators for feigning ignorance in light of the similarities between the oppressive nature of the Church of God and the oppressive nature of the church of beauty. Recounting her experience in an American department store, where she was deemed "too big" for its elegant selection, Mernissi revealed parallels between the violence of the veil that restricts women's movement and the violence of Western beauty norms that compel women to follow strict diet regimes and undergo dangerous surgeries.

Mernissi's rhetoric is simplistic, but the simplicity helps drive home a more sophisticated claim: the "God is bad for women" formulation is not the

25

truism many believe. Instead, it's a myth that hinges on assumptions about the nature of religion, personhood, freedom, and choice.

Overall, then, *is* God bad for women? Research over the past twenty years has shattered conventional views of conservative religions as monolithic sources of oppression. Social scientists have demonstrated that women can be empowered by their religion, that compliance is often strategic, that religion is a site where gender rules are constantly being rewritten, and that religiosity is produced through acts of devotion. More than anything, these studies show that asking "Is God bad for women?" is misguided, based on ideological assumptions rather than on sound empirical evidence. Ultimately, like most questions about culture and society, the answer can only be "it depends." Context—social, cultural, historical—is paramount, and it's impossible to assess the implications of women's involvement with religion without taking into account the diverse circumstances in which women encounter conservative religions. It's not God, but man, who's detrimental to or affirming of women's interests, both in the practices and behaviors we condemn and condone.

MLA CITATION

Avishai, Orit. "Women of God." *The Norton Reader: An Anthology of Nonfiction*,
    edited by Melissa A. Goldthwaite et al., 15th ed., W. W. Norton, 2020,
    pp. 837–44.

QUESTIONS

1. What is Orit Avishai's answer to the question of whether God is bad for women? What sources does she use to answer that question?

2. In paragraph 24, Avishai makes a generalization about what students on American college campuses believe about conservative religion. Do you agree with her assessment? Why or why not?

3. Avishai emphasizes the importance of context in evaluating whether conservative religions are bad or good for women. Choose a particular practice or doctrine from a religious group, making an argument about how it affects a specific group of women for good, ill, or in a more complicated way.

ANITA DIAMANT
The Orange on the Seder Plate

VERY JEWISH FAMILY produces a unique version of the Passover seder—the big ritual meal of traditional foods, served after and amid liturgy, storytelling, and song. We're all surprised at each other's customs: You eat lamb? You don't sing "Chad Gad Ya"?

And yet, virtually every seder does share a few common elements. Matzoh crumbs all over the floor. Wine stains on the tablecloth. A seder plate containing the traditional symbols of the holiday: a roasted shank bone and hardboiled egg, recalling the days of the Temple sacrifices; horseradish and salt water for the bitterness of oppression; parsley for spring; *haroset,* a mixture of wine, nuts, and fruit symbolizing mortar and the heavy labor performed by the Israelite slaves.

And for lots of us, an orange.

The ancient Hebrews who fled into the wilderness didn't know from citrus fruit, and there certainly weren't any Valencias on Grandma's seder plate. Starting in the 1980s, the new holiday symbol has been showing up on an ever-increasing number of Passover tables.

The custom originated with the teacher and writer Susannah Heschel, who first set it out as a symbol of inclusion for lesbian and gay Jews, and in following years for all those who have been marginalized in the Jewish community. Thanks largely to the Internet, Jewish women adopted the fruit as a symbol of their inclusion, and now there are oranges on seder plates all over the world, as well as alternative stories about how they got there in the first place.

Regardless of its genesis, that orange now makes several subtle spiritual and political statements. For one thing, it represents the creative piety of liberal Jews, who honor tradition by adding new elements to the old. The orange also announces that those on the margins have fully arrived as coauthors of Jewish history, as does the presence of another new ritual item, the Miriam's Cup, which acknowledges the role of Moses' sister, the singer-songwriter-prophet, in the story.

The orange is a living part of the ancient pedagogic strategy of Passover. We are commanded to teach our children about the Exodus from Egypt in a manner so vivid that everyone at the table—but especially the kids—remembers (not merely imagines but actually remembers) what it feels like to be a hungry, hunted slave. The seder makes memory manifest, tangible, and solid as Grandpa's kiddush cup.

Just like the shank bone, the orange is there so that someone under the age of thirteen will ask, "What's that thing doing on the seder plate?"

The orange is there so that Mom or Dad can say, "I'm so glad you asked that question. The orange is a symbol of the struggle by Jews who used to be

5

Published in Pitching My Tent: On Marriage, Motherhood, Friendship, and Other Leaps of Faith (2003), *Anita Diamant's collection of essays and reflections.*

ignored by our tradition—like gays and lesbians, and women, and Jews by choice—to become full partners in religious and community life. The orange is a sign of change, too, because now all kinds of Jews are rabbis and cantors and teachers and leaders. And the orange is a mark of our confidence in the Jewish future, which means that someday maybe you too will bring something new to the seder plate."

10   The orange on the seder plate is both a playful and a reverent symbol of Judaism's ability to adapt and thrive. It also celebrates the abundant diversity of creation. After all, God, who made the heavens and the earth, and dinosaurs and lemurs and human beings, is clearly a lover of variety and change—not to mention oranges.

MLA CITATION

Diamant, Anita. "The Orange on the Seder Plate." *The Norton Reader: An Anthology of Nonfiction*, edited by Melissa A. Goldthwaite et al., 15th ed., W. W. Norton, 2020, pp. 845–46.

QUESTIONS

1. Why do some Jewish families include an orange on the Passover seder plate? Why might other families not include an orange?

2. In "Women of God" (pp. 837–44), Orit Avishai describes several studies that consider gender and religious practices. Do any of the studies Avishai cites seem similar to the practice Anita Diamant describes? Or is Diamant's approach to religion somehow different? Explain the differences or similarities you see.

3. Write an essay in which you describe a tradition you follow or have changed.

ANNIE DILLARD
Sight into Insight

W HEN I WAS SIX OR SEVEN YEARS OLD, growing up in Pittsburgh, I used to take a penny of my own and hide it for someone else to find. It was a curious compulsion; sadly, I've never been seized by it since. For some reason I always "hid" the penny along the same stretch of sidewalk up the street. I'd cradle it at the roots of a maple, say, or in a hole left by a chipped-off piece of sidewalk. Then I'd take a piece of chalk and, starting at either end of the block, draw huge arrows leading up to the penny from both directions. After I learned to write I labeled the arrows "SURPRISE AHEAD" or "MONEY THIS WAY."

Originally published in Harper's Magazine *(1974), an American monthly covering politics, society, culture, and the environment; included in Annie Dillard's Pulitzer Prize–winning book,* Pilgrim at Tinker Creek *(1974).*

I was greatly excited, during all this arrowdrawing, at the thought of the first lucky passerby who would receive in this way, regardless of merit, a free gift from the universe. But I never lurked about. I'd go straight home and not give the matter another thought, until, some months later, I would be gripped by the impulse to hide another penny.

There are lots of things to see, unwrapped gifts and free surprises. The world is fairly studded and strewn with pennies cast broadside from a generous hand. But—and this is the point—who gets excited by a mere penny? If you follow one arrow, if you crouch motionless on a bank to watch a tremulous ripple thrill on the water, and are rewarded by the sight of a muskrat kit paddling from its den, will you count that sight a chip of copper only, and go your rueful way? It is very dire poverty indeed for a man to be so malnourished and fatigued that he won't stoop to pick up a penny. But if you cultivate a healthy poverty and simplicity, so that finding a penny will make your day, then, since the world is in fact planted in pennies, you have with your poverty bought a lifetime of days. What you see is what you get.

Unfortunately, nature is very much a now-you-see-it, now-you-don't affair. A fish flashes, then dissolves in the water before my eyes like so much salt. Deer apparently ascend bodily into heaven; the brightest oriole fades into leaves. These disappearances stun me into stillness and concentration; they say of nature that it conceals with a grand nonchalance, and they say of vision that it is a deliberate gift, the revelation of a dancer who for my eyes only flings away her seven veils.

For nature does reveal as well as conceal: now-you-don't-see-it, now-you-do. For a week this September migrating red-winged blackbirds were feeding heavily down by Tinker Creek at the back of the house. One day I went out to investigate the racket; I walked up to a tree, an Osage orange, and a hundred birds flew away. They simply materialized out of the tree. I saw a tree, then a whisk of color, then a tree again. I walked closer and another hundred blackbirds took flight. Not a branch, not a twig budged: the birds were apparently weightless as well as invisible. Or, it was as if the leaves of the Osage orange had been freed from a spell in the form of redwinged blackbirds; they flew from the tree, caught my eye in the sky, and vanished. When I looked again at the tree, the leaves had reassembled as if nothing had happened. Finally I walked directly to the trunk of the tree and a final hundred, the real diehards, appeared, spread, and vanished. How could so many hide in the tree without my seeing them? The Osage orange, unruffled, looked just as it had looked from the house, when three hundred red-winged blackbirds cried from its crown. I looked upstream where they flew, and they were gone. Searching, I couldn't spot one. I wandered upstream to force them to play their hand, but they'd crossed the creek and scattered. One show to a customer. These appearances catch at my throat; they are the free gifts, the bright coppers at the roots of trees.

It's all a matter of keeping my eyes open. Nature is like one of those line drawings that are puzzles for children: Can you find hidden in the tree a duck, a house, a boy, a bucket, a giraffe, and a boot? Specialists can find the most

5

incredibly hidden things. A book I read when I was young recommended an easy way to find caterpillars: you simply find some fresh caterpillar droppings, look up, and there's your caterpillar. More recently an author advised me to set my mind at ease about those piles of cut stems on the ground in grassy fields. Field mice make them; they cut the grass down by degrees to reach the seeds at the head. It seems that when the grass is tightly packed, as in a field of ripe grain, the blade won't topple at a single cut through the stem; instead, the cut stem simply drops vertically, held in the crush of grain. The mouse severs the bottom again and again, the stem keeps dropping an inch at a time, and finally the head is low enough for the mouse to reach the seeds. Meanwhile the mouse is positively littering the field with its little piles of cut stems into which, pre-sumably, the author is constantly stumbling.

If I can't see these minutiae, I still try to keep my eyes open. I'm always on the lookout for ant lion traps in sandy soil, monarch pupae near milkweed, skip-per larvae in locust leaves. These things are utterly common, and I've not seen one. I bang on hollow trees near water, but so far no flying squirrels have appeared. In flat country I watch every sunset in hopes of seeing the green ray. The green ray is a seldom-seen streak of light that rises from the sun like a spurting fountain at the moment of sunset; it throbs into the sky for two sec-onds and disappears. One more reason to keep my eyes open. A photography professor at the University of Florida just happened to see a bird die in mid-flight; it jerked, died, dropped, and smashed on the ground.

I squint at the wind because I read Stewart Edward White: "I have always maintained that if you looked closely enough you could *see* the wind—the dim, hardly-made-out, fine débris fleeing high in the air." White was an excellent observer, and devoted an entire chapter of *The Mountains* to the subject of see-ing deer: "As soon as you can forget the naturally obvious and construct an artificial obvious, then you too will see deer."

But the artificial obvious is hard to see. My eyes account for less than 1 per-cent of the weight of my head; I'm bony and dense; I see what I expect. I once spent a full three minutes looking at a bullfrog that was so unexpectedly large I couldn't see it even though a dozen enthusiastic campers were shouting direc-tions. Finally I asked, "What color am I looking for?" and a fellow said, "Green." When at last I picked out the frog, I saw what painters are up against: the thing wasn't green at all, but the color of wet hickory bark.

The lover can see, and the knowledgeable. I visited an aunt and uncle at a quarter-horse ranch in Cody, Wyoming. I couldn't do much of anything useful, but I could, I thought, draw. So, as we all sat around the kitchen table after supper, I produced a sheet of paper and drew a horse. "That's one lame horse," my aunt volunteered. The rest of the family joined in: "Only place to saddle that one is his neck"; "Looks like we better shoot the poor thing, on account of those terrible growths." Meekly, I slid the pencil and paper down the table. Everyone in that family, including my three young cousins, could draw a horse. Beautifully. When the paper came back it looked as though five shining, real quarter horses had been corraled by mistake with a papier-mâché moose; the real horses seemed to gaze at the monster with a steady, puzzled air. I stay away from horses now, but I can do a creditable goldfish. The point is that I just don't know what the lover knows; I just can't see the artificial obvious that those in the know construct. The herpetologist asks the native, "Are there snakes in that ravine?" "Nosir." And the herpetologist comes home with, yessir, three bags full. Are there butterflies on that mountain? Are the bluets in bloom, are there arrowheads here, or fossil shells in the shale?

Peeping through my keyhole I see within the range of only about 30 per-   10
cent of the light that comes from the sun; the rest is infrared and some little ultraviolet, perfectly apparent to many animals, but invisible to me. A night-mare network of ganglia, charged and firing without my knowledge, cuts and splices what I do see, editing it for my brain. Donald E. Carr[1] points out that the sense impressions of one-celled animals are *not* edited for the brain: "This is philosophically interesting in a rather mournful way, since it means that only the simplest animals perceive the universe as it is."

A fog that won't burn away drifts and flows across my field of vision. When you see fog move against a backdrop of deep pines, you don't see the fog itself, but streaks of clearness floating across the air in dark shreds. So I see only tat-ters of clearness through a pervading obscurity. I can't distinguish the fog from the overcast sky; I can't be sure if the light is direct or reflected. Everywhere darkness and the presence of the unseen appalls. We estimate now that only one atom dances alone in every cubic meter of intergalactic space. I blink and squint. What planet or power yanks Halley's Comet out of orbit? We haven't seen it yet; it's a question of distance, density, and the pallor of reflected light. We rock, cradled in the swaddling band of darkness. Even the simple darkness of night whispers suggestions to the mind. This summer, in August, I stayed at the creek too late.

Where Tinker Creek flows under the sycamore log bridge to the tear-shaped island, it is slow and shallow, fringed thinly in cattail marsh. At this spot an astonishing bloom of life supports vast breeding populations of insects, fish, reptiles, birds, and mammals. On windless summer evenings I stalk along the creek bank or straddle the sycamore log in absolute stillness, watching for musk-rats. The night I stayed too late I was hunched on the log staring spellbound at spreading, reflected stains of lilac on the water. A cloud in the sky suddenly lighted as if turned on by a switch; its reflection just as suddenly materialized on the water upstream, flat and floating, so that I couldn't see the creek bot-tom, or life in the water under the cloud. Downstream, away from the cloud on the water, water turtles smooth as beans were gliding down with the current in a series of easy, weightless push-offs, as men bound on the moon. I didn't know whether to trace the progress of one turtle I was sure of, risking sticking my face in one of the bridge's spider webs made invisible by the gathering dark, or take a chance on seeing the carp, or scan the mudbank in hope of seeing a muskrat, or follow the last of the swallows who caught at my heart and trailed it after them like streamers as they appeared from directly below, under the log, flying upstream with their tails forked, so fast.

1. American research chemist and science journalist (1903–1986).

But shadows spread and deepened and stayed. After thousands of years we're still strangers to darkness, fearful aliens in an enemy camp with our arms crossed over our chests. I stirred. A land turtle on the bank, startled, hissed the air from its lungs and withdrew to its shell. An uneasy pink here, an unfathomable blue there, gave great suggestion of lurking beings. Things were going on. I couldn't see whether that rustle I heard was a distant rattlesnake, slit-eyed, or a nearby sparrow kicking in the dry flood debris slung at the foot of a willow. Tremendous action roiled the water everywhere I looked, big action, inexplicable. A tremor welled up beside a gaping muskrat burrow in the bank and I caught my breath, but no muskrat appeared. The ripples continued to fan upstream with a steady, powerful thrust. Night was knitting an eyeless mask over my face, and I still sat transfixed. A distant airplane, a delta wing out of nightmare, made a gliding shadow on the creek's bottom that looked like a stingray cruising upstream. At once a black fin slit the pink cloud on the water, shearing it in two. The two halves merged together and seemed to dissolve before my eyes. Darkness pooled in the cleft of the creek and rose, as water collects in a well. Untamed, dreaming lights flickered over the sky. I saw hints of hulking underwater shadows, two pale splashes out of the water, and round ripples rolling close together from a blackened center.

At last I stared upstream where only the deepest violet remained of the cloud, a cloud so high its underbelly still glowed, its feeble color reflected from a hidden sky lighted in turn by a sun halfway to China. And out of that violet, a sudden enormous black body arced over the water. Head and tail, if there was a head and tail, were both submerged in cloud. I saw only one ebony fling, a headlong dive to darkness; then the waters closed, and the lights went out.

15   I walked home in a shivering daze, up hill and down. Later I lay open-mouthed in bed, my arms flung wide at my sides to steady the whirling darkness. At this latitude I'm spinning 836 miles an hour round the earth's axis; I feel my sweeping fall as a breakneck arc like the dive of dolphins, and the hollow rushing of wind raises the hairs on my neck and the side of my face. In orbit around the sun I'm moving 64,800 miles an hour. The solar system as a whole, like a merry-go-round unhinged, spins, bobs, and blinks at the speed of 43,200 miles an hour along a course set east of Hercules. Someone has piped, and we are dancing a tarantella until the sweat pours. I open my eyes and I see dark, muscled forms curl out of water, with flapping gills and flattened eyes. I close my eyes and I see stars, deep stars giving way to deeper stars, deeper stars bowing to deepest stars at the crown of an infinite cone.

"Still," wrote Van Gogh[2] in a letter, "a great deal of light falls on everything." If we are blinded by darkness, we are also blinded by light. Sometimes here in Virginia at sunset low clouds on the southern or northern horizon are completely invisible in the lighted sky. I only know one is there because I can see its reflection in still water. The first time I discovered this mystery I looked from

_____

2. Vincent van Gogh (1853–1890), Dutch Postimpressionist painter.

cloud to no-cloud in bewilderment, checking my bearings over and over, thinking maybe the ark of the covenant[3] was just passing by south of Dead Man Mountain. Only much later did I learn the explanation: polarized light from the sky is very much weakened by reflection, but the light in clouds isn't polarized. So invisible clouds pass among visible clouds, till all slide over the mountains; so a greater light extinguishes a lesser as though it didn't exist.

In the great meteor shower of August, the Perseid, I wail all day for the shooting stars I miss. They're out there showering down committing hara-kiri in a flame of fatal attraction, and hissing perhaps at last into the ocean. But at dawn what looks like a blue dome clamps down over me like a lid on a pot. The stars and planets could smash and I'd never know. Only a piece of ashen moon occasionally climbs up or down the inside of the dome, and our local star without surcease explodes on our heads. We have really only that one light, one source for all power, and yet we must turn away from it by universal decree. Nobody here on the planet seems aware of this strange, powerful taboo, that we all walk about carefully averting our faces, this way and that, lest our eyes be blasted forever.

Darkness appalls and light dazzles; the scrap of visible light that doesn't hurt my eyes hurts my brain. What I see sets me swaying. Size and distance and the sudden swelling of meanings confuse me, bowl me over. I straddle the sycamore log bridge over Tinker Creek in the summer. I look at the lighted creek bottom: snail tracks tunnel the mud in quavering curves. A crayfish jerks, but by the time I absorb what has happened, he's gone in a billowing smoke screen of silt. I look at the water; minnows and shiners. If I'm thinking minnows, a carp will fill my brain till I scream. I look at the water's surface: skaters, bubbles, and leaves sliding down. Suddenly, my own face, reflected, startles me witless. Those snails have been tracking my face! Finally, with a shuddering wrench of the will, I see clouds, cirrus clouds. I'm dizzy, I fall in.

This looking business is risky. Once I stood on a humped rock on nearby Purgatory Mountain, watching through binoculars the great autumn hawk migration below, until I discovered that I was in danger of joining the hawks on a vertical migration of my own. I was used to binoculars, but not, apparently, to balancing on humped rocks while looking through them. I reeled. Everything advanced and receded by turns; the world was full of unexplained foreshortenings and depths. A distant huge object, a hawk the size of an elephant, turned out to be the browned bough of a nearby loblolly pine. I followed a sharp-shinned hawk against a featureless sky, rotating my head unawares as it flew, and when I lowered the glass a glimpse of my own looming shoulder sent me staggering. What prevents the men at Palomar[4] from falling, voiceless and blinded, from their tiny, vaulted chairs?

I reel in confusion: I don't understand what I see. With the naked eye I can see two million light-years to the Andromeda galaxy. Often I slop some

20

3. Repository for the stone tablets of the Ten Commandments, carried by the ancient Israelites during their desert wanderings.
4. Astronomical observatory in California.

creek water in a jar, and when I get home I dump it in a white china bowl. After the silt settles I return and see tracings of minute snails on the bottom, a planarian or two winding round the rim of water, roundworms shimmying, frantically, and finally, when my eyes have adjusted to these dimensions, amoebae. At first the amoebae look like *muscae volitantes,* those curled moving spots you seem to see in your eyes when you stare at a distant wall. Then I see the amoebae as drops of water congealed, bluish, translucent, like chips of sky in the bowl. At length I choose one individual and give myself over to its idea of an evening. I see it dribble a grainy foot before it on its wet, unfathomable way. Do its unedited sense impressions include the fierce focus of my eyes? Shall I take it outside and show it Andromeda, and blow its little endoplasm? I stir the water with a finger, in case it's running out of oxygen. Maybe I should get a tropical aquarium with motorized bubblers and lights, and keep this one for a pet. Yes, it would tell its fissioned descendants, the universe is two feet by five, and if you listen closely you can hear the buzzing music of the spheres.

Oh, it's mysterious, lamplit evenings here in the galaxy, one after the other. It's one of those nights when I wander from window to window, looking for a sign. But I can't see. Terror and a beauty insoluble are a riband of blue woven into the fringe of garments of things both great and small. No culture explains, no bivouac offers real haven or rest. But it could be that we are not seeing something. Galileo[5] thought comets were an optical illusion. This is fertile ground: since we are certain that they're not, we can look at what our scientists have been saying with fresh hope. What if there are *really* gleaming, castellated cities hung up-side-down over the desert sand? What limpid lakes and cool date palms have our caravans always passed untried? Until, one by one, by the blindest of leaps, we light on the road to these places, we must stumble in darkness and hunger. I turn from the window. I'm blind as a bat, sensing only from every direction the echo of my own thin cries.

I chanced on a wonderful book called *Space and Sight,* by Marius Von Senden. When Western surgeons discovered how to perform safe cataract operations, they ranged across Europe and America operating on dozens of men and women of all ages who had been blinded by cataracts since birth. Von Senden collected accounts of such cases; the histories are fascinating. Many doctors had tested their patients' sense perceptions and ideas of space both before and after the operations. The vast majority of patients, of both sexes and all ages, had, in Von Senden's opinion, no idea of space whatsoever. Form, distance, and size were so many meaningless syllables. A patient "had no idea of depth, confusing it with roundness." Before the operation a doctor would give a blind patient a cube and a sphere; the patient would tongue it or feel it with his hands, and name it correctly. After the operation the doctor would show the same objects to the patient without letting him touch them; now he had no clue whatsoever to what he was seeing. One patient called lemonade "square" because it pricked on his tongue as a square shape pricked on the touch of his hands. Of another

5. Galileo Galilei (1564–1642), Italian astronomer and mathematician.

post-operative patient the doctor writes, "I have found in her no notion of size, for example, not even within the narrow limits which she might have encompassed with the aid of touch. Thus when I asked her to show me how big her mother was, she did not stretch out her hands, but set her two index fingers a few inches apart."

For the newly sighted, vision is pure sensation unencumbered by meaning. When a newly sighted girl saw photographs and paintings, she asked, "'Why do they put those dark marks all over them?' 'Those aren't dark marks,' her mother explained, 'those are shadows. That is one of the ways the eye knows that things have shape. If it were not for shadows, many things would look flat.' 'Well, that's how things do look,' Joan answered. 'Everything looks flat with dark patches.'"

In general the newly sighted see the world as a dazzle of "color-patches." They are pleased by the sensation of color, and learn quickly to name the colors, but the rest of seeing is tormentingly difficult. Soon after his operation a patient "generally bumps into one of these color-patches and observes them to be substantial, since they resist him as tactual objects do. In walking about it also strikes him—or can if he pays attention—that he is continually passing in between the colors he sees, that he can go past a visual object, that a part of it then steadily disappears from view; and that in spite of this, however he twists and turns—whether entering the room from the door, for example, or returning back to it—he always has a visual space in front of him. Thus he gradually comes to realize that there is also a space behind him, which he does not see."

The mental effort involved in these reasonings proves overwhelming for many patients. It oppresses them to realize that they have been visible to people all along, perhaps unattractively so, without their knowledge or consent. A disheartening number of them refuse to use their new vision, continuing to go over objects with their tongues, and lapsing into apathy and despair.

On the other hand, many newly sighted people speak well of the world, and teach us how dull our own vision is. To one patient, a human hand, unrecognized, is "something bright and then holes." Shown a bunch of grapes, a boy calls out, "It is dark, blue and shiny. . . . It isn't smooth, it has bumps and hollows." A little girl visits a garden. "She is greatly astonished, and can scarcely be persuaded to answer, stands speechless in front of the tree, which she only names on taking hold of it, and then as 'the tree with the lights in it.'" Another patient, a twenty-two-year-old girl, was dazzled by the world's brightness and kept her eyes shut for two weeks. When at the end of that time she opened her eyes again, she did not recognize any objects, but "the more she now directed her gaze upon everything about her, the more it could be seen how an expression of gratification and astonishment overspread her features; she repeatedly exclaimed: 'Oh God! How beautiful!'"

I saw color-patches for weeks after I read this wonderful book. It was summer; the peaches were ripe in the valley orchards. When I woke in the morning, color-patches wrapped round my eyes, intricately, leaving not one unfilled spot. All day long I walked among shifting color-patches that parted before me

25

like the Red Sea and closed again in silence,[6] transfigured, wherever I looked back. Some patches swelled and loomed, while others vanished utterly, and dark marks flitted at random over the whole dazzling sweep. But I couldn't sustain the illusion of flatness. I've been around for too long. Form is condemned to an eternal danse macabre with meaning: I couldn't unpeach the peaches. Nor can I remember ever having seen without understanding; the color-patches of infancy are lost. My brain then must have been smooth as any balloon. I'm told I reached for the moon; many babies do. But the color-patches of infancy swelled as meaning filled them; they arrayed themselves in solemn ranks down distance which unrolled and stretched before me like a plain. The moon rocketed away. I live now in a world of shadows that shape and distance color, a world where space makes a kind of terrible sense. What Gnosticism[7] is this, and what physics? The fluttering patch I saw in my nursery window—silver and green and shape-shifting blue—is gone; a row of Lombardy poplars takes its place, mute, across the distant lawn. That humming oblong creature pale as light that stole along the walls of my room at night, stretching exhilaratingly around the corners, is gone, too, gone the night I ate of the bittersweet fruit, put two and two together and puckered forever my brain. Martin Buber[8] tells this tale: "Rabbi Mendel once boasted to his teacher Rabbi Elimelekh that evenings he saw the angel who rolls away the light before the darkness, and mornings the angel who rolls away the darkness before the light. 'Yes,' said Rabbi Elimelekh, 'in my youth I saw that too. Later on you don't see these things anymore.'"

Why didn't someone hand those newly sighted people paints and brushes from the start, when they still didn't know what anything was? Then maybe we all could see color-patches too, the world unraveled from reason, Eden before Adam gave names. The scales would drop from my eyes; I'd see trees like men walking; I'd run down the road against all orders, hallooing and leaping.

Seeing is of course very much a matter of verbalization. Unless I call my attention to what passes before my eyes, I simply won't see it. If Tinker Mountain erupted, I'd be likely to notice. But if I want to notice the lesser cataclysms of valley life, I have to maintain in my head a running description of the present. It's not that I'm observant; it's just that I talk too much. Otherwise, especially in a strange place, I'll never know what's happening. Like a blind man at the ball game, I need a radio.

30   When I see this way I analyze and pry. I hurl over logs and roll away stones; I study the bank a square foot at a time, probing and tilting my head. Some days when a mist covers the mountains, when the muskrats won't show and the microscope's mirror shatters, I want to climb up the blank blue dome as a man would storm the inside of a circus tent, wildly, dangling, and with a steel knife claw a rent in the top, peep, and, if I must, fall.

6. According to the book of Exodus in the Bible, the Red Sea parted for the Israelites and closed over the Egyptians pursuing them.

7. Promise of secret knowledge of the divine.

8. Jewish religious philosopher (1878–1965).

But there is another kind of seeing that involves a letting go. When I see this way I sway transfixed and emptied. The difference between the two ways of seeing is the difference between walking with and without a camera. When I walk with a camera I walk from shot to shot, reading the light on a calibrated meter. When I walk without a camera, my own shutter opens, and the moment's light prints on my own silver gut. When I see this second way I am above all an unscrupulous observer.

It was sunny one evening last summer at Tinker Creek; the sun was low in the sky, upstream. I was sitting on the sycamore log bridge with the sunset at my back, watching the shiners the size of minnows who were feeding over the muddy sand in skittery schools. Again and again, one fish, then another, turned for a split second across the current and flash! the sun shot out from its silver side. I couldn't watch for it. It was always just happening somewhere else, and it drew my vision just as it disappeared: flash! like a sudden dazzle of the thinnest blade, a sparking over a dun and olive ground at chance intervals from every direction. Then I noticed white specks, some sort of pale petals, small, floating from under my feet on the creek's surface, very slow and steady. So I blurred my eyes and gazed toward the brim of my hat and saw a new world. I saw the pale white circles roll up, roll up, like the world's turning, mute and perfect, and I saw the linear flashes, gleaming silver, like stars being born at random down a rolling scroll of time. Something broke and something opened. I filled up like a new wineskin. I breathed an air like light; I saw a light like water. I was the lip of a fountain the creek filled forever; I was ether, the leaf in the zephyr; I was flesh-flake, feather, bone.

When I see this way I see truly. As Thoreau[9] says, I return to my senses. I am the man who watches the baseball game in silence in an empty stadium. I see the game purely; I'm abstracted and dazed. When it's all over and the white-suited players lope off the green field to their shadowed dugouts, I leap to my feet, I cheer and cheer.

But I can't go out and try to see this way. I'll fail, I'll go mad. All I can do is try to gag the commentator, to hush the noise of useless interior babble that keeps me from seeing just as surely as a newspaper dangled before my eyes. The effort is really a discipline requiring a lifetime of dedicated struggle; it marks the literature of saints and monks of every order east and west, under every rule and no rule, discalced[10] and shod. The world's spiritual geniuses seem to discover universally that the mind's muddy river, this ceaseless flow of trivia and trash, cannot be dammed, and that trying to dam it is a waste of effort that might lead to madness. Instead you must allow the muddy river to flow unheeded in the dim channels of consciousness; you raise your sights; you look along it, mildly, acknowledging its presence without interest and gazing beyond it into

9. Henry David Thoreau (1817–1862), American writer; see "Where I Lived, and What I Lived For" (pp. 481–89) and "The Battle of the Ants" (pp. 725–27).
10. Shoeless, as in the order of the Discalced Carmelites.

the realm of the real where subjects and objects act and rest purely, without utterance. "Launch into the deep," says Jacques Ellul,[11] "and you shall see."

35 The secret of seeing, then, is the pearl of great price. If I thought he could teach me to find it and keep it forever I would stagger barefoot across a hundred deserts after any lunatic at all. But although the pearl may be found, it may not be sought. The literature of illumination reveals this above all: although it comes to those who wait for it, it is always, even to the most practiced and adept, a gift and a total surprise. I return from one walk knowing where the killdeer nests in the field by the creek and the hour the laurel blooms. I return from the same walk a day later scarcely knowing my own name. Litanies hum in my ears; my tongue flaps in my mouth, *Alim non,* alleluia! I cannot cause light; the most I can do is try to put myself in the path of its beam. It is possible, in deep space, to sail on solar wind. Light, be it particle or wave, has force: you rig a giant sail and go. The secret of seeing is to sail on solar wind. Hone and spread your spirit till you yourself are a sail, whetted, translucent, broadside to the merest puff.

When her doctor took her bandages off and led her into the garden, the girl who was no longer blind saw "the tree with the lights in it." It was for this tree I searched through the peach orchards of summer, in the forests of fall and down winter and spring for years. Then one day I was walking along Tinker Creek thinking of nothing at all and I saw the tree with the lights in it. I saw the backyard cedar where the mourning doves roost charged and transfigured, each cell buzzing with flame. I stood on the grass with the lights in it, grass that was wholly fire, utterly focused and utterly dreamed. It was less like seeing than like being for the first time seen, knocked breathless by a powerful glance. The flood of fire abated, but I'm still spending the power. Gradually the lights went out in the cedar, the colors died, the cells unflamed and disappeared. I was still ringing. I had been my whole life a bell, and never knew it until at that moment I was lifted and struck. I have since only very rarely seen the tree with the lights in it. The vision comes and goes, mostly goes, but I live for it, for the moment when the mountains open and a new light roars in spate through the crack, and the mountains slam.

MLA CITATION

Dillard, Annie. "Sight into Insight." *The Norton Reader: An Anthology of Nonfiction,* edited by Melissa A. Goldthwaite et al., 15th ed., W. W. Norton, 2020, pp. 846–56.

QUESTIONS

1. Annie Dillard often uses several examples to support a general claim. In paragraph 3, for instance, she writes, "nature is very much a now-you-see-it, now-you-don't affair" and follows with "[a] fish flashes, then dissolves" and "the brightest

---

11. French Protestant theologian and critic of technology (1912–1994).

oriole fades into leaves." Locate other examples of this technique, marking the general statements and examples that accompany them. What purpose does this technique serve? In what kinds of writing is it appropriate, in what kinds inappropriate?

2. How does the kind of seeing Dillard describes at the end of her essay differ from the kind of seeing she describes at the beginning?

3. Take one of Dillard's general statements and come up with supporting examples of your own.

4. Dillard says, "I see what I expect" (paragraph 8). Write a description of something familiar, paying attention to how you "edit" your seeing. Then write a parallel description of it as if you were seeing it "unedited," as Dillard tries to see "color-patches" like the newly sighted do (paragraph 27).

16 IN CONVERSATION

> The most fruitful and natural exercise of the mind, in my
> opinion, is conversation.
> —MICHEL DE MONTAIGNE

For Michel de Montaigne, the sixteenth-century philosopher and statesman who more than any other author is responsible for inventing the modern essay, conversation was the ultimate pleasure: "I find the use of it," he says, "more sweet than of any other action of life." He especially celebrates a kind of vigorous, intellectual conversation that edifies as it delights: "When any one contradicts me, he raises my attention, not my anger: I advance towards him who controverts, who instructs me; the cause of truth ought to be the common cause both of the one and the other." This perspective on argument—that our interlocutors are not enemies to be defeated but partners in a mutual quest for understanding and knowledge—is one we should all embrace. And as Montaigne recognized, it pertains not just to literal conversations but also to those virtual "conversations" we can create for ourselves. By reading the books of "those who only live in the records of history," Montaigne observes, we "converse with the great and heroic souls of the best ages." This approach to reading the great authors of the past applies to contemporary authors as well. It informs every chapter of *The Norton Reader* and especially this one, which orchestrates and invites students to enter into "conversations" on three subjects of great contemporary significance: the implications of the brain sciences, the controversies around gun control, and the debates over free speech on college campuses.

The first three essays in the chapter—journalist Ben Yagoda's "Your Lying Mind," psychologist Jennifer L. Eberhardt's "Seeing Each Other," and philosopher Noga Arikha's "How Evil Happens"—invite you to consider some of the ways in which our brains shape our reasoning, our perceptions of others, and our behavior. Yagoda focuses on our cognitive biases, "the collection of faulty ways of thinking that is apparently hardwired into the human brain," asking how or even whether we can resist them. Eberhardt writes about the "other-race effect," the finding "that people are much better at recognizing faces of their own race than faces of other races"; she explains the science supporting it and considers some of its social and political implications, such as its bearing on the relationship among race, crime, and justice. Arikha ponders the extent to which human beings' capacity for evil—for violence, murder, genocide—might have a basis in the anatomy and functioning of the brain. Together, these essays raise a number of challenging and important questions: What can we do about the fact that our reasoning is predictably flawed? What does it mean for us, as individuals and collectively, that our perceptions of others seem to be inherently affected by race? Do we need to reconsider such fundamental concepts as good and evil, responsibility, and free will in light of what the brain sciences are teaching us? As you read these essays, consider as well how their authors' respective areas of expertise inform their approaches to their common subject: What does it matter that Yagoda is a journalist, Eberhardt a psychologist, Arikha a philosopher?

The chapter's next three selections—memoirist Joy Castro's "Grip," gun-control activist Emma González's "Fighting for Gun Control," and conservative journalist and gun-rights advocate David French's "What Critics Don't Understand about Gun Culture"—ask you to consider different perspectives on the controversial question of gun control. All three of these selections are personal as well as political. Castro offers an intimate and lyrical meditation on her complex feelings about her handgun. González, a survivor of a school shooting, delivers a powerful indictment of gun violence and call for effective gun regulation. French, a veteran and gun owner, explains and defends what he terms America's "gun culture." As you read these essays, you will probably find yourself strongly agreeing with one or another of them. Remember Montaigne, and resist the impulse to take sides, at least as first. Imagine yourself conversing with their authors in the common "cause of truth," and allow these essays to enrich and deepen your own thinking about guns, gun control, and gun rights. Castro's essay shows that people's perspectives toward guns can be subtly complex; she asks her readers not for their agreement, but for their understanding. So start by trying to appreciate the perspectives of each author: What about their histories and experiences makes them believe what they do? But don't stop there. González and French also write about their personal experiences but with an intention to persuade. So critically assess their arguments, and decide what you believe.

The chapter's final four selections—political theorist Teresa M. Bejan's essay "The Two Clashing Meanings of 'Free Speech,'" psychologist and neuroscientist Lisa Feldman Barrett's op-ed "When Is Speech Violence?," free-speech activists Hadar Harris and Mary Beth Tinker's op-ed "Hate Speech Is Showing Up in Schools," and legal scholars Erwin Chemerinsky and Howard Gillman's essay "What Students Think about Free Speech"—address a contemporary issue that also bears on the premise of this chapter, that we think best in "conversation" with others. Bejan considers conflicting concepts of free speech from ancient Greece to the present and offers a historical perspective on today's debates over the nature and boundaries of free speech on campuses. Barrett argues on scientific grounds that some speech causes real physical harm, which differentiates it from speech that is "merely offensive." Harris and Tinker, who focus on students' free-speech rights as guaranteed by the First Amendment, are concerned with the racial disparities in the protection of these rights. Chemerinsky and Gillman, two self-professed "baby boomer" professors, describe what they learned about the attitudes of today's students toward free speech from teaching a course on the subject. As you read these selections, consider the kinds of reasoning and evidence their authors use to make their arguments: historical analysis, scientific findings, legal standards, personal experience. Also, consider the selections in conversation with each another. How, for example, does Bejan's historical perspective illuminate the generational divide described by Chemerinsky and Gillman? How is Barrett's scientific justification for curtailing some forms of speech related to the legal standards Harris and Tinker explore? Ultimately, all of these selections ask a common question: How should we distinguish between speech and expression that should be protected, even when it is offensive or controversial, and speech and expression that should properly be constrained? As you enter into conversation with these authors, consider how you would answer this question, and on what grounds.

BEN YAGODA

Your Lying Mind

I AM STARING AT A PHOTOGRAPH of myself that shows me 20 years older than I am now. I have not stepped into the twilight zone.[1] Rather, I am trying to rid myself of some measure of my present bias, which is the tendency people have, when considering a trade-off between two future moments, to more heavily weight the one closer to the present. A great many academic studies have shown this bias—also known as hyperbolic discounting—to be robust and persistent.

Most of them have focused on money. When asked whether they would prefer to have, say, $150 today or $180 in one month, people tend to choose the $150. Giving up a 20 percent return on investment is a bad move—which is easy to recognize when the question is thrust away from the present. Asked whether they would take $150 a year from now or $180 in 13 months, people are overwhelmingly willing to wait an extra month for the extra $30 (Laibson, 1997).

Present bias shows up not just in experiments, of course, but in the real world. Especially in the United States, people egregiously undersave for retirement—even when they make enough money to not spend their whole paycheck on expenses, and even when they work for a company that will kick in additional funds to retirement plans when they contribute.

That state of affairs led a scholar named Hal Hershfield to play around with photographs. Hershfield is a marketing professor at UCLA whose research starts from the idea that people are "estranged" from their future self. As a result, Hershfield explained in a 2011 paper, "saving is like a choice between spending money today or giving it to a stranger years from now" (p. 24). The paper described an attempt by Hershfield and several colleagues to modify that state of mind in their students. They had the students observe, for a minute or so, virtual-reality avatars showing what they would look like at age 70. Then they asked the students what they would do if they unexpectedly came into $1,000. The students who had looked their older self in the eye said they would put an aver-

Published in the Atlantic *(2018), a magazine covering literature, culture, and politics.*

1. An alternate reality; the phrase derives from *The Twilight Zone* television show (1959–64).

age of $172 into a retirement account. That's more than double the amount that would have been invested by members of the control group, who were willing to sock away an average of only $80 (Hershfield, 2011).

I am already old—in my early 60s, if you must know—so Hershfield fur-   5
nished me not only with an image of myself in my 80s (complete with age spots, an exorbitantly asymmetrical face, and wrinkles as deep as a Manhattan pothole) but also with an image of my daughter as she'll look decades from now. What this did, he explained, was make me ask myself, *How will I feel toward the end of my life if my offspring are not taken care of?*

When people hear the word *bias*, many if not most will think of either racial prejudice or news organizations that slant their coverage to favor one political position over another. Present bias, by contrast, is an example of cognitive bias—the collection of faulty ways of thinking that is apparently hardwired into the human brain. The collection is large. *Wikipedia*'s "List of Cognitive Biases" (2017) contains 185 entries, from actor-observer bias ("the tendency for explanations of other individuals' behaviors to overemphasize the influence of their personality and underemphasize the influence of their situation . . . and for explanations of one's own behaviors to do the opposite") to the Zeigarnik effect ("uncompleted or interrupted tasks are remembered better than completed ones"; "List of Cognitive Biases," 2017).

Some of the 185 are dubious or trivial. The IKEA effect, for instance, is defined as "the tendency for people to place a disproportionately high value on objects that they partially assembled themselves" ("List of Cognitive Biases," 2017). And others closely resemble one another to the point of redundancy. But a solid group of 100 or so biases has been repeatedly shown to exist, and can make a hash of our lives.

The gambler's fallacy makes us absolutely certain that, if a coin has landed heads up five times in a row, it's more likely to land tails up the sixth time. In fact, the odds are still 50–50. Optimism bias leads us to consistently underestimate the costs and the duration of basically every project we undertake. Availability bias makes us think that, say, traveling by plane is more dangerous than traveling by car. (Images of plane crashes are more vivid and dramatic in our memory and imagination, and hence more available to our consciousness.)

The anchoring effect is our tendency to rely too heavily on the first piece of information offered, particularly if that information is presented in numeric form, when making decisions, estimates, or predictions. This is the reason negotiators start with a number that is deliberately too low or too high: They know that number will "anchor" the subsequent dealings. A striking illustration of anchoring is an experiment in which participants observed a roulette-style wheel that stopped on either 10 or 65, then were asked to guess what percentage of United Nations countries is African. The ones who saw the wheel stop on 10 guessed 25 percent, on average; the ones who saw the wheel stop on 65 guessed 45 percent. (The correct percentage at the time of the experiment was about 28 percent; Kahneman, 2011, p. 119).

10   The effects of biases do not play out just on an individual level. Last year, President Donald Trump decided to send more troops to Afghanistan,[2] and thereby walked right into the sunk-cost fallacy. He said, "Our nation must seek an honorable and enduring outcome worthy of the tremendous sacrifices that have been made, especially the sacrifices of lives" (Trump, 2017). Sunk-cost thinking tells us to stick with a bad investment because of the money we have already lost on it; to finish an unappetizing restaurant meal because, after all, we're paying for it; to prosecute an unwinnable war because of the investment of blood and treasure. In all cases, this way of thinking is rubbish.

          If I had to single out a particular bias as the most pervasive and damaging, it would probably be confirmation bias. That's the effect that leads us to look for evidence confirming what we already think or suspect, to view facts and ideas we encounter as further confirmation, and to discount or ignore any piece of evidence that seems to support an alternate view. Confirmation bias shows up most blatantly in our current political divide, where each side seems unable to allow that the other side is right about anything. Confirmation bias plays out in lots of other circumstances, sometimes with terrible consequences. To quote the 2005 report to the president on the lead-up to the Iraq War:[3] "When confronted with evidence that indicated Iraq did not have [weapons of mass destruction], analysts tended to discount such information. Rather than weighing the evidence independently, analysts accepted information that fit the prevailing theory and rejected information that contradicted it" (Commission on the Intelligence Capabilities of the United States Regarding Weapons of Mass Destruction, 2005).

The whole idea of cognitive biases and faulty heuristics—the shortcuts and rules of thumb by which we make judgments and predictions—was more or less invented in the 1970s by Amos Tversky and Daniel Kahneman, social scientists who started their careers in Israel and eventually moved to the United States. They were the researchers who conducted the African-countries-in-the-UN experiment. Tversky died in 1996. Kahneman won the 2002 Nobel Prize in Economics[4] for the work the two men did together, which he summarized in his 2011 best seller, *Thinking, Fast and Slow*. Another best seller, last

2. Donald Trump (b. 1946), 45th president of the United States; the United States has been at war in Afghanistan since 2001.

3. The lead-up to the Iraq War (2003–11) began after the September 11, 2001, terrorist attacks on the World Trade Center and the Pentagon, with the administration of President George W. Bush accusing Iraq of supporting terrorism and harboring "weapons of mass destruction," a charge later proven untrue.

4. The Nobel Prize in Economics, formally the Sveriges Riksbank Prize in Economic Sciences in Memory of Alfred Nobel, is sometimes given to social scientists who are not economists.

year's *The Undoing Project*, by Michael Lewis[5] (2016), tells the story of the sometimes contentious collaboration between Tversky and Kahneman. Lewis's earlier
book *Moneyball* (2003) was really about how his hero, the baseball executive Billy
Beane, countered the cognitive biases of old-school scouts—notably fundamental attribution error, whereby, when assessing someone's behavior, we put
too much weight on his or her personal attributes and too little on external
factors, many of which can be measured with statistics.

Another key figure in the field is the University of Chicago economist
Richard Thaler. One of the biases he's most linked with is the endowment
effect, which leads us to place an irrationally high value on our possessions. In
an experiment conducted by Thaler, Kahneman, and Jack L. Knetsch in 1991,
half the participants were given a mug and then asked how much they would
sell it for. The average answer was $5.78. The rest of the group said they would
spend, on average, $2.21 for the same mug (Kahneman et al., 1991, pp. 195–196).
This flew in the face of classic economic theory, which says that at a given time
and among a certain population, an item has a market value that does *not* depend
on whether one owns it or not. Thaler won the 2017 Nobel Prize in Economics.

Most books and articles about cognitive bias contain a brief passage, typically toward the end, similar to this one in *Thinking, Fast and Slow*: "The
question that is most often asked about cognitive illusions is whether they can
be overcome. The message . . . is not encouraging" (Kahneman, 2011, p. 28).

Kahneman and others draw an analogy based on an understanding of the   15
Müller-Lyer illusion, two parallel lines with arrows at each end.[6] One line's
arrows point in; the other line's arrows point out. Because of the direction of
the arrows, the latter line appears shorter than the former, but in fact the two
lines are the same length. Here's the key: Even after we have measured the
lines and found them to be equal, and have had the neurological basis of the
illusion explained to us, we still perceive one line to be shorter than the other.

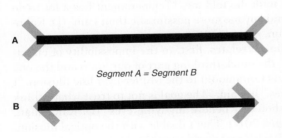

Segment A = Segment B

At least with the optical
illusion, our slow-thinking,
analytic mind—what Kahne-
man calls System 2—will
recognize a Müller-Lyer situation and convince itself not
to trust the fast-twitch System 1's perception. But that's
not so easy in the real world,
when we're dealing with
people and situations rather than lines. "Unfortunately, this sensible procedure is
least likely to be applied when it is needed most," writes Kahneman (2011, p. 417).

5. American journalist and author (b. 1960) who writes mainly about business and
sports; see pp. 291–98 for a selection from his book *The Blind Side: Evolution of a
Game* (2006).
6. Named for the German psychologist Franz Carl Müller-Lyer (1857–1916).

"We would all like to have a warning bell that rings loudly whenever we are about to make a serious error, but no such bell is available" (Kahneman, 2011, p. 417).

Because biases appear to be so hardwired and inalterable, most of the attention paid to countering them hasn't dealt with the problematic thoughts, judgments, or predictions themselves. Instead, it has been devoted to changing *behavior*, in the form of incentives or "nudges." For example, while present bias has so far proved intractable, employers have been able to nudge employees into contributing to retirement plans by making saving the default option; you have to actively take steps in order to *not* participate. That is, laziness or inertia can be more powerful than bias. Procedures can also be organized in a way that dissuades or prevents people from acting on biased thoughts. A well-known example: the checklists for doctors and nurses put forward by Atul Gawande in his 2010 book *The Checklist Manifesto*.[7]

Is it really impossible, however, to shed or significantly mitigate one's biases? Some studies have tentatively answered that question in the affirmative. These experiments are based on the reactions and responses of randomly chosen subjects, many of them college undergraduates: people, that is, who care about the $20 they are being paid to participate, not about modifying or even learning about their behavior and thinking. But what if the person undergoing the de-biasing strategies was highly motivated and self-selected? In other words, what if it was me?

Naturally, I wrote to Daniel Kahneman, who at 84 still holds an appointment at the Woodrow Wilson School of Public and International Affairs, at Princeton, but spends most of his time in Manhattan. He answered swiftly and agreed to meet. "I should," he said, "at least try to talk you out of your project" (D. Kahneman, personal communication, August 2017).

20   I met with Kahneman at a Le Pain Quotidien[8] in Lower Manhattan. He is tall, soft-spoken, and affable, with a pronounced accent and a wry smile. Over an apple pastry and tea with milk, he told me, "Temperament has a lot to do with my position. You won't find anyone more pessimistic than I am" (D. Kahneman, personal communication, August 2017).

In this context, his pessimism relates, first, to the impossibility of effecting any changes to System 1—the quick-thinking part of our brain and the one that makes mistaken judgments tantamount to the Müller-Lyer line illusion. "I see the picture as unequal lines," he said. "The goal is not to trust what I think I see. To understand that I shouldn't believe my lying eyes" (D. Kahneman, personal communication, August 2017). That's doable with the optical illusion, he said, but extremely difficult with real-world cognitive biases.

The most effective check against them, as Kahneman says, is from the outside: Others can perceive our errors more readily than we can. And "slow-thinking organizations," as he puts it, can institute policies that include the monitoring of individual decisions and predictions (D. Kahneman, personal

7. American surgeon and author (b. 1965); see pp. 639–56 for his essay "When Doctors Make Mistakes" (1999).
8. "The daily bread" in French, a restaurant chain serving bakery items and light food.

communication, August 2017). They can also require procedures such as check-lists and "premortems," an idea and term thought up by Gary Klein, a cognitive psychologist. A premortem attempts to counter optimism bias by requiring team members to imagine that a project has gone very, very badly and write a sen-tence or two describing how that happened. Conducting this exercise, it turns out, helps people think ahead.

"My position is that none of these things have any effect on System 1," Kahneman said. "You can't improve intuition. Perhaps, with very long-term training, lots of talk, and exposure to behavioral economics, what you can do is *cue* reasoning, so you can engage System 2 to follow rules. Unfortunately, the world doesn't provide cues. And for most people, in the heat of argument the rules go out the window.

"That's my story. I really hope I don't have to stick to it" (D. Kahneman, personal communication, August 2017).

As it happened, right around the same time I was communicating and meeting   25
with Kahneman, he was exchanging emails with Richard E. Nisbett, a social psy-chologist at the University of Michigan. The two men had been professionally connected for decades. Nisbett was instrumental in disseminating Kahneman and Tversky's work, in a 1980 book called *Human Inference: Strategies and Short-comings of Social Judgment.* And in *Thinking, Fast and Slow,* Kahneman (2011) describes an even earlier Nisbett article that showed subjects' disinclination to believe statistical and other general evidence, basing their judgments instead on individual examples and vivid anecdotes. (This bias is known as base-rate neglect.)

But over the years, Nisbett had come to emphasize in his research and thinking the possibility of training people to overcome or avoid a number of pitfalls, including base-rate neglect, fundamental attribution error, and the sunk-cost fallacy. He had emailed Kahneman in part because he had been working on a memoir, and wanted to discuss a conversation he'd had with Kahneman and Tversky at a long-ago conference. Nisbett had the distinct impression that Kahneman and Tversky had been angry—that they'd thought what he had been saying and doing was an implicit criticism of them. Kahne-man recalled the interaction, emailing back: "Yes, I remember we were (some-what) annoyed by your work on the ease of training statistical intuitions (angry is much too strong)" (D. Kahneman, personal communication, August 2017).

When R. Nisbett (personal communication, September 2017) has to give an example of his approach, he usually brings up the baseball-phenom survey. This involved telephoning University of Michigan students on the pretense of con-ducting a poll about sports, and asking them why there are always several Major League batters with .450 batting averages early in a season, yet no player has ever finished a season with an average that high. When he talks with students who haven't taken Introduction to Statistics, roughly half give erroneous rea-sons such as "the pitchers get used to the batters," "the batters get tired as the season wears on," and so on. And about half give the right answer: the law of large numbers, which holds that outlier results are much more frequent when the sample size (at bats, in this case) is small. Over the course of the season, as the number of at bats increases, regression to the mean is inevitable. When Nisbett asks the same question of students who have completed the statistics course, about 70 percent give the right answer. He believes this result shows, pace Kahneman, that the law of large numbers can be absorbed into System 2—and maybe into System 1 as well, even when there are minimal cues.

Nisbett's second-favorite example is that economists, who have absorbed the lessons of the sunk-cost fallacy, routinely walk out of bad movies and leave bad restaurant meals uneaten.

I spoke with Nisbett by phone and asked him about his disagreement with Kahneman. He still sounded a bit uncertain. "Danny seemed to be convinced that what I was showing was trivial," he said. "To him it was clear: Training was hopeless for all kinds of judgments. But we've tested Michigan students over four years, and they show a huge increase in ability to solve problems. Graduate students in psychology also show a huge gain" (R. Nisbett, personal communication, September 2017).

30   Nisbett writes in his 2015 book, *Mindware: Tools for Smart Thinking*, "I know from my own research on teaching people how to reason statistically that just a few examples in two or three domains are sufficient to improve people's reasoning for an indefinitely large number of events" (p. 144).

In one of his emails to Nisbett, Kahneman had suggested that the difference between them was to a significant extent a result of temperament: pessimist versus optimist. In a response, Nisbett suggested another factor: "You and Amos specialized in hard problems for which you were drawn to the wrong answer. I began to study easy problems, which you guys would never get wrong but untutored people routinely do. . . . Then you can look at the effects of instruction on such easy problems, which turn out to be huge" (R. Nisbett, personal communication, September 2017).

An example of an easy problem is the .450 hitter early in a baseball season. An example of a hard one is "the Linda problem," which was the basis of one of the early articles by Kahneman and Tversky (1983). Simplified, the experiment presented subjects with the characteristics of a fictional woman, "Linda," including her commitment to social justice, college major in philosophy, participation in antinuclear demonstrations, and so on. Then the subjects were asked which was more likely: (a) that Linda was a bank teller, or (b) that she was a bank teller and active in the feminist movement. The correct answer is (a), because it is always more likely that one condition will be satisfied in a situation than that the condition *plus* a second one will be satisfied. But because of the conjunction fallacy (the assumption that multiple specific conditions are more probable than a single general one) and the representativeness heuristic (our strong desire to apply stereotypes), more than 80 percent of undergraduates surveyed answered (b).

Nisbett justifiably asks how often in real life we need to make a judgment like the one called for in the Linda problem. I cannot think of any applicable scenarios in my life. It is a bit of a logical parlor trick.

R. Nisbett (personal communication, September 2017) suggested that I take "Mindware: Critical Thinking for the Information Age," an online Coursera course in which he goes over what he considers the most effective de-biasing skills and concepts. Then, to see how much I had learned, I would take a survey he gives to Michigan undergraduates. So I did.

The course consists of eight lessons by Nisbett—who comes across on-screen as the authoritative but approachable psych professor we all would like to have had—interspersed with some graphics and quizzes. I recommend it. Nisbett (2017) explains the availability heuristic this way: "People are surprised that suicides outnumber homicides, and drownings outnumber deaths by fire. People always think crime is increasing" even if it's not.

He addresses the logical fallacy of confirmation bias, explaining that people's tendency, when testing a hypothesis they're inclined to believe, is to seek examples confirming it. But Nisbett (2017) points out that no matter how many such examples we gather, we can never prove the proposition. The right thing to do is to look for cases that would disprove it.

And he approaches base-rate neglect by means of his own strategy for choosing which movies to see. His decision is never dependent on ads, or a particular review, or whether a film sounds like something he would enjoy. Instead, he says, "I live by base rates. I don't read a book or see a movie unless it's highly recommended by people I trust.

"Most people think they're not like other people. But they are" (Nisbett, 2017).

When I finished the course, Nisbett sent me the survey he and colleagues administer to Michigan undergrads. It contains a few dozen problems meant to measure the subjects' resistance to cognitive biases. For example:

Below are four cards. They are randomly chosen from a deck of cards in which every card has a letter on one side and a number on the other side. Your task is to say which of the cards you need to turn over in order to find out whether the following rule is true or false. The rule is: "If a card has an 'A' on one side, then it has a '4' on the other side." Turn over only those cards that you need to check the rule.

Box 1	Box 2	Box 3	Box 4
4	B	A	7

(a) Box 3 only
(b) Boxes 1, 2, 3 and 4
(c) Boxes 3 and 4
(d) Boxes 1, 3 and 4
(e) Boxes 1 and 3

Because of confirmation bias, many people who haven't been trained answer (e). But the correct answer is (c). The only thing you can hope to do in this situation is *disprove* the rule, and the only way to do that is to turn over the cards displaying the letter A (the rule is disproved if a number other than 4 is on the other side) and the number 7 (the rule is disproved if an A is on the other side).

I got it right. Indeed, when I emailed my completed test, Nisbett replied, "My guess is that very few if any UM seniors did as well as you. I'm sure at least some psych students, at least after 2 years in school, did as well. But note that you came fairly close to a perfect score" (R. Nisbett, personal communication, September 22, 2017).

Nevertheless, I did not feel that reading *Mindware* and taking the Coursera course had necessarily rid me of my biases. For one thing, I hadn't been tested beforehand, so I might just be a comparatively unbiased guy. For another, many of the test questions, including the one above, seemed somewhat remote from scenarios one might encounter in day-to-day life. They seemed to be "hard" problems, not unlike the one about Linda the bank teller. Further, I had been, as Kahneman would say, "cued." In contrast to the Michigan seniors, I knew exactly why I was being asked these questions, and approached them accordingly.

For his part, Nisbett insisted that the results were meaningful. "If you're doing better in a testing context," he told me, "you'll jolly well be doing better in the real world" (R. Nisbett, personal communication, September 22, 2017).

Nisbett's Coursera course and Hal Hershfield's close encounters with one's older self are hardly the only de-biasing methods out there. The New York–based NeuroLeadership Institute offers organizations and individuals a variety of training sessions, webinars, and conferences that promise, among other things, to use brain science to teach participants to counter bias. This year's two-day summit will be held in New York next month; for $2,845, you could learn, for example, "why are our brains so bad at thinking about the future, and how do we do it better?" (Smith & Inge, 2018).

45 Philip E. Tetlock, a professor at the University of Pennsylvania's Wharton School, and his wife and research partner, Barbara Mellers, have for years been studying what they call "superforecasters": people who manage to side-step cognitive biases and predict future events with far more accuracy than the pundits and so-called experts who show up on TV. In Tetlock's book *Super-forecasting: The Art and Science of Prediction* (co-written with Dan Gardner in 2015), and in the commercial venture he and Mellers co-founded, Good Judgment, they share the superforecasters' secret sauce.

One of the most important ingredients is what P. Tetlock (personal communication, August 2017) calls "the outside view." The inside view is a product of fundamental attribution error, base-rate neglect, and other biases that are constantly cajoling us into resting our judgments and predictions on good or vivid stories instead of on data and statistics. Tetlock explains, "At a wedding, someone sidles up to you and says, 'How long do you give them?' If you're shocked because you've seen the devotion they show each other, you've been sucked into the inside view" (P. Tetlock, personal communication, August 2017). Something like 40 percent of marriages end in divorce, and that statistic is far more predictive of the fate of any particular marriage than a mutually adoring gaze. Not that you want to share that insight at the reception.

The recent de-biasing interventions that scholars in the field have deemed the most promising are a handful of video games. Their genesis was in the Iraq War and the catastrophic weapons-of-mass-destruction blunder that led to it, which left the intelligence community reeling. In 2006, seeking to prevent another mistake of that magnitude, the U.S. government created the Intelligence Advanced Research Projects Activity (IARPA), an agency designed to use cutting-edge research and technology to improve intelligence-gathering and analysis. In 2011, IARPA initiated a program, Sirius, to fund the development of "serious" video games that could combat or mitigate what were deemed to be the six most damaging biases: confirmation bias, fundamental attribution error, the bias blind spot (the feeling that one is less biased than the average person), the anchoring effect, the representativeness heuristic, and projection bias (the assumption that everybody else's thinking is the same as one's own).

Six teams set out to develop such games, and two of them completed the process. The team that has gotten the most attention was led by Carey K. Morewedge, now a professor at Boston University. Together with collaborators who included staff from Creative Technologies, a company specializing in games and other simulations, and Leidos, a defense, intelligence, and health research company that does a lot of government work, Morewedge devised Missing. Some subjects played the game, which takes about three hours to complete, while others watched a video about cognitive bias. All were tested on bias-mitigation skills before the training, immediately afterward, and then finally after eight to twelve weeks had passed.

After taking the test, I played the game, which has the production value of a late-2000s PlayStation 3 first-person offering, with large-chested women and men, all of whom wear form-fitting clothes and navigate the landscape a bit tentatively. The player adopts the persona of a neighbor of a woman named Terry Hughes, who, in the first part of the game, has mysteriously gone missing. In the second, she has reemerged and needs your help to look into some skullduggery at her company. Along the way, you're asked to make judgments and predictions—some having to do with the story and some about unrelated issues—which are designed to call your biases into play. You're given immediate feedback on your answers.

For example, as you're searching Terry's apartment, the building superintendent knocks on the door and asks you, apropos of nothing, about Mary, another tenant, whom he describes as "not a jock." He says 70 percent of the tenants go to Rocky's Gym, 10 percent go to Entropy Fitness, and 20 percent just stay at home and watch Netflix. Which gym, he asks, do you think Mary probably goes to? A wrong answer, reached thanks to base-rate neglect (a form of the representativeness heuristic) is "None. Mary is a couch potato." The right answer—based on the data the super has helpfully provided—is Rocky's Gym (Creative Technologies Incorporated, 2014). When the participants in the study were tested immediately after playing the game or watching the video and then a couple of months later, everybody improved, but the game players improved more than the video watchers (Morewedge et al., 2015).

When I spoke with Morewedge, he said he saw the results as supporting the research and insights of Richard Nisbett. "Nisbett's work was largely written off by the field, the assumption being that training can't reduce bias," he told me. "The literature on training suggests books and classes are fine entertainment but largely ineffectual. But the game has very large effects. It surprised everyone" (C. Morewedge, personal communication, September 2017).

I took the test again soon after playing the game, with mixed results. I showed notable improvement in confirmation bias, fundamental attribution error, and the representativeness heuristic, and improved slightly in bias blind spot and anchoring bias. My lowest initial score—44.8 percent—was in projection bias. It actually dropped a bit after I played the game. (I really need to stop assuming that everybody thinks like me.) But even the positive results reminded me of something Daniel Kahneman had told me. "Pencil-and-paper doesn't convince me," he said. "A test can be given even a couple of years later. But the test cues the test-taker. It reminds him what it's all about" (D. Kahneman, personal communication, August 2017).

I had taken Nisbett's and Morewedge's tests on a computer screen, not on paper, but the point remains. It's one thing for the effects of training to show up in the form of improved results on a test—when you're on your guard, maybe even looking for tricks—and quite another for the effects to show up in the form of real-life behavior. Morewedge told me that some tentative real-world scenarios along the lines of Missing have shown "promising results," but that it's too soon to talk about them (C. Morewedge, personal communication, September 2017).

I am neither as much of a pessimist as Daniel Kahneman nor as much of an optimist as Richard Nisbett. Since immersing myself in the field, I have noticed a few changes in my behavior. For example, one hot day recently, I decided to buy a bottle of water in a vending machine for $2. The bottle didn't come out; upon inspection, I realized that the mechanism holding the bottle in place was broken. However, right next to it was another row of water bottles, and clearly the mechanism in that row was in order. My instinct was to not buy a bottle from the "good" row, because $4 for a bottle of water is too much. But all of my training in cognitive biases told me that was faulty thinking. I would be spending $2 for the water—a price I was willing to pay, as had already been established. So I put the money in and got the water, which I happily drank.

55   In the future, I will monitor my thoughts and reactions as best I can. Let's say I'm looking to hire a research assistant. Candidate A has sterling references and experience but appears tongue-tied and can't look me in the eye; Candidate B loves to talk NBA basketball—my favorite topic!—but his recommendations are mediocre at best. Will I have what it takes to overcome fundamental attribution error and hire Candidate A?

Or let's say there is an officeholder I despise for reasons of temperament, behavior, and ideology. And let's further say that under this person's administration, the national economy is performing well. Will I be able to dislodge my powerful confirmation bias and allow the possibility that the person deserves some credit?

As for the matter that Hal Hershfield brought up in the first place—estate planning—I have always been the proverbial ant, storing up my food for winter while the grasshoppers sing and play. In other words, I have always maxed out contributions to 401(k)s, Roth IRAs, Simplified Employee Pensions, 403(b)s, 457(b)s, and pretty much every alphabet-soup savings choice presented to me.[9] But as good a saver as I am, I am that bad a procrastinator. Months ago, my financial adviser offered to evaluate, for free, my will, which was put together

9. Varieties of tax-advantaged retirement accounts.

a couple of decades ago and surely needs revising. There's something about drawing up a will that creates a perfect storm of biases,[10] from the ambiguity effect ("the tendency to avoid options for which missing information makes the probability seem 'unknown,'" as *Wikipedia* defines it; "List of Cognitive Biases," 2017) to normalcy bias ("the refusal to plan for, or react to, a disaster which has never happened before"; "List of Cognitive Biases," 2017), all of them culminating in the ostrich effect (do I really need to explain?). My adviser sent me a prepaid FedEx envelope, which has been lying on the floor of my office gathering dust. It is still there. As hindsight bias tells me, I knew that would happen.

References

Commission on the Intelligence Capabilities of the United States Regarding Weapons of Mass Destruction. (2005). *Report to the president of the United States.* https://fas.org/irp/offdocs/wmd_report.pdf

Creative Technologies Incorporated. (2014). *Missing: The pursuit of Terry Hughes* [Video Game].

Gawande, A. (2010). *The checklist manifesto: How to get things right.* Metropolitan Books.

Hershfield, H. (2011). Increasing saving behavior through age-progressed renderings of the future self. *Journal of Marketing Research, 48,* 23–36. http://doi.org/fhp59x

Kahneman, D. (2011). *Thinking, fast and slow.* Farrar, Straus and Giroux.

Kahneman, D., Knetsch, J. L., & Thaler, R. H. (1991). Anomalies: The endowment effect, loss aversion, and status quo bias. *The Journal of Economic Perspectives, 5*(1), 193–206. http://doi.org/gfn5gr

Kahneman, D., & Tversky, A. (1983). Extensional versus intuitive reasoning: The conjunction fallacy in probability judgement. *Psychological Review, 90,* 293–315.

Laibson, D. (1997). Golden eggs and hyperbolic discounting. *The Quarterly Journal of Economics, 112*(2), 443–478. http://doi.org/bxxp5d

Lewis, M. (2003). *Moneyball: The art of winning an unfair game.* Norton.

Lewis, M. (2016). *The undoing project: A friendship that changed the world.* Norton.

List of cognitive biases. (2017, July). In *Wikipedia.* https://en.wikipedia.org/w/index.php?title=List_of_Cognitive_biases&oldid=792649878

Morewedge, C. K., Yoon, H., Scopelliti, I., Symborski, C. W., Korris, J. H., & Kassam, K. S. (2015). Debiasing decisions: Improved decision making with a single training intervention. *Policy Insights from Cognitive Psychology, 2*(1), 129–140. http://doi.org/gf3fkq

Nisbett, R. (2015). *Mindware: Tools for smart thinking.* Farrar, Straus and Giroux.

Nisbett, R. (Instructor). (2017). *Mindware: Critical thinking for the information age* [Online course]. Coursera. https://www.coursera.org/learn/mindware

10. Derived from the title of Sebastian Junger's book *The Perfect Storm* (1997).

Nisbett, R., & Ross, L. (1980). *Human inference: Strategies and shortcomings of social judgment*. Prentice Hall.

Smith, K., & Inge, C. (2018, July 25). *Preview of the 2018 NeuroLeadership summit* [Webinar]. NeuroLeadership Institute. https://neuroleadership.com /portfolio-items/preview-the-2018-neuroleadership-summit/

Tetlock, P. E., & Gardner, D. (2015). *Superforecasting: The art and science of prediction*. Broadway Books.

Trump, D. (2017, August 21). *Remarks by President Trump on the strategy in Afghanistan and South Asia*. National Security & Defense. https://www .whitehouse.gov/briefings-statements/remarks-president-trump-strategy -afghanistan-south-asia/

MLA CITATION

Yagoda, Ben. "Your Lying Mind." *The Norton Reader: An Anthology of Nonfiction*, edited by Melissa A. Goldthwaite et al., 15th ed., W. W. Norton, 2020, pp. 860–72.

QUESTIONS

1. Ben Yagoda asserts that cognitive biases "can make a hash of our lives" (paragraph 7). How do cognitive biases differ from other forms of bias, and why are they so troublesome or alarming?

2. As a journalist, Yagoda depends on the authority of experts for his information about cognitive bias. Two of these experts, Daniel Kahneman and Richard E. Nisbett, disagree about whether we can do much to resist these biases in ordinary life. Whom does Yagoda agree with? How can you tell? Whom do you agree with? Why?

3. How does Yagoda make the scientific concepts in his essay accessible to general readers?

4. Select one of the cognitive biases Yagoda identifies and write an essay about your own experience with it.

JENNIFER EBERHARDT
Seeing Each Other

I SPENT THE FIRST TWELVE YEARS of my life in Cleveland, Ohio, in an all-black world. My family, my neighbors, my teachers, my classmates, my friends—every person I had any meaningful contact with until that point was black. So when my parents announced we were moving to a nearly all-white suburb called Beachwood, I was excited about living in

Published as the first chapter of Jennifer L. Eberhardt's book Biased: Uncovering the Hidden Prejudice That Shapes What We See, Think, and Do *(2019). Eberhardt is a social psychologist and Stanford professor who studies racial perception, racial bias, and race and crime.*

a bigger house but worried about how I would be greeted by my new middle school classmates.

I worried they would make fun of me—my brown skin, my wiry hair, my large dark eyes. I worried about my way of speaking—my cadence, my word choice, my voice.

Yet when I arrived that fall, white students went out of their way to welcome me. They introduced themselves. They invited me to eat with them at lunch. They showed me around the school and loaded me up with details on the dizzying array of activities now open to me. It was what my parents had always dreamed of. I could sing in the choir or act in a play. I could study sign language or learn gymnastics. I could try out for the volleyball team or run for a seat on the student council.

My classmates seemed genuinely interested in helping me transition to this new place. I was grateful, and yet I struggled to make new friends. I'd call students by the wrong name, walk past a classmate in the hall without speaking, fail to remember the girl I'd shared a lunch table with in the cafeteria the day before. They didn't seem to hold it against me. They understood that I was meeting people every day and it was a lot to take in. But I knew there was something more going on. Every day I was confronted with a mass of white faces that I could not distinguish from one another. I didn't know how to do it or even where to start.

I'd had no practice recognizing white faces. They all looked alike to me.   5
I could describe in detail the face of the black woman I happened to pass in a shopping mall. But I could not pick out from a crowd the white girl who sat next to me in English class every day.

I found myself constantly seduced by the easiest way to sort people. I would hold on to the fact that the girl in the red sweater said this and the girl in the gray sweatshirt said that. This helped me to track a conversation in the moment, but I would be at a loss again the very next day.

I tried training myself to pay attention to features that I'd never needed to notice in my black neighborhood—eye color, various shades of blond hair, freckles. I tried remembering the most distinctive feature about each person I encountered. But all the faces would ultimately blend together again in my mind.

As time went on, I worried that my new friends would begin to drift away. Who would want to be friends with a girl who had to be reminded to whom she was talking from one day to the next?

Stripped of this most basic skill, I became a different person in my new neighborhood—awkward, uncertain, hesitant, withdrawn. I was afraid of making a mistake, of embarrassing myself or hurting the feelings of people I'd grown to like.

By springtime, whenever I saw girls whispering among themselves, I'd   10 wonder whether their patience was finally wearing thin. *Are they talking about me?* I'd sidle over to try to join the conversation, but they'd fall silent whenever I showed up.

I was relieved when one of the popular girls invited me to lunch at a restaurant one weekend. When I walked in, she was sitting at a table with a group of girls I didn't recognize, until they all yelled out, "Happy birthday!" I scanned their faces and realized that these were the classmates I'd seen whispering in the hall, planning a surprise party for the new girl who still hadn't managed to get their names right.

They'd brought gifts that reflected touchstones in their lives, including albums by musicians I'd never heard of: Bruce Springsteen, Billy Joel. I was moved beyond words by the gesture; no one had ever planned a surprise party for me. But when we finished the cake, hugged good-bye, and parted ways, I still was not confident I could tell those faces apart.

The irony of that school year always troubled me. I worried about being ostracized because I wasn't one of them. But I was the one stumbling over our racial differences. They wanted to connect, and so did I. But I had suddenly acquired a deficiency that they were not aware of and that I did not understand.

Decades later, I would realize that I was not alone.

THE SCIENCE OF RECOGNITION

15   For nearly fifty years, scientists have been documenting the fact that people are much better at recognizing faces of their own race than faces of other races—a finding dubbed the "other-race effect."

It's a universal phenomenon, and it shows up in different racial groups across the United States and in countries all over the world. It appears early and intensifies over time. By the time babies are three months old, their brains react more strongly to faces of their own race than to faces of people unlike them. That race-selective response only grows stronger as children move into adolescence, which suggests it is driven, in part, by the circumstances of our lives.

We learn what's important—the faces we see every day—and over time our brain builds a preference for those faces, at the expense of skills needed to recognize others less relevant. That experience-driven evolution of face perception skills remodels our brains so they can operate more efficiently.

Scientists see the other-race effect as a sign that our perceptive powers are shaped by what we see. That cringe-worthy expression *"They all look alike"* has long been considered the province of the bigot. But it is actually a function of biology and exposure. Our brains are better at processing faces that evoke a sense of familiarity.

I'd struggled to recognize my white classmates' faces because black faces were all I'd been routinely exposed to in the twelve years before I moved to the suburbs. My adolescent brain took some time to catch up to the new world I was navigating, but I would soon develop new skills to function in that world.

20   Race is not a pure dividing line. Children who are adopted by parents of a different race do not exhibit the classic other-race effect. For example, researchers in Belgium found that white children were better at recognizing white faces than Asian faces. But Chinese and Vietnamese children who'd

been adopted by white families were equally good at recognizing white and Asian faces.

Age and familiarity with various age-groups can also be factors. In England, a study of primary school teachers found that they were better at recognizing the faces of random eight- to eleven-year-olds than were college students who spent most of their time around other college students. And scientists in Italy found that maternity-ward nurses were better at telling infants apart by looking at their faces than were people from other professions—a proficiency that helps to ensure "mix-ups don't happen in the nursery," the researchers suggest.

Our experiences in the world seep into our brain over time, and without our awareness they conspire to reshape the workings of our mind.

IMAGING RACE

I couldn't have known back in middle school that my own brain development played a part in my struggle to connect. But I was convinced that skin color had a role in the dislocation I felt. That's ultimately what drew me to the field of social psychology. It offered the perspective I needed to address a question fundamental to my own adolescent experience: *How does race shape who we are and how we experience the world?* That question is the starting point of bigger questions about identity, power, and privilege that have molded our country and roiled the world for centuries.

Today, I am a professor and a researcher at Stanford University, a campus nestled in Silicon Valley, the heart of the start-up economy and a magnet for bright, energetic young people eager to tap the rich vein of technology for scientific solutions to social problems. When I arrived at Stanford, I was enticed by the tools of neuroscience research and began exploring the ways that race might influence basic brain functioning.

The brain is not a hardwired machine. It's a malleable organ that responds   25
to the environments we are placed in and the challenges we face. This view of the brain runs counter to what most of us learned in science class. In fact, the whole idea of neuroplasticity runs counter to what scientists believed to be true about the brain for centuries. Only fairly recent advances in neuroscience have allowed us to peek inside the brain and track its adaptation over time. Slowly, we're beginning to understand the many ways the brain can be altered by experience.

For example, in the last several decades, we have learned that when someone becomes blind, the occipital lobe, typically dedicated to processing visual stimuli, can dedicate itself instead to processing other types of stimuli, including sound and touch. When someone has a stroke, they might be able to learn to speak again, despite massive damage to specific areas of the temporal lobe that are dedicated to processing language. We don't know yet the extent of this neuroplasticity. And some of the most intriguing lessons come not only from studying damaged brains but also from watching people with normal brain function acquire unusual skills.

Research has shown that something as simple as driving a taxi can offer lessons in how basic practice and repetition can retrain our brains to function differently. In 2000, not long after I arrived at Stanford, a team led by Professor Eleanor Maguire published a paper that caused quite a stir in the neuroscience community. They'd scanned the brains of London cabdrivers in an effort to examine how the hippocampus—a horseshoe-shaped structure in the medial temporal lobe—might grow in response to demands placed upon it by the taxing experience of driving through the London city streets day in and day out.

Maguire's team found that the brains of taxicab drivers—who had by necessity learned the structural layout of more than twenty-five thousand London streets—showed significant differences in the hippocampus, the part of the brain that plays a critical role in spatial memory and navigation. The taxi drivers' navigational expertise was associated with increased gray matter. They had enlarged posterior hippocampal regions, in comparison with a control group of people who didn't drive cabs for a living. In fact, the longer the drivers had been on the job and the more experience they had, the larger their posterior hippocampus.

I found this all remarkable because it seemed to show not only how powerful our experiences must be to fundamentally change our brain but also how swiftly the transformation can take place. In the case of the taxi drivers, developing a deep structural knowledge of their environment forced a striking structural change in their brains. And that change happened not over hundreds of thousands of years but within a few years of an individual's life. Individual expertise, as it turns out, has its own neurobiological signature.

30 That revelation led me to pose another question, driven by both scientific curiosity and personal memories of my own adolescent lapse: *Because our experiences in the world are reflected in our brains, might our expertise in recognizing faces of our own race—and failing to recognize those of others—display its own neurobiological signature as well?*

Neuroscientists were initially skeptical about the prospect of race having an influence on something as basic, ancient, and important as how faces register in our brains. The act of perceiving faces is both critical and complicated, which may be why the task is distributed across multiple areas of the occipito-temporal region, stretching across two of four major lobes of the brain. The superior temporal sulcus—a trench-like structure in the temporal lobe that's vital to social competence—helps us to read the many different expressions that can suddenly emerge on someone's face, signaling us to approach, to smile, to share, to flee, or to quickly arm ourselves. A region known as the fusiform face area, buried deep near the base of the brain, helps us distinguish the familiar from the unfamiliar, friend from foe.

The fusiform face area, known as the FFA, is widely thought to be both primitive and fundamental to our survival as a species. Affiliation is a basic human need. Without the ability to track the identity of those around us, we are left alone, vulnerable, and exposed.

The FFA has been studied extensively, yet despite decades of research there had been little attention paid to whether race might influence FFA functioning. From the narrow perspective of brain science, the primary function of the FFA is to detect faces. Race, most scientists felt, should have nothing to do with that.

Against that backdrop, I began working with a team of Stanford neuroscientists who specialized in human memory to look further into the matter. Together, we recruited dozens of white and black volunteers and subjected them to functional magnetic resonance imaging (fMRI) scans that allowed us to track the blood flow changes in the brain that illustrate neural activity.

As is common, our study participants had giant coils wrapped around their heads to transmit the images. We slid them into a tube-like scanner (a giant magnet, actually) and showed them a series of faces of black and white strangers. We monitored the process from a control room nearby, taking whole-brain pictures as each face appeared before their eyes. The stronger their response to a face, the more oxygen flooded the targeted part of their brain and the brighter our measuring sensors shined.

35

By tracking the activation of the FFA over multiple displays of strangers' faces, we found that the FFA was responding more vigorously to faces that were the same race as the study participant. That finding held true for both the black and the white people we scanned. We also found that the more dramatic the FFA response to a specific face, the more likely the study participants were able to recognize that stranger's face when they were shown the photograph again later, outside the scanner.

Ours was the first neuroimaging study to demonstrate that there is a neural component to the same-race advantage in the face-recognition process. It offered support for the emerging notion that the brain tunes itself to our experiences as we move through life. And we learned that race can serve as a powerful interpretive lens in that tuning process. Race, as it turns out, could exert influence over one of the brain's most basic functions. The FFA, with its bright colors on our imaging scans, provided us with a clear picture of how in- and out-group distinctions—set in motion by our relationship to the world around us—are mapped onto the inner workings of our brains.

The Purse Snatchers

Call it scientific progress or streetwise knowledge. But what it took me decades to learn about the role of race in face recognition turned out to be common knowledge among an opportunistic band of young men on a crime spree in Oakland.

It was 2014 and I had just begun analyzing racial disparities in policing with the Oakland Police Department when the story made its rounds: Despite a substantial decline in crime across the city, the shopping district in Chinatown had registered an alarming rise in strong-arm robberies. Apparently, black teenage boys were roaming the streets, snatching the purses of middle-aged Asian women.

40   The police developed leads, made arrests, and even recovered some stolen property. But the cases fell apart before the suspects could be prosecuted, because even if a victim had seen the robber's face as he grabbed her purse and ran, none of the women could pick the culprits out of a police lineup.

"We would make stops on the suspect," recalled Captain Le-Ronne Armstrong from the police department. "Yet the victim could not ID. Absent the ID, you couldn't charge the case. This made it impossible to prosecute."

As the young men began to figure out that Asian women couldn't tell them apart, it turned into a license to steal, Armstrong explained to me years later, after some of the crimes were solved and the robbers who were bound for jail had confessed the details. "When we'd ask, 'Why'd you focus in on this particular woman?' they'd say to us very openly, 'The Asian people can't ID. They just can't tell brothers apart.' They'd tell us, 'Like, this is our dream. That's why we go.'"

There was a clear pattern to whom the teens targeted and where and how they struck. They focused on a neighborhood crowded with female, middle-aged Chinese shoppers. They approached from behind, grabbed the purses, and fled, so the victim didn't have much time to study their faces. And sure enough, Armstrong said, in nearly 80 percent of the cases tracked by Oakland police, the Asian victims could not identify the young men who robbed them. Black women, on the other hand, could identify black robbery suspects at a much higher rate, even after a mere glance.

The challenges of cross-racial identification are as well known to law enforcement officials as they are to scientists. Research and real-life experience have shown that the chance of false alarms—of identifying someone as the culprit who is not—goes way up when the suspect is of a different race from the victim. That's the practical fallout of the other-race effect.

45   Oakland investigators worked to minimize the possibility of misidentification. They followed scientific guidelines on how to construct and use lineups with textbook precision. They even tried offering the victims training, directing them "to focus on anything at all that was distinctive," Armstrong told me. *Was his skin dark or light? Did he have gold teeth? Was his hair in dreadlocks or braids?* "We needed them to move beyond the generic 'male black' description." But for the most part, the Asian women couldn't move beyond it. Even with all the training, they were still unable to distinguish one black teenager's face from another.

Ultimately, what did help put an end to the crime spree was technology. When cameras were placed outside the businesses that lined the busy streets of Chinatown, the risks of being caught suddenly shot up. The camera could capture what the women could not. The boys knew the jig was up.

Captain Armstrong's description of the situation led me to recall my own as a newcomer to Beachwood. I too tried the "remember what's distinctive" strategy. I failed and the Asian women failed, despite our strong desire to get it right. Yet the women's inability to remember those black male faces went beyond awkward moments and insecurities about conversations held in hushed tones. Their inability to remember those faces stymied the police and spread fear across the Chinatown community for months and months before the cameras were installed. These teenagers could rob them at will—even in broad daylight. They needed no mask. Their face was their mask.

MLA CITATION

Eberhardt, Jennifer L. "Seeing Each Other." *The Norton Reader: An Anthology of Nonfiction*, edited by Melissa A. Goldthwaite et al., 15th ed., W. W. Norton, 2020, pp. 872–79.

QUESTIONS

1. Jennifer L. Eberhardt's chapter explains the "other-race effect" for a general readership. What is this effect, and how does Eberhardt present it so that non-scientists can understand it?

2. Eberhardt introduces her chapter by recounting her own struggles as an African American child to identify her white classmates after transferring to a middle school. How does this anecdote complicate conventional assumptions about racial bias? Why might Eberhardt have chosen to open her chapter with it?

3. In what ways is the "other-race effect" like the various cognitive biases Ben Yagoda describes in "Your Lying Mind" (pp. 860–72)? In what ways is it different?

4. One of Eberhardt's research interests is the connection between race and crime, and in the final section of her chapter she presents an episode that touches on this theme, telling of "black teenage boys" (paragraphs 38–39) who deliberately targeted Asian women for robberies because such women would struggle to identify them. Write an essay in which you analyze Eberhardt's account of this episode and reflect on its significance. Why might she have chosen to end her chapter with it? What inferences can we draw (and not draw) from it? What are its practical implications for such issues as public safety, policing, or the administration of criminal justice?

NOGA ARIKHA
How Evil Happens

I N 1941, *EN ROUTE* FROM A GHETTO to a concentration camp in Ukraine, a Nazi soldier beat my grandfather to death.[1] My father witnessed this murder. His is just one of millions of similar stories, of course, and I grew up aware of how death hovered on the other side of life, and brutality on the underside of humanity. The "sapiens" in *Homo sapiens* does not fully describe our species: we are as violent as we are smart. This might be why we are the only *Homo* genus left over in the first place, and why we have been so destructively successful at dominating our planet. But still the question nags away: how are ordinary people capable of such obscene acts of violence?

This duality is also a puzzle to ourselves, at the heart of cosmologies, theologies and tragedies, the motor of moral codes and the tension at the heart of socio-political systems. We know light and we know dark. We are capable of doing terrible things, but also of asking ourselves contemplatively and creatively how that is. The self-consciousness that characterizes the human mind is nowhere more baffling than in this problem of evil, which philosophers have been discussing since Plato.[2] An obvious place to look for explanations of evil is in the patterns of behavior that those who commit atrocities display.

This is what the neurosurgeon Itzhak Fried at the University of California, Los Angeles did with his article "Syndrome E" (1997) in *The Lancet*.[3] A syndrome is a group of biological symptoms that together constitute a clinical picture. And E stands for evil. With Syndrome E, Fried identified a cluster of 10 neuropsychological symptoms that are often present when evil acts are committed—when, as he puts it, "groups of previously nonviolent individuals" turn "into repetitive killers of defenseless members of society." The 10 neuropsychological symptoms are:

1.   Repetition: the aggression is repeated compulsively.

2.   Obsessive ideation: the perpetrators are obsessed with ideas that justify their aggression and underlie missions of ethnic cleansing, for instance that all Westerners, or all Muslims, or all Jews, or all Tutsis[4] are evil.

Published in Aeon *(2018), an online magazine dedicated to addressing "big questions" about science, culture, and the arts. Noga Arikha is an intellectual historian and philosopher whose recent work concerns intersections of neuroscience and the humanities.*

1. References the Holocaust (1941–45), the systematic murder of six million Jews by Nazi Germany during World War II.
2. Ancient Athenian philosopher (c. 429–347 B.C.E.).
3. Prestigious British medical journal.
4. Ethnic cleansing, the systematic removal or eradication of an ethnic group from a region; Tutsis, Rwandan ethnic group subject to a genocide during the Rwandan Civil War (1990–94).

3. Perseveration: circumstances have no impact on the perpetrator's behavior, who perseveres even if the action is self-destructive.

4. Diminished affective reactivity: the perpetrator has no emotional affect.

5. Hyperarousal: the elation experienced by the perpetrator is a high induced by repetition, and a function of the number of victims.

6. Intact language, memory and problem-solving skills: the syndrome has no impact on higher cognitive abilities.

7. Rapid habituation: the perpetrator becomes desensitized to the violence.

8. Compartmentalization: the violence can take place in parallel to an ordinary, affectionate family life.

9. Environmental dependency: the context, especially identification with a group and obedience to an authority, determines what actions are possible.

10. Group contagion: belonging to the group enables the action, each member mapping his behavior on the other. Fried's assumption was that all these ways of behaving had underlying neurophysiological causes that were worth investigating.

Note that the syndrome applies to those previously normal individuals who become able to kill. It excludes the wartime, sanctioned killing by and of military recruits that leads many soldiers to return home (if they ever do) with post-traumatic stress disorder (PTSD); recognized psychopathologies such as sociopathic personality disorder that can lead someone to shoot schoolchildren; and crimes of passion or the sadistic pleasure in inflicting pain. When Hannah Arendt coined her expression "the banality of evil" in *Eichmann in Jerusalem* (1963),[5] she meant that the people responsible for actions that led to mass murder can be ordinary, obeying orders for banal reasons, such as not losing their jobs. The very notion of ordinariness was tested by social psychologists. In 1971, the prison experiment by the psychologist Philip Zimbardo at Stanford University played with this notion that "ordinary students" could turn into abusive mock "prison guards"—though it was largely unfounded, given evidence of flaws in the never-replicated experiment.[6] Still, those afflicted with Syndrome E are indeed ordinary insofar as that they are not affected by any evident psychopathology. The historian Christopher Browning wrote of equally "ordinary men" in the 1992 book of that name (referenced by

5. German-born Jewish American philosopher and political theorist (1906–1975); her book, subtitled *A Report on the Banality of Evil* reports and reflects on the trial of Adolf Eichmann (1906–1962), chief architect of the Holocaust, by Israel in 1961. Eichmann was hanged in 1962.
6. In this experiment, subjects were assigned to act either as guards or as prisoners.

Fried) who became Nazi soldiers. The soldier who killed my grandfather was very probably an ordinary man too.

5   Today, biology is a powerful explanatory force for much human behavior, though it alone cannot account for horror. Much as the neurosciences are an exciting new tool for human self-understanding, they will not explain away our brutishness. Causal accounts of the destruction that humans inflict on each other are best provided by political history—not science, nor metaphysics. The past century alone is heavy with atrocities of unfathomable scale, albeit fathomable political genesis. But it was the advent of ISIS and the surge in youthful, enthusiastic recruits to it that gave Fried's hypothesis a new urgency,[7] and prompted him to organize, with the neurophysiologist Alain Berthoz at the Collège de France in Paris, three conferences around Syndrome E that between 2015 and 2017 gathered cognitive neuroscientists, social psychologists, neurophysiologists, psychiatrists, terrorism specialists and jurists, some of whose theories and insights I share here. Syndrome E is a useful provocation to an innovative, interdisciplinary discussion of this old problem—and a powerful example of how to frame neuroscientific output in human terms. Already this approach is giving rise to interesting hypotheses and explanations.

As the brain's functional anatomy reveals itself in increasingly precise ways, neuroscience is growing in its ability to address the complexities underlying our behavior, violence included. But since we are evolved animals, to investigate the biological bases for behavior is to look both at the embodied results of evolutionary time and at historical time—at how the evolved circuits of the brain are recruited by cultures, as well as producing cultures. Given that we evolved as inherently social, interactive creatures, neuroscience requires dialogue with other disciplines—the brain has not evolved in isolation, and action always takes place at a moment in time in a particular place with particular meaning. The psychological and cultural environment is central in determining whether and how given biological processes will play out. The traits enumerated by Fried thus encompass a combination of neurological and environmental conditions.

Central to Syndrome E is the symptom of "diminished affect." Most people—except, precisely, psychopaths—shy away from or are extremely reluctant to inflict pain, let alone kill. As the psychiatrist Robert Jay Lifton has shown, it takes brainwashing and coercion to dull our emotional response and to overcome our reticence to cross the line beyond which "habituation" sets in—the Syndrome E symptom whereby the repetition of the act makes it easier to perform. Perpetrators of mass murder and torturers can also love and want the best for their children, while feeling nothing for their victims—an instance of the "compartmentalization" symptom of Syndrome E. This was probably the

7. ISIS, the Islamic State of Iraq and the Levant, a militant Sunni group that emerged in 2013 and until 2017 controlled territory in western Syria and eastern Iraq; ISIS recruited members internationally through the internet and social media.

case for the anonymous Nazi soldier who killed my grandfather. Family belonging and social belonging are separate. When they meet, as happened in Bosnia and Rwanda when families turned on each other, the group identity prevails. Empathy is rarely universal.

The social neuroscientist Tania Singer at the Max Planck Institute in Leipzig[8] in Germany defines empathy as the ability to "resonate" with the feelings of the other. It develops from babyhood on—as imitation at first, then joint attention—into the ability to adopt the point of view of another, along with a shift in spatial perception from self to other, as if one were literally stepping into another's shoes. This requires an ability to distinguish between self and other in the first place, an aspect of the so-called "theory of mind"[9] that one acquires over the first five years of life. The developmental psychologist Philippe Rochat at Emory University in Atlanta has shown how children develop an ethical stance by that time as well, and become aware of how their actions can be perceived by others.

But while empathy ensures the cohesion of a group or a society, it is also biased and parochial. Revenge thrives on it. The social psychologist Emile Bruneau at the University of Pennsylvania has demonstrated how it is easily directed at an "in-group" at the expense of an "out-group" that can then be targeted as an enemy, and dehumanized. Its selectivity also explains how we can walk by a homeless person without feeling the need to offer help, or rejoice in nasty gossip about a disliked absentee. Inevitably, we all practice selective empathy, its absence manifest in everyday, non-lethal instances of violence that occur in social and family life, in business and politics. What the psychologist Simon Baron-Cohen at the University of Cambridge calls "empathy erosion" in *The Science of Evil: On Empathy and the Origins of Cruelty* (2011) is therefore not a sufficient ingredient in the outbreak of extreme violence. But it is a necessary one, opening the way to discrimination and ultimately genocide. As the social neuroscientist Jean Decety at the University of Chicago put it, "our hypersociality has a dark side."

This developmental account can dispel, in part, the mystery of our two faces—of our ability at once to help each other and to kill each other, or to argue ourselves into "just wars." In common with other hominins such as chimpanzees, we have evolved the capacity to cement relationships, communicate and cooperate with those in our immediate environment—and also to attack outsiders and members of other tribes. But our evolved self-consciousness is what defines our humanity even apart from other hominins. What remains puzzling is our continued ability to destroy even as we are able to understand ourselves and to create sophisticated scientific models of our own minds.

Neuroscience gives an interesting physiological model of the emotion of empathy as a complex, dynamic process that unites executive, premotor and

10

8. Max Planck Institute for Evolutionary Anthropology, one of several research institutes supported by the Max Planck Society for the Advancement of Science.

9. The ability to attribute mental states such as thoughts, feelings, and intentions to oneself and others.

sensorimotor functions. It recruits, in particular, the ventromedial prefrontal cortex (vmPFC) and the orbitofrontal cortex (OFC), with which the vmPFC overlaps in part, and which is crucial for the processing of emotions generated in the amygdala—an evolutionary ancient structure within the limbic system. Lesion to the OFC impairs emotional feeling—and with it, decision-making. With his "somatic marker hypothesis," the neuroscientist Antonio Damasio at the University of Southern California in Los Angeles has shown how bodily feelings that participate in signaling emotions, processed in the OFC and vmPFC, enable appropriate, socially situated decision-making, thereby informing our evaluations of the world, including our moral sense.

In the phenomenon of diminished affect, hyperactivity in these same areas of the frontal lobe inhibits activation of the amygdala. Studies have shown dysfunctional activity of the OFC in people with obsessive-compulsive disorder. It thus might also be involved in the obsessive nature of ideas about one group that justify murderous intent against its members. And the sense of elated hyperarousal—such as that induced by cocaine—that entrains action upon these ideas involves processing in the medial prefrontal cortex (mPFC). In short, in cases of Syndrome E emotional pathways in the brain no longer regulate judgment and action. A breakdown occurs in the feedback between the amygdala and higher, cognitive cortical structures. The acting self splits away from the feeling self, a phenomenon that Fried calls "cognitive fracture." He believes that, under given circumstances, about 70 per cent of the population can be subject to it and be able to take part in crimes as part of a group—as might have happened in the Stanford prison experiment, despite caveats regarding its results.

The acting self of the individual with cognitive fracture feels no empathy. But empathy is not always a reliable guide to appropriate behavior—we don't feel empathy for the insects dying because of climate change, for instance, but we can decide rationally to act against the disaster. It can even lead to bad decisions with regard to those at whom it is directed—a surgeon who feels empathy for the patient under drapes should really not operate. There is such a thing as a surfeit of feeling. The psychologist Paul Bloom at Yale University has argued "against empathy," in a 2016 book of that title and elsewhere, suggesting that "rational compassion" is a better barometer with which to evaluate our environment and how we should act upon it. That is to say, members of a group whose mission is to kill its perceived enemies might have the ability for emotional empathy for their group, and no rational compassion for their perceived enemy.

An account of the inability to feel any emotion for such perceived enemies can take us closer to understanding what it is like to have crossed the line beyond which one can maim and kill in cold blood. Observers at the International Criminal Court (ICC) at the Hague note frequently the absence of remorse displayed by perpetrators. The clinical psychologist Françoise Sironi, who assesses perpetrators for the ICC and treats them and their victims, has directly seen what Lifton called the "murder of the self" at work—notably with

Kang Kek Iew, the man known as "Duch," who proudly created and directed the Khmer Rouge S-21 centre for torture and extermination in Cambodia. Duch was one of those who felt absolutely no remorse. His sole identity was his role, dutifully kept up for fear of losing himself and falling into impotence. He did not comprehend what Sironi meant when she asked him: "What happened to your conscience?" The very question was gibberish to him.

Along with what Fried calls this "catastrophic" desensitization to emotional cues, cognitive functions remain intact—another Syndrome E symptom. A torturer knows exactly how to hurt, in full recognition of the victim's pain. He—usually he—has the cognitive capacity, necessary but not sufficient for empathy, to understand the victim's experience. He just does not care about the other's pain except instrumentally. Further, he does not care that he does not care. Finally, he does not care that caring does, in fact, matter. The emotionally inflected judgment that underlies the moral sense is gone.   15

Such a state involves the fusion of identity with a larger system within which occurs the splitting of the feeling self and the cognitive self, and the concomitant replacement of individual moral values with that system's norms and rules. Chemistry is operative throughout, as it is in all cerebral and somatic functions—and tweakable by pharmaceuticals. The neuroscientist Trevor Robbins at the University of Cambridge has studied "pharmacoterrorism," and how, for instance, the amphetamine Captagon—used, inter alia, by ISIS members—affects dopamine function, depletes serotonin in the OFC, and leads to rigid, psychopathic-like behavior, increasing aggression and leading to the perseverance that Fried lists among the Syndrome E symptoms. It shuts off social attachment, and disables all emotional feeling (empathy included), a condition called alexithymia.

This is one simplified neurological account of how murderous action becomes possible. The neuroscience of value and action can help to further explain what might be going on. The OFC is exceptionally developed in humans and primates. As Edmund Rolls at the Oxford Centre for Computational Neuroscience has shown, it plays a crucial role in representing reward value in response to a stimulus: we make choices based on the assignation of value—to an object, an idea, an action, a norm, a person. Our emotions are value-rich, and our actions vary and can be updated according to how they are met in the world, in turn motivating us to seek or avoid a stimulus. Our behavior can continue in the search of an absent reward—this would be one account of compulsive action, a Syndrome E symptom. The neuroscientist Mathias Pesiglione and his team in Paris have also shown a central role for vmPFC in value-attribution to a stimulus or an idea, whereby we choose to undertake an action based on its attractive reward or its aversive outcome. But when this function is overstimulated, new inputs—such as cries for mercy—have no impact on the attribution of value to the idea, for instance that "all you people deserve to die," and action cannot change. It becomes automatic, controllable by an external agent or leader, independently of any sense of value.

But these neurological events signify criminal action only under particular environmental circumstances. The psychiatrist David Cohen and his team at the Pitié-Salpêtrière hospital in Paris evaluated teenage candidates for radicalization. They found that certain socio-psychological conditions in childhood—such as an absent father or an unstable mother, and a history of foster care—affected the development of identity, in some cases eventually leading to the need to subsume it into a wider group with a transcendental message. Again, group trumps family. As the anthropologist Scott Atran has shown, conflicts are often intractable and non-negotiable because they are conducted in the name of absolute, spiritual values—secular or religious—and not for any utilitarian outcome. These values can seem highly attractive—stronger than family ties.

In her novel *Home Fire* (2017), the British Pakistani writer Kamila Shamsie showed how a loving, innocent but maladjusted and lost young man of Pakistani origin could fall prey to an ISIS recruiter's siren call to rejoin a lost father and find fulfillment and belonging in a community depicted as devoted to a greater good. Our narratives, inner and outer, inform and justify the choices we make, conferring on them a coherence that is reassuring and can seem good and right. Coherence rides on the moral sense and masquerades as it, bringing on a cognitive dissonance "between what we think and what we do," as Zimbardo once put it—between what we convince ourselves was an appropriate action, and our deeply held, prior beliefs. Shamsie's character soon regrets his choice and tries to get away from a violence he cannot stomach, unable to withstand the cognitive dissonance. Not so Nazi doctors, say, who convinced themselves that they were acting for a greater good—in a perverse twist to the equivalence of morality with a concern for the good of others. Heinrich Himmler's speech in Poznan in 1943 is a chilling instance of this high-minded justification of criminal behavior: "We have the moral right, we had the duty to our people to do it, to kill this people who wanted to kill us." Once moral justification is divorced from an emotionally calibrated response to the other, violence can be deployed on rationalized grounds. This has happened time and again throughout history.

20   But "ordinary men" must cross a line into that zone where the Syndrome E symptoms operate—pushed by circumstance. A noteworthy insight into what happens during the crossing is provided by the neuroscientist Patrick Haggard at University College London. He has shown how powerful is the initial coercion that allows us to step beyond the line. In the wake of the 1961 trial in Jerusalem of Adolf Eichmann, who invoked the "Nuremberg Defense" that he was "just obeying orders"—so-called because it was first used by the Nazi defendants in the Nuremberg Trials of 1945–46—the psychologist Stanley Milgram at Yale University showed, or rather exaggeratedly claimed, that most people will obey orders from an authority even if the order is to harm another person. Milgram was interested in obedience. Haggard, who has been studying the sense of agency—the sense that we initiate and own our actions, which is central to our lives, and also to legal arguments about criminal accountability—asked instead what it feels like to be coerced and have one's autonomy removed to some degree. Through an experiment that partly takes its cue from Milgram's (but addresses some of its ethical and methodological

issues) and uses the intentional binding effect, Haggard found that people do feel a notable reduction in their sense of agency when they are coerced into an action. Coercion switches off the sense of responsibility—a chilling finding.

The neurological correlates of what can lead to our worst actions do not indicate a clinical condition. Syndrome E is not a disease, nor quite a disorder eligible for integration into the *Diagnostic and Statistical Manual of Mental Disorders* or the International Statistical Classification of Diseases and Related Problems.[10] If it were officialized as such, it would have intricate juridical ramifications: the use of neurological evidence in court is problematic, as the jurist Jean-Paul Costa, a former president of the European Court of Human Rights,[11] has pointed out, because it requires the expert reading of imprecise and opaque data. It is hard to establish exactly which brain events—including those underlying the sense of agency—could or should constitute legally mitigating factors.

But introducing, as Fried has done, a set of features that characterize our most beastly nature, and kickstarting a wide-ranging discussion across the fields relevant to their study, particularly in the area of neuroscience, can only help to enrich programmes of prevention and remediation at a time when these are sorely needed. The devil might be dead, but evil actions will always exist. The "Why?" remains a metaphysical puzzle, and I am one of the millions whose life is lived under this question mark, passed on by my survivor father. But at least some answers to the "How?" are now within our reach.

MLA CITATION

Arikha, Noga. "How Evil Happens." *The Norton Reader: An Anthology of Nonfiction*, edited by Melissa A. Goldthwaite et al., 15th ed., W. W. Norton, 2020, pp. 880–87.

QUESTIONS

1. Noga Arikha's essay considers possible scientific explanations for the problem she identifies in her title phrase: "How Evil Happens." What does she mean by "evil," and what do neuroscience and psychology tell us about it?

2. How does Arikha understand the relationship between human biology and culture? How does this understanding inform her attitude toward the potential of science to address the "problem of evil" (paragraph 2)?

3. In her opening paragraphs, Arikha notes that as a species, "we are as violent as we are smart" (paragraph 1) and suggests that understanding and navigating this "duality" has been the principal project of human thought and culture (paragraph 2).

10. Standard manuals or tools that define and allow the diagnosis of psychiatric and other diseases and conditions.

11. International court established in 1959 via the European Convention on Human Rights.

What specific "dualities," tensions, or paradoxes does Arikha explore in her essay? How does "duality" function as an organizing principle for her argument?

4. In their essays, Ben Yagoda (pp. 860–72), Jennifer L. Eberhardt (pp. 872–79), and Arikha each explore a common insight emerging from contemporary psychology and neuroscience: that our judgments, reasoning, perceptions, emotions, and actions are profoundly shaped, if not determined, by how our brains work. Write a dialogue among these three authors in which they discuss the practical ramifications of this insight. What are its implications for medicine, law, education, politics, or other areas of human activity and endeavor?

JOY CASTRO
Grip

OVER THE CRIB in the tiny apartment, there hung a bullet-holed paper target, the size and dark shape of a man—its heart zone, head zone, perforated where my aim had torn through: 36 little rips, no strays, centered on spots that would make a man die.

Beginner's luck, said the guys at the shooting range, at first. *Little lady*, they'd said, until the silhouette slid back and farther back. They'd cleared their throats, fallen silent.

A bad neighborhood. An infant child. A Ruger GP .357 with speed-loader.[1]

It's not as morbid as it sounds, a target pinned above a crib: the place was small, the walls already plastered full with paintings, sketches, pretty leaves, hand-illuminated psychedelic broadsides of poems by my friends. I masking-taped my paper massacre to the only empty space, a door I'd closed to form a wall.

5   When my stepfather got out of prison, he tracked my mother down. He found the city where she'd moved. He broke a basement window and crawled in. She never saw his car, halfway up the dark block, stuffed behind a bush.

My mother lived. She wouldn't say what happened in the house that night. Cops came: that's what I know. Silent, she hung a screen between that scene and me. It's what a mother does.

She lived—as lived the violence of our years with him, knifed into us like scrimshaw cut in living bone.

Carved but alive, we learned to hold our breath, dive deep, bare our teeth to what fed us.

First published in the journal Fourth Genre: Explorations in Nonfiction (2009).

1. Ruger GP .357, revolver manufactured by Sturm, Ruger & Company; speed-loader, a device used to reload a revolver rapidly.

When I was 21, my son slept under the outline of what I could do, a death I could hold in my hands.

At the time, I'd have denied its locale any meaning, called its placement   10 coincidence, pointing to walls crowded with other kinds of dreams.

But that dark, torn thing did hang there, its lower edge obscured behind the wooden slats, the flannel duck, the stuffed white bear.

It hung there like a promise, like a headboard, like a *No*, like a terrible poem, like these lines I will never show you, shielding you from the fear I carry—like a sort of oath I swore over your quiet sleep.

MLA CITATION

Castro, Joy. "Grip." *The Norton Reader: An Anthology of Nonfiction*, edited by
    Melissa A. Goldthwaite et al., 15th ed., W. W. Norton, 2020, pp. 888–89.

QUESTIONS

1. Joy Castro opens her essay with an arresting image: a bullet-riddled paper target pinned over a crib. Why did she decide to hang the target there? How does her explanation evolve between the essay's beginning and end?

2. In her short essay, Castro implies rather than states many details about her life. What can you infer about her family, history, and circumstances?

3. In her final sentence, Castro uses the pronouns "you" and "your" for the first time in the essay (paragraph 12). Who is the "you" she addresses? How does this shift into the second person change your understanding and response to the essay? (To spur your thinking, try imagining the essay without that final sentence.)

4. Castro's essay is only 363 words long, and much of its power derives from its compactness. Using Castro's essay as a model, write a similarly compact essay about a meaningful moment from your own life. Write a first draft of at least one thousand words. Revise it down to five hundred words, then to three hundred and fifty words (about the length of Castro's essay). What changes did you make with each of these revisions? Why?

EMMA GONZÁLEZ
Fighting for Gun Control

MY NAME IS EMMA GONZÁLEZ. I'm 18 years old, Cuban and bisexual. I'm so indecisive that I can't pick a favorite color, and I'm allergic to 12 things. I draw, paint, crochet, sew, embroider—anything productive I can do with my hands while watching Netflix.

But none of this matters anymore.

What matters is that the majority of American people have become complacent in a senseless injustice that occurs all around them. What matters is that most American politicians have become more easily swayed by money than by the people who voted them into office. What matters is that my friends are dead, along with hundreds upon hundreds of others all over the United States.

This started with, has been about, will always be for, all of us. And who are we? We are the people who died in the freshman building on Valentine's Day at Douglas High, and the people who died in every mass shooting in U.S. history. We are everyone who has been shot at, grazed or pierced by bullets, terrorized by the presence of guns and gun violence in America. We are kids, we are parents, we are students, we are teachers. We are tired of practicing school shooter drills and feeling scared of something we should never have to think about. We are tired of being ignored. So we are speaking up for those who don't have anyone listening to them, for those who can't talk about it just yet, and for those who will never speak again. We are grieving, we are furious, and we are using our words fiercely and desperately because that's the only thing standing between us and this happening again.

5   I have talked so much in the past few days that sometimes I feel like I might have used up all my words and I'll never speak again. And then I hear someone say something really stupid and I can barely keep myself from snapping in two.

"If you have ever lost someone very important to you, then you already know how it feels, and if you haven't, then you cannot possibly imagine it," wrote Lemony Snicket in *The Bad Beginning: A Series of Unfortunate Events.*[1] There are people who do not know, and will never know, what it feels like to go through this. For that I am eternally thankful. But to the people out there who disagree with us: if you have ever felt what it's like to deal with all of this, you would know we aren't doing this for attention. If these funerals were for your friends, you would know this grief is real, not paid for. We are children who

---

Published online in Harper's Bazaar *on February 26, 2018, twelve days after a school shooting at Marjory Stoneman Douglas High School in Parkland, Florida, and one month before the March for Our Lives, a student-led protest against gun violence. González, a Stoneman Douglas student and survivor of the shooting, helped to organize and spoke at the march.*

1. Published in 1999, the first of a series of thirteen novels by Daniel Handler, using the pen name Lemony Snicket.

are being expected to act like adults, while the adults are proving themselves to behave like children.

When did *children* become such a dirty word? Adults are saying that children are lazy, meanwhile Jaclyn Corin organized an entire trip to Tallahassee, three busses stuffed with 100 kids and reporters who went to discuss our pitiful firearm legislation with the people who can—but won't—do something about it.

Adults are saying that children are emotional. I should hope so—some of our closest friends were taken before their time because of a senseless act of violence that should never have occurred. If we weren't emotional, they would criticize us for that, as well. Adults are saying that children are disrespectful. But how can we respect people who don't respect us? We have always been told that if we see something wrong, we need to speak up; but now that we are, all we're getting is disrespect from the people who made the rules in the first place. Adults like us when we have strong test scores, but they hate us when we have strong opinions.

I'm constantly torn between being thankful for the endless opportunities to share my voice, and wishing I were a tree so that I'd never have had to deal with this in the first place. I'd like to think that it would be nice to be a tree.

Still, if I'm able to communicate one thing to adults, it would be this: it should not be easier to purchase a gun than it is to obtain a driver's license, and military-grade weapons should not be accessible in civilian settings. You don't drive a NASCAR on the street, no matter how fun it might be, just like you don't need an AR-15 to protect yourself when walking home at night. No one does.[2]

At the end of the day, we don't want people to have their guns taken away. We just want the people to be more responsible. We want civilians to have to go through more rolls of red tape to get what they want, because if any of that tape can stop those who shouldn't own a gun from owning a gun, then our government will have done something right. All we want to do is go back to school. But we want to know that when we walk onto campus, we won't have to worry about the possibility of staring down the barrel of a gun. We want to fix this problem so it doesn't occur again, but mostly we want people to forget about us once this is over. We want to go back to our lives and live them to the fullest in respect for the dead.

Teachers do not need to be armed with guns to protect their classes, they need to be armed with a solid education in order to teach their classes. That's the only thing that needs to be in their job description. People say metal detectors would help. Tell that to the kids who already have metal detectors at school and are still victims of gun violence. If you want to help arm the schools, arm them with school supplies, books, therapists, things they actually need and can make use of.

10

2. NASCAR, National Association for Stock Car Auto Racing; AR-15, military-style semiautomatic rifle.

One more thing. We want increased mental health care for all those who need it—including the angry, frustrated men who almost always commit these crimes. Mental illness and gun violence are not directly correlated, but when the two go hand in hand, Americans—often children—lose their lives. We don't need the NRA's excuses, we need the NRA[3] to finally stand up and use its power to supply the American people with something they deserve. (And please note, when members of the March for Our Lives movement talk about the NRA, we are referring to the organization itself, not the members. Many of the members understand and support our fight for responsible gun ownership, despite the organization preventing common sense gun laws from being instituted in the name of protecting the second amendment—rather than the American people.)

So march with us on March 24.[4] Register to vote. Actually show up to the polls. Because we need to relieve the NRA of its talking points, once and for all.

MLA CITATION

González, Emma. "Fighting for Gun Control." *The Norton Reader: An Anthology of Nonfiction*, edited by Melissa A. Goldthwaite et al., 15th ed., W. W. Norton, 2020, pp. 890–92.

QUESTIONS

1. In the last third of her essay, beginning with paragraph 10, Emma González offers a series of proposals for curtailing gun violence. Which of her proposals do you support? Why? Which do you oppose? Why?

2. According to classical rhetoric, there are three main ways a speaker or writer might connect with or persuade an audience: by establishing her own character, credibility, or authority on a subject (*ethos*), by appealing to emotions (*pathos*), or by offering reasoned arguments (*logos*). In her essay, González relies on all three

---

3. National Rifle Association, a pro-gun lobbying organization.
4. March 24, 2018, the date of the March for Our Lives protest.

types of appeal. Where and how does she use each of them? Why might she have chosen to organize her essay as she did?

3. González uses several "figures of speech," including *analogy*, the likening of one thing to another; *anaphora*, the repetition of words at the beginnings of a series of sentences or clauses; *chiasmus*, the repetition of concepts in reverse order but without a repetition or words; and *antimetabole*, the repetition of specific words in reverse order. Find examples of each of these figures of speech in González's essay. How do they enhance its effectiveness?

4. Using González's essay as a model, write an essay of your own in which you inform your audience about a problem that concerns you and endeavor to persuade them to take some action to remedy it.

DAVID FRENCH
What Critics Don't Understand about Gun Culture

MY WIFE KNEW SOMETHING WAS AMISS when the car blocked our driveway. She was outside our house, playing with our kids on our trampoline, when a car drove slowly down our rural Tennessee street. As it reached our house, it pulled partially in the driveway, and stopped.

A man got out and walked up to my wife and kids. Strangely enough, at his hip was an empty gun holster. She'd never seen him before. She had no idea who he was. He demanded to see me.

I wasn't there. I was at my office, a 50-minute drive from my house. My wife didn't have her phone with her. She didn't have one of our guns with her outside. She was alone with our three children. Even if she had her phone, the police were minutes away. My wife cleverly defused the confrontation before it escalated, but we later learned that this same person had been seen, hours before, slowly driving through the parking lot of our kids' school.

That wasn't the first disturbing incident in our lives, nor would it be the last. My wife is a sex-abuse survivor and was almost choked to death in college by a furious boyfriend. In just the last five years, we've faced multiple threats— so much so that neighbors have expressed concern for our safety, and theirs. They didn't want an angry person to show up at their house by mistake. We've learned the same lesson that so many others have learned. There are evil men in this world, and sometimes they wish you harm.

Miles's law states, "Where you stand is based on where you sit." In other words, your political opinions are shaped by your environment and your experience. We're products of our place, our time, and our people. Each of these   5

Published in the Atlantic *(2018), a magazine covering literature, culture, and politics. David French is a veteran of the Iraq War and a senior writer for* National Review, *a magazine of conservative opinion.*

things is far more important to shaping hearts and minds than any think piece, any study, or certainly any tweet. And it strikes me that many millions of Americans don't truly understand how "gun culture" is built, how the process of first becoming a gun owner, then a concealed-carrier, changes your life.

It starts with the consciousness of a threat. Perhaps not the kind of threat my family has experienced. Some people experience more. Some less. And some people don't experience a threat at all—but they're aware of those who do. With the consciousness of a threat comes the awareness of a vulnerability. The police can only protect the people you love in the most limited of circumstances (with those limits growing ever-more-severe the farther you live from a city center). You want to stand in that gap.

So you take a big step. You walk into a gun store. Unless you're the kind of person who grew up shooting, this is where you begin your encounter with American gun culture. The first thing you'll notice—and I've seen this without fail—is that the person behind that counter is ready to listen. They want to hear your experience. They'll share their own. They'll point you immediately to a potential solution. Often the person behind the counter is a veteran. Often they're a retired cop. Always they're well-informed. Always they're ready to teach.

Your first brush with this new world is positive, but it's just a start. The next place the responsible adult goes is to the gun range, a place that's often located in the store. Sometimes you buy the gun and walk straight to the range. You put on eye protection. You put on ear protection. And if you're honest with yourself, you're nervous.

But, again, there's a person beside you. They show you how to load the gun. They teach you the basics of marksmanship. They teach you gun safety. Always treat the gun as if it's loaded, even if you think you know it's not. Keep your finger off the trigger unless you intend to fire the weapon. Only point it at objects you intend to shoot.

10   You do it. You fire. It's loud, but if the salesman has done his job, then he's matched you with a gun you can handle. In an instant, the gun is demystified. You buy a box of ammunition and shoot it all. Then you buy another box. For most people there's an undeniable thrill when they realize that they can actually master so potent a tool.

But something else happens to you, something that's deeper than the fun of shooting a paper target. Your thought-process starts to change. Yes, if someone tried to break into your house, you know that you'd call 911 and pray for the police to come quickly, but you also start to think of exactly what else you'd do. If you heard that "bump" in the night, how would you protect yourself until the police arrived? You're surprised at how much safer you feel with the gun in the house.

Next, you realize that you want that sense of safety to travel with you. So you sign up for a concealed-carry permit class. You gather one night with friends and neighbors and spend the next eight hours combining a self-defense class with a dash of world-view training. And when you carry your weapon, you don't feel intimidated, you feel empowered. In a way that's tough to explain, the fact that you're so much less dependent on the state for your personal security and safety makes you feel more "free" than you've ever felt before.

And as your worldview changes, you expand your knowledge. You learn that people defend themselves with guns all the time, usually without pulling the trigger. You share the stories and your own experience with your friends, and soon they walk into gun stores. They start their own journey into America's "gun culture."

At the end of this process, your life has changed for the better. Your community has expanded to include people you truly like, who've perhaps helped you through a tough time in your life, and you treasure these relationships. You feel a sense of burning conviction that you, your family, and your community are safer and freer because you own and carry a gun.

It's a myth that gun owners despise regulation. Instead, they tend to believe   15
that government regulation should have two purposes—deny guns to the dangerous while protecting rights of access for the law-abiding. The formula is simple: Criminals and the dangerously mentally ill make our nation more violent. Law-abiding gun owners save and protect lives.

Thus the overwhelming support for background checks, the insistence from gun-rights supporters that the government enforce existing laws and lock up violent offenders, and the openness to solutions—like so-called "gun violence restraining orders" that specifically target troubled individuals for intervention.

Progressive policy prescriptions, like assault-weapons bans and bans on large-capacity magazines, are opposed because they're perceived to have exactly the wrong effect. They'll present only the most minor of hurdles for the lawless, while the law-abiding experience the law's full effect. It's a form of collective punishment for the innocent, a mere annoyance—at best—for the lawless.

Many gun-rights supporters were appalled to learn after the Sutherland Springs shooting that the military was systematically underreporting disqualifying convictions to the federal background check database. Under pressure, the military has added more than 4,000 new names in just three months. Similarly, law-enforcement failures or background-check failures that preceded, for example, the Virginia Tech, Charleston, Orlando, Sutherland Springs, and Parkland shootings[1] are spurring serious new consideration of the gun violence restraining order, a move that would allow family members and others close to a potential shooter to get in front of a judge to request that the court direct law enforcement to temporarily seize a dangerous person's weapons. It gives ordinary citizens a chance to "do something" after they "see something" and "say something."

1. Various mass shootings: On April 16, 2007, a gunman at Virginia Polytechnic Institute and State University shot forty-nine people, killing thirty-two; on June 17, 2015, a racially motivated gunman shot and killed nine African Americans at a prayer group meeting at the Emanuel African Methodist Episcopal Church in Charleston, South Carolina; on June 12, 2016, a gunman entered a gay nightclub and shot 102 people, killing forty-nine; on November 5, 2017, a gunman shot forty-six people at the First Baptist Church in Sutherland Springs, Texas, killing twenty-six; on February 14, 2018, a gunman shot thirty-four people at Marjory Stoneman Douglas High School in Parkland, Florida, killing seventeen.

It's against this backdrop of experience and sincere belief that gun owners experience the extraordinarily toxic rhetoric of the public gun debate. People who want to stop murders are compared to terrorists. People who want to prevent guns from falling into the wrong hands are compared to mass shooters. People are told they have "blood on their hands," when they aspire to have all the courage that Broward County School Resource Officer Scot Peterson[2] so clearly lacked.

20   And make no mistake, when it comes to rhetoric, the gun-owning community can give as good as it gets. A movement that's kind and generous to its friends and allies turns instantly on its enemies, eager to believe the absolute worst about political opponents who are genuinely stricken by the carnage in places like Parkland and Sandy Hook.[3]

Because of the threats against my family—and because I don't want to be dependent on a sometimes shockingly incompetent government for my family's security—I carry a weapon. My wife does as well. We're not scared. We're prepared, and that sense of preparation is contagious. Confidence is contagious. People want to be empowered. That's how gun culture is built. Not by the NRA[4] and not by Congress, but by gun owners, one free citizen at a time.

MLA CITATION

French, David. "What Critics Don't Understand about Gun Culture." *The Norton Reader: An Anthology of Nonfiction*, edited by Melissa A. Goldthwaite et al., 15th ed., W. W. Norton, 2020, pp. 893–96.

QUESTIONS

1. What, according to David French, is "gun culture?" Why are people drawn to it? What are the feelings, values, and opinions that characterize it?

2. French refers throughout his essay to the multiple "threats" he and his family have received, but except for his opening anecdote (paragraphs 1–3), he offers no details about them. Does his choice to leave the nature of these "threats" unspecified make his essay more or less persuasive? Why?

3. Compare David French's stance on gun control with Emma González's "Fighting for Gun Control" (pp. 890–92). Where do they disagree? Where do they find common ground? Compare French's essay with Joy Castro's "Grip" (pp. 888–89). In what ways does Castro fit French's portrait of a typical gun owner? In what ways does she differ from or complicate it?

4. Would you want to own a gun? Write an essay explaining why or why not.

---

2. During the Parkland shooting, this police deputy remained outside the school, rather than entering to confront the shooter.

3. On December 14, 2012, a gunman entered the Sandy Hook Elementary School in Newtown, Connecticut, and killed twenty-six people, twenty of them young children.

4. National Rifle Association, a pro-gun lobbying organization.

TERESA M. BEJAN

The Two Clashing Meanings of "Free Speech"

L ITTLE DISTINGUISHES DEMOCRACY IN AMERICA more sharply from Europe than the primacy—and permissiveness—of our commitment to free speech. Yet ongoing controversies at American universities suggest that free speech is becoming a partisan issue. While conservative students defend the importance of inviting controversial speakers to campus and giving offense, many self-identified liberals are engaged in increasingly disruptive, even violent, efforts to shut them down. Free speech for some, they argue, serves only to silence and exclude others. Denying hateful or historically "privileged" voices a platform is thus necessary to make *equality* effective, so that the marginalized and vulnerable can finally speak up—and be heard.

The reason that appeals to the First Amendment cannot decide these campus controversies is because there is a more fundamental conflict between two, very different concepts of free speech at stake. The conflict between what the ancient Greeks called *isegoria*, on the one hand, and *parrhesia*, on the other, is as old as democracy itself. Today, both terms are often translated as "freedom of speech," but their meanings were and are importantly distinct. In ancient Athens, *isegoria* described the equal right of citizens to participate in public debate in the democratic assembly; *parrhesia*, the license to say what one pleased, how and when one pleased, and to whom.

When it comes to private universities, businesses, or social media, the would-be censors are our fellow-citizens, not the state. Private entities like Facebook or Twitter, not to mention Yale or Middlebury, have broad rights to regulate and exclude the speech of their members. Likewise, online mobs are made up of outraged individuals exercising their own right to speak freely. To invoke the First Amendment in such cases is not a knock-down argument, it's a non sequitur.[1]

John Stuart Mill[2] argued that the chief threat to free speech in democracies was not the state, but the "social tyranny" of one's fellow citizens. And yet today, the civil libertarians who style themselves as Mill's inheritors have for the most part failed to refute, or even address, the arguments about free speech and equality that their opponents are making.

The two ancient concepts of free speech came to shape our modern liberal   5 democratic notions in fascinating and forgotten ways. But more importantly, understanding that there is not one, but *two* concepts of freedom of speech,

Published in the Atlantic *(2017), a magazine covering literature, culture, and politics. Teresa M. Bejan is the author of* Mere Civility: Disagreement and the Limits of Toleration *(2017).*

1. Latin for "does not follow," a logically invalid argument.

2. British utilitarian philosopher, economist, and political theorist (1806–1873); author of *On Liberty* (1859).

and that these are often in tension if not outright conflict, helps explain the frustrating shape of contemporary debates, both in the U.S. and in Europe— and why it so often feels as though we are talking past each other when it comes to the things that matter most.

Of the two ancient concepts of free speech, *isegoria* is the older. The term dates back to the fifth century B.C.E., although historians disagree as to when the democratic practice of permitting any citizen who wanted to address the assembly actually began. Despite the common translation "freedom of speech," the Greek literally means something more like "equal speech in public." The verb *agoreuein*, from which it derives, shares a root with the word *agora* or marketplace—that is, a public place where people, including philosophers like Socrates,[3] would gather together and talk.

In the democracy of Athens, this idea of addressing an informal gathering in the *agora* carried over into the more formal setting of the *ekklesia* or political assembly. The herald would ask, "Who will address the assemblymen?" and then the volunteer would ascend the *bema*, or speaker's platform. In theory, *isegoria* meant that any Athenian citizen in good standing had the right to participate in debate and try to persuade his fellow citizens. In practice, the number of participants was fairly small, limited to the practiced rhetoricians and elder statesmen seated near the front. (Disqualifying offenses included prostitution and taking bribes.)

Although Athens was not the only democracy in the ancient world, from the beginning the Athenian principle of *isegoria* was seen as something special. The historian Herodotus[4] even described the form of government at Athens not as *demokratia*, but as *isegoria* itself. According to the fourth-century orator and patriot Demosthenes, the Athenian constitution was based on speeches (*politeia en logois*) and its citizens had chosen *isegoria* as a way of life. But for its critics, this was a bug, as well as a feature. One critic, the so-called "Old Oligarch,"[5] complained that even slaves and foreigners enjoyed *isegoria* at Athens, hence one could not beat them as one might elsewhere.

Critics like the Old Oligarch may have been exaggerating for comic effect, but they also had a point: as its etymology suggests, *isegoria* was fundamentally about equality, not freedom. As such, it would become the hallmark of Athenian democracy, which distinguished itself from the other Greek city-states *not* because it excluded slaves and women from citizenship (as did every society in the history of humankind until quite recently), but rather because it *included the poor*. Athens even took positive steps to render this equality of public speech effective by introducing pay for the poorest citizens to attend the assembly and to serve as jurors in the courts.

---

3. Greek philosopher (470–399 B.C.E.).

4. Greek historian (484–c. 430/420 B.C.E.) whose *History* documents the Greco-Persian Wars (492–449 B.C.E.).

5. Unknown author of the political treatise "Constitution of the Athenians."

As a form of free speech then, *isegoria* was essentially political. Its competitor, *parrhesia*, was more expansive. Here again, the common English translation "freedom of speech" can be deceptive. The Greek means something like "all saying" and comes closer to the idea of speaking freely or "frankly." *Parrhesia* thus implied openness, honesty, and the courage to tell the truth, even when it meant causing offense. The practitioner of *parrhesia* (or *parrhesiastes*) was, quite literally, a "say-it-all."

Parrhesia could have a political aspect. Demosthenes and other orators stressed the duty of those exercising *isegoria* in the assembly to speak their minds. But the concept applied more often outside of the *ekklesia* in more and less informal settings. In the theater, *parrhesiastic* playwrights like Aristophanes offended all and sundry by skewering their fellow citizens, including Socrates, by name. But the paradigmatic *parrhesiastes* in the ancient world were the Philosophers, self-styled "lovers of wisdom" like Socrates himself who would confront their fellow citizens in the *agora* and tell them whatever hard truths they least liked to hear. Among these was Diogenes the Cynic,[6] who famously lived in a barrel, masturbated in public, and told Alexander the Great[7] to get out of his light—all, so he said, to reveal the truth to his fellow Greeks about the arbitrariness of their customs.

The danger intrinsic in *parrhesia*'s offensiveness to the powers-that-be—be they monarchs like Alexander or the democratic majority—fascinated Michel Foucault, who made it the subject of a series of lectures at Berkeley (home of the original campus Free Speech Movement) in the 1980s.[8] Foucault noticed that the practice of *parrhesia* necessarily entailed an asymmetry of power, hence a "contract" between the audience (whether one or many), who pledged to tolerate any offense, and the speaker, who agreed to tell them the truth and risk the consequences.

If *isegoria* was fundamentally about equality, then, *parrhesia* was about liberty in the sense of *license*—not a right, but rather an unstable privilege enjoyed at the pleasure of the powerful. In Athenian democracy, that usually meant the majority of one's fellow citizens, who were known to shout down or even drag speakers they disliked (including Plato's brother, Glaucon[9]) off the *bema*. This ancient version of "no-platforming" speakers who offended popular sensibilities could have deadly consequences—as the trial and death of Socrates, Plato's friend and teacher, attests.[10]

Noting the lack of success that Plato's loved ones enjoyed with both *isegoria* and *parrhesia* during his lifetime may help explain why the father of Western philosophy didn't set great store by either concept in his works. Plato no doubt

6. Greek philosopher (unknown–c. 320 B.C.E.).

7. King of Macedonia (356–323 B.C.E.) whose conquests resulted in a vast empire stretching from Greece to India.

8. Michel Foucault (1926–1984), French philosopher, historian, and political theorist; Free Speech Movement, student-led protest movement in the 1960s.

9. Plato, Greek philosopher (c. 429–347 B.C.E.).

10. Socrates was condemned to death for the crime of corrupting Athenian youth.

would have noticed that, despite their differences, *neither* concept relied upon the most famous and distinctively Greek understanding of speech as *logos*— that is, reason or logical argument. Plato's student, Aristotle,[11] would identify *logos* as the capacity that made human beings essentially *political* animals in the first place. And yet neither *isegoria* nor *parrhesia* identified the reasoned speech and arguments of *logos* as uniquely deserving of equal liberty *or* license. Which seems to have been Plato's point—how was it that a democratic city that prided itself on free speech, in all of its forms, put to death the one Athenian ruled by *logos* for speaking it?

15   Unsurprisingly perhaps, *parrhesia* survived the demise of Athenian democracy more easily than *isegoria*. As Greek democratic institutions were crushed by the Macedonian empire,[12] then the Roman, *parrhesia* persisted as a rhetorical trope. A thousand years after the fall of Rome, Renaissance humanists[13] would revive *parrhesia* as the distinctive virtue of the counselor speaking to a powerful prince in need of frank advice. While often couched in apologetics, this *parrhesia* retained its capacity to shock. The hard truths presented by Machiavelli and Hobbes to their would-be sovereigns would inspire generations of "libertine" thinkers to come.[14]

Still, there was another adaptation of the *parrhesiastic* tradition of speaking truth to power available to early modern Europeans. The early Christians took a page from Diogenes's book in spreading the "good news" of the Gospel throughout the Greco-Roman world—news that may not have sounded all that great to the Roman authorities. Many of the Christians who styled themselves as "Protestants" after the Reformation thought that a return to an authentically *parrhesiastic* and deliberately offensive form of evangelism was necessary to restore the Church to the purity of "primitive" Christianity. The early Quakers, for example, were known to interrupt Anglican services by shouting down the minister and to go naked in public "for a sign."[15]

Isegoria, too, had its early modern inheritors. But in the absence of democratic institutions like the Athenian *ekklesia*, it necessarily took a different form. The 1689 English Bill of Rights secured "the freedom of speech and debates in Parliament," and so applied to members of Parliament only, and only when they were present in the chamber. For the many who lacked access to formal political participation, the idea of *isegoria* as an equal right of public

---

11. Greek philosopher (384–322 B.C.E.).

12. Created by Alexander the Great.

13. Fall of Rome, traditionally dated to 476 C.E.; Renaissance humanism, early modern European intellectual and cultural movement valuing classical learning and individual thought and expression.

14. Niccolò Machiavelli (1469–1527), Florentine statesman and political philosopher; Thomas Hobbes (1588–1679), English political philosopher.

15. Quakers, dissenting Protestant group that emerged in England in the 1600s; Anglicanism, the official Church of England.

speech belonging to all citizens would eventually migrate from the concrete public forum to the virtual public sphere.

For philosophers like Spinoza and Immanuel Kant,[16] "free speech" meant primarily the intellectual freedom to participate in the public exchange of arguments. In 1784, five years before the French Revolution,[17] Kant would insist that "the freedom to make public use of one's reason" was the fundamental and equal right of any human being or citizen. Similarly, when Mill wrote *On Liberty* less than a century later, he did not defend the freedom of speech as such, but rather the individual "freedom of thought and discussion" in the collective pursuit of truth. While the equal liberty of *isegoria* remained essential for these thinkers, they shifted focus from actual *speech*—that is, the physical act of addressing others and participating in debate—to the mental exercise of *reason* and the exchange of ideas and arguments, very often in print. And so, over the course of two millennia, the Enlightenment finally united *isegoria* and *logos* in an idealized concept of free speech as freedom only for *reasoned* speech and rational deliberation that would have made Plato proud.

This logo-centric Enlightenment ideal remains central to the European understanding of free speech today. Efforts in Europe to criminalize hate speech owe an obvious debt to Kant, who described the freedom of (reasoned) speech in public as "the most harmless" of all. The same could never be said of ancient or early modern *parrhesia*, which was always threatening to speakers and listeners alike. Indeed, it was the obvious harm caused by their *parrhesiastic* evangelism to their neighbors' religious sensibilities that led so many evangelical Protestants to flee prosecution (or persecution, as they saw it) in Europe for the greater liberty—or license—of the New World. American exceptionalism can thus be traced all the way back to the seventeenth and eighteenth centuries: while America got the evangelicals and libertines, Europe kept the philosophers.

Debates about free speech on American campuses today suggest that the rival concepts of *isegoria* and *parrhesia* are alive and well. When student protesters claim that they are silencing certain voices—via no-platforming, social pressure, or outright censorship—in the name of free speech itself, it may be tempting to dismiss them as insincere, or at best confused. As I witnessed at an event at Kenyon College in September, when confronted with such arguments the response from gray-bearded free-speech fundamentalists like myself is to continue to preach to the converted about the First Amendment, but with an undercurrent of solidaristic despair about "kids these days" and their failure to understand the fundamentals of liberal democracy.

No wonder the "kids" are unpersuaded. While trigger warnings, safe spaces, and no-platforming grab headlines, poll after poll suggests that a more

20

16. Benedict de Spinoza (1632–1677), Dutch Jewish philosopher; Immanuel Kant (1724–1804), German philosopher.

17. Revolution resulting in the end of the *ancien régime* or "old order."

TERESA M. BEJAN

subtle, shift in mores is afoot. To a generation convinced that hateful speech is itself a form of violence or "silencing," pleading the First Amendment is to miss the point. Most of these students do not see themselves as standing against free speech at all. What they care about is the *equal right* to speech, and equal access to a public forum in which the historically marginalized and excluded can be heard and count equally with the privileged. This is a claim to *isegoria*, and once one recognizes it as such, much else becomes clear—including the contrasting appeal to *parrhesia* by their opponents, who sometimes seem determined to reduce "free speech" to a license to offend.

Recognizing the ancient ideas at work in these modern arguments puts those of us committed to America's *parrhesiastic* tradition of speaking truth to power in a better position to defend it. It suggests that to defeat the modern proponents of *isegoria*—and remind the modern *parrhesiastes* what they are fighting for—one must go beyond the First Amendment to the other, orienting principle of American democracy behind it, namely *equality*. After all, the genius of the First Amendment lies in bringing *isegoria* and *parrhesia* together, by securing the equal right and liberty of citizens not simply to "exercise their reason" but to speak their minds. It does so because the alternative is to allow the powers-that-happen-to-be to grant that liberty as a *license* to some individuals while denying it to others.

In contexts where the Constitution does not apply, like a private university, this opposition to arbitrariness is a matter of culture, not law, but it is no less pressing and important for that. As the evangelicals, protesters, and provocateurs who founded America's *parrhesiastic* tradition knew well: When the rights of all become the privilege of a few, neither liberty nor equality can last.

MLA CITATION

Bejan, Teresa M. "The Two Clashing Meanings of 'Free Speech.'" *The Norton Reader: An Anthology of Nonfiction*, edited by Melissa A. Goldthwaite et al., 15th ed., W. W. Norton, 2020, pp. 897–902.

QUESTIONS

1. In her essay "The Two Clashing Meanings of 'Free Speech,'" Teresa M. Bejan argues that conflicts over "free speech" on campuses today have their roots in two competing concepts of "free speech" from ancient Athens: *isegoria* and *parrhesia*. How would you explain these concepts to a peer who has not read Bejan's essay? Why is it important to recover them? (Couldn't Bejan simply have noted that people today understand "free speech" in two conflicting ways?)

2. At least twice, Bejan distinguishes between social and legal constraints on speech. Why does this distinction matter?

3. Most of Bejan's essay is devoted to developing the claim she makes at the end of her introduction, that recognizing that "free speech" has two competing meanings can help to explain why present-day debates over "free speech" seem so intractable (paragraph 5). She waits until the final section of her essay, however,

to state her own perspective. What is that perspective, and why might Bejan have waited until her conclusion to state it explicitly? Can you detect hints of it earlier in her essay?

4. Use Bejan's distinction between *isegoria* and *parrhesia* to analyze a specific instance of conflict over free speech on campus. You may write about an instance described in one of this chapter's other readings or identify one of your own.

LISA FELDMAN BARRETT
When Is Speech Violence?

IMAGINE THAT A BULLY threatens to punch you in the face. A week later, he walks up to you and breaks your nose with his fist. Which is more harmful: the punch or the threat?

The answer might seem obvious: Physical violence is physically damaging; verbal statements aren't. "Sticks and stones can break my bones, but words will never hurt me."[1]

But scientifically speaking, it's not that simple. Words can have a powerful effect on your nervous system. Certain types of adversity, even those involving no physical contact, can make you sick, alter your brain—even kill neurons—and shorten your life.

Your body's immune system includes little proteins called proinflammatory cytokines that cause inflammation when you're physically injured. Under certain conditions, however, these cytokines themselves can cause physical illness. What are those conditions? One of them is chronic stress.

Your body also contains little packets of genetic material that sit on the ends of your chromosomes. They're called telomeres. Each time your cells divide, their telomeres get a little shorter, and when they become too short, you die. This is normal aging. But guess what else shrinks your telomeres? Chronic stress.

If words can cause stress, and if prolonged stress can cause physical harm, then it seems that speech—at least certain types of speech—can be a form of violence. But which types?

This question has taken on some urgency in the past few years, as professed defenders of social justice have clashed with professed defenders of free speech on college campuses. Student advocates have protested vigorously, even violently, against invited speakers whose views they consider not just offensive but harmful—hence the desire to silence, not debate, the speaker. "Trigger warnings" are based on a similar principle: that discussions of certain

5

Published in the New York Times *(2017). Lisa Feldman Barrett is a psychologist and neuroscientist who studies human emotion*

1. Common childhood saying in the English-speaking world.

topics will trigger, or reproduce, past trauma—as opposed to merely challenging or discomfiting the student. The same goes for "microaggressions."[2]

This idea—that there is often no difference between speech and violence—has struck many as a coddling or infantilizing of students, as well as a corrosive influence on the freedom of expression necessary for intellectual progress. It's a safe bet that the Pew survey data released on Monday,[3] which showed that Republicans' views of colleges and universities have taken a sharp negative turn since 2015, results in part from exasperation with the "speech equals violence" equation.

The scientific findings I described above provide empirical guidance for which kinds of controversial speech should and shouldn't be acceptable on campus and in civil society. In short, the answer depends on whether the speech is abusive or merely offensive.

10   Offensiveness is not bad for your body and brain. Your nervous system evolved to withstand periodic bouts of stress, such as fleeing from a tiger, taking a punch or encountering an odious idea in a university lecture.

Entertaining someone else's distasteful perspective can be educational. Early in my career, I taught a course that covered the eugenics movement, which advocated the selective breeding of humans. Eugenics, in its time, became a scientific justification for racism. To help my students understand this ugly part of scientific history, I assigned them to debate its pros and cons. The students refused. No one was willing to argue, even as part of a classroom exercise, that certain races were genetically superior to others.

So I enlisted an African-American faculty member in my department to argue in favor of eugenics while I argued against; halfway through the debate, we switched sides. We were modeling for the students a fundamental principle of a university education, as well as civil society: When you're forced to engage a position you strongly disagree with, you learn something about the other perspective as well as your own. The process feels unpleasant, but it's a good kind of stress—temporary and not harmful to your body—and you reap the longer-term benefits of learning.

What's bad for your nervous system, in contrast, are long stretches of simmering stress. If you spend a lot of time in a harsh environment worrying about your safety, that's the kind of stress that brings on illness and remodels your brain. That's also true of a political climate in which groups of people endlessly hurl hateful words at one another, and of rampant bullying in school or on social media. A culture of constant, casual brutality is toxic to the body, and we suffer for it.

2. Term coined by psychiatrist Chester M. Pierce in 1970 for small, perhaps even unintentional, slights directed to a member of a minority group.

3. The Pew Research Center is a "nonpartisan fact tank" that conducts public opinion research; this survey was released on Monday, July 10, 2017.

That's why it's reasonable, scientifically speaking, not to allow a provocateur and hatemonger like Milo Yiannopoulos[4] to speak at your school. He is part of something noxious, a campaign of abuse. There is nothing to be gained from debating him, for debate is not what he is offering.

On the other hand, when the political scientist Charles Murray[5] argues   15
that genetic factors help account for racial disparities in I.Q. scores, you might find his view to be repugnant and misguided, but it's only offensive. It is offered as a scholarly hypothesis to be debated, not thrown like a grenade. There is a difference between permitting a culture of casual brutality and entertaining an opinion you strongly oppose. The former is a danger to a civil society (and to our health); the latter is the lifeblood of democracy.

By all means, we should have open conversations and vigorous debate about controversial or offensive topics. But we must also halt speech that bullies and torments. From the perspective of our brain cells, the latter is literally a form of violence.

MLA CITATION

Barrett, Lisa Feldman. "When Is Speech Violence?" *The Norton Reader: An Anthology of Nonfiction*, edited by Melissa A. Goldthwaite et al., 15th ed., W. W. Norton, 2020, pp. 903–05.

QUESTIONS

1. Lisa Feldman Barrett's argument—"If words can cause stress, and if prolonged stress can cause physical harm, then it seems that speech—at least certain types of speech—can be a form of violence" (paragraph 6)—depends on four terms: *speech*, *harm*, *stress*, and *violence*. How does Barrett understand each of these terms, and how do these understandings inform her reasoning?

2. Does Barrett's appeal to science make her argument more or less persuasive? Why?

3. Barrett illustrates the distinction between speech that is "abusive" and speech that is "merely offensive" (paragraph 9) with an anecdote about her own teaching: she and another professor took up opposing views on a controversial topic and then switched sides. What was the point of this demonstration, and how might you have responded to it if you were one of Barrett's students?

4. Write two responses to Barrett's op-ed, one in which you offer further support for her argument and another in which you challenge it.

4. British political commentator and speaker (b. 1984) known for his aggressively provocative statements; associated with the "alt-right."
5. F. A. Hayek Emeritus Chair in Cultural Studies (b. 1943) at the American Enterprise Institute, a conservative think tank.

HADAR HARRIS AND MARY BETH TINKER
Hate Speech Is Showing Up in Schools

Black HIGH SCHOOL STUDENTS demonstrate during the national anthem to protest police brutality and racism. They are punished. A group of predominantly white students smile and laugh as they appear to give the Nazi salute in a pre-prom photo. That school district says the students are protected by free-speech rights.

Same First Amendment, different outcomes.

Many have cited these incidents as evidence that white students receive more free-speech protections than students of color. While that is generally true, it's not uniform. At one Maryland school, a football coach supported the decision of his team—predominantly black players—to kneel.[1] At another, the superintendent is supporting a ban on the Confederate flag in the school dress code.[2]

Students' free-speech rights are constantly evolving, in the courts and in society. Despite legal precedents, students' rights are applied in a hodgepodge, unpredictable way. Although school districts are advised by an army of lawyers dedicated to keeping school communities in compliance, schools are made up of humans who often react to student speech with human emotion and their own internalized biases.

5   The result is that students do not enjoy equal speech rights. And too often, that means students of color and low-income students are slighted. We must change that—not by reducing the rights of some students, but by expanding the rights of all.

Race often has been implicated when students' free speech rights have been restricted. Ironically, the legal standard that expanded those rights is rooted in black student activism. During the civil rights movement's Mississippi Freedom Summer—when three young activists were murdered by members of the Ku Klux Klan[3]—black high school students protested by wearing buttons to school that read "One Man One Vote." For that, they were suspended.

The students took their case, *Burnside v. Byars*, to court and won at the U.S. Court of Appeals for the 5th Circuit in 1966. The ruling established that students have free speech rights in public schools if they do not substantially disrupt the learning environment.

Published in the Washington Post *(2018). Hadar Harris, an attorney specializing in human rights issues, is the executive director of the Student Press Law Center, which defends the First Amendment rights of student journalists; Mary Beth Tinker is a free-speech advocate and, at age 13, was the plaintiff in an important student free-speech case,* Tinker v. Des Moines Independent Community School District *(1969).*

1. Capital Christian Academy, an African American–run school in Lanham, Maryland; the team was emulating Colin Kaepernick, then quarterback of the San Francisco 49ers, who originated the gesture of kneeling during the national anthem in 2016.

2. A number of schools, including schools in Indiana, Montana, North Carolina, and South Carolina, have instituted such bans.

3. White supremacist group with a history of violence toward African Americans.

The "substantial disruption" standard came into play soon after in Mary Beth's own free speech case. She, her brother, John, and their friend Chris Eckhart wore black armbands to school to protest the Vietnam War. That peaceful protest led to their suspension and then a lawsuit by the American Civil Liberties Union. The 1969 Supreme Court ruling established a core principle of First Amendment law: that public school students do not "shed their constitutional rights to freedom of speech or expression at the schoolhouse gate." But, as with any rights, there would be limits. In establishing the Tinker standard, the Supreme Court reaffirmed that students' speech cannot cause "material and substantial" disruption of normal school activities or impinge on the rights of others.

Over the past 50 years, that standard has been applied inconsistently. While there are no statistics on how schools enforce students' free speech rights based on race, we know that schools generally punish students of color more severely than white students for similar behaviors.

Black students are suspended and expelled three times more often than white students, according to a U.S. Department of Education report. On average, 5 percent of white students are suspended, compared with 16 percent of black students. Black girls are suspended at a higher rate, 12 percent, than girls of any other race or ethnicity and more than most boys. The disparate rates also apply to American Indian and Native Alaskan students.

Even before getting to discipline, there is a sliding scale when it comes to the free speech rights that youth enjoy. We visit schools throughout the country, and it is undeniable that white students and higher-income students have more rights than others. They are much less likely to have strict dress code restrictions and much more likely to have outlets for expression such as school newspapers and journalism programs. Because of systemic racism and poverty, some students' speech is more privileged over others.

Some people want schools to even the playing field by taking a more forceful position against hateful comments and symbols. Speech that attacks a person or a group on the basis of race, religion, ethnic or national origin, gender, disability, sexual orientation or gender identity may impinge on the rights of others or, if it's serious enough, disrupt school, in violation of the Tinker ruling.

In one 2014 case, students who wore American flag shirts to school to mock Hispanic students on Cinco de Mayo were required to change their shirts or leave, because school officials anticipated they would cause substantial disruption because of previous altercations. The 9th Circuit Court upheld the school's decision because the provocation of the shirts would lead to a "material and substantial disruption."

Many critical race theorists and human rights advocates question why such hate speech should have First Amendment protection when its aim is to harm marginalized groups.

The Baraboo school district in Wisconsin, where students were photographed making an apparent Nazi salute, has been criticized for not punishing hateful speech. But we believe the district was correct. Instead of leaning on censorship, the district is addressing the problem in a way that will be ultimately more effective—holding community meetings and workshops, encouraging dialogue, and planning curricular interventions. Along the same lines, instead of disciplining students who kneel during the national anthem, many school districts have facilitated discussions about police brutality and racism.

Some believe that the damage caused by hate speech can't be countered by more "good" speech because unequal power relationships inhibit vulnerable groups' ability to respond effectively. But the response shouldn't be on the shoulders of marginalized groups alone. In Baraboo, school officials are using the pre-prom photo as a starting point to involve the entire community in grappling with the core issues of racism and anti-Semitism.

Many school districts have implemented anti-racism and anti-Semitism programs for their students, and there are good programs available like "Teaching Tolerance" of the Southern Poverty Law Center or Facing History and Ourselves.[4] For schools seeking to help their students deal with these issues, and to use their free speech rights in productive ways, these are a good place to start.

Education and democracy are controversial. Without controversy, there is no democracy or education. As advocates of student free speech, we believe that schools need to face controversy. And we need to deal with the inequalities in schools and communities that prevent equal access to free speech.

MLA CITATION

Harris, Hadar, and Mary Beth Tinker. "Hate Speech Is Showing Up in Schools." *The Norton Reader: An Anthology of Nonfiction*, edited by Melissa A. Goldthwaite et al., 15th ed., W. W. Norton, 2020, pp. 906–08.

QUESTIONS

1. Hadar Harris and Mary Beth Tinker note, "Despite legal precedents, students' [free-speech] rights are applied in a hodgepodge, unpredictable way" (paragraph 4). According to their op-ed, what factors contribute to this disparity, and how are they related?

2. Harris and Tinker argue for expanding the free-speech rights of all students. How do they answer those who would address the problem of "hate speech" by further constraining or censoring students' speech?

3. Do some research to learn more about one of the free-speech controversies that Harris and Tinker discuss. In an essay of your own, explain the episode and assess the way it was handled. What happened? How did the school, students, parents, legal authorities, or others respond? Were these responses justified or appropriate? What larger lessons about free speech can this episode teach us?

---

4. Southern Poverty Law Center, American civil rights legal and advocacy organization; Facing History and Ourselves, non-profit organization that develops education materials addressing anti-Semitism, racism, and other forms of intolerance.

ERWIN CHEMERINSKY AND HOWARD GILLMAN

What Students Think about Free Speech

A LTHOUGH IT IS FOOLHARDY to generalize about a generation of college students, their understanding and attitude about freedom of speech was strikingly different from what we, two baby-boomers,[1] expected when we began teaching a course on free speech on college campuses to 15 freshmen at the University of California at Irvine.

In the course we studied the basic principles of freedom of speech, including its history through Supreme Court decisions addressing restrictions on speech during World War I, World War II, the McCarthy era, the civil-rights movement, and the Vietnam War.[2] We discussed categories of speech that have been traditionally considered outside of First Amendment protection—such as incitement, fighting words, true threats, harassment, and defamation. We also looked at all of the decisions on student speech and focused a great deal of attention on recent controversies on college campuses.

At the very beginning of the course we discussed the story of the Sigma Alpha Epsilon fraternity members at the University of Oklahoma who had been videotaped chanting racist slurs aboard a bus. We had the students consider a hypothetical scenario in which one of the expelled students sues the university, claiming a violation of First Amendment rights. When asked to vote whether the student or university should win the lawsuit, our students voted unanimously in favor of the university and against free-speech rights. We concluded the course by polling them again on the same problem, and then the students split almost evenly. The difference in the discussion was remarkable; the instinctive desire to eradicate racist speech was replaced by all of the students seeing the need to strike a balance between free speech and creating a positive learning environment for all on campus.

Still, despite some evolution in their thinking, our students were skeptical of well-established precedents for the protection of offensive or hateful speech. Why? Here's what we learned from them:

Published in the Chronicle of Higher Education *(2016). Erwin Chemerinsky and Howard Gillman, both distinguished scholars of Constitutional law, are the authors of* Free Speech on Campus *(2017), among many other books. Chemerinsky is also dean of Berkeley Law, and Gillman is chancellor of the University of California at Irvine, where the course they describe in this essay was taught.*

1. People born from 1946 to 1964.
2. World War I, 1914–1918; World War II, 1939–1945; McCarthy Era, 1950–1954, Joseph McCarthy (1908–1957) was a United States senator and vehement anti-Communist; civil-rights movement, mid-1950s–mid-1960s, American protest movement challenging racial discrimination; Vietnam War, 1954–1975, the United States' military involvement in Vietnam expanded through the early 1960s and prompted widespread protests and civil unrest in the United States.

5   This generation has a very strong and persistent instinct to protect others against hateful, discriminatory, or intolerant speech, especially in educational settings.

This is the first generation of students to be educated, from a young age, not to bully. For as long as they can remember, their schools have organized "tolerance weeks." Their teachers and coaches are (thankfully) less likely to mock or shame students for poor performance. Compared to when the two of us were in middle and high school in the 1960s and '70s, there are much greater efforts to avoid making young people feel bad about themselves.

Our students often related personal stories of how bullying at school and on social media had affected people they cared about. They are deeply sensitized to the psychological harm associated with hateful or intolerant speech, and their instinct is to be protective. We realized that common descriptions of this generation of college students too often omits this sense of compassion and the admirable desire to protect their fellow students.

Additionally, arguments about the social value of freedom of speech are very abstract to today's undergraduates because they did not grow up at a time when the act of punishing speech was associated with hurting people and undermining other worthwhile values. Our students knew little about the history of free speech in the United States and had no awareness of how speech often had been directed to helping vulnerable political minorities: anti-imperialists, workers' rights advocates, and progressives in the 1910s and '20s; religious minorities during World War II; leftists during the McCarthy era; civil-rights advocates; anti-war protesters during the Vietnam War; student free-speech advocates.

The two of us grew up during the time of civil-rights and anti–Vietnam War protests. Much of the speech that was considered important to protect was raucous and even profane. Protesters burned draft cards, flags, and bras; cities prosecuted people who wore T-shirts that expressed obscene sentiments about the draft; authors, publishers, and even comedians risked jail by pushing against historic prohibitions against indecency or obscenity. We saw firsthand how officials attempted to stifle or punish protesters by claiming that they were defending community values or responding to threats to the public peace. We also saw how stronger principles of free speech assisted the drive for desegregation, the push to end the war, and the efforts of historically marginalized people to challenge convention and express their identities in new ways. In our experience, speech that was sometimes considered offensive, or that made people uncomfortable, was a good and necessary thing for progress.

10   For today's students, the historic link between free speech and the protection of dissenters and vulnerable groups is outside their direct experience, and too distant to affect their feelings about freedom of speech. As a result, their initial instinct was to be more trusting of the government and other public institutions, including the university, to regulate speech to protect students and prevent disruptions of the educational environment.

As the course went on, our students gained a deeper understanding of the potential for the abuse of power when officials are authorized to restrict unpopular speech. However, they continued to be concerned that the court's categories of unprotected speech were not broad enough to deal with certain harms that concerned them. For example, they worried that the definition of "incitement" was not broad enough to allow the government to stop international terrorists from using the Internet to recruit converts and help those recruits plan terrorist attacks.

They supported the rights of Westboro Baptist Church protesters,[3] known for staging antigay protests at military funerals, among other spectacles, even though that speech was deeply offensive and inflicted emotional harm. But in educational settings, they wanted officials to do all they can to create a supportive learning environment. There was no support among our students for the right of a faculty member to resist a university requirement to include "trigger warnings" on syllabi. They acknowledged the right of a faculty member to criticize such a mandate, but as was the case with their K-12 teachers, they thought the main role of the faculty member was to create a nurturing learning environment, not to be confrontational. They were not used to teachers who believed that learning could take place in an environment where students were made uncomfortable, or were forced to reflect on disturbing topics, or had their views challenged rather than always validated.

Studying free-speech law made them much more nuanced in drawing distinctions as to what speech to allow and what to punish. Some drew a distinction based on whether the hateful speech was directed to others or expressed more generally. This accounts for some of the change in votes regarding the Sigma Alpha Epsilon fraternity example. But they worried that if the university only restricted speech that amounted to "harassment" or "true threats," there would still be too much room for exclusionary, discriminatory, or insulting speech by people on campus.

The students came to recognize that campus officials should not protect people from being made uncomfortable by the expression of strongly held political or religious views. They agreed that campuses should not be cleansed of all controversial opinions or all expressions that some might consider offensive.

Still, they remained skeptical of the value of defending hateful or discriminatory speech that was not clearly tied to deeply held beliefs about religion or politics. Divisive ideas that were sincerely held seemed like a different thing than being mean, trying to make people feel bad, or other speech acts that seemed to have no social value worth protecting. The on-campus presence of people who had hateful or judgmental opinions—even if those opinions were expressed off campus or online—was a serious matter of concern. Our students acknowledged that one could decide to deal with this problem

15

3. Church based in Topeka, Kansas; identified as a "hate group" by multiple civil rights organizations.

with more speech rather than restrictions or punishments, but they were not sure this was enough to protect their peers from psychological distress.

Finally, we realized that current debates about the appropriate boundaries of campus free speech will not be a mere replay of 1990s battles over campus "hate speech" codes. We found what has recently been reported by the Pew Research Center[4] to be true: Millennials[5] are much more supportive of censoring offensive statements about minorities. They are also much less amenable to being persuaded by countervailing arguments about the need to protect hateful speech. This is not just a matter of not being exposed to pro-speech arguments or not taking them seriously. These were bright and thoughtful students at a leading research university, and they are thinking about these issues in fresh ways.

As debates continue about the appropriate boundaries of free speech on college campuses, strong free-speech advocates—and we consider ourselves in this category—cannot assume that the social benefits of broad free-speech protections will be automatically appreciated by a generation that has not lived through decades-long struggles against censorship and punishment of protesters, dissenters, and iconoclasts. As American history has demonstrated, there is no natural or inevitable instinct to support speech that many people consider disruptive, offensive, or even countercultural. The country has a much longer history of suppressing unpopular speakers than protecting them. The pro-free-speech case needs to be made anew, and it is not the responsibility of incoming students to have already internalized the arguments.

In making the case, pro-speech advocates will not win any new friends if they are dismissive of this generation's expectation that we care about the psychological impact that hateful and intolerant speech has on its victims. The necessity of creating supportive and nondiscriminatory learning environments must be acknowledged, and advocates will need to be explicit about how broad protections for speech—including offensive and hateful speech—can be reconciled with this commitment.

MLA CITATION

Chemerinsky, Erwin, and Howard Gillman. "What Students Think about Free
    Speech." *The Norton Reader: An Anthology of Nonfiction*, edited by Melissa A.
    Goldthwaite et al., 15th ed., W. W. Norton, 2020, pp. 909–12.

QUESTIONS

1. What, according to Erwin Chemerinsky and Howard Gillman, is the attitude of today's college students toward free speech? What values and experiences do they believe this attitude reflects?

---

4. Pew Research Center, a "nonpartisan fact tank" that conducts public opinion research.

5. People born from 1981 to 1996, according to the Pew Research Center; in their use of the term, Chemerinsky and Gillman are including students born somewhat later as well.

2. Why, according to Chemerinsky and Gillman, do today's students find arguments for the "social value of freedom of speech" (paragraph 8) unpersuasive?

3. Toward the end of their essay, Chemerinsky and Gillman note that "[t]he pro-free-speech case needs to be made anew" (paragraph 17) to today's college students. Teresa M. Bejan, in her essay "The Two Clashing Meanings of 'Free Speech'" (pp. 897–902), similarly observes that "the 'kids' are unpersuaded" by the pro-free-speech arguments of "gray-bearded free-speech fundamentalists" (paragraphs 20–23). Compare Chemerinsky and Gillman's suggestions for how older free-speech advocates might productively engage today's students. What do they have in common? How do they differ? Which seems most promising?

4. Write a response to Chemerinsky and Gillman from the perspective of your own generation.

Author Biographies

Edward Abbey (1927–1989)
American essayist, novelist, and self-described "agrarian anarchist." Born in Pennsylvania, Abbey lived in the Southwest from 1948, when he began his studies at the University of New Mexico, until his death. He took as his most pervasive theme the beauty of the Southwestern desert and the ways it has been despoiled by government, business, and tourism. Abbey's novels include *Fire on the Mountain* (1963), *Good News* (1980), and *The Monkey Wrench Gang* (1975), which is credited with helping to inspire the radical environmentalist movement. He published several collections of essays, among them *Abbey's Road* (1979), *Beyond the Wall: Essays from the Outside* (1984), *One Life at a Time, Please* (1988), and, most famously, *Desert Solitaire: A Season in the Wilderness* (1968), drawing on his years as a ranger in the national parks of southern Utah. See also abbeyweb.net.

Diana Abu-Jaber (b. 1960)
American author and teacher. The daughter of a Jordanian father and an American mother, Abu-Jaber grew up in both Jordan and Upstate New York, eventually earning a Ph.D. in English and creative writing from the State University of New York at Binghamton. The six award-winning books she has written since then, including the novels *Crescent* (2003), *Origin* (2007), and *Birds of Paradise* (2011), as well as her memoirs *The Language of Baklava* (2005) and *Life without a Recipe* (2016), explore her Arab American identity and the Arab culture she knows firsthand, with a particular focus on the outsize role played by food as a cultural centerpiece. She currently teaches creative writing at Portland State University. See also dianaabujaber.com.

Chimamanda Ngozi Adichie (b. 1977)
Nigerian novelist and essayist. Adichie grew up in Nsukka, where her parents worked at the University of Nigeria. As a child, she immersed herself in British and American literature, and would eventually earn two master's degrees in the United States. But it was reading the Nigerian novelist Chinua Achebe, author of *Things Fall Apart* (1958), that convinced Adichie that Africa, too, could be a setting for great literature. Her first two novels, *Purple Hibiscus* (2003) and *Half of a Yellow Sun* (2006), as well as her short story collection *The Thing Around Your Neck* (2009), feature postcolonial Nigeria and the disastrous civil war (1967–70) in which Adichie's Igbo people attempted unsuccessfully to secede from the rest of Nigeria. Her autobiographical third novel, *Americanah* (2013), depicts a young African woman pursuing an education in the United States. Adichie was awarded a MacArthur ("Genius") Fellowship in 2008. See also www.cerep.ulg.ac.be/adichie.

Roger Angell (b. 1920)
American sportswriter and essayist. The son of *New Yorker* fiction editor Katharine Angell White and the stepson of *New Yorker* essayist E. B. White, Angell became the *New Yorker*'s fiction editor and made a name for himself as the "Poet Laureate of Baseball" for his witty and lyrical essays about the national pastime, which have appeared regularly in the *New Yorker* since 1962. His many collections of baseball writing include *Season Ticket: A Baseball Companion* (1988) and *Game Time: A Baseball Companion* (2003); his autobiography, *Let Me Finish* (2006), describes a boyhood dominated by the literary world and baseball. *This Old Man: All in Pieces* (2015) collects writings from his tenth decade. See also newyorker.com/contributors/roger-angell.

Maya Angelou (1928–2014)
American memoirist, poet, essayist, and playwright. Born Marguerite Annie Johnson in St. Louis, Missouri, Angelou attended public schools in Arkansas and California before studying music and dance. In her lifetime, she worked as a cook, streetcar conductor, singer, actress, dancer, teacher, and director, with her debut film *Down in the Delta* (1998). Author of numerous volumes of poetry (her *Complete Collected Poems*

was published in 1994) and ten plays (stage, screen, and television), Angelou may be best known for *I Know Why the Caged Bird Sings* (1969), the first volume of her autobiography and one of the most influential accounts of an African American woman's experience in contemporary literature. Angelou published her seventh and final volume of her autobiography, *Mom & Me & Mom*, in 2013. See also mayaangelou.com.

Kwame Anthony Appiah (b. 1954)
Ghanaian British philosopher, scholar, and novelist. The son of a prominent Ghanaian politician father and an English novelist mother, Appiah was educated in both Ghana and England before earning his B.A. and then his Ph.D. in philosophy at Cambridge University. He has taught at many of the world's leading universities; currently he is a professor of philosophy at New York University. His first book, *In My Father's House* (1992), examined the roots of contemporary African culture. Since then his many publications have included three novels and such scholarly works as *Color Conscious: The Political Morality of Race*, co-authored with Amy Gutmann (1996), *The Ethics of Identity* (2005), *Cosmopolitanism: Ethics in a World of Strangers* (2006), and *The Honor Code: How Moral Revolutions Happen* (2010). In 2009, the president of Princeton University included Appiah in her *Forbes* list of the world's seven "most powerful thinkers." See also appiah.net.

Noga Arikha (b. 1969)
Franco-American essayist, philosopher, and historian of ideas. The daughter of a poet and a painter, Arikha was raised in Paris, earned her B.A. at Kings College, London, and her M.A. and Ph.D. in the early modern history of ideas at London's Warburg Institute. She has taught at Bard College and now lives in Paris, where she is affiliated with the Institut Jean Nicod (École Normale Supérieure) and SPHERE (Université Paris 7). Arikha's essays have appeared in publications such as *Aeon* and *Lapham's Quarterly*. Her first book, the critically acclaimed *Passions and Tempers* (2007), is a history of the theory of the four bodily "humors," or fluids, that sustained Western medicine and psychology for 2,000 years. Arikha has recently completed a book about the embodied mind and self based on neuropsychiatric case studies; she is presently at work on a book about Franz Boas and the history of anthropology. See also nogaarikha.com.

Margaret Atwood (b. 1939)
Canadian novelist, poet, and essayist. Atwood was born in Ottawa, grew up in Ontario and Québec, earned her B.A. at Victoria College, part of the University of Toronto, and earned her master's degree from Harvard University. The author of more than forty books, Atwood has long been a literary superstar and feminist icon. She was only twenty-two when she published her first book, *Double Persephone* (1961), an award-winning collection of poems. Since then her prodigious output has included *The Edible Woman* (1969), her first novel; *Surfacing* (1972), a novel exploring gender identities and sexual politics; and *Survival: A Thematic Guide to Canadian Literature* (1972), her first foray into nonfiction. Her tenth novel, *The Blind Assassin*, won England's prestigious Booker Prize in 2000. Many of her works have been adapted for film and television, most notably *The Handmaid's Tale* (1985), her dystopian novel depicting a harsh patriarchal theocracy. See also margaretatwood.ca.

Orit Avishai (b. 1969)
Israeli ethnographer and sociologist. Born in Israel, Avishai graduated from the law school of Tel Aviv University before earning postgraduate degrees at both Yale Law School and the University of California, Berkeley. She currently teaches sociology at Fordham University in New York. Despite her secular upbringing and her education in what she calls these "bastions" of secular thought, she explains, "I became fascinated with how religious women experience their faith, precisely because I felt that feminist discourse was too dismissive of these experiences, these narratives. So I've made a career out of studying the intersection of gender, religion, and sexuality from a critical feminist perspective." Avishai is a co-author of *A Gender Lens on Religion* (2015) and is presently engaged in research on "visibility and acceptance for Orthodox Jewish LGBTQ+ persons and communities." See also fordham.edu; search for "Avishai."

James Baldwin (1924–1987)
American essayist, novelist, and social activist. Baldwin was born in Harlem, became a minister at fourteen, and grew to maturity in an America plagued by racism and homophobia. He moved to Paris in 1948 believing that only outside the United States could he be read as "not merely a Negro; or, even, merely a Negro writer." His first published novel, *Go Tell*

It on the Mountain (1953), and his first play, *The Amen Corner* (1954), are autobiographical explorations of race and identity. Although he would write other plays, Baldwin concentrated his energies on essays and on novels such as *Giovanni's Room* (1956) and *Another Country* (1962). His stories are collected in *Going to Meet the Man* (1965); his essay collections, including *Notes of a Native Son* (1955) and *The Fire Next Time* (1963), demonstrate Baldwin's skills as a social critic. See also "James Baldwin, The Art of Fiction" at parisreview.org.

Dan Barber (b. 1969)
American chef, restauranteur, and food writer. A graduate of both Tufts University, where he earned a B.A. in English, and the French Culinary Institute, Barber has combined cooking and writing throughout his career. He is a multiple winner of the prestigious James Beard Award (including Best Chef: New York City in 2006, and Outstanding Chef of the United States in 2009). Barber has become a leading voice in the local foods movement; his articles about food's origins, the consequences of certain food choices, and the sustainability of modern food production have appeared in the *New York Times*, *Gourmet*, and *Food & Wine*. His book *The Third Plate: Field Notes on the Future of Food* was published in 2014. Barber is chef and co-owner of Blue Hill in Manhattan and Blue Hill at Stone Barns in Pocantico Hills, New York. See also bluehillfarm.com.

Lisa Feldman Barrett (b. 1963)
Canadian American psychologist, neuroscientist, and author. Born in Toronto, Barrett earned her B.S. degree at the University of Toronto and her Ph.D. in clinical psychology at the University of Waterloo, also in Ontario. She has devoted her career to the scientific study of human emotions—how they evolved, how they arise in an individual, how they affect groups and even entire populations. While still a graduate student, she began to develop her theory of constructed emotion to explain the way the brain assembles what we experience as emotion from sensory stimuli, past experience, and social cues. Barrett has presented her ideas in over 200 peer-reviewed scientific articles, in testimony before Congress, on television programs such as *The Today Show*, in a popular TED talk, and in six books, including the acclaimed *How Emotions Are Made:*

The Secret Life of the Brain (2017). See also lisafeldmanbarrett.com.

Lynda Barry (b. 1956)
American cartoonist and author. Born in Wisconsin, Barry grew up in Seattle and attended The Evergreen State College in Olympia, Washington, where she began to draw comic strips. Without her knowledge, a friend and fellow cartoonist, Matt Groening (creator of *The Simpsons*), launched her career by publishing Barry's strips in the *University of Washington Daily*. Since then her weekly comic strip, *Ernie Pook's Comeek*, has appeared in more than fifty publications; her many books include such collections as *The Fun House* (1987) and *Down the Street* (1988); the illustrated novels *The Good Times Are Killing Me* (1988) and *Cruddy* (1999); and *What It Is* (2008), a graphic novel that is part memoir and part how-to guide for creating graphic novels. Barry's most recent work is *Syllabus: Notes from an Accidental Professor* (2014). She teaches interdisciplinary creativity at the University of Wisconsin–Madison. See also drawnandquarterly.com/author/lynda-barry.

Alison Bechdel (b. 1960)
American cartoonist. Bechdel was born and raised in Lock Haven, Pennsylvania, and attended Simon's Rock College and Oberlin University, where she earned her B.A. degree. In 1983 she began her long-running comic strip *Dykes to Watch Out For*, first published in the feminist weekly *WomaNews*. Over the next twenty-five years, *Dykes* evolved from a single panel to a multi-panel strip featuring a growing cast of characters and a complex web of relationships. Bechdel's best-selling graphic memoir *Fun Home* (2006) was adapted into the Tony award–winning musical play (2015); she followed it with *Are You My Mother?: A Comic Drama* (2012), another commercial and critical success. In 2014 Bechdel received a MacArthur ("Genius") Fellowship. She presently lives, draws, and blogs in Vermont. See also dykestowatchoutfor.com.

Teresa M. Bejan (b. 1984)
American political theorist and author. Bejan earned degrees at both the University of Chicago and the University of Cambridge before receiving her Ph.D. in political science from Yale University in 2013. Much of her subsequent career in academia has been devoted to the study of the way civility, as a fundamental

aspect of any political system, has evolved historically. She has published widely in academic journals as well as the *Atlantic* and the *New York Times*; her first book, *Mere Civility: Disagreement and the Limits of Toleration* (2017), has made Bejan a familiar presence in television and radio debates about the meaning of "civility" in our contentious political era. She is presently working on a book on the history of equality before modern egalitarianism took root. Bejan teaches and conducts research at Oriel College, Oxford. See also teresabejan.com.

Eula Biss (b. 1977)
American nonfiction writer. Upon graduating from Hampshire College, Biss moved to New York City, where she taught in public schools for several years before leaving to earn an M.F.A. degree in the University of Iowa's nonfiction writing program. Since then she has published three books: *The Balloonists* (2002), a collection of autobiographical prose poems; *Notes from No Man's Land* (2009), a volume of essays about race in America; and *On Immunity: An Inoculation* (2014), an exploration of vaccination, vampires, and the value we place on health. Acknowledging the influence of poets Adrienne Rich and Sylvia Plath, Biss has written: "I count that as one of the reasons why I tend to think of personal narrative—particularly when it concerns the body or domesticity—as a perfectly viable space for intellectual exploration." Currently Biss teaches at Northwestern University. See also eulabiss.net.

Tom Bissell (b. 1974)
American journalist and author. After graduating from Michigan State University in 1996 with a degree in English, Bissell served as a Peace Corps volunteer in Uzbekistan; he then turned to the travel writing that made his name as a journalist. In addition to his widely anthologized short stories and feature articles, Bissell has published a number of books, including *Chasing the Sea: Lost among the Ghosts of Empire in Central Asia* (2003), *God Lives in St. Petersburg and Other Stories* (2005), and *Apostle: Travels Among the Tombs of the Twelve* (2016). His 2010 book, *Extra Lives: Why Video Games Matter*, stems from Bissell's deep involvement with video games; he has written scripts for six games, including *Gears of War: Judgment* (2013), of which he is co-author. See also compasstalent.com/tom-bissell.

Jaswinder Bolina (b. 1978)
American poet and essayist. Bolina's parents immigrated to the United States from northern India; he was born and grew up in Chicago. He earned a B.A. in philosophy from Loyola University Chicago before going on to the University of Michigan for his M.F.A. in creative writing and Ohio University for his Ph.D. in English. In his poems and essays, Bolina illuminates and challenges the hidden premises behind any too-easy understandings of the world, or of words. Bolina's poems have been collected in the volumes *Carrier Wave* (2006), *Phantom Camera* (2012), and *The 44th of July* (2019), as well as the chapbook *The Tallest Building in America* (2014). He teaches in the M.F.A. Program in Creative Writing at the University of Miami. See also jaswinderbolina.com.

Anthony Bourdain (1956–2018)
American chef, restauranteur, and writer. A native New Yorker, Bourdain studied at both Vassar College and the Culinary Institute of America before embarking on a legendary career as a chef and food celebrity. He worked his way up through the kitchens of some of New York's finest restaurants before becoming executive chef of Brasserie Les Halles in 1998; international food stardom came with the publication of his first book, the bestselling *Kitchen Confidential: Adventures in the Culinary Underbelly* (2000). A stream of other books followed, including novels and cookbooks. *A Cook's Tour: In Search of the Perfect Meal* (2001) accompanied Bourdain's television series in which he samples some of the world's most extreme cuisine. *The Nasty Bits* (2006), another best seller, collected some of his finest essays about food. *No Reservations: Around the World on an Empty Stomach* (2007) was the companion to another popular television series centered on Bourdain's adventure-eating. See also anthonybourdain.net.

Garnette Cadogan (b. 1971)
Garnette Cadogan is an essayist. But, if pressed, he would describe himself as a wanderer. His belief that walking opens up the world and draws one closer to it regularly leads him to look for opportunities to wander. Most of his meandering is done in cities, and so his work often focuses on cities, particularly the great challenge of pluralism—how do we co-exist? At the time of publication, he

holds fellowships or appointments at the Department of Urban Studies and Planning at Massachusetts Institute of Technology, the Institute for Advanced Studies in Culture at the University of Virginia, the Institute for Public Knowledge at New York University, and the Yale School of Art. He is editor-at-large for *Nonstop Metropolis: A New York City Atlas* (co-edited by Rebecca Solnit and Joshua Jelly-Schapiro) and, to no one's surprise, is at work on a book on walking. See also lithub.com/the-future-of-new-writing-garnette-cadogan.

Nicholas Carr (b. 1959)
American journalist and author. Carr received his B.A. from Dartmouth College and an M.A. in English from Harvard University, where he was executive editor of the *Harvard Business Review*. After nearly two decades as a management consultant, Carr published his first book, *Does IT Matter? Information Technology and the Corrosion of Competitive Advantage* (2004), earning him a reputation as a contrarian in an age of great excitement about technological change. *The Big Switch: Rewiring the World, from Edison to Google* (2008) and *The Shallows: What the Internet Is Doing to Our Brains* (2010) both argue that the explosion of innovation in information technology is already having widespread and unforeseen effects—not necessarily for the better—on commerce, culture, and human intelligence. His most recent books are *The Glass Cage: Automation and Us* (2014) and *Utopia Is Creepy and Other Provocations* (2016). See also nicholascarr.com.

Joy Castro (b. 1967)
American memoirist, novelist, and essayist. Castro was born in Miami and strictly raised as a Jehovah's Witness in London and West Virginia. After her parents divorced, her mother married a man who turned violently abusive. At fourteen, she ran away to live with her father and eventually graduated from Trinity University in Texas. Allowed as a child to read only religious literature, in adulthood she has blossomed into an eclectic writer of both fiction and nonfiction. Her best-known books are her memoirs, *The Truth Book: Escaping a Childhood of Abuse among Jehovah's Witnesses* (2005) and *Island of Bones* (2012). Both of her novels, *Hell or High Water* (2012) and *Nearer Home* (2013), are mysteries set in New Orleans after the catastrophic flooding caused by

Hurricane Katrina in 2005. Her most recent book is *How Winter Began* (2015), a collection of short stories. See also joycastro.com.

Erwin Chemerinsky (b. 1953)
American attorney and legal scholar. Born and raised in Chicago, Chemerinsky earned his B.S. from Northwestern University in 1975 before attending the Harvard Law School, graduating with a J.D. in 1978. Since that time he has distinguished himself both as a lawyer specializing in appellate cases and as a scholar of constitutional law, criminal procedure, and federal jurisdiction. Chemerinsky has authored over 200 articles in law reviews as well as eleven books, including *Closing the Courthouse Door: How Your Constitutional Rights Became Unenforceable* (2017) and *We the People: A Progressive Reading of the Constitution for the Twenty-First Century* (2018). A passionate believer in freedom of speech, Chemerinsky and his collaborator Howard Gillman co-authored *Free Speech on Campus* (2017). He is presently dean of the law school of the University of California, Berkeley. See also law.berkeley.edu; search for "Chemerinsky."

Durga Chew-Bose (b. 1986)
Canadian journalist and author. Born in Montreal to parents who had immigrated from Kolkata, India, Chew-Bose attended Sarah Lawrence College and spent a year at the University of Oxford before establishing herself as a writer in Brooklyn. Her journalism has covered a diverse range of topics from pop music and the latest movies to perfume, poets, and old movies; her articles have appeared in such publications as *BuzzFeed, Rolling Stone, GQ, Interview*, the *New York Times*, and the *Guardian*. In 2017 she published her widely acclaimed first book, *Too Much and Not the Mood*—a collection of personal essays that draw upon her experiences of the world around her and what she calls the "self-spectatorship" of deep introspection. Today she is back in Montreal, where she is a senior editor at *SSENSE*, a fashion platform that also publishes original content. See also muckrack.com/durga-chew-bose/articles.

Judith Ortiz Cofer (1952–2016)
American novelist, poet, and essayist. Born in Hormigueros, Puerto Rico, Cofer spent much of her childhood traveling between her Puerto Rican home and Paterson, New Jersey. Educated at Augusta

College, Florida Atlantic University, and Oxford University, Cofer was a longtime professor of English and creative writing at the University of Georgia. *Silent Dancing: A Partial Remembrance of a Puerto Rican Childhood* (1990) reflects her lifelong efforts to explore her bicultural and bilingual roots as a member of what she calls "the Puerto Rican diaspora." Her other books include *The Latin Deli: Prose and Poetry* (1993), *Woman in Front of the Sun: On Becoming a Writer* (2000), *The Meaning of Consuelo* (2003), the young adult novel *Call Me María* (2004), and *A Love Story Beginning in Spanish: Poems* (2005). See also georgiaencyclopedia.org; search for "Cofer."

Teju Cole (b. 1975)
American writer, photographer, and art historian. Born to Nigerian parents in Kalamazoo, Michigan, Cole grew up in Lagos, Nigeria, and returned to the United States at age seventeen to pursue his education. He earned a bachelor's degree at Kalamazoo College, then cut medical studies short and turned to art history, eventually receiving a Ph.D. at Columbia University. His essays and fiction have appeared in the *New York Times*, the *New Yorker*, *Granta*, *Brick*, and many other periodicals; his "On Photography" column in the *New York Times Magazine* was a finalist for a 2016 National Magazine Award. In addition to a book of his own photographs and writings, *Blind Spot* (2017), Cole has authored an autobiographical novella, *Every Day Is for the Thief* (2007); a novel, *Open City* (2011); and a collection of essays, *Known and Strange Things* (2016). Presently Cole teaches creative writing at Harvard University. See also tejucole.com.

William Cronon (b. 1954)
American environmental historian. Born in Connecticut and raised in Wisconsin, Cronon was a double major in history and English at the University of Wisconsin–Madison. After winning a Rhodes scholarship and completing a degree at Oxford University, in 1985 Cronon was granted a MacArthur ("Genius") Fellowship. He earned a Ph.D. in 1990 from Yale University, where he taught for over a decade. Cronon later returned to the University of Wisconsin–Madison, where he teaches American environmental history and the history of the American West. His books, all of which concern the way humans shape the natural world and are in turn shaped by it, include *Changes in the Land:*

Indians, Colonists, and the Ecology of New England (1983), *Nature's Metropolis: Chicago and the Great West* (1991), *Under an Open Sky: Rethinking America's Western Past* (1992), and *Uncommon Ground: Rethinking the Human Place in Nature* (1995). See also williamcronon.net.

Sloane Crosley (b. 1978)
American essayist and novelist. Since growing up in White Plains, New York, and graduating from Connecticut College in 2000, Crosley has devoted herself as a writer to making people laugh. Her personal essays—sometimes poignant, sometimes ironic, always funny—have appeared in magazines ranging from *Elle* and *Vogue* to *Esquire*, *Playboy*, and *Vanity Fair*. An icon among New York writers, she has produced columns for the *New York Observer* and the *Village Voice*; she was the inaugural columnist for the *New York Times* "Townies" series. Her work has been collected in best-selling books such as *I Was Told There'd Be Cake* (2008), *How Did You Get This Number* (2010), and, most recently, *Look Alive Out There* (2018). Her debut novel, *The Clasp* (2015), as witty and sharply observant as her essays, was met with rapturous acclaim. Crosley lives in Manhattan—of course. See also sloanecrosley.com.

Cormac Cullinan (b. 1962)
South African environmental attorney and author. Cullinan grew up wandering the hills near Pietermaritzburg, South Africa, with a keen sense that modern "monoculture" has disordered our relationship with nature. He received his legal education at the University of Natal and King's College London. Since 1992, the former anti-apartheid activist has turned his legal expertise to the drafting of a broad range of environmental treaties, laws, and policies in more than twenty countries. Cullinan's clients have included national and municipal governments, businesses, and NGOs such as Greenpeace Africa. A founding member of the executive committee of the Global Alliance for Rights of Nature, he oversaw the establishment of the International Tribunal on the Rights of Nature and was the presiding judge at the tribunal hearings in December 2015 in Paris. Cullinan's *Wild Law: A Manifesto for Earth Justice* (2nd ed., 2011) provides a blueprint for what he calls Earth Jurisprudence. See also vermontlaw.edu/directory /person/cullinan-cormac.

Edwidge Danticat (b. 1969)

Haitian American author. Raised for much of her childhood by an aunt and uncle in Port-au-Prince, Haiti, Danticat was educated in French and began writing in her native Creole when she was only nine years old. At twelve she joined her immigrant parents in Brooklyn; within two years she published her first work in English. After earning a B.A. at Barnard College and an M.F.A. in creative writing from Brown University, she turned her thesis into her first novel, *Breath, Eyes, Memory* (1994). The themes of that novel—Haitian identity, the immigrant experience, mothers and daughters—have informed her work ever since. She has published more than twenty books, including novels and collections of both short stories and essays. Her most recent books include the novel *Claire of the Sea Light* (2013) and *Everything Inside: Stories* (2019). In 2009 Danticat was granted a MacArthur ("Genius") Fellowship. See also edwidgedanticat.com.

Matt de la Peña (b. 1973)

American author of books for children and young adults. De la Peña grew up in San Diego, California, and attended the University of the Pacific on a basketball scholarship before earning an M.F.A. from San Diego State University. His very first book, the young adult novel *Ball Don't Lie* (2005), was made into a movie starring Ludacris. His next book, *Mexican WhiteBoy* (2008), was banned from classrooms in Tucson, Arizona, because it was alleged to contain "critical race theory"; in 2017 a court ruled that this was a violation of the constitutional rights of Mexican American students. In 2016, de la Peña's picture book *Last Stop on Market Street* (illustrated by Christian Robinson) won the Newbery Medal for the year's "most distinguished contribution to American literature for children," and the National Council of Teachers of English honored de la Peña with its National Intellectual Freedom Award. See also mattdelapena.com.

Anita Diamant (b. 1951)

American novelist and blogger. Born in Brooklyn, Diamant grew up in Newark, New Jersey, and Denver, Colorado. She earned her B.A. at Washington University in St. Louis, Missouri, and her M.A. in American literature at the State University of New York at Binghamton. She embarked on her writing career as a journalist in Boston before publishing her feature articles—about everything from medical ethics to pet ownership—in such national publications as *Self*, *McCall's*, and *Ms*. Her first book, *The New Jewish Wedding* (1985), has been followed by a number of other Jewish guidebooks, including *The New Jewish Baby Book* (1988). The first of Diamant's five historical novels, *The Red Tent* (1997), gave life to an obscure biblical figure named Dinah; the book was adapted into a television miniseries in 2014. Diamant's most recent novel is *The Boston Girl* (2014), depicting the struggles of immigrant life in the early twentieth century. See also anitadiamant.com.

Kate DiCamillo (b. 1964)

American author of books for children and young adults. Born in Philadelphia and raised in Florida, DiCamillo now resides in Minneapolis, Minnesota. She describes herself as "an enormously lucky person: I get to tell stories for a living." She has written picture books for young children, such as *Louise, the Adventures of a Chicken* (2008, illustrated by Harry Bliss), and chapter books for children learning to read, including her beloved Mercy Watson series. Her first children's novel, *Because of Winn-Dixie* (2000), was named one of "Teachers' Top 100 Books for Children" by the National Education Association. Seven children's novels have followed; two of these have made DiCamillo one of only six authors ever to win the prestigious Newbery Medal twice: first for *The Tale of Despereaux* (2003) and then for *Flora & Ulysses* (2013). Her most recent book is another children's novel, *Louisiana's Way Home* (2018). See also katedicamillo.com.

Joan Didion (b. 1934)

American novelist, essayist, and screenwriter. A native Californian, Didion studied at the University of California, Berkeley. After winning *Vogue* magazine's Prix de Paris contest for excellence in writing, she worked for the magazine until 1963, the year her first novel, *Run River*, was published. Since then, she has written five more novels, most recently *The Last Thing He Wanted* (1996). The essays collected in *Slouching Towards Bethlehem* (1968) and *The White Album* (1979) captured the spirit of the 1960s and 1970s, respectively, and put Didion in the forefront of American essayists. Her recent works of nonfiction include *Fixed Ideas: America since 9.11* (2003), *The Year of Magical Thinking* (2005 winner of the National Book Award), and *South and West: From a Notebook* (2017). *We Tell Ourselves Stories in Order to Live* (2006) collects her first seven volumes of nonfiction. See also thejoandidion.com.

Annie Dillard (b. 1945)
American nature writer, poet, and novelist. Born in Pittsburgh, Pennsylvania, Dillard received her B.A. and M.A. in English from Hollins College. She has published books that range from the poetry of her first book, *Tickets for a Prayer Wheel* (1974), to the nature meditation *Holy the Firm* (1977), the memoir *An American Childhood* (1987), the literary theory in *Living by Fiction* (1982), the essay collections *Teaching a Stone to Talk* (1982) and *The Abundance: Narrative Essays Old & New* (2016), and the novels *The Living* (1992) and *The Maytrees* (2007). In her Pulitzer Prize–winning nonfiction narrative *Pilgrim at Tinker Creek* (1974), Dillard recounts years she spent living in seclusion in the natural world, much like Henry David Thoreau. In *The Writing Life* (1989) she muses on her life's work—"to examine all things intensely and relentlessly." See also anniedillard.com.

Matt Dinan (b. 1984)
Canadian scholar and essayist. Dinan grew up in Miramichi, New Brunswick, and earned his B.A. in Great Ideas at St. Thomas University in Fredericton, New Brunswick. After receiving his Ph.D. in political theory at Baylor University in Waco, Texas, in 2012, he taught for three years at the College of the Holy Cross in Worcester, Massachusetts, before returning to St. Thomas University, where he now teaches in the Great Books program and conducts research in ancient and contemporary political thought. "I study and teach about Aristotle," he writes, noting that Aristotle "rates the social virtues and friendship as especially important for a happy human life"—elements of life he finds to be understudied in academia and underappreciated in the culture more broadly. Dinan is presently working on a book to be called *Less than Our Due: Responsibility and Forgiveness in Political Theory*. See also stu.ca/greatbooks/matt-dinan.

Frederick Douglass (c. 1818–1895)
American abolitionist, orator, journalist, and memoirist. Born a slave in Maryland, Douglass learned at a young age how to read and write, even though it was against the law to teach literacy to a slave. In 1836 he escaped from his master and fled to the North with Anna Murray, also a former slave, whom he later married. Douglass soon became an important orator in the abolitionist movement and, with the publication of his first autobiography, *A Narrative of the Life of Frederick Douglass* (1845), an international spokesman for freedom. Douglass founded the antislavery newspaper the *North Star* in 1847 and actively recruited black soldiers to join the Union Army at the outbreak of the Civil War. He continued his autobiography in *My Bondage and My Freedom* (1855) and *Life and Times of Frederick Douglass* (1881, rev. 1892). See also docsouth.unc.edu/neh/douglass/bio.html.

Brian Doyle (1956–2017)
American novelist, essayist, and editor. Born in New York City, Doyle received his B.A. from the University of Notre Dame in 1978. He worked on various magazines and newspapers in Chicago and Boston, and for twenty-six years edited the University of Portland's *Portland Magazine*. A passionate storyteller and a prolific writer of essays, stories, and the prose poems he called "proems," Doyle published sixteen books, including the essay collection *Spirited Men* (2004), about male musicians and writers, and *The Wet Engine* (2005), about "hearts and how they work and do not work and get repaired and patched, for a while." As his life neared its end, Doyle produced a flurry of award-winning novels: *Mink River* (2010), *The Plover* (2014), *Martin Marten* (2015), and *The Adventures of John Carson in Several Quarters of the World* (2017). See also ruminatemagazine.com; search for "Doyle."

Geoff Dyer (b. 1958)
English critic, novelist, and author. Born to working-class parents in Cheltenham, England, Dyer attended the University of Oxford as a scholarship student. He soon developed into a writer of unparalleled range. Dyer has written four novels, including *The Colour of Memory* (1989) and *Jeff in Venice, Death in Varanasi* (2009), as well as award-winning collections of art criticism such as *Otherwise Known as the Human Condition* (2011). Many of his best-known books are impossible to categorize. There's *But Beautiful* (1991), a fictionalized history of jazz; *Yoga for People Who Can't Be Bothered to Do It*

(2003); *Zona* (2012), subtitled "A Book about a Film about a Journey to a Room"; and *Another Great Day at Sea* (2014), describing life aboard a U.S. warship. Dyer's most recent book is *Broadsword Calling Danny Boy* (2018), a meditation on the 1968 war movie *Where Eagles Dare*. See also geoffdyer.com.

Jennifer Eberhardt (b. 1965)
American social psychologist and scholar. Eberhardt grew up in Cleveland, Ohio, and earned her B.A. at the University of Cincinnati. After receiving her Ph.D. in psychology from Harvard University and then teaching for several years at Yale University, she joined the faculty at Stanford University, where she teaches, conducts research, and acts as co-director of SPARQ (Social Psychological Answers to Real-World Questions). Much of her work centers on the psychological underpinnings of racial consciousness and racial bias, especially as they play out in economic inequality and the criminal justice system. Her first book, *Biased: Uncovering the Hidden Prejudice That Shapes What We, See, Think, and Do*, was published in 2019. In 2014 she received a MacArthur ("Genius") Fellowship, and in that same year she was recognized in *Foreign Policy* magazine's list of "100 Leading Global Thinkers." See also stanford.edu /~eberhard.

Barbara Ehrenreich (b. 1941)
American journalist, political activist, and author. Ehrenreich grew up in a working-class family in Butte, Montana. At Reed College she started out as a chemistry major, but then switched to physics; by the time she emerged from Rockefeller University with a Ph.D., she was a cell biologist. In the early 1970s, her involvement with what was then called the "women's health movement" led her to journalism and social activism. She has published countless essays and feature articles in the *Washington Post*, *Mother Jones*, *Ms.*, the *Atlantic*, the *Nation*, and many other newspapers and magazines. The twenty-one books she has authored or co-authored include the best-selling *Nickeled and Dimed: On (Not) Getting By in America* (2001), based on a number of menial jobs she took on as research, and, most recently, *Natural Causes: An Epidemic of Wellness, the Certainty of Dying, and Killing Ourselves to Live Longer* (2018). See also barbaraehrenreich.com.

Lars Eighner (b. 1948)
American writer. Born in Corpus Christi, Texas, Eighner attended the University of Texas at Austin, where he now lives. A self-described "skeptical Democrat," Eighner has worked in hospitals and drug-crisis programs despite ongoing struggles with illness and homelessness. His book *Travels with Lizbeth* (1993), which describes his three years of surviving on the streets with his dog, was a best seller. He has also published *Elements of Arousal* (1994), a how-to guide on writing gay erotica, and the comic novel *Pawn to Queen Four* (1995), about the gay subculture of a Texas town. See also larseighner.com.

Nora Ephron (1941–2012)
American journalist, director, and screenwriter. Born in New York City, Ephron grew up in Beverly Hills, California, the daughter of two screenwriters. Soon after graduating from Wellesley College in 1962, she began writing for the *New York Post*, *Esquire*, the *New York Times Magazine*, and *New York* magazine. In the mid-1970s she turned from journalism to screenplays and was nominated for three Academy Awards for best original screenplay, for *Silkwood* (1983), *When Harry Met Sally* (1989), and *Sleepless in Seattle* (1993). In the 1990s she began directing films, including *You've Got Mail* (1998), *Lucky Numbers* (2000), and *Julie & Julia* (2009). Her books include the novel *Heartburn* (1983) and the essay collections *Wallflower at the Orgy* (1970), *Crazy Salad* (1975), *Scribble, Scribble: Notes on the Media* (1978), and *I Remember Nothing: And Other Reflections* (2010). See also longreads .com; search for "Ephron."

David Epstein (b. 1983)
American journalist and author. Epstein earned his B.S. degree in environmental science and astronomy at Columbia University; he also holds master's degrees from Columbia in both environmental science and journalism. After a stint as a crime reporter for the *New York Daily News*, he wrote for *Sports Illustrated*, where he produced award-winning articles on the abuse of steroids, the particular dangers of heart failure faced by athletes, and painkiller addiction in sports. He is the author of *The Sports Gene: Inside the Science of Extraordinary Athletic Performance* (2013), about the role of genetics in the making of top-flight athletes, and *Range: Why Generalists*

Triumph in a Specialized World (2019), which argues that broad experience is the surest route to success. See also davidepstein.com.

Kathy Fish (b. 1960)
American short story writer. Born in Waterloo, Iowa, Fish earned a B.A. in psychology at the University of Northern Iowa in Cedar Falls. She is a master of the so-called short short story—also called flash fiction—and her work has been called prose poetry: minimalist, dreamlike stories ("Strong Tongue") or, sometimes, steel-trap mini-essays of astonishing power ("Collective Nouns for Humans in the Wild"). A frequent award winner in the literary subgenre of flash fiction, she has published her work in *Guernica*, the *Indiana Review*, the *Mississippi Review*, *Quick Fiction*, the *Denver Quarterly*, and many others, especially online. Her stories have been collected in five volumes, including her first, *Together We Can Bury It* (2012), and, most recently, *Wild Life: Collected Works from 2003–2018* (2018). Fish teaches fiction and mentors students in the Mile High M.F.A. program at Denver's Regis University. See also kathy-fish.com.

Benjamin Franklin (1706–1790)
American statesman, inventor, writer, and diplomat. Born in Boston, Franklin was apprenticed at twelve to his brother, a printer. He resettled in Philadelphia and at twenty-four was editor and publisher of the *Pennsylvania Gazette*. In 1733 he began writing *Poor Richard's Almanack*, a collection of aphorisms and advice. Retiring from business at forty-two to devote himself to study and research, he soon found himself involved in colonial politics. From 1757 until 1763 he represented the colonies in England. He served on the committee appointed to draft the Declaration of Independence and later was both minister to France and delegate to the Paris peace conference that officially concluded the Revolutionary War. Revered as "the First American," late in his life he became an advocate for the abolition of slavery. His posthumously published *Autobiography* is a classic memoir. See also fi.edu/benjamin-franklin/resources.

Joey Franklin (b. 1980)
American essayist. Franklin grew up in Beaverton, Oregon, and after a two-year stint as a Mormon missionary in Japan he earned a B.A. in English at Brigham Young University, an M.A. in creative nonfiction at Ohio University, and a Ph.D. in literature and creative writing from Texas Tech University. A specialist in creative nonfiction, Franklin professes an interest in "memory, identity, and self-representation." His essays have appeared in *American Literary Review, Gettysburg Review*, and the *Writer's Chronicle*; many of these are collected in his first book, *My Wife Wants You to Know I'm Happily Married* (2015). Franklin teaches creative writing at Brigham Young University. See also joeyfranklin.com.

Ian Frazier (b. 1951)
American essayist, humorist, and novelist. Born in Cleveland and raised in Hudson, Ohio, Frazier studied at Western Reserve Academy and Harvard University, where he worked at the satirical *Harvard Lampoon*. Since then he has written eleven books. Many of the humorous pieces he has published in the *New Yorker* have been collected in such volumes as *Dating Your Mom* (1986), *Coyote v. Acme* (1996), and *Lamentations of the Father* (2000). Frazier's best-known work of nonfiction, *Great Plains* (1989), like *Family* (1994) and *On the Rez* (2000), is based on both extensive research and his own experiences after moving to Montana in 1982. Since relocating to the East Coast he has published *Gone to New York: Adventures in the City* (2005), the bestselling *Travels in Siberia* (2010), *The Cursing Mommy's Book of Days* (2012—a novel), and *Hogs Wild: Selected Reporting Pieces* (2016). See also newyorker.com/contributors/ian-frazier.

David French (b. 1969)
American attorney, journalist, and essayist. A graduate of Harvard Law School, in 2007 French interrupted his legal career to deploy with the U.S. Army in Iraq, where he served as a judge advocate and was awarded the Bronze Star. He is a senior fellow of the National Review Institute and a familiar figure among the conservative commentariat; his articles and essays have appeared in the *National Review* as well as *Time* magazine and the *Atlantic*. French is the author of *A Season for Justice: Defending the Rights of the Christian Church, Home, and School* (2002) and *The Rise of ISIS: A Threat We Can't Ignore* (2014), a best seller. Along with his wife, Nancy, French co-authored *Home and Away: A Story of Family in a Time of War* (2011), based on the period of his service in Iraq. See also patheos.com/blogs/frenchrevolution.

Henry Louis Gates Jr. (b. 1950)
American scholar and literary critic. Born and raised in West Virginia, Gates was educated at both Yale and Cambridge Universities. Now a professor at Harvard University, Gates edits African American literature, composes literary criticism, and writes for general audiences. He has created a number of television documentaries, including *African American Lives* (2006) and *Finding Your Roots* (2012–19); his essays have appeared in the *New Yorker*, *Newsweek*, *Sports Illustrated*, and the *New York Times*. Gates's many books include *Figures in Black: Words, Signs, and the "Racial" Self* (1987); *The Signifying Monkey* (1988), winner of the National Book Award; *Colored People* (1994), his best-selling autobiography; *The Henry Louis Gates Jr. Reader* (2012), a collection of his writings; and, most recently, *Stony the Road: Reconstruction, White Supremacy, and the Rise of Jim Crow* (2019). Gates is the general co-editor of *The Norton Anthology of African American Literature* (3rd ed., 2014). See also aaas.fas.harvard.edu/people/henry-louis-gates-jr.

Atul Gawande (b. 1965)
American surgeon, teacher, and essayist. Born in Brooklyn to Indian immigrant parents, Gawande grew up in Athens, Ohio. He earned his B.A. at Stanford University, studied at Oxford University as a Rhodes Scholar, and then earned his M.D. from Harvard Medical School. In addition to scholarly studies published in the *New England Journal of Medicine*, his articles about health care and the medical profession have appeared frequently in *Slate* and the *New Yorker*. Gawande's four books, including *Complications: A Surgeon's Notes on an Imperfect Science* (2002), and *The Checklist Manifesto: How to Get Things Right* (2009), have been widely praised for the clarity with which they illuminate a complex technical subject for a general readership. His most recent book is *Being Mortal: Medicine and What Matters in the End* (2014). See also gawande.com.

Roxane Gay (b. 1974)
American writer and commentator. Born in Omaha, Nebraska, Gay earned an M.A. at the University of Nebraska at Lincoln and a Ph.D. in rhetoric and technical communications from Michigan Technological University. She has taught at Eastern Illinois University; Purdue University, where she was an associate professor of English; and, most recently, Yale University, where she was a Presidential Fellow. Her short stories and essays have appeared in such publications as *Time*, *McSweeney's*, and the *Nation*, as well as in a broad range of anthologies, from *Best Sex Writing* (2012) to *Best American Mystery Stories* (2014). Her books include *Ayiti* (2011), a short story collection; *An Untamed State* (2014), a novel; *Bad Feminist* (2014), a volume of essays that discusses the difficulties of being a woman in a world without perfect role models; *Difficult Women* (2017), a story collection; and *Hunger* (2017), a memoir. Gay is also the founder of Tiny Hardcore Press and the editor of the online *Gay Mag*. See also roxanegay.com.

A. Bartlett Giamatti (1938–1989)
American scholar and author. Born in Boston and raised in South Hadley, Massachusetts, Giamatti spent much of his life at Yale University. There he earned his B.A. and Ph.D., was a professor of English, and, in 1978, began his tenure as Yale's youngest-ever president. Eight years later he left Yale and turned to his first love: baseball. Giamatti was named president of the National League in 1986 and commissioner of Major League Baseball in 1989. Just five months after assuming his dream job, he died suddenly of a heart attack at the age of fifty-one. Author of eight books, Giamatti published influential scholarly volumes such as *Play of Double Senses: Spenser's Faerie Queene* (1975) and books about academia's role in American culture like *The University and the Public Interest* (1981). His lyrical essays about baseball are collected in *A Great and Glorious Game* (1998). See also https://www.mlb.com/official-information/commissioners/giamatti.

Howard Gillman (b. 1959)
American legal scholar and educator. Gillman grew up in Southern California and earned his B.A., M.A., and Ph.D. in political science at the University of California, Los Angeles, before embarking on a distinguished career of teaching and scholarship in political science. A specialist in the American Constitution and the Supreme Court, Gillman has written many articles as well as books that include *The Constitution Besieged* (1993), *The Votes That Counted: How the Court Decided the 2000 Presidential Election* (2001), and most recently *Free Speech on Campus* (2018, co-authored

with Erwin Chemerinsky). Gillman is presently chancellor of the University of California, Irvine, where he also holds faculty appointments in the departments of political science, history, and criminology, as well as the school of law. See also chancellor.uci.edu/about.

Malcolm Gladwell (b. 1963)
Canadian journalist and essayist. Born in England and raised in Canada, Gladwell graduated from the University of Toronto in 1984 and soon began his career as a journalist, writing for various publications including the *Washington Post*. Since joining the staff of the *New Yorker* in 1996, he has contributed articles on a wide array of topics, from the "science of shopping" to highway safety to mammography to the SAT. His books, all international best sellers, include *The Tipping Point: How Little Things Can Make a Big Difference* (2000), *Blink: The Power of Thinking without Thinking* (2005), *Outliers: The Story of Success* (2008), *What the Dog Saw* (2009), *David and Goliath: Underdogs, Misfits, and the Art of Battling Giants* (2013), and, most recently, *Talking to Strangers: What We Should Know about the People We Don't Know* (2019). See also gladwell.com.

Thomas Goetz (b. 1968)
American author and health care entrepreneur. Goetz holds a B.A. from Bates College, an M.P.H. from the University of California, Berkeley, and an M.A. in American literature from the University of Virginia. At *WIRED* magazine, where he was a longtime executive editor, he wrote articles about genomics, medical technology, and behavior change that have been widely anthologized; his popular TED talk about redesigning medical data led up to his co-founding of Iodine, "a health technology company with the mission of turning medical research data into clear and actionable tools for ordinary people to make better decisions about their health." Goetz is the author of two books: *The Decision Tree: Taking Control of Your Health in the New Era of Personalized Medicine* (2010) and *The Remedy* (2014), which chronicles the story of the battle against tuberculosis. See also thomasgoetz.com.

Emma González (b. 1999)
American activist and gun-control advocate. The daughter of Cuban immigrant parents, González grew up in the Miami suburb of Parkland, Florida, and was a high school senior on Valentine's Day, 2018, when a former student, armed with a semi-automatic assault rifle, entered Marjory Stoneman Douglas High School and shot thirty-four people, killing seventeen of them. When it was subsequently learned that the gunman had purchased his weapon legally, González channeled nationwide outrage with an impassioned eleven-minute speech delivered at a rally in front of the Broward County Courthouse. "We call B.S.," she declared, on the gun industry and pro-gun politicians. A video of the speech immediately went viral and González, suddenly the face of American gun-control advocacy, responded by cofounding Never Again MSD, a political action committee whose activism led the Florida legislature, less than a month after the shootings, to enact tighter gun regulations. See also marchforourlives.com.

JJ Goode (b. 1981)
American food and travel writer. Goode grew up in New Jersey eating supermarket mac and cheese, frozen pizza, and tuna noodle casserole. He is a graduate of Vassar College, where he studied psychology because, he says, he was afraid of taking writing classes. Now Goode writes about every aspect of food and drink: pancakes and pasta, salsa and sushi, cocktails and coffee. He has written for the *New York Times*, *Gourmet*, *Bon Appétit*, *Saveur*, and numerous other publications. He has co-authored many cookbooks, including *Truly Mexican* (2011) and *Tacos, Tortas, and Tamales* (2013), both with Roberto Santibañez; *A Girl and Her Pig* (2012); *A Girl and Her Greens* (2015); *Munchies* (2017) with Helen Hollyman; *Pok Pok: The Drinking Food of Thailand* (2017) with Andy Ricker; and, most recently, *State Bird Provisions* (2017) with Stuart Brioza and Nicole Krasinsky of the famed San Francisco restaurant. See also jjgoode.com.

Jonathan Gottschall (b. 1972)
American literary scholar and author. Since earning his Ph.D. in English at the State University of New York at Binghamton, Gottschall has devoted himself to the study of literature as a phenomenon of evolutionary psychology. Using scientific techniques, even brain scanning, to probe the human fascination with stories and fantasy is like "mapping wonderland," he has said—an entirely new approach to the study of literature. His work has been profiled in such publications as the *New York Times*, *Scientific*

American, and *Nature.* Gottschall has authored seven books, including *Literature, Science, and a New Humanities* (2008); *The Storytelling Animal: How Stories Make Us Human* (2012); and, most recently, *The Professor in the Cage: Why Men Fight and Why We Like to Watch* (2015), based on what Gottschall learned when he took up mixed martial arts. He teaches at Washington & Jefferson College in Pennsylvania. See also jonathangottschall.com.

Gerald Graff (b. 1937)
American scholar and author. Born and raised in Chicago, Graff earned his B.A. in English from the University of Chicago. After receiving his Ph.D. in English and American literature from Stanford University, he taught at a number of universities before settling at the University of Illinois at Chicago, where he has taught writing and literature since 2000. Graff has authored books such as *Literature against Itself: Literary Ideas in Modern Society* (1979) and *Professing Literature: An Institutional History* (1987) that champion what he calls "literature's rational, discursive qualities"; his books critiquing American intellectual culture include *Beyond the Culture Wars: How Teaching the Conflicts Can Revitalize American Education* (1993) and *Clueless in Academe: How Schooling Obscures the Life of the Mind* (2004). Most recently, Graff and his wife, writer Cathy Birkenstein, have coauthored *"They Say / I Say": The Moves That Matter in Academic Writing* (2018). See also geraldgraff.com.

Michael Hamad (b. 1972)
American music critic and visual artist. Hamad holds a master's degree in music theory from the Hartt School and a doctorate in musicology from Brandeis University. As a staff music writer for the *Hartford Courant* from 2013 to 2018, he covered popular music, jazz, "and whatever else sounds interesting." Hamad is also a guitarist and a visual artist who has devised a unique way of visually reimagining music in the form of "schematics"— assemblages of words and symbols, created in real time, that graph his aural experience in two or even three dimensions. Hamad's artwork has appeared in the *Village Voice,* the *Believer,* and the *New York Times;* he is currently the host/producer of the Hartford-based *Capitol Watch* podcast. See also setlistschematics.tumblr.com.

Jack Hamilton (b. 1979)
American music historian and cultural critic. Born and raised near Boston, Hamilton was a professional musician for several years before earning a B.A. in English at New York University and then, in 2013, a Ph.D. in American studies at Harvard University. He is the pop critic for *Slate,* where he writes about music, movies, television, books, and sports; his work has also appeared in the *Atlantic,* the *New Yorker,* and many other publications. His first book, *Just around Midnight: Rock and Roll and the Racial Imagination,* came out in 2016; he is presently at work on a book about the way innovations like the synthesizer and digital sampling have changed the way music is made. Hamilton teaches in the departments of media studies and American studies at the University of Virginia. See also jack-hamilton.com.

Hadar Harris (b. 1966)
American civil rights attorney and activist. A graduate of both Brown University and the law school at the University of California, Los Angeles, Harris has devoted her legal career to human rights activism in the United States and around the world. She has served as director of a number of rights advocacy organizations, including the Congressional Human Rights Caucus, the Center for Human Rights & Humanitarian Law, and the Student Press Law Center, "the nation's only legal assistance organization devoted exclusively to supporting student news media in their struggle to cover important issues free from censorship." More recently Harris has served as executive director of the Northern California Innocence Project, an organization devoted to exonerating innocent prisoners and advocating for reform of the criminal justice system. See also womensmediacenter.com/shesource/expert/hadar-harris.

Daisy Hernández (b. 1975)
American journalist, author, and social activist. Daughter of a Colombian mother and a Cuban father, Hernández grew up in New Jersey and earned an M.A. at New York University's school of journalism. She has reported for the *New York Times,* the *Atlantic,* and *Slate;* her essays and fiction have appeared in the *Bellingham Review, Fourth Genre, Rumpus,* and many other journals. An ardent feminist, she has been a columnist for *Ms.* magazine and was a coeditor of *Colonize This! Young Women of*

Color on Today's Feminism (2002). Hernández is the author of *A Cup of Water under My Bed* (2014), her coming-of-age memoir of "learning about feminism, queer identity, race, and immigration in the Americas." Presently she is a contributing editor for the Buddhist magazine *Tricycle* and teaches writing at Miami University in Ohio. See also daisyhernandez.com.

Kate Holbrook (b. 1972)
American historian. Born in Santa Barbara, California, Holbrook grew up in Utah, where she earned a B.A. in English and Russian literature from Brigham Young University. She went on to obtain an M.T.S. degree from the Harvard Divinity School and a Ph.D. in religious studies from Boston University. A devout Mormon, she served as a missionary for the Church of Jesus Christ of Latter-day Saints (LDS) in Samara, Russia. Presently she is a managing historian of the LDS Church History Department; her own research focuses on religion, gender, and food—revealing, she writes, people's "everyday attempts to prioritize and live their dearest values." Holbrook co-authored the chapter "Sexuality and Embodiment" in *The Oxford Handbook of Mormonism* (2015); she co-edited *Women and Mormonism* (2016). Her articles and essays have appeared in *Patheos* and the *Mormon Studies Review*. She is presently at work on a book about Mormon foodways. See also kateholbrook.org.

Langston Hughes (1902–1967)
American poet, playwright, and fiction writer. Born in Joplin, Missouri, Hughes grew up in the American Midwest before coming to New York City to attend Columbia University. Appalled by the racial discrimination there, he left Columbia to pursue his own writing, especially the "jazz poetry" that became his hallmark. After a period of travel and living abroad, he returned to the United States to complete his B.A. at Pennsylvania's Lincoln University. He returned to New York and soon emerged as a key figure in the Harlem Renaissance of the 1920s and 1930s, beginning with his collection of poems *The Weary Blues* in 1926. In his lifetime he would publish sixteen more volumes of poetry as well as two novels, seven collections of short stories, twenty-six plays, and seven works of nonfiction, including the memoir *The Big Sea* (1940). See also poetryfoundation.org/bio/langston-hughes.

Pico Iyer (b. 1957)
American essayist, travel writer, and novelist. Born Siddhart Pico Raghavan Iyer to Indian parents in Oxford, England, where his father taught philosophy, Iyer grew up there and in Santa Barbara, California, after his father began teaching at the University of California. He was educated at Eton College and the University of Oxford before earning a second master's degree at Harvard University. In 1982 he began to write for *Time* magazine on world affairs, and since then has traveled widely; the best known of his eight works of nonfiction, including *Video Night in Kathmandu* (1988) and *The Global Soul: Jet Lag, Shopping Malls, and the Search for Home* (2000), are extended essays derived from his excursions abroad. His most recent book, *Autumn Light: Season of Fire and Farewells* (2019), is, characteristically, a meditation on spirit and mortality. Iyer has lived in Nara, Japan, for many years. See also picoiyerjourneys.com.

Lauren Michele Jackson (b. 1991)
American essayist, and scholar. A native of Batavia, Illinois, Jackson graduated from the University of Illinois at Urbana-Champaign in 2013 and received her Ph.D. in English language and literature from the University of Chicago. Much of her criticism, which has appeared in a broad range of publications including the *Atlantic*, the *Paris Review*, *Rolling Stone*, and the *New Yorker*, investigates racial aesthetics in contemporary American culture. Her first book, an essay collection, is *White Negroes: When Cornrows Were in Vogue . . . and Other Thoughts on Cultural Appropriation* (2019). Jackson has recently joined the faculties of both the English and African American Studies departments at Northwestern University. See also laurjackson.com.

Leslie Jamison (b. 1983)
American novelist and essayist. Jamison was born in Washington, DC, and grew up in Los Angeles. She earned a B.A. in English at Harvard University, an M.F.A. at the University of Iowa Writers' Workshop, and a Ph.D. in English literature at Yale University. Her own writing has appeared in such publications as *Harper's*, *Oxford American*, the *Believer*, and the *New York Times Book Review*, where she is a frequent contributor. She is the author of four books: a highly acclaimed novel, *The Gin Closet* (2010); *The Empathy Exams* (2014), a collection of essays that

explore responses to both our own pain and the pain of others; *The Recovering: Intoxication and Its Aftermath* (2018), a memoir; and *Make It Scream, Make It Burn* (2019), fourteen explorations of "the dynamics of haunting and obsession." Jamison teaches writing at Columbia University. See also lesliejamison.com.

Thomas Jefferson (1743–1826)
American lawyer, architect, and writer; governor of Virginia (1779–81), secretary of state to George Washington (1790–93), vice president to John Adams (1797–1801), and third president of the United States (1801–1809). A learned man of significant accomplishments in many fields, Jefferson became a lawyer and was elected to Virginia's House of Burgesses, where he argued the cause of American independence. After completing his second term as president of the United States, he founded the University of Virginia, designing both the buildings and the curriculum. A fluent prose stylist, Jefferson authored Virginia's Statute of Religious Freedom and wrote books on science, religion, architecture, and even Anglo-Saxon grammar. He is best known for writing the Declaration of Independence; his preliminary drafts were edited by a committee that included Benjamin Franklin and John Adams before Jefferson prepared the final revision. See also monticello.org.

Rachel Pieh Jones (b. 1978)
American author and blogger. Born and raised in Minnesota, Jones and her husband, an English professor, settled in Djibouti in 2004. A few years later she started her blog *Djibouti Jones* with the mission "to help you live the best expatriate life possible." Soon her articles began to appear in periodicals such as the *New York Times*, *Christianity Today*, and even *Runner's World* (she's an avid runner). Her cookbook, *Djiboutilicious* (2006), features recipes from the Horn of Africa. A practicing Christian living in a Muslim country, Jones writes with respect and insight about spirituality and religion, calling herself a witness: "I aim to observe beautiful, creative aspects of our world and call out the good in them." Her most recent book is *Stronger than Death: How Annalena Tonelli Defied Terror and Tuberculosis in the Horn of Africa* (2019). See also djiboutijones.com.

David Joy (b. 1983)
American author of fiction and nonfiction. Born in Charlotte, North Carolina,

Joy holds a B.A. from Western Carolina University. He debuted with a memoir, *Growing Gills: A Fly Fisherman's Journey* (2011). His first novel, *Where All Light Tends to Go* (2015), is set in the hardscrabble Appalachia of western North Carolina; it was a finalist for the Edgar Award for best first novel by an American and was long-listed for the International Dublin Literary Award. Joy followed with two more novels: *The Weight of This World* (2017) and *The Line That Held Us* (2018). More recently, Joy co-edited *Gather at the River: Twenty-Five Authors on Fishing* (2019). His short stories and essays have appeared in numerous periodicals, including *Drafthorse*, *Smoky Mountain Living*, *Time*, and the *New York Times Magazine*. He lives in Webster, North Carolina. See also david-joy.com.

John F. Kennedy (1917–1963)
American author, politician, and thirty-fifth president of the United States. Born in Brookline, Massachusetts, Kennedy graduated from Harvard University and developed his senior thesis into the best-selling *Why England Slept* (1940). He received the Navy and Marine Corps Medal for his service in World War II. At twenty-nine Kennedy was elected to the U.S. House of Representatives; six years later he narrowly won a seat in the U.S. Senate, representing Massachusetts. His book *Profiles in Courage* (1956), detailing notable instances of political integrity by U.S. senators, won the Pulitzer Prize for biography and added to his growing fame. In 1960 his eloquence and poise in televised debates against Richard Nixon helped Kennedy win the presidency. His inaugural address, calling for all citizens' participation in the affairs of their nation, is one of the best-known speeches in American history. On November 22, 1963, Kennedy was assassinated in Dallas, Texas. See also jfklibrary.org.

Philip Kennicott (b. 1966)
American music, art, and architecture critic. Kennicott grew up in Schenectady, New York, attended Deep Springs College, and graduated from Yale University with a degree in philosophy. He began his career in journalism as the classical music critic for the *Detroit News* before moving on to the *St. Louis Post-Dispatch* and then the *Washington Post*, where he now serves as chief art and architecture critic. His articles about classical music have appeared in the *New Republic*, *Gramophone*, and *Opera News*. In addition to

music, he has written on a broad array of topics, including gun control, Abraham Lincoln, and the U.S. Holocaust Memorial Museum. His essay "Smuggler," first published in the *Virginia Quarterly Review*, was selected for *Best American Essays* (2015). In 2013 Kennicott was awarded the Pulitzer Prize for criticism in recognition of "his eloquent and passionate essays on art and the social forces that underlie it." See also philipkennicott.com.

Robin Wall Kimmerer (b. 1953)
American botanist and ecologist. Kimmerer was born in Upstate New York to parents of both European and Native American ancestry. She earned her B.S. in botany at the State University of New York's College of Environmental Science and Forestry in Syracuse, and her M.S. and Ph.D. at the University of Wisconsin. She has devoted her career to combining two ways of understanding the natural world—through the lens of modern science and also through a broader view incorporating traditional and cultural knowledge. In 2002 she co-founded the Traditional Ecological Knowledge section of the Ecological Society of America. An expert on mosses, she has authored two award-winning books: *Gathering Moss: A Natural and Cultural History of Mosses* (2003) and *Braiding Sweetgrass: Indigenous Wisdom, Scientific Knowledge, and the Teachings of Plants* (2013). Kimmerer is director of the Center for Native Peoples and the Environment at SUNY-ESF. See also www.esf.edu/faculty/kimmerer.

Martin Luther King Jr. (1929–1968)
American clergyman and civil rights leader. By the age of twenty-six, the Atlanta-born King had completed his undergraduate education, finished divinity school, and received a Ph.D. in religion from Boston University. In 1956 King took a public stand to support blacks boycotting segregated buses in Montgomery, Alabama, marking his entry into the struggle for equality. Soon he became a major figure in the civil rights movement, advocating nonviolent protest in the spirit of Jesus' teachings and Mahatma Gandhi's principles of passive resistance. In 1963, Birmingham, Alabama, one of the most segregated cities in the South, became the focal point for violent racial confrontations: over 2,400 civil rights workers, King among them, were jailed, occasioning his now-famous "Letter from Birmingham Jail." In 1964, at thirty-five,

he became the youngest recipient of the Nobel Peace Prize. King was assassinated on April 4, 1968, in Memphis, Tennessee. See also thekingcenter.org.

Stephen King (b. 1947)
American fiction writer. Born in Portland, Maine, King grew up fascinated with horror comics and began writing macabre tales while still a teenager. Not long after graduating with a B.A. in English from the University of Maine in 1970, he began writing short stories, one of which he threw away but then developed—on the advice of his wife Tabitha—into his first published novel, *Carrie* (1973). This bestselling supernatural thriller was soon followed by *Salem's Lot* (1975), *The Shining* (1977), and the serialized fantasy *The Dark Tower: The Gunslinger* (1977–81). Today King is a publishing phenomenon; his sixty novels, six nonfiction books, and ten collections of short stories have sold more than 350 million copies worldwide. Even after sustaining severe injuries in a 1999 road accident, he has managed to fulfill his daily quota of 2,000 words. See also stephenking.com.

Barbara Kingsolver (b. 1955)
American novelist and essayist. Born in Maryland, Kingsolver grew up in rural Kentucky and earned degrees in biology from DePauw University and the University of Arizona. She began her career as a freelance science writer, but later, as a novelist, she has made greater use of her experience living and working all over the world. Her first novel, *The Bean Trees* (1988), is set in Tucson, where she spent two decades; *The Poisonwood Bible* (1998) takes place in the Congo, where she spent a year of her childhood. In the memoir *Animal, Vegetable, Miracle* (2007), Kingsolver describes her yearlong attempt to feed her family with foods produced near her farm in rural Virginia. Her most recent novel, *Unsheltered* (2018), confronts the unsettling personal and professional circumstances of modern American life. In 2000 Kingsolver established the Bellwether Prize for writers whose fiction "engages visions of social change and human justice." See also kingsolver.com.

Elizabeth Kolbert (b. 1961)
American journalist and author. Kolbert grew up in New York, first in the Bronx and then in nearby Larchmont. After earning her B.A. at Yale University, she studied at the Universität Hamburg in Germany on a Fulbright scholarship;

while there she began working as a "stringer" (freelance reporter) for the *New York Times*. She joined the *Times* Metro desk in 1985; by 1997 she was writing the *Times* "Metro Matters" column. Since 1999 she has been a staff writer for the *New Yorker*, producing award-winning feature articles on science subjects ranging from bed bugs to mastodons. Her first book, *The Prophet of Love* (2004), dissected New York City politics. Much of her recent work, including *Field Notes from a Catastrophe* (2006) and *The Sixth Extinction: An Unnatural History* (2014), winner of the Pulitzer Prize for nonfiction, focuses on the increasingly hard-to-ignore effects of climate change. See also newyorker.com/contributors/elizabeth -kolbert.

Tim Kreider (b. 1967)
American essayist and cartoonist. Kreider grew up in Baltimore, where he went to public schools before attending Johns Hopkins University's Writing Seminars program. For twelve years his satirical cartoons ran in the *Baltimore City Paper* and other alternative weeklies; these have been collected in three volumes as *The Pain—When Will It End?* (2004), *Why Do They Kill Me?* (2005), and *Twilight of the Assholes* (2011). His cartoons and essays—about politics, books, movies, and life in general—have appeared in many periodicals, including *Men's Journal*, the *Comics Journal*, and the *New York Times*. Kreider's most recent books are collections of essays: *We Learn Nothing* (2012) and *I Wrote This Book Because I Love You* (2018). See also timkreider.com.

Jhumpa Lahiri (b. 1967)
American short story writer and novelist. Lahiri was born in London to Bengali Indian immigrant parents who, when she was three years old, moved the family to the United States and settled in Kingston, Rhode Island. She earned her bachelor's degree from Barnard College; at Boston University she earned three master's degrees as well as a doctorate in Renaissance studies. Her short stories were collected in *The Interpreter of Maladies* (1999), winner of the 2000 Pulitzer Prize for fiction. In her second story collection, *Unaccustomed Earth* (2008), as well as her novels *The Namesake* (2003) and *The Lowland* (2013), Lahiri has continued to focus on the experience of Indian immigrants and their children. Her memoir, *In Other Words* (2016), tells her story of cultural displacement from a fresh angle—she originally composed it in Italian. See also jhumpalahiri.net.

Chang-rae Lee (b. 1965)
American novelist. When he was three, Lee and his family left South Korea for the United States, settling in Westchester, New York. He received his B.A. from Yale in 1987 and spent a year as an equities analyst before pursuing his M.F.A. at the University of Oregon. Beginning with *Native Speaker* (1995), Lee's five novels all explore various aspects of identity—race, ethnicity, and "Americanness." *A Gesture Life* (1999) focuses on a Japanese American former medic who recalls treating "comfort women"—Korean women forced into sexual slavery by Japanese soldiers in World War II. *The Surrendered* (2010), set in the Korean War, was a Pulitzer Prize finalist. Lee's most recent novel, *On Such a Full Sea* (2014), features a Chinese American fish farmer living in a dystopian Baltimore—"B-Mor." Presently Lee teaches at Stanford University. See also newyorker.com/cont ributors/chang-rae-lee.

Jill Lepore (b. 1966)
American historian and author. Born the daughter of educators in West Boylston, Massachusetts, Lepore earned a B.A. in English at Tufts University, an M.A. in American culture at the University of Michigan, and a Ph.D. in American studies at Harvard University. She is the author of twelve award-winning books based on careful research; "history," she has written, "is the art of making an argument about the past by telling a story accountable to evidence." Her life's project is telling America's story, often on a grand scale, in books such as *The Name of War* (1998), *New York Burning* (2005), *The Story of America* (2012), and the massively ambitious *These Truths: A History of the United States* (2018). Her latest book is *This America: The Case for the Nation* (2019). Lepore has been a staff writer for the *New Yorker* since 2005 and teaches history at Harvard. See also newyorker.com /contributors/jill-lepore.

Michael Lewis (b. 1960)
American journalist and author. Born in New Orleans, Lewis earned a B.A. in art history at Princeton University and an M.A. in economics at the London School of Economics. His work in the financial industry provided the background for his first book, *Liar's Poker: Rising through*

the Wreckage on Wall Street (1989).
Since then Lewis has produced thirteen
more nonfiction best sellers that shed
light on the inner workings of a particular industry. *The New New Thing* (1999),
for example, tells the story of Silicon
Valley's rise to tech dominance; *Moneyball: The Art of Winning an Unfair Game*
(2003) describes the "sabermetric"
approach to creating a winning pro baseball team; *The Big Short: Inside the
Doomsday Machine* (2010), analyzes the
causes of the 2008 financial crisis; and
Lewis's latest book, *The Fifth Risk*
(2018), examines the inner workings of
the Trump administration. See also
michaellewiswrites.com.

Alan Lightman (b. 1948)
American physicist, author, and humanitarian. As a Memphis, Tennessee, high
school student, Lightman won both science fairs and literary awards; he studied
physics at Princeton University and
earned his Ph.D. at the California Institute of Technology. Lightman has made
fundamental contributions to the field of
astrophysics while also writing poems,
short stories, and essays on science
appearing in such journals as *Harper's*,
Granta, *Smithsonian*, *Story*, and the *New
Yorker*. His many books include the novels *Einstein's Dreams* (1993), an international best seller, and *The Diagnosis*
(2000), a National Book Award finalist.
His latest book, *Searching for Stars on an
Island in Maine* (2018), is a deep meditation on the yearning to discover scientific
grounds for human spiritual experience.
Lightman currently teaches humanities
at the Massachusetts Institute of Technology. In 2003 he founded the Harp-
swell Foundation to foster a new
generation of women leaders in the
developing world. See also cmsw.mit.edu
/alan-lightman.

Abraham Lincoln (1809–1865)
American lawyer, orator, legislator, and
sixteenth president of the United States.
Born in Kentucky, Lincoln was largely
self-made and self taught. In 1830 his
family moved to Illinois, where Lincoln
prepared himself for a career in law. In
1834 he was elected to the first of four
terms in the Illinois state legislature, and
in 1847, to the U.S. Congress. Elected
president in 1860, Lincoln guided the
Union through the Civil War while pressing for passage of the Thirteenth Amendment (1865), which outlawed slavery
"everywhere and forever" in the United

States. His most famous speech, the Gettysburg Address (1863), was delivered at
the site of one of the Civil War's bloodi-
est battles. Shortly after his reelection
and with the war drawing to a close, Lincoln gave his Second Inaugural Address
(1865), an eloquent appeal for reconciliation and peace. He was assassinated a
little more than a month later. See also
whitehouse.gov/1600/presidents/abraham
-lincoln.

Teresa Lust (b. 1964)
American chef, food writer, and editor.
Lust grew up in Yakima, Washington, and
earned a B.S. in biology at Washington
State University before earning her M.A.
in liberal studies at Dartmouth College.
Her first book, *Pass the Polenta: And
Other Writings from the Kitchen, with
Recipes* (1998), is a blend of memoir,
thoughts about food and its meaning in
our lives, and the recipes of her Italian
immigrant grandmother, for whom food
was family, love, and life itself. *The Bread
of Kings* (2015) traces the surprisingly rich
history of *grissini*—Italian breadsticks. A
professional chef and an Italian teacher,
Lust is also the translator of Italian author
Alessandra Lavagnino's novel *Librarians
of Alexandria: A Tale of Two Sisters* (2006).
See also teresalust.com.

Niccolò Machiavelli (1469–1527)
Italian statesman and political philosopher. An aristocrat who held public office
while Florence was a republic, Machiavelli fell from favor when the Medici
family returned to power in 1512. He was
tortured during a brief imprisonment;
upon his release he retired to a life of
studying philosophy and writing the treatises that would become seminal works
of modern political science. Machiavelli's most famous work, *The Prince*, composed in 1513 but not published until
after his death, has exerted considerable
literary and political influence within the
Western tradition. Because *The Prince* is
such a clear-eyed, unsentimental depic-
tion of the politics of the author's era, the
term *Machiavellian* has come to mean
manipulative, deceitful, and amoral. In
fact, Machiavelli himself was a trusted
civil servant and an admired philosopher. See also plato.stanford.edu/entries
/machiavelli.

Nancy Mairs (1943–2016)
American poet and essayist. Mairs was
born in Long Beach, California, and grew
up in Boston. Married at nineteen, she

completed her B.A. at Wheaton College, had a child, and earned M.F.A. and Ph.D. degrees from the University of Arizona. The personal difficulties that inform her writing include a near-suicidal bout of agoraphobia and anorexia, and the later discovery that she was afflicted with multiple sclerosis. She found salvation both in writing and in Roman Catholicism, to which she converted in her thirties. Her first book was a collection of poems, *In All the Rooms in the Yellow House* (1984). Her eight books of essays and memoirs include *Plaintext: Deciphering a Woman's Life* (1986), *Carnal Acts* (1990), *Voice Lessons: On Becoming a (Woman) Writer* (1994), *Waist-High in the World: A Life Among the Nondisabled* (1996), and *A Dynamic God: Living an Unconventional Catholic Faith* (2007). See also nytimes.com/2016/12/07 /books/nancy-mairs-dead-author.html.

Jane McGonigal (b. 1977)
American game designer and author. McGonigal grew up in New Jersey and earned a B.A. in English from Fordham University. Even before she had gone on to complete her Ph.D. in performance studies from the University of California, Berkeley, she had designed commercial video games such as *I Love Bees* (2004) and *Last Call Poker* (2005). Now known for alternative-reality games like *World without Oil* (2007), McGonigal believes that online gaming can help to make the world a better place by generating and focusing collective human intelligence for the common good. She is the author of *Reality Is Broken: Why Games Make Us Better and How They Can Change the World* (2011). McGonigal's most recent game is *SuperBetter* (2012); she followed it up with the best-selling book *SuperBetter: A Revolutionary Approach to Getting Stronger, Happier, Braver, and More Resilient* (2015). See also janemcgonigal.com.

John McPhee (b. 1931)
American nonfiction author. McPhee was born in Princeton, New Jersey, and educated at both Princeton and Cambridge Universities. He began his writing career at *Time* magazine; since 1965 he has been a staff writer for the *New Yorker*, which has serialized many of the thirty-nine books that have made him a leading light of what is now called "creative nonfiction." His first book, *A Sense of Where You Are* (1965), profiled then—college basketball player Bill Bradley. His subsequent books include *Encounters with the Archdruid* (1971), a portrait of Sierra Club founder David Brower; *Coming into the Country* (1977), a look at life in Alaska; and *Annals of the Former World* (1998), a five-book collection about geology, which was awarded the Pulitzer Prize for nonfiction. His most recent book is *The Patch* (2018). For decades he has taught a renowned creative writing course, "The Literature of Fact," at Princeton. See also www.newyorker.com/contributors/john -mcphee.

Mary Midgley (1919–2018)
English philosopher and author. Born in London, Midgley was raised in the intellectual atmosphere of her father's various postings, which included the chaplaincy at King's College, Cambridge. She studied Classics at Oxford University in preparation for a long and distinguished teaching career, much of it spent at Newcastle University. When she was fifty-nine she published the first of her fifteen books, *Beast and Man: The Roots of Human Nature* (1978); subsequent books include *Wickedness* (1984), a study of the nature of evil, and *The Owl of Minerva* (2005), her memoir. Throughout her career she advocated a holistic, humanistic understanding of the world as opposed to what she dismissed as the "reductionism" typical of science; she was a fierce champion of animal rights and said that her "principal passion" was "reviving our reverence for the earth." See also theguardian.com /education/2018/oct/12/mary-midgley -obituary.

John Muir (1838–1914)
American naturalist, preservationist, and writer. Muir's family emigrated from Scotland to the United States in 1849 and settled in Wisconsin. An avid student of nature, Muir studied geology and botany at the University of Wisconsin, though he left without taking a degree. As a young man, Muir traveled widely in the western United States to study its flora and fauna. He became a vocal advocate for what was then called "preservationism," co-founding the Sierra Club in 1892 to promote the protection of wilderness areas from development. Muir's efforts are largely responsible for the creation of Yosemite National Park; in 1976 the California Historical Society voted him "The Greatest Californian." His writings, which celebrate wilderness and extol the natural beauty of the American West, include such classics as *The Mountains of California* (1894) and *My First Summer in the Sierra* (1911). See also sierraclub.org/john_muir_exhibit.

Marion Nestle (b. 1936)

American food researcher and author. A tireless advocate of food safety and healthy eating, Nestle holds three degrees from the University of California, Berkeley—a B.A. in bacteriology, an M.P.H. in public health nutrition, and a Ph.D. in molecular biology—and for many years she taught nutrition, food studies, and public health at New York University. Nestle is renowned for her pugnacious opposition to the corporate interests that dominate the production and marketing of food in America. A prolific writer (and blogger), she was a longtime food columnist for the *San Francisco Chronicle*. Her nine books include *Food Politics: How the Food Industry Influences Nutrition and Health* (2002), *What to Eat* (2006), *Pet Food Politics: The Chihuahua in the Coal Mine* (2008), *Soda Politics: Taking on Big Soda (and Winning)* (2015), and, most recently, *Unsavory Truth: How Food Companies Skew the Science of What We Eat* (2018). See also foodpolitics.com.

Aimee Nezhukumatathil (b. 1974)

American poet and essayist. Born in Chicago to Asian immigrant parents, Nezhukumatathil earned both her B.A. in English and her M.F.A. in poetry and creative nonfiction at The Ohio State University. She now teaches in the University of Mississippi's M.F.A. program. Her elegant, warm-hearted, and often very funny poems have appeared widely and won her a Pushcart Prize and inclusion in the *Best American Poetry* series. Nezhukumatathil's seven volumes of poems include *Miracle Fruit* (2003), *At the Drive-in Volcano* (2007), *Lucky Fish* (2011), and, most recently, *Oceanic* (2018). Her next book is the forthcoming *World of Wonder*, an illustrated collection of nature essays. See also aimeenez.net.

Ngũgĩ wa Thiong'o (b. 1938)

Kenyan novelist, playwright, and social critic. Born in what was then British East Africa, Ngũgĩ grew up amid colonialism, revolution, and the emergence of independent Kenya in 1963. His first novel, *Weep Not, Child* (1964), and his second, *A Grain of Wheat* (1967), depict the Mau Mau Uprising against the British. His 1977 play, *Ngaahika Ndeenda*, written in his native Gĩkũyũ and translated by the author as *I Will Marry When I Want* (1982), was critical of the Kenyan government, resulting in Ngũgĩ's yearlong imprisonment. He has since lived in self-imposed exile in the United States and is currently a professor of comparative literature at the University of California, Irvine. His books include *Decolonising the Mind* (1986), which argues for the use of native languages; his masterpiece, *Wizard of the Crow* (2006), a novel; and *Dreams in a Time of War: A Childhood Memoir* (2010). See also ngugiwathiongo.com.

Viet Thanh Nguyen (b. 1971)

American author of fiction and nonfiction. Born in Vietnam, at the age of four Nguyen and his family fled the communist takeover of South Vietnam and eventually found refuge in San Jose, California. Nguyen holds two B.A. degrees, in English and ethnic studies, and a Ph.D. in English from the University of California, Berkeley. He had already distinguished himself as a professor at the University of Southern California when, in 2015, his first novel, *The Sympathizer*, was published to great acclaim, becoming a number-one best seller and winner of the Pulitzer Prize for fiction. His follow-up, the nonfiction *Nothing Ever Dies: Vietnam and the Memory of War* (2016), was a finalist for the National Book Award. *The Refugees*, a short story collection, appeared in 2017. Most recently, Nguyen co-edited *The Displaced: Refugee Writers on Refugee Lives* (2018). He is the recipient of both Guggenheim and MacArthur fellowships. See also vietnguyen.info.

Michelle Nijhuis (b. 1974)

American science journalist and author. A graduate of Reed College with a B.A. in biology, Nijhuis (pronounced NYE-house) now describes herself as a "lapsed biologist." She began her career in journalism as an intern at *High Country News*, where she is now a contributing editor. Her articles about conservation and climate change have appeared in many publications, including *Audubon*, *Orion*, *Smithsonian*, *National Geographic*, and the *Atlantic*, where she is now project editor. Nijhuis has won awards for articles on white-nose syndrome in bats, the human-assisted migration of threatened species, and the "doubt industry's" attempts to thwart the work of legitimate scientists. Her work has appeared in *Best American Science Writing* (2003) and *Best American Science and Nature Writing* (2009, 2013, 2017); she is also the co-editor, with journalist Thomas Hayden, of *The Science Writers' Handbook* (2013). She and her family live in White Salmon, Washington. See also michellenijhuis.com.

Barack Obama (b. 1961)
American author, politician, and forty-fourth president of the United States. Born in Honolulu to an American mother and a Kenyan father, Obama grew up in Hawaii and Indonesia before earning degrees at Columbia University and the Harvard Law School. He worked as a community organizer in Chicago and taught constitutional law at the University of Chicago Law School. Before his election to the U.S. presidency, he served in the Illinois State Senate and the U.S. Senate. Obama is the author of two books: his memoir, *Dreams from My Father* (1995), and a political manifesto, *The Audacity of Hope* (2006). His keynote speech at the 2004 Democratic National Convention catapulted him to national attention; his speech at Cairo University, soon after his inauguration, marked a "new beginning" in U.S. relations with the rest of the world. In 2009 Obama was awarded the Nobel Peace Prize. See also barackobama.com.

George Orwell (1903–1950)
Pen name of Eric Blair, English journalist, essayist, novelist, and social critic. Born in India and educated in England, Orwell was an officer in the Indian Imperial Police in Burma, an experience he later recounted in the novel *Burmese Days* (1934). In 1927 he went to Europe to pursue his career as a writer. His first book, *Down and Out in Paris and London* (1933), depicts his years of poverty and struggle while working as a dishwasher and day laborer. Orwell's experiences fighting in the Spanish Civil War are the subject of the memoir *Homage to Catalonia* (1938). Of his seven novels, the satiric *Animal Farm* (1945) and the dystopian *Nineteen Eighty-Four* (1949), both indictments of totalitarianism, have become classics. Orwell, one of the most polished and respected stylists in the English language, published five collections of essays, including *Shooting an Elephant and Other Essays* (1950). See also george-orwell.org.

Amanda Petrusich (b. 1980)
American music journalist and author. A native of the New York area, Petrusich earned a B.A. in English and film studies from the College of William and Mary and an M.F.A. in nonfiction writing from Columbia University. "My growth as a writer," she says, was unlearning the habits of what she calls the "music snob archetype." Her review and feature articles have appeared in many periodicals,

including the *New York Times*, *Spin*, *Esquire*, and the *Atlantic*; presently she is a staff writer for the *New Yorker* and teaches writing at New York University. Petrusich is the author three books: *Pink Moon* (2007), *It Still Moves: Lost Songs, Lost Highways, and the Search for the Next American Music* (2008), and *Do Not Sell at Any Price: The Wild, Obsessive Hunt for the World's Rarest 78rpm Records* (2014). In 2019 she was nominated for a Grammy for the notes she wrote to accompany Bob Dylan's *Trouble No More* box set. See also newyorker.com/contributors/amanda-petrusich.

Michael Pollan (b. 1955)
American author, environmental journalist, and educator. The son of two writers, Pollan was educated at Bennington College, Oxford University, and Columbia University, where he earned his M.A. in English. Pollan's first book, *Second Nature: A Gardener's Education* (1991), sets the template for a career focused mainly on food—as a source of nutrition and pleasure for the individual as well as a critical factor in science, economics, politics, and culture. An outspoken critic of modern industrial agriculture, he has explored these themes in books such as *The Botany of Desire: A Plant's-Eye View of the World* (2001), *In Defense of Food: An Eater's Manifesto* (2008), *Food Rules: An Eater's Manual* (2009), and, most recently, *How to Change Your Mind* (2018), an inquiry into psychedelic drugs. Pollan is a professor of nonfiction writing at Harvard University and of journalism at the University of California at Berkeley. See also michaelpollan.com.

Claudia Rankine (b. 1963)
American poet, playwright, and essayist. Born in Kingston, Jamaica, Rankine holds a B.A. from Williams College and an M.F.A. from Columbia University. Her poems have been published in five collections, including *Nothing in Nature Is Private* (1994) and *Don't Let Me Be Lonely: An American Lyric* (2004). Her best-known book, *Citizen: An American Lyric* (2014), combining poetry, prose, and visual images, was a finalist for the National Book Award; not only did it win the National Book Critics Circle Award for Poetry, but it was the first book ever to be named a finalist in both the poetry and criticism categories. She has co-edited a number of books, most recently *The Racial Imaginary: Writers on Race in the Life of the Mind* (2014). Rankine teaches

poetry at Yale University. With the money she won as a MacArthur ("Genius") fellow, in 2017 she established the Racial Imaginary Institute. See also claudiarankine.com.

Fariha Róisín (b. 1990)
Australian Canadian writer and podcaster. Born in Canada to Pakistani immigrant parents, Róisín grew up in Brisbane, Australia, feeling that her religion, her skin color, and even her body type required her to "whitewash" herself to conform with the culture around her. From an early age, she has turned to writing as a means of exploring her intersectional identity. Her smart, insightful essays have appeared in the *New York Times*, *Vice*, and *Al Jazeera*, and she is currently writer-at-large and culture editor for *The Juggernaut*, a digital publication that focuses on South Asian and South Asians. Róisín was a co-writer of the television series *Samara*, and as a podcaster she has co-hosted *Two Brown Girls*, *Yo Adrian*, and *How Do You Solve a Problem Like*. She has written a collection of poems, *How to Cure a Ghost* (2019), and is finishing her first novel, *Like a Bird*. See also fariharoisin.com.

Mike Rose (b. 1944)
American educator and author. Born to Italian immigrant parents in Altoona, Pennsylvania, Rose grew up in Los Angeles. In high school, he was wrongly placed on the "vocational track" for academic underachievers; a teacher discovered the error, and Rose went on to excel as a student, earning his B.A. from Loyola University and a Ph.D. in education from UCLA, as well as two master's degrees. Rose has made a career of championing the academic potential of the poor and underprivileged. A longtime teacher, he is presently a professor at the UCLA Graduate School of Education and Information Studies. His books include *Lives on the Boundary* (1989), which argues that poor preparation, not lack of intelligence, hampers most underachieving students; *The Mind at Work: Valuing the Intelligence of the American Worker* (2004); *Why School? Reclaiming Education for All of Us* (2009); and *Back to School: Why Everyone Deserves a Second Chance at Education* (2012). See also mikerosebooks.com.

Scott Russell Sanders (b. 1945)
American novelist, essayist, and teacher. Born in Memphis, Tennessee, and edu-

cated at both Brown and Cambridge Universities, Sanders has spent his teaching career at Indiana University at Bloomington, where he is professor of English. The author of four novels, two short story collections, and seven children's books, he is best known for his nature writing and his personal essays. Among his many books are *Wilderness Plots: Tales about the Settlement of the American Land* (1983, 2007); *The Paradise of Bombs* (1987), a collection of essays about violence in the United States; *Staying Put: Making a Home in a Restless World* (1993); *The Force of Spirit* (2000), a collection of meditations on family and the passage of time; *A Private History of Awe* (2006), a spiritual memoir; *A Conservationist Manifesto* (2009); *Earth Works: Selected Essays* (2012); and the novels *Divine Animal* (2014) and *The Engineer of Beasts* (2019). See also scottrussellsanders.com.

Chief Seattle (c. 1780–1866)
Native American leader. Seattle (also Seathl or Sealth) was chief of the Suquamish, Duwamish, and allied Salish tribes of the Pacific Northwest. He was baptized a Roman Catholic in 1848 and, foreseeing the unstoppable influx of whites, became an advocate of peace. Local settlers honored him and his work by naming their town Seattle, an Anglicization of Si'ahl (his name in his native language, Lushootseal). His famous address is a reply to an offer to buy over two million acres of Indian land around Puget Sound, proffered in 1854 by Isaac Stevens, governor of the newly created Washington Territory. (No authenticated translation of the speech exists; the most common version was first published thirty-three years after the fact.) Because of Seattle's example, his people avoided the bloody warfare that afflicted the territory from 1855 until 1870. See also duwamishtribe.org /chief-siahl.

David Sedaris (b. 1956)
American humorist and author. Born in Johnson City, New York, Sedaris grew up in Raleigh, North Carolina, graduated from Kent State University in Ohio, and moved to Chicago, where he did odd jobs until radio host Ira Glass happened to hear him at a comedy club reading from his diary about his experience as a Christmas elf at Macy's department store in New York. Glass invited Sedaris to read his "Santaland Diaries" on Glass's local show, *The Wild Room*, in 1992, a performance he soon followed up on National

Public Radio's *Morning Edition*. Sedaris became a star overnight. His first book, *Barrel Fever* (1994), a collection of drolly funny short stories and autobiographical essays, became a best seller, and Sedaris soon became a familiar voice on Glass's new NPR program, *This American Life*. Since then he has published ten more collections, the latest being *Calypso* (2018). See also davidsedarisbooks.com.

Amy Sequenzia (b. 1983)
American poet, essayist, and disability and human rights activist. Born autistic, with epilepsy and cerebral palsy, Florida native Sequenzia grew up being labeled "low-functioning" and even "retarded." Because she does not speak, it wasn't until she learned to type that she found her "voice" and was able to become a fierce advocate for herself and for neurodiversity in general. "Today," she writes, "I cannot imagine being silenced again." Her poem "Being Proudly Autistic" begins: "Being proudly Autistic. / Being proudly Disabled. / Being me. / . . . / I define myself." Co-editor of *Typed Words, Loud Voices* (2015), a book about typed communication, Sequenzia currently serves on the board of directors of the Autistic Self-Advocacy Network (ASAN). See also peoplepill.com /people/amy-sequenzia.

Laura Shapiro (b. 1946)
American food historian. Shapiro was born and raised in the Boston area and earned her B.A. at Radcliffe College, Harvard University. She began her writing career at Boston's *Real Paper*; covering the women's movement led her to women's history and then to culinary history. For sixteen years she was a columnist for *Newsweek* magazine, writing about food, women's issues, and the arts. Her work has also appeared in such publications as *Gourmet*, *Slate*, the *New York Times*, the *New Yorker*, and *Best Food Writing* (2002). Shapiro's first book, *Perfection Salad: Women and Cooking at the Turn of the Century* (1986), was followed by *Something from the Oven: Reinventing Dinner in 1950s America* (2004) and the award-winning *Julia Child* (2007), a biography of America's best-known television cook. Her most recent book is *What She Ate: Six Remarkable Women and the Food That Tells Their Stories* (2017). See also laurashapirowriter.com.

David Shields (b. 1956)
American author and filmmaker. Born in Los Angeles, Shields holds a B.A. in English from Brown University and an M.F.A. from the University of Iowa Writers' Workshop. His first two books, *Heroes* (1984) and *Dead Languages* (1989), were both more or less traditional literary novels; since then he's written another twenty books, many of them genre-blurring, "self-deconstructing nonfiction" such as *Remote: Reflections on Life in the Shadow of Celebrity* (1996), *Reality Hunger* (2010), and *How Literature Saved My Life* (2013). His most recent books are *Nobody Hates Trump More than Trump: An Intervention* (2018) and *The Trouble with Men: Reflections on Sex, Love, Marriage, Porn, and Power* (2019). Shields is also a documentary filmmaker; his latest film is *Lynch: A History* (2018), about the pro football player Marshawn Lynch. Shields teaches at the University of Washington and Warren Wilson College. See also davidshields.com.

Rebecca Skloot (b. 1972)
American science journalist and author. Skloot grew up in Portland, Oregon, and attended Portland Community College to become a veterinary technician; she then earned a B.S. in biology from Colorado State University and an M.F.A. in creative nonfiction from the University of Pittsburgh. Her more than 200 feature articles and essays have appeared in such publications as *Discover*, *O: The Oprah Magazine*, the *New York Times Magazine*, and *Popular Science*, where she is a contributing editor. Skloot's first book, *The Immortal Life of Henrietta Lacks* (2010), the story of a line of cells taken from an unwitting subject and used in revolutionary biological research, is a case study in social class, race relations, and modern science. A publishing phenomenon, the book took ten years to research and write, was a number-one *New York Times* best seller, and has been translated into more than twenty-five languages. See also rebeccaskloot.com.

Anna Deavere Smith (b. 1950)
American actor, playwright, and educator. Smith was born in Baltimore and studied acting at Beaver College (now Arcadia University) in Glenside, Pennsylvania, and at the American Conservatory Theater in San Francisco, where she earned an M.F.A. degree. Although she is a familiar presence on television (*The West Wing*, *Black-ish*) and in movies (*Philadelphia*, *Rent*), it is her unique approach to live theater that has won her great acclaim and honors such as a

MacArthur ("Genius") Fellowship. Smith's tour de force performances feature her playing numerous characters, based on personal interviews, whose words tell the story of a particular incident, often one that exposes America's racial fault lines. Such plays include *Fires in the Mirror* (1992), *Twilight: Los Angeles, 1992* (1994), about the so-called Rodney King riots, and most recently *Notes from the Field* (2015). The author of *Letters to a Young Artist* (2006), Smith teaches at New York University. See also annadeaveresmith.org.

Gwendolyn Ann Smith (b. 1967)
American activist and journalist. Smith has written the "Transmissions" column for the *Bay Area Reporter* since 2000, and is the managing editor for *Genderfork*, an online forum for the transgender community. A transgender woman herself, Smith initiated Transgender Day of Remembrance (November 20) as an annual memorial to victims of anti-transgender hatred and violence. In 2017, author Sophia Cecilia Leveque published *Trans / Active: A Biography of Gwendolyn Ann Smith*. See also genderfork.com.

Rebecca Solnit (b. 1961)
American essayist and author. Born in Bridgeport, Connecticut, Solnit grew up in Novato, California, and received all of her formal education in California public schools, even through college—San Francisco State University—and graduate school—the University of California, Berkeley, where she earned a master's degree in journalism. She has combined activism in an array of environmental and human rights causes with writing that has appeared in many periodicals, most notably *Harper's*, where she is a regular columnist, and in seventeen books. *A Paradise Built in Hell: The Extraordinary Communities That Arise in Disaster* (2009) explores people's resilience in the face of catastrophe. *Savage Dreams* (2014) argues that the suppression of American Indians has never stopped. The essays in her collections *Men Explain Things to Me* (2014) and *The Mother of All Questions* (2017) provide a feminist take on intergender communication. See also rebeccasolnit.net.

Kory Stamper (b. 1975)
American lexicographer and author. Stamper grew up in Colorado, but it was at Smith College that she found her calling—languages. A course on medi-

eval Icelandic family sagas led her to a study of Latin, Greek, Norse, Old English, and Middle English. For twenty years she worked as a lexicographer for Merriam-Webster where, in addition to her editorial duties, she also presented "Ask the Editor" videos that discuss words and the way they're used. Since 2018 she has served as executive director of the Dictionary Society of North America. Stamper keeps up a blog, *Harmless Drudgery: Defining the Words That Define Us*, and she provides commentary on language for the *Chicago Tribune*. She is acclaimed as the author of *Word by Word: The Secret Life of Dictionaries* (2017) and is at work on a book about the words we use for colors. See also korystamper.wordpress.com.

Elizabeth Cady Stanton (1815–1902)
American abolitionist and women's rights activist. Born in Johnstown, New York, she excelled academically at Johnstown Academy but, because of her sex, was barred from nearby Union College. She married the prominent abolitionist Henry B. Stanton, and the two spent their honeymoon at the World's Anti-Slavery Convention in London. In 1848 Stanton joined Lucretia Mott and others to organize the first American convention for women's rights, held in Seneca Falls, New York, where Stanton presented her draft of the "Declaration of Sentiments and Resolutions," now seen as a founding document of modern feminism. Three years later she was introduced to Susan B. Anthony, who became her lifelong friend and colleague; together they founded the National Woman Suffrage Association in 1869. Stanton spent the rest of her life campaigning for women's suffrage and legislation that would make divorce laws more favorable to women. See also nps .gov; search for "Stanton."

Sandra Steingraber (b. 1959)
American biologist, poet, and essayist. A native of Illinois, Steingraber received her B.A. in biology from Illinois Wesleyan University, her M.A. in English from Illinois State University, and her Ph.D. in biology from the University of Michigan. Since a near-fatal bout with bladder cancer when she was in her twenties, Steingraber has devoted her career to exploring the connections between the environment and human health. Her first book was a volume of intimately personal poems, *Post-Diagnosis* (1995). In *Living Downstream: An Ecolo-*

gist *Looks at Cancer and the Environment* (1997), she examines the links between industrial chemicals and increased risks of cancer; following its publication, Steingraber was hailed as "the new Rachel Carson" by the Sierra Club. Her most recent book is *Raising Elijah: Protecting Our Children in an Age of Environmental Crisis* (2011). Steingraber currently teaches at Ithaca College. See also steingraber.com.

Jonathan Swift (1667–1745)
Anglo-Irish poet, satirist, and cleric. Born to English parents who resided in Ireland, Swift studied at Trinity College, Dublin, and then moved to London in 1689. There he became part of the literary and political worlds, beginning his career by writing political pamphlets in support first of the Whigs, then the Tories. Swift earned a master's degree at Oxford University before returning to Ireland. Ordained in the Church of Ireland in 1695, he was appointed dean of St. Patrick's Cathedral, Dublin, in 1713 and held the post until his death. One of the master satirists of the English language, he wrote several scathing attacks on extremism and anti-Irish bigotry, including *The Battle of the Books* (1704), *A Tale of a Tub* (1704), and *A Modest Proposal* (1729), but he is probably best known for the imaginative worlds he created in *Gulliver's Travels* (1726). See also poetryfoundation.org/poets/jonathan-swift.

Nicholas Tampio (b. 1973)
American professor of political science and author. After growing up in the Washington, DC, area, Tampio earned his B.A. at New College of Florida, his M.A. at Indiana University, and his Ph.D. at Johns Hopkins University; since then his career has been devoted to research in the history of political thought, contemporary political theory, and education policy. His first book, *Kantian Courage* (2012), explores the continuing influence of eighteenth-century philosopher Immanuel Kant on political thinking. His second book, *Deleuze's Political Vision* (2015), is a reconsideration of the political theories of French philosopher Gilles Deleuze. Tampio's two most recent books, *Common Core: National Education Standards and the Threat to Democracy* (2018), and *Learning versus the Common Core* (2019), both argue against the "common core" standards that dominate much of American educational policy today. Since 2008, Tampio has taught political

theory at Fordham University. See also faculty.fordham.edu/tampio.

Henry David Thoreau (1817–1862)
American philosopher, essayist, naturalist, and poet. A graduate of Harvard University, Thoreau worked at a number of jobs—schoolmaster, house painter, employee in his father's pencil factory—before becoming a writer. He befriended Emerson and joined the Transcendental Club, contributing frequently to its journal, the *Dial*. Drawn to the natural world, he wrote his first book, *A Week on the Concord and Merrimack Rivers* (1849), about a canoe trip with his brother. Thoreau's abolitionist stance against slavery led to his arrest for refusing to pay the Massachusetts poll tax (an act of protest against the Mexican War, which he viewed as serving the interests of slaveholders). His essay defending this act, "Civil Disobedience" (1849), his book on the solitary life, *Walden* (1854), and his speech "A Plea for Captain John Brown" (1859) are classics of American literature. See also thoreausociety.org.

Mary Beth Tinker (b. 1952)
American pediatric nurse and free-speech activist. Tinker's name has been a touchstone of free-expression advocacy since 1969, when the U.S. Supreme Court ruled in her favor in the case of *Tinker v. Des Moines Independent Community School District*. Three years earlier, as a junior high school student in Des Moines, Iowa, Tinker had been one of two dozen Des Moines–area students who wore black armbands to school as part of a nationwide protest against American involvement in the war in Vietnam. Local school principals responded with a no-armbands policy. Tinker and four others refused to comply, and were suspended. The American Civil Liberties Union filed suit on their behalf, and the case eventually reached the Supreme Court, which ruled that the school district had violated the students' First Amendment rights to free expression. Since then, Tinker has pursued two careers: pediatric nursing and youth rights activism. See also tinkertourusa.org/about/tinkerbio.

Sojourner Truth (c. 1797–1883)
American abolitionist and women's rights activist. Born into slavery as Isabella Baumfree in Swartekill, New York, she escaped to freedom with her infant daughter in 1826, just a year before slavery was abolished in New York State,

and then won a court battle to free one of her sons—the first such legal victory of a black woman over a white man. In 1843, declaring that "the Spirit calls me, and I must go," she adopted the name Sojourner Truth and became an itinerant preacher, condemning the institution of slavery. The famed abolitionist William Lloyd Garrison encouraged her to dictate her memoirs, which he then published as *The Narrative of Sojourner Truth: A Northern Slave* in 1850. A year later, while attending the Women's Rights Convention in Akron, Ohio, she extemporaneously delivered the speech that became known as "Ain't I a Woman?" See also sojournertruth.org.

Sherry Turkle (b. 1948)
American sociologist and author. Turkle grew up in Brooklyn and earned her B.A. degree at Radcliffe College; she received her M.A. as well as a joint Ph.D. degree in sociology and personal psychology at Harvard University. Much of her work has centered on the relationship between people and technology. Her nine books include *The Second Self: Computers and the Human Spirit* (1984) and *Life on the Screen: Identity in the Age of the Internet* (1995); both explore the transformative effect of computers on our lives today. *Alone Together: Why We Expect More from Technology and Less from Each Other* (2011) and *Reclaiming Conversation: The Power of Talk in a Digital Age* (2015) are cautionary examinations of what is lost when we communicate through digital intermediaries. Turkle is a licensed clinical psychologist; she teaches in the sociology department of the Massachusetts Institute of Technology. See also www.mit.edu/~sturkle.

Mark Twain (1835–1910)
Pen name of Samuel Clemens, American journalist, novelist, and humorist. Twain grew up in Hannibal, Missouri, beside the river that he would later celebrate in the memoir *Life on the Mississippi* (1883) and in *Adventures of Huckleberry Finn* (1885), regarded by many as one of the greatest American novels. First apprenticed as a printer, he was by turns a riverboat pilot, a Confederate soldier (for two weeks), a gold prospector, and a journalist. His short story "The Celebrated Jumping Frog of Calaveras County" (1867) made him famous; during his lifetime he was enormously popular, lecturing widely to great acclaim and publishing a flood of

articles, essays, stories, and novels. Many of his books, including the memoir *Roughing It* (1872) and the novel *Adventures of Tom Sawyer* (1876), are classics. William Faulkner called Twain "the father of American literature." See also cmgww.com/historic/twain.

Jean M. Twenge (b. 1971)
American psychologist and author. Twenge earned both a B.A. and an M.A. from the University of Chicago before receiving her Ph.D. in psychology and sociology from the University of Michigan. She has devoted her career to studying the ways one generation differs from another in terms of their behaviors, attitudes, goals, and mental health. In addition to co-authoring two psychology textbooks and publishing scores of articles in professional journals, she has written four books for a more general readership, including *The Narcissism Epidemic: Living in the Age of Entitlement* (2010), *Generation Me: Why Today's Young Americans Are More Confident, Assertive, Entitled—and More Miserable than Ever Before* (2014), and most recently *iGen: Why Today's Super-Connected Kids Are Growing Up Less Rebellious, More Tolerant, Less Happy and Completely Unprepared for Adulthood* (2017). Twenge teaches at San Diego State University. See also jeantwenge.com.

Jose Antonio Vargas (b. 1981)
American journalist, filmmaker, and author. Born in the Philippines, as a twelve-year-old Vargas was sent to live with his grandparents in California, where he learned English, excelled in school, and then, at age sixteen, discovered that his identity documents were false—he was "illegal." His life since then has had two phases. While living in the shadows he graduated from San Francisco State University and established himself as a journalist, even winning a Pulitzer Prize for breaking news reporting as a member of a *Washington Post* team. Then, in 2011, he published his life story in the *New York Times Magazine*. Since then he has become the public face of the undocumented in America, founding the advocacy organization Define American for those who "just don't have the right papers." He has told his story in the 2013 film *Documented* and in his memoir, *Dear America: Notes of an Undocumented Citizen* (2018). See also joseantoniovargas.com.

Taté Walker (b. 1983)

Two Spirit storyteller and Indigenous rights activist. A citizen of the Cheyenne River Sioux Tribe of South Dakota, Walker is Mniconjou Lakota and an award-winning writer, photographer, and videographer for outlets like *Native Peoples* magazine, *Everyday Feminism*, *Indian Country Today*, and more. Their work can also be found in *FIERCE: Essays by and about Dauntless Women* (2018); their first book, *Thunder Thighs & Trickster Vibes*, will appear in the fall of 2020. Walker uses their fifteen years of experience working for news media, social justice organizations, and tribal education systems to organize students and professionals around issues of critical cultural competency, anti-racism/anti-bias, and inclusive community building. See also jtatewalker.com.

David Wallace-Wells (b. 1982)

American journalist and author. A New York native, Wallace-Wells began his college education at the University of Chicago and graduated with a B.A. in history from Brown University. As a self-described "general interest journalist," he has written articles on many subjects for *New York* magazine, where he is now deputy editor. In recent years, though, he has increasingly focused his journalistic work on the threats posed by climate change. His July 2017 cover story, "The Uninhabitable Earth," drew tremendous response from readers—some horrified by its dire implications, some grateful for its guarded optimism, some skeptical of either its grim predictions or the hope its author places in human engineering to get us out of the predicament that human activity got us into. That article became the basis for Wallace-Wells's best-selling book *The Uninhabitable Earth* (2019) with its unforgettable opening line: "It is worse, much worse, than you think." See also newamerica.org/our-people/david-wallace-wells.

Tara Westover (b. 1986)

American historian and memoirist. Born the youngest of seven children in a fundamentalist Mormon family in Clifton, Idaho, Westover was homeschooled by her survivalist family and was seventeen years old the first time she entered a formal classroom. She soon realized the deficits in her knowledge of the world and determined to teach herself enough about grammar and mathematics to get into college. Ten years later, after graduating *magna cum laude* from Brigham Young University, earning a master's degree as a scholarship student at Cambridge University, and spending a year as a teaching fellow at Harvard University, she received a Ph.D. in history from Cambridge. Her remarkable memoir, *Educated*, created an immediate sensation when it was published in 2018, becoming a number-one *New York Times* best seller. Writing in *Time* magazine, Bill Gates included her in a list of the 100 most influential people of 2019. See also tarawestover.com.

E. B. White (1899–1985)

American poet, journalist, editor, and essayist. Elwyn Brooks White was born in Mount Vernon, New York. Just three years after graduating from Cornell University in 1921, he began a sixty-year career on the staff of the *New Yorker*, contributing poems and articles and serving as a discreet and helpful editor. Among his many books, three written for children earned him lasting fame: *Stuart Little* (1945), *Charlotte's Web* (1952), and *The Trumpet of the Swan* (1970). Renowned for his graceful prose, White revised and edited William Strunk's text *The Elements of Style* (1919, 1959), a classic guide to writing still widely known as "Strunk and White." The collection *Essays of E. B. White* was published in 1977; a year later White was awarded a Pulitzer Prize for a lifetime of literary achievement. See also britannica.com/biography/E-B-White.

Colson Whitehead (b. 1969)

American novelist. Born in New York City, Whitehead grew up as a dedicated bookworm in Manhattan before earning his B.A. in English at Harvard University. He began his career writing movie and record reviews for the *Village Voice*. *The Intuitionist* (1999), his first novel, was a critical and commercial success, and was soon followed by his second, *John Henry Days* (2001), about the "steel-drivin' man" of folklore. The five novels he has written since then include *The Underground Railroad* (2016), winner of both the National Book Award and the Pulitzer Prize for fiction, and his latest, *Nickel Boys* (2019), about a hellish "reform school" in Florida. *The Colossus of New York* (2003) is a collection of essays; *The Noble Hustle* (2014) is an account of the 2011 World Series of Poker. In 2002 Whitehead was awarded a MacArthur ("Genius") Fellowship. See also colsonwhitehead.com.

Chris Wiewiora (b. 1987)
Born in Buckhannon, West Virginia, Wiewiora grew up first in Warsaw, Poland, where his parents were missionaries, and then in Orlando, Florida. He earned his B.A. in English at the University of Central Florida, where he served as an editor at the *Florida Review*. His essay "The Gift of Nothing" led to his acceptance into Iowa State University's Creative Writing and Environment Program, where he was managing editor of *Flyway*; the essay, first published in *Stymie*, has since been cited as "Notable" in *Best American Sports Writing* (2012). Wiewiora has held a variety of jobs; his stint as a pizza maker led to his essay "This Is Tossing," which was published in the literary magazine *MAKE* as well as the anthology *Best Food Writing* (2013). Many of his essays have appeared on *The Good Men Project*, an online review. Wiewiora's website features an astonishing list of the books he reads—nearly a hundred each year. See also chriswiewiora.com.

Florence Williams (b. 1967)
American journalist and author. Williams grew up in New York City, spending her summers camping in the West and Canada. "From an early age," she recalls, "I learned that forests and rivers and big landscapes provided fun and excitement, as well as peace and reflection." She graduated from both Yale University and the University of Montana, where she earned an M.F.A. degree. Always an avid outdoorswoman, she has been a staff writer for *High Country News* and is presently a contributing editor for *Outside* magazine; her feature journalism has also appeared in *National Geographic*, *Slate*, *Mother Jones*, *Bicycling*, and the *New York Times Magazine*. Her first book, *Breasts: A Natural and Unnatural History* (2012), won the *Los Angeles Times* Book Prize in science and technology. Williams's latest book is *The Nature Fix: Why Nature Makes Us Happier, Healthier, and More Creative* (2017). See also florencewilliams.com.

Patricia Williams (b. 1951)
American legal scholar and critic. Williams received her B.A. from Wellesley College and her J.D. from Harvard Law School. She is a leading proponent of critical race theory, which argues that race is a principal determinant in the legal system and in culture generally. Her monthly column, "Diary of a Mad Law Professor," appears in the *Nation*. Her books include *The Alchemy of Race and Rights: Diary of a Law Professor* (1991), *The Rooster's Egg* (1995), *Seeing a Color-Blind Future: The Paradox of Race* (1997), and *Open House: Of Family, Friends, Food, Piano Lessons, and the Search for a Room of My Own* (2004). Williams also co-edited *The Blind Goddess: A Reader on Race and Justice* (2011). She has received a MacArthur "Genius" Fellowship along with numerous other honors. Williams is a professor of law and humanities at Northeastern University. See also thenation.com/authors/patricia-j-williams.

Terry Tempest Williams (b. 1955)
American poet, nature writer, and environmental activist. Born to a Mormon family in Corona, California, Williams grew up surrounded by the vast desert landscape of Utah; she holds a bachelor's degree in English and a master's degree in environmental education from the University of Utah. Her book *Pieces of White Shell: A Journey to Navajoland* (1984) is a personal exploration of Native American myths; her much-reprinted essay "The Clan of One-Breasted Women" became the final section of the autobiographical *Refuge: An Unnatural History of Family and Place* (1991). Her subsequent books include *Red: Passion and Patience in the Desert* (2001), *The Open Space of Democracy* (2004), *When Women Were Birds* (2012), and, most recently, *The Hour of Land: A Personal Topography of America's National Parks* (2016). Williams is a frequent contributor to publications such as the *New York Times*, the *New Yorker*, and *Orion*. She is a columnist at the *Progressive*. See also coyoteclan.com.

Tom Wolfe (1930–2018)
American journalist, essayist, and novelist. A native of Richmond, Virginia, Wolfe earned a B.A. at Washington and Lee University and a Ph.D. in American studies from Yale University. Working as a traditional journalist at the *Washington Post* and the *New York Herald Tribune*, Wolfe started to utilize techniques derived from narrative fiction, creating what became known as "the New Journalism." Books such as *The Kandy-Kolored Tangerine-Flake Streamline Baby* (1965), *The Electric Kool-Aid Acid Test* (1968), and *The Purple Decades* (1982) established his reputation as a witty social critic and historian of popular culture. Wolfe's chronicle of the American space program, *The*

Right Stuff (1979), became a popular film. His satiric novels, including *The Bonfire of the Vanities* (1987) and *A Man in Full* (1998), aim to depict the breadth of American society. Wolfe's last book, *The Kingdom of Speech* (2016), questions modern theories about the origins of language. See also tomwolfe.com.

Virginia Woolf (1882–1941)
English novelist, critic, and essayist. The London-born daughter of the eminent philosopher Sir Leslie Stephen, Woolf was mainly self-educated through access to her father's substantial library. For decades she was at the center of the Bloomsbury Group, a celebrated collection of artists, scholars, and writers that included both Woolf and her husband, socialist writer Leonard Woolf. Together, the Woolfs founded and operated the Hogarth Press, whose publications included many of her works. A foremost modernist, Woolf employed psychological insight, lyricism, and experimental literary techniques in her fiction; her nine novels include the now-classic *Mrs. Dalloway* (1925), *To the Lighthouse* (1927), and *The Waves* (1931). Her numerous essays are collected in four volumes, including *A Room of One's Own* (1929), a historical investigation of women and creativity; and *Three Guineas* (1938), philosophical dialogues that explore issues of war and feminism. See also virginiawoolfsociety.co.uk.

Ben Yagoda (b. 1954)
American journalist, author, and educator. Yagoda grew up in New Rochelle, New York, earned his B.A. in English at Yale University and an M.A. in American civilization from the University of Pennsylvania. Before his quarter-century-long career teaching at the University of Delaware, Yagoda was a film critic for the *Philadelphia Daily News* and an editor at *Philadelphia* and other magazines. His articles have appeared in *Slate*, the *New York Times Magazine*, *Rolling Stone*, *Esquire*, and many other publications; he is a longtime contributor to *Lingua Franca*, a blog about language and writing. Yagoda has authored, edited, or co-edited twelve books, notably *Will Rogers: A Biography* (1993) and *How to Not Write Bad: The Most Common Writing Problems and How to Avoid Them* (2013). His most recent book is *The B-Side: The Death of Tin Pan Alley and the Rebirth of the Great American Song* (2015). See also benyagoda.com.

William Zinsser (1922–2015)
American journalist, writer, editor, and educator. Born in New York City, Zinsser graduated from Princeton University and then served in the army for two years at the end of World War II. In 1946 he joined the staff of the *New York Herald Tribune*, eventually becoming an editorial writer. A freelancer throughout the 1960s, Zinsser contributed to periodicals such as *Life*, *Look*, and the *New York Times Magazine*. In the 1970s he joined the English faculty at Yale University, where he taught nonfiction writing and edited the alumni magazine. Zinsser's nineteen books range in subject from travel to jazz to baseball, but he is best known for *On Writing Well* (1976, 1998), a classic guide to clear, economical nonfiction writing, as well as the memoir *Writing Places: The Life Journey of a Writer and Teacher* (2009). His award-winning columns from the *American Scholar* have been collected in *The Writer Who Stayed* (2012). See also williamzinsserwriter.com.

CREDITS

CHRONOLOGICAL INDEX

GENRES INDEX

CULTURAL ANALYSIS

Humor and Satire

Nature Writing

Op-Eds

VISUAL ANALYSIS

RHETORICAL MODES INDEX

DESCRIPTION

EXEMPLIFICATION

CLASSIFYING AND DIVIDING

EXPLAINING A PROCESS

Comparing and Contrasting

Defining

ANALYZING CAUSE AND EFFECT

PERSUASION / ARGUMENT

THEMATIC INDEX

POP CULTURE

RACE AND ETHNICITY

WORK

INDEX

ABOUT THE AUTHORS

Melissa A. Goldthwaite (Ph.D., The Ohio State University), General Editor, is professor of English at Saint Joseph's University, where she teaches composition, creative writing, and rhetorical theory. Her books include *Food, Feminisms, Rhetorics* (Southern Illinois University Press, 2017), *Books That Cook: The Making of a Literary Meal* (New York University Press, 2014), *The Norton Pocketbook of Writing by Students* (2010), *Surveying the Literary Landscapes of Terry Tempest Williams* (University of Utah Press, 2003), and *The St. Martin's Guide to Teaching Writing* (Bedford/St. Martin's, 2003, 2008, 2014).

Joseph Bizup (Ph.D., Indiana University) is Associate Dean for Undergraduate Academic Programs and Policies of the College of Arts & Sciences and associate professor of English at Boston University. He previously served as Director of the Arts & Sciences Writing Program and also of writing programs at Yale University and Columbia University in the City of New York. His scholarly interests include nineteenth-century literature, especially nonfiction prose, and writing studies, especially genre, style, and argumentation.

Anne E. Fernald (Ph.D., Yale University) is professor of English at Fordham University. She is the editor of the Cambridge University Press *Mrs. Dalloway* (2014) and the author of *Virginia Woolf: Feminism and the Reader* (2006) as well as articles and reviews on Woolf and feminist modernism. Since 2018, she has been Special Advisor to the Provost for Faculty Development and co-chair of the university council on Diversity, Equity, and Inclusion, spearheading the Provost's Office Initiative on Inclusive Pedagogy and Student Engagement. For more than ten years, she directed first-year writing at Fordham's Lincoln Center campus.

John Brereton (Ph.D., Rutgers University) is professor of English, Emeritus, at the University of Massachusetts, Boston. Previously he served as executive director of the Calderwood Writing Initiative at the Boston Athenæum. He has taught writing at Harvard University, Wayne State University, Brandeis University, and the City University of New York. His scholarship focuses on the history of teaching English literature and composition.